ONCOOKING

ON COOKING

▶ TECHNIQUES FROM EXPERT CHEFS

THIRD EDITION

SARAH R. LABENSKY, CCP
ALAN M. HAUSE

With Steven Labensky
Photographs by Richard Embery
Drawings by Stacey Winters Quattrone and William E. Ingram

Prentice
Hall

Upper Saddle River, New Jersey 07458

Library of Congress Cataloging-in-Publication Data

Labensky, Sarah R.
On cooking: techniques from expert chefs / Sarah R.
Labensky, Alan M. Hause; photographs by Richard Embery; drawings
by Stacey Winters Quattrone and William E. Ingram. —3rd ed.
p. cm.
Includes index.
ISBN 0-13-061865-9
1. Cookery. I. Hause, Alan M. II. Title.
TX651 .L328 2003
641.5—dc21

2002022987

Editor in Chief: Stephen Helba
Executive Editor: Vernon R. Anthony
Associate Editor: Marion Gottlieb
Executive Assistant: Nancy Kesterson
Editorial Assistant: Ann Brunner
Director of Manufacturing and Production: Bruce Johnson
Managing Editor: Mary Carnis
Creative Director: Cheryl Asherman
Interior Design: Cheryl Asherman
Manufacturing Buyer: Ilene Sanford
Production Editor: Linda Zuk
Production Management: WordCrafters

Senior Production Editor: Adele M. Kupchik
Formatting: Clarinda Company
Marketing Manager: Ryan DeGrote
Marketing Assistant: Elizabeth Farrell
Marketing Coordinator: Adam Kloza
Printer/Binder: R. R. Donnelley & Sons, Willard
Copy Editor: Amy Schneider
Proofreader: Kerry Stinson
Indexer: Karen Winget
Cover Design: Cheryl Asherman
Cover Illustration: Richard Embery and Marjory Dressler
Cover Printer: Lehigh

Photo Credits:

Portrait of Fannie Farmer—courtesy of The Schlesinger Library, Radcliffe College
Portrait of Auguste Escoffier—courtesy of Musée de l'Art Culinaire, Villeneuve-Loubet (Village) France
Portraits of Alexis Soyer and Antonin Carême—courtesy of Barbara Wheaton
Drawing of the Reform Club's Kitchen—courtesy of the Reform Club, London, England

Pearson Education, Ltd.
Pearson Education Australia Pty., Limited
Pearson Education Singapore, Pte. Ltd.
Pearson Education North Asia Ltd.
Pearson Education Canada Ltd.
Pearson Educación de Mexico, S.A. de C.V.
Pearson Education — Japan
Pearson Education Malaysia, Pte. Ltd.

10 9 8 7 6 5 4 3 2 1

ISBN 0-13-061865-9

CONTENTS

PART 5   BAKING

PREFACE

Learning to cook is much more than simply learning to follow a recipe. Consequently, this is not a cookbook or a collection of recipes. It is a carefully designed text intended to teach you the fundamentals of the culinary arts and to prepare you for a rewarding career in the food service industry.

Many chapters have extensive illustrated sections identifying foods and equipment. Throughout the book, we emphasize culinary principles, not recipes (although we include more than 750 of them). Whenever possible, we focus on the general procedure highlighting fundamental principles and skills, whether it be for preparing a yeast bread or grilling a piece of fish. We discuss both the how and why of cooking. Only then are specific applications and sample recipes given.

Numerous hotel and restaurant chefs throughout the country have contributed recipes to this book, usually accompanied by photographs of the dishes as prepared in their kitchens. These recipes and illustrations allow you to explore different techniques and presentation styles.

In order to provide you with a sense of the rich traditions of cookery, informative sidebars on food history, chef biographies and other topics are scattered throughout the book. Also included are several short essays written by prominent culinarians on topics ranging from tempering chocolate to tasting spicy foods.

We wish you much success in your culinary career and hope that this text will continue to inform and inspire you long after graduation.

▶ A NOTE ON RECIPES

Recipes are important and useful as a means of standardizing food preparation and recording information. We include recipes that are designed primarily to reinforce and explain techniques and procedures presented in the text. Many recipe yields are intentionally low in order to be less intimidating to beginning cooks and more useful in small schools and kitchens.

All ingredients are listed in both U.S. and metric measurements. The metric equivalents are rounded off to even, easily measured amounts. So, you should consider these ingredient lists as separate recipes or formulas; do not measure some ingredients according to the metric amounts and other ingredients according to the U.S. amount or the proportions will not be accurate and the intended result will not be achieved.

Throughout this book, unless otherwise noted:

▶ *mirepoix* refers to a preparation of 2 parts onion, 1 part celery and 1 part carrot by weight

▶ *pepper* refers to ground black pepper, preferably freshly ground

▶ *butter* refers to whole, unsalted butter

▶ *milk* refers to whole or reduced fat (not nonfat) milk, and

▶ *TT* means "to taste"

A registered dietician analyzed all of the recipes in this book using nutritional analysis software that incorporates data from the U.S. Department of Agriculture, research laboratories and food manufacturers. The nutrient information provided here should be used only as a reference, however. A margin of error of approximately 20% can be expected because of natural variations in ingredients. Preparation techniques and serving sizes may also significantly alter the values of many nutrients. For the nutritional analysis, if a recipe offers a choice of ingredients, the first-mentioned ingredient is the one used. Ingredients listed as "to taste" (TT) and "as needed" are omitted from the analysis. Corn oil and whole milk are used throughout for "vegetable oil" and "milk," respectively. In cases of a range of ingredient quantities or numbers of servings, the average is used.

Throughout this book various recipes are marked with the pyramid symbol. This symbol identifies dishes that are particularly low in calories, fat, saturated fat or sodium; if appropriate, they may also be a good source of vitamins, protein, fiber or calcium.

Vegetarian dishes are indicated with a vegetable symbol. These recipes do not contain meat, fish, shellfish or poultry, but may contain dairy products and/or eggs. Vegetarian dishes are not necessarily low in calories, fat or sodium; nor are they automatically good sources of vitamins, protein, fiber or calcium.

The World Wide Web icon appears next to end-of-chapter questions for discussion whose answers may be researched on the web.

Detailed procedures for standard techniques are presented in the text and generally are not repeated in each recipe (for example, "deglaze the pan" or "monté au beurre"). No matter how detailed the written recipe, however, we must assume that you have certain knowledge, skills and judgment.

Variations appear at the end of selected recipes. These variations give you the opportunity to see how one set of techniques or procedures can be used to prepare different dishes with only minor modifications.

You should also rely upon the knowledge and skills of your instructor for guidance. Although some skills and an understanding of theory can be acquired through reading and study, no book can substitute for repeated, hands-on preparation and observation.

▶ ACKNOWLEDGMENTS

This book would not have been possible without the assistance and support of many people. We are particularly indebted to Steve Labensky for his countless hours with a sharp pencil, his comments and criticism and his constant support. Special thanks to our photographer, Richard Embery, for his talent, professionalism and commitment to quality; and to Sharon Salomon, MS, RD, for preparation of the Nutrition chapter. The nutritional analysis for this edition was prepared by Mindy Hermann, MS, RD, whose thoroughness and prompt replies were greatly appreciated. Thanks also to Stacey Winters Quattrone and Bill Ingram for their artistry. We are also grateful to the many chefs, restaurateurs, writers and culinary professionals who provided recipes and essays for this book.

Alan would also like to thank his wife Chantal for her guidance, support, advice and patience throughout this project. He also thanks the many coworkers and friends who contributed to the success of the text including: Charlie Blonkenfeld, Tom Klarstrom, Reynalda Montes, Bryan Elliott, Rosalino Morales, Estela Morales, Margarita Nava, Gregoria Alvizo, Linda Proffitt, Marty van de Brug and Jimmy Curry.

Sarah especially wishes to thank Mississippi University for Women for granting her a break from her teaching duties. She would also like to thank her husband Dave Moline and her administrative assistant Cheryl Brown for their patience and for keeping the real world on track during this project.

The authors wish to thank the following companies for their generous donations of equipment and supplies: J.A. Henckels Zwillingswerk, Inc., All-Clad Metalcrafters, Inc. and Parrish's Cake Decorating Supplies, Inc. We also wish to thank Shamrock Foods Company, East Coast Seafood of Phoenix Inc., KitchenAid Home Appliances, Taylor Environmental Instruments, Hobart Corporation, Jeff and Sue Reising of Arizona Ostrich Fillet and Randy Dougherty of ISF International.

Finally, we wish to thank everyone involved in this project at Prentice Hall, including Vernon Anthony, Executive Editor; Linda Zuk, Production Editor; Marion Gottlieb, Associate Editor; Cheryl Asherman, Creative Director; Mary Carnis, Managing Editor; Adele Kupchik, Senior Production Editor; and Ryan DeGrote, Marketing Manager. We also remain indebted to Robin Baliszewski, Acquisitions Editor of the first edition and current President of Career, Health, Education & Technology Division, for her support and friendship.

The authors would also like to acknowledge the following reviewers for their comments and assistance with this third edition. The reviewers of *On Cooking* provided many excellent suggestions and ideas for improving the text. The quality of the reviews was outstanding and played a major role in the preparation of this revision. Their assistance and expertise is greatly appreciated.

Michael Baskette, CEC, CCE, AAC
American Culinary Federation
St. Augustine, FL

Carl A. Behnke, CEC
Purdue University
West Lafayette, IN

Brian C. Bergquist Ed.S., CFE, COI
University of Wisconsin-Stout
Menomonie, WI

Charlotte Britto, RD, FADA
San Joaquin Delta College
Stockton, CA

Scott H. Doughty
Newbury College
Brookline, MA

Nancy Graves
University of Houston
Houston, TX

William C. Jarvie
Johnson & Wales University
The Hospitality College
Providence, RI

Jerrold K. Leong
Oklahoma State University
Stillwater, OK

Brian McDonald, CEC, CCE
Asheville-Buncombe Technical
    Community College
Asheville, NC

Michael J. McGreal
Joliet Junior College
Joliet, IL

James W. Paul, II, CSC, CCE, FMP
Caroline Edenfield
Jim Morris, CCE
Joe Costa
The Art Institute of Atlanta—
    Culinary Arts
Atlanta, GA

Gary J. Prell, CEC, CCE, AAC
General Manager for the Colorado
    Convention Center & the Denver
    Performing Arts Complex
Denver, CO

Urbano Salvati, CEC
Brown Institute Le Cordon Bleu
Mendota Heights, MN

Raymond J. Wesolowski, CCC
Pennsylvania Culinary
Pittsburgh, PA

▶ ADDITIONAL CREDITS

We wish to extend our thanks to the many chefs and instructors who took the time to complete our general survey regarding introductory cooking textbooks. Their feedback has contributed greatly to the production of our text.

Henry Anderson, Macomb Community College; Mike Artlip, Kendall College; Allen Asch, University of Nevada–Las Vegas; Claire Berg, Brookdale Community College; Nancy Berkoff, Los Angeles Trade-Technical College; LeRoy Blanchard, Los Angeles Trade-Technical College; Char Britto, San Joaquin Delta College; Laura Bullen, College of Sequoias; Stephen Burgeson, Buffalo State College; Paul Cannamela, Erie Community College–City Campus; Michael Carmel, The Illinois Institute of Art; Jeanne Curtis, Newbury College; W. Haze Dennis, Mission College; Randy Doescher, Mitchell Technical Institute; Timothy Farley, Milwaukee Area Technical College; Andrew Feldman, Glendale Community College; Jo-Ann Foley, Sacramento City College; Gregory Forte, Utah Valley State College; Deborah Foster, Ball State University; Maureen Garfolo, Pennsylvania Culinary; Richard Ghiseli, Purdue University; Nancy Graves, University of Houston; Richard Grigsby, Florida Community College; Carol Gunter, Nicholls State University; Jeffrey Hamblin, Ricks College; John Harrison, Mercyhurst College–North East; Joe Harrold, Florida Community College at Jacksonville; John Head, Johnson County Community College; Carolyn Himes, Pueblo Community College; Roger Holden, Oakland Community College; Connie Holt, Widener University; James Hughes, Travel Institute of the Pacific; William Jarvie, Johnson & Wales University; Ken Jarvis, Anne Arundel Community College; Ron Jones, Atlantic Culinary Academy; Lisa Kennon, University of North Texas; Lind Kinney, University of Massachusetts; Jerrold Leong, Oklahoma State University; Wesley Luckhardt, Central Michigan University; Elaine Madden, Anne Arundel Community College; Brian McDonald, Asheville-Buncombe Technical Community College; Michael McGreal, Joliet Junior College; Robert Menne, Hennepin Technical College; Kenneth Morlino, Nashville State Tech; Robert Nelson, University of Delaware; Becky Noto, University of Louisiana at Lafayette; David Pavesic, Georgia State University; Jayne Pearson, Manchester Community College; Deborah Peterson, Victor Valley College; Rose Postel, East Carolina University; Mary Rhiner, Kirkwood Community College; Warren Sackler, Rochester Institute of Technology; Barbara Scheule, Kent State University; David Schneider, Macomb Community College; Doris Schomberg, Alamance Community College; Leslie Cory Shoemaker, Northern Michigan University; Nancy Simonds-Ruderman, Berkshire Community College; Beth Sonnier, El Centro College; Carl Statford, Manchester Community College; Jim Trebbien, Metro College–Omaha; Mary Trometter, Pennsylvania School of Technology; Keith Vonhoff, Joliet Junior College; Erich Wagner, Scottsdale Community College; Cliff Wener, College of Lake County; Raymond Weslowski, Pennsylvania Culinary; Mark Wright, Erie Community College; George Yackey, Grossmont College.

ONCOOKING

COOKERY IS BECOME AN ART,
A NOBLE SCIENCE; COOKS ARE GENTLEMEN.

—*Robert Burton, British author (1577–1640)*

PROFESSIONALISM

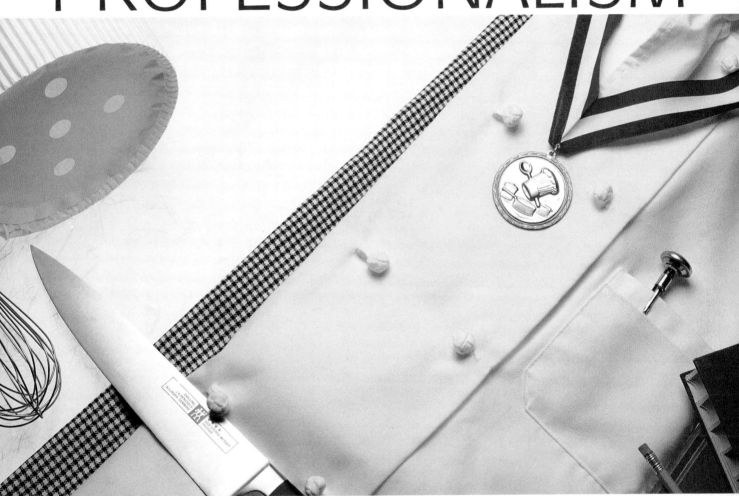

AFTER STUDYING THIS CHAPTER, YOU WILL BE ABLE TO:

▶ discuss the development of the modern food service industry

▶ name key historical figures responsible for developing food service professionalism

▶ explain the organization of classic and modern kitchen brigades

▶ appreciate the role of the professional chef in modern food service operations

▶ understand the attributes a student chef needs to become a professional chef

▶ **cooking** (1) the transfer of energy from a heat source to a food; this energy alters the food's molecular structure, changing its texture, flavor, aroma and appearance; (2) the preparation of food for consumption

▶ **cookery** the art, practice or work of cooking

▶ **professional cooking** a system of cooking based on a knowledge of and appreciation for ingredients and procedures

Like any fine art, great cookery requires taste and creativity, an appreciation of beauty and a mastery of technique. Like the sciences, successful cookery demands knowledge and an understanding of basic principles. And like any successful leader, today's professional chefs must exercise sound judgment and be committed to achieving excellence in their endeavors.

This book describes foods and cooking equipment, explains culinary principles and cooking techniques and provides recipes using these principles and techniques. No book , however, can provide taste, creativity, commitment and judgment. For these, you must rely upon yourself.

▶ CHEFS AND RESTAURANTS

Cooks have produced food in quantity for as long as people have eaten together. For millennia, chefs have catered to the often elaborate dining needs of the wealthy and powerful, whether they be Asian, Native American, European or African. And for centuries, vendors in China, Europe and elsewhere have sold to the public foods that they prepared themselves or bought from others.

But the history of the professional chef is of relatively recent origin. Its cast is mostly French, and it is intertwined with the history of restaurants—for only with the development of restaurants during the late 18th and early 19th centuries were chefs expected to produce, efficiently and economically, different dishes at different times for different diners.

THE 18TH CENTURY—BOULANGER'S RESTAURANT

The word *restaurant* is derived from the French word *restaurer* ("to restore"). Since the 16th century, the word *restorative* had been used to describe rich and highly flavored soups or stews capable of restoring lost strength. Restoratives, like all other cooked foods offered and purchased outside the home, were made by guild members. Each guild had a monopoly on preparing certain food items. For example, during the reign of Henri IV of France (1553–1610), there were separate guilds for *rotisseurs* (who cooked *la grosse viande*, the main cuts of meat), *patissiers* (who cooked poultry, pies and tarts), *tamisiers* (who baked breads), *vinaigriers* (who made sauces and some stews, including some restoratives), *traiteurs* (who made ragouts) and *porte-chapes* (caterers who organized feasts and celebrations).

The French claim that the first modern restaurant opened one day in 1765 when a Parisian tavernkeeper, a Monsieur Boulanger, hung a sign advertising the sale of his special restorative, a dish of sheep feet in white sauce. His establishment closed shortly thereafter as the result of a lawsuit brought by a guild whose members claimed that Boulanger was infringing on their exclusive right to sell prepared dishes. Boulanger triumphed in court and later reopened.

Boulanger's establishment differed from the inns and taverns that had existed throughout Europe for centuries. These inns and taverns served foods prepared (usually off premises) by the appropriate guild. The food—of which there was little choice—was offered by the keeper as incidental to the establishment's primary function: providing sleeping accommodations or drink. Customers were served family style and ate at communal tables. Boulanger's contribution to the food service industry was to serve a variety of foods prepared on premises to customers whose primary interest was dining.

Several other restaurants opened in Paris during the succeeding decades, including the Grande Taverne de Londres in 1782. Its owner, Antoine Beauvilliers (1754–1817), was the former steward to the Comte de Provence, later King Louis XVIII of France. He advanced the development of the modern restaurant by offering his wealthy patrons a menu listing available dishes during fixed hours. Beauvilliers's impeccably trained wait staff served patrons at small, individual tables in an elegant setting.

The French Revolution (1789–1799) had a significant effect on the budding restaurant industry. Along with the aristocracy, guilds and their monopolies were generally abolished. The revolution also allowed the public access to the skills and creativity of the well-trained, sophisticated chefs who had worked in the aristocracy's private kitchens. Although many of the aristocracy's chefs either left the country or lost their jobs (and some their heads), a few opened restaurants catering to the growing urbanized middle class.

THE EARLY 19TH CENTURY—CARÊME AND *GRANDE CUISINE*

As the 19th century progressed, more restaurants opened, serving a greater selection of items and catering to a wider clientele. By mid-century, several large, grand restaurants in Paris were serving elaborate meals, decidedly reminiscent of the *grande cuisine* (also known as *haute cuisine*) of the aristocracy. **Grande cuisine**, which arguably reached its peak of perfection in the hands of Antonin Carême, was characterized by meals consisting of dozens of courses of elaborately and intricately prepared, presented, garnished and sauced foods. Other restaurateurs blended the techniques and styles of *grande cuisine* with the simpler foods and tastes of the middle class (*cuisine bourgeoisie*) to create a new cuisine simpler than *grande cuisine* but more than mere home cooking.

> ▶ *grande cuisine* the rich, intricate and elaborate cuisine of the 18th- and 19th-century French aristocracy and upper classes. It is based on the rational identification, development and adoption of strict culinary principles. By emphasizing the how and why of cooking, *grande cuisine* was the first to distinguish itself from regional cuisines, which tend to emphasize the tradition of cooking.

THE LATE 19TH CENTURY—ESCOFFIER AND *CUISINE CLASSIQUE*

Following the lead set by the French in both culinary style and the restaurant business, restaurants opened in the United States and throughout Europe during the 19th century. Charles Ranhofer (1836–1899) was the first internationally renowned chef of an American restaurant, Delmonico's in New York City. In 1893, Ranhofer published his "franco-american" encyclopedia of cooking, *The Epicurean*, containing more than 3500 recipes.

One of the finest restaurants outside France was the dining room at London's Savoy Hotel, opened in 1898 under the directions of Cesar Ritz (1850–1918) and Auguste Escoffier. Escoffier is generally credited with refining the *grande cuisine* of Carême to create *cuisine classique* or **classic cuisine**. By doing so, he brought French cuisine into the 20th century.

> ▶ *classic cuisine* a late 19th- and early 20th-century refinement and simplification of French *grande cuisine*. Classic (or classical) cuisine relies on the thorough exploration of culinary principles and techniques, and emphasizes the refined preparation and presentation of superb ingredients.

THE MID-20TH CENTURY—POINT AND *NOUVELLE CUISINE*

The mid 20th century witnessed a trend toward lighter, more naturally flavored and more simply prepared foods. Fernand Point was a master practitioner of this movement. But this master's goal of simplicity and refinement was carried to even greater heights by a generation of chefs Point trained: principally, Paul Bocuse, Jean and Pierre Troisgros, Alain Chapel, Francois Bise and Louis Outhier. They, along with Michel Guérard and Roger Vergé, were the pioneers of **nouvelle cuisine** in the early 1970s.

Their culinary philosophy was principled on the rejection of overly rich, needlessly complicated dishes. These chefs emphasized healthful eating. The ingredients must be absolutely fresh and of the highest possible quality; the

> ▶ *nouvelle cuisine* French for "new cooking"; a mid-20th-century movement away from many classic cuisine principles and toward a lighter cuisine based on natural flavors, shortened cooking times and innovative combinations

MARIE-ANTOIN (ANTONIN) CARÊME (1783–1833)

Carême, known as the "cook of kings and the king of cooks," was an acknowledged master of French grande cuisine. Abandoned on the streets of Paris as a child, he worked his way from cook's helper in a working-class restaurant to become one of the most prestigious chefs of his (or, arguably, any other) time. During his career, he was chef to the famous French diplomat and gourmand Prince de Talleyrand, the Prince Regent of England (who became King George IV), Tsar Alexander I of Russia and Baron de Rothschild, among others.

His stated goal was to achieve "lightness," "grace," "order" and "perspicuity" in the preparation and presentation of food. As a *patissier*, he designed and prepared elaborate and elegant pastry and confectionery creations, many of which were based on architectural designs. (He wrote that "the fine arts are five in number, namely: painting, sculpture, poetry, music, architecture–the main branch of which is confectionery.") As a showman, he garnished his dishes with ornamental hatelets (skewers) threaded with colorful ingredients such as crayfish and intricately carved vegetables, and presented his creations on elaborate socles (bases). As a *saucier*, he standardized the use of roux as a thickening agent, perfected recipes and devised a system for classifying sauces. As a *garde-manger*, Carême popularized cold cuisine, emphasizing molds and aspic dishes. As a culinary professional, he designed kitchen tools, equipment and uniforms.

As an author, he wrote and illustrated important texts on the culinary arts, including *Le*

Courtesy of Barbara Wheaton

Maitre d'hotel francais (1822), describing the hundreds of dishes he personally created and cooked in the capitals of Europe; *Le Patissier royal parisian* (1825), containing fanciful designs for *les pieces montées*, the great decorative centerpieces that were the crowning glory of grand dinners; and his five-volume masterpiece on the state of his profession, *L'Art de la cuisine au XIXe siecle* (1833), the last two volumes of which were completed after his death by his associate Plumerey. Carême's writings almost single-handedly refined and summarized five hundred years of culinary evolution. But his treatises were not mere cookbooks. Rather, he analyzed cooking, old and new, emphasizing procedure and order and covering every aspect of the art known as *grande cuisine*.

Carême died before age 50, burnt out, according to Laurent Tailhade, "by the flame of his genius and the coal of the spits." But this may have been the glory he sought, for he once wrote:

> Imagine yourself in a large kitchen at the moment of a great dinner. . . . [S]ee twenty chefs coming, going, moving with speed in this cauldron of heat, look at the great mass of charcoal, a cubic meter for the cooking of entrées, and another mass on the ovens for the cooking of soups, sauces, ragouts, for frying and the water baths. Add to that a heap of burning wood in front of which four spits are turning, one which bears a sirloin weighing 45–50 pounds, the other fowl or game. In this furnace everyone moves with speed; not a sound is heard, only the chef has a right to speak, and at the sound of his voice, everyone obeys. Finally, the last straw; for about half an hour, all windows are closed so that the air does not cool the dishes as they are being served. This is the way we spend the best years of our lives. We must obey even when physical strength fails, but it is the burning charcoal that kills us. . . . [C]harcoal kills us but what does it matter? The shorter the life, the greater the glory.

cooking methods should be simple and direct whenever possible. The accompaniments and garnishes must be light and contribute to an overall harmony; the completed plates must be elegantly designed and decorated. Following these guidelines, some traditional cooking methods have been applied to untraditional ingredients, and ingredients have been combined in new and previously unorthodox fashions. For chefs with knowledge, skill, taste and judgment, this works.

THE LATE 20TH CENTURY—AN AMERICAN CULINARY REVOLUTION

During the last 30 years or so, two distinct culinary trends have emerged in the United States: "the hotter, the better" and "fresh food, simply prepared."

AUGUSTE ESCOFFIER (1846–1935)

Escoffier's brilliant culinary career began at the age of 13 in his uncle's restaurant and continued until his death at the age of 89. Called the "emperor of the world's kitchens," he is perhaps best known for defining French cuisine and dining during La Belle Époque (the "Gay Nineties").

Unlike Carême, Escoffier never worked in an aristocratic household. Rather, he exhibited his culinary skills in the dining rooms of the finest hotels in Europe, including the Place Vendôme in Paris and the Savoy and Carlton Hotels in London.

Escoffier did much to enhance the *grande cuisine* that arguably reached its perfection under Carême. Crediting Carême with providing the foundation for great–that is, French–cooking, Escoffier simplified the profusion of flavors, dishes and garnishes typifying Carême's work. He also streamlined some of Carême's overly elaborate and fussy procedures and classifications. For example, he reduced Carême's elaborate system of classifying sauces into the five

families of sauces still recognized today. Escoffier sought simplicity and aimed for the perfect balance of a few superb ingredients. Some consider his refinement of *grande cuisine* to have been so radical as to credit him with the development of a new cuisine referred to as *cuisine classique* (classic or classical cuisine).

His many writings include *Le Livre des menus* (1912), in which, discussing the principles of a well-planned meal, he analogizes a great dinner to a symphony with contrasting movements that should be appropriate to the occasion, the guests and the season, and *Ma cuisine* (1934), surveying *cuisine bourgeoisie*. But his most important contribution is a culinary treatise intended for the professional chef entitled *Le Guide culinaire* (1903). Still in use today, it is an astounding collection of more than 5000 classic cuisine recipes and garnishes. In it, Escoffier emphasizes the mastery of techniques, the thorough understanding of cooking, principles and the appreciation of ingredients– attributes he considered to be the building blocks professional chefs should use to create great dishes.

Escoffier was honored as a Chevalier of the French Legion of Honour in 1920 for his work in enhancing the reputation of French cuisine.

The first trend is due, in large part, to an unlikely source: the Immigration Act of 1965. Under its provisions, a large number of Asians immigrated to this country. They brought with them their rich culinary traditions and they ignited America's love affair with fiery hot cuisines. By the late 1970s, many Americans were no longer content with bland or overly salty pseudo-Chinese dishes such as chop suey and chow mein. They demanded authenticity and developed cravings for spicy dishes from Szechuan and Hunan provinces, Vietnam and Thailand. At the same time, Mexican food left the barrio and became mainstream. Burritos and tacos became routine menu items, while authentic regional Mexican dishes were sought out by middle America. Indeed, by the 1990s, people used more salsa than ketchup as a condiment.

During this same time period, restaurateurs and chefs began Americanizing the principles of French *nouvelle cuisine*. When Alice Waters opened Chez Panisse in Berkeley, California, in 1971, her goal was to serve fresh food, simply prepared. Rejecting the growing popularity of processed and packaged foods, Waters wanted to use fresh, seasonal and locally grown produce in simple preparations that preserved and emphasized the foods' natural flavors. Chez Panisse and the many chefs who passed through its kitchen launched a new style of cuisine that became known as **New American cuisine**. As Waters's culinary philosophy spread across the United States, farmers and chefs began working together to make fresh, locally grown foods available, and producers and suppliers began developing domestic sources for some of the high-quality ingredients that were once available only from overseas. Excellent foie gras from Long Island, New York, and goat cheese from Sonoma County, California, are just two examples.

By the mid-1980s, American chefs began to combine aspects of these two trends. Their work resulted in **fusion cuisine**. With fusion cuisine, ingredients or preparation methods associated with one ethnic or regional cuisine are combined with those of another. A fillet of Norwegian salmon might be grilled over hickory wood, then served on a bed of Japanese soba noodles with pesto cream

▶ **New American cuisine** a late-20th-century movement that began in California but has spread across the United States; it stresses the use of fresh, locally grown, seasonal produce and high-quality ingredients simply prepared in a fashion that preserves and emphasizes natural flavors

▶ **fusion cuisine** the blending or use of ingredients and/or preparation methods from various ethnic, regional or national cuisines in the same dish; also known as transnational cuisine

FERNAND POINT (1897–1955)

A massive man with a monumental personality, Point refined and modernized the classic cuisine of Escoffier. By doing so, he laid the foundations for *nouvelle cuisine*.

Point received his early training in some of the finest hotel-restaurant kitchens in Paris. In 1922, he and his family moved to Vienne, a city in southwest France near Lyon, and opened a restaurant. Two years later his father left the restaurant to Fernand, who renamed it *La Pyra-* *mide*. During the succeeding years, it became one of the culinary wonders of the world.

Point disdained dominating sauces and distracting accompaniments and garnishes. He believed that each dish should have a single dominant ingredient, flavor or theme; garnishes must be simple and match "like a tie to a suit." Procedure was of great importance. He devoted equal efforts to frying an egg and creating the marjolaine (a light almond and hazelnut spongecake filled with chocolate and praline buttercreams). His goal was to use the finest of raw ingredients to produce perfect food that looked elegant and simple. But simplicity was not easy to achieve. As he once said, "a bearnaise sauce is simply an egg yolk, a shallot, a little tarragon vinegar, and butter, but it takes years of practice for the result to be perfect."

sauce, for example, while duck confit prepared by the traditional French method is seasoned with lemongrass, ginger and chiles.

Along with this new interest in and appreciation for American ingredients and American tastes has come a new respect for American chefs. Many European and American food writers and pundits now consider American chefs to be among the best in the world, a fact they often triumph at the same time they express their concern about the general decline of French cuisine and the exodus of European chefs to America. In addition, the American public has taken food to heart.

Many chefs have been elevated to celebrity status; an entire cable television network is devoted to cooking. Bookstore and library shelves are jammed with cookbooks, and newspapers and magazines regularly review restaurants or report on culinary trends. With gourmet shops and cookware stores in most malls, cooking has become both a hobby and a spectator sport. All this has helped to inspire a generation of American teenagers to pursue careers behind the stove—and in front of the camera.

▶ INFLUENCES ON MODERN FOOD SERVICE OPERATIONS

From Monsieur Boulanger's humble establishment, a great industry has grown. Today, almost 850,000 public dining facilities operate in the United States alone. The dramatic growth and diversification of the food service industry is due in part to the Industrial Revolution and the social and economic changes it wrought, including the introduction of new technologies, foods, concerns and consumers.

NEW TECHNOLOGIES

Technology has always had a profound effect on cooking. For example, the development of clay and, later, metal vessels that could contain liquids and withstand as well as conduct heat offered prehistoric cooks the opportunity to stew, make soups and porridge, pickle and brine foods and control fermentation. But it was not until the rapid technological advances fostered by the Industrial Revolution that anything approaching the modern kitchen was possible.

One of the most important advancements was the introduction of the cast-iron stove. Prior to the 19th century, most cooking was done on spits or grills or in cauldrons or pots set on or in a wood- or coal-burning hearth. Hearthside cooking did not lend itself well to the simultaneous preparation of many items or to items requiring constant and delicate attention. With the introduction of cast-iron stoves during the 1800s (first wood- and coal-burning; by midcentury, gas; and by the early 20th century, electric), cooks could more comfortably and safely approach the heat source and control its temperatures. They were also able to efficiently prepare and hold for later use or service a multitude of smaller amounts of items requiring different cooking methods or ingredients, a necessity at a restaurant simultaneously catering to different diners' demands.

Also of great importance were developments in food preservation and storage techniques. For thousands of years, food had been preserved by sun-drying, salting, smoking, pickling, sugar-curing or fermenting. Although useful, these procedures destroy or distort the appearance and flavor of most foods. By the early 19th century, preserving techniques that had minimal effect on appearance and flavor began to emerge. For example, by 1800, the Frenchman François Appert successfully "canned" foods by subjecting foods stored in sterilized glass jars to very high heat. An early mechanical refrigerator was developed by the mid-1800s; soon reliable iceboxes, refrigerators and, later, freezers were available. During the 20th century, freeze-drying, vacuum-packing and irradiation became common preservation techniques.

While advancements were being made in preservation and storage techniques, developments in transportation technology were also underway. During the 19th century, steam-powered ships and railroads were able to bring foods quickly to market from distant suppliers. Indeed, by the 1870s, Chicago meat-packers were routinely supplying Europe with beef from the western Great Plains. During the 20th century, temperature-controlled cargo ships, trains, trucks and airplanes all were used as part of an integrated worldwide food transportation network. Combined with dependable food preservation and storage techniques, improved transportation networks have freed chefs from seasonal and geographic limitations in their choice of foods and have expanded consumers' culinary horizons.

Engineering advancements also have facilitated or even eliminated much routine kitchen work. Since the start of the Industrial Revolution, chefs have come to rely increasingly on mechanical and motorized food processors, mixers and cutters as well as a wealth of sophisticated kitchen equipment such as high-carbon stainless steel knife blades, infrared thermometers and induction cooktops.

NEW FOODS

Modern food preservation, storage and transportation techniques have made both fresh and exotic foods regularly available to chefs and consumers.

Advancements in agriculture such as the switch from organic to chemical fertilizers and the introduction of pesticides and drought- or pest-resistant strains have resulted in increased yields of healthy crops. Traditional hybridization techniques and, more recently, genetic engineering have produced new or improved grains and, for better or for worse, fruits and vegetables that have a longer shelf life and are more amenable to mass-production handling, storage and transportation methods.

Likewise, advancements in animal husbandry and aquaculture have led to a more reliable supply of leaner meat, poultry and fish. Moreover, foods found traditionally only in the wild (for example, game, wild rice and many mushrooms) are now being raised commercially and are routinely available.

Food preservation and processing techniques have also led to the development of prepackaged, prepared convenience foods, some of which are actually quite good. After careful thought and testing, today's chef can rely on some of these products. Doing so allows greater flexibility and more time to devote to other preparations.

NEW CONCERNS

Consumer concerns about nutrition and diet have fueled changes in the food service industry. Obviously, what we eat affects our health. Adequate amounts of certain nutrients promote good health by preventing deficiencies; good nutrition

A VERY BIG BUSINESS INDEED

The National Restaurant Association, which closely monitors the economic impact of the U.S. food service industry, issued the following statistics for 2001:

- Daily food service industry sales averaged $1.1 billion; annual sales were approximately $400 billion.
- More than 54 billion meals were eaten in restaurants and school and work cafeterias.
- The food service industry claimed approximately 45 percent of the U.S. food dollar.
- More than 11 million people were employed in the industry, making it the second-largest employer after the government.
- One-third of all American adults have worked in the food service industry at some time during their lives.

also helps prevent chronic diseases and increases longevity. Chefs should provide their customers with nutritious foods.

The public has long been concerned about food safety. Federal, state and local governments have helped promote food safety by inspecting and grading meats and poultry, regulating label contents for packaged foods and setting sanitation standards. All these standards, especially sanitation standards, affect the way foods are prepared, stored and served.

Concerns about nutrition and food safety have also resulted in renewed interest in organically grown fruits and vegetables and free-range-raised animals.

NEW CONSUMERS

▶ **global cuisine** foods (often commercially produced items) or preparation methods that have become ubiquitous throughout the world; for example, curries and French-fried potatoes

▶ **national cuisine** the characteristic cuisine of a nation

▶ **regional cuisine** a set of recipes based upon local ingredients, traditions and practices; within a larger geographical, political, cultural or social unit, regional cuisines are often variations of one another that blend together to create a national cuisine

▶ **ethnic cuisine** the cuisine of a group of people having a common cultural heritage, as opposed to the cuisine of a group of people bound together by geography or political factors

Demographic and social changes have contributed to the diversification of the food service industry by creating or identifying new consumer groups with their own desires or needs. By tailoring their menu, prices and décor accordingly, food service operations can cater to consumers defined by age (baby boomers and seniors, in particular), type of household (singles, couples and families), income, education and geography.

Since World War II, there has also been a rapid increase in the number and types of institutions providing food services. These include hospitals, schools, retirement centers, hotels and resorts (which may in turn have fine dining, coffee shop, banquet and room service facilities), factories and office complexes. Each of these institutions presents the professional chef with unique challenges, whether they be culinary, dietary or budgetary.

Through travel or exposure to the many books and magazines about food, consumers are becoming better educated and more sophisticated. Educated consumers provide a market for new foods and cuisines as well as an appreciation for a job well done.

Although some consumers may frequent a particular restaurant because its chef or owner is a celebrity or the restaurant is riding high on a crest of fad or fashion, most consumers choose a restaurant—whether it be a fast-food burger place or an elegant French restaurant—because it provides quality food at a cost they are willing to pay. To remain successful, then, the restaurant must carefully balance its commitment to quality with marketplace realities.

▶ THE FOOD SERVICE OPERATION

▶ **brigade** a system of staffing a kitchen so that each worker is assigned a set of specific tasks; these tasks are often related by cooking method, equipment or the types of foods being produced

To function efficiently, a food service operation must be well organized and staffed with appropriate personnel. This staff is sometimes called a **brigade**. Although a chef will be most familiar with the back-of-the-house or kitchen brigade, he or she should also understand how the dining room or front of the house operates.

THE CLASSIC KITCHEN BRIGADE

Escoffier is credited with developing the kitchen brigade system used in large restaurant kitchens. From the chaos and redundancy found in the private kitchens of the aristocracy, he created a distinct hierarchy of responsibilities and functions for commercial food service operations.

At the top is the *chef de cuisine* or *chef*, who is responsible for all kitchen operations, developing menu items and setting the kitchen's tone and tempo.

His or her principal assistant is the *sous-chef* (the under chef or second chef), who is responsible for scheduling personnel and replacing the chef and station chefs as necessary. The *sous-chef* also often functions as the *aboyeur* (expediter or announcer), who accepts the orders from the dining room, relays them to the various station chefs and then reviews the dishes before service.

The *chefs de partie* (station chefs) produce the menu items and are under the direct supervision of the chef or *sous-chef*. Previously, whenever a cook needed an item, he or his assistants produced it; thus several cooks could be making the same sauce or basic preparation. Under Escoffier's system, each station chef is assigned a specific task based on either the cooking method and equipment or the category of items to be produced. They include the following:

▶ The *saucier* (sauté station chef), who holds one of the most demanding jobs in the kitchen, is responsible for all sautéed items and most sauces.

▶ The *poissonier* (fish station chef) is responsible for fish and shellfish items and their sauces. This position is occasionally combined with the sauce station.

▶ The *grillardin* (grill station chef) is responsible for all grilled items.

▶ The *friturier* (fry station chef) is responsible for all fried items.

▶ The *rotisseur* (roast station chef) is responsible for all roasted items and jus or other related sauces. The grill and fry stations are sometimes subsumed into the roast station.

▶ The *potager* (soup station chef) is responsible for soups and stocks.

▶ The *legumier* (vegetable station chef) is responsible for all vegetable and starch items.

▶ The *potager* and *legumier* functions are often combined into a single vegetable station whose chef is known as the *entremetier*. *Entremets* were the courses served after the roast and usually comprised vegetables, fruits, fritters or sweet items (the sorbet served before the main course in some contemporary restaurants is a vestigial *entremet*).

▶ The *garde-manger* (pantry chef) is responsible for cold food preparations, including salads and salad dressings, cold appetizers, charcuterie items, pâtés, terrines and similar dishes. The *garde-manger* supervises the *boucher* (butcher), who is responsible for butchering meats and poultry (fish and shellfish are usually fabricated by the fish station chef), as well as the chefs responsible for hors d'oeuvre and breakfast items.

▶ The *tournant*, also known as the roundsman or swing cook, works where needed.

▶ The *patissier* (pastry chef) is responsible for all baked items, including breads, pastries and desserts. Unlike the several station chefs, the *patissier* is not necessarily under the *sous-chef*'s direct supervision. The *patissier* supervises the *boulanger* (bread baker), who makes the breads, rolls and baked dough containers used for other menu items (for example, *bouchées* and *feuilletés*); the *confiseur*, who makes candies and petits fours; the *glacier*, who makes all chilled and frozen desserts; and the *decorateur*, who makes showpieces and special cakes.

▶ Depending upon the size and needs of any station or area, there are one or more *demi-chefs* (assistants) and *commis* (apprentices) who work with the station chef or pastry chef to learn the area.

THE MODERN KITCHEN BRIGADE

Today, most food service operations use a simplified version of Escoffier's kitchen brigade.

The **executive chef** coordinates kitchen activities and directs the kitchen staff's training and work efforts. The executive chef plans menus and creates recipes. He or she sets and enforces nutrition, safety and sanitation standards and participates in (or at least observes) the preparation and presentation of menu items to ensure that quality standards are rigorously and consistently maintained. He or she is also responsible for purchasing food items and, often, equipment. In some food service operations, the executive chef may assist in designing the menu, dining room and kitchen. He or she trains the dining room staff so that

THE DINING ROOM

Like the back-of-the-house (that is, kitchen) staff, the front-of-the-house (that is, dining room) staff is also organized into a brigade. A traditional dining room brigade is led by the **dining room manager** (French *maître d'hotel* or *maître d'*), who generally trains all service personnel, oversees wine selections and works with the chef to develop the menu. He or she organizes the seating chart and may also seat the guests. Working subordinate to him or her are:

- The **wine steward** (French *chef de vin* or *sommelier*), who is responsible for the wine service, including purchasing wines, assisting guests in selecting wines and serving the wines.
- The **headwaiter** (French *chef de salle*), who is responsible for service throughout the dining room or a section of it. In smaller operations, his or her role may be assumed by the *maître d'* or a captain.

- The **captains** (French *chefs d'étage*), who are responsible for explaining the menu to guests and taking their orders. They are also responsible for any tableside preparations.
- The **front waiters** (French *chefs de rang*), who are responsible for assuring that the tables are set properly for each course, foods are delivered properly to the proper tables and the needs of the guests are met.
- The **back waiters** (French *demi-chefs de rang* or *commis de rang*, also known as dining room attendants or buspersons), who are responsible for clearing plates, refilling water glasses and other general tasks appropriate for new dining room workers.

Whether a restaurant uses this entire array of staff depends upon the nature and size of the restaurant and the type of service provided. With **American service,** there is one waiter (also called a server) who takes the order and

brings the food to the table. The table is then cleaned by a dining room attendant. With **French service**, there are two waiters: a captain and a waiter. The captain takes the order, does the tableside cooking and brings the drinks, appetizers, entrées and desserts to the table. The waiter serves bread and water, clears each course, crumbs the table and serves the coffee. With **Russian service**, the entrée, vegetables and potatoes are served from a platter onto a plate by the waiter. With **buffet service**, usually found in specialty restaurants and some institutional settings such as schools and correctional facilities, diners generally serve themselves or are served by workers assigned to specific areas of the buffet. Restaurants offering buffet service generally charge by the meal; if they charge by the dish, they are known as cafeterias.

they can correctly answer questions about the menu. He or she may also work with food purveyors to learn about new food items and products, as well as with catering directors, equipment vendors, food stylists, restaurant consultants, public relations specialists, sanitation engineers, nutritionists and dietitians.

The executive chef is assisted by a **sous-chef** or **executive sous-chef**, who participates in, supervises and coordinates the preparation of menu items. His or her primary responsibility is to make sure that the food is prepared, portioned, garnished and presented according to the executive chef's standards. The sous-chef may be the cook principally responsible for producing menu items and supervising the kitchen.

Large hotels and conference centers with multiple dining facilities may have one or more **area chefs**, each responsible for a specific facility or function. There could be, for instance, a restaurant chef and a banquet chef. Area chefs usually report to the executive chef. Each area chef, in turn, has a brigade working under him or her.

Like Escoffier's station chefs, **line cooks** (or section cooks) are responsible for preparing menu items according to recipe specifications. Making the most of time, talent, space and equipment, the chef assigns responsibilities to each of the line cooks.

The **pastry chef** is responsible for developing recipes for and preparing desserts, pastries, frozen desserts and breads. He or she is usually responsible for purchasing the food items used in the bakeshop.

And, as in Escoffier's days, **assistants** and **apprentices** are assigned where needed in today's kitchens.

New styles of dining have created new positions since Escoffier's days. The most notable is the **short-order cook**, who is responsible for quickly preparing foods to order in smaller operations. He or she will work the broiler, deep-fat fryer and griddle as well as make sandwiches and even some sautéed items. Another is the **institutional cook**, who generally works with large quantities of prepackaged or prepared foods for a captive market such as a school, hospital or prison.

▶ THE PROFESSIONAL CHEF

Although there is no one recipe for producing a good professional chef, we believe that with knowledge, skill, taste, judgment, dedication and pride a student chef will mature into a professional chef.

KNOWLEDGE

Chefs must be able to identify, purchase, utilize and prepare a wide variety of foods. They should be able to train and supervise a safe, skilled and efficient staff. To do all this successfully, chefs must possess a body of knowledge and understand and apply certain scientific and business principles. Schooling helps. A professional culinary program should, at a minimum, provide the student chef with a basic knowledge of foods, food styles and the methods used to prepare foods. Student chefs should also have an understanding of sanitation, nutrition and business procedures such as food costing.

This book is designed to help you learn these basics. Many chapters have extensive sections identifying foods and equipment. Throughout this book, we emphasize culinary principles, not recipes. Whenever possible, whether it be preparing puff pastry or grilling a steak, we focus on the general procedure, highlighting fundamental principles and skills; we discuss both the how and why of cooking. Only then are specific applications and sample recipes given. We also want you to have a sense of the rich tradition of cookery, so informative sidebars on food history, chef biographies and other topics are scattered throughout the book.

In this way, we follow the trail blazed by Escoffier, who wrote in the introduction to *Le Guide culinaire* that his book is not intended to be a compendium of recipes slavishly followed, but rather his treatise should be a tool that leaves his colleagues "free to develop their own methods and follow their own inspiration; . . . the art of cooking . . . will evolve as a society evolves, . . . only basic rules remain unaltered."

As with any profession, an education does not stop at graduation. The acquisition of knowledge continues after the student chef joins the ranks of the employed. He or she should take additional classes on unique or ethnic cuisines, nutrition, business management or specialized skills. He or she should regularly review some of the many periodicals and books devoted to cooking, should travel and should try new dishes to broaden his or her culinary horizons. The professional chef should also become involved in professional organizations (see Appendix I) in order to meet his or her peers and exchange ideas.

SKILL

Culinary schooling alone does not make a student a chef. Nothing but practical, hands-on experience will provide even the most academically gifted student with the skills needed to produce, consistently and efficiently, quality foods or to organize, train, motivate and supervise a staff.

Many food service operations recognize that new workers, even those who have graduated from culinary programs, need time and experience to develop and hone their skills. Therefore, many graduates start in entry-level positions. Do not be discouraged; advancement will come, and the training pays off in the long run. Today, culinary styles and fashions change frequently. What does not go out of fashion are well-trained, skilled and knowledgeable chefs. They can adapt.

TASTE

No matter how knowledgeable or skilled the chef, he or she must be able to produce foods that taste great, or the consumer will not return. A chef can do so only if he or she is confident about his or her own sense of taste.

ON TASTE

Taste is composed of about ten thousand compounds. When we think of taste, we normally think in terms of the language we are familiar with and the foods we grew up with. The structure of our taste is formed very early, basically when we start eating baby food. As Westerners, we divide taste into four major groups: sweet, salty, bitter and sour. The Chinese include a fifth, hot (spicy), and Southeast Asians add aromatic and pungent. So there are actually seven or more types. Americans, however, largely rely on sweet and salty. They don't use sour and bitter very much. They certainly don't use hot very much. Nor do they use aromatic or strong pungent things like fish paste very often. We really use only about 30 percent of our palate. To compare this to sight, it's as if we are colorblind, unable to perceive and enjoy fully five out of every seven colors we see. This is why we sometimes have trouble "acquiring" a taste for ethnic foods.

Westerners have a lineal palate, which is set up on sweet and salty with very few counterpoints and harmonies. For instance, if you eat in the European manner, you usually begin with an appetizer, which may be salty or hot. Then you have soup, then a fish course, then a meat course, then a sweet. You are using different parts of your palate, but one after another, or linearly. Asian cuisines, however, use sweet, hot, bitter and sour at the same time. You're eating circularly. The meal is not a lineal progress to some point, like dessert. You may have already had fruit or a sweet in the meal, which is a much more satisfying and actually much more healthy way to eat. European food, like European art, is more concerned with finished form. Most ethnic things are concerned with process and expression.

You must train your mind to go after flavor characteristics and become involved in the process of eating. You must look for flavors in different parts of your mouth. Think about how quickly flavors appear in the mouth and how long the flavors are. Think about the finish. You must develop a very good sensitivity to the finish of the product; otherwise, you overseason and lose the compositional balance.

MARK MILLER, Chef/Owner, Red Sage, Washington, D.C.,
and Coyote Cafe, Santa Fe, NM

▶ **gastronomy** the art and science of eating well

▶ **gourmet** a connoisseur of fine food and drink

▶ **gourmand** a connoisseur of fine food and drink, often to excess

▶ **gourmet foods** foods of the highest quality, perfectly prepared and beautifully presented

Our total perception of taste is a complex combination of smell, taste, sight, sound and texture. All senses are involved in the enjoyment of eating; all must be considered in creating or preparing a dish. The chef should develop a taste memory by sampling foods, both familiar and unfamiliar. The chef should also think about what he or she tastes, making notes and experimenting with flavor combinations and cooking methods. But a chef should not be inventive simply for the sake of invention. Rather, he or she must consider how the flavors, appearances, textures and aromas of various foods will interact to create a total taste experience.

JUDGMENT

Selecting menu items, determining how much of what item to order, deciding whether and how to combine ingredients and approving finished items for service are all matters of judgment. Although knowledge and skill play a role in developing judgment, sound judgment comes only with experience. And real experience is often accompanied by failure. Do not be upset or surprised when a dish does not turn out as you expected. Learn from your mistakes as well as from your successes; only then will you develop sound judgment.

DEDICATION

Becoming a chef is hard work; so is being one. The work is often physically taxing, the hours are usually long and the pace is frequently hectic. Despite these pressures, the chef is expected to efficiently produce consistently fine foods that are properly prepared, seasoned, garnished and presented. To do so, the chef must be dedicated to the job.

The dedicated chef should never falter. The food service industry is competitive and depends upon the continuing goodwill of an often fickle public. One bad dish or one off night can result in a disgruntled diner and lost business. The chef should always be mindful of the food prepared and the customer served.

The chef must also be dedicated to his or her staff. Virtually all food service operations rely on teamwork to get the job done well. Good teamwork requires a positive attitude and dedication to a shared goal.

PRIDE

Not only is it important that the job be well done, but the professional chef should have a sense of pride in doing it well. Pride should also extend to personal appearance and behavior in and around the kitchen. The professional chef should be well-groomed and in uniform when working.

The professional chef's uniform consists of comfortable shoes, trousers (either solid white, solid black, black-and-white checked or black-and-white striped), a white double-breasted jacket, an apron and a neckerchief usually knotted or tied cravat style. The uniform has certain utilitarian aspects: Checked trousers disguise stains; the double-breasted white jacket can be rebuttoned to hide dirt, and the double layer of fabric protects from scalds and burns; the neckerchief absorbs facial perspiration; and the apron protects the uniform and insulates the body. This uniform should be worn with pride. Shoes should be polished; trousers and jacket should be pressed.

The crowning element of the uniform is the toque. A toque is the tall white hat worn by chefs almost everywhere. Although the toque traces its origin to the monasteries of the 6th century, the style worn today was introduced at the end of the 19th century. Most chefs now wear a standard six- or nine-inch-high toque, but historically, a cook's rank in the kitchen dictated the type of hat worn. Beginners wore flat-topped calottes; cooks with more advanced skills wore low toques and the master chefs wore high toques called dodin-bouffants. Culinary lore holds that the toque's pleats—101 in all—represent the 101 ways its wearer can successfully prepare eggs.

CONCLUSION

The art and science of cookery form a noble profession with a rich history and long traditions. With knowledge, skill, taste, judgment, dedication and pride, the student chef can become part of this profession. In this book, we provide you with the basic knowledge and describe the techniques in which you must become skilled. Dedicate yourself to learning this information and mastering your skills. Once you have done so, take pride in your accomplishments. Good luck.

QUESTIONS FOR DISCUSSION

1 Describe the kitchen brigade system. What is its significance in today's professional kitchens?
2 What are the roles of a chef, sous-chef and line cook in a modern kitchen?
3 Describe the differences in a meal prepared by Carême and one prepared by Point.
4 List and explain three technological advances affecting food preparation.
5 Discuss the societal changes that have contributed to diversification in the modern food service industry.
6 The newspapers in most large cities publish restaurant reviews. Use the Internet to find restaurant reviews from a city other than the one in which you live. Select one or two restaurants where you would like to dine the next time you visit that city. Why did you select these particular establishments?
7 The James Beard Foundation recognizes and honors outstanding American chefs each year. Who was James Beard? Which chefs are currently considered some of the most outstanding in the United States? Why?

OUR LIVES ARE NOT IN THE LAP OF THE GODS, BUT IN THE LAP OF OUR COOKS.
—*Lin Yutang, Chinese-American writer, in* The Importance of Living, *1937*

2

FOOD SAFETY AND SANITATION

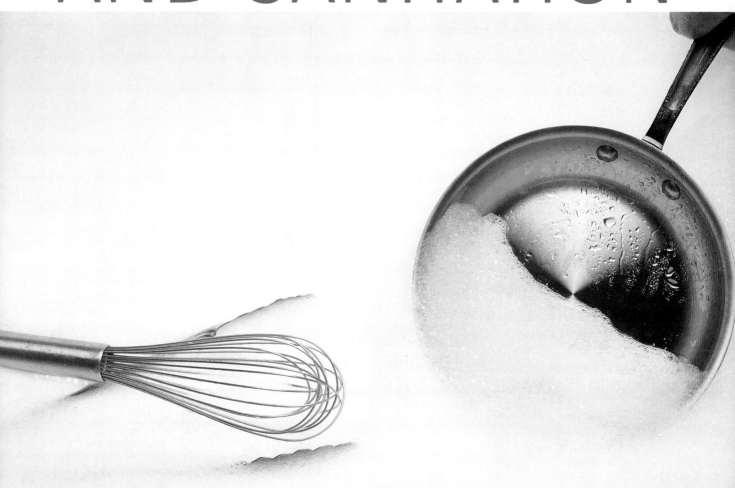

AFTER STUDYING THIS CHAPTER, YOU WILL BE ABLE TO:

▶ identify the causes of food-borne illnesses

▶ handle foods in a safe manner

▶ explain and follow a HACCP system

▶ take appropriate actions to create and maintain a safe and sanitary working environment

The U.S. Public Health Service identifies more than 40 diseases that can be transmitted through food. Many can cause serious illness; some are even deadly. Therefore, providing consumers with safe food is the food handler's most important responsibility. Unfortunately, food handlers are also the primary cause of food-related illnesses.

By understanding what causes food-borne illnesses and what can be done to prevent them, you will be better able to protect your customers. This chapter, however, is not meant to be a complete discussion of sanitation in food service operations. But it should alert you to practices that can result in food-borne illnesses.

Federal, state, county and municipal health, building and other codes are designed in part to ensure that food is handled in a safe and proper manner. Always consult your local health department for information and guidance. And always be conscious of what you can do to create and maintain a safe product as well as a safe environment for your customers, your fellow employees and yourself.

▶ **biological hazard** a danger to the safety of food caused by disease-causing microorganisms such as bacteria, molds, yeasts, viruses or fungi

▶ **chemical hazard** a danger to the safety of food caused by chemical substances, especially cleaning agents, pesticides and toxic metals

▶ **physical hazard** a danger to the safety of food caused by particles such as glass chips, metal shavings, bits of wood or other foreign matter

Sanitation refers to the creation and maintenance of conditions that will prevent food contamination or food-borne illness. **Contamination** refers to the presence, generally unintended, of harmful organisms or substances. Contaminants can be (1) biological, (2) chemical or (3) physical. When consumed in sufficient quantities, food-borne contaminants can cause illness or injury, long-lasting disease or even death.

Contamination occurs in two ways: direct contamination and cross-contamination. **Direct contamination** is the contamination of raw foods, or the plants or animals from which they come, in their natural settings or habitats. Chemical and biological contaminants such as bacteria and fungi are present in the air, soil and water. So foods can be easily contaminated by their general exposure to the environment: Grains can become contaminated by soil fumigants in the field, and shellfish can become contaminated by ingesting toxic marine algae.

Chemicals and microorganisms generally cannot move on their own, however. They need to be transported, an event known as **cross-contamination**. The major cause of cross-contamination is people. Food handlers can transfer biological, chemical and physical contaminants to food while processing, preparing, cooking or serving it. It is therefore necessary to view sanitation as the correction of problems caused by direct contamination and the prevention of problems caused by cross-contamination during processing and service.

▶ DIRECT CONTAMINATION

BIOLOGICAL CONTAMINANTS

▶ **microorganisms** single-celled organisms as well as tiny plants and animals that can be seen only through a microscope

Several **microorganisms**, primarily bacteria, parasites, viruses and fungi, can cause biologically based food-borne illnesses. By understanding how these organisms live and reproduce, you can better understand how to protect food from them.

BACTERIA

Bacteria, which are single-celled microorganisms, are the leading cause of food-borne illnesses. See Figure 2.1. Some bacteria are beneficial, such as those that aid in digesting food or decomposing garbage. Other bacteria spoil food, but without rendering it unfit for human consumption. These bacteria, called **putrefactives**, are not a sanitation concern. (Indeed, in some cultures, they are not even a culinary concern. Cultures differ on what constitutes "bad" meat, for example, and game is sometimes hung for a time to allow bacteria to grow.) The bacteria that are dangerous when consumed by humans are called **pathogenic**. These bacteria must be destroyed or controlled in a food service operation.

Most bacteria reproduce by binary fission: Their genetic material is first duplicated and the nucleus then splits, each new nucleus taking some of the cellular material with it. See Figure 2.2. Under favorable conditions each bacterium can divide every 15–30 minutes. Within 12 hours, one bacterium can become a colony of 72 billion bacteria, more than enough to cause serious illness.

Some rod-shaped bacteria are capable of forming spores. Spores are thick-walled structures used as protection against a hostile environment. The bacteria essentially hibernate within their spores, where they can survive extreme conditions that would otherwise destroy them. When conditions become favorable, the bacteria return to a viable state. This is important in food sanitation because heating or sanitizing techniques may not destroy bacterial spores.

Intoxications and Infections

Depending upon the particular microorganism, pathogenic bacteria can cause illnesses in humans in one of three ways: by intoxication, infection or toxin-mediated infection. See Table 2.1.

Botulism is a well-known example of an **intoxication**. Certain bacteria produce **toxins**, byproducts of their life processes. You cannot smell, see or taste toxins. Ingesting these toxin-producing bacteria by themselves does not cause illness. But when their toxins are ingested, the toxins can poison the consumer. Proper food-handling techniques are critical in preventing an intoxication because even if a food is cooked to a sufficiently high temperature to kill all bacteria present, the toxins they leave behind are usually not destroyed.

The second type of bacterial illness is an **infection**. Salmonella is an especially well-known example. An infection occurs when live pathogenic bacteria (infectants) are ingested. The bacteria then live in the consumer's intestinal tract.

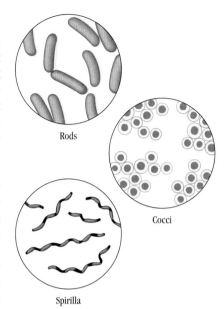

Rods

Cocci

Spirilla

FIGURE 2.1 ▶ **Bacteria can be classified by shape: Rods are short, tubular structures; cocci are discs, some of which form clusters; and spirilla are corkscrews.**

▶ **pathogen** any organism that causes disease; usually refers to bacteria

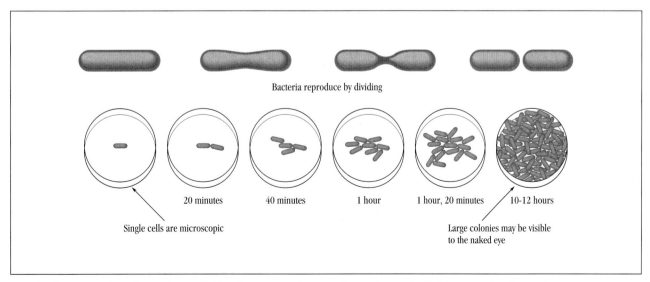

Bacteria reproduce by dividing

Single cells are microscopic

20 minutes   40 minutes   1 hour   1 hour, 20 minutes   10-12 hours

Large colonies may be visible to the naked eye

FIGURE 2.2 ▶ **One bacterium divides into two; the two bacteria each divide, creating four; the four become 16 and so on. It takes only a very short time for one bacterium to produce millions more.**

Table 2.1 CHARACTERISTICS OF BACTERIAL ILLNESSES

COMMON NAME	ORGANISM	FORM	COMMON SOURCES	PREVENTION
Staph	*Staphylococcus aureus*	Toxin	Starchy foods, cold meats, bakery items, custards, milk products, humans with infected wounds or sores	Wash hands and utensils before use; exclude unhealthy food handlers; avoid having foods at room temperature
Perfringens or CP	*Clostridium perfringens*	Cells and toxin	Reheated meats, sauces, stews, casseroles	Keep cooked foods at an internal temperature of 140°F (60°C) or higher; reheat leftovers to an internal temperature of 165°F (74°C) or higher
Botulism	*Clostridium botulinum*	Toxin, cells, spores	Cooked foods held for an extended time at warm temperatures with limited oxygen, rice, potatoes, smoked fish, canned vegetables	Keep cooked foods at an internal temperature of 140°F (60°C) or higher or 40°F (4°C) or lower; reheat leftovers thoroughly; discard swollen cans
Salmonella	*Salmonella*	Cells	Poultry, eggs, milk, meats, fecal contamination	Thoroughly cook all meat, poultry, fish and eggs; avoid cross-contamination with raw foods; maintain good personal hygiene
Strep	*Streptococcus*	Cells	Infected food handlers	Do not allow employees to work if ill; protect foods from customers' coughs and sneezes
E. coli or 0157	*Escherichia coli* 0157:H7 (enteropathogenic strains)	Cells and toxins	Any food, especially raw milk, raw vegetables, raw or rare beef, humans	Thoroughly cook or reheat items
Listeria	*Listeria monocytogenes*	Cells	Milk products, humans, deli meats	Avoid raw milk and cheese made from unpasteurized milk; keep storage areas clean

POTENTIALLY HAZARDOUS FOODS

A potentially hazardous food (PHF) is any food or food ingredient that will support the rapid growth of infectious or toxigenic microorganisms, or the slower growth of *Clostridium botulinum*. Potentially hazardous foods include the following:

- Food from an animal source (for example, meat, fish, shellfish, poultry, milk and eggs)
- Food from a plant that has been heat-treated (for example, cooked rice, beans, potatoes, soy products and pasta)
- Raw seed sprouts
- Cut melons
- Garlic in oil mixtures that are not acidified or otherwise appropriately modified at a processing plant
- Foods containing any of the preceding items (for example, custards, sauces and casseroles)

It is the living bacteria, not their waste products, that cause an illness. Infectants must be alive when eaten for them to do any harm. Fortunately, these bacteria can be destroyed by cooking foods to sufficiently high temperatures, usually 165°F (74°C) or higher.

The third type of bacterial illness has characteristics of both an intoxication and an infection, and is referred to as a **toxin-mediated infection**. Examples are *Clostridium perfringens* and *Escherichia coli* 0157:H7. When these living organisms are ingested, they establish colonies in human or animal intestinal tracts where they then produce toxins. These bacteria are particularly dangerous for young children, the elderly and the infirm.

Preventing Bacterial Intoxications and Infections

All bacteria, like other living things, need certain conditions in order to complete their life cycles. Like humans, they need food, a comfortable temperature, moisture, the proper pH, the proper atmosphere and time. The best way to prevent bacterial intoxications and infections is to attack the factors bacteria need to survive and multiply.

FOOD Bacteria need food for energy and growth. The foods on which bacteria thrive are referred to as **potentially hazardous foods (PHF)**. They are generally high in protein and include animal-based products, cooked grains and some cooked vegetables. These foods and items containing these foods must be handled with great care.

THE FOOD-BORNE ILLNESS CRISIS IN AMERICA

America is confronted with a food-related health crisis of unprecedented proportions. The Centers for Disease Control and Prevention (CDC) have estimated that there are some 76 million incidents of food-related illness in the United States annually. Of these, an estimated 325,000 Americans are hospitalized and 5,000 die each year. Yet most Americans are unaware of this crisis and, indeed, many who suffer from food poisoning are not even aware of the cause. Symptoms may take a week or longer to appear, and victims frequently incorrectly attribute the distress and discomfort to stomach flu. It is not until the victims' afflictions become acute that tests are taken to determine the real cause. For those at risk—children, the elderly and anyone with a compromised immune system—this is frequently too late and the consequences can be deadly.

In his best-selling book, *Fast Food Nation*, Eric Schlosser points out that one cause for this increase in food-borne illnesses is the vast expansion of the meat-packing industry due to increased demand from the fast-food industry. Indeed, recent *E. coli* outbreaks have been traced to meat processors' operations, just as *Salmonella* has increasingly been traced to poultry operations.

While the health problems that Schlosser raises are important and should not be glossed over, they should not be exaggerated either. The Food Safety and Inspection Service (FSIS), a branch of the U.S. Department of Agriculture (USDA), has tested more than 26,000 samples of ground beef since 1996. Of these, only 25 tested positive for *E. coli* and none of these samples were associated with any outbreak of illness. Even if health problems in the meat-packing industry were somehow solved tomorrow, food-borne illnesses would likely still be on the rise. The Government Accounting Office has estimated that 85 percent of food-borne illnesses comes from fruits, vegetables, seafood and cheeses—not meat or poultry.

Schlosser also raises concerns about the fat and nutritional content of the food served in fast-food establishments. Obesity and high cholesterol can cause health problems, and consuming vast quantities of fast food can contribute to potential illness. However, for most Americans an occasional trip to McDonald's is not hazardous to their health. It just depends on the rest of their diet. And popular images to the contrary, fast-food establishments have a good record of cleanliness when compared with other restaurants—and particularly when compared with home kitchens.

In fact, food safety experts have concluded that the home is the number one place where food-borne illnesses originate. Indeed, most home kitchens would not pass food inspections that public facilities regularly pass with flying colors. And most cases of illnesses caused by *E. coli* and *Salmonella*, even those originating at meat and poultry packers, could have been averted if home cooks had followed basic health procedures: properly storing meat and poultry, frequently washing their hands, promptly disinfecting all areas touched by raw meat or poultry and correctly cooking foods at the appropriate high temperatures for the appropriate period of time.

Of course, food inspections need to be increased and conditions improved at some meat and poultry packing plants. However, while blaming particular elements in the food system may bring visibility to serious problems, contamination can occur at many points along the way in the food system. If this food-related health crisis is to be controlled, it must be approached systemically from the farm to the fork.

ANDREW F. SMITH teaches culinary history at the New School University and is the author of eight books on culinary topics. He is editor-in-chief of the forthcoming *Oxford Encyclopedia of American Food and Drink*.

TEMPERATURE Temperature is the most important factor in the pathogenic bacteria's environment because it is the factor most easily controlled by food service workers. Most microorganisms are destroyed at high temperatures. Freezing slows but does not stop growth, nor does it destroy bacteria.

Most bacteria that cause food-borne illnesses multiply rapidly at temperatures between 60°F and 120°F (16°C and 49°C). Therefore, the broad range of temperatures between 40°F and 140°F (4°C and 60°C) is referred to as the **temperature danger zone**. See Figure 2.3. By keeping foods out of the temperature danger zone, you decrease the bacteria's ability to thrive and reproduce.

To control the growth of any bacteria that may be present, it is important to maintain the internal temperature of food at 140°F (60°C) or above or 40°F (4°C) or below. Simply stated: *Keep hot foods hot and cold foods cold*. Potentially hazardous foods should be heated or cooled quickly so that they are within the temperature danger zone as briefly as possible. This is known as the **time-and-temperature principle**.

Keep hot foods hot. The high internal temperatures reached during proper cooking kill most of the bacteria that can cause food-borne illnesses. (See Table 2.2.) When foods are reheated, the internal temperature should quickly reach or exceed 165°F (74°C) in order to kill any bacteria that may have grown during storage. Once properly heated, hot foods must be held at temperatures of 140°F (60°C) or above. Foods that are to be displayed or served hot must be heated

THE TEMPERATURE DANGER ZONE

The temperature danger zone is a broad range of temperatures in which most of the bacteria that cause food-borne illnesses multiply rapidly. The *2001 Model Food Code* of the Food and Drug Administration (FDA) indicates that the temperature danger zone begins at 41°F (5°C) and ends at 140°F (60°C). Regulations in some localities state that the danger zone begins at 45°F (7°C) or ends at 130°F (54°C), however. Here we use the broader range recommended by the U.S. Department of Agriculture (USDA)—40°F to 140°F (4°C to 60°C)—since this provides a slightly greater margin of safety.

CELSIUS   FAHRENHEIT

100°C ← → 212°F

74°C ← → 165°F

60°C ← → 140°F

4°C ← → 40°F
0°C ← → 32°F

-18°C ← → 0°F

FIGURE 2.3 ▶ **The temperature danger zone**

rapidly to reduce the time within the temperature danger zone. When heating or reheating foods:

▶ Heat small quantities at a time.
▶ Stir frequently.
▶ Heat foods as close to service time as possible.
▶ Use preheated ingredients whenever possible to prepare hot foods.
▶ Never use a steam table for heating or reheating foods. Bring reheated food to an appropriate internal temperature (at least 165°F/74°C) before placing it in the steam table for holding.

Keep cold foods cold. Foods that are to be displayed, stored or served cold must be cooled rapidly. When cooling foods:

▶ Refrigerate semisolid foods at 40°F (4°C) or below in containers that are less than 2 inches deep. (Increased surface area decreases cooling time.)
▶ Avoid crowding the refrigerator; allow air to circulate around foods.
▶ Vent hot foods in an ice-water bath, as illustrated in Chapter 11, Stocks and Sauces.
▶ Prechill ingredients such as mayonnaise before preparing cold foods.
▶ Store cooked foods above raw foods to prevent cross-contamination.

Keep frozen foods frozen. Freezing at 0°F (−18°C) or below essentially stops bacterial growth but will not kill the bacteria. Do not place hot foods in a standard freezer. This will not cool the food any faster, and the release of heat can raise the temperature of other foods in the freezer. Only a special blast freezer can be used for chilling hot items. If one is not available, cool hot foods as mentioned earlier before freezing them. When frozen foods are thawed, bacteria that are present will begin to grow. Therefore:

▶ Never thaw foods at room temperature.
▶ Thaw foods gradually under refrigeration to maintain the food's temperature at 40°F (4°C) or less. Place thawing foods in a container to prevent cross-contamination from dripping or leaking liquids.
▶ Thaw foods under running water at a temperature of 70°F (21°C) or cooler.
▶ Thaw foods in a microwave only if the food will be prepared and served immediately.

TIME When bacteria are moved from one place to another, they require time to adjust to new conditions. This resting period, during which very little growth occurs, is known as the **lag phase** and may last from one to four hours. It is followed by the **log phase**, a period of accelerated growth, and then by the **stationary phase**, which lasts until the bacteria begin to crowd others within their colony, creating competition for food, space and moisture. This begins the **decline** or **negative growth phase**, during which bacteria die at an accelerated rate. See Figure 2.4.

Because of the lag phase, foods can be in the temperature danger zone for *very short periods* during preparation without an unacceptable increase in bacterial growth. Exposure to the temperature danger zone is cumulative, however, and should not exceed four hours total. The less time food is in the temperature danger zone, the less opportunity bacteria have to multiply.

MOISTURE Bacteria need a certain amount of moisture, which is expressed as water activity or A_w. Water it-

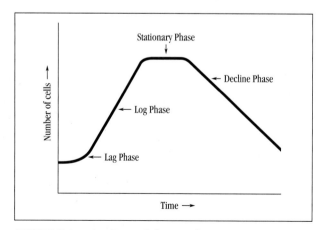

FIGURE 2.4 ▶ **Bacterial growth curve**

TABLE 2.2 RECOMMENDED INTERNAL COOKING TEMPERATURES

PRODUCT	TEMPERATURE
Beef, veal or lamb steaks, chops and roasts	Cook to 145°F/63°C
Egg dishes	Cook to 160°F/71°C; if the dish is uncooked, use only pasteurized eggs
Eggs	Cook until the yolk and white are firm OR cook to 145°F/63°C for 15 seconds if prepared for a customer's immediate order*
Fish	Cook until opaque and flakes easily OR cook to 145°F/63°C for 15 seconds*
Game, commercial	Cook to 165°F/74°C
Ground beef, veal, pork or lamb	Cook to 160°F/71°C
Ground turkey or chicken	Cook to 165°F/74°C
Pork, ham and bacon	Cook to 145°F/63°C for 15 seconds*
Poultry	Cook to 180°F/82°C (in thigh); 170°F/77°C (in breast)
Ratites and injected meats (commercially flavored with marinade or brine)	Cook to 155°F/68°C for 15 seconds*
Shellfish	Cook until opaque and firm; shells should open
Stuffing, stuffed meat, stuffed pasta and casseroles	Cook to 165°F/74°C

SOURCE: USDA Food Safety and Inspection Service
*FDA 2001 Model Food Code

self has an A_w of 1.0. Any food with an A_w of 0.85 or greater is considered potentially hazardous. Bacteria cannot flourish where the A_w is too low, usually below 0.85. This explains why dry foods such as flour, sugar or crackers are rarely subject to bacterial infestations. A low A_w only halts bacterial growth, however; it does not kill the microorganisms. When dried foods such as beans or rice are rehydrated, any bacteria present can flourish and the food may become potentially hazardous.

ACID/ALKALI BALANCE   Bacteria are affected by the **pH** of their environment. Although they can survive in a wider range, they prefer a neutral environment with a pH of 6.6 to 7.5. Growth is usually halted if the pH is 4.6 or less. So acidic foods such as lemon juice, tomatoes and vinegar create an unfavorable environment for bacteria. Simply adding an acidic ingredient to foods should not, however, be relied upon to destroy bacteria or preserve foods. The amount of acidity appropriate for flavoring is not sufficient to ensure the destruction of bacteria.

ATMOSPHERE   Bacteria need an appropriate atmosphere. Some bacteria, known as **aerobic**, thrive on oxygen, whereas others, known as **anaerobic**, cannot survive in its presence. Still others, known as **facultative**, can adapt and will survive with or without oxygen. Unfortunately, most pathogenic bacteria are facultative.

Canning, which creates an anaerobic atmosphere, destroys bacteria that need oxygen. But it also creates a favorable atmosphere for anaerobic and facultative bacteria. A complete vacuum need not be formed for anaerobic bacteria to thrive, however. A tight foil covering, a complete layer of fat, even a well-fitting lid can create an atmosphere sufficiently devoid of oxygen to permit the growth of anaerobic bacteria.

PARASITES

Parasites are tiny organisms that depend on nutrients from a living host to complete their life cycle. Animals, poultry, fish, shellfish and humans can all play host to parasites. Several types of very small parasitic worms can enter an

▶ **pH** a measurement of the acid or alkali content of a solution, expressed on a scale of 0 to 14.0. A pH of 7.0 is considered neutral or balanced. The lower the pH value, the more acidic the substance. The higher the pH value, the more alkaline the substance.

MAD COW DISEASE

During the past several years, medical authorities have found links between a disease in cattle called **bovine spongiform encephalopathy** (**BSE**, popularly known as "mad cow disease") and an extremely rare disease in humans called **new variant Creutzfeldt-Jakob disease** (**nvCJD**). Both BSE and nvCJD are slowly degenerative and invariably fatal diseases affecting the central nervous system. Researchers know that these diseases have unusually long incubation periods, but do not know exactly what causes them. They believe that BSE is spread in cattle through feed that has been made, in part, with processed ingredients from slaughtered animals that carried the unknown infectious agent. They also believe that nvCJD is probably contracted by eating meat or other products processed from infected animals. So far, the worst of the known BSE outbreaks has been confined to Europe, principally Great Britain, and even there only a few people have been diagnosed with nvCJD.

There have been no reported cases of BSE or nvCJD in the United States. For more than a decade, federal authorities have restricted the importation of certain species of live animals and products derived from them originating in countries suffering or suspected of suffering from outbreaks of BSE. They also actively monitor American meat-packing facilities for any signs of BSE in cattle waiting to be slaughtered, and long ago banned the sale of the type of feed associated with BSE in Europe.

Responsible government and nongovernmental authorities continue to assure the American public that it is safe to eat American beef.

---

animal through contaminated feed, then settle in the host's intestinal tract or muscles, where they grow and reproduce.

Trichinosis is caused by eating undercooked meat (usually game or pork) infected with trichina larvae. Although trichinosis has been virtually eradicated by grain-feeding hogs and testing them before slaughter, some cases still occur each year. Traditionally, it was thought that pork must be cooked to internal temperatures of 170°F (77°C) or higher to eradicate the larvae. This generally resulted in a dry, tough product. Scientists have now determined that trichina larvae are killed if held at 137°F (58°C) for 10 seconds. The FDA currently recommends cooking pork products to an internal temperature of 145°F (63°C) or above for 15 seconds. The National Livestock and Meat Board and the USDA recommend cooking all pork products to 160°F (71°C), however.

Anisakiasis is another illness caused by parasitic roundworms. *Anisakis* worms reside in the organs of fish, especially bottom feeders or those taken from contaminated waters. Raw or undercooked fish are most often implicated in anisakiasis. Fish should be thoroughly cleaned immediately after being caught so that the parasites do not have an opportunity to spread. Thorough cooking to a minimum internal temperature of 140°F (60°C) is the only way to destroy the larvae since they can survive even highly acidic marinades.

Cyclospora infections are caused by a single-celled parasite found in water or food contaminated by infected feces. Produce from undeveloped countries is a common source of *Cyclospora* parasites, as is untreated water. Avoiding such products is the best prevention method.

VIRUSES

Viruses cause other biologically based food-borne illnesses such as hepatitis A and the Norwalk virus. Viruses are among the smallest known forms of life. They invade the living cells of a host, take over those cells' genetic material, and cause the cells to produce more viruses.

Viruses do not require a host to survive, however. They can survive—but not multiply—while lying on any food or food contact surface. Unlike bacteria, viruses can be present on any food, not just a potentially hazardous food. The food or food contact surface simply becomes a means of transportation between hosts.

Unlike bacteria, viruses are not affected by the water activity, pH or oxygen content of their environment. Some, however, can be destroyed by temperatures higher than 176°F (80°C). Basically, the only way to prevent food-borne viral illnesses is to prevent contamination in the first place.

FOOT-AND-MOUTH DISEASE

Although humans are not susceptible to **foot-and-mouth disease** (**FMD**; also known as hoof-and-mouth disease), it could have a severe impact on our food supply. Foot-and-mouth disease affects animals with cloven hooves such as cattle, swine, sheep, goats and deer. Nearly 100 percent of the animals exposed to the virus ultimately become infected. The disease is rarely fatal, but those that survive are often debilitated and experience severe loss in milk or meat production.

Fortunately, there has not been a reported case of FMD in the United States for more than 70 years. But in recent years, there has been an FMD epidemic in Europe. Hundreds of thousands of cattle, pigs and sheep have been destroyed. Milk and meat production has declined and farmers and meat packers are suffering tremendous economic loses.

The U.S. government is taking steps to ensure that a similar outbreak does not take place here. It has temporarily prohibited the importa-tion of certain animals and animal products from countries with infected animal populations. In addition, as the FMD virus can be transported by humans and on their clothes and possessions, travelers from countries with infected animal populations are prohibited from bringing with them most agricultural products, and they and their possessions can be subjected to varying degrees of decontamination procedures.

Hepatitis A often enters the food supply through shellfish harvested from polluted waters. The virus is carried by humans, some of whom may never know they are infected, and is transmitted by poor personal hygiene and cross-contamination. The actual source of contamination may be hard to establish, though, because it sometimes takes months for symptoms to appear.

The **Norwalk virus** is spread almost entirely by poor personal hygiene among infected food handlers. The virus is found in human feces, contaminated water or vegetables fertilized by manure. The virus can be destroyed by high cooking temperatures but not by sanitizing solutions or freezing. In fact, the Norwalk virus has even been found in ice cubes.

Foods most likely to transmit viral diseases are those that are not heated after handling. These include salads, sandwiches, milk, baked products, uncooked fish and shellfish and sliced meats. The best techniques for avoiding viral food-borne illnesses are to observe good personal hygiene habits, avoid cross-contamination and use only foods obtained from reputable sources.

FUNGI

Fungi are a large group of plants ranging from single-celled organisms to giant mushrooms. Fungi are everywhere: in the soil, air and water. Poisonous mushrooms, a type of fungus, can cause illness or death if consumed. The most common fungi, however, are molds and yeasts.

Molds

Molds are algaelike fungi that form long filaments or strands. These filaments often extend into the air, appearing as cottony or velvety masses on food. Large colonies of mold are easily visible to the naked eye. Although many food molds are not dangerous, and some are even very beneficial, rare types known as *mycotoxicoses* form toxins that have been linked to food-borne illnesses. For the most part, however, molds affect only the appearance and flavor of foods. They cause discoloration, odors and off-flavors.

Unlike bacteria, molds can grow on almost any food at almost any temperature, moist or dry, acidic or alkaline. Mold cells can be destroyed by heating to 140°F (60°C) for 10 minutes. Their toxins are heat resistant, however, and are not destroyed by normal cooking methods. Therefore, foods that develop mold should be discarded, and any container or storage area cleaned and sanitized.

Yeasts

Yeasts require water and carbohydrates (sugar or starch) for survival. As the organisms consume carbohydrates, they expel alcohol and carbon dioxide gas through a process known as **fermentation**. Fermentation is of great benefit in making breads and alcoholic beverages.

Although naturally occurring yeasts have not been proved to be harmful to humans, they can cause foods to spoil and develop off-flavors, odors and discoloration. Yeasts are killed at temperatures of 136°F (58°C) or above.

CHEMICAL CONTAMINANTS

Contamination of foods by a wide variety of chemicals is a very real and serious danger in which the public has shown a strong interest. Chemical contamination is usually inadvertent and invisible, making it extremely difficult to detect. The only way to avoid such hazards is for everyone working in a food service operation to follow proper procedures when handling foods or chemicals.

Chemical hazards include contamination with (1) residual chemicals used in growing the food supply, (2) food service chemicals and (3) toxic metals.

RESIDUAL CHEMICALS

Chemicals such as antibiotics, fertilizers, insecticides and herbicides have brought about great progress in controlling plant, animal and human diseases, permitting greater food yields and stimulating animal growth. The benefits derived from these chemicals, however, must be contrasted with the adverse effects on humans when they are used indiscriminately or improperly.

The danger of these chemicals lies in the possible contamination of human foods, which occurs when chemical residues remain after the intended goal is achieved. Fruits and vegetables must be washed and peeled properly to reduce the risk of consuming residual chemicals.

FOOD SERVICE CHEMICALS

A more common contamination problem involves the common chemicals found in most every food service operation. Cleaners, polishes, pesticides and abrasives are often poisonous to humans. Illness and even death can result from foods contaminated by such common items as bug spray, drain cleaner, oven cleaner or silver polish. These chemicals pose a hazard if used or stored near food supplies. Even improperly washing or rinsing dishes and utensils leaves a soap residue, which is then transmitted via food to anyone using the item.

To avoid food service chemical contamination, make sure all cleaning chemicals are clearly labeled and stored well away from food preparation and storage areas. Always use these products as directed by the manufacturer; never reuse a chemical container or package.

TOXIC METALS

Another type of chemical contamination occurs when metals such as lead, mercury, copper, zinc and antimony are dispersed in food or water. For example:

▶ Metals can accumulate in fish and shellfish living in polluted waters or in plants grown in soil contaminated by the metals.

▶ Using an acidic food such as tomatoes or wine in a zinc (galvanized) or unlined copper container causes metal ions to be released into the food.

▶ Antimony is used in bonding enamelware; it can be released into food when the enamel is chipped or cracked, so the use of enamelware is prohibited in food service facilities.

▶ Lead enters the water supply from lead pipes and solder, and is found in the glaze on some imported ceramic items.

Consuming any of these metals can cause poisoning.

To prevent metal contamination, use only approved food service equipment and utensils and re-tin copper cookware as needed. Never serve fish or shellfish that was illegally harvested or obtained from uninspected sources.

PHYSICAL CONTAMINANTS

Physical contaminants include foreign objects that find their way into foods by mistake. Examples include metal shavings created by a worn can opener, pieces of glass from a broken container, hair and dirt. Physical contaminants may be created by intentional tampering, but they are most likely the result of poor safety and sanitation practices or a lack of training.

▶ CROSS-CONTAMINATION

Generally, microorganisms and other contaminants cannot move by themselves. Rather, they are carried to foods and food contact surfaces by humans, rodents or insects. This transfer is referred to as cross-contamination.

Cross-contamination is the process by which one item, such as your finger or a cutting board, becomes contaminated and then contaminates another food or tool. For example, suppose a chef's knife and cutting board are used in butchering a potentially hazardous food such as a chicken, and the chicken was directly contaminated with salmonella at the hatchery. If the knife and board are not cleaned *and sanitized* properly, anything that touches them can also become contaminated. So even though cooking the chicken to an appropriate internal temperature may destroy the salmonella in the chicken, the uncooked salad greens cut on the same cutting board or with the same knife can contain live bacteria.

Cross-contamination can occur with bacteria or other microorganisms, chemicals, dirt and debris. Side towels are an especially common source of cross-contamination. If a cook uses a side towel to wipe a spill off the floor, then uses that same towel to dry his hands after visiting the restroom, he has recontaminated his hands with whatever bacteria or dirt was on the floor. Cross-contamination also occurs when raw foods come in contact with cooked foods. Never store cooked food below raw food in a refrigerator, and never return cooked food to the container that held the raw food. Cross-contamination can also occur easily from smoking, drinking or eating, unless hands are properly washed after each of these activities.

Even with proper hand washing, food service workers should strive to minimize direct contact with prepared food by using single-use gloves, clean tongs, tasting spoons, bakery tissue paper and other appropriate tools whenever possible.

REDUCING CROSS-CONTAMINATION

Cross-contamination can be reduced or even prevented by (1) personal cleanliness, (2) dish and equipment cleanliness and (3) pest management.

PERSONAL CLEANLINESS

To produce clean, sanitary food, all food handlers must maintain high standards of personal cleanliness and hygiene. This begins with good grooming.

Humans provide the ideal environment for the growth of microorganisms. Everyone harbors bacteria in the nose and mouth. These bacteria are easily spread by sneezing or coughing, by not disposing of tissues properly and by not washing hands frequently and properly. Touching your body and then touching food or utensils transfers bacteria. Human waste carries many dangerous microorganisms, so it is especially important to wash your hands thoroughly after visiting the restroom. An employee who is ill should not be allowed in the kitchen.

Current research shows that the human immunodeficiency virus (HIV), the causative agent of AIDS, is not spread by food. According to the Centers for Disease Control and Prevention (CDC), food service workers infected with HIV should not be restricted from work unless there is another infection or illness.

PROPER HAND-WASHING PROCEDURE

- Use hot running water.
- Wet hands and forearms.
- Apply an antibacterial soap.
- Rub hands and arms briskly with soapy lather for at least 20 seconds.
- Scrub between fingers and clean nails with a clean nail brush.
- Rinse thoroughly under hot running water.
- Reapply soap and scrub hands and forearms for another 5–10 seconds.
- Rinse again.
- Dry hands and arms using a single-use towel.
- Use the towel to turn off the water.
- Discard the towel in a trash receptacle.

You can do several things to decrease the risk of an illness being spread by poor personal hygiene:

▶ Wash your hands frequently and thoroughly. Gloves are not a substitute for proper hand washing.

▶ Keep your fingernails short, clean and neat. Do not bite your nails or wear nail polish.

▶ Keep any cut or wound antiseptically bandaged. An injured hand should also be covered with a disposable glove.

▶ Bathe daily, or more often if required.

▶ Keep your hair clean and restrained.

▶ Wear work clothes that are clean and neat. Avoid wearing jewelry or watches.

▶ Do not eat, drink, smoke or chew gum in food preparation areas.

DISH AND EQUIPMENT CLEANLINESS

One of the requirements for any food service facility is cleanability. But there is an important difference between *clean* and *sanitary*. **Clean** means that the item has no visible soil on it. **Sanitary** means that harmful substances are reduced to safe levels. Thus, something may be clean without being sanitary; the visible dirt can be removed, but disease-causing microorganisms can remain.

The cleaning of dishes, pots, pans and utensils in a food service operation involves both removing soil and sanitizing. Soil can be removed manually or by machine. Sanitizing can be accomplished with heat or chemical disinfectants.

Procedures for manually washing, rinsing and sanitizing dishes and equipment generally follow the three-compartment sink setup shown in Figure 2.5. The dishwasher must do the following:

1 Scrape and spray the item to remove soil.

2 Wash the item in the first sink compartment using an approved detergent. A brush or cloth may be used to remove any remaining soil.

3 Rinse the item in the second sink compartment using clear, hot water.

4 Sanitize the item in the third sink compartment by either:
    a. immersing it in 171°F (77°C) water for at least 30 seconds, or
    b. immersing it in an approved chemical sanitizing solution used according to the manufacturer's directions.

5 Empty, clean and refill each sink compartment as necessary, and check the water temperature regularly.

Food service items, dishes, silverware and utensils should always be allowed to air-dry, as towel-drying might recontaminate them.

▶ **clean** to remove visible dirt and soil

▶ **sanitize** to reduce pathogenic organisms to safe levels

▶ **sterilize** to destroy all living microorganisms

FIGURE 2.5 ▶ The three-compartment sink procedure—scrape, spray, wash, rinse, sanitize and air-dry each item.

Machine-washing dishes or utensils follows a similar procedure. The dishwasher should first scrape and rinse items as needed, then load the items into dishwasher racks so that the spray of water will reach all surfaces. The machine cleans the items with a detergent, then sanitizes them with either a hot-water rinse (at least 180°F/82°C) or a chemical disinfectant. When the machine cycle is complete, items should be inspected for residual soil, allowed to air-dry and stored in a clean area.

Work tables and stationary equipment must also be cleaned and sanitized properly. Equipment and surfaces, including floors, walls and work tables, should be easily exposed for inspection and cleaning and should be constructed so that soil can be removed effectively and efficiently with normal cleaning procedures. A thorough cleaning schedule should be implemented and closely monitored to prevent problems from developing.

The following points are important to the safety and cleanliness of any food service facility:

▶ Equipment should be disassembled for cleaning; any immersible pieces should be cleaned and sanitized like other items.

▶ All work tables or other food contact surfaces should be cleaned with detergent, then sanitized with a clean cloth dipped in a sanitizing solution. Combining 1 gallon (4 liters) of lukewarm water with 1 tablespoon (15 milliliters) of chlorine bleach makes an acceptable sanitizing solution. This solution must be replaced every two hours. Other chemical sanitizers should be prepared and used according to health department and manufacturer's directions.

▶ Surfaces, especially work surfaces with which food may come in contact, should be smooth and free of cracks, crevices or seams in which soil and microorganisms can hide.

▶ Floors should be nonabsorbent and should not become slippery when wet.

▶ Walls and ceilings should be smooth and light-colored so that soil is easier to see.

▶ Light should be ample and well located throughout food preparation and storage areas. All light bulbs should be covered with a sleeve or globe to protect surroundings from shattered glass.

A kitchen's design can also affect food safety and sanitation. Food preparation equipment should be arranged in such a way as to decrease the chances of cross-contamination. The workflow should eliminate crisscrossing and backtracking. Employees should be able to reach storage, refrigeration and cleanup areas easily. Dish- and pot-washing areas and garbage facilities should be kept as far from food preparation and storage areas as possible. Cleaning supplies and other chemicals should be stored away from foods.

PEST MANAGEMENT

Food can be contaminated by insects (for example, roaches and flies) and rodents (for example, mice and rats). These pests carry many harmful bacteria on their bodies, thus contaminating any surface with which they come in contact. An insect or rodent infestation is usually considered a serious health risk and should be dealt with immediately and thoroughly. Pests must be controlled by (1) building them out of the facility, (2) creating an environment in which they cannot find food, water or shelter, and (3) relying on professional extermination.

The best defense against pests is to prevent infestations in the first place by building them out. Any crack—no matter how small—in door frames, walls or window sills should be repaired immediately, and all drains, pipes and vents should be well sealed. Inspect all deliveries thoroughly, and reject any packages or containers found to contain evidence of pests.

SAFETY ALERT

Use a clean cloth dipped in sanitizing solution when wiping off your knives, utensils or cutting board during work. An acceptable solution can be made by combining 1 gallon of lukewarm water with 1 tablespoon of chlorine bleach. Replace this solution every two hours.

Flies are a perfect method of transportation for bacteria because they feed and breed on human waste and garbage. Use screens or "fly fans" (also known as air curtains) to keep them out in the first place. Controlling garbage is also essential because moist, warm, decaying organic material attracts flies and provides favorable conditions for eggs to hatch and larvae to grow.

Pest management also requires creating an inhospitable environment for pests. Store all food and supplies at least 6 inches off the floor and 6 inches away from walls. **Rotate stock** often to disrupt nesting places and breeding habits. Provide good ventilation in storerooms to remove humidity, airborne contaminants, grease and fumes. Do not allow water to stand in drains, sinks or buckets, as cockroaches are attracted to moisture. Clean up spills and crumbs immediately and completely to reduce their food supply.

Despite your best efforts to build pests out and maintain proper housekeeping standards, it is still important to watch for the presence of pests. For example, cockroaches leave a strong, oily odor and feces that look like large grains of pepper. Cockroaches prefer to search for food and water in the dark, so seeing any cockroach on the move in the daylight is an indication of a large infestation.

Rodents (mice and rats) tend to hide during the day, so an infestation may be rather serious before any creature is actually seen. Rodent droppings, which are shiny black to brownish gray, may be evident, however. Rodent nests made from scraps of paper, hair or other soft materials may be spotted.

Should an infestation occur, consult a licensed pest control operator immediately. With early detection and proper treatment, infestations can be eliminated. Be very careful in attempting to use pesticides or insecticides yourself. These chemicals are toxic to humans as well as to pests. Great care must be used to prevent contaminating food or exposing workers or customers to the chemicals.

▶ **rotate stock** to use products in the order in which they were received; all perishable and semi-perishable goods, whether fresh, frozen, canned or dry, should be used according to the first in, first out (FIFO) principle

▶ HACCP Systems

Now that you understand what contaminants are and how they can be destroyed or controlled, it is necessary to put this information into practice during day-to-day operations. Although local health departments regularly inspect all food service facilities, continual self-inspection and control are essential for maintaining sanitary conditions.

Hazard Analysis Critical Control Points (HACCP) is proving to be an effective and efficient system for managing and maintaining sanitary conditions in all types of food service operations. Developed in 1971 for NASA to ensure food safety for astronauts, HACCP (pronounced HASS-ip) is a rigorous system of self-inspection. It focuses on the flow of food through the food service facility, from the decision to include an item on the menu through service to the consumer. A critical control point in that flow is any step during the processing of a food when a mistake can result in the transmission, growth or survival of pathogenic bacteria.

The HACCP process begins by identifying the steps and evaluating the type and severity of hazard that can occur. It then identifies what actions can be taken to reduce or prevent each risk of hazard. See Table 2.3. The activities that present the highest risk of hazard should be monitored most closely. For example, a cook's failure to wash his or her hands before handling cooked food presents a greater risk of hazard than a dirty floor. In other words, hazards must be prioritized, and the correction of critical concerns should take priority.

Note that the standards (or what some might call boundaries) applied in a formal HACCP system are no different from those that should be rigorously followed in any food service operation.

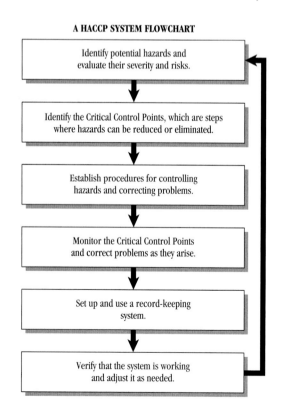

A HACCP SYSTEM FLOWCHART

Identify potential hazards and evaluate their severity and risks.

Identify the Critical Control Points, which are steps where hazards can be reduced or eliminated.

Establish procedures for controlling hazards and correcting problems.

Monitor the Critical Control Points and correct problems as they arise.

Set up and use a record-keeping system.

Verify that the system is working and adjust it as needed.

Table 2.3 HACCP ANALYSIS—THE FLOW OF FOOD

CONTROL POINT	HAZARDS	STANDARDS	CRITICAL ACTIONS
Selecting the menu and recipes	PHF; human hands involved in food preparation	Analyze menus and recipes for control points; wash hands frequently; use single-use gloves as appropriate	Plan physical work flow; train employees
Receiving	Contaminated or spoiled goods; PHF in the temperature danger zone	Do not accept torn bags, dented cans, broken glass containers or leaking or damaged packages; frozen food should be received at 0°F (−18°C) or below and refrigerated food at 40°F (4°C) or below	Inspect all deliveries and reject as necessary
Storing	Cross-contamination to and from other foods; bacterial growth; spoilage; improper holding temperatures	Avoid crowding and allow air to circulate in freezers and refrigerators; rotate stock and keep storage areas clean, dry and well lit; store frozen food at 0°F (−18°C) or below and refrigerated food at 40°F (4°C) or below	Maintain proper temperatures and other storage conditions; discard if necessary
Preparing	Cross-contamination; bacterial growth	Keep PHF at 40°F (4°C) or below or 140°F (60°C) or above; thaw frozen foods under refrigeration or under cold running water (70°F/21°C) for no more than 2 hours	Avoid the temperature danger zone; maintain good personal hygiene and use sanitary utensils
Cooking	Bacterial survival; physical or chemical contamination	Heat foods to the appropriate internal temperature; reheat leftover foods to at least 165°F (74°C)	Cook foods to their proper temperatures
Holding and service	Bacterial growth; contamination	Maintain hot holding temperatures at 140°F (60°C) or above and cold holding temperatures at 40°F (4°C) or below; do not mix new product with old and discard food after 2 hours of being held at room temperature	Maintain proper temperatures and use sanitary equipment
Cooling leftovers	Bacterial growth	Spread food into clean, shallow, metal containers; use an ice bath; stir periodically during cooling; cool to 70°F (21°C) within 2 hours, then cool to 40°F (4°C) or below within 4 hours; cover and refrigerate; store cooked food above raw	Cool foods quickly; label and store them properly
Reheating	Bacterial survival and growth	Use leftovers within 4 days; heat leftovers to 165°F (74°C) within 2 hours; do not mix old product with new and discard secondary leftovers	Reheat food quickly (do not use a steam table) and as close to serving time as possible; reheat smaller quantities as needed; discard if necessary

HACCP does not impose new or different food safety standards; it is merely a system for assuring that those standards are actually followed.

One way to assure compliance is to frequently check and record the temperature of PHF during cooking, cooling and holding. Maintaining written time-and-temperature logs allows management to evaluate and adjust procedures as necessary. Whatever system is followed, all personnel must be constantly aware of and responsive to risks and problems associated with the safety of the food they serve.

BEEF STROGANOFF

Yield: 8 Servings, 8 oz. (250 g) each   **Method:** Sautéing

Tenderloin tips, émincé	2 lb.	1 kg
Clarified butter	3 Tbsp.	45 ml
Onion, medium dice	4 oz.	120 g
Mushrooms, halved	1 lb.	450 g
Demi-glace	10 fl. oz.	300 ml
Heavy cream	10 fl. oz.	300 ml
Sour cream	8 oz.	250 g
Dijon mustard	1 Tbsp.	15 ml
Fresh dill, chopped	1 Tbsp.	15 ml
Fresh parsley, chopped	1 Tbsp.	15 ml
Salt and pepper	TT	TT
Egg noodles, cooked	24 oz.	700 g

PRE-PREPARATION

A. Wash hands before handling food, after handling raw foods and after any interruptions in work.

B. Cut the beef tenderloin using a clean, sanitized knife and cutting board. Place the émincé into a clean container, cover and refrigerate until ready to use. If work is interrupted, return the beef to refrigerated storage during the interruption.

C. Measure the demi-glace, cream and sour cream, cover and keep refrigerated until ready to use.

D. Chop the onions and herbs using a clean, sanitized knife and cutting board.

PREPARATION

CCP 1. Sauté the tenderloin tips in the butter, searing on all sides. Remove the meat **to a clean container and hold at 140°F (60°C) or higher for no more than 2 hours.**

2. Add the onions to the pan and sauté lightly. Add the mushrooms and sauté until dry.

3. Add the demi-glace. Bring to a boil, reduce to a simmer and cook for 10 minutes.

CCP 4. Add the cream, sour cream, mustard and any meat juices that accumulated while holding the meat. **Cook until an internal temperature of 145°F (63°C) is maintained for at least 15 seconds.**

CCP 5. Return the meat to the sauce. **Cook until the meat reaches an internal temperature of 145°F (63°C).** Stir in the dill and parsley. Adjust the seasonings and serve over hot egg noodles.

HOLDING

CCP   Transfer the sauce to a clean steam table pan and cover. Hold for service in a preheated steam table at **140°F (60°C) or higher. Use within 4 hours.**

LEFTOVERS

CCP   Place in shallow metal pans with a product depth of no more than 2 inches. **Cool from 140°F (60°C) to 70°F (21°C) within 2 hours and from 70°F (21°C) to 40°F (4°C) within 4 additional hours,** for a total cooling time of not more than 6 hours. Cover and store in a refrigerator so that the internal product temperature is 40°F (4°C) or less. Use leftovers within 4 days.

REHEATING

CCP   Reheat Stroganoff to an internal temperature of **165°F (74°C) or higher within 2 hours;** discard any product that is not consumed within 4 hours.

NOTES:
Measure all internal temperatures with a clean, sanitized thermocouple or thermometer.
Once cooked, egg noodles are a potentially hazardous food and should be held and stored accordingly.

FIGURE 2.6 ▶ A recipe showing critical control points (CCP).

One way that a food service operation can make workers aware of potential hazards and the critical actions that are necessary to avoid those hazards is by including detailed safety information in every recipe. Figure 2.6 shows the recipe for Beef Stroganoff from page 328, as it would appear with all critical control points (CCP) noted. When an operation writes this much detail into every one of its standardized recipes, it serves as a constant reminder to employees of both the specific actions necessary and the importance of food safety to the operation.

► THE SAFE WORKER

Kitchens are filled with objects that can cut, burn, break, crush or sprain the human body. The best ways to prevent work-related injuries are proper training, good work habits and careful supervision.

The federal government enacted legislation designed to reduce hazards in the work area, thereby reducing accidents. The Occupational Safety and Health Act (OSHA) covers a broad range of safety matters. Employers who fail to follow its rules can be severely fined. Unfortunately, human error is the leading cause of accidents, and no amount of legislation can protect someone who doesn't work in a safe manner.

Safe behavior on the job reflects pride, professionalism and consideration for fellow workers. The following list should alert you to conditions and activities aimed at preventing accidents and injuries:

- ► Clean up spills as soon as they occur.
- ► Learn to operate equipment properly; always use guards and safety devices.
- ► Wear clothing that fits properly; avoid wearing jewelry, which may get caught in equipment.
- ► Use knives and other equipment for their intended purposes only.
- ► Walk, do not run.
- ► Keep exits, aisles and stairs clear and unobstructed.
- ► Always assume pots and pans are hot; handle them with dry towels.
- ► Position pot and pan handles out of the aisles so that they do not get bumped.
- ► Get help or use a cart when lifting or moving heavy objects.
- ► Avoid back injury by lifting with your leg muscles; stoop, don't bend, when lifting.
- ► Use an appropriately placed ladder or stool for climbing; do not use a chair, box, drawer or shelf.
- ► Keep breakable items away from food storage or production areas.
- ► Warn people when you must walk behind them, especially when carrying a hot pan.

Some accidents will inevitably occur, and it is important to act appropriately in the event of an injury or emergency. This may mean calling for help or providing first aid. Every food service operation should be equipped with a complete first-aid kit. Municipal regulations may specify the exact contents of the kit. Be sure that the kit is conveniently located and well stocked at all times.

The American Red Cross and local public health departments offer training in first aid, cardiopulmonary resuscitation (CPR) and the Heimlich maneuver used for choking victims. All employees should be trained in basic emergency procedures. A list of emergency telephone numbers should be posted by each telephone.

CONCLUSION

All food service workers are responsible for supplying food that is safe to eat. Microorganisms that cause food-borne illnesses can be destroyed or their growth severely limited by proper food-handling procedures. By learning about food contaminants, how they are spread and how they can be prevented or controlled, you can help ensure customer safety. You are also responsible for your own physical safety as well as that of your customers and fellow workers. Maintaining sanitary and safe facilities as well as high standards of personal hygiene are necessary parts of this responsibility.

QUESTIONS FOR DISCUSSION

1 Foods can be contaminated in several ways. Explain the differences between biological, chemical and physical contamination. Give an example of each.

2 Under what conditions will bacteria thrive? Explain what you can do to alter these conditions.

3 What is the temperature danger zone? What is its significance in food preparation?

4 Explain how improper or inadequate pest management can lead to food-borne illnesses.

5 Define HACCP. How is this system used in a typical food service facility?

 6 Visit the Web sites of the U.S. Department of Agriculture and the Food and Drug Administration. What is the Model Food Code? What types of programs do these agencies offer for training consumers about food safety?

IF WE COULD GIVE EVERY INDIVIDUAL THE RIGHT AMOUNT OF NOURISHMENT AND EXERCISE, NOT TOO LITTLE AND NOT TOO MUCH, WE WOULD HAVE FOUND THE SAFEST WAY TO HEALTH.

—*Hippocrates, Greek physician and father of medicine (c. 460–377 B.C.E.)*

NUTRITION

3

AFTER STUDYING THIS CHAPTER, YOU WILL BE ABLE TO:

▶ identify categories of nutrients and explain their importance in a balanced diet

▶ understand the effects that storage and preparation techniques have on various foods' nutritional values

▶ appreciate the use of ingredient substitutes and alternatives

▶ provide diners with nutritious foods

Since the days of prehistoric hunters and gatherers, people have understood that some animals and plants are good to eat and others are not. For thousands of years, cultures worldwide have attributed medicinal or beneficial effects to certain foods, particularly plants, and have recognized that foods that would otherwise be fine to eat may be unhealthy if improperly prepared or stored.

But not until the past few decades have people become increasingly concerned about understanding how all foods affect their health and what foods can and should be consumed in order to promote good health. These concerns compose the study of nutrition.

This chapter cannot provide an in-depth study of the nutritional sciences. Rather, it sets forth basic information about nutrients and guidelines for planning a healthy diet. The chapter also introduces the framework for understanding ingredient substitution and for preparing more nutritious meals.

Detailed nutritional information about many specific foods is found throughout the book. All recipes are accompanied by a nutritional analysis; recipes for dishes particularly low in calories, fat or sodium are marked with a ◢◣.

Nutrition is the science that studies nutrients—(chemical) substances found in food that nourish the body by promoting growth, maintenance and repair and by facilitating body functions. Some nutrients also provide energy.

The six categories of nutrients are carbohydrates, lipids (fats), proteins, vitamins, minerals and water. **Essential nutrients** are those that must be provided by food because the body does not produce them in sufficient quantities or cannot make them at all. See Table 3.1. Some nutritional components are consid-

Table 3.1 ESSENTIAL NUTRIENTS

Essential nutrients are those that must be provided because the human body does not produce them in sufficient quantities. They are the following:

Energy Nutrients
  Carbohydrates
  Fats (linoleic and linolenic acids)
  Proteins (the amino acids: histidine, isoleucine, leucine, lysine, methionine, phenylalanine, threonine, tryptophan and valine)

Vitamins (thiamine, riboflavin, niacin, pantothenic acid, biotin, vitamin B_6, vitamin B_{12}, folate, vitamin C, vitamin A, vitamin D, vitamin E and vitamin K)

Minerals (calcium, chloride, magnesium, phosphorous, potassium, sodium, sulfur, selenium, zinc, chromium, copper, fluoride, iodide, iron, manganese, and molybdenum)

Water

SHARON SALOMON, MS, RD

This chapter was researched and written by Sharon Salomon, a registered dietitian with a masters of science degree in clinical nutrition. As an undergraduate at Queens College in Flushing, New York, Ms. Salomon majored in cultural anthropology and traveled to Mexico, Turkey and Europe as part of her education. On these trips she enjoyed the benefits of living with local people in their homes, where she spent most of her free time in the families' kitchens learning authentic preparation of their native cuisines. Ms. Salomon has also studied at La Varenne Cooking School in Burgundy, France, and attended the Culinary Institute of America at Greystone for certification in nutritional cuisine.

Ms. Salomon has combined her love of food and cooking with her nutrition education in a variety of ways. She has taught nutrition and culinary nutrition courses and has worked as a caterer as well as a spokesperson for the Arizona Beef Council, the National Pork Producers Council and the California Kiwi Association. She appears regularly on Phoenix-area television and has written magazine and newspaper columns on sports nutrition and cooking with children.

ered nonessential because healthy, well-nourished bodies can make them in sufficient quantities to satisfy their needs.

Our bodies depend upon the various nutrients for different purposes and require different amounts of each depending on age, sex and health. In addition, some nutrients depend on one another for proper functioning. For example, calcium and vitamin D work together in the body: Vitamin D promotes the absorption of the calcium that the body utilizes for proper bone growth. Because foods differ with regard to their nutritional content, it is important to eat a variety of foods in order to achieve proper nutritional balance.

▶ ESSENTIAL NUTRIENTS

Three of the essential nutrients provide calories or energy. Sometimes referred to as **macronutrients** because they are needed in larger quantities than other nutrients, they are carbohydrates, lipids (fats) and proteins.

A **calorie** (abbreviated kcal) is the way we describe the amount of energy in food. The number of calories in a food is measured in a laboratory by a device called a calorimeter, which burns the food and measures the heat the food gives off. From that measurement, an estimate for how the food would be burned in the body is calculated. The results of that calculation are the calorie designations assigned to the energy nutrients.

One gram of pure fat supplies 9 kcal; one gram of pure carbohydrate supplies 4 kcal, as does one gram of pure protein. Most foods are a combination of carbohydrates, proteins and fats; their calorie content may not be easily determined unless we know how much of each nutrient the food contains.

Vitamins and minerals, sometimes referred to as **micronutrients** because they are needed in small quantities, are essential nutrients and must be provided through the diet because the body cannot manufacture them in quantities adequate to ensure good health. They provide no calories but are important to the body in generating energy from the foods we eat.

▶ **calorie** the unit of energy measured by the amount of heat required to raise 1000 grams of water one degree Celsius; it is also written as kilocalorie or kcal

CARBOHYDRATES

Carbohydrates comprise carbon, hydrogen and oxygen and are found exclusively in plant foods and milk sugars. Simple carbohydrates include monosaccharides (single sugars) and disaccharides (double sugars). See Table 3.2. **Simple carbohydrates** are found in the naturally occurring sugars in fruit, vegetables and milk, as well as sweeteners such as honey, corn syrup and table sugar. **Complex carbohydrates** are composed of long chains of the monosaccharide glucose. Starch is a complex carbohydrate. Complex carbohydrates are found in fruit, vegetables and cereal grains such as wheat, barley and oats. The

Table 3.2 **SUGARS**	
MONOSACCHARIDES	**DISACCHARIDES**
Glucose (blood sugar)	Lactose (milk sugar)
Fructose (fruit sugar)	Maltose (malt sugar)
Galactose (part of milk sugar)	Sucrose (table sugar)

body digests (or breaks down) these sugars and starches into glucose. Glucose, also known as blood sugar, is a very important source of energy for the body.

Another complex carbohydrate is fiber. Fiber is a unique carbohydrate because humans cannot digest it, so they do not derive calories from it. **Dietary fiber,** which generally comes from the seeds and cell walls of fruit, vegetables and cereal grains, plays an important role in health. There are two types of fiber: soluble and insoluble. Fiber-containing foods are usually composed of both kinds with one kind predominating. Because the body cannot digest dietary fiber, it passes through the digestive system almost completely unchanged. This helps keep the digestive tract running smoothly. Insoluble fiber, such as that found in whole wheat, increases fecal bulk, which encourages proper elimination of waste products from the large intestines and helps avoid some forms of gastrointestinal distress. Some forms of fiber also reduce serum cholesterol. In addition, because of its action in speeding up the passage of waste materials, it is believed that insoluble fiber may prevent colon cancer. Soluble fiber, found in oats and beans, reduces serum cholesterol, thereby lessening the risk for heart disease.

LIPIDS

Lipids, like carbohydrates, are composed of carbon, hydrogen and oxygen. The differences between carbohydrates and lipids are the number and arrangement of the carbon, hydrogen and oxygen atoms. Fats and cholesterol are considered lipids. Fats are found in both animal and plant foods, although fruits contain very little fat. Fats provide calories, help carry fat-soluble vitamins and give food a creamy, pleasant mouth-feel. A healthy diet contains a moderate amount of fat; in fact, some forms of fat are considered essential.

Cholesterol, also a lipid, is found only in foods of animal origin. Cholesterol is not considered an essential nutrient nor does it contribute calories. Cholesterol is, however, an important component of the body, although it is not necessary to eat foods containing cholesterol as the body can manufacture all it needs from the fat in the diet.

Depending upon their structure, the fats in foods can be classified as saturated, monounsaturated or polyunsaturated. Most foods contain a combination of the three kinds of fats, although one kind may predominate. If saturated fat is the most abundant kind (as in the fat surrounding muscle meats), the food is classified as being high in saturated fat even though it contains a mixture of all three kinds of fats.

Saturated fats are found mainly in animal products such as milk, eggs and meats, as well as in tropical oils such as coconut and palm. Monounsaturated fats come primarily from plants and plant foods such as avocados and olives and the oils made from them. Polyunsaturated fats come from plants (soy and corn, for example) and fish.

Vegetable oils such as rapeseed (canola) and olive are high in monounsaturated fat. Cottonseed, sunflower, corn and safflower oils are high in polyunsaturated fat. All oils, however, are a combination of the three kinds of fat. All vegetable oils are cholesterol-free, however, as cholesterol is not found in plants.

Saturated fats such as butter, lard and other animal fats are usually solid at room temperature. Monounsaturated and polyunsaturated fats are usually soft or liquid at room temperature. Hydrogenation is a process by which a liquid fat is made more solid (or saturated) by the addition of hydrogen atoms. Hydrogenation increases the percentage of saturated fatty acids, resulting in a more solid product (such as margarine made from a liquid polyunsaturated oil such as corn oil). Hydrogenation has positive effects as well; it reduces the tendency to rancidity, thus increasing shelf life. For this reason, it is a process used frequently in the food manufacturing industry.

Research suggests that high-fat diets, especially diets high in saturated fat, may be linked to heart disease, obesity and certain forms of cancer. Saturated fats are also linked to high levels of blood cholesterol, which are associated with arteriosclerosis (hardening of the arteries). Although the liver can produce all the cholesterol the body needs, additional cholesterol is often provided in the diet from meats, poultry, fish, eggs and dairy products. The combination of a diet high in saturated fat and a diet high in cholesterol can increase the risk of heart disease.

PROTEINS

Proteins are found in both animal and plant foods. They differ from carbohydrates and lipids in that they contain nitrogen as well as carbon, hydrogen and oxygen. Protein chains consist of amino acids, the building blocks of protein. There are 20 amino acids, 9 of which are essential. People who eat a varied diet with adequate calories and protein can easily get all the essential amino acids even if they do not eat any animal foods. The specific combination of amino acids gives each protein its unique characteristics and properties.

Proteins are necessary for manufacturing, maintaining and repairing body tissues. They are essential for the periodic replacement of the outer layer of skin as well as for blood clotting and scar tissue formation. Hair and nails, which provide a protective cover for the body, are composed of proteins.

Another important function of protein is the regulation of body processes. Proteins regulate the balance of water, acids and bases, and move nutrients in and out of cells. Proteins contribute to the immune system by producing antibodies, which are necessary for combating diseases. Proteins also form the enzymes that act as catalysts for body functions and the hormones that help direct body processes.

VITAMINS

Vitamins are vital dietary substances needed to regulate **metabolism** and for normal growth and body functions. They are essential and noncaloric, and are needed in the body in small amounts.

There are 13 vitamins. Table 3.3 lists them, their known functions in the human body, the foods that contain high concentrations of these nutrients and some of the preparation and storage techniques that help retain the maximum amount of the various vitamins in their food sources.

Vitamins are divided into two categories: fat-soluble and water-soluble. The fat-soluble vitamins are A, D, E and K and are found in foods containing fat. Excess supplies of these vitamins may be stored in fatty tissues and the liver. Water-soluble vitamins are vitamin C and the B-complex vitamins, including thiamin (B_1), riboflavin (B_2), niacin (B_3), cyano-cobalamin (B_{12}), pyridoxine (B_6), pantothenic acid, biotin and folate. Vitamins B_1 and B_2 are commonly referred to by their names (thiamin and riboflavin, respectively), whereas cobalamin and pyridoxine are commonly referred to by their letter designations (B_{12} and B_6, respectively). Water-soluble vitamins are not stored to the extent that fat-soluble vitamins are, and excesses may be excreted in the urine. Because of these differences, deficiencies in water-soluble vitamins usually develop more rapidly.

▶ **metabolism** all the chemical reactions and physical processes that occur continuously in living cells and organisms

Table 3.3 **VITAMINS: THEIR FUNCTIONS, SOURCES AND TECHNIQUES FOR RETAINING MAXIMUM NUTRIENT CONTENT**

VITAMIN	KNOWN FUNCTIONS IN THE HUMAN BODY	SOURCES	TECHNIQUES FOR NUTRIENT REACTION
Vitamin A	Keeps skin healthy; protects eyes; protects mouth and nose linings; supports immune functioning	Deep yellow and orange vegetables, leafy green vegetables, deep orange fruits, egg yolks, liver, fortified milk	Serve fruits and vegetables raw or lightly cooked; store vegetables covered and refrigerated; steam vegetables; roast or broil meats
Vitamin D	Helps body absorb calcium; regulates calcium and phosphorus in the bones; assists bone mineralization	Fortified milk, butter, some fish oils, egg yolks (exposure to sunlight produces vitamin D in the body)	Stable under heat and insoluble in water; therefore unaffected by cooking
Vitamin E	Antioxidant; protects membranes and cell walls	Vegetable oils, whole grains, dark leafy vegetables, wheat germ, nuts, seeds, whole grains	Use whole-grain flours, store foods in airtight containers; avoid exposing food to light and air
Vitamin K	Assists blood-clotting proteins	Liver, dark green leafy vegetables (bacteria in the intestinal tract also produce some vitamin K)	Steam or microwave vegetables; do not overcook meats
Vitamin C (ascorbic acid)	Supports immune system functioning; repairs connective tissues; promotes healing; assists amino acid metabolism	Citrus fruits, green vegetables, strawberries, cantaloupes, tomatoes, broccoli, potatoes	Serve fruits and vegetables raw; steam or microwave vegetables
Thiamin (vitamin B_1)	Assists energy metabolism; supports nervous system functioning	Meats (especially pork), legumes, whole grains	Use enriched or whole grain pasta or rice; do not wash whole grains before cooking or rinse afterward; steam or microwave vegetables; roast meats at moderate temperatures; cook meats only until done
Riboflavin (vitamin B_2)	Assists energy metabolism	Milk, cheese, yogurt, fish, enriched grain breads and cereals, dark green leafy vegetables	Store foods in opaque containers; roast or broil meats or poultry
Niacin (vitamin B_3)	Promotes normal digestion; supports nervous system functioning; assists energy metabolism	Meats, poultry, fish, dark green leafy vegetables, whole-grain or enriched breads and cereals, nuts	Steam or microwave vegetables; roast or broil beef, veal, lamb and poultry (pork retains about the same amount of niacin regardless of cooking method)
Vitamin B_6	Necessary for protein metabolism and red blood cell formation	Meats, fish, poultry, shellfish, whole grains, dark green vegetables, potatoes, liver	Serve vegetables raw; cook foods in a minimum amount of water and for the shortest possible time; roast or broil meats and fish
Vitamin B_{12}	Helps produce red blood cells; assists metabolism	Animal foods only, particularly milk, eggs, poultry and fish	Roast or broil meats, poultry and fish
Folate	Necessary for protein metabolism and red blood cell formation	Orange juice, dark green leafy vegetables, organ meats, legumes, seeds	Serve vegetables raw; steam or microwave vegetables; store vegetables covered and refrigerated
Biotin	Coenzyme in energy metabolism, glycogen synthesis and fat metabolism	Widespread in foods	
Pantothenic acid	Coenzyme in energy metabolism	Widespread in foods	

Virtually all foods contain some vitamins. Many factors contribute to a particular food's vitamin concentration. An animal's feed; the manner by which the produce is harvested, stored or processed; and even the type of soil, sunlight, rainfall and temperature have significant effects on a food's vitamin content. For example, tomatoes have a higher concentration of vitamin C when picked ripe from the vine than when picked green. Furthermore, different varieties of fruit and vegetables have different vitamin contents. A Wegener apple, for example, has 19 mg of vitamin C, whereas a Red Delicious has only 6 mg.

You can control vitamin concentration and retention through careful food preparation:

1 Try to prepare vegetables as close to service time as possible; vegetables cut long before service lose more vitamins than those cut immediately before cooking.

2 Whether a vegetable is boiled, steamed or microwaved also determines the amount of vitamins it retains. Because the B-complex vitamins and vitamin C are water-soluble, they are easily leached (washed out) or destroyed by food processing and preparation techniques involving high temperatures and water. Steaming and microwaving help retain nutrients (when steaming, keep the water level below the vegetables). But microwave cooking is best because it cooks vegetables with minimal water in less time.

3 In general, roasting and grilling meats, poultry, fish and shellfish preserve more vitamins than stewing and braising. The temperatures to which foods are cooked and the length of time they are cooked may affect vitamin retention as well.

4 Storage affects vitamin concentrations. For example, long exposure to air may destroy vitamin C. Using airtight containers prevents some of this loss. Riboflavin is sensitive to light, so milk products (which are good sources of riboflavin) should be stored in opaque containers.

MINERALS

Minerals cannot be manufactured by the body. They are obtained by eating plants that have drawn minerals from the ground or the flesh of animals that have eaten such plants.

Minerals are a critical component in hard and soft tissues (for example, the calcium, magnesium and phosphorus present in bones and teeth). Minerals also regulate certain necessary body functions. For example, nerve impulses are transmitted through an exchange of sodium and potassium ions in the nerve cells.

Minerals are divided into two categories: trace minerals and major minerals. Trace minerals such as iron are needed in only very small amounts. Major minerals such as calcium are needed in relatively larger quantities. Table 3.4 lists some minerals, their known functions in the human body and the foods that contain high concentrations of these nutrients.

As with vitamins, food processing and preparation can reduce a food's mineral content. Soaking or cooking in large amounts of water can leach out small quantities of water-soluble minerals. Processing or refining grains, such as the wheat used to make white flour, also removes minerals.

WATER

The human body is approximately 60 percent water. Water is necessary for transporting nutrients and wastes throughout the body. It cushions the cells, lubricates the joints, maintains stable body temperatures and assists waste elimination. It also promotes functioning of the nervous system and muscles.

Although the principal sources of water are beverages, water is also the predominant nutrient by weight in most foods. Some foods such as tomatoes,

▶ **acidulated water** a mildly acidic solution of water and lemon juice or vinegar used to prevent cut fruits and vegetables from darkening

▶ **artesian-well water** water obtained from an underground source; the water rises to the surface under pressure

▶ **bottled water** any water, either still or sparkling, that is bottled and sold

▶ **deionized water** water that has had the cations and anions removed by passing it over a bed of ion-exchange resins

▶ **demineralized water** water that has had all the minerals and impurities removed by passing it over a bed of ion-exchange resins

▶ **distilled water** water that has had all the minerals and impurities removed through distillation; it is generally used for pharmaceutical purposes

▶ **drinking water** water that comes from a government-approved source and has undergone some treatment and filtration; it can be bottled or available on tap and is used for drinking and general culinary purposes

▶ **fluoridated water** water, either naturally fluoridated or treated with a fluorine-containing compound, intended to promote healthy teeth by preventing tooth decay

▶ **hard water** water with relatively high calcium and magnesium concentrations

▶ **mineral water** drinking water that comes from a protected underground water source and contains at least 250 parts per million of total dissolved solids such as calcium

▶ **natural water** bottled drinking water not derived from a municipal water supply; it can be mineral, spring, well or artesian-well water

▶ **purified water** bottled water produced by distillation, reverse osmosis, deionization or suitable processes that meet governmental standards

▶ **seltzer water** a flavorless natural mineral water with carbonation, originally from the German town of Nieder Selters

Table 3.4   **MINERALS: THEIR FUNCTIONS AND SOURCES**

MINERAL	KNOWN FUNCTIONS IN THE HUMAN BODY	SOURCES
Major Minerals		
Calcium	Helps build bones and teeth; helps blood clot, promotes muscle and nerve functions	Dairy products, canned salmon and sardines, broccoli, kale, tofu, turnips
Magnesium	Muscle contraction; assists energy metabolism, bone formation	Green leafy vegetables, whole grains, legumes, fish, shellfish, cocoa
Phosphorus	Helps build bones and teeth; assists energy metabolism; formation of DNA	All animal tissues, milk, legumes, nuts
Potassium	Maintains electrolyte and fluid balance; promotes normal body functions; assists protein metabolism	Meats, poultry, fish, fruits (especially bananas, oranges, and cantaloupes), legumes, vegetables
Sodium	Maintains normal fluid balance; necessary for nerve impulse transmission	Salt, soy sauce, processed foods, MSG
Chloride	With sodium, involved in fluid balance; component of stomach acid	Salt, soy sauce, meats, milk, processed foods
Sulfur	A component of some proteins, insulin, and the vitamins biotin and thiamin	All protein-containing foods
Trace Minerals		
Iron	Part of hemoglobin (the red substance in blood that carries oxygen); prevents anemia	Liver, meats, shellfish, enriched breads and cereals, legumes
Zinc	A component of insulin, enhances healing, a component of many enzymes; involved in taste perception; bone formation	Protein foods, whole-grain breads and cereals, fish, shellfish, poultry, vegetables
Selenium	Antioxidant	Fish, shellfish, meats, eggs, grains (depends on soil conditions)
Iodine	Component of thyroid hormone	Iodized salt, fish, shellfish, bread, plants grown in iodide-rich soil
Copper	Facilitates iron absorption; part of enzymes	Meats, fish, shellfish, nuts, seeds
Fluoride	Necessary for bone and teeth formation; helps teeth resist tooth decay	Fluoridated drinking water, fish, shellfish
Chromium	Insulin cofactor	Liver, whole grains, brewer's yeast, nuts, oils
Molybdenum	Cofactor in metabolism	Legumes, cereals
Manganese	Cofactor in metabolism	Whole grains, nuts, organ meats
Cobalt	Component of vitamin B_{12} (cobalamin)	

▶ **soda water** a flavorless water with induced carbonation, consumed plain or used as a mixer for alcoholic drinks or soda fountain confections; also known as club soda and seltzer

▶ **soft water** water with a relatively high sodium concentration

▶ **spring water** water obtained from an underground source that flows naturally to the earth's surface

oranges, watermelon and iceberg lettuce are particularly high in water. Others such as dried fruits, nuts and seeds are lower. Even foods such as chicken and bread provide some water. The body also forms water when other nutrients are metabolized for energy.

The average adult should consume at least 8 to 10 glasses (64 fluid ounces or 2 liters) of water a day to ensure adequate intake. People who exercise, those who live in a warm climate and the elderly should replace body water lost through sweat by drinking even more.

PHYTOCHEMICALS

Recent scientific research has identified nonnutritive components of plant foods called phytochemicals, which may be important in preventing some forms of cancer and heart disease. More than nine hundred of these chemicals have been identified, including plant estrogens, carotenoids and flavonoids. The health benefits of these substances appear to depend on consumption of a varied diet

LIGHTEN UP!

On the night before their trials on the Colosseum floor, gladiators ate meat to make themselves strong. Until a few years ago, modern-day gladiators and coaches insisted that athletes needed meat the night before the game. Of course, being more scientific, they referred to their training-table steak as protein.

Times change, the pendulum swings, and whoever thought a brawny athlete would admit to being a vegetarian? The new message from the American Heart Association and the USDA's U.S. Dietary Goals is that we needn't stop eating meat entirely. Instead, we should reduce our consumption of beef, turning to alternative sources of protein such as fish, poultry, low-fat dairy products, nuts, beans and seeds, and increase our consumption of fresh fruit, vegetables, grains and other complex carbohydrates. The results: fewer fats, more fiber and lower cholesterol, helping to create a slimmer, energetic, longer-lasting body.

This new "fresh," "nutrient-dense," "light," "natural," "heart-healthy" approach to dining has gone from fad to fashion to fact of life.

From formal French to Mexican fast food, facilities offering portions of innovative, tasty, eye-catching healthy cuisine will surely win allegiance and accolades from patrons. So lighten up. Replace the deep-fat fryer with a griddle. Garnish with fresh fruit. Serve whole-grain bread, but take heed: Balance is paramount. An occasional indulgence is a joy. There will always be room for chocolate.

HARRIS GOLDEN, formerly executive chef of Elizabeth Arden's Maine Chance Health Resort, is the author of two cookbooks.

that includes plenty of grains, fruits and vegetables. The importance of phytochemicals to human health and well-being should not be minimized even though they do not constitute a nutrient category nor are there established recommendations for their intake.

▶ EATING FOR HEALTH

It is generally recognized that a balanced diet is an important component of a healthy lifestyle. Eating well and exercising, getting adequate sleep and living moderately all can contribute to a longer, healthier life.

HEALTH ORGANIZATION RECOMMENDATIONS

Planning a diet to enhance health is made simpler by diet and exercise recommendations from organizations such as the American Heart Association and the American Cancer Society. Both stress the importance of controlling the amount of fat in the diet and consuming plant foods such as vegetables, fruits and whole grains in greater quantities.

Another useful planning tool is *Dietary Guidelines for Americans*, jointly published by the USDA and the U.S. Department of Health and Human Services. The fifth edition (2000) presents health messages called the "ABCs of Good Health":

▶ *Aim for fitness* by maintaining a healthy weight and being physically active.
▶ *Build a healthy base* using the Food Guide Pyramid and keeping food safe to eat.
▶ *Choose sensibly* by eating a diet low in saturated fat, cholesterol, sugar and salt and drinking alcoholic beverages in moderation.

ESTABLISHING NUTRIENT REQUIREMENTS

In the past, the RDAs (Recommended Dietary Allowances), standards developed by the federal government, were used to establish guidelines for school lunch programs, food labeling regulations, government nutrition policies,

FOOD GROUPIES

For many years, nutritionists and others have attempted to define a healthy, balanced diet. Most plans divide foods into general categories and recommend that a certain number of servings or calories be consumed from each category for a balanced diet.

Before 1956, the USDA recognized seven food groups: (1) meats, eggs, dried peas and beans, (2) milk, cheese and ice cream, (3) potatoes and other vegetables and fruit, (4) green leafy and yellow vegetables, (5) citrus fruit, tomatoes and raw cabbage, (6) breads and flours and (7) butter and fortified margarine.

In 1956, the USDA reduced the seven groups to four: (1) milk and cheese, (2) meats and fish, (3) fruit and vegetables and (4) grains. An optional fifth category was sweets and fats. From these Four Basic Food Groups, the USDA recommended that the average adult eat a total of 12 servings daily. Two or more servings were to come from each of the meat and milk groups, and four or more servings from each of the other two groups.

In 1992, the USDA replaced the Four Basic Food Groups with the Food Guide Pyramid. The Food Guide Pyramid prioritizes and proportions the food choices among six food categories and gives a visual presentation of proper daily nutrition. The pyramid emphasizes flexibility and is designed to be used by people of all ages and backgrounds.

educational campaigns and the like. During the last decade, however, research regarding the nutrient needs of children, adults and the elderly has raised questions and concerns about the adequacy of the RDAs. Scientists are currently reviewing the pertinent literature to determine how the government can best revise these nutrient recommendations. An important criterion for making nutrient recommendations is the recognition that each person's body is unique and as health and growth status change, so do nutrient needs. The committee, therefore, has proposed different categories to include average needs, estimated needs and adequate needs to more fully meet the needs of different people. Some new recommendations have already been made. For the most up-to-date data, check with government nutrition Web sites.

THE FOOD GUIDE PYRAMID

The most useful diet planning tool available is the Food Guide Pyramid developed by the USDA. See Figure 3.1. It prioritizes and proportions food according to groupings that provide similar nutrients. The size of each section of the pyramid visually represents the number of daily servings recommended.

The base or foundation of the pyramid conveys the idea that a healthy diet is based on the consumption of adequate whole grains and cereals. As you move up the pyramid, fruit and vegetables are next in amount. Meats, poultry, fish, beans, eggs and nuts, as well as milk, yogurt and cheese are allotted smaller sections above the fruit and vegetables. Although they provide essential nutrients such as protein, vitamins and minerals, these foods may be high in fat and calories, and their intake should be moderated. The small tip of the pyramid includes fats, oils and sweets. The size and placement of these indicate that they can be a part of a healthy diet if used sparingly.

Pay careful attention to the serving sizes in Table 3.5. One of the principal complaints consumer health groups have about restaurant meals is the "supersizing" of portions. Often restaurant portions are two or more times what the Food Guide Pyramid recommends for a serving. Portion size represents a dilemma for the restaurateur because the public views larger portions as offering more value for their money. Health education messages, however, allow the dining public to eat out without guilt by teaching strategies such as eating only half of what is served and taking the other half home for another meal or sharing entrées to ensure more reasonable portion sizes.

FIGURE 3.1 ▶ The Food Guide Pyramid

Table 3.5   SERVINGS AND SELECTIONS FROM THE FOOD GUIDE PYRAMID

FOOD GROUP AND SERVICE SIZE	NUTRIENTS PROVIDED	SELECTION TIPS
Bread, Cereal, Rice and Pasta Group *(6–11 Servings)*		
½ cup cooked cereal 1 ounce dry cereal 1 slice bread 2 cookies ½ medium doughnut	B vitamins, fiber, iron, magnesium, zinc	Choose whole-grain breads, cereals and grains such as whole-wheat or rye bread, oatmeal and brown rice. Moderate the intake of high-fat, high-sugar baked goods such as cakes, cookies and pastries. Limit fats and sugars added as spreads, sauces or toppings.
Vegetable Group *(3–5 Servings)*		
½ cup cooked or raw chopped vegetables 1 cup raw leafy vegetables ¾ cup vegetable juice 10 French fries	Vitamin A, vitamin C, folate, magnesium, iron, fiber	Eat a variety of vegetables, including dark green leafy vegetables (for example, spinach and broccoli), deep yellow vegetables (for example, carrots and sweet potatoes), starchy vegetables (for example, potatoes and corn), legumes (for example, kidney beans) and other vegetables such as green beans and tomatoes. Cook vegetables by steaming or baking. Avoid frying and limit high-fat spreads or dressings.
Fruit Group *(2–4 Servings)*		
1 medium apple, banana or orange ½ cup chopped, cooked or canned fruit ¾ cup fruit juice ¼ cup dried fruit	Vitamin A, vitamin C, potassium, fiber	Choose fresh fruit, fruit frozen without sugar, dried fruit or fruit canned in water or juice. If canned in heavy syrup, rinse with water before eating. Eat whole fruits more often than juices since they are higher in fiber. Regularly eat citrus fruits, melons or berries rich in vitamin C. Only 100 percent fruit juice should be counted as a fruit.
Milk, Yogurt and Cheese Group *(2–3 Servings)*		
1 cup milk or yogurt 1½ ounces natural cheese 2 ounces processed cheese 2 cups cottage cheese 1½ cups ice cream 1 cup frozen yogurt	Protein, calcium, riboflavin	Use skim or low-fat milk for healthy people older than two years of age. Choose low-fat and nonfat yogurt, part-skim and low-fat cheeses and lower-fat frozen desserts such as ice milk and frozen yogurt. Limit high-fat cheeses and ice cream.
Meat, Poultry, Fish, Dry Beans, Eggs and Nuts Group *(2–3 Servings)*		
2–3 ounces cooked lean meat, fish or poultry 2–3 eggs 4–6 tablespoons peanut butter 1½ cups cooked dry beans 1 cup nuts	Protein, niacin, vitamin B_{12}, iron, zinc	Select lean meat, poultry without skin, fish and dry beans. Trim fat and cook by broiling, roasting, grilling or boiling rather than frying. Limit egg yolks, which are high in cholesterol, and nuts and seeds, which are high in fat. Be aware of serving size; 3 ounces of meat is the size of an average hamburger.
Fats, Oils and Sweets *(use sparingly)*		
Butter, mayonnaise, salad dressing, cream cheese, sour cream, jam, jelly		These are high in energy and low in micronutrients. Substitute low-fat dressings and spreads.

Source: U.S. Department of Agriculture. *The Food Guide Pyramid. Home and Garden Bulletin No. 252.* Hyattsville, MD: Human Nutrition Information Service, 1992

THE FEDERAL GOVERNMENT GUARDS OUR LARDER

The federal government plays an important role in the way various foodstuffs are grown, raised, slaughtered, processed, marketed, stored and transported. The principal actors are the Food and Drug Administration of the U.S. Department of Health and Human Services (FDA) and the U.S. Department of Agriculture (USDA).

The FDA's activities are directed toward protecting the nation's health against impure and unsafe foods, as well as drugs, cosmetics, medical devices and other things. It develops and administers programs addressing food safety. For example, the FDA must approve any new food additive before a manufacturer markets it to food producers and processors. To gain FDA approval, the manufacturer must prove to the FDA's satisfaction that the additive (1) is effective for the intended purpose, (2) can be detected and measured in the final product and (3) is safe. The FDA holds public hearings during which experts and consumers provide evidence and opinions before it decides to grant or deny approval. If it grants approval, the FDA issues regulations identifying the amount of the additive that can be used and the foods to which it can be added. The FDA also sets standards for labeling foods, including nutrition labels. Labeling regulations not only address the type of information that must be conveyed, but also the way it is presented.

The USDA's principal responsibility is to make sure that individual food items are safe, wholesome and accurately labeled. It attempts to meet these responsibilities through inspection and grading procedures. The USDA also provides consumer services. It conducts and publishes research on nutrition and assists those producing our food to do so efficiently and effectively.

Other federal agencies that have a role in the nation's health and food supply include the U.S. Centers for Disease Control and Prevention (CDC), which tracks illnesses, including those caused by food-borne pathogens; the National Institutes of Health (NIH), which does basic biological and nutritional research; and the Department of the Interior, which sets environmental and land-use standards.

▶ INGREDIENT SUBSTITUTES AND ALTERNATIVES

More and more people are becoming health-conscious consumers. Many are trying to cut down on foods high in salt, fat, added sugar and cholesterol. To a degree, people can accomplish their goals—and chefs can assist them—by turning to ingredient substitutes and alternatives where possible.

Here we use the term **ingredient substitute** to mean the replacement of one ingredient with another of presumably similar—although not necessarily identical—flavor, texture, appearance and other sensory characteristics. The substitute may be more nutritious, however. So someone who is avoiding fats can use reduced-fat or nonfat sour cream in place of regular sour cream when baking quick breads. The differences in flavor, texture, appearance and baking quality should be minimal.

We use the term **ingredient alternative** to mean the replacement of one ingredient with another of different flavor, texture, appearance or other characteristic, but one that will not compromise—although it may change—the flavor of the dish. As with the ingredient substitute, the ingredient alternative may be more nutritious. Lemon juice and herbs, for instance, can be used as flavoring alternatives to salt; a salsa of fresh vegetables can replace a cream-based sauce. The dishes will not taste the same, but they will still taste good.

In attempting to modify a recipe, the chef should first identify the ingredient(s) or cooking method(s) that may need to be changed. He or she can then use the following principles—reduce, replace or eliminate—to make a dish healthier:

1 Reduce the amounts of the ingredient(s).
2 Replace the ingredient(s) with a substitute that will do the least to change the flavor and appearance of the dish.
3 Eliminate the ingredient(s).

SALT SUBSTITUTES AND ALTERNATIVES

A concern in the American diet is excessive sodium (salt). The average American consumes 3000 to 7000 mg of sodium per day, well in excess of daily needs. Research has linked excessive amounts of sodium to hypertension (high blood pressure), heart and kidney diseases and strokes.

Chefs are sometimes taught to use salt liberally to enhance flavors. Most salt substitutes (which are potassium chloride instead of sodium chloride), however, neither enhance flavors like salt nor are even palatable to many people. In trying to moderate the amount of salt in a dish, the chef should reduce the quantity of the sodium-containing ingredients or use a lower-sodium choice. Soy sauce is a good example; often the quantity can be reduced, and excellent low-sodium soy products are available. In addition, pepper, lemon, herbs, spices, fruit and flavored vinegars can be used as salt alternatives to heighten flavor.

ARTIFICIAL SWEETENERS

Saccharin, the oldest artificial sugar substitute, has been used for more than a century. It has no calories and tastes 300 times sweeter than table sugar. Saccharin has a bitter aftertaste, however, and many people find it unpalatable.

Aspartame (brand name NutraSweet), approved by the FDA in 1981, comprises the amino acids aspartic acid and phenylalanine. Unlike saccharin, aspartame does not have an aftertaste. It is 180 times sweeter than table sugar. It is now widely used in soft drinks, frozen yogurts, fruit spreads, candies and similar products. Aspartame breaks down when heated, so it cannot be used in cooked foods. According to the FDA, aspartame is a safe substitute for sugar, although it is a risk for those people with the rare disorder phenylketonuria (PKU), who cannot metabolize the phenylalanine in aspartame. Appropriate warnings are printed on all aspartame-sweetened foods.

Another sugar substitute is acesulfame-K (brand name Sunnette), which the FDA approved in 1988. The body cannot metabolize acesulfame-K, so it passes through the digestive system unchanged. Like aspartame, it has no aftertaste. Acesulfame-K is used in chewing gum, dry beverage mixes, instant coffees and teas, gelatins and nondairy creamers. It is more stable than aspartame, so it can be used in baking.

The latest alternative sweetener approved by the FDA, sucralose (brand name Splenda) was discovered in 1976. It is 600 times sweeter than sugar and can be used like sugar in some baked goods. Sucralose, a derivative of table sugar, is virtually calorie-free because its sweetness is so intense that only minute amounts are needed to replace the sweetness of sugar.

FAT SUBSTITUTES AND ALTERNATIVES

Several types of FDA-approved fat substitutes have been used with varying degrees of success in the food industry. They include olestra (brand name Olean), Simplesse, caprenin, salatrim (brand name Benefat) and oatrim (hydrolyzed oat flour; brand name Replace). Some are synthetic, others are derived from naturally occurring food substances.

Olestra is made of sucrose and vegetable oil. The two are bonded together, and the final product consists of molecules too large to be digested. Because it cannot be digested, olestra does not add any calories. Currently, olestra is used in snack foods such as potato chips. It may become a useful substitute for fats in baking or cooking, but health concerns have kept it from being widely available.

Simplesse is a fat substitute used in frozen desserts such as ice creams and yogurt. Simplesse, made from egg whites or milk proteins, has a rich, creamy texture similar to fat but is fat-free. Products made with Simplesse are not usually fat-free because other fat-containing ingredients are added.

Caprenin and salatrim are fat substitutes used in the candy industry and not available for home or restaurant use. Oatrim is used in baked goods and dairy products. It has also been found to have antioxidant properties and is available for home or restaurant use.

Table 3.6	**INGREDIENT SUBSTITUTES**
INSTEAD OF	**USE**
Bacon	Canadian bacon or well-cooked, drained bacon
Butter	Powdered butter granules plus liquid (either fat-free milk or water) or butter-flavored oil sprays
Chocolate	Cocoa (vegetable oil may be added as needed)
Cream cheese	Reduced-fat cream cheese or fat-free cream cheese
Emulsified salad dressing	Start with a base of reduced-fat or nonfat yogurt, sour cream or mayonnaise, then thin with fat-free milk; *or* use a slurry-thickened broth or juice as the oil and add vinegar and other seasonings; *or* blend silken tofu with other ingredients for a creamy dressing
Ground beef	Textured soy protein; tempeh; seitan, a form of wheat gluten
Light cream	Equal portions of low-fat milk and fat-free evaporated milk
Mayonnaise	Reduced-fat mayonnaise (it can be mixed with reduced-fat or nonfat sour cream)
Sour cream	Reduced-fat or nonfat sour cream; drained reduced-fat or nonfat plain yogurt without gelatin
Whipped cream	Whipped chilled evaporated fat-free milk; the milk and beaters need to be very cold (needs to be stabilized)

OTHER INGREDIENT SUBSTITUTES AND ALTERNATIVES

▶ **additives** substances added to many foods to prevent spoilage or improve appearance, texture, flavor or nutritional value; they may be synthetic materials copied from nature (for example, sugar substitutes) or naturally occurring substances (for example, lecithin). Some food additives may cause allergic reactions in sensitive people.

▶ **incidental food additives** those inadvertently or unintentionally added to foods during processing, such as pesticide residues on fruits

▶ **intentional food additives** those added to foods on purpose, such as the chemicals used to ensure longer shelf life or food colorings

There are many other ingredient substitutes, some of which are identified in Table 3.6. Often ingredient substitutes and alternatives will have a dramatic impact on the nutritional values of a completed dish. Compare, for example, Recipes 33.25 and 33.26 in Chapter 33; the former brownie recipe is made with traditional ingredients, while the latter uses ingredient substitutes. Note the differences, especially in the values for fat and cholesterol.

Ingredient substitutes and, especially, ingredient alternatives change the nutritional values of a dish; they may also change its flavor, texture or appearance. Sometimes these changes are acceptable; sometimes they are not. Because some changes result in unsatisfactory flavors, textures or appearance, many recipes are not suitable for substitution or alteration. Use your judgment.

▶ NUTRITION LABELING

In an effort to provide chefs and consumers with greater information about the nutritional values of foods they purchase, the FDA requires that most food products be clearly labeled. The FDA also closely regulates the language used on these labels. Terms such as "low fat" and "lite" have specific legal definitions. The FDA also closely monitors health claims on food labels. A cereal, for instance, may claim that its fiber content may reduce the incidence of heart disease only if it meets the criteria set forth by the FDA.

The FDA also sets standards for the nutrition claims that can be made on restaurant menus. The language for menus is the same as that for product labels. Restaurateurs, however, are required to supply nutrition information only if they make a claim about a specific dish. For example, if a menu selection is described as "low fat," the dish must have 3 grams or less of fat per serving and the nutrition information (nutrient analysis) should be available to anyone who requests it. Restaurateurs and chefs should consult the FDA and the National Restaurant Association for guidance in complying with these labeling regulations.

PRODUCT CLAIMS

The FDA requires that words such as "low fat" and "fat free" be used according to the following specific standards:

- *Free*—The food contains no or only "physiologically inconsequential" amounts of fat, saturated fat, cholesterol, sodium, sugars or calories.
- *Low, little, few* and *low source of*—The food can be eaten frequently without exceeding dietary guidelines for fat, saturated fat, cholesterol, sodium or calories.

Specific uses include the following:

- *Low fat*—The food has 3 grams or less of fat per serving.
- *Low saturated fat*—The food has 1 gram or less of saturated fat per serving; not more than 15 percent of a serving's calories are from saturated fat.
- *Low sodium*—The food has 140 mg or less of salt per serving.

- *Very low sodium*—The food has 35 mg or less of salt per serving.
- *Low cholesterol*—The food has 20 mg or less of cholesterol per serving.
- *Low calorie*—The food has 40 calories or fewer per serving.
- *Reduced, less* and *fewer*—The nutritionally altered product contains at least 25 percent fewer calories than the regular or reference (that is, FDA standard) food product.
- *Light* or *lite*—The nutritionally altered product contains at least one-third or 50 percent less fat than the reference product. *Light in sodium* means that the nutritionally altered product contains 50 percent or less sodium than the regular or reference product. *Light* may still be used to describe color, as in "light brown sugar."
- *High*—The food contains 20 percent or more of the daily value for a desirable nutrient per serving.

- *More*—The food contains at least 10 percent or more of the daily value for protein, vitamins, minerals, dietary fiber or potassium than the reference product.
- *Good source*—The food contains 10 to 19 percent of the daily value per serving for the specific nutrient such as calcium or dietary fiber.
- *Lean*—The meat, poultry, game, fish or shellfish item contains less than 10 grams of fat, less than 4 grams of saturated fat and less than 95 mg of cholesterol per serving and per 100 grams.
- *Extra lean*—The meat, poultry, game, fish or shellfish item contains less than 5 grams of fat, less than 2 grams of saturated fat and less than 95 mg of cholesterol per serving and per 100 grams.

► CONSUMER CONCERNS ABOUT FOOD AND NUTRITION

Many food ingredients have been linked to medical conditions. Some of the links are tenuous at best; others may be well supported by research. Nutrition is a science, and new information about the relationship of food to health and disease is always changing.

Americans have voiced concerns about the possible links of certain fats and dietary cholesterol to heart disease; they want to know if sugar intake is related to obesity, diabetes and heart disease. Some people are concerned that pesticide residues in produce may be dangerous, and they will seek out restaurants that serve organically grown produce. Some people are worried about the increasing prevalence of genetically modified organisms and other products of biotechnology in our food supply and would prefer not to consume foods made with these ingredients. Others are curious about the alleged medicinal or health benefits of foods. Others have metabolic or digestive conditions that make it difficult or even dangerous for them to eat specific ingredients. Because of these concerns, patrons may request that their meals be prepared in special ways or that ingredients be deleted from or added to a dish. Patrons who question the wait staff about ingredients expect complete and accurate information.

A food service operation must train its servers to accurately answer customers' questions about ingredients, especially those commonly known to cause allergic reactions. Some people are so dangerously allergic that even the smallest amount of a particular ingredient could cause a deadly reaction. Common allergens include peanuts, soy, eggs, wheat, shellfish, mushrooms and milk. When using prepared or packaged ingredients in the kitchen, be sure to study the ingredient list and learn to recognize disguised ingredients or ingredients that are not used in their common form. For example, miso and lecithin are soy derivatives. If a customer wants to know whether a dish contains soy, the well-trained server should be able to answer correctly.

The tremendous public interest in nutrition presents a special challenge to chefs. They should be able to prepare and serve food that meets the high standards for health demanded by some patrons, while maintaining the flavor and appearance important to everyone.

▶ NUTRITION, EATING OUT AND THE CHEF

On a typical day, almost half of all American adults eat at least one meal in a food service establishment. Yet even though eating out has become an integral part of everyday life, Americans still treat a restaurant meal as a special occasion. The quantity and choices of foods offered by many restaurants has wreaked havoc with the American diet. Restaurant meals typically have more calories, sodium, fat and cholesterol and less fiber, vitamins and minerals than meals prepared at home. A recent study found that people who eat out most often tend to weigh more than those who usually eat at home.

Ultimately, it is the consumer's responsibility to choose wisely and eat moderately. Nevertheless, restaurateurs complain that customers do not usually order heart-healthy or low-fat dishes, perhaps viewing such menu items as less-tasty options than the traditional fare.

Patrons concerned with calories and fat may choose to order appetizers in place of entrées to control quantity and thereby reduce calories and fat. They may request half-orders or split a full order with a companion. They can ask that dressings and sauces be served on the side or that a different cooking method be used—for instance, that a fish be broiled or baked instead of deep-fried or sautéed. Chefs and restaurateurs should be flexible and willing to accommodate these patrons.

The Food Guide Pyramid was designed to guide food consumption for a more healthful life. It presents a plan for a balanced diet. Chefs can use it to plan balanced menus as well. As the Food Guide Pyramid suggests, chefs do not need to use only meat as the center of the plate presentation. The pyramid demands that a variety of breads, pasta and grains be included on the menu along with an interesting selection of vegetable dishes. And it cautions against the use of too much fat and sugar.

Although not every food service operation can (or should) be devoted to "health food," to the extent appropriate you should offer healthful dining alternatives. Your ability to do so depends, of course, upon your facility. Chefs at hospitals, prisons and schools have much greater control over the foods their guests consume. Therefore, they have a far greater opportunity and responsibility to provide selections for a well-balanced diet. Chefs at most restaurants, however, do not have such captive audiences. But that does not mean that you can shirk your responsibilities. You assist customers when you do the following:

1 Use proper purchasing and storage techniques in order to preserve nutrients.
2 Offer a variety of foods from each tier of the Food Guide Pyramid so that customers have a choice.
3 Offer entrées that emphasize plant instead of animal foods.
4 Offer low-salt and low-fat dishes.
5 Use cooking procedures that preserve rather than destroy nutrients.
6 Use cooking procedures that minimize the use of added fat (for example, stocks, sauces and soups can be cooled and the congealed fats removed; foods can be browned in the oven instead of being sautéed in hot fat).
7 Use equipment that minimizes the use of added fat (e.g., nonstick pans).
8 Train the wait staff to respond properly to nutritional questions diners may have about menu items.
9 Use ingredient alternatives or substitutes where appropriate. If a dish does not lend itself to ingredient alternatives or substitutes, consider creating a new

dish that replaces less-nutritious traditional foods or preparations with more-nutritious ones. For example, instead of serving a sauce made with butter, flour and cream, you can reduce an appropriately seasoned wine, stock or juice and then thicken it with fruit or vegetable purées or cornstarch.

A registered dietician has analyzed all of the recipes in this book using nutritional analysis software that incorporates data from the USDA, research laboratories and food manufacturers. The nutrient information provided here should be used only as a reference, however. A margin of error of approximately 20 percent can be expected because of natural variations in ingredients; the federal government permits food manufacturers and other suppliers to use this same margin of error in their food labeling efforts. Preparation techniques and serving sizes may also significantly alter the values of many nutrients. For the nutritional analysis, if a recipe offers a choice of ingredients, the first-mentioned ingredient was the one used. Ingredients listed as "to taste" (TT) and "as needed" were omitted from the analysis. Corn oil and whole milk were used throughout for "vegetable oil" and "milk," respectively. When given a range of ingredient quantities or numbers of servings, the average was used.

Throughout this book various recipes are marked with the pyramid symbol illustrated in Figure 3.2. This symbol identifies dishes that are particularly low in calories, fat, saturated fat or sodium; if appropriate, they may also be a good source of vitamins, protein, fiber or calcium.

Vegetarian dishes are indicated with the symbol illustrated in Figure 3.3. These recipes do not contain any meat, fish, shellfish or poultry, but may contain dairy products and/or eggs. Vegetarian dishes are not necessarily low in calories, fat or sodium, nor are they automatically good sources of vitamins, protein, fiber or calcium, as defined by government standards.

FIGURE 3.2 ▶ Symbol for a healthy recipe

FIGURE 3.3 ▶ Symbol for a vegetarian recipe

CONCLUSION

A basic understanding and appreciation of nutrition are important for both the consumer and those who prepare the foods consumed.

What you serve is important. Carbohydrates, proteins, lipids (fats), vitamins, minerals, and water, in varying amounts, are all necessary for good health. The Food Guide Pyramid can guide selections to create and maintain a healthful diet.

How foods are prepared is also important. Remember that some cooking and storage techniques preserve nutrients; others do not. In addition, by substituting or modifying ingredients and preparation methods, many dishes can be made more nutritious.

QUESTIONS FOR DISCUSSION

1 Identify the six categories of nutrients and list two sources for each.
2 What are the differences between saturated fats and unsaturated fats? Identify two sources for each.
3 List four ways to reduce mineral and vitamin loss when storing or preparing foods.
4 Describe the Food Guide Pyramid. Explain how a chef can use it to plan well-balanced meals and how a consumer can use it to establish a healthful diet. What other diet-planning tools can be used along with the pyramid?
5 Locate the latest information on the U.S. government's standards for organic certification.
6 Find the address and contact information for your local extension service. Determine what nutritional guidance they offer consumers.

My mother's [recipes] don't do me as much good as they might because she never included directions. Her reasoning, often expressed, was that any cook worth her salt would know, given a list of ingredients, what to do with them, and if she did come to a momentary loss while stirring up a dish—*TASTE* it! Cooking was a matter of born sense, ordinary good judgment, enough experience, materials worth the bothering about, and tasting.

—*Eudora Welty, American author (1909–2001)*
in her introduction to The Jackson Cookbook,
1971

MENUS AND RECIPES

4

AFTER STUDYING THIS CHAPTER, YOU WILL BE ABLE TO:

▶ appreciate the different types and styles of menus

▶ understand the purpose of standardized recipes

▶ convert recipe yield amounts

▶ appreciate the need for cost controls in any food service operation

▶ **entrée** the main dish of an American meal, usually meat, poultry, fish or shellfish accompanied by a vegetable and starch; in France, the first course, served before the fish and meat courses

Today's professional chef must master more than the basics of béchamel, butchering and bread baking. You must be equally skilled in the business of food services. This means knowing what products cost and how to control and maintain food costs. It also means understanding how accurate measurements, portion control and proper food handling directly affect the food service operation's bottom line.

This chapter introduces you to various types and styles of menus. It then explains a standardized recipe format and presents information on measurements and techniques for changing or converting recipe yields. It then describes methods for determining unit and recipe costs and concludes with a discussion of methods for controlling food costs.

▶ THE MENU

Whether it lists Spanish dishes, hamburgers, just desserts or classic cuisine, and whether the prices range from inexpensive to exorbitant, the menu is the soul of every food service operation. Its purposes are to identify for the consumer the foods and beverages the operation offers, to create consumer enthusiasm and to increase sales. When combined with good food and good service, a good menu helps ensure success.

Most menus offer consumers sufficient selections to build an entire meal. A typical North American meal consists of three courses. The first course may be a hot or cold appetizer, soup or salad. The second course is the **entrée** or main dish, usually meat, poultry, fish or shellfish accompanied by a vegetable and starch. The third course is dessert, either a sweet preparation or fruit and cheese. For a more formal meal, there may be a progression of first courses, including a hot or cold appetizer and soup, as well as a fish course served before the main dish (which, in this case, would not be fish). For a meal served in the European tradition, the salad would be presented as a palate cleanser after the main dish and before the dessert.

TYPES OF MENUS

Menus are classified according to the regularity with which the foods are offered:

1 **Static menu**—All patrons are offered the same foods every day. Once a static menu is developed and established, it rarely changes. Static menus are typically found in fast-food operations, ethnic restaurants, steakhouses and the like. Static menus can also be used in institutional settings. For example, a static menu at an elementary school could offer students, along with a vegetable and dessert, the same luncheon choices every school day: a cheeseburger, fish sticks, chicken tacos, pizza wedges or a sandwich.

2 **Cycle menu**—A cycle menu is developed for a set period; at the end of that period it repeats itself (that is, on a seven-day cycle, the same menu is used every Monday). Some cycle menus are written on a seasonal basis, with a new menu for each season to take advantage of product availability. Cycle menus are used commonly in schools, hospitals and other institutions. Although cycle menus may be repetitive, the

FOOD IN FLICKS

Growing up in New York City afforded me a wide array of cultural experiences. East 86th Street had everything I needed: bookstores, record stores, pizza places, and my beloved movies. Ah, the movies. Remember that bygone era before the VCR when waiting on line at the cinema was a sociable experience?

A sojourn to the movies also meant a fine dining experience: a hot dog and a papaya drink at Papaya King. Laugh if you must, but Papaya King, just like Gramercy Tavern, is also listed in the Zagat guide. Even though I'm no longer a kid, I still occassionaly sneak in a contraband cheeseburger, as Woody Allen did at the now-defunct Bleecker Street Cinema in his 1989 film *Crimes and Misdemeanors.*

Movies have always embraced food as well; over the years, food has been celebrated, created, thrown, questionably digested and even animated. The combination of food and film could be considered, as Humphrey Bogart said to Claude Rains at the end of *Casablanca,* "the beginning of a beautiful friendship." Here's a list of some films and, if you'll allow, some editorial remarks to give you food for thought the next time you visit a video emporium.

Animal House (1978)—John Belushi at the cafeteria. His imitation of a zit, and ultimately the food fight.

Blazing Saddles (1974)—Mel Brooks. The campfire scene. Enough said.

Big Night (1996)—The creation of that amazing Timpano in hopes that Louis Prima would soon arrive to share in what would sadly be the restaurant's final night.

Diner (1982)—"You gonna finish that sandwich?"

Monty Python's The Meaning of Life (1983)—"One tiny wafer-thin mint?"

Italianamerican (1974)—Martin Scorsese's look at his parents' history from the old country and the secret to great sauce making.

Tom Jones (1963)—Food as seduction in Tony Richardson's Oscar winner.

My Dinner with André (1981)—The sharing of a meal and life lessons and philosophy between André Gregory and Wallace Shawn.

Fried Green Tomatoes (1991)—Secret-recipe barbecue and blackberry cobbler.

Tampopo (1986)—The quest of a truck driver to help a widow improve a noodle shop.

The Big Chill (1983)—Preparing dinner to the strains of the Temptations' "Ain't Too Proud to Beg."

Chocolat (2000)

The Godfather (1972)—Clemenza teaches the young Michael Corleone the secret to a good spaghetti sauce: "Ya might have to cook for twenty, thirty guys someday." Or Clemenza's instructions to one of his henchmen after dispatching a traitor: "Leave the gun . . . take the cannoli."

Like Water for Chocolate (1992)

Kramer vs. Kramer (1979)—Dustin Hoffman trying in vain to make French toast for his son the morning after his wife, Meryl Streep, has left them.

Eat Drink, Man Woman (1994)

Babe (1995)—Ferdinand the Duck's rant: "Christmas means dinner; dinner means death. Death means carnage; Christmas is carnage!"

Willy Wonka and the Chocolate Factory (1971)—Everlasting Gobstoppers, fizzy-lifting drink, a chocolate river . . . pure imagination.

Goodfellas (1990)—Paul Sorvino slicing garlic with a razor blade to enhance his jail cell cooking.

Soul Food (1997)

Five Easy Pieces (1970)—Jack Nicholson and the chicken salad sandwich.

The Silence of the Lambs (1991)—"A census taker once tried to test me. I ate his liver with some fava beans and a nice Chianti."

The Gold Rush (1925)—Charlie Chaplin's classic includes the dance of the dinner rolls and the preparation of a leather boot for dinner.

L.A. Story (1991)—"I'll have a half double decaffeinated half-caf, with a twist of lemon."

Babette's Feast (1987)—Oscar winner for Best Foreign Film in which the spoils of a lottery winning goes entirely towards a celebratory feast.

I would be remiss if I neglected Bugs Bunny, hence *French Rarebit* (1951). French chefs Louie and François argue over who will have Bugs on the menu. Bugs's suggestion: "Of course if you want something really good, you can't beat a Louisiana Back Bay Bayou Bunny Bordelaise . . . à la Antoine." Chef Louie: "À la Antoine? You mean Antoine of New Orleans?" Bugs: "I don't mean Antoine of Flatbush."

That's all folks!

ROGER RAINES, an actor and writer who also works at Gramercy Tavern, New York, NY

repetition is not necessarily noticeable to diners because of the length of the cycles.

3 Market menu—A market menu is based upon product availability during a specific period; it is written to use foods when they are in peak season or readily available. Market menus are becoming increasingly popular with chefs (and consumers) since they challenge the chef's ingenuity in using fresh, seasonal products. Market menus are short-lived, however, because of limited product availability and perishability. In fact, they often change daily.

4 Hybrid menu—A hybrid menu combines a static menu with a cycle menu or a market menu of specials.

Food service operations may have separate menus for breakfast, lunch or dinner. If all three meals are available all day and are listed on the same menu, the menu is often called a **California menu;** California menus are typically found in 24-hour restaurants. Depending on the food service operation's objectives, separate specialty menus for drinks, hors d'oeuvres, desserts, brunch or afternoon tea, for example, are used.

Regardless of whether the menu is static, cycle, market or hybrid, it can offer consumers the opportunity to purchase their selections à la carte, semi à la carte, table d'hôte or some combination of the three.

1 **À la carte**—Every food and beverage item is priced and ordered separately.

2 **Semi à la carte**—With this popular menu style, some food items (particularly appetizers and desserts) are priced and ordered separately, while the entrée is accompanied by and priced to include other items, such as a salad, starch or vegetable.

3 **Table d'hôte** or **prix fixe**—This menu offers a complete meal at a set price. (The term *table d'hôte* is French for "host's table" and is derived from the innkeeper's practice of seating all guests at a large communal table and serving them all the same meal.) A table d'hôte meal can range from very elegant to a diner's blue-plate special.

Many menus combine à la carte, semi à la carte and table d'hôte choices. For example, appetizers, salads and desserts may be available à la carte; entrées may be offered semi à la carte (served with a salad, starch and vegetable), while the daily special is a complete (table d'hôte or prix fixe) meal.

MENU LANGUAGE

The menu is the principal way in which the food service operation, including the chef, communicates with the consumer. A well-designed menu often reflects the input of design, marketing, art and other consultants as well as the chef and management. The type of folds, cover, artwork, layout, typefaces, colors and paper are all important considerations. But the most important consideration is the language.

The menu should list the foods offered. It may include descriptions such as the preparation method, essential ingredients and service method as well as the quality, cut and quantity of product. For example, the menu can list "Porterhouse Steak" or "Mesquite Grilled 16-oz. Angus Beef Porterhouse Steak."

TRUTH IN ADVERTISING

Federal as well as some state and local laws require that certain menu language be accurate. Areas of particular concern include statements about quantity, quality, grade and freshness. Accurate references to an item's source are also important. If brand names are used, those brands must be served. If the restaurant claims to be serving "Fresh Dover Sole," it must be just that, not frozen sole from New England. (On the other hand, like French or Russian dressing, "English mint sauce" is a generic name for a style of food, so using that geographical adjective is appropriate even if the mint sauce is made in Arizona.) A reference to "our own fresh-baked" desserts means that the restaurant regularly bakes the desserts on premises, serves them soon after baking and does not substitute commercially prepared or frozen goods.

NUTRITIONAL STATEMENTS

As discussed in Chapter 3, Nutrition, the FDA carefully regulates the language used on packaged food labels. In 1997, the FDA extended its nutrition labeling regulations to restaurant menus. These regulations are intended to prevent restaurants from making misleading health or nutrition claims. For example, terms such as "light," "healthy" or "heart healthy" must be accurate and documented. The standards for calculating and presenting that information are far less stringent than the regulations for packaged foods, however. Restaurants may support their claims with data from any "reasonable" source, and may present that information in any format, including verbally. Nutritional data is not required for menu items that do not carry a nutritional content or health claim.

▶ STANDARDIZED RECIPES

Menu writing and **recipe** development are mutually dependent activities. Once the menu is created, standardized recipes should be prepared for each item. A **standardized recipe** is one that will produce a known quality and quantity of food for a specific operation. It specifies (1) the type and amount of each ingredient, (2) the preparation and cooking procedures and (3) the yield and portion size.

Standardized recipes are not found in books or provided by manufacturers; they are recipes customized to your operation—cooking time, temperature and utensils should be based on the equipment actually available. Yield should be adjusted to an amount appropriate for your operation. A recipe must be tested repeatedly and adjusted to fit your facility and your needs before it can be considered standardized.

Standardized recipes are a tool for the chef and management. The written forms assist with training cooks, educating service staff and controlling financial matters. They help ensure that customers receive a consistent quality and quantity of product. And they are essential for accurate recipe costing and menu pricing. Each recipe should be complete, consistent and simple to read and follow. These recipe forms should be stored in a readily accessible place. Index cards, notebook binders or a computerized database may be used, depending on the size and complexity of the operation.

▶ **recipe** a set of written instructions for producing a specific food or beverage; also known as a formula

▶ **standardized recipe** a recipe producing a known quality and quantity of food for a specific operation

Table 4.1 COMMON ABBREVIATIONS

teaspoon	= tsp.
tablespoon	= Tbsp.
cup	= c.
pint	= pt.
quart	= qt.
gram	= g
milliliter	= ml
liter	= lt
ounce	= oz.
fluid ounce	= fl. oz.
pound	= lb.
kilogram	= kg

▶ MEASUREMENTS AND CONVERSIONS

MEASUREMENT FORMATS

Accurate measurements are among the most important aspects of food production. Ingredients and portions must be measured correctly to ensure consistent product quality. In other words, the chef must be able to prepare a recipe the same way each time, and portion sizes must be the same from one order to the next. In a kitchen, measurements may be made in three ways: weight, volume and count.

Weight refers to the mass or heaviness of a substance. It is expressed in terms such as grams, ounces, pounds and tons. Weight may be used to measure liquid or dry ingredients (for example, 2 pounds of eggs for a bread recipe) and portions (for example, 4 ounces of sliced turkey for a sandwich). Since weight is generally the most accurate form of measurement, portion scales or balance scales are commonly used in kitchens.

Volume refers to the space occupied by a substance. This is mathematically expressed as *height × width × length*. It is expressed in terms such as cups, quarts, gallons, teaspoons, fluid ounces, bushels and liters. Volume is most commonly used to measure liquids. It may also be used for dry ingredients when the amount is too small to be weighed accurately (for example, ¼ teaspoon of salt). Although measuring by volume is somewhat less accurate than measuring by weight, volume measurements are generally quicker to do.

Frequently, mistakes are made in food preparation by chefs who assume wrongly that weight and volume are equal. Do not be fooled! One cup does not always equal 8 ounces. Although it is true that 1 standard cup contains 8 *fluid* ounces, it is not true that the contents of that standard cup will *weigh* 8 ounces. For example, the weight of 1 cup of diced apples will vary depending on the size of the apple pieces. Errors are commonly made in the bakeshop by cooks who assume that 8 ounces of flour is the same as 1 cup of flour. In fact, 1 cup of flour weighs only about 4 ½ ounces.

It is not unusual to see both weight and volume measurements used in a single recipe. When a recipe ingredient is expressed in weight, weigh it. When it is expressed as a volume, measure it. Like most rules, however, this one has exceptions. The weight and volume of water, butter, eggs and milk are, in each case, the same. For these ingredients you may use whichever measurement is most convenient.

Count refers to the number of individual items. Count is used in recipes (for example, 4 eggs) and in portion control (for example, 2 fish fillets or 1 ear of corn). Count is also commonly used in purchasing to indicate the size of the individual items. For example, a "96 count" case of lemons means that a 40-pound case contains 96 individual lemons; a "115 count" case means that the same 40-pound case contains 115 individual lemons. So, each lemon in the 96-count case is larger than those in the 115-count case. Shrimp is another item commonly sold by count. One pound of shrimp may contain from eight to several hundred shrimp, depending on the size of the individual pieces. When placing an order, the chef must specify the desired count. For example, when ordering one pound of 21–25-count shrimp, the chef expects to receive not fewer than 21 nor more than 25 pieces.

MEASUREMENT SYSTEMS

The measurement formats of weight, volume and count are used in both the U.S. and metric measurement systems. Both of these systems are used in modern food service operations, so you should be able to prepare recipes written in either one.

The **U.S. system,** with which you are probably familiar, is actually the more difficult system to understand. It uses pounds for weight and cups for volume.

The **metric system** is the most commonly used system in the world. Developed in France during the late 18th century, it was intended to fill the need for a mathematically rational and uniform system of measurement. The metric system is a decimal system in which the gram, liter and meter are the basic units of weight, volume and length, respectively. Larger or smaller units of weight, volume and length are formed by adding a prefix to the words *gram, liter* or *meter.* Some of the more commonly used prefixes in food service operations are *deca-* (10), *kilo-* (1000), *deci-* (¹⁄₁₀) and *milli-* (¹⁄₁₀₀₀). Thus, a kilogram is 1000 grams; a decameter is 10 meters; a milliliter is ¹⁄₁₀₀₀ of a liter. Because the metric system is based on multiples of 10, it is extremely easy to increase or decrease amounts.

The most important thing for a chef to know about the metric system is that *you do not need to convert between the metric system and the U.S. system in recipe preparation.* If a recipe is written in metric units, use metric measuring equipment; if it is written in U.S. units, use U.S. measuring equipment. Luckily, most modern measuring equipment is calibrated in both U.S. and metric increments. The need to convert amounts will arise only if the proper equipment is unavailable.

CONVERTING GRAMS AND OUNCES

As you can see from Table 4.2, 1 ounce equals 28.35 grams. Likewise, 1 fluid ounce equals 28.35 milliliters. So, to convert ounces/fluid ounces to grams/milliliters, multiply the number of ounces by 28 (rounded for convenience).

FANNIE MERRITT FARMER (1857–1915)

Fannie Farmer is more than the name on a cookbook. She was an early, vigorous and influential proponent of scientific cooking, nutrition and academic training for culinary professionals.

At age 30, Farmer enrolled in the Boston Cooking School. The school's curriculum was not designed to graduate chefs, but rather to produce cooking teachers. After graduating from the two-year course, Farmer stayed on, first as assistant principal and then as principal.

During her years there (and, indeed, for the rest of her career) she was obsessed with accurate measurements. She waged a campaign to eliminate measurements such as a "wine glass" of liquid, a "handful" of flour, a chunk of butter the "size of an egg" or a "heaping spoonful" of salt. For, as she once wrote, "correct measurements are absolutely necessary to insure the best results." Farmer also sought to replace the European system of measuring ingredients by weight with, for her, a more scientific measurement system based on volume and level measures (for example, a level tablespoon). To a great degree, she succeeded.

Her writings reflect her concern for accurate measurements. Her first book, *The Boston Cooking School Cookbook* (1896), includes clearly written recipes with precise measurements. Later editions add recipe yields, oven temperatures and baking times.

After leaving the Boston Cooking School, she opened Miss Farmer's School of Cookery.

The curriculum listed 60 lessons divided into six courses. The first course covered the basics: laying a fire and using a gas stove; making breads, eggs, soups, potatoes and coffee. The second and third courses emphasized more advanced cooking. Pastry, desserts and salads were taught during the fourth course; presentation and service were taught during the fifth course. Quite progressively for the time, her sixth course taught cooking for nurses and emphasized nutrition and the dietary needs of the sick and elderly. (This may have reflected Farmer's personal interests, for she was partially disabled and in poor health from time to time.)

Farmer wrote other cookbooks, including *Food and Cookery for the Sick and Convalescent* (1904) and *A New Book of Cookery* (first published in 1912 and republished in several revised versions). Her writings never address the joys of cooking and eating; rather, they reflect a scientific approach to cooking and rely on clearly written, accurately measured recipes for good, solid food.

$$8 \text{ oz.} \times 28 = 224 \text{ g}$$

$$8 \text{ fl. oz.} \times 28 = 224 \text{ ml}$$

To convert grams/milliliters to ounces/fluid ounces, divide the number of grams/milliliters by 28.

$$224 \text{ g} \div 28 = 8 \text{ oz.}$$

$$224 \text{ ml} \div 28 = 8 \text{ fl. oz.}$$

To help you develop a framework for judging conversions, remember that:

► A kilogram is about 2.2 pounds
► A gram is about 1/30 ounce
► A pound is about 450 grams
► A liter is slightly more than a quart
► A centimeter is slightly less than ½ inch
► 0°C (32°F) is the freezing point of water
► 100°C (212°F) is the boiling point of water

These approximations are not a substitute for accurate conversions, however. Appendix II contains additional information on equivalents and metric conversions. There is no substitute for knowing this information. In fact, it should become second nature to you.

Table 4.2	**COMMON EQUIVALENTS**
dash	= 1/8 teaspoon
3 teaspoons	= 1 tablespoon
2 tablespoons	= 1 fl. oz.
4 tablespoons	= 1/4 cup (2 fl. oz.)
5⅓ tablespoons	= 1/3 cup (2⅔ fl. oz.)
16 tablespoons	= 1 cup (8 fl. oz.)
2 cups	= 1 pint (16 fl. oz.)
2 pints	= 1 quart (32 fl. oz.)
4 quarts	= 1 gallon (128 fl. oz.)
2 gallons	= 1 peck
4 pecks	= 1 bushel
1 gram	= 0.035 ounce (1/30 oz.)
1 ounce	= 28.35 grams
454 grams	= 1 pound
2.2 pounds	= 1 kilogram (1000 grams)
1 teaspoon	= 5 milliliters
1 tablespoon	= 15 milliliters
1 fluid ounce	= 28.35 milliliters
1 cup	= 0.24 liters
1 gallon	= 3.80 liters

▶ **yield** the total amount of a product made from a specific recipe; also, the amount of a food item remaining after cleaning or processing

▶ **conversion factor (C.F.)** the number used to increase or decrease ingredient quantities and recipe yields

$$\frac{\text{New}}{\text{Old}} = \text{C.F.}$$

$$\frac{\text{Old Recipe}}{\text{X} \quad \text{C.F.}}$$
$$\text{New Recipe}$$

▶ RECIPE CONVERSIONS

Whether 6 servings or 60, every recipe is designed to produce or **yield** a specific amount of product. A recipe's yield may be expressed in *volume, weight* or *servings* (for example, 1 quart of sauce; 8 pounds of bread dough; 8 half-cup servings). If the expected yield does not meet your needs, you must convert (that is, increase or decrease) the ingredient amounts. Recipe conversion is sometimes complicated by *portion size conversion.* For example, it may be necessary to convert a recipe that initially produces 24 8-ounce servings of soup into a recipe that produces 62 6-ounce servings.

It is just as easy to change yields by uneven amounts as it is to double or halve recipes. The mathematical principle is the same: *Each ingredient is multiplied by a* **conversion factor.** Do not take shortcuts by estimating recipe amounts or conversion factors. Inaccurate conversions lead to inedible foods, embarrassing shortages or wasteful excesses. Take the time to learn and apply proper conversion techniques.

CONVERTING TOTAL YIELD

When portion size is unimportant or remains the same, recipe yield is converted by a simple two-step process:

STEP 1 Divide the desired (new) yield by the recipe (old) yield to obtain the conversion factor (C.F.).

new yield ÷ old yield = conversion factor

STEP 2 Multiply each ingredient quantity by the conversion factor to obtain the new quantity.

old quantity × conversion factor = new quantity

EXAMPLE 4.1

You need to convert a recipe for cauliflower soup. The present recipe yields 1½ gallons. You need to make only ¾ gallon.

STEP 1 Determine the conversion factor:

0.75 gallon ÷ 1.5 gallons = 0.5

Note that any unit can be used, as long as the *same* unit is used with *both* the new and the old recipes. For example, the same conversion factor would be obtained if the recipe amounts were converted to fluid ounces:

96 fluid ounces ÷ 192 fluid ounces = 0.5

STEP 2 Apply the conversion factor to each ingredient in the soup recipe:

CAULIFLOWER SOUP

	old quantity	×	C.F.	=	new quantity
Cauliflower, chopped	5 lb.	×	0.5	=	2½ lb.
Celery stalks	4	×	0.5	=	2
Onion	1	×	0.5	=	½
Chicken stock	2 qt.	×	0.5	=	1 qt.
Heavy cream	3 pt.	×	0.5	=	1½ pt.

CONVERTING PORTION SIZE

Sometimes the amount of food served as a portion must be changed. For example, new soup cups may hold less than cups now being used, or a banquet menu may require a smaller entrée portion than is normally served à la carte. A few additional steps are necessary to convert recipes when portion sizes must also be changed. This is easy to understand if you think in terms of the total amount of a food item that is needed in relation to the total amount of that item (yield) produced by the current recipe. The key is to find a common denominator for the new and old recipes: ounces, grams, cups, servings and so on. Any unit can be used, as long as the *same* unit is used with *both* the new and the old recipes.

STEP 1 Determine the total yield of the existing recipe by multiplying the number of portions by the portion size.

original portions × original portion size = total (old) yield

STEP 2 Determine the total yield desired by multiplying the new number of portions by the new portion size.

desired portions × desired portion size = total (new) yield

STEP 3 Obtain the conversion factor as described earlier.

total (new) yield ÷ total (old) yield = conversion factor

STEP 4 Multiply each ingredient quantity by the conversion factor.

old quantity × conversion factor = new quantity

$$\frac{\text{No. of Portions} \times \text{Portion Size}}{\text{Yield}}$$

$$\frac{\text{New Yield}}{\text{Old Yield}} = \text{C.F.}$$

EXAMPLE 4.2

Returning to the cauliflower soup: The original recipe produced 1½ gallons or 48 4-ounce servings. Now you need 72 6-ounce servings.

STEP 1 Total original yield is 48 × 4 = 192 ounces.
STEP 2 Total desired yield is 72 × 6 = 432 ounces.
STEP 3 The conversion factor is calculated by dividing total new yield by total old yield:

432 ÷ 192 = 2.25

STEP 4 Old ingredient quantities are multiplied by the conversion factor to determine the new quantities:

CAULIFLOWER SOUP

	old quantity	×	C.F.	=	new quantity
Cauliflower, chopped	5 lb.	×	2.25	=	11.25 lb.
Celery stalks	4	×	2.25	=	9
Onion	1	×	2.25	=	2.25
Chicken stock	2 qt.	×	2.25	=	4.5 qt.
Heavy cream	3 pt.	×	2.25	=	6.75 pt.

ADDITIONAL CONVERSION PROBLEMS

When making large recipe changes—for example, from 5 to 25 portions or 600 to 300 portions—you may encounter additional problems. The mathematical conversions described here do not take into account changes in equipment, evaporation rates, unforeseen recipe errors or cooking times. Chefs learn to use their judgment, knowledge of cooking principles and skills to compensate for these factors.

EQUIPMENT

When you change the size of a recipe, you must often change the equipment used as well. Problems arise, however, when the production techniques previously used no longer work with the new quantity of ingredients. For example, if you normally make a muffin recipe in small quantities by hand and you increase the recipe size, it may be necessary to prepare the batter in a mixer. But if mixing time remains the same, the batter may become overmixed, resulting in poor-quality muffins. Trying to prepare a small amount of product in equipment that is too large for the task can also affect its quality.

EVAPORATION

Equipment changes can also affect product quality because of changes in evaporation rates. Increasing a soup recipe may require substituting a tilt skillet for a saucepan. But because a tilt skillet provides more surface area for evaporation than does a saucepan, reduction time must be decreased to prevent overthickening the soup. The increased evaporation caused by increased surface area may also alter the strength of the seasonings.

RECIPE ERRORS

A recipe may contain errors in ingredients or techniques that are not obvious when it is prepared in small quantities. When increased, however, small mistakes often become big (and obvious) ones, and the final product suffers. The only solution is to test recipes carefully and rely on your knowledge of cooking principles to compensate for unexpected problems.

TIME

Do not multiply time specifications given in a recipe by the conversion factor used with the recipe's ingredients. All things being equal, *cooking time* will not change when recipe size changes. For example, a muffin requires the same amount of baking time whether you prepare 1 dozen or 14 dozen. Cooking time will be affected, however, by changes in evaporation rate or heat conduction caused by equipment changes. *Mixing time* may change when recipe size is changed. Different equipment may perform mixing tasks more or less efficiently than previously used equipment. Again, rely on experience and good judgment.

▶ CALCULATING UNIT COSTS AND RECIPE COSTS

UNIT COSTS

Food service operations purchase most foods from suppliers in bulk or wholesale packages. For example, canned goods are purchased by the case; produce by the flat, case or lug; and flour and sugar by 25- or 50-pound bags. Even fish and meats are often purchased in large cuts, not individual serving-sized portions. The purchased amount is rarely used for a single recipe, however. It must be broken down into smaller units such as pounds, cups, quarts or ounces.

In order to allocate the proper ingredient costs to the recipe being prepared, it is necessary to convert **as-purchased (A.P.) costs or prices** to **unit costs or**

▶ **as purchased (A.P.)** the condition or cost of an item as it is purchased or received from the supplier

▶ **unit cost** the price paid to acquire one of the specified units

prices. To find the unit cost (that is, the cost of a particular unit, say, a single egg) in a package containing multiple units (for example, a 30-dozen case), divide the A.P. cost of the package by the number of units in the package.

A.P. cost ÷ number of units = cost per unit

$$\frac{\text{A.P. \$}}{\text{\# of Units}} = \text{\$ per Unit}$$

EXAMPLE 4.3

A case of #10 cans contains six individual cans. If a case of tomato paste costs $23.50, then each can costs $3.92.

$23.50 ÷ 6 = $3.92

If your recipe uses less than the total can, you must continue dividing the cost of the can until you arrive at the appropriate unit amount. Continuing with the tomato paste example, if you need only 1 cup of tomato paste, divide the can price ($3.92) by the total number of cups contained in the can to arrive at the cost per cup (unit). The list of canned-good sizes in Appendix II shows that a #10 can contains approximately 13 cups. Using the formula, each cup costs $0.30.

$3.92 ÷ 13 = $0.30

The cost of one cup can be reduced even further if necessary. If the recipe uses only 1 tablespoon of tomato paste, divide the cost per cup by the number of tablespoons in a cup. As you can see, the cost for 1 tablespoon of this tomato paste is $0.018.

$0.30 ÷ 16 = $.018

So when you are calculating the total cost of a recipe containing a tablespoon of tomato paste, the unit cost will be $.018 or 1.8¢.

Cost information is usually provided to the chef or manager from purchase invoices. It may also be necessary to examine a product's label or package to determine some information such as actual weight or size.

RECIPE COSTS

A standard recipe, listing the ingredients and their amounts, as well as the number and size of the portions, must be established in order to determine the cost of a completed menu item. Once an accurate recipe is written, the **total recipe cost** is calculated with the following two-step procedure:

STEP 1 Determine the cost for the given quantity of each recipe ingredient with the unit costing procedures described earlier.

STEP 2 Add all the ingredient costs together to obtain the total recipe cost.

▶ **total recipe cost** the total cost of ingredients for a particular recipe; it does not reflect overhead, labor, fixed expenses or profit

The total recipe cost can then be broken down into the **cost per portion,** which is the most useful figure for food cost controls. To arrive at cost per portion, divide the total recipe cost by the total number of servings or portions produced by that recipe.

total recipe cost ÷ number of portions = cost per portion

▶ **cost per portion** the amount of the total recipe cost divided by the number of portions produced from that recipe; the cost of one serving

$$\frac{\text{Recipe \$}}{\text{\# of Portions}} = \text{\$ per Portion}$$

The Recipe Costing Form shown in Figure 4.1 is useful for organizing recipe costing information. It provides space for listing each ingredient, the quantity of each ingredient needed, the cost of each unit (known as **edible portion** or **E.P**), and the total cost for the ingredient. Total yield, portion size and cost per portion are listed at the bottom of the form. Note that there is no space for recipe procedures, since these are generally irrelevant in recipe costing.

▶ **edible portion (E.P.)** the amount of a food item available for consumption or use after trimming or fabrication; a smaller, more convenient portion of a larger or bulk unit

RECIPE COSTING FORM

Menu Item ___Beef Stew___ Date _____

Total Yield ___200 fl. oz.___ Portion Size ___4 fl. oz.___

INGREDIENT	QUANTITY	A.P. $	Yield %*	E.P. $	RECIPE COST
Beef, cubes	6 lb.	1.60/lb.		1.60/lb.	9.60
Corn oil	3 Tbsp.	4.58/gal.		.29/c.	.05
Flour	1 1/2 oz.	11.20/50#		.22/lb.	.02
Beef stock	2 qt.	1.50/gal.		.375/qt.	.75
Carrots, diced	1 lb.	.26/lb.	82%	.32/lb.	.32
Potatoes, diced	2 lb.	.28/lb.	80%	.35/lb.	.70
Onions	2	.10 each		.10 each	.20
Salt	TT				-0-

TOTAL RECIPE COST $ ___11.64___

Number of Portions ___25___

Cost per Portion $ ___.465___

*The yield percentage is used to calculate the amount of waste that naturally occurs when cleaning, peeling and processing certain foods. Calculating and applying yield factors is beyond the scope of this text.

FIGURE 4.1 ▶ Recipe costing form

▶ CONTROLLING FOOD COSTS

Many things affect food costs in any given operation; most can be controlled by the chef or manager. These controls do not require mathematical calculations or formulas, just basic management skills and a good dose of common sense. The following factors all have an impact on the operation's bottom line:

▶ Menu
▶ Purchasing/ordering
▶ Receiving
▶ Storing
▶ Issuing
▶ Kitchen procedures
   Establishing standard portions
   Waste
▶ Sales and service

Chefs tend to focus their control efforts in the area of kitchen preparation. Although this may seem logical, it is not adequate. A good chef will be involved in all aspects of the operation to help prevent problems from arising or to correct those that may occur.

MENU

A profitable menu is based upon many variables, including customer desires, physical space and equipment, ingredient availability, cost of goods sold, employee skills and competition. All management personnel, including the chef, should be consulted when planning the menu. Menu changes, though possibly desirable, must be executed with as much care as the original design.

PURCHASING/ORDERING

Purchasing techniques have a direct impact on cost controls. On the one hand, **parstock** must be adequate for efficient operations; on the other hand, too much inventory wastes space and resources and may spoil. Before any items are ordered, purchasing specifications should be established and communicated to potential purveyors. Specifications should precisely describe the item, including grade, quality, packaging and unit size. Each operation should design its own form to best meet its specific needs. A sample specification form is shown in Figure 4.2. This information can be used to obtain price quotes from several purveyors. Update these quotes periodically to ensure that you are getting the best value for your money.

▶ **parstock (par)** the amount of stock necessary to cover operating needs between deliveries

RECEIVING

Whether goods are received by a full-time clerk, as they are in a large hotel, or by the chef or kitchen manager, certain standards should be observed. The person signing for merchandise should first confirm that the items were actually ordered. Second, determine whether the items listed on the invoice are the ones being delivered and that the price and quantity listed are accurate. Third, the items, especially meats and produce, should be checked for quality, freshness and weight. The temperature of all perishable items should be carefully checked at the time of delivery to ensure compliance with food safety standards. Established purchase specifications should be readily available for anyone responsible for receiving goods.

STORING

Proper storage of foodstuffs is crucial in order to prevent spoilage, pilferage and waste. Stock must be rotated so that the older items are used first. Such a system for rotating stock is referred to as **FIFO:** first in, first out. Dry storage areas should be well ventilated and lit to prevent pest infestation and mold. Freezers and refrigerators should be easily accessible, operating properly, and kept clean and organized.

▶ **FIFO** first in, first out; a system of rotating inventory, particularly perishable and semiperishable goods, in which items are used in the order in which they are received

ISSUING

It may be necessary, particularly in larger operations, to limit storeroom access to specific personnel. Maintaining ongoing inventory records or parstock sheets helps the or-

MEAT PURCHASING SPECIFICATIONS	
Product:	
Menu Item:	
Grade/Quality:	NAMP/IMPS#:
Packaging:	
Pricing Unit:	
Delivery Conditions:	
Comments:	

FIGURE 4.2 ▶ Specification form

dering process. Controlling issuances eliminates waste caused by multiple opened containers and ensures proper stock rotation.

KITCHEN PROCEDURES: ESTABLISHING STANDARD PORTIONS

Standardizing portions is essential to controlling food costs. Unless portion quantity is uniform, it will be impossible to compute portion costs accurately. Portion discrepancies can also confuse or mislead customers.

Actual portion sizes depend on the food service operation itself, the menu, the prices and the customers' desires. Some items are generally purchased pre-portioned for convenience (for example, steaks are sold in uniform cuts, baking potatoes are available in uniform sizes, butter comes in preportioned pats and bread comes sliced for service). Other items must be portioned by the establishment prior to service. Special equipment makes consistent portioning easy. There are machines to slice meats, cutting guides for cakes and pies and portion scales for weighing quantities. Standardized portion scoops and ladles are indispensable for serving vegetables, soups, stews, salads and similar foods. Many of these items are discussed and illustrated in Chapter 5, Tools and Equipment.

Once acceptable portion sizes are established, employees must be properly trained to present them. If each employee of a sandwich shop prepared sandwiches the way he or she would like to eat them, customers would probably never receive the same sandwich twice. Customers may become confused and decide not to risk a repeat visit. Obviously, carelessness in portioning can also drastically affect food cost.

KITCHEN PROCEDURES: WASTE

The chef must also control waste from overproduction or failure to use leftovers. With an adequate sales history, the chef can accurately estimate the quantity of food to prepare for each week, day or meal. If the menu is designed properly, the chef can also use leftovers and trim from product fabrication. The less waste generated in food preparation, the lower the overall food cost will be.

SALES AND SERVICE

An improperly trained sales staff can undo even the most rigorous of food cost controls. Front-of-the-house personnel are, after all, ultimately responsible for the *sales* portion of the food cost equation. Prices charged must be accurate and complete. Poor service can lead to the need to "comp" (serve for free) an excessive amount of food. Dropped or spilled foods do not generate revenues. Proper training is once again critical. The dining room manager and the chef should work together to educate servers about menu items and sales techniques.

CONCLUSION

No food service operation becomes a success on the chef's cooking ability alone. A well-designed, enticing and accurately priced menu is also necessary. By following a standardized recipe, you should be able to repeatedly produce a known quality and quantity of food for your specific food service operation. Based upon the regularity with which you offer these foods, your menu can be classified as static, cycle, market or hybrid. You can offer your menu items either à la carte, semi à la carte or table d'hôte.

You must be able to understand and apply proper techniques for converting recipes, food costing and loss control. Although computers are useful and are becoming more common in kitchens, no machine can substitute for a chef's watchful eye and hands-on controls.

1 Describe the four types of menus. Can each type of menu offer foods à la carte, semi à la carte and/or table d'hôte? Explain your answer.
2 Discuss three factors in food preparation that affect successful recipe size changes.
3 Why is it important to calculate the portion cost of a recipe in professional food service operations? Why is the full recipe cost inadequate?
4 List several factors, other than kitchen procedures, that a chef should examine when looking for ways to control food costs.
5 Several recipe costing software programs are available online, or are sold through the Internet. Research two of these programs. What are their advantages and disadvantages? Why is it important for cooks to learn to calculate recipe costs without the aid of a computer?

AND, INDEED, IS THERE NOT SOMETHING HOLY ABOUT A GREAT KITCHEN? . . . THE SCOURED GLEAM OF ROW UPON ROW OF METAL VESSELS DANGLING FROM HOOKS OR REPOSING ON THEIR SHELVES TILL NEEDED WITH THE AIR OF SO MANY CHALICES WAITING FOR THE CELEBRATION OF THE SACRAMENT OF FOOD.

—*Angela Carter, British novelist (1940–1992)*

5

TOOLS
AND EQUIPMENT

AFTER STUDYING THIS
CHAPTER, YOU WILL BE
ABLE TO:

▶ recognize a variety of
professional kitchen tools and
equipment

▶ select and care for knives

▶ understand how a professional
kitchen is organized

Having the proper tools and equipment for a particular task may mean the difference between a job well done and one done carelessly, incorrectly or even dangerously. This chapter introduces most of the tools and equipment typically used in a professional kitchen. Items are divided into categories according to their function: hand tools, knives, measuring and portioning devices, cookware, strainers and sieves, processing equipment, storage containers, heavy equipment, buffet equipment and safety equipment.

A wide variety of specialized tools and equipment is available to today's chef. Breading machines, croissant shapers and doughnut glazers are designed to speed production by reducing handwork. Other devices —for instance, a duck press or a couscousière—are used only for unique tasks in preparing a few menu items. Much of this specialized equipment is quite expensive and found only in food manufacturing operations or specialized kitchens; a discussion of it is beyond the scope of this chapter. Brief descriptions of some of these specialized devices are, however, found in the Glossary. Baking pans and tools are discussed in Chapter 29, Principles of the Bakeshop.

Before using any equipment, study the operator's manual or have someone experienced with the particular item instruct you on proper procedures for its use and cleaning. And remember, always think safety first.

▶ STANDARDS FOR TOOLS AND EQUIPMENT

NSF International (NSF), previously known as the National Sanitation Foundation, promulgates consensus standards for the design, construction and installation of kitchen tools, cookware and equipment. Many states and municipalities require that food service operations use only NSF-certified equipment. Although NSF certification is voluntary, most manufacturers submit their designs to NSF for certification to show that they are suitable for use in professional food service operations. Certified equipment bears the NSF mark shown in Figure 5.1.

NSF standards reflect the following requirements:

1 Equipment must be easily cleaned.
2 All food contact surfaces must be nontoxic (under intended end-use conditions), nonabsorbent, corrosion resistant and nonreactive.
3 All food contact surfaces must be smooth—that is, free of pits, cracks, crevices, ledges, rivet heads and bolts.
4 Internal corners and edges must be rounded and smooth; external corners and angles must be smooth and sealed.
5 Coating materials must be nontoxic and easily cleaned; coatings must resist chipping and cracking.
6 Waste and waste liquids must be easily removed.

FIGURE 5.1 ▶ The NSF mark

► SELECTING TOOLS AND EQUIPMENT

In general, only commercial food service tools and equipment should be used in a professional kitchen. Household tools and appliances that are not NSF-certified may not withstand the rigors of a professional kitchen. Look for tools that are well constructed. For example, joints should be welded, not bonded with solder; handles should be comfortable, with rounded borders; plastic and rubber parts should be seamless.

Before purchasing or leasing any equipment, you should evaluate several factors:

1 Is this equipment necessary for producing menu items?

2 Will this equipment perform the job required in the space available?

3 Is this equipment the most economical for the operation's specific needs?

4 Is this equipment easy to clean, maintain and repair?

Table-Mounted Can Opener

► HAND TOOLS

Hand tools are designed to aid in cutting, shaping, moving or combining foods. They have few, if any, moving parts. Knives, discussed separately later, are the most important hand tools. Others are metal or rubber spatulas, spoons, whisks, tongs and specialized cutters. In addition to the items shown here, many hand tools designed for specific tasks, such as pressing tortillas or pitting cherries, are available. Sturdiness, durability and safety are the watchwords when selecting hand tools. Choose tools that can withstand the heavy use of a professional kitchen and those that are easily cleaned.

Chef's Fork

Meat Mallet

Vegetable Peeler

Perforated, Plain and Slotted Spoons

Balloon and Rigid Whisks

Melon Ball Cutter

Zester

Grill Spatula

Rubber Spatula

Straight-Spatula (Cake Spatula)

Straight Tongs

▶ KNIVES

Knives are the most important items in your tool kit. With a sharp knife, the skilled chef can accomplish a number of tasks more quickly and efficiently than any machine. Good-quality knives are expensive but will last for many years with proper care. Select easily sharpened, well-constructed knives that are comfortable and balanced in your hand. Knife construction and commonly used knives are discussed here; knife safety and care as well as cutting techniques are discussed in Chapter 6, Knife Skills.

KNIFE CONSTRUCTION

A good knife begins with a single piece of metal, stamped, cut or—best of all—forged and tempered into a blade of the desired shape. The metals generally used for knife blades are:

1 **Carbon steel**—An alloy of carbon and iron, carbon steel is traditionally used for blades because it is soft enough to be sharpened easily. It corrodes and discolors easily, however, especially when used with acidic foods.

2 **Stainless steel**—Stainless steel will not rust, corrode or discolor and is extremely durable. A stainless steel blade is much more difficult to sharpen than a carbon steel one, although once an edge is established, it lasts longer than the edge on a carbon steel blade.

3 **High-carbon stainless steel**—An alloy combining the best features of carbon steel and stainless steel, high-carbon stainless steel neither corrodes nor discolors and can be sharpened almost as easily as carbon steel. It is now the most frequently used metal for blades.

4 **Ceramic**—A ceramic called zirconium oxide is now used to make knife blades that are extremely sharp, very easy to clean, rustproof and nonreactive. With proper care, ceramic blades will remain sharp for years, but when sharpening is needed, it must be done professionally on special diamond wheels. Material costs and tariffs make ceramic-bladed knives very expensive. Although this ceramic is highly durable, it does not have the flexibility of metal, so never use a ceramic knife to pry anything, to strike a hard surface (for example, when crushing garlic or chopping through bones) or to cut against a china or ceramic surface.

A portion of the blade, known as the tang, fits inside the handle. The best knives are constructed with a full tang running the length of the handle; they also have a bolster where the blade meets the handle (the bolster is part of the blade, not a separate collar). Less expensive knives may have a ¾-length tang or a thin "rattail" tang. Neither provides as much support, durability or balance as a full tang.

Knife handles are often made of hard woods infused with plastic and riveted to the tang. Molded polypropylene handles are permanently bonded to a tang without seams or rivets. Stainless steel handles welded directly to the blade are durable but very lightweight. Any handle should be shaped for comfort and ground smooth to eliminate crevices where bacteria can grow.

tip   spine   bolster   tang

cutting edge   heel   rivets

FIGURE 5.2 ▶ The parts of a chef's knife

KNIFE SHAPES AND SHARPENING EQUIPMENT

You will collect many knives during your career, many with specialized functions not described here. This list includes only the most basic knives and sharpening equipment.

French or Chef's Knife

FRENCH OR CHEF'S KNIFE

An all-purpose knife used for chopping, slicing and mincing. Its rigid 8- to 14-inch-long blade is wide at the heel and tapers to a point at the tip.

Utility Knife

UTILITY KNIFE

An all-purpose knife used for cutting fruits and vegetables and carving poultry. Its rigid 6- to 8-inch-long blade is shaped like a chef's knife but narrower.

Rigid Boning Knife

BONING KNIFE

A smaller knife with a thin blade used to separate meat from bone. The blade is usually 5 to 7 inches long and may be flexible or rigid.

Paring Knife

PARING KNIFE

A short knife used for detail work or cutting fruits and vegetables. The rigid blade is from 2 to 4 inches long. A tournée or **bird's-beak knife** is similar to a paring knife but with a curved blade; it is used to cut curved surfaces or tournée vegetables.

Cleaver

CLEAVER

A knife with a large, heavy rectangular blade used for chopping or cutting through bones.

Flexible Slicer

SLICER

A knife with a long, thin blade used primarily for slicing cooked meat. The tip may be round or pointed, and the blade may be flexible or rigid. A similar knife with a serrated edge is used for slicing bread or pastry items.

Serrated Slicer

Butcher Knive or Scimitar

BUTCHER KNIFE

Sometimes known as a **scimitar** because the rigid blade curves up in a 25-degree angle at the tip, it is used for fabricating raw meat and is available with 6- to 14-inch blades.

Oyster Knife

OYSTER AND CLAM KNIVES

The short, rigid blades of these knives are used to open oyster and clam shells. The tips are blunt; only the clam knife has a sharp edge.

Clam Knife

Three-Sided Sharpening or Whetstone

Steel

SHARPENING STONE

Also known as a **whetstone,** a flat brick of synthetic abrasives that is used to put an edge on a dull blade. Various grit sizes are available. The most practical sets include both coarse- and fine-grit stones.

STEEL

A scored, slightly abrasive steel rod used to hone or straighten a blade immediately after and between sharpenings.

▶ MEASURING AND PORTIONING DEVICES

Recipe ingredients must be measured precisely, especially in the bakeshop, and foods should be measured when served to control portion size and cost. The devices used to measure and portion foods are, for the most part, hand tools designed to make food preparation and service easier and more precise. The accuracy they afford prevents the cost of mistakes made when accurate measurements are ignored.

Measurements may be based upon weight (for example, grams, ounces, pounds) or volume (for example, teaspoons, cups, gallons). Therefore, it is necessary to have available several measuring devices, including liquid and dry measuring cups and a variety of scales. Thermometers and timers are also measuring devices and are discussed here. When purchasing measuring devices, look for quality construction and accurate markings.

SCALES

Scales are necessary to determine the weight of an ingredient or a portion of food (for example, the sliced meat for a sandwich). Portion scales use a spring mechanism, round dial and single flat tray. They are available calibrated in grams, ounces or pounds. Electronic scales also use a spring mechanism but provide digital readouts. They are often required where foods are priced for sale by weight. Balance scales (also known as baker's scales) use a two-tray, free-weight counterbalance system. A balance scale allows more weight to be measured at one time because it is not limited by spring capacity.

Any scale must be properly used and maintained to provide an accurate reading. Never pick up a scale by its platform as this can damage the balancing mechanism.

Portion Scale

Balance or Baker's Scale

VOLUME MEASURES

Ingredients may be measured by volume using measuring spoons and measuring cups. Measuring spoons sold as a set usually include ¼-teaspoon, ½-teaspoon, 1-teaspoon and 1-tablespoon units (or the metric equivalent). Liquid measuring cups are available in capacities from 1 cup to 1 gallon. They have a lip or pour spout above the top line of measurement to prevent spills. Measuring cups for dry ingredients are usually sold in sets of ¼-, ⅓-, ½-, and 1-cup units. They do not have pour spouts, so the top of the cup is level with the top measurement specified. Glass measuring cups are not recommended because they can break. Avoid using bent or dented measuring cups as the damage may distort the measurement capacity.

Measuring Spoons

Liquid Measuring Cup

Dry Measuring Cups

LADLES

Long-handled ladles are useful for portioning liquids such as stocks, sauces and soups. The capacity, in ounces or milliliters, is stamped on the handle.

PORTION SCOOPS

Portion scoops (also known as dishers) resemble ice cream scoops. They come in a range of standardized sizes and have a lever-operated blade for releasing their contents. Scoops are useful for portioning salads, vegetables, muffin batters or other soft foods. A number, stamped on either the handle or the release mechanism, indicates the number of level scoopfuls per quart. The higher the scoop number, the smaller the scoop's capacity. See Table 5.1.

THERMOMETERS

Various types of thermometers are used in the kitchen.

Stem-type thermometers, including instant-read models, are inserted into foods to obtain temperature readings. Temperatures are shown on either a dial noted by an arrow or a digital readout. An instant-read thermometer is a small stem-type model, designed to be carried in a pocket and used to provide quick temperature readings. An instant-read thermometer should not be left in foods that are cooking because doing so damages the thermometer. Sanitize the stem of any thermometer before use in order to avoid cross-contamination.

Candy and fat thermometers measure temperatures up to 400°F (204°C) using mercury in a column of glass. A back clip attaches the thermometer to the

Portion Scoop

Ladles

Instant-Read Thermometer

Candy Thermometer

Table 5.1	PORTION SCOOP CAPACITIES			
	VOLUME		**APPROXIMATE WEIGHT***	
SCOOP NUMBER	**U.S.**	**METRIC**	**U.S.**	**METRIC**
6	⅔ c.	160 ml	5 oz.	160 g
8	½ c.	120 ml	4 oz.	120 g
10	3 fl. oz.	90 ml	3–3½ oz.	85–100 g
12	⅓ c.	80 ml	2½–3 oz.	75–85 g
16	¼ c.	60 ml	2 oz.	60 g
20	1½ fl. oz.	45 ml	1¾ oz.	50 g
24	1⅓ oz.	40 ml	1⅓ oz.	40 g
30	1 fl. oz.	30 ml	1 oz.	30 g
40	0.8 fl. oz.	24 ml	0.8 oz.	23 g
60	½ fl. oz.	15 ml	½ oz.	15 g

*Weights are approximate because they vary by food.

HOW TO CALIBRATE A STEM-TYPE THERMOMETER

All stem-type thermometers should be calibrated at least weekly as well as whenever they are dropped. To calibrate a stem-type thermometer, fill a glass with shaved ice, then add water. Place the thermometer in the ice slush and wait until the temperature reading stabilizes. Following the manufacturer's directions, adjust the thermometer's calibration nut until the temperature reads 32°F (0°C). Check the calibration by returning the thermometer to the slush. Then repeat the procedure, substituting boiling water for the ice slush, and calibrate the thermometer at 212°F (100°C).

pan, keeping the chef's hands free. Be careful not to subject glass thermometers to quick temperature changes as the glass may shatter.

Electronic probe thermometers are now reasonably priced and commonly used in food service facilities. These thermometers provide immediate, clear, digital readouts from a handheld unit attached to a metal probe (some are conveniently designed so that the probe is imbedded in the tines of a long-handled fork or the bowl of a ladle). A detachable probe is especially useful inside an oven and for deep-frying and grilling.

The latest advancement in thermometers relies on infrared sensors with laser sightings. Infrared thermometers can instantly monitor the surface temperature of foods during cooking or holding, and the temperature of goods at receiving and in storage. Units can respond to a wide range of temperatures in less than a second without actually touching the food, thus avoiding any risk of cross-contamination.

Because proper temperatures must be maintained for holding and storing foods, oven and refrigerator thermometers are also useful. Select thermometers with easy-to-read dials or column divisions.

TIMERS

Portable kitchen timers are useful for any busy chef. Small digital timers can be carried in a pocket; some even time three functions at once. Select a timer with a loud alarm signal and long timing capability.

▶ COOKWARE

Cookware includes the sauté pans and stockpots used on the stove top as well as the roasting pans, hotel pans and specialty molds used inside the oven. Cookware should be selected for its size, shape, ability to conduct heat evenly and overall quality of construction.

METALS AND HEAT CONDUCTION

Cookware that fails to distribute heat evenly may cause hot spots that burn foods. Because different metals conduct heat at different rates, and thicker layers of metal conduct heat more evenly than thinner ones, the most important considerations when choosing cookware are the type and thickness (known as the *gauge*) of the material used. No one cookware or material suits every process or need, however; always select the most appropriate material for the task at hand.

COPPER

Copper is an excellent conductor: It heats rapidly and evenly and cools quickly. Indeed, unlined copper pots are unsurpassed for cooking sugar and fruit mixtures. But copper cookware is extremely expensive. It also requires a great deal of care and is often quite heavy. Moreover, because copper may react with some foods, copper cookware usually has a tin lining, which is soft and easily scratched. Because of these problems, copper is now often sandwiched between layers of stainless steel or aluminum in the bottom of pots and pans.

ALUMINUM

Aluminum is the metal used most commonly in commercial utensils. It is lightweight and, after copper, conducts heat best. Aluminum is a soft metal, though, so it should be treated with care to avoid dents. Do not use aluminum containers for storage or for cooking acidic foods because the metal reacts chemically with many foods. Light-colored foods, such as soups or sauces, may be discolored when cooked in aluminum, especially if stirred with a metal whisk or spoon.

Anodized aluminum has a hard, dark, corrosion-resistant surface that helps prevent sticking and discoloration.

STAINLESS STEEL

Although stainless steel conducts and retains heat poorly, it is a hard, durable metal particularly useful for holding foods and for low-temperature cooking where hot spots and scorching are not problems. Stainless steel pots and pans are available with aluminum or copper bonded to the bottom or with an aluminum-layered core. Although expensive, such cookware combines the rapid, uniform heat conductivity of copper and aluminum with the strength, durability and non-reactivity of stainless steel. Stainless steel is also ideal for storage containers because it does not react with foods.

CAST IRON

Cast-iron cookware distributes heat evenly and holds high temperatures well. It is often used in griddles and large skillets. Although relatively inexpensive, cast iron is extremely heavy and brittle. It must be kept properly conditioned and dry to prevent rust and pitting.

GLASS

Glass retains heat well but conducts it poorly. It does not react with foods. Tempered glass is suitable for microwave cooking provided it does not have any metal band or decoration. Commercial operations rarely use glass cookware because of the danger of breakage.

CERAMICS

Ceramics, including earthenware, porcelain and stoneware, are used primarily for baking dishes, casseroles and baking stones because they conduct heat uniformly and retain temperatures well. Ceramics are nonreactive, inexpensive and generally suitable for use in a microwave oven (provided there is no metal in the glaze). Ceramics are easily chipped or cracked, however, and should not be used over a direct flame. Also, quick temperature changes may cause the cookware to crack or shatter.

PLASTIC

Plastic containers are frequently used in commercial kitchens for food storage or service, but they cannot be used for heating or cooking except in a microwave oven. Plastic microwave cookware is made of phenolic resin. It is easy to clean, relatively inexpensive and rigidly shaped, but its glasslike structure is brittle, and it can crack or shatter.

ENAMELWARE

Pans lined with enamel should not be used for cooking; in many areas, their use in commercial kitchens is prohibited by law. The enamel can chip or crack easily, providing good places for bacteria to grow. Also, the chemicals used to bond the enamel to the cookware can cause food poisoning if ingested.

NONSTICK COATINGS

Without affecting a metal's ability to conduct heat, a polymer (plastic) known as polytetrafluoroethylene (PTFE) and marketed under the trade names Teflon and Silverstone may be applied to many types of cookware. It provides a slippery, nonreactive finish that prevents food from sticking and allows the use of less fat in cooking. Cookware with nonstick coatings requires a great deal of care, however, since the coatings can scratch, chip and blister. Do not use metal spoons or spatulas in cookware with nonstick coatings.

ROMAN POTS, SOUTHERN STILLS AND CRAFT FAIRS

Lead is poisonous. Ingesting it can cause severe gastrointestinal pains, anemia and central nervous system disorders, including intelligence and memory deficits and behavioral changes.

The unwitting and dangerous consumption of lead is not limited to children eating peeling paint chips. Some historians suggest that the use of lead cookware and lead-lined storage vessels and water pipes may have caused pervasive lead poisoning among the elite of the Roman Empire and thus contributed to the empire's decline. There is also ample evidence that from ancient times until just a few hundred years ago, wine was heated in lead vessels to sweeten it. This had a disastrous effect on the drinker and, for several centuries in countries throughout Europe, on the wine purveyor as well. The former could be poisoned, and the latter could be punished by death for selling adulterated wine. More recently, it was found that much of the moonshine whiskey produced in the American South contained lead in potentially toxic ranges. The source was determined to be the lead solder used in homemade stills, some of which even included old lead-containing car radiators as condensers.

Although commercially available cookware does not contain lead, be careful of imported pottery and those lovely hand-thrown pots found at craft fairs—there could be lead in the glaze.

COMMON COOKWARE

POTS

Pots are large round vessels with straight sides and two loop handles. Available in a range of sizes based on volume, they are used on the stove top for making stocks or soups, or for boiling or simmering foods, particularly where rapid evaporation is not desired. Flat or fitted lids are available.

PANS

Pans are round vessels with one long handle and straight or sloped sides. They are usually smaller and shallower than pots. Pans are available in a range of diameters and are used for general stove top cooking, especially sautéing, frying or reducing liquids rapidly.

Stockpot with Spigot

Saucepan

Sautoir (Straight Sides)

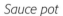
Sauce pot

Cast-Iron Skillet (Griswold)

Rondeau/Brazier

Sauteuse (Sloped Sides)

WOKS

Originally used to prepare Asian foods, woks are now found in many professional kitchens. Their round bottoms and curved sides diffuse heat and make it easy to toss or stir contents. Their large domed lids retain heat for steaming vegetables. Woks are useful for quickly sautéing strips of meat, simmering a whole fish or deep-frying appetizers. Stove top woks range in diameter from 12 to 30 inches; larger built-in gas or electric models are also available.

Wok

HOTEL PANS

Hotel pans (also known as steam table pans) are rectangular stainless steel pans designed to hold food for service in steam tables. Hotel pans are also used for baking, roasting or poaching inside an oven. Perforated pans useful for draining, steaming or icing down foods are also available. The standard full-size pan is 12 by 20 inches, with pans one-half, one-third, one-sixth and other fractions of this size available. Hotel pan depth is standardized at 2 inches (referred to as a "200 pan"), 4, 6 and 8 inches.

MOLDS

Pâté molds are available in several shapes and sizes, and are usually made from tinned steel. Those with hinged sides, whether smooth or patterned, are more properly referred to as *pâté en croûte* molds. The hinged sides make it easier to remove the baked pâté. Terrine molds are traditionally lidded earthenware or enameled cast-iron containers used for baking ground meat mixtures. They may be round, oval or rectangular. Timbale molds are small (about 4 ounces) metal or ceramic containers used for molding aspic or baking individual portions of mousse, custard or vegetables. Their slightly flared sides allow the contents to release cleanly when inverted.

Hotel Pans

Timbales

Pâté en Croûte Mold

Colander

Round Mesh Strainer

▶ STRAINERS AND SIEVES

Strainers and sieves are used primarily to aerate and remove impurities from dry ingredients and drain or purée cooked foods. Strainers, colanders, drum sieves, china caps and chinois are nonmechanical devices with a stainless steel mesh or screen through which food passes. The size of the mesh or screen varies from extremely fine to several millimeters wide; select the fineness best suited for the task at hand.

Drum sieve (Tamis)

CHINOIS AND CHINA CAP

Both the chinois and china cap are cone-shaped metal strainers. The conical shape allows liquids to filter through small openings. The body of a chinois is made from a very fine mesh screen, while a china cap has a perforated metal body. Both are used for straining stocks and sauces, with the chinois being particularly useful for consommé. A china cap can also be used with a pestle to purée soft foods.

Chinois

China Cap

SKIMMER AND SPIDER

Both the skimmer and spider are long-handled tools used to remove foods or impurities from liquids. The flat, perforated disk of a skimmer is used for skimming stocks or removing foods from soups or stocks. The spider has a finer mesh disk, which makes it better for retrieving items from hot fat. Wooden-handled spiders are available but are less sturdy and harder to clean than all-metal designs.

CHEESECLOTH

Cheesecloth is a loosely woven cotton gauze used for straining stocks and sauces and wrapping poultry or fish for poaching. Cheesecloth is also indispensable for making sachets. Always rinse cheesecloth thoroughly before use; this removes lint and prevents the cheesecloth from absorbing other liquids.

FOOD MILL

A food mill purées and strains food at the same time. Food is placed in the hopper and a hand-crank mechanism turns a blade in the hopper against a perforated disk, forcing the food through the disk. Most models have interchangeable disks with various-sized holes. Choose a mill that can be taken apart easily for cleaning.

FLOUR SIFTER

A sifter is used for aerating, blending and removing impurities from dry ingredients such as flour, cocoa and leavening agents. The 8-cup hand-crank sifter shown here uses four curved rods to brush the contents through a curved mesh screen. The sifter should have a medium-fine screen and a comfortable handle.

Skimmer

Spider

Food Mill

Flour Sifter

▶ PROCESSING EQUIPMENT

Processing equipment includes both electrical and nonelectrical mechanical devices used to chop, purée, slice, grind or mix foods. Before using any such equipment, be sure to review its operating procedures and ask for assistance if necessary. Always turn the equipment off and disconnect the power before disassembling, cleaning or moving the appliance. Any problems or malfunctions should be reported immediately. *Never place your hand into any machinery when the power is on. Processing equipment is powerful and can cause serious injury.*

Slicer

SLICER

An electric slicer is used to cut meat, bread, cheese or raw vegetables into uniform slices. It has a circular blade that rotates at high speed. Food is placed in a carrier, then passed (manually or by an electric motor) against the blade. Slice thickness is determined by the distance between the blade and the carrier. Because of the speed with which the blade rotates, foods can be cut into extremely thin slices very quickly. An electric slicer is convenient for preparing moderate to large quantities of food, but the time required to disassemble and clean the equipment makes it impractical when slicing only a few items.

MANDOLINE

Mandoline

A mandoline is a manually operated slicer made of stainless steel with adjustable slicing blades. It is also used to make julienne and waffle-cut slices. Its narrow, rectangular body sits on the work counter at a 45-degree angle. Foods are passed against a blade to obtain uniform slices. It is useful for slicing small quantities of fruits or vegetables when using a large electric slicer would be unwarranted. To avoid injury, always use a hand guard or steel glove when using a mandoline.

FOOD CHOPPER OR BUFFALO CHOPPER

This chopper is used to process moderate to large quantities of food to a uniform size, such as chopping onions or grinding bread for crumbs. The food is placed in a large bowl rotating beneath a hood where curved blades chop it. The size of the cut depends on how long the food is left in the machine. Buffalo choppers are available in floor or tabletop models. The motor can usually be fitted with a variety of other tools such as a meat grinder or a slicer/shredder, making it even more useful.

FOOD PROCESSOR

A food processor has a motor housing with a removable bowl and S-shaped blade. It is used, for example, to purée cooked foods, chop nuts, prepare compound butters and emulsify sauces. Special disks can be added that slice, shred or julienne foods. Bowl capacity and motor power vary; select a model large enough for your most common tasks.

Food Processor

Buffalo Chopper with Slicer and Meat Grinder Attachments

BLENDER

Though similar in principle to a food processor, a blender has a tall, narrow food container and a four-pronged blade. Its design and whirlpool action is better for processing liquids or lique-fying foods quickly. A blender is used to prepare smooth drinks, purée soups and sauces, blend batters and chop ice. A **vertical cutter/mixer (VCM)** operates like a very large, powerful blender. A VCM is usually floor-mounted and has a capacity of 15 to 80 quarts.

Heavy-Duty Blender

IMMERSION BLENDER

An immersion blender—as well as its household counterpart called a hand blender or wand—is a long shaft fitted with a rotating four-pronged blade at the bottom. Operated by pressing a button in the handle, an immersion blender is used to purée a soft food, soup or sauce directly in the container in which it was prepared, eliminating the need to transfer the food from one container to another. This is especially use-ful when working with hot foods. Small cord-less, rechargeable models are convenient for puréeing or mixing small quantities or beverages, but larger heavy-duty electric models are more practical in commercial kitchens.

Immersion Blender

MIXER

A vertical mixer is indispensable in the bakeshop and most kitchens. The U- shaped arms hold a metal mixing bowl in place; the selected mixing attachment fits onto the rotating head. The three common mix-ing attachments are the whip (used for whipping eggs or cream), the paddle (used for gen-eral mixing) and the dough hook (used for kneading bread). Most mixers have several operating speeds. Bench models range in capacity from 4.5 to 20 quarts, while floor mixers can hold as much as 140 quarts. Some mixers can be fitted with shredder/ slicers, meat grinders, juicers or power strainers, making the equipment more versatile.

Flat Paddle

Whip

Dough Hook

20-Quart Mixer and Attachments

JUICER

Two types of juicers are available: reamers and ex-tractors. Reamers, also known as citrus juicers, re-move juice from citrus fruits. They can be manual or electric. Manual models use a lever arm to squeeze the fruit with increased pressure. They are most often used to prepare small to moderate

Citrus Juicer

amounts of juice for cooking or beverages. Juice extractors are electrical devices that create juice by liquefying raw fruits, vegetables and herbs. They use centrifugal force to filter out fiber and pulp.

► STORAGE CONTAINERS

Storage Containers

Proper storage containers are necessary for keeping leftovers and opened packages of food safe for consumption. Proper storage can also reduce the costs incurred by waste or spoilage.

Although stainless steel pans such as hotel pans are suitable and useful for some items, the expense of stainless steel and the lack of airtight lids makes these pans impractical for general storage purposes. Aluminum containers are not recommended because the metal can react with even mildly acidic items. Glass containers are generally not allowed in commercial kitchens because of the hazards of broken glass. The most useful storage containers are those made of high-density plastic such as polyethylene and polypropylene.

Storage containers must have well-fitting lids and should be available in a variety of sizes, including some that are small enough to hold even minimal quantities of food without allowing too much exposure to oxygen. Round and square plastic containers are widely available. Flat, snap-on lids allow containers to be stacked for more efficient storage. Containers may be clear or opaque white, which helps protect light-sensitive foods. Larger containers may be fitted with handles and spigots, making them especially suited for storing stock. Some storage containers are marked with graduated measurements so that content quantity can be determined at a glance.

Large quantities of dry ingredients, such as flour, sugar and rice, can be stored in rolling bins. The bins should be seamless with rounded corners for easy cleaning. They should have well-fitting but easy-to-open lids and should move easily on well-balanced casters.

► HEAVY EQUIPMENT

Heavy equipment includes the gas-, electric- or steam-operated appliances used for cooking, reheating or holding foods. It also includes dishwashers and refrigeration units. These items are usually installed in a fixed location determined by the kitchen's traffic flow and space limitations.

Heavy equipment may be purchased or leased new or used. Used equipment is most often purchased in an effort to save money. Although the initial cost is generally less for used equipment, the buyer should also consider the lack of a manufacturer's warranty or dealership guarantee and how the equipment was maintained by the prior owner. Functional used equipment is satisfactory for back-of-the-house areas, but it is usually better to purchase new equipment if it will be visible to the customer. Leasing equipment may be appropriate for some operations. The cost of leasing is less than purchasing and, if something goes wrong with the equipment, the operator is generally not responsible for repairs or service charges.

STOVE TOPS

Stove tops or ranges are often the most important cooking equipment in the kitchen. They have one or more burners powered by gas or electricity. The burners may be open or covered with a cast-iron or steel plate. Open burners supply quick, direct heat that is easy to regulate. A steel plate, known as a **flat top,** supplies even but less intense heat. Although it takes longer to heat than a burner, the flat top supports heavier weights and makes a larger area available for cooking. Many stoves include both flat tops and open burner arrangements.

INDUCTION—A NEW HEAT WAVE

Induction cooking uses special conductive coils called inductors placed below the stove top's surface in combination with cookware made of cast iron or magnetic stainless steel. The coil generates a magnetic current so that the cookware is heated rapidly with magnetic friction. Heat energy is then transferred from the cookware to the food by conduction. The cooking surface, which is made of a solid ceramic material, remains cool. Only the cookware and its contents get hot. This means that induction systems are extremely efficient with instant response time because power is directed into the cooking utensil, not the surrounding air.

Induction cooking is gaining acceptance in professional kitchens because of the speed with which foods can be heated and the ease of cleanup. Portable induction burners are useful on buffets, and cafeteria lines and for tableside cooking because they maintain a safer, cooler environment for both chefs and customers.

Induction Cooktop

Wood-Burning Oven

Griddles are similar to flat tops except they are made of a thinner metal plate. Foods are usually cooked directly on the griddle's surface, not in pots or pans, which can nick or scratch the surface. The surface should be properly cleaned and conditioned after each use. Griddles are popular for short-order and fast-food-type operations.

Griddle

OVENS

An oven is an enclosed space where food is cooked by being surrounded with hot, dry air. Conventional ovens are often located beneath the stove top. They have a heating element located at the unit's bottom or floor, and pans are placed on adjustable wire racks inside the oven's cavity. See Figure 5.3. Conventional ovens may also be separate, freestanding units or decks stacked one on top of the other. In stack ovens, pans are placed directly on the deck or floor and not on wire racks.

Convection ovens use internal fans to circulate the hot air. This tends to cook foods more quickly and evenly. Convection ovens are almost always freestanding units, powered either by gas or electricity. Because convection ovens cook foods more quickly, temperatures may need to be reduced by 25°F to 50°F (10°C to 20°C) from those recommended for conventional ovens.

Stack Oven

WOOD-BURNING OVENS

The ancient practice of baking in a retained-heat masonry oven has been revived in recent years, with many upscale restaurants and artesian bakeries installing brick or adobe ovens for baking pizzas and breads as well as for roasting fish, poultry and vegetables. These ovens have a curved interior chamber that is usually recessed into a wall. Although gas-fired models are available, wood-firing is more traditional and provides the aromas and flavors associated with brick ovens. A wood fire is built inside the oven to heat the brick chamber. The ashes are then swept out and the food is placed on the flat oven floor. The combination of high heat and wood smoke adds distinctive flavors to foods.

MICROWAVE OVENS

Microwave ovens are electrically powered ovens used to cook or reheat foods. They are available in a range of sizes and power settings. Microwave ovens will not brown foods unless fitted with special browning elements. Microwave cooking is discussed in more detail in Chapter 10, Principles of Cooking.

FIGURE 5.3 ▶ Gas burner and flat-top range with dual ovens and an overhead broiler (salamander).

Overhead Broiler

BROILERS AND GRILLS

Broilers and grills are generally used to prepare meats, fish and poultry. For a grill, the heat source is beneath the rack on which the food is placed. For a broiler, the heat source is above the food. Most broilers are gas powered; grills may be gas or electric or may burn wood or charcoal. A **salamander** is a small overhead broiler primarily used to finish or top-brown foods. See Figure 5.3. A **rotisserie** is similar to a broiler except that the food is placed on a revolving spit in front of the heat source. The unit may be open or enclosed like an oven; it is most often used for cooking poultry or meats.

Gas Grill

TILTING SKILLETS

Tilting skillets are large, freestanding, flat-bottomed pans about 6 inches deep with an internal heating element below the pan's bottom. They are usually made of stainless steel with a cover, and have a hand-crank mechanism that turns or tilts the pan to pour out the contents. Tilting

Tilting Skillet

Rotisserie

Steam Kettle

Convection Steamer

Deep-Fat Fryer

skillets can be used as stockpots, braziers, fry pans, griddles or steam tables, making them one of the most versatile of commercial appliances.

STEAM KETTLES

Steam kettles (also known as steam-jacketed kettles) are similar to stockpots except they are heated from the bottom and sides by steam circulating between layers of stainless steel. The steam may be generated internally or from an outside source. Because steam heats the kettle's sides, foods cook more quickly and evenly than they would in a pot sitting on the stove top. Steam kettles are most often used for making sauces, soups, custards or stocks. Steam kettles are available in a range of sizes, from a 2-gallon tabletop model to a 100-gallon floor model. Some models have a tilting mechanism that allows the contents to be poured out; others have a spigot near the bottom through which liquids can be drained.

STEAMERS

Pressure and convection steamers are used to cook foods rapidly and evenly, using direct contact with steam. Pressure steamers heat water above the boiling point in sealed compartments; the high temperature and sealed compartment increase the internal pressure in a range of 4 to 15 pounds per square inch. The increased pressure and temperature cook the foods rapidly. Convection steamers generate steam in an internal boiler, then release it over the foods in a cooking chamber. Both types of steamer are ideal for cooking vegetables with minimal loss of flavor or nutrients.

DEEP-FAT FRYERS

Deep-fat fryers are used to cook foods in a large amount of hot fat. Fryers are sized by the amount of fat they hold. Most commercial fryers range between 15 and 82 pounds. Fryers can be either gas or electric and are thermostatically controlled for temperatures between 200°F and 400°F (90°C and 200°C).

When choosing a fryer, look for a fry tank with curved, easy-to-clean sloping sides. Some fryers have a cold zone (an area of reduced temperature) at the bottom of the fry tank to trap particles. This prevents them from burning, creating off-flavors and shortening the life of the fryer fat.

Deep-fryers usually come with steel wire baskets to hold the food during cooking. Fryer baskets are usually lowered into the fat and raised manually, although some models have automatic basket mechanisms. The most important factor when choosing a deep-fryer is **recovery time.** Recovery time is the length of time it takes the fat to return to the desired cooking temperature after food is submerged in it. When food is submerged, heat is immediately transferred to the food from the fat. This heat transfer lowers the fat's temperature. The more food added at one time, the greater the drop in the fat's temperature. If the temperature drops too much or does not return quickly to the proper cooking temperature, the food may absorb excess fat and become greasy.

REFRIGERATORS

Proper refrigeration space is an essential component of any kitchen. Many foods must be stored at low temperatures to maintain quality and safety. Most commercial refrigeration is of two types: walk-in units and reach-in or upright units.

A walk-in is a large, room-sized box capable of holding hundreds of pounds of food on adjustable shelves. A separate freezer walk-in may be positioned nearby or even inside a refrigerated walk-in.

Reach-ins may be individual units or parts of a bank of units, each with shelves approximately the size of a full sheet pan. Reach-in refrigerators and freezers are usually located throughout the kitchen to provide quick access to foods. Small units may also be placed beneath the work counters. Freezers and refrigerators are available in a wide range of sizes and door designs to suit any operation.

Other forms of commercial refrigeration include chilled drawers located beneath a work area that are just large enough to accommodate a hotel pan, and display cases used to show foods to the customer.

DISHWASHERS

Mechanical dishwashers are available to wash, rinse and sanitize dishware, glassware, cookware and utensils. Small models clean one rack of items at a time, while larger models can handle several racks simultaneously on a conveyor belt system. Sanitation is accomplished either with extremely hot water (180°F/82°C) or with chemicals automatically dispensed during the final rinse cycle. Any dishwashing area should be carefully organized for efficient use of equipment and employees, and to prevent recontamination of clean items.

Insulated Carrier

▶ BUFFET EQUIPMENT

Food service operations that prepare buffets or cater off-premise events need a variety of specialized equipment to ensure that food is handled safely and efficiently and displayed appropriately. Proper temperatures must be maintained during transportation, display and service.

Insulated carriers hold food at its current temperature for a time. They are designed to hold hotel pans or sheet pans, and are available with wheels for easy movement. Some are available with a spigot for serving hot or cold beverages. Any carrier should be easy to clean and of a convenient size for the space available and the type of operation.

Temperature remains a concern when arranging food on a buffet table. **Chafing dishes** are commonly used for keeping hot foods hot during service. Chafing dishes are designed so that cans of solid fuel can be placed under a deep hotel pan of hot water. Like a double boiler or bain marie, the hot water then helps maintain the temperature of food placed in a second hotel pan suspended over the first. Chafing dishes, however, should never be used to heat food. Chafing dishes are available in several sizes and shapes, but the most convenient are those based on the size of a standard hotel pan. Round, deep chafing dishes are useful for serving soups or sauces. Exteriors can be plain or ornate, and made of silver, copper or stainless steel.

Roast beef, turkey, ham or other large cuts of meat are sometimes carved on a buffet in front of guests. **Heat lamps** can be used to keep these foods warm. Heat lamps are also useful for maintaining the temperature of pizza or fried foods, which might become soggy if held in a chafing dish.

Pastries, breads and cold foods can be arranged on a variety of platters, trays, baskets and serving pieces, depending on the size and style of the buffet. Some of the most elegant and traditional serving pieces are flat display mirrors. These may be plastic or glass and are available in a wide variety of shapes and sizes. The edges should be sealed in an easy-to-clean plastic to prevent chipping.

Although many of these items can be rented, operations that regularly serve buffets may prefer to invest in their own transportation and serving equipment.

Heat Lamp

Chafing Dish

▶ SAFETY EQUIPMENT

Safety devices, many of which are required by federal, state or local law, are critical to the well-being of a food service operation although they are not used in food preparation. Failing to include safety equipment in a kitchen or failing to maintain it properly endangers workers and customers.

Table 5.2	FIRE EXTINGUISHERS	
CLASS	**SYMBOL**	**USE**
Class A	▲	Fires involving wood, paper, cloth or plastic
Class B	■	Fires involving oil, grease or flammable chemicals
Class C	●	Fires involving electrical equipment or wiring

Combination extinguishers—AB, BC and ABC—are also available.

FIRE EXTINGUISHERS

Fire extinguishers are canisters of foam, dry chemicals (such as sodium bicarbonate or potassium bicarbonate) or pressurized water used to extinguish small fires. They must be placed within sight of and easily reached from the work areas in which fires are likely to occur. Different classes of extinguishers use different chemicals to fight different types of fires. The appropriate class must be used for the specific fire. See Table 5.2. Fire extinguishers must be recharged and checked from time to time. Be sure they have not been discharged, tampered with or otherwise damaged.

VENTILATION SYSTEMS

Ventilation systems (also called ventilation hoods) are commonly installed over cooking equipment to remove vapors, heat and smoke. Some systems include fire extinguishing agents or sprinklers. A properly operating hood makes the kitchen more comfortable for the staff and reduces the danger of fire. The system should be designed, installed and inspected by professionals, then cleaned and maintained regularly.

FIRST-AID KITS

First-aid supplies should be stored in a clearly marked box, conspicuously located near food preparation areas. State and local laws may specify the kit's exact contents. Generally, they should include a first-aid manual, bandages, gauze dressings, adhesive tape, antiseptics, scissors, cold packs and other supplies. The kit should be checked regularly and items replaced as needed. In addition, cards with emergency telephone numbers should be placed inside the first-aid kit and near a telephone.

▶ THE PROFESSIONAL KITCHEN

The kitchen is the heart of the food service operation. There, food and other items are received, stored, prepared and plated for service; dining room staff places orders, retrieves foods that are ready for service and returns dirty service items; dishes and other wares are cleaned and stored; and the chef conducts business. But commercial space is expensive, and most food service operators recognize that the greater number of customers served, the greater the revenues. Often this translates into a large dining area and small kitchen and storage facilities. Therefore, when designing a kitchen, it is important to use the space wisely so that each of its functions can be accomplished efficiently.

Kitchen design begins with a consideration of the tasks to be performed. Analyzing the menu identifies these tasks. A restaurant featuring steaks and chops, for example, will need areas to fabricate and grill meats. If it relies on commercially prepared desserts and breads, it will not need a bakeshop but will still need space to store and plate baked goods.

Once all food preparation tasks are identified, a work area for each particular task is designated. These work areas are called **work stations.** At a steak restaurant, an important work station is the broiler. If the restaurant serves fried foods, it will also need a fry station. The size and design of each work station is determined by the volume of food the operation intends to produce.

Usually work stations using the same or similar equipment for related tasks are grouped into **work sections.** See Table 5.3. (Note that work stations correspond to the kitchen brigade system discussed in Chapter 1, Professionalism.) For example, in a typical full-service restaurant, there will be a hot-foods section that includes broiler, fry, griddle, sauté and sauce stations. The principal cooking equipment (a range, broiler, deep-fat fryer, oven, griddle, and so on) will be arranged in a line under a ventilation hood. During service each work station within the hot-foods section may be staffed by a different line cook, but the proximity of the stations allows one line cook to cover more than one station if the kitchen is shorthanded or when business is slow.

When designing the work area, one must also consider what equipment and storage facilities can be placed beneath or on top of other equipment. For example, in a bakeshop, rolling storage bins for flour and sugar may be located beneath the work surface, while mixing bowls and dry ingredients are stored on shelves above. Ideally, each station should be designed so that the cook takes no more than three steps in any direction to perform all of his or her assigned station tasks.

In addition to the work sections where the menu items are produced, a typical restaurant kitchen includes areas dedicated to the following functions:

Table 5.3	WORK SECTIONS AND THEIR STATIONS
SECTIONS	**STATIONS**
Hot-foods section	Broiler station Fry station Griddle station Sauté/sauce station Holding
Garde-manger section	Salad greens cleaning Salad preparation Cold foods preparation Sandwich station Showpiece preparation
Bakery section	Mixing station Dough holding and proofing Dough rolling and forming Baking and cooling Dessert preparation* Frozen desert preparation* Plating desserts*
Banquet section	Steam cooking Dry-heat cooking (roasting, broiling) Holding and plating
Short-order section	Griddle station Fry station Broiler station
Beverage section	Hot beverage station Cold beverage station Alcoholic beverage station

*These stations are sometimes found in the garde-manger section.

1 *Receiving and storing foods and other items.* Most kitchens will need freezer, refrigerator and dry-goods storage facilities. Each should have proper temperature, humidity and light controls in order to properly and safely maintain the stored items. Typically there is a combination of central and section storage. For example, up to 100 pounds of flour and sugar can be stored in rolling bins under a work table in the bakeshop, while several hundreds of pounds more remain in a central dry-goods area. Similarly, one box of salt can be stored near the hot line for immediate use, while the remainder of the case is stored in a central dry-goods area. Additional storage space will be needed for cleaning and paper supplies, dishes and other service ware.

2 *Washing dishes and other equipment.* These dish- and equipment-washing facilities should have their own sinks. Food-preparation and hand-washing sinks must be separate.

3 *Employee use.* Restrooms, locker facilities and an office are also found in most food service facilities.

The guiding principle behind a good kitchen design is to maximize the flow of goods and staff from one area to the next and within each area itself. Maximizing flow creates an efficient work environment and helps reduce preparation and service time.

SAFETY ALERT

STORAGE

▶ Never store cleaning supplies or other chemicals with or near foods.

▶ Never store chemicals in a container that originally held food; never store food in a container that once held a chemical.

▶ Keep chemicals and cleaners in properly labeled containers.

ALEXIS SOYER (1809–1858)

The father of the contemporary celebrity chef was Alexis Soyer, a Frenchman whose tragically short working life was spent mostly in London. He was a flamboyant, talented and egocentric showman. He was also a renowned chef, restaurateur, social activist, author, purveyor of prepared foods and inventor.

In 1831, Soyer left his thriving catering business and restaurant in Paris for London. (A scandal was rumored to be behind his sudden departure.) There he quickly established a reputation as a talented chef in the latest French fashion. By

Alexis Soyer
Photo courtesy of Barbara Wheaton.

1838, he was employed at a gentlemen's club called the Reform. Able to assist in planning the club's new kitchen facility, Soyer installed the most modern equipment: gas ovens with temperature controls, a steam-driven mechanical spit and a storage locker cooled by running water. From this modern kitchen he produced his signature dish: lamb chops Reform.

The Reform was founded by members of the Liberal party, a political party interested in social reform. Their chef soon joined the party ranks. He developed recipes for inexpensive,

"The Kitchen Department of the Reform Club" (1841). "To show them at one glance," wrote the *Spectator,* "the partition walls are cut away, and a bird's eye view is given of the several kitchens, larders, sculleries, and batterie de cuisine; the different functionaries are at their posts, and the accomplished chef, Monsieur Soyer, is in the act of pointing out to a favoured visitor the various contrivances suggested by his ingenuity and experience."

nutritious soups for the working class and in 1847 went to Ireland and opened soup kitchens to feed those who were starving as a result of the potato famine.

His most important writings reflect his interests in good food for the masses. The intended audience for *The Modern Housewife* (1849) was the middle class; the growing urban working class was the intended audience for his second book, *A Schilling Cookery for the People* (1855).

In 1851, Soyer opened his own lavishly decorated and expensively equipped restaurant called the Gastronomic Symposium of All Nations. It closed shortly thereafter, in part because of Soyer's debts, in part because he lost his operating license as a result of the rowdiness in the restaurant's American-style bar, at which customers were publicly served cocktails for the first time in London.

In addition to cooking and writing, Soyer created and marketed several prepared food items: Soyer's Sauce, Soyer's Nectar and Soyer's Relish. He was also fascinated with kitchen gadgets and invented several, including a sink stopper, jelly mold, egg cooker and coffeepot. The most notable, however, was a portable "Magic Stove" weighing less than 4 pounds, similar to a modern chafing dish. Soyer's final triumph was in the Crimean War (1854–1857). He developed army rations, reorganized field and hospital kitchens and introduced one of his last inventions, the campaign stove. Portable, efficient and requiring little fuel, it was used by the British army for the next 90 years.

Governmental building, health, fire and safety codes will dictate, to a degree, certain aspects of a professional kitchen's design. But to make the most of these spaces, the well-designed kitchen should reflect a sound understanding of the tasks to be performed and the equipment necessary to perform them efficiently.

CONCLUSION

Hundreds of tools and pieces of equipment can help you prepare, cook, store and present food. Every year, manufacturers offer new or improved items. Throughout your career, you will use many of them. Select those that are well constructed, durable and best suited for the task at hand. Then use them in a safe and efficient manner.

The way in which equipment is arranged and stored in a kitchen is also important. Good kitchen design emphasizes the efficient flow of goods and staff from one work section to another as well as within each work section or station.

QUESTIONS FOR DISCUSSION

1 What is NSF International? What is its significance with regard to commercial kitchen equipment?

2 List the parts of a chef's knife and describe the knife's construction.

3 List six materials used to make commercial cookware and describe the advantages and disadvantages of each.

4 Describe six pieces of equipment that can be used to slice or chop foods.

5 List three classes of fire extinguishers. For each one, describe its designating symbol and identify the type or types of fire it should be used to extinguish.

6 Explain the relationship between work sections and work stations and the kitchen brigade system discussed in Chapter 1, Professionalism.

7 Use the Internet to locate vendors, obtain specifications, and compare warranties and prices for a piece of commercial kitchen equipment.

8 Research information on selecting and installing a wood-burning oven in a commercial kitchen.

EVERY MORNING ONE MUST START FROM SCRATCH,
WITH NOTHING ON THE STOVES. THAT IS CUISINE.
—Fernand Point, French restaurateur (1897–
1955)

KNIFE SKILLS

AFTER STUDYING THIS CHAPTER, YOU WILL BE ABLE TO:

▶ care for knives properly
▶ use knives properly
▶ cut foods into a variety of classic shapes

Every professional must become skilled in the use of certain tools. The professional chef is no exception. One of the most important tools the student chef must master is the knife. Good knife skills are critical to a chef's success because the knife is the most commonly used tool in the kitchen. Every chef spends countless hours slicing, dicing, mincing and chopping. Learning to perform these tasks safely and efficiently is an essential part of your training.

At first, professional knives may feel large and awkward and the techniques discussed in this chapter may not seem all that efficient. But as you become familiar with knives and practice your knife skills, using knives correctly will become second nature.

Knives are identified in Chapter 5, Tools and Equipment. Here we show how they are used to cut vegetables. The techniques presented, however, can be used for most any food that holds its shape when cut. Knife skills for butchering and fabricating meat, poultry, fish and shellfish are discussed in Chapter 13, Principles of Meat Cookery, through Chapter 20, Fish and Shellfish.

A note about language: Many of the classic cuts are known by their French names: julienne, for example. Although these words are nouns and entered the English language as nouns (for example, a julienne of carrot), they are also used as verbs (to julienne a carrot) and adjectives (julienned carrots).

▶ USING YOUR KNIFE SAFELY

The first rule of knife safety is to think about what you are doing. Other basic rules of knife safety are as follows:

1 Use the correct knife for the task at hand.
2 Always cut away from yourself.
3 Always cut on a cutting board. Do not cut on glass, marble or metal.
4 Keep knives sharp; a dull knife is more dangerous than a sharp one.
5 When carrying a knife, hold it point down, parallel and close to your leg as you walk.
6 A falling knife has no handle. Do not attempt to catch a falling knife; step back and allow it to fall.
7 Never leave a knife in a sink of water; anyone reaching into the sink could be injured or the knife could be dented by pots or other utensils.

► CARING FOR YOUR KNIFE

KNIFE SHARPENING

A sharpening stone called a **whetstone** is used to put an edge on a dull knife blade. To use a whetstone, place the heel of the blade against the whetstone at a 20-degree angle. Keeping that angle, press down on the blade while pushing it away from you in one long arc, as if to slice off a thin piece of the stone. The entire length of the blade should come in contact with the stone during each sweep. Repeat the procedure on both sides of the blade until sufficiently sharp. With a triple-faced stone, such as that shown here, you progress from the coarsest to the finest surface. Any whetstone can be moistened with either water or mineral oil, but not both. Do not use vegetable oil on a whetstone since it will soon become rancid and gummy.

A **steel** does not sharpen a knife. Rather, it is used to hone or straighten the blade immediately after and between sharpenings. To use a steel, place the blade against the steel at a 20-degree angle. Then draw the blade along the entire length of the steel. Repeat the technique several times on each side of the blade.

A final note on knife care: Do not wash knives in commercial dishwashers. The heat and harsh chemicals can damage the edge and the handle. The blade can also be damaged if it knocks against cookware or utensils. In addition, the knife could injure an unsuspecting worker. Always wash and dry your knives by hand immediately after each use.

When sharpening a knife against a three-sided whetstone, go from the coarsest to the finest surface.

Honing a knife against a steel straightens the blade between sharpenings.

► GRIPPING YOUR KNIFE

There are several different ways to grip a knife. Use the grip that is most comfortable for you or the one dictated by the job at hand. Whichever grip you use should be firm but not so tight that your hand becomes tired. Gripping styles are shown here.

The most common grip: Hold the handle with three fingers while gripping the blade between the thumb and index finger.

A variation on the most common grip: Grip the handle with four fingers and place the thumb on the front of the handle.

The underhand grip for a rigid boning knife: Grip the handle in a fist with four fingers and thumb. This grip allows you to use the knife tip to cut around joints and separate flesh from bone when boning meat and poultry.

▶ CONTROLLING YOUR KNIFE

To safely produce even cuts, you must control (or guide) your knife with one hand and hold the item being cut with the other. Always allow the blade's sharp edge to do the cutting. Never force the blade through the item being cut. Use smooth, even strokes. Using a dull knife or excessive force with any knife produces, at best, poor results and, at worst, a significant safety risk. Cutting without using your hand as a guide may also be dangerous. Two safe cutting methods that produce good results are shown here.

Method A

1 Keeping your fingertips curled back, grip the item being cut with three fingertips and your thumb. Hold the knife in the other hand. While keeping the knife's tip on the cutting board, lift the heel of the knife.

2 Using the second joint of your index finger as a guide, cut a slice using a smooth, even, downward stroke. Adjust the position of the guiding finger after each slice to produce slices of equal size. After a few cuts, slide your fingertips and thumb down the length of the item and continue slicing. For this slicing technique, the knife's tip acts as the fulcrum.

Method B

1 Grip the item as described above. Using the second joint of your index finger as a guide, lift the knife's tip and slice by drawing the knife slightly back toward you and down through the item, cutting the item to the desired thickness.

2 The motion of the knife should come almost entirely from the wrist, not the elbow. Allow the weight of the knife to do most of the work; very little downward pressure needs to be applied to the knife. For this slicing technique, your wrist should act as the fulcrum.

► CUTTING WITH YOUR KNIFE

A knife is used to shape and reduce an item's size. Uniformity of size and shape ensures even cooking and enhances the appearance of the finished product. Items are shaped by slicing, chopping, dicing, mincing and other special cutting techniques.

SLICING

To slice is to cut an item into relatively broad, thin pieces. Slices may be either the finished cut or the first step in producing other cuts. Slicing is typically used to create three specialty cuts: chiffonade, rondelle and diagonal. Slicing skills are also used to produce oblique or roll cuts and lozenges.

A **chiffonade** is a preparation of finely sliced or shredded leafy vegetables used as a garnish or a base under cold presentations. As shown here, slicing spinach en chiffonade is a relatively simple process.

► **chiffonade** (chef-fon-nahd) to finely slice or shred leafy vegetables or herbs

1 Wash and destem the leaves as necessary. Stack several leaves on top of each other and roll them tightly like a cigar.

2 Make fine slices across the leaves while holding the leaf roll tightly.

As seen here, **rondelles** or **rounds** are easily made disk-shaped slices of cylindrical vegetables or fruits.

► **rondelles** (ron-dellz) disk-shaped slices

Peel the item (if desired) and place it on a cutting board. Make even slices perpendicular to the item being cut.

Diagonals are elongated or oval-shaped slices of cylindrical vegetables or fruits. They are produced with a cut similar to that used to cut rondelles except that the knife is held at an angle to the item being cut.

► **diagonals** oval-shaped slices

Peel the item (if desired) and place it on a cutting board. Position the knife at the desired angle to the item being cut and slice it evenly.

▶ **oblique cuts** (oh-BLEEK) small pieces with two angle-cut sides

Oblique-cut or **roll-cut** items are small pieces with two angle-cut sides. It is a relatively simple cut most often used on carrots and parsnips.

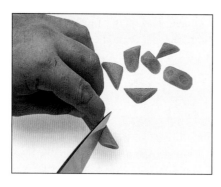

Place the peeled item on a cutting board. Holding the knife at a 45-degree angle, make the first cut. Roll the item a half turn, keeping the knife at the same angle, and make another cut. The result is a wedge-shaped piece with two angled sides.

▶ **lozenges** diamond-shaped pieces, usually of firm vegetables

Lozenges are diamond-shaped cuts prepared from firm vegetables such as carrots, turnips, rutabagas and potatoes.

1 Slice the item into long slices of the desired thickness. Then cut the slices into strips of the desired width.

2 Cut the strips at an angle to produce diamond shapes.

HORIZONTAL SLICING

▶ **butterfly** to slice boneless meat, poultry or fish nearly in half lengthwise so that it spreads open like a book

To horizontal slice is to **butterfly** or cut a pocket into meats, poultry or fish. It is also a method of cutting used to thinly slice soft vegetables.

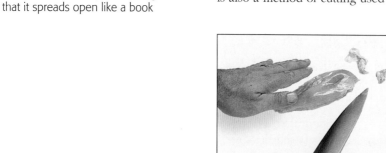

1 With your hand opened and your fingers arched upward, hold the item to be cut firmly in the center of your palm.

2 Holding the knife parallel to the table, slice a pocket to the desired depth, or cut through the item completely.

CHOPPING

To **chop** is to cut an item into small pieces where uniformity of size and shape is neither necessary (for example, coarsely chopped onions for a mirepoix that will be removed from the stock before service) nor feasible (for example, parsley).

► **chop** to cut into pieces where uniformity of size and shape is not important

COARSE CHOPPING

Coarse chopping does not mean carelessly hacking up food. Rather, the procedure is identical to that used for slicing but without the emphasis on uniformity. Coarsely chopped pieces should measure approximately ¾ inch × ¾ inch × ¾ inch (2 cm × 2 cm × 2 cm).

Grip the knife as for slicing. Hold the item being chopped with your other hand. It may not be necessary to use your finger as a guide because uniformity is not crucial.

CHOPPING PARSLEY AND SIMILAR FOODS

Parsley can be cut very coarsely or very finely. As shown here, it is easy to chop parsley and similar foods properly regardless of the desired fineness.

1 Wash the parsley in cold water; drain well. Remove the parsley sprigs from the stems.

2 Grip the knife in one hand. With the other hand spread flat, hold the knife's tip on the cutting board. Keeping the knife's tip on the board, chop the parsley sprigs by rocking the curved blade of the knife up and down while moving the knife back and forth over the parsley.

3 Place the chopped parsley in a clean kitchen towel or a double layer of cheesecloth. Rinse it under cold water and squeeze out as much water as possible. The chopped parsley should be dry and fluffy.

CHOPPING GARLIC

A daily chore in many food service facilities, peeling and chopping garlic is a simple job made easy with the procedure shown here.

1 Break the head of garlic into individual cloves with your hands. Lightly crush the cloves using the flat edge of a chef's knife or a mallet. They will break open and the peel can be separated easily from the garlic flesh.

2 With a flat hand, hold the knife's tip on the cutting board. Using a rocking motion, chop the garlic cloves to the desired size. Garlic is usually chopped very finely.

3 Garlic paste can be made by first finely chopping the garlic and then turning the knife on an angle and repeatedly dragging the edge of the knife along the cutting board, mashing the garlic.

CUTTING STICKS AND DICING

▶ **dice** to cut into cubes with six equal-sized sides

To **dice** is to cut an item into cubes. The techniques described here are most often used when uniformity of size and shape is important (for example, julienned carrots for a salad or brunoised vegetables for a garnish).

Before an item can be diced, it must be cut into sticks such as juliennes and batonnets. These sticks are then reduced through dicing into the classic cuts known as brunoise, small dice, medium dice, large dice and paysanne. Although most cooks have some notion of what size and shape "small diced" potatoes or julienne carrots may be, there are specific sizes and shapes for these cuts. They are:

Julienne—(ju-lee-en) a stick-shaped item with dimensions of ⅛ inch × ⅛ inch × 2 inches (3 mm × 3 mm × 5 cm). When used with potatoes, this cut is sometimes referred to as an **allumette** (al-yoo-MEHT). A **fine julienne** has dimensions of ¹⁄₁₆ inch × ¹⁄₁₆ inch × 2 inches (1.5 mm × 1.5 mm × 5 cm).

Batonnet—(bah-toh-nah) a stick-shaped item with dimensions of ¼ inch × ¼ inch × 2 inches (6 mm × 6 mm × 5 cm).

Brunoise—(broo-nwaz) a cube-shaped item with dimensions of ⅛ inch × ⅛ inch × ⅛ inch (3 mm × 3 mm × 3 mm). A ¹⁄₁₆-inch (1.5-mm) cube is referred to as a **fine brunoise.**

Small dice—a cube-shaped item with dimensions of ¼ inch × ¼ inch × ¼ inch (6 mm × 6 mm × 6 mm).

Medium dice—a cube-shaped item with dimensions of ½ inch × ½ inch × ½ inch (1.2 cm × 1.2 cm × 1.2 cm).

Large dice—a cube-shaped item with dimensions of ¾ inch × ¾ inch × ¾ inch (2 cm × 2 cm × 2 cm).

Paysanne—(pahy-sahn) a flat, square, round or triangular item with dimensions of ½ inch × ½ inch × ⅛ inch (1.2 cm × 1.2 cm × 3 mm).

CUTTING JULIENNE AND BATONNET

Julienne and batonnet are matchstick-shaped cuts prepared using the same procedure as cutting sticks for dicing.

1 Peel the item (if desired) and square off the sides. Trim the item so that the slices cut from it will be the proper length. Cut even slices of the desired thickness, ⅛ inch (3 mm) for julienne or ¼ inch (6 mm) for batonnet.

2 Stack the slices and cut them evenly into sticks (also referred to as "planks") that are the same thickness as the slices.

CUTTING BRUNOISE AND SMALL, MEDIUM AND LARGE DICE

Brunoise as well as small, medium and large dice are made by first cutting the item into sticks following the procedure for cutting julienne or batonnet, then making cuts perpendicular to the length of the sticks to produce small cubes. Making a ⅛-inch (3-mm) cut perpendicular to the length of a julienne produces a brunoise. Similarly, a fine julienne (1/16 inch × 1/16 inch × 2 inches) is used to produce a fine brunoise. Making a ¼-inch (6-mm) cut perpendicular to the length of a batonnet produces a small dice. A ½-inch (1.2-cm) cut from a ½-inch (1.2-cm) stick produces a medium dice, and a ¾-inch (1.8-cm) cut from a ¾-inch (1.8-cm) stick produces a large dice.

Batonnet and julienne sticks and the large, medium, small and brunoise dices cut from them.

CUTTING PAYSANNE

Paysanne is a classic vegetable cut for garnishing soups and other dishes. It could be described as a very thin ½-inch cube. It is produced by following the procedures for dicing, but in the final step the ½-inch × ½-inch (1.2-cm × 1.2-cm) sticks are cut into slices ⅛ inch (3 mm) thick. The term *paysanne* is also used to refer to similarly sized round or triangular pieces.

Cutting paysanne from a ½-inch × ½-inch (6-mm × 6-mm) stick.

DICING AN ONION

Onions are easily peeled and diced to any size desired using the procedure shown here.

1 Using a paring knife, remove the stem end. Trim the root end but leave it nearly intact (this helps prevent the onion from falling apart while dicing). Peel away the outer skin; be careful not to remove and waste too much onion.

2 Cut the onion in half through the stem and root. Place the cut side down on the cutting board.

3 Cut parallel slices of the desired thickness vertically through the onion from the root toward the stem end without cutting completely through the root end.

4 Make a single horizontal cut on a small onion or two horizontal cuts on a large onion through the width of the onion, again without cutting through the root end.

5 Turn the onion and cut slices perpendicular to the other slices to produce diced onion.

▶ **mince** to cut into very small pieces where uniformity of shape is not important

MINCING

To **mince** is to cut an item into very small pieces. The terms *finely chopped* and *minced* are often used interchangeably and are most often used when referring to garlic, shallots, herbs and other foods that do not have to be uniform in shape.

MINCING SHALLOTS

The procedure for mincing shallots is shown here.

1 Peel and dice the shallots, following the procedure for peeling and dicing an onion.

2 With a flat hand, hold the knife's tip on the cutting board. Using a rocking motion, mince the shallots with the heel of the knife.

TOURNER

▶ **tourner** (toor-nay) to cut into football-shaped pieces with seven equal sides and blunt ends

Tourner (toor-nay; "to turn" in French) is a cutting technique that results in a football-shaped finished product with seven equal sides and flat ends. The size of the finished product may vary, the most common being 2 inches (5 cm) long and 1 to 1½ inches in diameter. This is a more complicated procedure than other cuts and it takes considerable practice to produce good, consistent results.

1 Cut the item being "turned" into pieces 2 inches (5 cm) × ¾ to 1 inch (2 to 2.5 cm). Each piece should have flat ends. (Potatoes, turnips and beets may be cut into as many as six or eight pieces; carrots can simply be cut into 2-inch lengths.) Peeling is optional because in most cases the item's entire surface area is trimmed away.

2 Holding the item between the thumb and forefinger, use a tourné knife or a paring knife to cut seven curved sides on the item, creating a flat-ended, football-shaped product.

PARISIENNES

A melon ball cutter or Parisienne scoop can be used to cut fruits and vegetables into uniform spheres, or **Parisiennes.** Small balls or spheres of fresh melon can be used in fruit salad, while tiny spheres of carrot, turnip, squash and so on can be used as a side dish or to garnish soup or an entrée. Melon ball cutters are available in a range of sizes, the smallest of which has an approximately ⅜-inch (9-mm) diameter and is known as a Parisienne (or Parisian) scoop.

▶ **parisienne** (pah-ree-zee-en) spheres of fruits or vegetables cut with a small melon ball cutter

1 Cut each scoop with a pressing and twisting motion.

2 Make the cuts as close together as possible in order to minimize trim loss.

USING A MANDOLINE

The mandoline is a nonmechanical cutting tool. It does jobs that can be done with a chef's knife, such as very thinly sliced apples or large quantities of julienned vegetables, quickly, easily, and very accurately. It can also produce cuts such as a ridged slice or **gaufrette** that cannot be done with a conventional chef's knife.

When using the mandoline, always use the guard or a steel-mesh glove to protect your hand.

▶ **gaufrette** (goh-FREHT) a thin lattice or waffle-textured slice of vegetable cut on a mandoline

1 To use a mandoline, position the legs and set the blade to the desired shape and thickness.

2 Slide the guard into place.

3 To slice, slide the item against the blade with a single, smooth stroke.

4 To cut gaufrette, select the ridged blade and set it to the desired thickness. Make the first slice, turn the item 60° to 90° and make a second slice. Turn the item back to the original position and make another slice, and so on.

CONCLUSION

Although many slicing and dicing machines are available, none can ever completely replace a skilled chef with a sharp knife. As a student chef, you should make becoming efficient with your knives a high priority. Possessing good knife skills allows you to produce more attractive products in a safe and efficient manner. You will use the classic cuts and techniques outlined in this chapter throughout your career. You should memorize the procedures and practice them often. And remember, a dull or carelessly handled knife is dangerous.

QUESTIONS FOR DISCUSSION

1 Explain the step-by-step procedures for sharpening a knife using a three-sided whetstone.
2 What is the purpose of a steel? How is it used?
3 Why is it necessary to cut vegetables into uniform shapes and sizes?
4 Describe the following cutting procedures: slicing, chopping and dicing.
5 Identify the dimensions of the following cuts: julienne, batonnet, brunoise, small dice, medium dice, large dice and paysanne.
6 Describe the procedure for making tournéed vegetables.
7 Describe three preparations for which a mandoline would be useful.
8 A large number of vendors sell professional-quality knives through their Web sites. What are the advantages and disadvantages of buying knives from an online source?

SOME PEOPLE LIKE TO PAINT PICTURES, OR DO
GARDENING, OR BUILD A BOAT IN THE BASEMENT.
OTHER PEOPLE GET A TREMENDOUS PLEASURE OUT
OF THE KITCHEN, BECAUSE COOKING IS JUST AS
CREATIVE AND IMAGINATIVE AN ACTIVITY AS
DRAWING, OR WOOD CARVING, OR MUSIC.
—*Julia Child, American cooking teacher and
author (1912–)*

KITCHEN STAPLES

AFTER STUDYING THIS
CHAPTER, YOU WILL BE
ABLE TO:

▶ recognize and use a variety of
herbs, spices, nuts, oils,
vinegars and condiments

▶ prepare and serve quality
coffees and teas

▶ **seasoning** an item added to enhance the natural flavors of a food without dramatically changing its taste; salt is the most common seasoning

▶ **flavoring** an item that adds a new taste to a food and alters its natural flavors; flavorings include herbs, spices, vinegars and condiments. The terms *seasoning* and *flavoring* are often used interchangeably.

▶ **herb** any of a large group of aromatic plants whose leaves, stems or flowers are used as a flavoring; used either dried or fresh

▶ **aromatic** a food added to enhance the natural aromas of another food; aromatics include most flavorings, such as herbs and spices, as well as some vegetables

▶ **spice** any of a large group of aromatic plants whose bark, roots, seeds, buds or berries are used as a flavoring; usually used in dried form, either whole or ground

▶ **condiment** traditionally, any item added to a dish for flavor, including herbs, spices and vinegars; now also refers to cooked or prepared flavorings such as prepared mustards, relishes, bottled sauces and pickles

Certain foods are used in almost all stations of the kitchen with such regularity that they have become known as staples. Included are many of the processed, packaged items we often take for granted: salt, pepper, flour, sugar, oil and flavorings. There is, however, no single list of staples. Each food service operation will have its own list, depending on the menu and the cooking methods used.

This chapter identifies and discusses selected herbs and spices, salt, nuts, oils, vinegars and condiments as well as two popular beverages, coffee and tea. We provide identifying characteristics for some of the more common staples and set forth standards of quality and usage. Other staples, such as flour and sugar, are covered in Chapter 29, Principles of the Bakeshop.

▶ HERBS AND SPICES

Herbs and spices are the kitchen staples used as **flavorings. Herbs** refer to the large group of **aromatic** plants whose leaves, stems or flowers are used to add flavors to other foods. Most herbs are available fresh or dried. Because drying alters their flavors and aromas, fresh herbs are generally preferred and should be used if possible. **Spices** are strongly flavored or aromatic portions of plants used as flavorings, **condiments** or aromatics. Spices are the bark, roots, seeds, buds or berries of plants, most of which grow naturally only in tropical climates. Spices are almost always used in their dried form, rarely fresh, and can usually be purchased whole or ground. Some plants—dill, for example—can be used as both an herb (its leaves) and a spice (its seeds).

HERBS

Basil (Fr. *basilique*) is considered one of the great culinary herbs. It is available in a variety of "flavors"—cinnamon, garlic, lemon, even chocolate—but the most common is sweet basil. **Sweet basil** has light green, tender leaves and small white flowers. Its flavor is strong, warm and slightly peppery, with a hint of cloves. Basil is used in Mediterranean cuisines and has a special affinity for garlic and tomatoes. When purchasing fresh basil, look for bright green leaves; avoid flower buds and wilted or rust-colored leaves. Dried sweet basil is readily available but has a decidedly weaker flavor.

Basil

Opal basil is named for its vivid purple color. It has a tougher, crinkled leaf and a medium-strong flavor. Opal basil may be substituted for sweet basil in cooking, and its appearance makes it a distinctive garnish.

Opal Basil

Bay (Fr. *laurier*), also known as sweet laurel, is a small tree from Asia that produces tough, glossy leaves with a sweet balsamic aroma and peppery flavor. Bay symbolized wisdom and glory in ancient Rome; the leaves were used to form crowns or "laurels" worn by emperors and victorious athletes. In cooking, dried bay leaves are often preferred over the more bitter fresh leaves. Essential in French cuisine, bay leaves are part of the traditional bouquet garni and court bouillon. Whole dried leaves are usually added to a dish at the start of cooking, then removed when sufficient flavor has been extracted.

Bay Leaves

Chervil (Fr. *cerfeuil*), also known as sweet cicely, is native to Russia and the Middle East. Its lacy, fernlike leaves are similar to parsley and can be used as a garnish. Chervil's flavor is delicate, similar to parsley but with the distinctive aroma of anise. It should not be heated for long periods. Chervil is commonly used in French cuisine and is one of the traditional fines herbes.

Chives (Fr. *ciboulette*) are perhaps the most delicate and sophisticated members of the onion family. Their hollow, thin grass-green stems grow in clumps and produce round, pale purple flowers, which are used as a garnish. Chives may be purchased dried, quick-frozen or fresh. They have a mild onion flavor and bright green color. Chives complement eggs, poultry, potatoes, fish and shellfish. They should not be cooked for long periods or at high temperatures. Chives make an excellent garnish when snipped with scissors or carefully chopped and sprinkled over finished soups or sauces.

Garlic chives, also known as Chinese chives, actually belong to another plant species. They have flat, solid (not hollow) stems and a mild garlic flavor. They may be used in place of regular chives if their garlic flavor is desired.

Cilantro (Fr. *coriander*) is the green leafy portion of the plant that yields seeds known as coriander. The flavors of the two portions of this plant are very different and cannot be substituted for each other.

Cilantro, also known as Chinese parsley, is sharp and tangy with a strong aroma and an almost citrus flavor. It is widely used in Asian, Mexican and South American cuisines, especially in salads and sauces. It should not be subjected to heat, and cilantro's flavor is completely destroyed by drying. Do not use yellow or discolored leaves or the tough stems.

Curry leaves (Hindi *karipatta; kitha neem*) are the distinctively flavored leaves of a small tree that grows wild in the Himalayan foothills, southern India and Sri Lanka. They look like small shiny bay leaves and have a strong currylike fragrance and a citrus-curry flavor. Often added to a preparation whole, then removed before serving, they can also be minced or finely chopped for marinades and sauces. Choose fresh bright green leaves, if possible, or frozen leaves; dried leaves have virtually no flavor. Although used in making southern Indian and Thai dishes, curry leaves (also known as neem leaves) must not be confused with curry powder, which is discussed later.

Dill (Fr. *aneth*), a member of the parsley family, has tiny, aromatic, yellow flowers and feathery, delicate blue-green leaves. The leaves taste like parsley, but sharper, with a touch of anise. Dill seeds are flat, oval and brown, with a bitter flavor similar to caraway. Both the seeds and the leaves of the dill plant are used in cooking. Dill is commonly used in Scandinavian and central European cuisines, particularly with fish and potatoes. Both leaves and seeds

Chervil

Chives

Garlic Chives

Cilantro

Curry Leaves

Dill

Epazote

Lemongrass

Marjoram

Peppermint

are used in pickling and sour dishes. Dill leaves are available fresh or dried but lose their aroma and flavor during cooking, so add them only after the dish is removed from the heat. Dill seeds are available whole or ground and are used in fish dishes, pickles and breads.

Epazote, also known as wormseed or stinkweed, grows wild throughout the Americas. It has a strong aroma similar to kerosene and a wild flavor. Fresh epazote is used in salads and as a flavoring in Mexican and Southwestern cuisines. It is often cooked with beans to reduce their gaseousness. Dried epazote is brewed to make a beverage.

Lavender is an evergreen with thin leaves and tall stems bearing spikes of tiny purple flowers. Although lavender is known primarily for its aroma, which is widely used in perfumes, soaps and cosmetics, the flowers are also used as a flavoring, particularly in Middle Eastern and Provençal cuisines. These flowers have a sweet, lemony flavor and can be crystallized and used as a garnish. Lavender is also used in jams and preserves and to flavor teas and tisanes.

Lavender

Lemongrass (Fr. *herbe de citron*), also known as citronella grass, is a tropical grass with the strong aroma and flavor of a lemon. It is similar to scallions in appearance but with a woody texture. Only the lower base and white leaf stalks are used. Available fresh or quick-frozen, lemongrass is widely used in Southeast Asian cuisines.

Lovage (Fr. *celeri bâtard,* "false celery") has tall stalks and large dark green celery-like leaves. The leaves, stalks and seeds (which are commonly known as **celery seeds**) have a strong celery flavor. Also known as sea parsley and smallage, the leaves and stalks are used in salads and stews and the seeds are used for flavoring.

Marjoram (Fr. *marjolaine*), also known as sweet marjoram, is a flowering herb native to the Mediterranean and used since ancient times. Its flavor is similar to thyme but sweeter; it also has a stronger aroma. Marjoram is now used in many European cuisines. Although it is available fresh, marjoram is one of the few herbs whose flavor increases when dried. Wild marjoram is more commonly known as oregano.

Mint (Fr. *menthe*), a large family of herbs, includes many species and flavors (even chocolate). **Spearmint** is the most common garden and commercial variety. It has soft, bright green leaves and a tart aroma and flavor. Mint does not blend well with other herbs, so its use is confined to specific dishes, usually fruits or fatty meats such as lamb. Mint has an affinity for chocolate. It can also be brewed into a beverage or used as a garnish.

Spearmint

Peppermint has thin, stiff, pointed leaves and a sharper menthol flavor and aroma. Fresh peppermint is used less often in cooking or as a garnish than spearmint, but peppermint oil is a common flavoring in sweets and candies.

Oregano (Fr. *origan*), also known as wild marjoram, is a pungent, peppery herb used in Mediterranean cuisines, particularly Greek and Italian, as well as in Mexican cuisine. It is a classic complement to tomatoes. Oregano's thin, woody stalks bear clumps of tiny, dark green leaves, which are available dried and crushed.

Oregano

Parsley (Fr. *persil*) is probably the best known and most widely used herb in the world. It grows in almost all climates and is available in many varieties, all of which are rich in vitamins and minerals. The most common type in the United States and Northern Europe is **curly parsley.** It has small curly leaves and a bright green color. Its flavor is tangy and clean. Other cuisines use a variety sometimes known as **Italian parsley,** which has flat leaves, a darker color and coarser flavor. Curly parsley is a ubiquitous garnish; both types can be used in virtually any food except sweets. Parsley stalks have a stronger flavor than the leaves and are part of the standard bouquet garni. Chopped parsley forms the basis of any fine herb blend.

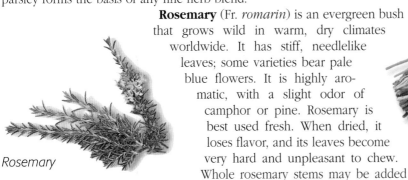

Parsley

Italian Parsley

Rosemary (Fr. *romarin*) is an evergreen bush that grows wild in warm, dry climates worldwide. It has stiff, needlelike leaves; some varieties bear pale blue flowers. It is highly aromatic, with a slight odor of camphor or pine. Rosemary is best used fresh. When dried, it loses flavor, and its leaves become very hard and unpleasant to chew. Whole rosemary stems may be added to a dish such as a stew and then removed when enough flavor has been imparted. They may also be added to a bouquet garni. Rosemary has a great affinity for roasted and grilled meats, especially lamb.

Rosemary

Sage (Fr. *sauge*) was used as a medicine for centuries before it entered the kitchen as a culinary herb. Culinary sage has narrow, fuzzy, gray-green leaves and blue flowers. Its flavor is strong and balsamic, with notes of camphor. Sage is used in poultry dishes, with fatty meats or brewed as a beverage. Sage's strong flavor does not blend well with other herbs. It dries well and is available in whole or chopped leaves or rubbed (coarsely ground).

Sage

Savory (Fr. *sariette*), also known as summer savory, has been used since ancient times. Its leaves are small and narrow, and it has a sharp, bitter flavor, vaguely like thyme. It dries well and is used in bean dishes, sausages and fine herb blends.

Tarragon (Fr. *estragon*), another of the great culinary herbs, is native to Siberia. It is a bushy plant with long, narrow, dark green leaves and tiny gray flowers. Tarragon goes well with fish and tomatoes and is essential in many French dishes such as béarnaise sauce and fine herb blends. Its flavor is strong and diffuses quickly through foods. It is available dried, but drying may cause haylike flavors to develop.

Savory

Tarragon

Thyme (Fr. *thym*) has been popular since 3500 B.C., when Egyptians used it as a medicine and for embalming. Thyme is a small, bushy plant with woody stems, tiny green-gray leaves and purple flowers. Its flavor is strong but refined, with notes of sage. Thyme dries well and complements virtually all types of meat, poultry, fish, shellfish and vegetables. It is often included in a bouquet garni or added to stocks.

Thyme

Aleppo Pepper

Allspice

Star Anise

Capers

SPICES

Aleppo pepper (ah-LEHP-oh) is made from bright red chiles grown in Turkey and northern Syria. The sun-dried Aleppo chiles are seeded and crushed, then used as a condiment. It has a sharp, but sweet, fruity flavor, with only mild heat (15,000 Scoville units). Although a member of the *Capsicum* family, Aleppo pepper is used more like ground peppercorns (*piper nigrum*) than a chile. Also known as Halaby pepper, it adds an authentic Mediterranean flavor and fragrance to foods.

Allspice (Fr. *toute-épice*), also known as Jamaican pepper, is the dried berry of a tree that flourishes in Jamaica, and one of the few spices still grown exclusively in the New World. Allspice is available whole; in berries that look like large, rough, brown peppercorns; or ground. Ground allspice is not a mixture of spices although it does taste like a blend of cinnamon, cloves and nutmeg. Allspice is now used throughout the world, in everything from cakes to curries, and is often included in peppercorn blends.

Anise (Fr. *anis*) is native to the eastern Mediterranean, where it was widely used by ancient civilizations. Today, it is grown commercially in warm climates throughout India, North Africa and southern Europe. The tiny, gray-green egg-shaped seeds have a distinctively strong, sweet flavor, similar to licorice and fennel. When anise seeds turn brown, they are stale and should be discarded. Anise is used in pastries as well as fish, shellfish and vegetable dishes, and is commonly used in alcoholic beverages (for example, Pernod and ouzo). The green leaves of the anise plant are occasionally used fresh as an herb or in salads.

Anise Seeds

Star anise, also known as Chinese anise, is the dried, star-shaped fruit of a Chinese magnolia tree. Although it is botanically unrelated, its flavor is similar to anise seeds but more bitter and pungent. It is an essential flavor in many Chinese dishes and one of the components of five-spice powder.

Annatto seeds (Fr. *roucou*) are the small, brick-red triangular seeds of a shrub from South America and the Caribbean. Annatto seeds add a mild, peppery flavor to rice, fish and shellfish dishes and are crushed to make Mexican achiote paste. Because they impart a bright yellow-orange color to foods, annatto seeds are commonly used as a natural food coloring, especially in cheeses and margarine.

Annatto Seeds

Asafetida (ah-sah-FEH-teh-dah; also spelled *asafoetida*) is a pale brown resin made from the sap of a giant fennel-like plant native to India and Iran. Also known as devil's dung, it has a garlicky flavor and a strong unpleasant fetid aroma (the aroma is not transferred to food being flavored). Available powdered or in lump form, it is used—very sparingly—as a flavoring in Indian and Middle Eastern cuisines.

Capers (Fr. *capres*) come from a small bush that grows wild throughout the Mediterranean basin. Its unopened flower buds have been pickled and used as a condiment for thousands of years. Fresh capers are not used, as the sharp, salty-sour flavor develops only after curing in strongly salted white vinegar. The finest capers are the smallest, known as nonpareils, which are produced in France's Provence region. Capers are used in a variety of sauces (tartare, rémoulade) and are excellent with fish and game. Capers will keep for long periods if moistened by their original liquid. Do not add or substitute vinegar, however, as this causes the capers to spoil.

A PINCH OF HISTORY

Spices have been used for many purposes for thousands of years. Egyptian papyri dating back to 2800 B.C. identify several spices native to the Middle and Far East that were used by the ruling and priestly classes for therapeutic, cosmetic, medicinal, ritualistic and culinary purposes.

By A.D. 300, the Romans were regularly importing spices for use as perfumes, medicines, preservatives and ingredients from China and India via long, difficult caravan journeys over sea and land. Spices were extremely expensive and unavailable to all but the wealthiest citizens.

After Rome fell in the second half of the 5th century A.D., much of the overland route through southern Europe became prey to bandits; and after Constantinople fell in 1453, the spice routes through the Middle East were controlled by the Ottoman Turks. Spice costs soared, and economies based upon the spice trade, such as that of Venice, were at risk.

By then highly spiced food had become common, especially in wealthier households. So, in part to maintain their culinary norm, the Europeans set out to break the Ottoman Turk monopoly. These efforts led to Columbus's exploration of the Americas and Vasco da Gama's discovery of a sea route to India. Although the New World contained none of the spices for which Columbus was searching, it provided many previously unknown foods and flavorings that subsequently changed European tables forever, including chiles, vanilla, tomatoes, potatoes and chocolate.

Formation of the Dutch East India Company in 1602 marked the start of the Dutch colonial empire and made spices widely available to the growing European middle classes. The transplantation and cultivation of spice plants eventually weakened the once-powerful trading empires until, by the 19th century, no European country could monopolize trade. Prices fell dramatically.

Caraway Seeds

Caraway (Fr. *carvi*) is perhaps the world's oldest spice. Its use has been traced to the Stone Age, and seeds have been found in ancient Egyptian tombs. The caraway plant grows wild in Europe and temperate regions of Asia. It produces a small, crescent-shaped brown seed with the peppery flavor of rye. Seeds may be purchased whole or ground. (The leaves have a mild, bland flavor and are rarely used in cooking.) Caraway is a very European flavor, used extensively in German and Austrian dishes, particularly breads, meats and cabbage. It is also used in alcoholic beverages and cheeses.

Cardamom Seeds

Cardamom (Fr. *cardamome*) is one of the most expensive spices, second only to saffron in cost. Its seeds are encased in ¼-inch- (6-millimeter-) long light green or brown pods. Cardamom is highly aromatic. Its flavor, lemony with notes of camphor, is quite strong and is used in both sweet and savory dishes. Cardamom is widely used in Indian and Middle Eastern cuisines, where it is also used to flavor coffee. Scandinavians use cardamom to flavor breads and pastries. Ground cardamom loses its flavor rapidly and is easily adulterated, so it is best to purchase whole seeds and grind your own as needed.

▶ For our purposes, *chile* refers to the plant, *chili* refers to the stewlike dish containing chiles and *chilli* refers to the commercial spice powder

Chiles, including paprika, chile peppers, bell peppers and cayenne, are members of the **capsicum** plant family. Although cultivated for thousands of years in the West Indies and Americas, capsicum peppers were unknown in the Old World prior to Spanish explorations during the 15th century. Capsicum peppers come in all shapes and sizes, with a wide range of flavors, from sweet to extremely hot. Some capsicums are used as a vegetable, while others are dried, ground and used as a spice. Fresh chiles and bell peppers are discussed in Chapter 22, Vegetables. Capsicums are botanically unrelated to **piper nigrum,** the black peppercorns discussed later.

Cayenne Pepper

Cayenne, sometimes simply labeled "red pepper," is ground from a blend of several particularly hot types of dried red chile peppers. Its flavor is extremely hot and pungent; it has a bright orange-red color and fine texture.

Paprika

Paprika, also known as Hungarian pepper, is a bright red powder ground from specific varieties of red-ripened and dried chiles. Paprika's flavor ranges from sweet to pungent; its aroma is distinctive and strong. It is essential to many Spanish and eastern European dishes. Mild paprika is meant to be used in generous quantities and may be sprinkled on prepared foods as a garnish.

Chilli Powder

Crushed Chiles

Cloves

Cumin

Ground Cinnamon and Cinnamon Sticks

Coriander Seeds

Fennel

Chile powders are made from a wide variety of dried chile peppers, ranging from sweet and mild to extremely hot and pungent. The finest pure chile powders come from dried chiles that are simply roasted, ground and sieved. Commercial chilli powder, an American invention, is actually a combination of spices—oregano, cumin, garlic and other flavorings—intended for use in Mexican dishes. Each brand is different and should be sampled before using.

Crushed chiles, also known as chile flakes, are blended from dried, coarsely crushed chiles. They are quite hot and are used in sauces and meat dishes.

Cinnamon (Fr. *cannelle*) and its cousin **cassia** are among the oldest known spices: Cinnamon's use is recorded in China as early as 2500 B.C., and the Far East still produces most of these products. Both cinnamon and cassia come from the bark of small evergreen trees, peeled from branches in thin layers and dried in the sun. High-quality cinnamon should be pale brown and thin, rolled up like paper into sticks known as quills. Cassia is coarser and has a stronger, less subtle flavor than cinnamon. Consequently, it is cheaper than true cinnamon. Cinnamon is usually purchased ground because it is difficult to grind. Cinnamon sticks are used when long cooking times allow for sufficient flavor to be extracted (for example, in stews or curries). Cinnamon's flavor is most often associated with pastries and sweets, but it has a great affinity for lamb and spicy dishes. Labeling laws do not require that packages distinguish between cassia and cinnamon, so most of what is sold as cinnamon in the United States is actually cassia, blended for consistent flavor and aroma.

Cloves (Fr. *girofles*) are the unopened buds of evergreen trees that flourish in muggy tropical regions. When dried, whole cloves have hard, sharp prongs that can be used to push them into other foods, such as onions or fruit, in order to provide flavor. Cloves are extremely pungent, with a sweet, astringent aroma. A small amount provides a great deal of flavor. Cloves are used in desserts and meat dishes, preserves and liquors. They may be purchased whole or ground.

Coriander (Fr. *coriander*) seeds come from the cilantro plant. They are round and beige, with a distinctive sweet, spicy flavor and strong aroma. Unlike other plants in which the seeds and the leaves carry the same flavor and aroma, coriander and cilantro are very different. Coriander seeds are available whole or ground and are frequently used in Indian cuisine and pickling mixtures.

Cumin is the seed of a small delicate plant of the parsley family that grows in North Africa and the Middle East. The small seeds are available whole or ground and look (but do not taste) like caraway seeds. Cumin has a strong earthy flavor and tends to dominate any dish in which it is included. It is used in Indian, Middle Eastern and Mexican cuisines, in sausages and a few cheeses.

Fennel (Fr. *fenouil*) is a perennial plant with feathery leaves and tiny flowers long cultivated in India and China as a medicine and cure for witchcraft. Its seeds are greenish brown with prominent ridges and short, hairlike fibers. Their taste and aroma are similar to anise, though not as sweet. Whole seeds are widely used in Italian stews and sausages; central European cuisines use fennel with fish, pork, pickles and vegetables. Ground seeds can also be used in breads, cakes and cookies. The same plant produces a bulbous stalk used as a vegetable.

Fenugreek (Fr. *fenugrec*), grown in Mediterranean countries since ancient times, is a small, beanlike plant with a tiny flower. The seeds, available whole or ground, are pebble shaped and transfer their pale orange color to the foods with which they are cooked. Their flavor is bittersweet, like burnt sugar with a bitter aftertaste. Fenugreek is a staple in Indian cuisines, especially curries and chutneys.

Fenugreek

Filé powder (fee-LAY) is the dried, ground leaf of the sassafras plant. Long used by Choctaw Indians, it is now most commonly used as a thickener and flavoring in Cajun and Creole cuisines. Filé is also used as a table condiment to add a spicy note to stews, gumbo and the like. The powder forms strings if allowed to boil, so it should be added during the last minutes of cooking.

Filé Powder

Galangal (guh-LANG-guhl) is the rhizome of a plant native to India and Southeast Asia. The rhizome has a reddish skin, an orange or whitish flesh and a peppery, gingerlike flavor and piny aroma. Also known as galanga root, Thai ginger and Laos ginger, it is peeled and crushed for used in Thai and Indonesian cuisines. Fresh ginger is an appropriate substitute.

Ginger (Fr. *gingembre*) is a well-known spice obtained from the root of a tall, flowering tropical plant. Fresh ginger root is known as a "hand" because it looks vaguely like a group of knobby fingers. It has grayish-tan skin and a pale yellow, fibrous interior. Fresh ginger should be plump and firm with smooth skin. It should keep for about a month under refrigeration. Its flavor is fiery but sweet, with notes of lemon and rosemary. Fresh ginger is widely available and is used in Indian and Asian cuisines. It has a special affinity for chicken, beef and curries. Ginger is also available peeled and pickled in vinegar, candied in sugar or preserved in alcohol or syrup. Dried, ground ginger is a fine yellow powder widely used in pastries. Its flavor is spicier and not as sweet as fresh ginger.

Ginger Root

Grains of paradise are the seeds of a perennial reedlike plant indigenous to the West African coast. Related to cardamom, grains of paradise have a spicy, warm and slightly bitter flavor, similar to peppercorns. In fact, grains of paradise were traditionally used in place of black pepper and are also known as Guinea pepper or Melegueta pepper. Now enjoying a resurgence in popularity and increased availability, they are ground and used primarily in West African and Magreb dishes, and in the spice blend known as ras el hanout.

Grains of Paradise

Horseradish (Fr. *cranson de Bretagne*) is the large off-white taproot of a hardy perennial (unrelated to radishes) that flourishes in cool climates. Fresh roots should be firm and plump; they will not have the distinctive horseradish aroma unless cut or bruised. The outer skin and inner core of a fresh horseradish root can have an unpleasant flavor and should be discarded. Typically used in Russian and Central European cuisines, especially as an accompaniment to roasted meats and fish and shellfish dishes, horseradish is usually served grated, creamed into a sauce or as part of a compound butter or mustard preparation. If horseradish is cooked, heat can destroy its flavor and pungency, so any horseradish should be added near the end of cooking.

Horseradish Root

Juniper (Fr. *genièvre*) is an evergreen bush grown throughout the northern hemisphere. It produces round purple berries with a sweet flavor similar to pine. Juniper berries are used for flavoring gin and other alcoholic beverages, and are crushed and incorporated in game dishes, particularly venison and wild boar.

Juniper Berries

Mustard seeds (Fr. *moutarde*), available in black, brown and yellow, come from three different plants in the cabbage family. Mustard seeds are small, hard spheres with a bitter flavor. The seeds have no aroma, but their flavor is sharp and fiery hot. Yellow seeds have the mildest and black seeds the strongest flavor. All are sold whole and can be crushed for cooking. Mustard seeds are a standard component of pickling spices and are processed and blended for prepared mustards, which we discuss later. Ground or dry mustard is a bright yellow powder made from a blend of ground seeds, wheat flour and turmeric.

Mustard Seeds   *Ground Mustard*

Whole Nutmegs with Ground Mace (left) and Ground Nutmeg (right)

Mace

Green Peppercorns

Pink Peppercorns

Szechuan Pepper

Nutmeg (Fr. *muscade*) and **mace** come from the yellow plumlike fruit of a large tropical evergreen. These fruits are dried and opened to reveal the seed known as nutmeg. The seed is surrounded by a bright red lacy coating or *aril*; the aril is the spice mace. Whole nutmegs are oval and look rather like a piece of smooth wood. The flavor and aroma of nutmeg are strong and sweet, and a small quantity provides a great deal of flavor. Nutmeg should be grated directly into a dish as needed; once grated, flavor loss is rapid. Nutmeg is used in many European cuisines, mainly in pastries and sweets, but is also important in meat and savory dishes.

Mace is an expensive spice, with a flavor similar to nutmeg but more refined. It is almost always purchased ground and retains its flavor longer than other ground spices. Mace is used primarily in pastry items.

Peppercorns (Fr. *poivre*) are the berries of a vine plant (*piper nigrum*) native to tropical Asia. Peppercorns should not be confused with the chile (capsicum) peppers discussed earlier. Peppercorns vary in size, color, pungency and flavor. Many of these differences are the result of variations in climate and growing conditions. Good-quality pepper is expensive and should be purchased whole and ground fresh in a peppermill as needed. Whole peppercorns will last indefinitely if kept dry. They should be stored well covered in a cool, dark place.

Black and **white peppercorns** are produced from the same plant, but are picked and processed differently. For black peppercorns, the berries are picked when green and simply dried whole in the sun. Black pepper has a warm, pungent flavor and aroma. Tellicherry peppercorns from the southwest coast of India are generally considered the finest black peppercorns in the world and are priced accordingly.

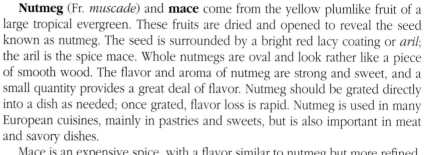

Black Pepper (left) and White Pepper (right)

For white peppercorns, the berries are allowed to ripen until they turn red. The ripened berries are allowed to ferment, then the outer layer of skin is washed off. Nowadays, white pepper may be produced by mechanically removing the outer skin from black peppercorns. This is not true white pepper, and the resulting product should be labeled "decorticated." White pepper has less aroma than black pepper but is useful in white sauces or where the appearance of black speckles is undesirable.

Green peppercorns are unripened berries that are either freeze-dried or pickled in brine or vinegar. Pickled green peppercorns are soft, with a fresh, sour flavor similar to capers. They are excellent in spiced butters and sauces or with fish.

Pink peppercorns are actually the berries of a South American tree, not a vine pepper plant. Pink peppercorns are available dried or pickled in vinegar. Although they are attractive, their flavor is bitter and pinelike, with less spiciness than true pepper.

Szechuan pepper (also spelled Szechwan and Sichuan) is the dried red berries of the prickly ash tree native to China. Also known as anise pepper and Chinese pepper, the berries have an extremely hot, peppery, spicy flavor with citrus overtones and are used in Chinese cuisines and as part of Chinese five-spice powder.

Poppy seeds (Fr. *pavot*) are the ripened seeds of the opium poppy, which flourishes in the Middle East and India. (When ripe, the seeds do not contain any of the medicinal alkaloids found elsewhere in the plant.) The tiny blue-gray seeds are round and hard with a sweet, nutty flavor. Poppy seeds are used in pastries and breads.

Poppy Seeds

Saffron (Fr. *safran*) comes from the dried stigmas of the saffron crocus. Each flower bears only three threadlike stigmas, and each must be picked by hand. It takes about 250,000 flowers to produce one pound of saffron, making it the most expensive spice in the world. Beware of bargains; there is no such thing as cheap saffron. Luckily, a tiny pinch is enough to color and flavor a large quantity of food. Good saffron should be a brilliant orange color, not yellow, with a strong aroma and a bitter, honeylike taste. Saffron produces a yellow dye that diffuses through any warm liquid. Valencia or Spanish saffron is considered the finest. It is commonly used with fish and shellfish (a necessity for bouillabaisse) and rice dishes such as paella and risotto. When using saffron threads, first crush them gently, then soak them in some hot liquid from the recipe. Powdered saffron is less expensive but more easily adulterated. It may be added directly to the other ingredients when cooking.

Saffron

Sesame seeds, also known as benne seeds, are native to India. They are small, flat ovals, with a creamy white color. Their taste is nutty and earthy, with a pronounced aroma when roasted or ground into a paste (known as tahini). Sesame seeds are the source of sesame oil, which has a mild, nutty flavor and does not go rancid easily. Sesame seeds are roasted and used in or as a garnish for breads and meat dishes. They are popular in Indian and Asian cuisines, with a black variety of seeds most popular as a Japanese condiment.

Sesame Seeds

Tamarind (Fr. *tamarin;* Sp. and It. *tamarindo*), also known as an Indian date, is the brown, bean-shaped pod of the tamarind tree, which is native to Africa. Although naturally sweet, tamarind also contains 12% tartaric acid, which makes it extremely tart. It is commonly used in Indian curries and Mediterranean cooking as a souring agent and in the West Indies in fruit drinks. Tamarind is sold as a concentrate or in sticky blocks of crushed pods, pulp and seeds, which should be soaked in warm water for about five minutes, then squeezed through a sieve. Tamarind's high pectin content is useful in chutneys and jams, and it is often included in barbeque sauces and marinades. It is a key ingredient in Worcestershire sauce.

Tamarind Pods *Tamarind Paste*

Turmeric (Fr. *curcuma*), also known as Indian saffron, is produced from the roots of a flowering tropical plant related to ginger. Unlike ginger, fresh turmeric is not used in cooking. It is only available dried and usually ground. Turmeric is renowned for its vibrant yellow color and is used as a food coloring and dye. Turmeric's flavor is distinctive and strong; it should not be substituted for saffron. Turmeric is a traditional ingredient in Indian curries, to which it imparts color as well as flavor.

Turmeric

Wasabi is a pale green root similar, but unrelated, to horseradish. It has a strong aroma and a sharp, cleansing flavor with herbal overtones that is a bit hotter than that of horseradish. Fresh wasabi is rarely found outside Japan, but tins of powder and tubes of paste are readily available. It is commonly served with sushi and sashimi and can be used to add a spicy Asian note to other dishes, such as mashed potatoes or a compound butter.

Wasabi

HERB AND SPICE BLENDS

Many cuisines have created recognizable combinations of flavors that are found in a variety of dishes. Although many of these blends are available ready-prepared for convenience, most can be mixed by the chef as needed. A few of the more common herb and spice blends are described here. In addition, a recipe for Cajun Spice Mix appears on page 541 and one for Creole Spice Mix appears on page 582.

Chinese five-spice powder is a combination of equal parts finely ground Szechuan pepper, star anise, cloves, cinnamon and fennel seeds. This blend is widely used in Chinese and some Vietnamese foods and is excellent with pork and in pâtés.

Curry powder is a European invention that probably took its name from the

Five-Spice Powder

Curry Powder

Herbes de Provence

Pickling Spice

Tamil word *kari*, meaning "sauce." Created by 19th-century Britons returning from colonial India, it was meant to be the complete spicing for a "curry" dish. There are as many different formulas for curry powder as there are manufacturers, some mild and sweet (Bombay or Chinese style), others hot and pungent (Madras style). Typical ingredients in curry powder are black pepper, cinnamon, cloves, coriander, cumin, ginger, mace and turmeric.

Fine herbs (Fr. *fines herbes*) are a combination of parsley, tarragon, chervil and chives widely used in French cuisine. The mixture is available dried, or you can create your own from fresh ingredients.

Masala (mah-SAH-lah) is a flavorful, aromatic blend of roasted and ground spices used in Indian cuisines. A **garam masala** (gah-RAHM) is a masala made with hot spices (*garam* means warm or hot). A dry garam masala usually contains peppercorns, cardamom, cinnamon, cloves, coriander, nutmeg, turmeric, bay leaves and fennel seeds and is added toward the end of cooking or sprinkled on the food just before service. A wet garam masala is made by adding coconut milk, oil or sometimes tamarind water to a dry garam masala. A wet garam masala is typically added at the start of cooking.

Herbes de Provence (airbs duh pro-VAWNS) is a blend of dried herbs commonly grown and used in southern France. Commercial blends usually include thyme, rosemary, bay leaf, basil, fennel seeds, savory and lavender. The herb blend is used with grilled or roasted meat, fish or chicken; in vegetable dishes; on pizza; and even in steamed rice and yeast breads.

Italian seasoning blend is a commercially prepared mixture of dried basil, oregano, sage, marjoram, rosemary, thyme, savory and other herbs associated with Italian cuisine.

Pickling spice, as with other blends, varies by manufacturer. Most pickling spice blends are based on black peppercorns and red chiles, with some or all of the following added: allspice, cloves, ginger, mustard seeds, coriander seeds, bay leaves and dill. These blends are useful in making cucumber or vegetable pickles as well as in stews and soups.

Quatre-épices (kah-tray-pees), literally "four spices" in French, is a peppery mixture of black peppercorns with lesser amounts of nutmeg, cloves and dried ginger. Sometimes cinnamon or allspice is included. Quatre-épices is used in charcuterie and long-simmered stews.

Ras el hanout (rass al ha-noot) is a common Moroccan spice blend varying greatly from supplier to supplier. It typically contains 20 or more spices, such as turmeric, cinnamon, cloves, grains of paradise, coriander, cumin, cardamom, peppercorns, dried chiles, dried flower petals and, allegedly, an aphrodisiac or two. It is sold whole and ground by the cook as necessary to flavor stews, rice, couscous and game dishes.

Seasoned salts are commercially blended products containing salt and one or more natural flavoring ingredients such as garlic, spices or celery seeds, and, often, monosodium glutamate.

STORING HERBS AND SPICES

Fresh herbs should be kept refrigerated at 34°F–40°F (2°C–4°C). Large bouquets can be stored upright, their leaves loosely covered with plastic wrap and their stems submerged in water. Smaller bunches should be stored loosely covered with a damp towel. Excess fresh herbs can be dried for later use in an electric dehydrator or spread out on baking sheets in a 100°F (38°C) oven.

Dried herbs and spices should be stored in airtight, opaque containers in a cool, dry place. Avoid light and heat, both of which destroy delicate flavors.

USING HERBS AND SPICES

Herbs and spices are a simple, inexpensive way to bring individuality and variety to foods. Their proper use leads to better-flavored and distinctively different dishes. They add neither fat nor sodium and virtually no calories to foods; most contain only 3 to 10 calories per teaspoon. Table 7.1 lists just a few uses for some of the more common herbs and spices.

Table 7.1	USES FOR SOME COMMON HERBS AND SPICES	
FLAVORING	**FORM**	**SUGGESTED USES**
Allspice	Whole or ground	Fruits, relishes, braised meats
Anise	Whole or ground	Asian cuisines, pastries, breads, cheeses
Basil	Fresh or dried	Tomatoes, salads, eggs, fish, chicken, lamb, cheeses
Caraway	Whole or ground	Rye bread, cabbage, beans, pork, beef, veal
Chervil	Fresh or dried	Chicken, fish, eggs, salads, soups, vegetables
Chives	Fresh or dried	Eggs, fish, chicken, soups, potatoes, cheeses
Cilantro	Fresh leaves	Salsa, salads, Mexican cuisine, fish, shellfish, chicken
Cloves	Whole or ground	Marinades, baked goods, braised meats, pickles, fruits, beverages, stocks
Cumin	Whole or ground	Chili, sausages, stews, eggs
Dill	Fresh or dried leaves; whole seeds	Leaves or seeds in soups, salads, fish, shellfish, vegetables, breads; seeds in pickles, potatoes, vegetables
Fennel	Whole seeds	Sausages, stews, sauces, pickling, lamb, eggs
Ginger	Fresh root or powder	Asian, Caribbean and Indian cuisines, pastries, curries, stews, meats
Marjoram	Fresh or dried	Sausages, pâtés, meats, poultry, stews, green vegetables, tomatoes, game
Nutmeg	Ground	Curries, relishes, rice, eggs, beverages
Rosemary	Fresh or dried	Lamb, veal, beef, poultry, game, marinades, stews
Saffron	Threads or ground	Rice, breads, potatoes, soups, stews, chicken, fish, shellfish
Sage	Fresh or dried	Poultry, charcuterie, pork, stuffings, pasta, beans, tomatoes
Tarragon	Fresh or dried	Chicken, fish, eggs, salad dressings, sauces, tomatoes
Thyme	Fresh or dried	Fish, chicken, meats, stews, charcuterie, soups, tomatoes
Turmeric	Ground	Curries, relishes, rice, eggs, breads

FLAVOR CONCEPTS

In *Ethnic Cuisine: The Flavor Principle Cookbook,* Elisabeth Rozin writes: "Every culture tends to combine a small number of flavoring ingredients so frequently and so consistently that they become definitive of that particular cuisine" (p. xiv). She calls these defining flavors "flavor principles" and notes that they are "designed to abstract what is absolutely fundamental about a cuisine and, thus, to serve as a guide in cooking and developing new recipes" (p. xvii). She identifies the following flavor principles:

Central Asia: cinnamon, fruit and nuts

China: generally—soy sauce, rice wine and ginger root

   Northern China (Mandarin/Peking)—miso and/or garlic and/or sesame

   Western China (Szechuan)—sweet, sour and hot

   Southern China (Canton)—black beans, garlic

Eastern Europe (Jewish): onion and chicken fat

Eastern and Northern Europe: sour cream and dill or paprika or allspice or caraway

France: generally—olive oil, garlic and basil or wine and herb or butter and/or sour cream and/or cheese plus wine and/or stock

   Provence—olive oil, thyme, rosemary, marjoram, sage plus tomato as a variation

   Normandy—apple, cider, Calvados

Greece: tomato, cinnamon or olive oil, lemon, oregano

India: Northern—cumin, ginger, garlic

   Southern—mustard seed, coconut, tamarind, chile

Italy: generally—olive oil, garlic, basil

   Northern Italy—wine vinegar, garlic

   Southern Italy—olive oil, garlic, parsley, anchovy, tomato

Japan: soy sauce, sake, sugar

Mexico: tomato and chile or lime and chile

North Africa: cumin, coriander, cinnamon, ginger, onion and/or tomato and/or fruit

Spain: olive oil, garlic, nut or olive oil, onion, pepper, tomato

Thailand: fish sauce, curry, chile

West Africa: tomato, peanut, chile

Although the flavors and aromas of fresh herbs are generally preferred, dried herbs are widely used because they are readily available and convenient. Purchase only the amount of dried herbs that can be used within a short time. If stored properly, dried herbs should last for two to three months.

Use less dried herbs than you would fresh herbs. The loss of moisture strengthens and concentrates the flavor in dried herbs. In general, you should use only one-half to one-third as much dried herb as fresh in any given recipe. For example, if a recipe calls for 1 tablespoon of fresh basil, you should substitute only 1 *teaspoon* of dried basil. You can usually add more later if necessary.

Spices are often available whole or ground. Once ground, they lose their flavors rapidly, however. Whole spices should keep their flavors for many months if stored properly. Stale spices lose their spicy aroma and develop a bitter or musty aftertaste. Discard them.

Because ground spices release their flavors quickly, they should be added to cooked dishes near the end of the cooking period. In uncooked dishes that call for ground spices (for example, salad dressings), the mixture should be allowed to stand for several hours to develop good flavor.

Although some combinations are timeless—rosemary with lamb, dill with salmon, nutmeg with spinach, caraway with rye bread—less common pairings can be equally delicious and far more exciting. A chef must be willing and able to experiment with new flavors. But first you must be familiar with the distinctive flavor and aroma of the herb or spice. Then you can experiment, always bearing in mind the following guidelines:

▶ Flavorings should not hide the taste or aroma of the primary ingredient.

▶ Flavorings should be combined in balance, so as not to overwhelm the palate.

▶ Flavorings should not be used to disguise poor quality or poorly prepared products.

Even in a well-tested recipe, the quantity of flavorings may need to be adjusted because of a change in brands or the condition of the ingredients. A chef should strive to develop his or her palate to recognize and correct subtle variances as necessary.

▶ SALT

Salt (Fr. *sel*) is the most basic seasoning, and its use is universal. It preserves foods, heightens their flavors and provides the distinctive taste of saltiness. The presence of salt can be tasted easily but not smelled. Salt suppresses bitter flavors, making the sweet and sour ones more prominent. The flavor of salt will not evaporate or dissipate during cooking so it should be added to foods carefully, according to taste. Remember, you can always add more salt, but you can neither remove nor mask it if you have added too much.

Culinary or **table salt** is sodium chloride (NaCl), one of the minerals essential to human life. Salt contains no calories, proteins, fats or carbohydrates. It is available from several sources, each with its own flavor and degree of saltiness.

Rock salt, mined from underground deposits, is available in both edible and nonedible forms. It is used in ice cream churns, for thawing frozen sidewalks and, in edible form, in salt mills.

Common kitchen or table salt is produced by pumping water through underground salt deposits, then bringing the brine to the surface to evaporate, leaving behind crystals. Chemicals are usually added to prevent table salt from absorbing moisture and thus keep it free-flowing. Iodized salt is commonly used in the United States. The iodine has no effect on the salt's flavor or use; it is simply added to provide an easily available source of iodine, an important nutrient, to a large number of people.

Rock Salt

ABOUT FLAVORS

Flavor is to food what hue is to color. It is what timbre is to music. Flavor is adjective; food is noun. Each ingredient has its own particular character, which is altered by every other ingredient it encounters. A secret ingredient is one that mysteriously improves the flavor of a dish without calling attention to itself. It is either undetectable or extremely subtle, but its presence is crucial because the dish would not be nearly as good without it.

Primary flavors are those that are obvious, such as the flavors of chicken and tarragon in a chicken tarragon, shrimp and garlic in a shrimp scampi, or beef and red wine in a beef à la Bourguignon. Secret ingredients belong to the realm of secondary flavors. However obvious it is that you need tarragon to prepare a chicken tarragon, you would not achieve the most interesting result using only tarragon. Tarragon, in this case, needs secondary ingredients—a hint of celery seed and anise—to make it taste more like quintessential tarragon and at the same

time more than tarragon. In this way, primary flavors often depend on secret ingredients to make them more interesting and complex. Using only one herb or spice to achieve a certain taste usually results in a lackluster dish—each mouthful tastes the same. Whether they function in a primary or secondary way, flavors combine in only three different ways: They marry, oppose, or juxtapose.

When flavors marry, they combine to form one taste. Some secondary flavors marry with primary ones to create a new flavor greater than the sum of its parts, and often two flavors can do the job better than one. It may sound like an eccentric combination, but vanilla marries with the flavor of lobster, making it taste more like the essence of lobster than lobster does on its own. And when ginger and molasses marry, they create a flavor superior to either alone.

Opposite flavors can highlight or cancel each other; they can cut or balance each other.

Sweet/sour, sweet/salty, sweet/hot, salty/sour, and salty/tart are all opposites. Salt and sugar are so opposed, in fact, that when used in equal amounts they cancel each other entirely. Sweet relish helps to cancel the salty flavor of hot dogs. Chinese sauces usually contain some sugar to help balance the saltiness of soy sauce.

Because flavors are sensed on different parts of the tongue and palate, and because they are tasted at different times, we can juxtapose them, using flavors side by side or in layers. The layering of flavors makes the food we taste more interesting because each mouthful is different.

Knowing how to combine many flavors and aromas to achieve a simple and pure result (and knowing when not to combine flavors) will make you a better, more confident cook. Good cooks over the centuries have known these things intuitively—but they've had neither the huge variety of ingredients nor the knowledge of world cuisines that we have today.

CHEF MICHAEL ROBERTS, *Secret Ingredients*

"Fleur de Sel" (Sea Salt)

Kosher Salt

Sea salt, also known as *fleur de sel* or *sel gris,* is obtained, not surprisingly, by evaporating seawater. Unlike other table salts, sea salt contains additional mineral salts such as magnesium, calcium and potassium, which give it a stronger, more complex flavor and a grayish-brown color. The region where it is produced can also affect its flavor. For example, salt from the Mediterranean Sea will taste different from salt obtained from the Indian Ocean or the English Channel. Sea salt is considerably more expensive than other table salts and is often reserved for finishing a dish or used as a condiment.

Kosher salt has large, irregular crystals and is used in the "koshering" or curing of meats. It is purified rock salt that contains no iodine or additives. It can be substituted for common kitchen salt.

Because it is nonorganic, salt keeps indefinitely. It will, however, absorb moisture from the atmosphere, which prevents it from flowing properly. Salt is a powerful preservative; its presence stops or greatly slows down the growth of many undesirable organisms. Salt is used to preserve meats, vegetables and fish. It is also used to develop desirable flavors in bacon, ham, cheeses and fish products as well as pickled vegetables

▶ NUTS

A **nut** (Fr. *noix*) is the edible single-seed kernel of a fruit surrounded by a hard shell. A hazelnut is an example of a true nut. The term is used more generally, however, to refer to any seed or fruit with an edible kernel in a hard shell. Walnuts and peanuts are examples of non-nut "nuts" (peanuts are legumes that grow underground; walnuts have two kernels). Nuts are a good source of protein and B vitamins but are high in fat. Their high fat content makes them especially susceptible to rancidity and odor absorption. Nuts should be stored in nonmetal, airtight containers in a cool, dark place. Most nuts may be kept frozen for up to one year.

Nuts are used in foods to provide texture and flavor. They are often roasted in a low (275°F/135°C) oven before being used in order to heighten their flavor. Allowing roasted nuts to cool to room temperature before grinding prevents them from releasing too much oil.

Almonds

Almonds (Fr. *almande*) are the seeds of a plumlike fruit. Native to western India, the almond was first cultivated by the ancient Greeks. It is now a major commercial crop in California. Almonds are available whole, sliced, slivered or ground. Blanched almonds have had their brown, textured skins removed; natural almonds retain their skins. Unless the brown color of natural almond skin is undesirable, the two types can be used interchangeably in recipes. Almonds are frequently used in pastries and candies and are the main ingredient in marzipan.

Brazil nuts (Fr. *noix du Brésil*), sometimes referred to as cream nuts, are the large, oval-shaped seeds of huge trees that grow wild in the rainforests of Central and South America. Their high oil content gives them a rich, buttery flavor and a tender texture. Brazil nuts are available both in-shell and shelled, and are eaten raw, roasted, salted and in ice creams and bakery and confectionery products.

Brazil Nuts

Cashews

Cashews (Fr. *noix de caju*), native to the Amazon, are now cultivated in India and east Africa. The cashew nut is actually the seed of a plant related to poison ivy. Because of toxins in the shell, cashews are always sold shelled. They are expensive and have a strong flavor. Cashews are used in some Asian cuisines and make a wonderful addition to cookies and candies.

Chestnuts (Fr. *marrons*) are true nuts that must be cooked before using. Available steamed, dried, boiled or roasted, they are often sold as a canned purée, with or without added sugar. Candied or glazed chestnuts are also available. Most chestnuts are grown in Europe, primarily Italy, but new varieties are beginning to flourish in North America. Their distinctive flavor is found in many sweet dishes and pastries. Because of their high starch content, chestnuts are also used in soups and sauces and may be served as a side dish.

Coconuts (Fr. *noix de coco*) are the seeds from one of the largest of all fruits. They grow on the tropical coconut palm tree. The nut is a dark brown oval, covered with coarse fibers. The shell is thick and hard; inside is a layer of white, moist flesh. The interior also contains a clear liquid known as **coconut water.**

Chestnuts

Coconuts

(This is not the same as **coconut milk** or **coconut cream,** both of which are prepared from the flesh.) Coconut has a mild aroma, a sweet, nutty flavor and a crunchy, chewy texture. Fresh coconuts are readily available but require some effort to use. Coconut flesh is available shredded or flaked, with or without added sugar. Coconut is most often used in pastries and candies and is also an important ingredient in Indian and Caribbean cuisines. A good fresh coconut should feel heavy; you should be able to hear the coconut water sloshing around inside. Avoid cracked, moist or moldy coconuts.

▶ **coconut water** the thin, slightly opaque liquid contained within a fresh coconut

▶ **coconut milk** a coconut-flavored liquid made by pouring boiling water over shredded coconut; may be sweetened or unsweetened. Do not substitute cream of coconut for coconut milk.

▶ **coconut cream** (1) a coconut-flavored liquid made like coconut milk but with less water; it is creamier and thicker than coconut milk; (2) the thick fatty portion that separates and rises to the top of canned or frozen coconut milk. Do not substitute cream of coconut for true coconut cream.

▶ **cream of coconut** a canned commercial product consisting of thick, sweetened coconut-flavored liquid; used for baking and in beverages

Hazelnuts (Fr. *noisette*) are true nuts that grow wild in the northeastern and upper midwestern states. The cultivated form, known as a **filbert,** is native to temperate regions throughout the Northern Hemisphere. A bit larger than the hazelnut, the filbert has a weaker flavor than its wild cousin. Both nuts look like smooth brown marbles. Filberts are more abundant, so are generally less expensive. Hazelnuts are often ground for use in cakes or pastries. Their distinctive flavor goes well with chocolate and coffee.

Hazelnuts

To remove the hazelnut's bitter skin, roast whole nuts in a 275°F (135°C) oven for 12 to 15 minutes. They should give off a good aroma and just begin to darken. While still hot, rub the nuts in a dry towel or against a mesh sifter to remove the skin.

Macadamias, although commercially significant in Hawaii, are actually native to Australia. This small round nut is creamy white with a sweet, rich flavor and high fat content. Its shell is extremely hard and must be removed by machine, so the macadamia is always sold out of the shell. Its flavor blends well with fruit, coconut and white and dark chocolate.

Macadamias

Peanuts (Fr. *arachide*), also known as groundnuts, are actually legumes that grow underground. The peanut is native to South America; it made its way into North America via Africa and the slave trade. Peanuts are a good source of protein and fat and became an important source of food and oil during World War II. They may be eaten raw or roasted and are available shelled or unshelled, with or without their thin red skins. Peanuts are used in Asian cuisines and are ubiquitous ground with a bit of oil into peanut butter.

Peanuts

Pecans (Fr. *noix de pacane*), native to the Mississippi River Valley, are perhaps the most popular nuts in America. Their flavor is rich and mapley and appears most often in breads, sweets and pastries. They are available whole in the shell or in various standard sizes and grades of pieces.

Pecans

Pine nuts (Fr. *pignon*), also known as piñon nuts and pignole, are the seeds of several species of pine tree. The small, creamy white, teardrop-shaped nuts are commonly used in dishes from Spain, Italy and the American Southwest. They are rarely chopped or ground because of their small size, and will need roasting only if being used in a dish that will not receive further cooking. Pine nuts are used in breads, pastries and salads and are essential to classic pesto sauce.

Pine Nuts

Pistachios (Fr. *pistaches*) are native to central Asia, where they have been cultivated for more than 3000 years. California now produces most of the pistachios marketed in this country. Pistachios are unique for the green color of their meat. When ripe, the shell opens naturally at one end, aptly referred to as "smiling," which makes shelling the nuts quite easy. Red pistachios are dyed, not natural. Pistachios are sold whole, shelled or unshelled, and are used in pastries and meat dishes, particularly pâtés.

Pistachios

Walnuts (Fr. *noix*), relatives of the pecan, are native to Asia, Europe and North America. The black walnut, native to Appalachia, has a dark brown meat and a strong flavor. The English walnut, now grown primarily in California, has a milder flavor, is easier to shell and is less expensive. Walnuts are more popular than pecans outside the United States. They are used in baked goods and are pressed for oil.

English Walnuts

▶ OILS

Oils (Fr. *huile*) are a type of fat that remains liquid at room temperature. Cooking oils are refined from various seeds, plants and vegetables. (Other fats, such as butter and margarine, are discussed in Chapter 8, Dairy Products; animal and solid fats are discussed in Chapter 29, Principles of the Bakeshop.)

When purchasing oils, you should consider their use, **smoke point,** flavor and cost. Fats, including oils and **shortenings,** are manufactured for specific purposes such as deep-frying, cake baking, salad dressings and sautéing. Most food service operations purchase different ones for each of these needs.

Fats break down at different temperatures. When fats break down, their chemical structure is altered; the triglyceride molecules that make up fat are converted into individual fatty acids. These acids add undesirable flavors to the

▶ **smoke point** the temperature at which a fat begins to break down and smoke

▶ **shortening** (1) a white, flavorless, solid fat formulated for baking or deep-frying; (2) any fat used in baking to tenderize the product by shortening gluten strands fat and can ruin the flavor of the food being cooked. The temperature at which a given fat begins to break down and smoke is known as its smoke point. Choose fats with higher smoke points for high-temperature cooking such as deep-frying and sautéing.

The flavor and cost of each oil must also be considered. For example, both corn oil and walnut oil can be used in a salad dressing. Their selection may depend on balancing cost (corn oil is less expensive) against flavor (walnut oil has a stronger, more distinctive flavor).

When fats spoil, they are said to go **rancid.** Rancidity is a chemical change caused by exposure to air, light or heat. It results in objectionable flavors and odors. Different fats turn rancid at different rates, but all fats benefit from refrigerated storage away from moisture, light and air. (Some oils are packaged in colored glass containers because certain tints of green and yellow block the damaging light rays that can cause an oil to go rancid.) Although oils may become thick and cloudy under refrigeration, this is not a cause for concern. The oils will return to their clear, liquid states at room temperature. Stored fats should also be covered to prevent them from absorbing odors.

Vegetable oils are extracted from a variety of plants, including corn, cottonseed, peanuts, grape seeds, sesame seeds and soybeans, by pressure or chemical solvents. The oil is then refined and cleaned to remove unwanted colors, odors or flavors. Vegetable oils are virtually odorless and have a neutral flavor. Because they contain no animal products, they are cholesterol-free. If a commercial product contains only one type of oil, it is labeled "pure" (as in "pure corn oil"). Products labeled "vegetable oil" are blended from several sources. Products labeled "salad oil" are highly refined blends of vegetable oil.

Canola oil is processed from rapeseeds. Its popularity is growing rapidly because it contains no cholesterol and has a high percentage of monounsaturated fat. Canola oil is useful for frying and general cooking because it has no flavor and a high smoke point.

Canola Oil

Nut oils are extracted from a variety of nuts and are almost always packaged as a "pure" product, never blended. A nut oil should have the strong flavor and aroma of the nut from which it was processed. Popular examples are walnut and hazelnut oils. These oils are used to give flavor to salad dressings, marinades and other dishes. But heat diminishes their flavor, so nut oils are not recommended for frying or baking. Nut oils tend to go rancid quickly and therefore are usually packaged in small containers.

Olive oil (Fr. *huile díolive*) is the only oil that is extracted from a fruit rather than a seed, nut or grain. Olive oil is produced primarily in Spain, Italy, France, Greece and North Africa; California produces a relatively minor amount of olive oil. Like wine, olive oils vary in color and flavor according to the variety of tree, the ripeness of the olives, the type of soil, the climate and the producer's preferences. Colors range from dark green to almost clear, depending on the ripeness of the olives at the time of pressing and the amount of subsequent refining. Color is not a good indication of flavor, however. Flavor is ultimately a matter of personal preference. A stronger-flavored oil may be desired for some foods, while a milder oil is better for others. Good olive oil should be thicker than refined vegetable oils, but not so thick that it has a fatty texture.

Hazelnut Oil

The label designations—extra virgin, virgin and pure—refer to the acidity of the oil (a low acid content is preferable) and the extent of processing used to extract the oil. The first cold-pressing of the olives results in virgin oil. (The designation "virgin" is used only when the oil is 100% unadulterated olive oil, unheated and without any chemical processing.) Virgin oil may still vary in

Extra Virgin Olive Oil

THE OLIVE

Olives (*Olea europaea*) are the fruit of a tree native to the Mediterranean area. Green olives are those harvested unripened; black olives are fully ripened. The raw fruit is inedibly bitter and must be washed, soaked and cured or pickled before eating. Green olives should have a smooth, tight skin. Ripe olives will be glossy but softer, with a slightly wrinkled skin. Many varieties and flavors are available, from the tiny black French niçoise to the large purplish Greek Kalamata. Ripe black olives are packaged in a range of seven sizes, from small to super colossal. Unripe green olives are available in eleven sizes, from subpetite to supercolossal. Both black and green olives are available whole (with the pit), pitted, sliced, halved or in pieces. Pitted green olives are often stuffed with strips of pimento, jalapeño pepper, almonds or other foods for flavor and appearance.

Olives are used as a finger food for snacks or hors d'oeuvre, or added to salads or pasta. They may even be cooked in breads, soups, sauces, stews and casseroles. A paste made of minced ripe olives, known as tapenade, is used as a dip or condiment.

Jumbo Spanish Olives

Ripe California Olives

Kalamata Olives

Niçoise Olives

quality depending on the level of free acidity, expressed as oleic acid. Extra virgin oil is virgin oil with not more than 1% free acidity (oleic acid); virgin oil may have up to 3%. Pure olive oil is processed from the pulp left after the first pressing using heat and chemicals. Pure oil is lighter in flavor and less expensive than virgin oil.

Flavored oils, also known as **infused oils,** are an interesting and increasingly popular condiment. These oils may be used as a dip for breads, a cooking medium or a flavoring accent in marinades, dressings, sauces or other dishes. Flavors include basil and other herbs, garlic, citrus and spice. Flavored oils are generally prepared with olive oil for additional flavor or canola oil, both considered more healthful than other fats.

Top-quality commercially flavored oils are prepared by extracting aromatic oils from the flavoring ingredients and then emulsifying them with a high-grade oil; any impurities are then removed by placing the oil in a centrifuge. Using the aromatic oils of the flavoring ingredients yields a more intense flavor than merely steeping the same ingredients in the oil. Flavored oils should be stored as you would any other high-quality oil.

▶ FATS FOR DEEP FRYING

Many types of fats can be used for deep-frying. Although animal fats, such as rendered beef fat, are sometimes used to impart their specific flavors to deep-fried foods, their low smoke points generally make them unsuitable for deep-frying unless blended with vegetable fats. By far the most common fats used for deep-frying are vegetable oils such as soybean, peanut and canola oil, all of which have high smoke points and are relatively inexpensive. See Table 7.2.

Specially formulated deep-frying compounds are also available. These are usually composed of a vegetable oil or oils to which antifoaming agents, antioxidants and preservatives have been added. These additives increase the oil's usable life and raise its smoke point.

Table 7.2 REACTION TEMPERATURES OF FATS

FAT	MELT POINT	SMOKE POINT	FLASH POINT
Butter	92–98°F/33–36°C	260°F/127°C	Possible at any temperature above 300°F/150°C
Butter, clarified	92–98°F/33–36°C	335–380°F/168–193°C	Possible at any temperature above 300°F/150°C
Lard	89–98°F/32–36°C	370°F/188°C	n/a
Deep-fryer shortening, heavy-duty, premium	102°F/39°C	440°F/227°C	690°F/365°C
Canola oil	n/a	430–448°F/220–230°C	553–560°F/275–290°C
Corn oil	40–50°F/5–7°C	410°F/210°C	610°F/321°C
Cocoa butter	88–93°F/31–34°C	n/a	n/a
Cottonseed oil	55°F/13°C	450°F/232°C	650°F/343°C
Margarine	94–98°F/34–36°C	410–430°F/210–221°C	Possible at any temperature above 300°F/150°C
Olive oil, extra virgin	32°F/0°C	250°F/121°C	n/a
Olive oil, pure or pumice	32°F/0°C	410°F/210°C	437°F/225°C
Peanut oil	28°F/–2°C	450°F/232°C	540°F/283°C
Shortening, vegetable, all-purpose	120°F/49°C	410°F/210°C	625°F/329°C
Soybean oil	–5°F/–20°C	495°F/257°C	540°F/282°C
Walnut oil	n/a	450°F/232°C	620°F/326°C

This data was compiled from a variety of sources and is meant as a guideline only. Because reaction temperatures depend on the exact type and ratio of fatty acids present, the actual temperatures will vary depending on the brand or manufacturer of the fat in question. Temperatures are for clean, previously unused fats. Heating a fat, even one time, can lower the smoke and flash points dramatically.

n/a = not available

Deep-fryer fats may also be hydrogenated. **Hydrogenation** is a chemical process that adds hydrogen to oil, turning the liquid oil into a solid (margarine is hydrogenated vegetable oil). Hydrogenated fats are more resistant to oxidation and chemical breakdown.

To choose the right fat, consider flavor, smoke point and resistance to chemical breakdown. High-quality frying fat should have a clean or natural flavor and a high smoke point and, when properly maintained, should be resistant to chemical breakdown.

Properly maintaining deep-fryer fat will greatly extend its useful life. To do so:

1 Store the fat in tightly sealed containers away from strong light; cover the deep fryer when not in use. Prolonged exposure to air and light turns fat rancid.

2 Skim and remove food particles from the fat's surface during frying. Food particles cause fat to break down; if they are not removed, they will accumulate in the fryer and burn.

3 Do not salt food over the fat. Salt causes fat to break down chemically.

4 Prevent excessive water from coming into contact with the fat; pat-dry moist foods as much as possible before cooking and dry the fryer, baskets and utensils well after cleaning. Water, like salt, causes fat to break down.

5 Do not overheat the fat (turn the fryer down or off if not in use). High temperatures break down the fat.

6 Filter the fat each day or after each shift if the fryer is heavily used. Best results are obtained by using a filtering machine designed specifically for this purpose. Many large commercial fryers even have built-in filter systems. Less well-equipped operations can simply pour the hot fat through a paper filter.

Table 7.3

FRYER FAT CAN BE DAMAGED BY:

Salt

Water

Overheating

Food particles

Oxygen

CHANGE FRYER FAT WHEN IT:

Becomes dark

Smokes

Foams

Develops off-flavors

▶ VINEGARS

Vinegar (Fr. *vinaigre*) is a thin, sour liquid used for thousands of years as a preservative, cooking ingredient, condiment and cleaning solution. Vinegar is obtained through the fermentation of wine or other alcoholic liquid. Bacteria attacks the alcohol in the solution, turning it into acetic acid. No alcohol will remain when the transformation is complete. The quality of vinegar depends upon the quality of the wine or other liquid on which it is based. Vinegar flavors are as varied as the liquids from which they are made.

Vinegars should be clear and clean-looking, never cloudy or muddy. Commercial vinegars are pasteurized, so an unopened bottle should last indefinitely in a cool, dark place. Once opened, vinegars should last about three months if tightly capped. Any sediment that develops can be strained out; if mold develops, discard the vinegar.

Wine vinegars are as old as wine itself. They may be made from white or red wine, sherry or even champagne, and should bear the color and flavor hallmarks of the wine used. Wine vinegars are preferred in French and Mediterranean cuisines.

Malt vinegar is produced from malted barley. Its slightly sweet, mild flavor is used as a condiment, especially with fried foods.

Distilled vinegar, made from grain alcohol, is completely clear with a stronger vinegary flavor and higher acid content than other vinegars. It is preferred for pickling and preserving.

Cider vinegar is produced from unpasteurized apple juice or cider. It is pale brown in color with a mild acidity and fruity aroma. Cider vinegar is particularly popular in the United States.

Rice vinegar is a clear, slightly sweet product brewed from rice wine. Its flavor is clean and elegant, making it useful in a variety of dishes.

Flavored vinegars are simply traditional vinegars in which herbs, spices, fruits or other foods are steeped to infuse their flavors. They are easily produced from commercial wine or distilled vinegars, using any herb, spice or fruit desired. The use of flavored vinegars is extremely popular but definitely not new. Clove, raspberry and fennel vinegars were sold on the streets of Paris during the 13th century. Making fruit-flavored vinegars was also one of the responsibilities of American housewives during the 18th and 19th centuries.

Balsamic vinegar (It. *aceto Balsamico*) is newly popular in the United States, though it has been produced in Italy for more than 800 years. To produce balsamic vinegar, red wine vinegar is aged in a succession of wooden barrels made from a variety of woods—oak, cherry, locust, ash, mulberry and juniper—for at least 4, but sometimes up to 50, years. The resulting liquid is dark reddish-brown and sweet. Balsamic has a high acid level, but the sweetness covers the tart flavor, making it very mellow. True balsamic is extremely expensive because of the long aging process and the small quantities available. Most of the commercial products imported from Italy are now made by a quick carmelization and flavoring process. Balsamic is excellent as a condiment or seasoning and has a remarkable affinity for tomatoes and strawberries.

Balsamic Vinegar, Raspberry Vinegar and Cider Vinegar

▶ **relish** a cooked or pickled sauce usually made with vegetables or fruits and often used as a condiment; can be smooth or chunky, sweet or savory and hot or mild

▶ **pickle** (1) to preserve food in a brine or vinegar solution; (2) food that has been preserved in a seasoned brine or vinegar, especially cucumbers. Pickled cucumbers are available whole, sliced, in wedges, or chopped as a relish, and may be sweet, sour, dill-flavored or hot and spicy.

▶ CONDIMENTS

Strictly speaking, a condiment is any food added to a dish for flavor, including herbs, spices and vinegars. Today, however, condiments more often refer to cooked or prepared flavorings, such as prepared mustards, **relishes,** bottled sauces and **pickles.** We discuss several frequently used condiments here. These staples may be used to alter or enhance the flavor of a dish during cooking or added to a completed dish at the table by the consumer.

Fermented black bean sauce is a Chinese condiment and flavoring ingredient made from black soybeans that have been heavily salted, then fermented and either slightly mashed (whole bean sauce) or puréed (paste). Both versions are usually mixed with hoisin, chile sauce or minced garlic to produce a sauce that has an intense, pungent, salty flavor. Yellow bean sauces are similar, but milder and sweeter.

Fish sauce (Viet. *nuoc mam;* Thai *nam pla*), is the liquid drained from fermenting salted anchovy-like fish. It is a thin, golden to light brown liquid with a very pungent, rotting odor and salty flavor. There is no substitute for the savory richness that it adds to food and it is considered an essential flavoring and condiment throughout Southeast Asia, where it is used in and served with most every sort of dish.

Ketchup (also known as catsup or catchup) originally referred to any salty extract from fish, fruits or vegetables. Prepared tomato ketchup is really a sauce, created in America and used worldwide as a flavoring ingredient or condiment. It is bright red and thick, with a tangy, sweet-sour flavor. Ketchup can be stored either in the refrigerator or at room temperature; it should keep well for up to four months after opening. Ketchup does not turn rancid or develop mold, but it will darken and lose flavor as it ages.

Prepared mustard is a mixture of crushed mustard seeds, vinegar or wine and salt or spices. It can be flavored in many ways—with herbs, onions, peppers and even citrus zest. It can be a smooth paste or coarse and chunky, depending on how finely the seeds are ground and whether the skins are strained out. Prepared mustard gets its tangy flavor from an essential oil that forms only when the seeds are crushed and mixed with water. Prepared mustard can be used as a condiment, particularly with meat and charcuterie items, or as a flavoring ingredient in sauces, stews and marinades.

Dijon mustard takes its name from a town and the surrounding region in France that produces about half of the world's mustard. French mustard labeled

Fermented Black Bean Sauce

Fish Sauce

Yellow Mustard

Dijon Mustard

FROM YOUR GROCER'S SHELF

Even the most sophisticated food service operation occasionally uses prepared condiments or flavorings. The products described here are widely used and available from grocery stores or wholesale purveyors. Some are brand-name items that have become almost synonymous with the product itself; others are available from several manufacturers.

Barbecue sauce—Commercial barbecue sauce is a mixture of tomatoes, vinegar and spices used primarily for marinating or basting meat, poultry or fish. A tremendous variety of barbecue sauces are available, with various flavors, textures and aromas. Sample several before selecting the most appropriate for your specific needs.

Chile sauce—Asian chile sauce, or hot sauce, varies somewhat depending on the country of origin or style, but all are thick, reddish-orange and extremely pungent and spicy. They usually contain pieces of chiles and/or garlic and less vinegar than Louisiana-style hot sauce. Asian

cuisines incorporate these bottled sauces in curries and other dishes, and use them as table condiments. One of the most popular and readily available brands is the Vietnamese-style Tuong ót Srirachar with its rooster logo.

Hoisin sauce—Hoisin sauce is a dark, thick, salty-sweet sauce made from fermented soy beans, vinegar, garlic and caramel. It is used in Chinese dishes or served as a dipping sauce.

Old Bay brand seasoning—Old Bay is a dry spice blend containing celery salt, dry mustard, paprika and other flavorings. It is widely used in shellfish preparations, especially boiled shrimp and crab.

Oyster sauce—Oyster sauce is a thick, dark sauce made from oyster extract. It has a salty-sweet flavor and a rich aroma. Oyster sauce is often used with stir-fried meats and poultry.

Pickapeppa brand sauce—Pickapeppa sauce is a dark, thick, sweet-hot blend of tomatoes, onions, sugar, vinegar, mango, raisins, tamarinds and spices. Produced in Jamaica, West In-

dies, it is used as a condiment for meat, game or fish and as a seasoning in sauces, soups and dressings.

Tabasco brand sauce—Tabasco sauce is a thin, bright red liquid blended from vinegar, chiles and salt. Its fiery flavor is widely used in sauces, soups and prepared dishes; it is a popular condiment for Mexican, southern and southwestern cuisines. Tabasco sauce has been produced in Louisiana since 1868. Other "Louisiana-style" hot sauces (those containing only peppers, vinegar and salt) may be substituted.

Worcestershire sauce – Worcestershire sauce is a thin, dark brown liquid made from malt vinegar, tamarind, molasses and spices. It is used as a condiment for beef and as a seasoning in sauces, soups, stews and prepared dishes. Its flavor should be rich and full, but not salty.

Whole-Grain Mustard

Brown Mustard

"Dijon" must, by law, be produced only in that region. Dijon and Dijon-style mustards are smooth with a rich, complex flavor.

English and Chinese mustards are made from mustard flour and cool water. They are extremely hot and powerful. American or "ballpark" mustard is mild and vinegary with a bright yellow color.

Mustard never really spoils; its flavor just fades away. Because of its high acid content, mustard does not turn rancid, but it will oxidize and develop a dark surface crust. Once opened, mustard should be kept well-covered and refrigerated.

Soy sauce is a thin, dark brown liquid fermented from cooked soy beans, wheat and salt. Available in several flavors and strengths, it is ubiquitous in most Asian cuisines. Light soy sauce is thin, with a light brown color and a very salty flavor. Dark soy sauce is thicker and dark brown, with a sweet, less salty flavor. Necessary for preparing many Asian dishes, soy sauce is also used in marinades and sauces and as an all-purpose condiment. Other soy-based condiments include tamari, teriyaki sauce and fermented bean paste (miso).

Soy Sauce

▶ COFFEES AND TEAS

Coffee and tea are the staples of most beverage menus. Despite their relatively low price, a good cup of coffee or tea can be extremely important to a customer's impression of your food service operation. A cup of coffee is often either the very first or the very last item consumed by a customer. Tea, whether iced or hot, is often consumed throughout the meal. Consequently, it is important that you learn to prepare and serve these beverages properly.

COFFEE

Coffee (Fr. *café*) begins as the fruit of a small tree grown in tropical and subtropical regions throughout the world. The fruit, referred to as a cherry, is bright red with translucent flesh surrounding two flat-sided seeds. These seeds are the coffee beans. When ripe, the cherries are harvested by hand, then cleaned, fermented and hulled, leaving the green coffee beans. The beans are then roasted, blended, ground and brewed. Note that any coffee bean can be roasted to any degree of darkness, ground to any degree of fineness and brewed by any number of methods.

Only two species of coffee bean are routinely used: arabica and robusta. Arabica beans are the most important commercially and the ones from which the finest coffees are produced. Robusta beans do not produce as flavorful a drink as arabica. Nevertheless, robusta beans are becoming increasingly significant commercially, in part because robusta trees are heartier and more fertile than arabica trees.

The conditions in which the beans are grown have almost as much effect on the final product as subsequent roasting, grinding and brewing. Because coffee takes much of its flavor and character from the soil, sunlight and air, the beans' origin is critical to the product's final quality. Each valley and mountain produces coffee distinct from all others, so geographic names are used to identify the beans whether they are from arabica or robusta trees. Thus, purveyors may offer beans known as Columbian, Chanchamayo (from Peru), Kilimanjaro (from Tanzania), Blue Mountain (from Jamaica), Java, Sumatra or Kona (from Hawaii), to name a few.

Although many so-called gourmet coffees are made from a single type of bean, nearly all coffee sold in the United States is a blend of various qualities and types of bean.

ROASTING COFFEE

Roasting releases and enhances the flavors in coffee. It also darkens the beans and brings natural oils to the surface. Traditionally, almost everyone roasted their own coffee beans because all coffee beans were sold green. Today, however, roasting is left to experts who possess the necessary equipment.

It is important to recognize and understand some of the standard descriptions used for various types of roasting. No single international organization controls the naming of roasted coffee, however, so a coffee roaster may refer to products by any name. The following descriptions are based on the most common terminology:

Green Coffee Beans

▶ **City roast:** Also called American or brown roast, city roast is the most widely used coffee style in this country. City roast produces a beverage that may lack brilliance or be a bit flat, yet it is the roast most Americans assume they prefer because it is the roast most often used in grocery store blends.

▶ **Brazilian:** Somewhat darker than a city roast, Brazilian roast should begin to show a hint of dark-roast flavor. The beans should show a trace of oil. In this context, the word *Brazilian* has no relationship to coffee grown in Brazil.

City-Roast Beans

▶ **Viennese:** Also called medium-dark roast, Viennese roast generally falls somewhere between a standard city roast and French roast.

▶ **French roast:** French roast, also called New Orleans or dark roast, approaches espresso in flavor without sacrificing smoothness. The beans should be the color of semisweet chocolate, with apparent oiliness on the surface.

▶ **Espresso roast:** Espresso roast, also called Italian roast, is the darkest of all. The beans are roasted until they are virtually burnt. The beans should be black with a shiny, oily surface.

French-Roast Beans

GRINDING COFFEE

Unlike roasting, which is best left to the experts, the grinding of coffee beans is best left to the consumer or food service operation. Whole coffee beans stay fresh longer than ground coffee. Ground coffee kept in an airtight container away from heat and light will stay fresh for three or four days. Whole beans will stay fresh for a few weeks and may be kept frozen for several months, as long as they are dry and protected from other flavors. Frozen coffee beans do not need to be thawed before grinding and brewing. Do not refrigerate coffee.

The fineness of the grind depends entirely on the type of coffee maker being used. The grind determines the length of time it takes to achieve the optimum (19%) extraction from the beans. The proper grind is simply whatever grind allows this to happen in the time it takes a specific coffee maker to complete its brewing cycle. Follow the directions for your coffee maker, or ask your specialty coffee purveyor for guidance.

BREWING COFFEE

Coffee is brewed by one of two methods: decoction or infusion. **Decoction** means boiling a substance until its flavor is removed. Boiling is the oldest method of making coffee, but is no longer used except in preparing extremely strong Turkish coffee. Infusion refers to the extraction of flavors at temperatures below boiling. **Infusion** techniques include steeping (mixing hot water with ground coffee), filtering (slowly pouring hot water over ground coffee held in a disposable cloth or paper filter) and dripping (pouring hot water over ground coffee and allowing the liquid to run through a strainer). Percolating is undesirable, as the continuous boiling ruins the coffee's flavor.

The secrets to brewing a good cup of coffee are knowing the exact proportion of coffee to water as well as the length of time to maintain contact between

DON'T WRECK
THE ENDING

Lots of time and thought are spent on selecting the wines to accompany the various savory courses of a meal, but too often at the sweet course the dessert wine finds itself up against its worst enemy: chocolate. A good sauterne, or a good-quality dessert wine of almost any kind, works best with a fruit tart or with noncitrus sorbets accompanied by "dry cookie-like things," to use Richard Olney's phrase. Chocolate, whether in the form of pastry or confection, belongs with coffee, whose aromatic bitterness is a perfect foil for it.

The late RICHARD H. GRAFF, Chairman
Chalone Wine Group

the two. The best results are nearly always achieved by using two level table-spoons of ground coffee per ¾ measuring cup (6 ounces) of water. (A standard cup of coffee is three-quarters the size of a standard measuring cup; one pound of coffee yields approximately 80 level tablespoons or enough for 40 "cups" of coffee.) An Approved Coffee Measure (ACM) was developed by the Coffee Brewing Institute to measure two level tablespoons accurately. ACM scoops are readily available and are often included with retail coffee packages.

Premeasured packages of ground coffee are generally used with commercial brewing equipment. These packages are available in a range of sizes for making single pots or large urns of coffee.

If stronger coffee is desired, use more coffee per cup of water, not a longer brewing time. For weaker coffee, prepare regular-strength coffee and dilute it with hot water. Never reuse coffee grounds.

Coffeepots and carafes should be cleaned well with hot water between each use; coffee makers should be disassembled and cleaned according to the manufacturer's directions. Unless equipment is properly cleaned, oils from coffee form an invisible film on the inside of the maker and pots, imparting a rancid or stale flavor to each subsequent batch.

Finally, coffee should be served as soon as it is brewed. Oxidation takes a toll on the aroma and flavor, which soon become flat and eventually bitter. Coffee may be held for a short time on the coffee maker's hot plate at temperatures of 185°F to 190°F (85°C to 88°C). A better holding method, however, is to immediately pour freshly brewed coffee into a thermal carafe. Never attempt to reheat cold coffee, as drastic temperature shifts destroy flavor.

TASTING COFFEE

Coffee can be judged on four characteristics: aroma, acidity, body and flavor.

As a general rule, coffee will taste the way it smells. Some coffees, particularly Colombian, are more fragrant than others, however.

Acidity, also called wininess, refers to the tartness of the coffee. Acidity is a desirable characteristic that indicates snap, life or thinness. Kenyan and Guatemalan are examples of particularly acidic coffees.

Body refers to the feeling of heaviness or thickness that coffee provides on the palate. Sumatran is generally the heaviest, with Mexican and Venezuelan being the lightest.

Flavor, of course, is the most ambiguous as well as the most important characteristic. Terms such as *mellow, harsh, grassy* or *earthy* are used to describe the rather subjective characteristics of flavor.

SERVING COFFEE

Coffee may be served unadorned, unsweetened and black (without milk or cream). The customer then adds the desired amount of sugar and milk. Other coffee beverages are made with specific additions and provide value-added menu alternatives. The most common ways of serving coffee are described here.

Espresso

▶ **steamed milk** milk that is heated with steam generated by an espresso machine; it should be approximately 150°F to 170°F (65°C to 76°C)

▶ *Espresso:* Espresso refers to a unique brewing method in which hot water is forced through finely ground and packed coffee under high pressure. Properly made, it will be strong, rich and smooth, not bitter or acidic. Espresso is usually made with beans that have been roasted very dark, but any type of bean may be used. A single serving of espresso uses about ¼ ounce (7 grams) of coffee to 1½ ounces (45 milliliters) of water. Americans tend to prefer a larger portion, known as espresso lungo, made with 2 to 3 ounces (60 to 90 grams) of water.

▶ *Espresso machiatto:* Espresso "marked" with a tiny portion of **steamed milk.**

▶ *Cappuccino:* One-third espresso, one-third steamed milk and one-third **foamed milk;** the total serving is still rather small, about 4 to 6 ounces (120 to 180 grams).

▶ *Caffè latte:* One-third espresso and two-thirds steamed milk without foam; usually served in a tall glass.

▶ *Café au lait:* The French version of the Italian caffè latte, café au lait (or café crème) is made with strong coffee instead of espresso and hot, not steamed, milk. It is traditionally served in a handleless bowl.

▶ *Caffè mocha:* One-third espresso and two-thirds steamed milk, flavored with chocolate syrup; usually topped with whipped cream and chocolate shavings or cocoa.

▶ *Flavored coffees:* Dried, ground chicory root has long been added to coffee, particularly by the French, who enjoy its bitter flavor. Toasted barley, dried figs and spices have also been used by various cultures for years. Coffees flavored with vanilla, chocolate, liquors, spices and nuts have recently become popular in the United States. These flavors are added to roasted coffee beans by tumbling the beans with special flavoring oils. The results are strongly aromatic flavors such as vanilla hazelnut, chocolate raspberry or maple walnut.

▶ **foamed milk** milk that is heated and frothed with air and steam generated by an espresso machine; it will be slightly cooler than steamed milk

Cappuccino

Caffè Latte

DECAFFEINATED COFFEE

Caffeine is an alkaloid found in coffee beans (as well as in tea leaves and cocoa beans). It is a stimulant that can improve alertness or reduce fatigue. In excess, however, caffeine can cause some people to suffer palpitations or insomnia. Regular filtered coffee contains from 85 to 100 milligrams of caffeine per cup. Robusta beans contain more caffeine than the better-quality arabica beans. Decaffeinated coffee (with 97 percent or more of the caffeine removed) is designed to meet consumer desires for a caffeine-free product.

OTHER USES

In addition to its use as a beverage, coffee is frequently an ingredient in mixed drinks such as Irish coffee (with whiskey and cream) or café brûlot (with

A CUP OF COFFEE HISTORY

Some anthropologists suggest that coffee was initially consumed by central African warriors in the form of a paste made from mashed coffee beans and animal fat rolled into balls. Eaten before battle, the animal fat and bean protein provided nourishment; the caffeine provided a stimulant.

A hot coffee drink may first have been consumed sometime during the 9th century A.D. in Persia. Made by a decoction of ripe beans, the drink was probably very thick and acrid. Nevertheless, by the year 1000, the elite of the Arab world were regularly drinking a decoction of dried coffee beans. The beans were harvested in Abyssinia (Ethiopia) and brought to market by Egyptian merchants. Within a century or so, *kahwa* became immensely popular with members of all strata of Arab society. Coffeehouses opened throughout the Levant, catering to cus-

tomers who sipped the thick, brown brew while discussing affairs of heart and state.

Although European travelers to the Ottoman Empire had tasted coffee, and a few Arab or Turkish merchants living in Marseilles offered their guests a chance to sample the rare drink, coffee did not become popular in Europe until the 17th century. Its popularity is due in great part to Suleiman Aga, the Grand Panjandrum of the Ottoman Empire. In 1669, he arrived at the court of King Louis XIV of France as ambassador, bringing with him many exotic treasures, including caffè. Offered at his opulent parties, caffè soon became the drink of choice for the French aristocracy.

Coffee became popular in Vienna as a fortune of war. By 1683, the Turks were at the gates of Vienna. A decisive battle was fought, and the Turks fled, leaving behind stores of

gold, equipment, supplies and a barely known provision—green coffee beans. One of the victorious leaders, Franz George Kolschitzky, recognized the treasure, took it as his own and soon opened the first coffeehouse in Vienna, The Blue Bottle.

Despite its growing popularity, coffee was exorbitantly expensive, in part, the result of the sultan's monopoly on coffee beans. His agents, principally in Marseilles, controlled the sale of beans. But the monopoly was not to survive. By the end of the 17th century, the Dutch had stolen coffee plants from Arabia and began cultivating them in Java. By the early 18th century, the French had transported seedlings to the West Indies; from there coffee plantations spread throughout the New World.

orange, cloves and brandy). Coffee is also used in stews, sauces and pan gravy. It may be added to breads, such as rye and pumpernickel, cakes, custards, ice creams, dessert sauces and frostings. The flavor of coffee has a strong affinity for chocolate, nuts and rum.

TEA

Tea (Fr. *thé*) is the name given to the leaves of *Camellia sinensis,* a tree or shrub that grows at high altitudes in damp tropical regions. Although tea comes from only one species of plant, there are three general types of tea—black, green and oolong. The differences among the three are the result of the manner in which the leaves are treated after picking.

Black tea is amber-brown and strongly flavored. Its color and flavor result from fermenting the leaves. Black tea leaves are named or graded by leaf size. Because larger leaves brew more slowly than smaller ones, teas are sorted by leaf size for efficient brewing. *Souchong* denotes large leaves, *pekoe* denotes medium-sized leaves and *orange pekoe* denotes the smallest whole leaves. (Note that *orange pekoe* does not refer to any type of orange flavor.) Broken tea, graded as either broken orange pekoe or broken pekoe, is smaller, resulting in a darker, stronger brew. Broken tea is most often used in tea bags. These grades apply to both Chinese and Indian black teas.

Green tea is yellowish-green in color with a bitter flavor. Leaves used for green tea are not fermented. Chinese green tea leaves are also graded according to leaf size and age. The finest green tea is Gunpowder, followed by Imperial and Hyson.

Oolong tea is partially fermented to combine the characteristics of black and green teas. Oolong is popular in China and Japan, often flavored with jasmine flowers. Oolong tea leaves are also graded by size and age.

As with coffee, tea takes much of its flavor from the geographic conditions in which it is grown. Teas are named for their place of origin—for example, Darjeeling, Ceylon (now Sri Lanka) or Assam. Many popular and commercially available teas are actually blends of leaves from various sources. Blended and unblended teas may also be flavored with oils, dried fruit, spices, flowers or herbs.

Fruit Tea

Gunpowder

Darjeeling

TEA FLAVORS

The following descriptions apply to some of the teas frequently available through wholesalers or gourmet suppliers. Taste several different ones to find the best for your purposes. Remember that the same tea from different blenders or distributors may taste different, and that different flavors will be more or less appropriate for different times of the day. You may wish to offer your patrons a selection of flavors.

Assam—a rich black tea with a reddish color from northeastern India. It is valued by connoisseurs, especially for breakfast.

Ceylon—a full-flavored black tea with a golden color and delicate fragrance. Ideal for serving iced, it does not become cloudy when cold.

Darjeeling—the champagne of teas, grown in the foothills of the Himalayas in northeastern India. It is a full-bodied, black tea with a muscat flavor.

Earl Grey—a blend of black teas, usually including Darjeeling, flavored with oil of bergamot. A popular choice for afternoon tea.

English Breakfast—an English blend of Indian and Sri Lankan black teas; it is full-bodied and robust, with a rich color.

Gunpowder—a green Chinese tea with a tightly curled leaf and gray-green color. It has a pungent flavor and a light straw color. It is often served after the evening meal.

Keemum—a mellow black Chinese tea with a strong aroma. It is less astringent than other teas and is delicious iced.

Lapsang Souchong—a large-leafed (souchong) tea from the Lapsang district of China. It has a distinctive tarry, smoky flavor and aroma, appropriate for afternoon tea or dinner.

Formosa Oolong—a unique and expensive large-leafed oolong tea with the flavor of ripe peaches. It is appropriate for breakfast or afternoon tea.

BREWING TEA

Tea may be brewed by the cup or the pot. In either case, it is important to use the following procedure:

1 Always begin with clean equipment and freshly drawn cold water. Water that has been sitting in a kettle or hot water tank contains less air and will taste flat or stale.

2 Warm the teapot by rinsing its interior with hot water. This begins to relax the tea leaves and ensures that the water will stay hot when it comes in contact with the tea.

3 Place 1 teaspoon (5 milliliters) of loose tea or one tea bag per ¾ cup (6 ounces/180 grams) of water capacity in the warmed teapot.

4 As soon as the water comes to a boil, pour the appropriate amount over the tea. Do not allow the water to continue boiling as this removes the oxygen, leaving a flat taste. The water should be at a full boil when it comes in contact with the tea so that the tea leaves will uncurl and release their flavor.

5 Replace the lid of the teapot and allow the tea to infuse for 3 to 5 minutes. Time the brew. Color is not a reliable indication of brewing time; tea leaves release color before flavor, and different types of tea will be different colors when properly brewed.

6 Remove the tea bags or loose tea from the water when brewing is complete. This can be accomplished easily if the teapot is fitted with a removable leaf basket or if a tea bag or a perforated tea ball is used. Otherwise, decant the tea through a strainer into a second warmed teapot.

7 Serve immediately, accompanied with sugar, lemon, milk (not cream) and honey as desired. Dilute the tea with hot water if necessary.

8 Do not reuse tea leaves. One pound of tea yields 200 cups, making it the most inexpensive beverage after tap water.

A CUP OF TEA HISTORY

Some believe that the Chinese Emperor Shen Nung discovered tea drinking in 2737 B.C. Legend holds that the emperor was boiling his drinking water beneath a tree when some leaves fell into the pot. Enchanted with the drink, he began to cultivate the plant. Whether this is myth or truth, it is known that a hot drink made from powdered dried tea leaves whipped into hot water was regularly consumed in China sometime after the 4th century. Later, decoctions of tea leaves (as well as rice, spices and nuts) became popular. But it was not until the Ming dynasty (A.D. 1368–1644) that infusions of tea leaves became commonplace.

By the 9th century, tea drinking had spread to Japan. In both Chinese and Japanese cultures, tea drinking developed into a ritual. For the Chinese, a cup of tea became the mirror of the soul. For the Japanese, it was the drink of immortality.

Tea was first transported from China to Europe by Dutch merchants during the early 1600s. By midcentury, it was introduced into England. In 1669, the British East India Company was granted a charter by Queen Elizabeth I to import tea, a monopoly it held until 1833. To ensure a steady supply, the English surreptitiously procured plants from China and started plantations throughout the Indian subcontinent, as did the Dutch.

Tea drinking became fashionable in England, at least in court circles, through Charles II (raised in exile at The Hague in Holland, he reigned from 1660 to 1685) and his Portuguese wife, Catherine of Braganza. Queen Anne of England (who reigned from 1702 to 1714) introduced several concepts that eventually became part of the English tea custom. For example, she substituted tea for ale at breakfast and began using large silver pots instead of tiny china pots.

The social custom of afternoon tea began in the late 1700s, thanks to Anna, Duchess of Bedford. Historians attribute to her the late-afternoon ritual of snacking on sandwiches and pastries accompanied by tea. She began the practice in order to quell her hunger pangs between breakfast and dinner (which was typically served at 9:30 or 10:00 P.M.).

Eventually, two distinct types of teatime evolved. Low tea was aristocratic in origin and consisted of a snack of pastries and sandwiches, with tea, served in the late afternoon as a prelude to the evening meal. High tea was bourgeois in origin, consisting of leftovers from the typically large middle-class lunch, such as cold meats, bread and cheeses. High tea became a substitute for the evening meal.

For iced tea, prepare regular brewed tea using 50 percent more tea. Then pour the tea into a pitcher or glass filled with ice. The stronger brew will hold its flavor better as the ice melts.

SERVING TEA

▶ **tisanes** herbal infusions that do not contain any "real" tea; examples include chamomile, ginseng and lemon balm. Tisanes are prepared in the same way as tea infusions.

Black and oolong tea may be served hot or cold, but green tea is best served hot. Black tea is served with milk or lemon and sugar; green and oolong tea are most often served plain. Adding milk to hot tea is a British preference (not normally followed in Europe or Asia) that reduces the astringency of the tea. Iced tea, an American invention, may be served plain or sweetened, and is often garnished with lemon, orange or fresh mint.

CONCLUSION

Kitchen staples include fresh and dried herbs, spices, salt, nuts, oils, vinegars, condiments, coffees and teas. You must be able to recognize, purchase, store and use many of these staples.

The only way to determine which brand or type of staple is best for your particular needs is to taste, smell, sample and use a variety of those available. Cost, convenience and storage factors must also be considered. By maintaining a supply of seasonings, flavorings, condiments and other staples, you will be able to create new dishes or enhance standard ones at a moment's notice.

QUESTIONS FOR DISCUSSION

1 What is a staple? Does every kitchen keep the same staples on hand? Explain your answer.
2 What are the differences between an herb and a spice? Give an example of a plant that is used as both an herb and a spice.
3 If a recipe calls for a fresh herb and you only have the herb dried, what do you do? Explain your answer.
4 How are condiments used by chefs and by customers?
5 What qualities should be considered when choosing a fat for deep-frying?
6 List three signs that fryer fat has broken down and should be replaced. What causes fryer fat to break down? What can you do to extend the life of fryer fat?
7 Discuss the importance of using proper preparation and service techniques for coffee and tea. How can these beverages be used to improve or enhance your food service operation?

8 Assume that you are interested in opening a coffeehouse in your local community. What resources are available to you on the Internet to assist in planning your new business? Research two potential vendors for the equipment and supplies that you will need.

FOOD HISTORY IS AS IMPORTANT AS A BAROQUE
CHURCH. GOVERNMENTS SHOULD RECOGNIZE
CULTURAL HERITAGE AND PROTECT TRADITIONAL
FOODS. A CHEESE IS AS WORTHY OF PRESERVING
AS A SIXTEENTH-CENTURY BUILDING.

—Carlo Petrini, Italian journalist (1950–)

DAIRY PRODUCTS

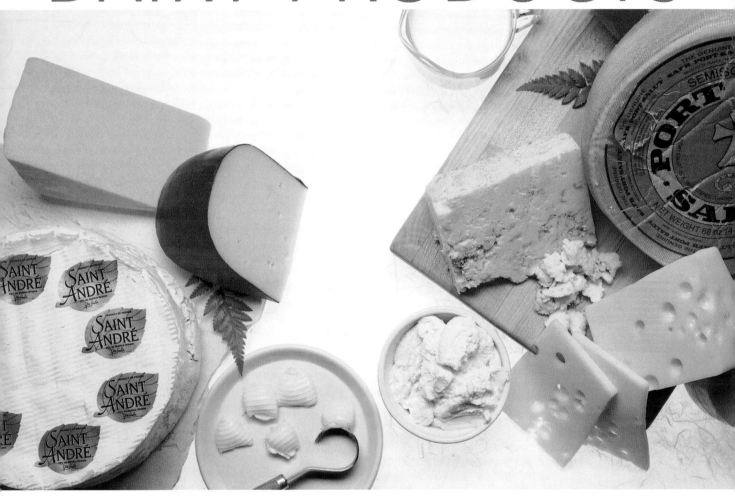

Dairy products include cow's milk and foods produced from cow's milk such as butter, yogurt, sour cream and cheese. The milk of other mammals, namely, goats, sheep (ewe) and buffaloes, is also made into cheeses that are used in commercial food service operations. Dairy products are extremely versatile and are used throughout the kitchen, served either as is or as ingredients in everything from soups and salads to breads and desserts.

▶ MILK

Milk is not only a popular beverage, it is also an ingredient in many dishes. It provides texture, flavor, color and nutritional value for cooked or baked items. Indeed, milk is one of the most nutritious foods available, providing proteins, vitamins and minerals (particularly calcium). But milk is also highly perishable and an excellent bacterial breeding ground. Care must be exercised when handling and storing milk and other dairy products.

Whole milk—that is, milk as it comes from the cow—consists of water primarily (about 88%). It contains approximately 3.5% milkfat and 8.5% other milk solids (proteins, milk sugar [lactose] and minerals).

Whole milk is graded A, B or C according to standards recommended by the U.S. Public Health Service. Grades are assigned based on bacterial count, with Grade A products having the lowest count. Grades B and C, though still safe and wholesome, are rarely available for retail or commercial use. Fresh whole milk is not available raw, but must be processed as we describe shortly.

PROCESSING TECHNIQUES

PASTEURIZATION

By law, all Grade A milk must be pasteurized prior to retail sale. Pasteurization is the process of heating milk to a sufficiently high temperature for a sufficient length of time to destroy pathogenic bacteria. This typically requires holding milk at a temperature of 161°F (72°C) for 15 seconds. Pasteurization also destroys enzymes that cause spoilage, thus increasing shelf life. Milk's nutritional value is not significantly affected by pasteurization.

ULTRA-PASTEURIZATION

Ultra-pasteurization is a process in which milk is heated to a very high temperature (275°F/135°C) for a very short time (2 to 4 seconds) in order to destroy virtually all bacteria. Ultra-pasteurization is most often used with whipping cream and individual creamers. Although the process may reduce cream's whipping properties, it extends its shelf life dramatically.

ULTRA-HIGH-TEMPERATURE PROCESSING

Ultra-high-temperature (UHT) processing is a form of ultra-pasteurization in which milk is held at a temperature of 280°F–300°F (138°C–150°C) for 2 to 6 seconds. It is then packed in sterile containers under sterile conditions and aseptically sealed to prevent bacteria from entering the container. Unopened UHT milk can be stored without refrigeration for at least three months. Although UHT milk can be stored unrefrigerated, it should be chilled before serving and stored like fresh milk once opened. UHT processing may give milk a slightly cooked taste, but it has no significant effect on milk's nutritional value. Long available in Europe, it is now gaining popularity in the United States.

HOMOGENIZATION

Homogenization is a process in which the fat globules in whole milk are reduced in size and permanently dispersed throughout the liquid. This prevents the fat from clumping together and rising to the surface as a layer of cream. Although homogenization is not required, milk sold commercially is generally homogenized because it ensures a uniform consistency, a whiter color and a richer taste.

MILKFAT REMOVAL

Whole milk can also be processed in a centrifuge to remove all or a portion of the milkfat, resulting in reduced-fat, low-fat and nonfat milks. All reduced-fat milks must still be nutritionally equivalent to full-fat milk and must provide at least the same amounts of the fat-soluble vitamins A and D as full-fat milk.

Reduced-fat or less-fat milk is whole milk from which sufficient milkfat has been removed to produce a liquid with 2% milkfat. **Low-fat** or little-fat milk contains 1% milkfat. **Nonfat** milk, also referred to as fat-free, no-fat or skim milk, has had as much milkfat removed as possible. The fat content must be less than 0.5%.

STORAGE

Fluid milk is a potentially hazardous food and should be kept refrigerated at or below 40°F (4°C). Its shelf life is reduced by half for every five-degree rise in temperature above 40°F (4°C). Keep milk containers closed to prevent absorption of odors and flavors. Freezing is not recommended.

CONCENTRATED MILKS

Concentrated or condensed milk products are produced by using a vacuum to remove all or part of the water from whole milk. The resulting products have a high concentration of milkfat and milk solids and an extended shelf life.

Evaporated milk is produced by removing approximately 60 percent of the water from whole, homogenized milk. The concentrated liquid is canned and heat-sterilized. This results in a cooked flavor and darker color. Evaporated skim milk, with a milkfat content of 0.5%, is also available. A can of evaporated milk requires no refrigeration until opened, although the can should be stored in a cool place. Evaporated milk can be reconstituted with an equal amount of water and used like whole milk for cooking or drinking.

Sweetened condensed milk is similar to evaporated milk in that 60 percent of the water has been removed. But unlike evaporated milk, sweetened condensed milk contains large amounts of sugar (40 to 45 percent). Sweetened condensed milk is also canned; the canning process darkens the color and adds a caramel flavor. Sweetened condensed milk cannot be substituted for whole milk or evaporated milk because of its sugar content. Its distinctive flavor is most often found in desserts and confections.

Dry milk powder is made by removing virtually all the moisture from pasteurized milk. Dry whole milk, nonfat milk and buttermilk are available. The lack of moisture prevents the growth of microorganisms and allows dry milk powders to be stored for extended periods without refrigeration. Powdered milks can be reconstituted with water and used like fresh milk. Milk powder may also be added to foods directly, with additional liquid included in the recipe. This procedure is typical in bread making and does not alter the function of the milk or the flavor in the finished product.

CREAM

Cream is a rich, liquid milk product containing at least 18% fat. It must be pasteurized or ultra-pasteurized and may be homogenized. Cream has a slight

IMITATION AND ARTIFICIAL DAIRY PRODUCTS

Coffee whiteners, imitation sour cream, whipped topping mixes and some whipped toppings in pressurized cans are made from nondairy products. These products usually consist of corn syrup, emulsifiers, vegetable fats, coloring agents and artificial flavors. These products are generally less expensive and have a longer shelf life than the real dairy products they replace, but their flavors are no match. Imitation and artificial products may be useful, however, for people who have allergies or are on a restricted diet. If you choose to use these products, you cannot claim to be using real dairy products on menus or labels.

SAFETY ALERT

MILK STORAGE

Canned milks, aseptically packaged milks and dry milk powders are shelf-stable products needing no refrigeration. After the can or box is opened or the powder is reconstituted with water, however, these become potentially hazardous foods and must be handled just as carefully as fresh milk. Do not store an open can of milk in its original container, and keep all milk products refrigerated at or below 40°F (4°C).

yellow or ivory color and is more viscous than milk. It is used throughout the kitchen to give flavor and body to sauces, soups and desserts. Whipping cream, containing not less than 30% milkfat, can be whipped into a stiff foam and used in pastries and desserts. Cream is marketed in several forms with different fat contents, as described here.

Half-and-half is a mixture of whole milk and cream containing between 10% and 18% milkfat. It is often served with cereal or coffee, but does not contain enough fat to whip into a foam.

Light cream, coffee cream and **table cream** are all products with more than 18% but less than 30% milkfat. These products are often used in baked goods or soups as well as with coffee, fruit and cereal.

Light whipping cream or, simply, **whipping cream,** contains between 30% and 36% milkfat. It is generally used for thickening and enriching sauces and making ice cream. It can be whipped into a foam and used as a dessert topping or folded into custards or mousses to add flavor and lightness.

Heavy whipping cream or, simply, **heavy cream,** contains not less than 36% milkfat. It whips easily and holds its whipped texture longer than other creams. It must be pasteurized, but is rarely homogenized. Heavy cream is used throughout the kitchen in the same ways as light whipping cream.

STORAGE

Ultra-pasteurized cream will keep for six to eight weeks if refrigerated at or below 40°F (4°C). Unwhipped cream should not be frozen. Keep cream away from strong odors and bright lights, as they can adversely affect its flavor.

CULTURED DAIRY PRODUCTS

Cultured dairy products such as yogurt, buttermilk and sour cream are produced by adding specific bacterial cultures to fluid dairy products. The bacteria convert the milk sugar **lactose** into lactic acid, giving these products their body and tangy, unique flavors. The acid content also retards the growth of undesirable microorganisms; thus cultured products have been used for centuries to preserve milk.

▶ **lactose** a disaccharide that occurs naturally in mammalian milk; milk sugar

Buttermilk originally referred to the liquid remaining after cream was churned into butter. Today, buttermilk is produced by adding a culture (*Streptococcus lactis*) to fresh, pasteurized skim or low-fat milk. This results in a tart milk with a thick texture. Buttermilk is most often used as a beverage or in baked goods.

Sour cream is produced by adding the same culture to pasteurized, homogenized light cream. The resulting product is a white, tangy gel used as a condiment or to give baked goods a distinctive flavor. Sour cream must have a milkfat content of not less than 18%.

Crème fraîche is a cultured cream popular in French cuisine. Although thinner and richer than sour cream, it has a similar tart, tangy flavor. It is used extensively in soups and sauces, especially with poultry, rabbit and lamb dishes. It is easily prepared from the following recipe.

Yogurt is a thick, tart, custardlike product made from milk (either whole, low-fat or nonfat) cultured with *Lactobacillus bulgaricus* and *Streptococcus thermophilus*. Though touted as a health or diet food, yogurt contains the same amount of milkfat as the milk from which it is made. Yogurt may also contain a variety of sweeteners, flavorings and fruits. Yogurt is generally eaten as is, but may be used in baked products, salad dressings and frozen desserts. It is used in many Middle Eastern cuisines.

STORAGE

Cultured products are potentially hazardous foods and should be kept refrigerated at or below 40°F (4°C). Under proper conditions, sour cream will last up to

CRÈME FRAÎCHE

Yield: 1 pint (500 ml)

Heavy cream	16 fl. oz.	500 g
Buttermilk, with active cultures	1 fl. oz.	30 g

1 Heat the cream (preferably not ultra-pasteurized) to approximately 100°F (43°C).
2 Remove the cream from the heat and stir in the buttermilk.
3 Allow the mixture to stand in a warm place, loosely covered, until it thickens, approximately 12 to 36 hours.
4 Chill thoroughly before using. Crème fraîche will keep for up to 10 days in the refrigerator.

Approximate values per 1-oz. (30-g) serving: **Calories** 90, **Total fat** 10 g, **Saturated fat** 6 g, **Cholesterol** 35 mg, **Sodium** 10 mg, **Total carbohydrates** 1 g, **Protein** 1 g, **Vitamin A** 10%, **Claims—**very low sodium

four weeks, yogurt up to three weeks and buttermilk up to two weeks. Freezing is not recommended for these products, but dishes prepared with cultured products generally can be frozen.

BUTTER

Butter is a fatty substance produced by agitating or churning cream. Its flavor is unequaled in sauces, breads and pastries. Butter contains at least 80% milkfat, not more than 16% water and 2–4% milk solids. It may or may not contain added salt. Butter is firm when chilled and soft at room temperature. It melts into a liquid at approximately 93°F (33°C) and reaches the smoke point at 260°F (127°C).

Government grading is not mandatory, but most processors submit their butters for testing. The USDA label on the package assures the buyer that the butter meets federal standards for the grade indicated:

▶ USDA Grade AA—butter of superior quality, with a fresh, sweet flavor and aroma, a smooth, creamy texture and good spreadability.
▶ USDA Grade A—butter of very good quality, with a pleasing flavor and fairly smooth texture.
▶ USDA Grade B—butter of standard quality, made from sour cream; has an acceptable flavor but lacks the flavor, texture and body of Grades AA and A. Grade B is most often used in the manufacturing of foods.

Salted butter is butter with up to 2.5% salt added. This not only changes the butter's flavor, it also extends its keeping qualities. When using salted butter in cooking or baking, the salt content must be considered in the total recipe.

European-style butter contains more milkfat than regular butter, usually from 82 to 86%, and very little or no added salt. It is often churned from cultured cream, giving it a more intense, buttery flavor. It may be used in lieu of any regular butter in cooking or baking.

Whipped butter is made by incorporating air into the butter. This increases its volume and spreadability, but also increases the speed with which the butter will become rancid. Because of the change in density, whipped butter should not be substituted in recipes calling for regular butter.

Clarified butter is butter that has had its water and milk solids removed by a process called clarification. Although **whole butter** can be used for cooking

▶ **whole butter** butter that is not clarified, whipped or reduced-fat

MARGARINE: FROM LABORATORY BENCH TO DINNER TABLE

Margarine was invented by a French chemist in 1869 after Napoleon III offered a prize for the development of a synthetic edible fat. Originally produced from animal fat and milk, margarine is now made almost exclusively from vegetable fats.

In *On Food and Cooking: The Science and Lore of the Kitchen,* Harold McGee recounts the history of margarine. He explains that margarine caught on quickly in Europe and America, with large-scale production underway by 1880. But the American dairy industry and the U.S. government put up fierce resistance. First, margarine was defined as a harmful drug and its sale restricted. Then it was heavily taxed; stores had to be licensed to sell it and, like alcohol and tobacco, it was bootlegged. The U.S. government refused to purchase it for use by the armed forces. And, in an attempt to hold it to its true colors, some states did not allow margarine to be dyed yellow (animal fats and vegetable oils are much paler than butter); the dye was sold separately and mixed in by the consumer. World War II, which brought butter rationing, probably did the most to establish margarine's respectability. But it was not until 1967 that yellow margarine could be sold in Wisconsin.

or sauce making, sometimes a more stable and consistent product will be achieved by using clarified butter. The clarification process is described in Chapter 9, Mise en Place.

STORAGE

Butter should be well wrapped and stored at temperatures between 32°F and 35°F (0°C and 2°C). Unsalted butter is best kept frozen until needed. If well wrapped, frozen butter will keep for up to nine months at a temperature of 0°F (18°C).

MARGARINE

Margarine is not a dairy product but is included in this section because it is so frequently substituted for butter in cooking, baking and table service. Margarine is manufactured from animal or vegetable fats or a combination of such fats. Flavorings, colorings, emulsifiers, preservatives and vitamins are added, and the mixture is firmed or solidified by exposure to hydrogen gas at very high temperatures, a process known as hydrogenation. Generally, the firmer the margarine, the greater the degree of hydrogenation and the longer its shelf life. Like butter, margarine is approximately 80% fat and 16% water. But even the finest margarine cannot match the flavor of butter.

Margarine packaged in tubs is softer and more spreadable than solid products and generally contains more water and air. Indeed, diet margarine is approximately 50% water. Because of their decreased density, these soft products should not be substituted for regular butter or margarine in cooking or baking.

Specially formulated and blended margarine is available for commercial use in making puff pastry, croissant doughs, frostings and the like.

▶ NUTRITION

Dairy products are naturally high in vitamins, minerals and protein. Often liquid products such as milk are fortified with additional vitamins and minerals, especially vitamins A and D. Because milk and butter are animal products, they do contain cholesterol. Their overall fat content varies depending upon the amount of milkfat left after processing.

► NATURAL CHEESES

Cheese (Fr. *fromage;* It. *fromaggio*) is one of the oldest and most widely used foods known to man. It is served alone or as a principal ingredient in or an accompaniment to countless dishes. Cheese is commonly used in commercial kitchens, appearing in everything from breakfast to snacks to desserts.

Literally hundreds of natural cheeses are produced worldwide. Although their shapes, ages and flavors vary according to local preferences and traditions, all natural cheeses are produced in the same basic fashion as has been used for centuries. Each starts with a mammal's milk; cows, goats and sheep are the most commonly used. The milk proteins (known as *casein*) are coagulated with the addition of an enzyme, usually rennet, which is found in calves' stomachs. As the milk coagulates, it separates into solid curds and liquid whey. After draining off the whey, either the curds are made into fresh cheese, such as ricotta or cottage cheese, or the curds are further processed by cutting, kneading and cooking. The resulting substance, known as "green cheese," is packed into molds to drain. Salt or special bacteria may be added to the molded cheeses, which are then allowed to age or ripen under controlled conditions to develop the desired texture, color and flavor.

Cheeses are a product of their environment, which is why most fine cheeses cannot be reproduced outside their native locale. The breed and feed of the milk animal, the wild spores and molds in the air and even the wind currents in a storage area can affect the manner in which a cheese develops. (Roquefort, for example, develops its distinctive flavor from aging in particular caves filled with crosscurrents of cool, moist air.)

Some cheeses develop a natural rind or surface because of the application of bacteria (bloomy rind) or by repeated washing with brine (washed rind). Most natural rinds may be eaten if desired. Other cheeses are coated with an inedible wax rind to prevent moisture loss. Fresh cheeses have no rind whatsoever.

Moisture and fat contents are good indicators of a cheese's texture and shelf life. The higher the moisture content, the softer the product and the more perishable it will be. Low-moisture cheeses may be used for grating and will keep for several weeks if properly stored. (Reduced water activity levels prohibit bacterial growth.) Fat content ranges from low fat (less than 20% fat) to double cream (at least 60% fat) and triple cream (at least 72% fat). Cheeses with a high fat content will be creamier and have a richer flavor and texture than low-fat products.

Most cheeses contain high percentages of fat and protein. Cheese is also rich in calcium, phosphorus and vitamin A. As animal products, natural cheeses contain cholesterol. Today, many low-fat and even nonfat processed cheeses are available. Sodium has also been reduced or eliminated from some modern products.

CHEESE VARIETIES

Cheeses can be classified by country of origin, ripening method, fat content or texture. Here we classify fine cheeses by texture and have adopted five categories: fresh or unripened, soft, semisoft, firm and hard. A separate section on goat's-milk cheeses is also included.

FRESH OR UNRIPENED CHEESES

Fresh cheeses are uncooked and unripened. Referred to as *fromage blanc* or *fromage frais* in French, they are generally mild and creamy with a tart tanginess. They should not taste acidic or bitter. Fresh cheeses have a moisture content of 40 to 80% and are highly perishable.

Cream cheese is a soft cow's-milk cheese from the United States containing approximately 35% fat. It is available in various-sized solid white blocks or

MAKING MOZZARELLA

In Italy, mozzarella is made every day; it is meant to be consumed just as often. Before there was refrigeration, the balls of mozzarella were stored in well water to keep them cool, which is where the tradition originated of storing fresh mozzarella in liquid.

Once the milk is coagulated and the curds are cut, the mass is slowly stirred to enhance the whey's expulsion. A few hours later, when the curds are mature, they are removed from the whey, chopped or shredded and then mixed with hot water.

To test the exact amount of maturity, a handful of curds is dipped into a bucket of hot water for 10 seconds. When the curds are removed, they should be kneaded briefly and then, holding the mass with two hands, it should be pulled and stretched out to determine its maturity. When it is exactly ready to be strung, it can be stretched as thin and opaque as tissue paper. At this point, small amounts of curd are dumped into a small vat and stirred with hot water using a paddle. This is known as "stringing" the cheese because as the curds are mixed with the water they begin to melt somewhat and become stringy. The more the cheese is stirred, the longer the strings are stretched. Eventually, all the strings come together to make a large mass of satiny-smooth cheese. In Italian, the word *filare* means "to string"; therefore, all cheeses that are strung are members of the *pasta filata* family.

When stringing is complete, the cheese is ready to be shaped and hand-formed into balls. The balls are tossed immediately into vats of cool water so they will maintain the desired shapes. When cool, the balls are immersed in brine solution and then wrapped in parchment paper.

PAULA LAMBERT, owner,
Mozzarella Company, Dallas, Texas

whipped and flavored. It is used throughout the kitchen in baking, dips, dressings and confections and is popular as a spread for bagels and toast.

Feta is a semisoft Greek or Italian product made from sheep's and/or goat's milk. It is a white, flaky cheese that is pickled (but not ripened) and stored in brine water, giving it a shelf life of four to six weeks. Its flavor becomes sharper and saltier with age. Feta is good for snacks and salads and melts easily for sauces and fillings.

Mascarpone (mas-cahr-POHN-ay) is a soft cow's-milk cheese originally from Italy's Lombard region. It contains 70 to 75% fat and is extremely smooth and creamy. Mascarpone is highly perishable and is available in bulk or in 8- or 16-ounce tubs. With its pale ivory color and rich, sweet flavor, it is useful in both sweet and savory sauces as well as desserts. It is also eaten plain, with fresh fruit or spread on bread and sprinkled with cocoa or sugar.

Mozzarella (maht-suh-REHL-lah) is a firm Italian cheese traditionally made with water buffalo's milk (today, cow's milk is more common) and containing 40 to 45% fat. Mozzarella becomes elastic when melted and is well known as "pizza cheese." Fresh mozzarella is excellent in salads or topped simply with olive oil and herbs. It is a very mild white cheese best eaten within hours of production. Commercial mozzarella is rather bland and rubbery and is best reserved for cooking, for which it may be purchased already shredded.

Queso Oaxaca (KEH-soh wah-HA-kaa), also known as Quesillo or Asadero, is one of the most popular cheeses of Mexico. It is a cow's-milk *pasta filata* or stretched-curd cheese that is kneaded and wound into balls, then soaked in brine for several minutes. It is pulled apart into thin strings before being used to fill tortillas or melted over cooked dishes. Queso Oaxaca is a good melting cheese with a smooth semisoft texture, white color and 45% fat content. It is invaluable in preparing Mexican and Mexican-American dishes such as quesadillas, nachos and tacos, and is also available blended with herbs, spices or chiles.

Ricotta (rih-COH-tah) is a soft Italian cheese, similar to American cottage cheese, made from the whey left when other cow's-milk cheeses are produced. It contains only 4 to 10% fat. It is white or ivory in color and fluffy, with a small grain and sweet flavor. Ricotta is an important ingredient in many pasta dishes and desserts. It can be made easily with the following recipe.

Feta

Mascarpone

Mozzarella

Queso Oaxaca

Ricotta

RICOTTA CHEESE   RECIPE 8.2

THE ART INSTITUTE OF WASHINGTON, ARLINGTON, VA
Chef John Harrison

Yield: 8 oz. (225 g)

Milk	1 qt.	950 ml
Fresh lime juice	3 fl. oz.	85 ml

1 Allow the milk to reach room temperature in a covered container.

2 In a stainless steel saucepan slowly heat the milk to 180°F (82°C), stirring often. Hold the heated milk at 180°F (82°C) for 5 minutes.

3 Remove the milk from the heat and gently stir it while adding the lime juice. Continue to stir until curds form.

4 Gently pour the curds into a strainer or china cap lined with new, rinsed cheesecloth. Allow the whey (liquid) to separate and drain away from the curds (solids). Discard the whey.

5 Allow the cheese to rest undisturbed for 1 hour. For a firm, dry ricotta, lift the corners of the cheesecloth and tie them together with twine. Suspend the bag in a tall, covered container, place it in the refrigerator and allow the cheese to drain for 4 hours or overnight.

6 Unwrap the cheese. Season it with salt if desired. Use the cheese as you would use commercially produced ricotta.

Approximate values per 1-oz. (30-g) serving: **Calories** 80, **Total fat** 4 g, **Saturated fat** 2.5 g, **Cholesterol** 15 mg, **Sodium** 60 mg, **Total carbohydrates** 7 g, **Protein** 4 g, **Calcium** 15%

1 Heat the milk to 180°F (82°C).

2 Gently stir in the lime juice.

3 Strain the mixture through cheesecloth.

4 The finished ricotta.

SOFT CHEESES

Soft cheeses are characterized by their thin skins and creamy centers. They are among the most delicious and popular of cheeses. They ripen quickly and are at their peak for only a few days, sometimes less. Moisture content ranges from 50 to 75%.

Bel Paese (bell pah-AYZ-eh) is a 20th-century Italian creation made from cow's milk and containing approximately 50% fat. It is mild and creamy with a fruity flavor. The inside is yellowish, and the outside is brown or gray. Bel Paese is excellent for snacking and melts easily.

Brie (bree) is a rind-ripened French cheese made with cow's milk and containing about 60% fat. Brie is made in round, flat disks weighing 2 or 4 pounds; it is coated with a bloomy white rind. At the peak of ripeness, it is creamy and rich, with a texture that oozes. Selecting a properly ripened Brie is a matter of judgment and experience. Select a cheese that is bulging a bit inside its rind; there should be just the beginning of a brown coloring on the rind. If underripe, Brie will be bland with a hard, chalky core. Once the cheese is cut, it will not ripen any further. If overripe, Brie will have a brownish rind that may be gummy or sagging and will smell strongly of ammonia. The rind is edible, but trim it off if preferred. The classic after-dinner cheese, Brie is also used in soups, sauces and hors d'oeuvres.

Brie

Boursin (boor-SAHN) is a triple-cream cow's-milk cheese from France containing approximately 75% fat. Boursin is usually flavored with peppers, herbs or garlic. It is rindless, with a smooth, creamy texture, and is packed in small, foil-wrapped cylinders. Boursin is a good breakfast cheese and a welcome addition to any cheese board. It is also a popular filling for baked chicken.

Boursin

Camembert (kam-uhm-BAIR) is a rind-ripened cheese from France containing approximately 45% fat. Bavaria also produces a Camembert, though of a somewhat lesser quality. Camembert is creamy, like Brie, but milder. It is shaped in small round or oval disks and is coated with a white bloomy rind. Selecting a properly ripened Camembert is similar to selecting a Brie, but Camembert will become overripe and ammoniated even more quickly than Brie. Camembert is an excellent dessert or after-dinner cheese and goes particularly well with fruit.

Taleggio (tahl-EH-zhee-oh) is a semisoft cheese that has been produced since the 10th century in a small town near Bergamo in the Lombardy region of Italy. Made with pasteurized or unpasteurized cow's milk, it contains 48% fat and is aged for one to two months. Taleggio has an orange-colored washed rind that is edible but pungent. It is molded in a distinctive 8-inch square, approximately 2 inches thick. Its nutty, salty flavor and strong aroma become softer, creamier and more piquant with age. Serve as a dessert cheese with a strong red wine, crusty bread and fruit, or with a salad at the end of a meal.

SEMISOFT CHEESES

Semisoft cheeses include many mild, buttery cheeses with smooth, sliceable textures. Some semisoft cheeses are also known as monastery or Trappist cheeses because their development is traced to monasteries, some recipes having originated during the Middle Ages. The moisture content of semisoft cheeses ranges from 40 to 50%.

Cabrales (kah-BRAH-layss) is a blue-veined Spanish cheese made primarily from a blend of raw goat's, ewe's and cow's milks and containing 45 to 48% fat. Its wrapper made from large maple, oak or sycamore leaves is easily recognized. The outer foil wrapper is marked with the *Denominación de Origen* (D.O.) logo, and each 5- to 9-pound (2.5- to 4.5-kg) wheel is stamped with a unique number. It is aged for three to six months under the cold, humid and breezy conditions in natural caves found in the Asturias region. Cabrales has a moist, crumbly interior with purple-blue veins and a rough, salt-cured rind. It has a thick, creamy texture, a strong aroma and a complex sour, piquant flavor. Cabrales is especially good with salami and a full-bodied red wine or for dessert with a sweet sherry such as Pedro Ximenex.

Cabrales

Doux de Montagne (doo duh mahn-tahn-yuh) is a cow's-milk cheese from France containing approximately 45% fat. Produced in the foothills of the Pyrenees, it is also referred to as **pain de Pyrenees.** Doux de Montagne is pale yellow with irregular holes and a mellow, sweet, nutty flavor. It is sometimes studded with green peppercorns, which provide a tangy flavor contrast. It is usually shaped in large, slightly squashed spheres and coated with brown wax. Doux de Montagne is good before dinner and for snacking.

Doux de Montagne

Fontina (fon-TEE-nah) is a cow's-milk cheese from Italy's Piedmont region containing approximately 45% fat. The original, known as **Fontina Val D'Aosta,** has a dark gold, crusty rind; the pale gold, dense interior has a few small holes. It is nutty and rich. The original must have a purple trademark stamped on the rind. Imitation Fontinas (properly known as **Fontal** or **Fontinella**) are produced in Denmark, France, Sweden, the United States and other regions of Italy. They tend to be softer, with less depth of flavor, and may have a rubbery texture. Real Fontina is a good after-dinner cheese; the imitations are often added to sauces, soups or sandwiches.

Gorgonzola (gohr-guhn-ZOH-lah) is a blue-veined cow's-milk cheese from Italy containing 48% fat. Gorgonzola has a white or ivory interior with bluish-green veins. It is creamier than other blues such as Stilton or Roquefort, with a somewhat more pungent, spicy, earthy flavor. White Gorgonzola has no veins but a similar flavor, while aged Gorgonzola is drier and crumbly with a very strong, sharp flavor. The milder Gorgonzolas are excellent with fresh peaches or pears or crumbled in a salad. Gorgonzola is also used in sauces and in torta con basilico, a cakelike cheese loaf composed of layers of cheese, fresh basil and pine nuts.

Gouda (GOO-dah) is a Dutch cheese containing approximately 48% fat. Gouda is sold in various-sized wheels covered with red or yellow wax. The cheese is yellow with a few small holes and a mild, buttery

LEFTOVER CHEESE

Never discard those little leftover bits and pieces of cheese lurking in your refrigerator. The tag ends of Brie, cheddar, farmer cheese, chevre, Roquefort, Mozzarella, and scores of other cheese can be quickly transformed into a tasty mixture that the thrifty French call *fromage fort* ("strong cheese"). Seasoned with fresh garlic and a few splashes of wine, it makes an assertively flavored topping for toast or thick slices of bread and tastes best when briefly melted under the broiler.

To make fromage fort, gather together 1 pound of leftover cheese (3 kinds is enough, 6 or 7 will be even better). Trim off any mold or very dried out parts from the surface. Toss 3 or 4 peeled cloves of garlic into a food processor and process for several seconds until coarsely chopped. Add the cheese to the garlic along with ½ cup dry white wine and at least 1 teaspoon of freshly ground black pepper. Process until the mixture becomes soft and creamy, about 30 seconds. Remove the mixture from the processor and transfer it to a crock or bowl. Cover tightly with plastic wrap and refrigerate.

STEVE JENKINS,
Steve Jenkins Cheese Primer

Gorgonzola

▶ **fondue** a Swiss specialty made with melted cheese, wine and flavorings; eaten by dipping pieces of bread into the hot mixture with long forks

flavor. Gouda may be sold soon after production, or it may be aged for several months, resulting in a firmer, more flavorful cheese. Gouda is widely popular for snacking and in **fondue.**

Havarti (hah-VAHR-tee) is a cow's-milk monastery-style cheese from Denmark containing 45 to 60% fat. Havarti is also known as **Danish Tilsit** or by the brand name **Dofino.** Pale yellow with many small, irregular holes, it is sold in small rounds, rectangular blocks or loaves. Havarti has a mild flavor and creamy texture. It is often flavored with dill, caraway seeds or peppers. Havarti is very popular for snacking and in sandwiches.

Port du Salut (por dah suh-LOO) is a monastery cow's-milk product from France containing approximately 50% fat. Port du Salut (also known as Port Salut) is smooth, rich and savory. It is shaped in thick wheels with a dense, pale yellow interior and an

Havarti

edible, bright orange rind. The Danish version is known as Esrom. One of the best and most authentic Port du Saluts has the initials S.A.F.R. stamped on the rind. Lesser-quality brands may be bland and rubbery. It is popular for breakfast and snacking, especially with fruit.

▶ **blue cheese** (1) a generic term for any cheese containing visible blue-green molds that contribute a characteristic tart, sharp flavor and aroma; also known as a blue-veined cheese or bleu; (2) a group of Roquefort-style cheeses made in the United States and Canada from cow's or goat's milk rather than ewe's milk and injected with molds that form blue-green veins; also known as blue mold cheese or blue-veined cheese

Roquefort (ROHK-fuhr) is a blue-veined sheep's-milk cheese from France containing approximately 45% fat. It was first mentioned in a text dated to 79 A.D. and Roquefort producers have held a legal monopoly over making this cheese since 1411. Roquefort is intensely pungent with a rich, salty flavor and strong aroma. It is a white paste with veins of blue mold and a thin natural rind shaped into thick, foil-wrapped cylinders. Roquefort is always aged for at least three months in the limestone caves of Mount Combalou. Since 1926, no producer outside this region can legally use the name Roquefort or even "Roquefort-style." Roquefort is an excellent choice for serving before or after dinner and is, of course, essential for Roquefort dressing.

Roquefort

Stilton is a blue-veined cow's-milk cheese from Great Britain containing 45% fat. Stilton is one of the oldest and grandest cheeses in the world. It has a white or pale yellow interior with evenly spaced blue veins. Stilton's distinctive flavor is pungent, rich and tangy, combining the best of blues and cheddars. It is aged in cool ripening rooms for four to six months to develop the blue veining; it is then sold in tall cylinders with a crusty, edible rind. Stilton should be wrapped in a cloth dampened with salt water and stored at cool temperatures, but not refrigerated. It is best served alone, with plain crackers, dried fruit or vintage port.

FIRM CHEESES

Firm cheeses are not hard or brittle. Some are close-textured and flaky, like Cheddar; others are dense, holey cheeses like Emmenthaler. Most firm cheeses are actually imitators of these two classics. Their moisture content ranges from 30 to 40%.

Stilton

Cheddars are produced in both North America and Great Britain. **American Cheddar** is a cow's-milk cheese made primarily in New York, Wisconsin, Vermont and Oregon, containing from 45 to 50% fat. The best cheddars are made from raw milk and aged for several months. (Raw milk may be used in the United States provided the cheese is then aged at least 60 days.) They have a dense, crumbly texture. Cheddars may be white or colored orange with vegetable dyes, depending on local preference. Flavors range from mild to very sharp, depending on the age of the cheese. **Colby** and **Longhorn** are two well-known mild, soft-textured Wisconsin Cheddars. Cheddars are sold in a variety of shapes and sizes, often coated with wax. Good-quality Cheddars are welcome additions to any cheese board, while those of lesser quality are better reserved for cooking and sandwiches. **English Cheddar** is a variety of cow's-milk cheese produced in Great Britain containing approximately 45% fat. Perhaps the most imitated cheese in the world, true English Cheddar is rarely seen in the United States because of import restrictions. It is a moist yet sliceable cheese, aged at least six months.

American Cheddar—Wisconsin Sharp, Vermont Cabot, Canadian Black Diamond

Emmenthaler (EM-en-tah-ler) is a cow's-milk cheese from Switzerland containing approximately 45% fat. Emmenthaler is the original Swiss cheese; it accounts for more than half of Switzerland's cheese production. It is mellow, rich and nutty with a natural rind and a light yellow interior full of large holes. It is ripened in three stages with the aid of fermenting bacteria. The holes or "eyes" are caused by gases expanding inside the cheese during fermentation. Authentic Emmenthaler is sold in 200-pound wheels with the word *Switzerland* stamped on the rind like the spokes of a wheel. Emmenthaler, one of the basic fondue cheeses, is also popular for sandwiches, snacks and after dinner with fruit and nuts.

Emmenthaler (Swiss)

Gruyère (groo-YAIR) is a cow's-milk cheese made near Fribourg in the Swiss Alps and containing approximately 45 to 50% fat. Gruyère is often imitated, as the name is not legally protected. True Gruyère is moist and highly flavorful, with a sweet nuttiness similar to Emmenthaler. Gruyère is aged for up to 12 months and then sold in huge wheels. It should have small, well-spaced holes and a brown, wrinkled rind. Gruyère melts easily and is often used with meats and in sauces, but it is also appropriate before or after dinner.

Jarlsberg (YAHRLZ-behrg) is a Swiss-type cow's-milk cheese from Norway containing approximately 45% fat. Jarlsberg closely resembles Emmenthaler in both flavor and appearance. It is mild with a delicate, sweet flavor and large holes. Jarlsberg has a pale yellow interior; it is coated with yellow wax and sold in huge wheels. It has a long shelf life and is popular for sandwiches and snacks and in cooking.

Gruyère

Manchego

Manchego (mahn-CHAY-goh) is the best-known and most widely available Spanish sheep's-milk cheese. Its ivory to pale yellow interior is firm and compact with a few small air pockets. It has a buttery and slightly piquant flavor with an aftertaste of sheep's milk. The inedible rind is black, gray or beige with a very distinctive zigzag pattern imprinted by the traditional esparto grass molds.

There are two types of Manchego: farmhouse style, made with unpasteurized sheep's milk, and industrial, made with pasteurized milk. For both, only milk from Manchega sheep raised in the La Mancha region is used. Manchego is aged from two months (*fresco*) to one year (*curado*) to two years (*añejo* or *viejo*) and contains 45 to 57% fat. Its intense flavor and crumbly texture make it excellent for eating as is, with bread or fruit, or as the focal point of antipasto with a robust red wine or a dry sherry.

Monterey Jack is a cheddarlike cow's-milk cheese from California containing 50% fat. It is very mild and rich, with a pale ivory interior. It is sold in wheels or loaves coated with dark wax. "Jack" is often flavored with peppers or herbs and is good for snacking and sandwiches and in Mexican dishes. Dry-aged Jack develops a tough, wrinkled brown rind and a rich, firm yellow interior. It has a nutty, sharp flavor and is dry enough for grating.

Monterey Jack

Provolone (pro-voh-LOH-nee) is a cow's-milk cheese from southern Italy containing approximately 45% fat. Provolone *dolce,* aged only two months, is mild, with a smooth texture. Provolone *piccante,* aged up to six months, is stronger and somewhat flaky or stringy. Smoked provolone is also popular, especially for snacking. Provolone is shaped in various ways, from huge salamis to plump spheres to tiny piglets shaped by hand. It is excellent in sandwiches and for cooking, and is often used for melting and in pizza and pasta dishes.

HARD CHEESES

Hard cheeses are not simply cheeses that have been allowed to dry out. Rather, they are carefully aged for extended periods and have a moisture content of about 30%. Hard cheeses are most often used for grating; the best flavor will come from cheeses grated as needed. Even the finest hard cheeses begin to lose their flavor within hours of grating. The most famous and popular of the hard cheeses are those from Italy, where they are known as *grana*. Hard cheeses can also be served as a table cheese or with a salad.

Provolone

Asiago (ah-zee-AH-go) is a cow's-milk cheese from Italy containing approximately 30% fat. After only one year of aging, Asiago is sharp and nutty with a cheddarlike texture. If aged for two years or more, Asiago becomes dry, brittle and suitable for grating. Either version should be an even white to pale yellow in color with no dark spots, cracks or strong aromas. Asiago melts easily and is often used in cooking.

Asiago

Parmigiano-Reggiano (Parmesan) (pahr-me-ZHAN-no reg-gee-AH-no) is a cow's-milk cheese made exclusively in the region near Parma, Italy, containing from 32 to 35% fat. Parmigiano-Reggiano is one of the world's oldest and most widely copied cheeses. Used primarily for grating and cooking, it is rich, spicy and sharp with a golden interior and a hard oily rind. It should not be overly salty or bitter. Reggiano, as it is known, is produced only from mid-April to mid-November. It is shaped into huge wheels of about 80 pounds (36 kilos) each, with the name stenciled repeatedly around the rind. Imitation Parmesan is produced in the United States, Argentina and elsewhere, but none can match the distinctive flavor of freshly grated Reggiano.

Pecorino Romano (peh-coh-REE-no roh-MAH-no) is a sheep's-milk cheese from central and southern Italy containing approximately 35% fat. Romano is very brittle and sharper than other grating cheeses, with a "sheepy" tang. Its light, grainy interior is whiter than Parmesan or Asiago. It is packed in large cylinders with a yellow rind. Romano is often substituted for, or combined with, Parmesan in cooking, but it is also good eaten with olives, sausages and red wine.

Parmigiano-Reggiano (Parmesan)

GOAT'S-MILK CHEESES

Because of their increasing popularity, cheeses made from goat's milk deserve a few words of their own. Although goats give less milk than cows, their milk is higher in fat and protein and richer and more concentrated in flavor. Cheeses made with goat's milk have a sharp, tangy flavor. They may range in texture from very soft and fresh to very hard, depending on age.

Chèvre (shehv; French for "goat") refers to small, soft, creamy cheeses produced in a variety of shapes: cones, disks, pyramids or logs. Chèvres are often coated with ash, herbs or seasonings. They are excellent for cooking and complement a wide variety of flavors. Unfortunately, they have a short shelf life, perhaps only two weeks. Cheese labeled *pur chèvre* must be made with 100% goat's milk, while others may be a mixture of cow's and goat's milk.

The finest goat's-milk cheeses usually come from France. Preferred brands include Bucheron, exported from France in 5-pound (2-kilograms) logs; Chevrotin, one of the mildest; and Montrachet, a tangy soft cheese from the

Goat's Milk Cheeses

AMERICAN CHEESE PRODUCTION

The first cheese factory in the United States was built in 1851 in Oneida County, New York. Herkimer County, which adjoins Oneida County, soon became the center of the American cheese industry and remained so for the next 50 years. During this time, the largest cheese market in the world was at Little Falls, New York, where farm-produced cheeses and cheeses from more than 200 factories were sold. At the turn of the century, as New York's population increased, there was a corresponding increase in demand for fluid milk. Because dairies could receive more money for fluid milk than for cheese, cheese production declined.

Although New York still produces some outstanding cheddars, the bulk of the American cheese industry gradually moved westward, eventually settling in Wisconsin's rich farmlands. The United States is now the world's largest manufacturer of cheeses, producing nearly twice as many pounds per year as its nearest competitor, France.

Burgundy wine region. Spurred on by the increased popularity of chèvre, several American producers have developed excellent goat's-milk cheeses in a wide variety of shapes and styles.

▶ PROCESSED CHEESES

Pasteurized processed cheese is made from a combination of aged and green cheeses mixed with emulsifiers and flavorings, pasteurized and poured into molds to solidify. Manufacturers can thus produce cheeses with consistent textures and flavors. Processed cheeses are commonly used in food service operations because they are less expensive than natural cheeses. And, because they will not age or ripen, their shelf life is greatly extended. Nutritionally, processed cheeses generally contain less protein, calcium and vitamin A and more sodium than natural cheeses.

Processed cheese food contains less natural cheese (but at least 51 precent by weight) and more moisture than regular processed cheese. Often vegetable oils and milk solids are added, making cheese food soft and spreadable.

Imitation cheese is usually manufactured with dairy by-products and soy products mixed with emulsifiers, colorings and flavoring agents and enzymes. Although considerably less expensive than natural cheese, imitation cheese tends to be dense and rubbery, with little flavor other than that of salt.

▶ SERVING CHEESES

Cheeses may be served at any time of day. In Northern Europe, they are common for breakfast; in Great Britain, they are a staple at lunch. Cheeses are widely used for sandwiches, snacks and cooking in America, and they are often served following the entrée or instead of dessert at formal dinners.

The flavor and texture of natural cheeses are best at room temperature. So, except for fresh cheeses, all cheeses should be removed from the refrigerator 30 minutes to an hour before service to allow them to come to room temperature. Fresh cheeses, such as cottage and cream, should be eaten chilled.

CHEESE TERMINOLOGY

The following terms often appear on cheese labels and may help you identify or appreciate new or unfamiliar cheeses:

Affiné—French term for a washed-rind cheese.

Bleu—French for "blue."

Brique or *briquette*—refers to a group of French brick-shaped cheeses.

Brosse—French term for cheeses that are brushed during ripening.

Capra—Italian for goat's-milk cheese.

Carré—French term for square, flat cheeses.

Cendré—French term for cheeses ripened in ashes.

Coulant—French for "flowing," used to describe Brie, Camembert and other cheeses when their interiors ooze or flow.

Ferme or *fermier*—French adjective used to indicate farm-produced cheeses.

Kaas—Dutch for "cheese."

Käse—German for "cheese."

Lait cru—French term for raw milk.

Laiterie or *laitier*—French for "dairy"; appears on factory-made cheeses.

Matières grasses—French term for dry matter.

Mi chevre—a French product so labeled must contain at least 25 percent goat's milk.

Ost—Scandinavian for "cheese."

Pecorino—Italian term for all sheep's-milk cheeses.

Queso—Spanish for "cheese."

Râpé—French term applied to cheeses that are suitable for grating.

Tome or *tomme*—term used by the French, Italians and Swiss to refer to mountain cheeses, particularly from the Pyrenees or Savoie regions.

Tyrophile—one who loves cheese.

Vaccino—Italian term for cow's-milk cheese.

Vache—French term for cow's-milk cheese.

Cheeseboard Ready for Service

Any selection of fine cheeses should include a variety of flavors and textures: from mild to sharp, from soft to creamy to firm. Use a variety of shapes and colors for visual appeal. Do not precut the cheeses, as this only causes them to become dry. Provide an adequate supply of serving knives so that stronger-flavored cheeses will not combine with and overpower milder ones. Fine cheeses are best appreciated with plain bread and crackers, as salted or seasoned crackers can mask the cheese's flavor. Noncitrus fruits are also a nice accompaniment.

STORAGE

Most cheeses are best kept refrigerated, well wrapped to keep odors out and moisture in. Firm and hard cheeses can be kept for several weeks; fresh cheeses will spoil in 7 to 10 days because of their high moisture content. Some cheeses that have become hard or dry may still be grated for cooking or baking. Freezing is possible but not recommended because it changes the cheese's texture, making it mealy or tough.

WINE AND CHEESE: CLASSIC COMBINATIONS

Some cheeses are delicious with beers or ales. Others are best with strong coffee or apple cider, and nothing accompanies a Cheddar cheese sandwich as well as ice-cold milk. For most cheeses, however, the ultimate partner is wine. Wine and cheese bring out the best in each other. The proteins and fats in cheeses take the edge off harsh or acidic wines, while the tannins and acids in wines bring out the creamy richness of cheeses.

Because of their natural affinity, certain pairings are universal favorites: Stilton with

port, Camembert with Bordeaux, Roquefort with Sauternes and English Cheddar with Burgundy. Although taste preferences are an individual matter, cheese-wine marriages follow two schools of thought: either pair likes or pair opposites.

Pairing like with like is simple: Cheeses are often best served with wines produced in the same region. For example, a white Burgundy such as Montrachet would be an excellent choice for cheeses from Burgundy; and goat cheeses from the Rhone Valley go well with

wines of that region. Hearty Italian wines such as Chianti, Barolo and Valpolicella are delicious with Italian cheese—Gorgonzola, Provolone, Taleggio. And a dry, aged Monterey Jack is perhaps the perfect mate for California Zinfandel.

Opposites do attract, however. Sweet wines such as Sauternes and Gewürztraminer go well with sharp, tangy blues, especially Roquefort. And light, sparkling wines such as Champagne or Spanish Cava are a nice complement to rich, creamy cheeses such as Brie and Camembert.

CONCLUSION

Dairy products are versatile foods used throughout the kitchen. They may be served as is or incorporated into many dishes, including soups, sauces, entrées, breads and desserts. Fine natural cheeses are useful in prepared dishes but are most important for buffets, as the cheese course during a meal or whenever cheese is the primary ingredient or dominant flavor. Dairy products spoil easily and must be handled and stored properly.

QUESTIONS FOR DISCUSSION

1 What is milkfat, and how is it used in classifying milk-based products?
2 If a recipe calls for whole milk and you have only dried milk, what do you do? Explain your answer.
3 What is clarified butter, and when is it used? Describe the procedure for clarifying butter.
4 The texture and shelf life of cheese depend on what two factors?
5 Cheeses are categorized as fresh, soft, semisoft, firm and hard. Give two examples of each, and explain how they are generally used.

6 The FDA has proposed extending the mandatory aging period for cheeses made from raw (unpasteurized) milk beyond the 60 days currently required. The FDA has also proposed banning importation of raw-milk cheeses altogether on food safety grounds. Several groups, including the American Cheese Society and Oldways Preservation & Exchange Trust, are fighting these proposals. What is the current status of the FDA proposals? What arguments are used in support of and in opposition to these proposals?

7 Use the Internet to locate a U.S. producer of European-style goat cheeses. What varieties of goat cheeses do they market?

WHEN YOU BECOME A GOOD COOK,
YOU BECOME A GOOD CRAFTSMAN, FIRST. YOU
REPEAT AND REPEAT AND REPEAT UNTIL YOUR
HANDS KNOW HOW TO MOVE WITHOUT THINKING
ABOUT IT.

—*Jacques Pepin, French chef and teacher*
(1935–)

MISE EN PLACE

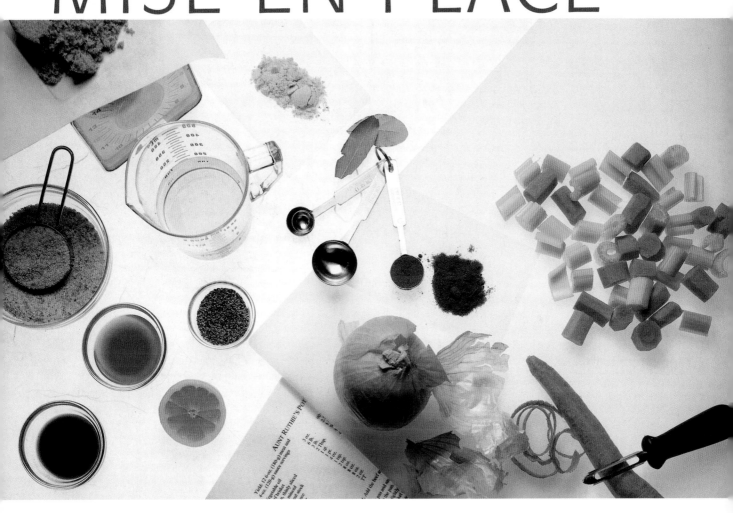

AFTER STUDYING THIS CHAPTER, YOU WILL BE ABLE TO:

▶ organize and plan your work more efficiently

▶ understand basic flavoring techniques

▶ prepare items needed prior to actual cooking

▶ set up and use the standard breading procedure

The French term *mise en place* (meez ahn plahs) literally means "to put in place" or "everything in its place." But in the culinary context, it means much more. Escoffier defined the phrase as "those elementary preparations that are constantly resorted to during the various steps of most culinary preparations." He meant, essentially, gathering and prepping the ingredients to be cooked as well as assembling the tools and equipment necessary to cook them.

In this chapter, we discuss many of the basics that must be in place before cooking begins: for example, creating bouquets garni, clarifying butter, making bread crumbs, toasting nuts and battering foods. Chopping, dicing, cutting and slicing—important techniques used to prepare foods as well—are discussed in Chapter 6, Knife Skills, while specific preparations, such as roasting peppers and trimming pineapples, are discussed elsewhere.

The concept of mise en place is simple: A chef should have at hand everything he or she needs to prepare and serve food in an organized and efficient manner.

Proper mise en place can consist of just a few items—for example, those needed to prepare a small quantity of chicken soup. Or it can be quite extensive —for example, when setting up the hot line for a busy restaurant with a large menu. A proper mise en place requires the chef to consider work patterns, ingredient lists and tool and equipment needs.

Mise en place will differ from one restaurant to another. A banquet chef's mise en place could include organizing large quantities of meats, vegetables, salad ingredients, breads, condiments and pastries for several dinners, all with different menus. Regardless of the specific menu, banquet mise en place may also include gathering hot boxes, plates, chafing dishes, tongs, spoons and ladles, and setting up the dish-up line. The mise en place for the broiler station at a steakhouse could include properly storing raw steaks and chops that will be cooked to order, as well as gathering the salt, pepper, pre-prepared sauces and accompaniments that are used during cooking or served with the finished items. The broiler cook could also be responsible for gathering plates, building a charcoal fire for the grill, and stocking his or her work area with hand tools, towels and sanitizing solution. In the restaurant situation, unlike in banquet work, the cook's mise en place is probably identical night after night. A waiter's mise en place could include brewing tea, cutting lemon wedges and refilling salt and pepper shakers—preparations that will make work go more smoothly during actual service. Regardless of the number of items used or the complexity of the recipes being prepared, completing a proper mise en place requires careful planning, efficient organization and attention to detail.

Coordination of multiple tasks is also important. An organized cook will think about everything that needs to be done and the most efficient way to complete those tasks before beginning the actual work. Taking the time to first plan the day's activities can eliminate unnecessary steps and conserve resources.

Proper mise en place also requires a good sense of timing. Knowing how long before service to begin a task, or how far in advance of service some preparations can be made, allows a cook to better plan for the efficient execution of his or her duties. In this type of planning, it is also important to consider food safety issues, such as those relating to time and temperature controls. See Chapter 2, Food Safety and Sanitation, for detailed information.

▶ SELECTING TOOLS AND EQUIPMENT

An important step in creating the proper mise en place is to identify and gather all of the tools and equipment that will be needed to prepare a recipe properly or to work a station efficiently. The tools and equipment used to prepare, cook and store foods are discussed in Chapter 5, Tools and Equipment. A few general rules to bear in mind:

- ▶ All tools, equipment and work surfaces must be clean and sanitized.
- ▶ Knives should be honed and sharpened.
- ▶ Measuring devices should be checked periodically for accuracy.
- ▶ Ovens and cooking surfaces should be preheated, as necessary.
- ▶ Mixing bowls, saucepans and storage containers should be the correct size for the task at hand.
- ▶ Serving plates, cookware, utensils, hand tools and other necessary smallwares should be gathered and stored nearby.
- ▶ Foods should be gathered and stored conveniently at the proper temperatures.
- ▶ Expiration dates on foods should be checked periodically for validity.
- ▶ Sanitizing solution, hand towels, disposable gloves and trash receptacles should be conveniently located.

▶ MEASURING INGREDIENTS

In order to reproduce foods consistently and for the same cost day after day, it is important that the ingredients be measured accurately each time. As explained in more detail in Chapter 4, Menus and Recipes, ingredients may be measured by weight, volume or count. Weight refers to the mass or heaviness of

1 To use a balance scale to weigh an ingredient, place an empty container on the left, then set a counterbalance to that container on the right. Use weights and the sliding beam weight to add an amount equal to the amount of the ingredient needed.

2 Place the ingredient on the left side of the scale until the two platforms are balanced.

Liquids should be measured in liquid measuring cups, which may be marked in U.S. and/or metric units.

Small amounts of dry ingredients are measured by overfilling the appropriate measuring spoon, then leveling the ingredient.

an item and is measured using a scale. Volume refers to the space occupied by a substance and is measured with graduated measuring cups and spoons. Count refers to the number of individual items. It is important to remember that foods do not weigh their volume. In other words, although 1 cup contains 8 *fluid ounces,* 1 cup of flour, honey, cinnamon, and so on does not *weigh* 8 ounces.

▶ PREPARING INGREDIENTS

Some ingredients that are used frequently throughout the kitchen are often prepared in large quantities so that they are ready when needed for a specific recipe. For example, dry bread crumbs can be made and stored whenever a supply of bread is available. Large quantities of butter can be clarified on a back burner while other operations proceed on the line. These chores may be simple, but they are time-consuming. As an entry-level cook, you may be assigned responsibility for this type of mise en place. Never feel that such chores are beneath you; consider, instead, how frustrating it would be for the chef to run out of a simple item just when it is needed during service.

CLARIFYING BUTTER

▶ **ghee** a form of clarified butter in which the milk solids remain with the fat and are allowed to brown; originating in India and now used worldwide as an ingredient and cooking medium, it has a long shelf life, a high smoke point and a nutty, caramel-like flavor

Unsalted whole butter is approximately 80% fat, 16% water and 4% milk solids. Although whole butter can be used for cooking or sauce making, sometimes a more stable and consistent product will be achieved by using butter that has had the water and milk solids removed by a process called **clarification.**

▶ PROCEDURE FOR CLARIFYING BUTTER

1 Slowly warm the butter in a saucepan over low heat without boiling or agitation. As the butter melts, the milk solids rise to the top as a foam and the water sinks to the bottom.

2 When the butter is completely melted, skim the milk solids from the top.

3 When all the milk solids have been removed, ladle the butterfat into a clean saucepan, being careful to leave the water in the bottom of the pan.

4 The clarified butter is now ready to use. One pound (454 grams) of whole butter will yield approximately 12 ounces (340 grams) of clarified butter—a yield of 75%.

Clarified butter will keep for extended periods in either the freezer or refrigerator.

Skimming milk solids from the surface of melted butter.

Ladling the butterfat into a clean pan.

TOASTING NUTS AND SPICES

Nuts are often toasted lightly before being used in baked goods, breadings, salads and sauces. Whole spices are sometimes toasted before being ground for a sauce or used as a garnish. Toasting not only browns the food, it brings out its flavor and makes it crispier and crunchier. Whether toasting nuts or spices in the oven or on the stove top, they should be watched closely as they can develop scorched flavors and burn easily.

MAKING BREAD CRUMBS

Most any bread can be used to make crumbs; the choice depends on how the crumbs will be used. **Fresh bread crumbs** are made from fresh bread that is slightly dried out, approximately two to four days old. If the bread is too fresh, the crumbs will be gummy and stick together; if the bread is too stale, the crumbs will taste stale as well. **Dry bread crumbs** are made from bread that has been lightly toasted in a warm oven. Do not make crumbs from stale or molding bread, as these undesirable flavors will be apparent when the crumbs are used.

To make crumbs, the bread is cubed or torn into pieces and ground in a food processor. Dried bread can be processed to a finer consistency than fresh bread. After processing, the crumbs should be passed through a tamis and stored in a tightly closed plastic container in a cool, dry place.

For additional flavors, dried herbs and spices can be mixed into the crumbs.

Toasting sesame seeds in a dry sauté pan on the stove top.

1 Grind chunks of bread in a food processor.

2 Pass the crumbs through a tamis or sieve so that they will be the same size.

CONVENIENCE PRODUCTS

Convenience products have now replaced many of the chores that were typically part of a cook's routine mise en place. For example, stock and sauce bases eliminate the time and labor necessary to make these products from scratch. Fresh onions and garlic can be purchased peeled, chopped and ready to use. Bread crumbs are available in bulk, and ready-to-use clarified butter is sold in refrigerated tubs. All this convenience comes at a price, of course. A chef must carefully consider whether the savings in employee time, along with the quality and consistency of available products, justify the higher cost of some of the convenience products now on the market.

▶ FLAVORING FOODS

Foods are often flavored with herbs or spices, marinades or rubs before they are actually cooked. This may require the chef to prepare various flavoring or seasoning mixtures and wait for a period of time between steps in a recipe.

BOUQUET GARNI AND SACHET

A bouquet garni and sachet are used to introduce flavorings, seasonings and aromatics into stocks, sauces, soups and stews.

A **bouquet garni** is a selection of herbs (usually fresh) and vegetables tied into a bundle with twine. A standard bouquet garni consists of parsley stems, celery, thyme, leeks and carrots.

A **sachet** (also known as a *sachet d'épices*) is made by tying seasonings together in cheesecloth. A standard sachet consists of peppercorns, bay leaves, parsley stems, thyme, cloves and, optionally, garlic. The exact quantity of these ingredients is determined by the amount of liquid the sachet is meant to flavor.

Bouquet Garni

Sachet

Oignon Piqué

Bouquets garni and sachets are used to add flavors in such a way that they can be easily removed from a dish when their flavors have been extracted. A similar technique, although less commonly used, is an **oignon piqué** (also known as an *onion piquet*). To prepare an oignon piqué, peel the onion and trim off the root end. Attach one or two dried bay leaves to the onion using whole cloves as pins. The oignon piqué is then simmered in milk or stock to extract flavors.

MARINADES

Marinating is the process of soaking meat or poultry in a seasoned liquid to flavor and tenderize it. Marinades can be a simple blend (herbs, seasonings and oil) or a complicated cooked recipe (red wine, fruit and other ingredients). Mild marinades should be used on more delicate meats, such as veal. Game and beef require strongly flavored marinades. In wine-based marinades, white wine is usually used for white meats and poultry, and red wine is used for red meats. Not only does the wine add a distinctive flavor, but the acids in it break down connective tissues and help tenderize the meat.

Poultry, veal and pork generally require less time to marinate than game, beef and lamb. Smaller pieces of meat take less time than larger pieces. When marinating, be sure to cover the meat or poultry completely and keep it refrigerated. Stir or turn it frequently so that the marinade can penetrate evenly.

Marinating chicken breasts

Some chefs prefer to marinate food in heavy-duty plastic food storage bags. These are useful for smaller quantities and allow for easy disposal of leftover marinades with less risk of cross-contamination. Label the bags properly and be sure to seal them tightly to prevent leaks.

RUBS AND PASTES

Additional flavors can be added to meat, fish and poultry by rubbing them with a mixture of fresh or dried herbs and spices ground together with a mortar and pestle or in a spice grinder. The flavoring blend, called a **rub,** can be used dried, or it can be mixed with a little oil, lemon juice, prepared mustard or ground fresh garlic or ginger to make a **paste** (also known as a **wet rub**). Rubs and pastes add flavor and, often, a bit of crispy crust. They do not, however, generally act as a tenderizer. They are most often used on foods that will be cooked with dry heat, especially by grilling, broiling, baking or roasting.

To apply a rub or paste, slather the mixture over the entire surface of the food to be flavored. Use enough pressure to make sure that the rub or paste adheres. (Pastes tend to adhere better than rubs.) The thicker the covering or the longer it remains on the food before cooking, the more pronounced the flavor. If the rubbed food is to be left for some time so that the flavors can be absorbed, it should be covered, refrigerated and turned from time to time.

It is best to wear disposable gloves when applying a rub or paste. Some spices can irritate or stain the skin, and cross-contamination can occur from handling raw meats.

Applying a dry rub to beef

STEEPING

Steeping is the process of soaking dry ingredients in a liquid (usually hot) in order to either soften a food or to infuse its flavor into the liquid. Spices, coffee beans and nuts are often steeped in hot milk to extract their flavors. The milk is then used to flavor other foods during cooking. For example, coffee beans can be steeped in hot milk and then strained out, with the coffee-flavored milk being used to make a custard sauce.

Steeping is also used for rehydrating dried fruits and vegetables such as raisins and mushrooms. Typically, the softened fruits or vegetables will be used in a recipe and the liquid discarded. Additional flavors can be achieved by using wine, spirits, stock or other flavored liquids as the rehydrating medium.

Note that in both situations, the steeping mixture is generally covered and removed from the heat to avoid evaporation or reduction of the liquid.

Steeping a vanilla bean and cinnamon sticks in warm milk to extract their flavors.

Steeping raisins in hot water to rehydrate.

▶ PREPARING TO COOK

Some techniques are done very close to or almost as a part of the final preparation of a dish.

BREADING AND BATTERING FOODS

BREADING

▶ **meal** (1) the coarsely ground seeds of any edible grain such as corn or oats; (2) any dried, ground substance (such as bonemeal)

A breaded item is any food that is coated with bread crumbs, cracker meal, cornmeal or other dry **meal** to protect it during cooking. Breaded foods can be seasoned before the breading is applied, or seasonings may be added to the flour, bread crumbs or meal before the main item is coated. Breaded foods are generally cooked by deep-frying or pan-frying. The breading makes a solid coating that seals during cooking and prevents the fat from coming in direct contact with the food, which would make it greasy.

▶ STANDARD BREADING PROCEDURE

For breading meats, poultry, fish, shellfish or vegetables, a three-step process is typically used. Called the **standard breading procedure,** it gives foods a relatively thick, crisp coating.

1 Pat the food dry and dredge it in seasoned flour. The flour adds seasoning to the food, helps seal it, and allows the egg wash to adhere.

2 Dip the floured food in an egg wash. The egg wash should contain whole eggs whisked together with approximately 1 tablespoon (15 milliliters) milk or water per egg. The egg wash will cause the crumbs or meal to completely coat the item and form a tight seal when the food is cooked.

3 Coat the food with bread crumbs, cracker crumbs or other dry meal. Shake off excess crumbs and place the breaded item in a pan. As additional breaded items are added to the pan, align them in a single layer; do not stack them or the breadings will get soggy and the foods will stick together.

Figure 9.1 shows the proper setup for breading foods using the standard breading procedure. The following procedure helps to bread foods more efficiently:

1 Assemble the mise en place as shown in Figure 9.1.

2 With your left hand, place the food to be breaded in the flour and coat it evenly. With the same hand, remove the floured item, shake off the excess flour and place it in the egg wash.

3 With your right hand, remove the item from the egg wash and place it in the bread crumbs or meal.

4 With your left hand, cover the item with crumbs or meal and press lightly to make sure the item is completely and evenly coated. Shake off the excess crumbs or meal and place the breaded food in the empty pan for finished product.

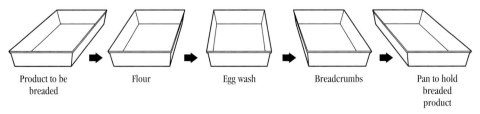

| Product to be breaded | Flour | Egg wash | Breadcrumbs | Pan to hold breaded product |

FIGURE 9.1 ▶ Setup for the standard breading procedure

Product to be battered   Flour   Floured product   Bowl of batter   Skillet or Deep fryer

FIGURE 9.2 ▶ Setup for the standard battering procedure

The key is to use one hand for the liquid ingredients and the other hand for the dry ingredients. This prevents your fingers from becoming coated with layer after layer of breading.

BATTERING

Batters, like breading, coat the food being cooked, keeping it moist and preventing it from becoming excessively greasy. Batters consist of a liquid such as water, milk or beer, combined with a starch such as flour or cornstarch. Many batters also contain a leavening agent such as baking powder or whipped egg whites. Two common batters are beer batter, which uses the beer for leavening as well as for flavor and is illustrated in the recipe for Beer Battered Onion Rings, page 650, and tempura batter, which is used in Tempura Vegetables with Dipping Sauce, page 673. Items coated with a batter are cooked immediately, usually by deep-frying or pan-frying.

▶ PROCEDURE FOR BATTERING FOODS

1 Prepare the batter.
2 Pat the food dry and dredge in flour if desired.
3 Dip the item in the batter and place it directly in the hot fat.

BLANCHING AND PARBOILING

Some foods, especially vegetables, are **blanched** or **parboiled** before being used in a recipe. To do so, they are immersed in a large quantity of a boiling or simmering liquid—oil or water—and partially cooked. This **parcooking** assists preparation (for example, it loosens peels from vegetables), removes undesirable flavors, softens firm foods, sets colors and shortens final cooking times. The only difference between blanching and parboiling is cooking time. Blanching is done quickly, usually only a few seconds. Parboiling lasts longer, usually several minutes. Foods that are blanched or parboiled in water (rather than fat) are often **shocked** or **refreshed** in ice water to halt the cooking process.

▶ **blanching** very briefly and partially cooking a food in boiling water or hot fat; used to assist preparation (for example, to loosen peels from vegetables), as part of a combination cooking method or to remove undesirable flavors

▶ **parboiling** partially cooking a food in boiling or simmering liquid; similar to blanching but the cooking time is longer

▶ **parcooking** partially cooking a food by any cooking method

▶ **shocking** also called refreshing; the technique of quickly chilling blanched or parcooked foods in ice water; prevents further cooking and sets colors

1 Blanch or parboil the food as desired in boiling water.

2 Remove the food from the cooking liquid and submerge it in ice water to refresh.

MAKING AN ICE BATH

Because of the risk of food-borne illness, it is important to cool hot foods quickly to a temperature below 41°F (4°C) before storing them in the refrigerator. An ice bath is an easy, efficient way to do so. An ice bath is also necessary for shocking or refreshing blanched or parcooked vegetables and for stopping the cooking of delicate mixtures such as custards.

An ice bath is simply a container of ice cubes and cold water. The combination of ice and water will chill foods more rapidly than a container of only ice. The food being chilled will also cool faster if it is in a metal container, rather than one made of plastic or glass.

Chilling sauce in an ice bath

CONCLUSION

As with most endeavors, consistently good cooking requires careful planning, preparation and organization. With these skills, you should be able to create a proper mise en place for most any occasion.

QUESTIONS FOR DISCUSSION

1 Explain the differences between breading and battering foods.

2 Describe the correct mise en place for the standard breading procedure.

3 Choose a dessert recipe from the baking chapters of this book and describe the proper mise en place for preparing that dish.

4 How can the concepts of mise en place be applied to activities outside of the kitchen?

THE QUALITIES OF AN EXCEPTIONAL COOK ARE AKIN
TO THOSE OF A SUCCESSFUL TIGHTROPE WALKER:
AN ABIDING PASSION FOR THE TASK, COURAGE
TO GO OUT ON A LIMB AND AN IMPECCABLE
SENSE OF BALANCE.

—Bryan Miller, American food writer

PRINCIPLES OF COOKING

AFTER STUDYING THIS
CHAPTER, YOU WILL BE
ABLE TO:

▶ understand how heat is
transferred to foods through
conduction, convection and
radiation

▶ understand how heat affects
foods

▶ understand the basic principles
of various cooking methods

Cooking can be defined as the transfer of energy from a heat source to a food. This energy alters the food's molecular structure, changing its texture, flavor, aroma and appearance. But why is food cooked at all? The obvious answer is that cooking makes food taste better. Cooking also destroys undesirable microorganisms and makes foods easier to ingest and digest.

To cook foods successfully, you must first understand the ways in which heat is transferred: conduction, convection and radiation. You should also understand what the application of heat does to the proteins, sugars, starches, water and fats in foods.

Perhaps most important, you must understand the cooking methods used to transfer heat: broiling, grilling, roasting and baking, sautéing, pan-frying, deep-frying, poaching, simmering, boiling, steaming, braising and stewing. Each method is used for many types of food, so you will be applying one or more of them every time you cook. The cooking method you select gives the finished product a specific texture, appearance, aroma and flavor. A thorough understanding of the basic procedures involved in each cooking method helps you produce consistent, high-quality products.

This chapter describes each of the cooking methods and uses photographs to outline their general procedures. Detailed procedures and recipes applying these methods to specific foods are found in subsequent chapters.

▶ HEAT TRANSFER

Heat is a type of energy. When a substance gets hot, its molecules have absorbed energy, which causes the molecules to vibrate rapidly, expand and bounce off one another. As the molecules move, they collide with nearby molecules, causing a transfer of heat energy. The faster the molecules within a substance move, the higher its temperature. This is true whether the substance is air, water, an aluminum pot or a sirloin steak.

Heat energy may be transferred *to* foods via conduction, convection or radiation. Heat then travels *through* foods by conduction. Only heat is transferred—cold is simply the absence of heat, so cold cannot be transferred from one substance to another.

CONDUCTION

Conduction is the most straightforward means of heat transfer. It is simply the movement of heat from one item to another through direct contact. For example, when the flame of a gas burner touches the bottom of a sauté pan, heat is conducted to the pan. The metal of the pan then conducts heat to the surface of the food lying in that pan.

Conduction

Convection

Infrared Radiation

Microwave Radiation

FIGURE 10.1 ▶ Arrows indicate heat patterns during conduction, convection and radiation

Some materials conduct heat better than others. Water is a better conductor of heat than air. This explains why a potato cooks much faster in boiling water than in an oven, and why you cannot place your hand in boiling water at a temperature of 212°F (100°C), but can place your hand, at least very briefly, into a 400°F (200°C) oven. Generally, metals are good conductors (as discussed in Chapter 5, Tools and Equipment, copper and aluminum are the best conductors), while liquids and gases are poor conductors.

Conduction is a relatively slow method of heat transfer because there must be physical contact to transfer energy from one molecule to adjacent molecules. Consider what happens when a metal spoon is placed in a pot of simmering soup. At first the spoon handle remains cool. Gradually, however, heat travels up the handle, making it warmer and warmer, until it becomes too hot to touch.

Conduction is important in all cooking methods because it is responsible for the movement of heat from the surface of a food to its interior. As the molecules near the food's exterior gather energy, they move more and more rapidly. As they move, they conduct heat to the molecules nearby, thus transferring heat *through* the food (from the exterior of the item to the interior).

In conventional heating methods (nonmicrowave), the heat source causes food molecules to react largely from the surface inward so that layers of molecules heat in succession. This produces a range of temperatures within the food, which means that the outside can brown and form a crust long before the interior is noticeably warmer. That is why a steak can be fully cooked on the outside but still rare on the inside.

CONVECTION

Convection refers to the transfer of heat through a fluid, which may be liquid or gas. Convection is actually a combination of conduction and a mixing in which molecules in a fluid (whether air, water or fat) move from a warmer area to a cooler one. There are two types of convection: natural and mechanical.

Natural convection occurs because of the tendency of warm liquids and gases to rise while cooler ones fall. This causes a constant natural circulation of heat. For example, when a pot of stock is placed over a gas burner, the molecules at the bottom of the pot are warmed. These molecules rise while cooler, heavier molecules sink. Upon reaching the pot's bottom, the cooler molecules are warmed and begin to rise. This ongoing cycle creates currents within the stock, and these currents distribute the heat throughout the stock.

Mechanical convection relies on fans or stirring to circulate heat more quickly and evenly. This explains why foods heat faster and more evenly when stirred. Convection ovens are equipped with fans to increase the circulation of air currents, thus speeding up the cooking process. But even conventional ovens (that is, not convection ovens) rely on the natural circulation patterns of heated air to transfer heat energy to items being baked or roasted.

RADIATION

Unlike conduction and convection, **radiation** does not require physical contact between the heat source and the food being cooked. Instead, energy is transferred by waves of heat or light striking the food. Two kinds of radiant heat are used in the kitchen: infrared and microwave.

Infrared cooking uses an electric or ceramic element heated to such a high temperature that it gives off waves of radiant heat that cook the food. Radiant heat waves travel at the speed of light in any direction (unlike convection heat, which only rises) until they are absorbed by a food. Infrared cooking is commonly used with toasters and broilers. The glowing coals of a fire are another example of radiant heat.

Microwave cooking relies on radiation generated by a special oven to penetrate the food, where it agitates water molecules, creating friction and heat. This energy then spreads throughout the food by conduction (and by convection in liquids). Microwave cooking is much faster than other methods because energy penetrates the food up to a depth of several centimeters, setting all water molecules in motion at the same time. Heat is generated quickly and uniformly throughout the food. Microwave cooking does not brown foods, however, and often gives meats a dry, mushy texture, making microwave ovens an unacceptable replacement for traditional ovens.

Because microwave radiation affects only water molecules, a completely waterless material (such as a plate) will not get hot. Any warmth felt in a plate used when microwaving food results from heat being conducted from the food to the plate.

Microwave cooking requires the use of certain types of utensils, usually heat-resistant glass or microwavable plastic. But even heat-resistant glass can shatter and is not recommended for professional use. The aluminum and stainless steel utensils most common in professional kitchens cannot be used because metal deflects microwaves, and this can damage the oven.

▶ THE EFFECTS OF HEAT

Foods are composed of proteins, carbohydrates (starches and sugars), water and fats, plus small amounts of minerals and vitamins. Changes in the shape, texture, color and flavor of foods may occur when heat is applied to each of these nutrients. By understanding these changes and learning to control them, you will be able to prepare foods with the characteristics desired. Although volumes are written on these subjects, it is sufficient for you to know the following processes as you begin your study of cooking.

PROTEINS COAGULATE

The proper term for the cooking of proteins is **coagulation.** Proteins are large, complex molecules found in every living cell, plant as well as animal. Coagulation refers to the irreversible transformation of proteins from a liquid or semi-liquid state to a solid state. As proteins cook, they lose moisture, shrink and become firm. Common examples of coagulation are the firming of meat fibers during cooking, egg whites changing from a clear liquid to a white solid when heated and the setting of the structure of wheat proteins (known as gluten) in bread during baking. Most proteins complete coagulation at 160°F to 185°F (71°C to 85°C).

STARCHES GELATINIZE

Gelatinization is the proper term for the cooking of starches. Starches are complex carbohydrates present in plants and grains such as potatoes, wheat, rice and corn. When a mixture of starch and liquid is heated, remarkable changes occur. The starch granules absorb water, causing them to swell, soften and clarify slightly. The liquid visibly thickens because of the water being absorbed into the starch granules and the granules themselves swelling to occupy more space.

Gelatinization occurs gradually over a range of temperatures—150°F to 212°F (66°C to 100°C)—depending on the type of starch used. Starch gelatinization affects not only sauces or liquids to which starches are added for the express purpose of thickening, but also any mixture of starch and liquid that is heated. For example, the flour (a starch) in cake batter gelatinizes by absorbing the water from eggs, milk or other ingredients as the batter bakes. This causes part of the firming and drying associated with baked goods.

SUGARS CARAMELIZE

The process of cooking sugars is properly known as **caramelization.** Sugars are simple carbohydrates used by all plants and animals to store energy. As sugars cook, they gradually turn brown and change flavor. Caramelized sugar is used in many sauces, candies and desserts. But caramelized sugar is also partly responsible for the flavor and color of bread crusts and the browning of meats and vegetables. In fact, the process of caramelization is responsible for most flavors we associate with cooking.

Sucrose (common table sugar) begins to brown at about 338°F (170°C). The naturally occurring sugars in other foods, such as maltose, lactose and fructose, also caramelize, but at varying temperatures. Because high temperatures are required for browning (that is, caramelizing), most foods will brown only on the outside and only through the application of dry heat. Because water cannot be heated above 212°F (100°C), foods cooked with moist-heat methods do not get hot enough to caramelize. Foods cooked with dry-heat methods, including those using fats, will reach the high temperatures at which browning occurs.

WATER EVAPORATES

All foods contain some water. Some foods, especially eggs, milk and leafy vegetables, are almost entirely water. Even as much as 75 percent of raw meat is water. As the internal temperature of a food increases, water molecules move faster and faster until the water turns to a gas (steam) and vaporizes. This **evaporation** of water is responsible for the drying of foods during cooking.

FATS MELT

Fat is an energy source for the plant or animal in which it is stored. Fats are smooth, greasy substances that do not dissolve in water. Their texture varies from very firm to liquid. Oils are simply fats that remain liquid at room temperature. Fats **melt** when heated; that is, they gradually soften, then liquefy. Fats will not evaporate. Most fats can be heated to very high temperatures without burning, so they can be used as a cooking medium to brown foods.

▶ COOKING METHODS

Foods can be cooked in air, fat, water or steam. These are collectively known as **cooking media.** There are two general types of cooking methods: dry heat and moist heat.

Dry-heat cooking methods are those using air or fat. They are broiling, grilling, roasting and baking, sautéing, pan-frying and deep-frying. Foods cooked using dry-heat cooking methods have a rich flavor caused by browning.

Moist-heat cooking methods are those using water or steam. They are poaching, simmering, boiling and steaming. Moist-heat cooking methods are used to tenderize and emphasize the natural flavors of food.

Other cooking methods employ a combination of dry- and moist-heat cooking methods. The two most significant of these **combination cooking methods** are braising and stewing.

Each of these cooking methods can be applied to a wide variety of foods—meats, fish, vegetables and even pastries. Here we describe each of the cooking methods and use photographs to outline their general procedures. Detailed procedures and recipes applying these methods to specific foods are found in subsequent chapters.

Table 10.1 COOKING METHODS

METHOD	MEDIUM	EQUIPMENT
Dry-Heat Cooking Methods		
Broiling	Air	Overhead broiler, salamander, rotisserie
Grilling	Air	Grill
Roasting	Air	Oven
Baking	Air	Oven
Sautéing	Fat	Stove top
Pan-frying	Fat	Stove top, tilt skillet
Deep-frying	Fat	Deep-fat fryer
Moist-Heat Cooking Methods		
Poaching	Water or other liquid	Stove top, oven, steam-jacketed kettle, tilt skillet
Simmering	Water or other liquid	Stove top, steam-jacketed kettle, tilt skillet
Boiling	Water or other liquid	Stove top, steam-jacketed kettle, tilt skillet
Steaming	Steam	Stove top, convection steamer
Combination Cooking Methods		
Braising	Fat, then liquid	Stove top, oven, tilt skillet
Stewing	Fat, then liquid	Stove top, oven, tilt skillet

DRY-HEAT COOKING METHODS

Cooking by dry heat is the process of applying heat either directly, by subjecting the food to the heat of a flame, or indirectly, by surrounding the food with heated air or heated fat.

BROILING

Broiling uses radiant heat from an overhead source to cook foods. The temperature at the heat source can be as high as 2000°F (1093°C). The food to be broiled is placed on a preheated metal grate. Radiant heat from overhead cooks the food, while the hot grate below marks it with attractive crosshatch marks.

Delicate foods that may be damaged by being placed directly on a metal grate or foods on which crosshatch marks are not desirable may be placed on a preheated heatproof platter and then placed under the broiler. Cooking will take place through indirect heat from the preheated platter as well as by direct heat from the broiler's overhead heat source.

► PROCEDURE FOR BROILING FOODS

1 Heat the broiler.

2 If necessary, use a wire brush to remove any charred or burnt particles that may be stuck to the broiler grate. The grate can be wiped with a lightly oiled towel to remove any remaining particles and to help season it.

3 Cut, trim or otherwise prepare the food to be broiled. Marinate, rub or season it, as desired. Many foods can be brushed lightly with oil to keep them from sticking to the grate.

4 Place the food in the broiler, presentation side down. If necessary, use tongs to turn or flip the item without piercing its surface.

1 Preheat the grate under the broiler, then pull it out and place the food on the hot grate, presentation side down. If the item is oblong, place it at a 45-degree angle to the bars on the cooking grate. Slide the grate back under the broiler and cook long enough for the food to develop lines where it touches the grate. Pull the sliding grate out again and turn the food over at a 90-degree angle, working from left to right.

2 Pull the sliding grate out of the broiler to turn the food as necessary in order to cook it evenly. Note the handle visible on the right, which can be used to adjust the distance between the grate and the heat source.

3 Remove the cooked item from the broiler grate.

5 Cook the food to the desired degree of doneness while developing the proper surface color. To do so, adjust the position of the item on the broiler, or adjust the distance between the grate and heat source. Doneness is often determined by touch, internal temperature or specific visual cues (for example, clear juices running from poultry).

GRILLING

Although similar to broiling, grilling uses a heat source located beneath the cooking surface. Grills may be electric or gas, or they can burn wood or charcoal, which will add a smoky flavor to the food. Specific woods such as mesquite, hickory or vine clippings can be used to create special flavors. Grilled foods are often identified by crosshatch markings.

▶ PROCEDURE FOR GRILLING FOODS

1 Heat the grill.

2 If necessary, use a wire brush to remove any charred or burnt particles that may be stuck to the grill grate. The grate can be wiped with a lightly oiled towel to remove any remaining particles and to help season it.

3 Cut, trim or otherwise prepare the food to be grilled. Marinate, rub or season it, as desired. Many foods can be brushed lightly with oil to keep them from sticking to the grate.

4 Place the food on the grill, presentation side down. If practical, turn the food to produce the attractive crosshatch marks associated with grilling. Use tongs to turn or flip the item without piercing its surface.

5 Cook the food to the desired degree of doneness while developing the proper surface color. To do so, adjust the position of the item on the grill, or adjust the distance between the grate and heat source. Doneness is often determined by touch, internal temperature or specific visual cues (for example, clear juices running from poultry).

1 Decide which side of the grilled food will be presented face up to the customer. Place the food on the hot grill with this side facing down. If the item is oblong, place it at a 45-degree angle to the bars on the cooking grate. Cook long enough for the food to develop dark charred lines where it touches the grate.

2 Rotate the food 90 degrees and allow it to cook long enough for the grates to char it to the same extent as in Step 1.

3 Turn the food over and finish cooking it. It is usually unnecessary to create the crosshatch markings on the reverse side since the customer will not see this side.

ROASTING AND BAKING

Roasting and baking are the processes of surrounding a food with dry, heated air in a closed environment. The term roasting is usually applied to meats and poultry, while baking is used when referring to fish, fruits, vegetables, starches, breads or pastry items. Heat is transferred by convection to the food's surface, and then penetrates the food by conduction. The surface dehydrates, and the food browns from caramelization, completing the cooking process.

Poêléing (pwah-lay-ing) is a cooking method similar to both roasting and braising. The food is cooked in an oven, but in a covered pot with aromatic vegetables and bacon fat or butter, so that it steams in its own juices. Also known as butter roasting, the French poêlé technique is perhaps most similar to pot-roasting. Like a typical roasted dish (and unlike a typical braised dish), this method is used for tender cuts of meats and poultry that do not require long, slow cooking, and no additional liquid is added during cooking. The meat or poultry can first be browned in hot fat or it can be browned toward the end of cooking by removing the lid of the cooking vessel. Doneness is determined using the same techniques as those used for roasting. The meat or poultry is usually served with a sauce made from the pan juices mixed with a liquid and finished in the same way as a sauce for a braised dish. A recipe for Poêlé of Chicken with Pearl Onions and Mushrooms is given on page 429.

▶ PROCEDURE FOR ROASTING OR BAKING FOODS

1 Preheat the oven.

2 Cut, trim or otherwise prepare the food to be roasted or baked. Marinate or season as desired. Brush with oil or butter, as appropriate.

3 Place the food on a rack or directly in a roasting pan or baking dish.

4 Roast the food, generally uncovered, at the desired temperature. **Baste** as necessary.

5 Cook to the desired internal temperature or doneness, remembering that many foods will undergo **carryover cooking** after they are removed from the oven.

▶ **baste** to moisten foods during cooking (usually grilling, broiling or roasting) with melted fat, pan drippings, a sauce or other liquids to prevent drying and to add flavor

▶ **carryover cooking** the cooking that occurs after a food is removed from a heat source; it is accomplished by the residual heat remaining in the food

1 Season the item to be roasted, arrange it in an uncovered pan and place it in a preheated oven.

2 Use a thermometer to check the internal temperature of the item being roasted.

SAUTÉING

Sautéing is a dry-heat cooking method that uses conduction to transfer heat from a hot sauté pan to food with the aid of a small amount of fat. Heat then penetrates the food through conduction. High temperatures are used to sauté, and the foods are usually cut into small pieces to promote even cooking.

To sauté foods properly, begin by heating a sauté pan on the stove top, then add a small amount of fat. The fat should just cover the bottom of the pan. Heat the fat to the point where it just begins to smoke. The food to be cooked should be as dry as possible when it is added to the pan to promote browning and to prevent excessive spattering. Place the food in the pan in a single layer. (The pan should be just large enough to hold the food in a single layer; a pan that is too large may cause the fat to burn.) The heat should be adjusted so that the food cooks thoroughly; it should not be so hot that the outside of the food burns before the inside is cooked. The food should be turned or tossed periodically to develop the proper color. Larger items should be turned using tongs without piercing the surface. Smaller items are often turned by using the sauteuse's sloped sides to flip them back on top of themselves. When tossing sautéed foods, keep the pan in contact with the heat source as much as possible to prevent it from cooling. Sautéing sometimes includes the preparation of a sauce directly in the pan after the main item has been removed.

Stir-frying is a variation of sautéing. A wok is used instead of a sauté pan; the curved sides and rounded bottom of the wok diffuse heat efficiently and facilitate tossing and stirring. Otherwise, stir-frying procedures are the same as those outlined for sautéing and will not be discussed separately here.

▶ PROCEDURE FOR SAUTÉING FOODS

1 Cut, pound or otherwise prepare the food to be sautéed. Season and dredge it in flour, if desired.

2 Heat a sauté pan and add enough fat (typically, oil or clarified butter) to just cover the pan's bottom.

3 Add the food to the sauté pan in a single layer, presentation side down. Do not crowd the pan.

4 Adjust the temperature so that the food's exterior browns properly without burning and the interior cooks. The heat should be high enough to complete the cooking process before the food begins to stew in its own juices.

5 Turn or toss the food as needed. Avoid burns by not splashing hot fat.

6 Cook until done. Doneness is usually determined by timing or touch.

1 Heat a small amount of oil in the sauté pan before adding the food.

2 The sloped edge of the pan can be used to toss the food. The item being sautéed should be cooked quickly.

PAN-FRYING

Pan-frying shares similarities with both sautéing and deep-frying. It is a dry-heat cooking method in which heat is transferred by conduction from the pan to the food, using a moderate amount of fat. Heat is also transferred to the food from the hot fat by convection. Foods to be pan-fried are usually coated in breading. This forms a seal that keeps the food moist and prevents the hot fat from penetrating the food and causing it to become greasy. (Breading procedures are explained in Chapter 9, Mise en Place.)

To pan-fry foods properly, first heat the fat in a sauté pan. Use enough fat so that when the food to be cooked is added, the fat comes one-third to halfway up the item being cooked. The fat should be at a temperature somewhat lower than that used for sautéing; it should not smoke but should be hot enough so that when the food is added it crackles and spatters from the rapid vaporization of moisture. If the temperature is too low, the food will absorb excessive amounts of fat; if it is too high, the food will burn on the outside before the interior is fully cooked. When the food is properly browned on one side, use tongs to turn it without piercing. Always turn the food away from you to prevent being burned by any fat that may splash. When the food is fully cooked, remove it from the pan, drain it on absorbent paper and serve it immediately.

▶ PROCEDURE FOR PAN-FRYING FOODS

1 Cut, pound or otherwise prepare the food to be pan-fried; then bread, batter or flour it as desired.

2 Heat a moderate amount of fat or oil in a heavy pan—usually enough to cover the item one-third to halfway up its sides.

3 Add the food to the pan, being careful not to splash the hot fat.

4 Fry the food on one side until brown. Using tongs, turn and brown the other side. Generally, pan-fried foods are fully cooked when they are well browned on both sides.

5 Remove the food from the pan and drain it on absorbent paper before serving.

1 Use tongs to carefully place the item being pan-fried into a moderate amount of hot oil.

2 Turn the item to brown the other side.

3 Drain the cooked item on absorbent paper.

DEEP-FRYING

Deep-frying is a dry-heat cooking method that uses conduction and convection to transfer heat to food submerged in hot fat. Although conceptually similar to boiling, deep-frying is not a moist-heat cooking method because the liquid fat

▶ **recovery time** the length of time it takes a cooking medium such as fat or water to return to the desired cooking temperature after food is submerged in it

contains no water. A key difference between boiling and deep-frying is the temperature of the cooking medium. The boiling point, 212°F (100°C), is the hottest temperature at which food can be cooked in water. At this temperature, most foods require a long cooking period and surface sugars cannot caramelize. With deep-frying, temperatures up to 400°F (200°C) are used. These high temperatures cook food more quickly and allow the food's surface to brown.

Foods to be deep-fried are usually first coated in batter or breading. This preserves moisture and prevents the food from absorbing excessive quantities of fat. Foods to be deep-fried should be of a size and shape that allows them to float freely in the fat. Foods that are to be deep-fried together should be of uniform size and shape. Delicately flavored foods should not be deep-fried in the same fat used for more strongly flavored ones, as the former could develop an odd taste from residual flavors left in the fat. Deep-fried foods should cook thoroughly while developing an attractive deep golden-brown color.

Today, most deep-frying is done in specially designed commercial fryers. These deep-fat fryers have built-in thermostats, making temperature control more precise. Deep-frying foods in a saucepan on the stove top is discouraged because it is both difficult and dangerous. **Recovery time** is usually very slow, and temperatures are difficult to control. Also, the fat can spill easily, leading to injuries or creating a fire hazard.

To deep-fry food, first heat the fat or oil to a temperature between 325°F and 375°F (160°C and 190°C). The cooking medium's temperature can be adjusted within this range to allow the interior of thicker foods or frozen foods to cook before their surfaces become too dark. The fat must be hot enough to quickly seal the surface of the food so that it does not become excessively greasy, yet it should not be so hot that the food's surface burns before the interior is cooked.

There are two methods of deep-frying: the basket method and the swimming method. The **basket method** uses a basket to hold foods that are breaded, are individually quick-frozen or otherwise will not tend to stick together during cooking. The basket is removed from the fryer and filled as much as two-thirds full of product. (Do not fill the basket while it is hanging over the fat, as this allows unnecessary salt and food particles to fall into the fat, shortening its life.) The filled basket is then submerged in the hot fat. When cooking is completed, the basket is used to remove the foods from the fat and hold them while excess fat drains off.

A variation on this procedure is the **double-basket method.** It is used because many foods float as they deep-fry. This may produce undesirable results because the portion of the food not submerged may not cook. To prevent this and to promote even cooking, a second basket is placed over the food held in the first basket, keeping the food submerged in the fat.

Most battered foods initially sink to the bottom when placed in hot fat, then rise to the top as they cook. Because they would stick to a basket, the **swimming method** is used for these foods. With the swimming method, battered foods are carefully dropped directly into the hot fat. (Baskets are not used.) They will rise to the top as they cook. When the surface that is in contact with the fat is properly browned, the food is turned over with a spider or a pair of tongs so that it can cook evenly on both sides. When done, the product is removed and drained, again using a spider or tongs.

The basket method of deep-frying.

The double-basket method of deep-frying.

The swimming method of deep-frying

▶ PROCEDURE FOR DEEP-FRYING FOODS

1 Cut, trim or otherwise prepare the food to be deep-fried. Bread or batter it, as desired.

2 Heat the oil or fat to the desired temperature.

3 Using either the basket method or swimming method, carefully place the food in the hot fat.

4 Deep-fry the food until done. Doneness is usually determined by timing, surface color or sampling.

5 Remove the deep-fried food from the fryer and hold it over the cooking fat, allowing the excess fat to drain off.

6 Transfer the food to a hotel pan either lined with absorbent paper or fitted with a rack.

7 If the deep-fried items are to be held for later service, place them under a heat lamp; steam tables will not keep fried foods properly hot.

MOIST-HEAT COOKING METHODS

Cooking with moist heat is the process of applying heat to food by submerging it directly into a hot liquid or by exposing it to steam.

POACHING

Poaching is a moist-heat cooking method that uses convection to transfer heat from a liquid to a food. It is most often associated with delicately flavored foods that do not require lengthy cooking times to tenderize them, such as eggs, fruit or fish.

For poaching, the food is placed in a liquid held at temperatures between 160°F and 180°F (71°C and 82°C). The surface of the liquid should show only slight movement, but no bubbles. It is important to maintain the desired temperature throughout the cooking process. Do not allow the liquid to reach a boil, since the agitation will cause meats to become tough and stringy and will destroy tender foods such as fresh fruit or fish.

The flavor of the poaching liquid strongly affects the ultimate flavor of the finished product, so stock, court bouillon or broth is generally used. The liquid used to poach a food is sometimes used to make an accompanying sauce.

There are two methods of poaching: submersion poaching and shallow poaching. For **submersion poaching,** the food is completely covered with the cooking liquid. There should not be too much excess liquid, however, as this could leach away much of the food's flavor. Nor should there be too little, as that could leave a portion of the food exposed, preventing it from cooking.

For **shallow poaching,** the food is placed in just enough liquid to come approximately halfway up its sides. The liquid, called a **cuisson,** is brought to a simmer on the stove top. The pan is then covered with a piece of buttered parchment paper or a lid, and cooking is completed either on the stove top or in the oven. Shallow poaching combines aspects of poaching and steaming.

Poaching (160°F–180°F/71°C–82°C)

Simmering (185°F–205°F/85°C–96°C)

▶ PROCEDURE FOR POACHING FOODS

1 Cut, trim or otherwise prepare the food to be poached.

2 Bring an adequate amount of cooking liquid to the desired starting temperature. (For some items, the cooking liquid is first brought to a boil and then reduced to the poaching temperature.) Place the food in the liquid.

3 For submersion poaching, the liquid should completely cover the food.

4 For shallow poaching, the liquid should come approximately halfway up the side of the food. If shallow poaching, cover the pan with a piece of buttered parchment paper or a lid.

5 Maintaining the proper temperature, poach the food to the desired doneness in the oven or on the stove top. Doneness is generally determined by timing, internal temperature or tenderness.

6 Remove the food and hold it for service in a portion of the cooking liquid or, using an ice bath, cool it in the cooking liquid.

7 The cooking liquid can sometimes be used to prepare an accompanying sauce or reserved for use in other dishes.

Boiling (212°F/100°C)

1 Season the poaching liquid as desired and bring it to the correct temperature.

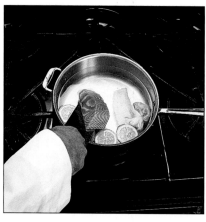

2 Carefully place the food item into the poaching liquid.

3 Remove the cooked food from the poaching liquid.

SIMMERING

Simmering is another moist-heat cooking method that uses convection to transfer heat from a liquid to a food. It is often associated with foods that need to be tenderized through long, slow, moist cooking, such as less tender cuts of meat. Properly simmered foods should be moist and very tender. For simmering, the food is submerged in a liquid held at temperatures between 185°F and 205°F (85°C and 96°C). Because simmering temperatures are slightly higher than those used for poaching, there should be more action on the liquid's surface, with a few air bubbles breaking through.

As with poaching, the liquid used for simmering has a great effect on the food's flavor. Be sure to use a well-flavored stock or broth and to add mirepoix, herbs and seasonings as needed.

▶ PROCEDURE FOR SIMMERING FOODS

1 Cut, trim or otherwise prepare the food to be simmered.

2 Bring an adequate amount of the cooking liquid to the appropriate temperature (some foods, especially smoked or cured items, are started in a cold liquid). There should be enough liquid to cover the food completely.

3 Add the food to the simmering liquid.

1 The item being simmered should be fully submerged in the seasoned liquid.

2 Remove the cooked item from the liquid.

4 Maintaining the proper cooking temperature throughout the process, simmer the food to the desired doneness. Doneness is generally determined by timing or tenderness.

5 Remove the item and hold it for service in a portion of the cooking liquid or, using an ice bath, cool the food in its cooking liquid.

BOILING

Boiling is another moist-heat cooking method that uses the process of convection to transfer heat from a liquid to a food. Boiling uses large amounts of rapidly bubbling liquid to cook foods. The turbulent waters and the relatively high temperatures cook foods more quickly than do poaching or simmering. Few foods, however, are cooked by true boiling. Most "boiled" meats are actually simmered. Even "hard-boiled" eggs are really only simmered. Starches such as pasta and potatoes are among the only types of food that are truly boiled.

Under normal atmospheric pressure at sea level, water boils at 212°F (100°C). The addition of other ingredients or a change in atmospheric pressure can change the boiling point, however. As altitude increases, the boiling point decreases because of the drop in atmospheric pressure. For every 1000 feet above sea level, the boiling point of water drops 2°F (1°C). In the mile-high city of Denver, for example, water boils at 203°F (95°C). Because the boiling temperature is lower, it will take longer to cook foods in Denver than in, for example, Miami.

The addition of alcohol also lowers the boiling point of water because alcohol boils at about 175°F (80°C). In contrast, the addition of salt, sugar or other substances raises the boiling point slightly. This means that foods cooked in salted water cook faster because the boiling point is one or two degrees higher than normal.

Use as much water as practical when boiling food. Whenever food is added to boiling water, it lowers the water's temperature. The greater the amount of water, however, the faster it will return to the boil.

1 Bring the cooking liquid to a full boil. When the item being cooked is added to the liquid, its temperature will fall.

▶ PROCEDURE FOR BOILING FOODS

1 Bring an appropriate amount of a liquid to a boil over high heat. Add oil or seasonings, if desired.

2 Add the food to be boiled to the rapidly boiling water. Bring the liquid back to a boil and adjust the temperature to maintain the boil.

3 Cook until done. Doneness is usually determined by timing or texture.

4 Remove the boiled food from the cooking liquid, draining any excess liquid.

5 Serve the boiled food immediately. Some boiled foods can be refreshed in cold water and held for later service.

2 After a boiled item such as pasta is cooked, it may be drained through a colander.

STEAMING

Steaming is a moist-heat cooking method that uses the process of convection to transfer heat from the steam to the food being cooked. It is most often associated with tender, delicately flavored foods, such as fish and vegetables, which do not require long cooking times. Steaming tends to enhance a food's natural flavor and helps to retain its nutrients. Properly steamed foods should be moist and tender. Additional flavor can be introduced by adding wine, stock, aromatics, spices or herbs to the liquid used as the steaming medium. The steaming liquid can also often be used to make a sauce to be served with the steamed food.

The food to be steamed is usually placed in a basket or rack above a boiling liquid. The food should not touch the liquid; it should be positioned so that the steam can circulate around it. (Some foods, such as shellfish and ears of corn,

Table 10.2	MOIST-HEAT COOKING METHODS		
METHOD	**LIQUID'S TEMPERATURE**	**LIQUID'S CONDITION**	**USES**
Poaching	160–180°F 71–82°C	Liquid moves slightly but no bubbles	Eggs, fish, fruits
Simmering	185–205°F 85–96°C	Small bubbles break through the liquid's surface	Meats, stews, chicken
Boiling	212°F 100°C	Large bubbles and rapid movement	Vegetables, pasta
Steaming	212°F or higher 100°C or higher	Food is in contact only with the steam generated by a boiling liquid	Vegetables, fish, shellfish

however, can be placed directly in a shallow pool of boiling water.) A lid should be placed on the steaming pot to trap the steam and also create a slight pressure within the pot, which speeds the cooking process.

Another type of steaming uses a convection steamer. Convection steamers use pressurized steam to cook food very quickly in an enclosed chamber. Convection steamer cooking does not result in a flavored liquid that can be used to make a sauce.

Steamed foods should be served immediately. If held for later service, they should be refreshed and refrigerated until used.

▶ PROCEDURE FOR STEAMING FOODS

1 Cut, trim or otherwise prepare the food to be steamed.
2 If a convection steamer is not being used, prepare a steaming liquid and bring it to a boil in a covered pan or double boiler.
3 Place the food to be steamed on a rack, in a basket or on a perforated pan in a single layer. Do not crowd the items. Place the rack, basket or pan over the boiling liquid.
4 Alternatively, place the food in a shallow pool of the cooking liquid.
5 Cover the cooking assemblage and cook to the desired doneness. Doneness is usually determined by timing, color or tenderness.

1 Trim items before steaming them so that they cook evenly.

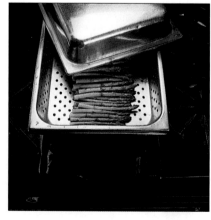

2 A perforated hotel pan can be set over a deeper pan of water, covered and used as a steamer.

COMBINATION COOKING METHODS

Some cooking methods employ both dry-heat and moist-heat cooking techniques. The two principal combination methods are braising and stewing. In both methods, the first step is usually to brown the main item using dry heat. The second step is to complete cooking by simmering the food in a liquid. Combination methods are often used for less tender but flavorful cuts of meat as well as for poultry and some vegetables.

BRAISING

Braised foods benefit from the best qualities of both dry- and moist-heat cooking methods. Foods to be braised are usually large pieces that are first browned in a small amount of fat at high temperatures. As with sautéing, heat is transferred from the pan to the food mainly by the process of conduction. Vegetables and seasonings are added, and enough sauce or liquid is added to come one-third to halfway up the item being cooked. The pan is covered, and the heat is reduced. The food is then cooked at low heat, using a combination of simmering and steaming to transfer heat from the liquid (conduction) and the air (convection) to the food. This can be done on the stove top or in the oven. A long, slow cooking period helps tenderize the main item. Braised foods are usually served with a sauce made from the cooking liquid.

1 The item being braised is first browned in fat.

▶ PROCEDURE FOR BRAISING FOODS

1 Cut, trim or otherwise prepare the food to be braised. Dredge it in flour, if desired.

2 Heat a small amount of fat in a heavy pan.

3 Sear the food on all sides. Some foods—notably, meats—should be removed from the pan after they are seared.

4 Add any other ingredients and sauté.

5 Add flour or roux, if used.

6 Add the cooking liquid; it should partially cover the food being braised.

7 Add aromatics and seasonings.

8 If the principal item was removed, return it to the pan.

9 Cover the pan and bring the cooking liquid to a simmer. Cook slowly, either on the stove top or in an oven at 250°F–300°F (120°C–150°C). Baste and turn the food as needed.

10 When the principal item is cooked, remove it from the pan and hold it in a warm place.

11 Prepare a sauce from the braising liquid if desired. This may be done by reducing the liquid on the stove top to intensify its flavors. If the food was braised in an unthickened stock, the stock may now be thickened using a roux, arrowroot or cornstarch. Strain the sauce or, if desired, purée the mirepoix and other ingredients and return them to the sauce. Adjust the sauce's consistency as desired.

2 Liquid is added to the pan.

STEWING

Stewing also uses a combination of dry- and moist-heat cooking methods. Stewing is most often associated with smaller pieces of food that are first cooked either by browning them in a small amount of fat or oil or by blanching them in a liquid. Cooking is then finished in a liquid or sauce. Stewed foods have enough liquid added to cover them completely and are simmered at a constant temperature until tender. Cooking time is generally shorter for stewing than for braising because the main items are smaller.

3 The item can be basted with the liquid during cooking.

▶ PROCEDURE FOR STEWING FOODS

1 Trim and cut the food to be stewed into small, uniform-sized pieces. Dredge the pieces in flour, if desired.

2 Heat a small amount of fat in a heavy pan. Then sear the food on all sides developing color as desired.

3 Add any other ingredients and sauté.

4 Add flour or roux.

5 Gradually add the cooking liquid, stirring to prevent lumps. The liquid should completely cover the principal items.

6 Bring the stew to the appropriate temperature. Cover and place in the oven at 250°F–300°F (120°C–150°C) or continue to simmer on the stove top until the principal items are tender.

7 Remove the principal items and hold them in a warm place.

8 Thicken the sauce as desired.

9 Return the principal items to the stew. If not added during the cooking process, vegetables and other garnishes may be cooked separately and added to the finished stew.

1 The item being stewed is first browned in a small amount of fat.

2 Flour is added to make a roux.

3 Liquid is added to the pan.

4 Degrease the finished stew as necessary.

CONCLUSION

Cooking is the transfer of heat energy to foods by conduction, convection or radiation. Cooking changes the molecular structure of certain nutrients. When heat is applied, proteins coagulate, starches gelatinize, sugars caramelize, fats melt and water evaporates. Foods can be cooked using a variety of methods. Some use dry heat: broiling, grilling, roasting and baking, sautéing, pan-frying and deep-frying. Others use moist heat: poaching, simmering, boiling and steaming. Still others use a combination of the two: braising and stewing. The method used affects the texture, appearance and flavor of the cooked foods. You must understand these principles in order to ensure that foods are cooked properly.

1 Describe the differences between conduction and convection. Identify four cooking methods that rely on both conduction and convection to heat foods. Explain your choices.

2 Identify two cooking methods that rely on infrared heat. What is the principal difference between these methods?

3 At the same temperature, will a food cook faster in a convection oven or a conventional oven? Explain your answer.

4 Describe the process of caramelization and its significance in food preparation. Will a braised food have a caramelized surface? Explain your answer.

5 Describe the process of coagulation and its significance in food preparation. Will a pure fat coagulate if heated? Explain your answer.

6 Describe the process of gelatinization and its significance in food preparation. Will a pure fat gelatinize? Explain your answer.

7 Name and describe two styles of deep-frying.

WHAT I LOVE ABOUT COOKING IS THAT AFTER A HARD DAY, THERE IS SOMETHING COMFORTING ABOUT THE FACT THAT IF YOU MELT BUTTER AND ADD FLOUR, THEN HOT STOCK, IT WILL GET THICK! IT'S A SURE THING. IT'S A SURE THING IN A WORLD WHERE NOTHING IS SURE!

—Nora Ephron, American author and filmmaker
  (1941–)

11

STOCKS
AND SAUCES

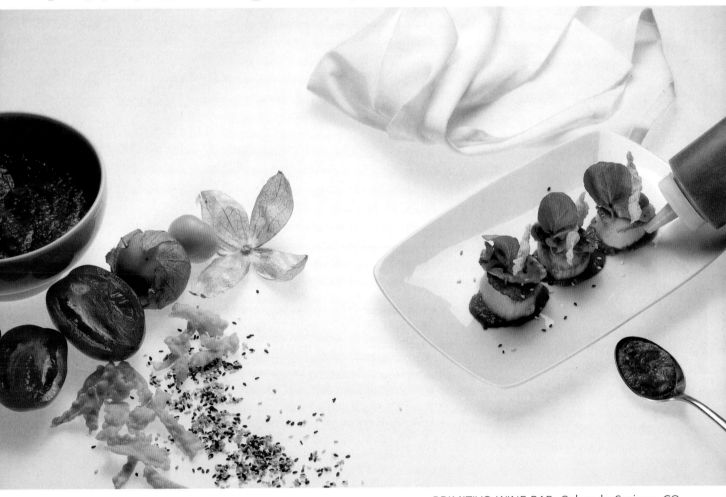

PRIMITIVO WINE BAR, Colorado Springs, CO
John Broening, Executive Chef

AFTER STUDYING THIS
CHAPTER, YOU WILL BE
ABLE TO:

▶ prepare a variety of stocks

▶ recognize and classify sauces

▶ use thickening agents properly

▶ prepare a variety of classic and
  modern sauces

A **stock** is a flavored liquid. A good stock is the key to a great soup, sauce or braised dish. The French appropriately call a stock *fond* ("base"), as stocks are the basis for many classic and modern dishes.

A **sauce** is a thickened liquid used to flavor and enhance other foods. A good sauce adds flavor, moisture, richness and visual appeal. A sauce should complement food; it should never disguise it. A sauce can be hot or cold, sweet or savory, smooth or chunky.

Although the thought of preparing stocks and sauces may be intimidating, the procedures are really quite simple. Carefully follow the basic procedures outlined in this chapter, use high-quality ingredients and, with practice and experience, you will soon be producing fine stocks and sauces.

This chapter addresses classical hot sauces as well as coulis, contemporary broths, flavored oils, salsas and relishes. Cold sauces, generally based on mayonnaise, are discussed in Chapter 24, Salads and Salad Dressings; dessert sauces are discussed in Chapter 34, Custards, Creams, Frozen Desserts and Dessert Sauces.

▶ STOCKS

There are several types of stocks. Although they are all made from a combination of bones, vegetables, seasonings and liquids, each type uses specific procedures to give it distinctive characteristics.

A **white stock** is made by simmering chicken, veal or beef bones in water with vegetables and seasonings. The stock remains relatively colorless during the cooking process.

A **brown stock** is made from chicken, veal, beef or game bones and vegetables, all of which are caramelized before being simmered in water with seasonings. The stock has a rich, dark color.

Both a **fish stock** and a **fumet** are made by slowly cooking fish bones or crustacean shells and vegetables without coloring them, then simmering them in water with seasonings for a short time. For a fumet, wine and lemon juice are also added. The resulting stock or fumet is a strongly flavored, relatively colorless liquid.

A **court bouillon** is made by simmering vegetables and seasonings in water and an acidic liquid such as vinegar or wine. It is used to poach fish or vegetables.

INGREDIENTS

The basic ingredients of any stock are bones, a vegetable mixture known as a **mirepoix,** seasonings and water.

BONES

Bones are the most important ingredient; they add flavor, richness and color to the stock. Traditionally, the kitchen or butcher shop saved the day's bones to make stock. But because many meats and poultry items are now purchased precut or portioned, food service operations often purchase bones specifically for stock making.

Different bones release their flavor at different rates. Even though the bones are cut into 3- to 4-inch (8- to 10-centimeter) pieces, a stock made entirely of beef and/or veal bones requires six to eight hours of cooking time, while a stock made entirely from chicken bones requires only five to six hours.

Beef and Veal Bones

The best bones for beef and veal stock are from younger animals. They contain a higher percentage of **cartilage** and other **connective tissue** than do bones from more mature animals. Connective tissue has a high **collagen** content. Through the cooking process, the collagen is converted into **gelatin** and water. The gelatin adds richness and body to the finished stock.

The best beef and veal bones are back, neck and shank bones, as they have high collagen contents. Beef and veal bones should be cut with a meat saw into small pieces, approximately 3 to 4 inches (8 to 10 centimeters) long, so that they can release as much flavor as possible while the stock cooks.

Chicken Bones

The best bones for chicken stock are from the neck and back. If a whole chicken carcass is used, it can be cut up for easier handling.

Fish Bones

The best bones for fish stock are from lean fish such as sole, flounder, whiting or turbot. Bones from fatty fish (for example, salmon, tuna and swordfish) do not produce good stock because of their high fat content and distinctive flavors. The entire fish carcass can be used, but it should be cut up with a cleaver or heavy knife for easy handling and even extraction of flavors. After cutting, the pieces should be rinsed in cold water to remove blood, loose scales and other impurities.

Other Bones

Lamb, turkey, game and ham bones can also be used for white or brown stocks. Although mixing bones is generally acceptable, be careful of blending strongly flavored bones, such as those from lamb or game, with beef, veal or chicken bones. The former's strong flavors may not be appropriate or desirable in the finished product.

MIREPOIX

A mirepoix is a mixture of onions, carrots and celery added to a stock to enhance its flavor and aroma. Although chefs differ on the ratio of vegetables, generally a mixture of 50 percent onions, 25 percent carrots and 25 percent celery, by weight, is used. (Unless otherwise noted, any reference to mirepoix in this book refers to this ratio.) For a brown stock, onion skins may be used to add color. It is not necessary to peel the carrots or celery because flavor, not aesthetics, is important.

The size in which the mirepoix is chopped is determined by the stock's cooking time: The shorter the cooking time, the smaller the vegetables must be chopped to ensure that all possible flavor is extracted. For white or brown stocks made from beef or veal bones, the vegetables should be coarsely chopped into large, 1- to 2-inch (2½- to 5-centimeter) pieces. For chicken and fish stocks, the vegetables should be more finely chopped into ½-inch (1¼-centimeter) pieces.

A white mirepoix is made by replacing the carrots in a standard mirepoix with parsnips and adding mushrooms and leeks. Some chefs prefer to use a white mirepoix when making a white stock, as it produces a lighter product. Sometimes parsnips, mushrooms and leeks are added to a standard mirepoix for additional flavors.

▶ **cartilage** also known as gristle, a tough, elastic, whitish connective tissue that helps give structure to an animal's body

▶ **connective tissue** tissue found throughout an animal's body that binds together and supports other tissues such as muscles

▶ **collagen** a protein found in nearly all connective tissue; it dissolves when cooked with moisture

▶ **gelatin** a tasteless and odorless mixture of proteins (especially collagen) extracted from boiling bones, connective tissue and other animal parts; when dissolved in a hot liquid and then cooled, it forms a jellylike substance used as a thickener and stabilizer

▶ **matignon** a standard mirepoix plus diced smoked bacon or smoked ham and, depending on the dish, mushrooms and herbs; sometimes called an edible mirepoix, it is usually cut more uniformly than a standard mirepoix and left in the finished dish as a garnish

Mirepoix Ingredients

SEASONINGS

Principal stock seasonings are peppercorns, bay leaves, thyme, parsley stems and optionally, garlic. These seasonings generally can be left whole. A stock is cooked long enough for all of their flavors to be extracted, so there is no reason to chop or grind them. Seasonings generally are added to the stock at the start of cooking. Some chefs do not add seasonings to beef or veal stock until midway through the cooking process, however, because of the extended cooking times. Seasonings can be added as a sachet d'épices or a bouquet garni.

Salt, an otherwise important seasoning, is not added to stock. Because a stock has a variety of uses, it is impossible for the chef to know how much salt to add when preparing it. If, for example, the stock was seasoned to taste with salt, the chef could not reduce it later; salt is not lost through reduction, and the concentrated product would taste too salty. Similarly, seasoning the stock to taste with salt could prevent the chef from adding other ingredients that are high in salt when finishing a recipe. Unlike many seasonings whose flavors must be incorporated into a product through lengthy cooking periods, salt can be added at any time during the cooking process with the same effect.

PRINCIPLES OF STOCK MAKING

The following principles, outlined in Figure 11.1, apply to all stocks. You should follow them in order to achieve the highest-quality stocks possible.

A. START THE STOCK IN COLD WATER

The ingredients should always be covered with cold water. When bones are covered with cold water, blood and other impurities dissolve. As the water heats, the impurities coagulate and rise to the surface, where they can be removed easily by skimming. If the bones were covered with hot water, the impurities would coagulate more quickly and remain dispersed in the stock without rising to the top, making the stock cloudy.

If the water level falls below the bones during cooking, add water to cover them. Flavor cannot be extracted from bones not under water, and bones exposed to the air will darken and discolor a white stock.

B. SIMMER THE STOCK GENTLY

The stock should be brought to a boil and then reduced to a simmer, a temperature of approximately 185°F (85°C). While simmering, the ingredients release their flavors into the liquid. If kept at a simmer, the liquid will remain clear as it reduces and the stock develops.

Never boil a stock for any length of time. Rapid boiling of a stock, even for a few minutes, causes impurities and fats to blend with the liquid, making it cloudy.

C. SKIM THE STOCK FREQUENTLY

A stock should be skimmed often to remove the fat and impurities that rise to the surface during cooking. If they are not removed, they may make the stock cloudy.

D. STRAIN THE STOCK CAREFULLY

Once a stock finishes cooking, the liquid must be separated from the bones, vegetables and other solid ingredients. In order to keep the liquid clear, it is important not to disturb the solid ingredients when removing the liquid. This is easily accomplished if the stock is cooked in a steam kettle or stockpot with a spigot at the bottom.

If the stock is cooked in a standard stockpot, to strain it:

1 Skim as much fat and as many impurities from the surface as possible before removing the stockpot from the heat.

Start the stock in cold water.

Simmer the stock gently.

Skim the stock frequently.

Strain the stock carefully.

Cool the stock quickly.

Store the stock properly.

Degrease the stock.

FIGURE 11.1 ▷ **Principles of stock making**

FIGURE 11.2 ▶ Venting a stockpot

2 After removing the pot from the heat, carefully ladle the stock from the pot without stirring it.

3 Strain the stock through a china cap lined with several layers of cheesecloth.

E. COOL THE STOCK QUICKLY

Most stocks are prepared in large quantities, cooled and held for later use. Great care must be taken when cooling a stock to prevent food-borne illnesses or souring. To cool a stock quickly and safely:

1 Keep the stock in a metal container. A plastic container insulates the stock and delays cooling.

2 Vent the stockpot in an empty sink by placing it on blocks or a rack. This allows water to circulate on all sides and below the pot when the sink is filled with water. See Figure 11.2.

3 Install an overflow pipe in the drain, and fill the sink with cold water or a combination of cold water and ice. Make sure that the weight of the stockpot is adequate to keep it from tipping over.

4 Let cold water run into the sink and drain out the overflow pipe. Stir the stock frequently to facilitate even, quick cooling.

In addition to this venting procedure, cooling wands can be used to speed the cooling of stocks, soups, sauces and other liquids. These wands (also known as ice paddles) are hollow plastic containers that can be filled with water or ice, sealed, frozen and then used to stir and cool liquids. Clean and sanitize the wand after each use to prevent cross-contamination.

F. STORE THE STOCK PROPERLY

Once the stock is cooled, transfer it to a sanitized covered container (either plastic or metal) and store it in the refrigerator. As the stock chills, fat rises to its surface and solidifies. If left intact, this layer of fat helps preserve the stock. Stocks can be stored for up to one week under refrigeration or frozen for several months.

G. DEGREASE THE STOCK

Degreasing a stock is simple: When a stock is refrigerated, fat rises to its surface, hardens and is easily lifted or scraped away before the stock is reheated.

Lifting fat from the surface of a cold stock.

▶ **degrease** to remove fat from the surface of a liquid such as a stock or sauce by skimming, scraping or lifting congealed fat

WHITE STOCK

A white or neutral stock may be made from beef, veal or chicken bones. The finished stock should have a good flavor, good clarity, high gelatin content and little or no color. Veal bones are most often used, but any combination of beef, veal or chicken bones may be used.

BLANCHING BONES

Chefs disagree on whether the bones for a white stock should be blanched to remove impurities. Some chefs argue that blanching keeps the stock as clear and colorless as possible; others argue that blanching removes nutrients and flavor.

▶ PROCEDURE FOR BLANCHING BONES

If you choose to blanch the bones:

1 Wash the cut-up bones, place them in a stockpot and cover them with cold water.
2 Bring the water to a boil over high heat.
3 As soon as the water boils, skim the rising impurities. Drain the water from the bones and discard it.
4 Refill the pot with cold water, and proceed with the stock recipe.

RECIPE 11.1   WHITE STOCK

Yield: 2 gal. (8 lt)

Bones, veal, chicken or beef	15 lb.	7 kg
Cold water	3 gal.	11 lt
Mirepoix	2 lb.	1 kg
Sachet:		
Bay leaves	2	2
Dried thyme	½ tsp.	2 ml
Peppercorns, crushed	½ tsp.	2 ml
Parsley stems	8	8

1 Cut the washed bones into pieces approximately 3–4 inches (8–10 centimeters) long.
2 Place the bones in a stockpot and cover them with cold water. If blanching, bring the water to a boil, skimming off the scum that rises to the surface. Drain off the water and the impurities. Then add the 3 gallons (11 liters) of cold water and bring to a boil. Reduce to a simmer.
3 If not blanching the bones, bring the cold water to a boil. Reduce to a simmer and skim the scum that forms.
4 Add the mirepoix and sachet to the simmering stock.
5 Continue simmering and skimming the stock for 6 to 8 hours. (If only chicken bones are used, simmer for 5 to 6 hours.)
6 Strain, cool and refrigerate.

Approximate values per 1-fl.-oz. (30-ml) serving: **Calories** 4, **Total fat** 0.1 g, **Saturated fat** 0.1 g, **Cholesterol** 0 mg, **Sodium** 5 mg, **Total carbohydrates** 0 g, **Protein** 0.2 g, **Claims**—fat free; very low sodium

BROWN STOCK

A brown stock is made from chicken, veal, beef or game bones. The finished stock should have a good flavor, rich dark brown color, good body and high gelatin content.

The primary differences between a brown stock and a white stock are that for a brown stock, the bones and mirepoix are caramelized before being simmered and a tomato product is added. These extra steps provide the finished stock with a rich dark color and a more intense flavor.

CARAMELIZING

Caramelization is the process of browning the sugars found on the surface of most foods. This gives the stock its characteristic flavor and color.

▶ PROCEDURE FOR CARAMELIZING BONES

For caramelizing, do not wash or blanch the bones as this retards browning. To caramelize:

1 Place the cut-up bones in a roasting pan one layer deep. It is better to roast several pans of bones than to overfill one pan.

2 Roast the bones for approximately 1 hour in a hot oven (375°F/190°C). Stirring occasionally, brown the bones thoroughly, but do not allow them to burn.

3 Transfer the roasted bones from the pan to the stockpot.

DEGLAZING THE PAN

After the bones are caramelized, the excess fat should be removed and reserved for future use. The caramelized and coagulated proteins remaining in the roasting pan are very flavorful. To utilize them, you **deglaze** the pan.

▶ **deglaze** to swirl or stir a liquid (usually wine or stock) in a sauté pan or other pan to dissolve cooked food particles remaining on the bottom; the resulting mixture often becomes the base for a sauce

▶ PROCEDURE FOR DEGLAZING THE PAN

1 Place the pan on the stove top over medium heat, and add enough water to cover the bottom of the pan approximately ½ inch (12 millimeters) deep.

2 Stir and scrape the pan bottom to dissolve and remove all the caramelized materials while the water heats.

3 Pour the deglazing liquid (also known as the deglazing liquor) over the bones in the stockpot.

▶ PROCEDURE FOR CARAMELIZING MIREPOIX

1 Add a little of the reserved fat from the roasted bones to the roasting pan after it has been deglazed. (Or use a sautoir large enough to contain all the mirepoix comfortably.)

2 Sauté the mirepoix, browning all the vegetables well and evenly without burning them.

3 Add the caramelized mirepoix to the stockpot.

▶ **remouillage** (rhur-moo-yahj) French for "rewetting"; a stock produced by reusing the bones left from making another stock. After draining the original stock from the stockpot, add fresh mirepoix, a new sachet and enough water to cover the bones and mirepoix, and a second stock can be made. A remouillage is treated like the original stock; allow it to simmer for four to five hours before straining. A remouillage will not be as clear or as flavorful as the original stock, however. It is often used to make glazes or in place of water when making stocks.

Most any tomato product can be used in a brown stock: fresh tomatoes, canned whole tomatoes, crushed tomatoes, tomato purée or paste. If using a concentrated tomato product such as paste or purée, use approximately half the amount by weight of fresh or canned tomatoes. The tomato product should be added to the stockpot when the mirepoix is added.

RECIPE 11.2   BROWN STOCK

Yield: 2 gal. (8 lt)

Bones, veal or beef, cut in 3- to 4-in. (8- to 10-cm) pieces	15 lb.	7 kg
Cold water	3 gal.	11 lt
Mirepoix	2 lb.	1 kg
Tomato paste	8 oz.	250 g
Sachet:		
Bay leaves	2	2
Dried thyme	½ tsp.	2 ml
Peppercorns, crushed	½ tsp.	2 ml
Garlic cloves, crushed	3	3
Parsley stems	12	12

1 Place the bones in a roasting pan, one layer deep, and brown in a 375°F (190°C) oven. Turn the bones occasionally to brown them evenly.
2 Remove the bones and place them in a stockpot. Pour off the fat from the roasting pan and reserve it.
3 Deglaze the roasting pan with part of the cold water.
4 Add the deglazing liquor and the rest of the cold water to the bones, covering them completely. Bring to a boil and reduce to a simmer.
5 Add a portion of the reserved fat to the roasting pan and sauté the mirepoix until evenly browned. Then add it to the simmering stock.
6 Add the tomato paste and sachet to the stock and continue to simmer for 6 to 8 hours, skimming as necessary.
7 Strain, cool and refrigerate.

Approximate values per 1-fl.-oz. (30-ml) serving: **Calories** 3, **Total fat** 0 g, **Saturated fat** 0 g, **Cholesterol** 0.3 mg, **Sodium** 105 mg, **Total carbohydrates** 0 g, **Protein** 0 g, **Claims**—fat free; low sodium

1 Caramelizing the bones.

2 Deglazing the pan with water.

3 Caramelizing the mirepoix.

4 Adding the proper amount of water.

FISH STOCK AND FISH FUMET

A fish stock and a fish fumet (foo-may) are similar and can be used interchangeably in most recipes. Both are clear with a pronounced fish flavor and very light body. A fumet, however, is more strongly flavored and aromatic and contains an acidic ingredient such as white wine and/or lemon juice.

The fish bones and crustacean shells used to make a fish stock or fumet should be washed but never blanched because blanching removes too much flavor. They may be **sweated** without browning if desired, however. Because of the size and structure of fish bones and crustacean shells, stocks and fumets made from them require much less cooking time than even a chicken stock; 30 to 45 minutes is usually sufficient to extract full flavor. Mirepoix or other vegetables should be cut small so that all of their flavors can be extracted during the short cooking time.

The procedure for making a fish stock is very similar to that for making a white stock.

► **sweat** to cook a food in a pan (usually covered), without browning, over low heat until the item softens and releases moisture; sweating allows the food to release its flavor more quickly when cooked with other foods

FISH STOCK

Yield: 1 gal. (4 lt)

Fish bones or crustacean shells	10 lb.	4.5 kg
Water	5 qts.	5 lt
Mirepoix, small dice	1 lb.	450 g
Mushroom trimmings	8 oz.	250 g
Sachet:		
Bay leaves	2	2
Dried thyme	½ tsp.	2 ml
Peppercorns, crushed	¼ tsp.	1 ml
Parsley stems	8	8

1 Combine all ingredients in a stockpot.

2 Bring to a simmer and skim impurities as necessary.

3 Simmer for 30 to 45 minutes.

4 Strain, cool and refrigerate.

Approximate values per 1-fl.-oz. (30-ml) serving: **Calories** 5, **Total fat** 0 g, **Saturated fat** 0 g, **Cholesterol** 0 mg, **Sodium** 100 mg, **Total carbohydrates** 0 g, **Protein** 1 g, **Claims**—fat free; low sodium

A fish stock is sometimes used to make a fish fumet; if so, the resulting product is very strongly flavored. A fish fumet is also flavored with white wine and lemon juice. When making a fumet, sweat the bones and vegetables before adding the cooking liquid and seasonings.

FISH FUMET

Yield: 2 gal. (8 lt)

Whole butter	2 oz.	60 g
Onion, small dice	1 lb.	500 g
Parsley stems	12	12
Fish bones	10 lb.	5 kg
Dry white wine	1½ pt.	750 ml
Lemon juice	2 fl. oz.	60 ml
Cold water or fish stock	7 qt.	7 lt
Mushroom trimmings	2 oz.	60 g
Fresh thyme	1 sprig	1 sprig
Lemon slices	10	10

1 Melt the butter in a stockpot.

2 Add the onion, parsley stems and fish bones. Cover the pot and sweat the bones over low heat.

3 Sprinkle the bones with the white wine and lemon juice.

4 Add the cold water or fish stock, mushroom trimmings, thyme and lemon slices. Bring to a boil, reduce to a simmer and cook approximately 30 minutes, skimming frequently.

5 Strain, cool and refrigerate.

Approximate values per 1-fl.-oz. (30-ml) serving: **Calories** 5, **Total fat** 0.7 g, **Saturated fat** 0.2 g, **Cholesterol** 0.5 mg, **Sodium** 90 g, **Total carbohydrates** 0 g, **Protein** 1 g, **Claims**—fat free; low sodium

1 Sweating the onions, parsley stems and fish bones.

2 Adding cold water and seasonings.

VEGETABLE STOCK

A good vegetable stock should be clear and light-colored. Because no animal products are used, it has no gelatin content. A vegetable stock can be used instead of a meat-based stock in most recipes. This substitution is useful when preparing vegetarian dishes or as a lighter, more healthful alternative when preparing sauces and soups. Although almost any combination of vegetables can be used for stock making, more variety is not always better. Sometimes a vegetable stock made with one or two vegetables that complement the finished dish particularly well will produce better results than a stock made with many vegetables.

RECIPE 11.5   VEGETABLE STOCK

Yield: 1 gal. (4 lt)

Vegetable oil	2 fl. oz.	60 ml
Mirepoix, small dice	2 lb.	900 g
Leek, whites and greens, chopped	8 oz.	250 g
Garlic cloves, chopped	4	4
Fennel, small dice	4 oz.	120 g
Turnip, diced	2 oz.	60 g
Tomato, diced	2 oz.	60 g
White wine	8 fl. oz.	250 ml
Water	1 gal.	4 lt
Sachet:		
Bay leaf	1	1
Dried thyme	½ tsp.	2 ml
Peppercorns, crushed	¼ tsp.	1 ml
Parsley stems	8	8

1 Heat the oil. Add the vegetables and sweat for 10 minutes.
2 Add the white wine, water and sachet.
3 Bring the mixture to a boil, reduce to a simmer and cook for 45 minutes.
4 Strain, cool and refrigerate.

Approximate values per 1-fl.-oz. (30-ml) serving: **Calories** 5, **Total fat** 0 g, **Saturated fat** 0 g, **Cholesterol** 0 mg, **Sodium** 0 mg, **Total carbohydrates** 0 g, **Protein** 0 g, **Claims**—fat free; low calorie

COURT BOUILLON

A court bouillon (bool-yawn), though not actually a stock, is prepared in much the same manner as stocks, so it is included here. A court bouillon (French for "short broth") is a flavored liquid, usually water and wine or vinegar, in which vegetables and seasonings have been simmered to impart their flavors and aromas.

Court bouillon is most commonly used to poach foods such as fish and shellfish. Recipes vary depending upon the foods to be poached. Although a court bouillon can be made in advance and refrigerated for later use, its simplicity lends itself to fresh preparation whenever needed.

COURT BOUILLON		RECIPE 11.6

Yield: 1 gal. (4 lt)

Water	1 gal.	4 lt
Vinegar	6 fl. oz.	180 ml
Lemon juice	2 fl. oz.	60 ml
Mirepoix	1 lb. 8 oz.	650 g
Peppercorns, crushed	1 tsp.	5 ml
Bay leaves	4	4
Dried thyme	pinch	pinch
Parsley stems	1 bunch	1 bunch

1 Combine all ingredients and bring to a boil.
2 Reduce to a simmer and cook for 45 minutes.
3 Strain and use immediately or cool and refrigerate.

Approximate values per 1-fl.-oz. (30-ml) serving: **Calories** 3, **Total fat** 0 g, **Saturated fat** 0 g, **Cholesterol** 0 mg, **Sodium** 0 mg, **Total carbohydrates** 0 g, **Protein** 0 g, **Claims**—fat free; low sodium

Note: This recipe can be used for poaching almost any fish, but it is particularly well suited to salmon, trout and shellfish. When poaching freshwater fish, replace the water and vinegar with equal parts white wine and water.

COMMERCIAL BASES

Commercially produced flavor (or convenience) bases are widely used in food service operations. They are powdered or paste flavorings added to water to create stocks or, when used in smaller amounts, to enhance the flavor of sauces and soups. These products are also sold as bouillon cubes or granules. Although inferior to well-made stocks, flavor bases do reduce the labor involved in the production of stocks, sauces and soups. Used properly, they also ensure a consistent product. Because bases do not contain gelatin, stocks and sauces made from them do not benefit from reduction.

Bases vary greatly in quality and price. Sodium (salt) is the main ingredient in many bases. Better bases are made primarily of meat, poultry or fish extracts. To judge the quality of a flavor base, prepare it according to package directions and compare the flavor to that of a well-made stock. The flavor base can be improved by adding a mirepoix, standard sachet and a few appropriate bones to the mixture, then simmering for one or two hours. It can then be strained, stored and used like a regular stock. Although convenience bases are widely used in the industry, it is important to remember that even the best base is a poor substitute for a well-made stock.

NAGE

An aromatic court bouillon is sometimes served as a light sauce or broth with fish or shellfish. This is known as a nage (nahj), and dishes served in this manner are described as *à la nage* (French for "swimming"). After the fish or shellfish is cooked, additional herbs and aromatic vegetables are added to the cooking liquid, which is then reduced slightly and strained.

Alternatively, the used court bouillon can be strained, chilled, and clarified with egg whites and aromatic vegetables in the same manner as a consommé. Finally, whole butter or cream may be added to a nage for richness.

1 A properly thickened glaze made from brown stock.

GLAZE

A glaze is the dramatic reduction and concentration of a stock. One gallon (4 liters) of stock produces only 1 to 2 cups (2½ to 5 deciliters) of glaze. *Glace de viande* is made from brown stock, reduced until it becomes dark and syrupy. *Glace de volaille* is made from chicken stock, and *glace de poisson* from fish stock.

Glazes are added to soups or sauces to increase and intensify flavors. They are also used as a source of intense flavoring for several of the small sauces discussed next.

▶ PROCEDURE FOR REDUCING A STOCK TO A GLAZE

1 Simmer the stock over very low heat. Be careful not to let it burn, and skim it often.

2 As it reduces and the volume decreases, transfer the liquid into progressively smaller saucepans. Strain the liquid each time it is transferred into a smaller saucepan.

3 Strain it a final time, cool and refrigerate. A properly made glaze will keep for several months under refrigeration.

2 Chilled glace de viande.

Table 11.1 **TROUBLESHOOTING CHART FOR STOCKS**

PROBLEM	REASON	SOLUTION
Cloudy	Impurities Stock boiled during cooking	Start stock in cold water Strain through layers of cheesecloth
Lack of flavor	Not cooked long enough Inadequate seasoning Improper ratio of bones to water	Increase cooking time Add more flavoring ingredients Add more bones
Lack of color	Improperly caramelized bones and mirepoix Not cooked long enough	Caramelize bones and mirepoix until darker Cook longer
Lack of body	Wrong bones used Insufficient reduction Improper ratio of bones to water	Use bones with a higher content of connective tissue Cook longer Add more bones
Too salty	Commercial base used Salt added during cooking	Change base or make own stock; do not salt stock

▶ SAUCES

With a few exceptions, a sauce is a liquid plus thickening agent plus seasonings. Any chef can produce fine sauces by learning to do the following:

1 Make good stocks

2 Use thickening agents properly to achieve the desired texture, flavor and appearance

3 Use seasonings properly to achieve the desired flavors

Classic hot sauces are divided into two groups: **mother** or **leading sauces** (Fr. *sauce mère*) and **small** or **compound sauces.** The five classic mother sauces are béchamel, velouté, espagnole (brown), tomato and hollandaise. Except for hollandaise, leading sauces are rarely served as is; more often they are used to create the many small sauces.

Not all sauces fall into the traditional classifications, however. Some sauces use purées of fruits or vegetables as their base; they are known as **coulis.** Others, such as **beurre blanc** (French for "white butter") and **beurre rouge** ("red butter"), are based on an acidic reduction in which whole butter is incorporated. **Flavored butters, flavored oils, salsas, relishes** and **pan gravy** are also used as sauces in modern food service operations.

THICKENING AGENTS

One of the most traditional and commonly used methods for thickening sauces is through the gelatinization of starches. As discussed in Chapter 10, Principles of Cooking, gelatinization is the process by which starch granules absorb moisture when placed in a liquid and heated. As the moisture is absorbed, the product thickens. Starches generally used to thicken sauces are flour, cornstarch and arrowroot. Gelatinization may sound easy, but it takes practice to produce a good sauce that:

▶ Is lump-free

▶ Has a good clean flavor that is not pasty or floury

▶ Has a consistency that will coat the back of a spoon (the French call this *nappe*)

▶ Will not separate or break when the sauce is held or reduced

ROUX

Roux (roo) is the principal means used to thicken sauces. It is a combination of equal parts, by weight, of flour and fat, cooked together to form a paste. Cooking the flour in fat coats the starch granules with the fat and prevents them from lumping together or forming lumps when introduced into a liquid. In large production kitchens, large amounts of roux are prepared and held for use as needed. Smaller operations may make roux as required for each recipe.

There are three types of roux:

1 White roux is cooked only briefly and should be removed from the heat as soon as it develops a frothy, bubbly appearance. It is used in white sauces, such as béchamel, or in dishes where little or no color is desired.

2 Blond roux is cooked slightly longer than white roux, and should begin to take on a little color as the flour caramelizes. It is used in ivory-colored sauces, such as velouté, or where a richer flavor is desired.

3 Brown roux is cooked until it develops a darker color and a nutty aroma and flavor. Brown roux is used in brown sauces and dishes where a dark color is desired. It is important to remember that cooking a starch before

White, Blond and Brown Roux

adding a liquid breaks down the starch granules and prevents gelatinization from occurring. Therefore, because brown roux is cooked longer than white roux, more brown roux is required to thicken a given quantity of liquid.

▶ PROCEDURE FOR PREPARING ROUX

Whether it will be white, blond or brown, the procedure for making a roux is the same:

1 Using a heavy saucepan to prevent scorching, heat the clarified butter or other fat.
2 Add all the flour and stir to form a paste. Although all-purpose flour can be used, it is better to use cake or pastry flour because they contain a higher percentage of starch. Do not use high-gluten flour because of its greatly reduced starch content. (Flours are discussed in Chapter 29, Principles of the Bakeshop.)
3 Cook the paste over medium heat until the desired color is achieved. Stir the roux often to avoid burning. Burnt roux will not thicken a liquid; it will simply add dark specks and an undesirable flavor.

Cooking the roux.

The temperature and amount of roux being prepared determine the exact length of cooking time. Generally, however, a white roux needs to cook for only a few minutes, long enough to minimize the raw flour taste. Blond roux is cooked longer, until the paste begins to change to a slightly darker color. Brown roux requires a much longer cooking time to develop its characteristic color and aroma. A good roux will be stiff, not runny or pourable.

▶ INCORPORATING ROUX INTO A LIQUID

There are two ways to incorporate roux into a liquid without causing lumps:

1 Cold stock can be added to the hot roux while stirring vigorously with a whisk.
2 Room-temperature roux can be added to a hot stock while stirring vigorously with a whisk.

When the roux and the liquid are completely incorporated and the sauce begins to boil, it is necessary to cook the sauce for a time to remove any raw flour taste that may remain. Most chefs feel a minimum of 20 minutes is necessary.

▶ GUIDELINES FOR USING ROUX

1 Avoid using aluminum pots. The scraping action of the whisk will turn light sauces gray and will impart a metallic flavor.
2 Use sufficiently heavy pots to prevent sauces from scorching or burning during extended cooking times.
3 Avoid extreme temperatures. Roux should be no colder than room temperature so that the fat is not fully solidified. Extremely hot roux is dangerous and can spatter when combined with a liquid. Stocks should not be ice cold when combined with roux; the roux will become very cold, and the solidified pieces may be very difficult to work out with a whisk.
4 Avoid overthickening. See Table 11.2. Roux does not begin to thicken a sauce until the sauce is almost at the boiling point; the thickening action continues for several minutes while the sauce simmers. If a sauce is to cook for a long time, it will also be thickened by reduction.

When thickening stock with roux, either
(a) **add cold stock to hot roux, or**
(b) **add cold roux to hot stock.**

A SAUCY HISTORY

The word *sauce* is derived from the Latin word *salus,* meaning "salted." This derivation is appropriate. For millennia, salt has been the basic condiment for enhancing or disguising the flavor of many foods. Over the centuries, sauces have also been used for these purposes.

Cooks of ancient Rome flavored many dishes with *garum,* a golden-colored sauce made from fermented fish entrails combined with brine, condiments, water and wine or vinegar. They also used a sauce referred to as a "single" made from oil, wine and brine. When boiled with herbs and saffron, it became a "double" sauce. To this the Byzantines later added pepper, cloves, cinnamon, cardamom and coriander or spikenard (a fragrant ointment made from grains).

During the Middle Ages, chefs (and their employers) were fond of either very spicy or sweet-and-sour sauces. A typical sauce for roasted meat consisted of powdered cinnamon, mustard, red wine and a sweetener such as honey. It was thickened, if at all, with bits of stale or grilled bread. Other sauces were based on verjuice, an acidic stock prepared from the juice of unripe grapes. To it were added other fruit juices, honey, flower petals and herbs or spices. Indeed, most medieval sauces were heavily spiced. Perhaps this was done to hide the taste of salt-cured or less-than-fresh meats. More likely, however, these sauces were served to showcase the host's wealth.

Guillaume Tirel (c. 1312–1395), who called himself **Taillevent,** was the master chef for Charles V of France. Around 1375, Taillevent wrote *Le Viandier,* the oldest known French cookbook. The cooking style he describes relies heavily on pounding, puréeing and spicing most foods so that the finished dish bears little resemblance in shape, texture or flavor to the

original ingredients. Included in his methods are 17 sauces. Among them is a recipe for a *cameline* sauce. It is made from grilled bread soaked in wine; the wine-soaked bread is then drained, squeeze-dried and ground with cinnamon, ginger, pepper, cloves and nutmeg; this mixture is then diluted with vinegar. There is also a recipe for a sauce called *taillemaslée,* made of fried onions, verjuice, vinegar and mustard. (Appropriately, on his grave marker, Taillevent is dressed as a sergeant-at-arms whose shield is decorated with three cooking pots.)

Recipes for some sauces of the Renaissance, such as poivrade or Robert, are recognizable today. Most sauces enjoyed in Renaissance-era Italy and France consisted of some combination of concentrated cooking juices, wines, herbs and spices (especially pepper), sometimes thickened with bread. Sweet, fruit-based sauces were also popular. Most important for the development of modern cuisine, however, was the growing use of sauces based on broths

thickened with cream, butter and egg yolks and flavored with herbs and spices.

Although he died in relative obscurity, many now consider **François Pierre de La Varenne** (1618–1678) to be one of the founding fathers of French cuisine. His treatises, especially *Le Cuisinier français* (1651), detail the early development, methods and manners of French cuisine. His analysis and recipes mark a departure from medieval cookery and a French cuisine heavily influenced by Italian traditions. His writings were uniquely modern in that he included recipes for new foods (especially fruits and vegetables native to the Americas or the Far East) and for indigenous foods (such as salt-water fish) that were gradually becoming more popular. La Varenne is credited with introducing roux as a thickening agent for sauces, especially velouté sauces. He emphasized the importance of properly prepared *fonds* and the reduction of cooking juices to concentrate flavors. He also popularized the use of bouquets garni to flavor stocks and sauces.

Sometime during the early 18th century, the chef to the French Duc de Levis-Mirepoix pioneered the use of onions, celery and carrots to enhance the flavor and aroma of stocks. The mixture, named for the chef's employer, soon became the standard way of enriching stocks. An enriched stock greatly improves the quality of the sauces derived from it.

During the early 19th century, **Antonin Carême** developed the modern system for classifying hundreds of sauces. It is unknown how many sauces Carême actually invented himself, but he wrote treatises containing the theories and recipes for many of the sauces still used today. Carême's extravagant lists of sauces were reduced and simplified by chefs later in the 19th century, most notably by **Auguste Escoffier.**

CORNSTARCH

Cornstarch, a very fine white powder, is a pure starch derived from corn. It is used widely as a thickening agent for hot and cold sauces and is especially popular in Asian cuisines for thickening sauces and soups. Liquids thickened with cornstarch have a glossy sheen that may or may not be desirable.

One unit of cornstarch thickens about twice as much liquid as an equal unit of flour. Sauces thickened with cornstarch are less stable than those thickened with roux because cornstarch can break down and lose its thickening power after prolonged heating. Products thickened with cornstarch should not be reheated.

Table 11.2		PROPORTIONS OF ROUX TO LIQUID					
FLOUR	**+**	**BUTTER**	**=**	**ROUX**	**+**	**LIQUID**	**=**	**SAUCE**
6 oz./190 g	+	6 oz./190 g	=	12 oz./375 g	+	1 gal./4 lt	=	light
8 oz./250 g	+	8 oz./250 g	=	1 lb./500 g	+	1 gal./4 lt	=	medium
12 oz./375 g	+	12 oz./375 g	=	24 oz./750 g	+	1 gal./4 lt	=	heavy

Variables: The starch content of a flour determines its thickening power. Cake flour, being lowest in protein and highest in starch, has more thickening power than bread flour, which is high in protein and low in starch. In addition, a dark roux has less thickening power than a lighter one, so more will be needed to thicken an equal amount of liquid.

▶ **slurry** a mixture of raw starch and cold liquid used for thickening

1 Kneading the butter and flour together.

2 Adding the beurre manié in small pieces to finish a sauce.

▶ **tempering** gradually raising the temperature of a cold liquid such as eggs by slowly stirring in a hot liquid

Incorporating Cornstarch

Cornstarch must be mixed with a cool liquid before it is introduced into a hot one. The cool liquid separates the grains of starch and allows them to begin absorbing liquid without lumping. A solution of a starch and a cool liquid is called a **slurry.**

The starch slurry may be added to either a hot or cold liquid. If added to a hot liquid, it must be stirred continuously during incorporation. Unlike roux, cornstarch begins to thicken almost immediately if the liquid is hot. Sauces thickened with cornstarch must be cooked gently until the raw starch flavor disappears, usually about five minutes.

ARROWROOT

Arrowroot, derived from the roots of several tropical plants, is similar in texture, appearance and thickening power to cornstarch and is used in exactly the same manner. Arrowroot does not break down as quickly as cornstarch, and it produces a slightly clearer finished product although it is much more expensive.

BEURRE MANIÉ

Beurre manié (burr mahn-yay) is a combination of equal amounts, by weight, of flour and soft whole butter. The flour and butter are kneaded together until smooth. The mixture is then formed into pea-sized balls and whisked into a simmering sauce. Beurre manié is used for quick thickening at the end of the cooking process. The butter also adds shine and flavor to the sauce as it melts.

LIAISON

Unlike the thickeners already described, a liaison (lee-yeh-zon) does not thicken a sauce through gelatinization. A liaison is a mixture of egg yolks and heavy cream; it adds richness and smoothness with minimal thickening. Special care must be taken to prevent the yolks from coagulating when they are added to a hot liquid because this could curdle the sauce.

▶ PROCEDURE FOR USING A LIAISON

1 Whisk together one part egg yolk and three parts whipping cream. Combining the yolk with cream raises the temperature at which the yolk's proteins coagulate, making it easier to incorporate them into a sauce without lumping or curdling.

2 **Temper** the egg yolk and cream mixture by slowly adding a small amount of the hot liquid while stirring continuously.

3 When enough of the hot liquid has been added to the liaison to warm it thoroughly, begin adding the warmed liaison to the remaining hot liquid.

Be sure to stir the mixture carefully to prevent the yolk from overcooking or lumping. Plain egg yolks coagulate at temperatures between 149°F and 158°F (65°C and 70°C). Mixing them with cream raises the temperatures at which they coagulate to approximately 180°F–185°F (82°C–85°C). Temperatures over 185°F (85°C) will cause the yolks to curdle. Great care must be taken to hold the sauce above 140°F (60°C) for food safety and sanitation reasons, yet below 185°F (85°C) to prevent curdling.

1 Adding hot liquid to the egg yolk and cream mixture.

FINISHING TECHNIQUES

REDUCTION

As sauces cook, moisture is released in the form of steam. As steam escapes, the remaining ingredients concentrate, thickening the sauce and strengthening the flavors. This process, known as **reduction,** is commonly used to thicken sauces because no starches or other flavor-altering ingredients are needed. Sauces are often finished by allowing them to reduce until the desired consistency is reached.

STRAINING

Smoothness is important to the success of most sauces. They can be strained through either a china cap lined with several layers of cheesecloth or a fine mesh chinois. As discussed later, often vegetables, herbs, spices and other seasonings are added to a sauce for flavor. Straining removes these ingredients as well as any lumps of roux or thickener remaining in the sauce after the desired flavor and consistency have been reached.

2 Adding the tempered egg yolk and cream liaison to the hot liquid.

▶ **reduction** cooking a liquid such as a sauce until its quantity decreases through evaporation. To reduce by one-half means that one-half of the original amount remains. To reduce by three-quarters means that only one-quarter of the original amount remains. To reduce au sec means that the liquid is cooked until nearly dry.

MONTER AU BEURRE

Monter au beurre (mohn-tay ah burr) is the process of swirling or whisking whole butter into a sauce to give it shine, flavor and richness. Compound or flavored butters, discussed later, can be used in place of whole butter to add specific flavors. Monter au beurre is widely used to enrich and finish small sauces.

SAUCE FAMILIES

Leading or **mother sauces** are the foundation for the entire classic repertoire of hot sauces. The five leading sauces—béchamel, velouté, espagnole (also known as brown), tomato and hollandaise—can be seasoned and garnished to create a wide variety of small or compound sauces. These five leading sauces are distinguished principally by the liquids and thickeners used to create them. See Table 11.3.

Table 11.3	SAUCE FAMILIES	
MOTHER SAUCE	**LIQUID**	**THICKENER**
Béchamel	Milk	Roux
Velouté	White Stock	Roux
Veal Velouté	Veal Stock	
Chicken Velouté	Chicken Stock	
Fish Velouté	Fish Stock	
Espagnole (Brown Sauce)	Brown Stock	Roux
Tomato Sauce	Tomato	Roux (optional)
Hollandaise	Butter	Egg yolks

Small or **compound sauces** are grouped into families based on their leading sauce. Some small sauces have a variety of uses; others are traditional accompaniments for specific foods. A small sauce may be named for its ingredients, place of origin or creator. Although there are numerous classic small sauces, we have included only a few of the more popular ones following each of the leading sauce recipes.

THE BÉCHAMEL FAMILY

Named for its creator, Louis de Béchameil (1630–1703), steward to Louis XIV of France, béchamel (bay-shah-mell) sauce is the easiest mother sauce to prepare. Traditionally, it is made by adding heavy cream to a thick veal velouté. Although some chefs still believe a béchamel should contain veal stock, today the sauce is almost always made by thickening scalded milk with a white roux and adding seasonings. Often used for vegetable, egg and gratin dishes, béchamel has fallen into relative disfavor recently because of its rich, heavy nature. It is nevertheless important to understand its production and its place in traditional sauce making.

A properly made béchamel is rich, creamy and absolutely smooth with no hint of graininess. The flavors of the onion and clove used to season it should be apparent but not overwhelm the sauce's clean, milky taste. The sauce should be the color of heavy cream and have a deep luster. It should be thick enough to coat foods lightly but should not taste like the roux used to thicken it.

RECIPE 11.7 BÉCHAMEL

Béchamel

Yield: 1 gal. (4 lt)

Onion piquet	1	1
Milk	1 gal.	4 lt
Flour	8 oz.	250 g
Clarified butter	8 fl. oz.	250 ml
Salt and white pepper	TT	TT
Nutmeg	TT	TT

1 Add the onion piquet to the milk in a heavy saucepan and simmer for 20 minutes.
2 In a separate pot, make a white roux with the flour and butter.
3 Remove the onion piquet from the milk. Gradually add the hot milk to the roux while stirring constantly with a whisk to prevent lumps. Bring to a boil.
4 Reduce the sauce to a simmer, add the seasonings and continue cooking for 30 minutes.
5 Strain the sauce through a china cap lined with cheesecloth. Melted butter can be carefully ladled over the surface of the sauce to prevent a skin from forming. Hold for service or cool in a water bath.

Approximate values per 6-fl.-oz. (180-ml) serving: **Calories** 240, **Total fat** 15 g, **Saturated fat** 9 g, **Cholesterol** 50 mg, **Sodium** 180 mg, **Total carbohydrates** 18 g, **Protein** 7 g, **Vitamin A** 15%, **Calcium** 25%

Small Béchamel Sauces

With a good béchamel, producing the small sauces in its family is quite simple. The quantities given are for 1 quart (1 liter) of béchamel. The final step for each recipe is to season to taste with salt and pepper.

CREAM SAUCE Add to béchamel 8–12 fluid ounces (250–360 milliliters) scalded cream and a few drops of lemon juice.

CHEESE Add to béchamel 8 ounces (250 grams) grated Cheddar or American cheese, a dash of Worcestershire sauce and 1 tablespoon (15 milliliters) dry mustard.

MORNAY   Add to béchamel 4 ounces (120 grams) grated Gruyère and 1 ounce (30 grams) grated Parmesan. Thin as desired with scalded cream. Remove the sauce from the heat and swirl in 2 ounces (60 grams) whole butter.

NANTUA   Add to béchamel 4 fluid ounces (120 milliliters) heavy cream and 6 ounces (180 grams) crayfish butter (page 223). Add paprika to achieve the desired color. Garnish the finished sauce with diced crayfish meat.

SOUBISE (MODERN)   Sweat 1 pound (500 grams) diced onion in 1 ounce (30 grams) whole butter without browning. Add béchamel and simmer until the onions are fully cooked. Strain through a fine chinois.

THE VELOUTÉ FAMILY

Velouté (veh-loo-TAY) sauces are made by thickening a white stock or fish stock with roux. The white stock can be made from veal or chicken bones. A fish velouté sauce, made from fish stock, is used to create a few small sauces. A velouté sauce made from veal or chicken stock is usually used to make one of two intermediary sauces—allemande and suprême—from which many small sauces are derived. **Allemande** sauce is made by adding lemon juice and a liaison to either a veal or chicken velouté. (The stock used depends upon the dish with which the sauce will be served.) **Suprême** sauce is made by adding cream to a chicken velouté. See Table 11.4.

A properly made velouté should be rich, smooth and lump-free. If made from chicken or fish stock, it should taste of chicken or fish. A velouté made from veal stock should have a more neutral flavor. The sauce should be ivory-colored, with a deep luster. It should be thick enough to cling to foods without tasting like the roux used to thicken it.

▶ **allemande** (ah-leh-MAHND) an intermediary sauce made by adding lemon juice and a liaison to chicken or veal velouté

▶ **suprême** (soo-prem) an intermediary sauce made by adding cream to chicken velouté

Table 11.4		VELOUTÉ SAUCES				
Fish stock	+ Roux	= Velouté				
Chicken stock	+ Roux	= Velouté	+ Cream		=	Suprême
Chicken stock	+ Roux	= Velouté	+ Liaison and lemon	=	Allemande
Veal stock	+ Roux	= Velouté	+ Liaison and lemon	=	Allemande

VELOUTÉ

RECIPE 11.8

Yield: 1 gal. (4 lt)

Clarified butter	8 fl. oz.	250 ml
Flour	8 oz.	250 g
Chicken, veal or fish stock	5 qt.	5 lt
Salt and white pepper	TT	TT

1 Heat the butter in a heavy saucepan. Add the flour and cook to make a blond roux.
2 Gradually add the stock to the roux, stirring constantly with a whisk to prevent lumps. Bring to a boil and reduce to a simmer. (Seasonings are optional; their use depends upon the seasonings in the stock and the sauce's intended use.)
3 Simmer and reduce to 1 gallon (4 liters), approximately 30 minutes.
4 Strain through a china cap lined with cheesecloth.
5 Melted butter may be carefully ladled over the surface of the sauce to prevent a skin from forming. Hold for service or cool in a water bath.

Velouté

Approximate values per 1-fl.-oz. (30-ml) serving: **Calories** 25, **Total fat** 1.5 g, **Saturated fat** 1 g, **Cholesterol** 5 mg, **Sodium** 140 mg, **Total carbohydrates** 2 g, **Protein** 1 g

Small Fish Velouté Sauces

A few small sauces can be made from fish velouté. The quantities given are for 1 quart (1 liter) fish velouté sauce. The final step for each recipe is to season to taste with salt and pepper.

BERCY   Sauté 2 ounces (60 grams) finely diced shallots in butter. Then add 8 fluid ounces (250 milliliters) dry white wine and 8 fluid ounces (250 milliliters) fish stock. Reduce this mixture by one-third and add the fish velouté. Finish with butter and garnish with chopped parsley.

CARDINAL   Add 8 fluid ounces (250 milliliters) fish stock to 1 quart (1 liter) fish velouté. Reduce this mixture by half and add 1 pint (500 milliliters) heavy cream and a dash of cayenne pepper. Bring to a boil and swirl in 1½ ounces (45 grams) lobster butter (page 223). Garnish with chopped lobster coral at service time.

NORMANDY   Add 4 ounces (120 grams) mushroom trimmings and 4 fluid ounces (120 milliliters) fish stock to 1 quart (1 liter) fish velouté. Reduce by one-third and finish with an egg yolk and cream liaison. Strain through a fine chinois.

RECIPE 11.9 — ALLEMANDE SAUCE

Yield: 1 gal. (4 lt)

Veal or chicken velouté sauce	1 gal.	4 lt
Egg yolks	8	8
Heavy cream	24 fl. oz.	675 ml
Lemon juice	1 fl. oz.	30 ml
Salt and white pepper	TT	TT

1   Bring the velouté to a simmer.
2   In a stainless steel bowl, whip the egg yolks with the cream to create a liaison. Ladle approximately one-third of the hot velouté sauce into this mixture, while whisking, to temper the yolk and cream mixture.
3   When one-third of the velouté has been incorporated into the now-warmed yolk and cream mixture, gradually add the liaison to the remaining velouté sauce while whisking continuously.
4   Reheat the sauce. Do not let it boil.
5   Add the lemon juice; season with salt and white pepper to taste.
6   Strain through a china cap lined with cheesecloth.

Approximate values per 1-fl.-oz. (30-ml) serving: **Calories** 40, **Total fat** 3.5 g, **Saturated fat** 2 g, **Cholesterol** 25 mg, **Sodium** 95 mg, **Total carbohydrates** 1 g, **Protein** 1 g, **Vitamin A** 4%

Small Allemande Sauces

Several small sauces are easily produced from an allemande sauce made with either a chicken or veal velouté. The quantities given are for 1 quart (1 liter) allemande. The final step for each recipe is to season to taste with salt and pepper.

AURORA   Add to allemande 2 ounces (60 grams) tomato paste and finish with 1 ounce (30 grams) butter.

HORSERADISH   Add to allemande 4 fluid ounces (120 milliliters) heavy cream and 1 teaspoon (5 milliliters) dry mustard. Just before service add 2 ounces (60 grams) freshly grated horseradish. The horseradish should not be cooked with the sauce.

MUSHROOM   Sauté 4 ounces (120 grams) sliced mushrooms in ½ ounce (15 grams) whole butter; add 2 teaspoons (10 milliliters) lemon juice. Then add the allemande to the mushrooms. Do not strain.

POULETTE   Sauté 8 ounces (250 grams) sliced mushrooms and ½ ounce (15 grams) diced shallots in 1 ounce (30 grams) whole butter. Add to the allemande; then add 2 fluid ounces (60 milliliters) heavy cream. Finish with lemon juice to taste and 1 tablespoon (15 milliliters) chopped parsley.

SUPRÊME SAUCE

RECIPE 11.10

Yield: 1 gal. (4 lt)

Chicken velouté sauce	1 gal.	4 lt
Mushroom trimmings	8 oz.	225 g
Heavy cream	1 qt.	1 lt
Salt and white pepper	TT	TT

1 Simmer the velouté sauce with the mushroom trimmings until reduced by one-fourth.
2 Gradually whisk in the heavy cream and return to a simmer.
3 Adjust the seasonings.
4 Strain through a china cap lined with cheesecloth.

Approximate values per 1-fl.-oz. (30-ml) serving: **Calories** 45, **Total fat** 4 g, **Saturated fat** 2.5 g, **Cholesterol** 15 mg, **Sodium** 95 mg, **Total carbohydrates** 1 g, **Protein** 1 g, **Vitamin A** 4%

Small Suprême Sauces

The following small sauces are easily made from a suprême sauce. The quantities given are for 1 quart (1 liter) suprême sauce. The final step for each recipe is to season to taste with salt and pepper.

ALBUFERA   Add to suprême 3 fluid ounces (90 milliliters) glace de volaille and 2 ounces (60 grams) red pepper butter (page 224).

HUNGARIAN   Sweat 2 ounces (60 grams) diced onion in 1 tablespoon (15 milliliters) whole butter. Add 1 tablespoon (15 milliliters) paprika. Stir in the suprême sauce. Cook for 2–3 minutes, strain and finish with whole butter.

IVORY   Add to suprême 3 fluid ounces (90 milliliters) glace de volaille.

THE ESPAGNOLE FAMILY

The mother sauce of the espagnole (ess-spah-nyol) or brown sauce family is full-bodied and rich. It is made from a brown stock to which brown roux, mirepoix and tomato purée have been added. Most often this sauce is used to produce demi-glace. Brown stock is also used to make jus lié. Demi-glace and jus lié are intermediary sauces used to create the small sauces of the espagnole family.

ESPAGNOLE (BROWN SAUCE)

RECIPE 11.11

Yield: 1 gal. (4 lt)

Mirepoix, medium dice	2 lb.	1 kg
Clarified butter	8 fl. oz.	250 ml
Flour	8 oz.	250 g
Brown stock	5 qt.	5 lt
Tomato purée	8 oz.	250 g
Sachet:		
Bay leaf	1	1
Dried thyme	½ tsp.	2 ml
Peppercorns, crushed	¼ tsp.	1 ml
Parsley stems	8	8
Salt and pepper	TT	TT

Espagnole

1 Sauté the mirepoix in butter until well caramelized.

2 Add the flour and cook to make a brown roux.

3 Add the brown stock and tomato purée. Stir to break up any lumps of roux. Bring to a boil; reduce to a simmer.

4 Add the sachet.

5 Simmer for approximately 1 ½ hours, allowing the sauce to reduce. Skim the surface as needed to remove impurities.

6 Strain the sauce through a china cap lined with several layers of cheesecloth. Adjust seasonings and cool in a water bath or hold for service.

Approximate values per 1-fl.-oz. (30-ml) serving: **Calories** 35, **Total fat** 2 g, **Saturated fat** 1 g, **Cholesterol** 5 mg, **Sodium** 150 mg, **Total carbohydrates** 4 g, **Protein** 1 g, **Vitamin A** 6%, **Claims**—low fat; low calorie

Demi-Glace

Brown stock is used to make the espagnole or brown sauce described earlier. Espagnole sauce can then be made into demi-glace, which in turn is used to make the small sauces of the espagnole family. Demi-glace is half brown sauce, half brown stock, reduced by half. It is usually finished with a small amount of Madeira or sherry wine. Because demi-glace creates a richer, more flavorful base, it produces finer small sauces than those made directly from a brown sauce.

A properly made demi-glace is rich, smooth and lump-free. Its prominent roasted flavor comes from the bones used for the brown stock. There should be no taste of roux. The caramelized bones and mirepoix as well as the tomato product contribute to its glossy dark brown, almost chocolate, color. It should be thick enough to cling to food without being pasty or heavy.

RECIPE 11.12

DEMI-GLACE

Demi-Glace

Yield: 1 qt. (1 lt)

Brown stock	1 qt.	1 lt
Brown sauce	1 qt.	1 lt

1 Combine the stock and sauce in a saucepan over medium heat.

2 Simmer until the mixture is reduced by half (a yield of 1 quart or 1 liter).

3 Strain and cool in a water bath.

Approximate values per 1-fl.-oz. (30-ml) serving: **Calories** 30, **Total fat** 1.5 g, **Saturated fat** 0.5 g, **Cholesterol** 5 mg, **Sodium** 200 mg, **Total carbohydrates** 4 g, **Protein** 1 g, **Vitamin A** 6%, **Claims**—low fat; low calorie

Jus Lié

Jus lié (zhoo lee-ay), also known as fond lié, is used like a demi-glace, especially to produce small sauces. Jus lié is lighter and easier to make than a demi-glace, however. It is made in one of two ways:

1 A rich brown stock is thickened with cornstarch or arrowroot and seasoned.

2 A rich brown stock is simmered and reduced so that it thickens naturally because of the concentrated amounts of gelatin and other proteins.

The starch-thickened method is a quick alternative to the long-simmering demi-glace. But because it is simply a brown stock thickened with cornstarch or arrowroot, it will only be as good as the stock with which it was begun. Sauces made from reduced stock usually have a better flavor but can be expensive to produce because of high food costs and lengthy reduction time.

A properly made jus lié is very rich and smooth. It shares many flavor characteristics with demi-glace. Its color should be dark brown and glossy from the concentrated gelatin content. Its consistency is somewhat lighter than demi-glace, but it should still cling lightly to foods.

Small Brown Sauces

Demi-glace and jus lié are used to produce many small sauces. The quantities given are for 1 quart (1 liter) demi-glace or jus lié. The final step for each recipe is to season to taste with salt and pepper.

BORDELAISE   Combine 1 pint (250 milliliters) dry red wine, 2 ounces (60 grams) chopped shallots, 1 bay leaf, 1 sprig thyme and a pinch of black pepper in a saucepan. Reduce by three-fourths, then add demi-glace and simmer for 15 minutes. Strain through a fine chinois. Finish with 2 ounces (60 grams) whole butter and garnish with sliced, poached beef marrow.

CHASSEUR (HUNTER'S SAUCE)   Sauté 4 ounces (120 grams) sliced mushrooms and 1 tablespoon (15 milliliters) diced shallots in whole butter. Add 8 fluid ounces (250 milliliters) white wine and reduce by three-fourths. Then add demi-glace and 6 ounces (170 grams) diced tomatoes; simmer for 5 minutes. Do not strain. Garnish with chopped parsley.

CHÂTEAUBRIAND   Combine 1 pint (500 milliliters) dry white wine and 2 ounces (60 grams) diced shallots. Reduce the mixture by two-thirds. Add demi-glace and reduce by half. Season to taste with lemon juice and cayenne pepper. Do not strain. Swirl in 4 ounces (120 grams) whole butter to finish and garnish with chopped fresh tarragon.

CHEVREUIL   Prepare a poivrade sauce but add 6 ounces (170 grams) bacon or game trimmings to the mirepoix. Finish with 4 fluid ounces (120 milliliters) red wine and a dash of cayenne pepper.

MADEIRA OR PORT   Bring demi-glace to a boil, reduce slightly. Then add 4 fluid ounces (120 milliliters) madeira wine or ruby port.

MARCHAND DE VIN   Reduce 8 fluid ounces (250 milliliters) dry red wine and 2 ounces (60 grams) diced shallots by two-thirds. Then add demi-glace, simmer and strain.

MUSHROOM   Blanch 8 ounces (250 grams) mushroom caps in 8 fluid ounces (250 milliliters) boiling water seasoned with salt and lemon juice. Drain the mushrooms, saving the liquid. Reduce this liquid to 2 tablespoons (30 milliliters) and add it to the demi-glace. Just before service stir in 2 ounces (60 grams) whole butter and the mushroom caps.

PÉRIGUEUX   Add finely diced truffles to Madeira sauce. **Périgourdine** sauce is the same, except that the truffles are cut into relatively thick slices.

PIQUANT   Combine 1 ounce (30 grams) shallots, 4 fluid ounces (120 milliliters) white wine and 4 fluid ounces (120 milliliters) white wine vinegar. Reduce the mixture by two-thirds. Then add demi-glace and simmer for 10 minutes. Add 2 ounces (60 grams) diced cornichons, 1 tablespoon (15 milliliters) fresh tarragon, 1 tablespoon (15 milliliters) fresh parsley and 1 tablespoon (15 milliliters) fresh chervil. Do not strain.

POIVRADE   Sweat 12 ounces (340 grams) mirepoix in 2 tablespoons (30 milliliters) oil. Add 1 bay leaf, 1 sprig thyme and 4 parsley stems. Then add 1 pint (500 milliliters) vinegar and 4 fluid ounces (120 milliliters) white wine. Reduce by half, add demi-glace and simmer for 40 minutes. Then add 20 crushed peppercorns and simmer for 5 more minutes. Strain through a fine chinois and finish with up to 2 ounces (60 grams) whole butter.

ROBERT   Sauté 8 ounces (250 grams) chopped onion in 1 ounce (30 grams) whole butter. Add 8 fluid ounces (250 milliliters) dry white wine and reduce by two-thirds. Add demi-glace and simmer for 10 minutes. Strain and then add 2 teaspoons (10 milliliters) prepared Dijon mustard and 1 tablespoon (15 milliliters) granulated sugar. If the finished Robert sauce is garnished with sliced sour pickles, preferably cornichons, it is known as **Charcuterie.**

POIVRADE POUR GIBIER

Poivrade is also the name given a flavorful sauce traditionally made with game stock and seasoned with peppercorns. It is used for the wonderful *Sauce Grand Veneur*, one of the most complex small sauces in the classic repertoire. For *Grand Veneur*, game stock is flavored with demi-glace and finished with cream and currant jelly. The sweetness balances the strong flavor of the game meats.

THE TOMATO SAUCE FAMILY

Classic tomato sauce is made from tomatoes, vegetables, seasonings and white stock and thickened with a blond or brown roux. In today's kitchens, however, most tomato sauces are not thickened with roux. Rather, they are created from tomatoes, herbs, spices, vegetables and other flavoring ingredients simmered together and puréed.

A **gastrique** is sometimes added to reduce the acidity of a tomato sauce. To prepare a gastrique, caramelize a small amount of sugar, then thin or deglaze with vinegar. This mixture is then used to finish the tomato sauce.

A properly made tomato sauce is thick, rich and full-flavored. Its texture should be grainier than most other classic sauces, but it should still be smooth. The vegetables and other seasonings should add flavor, but none should be pronounced. Tomato sauce should not be bitter, acidic or overly sweet. It should be deep red and thick enough to cling to foods.

▶ **gastrique** (gas-streek) caramelized sugar deglazed with vinegar; used to flavor tomato or savory fruit sauces

RECIPE 11.13

TOMATO SAUCE

Yield: 1 gal. (4 lt)

Salt pork, small dice	4 oz.	120 g
Mirepoix	1 lb. 8 oz.	750 g
Tomato, fresh or canned	3 qt.	3 lt
Tomato purée	2 qt.	2 lt
Sachet:		
Dried thyme	1 tsp.	5 ml
Bay leaves	3	3
Garlic cloves	3	3
Parsley stems	10	10
Peppercorns, crushed	½ tsp.	3 ml
Salt	1½ oz.	45 g
Granulated sugar	¾ oz.	20 g
White stock	3 qt.	3 lt
Pork bones	2 lb.	1 kg

1 Passing the sauce through a food mill.

1 Render the salt pork over medium heat.
2 Add the mirepoix and sauté, but do not brown.
3 Add the tomatoes and tomato purée, sachet, salt and sugar.
4 Add the white stock and bones.
5 Simmer slowly for ½ to 2 hours or until the desired consistency has been reached.
6 Remove the bones and sachet, and pass the sauce through a food mill. Cool in a water bath and refrigerate.

Approximate values per 1-fl.-oz. (30-ml) serving: **Calories** 30, **Total fat** 0.5 g, **Saturated fat** 0.2 g, **Cholesterol** 0.7 mg, **Sodium** 240 mg, **Total carbohydrates** 4 g, **Protein** 2 g, **Vitamin A** 6%, **Claims**—low fat; low calorie

2 The finished sauce.

Small Tomato Sauces

The following small sauces are made by adding the listed ingredients to 1 quart (1 liter) tomato sauce. The final step for each recipe is to season to taste with salt and pepper.

CREOLE Sauté 6 ounces (170 grams) finely diced onion, 4 ounces (120 grams) thinly sliced celery and 1 teaspoon (5 milliliters) garlic in 1 fluid ounce (30 milliliters) oil. Add tomato sauce, a bay leaf and a pinch of thyme; simmer for 15 minutes. Then add 4 ounces (120 grams) finely diced green pepper and a dash of hot pepper sauce; simmer for 15 minutes longer. Remove the bay leaf.

SPANISH Prepare creole sauce as directed, adding 4 ounces (120 grams) sliced mushrooms to the sautéed onions. Garnish with sliced black or green olives.

MILANAISE Sauté 5 ounces (140 grams) sliced mushrooms in ½ ounce (15 grams) whole butter. Add tomato sauce and then stir in 5 ounces (140 grams) cooked ham (julienne) and 5 ounces (140 grams) cooked tongue (julienne). Bring to a simmer.

THE HOLLANDAISE FAMILY

Hollandaise and the small sauces derived from it are **emulsified** sauces. Egg yolks, which contain large amounts of lecithin, a natural emulsifier, are used to emulsify warm butter and a small amount of water, lemon juice or vinegar. When the egg yolks are vigorously whipped with the liquid while the warm butter is slowly added, the lecithin coats the individual fat droplets and holds them in suspension in the liquid.

A properly made hollandaise is smooth, buttery, pale lemon-yellow-colored and very rich. It is lump-free and should not exhibit any signs of separation. The buttery flavor should dominate but not mask the flavors of the egg, lemon and vinegar. The sauce should be frothy and light, not heavy like a mayonnaise.

► **emulsification** the process by which generally unmixable liquids, such as oil and water, are forced into a uniform distribution

Temperatures and Sanitation Concerns

Temperatures play an important role in the proper production of a hollandaise sauce. As the egg yolks and liquid are whisked together, they are cooked over a bain marie until they thicken to the consistency of slightly whipped cream. Do not overheat this mixture, because even slightly cooked eggs lose their ability to emulsify. The clarified butter used to make the sauce should be warm but not so hot as to further cook the egg yolks. Although hollandaise sauce can be made from whole butter, a more stable and consistent product will be achieved by using clarified butter. (Clarification is described in Chapter 9, Mise en Place.)

Rescuing a Broken Hollandaise

Occasionally, a hollandaise will break or separate and appear thin, grainy or even lumpy. A sauce breaks when the emulsion has not formed or the emulsified butter, eggs and liquid have separated. This may happen for several reasons: The temperature of the eggs or butter may have been too high or too low; the butter may have been added too quickly; the egg yolks may have been overcooked; too much butter may have been added or the sauce may not have been whipped vigorously enough.

To rescue and re-emulsify broken hollandaise you must first determine if it is too hot or too cold. If it is too hot, allow the sauce to cool. If it is too cold, reheat the sauce over a double boiler before attempting to rescue it.

For 1 quart (1 liter) of broken sauce, place 1 tablespoon (15 milliliters) of water in a clean stainless steel bowl and slowly beat in the broken sauce. If the problem seems to be that the eggs were overcooked or too much butter was added, add a yolk to the water before incorporating the broken sauce.

SAFETY ALERT

HANDLING EMULSIFIED BUTTER SAUCES

Emulsified butter sauces must be held at the specific temperatures most conducive to bacterial growth: 40°F–140°F (4°C–60°C). If the sauce is heated above 150°F (65°C), the eggs will cook and the sauce will break and become grainy. If the sauce temperature falls below 45°F (7°C), the butter will solidify, making the sauce unusable. In order to minimize the risk of food-borne illnesses:

- Always use clean, sanitized utensils.
- Schedule sauce production as close to the time of service as possible. Never hold hollandaise-based sauces more than 1½ hours.
- Make small batches of sauce.
- Never mix an old batch of sauce with a new one.

HOLLANDAISE   RECIPE 11.14

Yield: 1½ qt. (1.5 lt)

White peppercorns, crushed	½ tsp.	2 ml
White wine vinegar	6 fl. oz.	180 ml
Water	4 fl. oz.	120 ml
Egg yolks	10	10
Lemon juice	2½ fl. oz.	75 ml
Clarified butter, warm	1 qt.	1 lt
Salt and white pepper	TT	TT
Cayenne pepper	TT	TT

1 Combining the egg yolks with the vinegar and pepper reduction in a stainless steel bowl.

2 Whipping the mixture over a double boiler until it is thick enough to leave a trail when the whip is removed.

3 Using a kitchen towel and saucepot to firmly hold the bowl containing the yolks, add the butter slowly while whipping continuously.

4 Hollandaise at the proper consistency.

1 Combine the peppercorns, vinegar and water in a small saucepan and reduce by one-half.

2 Place the egg yolks in a stainless steel bowl. Strain the vinegar and pepper reduction through a chinois, into the yolks.

3 Place the bowl over a double boiler, whipping the mixture continuously with a wire whip. As the yolks cook, the mixture will thicken. When the mixture is thick enough to leave a trail across the surface when the whip is drawn away, remove the bowl from the double boiler. Do not overcook the egg yolks.

4 Whip in 1 fluid ounce (30 milliliters) lemon juice to stop the yolks from cooking.

5 Begin to add the warm clarified butter to the egg yolk mixture a drop at a time, while constantly whipping the mixture to form an emulsion. Once the emulsion is started, the butter may be added more quickly. Continue until all the butter is incorporated.

6 Whip in the remaining lemon juice. Adjust the seasonings with salt, white pepper and cayenne pepper.

7 Strain the sauce through cheesecloth if necessary and hold for service in a warm (not simmering) bain marie.

Approximate values per 1-fl.-oz. (30-ml) serving: **Calories** 170, **Total fat** 18 g, **Saturated fat** 11 g, **Cholesterol** 90 mg, **Sodium** 180 mg, **Total carbohydrates** 0 g, **Protein** 1 g, **Vitamin A** 20%

RECIPE 11.15   HOLLANDAISE, BLENDER METHOD

Yield: 1 qt. (1 lt)

Egg yolks	9	9
Water, warm	3 fl. oz.	90 ml
Lemon juice	1 fl. oz.	30 ml
Cayenne pepper	TT	TT
Salt	1 tsp.	5 ml
White pepper	¼ tsp.	1 ml
Tabasco sauce	TT	TT
Whole butter	24 oz.	750 g

1 Place the egg yolks, water, lemon juice, cayenne pepper, salt, white pepper and Tabasco sauce in the bowl of the blender. Cover and blend on high speed for approximately 5 seconds.

2 Heat the butter to approximately 175°F (80°C). This allows the butter to cook the yolks as it is added to them.

3 Turn the blender on and immediately begin to add the butter in a steady stream. Incorporate all the butter in 20 to 30 seconds. Adjust the seasonings.

4 If any lumps are present, strain the sauce through a mesh strainer. Transfer the sauce to a stainless steel container and adjust the seasonings. Hold for service in a bain marie, remembering the sanitation precautions discussed earlier.

Approximate values per 1-fl.-oz. (30-ml) serving: **Calories** 120, **Total fat** 12 g, **Saturated fat** 7 g, **Cholesterol** 70 mg, **Sodium** 170 mg, **Total carbohydrates** 0 g, **Protein** 1 g, **Vitamin A** 15%

Small Hollandaise Sauces

The following small sauces are easily made by adding the listed ingredients to 1 quart (1 liter) of hollandaise. The final step for each recipe is to season to taste with salt and pepper. Béarnaise is presented here as a small sauce although some chefs consider it a leading sauce.

BÉARNAISE (bair-NAYZ) Combine 2 ounces (60 grams) chopped shallots, 5 tablespoons (75 milliliters) chopped fresh tarragon, 3 tablespoons (45 milliliters) chopped fresh chervil and 1 teaspoon (5 milliliters) crushed peppercorns with 8 fluid ounces (250 milliliters) white wine vinegar. Reduce to 2 fluid ounces (60 milliliters). Add this reduction to the egg yolks and proceed with the hollandaise recipe. Strain the finished sauce and season to taste with salt and cayenne pepper. Garnish with additional chopped fresh tarragon.

CHORON Combine 2 ounces (60 grams) tomato paste and 2 fluid ounces (60 milliliters) heavy cream; add the mixture to a béarnaise.

FOYOT Add to béarnaise 3 fluid ounces (90 milliliters) melted glace de viande.

GRIMROD Infuse a hollandaise sauce with saffron.

MALTAISE Add to hollandaise 2 fluid ounces (60 milliliters) orange juice and 2 teaspoons (10 milliliters) finely grated orange zest. Blood oranges are traditionally used for this sauce.

MOUSSELINE (CHANTILLY SAUCE) Whip 8 fluid ounces (250 milliliters) heavy cream until stiff. Fold it into the hollandaise just before service. Mousseline sauce is also used as a **glaçage** coating.

▶ **glaçage** (glah-sahge) browning or glazing a food, usually under a salamander or broiler

BEURRE BLANC AND BEURRE ROUGE

Beurre blanc (burr blahnk) and beurre rouge (burr rooge) are emulsified butter sauces made without egg yolks. The small amounts of lecithin and other emulsifiers naturally found in butter are used to form an oil-in-water emulsion. Although similar to hollandaise in concept, they are not considered either classic leading or compound sauces. Beurre blancs are thinner and lighter than hollandaise and béarnaise. They should be smooth and slightly thicker than heavy cream.

Beurre blanc and beurre rouge are made from three main ingredients: shallots, white (Fr. *blanc*) wine or red (Fr. *rouge*) wine and whole butter (not clarified). The shallots and wine provide flavor, while the butter becomes the sauce. A good beurre blanc or beurre rouge is rich and buttery, with a neutral flavor that responds well to other seasonings and flavorings, thereby lending itself to the addition of herbs, spices and vegetable purées to complement the dish with which it is served. Its pale color changes depending upon the flavorings added. It should be light and airy yet still liquid, while thick enough to cling to food.

▶ **beurre noir** (burr NWAR) French for "black butter"; used to describe whole butter cooked until dark brown (not black); sometimes flavored with vinegar or lemon juice, capers and parsley and served over fish, eggs and vegetables

▶ **beurre noisette** (burr nwah-ZEHT) French for "brown butter"; used to describe butter cooked until it is a light brown color; it is flavored and used in much the same manner as beurre noir

▶ PROCEDURE FOR PREPARING BEURRE BLANC OR BEURRE ROUGE

1 Use a nonaluminum pan to prevent discoloring the sauce. Do not use a thin-walled or nonstick pan, as heat is not evenly distributed in a thin-walled pan and a nonstick pan makes it difficult for an emulsion to set.

2 Over medium heat, reduce the wine, shallots and herbs or other seasonings, if used, until *au sec* (that is, nearly dry). Some chefs add a small amount of heavy cream at this point and reduce the mixture. Although not necessary, the added cream helps stabilize the finished sauce.

3 Whisk in cold butter a small amount at a time. The butter should be well chilled, as this allows the butterfat, water and milk solids to be gradually incorporated into the sauce as the butter melts and the mixture is whisked.

4 When all the butter is incorporated, strain and hold the sauce in a bain marie.

TEMPERATURE

Do not let the sauce become too hot. At 136°F (58°C) some of the emulsifying proteins begin to break down and release the butterfat they hold in emulsion. Extended periods at temperatures over 136°F (58°C) will cause the sauce to separate. If the sauce separates, it can be corrected by cooling to approximately 110°F–120°F (43°C–49°C) and whisking to reincorporate the butterfat.

If the sauce is allowed to cool below 85°F (30°C), the butterfat will solidify. If the sauce is reheated it will separate into butterfat and water; whisking will not re-emulsify it. Cold beurre blanc can be used as a soft, flavored butter, however, simply by whisking it at room temperature until it smoothes out to the consistency of mayonnaise.

RECIPE 11.16   **BEURRE BLANC**

Yield: 1 qt. (1 lt)

White wine	1 fl. oz.	30 ml
White wine vinegar	4 fl. oz.	120 ml
Salt	1 ½ tsp.	7 ml
White pepper	½ tsp.	2 ml
Shallot, minced	3 Tbsp.	45 ml
Whole butter, chilled	2 lb.	1 kg

1 Reducing the shallots and wine au sec.

2 Whisking in the cold butter a little at a time.

3 Straining the sauce.

1 Combine the white wine, white wine vinegar, salt, white pepper and shallot in a small saucepan. Reduce the mixture until approximately 2 tablespoons (30 milliliters) of liquid remain. If more than 2 tablespoons of liquid are allowed to remain, the resulting sauce will be too thin. For a thicker sauce, reduce the mixture au sec.

2 Cut the butter into pieces approximately 1 ounce (30 grams) in weight. Over low heat, whisk in the butter a few pieces at a time, using the chilled butter to keep the sauce between 100°F and 120°F (43°C and 49°C).

3 Once all the butter has been incorporated, remove the saucepan from the heat. Strain through a chinois and hold the sauce at a temperature between 100°F and 130°F (38°C and 54°C) for service.

Variations: *Beurre Rouge*—Substitute a dry red wine for the white wine and red wine vinegar for the white wine vinegar.

Lemon-Dill—Heat 2 tablespoons (30 milliliters) lemon juice and whisk it into the beurre blanc. Stir in 4 tablespoons (60 milliliters) chopped fresh dill.

Pink Peppercorn—Add 2 tablespoons (30 milliliters) coarsely crushed pink peppercorns to the shallot-wine reduction when making beurre rouge. Garnish the finished sauce with whole pink peppercorns.

Approximate values per 1-fl.-oz. (30-ml) serving: **Calories** 210, **Total fat** 23 g, **Saturated fat** 14 g, **Cholesterol** 60 mg, **Sodium** 340 mg, **Total carbohydrates** 0 g, **Protein** 0 g, **Vitamin A** 20%

COMPOUND BUTTERS

A compound butter is made by incorporating various seasonings into softened whole butter. These butters, also known as *beurres composés,* give flavor and color to small sauces or may be served as sauces in their own right. For example, a slice of maître d'hôtel butter (parsley butter) is often placed on a grilled steak or piece of fish at the time of service. The butter quickly melts, creating a sauce for the beef or fish.

Butter and flavoring ingredients can be combined with a blender, food processor or mixer. Using parchment paper or plastic wrap, the butter is then rolled into a cylinder, chilled and sliced as needed. Or it can be piped into rosettes and refrigerated until firm. Most compound butters will keep for two to three days in the refrigerator, or they can be frozen for longer storage.

1 Placing the butter on the plastic wrap.

RECIPES FOR COMPOUND BUTTERS

For each of the following butters, add the listed ingredients to 1 pound (500 grams) of softened, unsalted butter. The compound butter should then be seasoned with salt and pepper to taste.

BASIL BUTTER Mince 2 ounces (60 grams) basil and 2 ounces (60 grams) shallots; add to the butter with 2 teaspoons (10 milliliters) lemon juice.

HERB BUTTER Add to the butter up to 1 cup (250 milliliters) of mixed chopped fresh herbs such as parsley, dill, chives, tarragon or chervil.

LOBSTER OR CRAYFISH BUTTER Grind 8 ounces (250 grams) cooked lobster or crayfish meat, shells and/or coral with 1 pound (500 grams) butter. Place in a saucepan and clarify. Strain the butter through a fine chinois lined with cheesecloth. Refrigerate, then remove the butterfat when firm.

MAÎTRE D'HÔTEL BUTTER Mix into the butter 4 tablespoons (60 milliliters) finely chopped parsley, 3 tablespoons (45 milliliters) lemon juice and a dash of white pepper.

MONTPELIER BUTTER Blanch 1 ounce (30 grams) parsley, 1 ounce (30 grams) chervil, 1 ounce (30 grams) watercress and 1 ounce (30 grams)

2 Rolling the butter in the plastic wrap to form a cylinder.

tarragon in boiling water. Drain thoroughly. Mince 2 hard-boiled egg yolks, 2 garlic cloves and 2 gherkin pickles. Blend everything into the butter.

RED PEPPER BUTTER   Purée 8 ounces (250 grams) roasted, peeled red bell peppers until liquid, then add to the butter.

SHALLOT BUTTER   Blanch 8 ounces (250 grams) of peeled shallots in boiling water. Dry and finely dice them and mix with the butter.

PAN GRAVY

▶ **gravy** a sauce made from meat or poultry juices combined with a liquid and thickening agent; usually made in the pan in which the meat or poultry was cooked

Pan gravy is aptly named: It is made directly in the pan used to roast the poultry, beef, lamb or pork that the gravy will accompany. Pan gravy is actually a sauce; it is a liquid thickened with a roux. Pan gravy gains additional flavors from the drippings left in the roasting pan and by using a portion of the fat rendered during the roasting process to make the roux. This technique is used in the recipe for Roast Turkey with Chestnut Dressing and Giblet Gravy (page 425).

A properly made pan gravy should have all the characteristics of any brown sauce except that it has a meatier flavor as a result of the pan drippings.

▶ PROCEDURE FOR PREPARING PAN GRAVY

1 Remove the cooked meat or poultry from the roasting pan.
2 If mirepoix was not added during the roasting process, add it to the pan containing the drippings and fat.
3 Place the roasting pan on the stove top and clarify the fat by cooking off any remaining moisture.
4 Pour off the fat, reserving it to make the roux.
5 Deglaze the pan using an appropriate stock. The deglazing liquid may be transferred to a saucepan for easier handling, or the gravy may be finished directly in the roasting pan.
6 Add enough stock or water to the deglazing liquid to yield the proper amount of finished gravy.
7 Determine the amount of roux needed to thicken the liquid and prepare it in a separate pan, using a portion of the reserved fat.
8 Add the roux to the liquid and bring the mixture to a simmer. Simmer until the mirepoix is well cooked, the flavor is extracted and the flour taste is cooked out.
9 Strain the gravy and adjust the seasonings.

COULIS

▶ **coulis** (koo-lee) a sauce made from a purée of vegetables and/or fruit; may be served hot or cold

The term *coulis* most often refers to a sauce made from a purée of vegetables and/or fruit. A vegetable coulis can be served as either a hot or a cold accompaniment to other vegetables, starches, meat, poultry, fish or shellfish. It is often made from a single vegetable base (popular examples include broccoli, tomatoes and sweet red peppers) cooked with flavoring ingredients such as onions, garlic, shallots, herbs and spices and then puréed. An appropriate liquid (stock, water or cream) may be added to thin the purée if necessary. Vegetable coulis are often prepared with very little fat and served as a healthy alternative to a heavier, classic sauce.

A fruit coulis, often made from fresh or frozen berries, is generally used as a dessert sauce. It is usually as simple as puréed fruit thinned to the desired consistency with sugar syrup.

Typically, both vegetable and fruit coulis have a texture similar to that of a thin tomato sauce. But their textures can range from slightly grainy to almost lumpy, depending on their intended use. The flavor and color of a coulis should be that of the main ingredient. The flavors of herbs, spices and other flavoring ingredients should only complement and not dominate the coulis.

▶ PROCEDURE FOR PREPARING A COULIS

Here we include a procedure for making a vegetable coulis. Procedures for making fruit coulis are included as recipes in Chapter 34, Custards, Creams, Frozen Desserts and Dessert Sauces.

1 Cook the main ingredient and any additional flavoring ingredients with an appropriate liquid.

2 Purée the main ingredient and flavoring ingredients in a food mill, blender or food processor.

3 Combine the purée with the appropriate liquid and simmer to blend the flavors.

4 Thin and season the coulis as desired.

RED PEPPER COULIS

RECIPE 11.17

Yield: 1 qt. (1 lt)

Vegetable oil	1 fl. oz.	30 ml
Garlic, chopped	2 tsp.	10 ml
Onion, small dice	3 oz.	90 g
Red bell pepper, medium dice	3 lb.	1.25 kg
White wine	8 fl. oz.	250 ml
Chicken stock	1 pt.	450 ml
Salt and pepper	TT	TT

1 Heat the oil and sauté the garlic and onion until translucent, without browning.

2 Add the bell pepper and sauté until tender.

3 Deglaze the pan with the white wine.

4 Add the chicken stock, bring to a simmer and cook for 15 minutes. Season with salt and pepper.

5 Purée in a blender or food processor and strain through a china cap.

6 Adjust the consistency and seasonings and hold for service.

Approximate values per 1-fl.-oz. (30-ml) serving: **Calories** 20, **Total fat** 1 g, **Saturated fat** 0 g, **Cholesterol** 0 mg, **Sodium** 45 mg, **Total carbohydrates** 2 g, **Protein** 1 g, **Vitamin C** 50%, **Claims**—low fat; low sodium; low calorie

1 Sautéing the red peppers.

2 Puréeing the cooked peppers.

3 Straining the coulis.

CONTEMPORARY SAUCES

Modern chefs and menu writers are relying less on traditional sauces and more on salsas, relishes, juices, broths, essences and infused oils in their work. Unlike classic sauces, these modern accompaniments do not rely on meat-based stocks and starch thickeners, but rather on fresh vegetables, vegetable juices, aromatic broths and intensely flavored oils. The names for these sauces are not codified, as are those in the classic sauce repertoire. Chefs apply various terms freely, using whatever name best fits the dish and the overall menu. Most of these contemporary sauces can be prepared more quickly than their classic counterparts, and the use of fresh fruits and vegetables enhances the healthfulness of the dish. These so-called contemporary or modern sauces may have a lighter body and less fat than classic sauces, but they are still derived from classical culinary techniques and principles. The sauces should be appropriate in flavor, texture and appearance and should complement, not overwhelm, the food they accompany.

SALSA AND RELISH

Many people think of salsa (Spanish for "sauce") as a chunky mixture of raw vegetables and chiles eaten with chips or ladled over Mexican food; they think

▶ **chutney** a sweet-and-sour condiment made of fruits and/or vegetables cooked in vinegar with sugar and spices; some chutneys are reduced to a purée; others retain recognizable pieces of their ingredients.

of relish as a sweet green condiment spooned on a hot dog. But salsas and relishes—generally, cold chunky mixtures of herbs, spices, fruits and/or vegetables—can be used as sauces for many meat, poultry, fish and shellfish items. They can include ingredients such as oranges, pineapple, papaya, black beans, jicama, tomatillos and an array of other vegetables.

Although not members of any classic sauce family, salsas and relishes are currently enjoying great popularity because of their intense fresh flavors, ease of preparation and low fat and calorie content. Salsas and relishes are often a riot of colors, textures and flavors, simultaneously cool and hot, spicy and sweet.

▶ PROCEDURE FOR PREPARING A SALSA OR RELISH

1 Cut or chop the ingredients.
2 Precook and chill items as directed in the recipe.
3 Toss all ingredients together and refrigerate, allowing the flavors to combine for at least 30 minutes before service.

RECIPE 11.18

 TOMATO SALSA (PICO DE GALLO)

Mixing tomato salsa.

Yield: 1 qt. (1 lt)

Tomatoes, seeded, small dice	5	5
Green onions, sliced	1 bunch	1 bunch
Garlic cloves, minced	3	3
Cilantro, chopped	½ bunch	½ bunch
Jalapeño, chopped fine	3	3
Lemon juice	2 fl. oz.	60 ml
Cumin, ground	½ tsp.	2 ml
Salt and pepper	TT	TT

1 Combine all ingredients and gently toss. Adjust seasonings and refrigerate.

Approximate values per 1-fl.-oz. (30-ml) serving: **Calories** 5, **Total fat** 0 g, **Saturated fat** 0 g, **Cholesterol** 0 mg, **Sodium** 30 mg, **Total carbohydrates** 1 g, **Protein** 0 g, **Claims**—fat free; very low sodium; low calorie

VEGETABLE JUICE SAUCES

Juice extractors make it possible to prepare juice from fresh, uncooked vegetables such as carrots, beets and spinach. Thinner and smoother than a purée, vegetable juice can be heated, reduced, flavored and enriched with butter to create colorful, intensely flavored sauces. Cream or stock can be added to finish the sauce. Sauces made from vegetable juices are sometimes referred to as an **essence** or **tea** on menus.

Juice from a single type of vegetable provides the purest, most pronounced flavor, but two or more vegetables sometimes can be combined successfully. Be careful of mixing too many flavors and colors in the juice, however. Juiced vegetable sauces are particularly appropriate with pasta, fish, shellfish and poultry, and can be useful in vegetarian cuisine or as a healthier alternative to classic sauces.

▶ **essence** a sauce made from a concentrated vegetable juice

▶ PROCEDURE FOR PREPARING A VEGETABLE JUICE SAUCE

1 Wash and peel vegetables as needed.
2 Process the vegetables through a juice extractor.
3 Place the juice in a saucepan and add stock, lemon juice, herbs or other flavorings as desired.

4 Bring the sauce to a simmer and reduce as necessary.

5 Strain the sauce through a fine chinois.

6 Adjust the seasonings and whisk in whole butter to finish.

THYME-SCENTED CELERY ESSENCE

RECIPE 11.19

STOUFFER STANFORD COURT HOTEL, San Francisco, CA

Former Executive Chef Ercolino Crugnale

Yield: 1 qt. (1 lt)

Celery juice	1 qt.	1 lt
Tomato juice	1 pt.	500 ml
Fresh thyme, chopped	½ oz.	15 g
Whole butter	6 oz.	180 g
Salt	TT	TT
Tabasco sauce	TT	TT

1 Combine the celery juice, tomato juice and thyme. Bring to a simmer and reduce to 1½ pints (750 milliliters).

2 Whisk in the butter and adjust the seasonings with salt and Tabasco sauce.

3 Strain through a chinois.

Approximate values per 1-fl.-oz. (30-ml) serving: **Calories** 50, **Total fat** 4.5 g, **Saturated fat** 2.4 g, **Cholesterol** 10 mg, **Sodium** 200 mg, **Total carbohydrates** 2 g, **Protein** 0 g

BROTH

Broth, which also appears on menus as a **tea, au jus, essence** or **nage,** is a thin, flavorful liquid served in a pool beneath the main food. The broth should not be so abundant as to turn an entrée into a soup, but it should provide moisture and flavor. The essence, broth or nage is often made by simply reducing and straining the liquid in which the main food was cooked. Alternatively, a specifically flavored stock—tomato, for example—can be prepared, then clarified like consommé to create a broth or essence to accompany an appetizer or entrée.

▶ **essence** a sauce made from a concentrated vegetable juice

FLAVORED OIL

Small amounts of intensely flavored oils can be used to dress or garnish a variety of dishes. Salads, soups, vegetable and starch dishes and entrées can be enhanced with a drizzle of colorful, appropriately flavored oil. Because such small quantities are used, these oils provide flavor and moisture without adding too many calories or fat.

Unless the flavoring ingredient goes especially well with olive oil (for example, basil), select a high-quality but neutral oil such as peanut, safflower or canola. Although flavoring ingredients can be simply steeped in oil for a time, a better way to flavor oil is to crush, purée or cook the flavoring ingredients first.

▶ PROCEDURE FOR PREPARING A FLAVORED OIL

1 Purée or chop fresh herbs, fruits or vegetables. Sweat dry spices or seeds in a small amount of oil to form a paste.

2 Place the selected oil and the flavoring ingredients in a jar or other tightly lidded container.

Table 11.5 **USING SAUCES**

SAUCE	QUALITIES	SMALL SAUCE OR FLAVORINGS	USE
Béchamel	Smooth, rich and creamy; no graininess; cream-colored with rich sheen	Cream	Vegetables, pasta, eggs, fish
		Cheese	Vegetables, pasta
		Mornay	Fish, shellfish, poultry, vegetables
		Nantua	Fish, shellfish
		Soubise	Veal, pork, eggs
Velouté	Smooth and rich; ivory-colored; good flavor of the stock used; not pasty or heavy	Fish Velouté	
		Bercy	Poached fish
		Cardinal	Lobster, white fish, crab, eggs
		Normandy	Delicate white fish, oysters
		Allemande (veal or chicken)	
		Aurora	Eggs, chicken, sweetbreads
		Horseradish	Roast beef, corned beef, baked ham
		Mushroom	Sautéed poultry, white meats
		Poulette	Vegetables, sweetbreads
		Suprême (chicken)	
		Albufera	Braised poultry, sweetbreads
		Hungarian	Eggs, chicken, chops, sweetbreads
		Ivory	Eggs, braised poultry
Espagnole	Smooth and rich; dark brown color; good meat flavor	Bordelaise	Sautéed or grilled meats
		Chasseur	Sautéed or grilled meats and poultry
		Châteaubriand	Broiled meats
		Chevreuil	Roasted meats and game
		Madeira/Port	Grilled or roasted meats and game, ham
		Marchand de Vin	Grilled or roasted meats
		Mushroom	Sautéed or grilled meats and poultry
		Périgueux/Périgourdine	Sautéed poultry, grilled meats and game, sweetbreads
		Piquant	Pork
		Poivrade	Grilled or roasted meats, game
		Robert	Pork
Tomato	Thick and rich; slightly grainy; full-flavored	Tomato	Meats, poultry, vegetables, pasta and for making small sauces
		Creole	Fish, eggs, chicken
		Spanish	Eggs, fish
		Milanaise	Pasta, grilled or sautéed poultry and white meats
Hollandaise	Smooth and rich; buttery flavor; light and slightly frothy; pale yellow color; no signs of separating	Béarnaise	Grilled or sautéed meats and fish
		Choron	Grilled meats and fish
		Foyot	Grilled meats and fish
		Grimrod	Eggs, poached fish
		Maltaise	Poached fish
		Mousseline	Poached fish, eggs, vegetables
Beurre blanc and beurre rouge	Rich and buttery; thinner than hollandaise; light and airy; pale-colored	Wide variety of seasonings and flavorings may be used	Steamed, grilled or poached fish, chicken or vegetables
Compound butter	Flavor ingredients should be evenly distributed	Wide variety of seasonings and flavorings may be used	Grilled meats, poultry and fish; finishing sauces
Pan gravy	Smooth; deep rich color; meaty flavor	Made from pan drippings	Roasted meats and poultry
Coulis	Rich color; moderately thin, grainy texture; strongly flavored	Made with a wide variety of vegetables or fruits	Vegetables, grilled or poached meats, poultry and fish
Salsa and relish	Chunky; bright colors; not watery	Made with a wide variety of vegetables, fruits and seasonings	Meats, fish, vegetables and poultry; used as a sauce or condiment
Flavored oil	Smooth; bright colors; intense flavors	Made with a variety of herbs, spices and seasonings	Used as a garnish

3 Allow the mixture to stand at room temperature until sufficient flavor is extracted. This may take from 1 to 24 hours. Shake the jar periodically. Do not allow the flavoring ingredients to remain in the oil indefinitely, as it may become harsh or bitter.

4 Strain the oil through a chinois lined with a coffee filter.

5 Store the flavored oil in a covered container in the refrigerator.

SHALLOT CURRY OIL

RECIPE 11. 20

Yield: 8 fl. oz. (225 ml)

Canola oil	8 fl. oz.	225 ml
Shallot, minced	1	1
Curry powder	4 Tbsp.	60 ml
Water	2 fl. oz.	60 ml

1 In a small saucepan, heat 1 tablespoon (15 milliliters) of oil over medium heat. Add the shallot and sauté until softened and translucent. Do not allow the shallot to brown.

2 Add the curry powder and sauté for 1 to 2 minutes.

3 Stir in the water and bring the mixture to a boil. Reduce the heat and simmer until most of the water evaporates, leaving a paste of curry and shallots.

4 Remove from the heat and stir in the remaining oil.

5 Place the mixture in a lidded jar and set aside at room temperature for 6 to 8 hours. Shake the jar occasionally.

6 Strain the oil through a chinois lined with a coffee filter. Place the flavored oil in a covered container and refrigerate until ready to use.

Approximate values per 1-fl.-oz. (30-ml) serving: **Calories** 208, **Total fat** 23 g, **Saturated fat** 2 g, **Cholesterol** 0 mg, **Sodium** 1 mg, **Total carbohydrates** 1 g, **Protein** 0 g, **Claims**—no cholesterol; no sodium

CONCLUSION

In *Le Guide culinaire*, Auguste Escoffier wrote "Indeed, stock is everything in cooking . . . without it, nothing can be done. If one's stock is good, what remains of the work is easy; if, on the other hand, it is bad or merely mediocre, it is quite hopeless to expect anything approaching a satisfactory result." Because stocks and the sauces made from them are still the basis for much of contemporary cuisine, Escoffier's words are as true today as when he wrote them.

Both the classic mother sauces and the small sauces derived from them as well as sauces such as beurre blanc and beurre rouge, coulis, flavored oils, salsas and relishes that are not based on classic recipes all share two goals: to complement the foods with which they are served and neither mask nor disguise poorly prepared foods. With practice and care (and the right ingredients), you will be able to make great sauces.

QUESTIONS FOR DISCUSSION

1 Why are the bones of younger animals preferred for making stocks?

2 Why should a stock made from beef or veal bones cook longer than a stock made from fish bones? What is the result if a stock does not cook long enough?

3 What can cause a stock to become cloudy? How can you prevent this from happening?

4 List three differences in the production of a white stock and a brown stock.

5 List the five classic mother sauces, and explain how they are used to prepare small sauces.

6 Why is demi-glace preferred when making brown sauces? Is jus lié different from classic demi-glace? Can they be used interchangeably?

7 Why are temperatures important when making hollandaise sauce? What precautions must be taken when holding hollandaise for service?

8 Compare a beurre blanc and a hollandaise sauce. How are they similar? How are they different?

9 How are compound butters used in making sauces? What are the ingredients for a traditional maître d'hôtel butter?

10 What are the differences between a salsa, a chutney and a relish? Can these items be used in place of classic sauces? Explain your answer.

11 What are the differences between a vegetable juice sauce and a broth?

SEARED DIVER SCALLOPS WITH TOMATILLO SAUCE, AVOCADO RELISH AND TOMATO SYRUP

RECIPE 11.21

Note: This dish appears in the chapter opening photograph.

PRIMITIVO WINE BAR, Colorado Springs, CO

John Broening, Executive Chef

Yield: 8 Servings   **Method:** Sautéing

Scallops, 1 oz. (30 g) each	24	24
Salt and white pepper	TT	TT
Clarified butter	4 fl. oz.	120 ml
Tomatillo Sauce (recipe follows)	as needed	as needed
Tomato Syrup (recipe follows)	as needed	as needed
Avocado Relish (recipe follows)	as needed	as needed
Cilantro	24 sprigs	24 sprigs
Black and white sesame seeds, toasted	3 Tbsp.	45 ml
Curried Chickpea Crisps (recipe follows)	as needed	as needed

1 Season the scallops with salt and white pepper. Heat the clarified butter in a sauté pan until very hot. Sear the scallops until golden brown, approximately 2 minutes on each side. Remove the scallops when they are done and drain on paper towels.

2 Spoon three pools of Tomatillo Sauce on each of 8 plates. Place a pool of Tomato Syrup next to each pool of Tomatillo Sauce. Place a scallop in the center of each pool of Tomatillo Sauce. Top each scallop with a quenelle-shaped dollop of Avocado Relish. Top the relish with a sprig of cilantro. Sprinkle each plate with sesame seeds and garnish with Curried Chickpea Crisps.

Approximate values per serving: **Calories** 360, **Total fat** 27 g, **Saturated fat** 10 g, **Cholesterol** 60 mg, **Sodium** 370 mg, **Total carbohydrates** 17 g, **Protein** 17 g, **Vitamin A** 45%, **Vitamin C** 80%, **Iron** 15%

TOMATILLO SAUCE

Yield: 20 fl. oz. (570 ml)

Tomatillos, small	8	8
Olive oil	1 Tbsp.	15 ml
Lime	1	1
Cilantro leaves	2 c.	450 ml
Jalapeños, seeded, chopped fine	2	2
Garlic, minced	1 tsp.	5 ml
Cumin, ground, toasted	1 tsp.	5 ml
Honey	1 Tbsp.	15 ml
Salt and pepper	TT	TT

1 Remove the husks from the tomatillos. Soak them in warm water for 30 seconds. Drain and toss the tomatillos in the olive oil. Place the tomatillos on a half sheet pan and roast in a 300°F (150°C) oven until soft but not colored. Cool completely.

2 Juice the lime.

3 Combine the tomatillos with the other ingredients in the bowl of a blender and blend for a few seconds or until smooth.

Approximate values per 1-fl.-oz. (30-ml) serving: **Calories** 15, **Total fat** 1 g, **Saturated fat** 0 g, **Cholesterol** 0 mg, **Sodium** 0 mg, **Total carbohydrates** 2 g, **Protein** 0 g, **Vitamin C** 15%

CHEF JOHN BROENING

A graduate of Peter Kump's New York Cooking School, John Broening is executive chef of Primitivo Wine Bar in Colorado Springs. He is also a writer and the book reviewer for the Colorado Springs *Independent.*

Starting with a job at the Hit N Run Club in Baltimore's Memorial Stadium, Chef Broening moved on to such internationally known restaurants as Chef Patrick Clark's Metro in New York, Bistrot de l'Etoile and Le Grenadin in Paris and Bix, Roti, Grand Café and Obelisque in the San Francisco Bay area. He joined Primitivo Wine Bar in 1999 and has represented the restaurant at several James Beard House functions.

He advises students that "if you're in this profession for the long haul, take care of your health."

TOMATO SYRUP

Yield: 6 fl. oz. (180 ml)

Tomato juice	1 pt.	450 ml
Chipotle powder	1 pinch	1 pinch
Cumin, ground, toasted	1 pinch	1 pinch
Salt and pepper	TT	TT

1 In a nonreactive sauce pan, reduce the tomato juice by two-thirds. Add the remaining ingredients, stir well and strain through a chinois.

Approximate values per 1-fl.-oz. (30-ml) serving: **Calories** 15, **Total fat** 0 g, **Saturated fat** 0 g, **Cholesterol** 0 mg, **Sodium** 290 mg, **Total carbohydrates** 3 g, **Protein** 1 g, **Vitamin A** 10%, **Vitamin C** 25%

AVOCADO RELISH

Yield: 16 fl. oz. (450 ml)

Lime	1	1
Ripe avocados, peeled and chopped fine	2	2
Jalapeño, seeded, chopped fine	1	1
Cilantro leaves, chopped coarse	2 Tbsp.	30 ml
Cumin, ground, toasted	1/2 tsp.	3 ml
Olive oil	1 Tbsp.	15 ml
Tomato concassée	4 Tbsp.	60 ml
Salt and pepper	TT	TT
Onion, minced	3 Tbsp.	45 ml

1 Juice the lime.
2 Combine the lime juice with all of the ingredients and mix well.

Approximate values per 1-fl.-oz. (30-ml) serving: **Calories** 50, **Total fat** 4.5 g, **Saturated fat** 0.5 g, **Cholesterol** 0 mg, **Sodium** 0 mg, **Total carbohydrates** 3 g, **Protein** 1 g, **Vitamin C** 10%

CURRIED CHICKPEA CRISPS

Yield: 2 qt. (2 lt)

All-purpose flour	1 1/2 c.	350 ml
Chickpea flour	1 c.	240 ml
Turmeric	1 Tbsp.	15 ml
Cumin, ground	1 Tbsp.	15 ml
Coriander, ground	1 Tbsp.	15 ml
Cinnamon, ground	1 tsp.	5 ml
Cayenne pepper	1/2 tsp.	3 ml
Black pepper, ground	1 tsp.	5 ml
Salt	1 Tbsp.	15 ml
Granulated sugar	1 Tbsp.	15 ml
Water	3/4 c.	180 ml
Extra virgin olive oil	2 Tbsp.	30 ml

1 In a stainless steel bowl, stir together the dry ingredients. Form a pool in the middle of the mixture and add the liquid ingredients. Mix together by hand, adding additional flour if necessary. Knead until smooth and elastic, approximately 5 minutes.
2 Roll out the dough using a pasta machine to thickness number 6. Using a ravioli cutter, cut the dough into 2-inch × 1/4-inch (5-centimeter × 6-millimeter) strips.
3 Using the swimming method, deep-fry the strips at 275°F (135°C) for 3 minutes. Season with salt and hold warm.

MARCHAND DE VIN (RED-WINE SAUCE)

RECIPE 11.22

BRENNAN'S RESTAURANT, NEW ORLEANS, LA
Chef Michael Roussel

Yield: 24 fl. oz. (680 ml)   **Method:** Roux-thickened

Unsalted butter	3 oz.	90 g
Onion, chopped fine	2 oz.	60 g
Garlic, chopped fine	1½ tsp.	7 ml
Green onion, chopped fine	2 oz.	60 g
Boiled ham, chopped fine	2 oz.	60 g
Mushrooms, chopped fine	2 oz.	60 g
All-purpose flour	⅓ c.	75 ml
Worcestershire sauce	2 Tbsp.	30 ml
Beef stock	1 pt.	450 ml
Red wine	4 fl. oz.	120 ml
Thyme, dried leaves	1½ tsp.	7 ml
Bay leaf	1	1
Fresh parsley, chopped fine	1½ oz.	45 g
Salt and pepper	TT	TT

1 Melt the butter in a large saucepan and sauté the onion, garlic, green onions and ham for 5 minutes.
2 Add the mushrooms, reduce the heat to medium and cook for 2 minutes.
3 Blend in the flour and cook, stirring, for 4 minutes. Then add the Worcestershire sauce, stock, wine, thyme and bay leaf. Simmer until the sauce thickens, approximately 1 hour.
4 At service, remove the bay leaf and add the parsley. Season to taste with salt and pepper.
5 For a smoother texture, pass the sauce through a fine mesh strainer before adding the parsley.

Approximate values per 1½-fl.-oz. (45-ml) serving: **Calories** 45, **Total fat** 3 g, **Saturated fat** 2 g, **Cholesterol** 10 mg, **Sodium** 100 mg, **Total carbohydrates** 3 g, **Protein** 1 g, **Vitamin A** 15%

BRENNAN'S RED-WINE AND MUSHROOM SAUCE

RECIPE 11.23

BRENNAN'S RESTAURANT, NEW ORLEANS, LA
Chef Michael Roussel

Yield: 24 fl. oz. (680 ml)

Whole butter	4 oz.	120 g
Onion, diced	4 oz.	120 g
Tomato paste	4 oz.	120 g
Mushrooms, sliced	1 pt.	450 ml
Paprika	1½ Tbsp.	22 ml
All-purpose flour	1 oz.	30 g
Beef stock	24 fl. oz.	680 ml
Green onion, sliced	8 oz.	225 g
Worcestershire sauce	1 Tbsp.	15 ml
Burgundy wine	6 fl. oz.	180 ml
Garlic, minced	1 Tbsp.	15 ml
Salt and pepper	TT	TT

1 Melt the butter in a large saucepan. Add the onion and sauté until tender, approximately 3 minutes.

2 Stir in the tomato paste, mushrooms and paprika. Cook until the mushroom is tender, then add the flour. Stir until well blended.

3 Using a whisk, incorporate the stock. When the sauce is smooth, add the green onion, Worcestershire sauce, wine and garlic. Simmer until reduced and thickened, approximately 25 minutes. Season to taste with salt and pepper and hold for service.

Approximate values per 2-fl.-oz. (60-ml) serving: **Calories** 60, **Total fat** 4 g, **Saturated fat** 2.5 g, **Cholesterol** 10 mg, **Sodium** 95 mg, **Total carbohydrates** 5 g, **Protein** 1 g, **Vitamin A** 25%, **Vitamin C** 10%

RECIPE 11.24   ## RED-WINE THYME SAUCE

VINCENT ON CAMELBACK, Phoenix, AZ

Chef Vincent Guerithault

Yield: 1½ qt. (1.5 lt)   **Method:** Reduction

Red wine	8 fl. oz.	250 ml
Garlic, chopped	1 Tbsp.	15 ml
Shallot, chopped	2 oz.	60 g
Veal stock	1 qt.	1 lt
Fresh rosemary	1 sprig	1 sprig
Fresh thyme	1 sprig	1 sprig
Bay leaves	2	2
Unsalted butter	1 oz.	30 g

1 Reduce the red wine, garlic and shallot by one-quarter.

2 Add the veal stock, rosemary, thyme and bay leaves and reduce by one-quarter.

3 Remove from the heat and strain. Monter au beurre.

Approximate values per 1-fl.-oz. (30-ml) serving: **Calories** 40, **Total fat** 2 g, **Saturated fat** 1 g, **Cholesterol** 5 mg, **Sodium** 210 mg, **Total carbohydrates** 4 g, **Protein** 1 g, **Vitamin A** 10%, **Claims**—low fat; low calorie; no sugar

RECIPE 11.25   ## ROASTED GARLIC SAUCE

CHEF LELAND ATKINSON, Washington, DC

Yield: 12 fl. oz. (340 ml)

Shallot, minced	4 Tbsp.	60 ml
Clarified butter	1 Tbsp.	15 ml
Madeira	4 fl. oz.	120 ml
Fresh thyme	1 sprig	1 sprig
Bay leaf	1	1
Garlic head, trimmed and roasted	1	1
Demi-glace	1 pt.	450 ml
Roux	as needed	as needed
Salt and pepper	TT	TT

1 Sauté the shallot lightly in the clarified butter until slightly caramelized.

2 Add the Madeira, thyme and bay leaf and reduce by one-third.

3 Squeeze in the garlic, discarding the skins and root.

4 Add the demi-glace and reduce by one third.

5 Thicken slightly with roux if desired, adjust the seasonings and force through a fine strainer.

Approximate values per 1-fl.-oz. (30-ml) serving: **Calories** 15, **Total fat** 1 g, **Saturated fat** 0.5 g, **Cholesterol** 5 mg, **Sodium** 240 mg, **Total carbohydrates** 0 g, **Protein** 0 g

HORSERADISH CREAM SAUCE

RECIPE 11.26

BRENNAN'S RESTAURANT, New Orleans, LA
Chef Michael Roussel

Yield: 24 fl. oz. (680 ml)

Heavy cream	1 qt.	950 ml
Salt	½ tsp.	3 ml
White pepper	½ tsp.	3 ml
Whole butter	½ tsp.	3 ml
All-purpose flour	4 Tbsp.	60 ml
Horseradish, grated	4 Tbsp.	60 ml

1 Combine the cream, salt and pepper in a saucepan. Heat over medium heat. Do not allow the cream to boil.

2 Rub the butter and flour together to form small balls (beurre manié).

3 Add the beurre manié to the simmering cream. Cook until the sauce is smooth, then add the horseradish. Serve warm.

Approximate values per 1-fl.-oz. (30-ml) serving: **Calories** 140, **Total fat** 15 g, **Saturated fat** 9 g, **Cholesterol** 55 mg, **Sodium** 65 mg, **Total carbohydrates** 2 g, **Protein** 1 g, **Vitamin A** 10%

DUXELLES SAUCE

RECIPE 11.27

Yield: 1½ pt. (750 ml)

Mushroom, chopped fine	8 oz.	250 g
Shallot, chopped fine	3 oz.	90 g
Clarified butter	1 fl. oz.	30 ml
Olive oil	1 fl. oz.	30 ml
Dry white wine	12 fl. oz.	700 ml
Demi-glace	1 pt.	500 ml
Heavy cream	2 fl. oz.	60 ml
Salt and pepper	TT	TT
Parsley, chopped fine	1 Tbsp.	15 ml

1 Sauté the mushroom and shallot in the butter and oil. The mushrooms will release their liquid and darken. Cook until completely dry.

2 Deglaze with the white wine and reduce by two-thirds.

3 Add the demi-glace. Bring to a boil, then simmer for 5 minutes.

4 Stir in the cream. Adjust the seasonings. Garnish with parsley.

Approximate values per 1-fl.-oz. (30-ml) serving: **Calories** 100, **Total fat** 10 g, **Saturated fat** 6 g, **Cholesterol** 30 mg, **Sodium** 40 g, **Total carbohydrates** 2 g, **Protein** 1 g, **Vitamin A** 15%

FRESH TOMATO SAUCE FOR PASTA

RECIPE 11.28

Yield: 2½ qt. (2.5 lt)

Onion, small dice	8 oz.	250 g
Carrot, small dice	4 oz.	120 g
Garlic, minced	1 Tbsp.	15 ml
Olive oil	2 fl. oz.	60 ml
Tomato concassée	7 lb.	3.1 kg
Fresh oregano	1 Tbsp.	15 ml
Fresh thyme	2 tsp.	10 ml
Salt	1 tsp.	5 ml
Pepper	½ tsp.	2 ml
Fresh basil, chopped	½ oz.	15 g

1 Sweat the onion, carrot and garlic in the olive oil until tender.

2 Add the tomato concassée, oregano and thyme. Simmer for approximately 1 hour or until the desired consistency is reached.

3 Pass the sauce through a food mill if a smooth consistency is desired. Do not purée if a chunkier sauce is desired.

4 Adjust the seasonings and add the chopped basil.

Approximate values per 1-fl.-oz. (30-ml) serving: **Calories** 20, **Total fat** 1 g, **Saturated fat** 0 g, **Cholesterol** 0 mg, **Sodium** 35 mg, **Total carbohydrates** 2 g, **Protein** 0 g, **Vitamin** C 15%, **Claims**–low fat; low sodium; low calorie

---

RECIPE 11.29   BOLOGNESE SAUCE

Yield: 1 qt. (1 lt)

Mirepoix, fine dice	8 oz.	250 g
Olive oil	2 fl. oz.	60 ml
Whole butter	1 oz.	30 g
Ground beef	1 lb.	500 g
White wine	8 fl. oz.	250 ml
Milk	6 fl. oz.	180 ml
Nutmeg	TT	TT
Tomato concassée	2 lb.	1 kg
White stock	approx. 8 fl. oz.	approx. 250 ml
Salt and pepper	TT	TT

1 Sauté the mirepoix in the olive oil and butter until tender. Add the beef and cook until no pink remains. Drain fat if necessary.

2 Add the wine. Cook and reduce the wine until nearly dry.

3 Add the milk and season with nutmeg. Cook and reduce the milk until nearly dry.

4 Add the tomato concassée and 8 fluid ounces (250 milliliters) of stock; season with salt and pepper. Simmer for 3 to 4 hours, adding stock as needed to prevent scorching. Adjust the seasonings.

Approximate values per 1-fl.-oz. (30-ml) serving: **Calories** 50, **Total fat** 4 g, **Saturated fat** 1.5 g, **Cholesterol** 10 mg, **Sodium** 115 mg, **Total carbohydrates** 2 g, **Protein** 2 g, **Vitamin C** 10%

RECIPE 11.30   MOLE

Yield: 1 qt. (1 lt)

Cinnamon stick	1	1
Allspice	½ tsp.	3 ml
Guajillo chiles	2	2
Pasilla chiles	2	2
Sesame seeds	4 oz.	120 g
Pumpkin seeds	6 oz.	180 g
Cumin seeds	1 tsp.	5 ml
Onion, small	1	1
Olive oil	as needed	as needed
Plum tomatoes	4	4
Garlic cloves	4	4
Fresh thyme	1 sprig	1 sprig
Oregano, dried	1 tsp.	5 ml
Chicken stock	1 qt.	1 lt
Salt	TT	TT
Semisweet chocolate, chopped	2 oz.	60 g

1 Grind the cinnamon and allspice in a spice grinder.

2 Stem and seed the guajillo and pasilla chiles. Break them into small pieces and simmer them in water for 15 minutes. Drain well.

3 Combine the sesame seeds, pumpkin seeds and cumin seeds and fry them in a dry sauté pan until well toasted.

4 Slice the onion approximately ½ inch (1.2 centimeters) thick. Brush it with olive oil and grill it until well colored.

5 Roast the tomatoes in the flame of a gas burner until they are evenly charred and blistered. Remove the cores, peel the tomatoes and chop them coarsely.

6 Combine the cinnamon and allspice with the chiles, toasted seeds, onion, tomatoes, garlic, thyme, oregano and chicken stock in a saucepan. Season with salt and bring to a boil. Reduce to a simmer and cook for 15 minutes. Remove from the heat, cool and remove the sprig of thyme.

7 Blend the mixture in a blender until smooth. Strain through a china cap and stir in the chocolate until melted. Adjust the seasonings.

8 Serve the mole over grilled chicken, turkey, duck, quail or a meat such as pork or rabbit. Or, reheat cooked turkey or chicken pieces in the sauce until hot and serve with a portion of the sauce.

Approximate values per 1-fl.-oz. (30-ml) serving: **Calories** 70, **Total fat** 5 g, **Saturated fat** 1 g, **Cholesterol** 0 mg, **Sodium** 90 mg, **Total carbohydrates** 4 g, **Protein** 2 g, **Iron** 10%

FRESH TOMATO VINAIGRETTE FOR PASTA

RECIPE 11.31

Yield: 2 qt. (2 lt)

Tomato concassée	8 oz.	250 g
Fresh basil, thyme or marjoram	1 oz.	30 g
Balsamic vinegar	3 fl. oz.	90 ml
Shallot, minced	2 Tbsp.	30 ml
Olive oil	8 fl. oz.	250 ml
Salt and pepper	TT	TT

1 Combine all ingredients. Season to taste with salt and pepper. Set aside for 20 to 30 minutes to allow the flavors to blend.

2 Adjust the seasonings. Serve immediately or refrigerate and serve chilled.

Approximate values per 8-fl.-oz. (240-ml) serving: **Calories** 700, **Total fat** 58 g, **Saturated fat** 8 g, **Cholesterol** 35 mg, **Sodium** 600 mg, **Total carbohydrates** 38 g, **Protein** 7 g, **Vitamin C** 20%

PESTO SAUCE

RECIPE 11.32

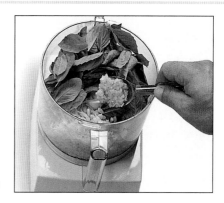

Yield: 1½ pt. (750 ml) **Method:** Puréeing

Olive oil	12 fl. oz.	360 ml
Pine nuts	3 oz.	90 g
Fresh basil leaves	6 oz.	180 g
Garlic, chopped	1 Tbsp.	15 ml
Parmesan, grated	4 oz.	120 g
Romano, grated	4 oz.	120 g
Salt and pepper	TT	TT

1 Place one-third of the olive oil in a blender or food processor and add all the remaining ingredients.

2 Blend or process until smooth. Add the remaining olive oil and blend a few seconds to incorporate.

1 Combining the pesto ingredients.

Variations: *Walnut Pesto*—Substitute walnuts for pine nuts in the recipe.

Sun-Dried Tomato Pesto—Add 1 ounce (30 grams) of sun-dried tomatoes that have been softened in oil or water. Add additional olive oil as necessary.

Approximate values per 1-fl.-oz. (30-ml) serving: **Calories** 200, **Total fat** 19 g, **Saturated fat** 4 g, **Cholesterol** 10 mg, **Sodium** 250 mg, **Total carbohydrates** 1 g, **Protein** 4 g, **Calcium** 15%

2 The finished pesto sauce.

RECIPE 11.33

BRENNAN'S LEMON BUTTER SAUCE

BRENNAN'S RESTAURANT, NEW ORLEANS, LA
Chef Michael Roussel

Yield: 1 qt. (1 lt)

Brown Sauce (page 215)	4 fl. oz.	120 ml
Fresh lemon juice	2 fl. oz.	60 ml
Whole butter, room temperature	2 lb.	900 g

1 Combine the brown sauce and lemon juice in a large saucepan.
2 Working the pan on and off the direct heat, add the butter a bit at a time, whisking the sauce smooth between additions.
3 Adjust the flavor with additional lemon juice if necessary. Transfer the sauce to a clean container and hold at room temperature for service. Use the sauce within 2 hours or discard it.

Approximate values per 1-fl.-oz. (30-ml) serving: **Calories** 210, **Total fat** 23 g, **Saturated fat** 14 g, **Cholesterol** 65 g, **Sodium** 20 mg, **Total carbohydrates** 1 g, **Protein** 0 g, **Vitamin A** 15%

RECIPE 11.34

CITRUS BEURRE BLANC

VINCENT ON CAMELBACK, PHOENIX, AZ
Chef Vincent Guerithault

Yield: 4 Servings, 5 fl. oz. (150 ml) each

Orange juice	8 fl. oz.	225 ml
Lime juice	1 Tbsp.	15 ml
Lemon juice	1 Tbsp.	15 ml
White wine	8 fl. oz.	225 ml
White wine vinegar	8 fl. oz.	225 ml
Shallot, chopped fine	1 Tbsp.	15 ml
Heavy cream	1 Tbsp.	15 ml
Unsalted butter	1 lb.	450 g
Salt and pepper	TT	TT
Orange rind, grated and blanched	1 Tbsp.	15 ml
Lime rind, grated and blanched	1 Tbsp.	15 ml
Lemon rind, grated and blanched	1 Tbsp.	15 ml

1 Combine the citrus juices, wine, vinegar and shallot and reduce au sec over moderate heat.
2 Whisk in the cream, then whisk in the butter 2 ounces (60 grams) at a time.

3 Strain the sauce, season with salt and pepper and stir in the citrus rinds. Keep hot for service.

Approximate values per 5-fl.-oz. (150-ml) serving: **Calories** 890, **Total fat** 94 g, **Saturated fat** 58 g, **Cholesterol** 255 mg, **Sodium** 600 mg, **Total carbohydrates** 9 g, **Protein** 2 g, **Vitamin A** 90%

CREAM BEURRE BLANC   RECIPE 11.35

THE ART INSTITUTE OF WASHINGTON, ARLINGTON, VA
Chef John Harrison

This version of beurre blanc is easier to master than a traditional beurre blanc. It is also less temperature-sensitive.

Yield: 12 fl. oz. (360 ml)

Shallot, chopped fine	1 Tbsp.	15 ml
Clarified butter	2 tsp.	10 ml
White wine	6 fl. oz.	180 ml
Heavy cream	8 fl. oz.	240 ml
Unsalted butter, softened	8 oz.	240 g
Salt and white pepper	TT	TT

1 Sauté the shallot in the clarified butter until translucent but not brown. Add the white wine and reduce by half.
2 Add the heavy cream, bring to a boil and reduce by two-thirds.
3 Remove from the heat and keep warm. Whisk the softened butter into the sauce in several batches. Move the pan back and forth over the heat to keep the sauce from becoming too hot or too cold.
4 Season the sauce with salt and white pepper. Strain if desired. Hold in a warm place for service.

Note: Like a traditional beurre blanc, this sauce can be flavored by adding any of a wide variety of herbs and spices. Beurre rouge may be prepared by substituting red wine for the white wine.

Approximate values per 2-fl.-oz. (60-ml) serving: **Calories** 220, **Total fat** 23 g, **Saturated fat** 15 g, **Cholesterol** 70 mg, **Sodium** 10 mg, **Total carbohydrates** 1 g, **Protein** 1 g, **Vitamin A** 20%

BEER BEURRE BLANC SAUCE   RECIPE 11.36

MISSISSIPPI UNIVERSITY FOR WOMEN, COLUMBUS, MS
Chef Jim Fitzgerald, Ph.D., CCP

Yield: 1½ qt. (1.4 lt)

Shallots, minced	4	4
Unsalted butter	1 Tbsp.	15 ml
Salt and pepper	TT	TT
White wine vinegar	3 fl. oz.	90 ml
Bay leaf	1	1
Fresh thyme	1 sprig	1 sprig
Beer	10 fl. oz.	300 ml
Unsalted butter, cold	1½ lb.	720 g

1 Sweat the shallots in the 1 tablespoon of butter over medium heat for approximately 2 minutes. Add the salt and pepper, vinegar, bay leaf, thyme and beer.
2 Reduce by two-thirds.

3 Whisk in the cold butter in pieces, moving the pan on and off the heat as necessary. Do not allow the sauce to boil. Adjust the seasonings, strain and hold in a bain marie for up to 2 hours. Serve with fried or grilled meat or poultry.

Approximate values per 1-fl.-oz. (30-ml) serving: **Calories** 110, **Total fat** 12 g, **Saturated fat** 7 g, **Cholesterol** 30 mg, **Sodium** 0, **Total carbohydrates** 0, **Protein** 0, **Vitamin A** 10%

RECIPE 11.37　　　**TOMATO BUTTER SAUCE WITH THYME**

NEWBURY COLLEGE, Brookline, MA
Senior Instructor Scott Doughty

Yield: 1 pt. (480 ml)

Plum tomato concassée, minced	2½ lb.	1.1 kg
Olive oil	1 fl. oz.	30 ml
White wine	2 fl. oz.	60 ml
Vermouth, dry, red or white	2 fl. oz.	60 ml
Wine vinegar, red or white	2 fl. oz.	60 ml
Shallot, minced	2 Tbsp.	30 ml
Heavy cream	2 fl. oz.	60 ml
Fresh thyme, chopped	1 Tbsp.	15 ml
Salt	¾ tsp.	4 ml
Black pepper	¼ tsp.	1 ml
Whole butter, cut into pieces	4 oz.	120 g
Fresh parsley, chopped	½ c.	180 ml

1 Sauté the tomato concassée in the olive oil for approximately 2 minutes. Lower the heat to a simmer and reduce the tomato until thick but not dry.

2 In a saucepan, combine the wine, vermouth, vinegar and shallot. Bring to a boil and reduce au sec. Add the cream and reduce by half.

3 Add the thyme, salt and pepper to the tomatoes. Stir in the wine, cream and shallot reduction.

4 Bring the sauce to a simmer. Add the butter pieces and stir until incorporated. Do not allow the sauce to boil or the butter will separate. Adjust the seasonings and stir in the parsley.

Approximate values per 3-fl.-oz. (90-ml) serving: **Calories** 100, **Total fat** 9 g, **Saturated fat** 4.5 g, **Cholesterol** 20 mg, **Sodium** 120 mg, **Total carbohydrates** 4 g, **Protein** 1 g, **Vitamin A** 15%, **Vitamin C** 25%

RECIPE 11.38　　　**SORREL SAUCE**

Yield: 1 qt. (1 lt)		**Method:** Puréeing
Shallot, coarsely chopped	1 Tbsp.	15 ml
Whole butter	1 oz.	30 g
White wine	8 fl. oz.	250 ml
Heavy cream	1 pt.	500 ml
Sorrel, stemmed	8 oz.	250 g
Spinach, stemmed	8 oz.	250 g
Salt and white pepper	TT	TT
Lemon juice	1 fl. oz.	30 ml

1 Sauté the shallot in the butter until tender.

2 Add the white wine and reduce by half.

3 Add the cream and reduce until it begins to thicken.

4 Add the sorrel and spinach to the cream and cook just until the leaves are wilted.

5 Purée the sauce in a blender or food processor and season with salt, white pepper and lemon juice. Serve the sauce with egg, chicken, veal or rich fish dishes.

Approximate values per 1-fl.-oz. (30-ml) serving: **Calories** 70, **Total fat** 7 g, **Saturated fat** 4 g, **Cholesterol** 25 mg, **Sodium** 90 mg, **Total carbohydrates** 1 g, **Protein** 1 g, **Vitamin A** 10%

BARBECUE SAUCE   RECIPE 11.39

Yield: 1½ qt. (1.5 lt)

Onion, small dice	8 oz.	250 g
Garlic, chopped	1 oz.	30 g
Vegetable oil	1 fl. oz.	30 ml
Red wine vinegar	6 fl. oz.	180 ml
Brown sugar	1 oz.	30 g
Honey	2 fl. oz.	60 ml
Beef stock	8 fl. oz.	250 ml
Ketchup	10 oz.	300 g
Dry mustard	1 oz.	30 g
Worcestershire sauce	2 Tbsp.	30 ml
Salt and pepper	TT	TT
Cayenne pepper	TT	TT

1 Sweat the onions and garlic in the oil until tender.

2 Combine the remaining ingredients and simmer for 30 minutes.

Approximate values per 1-fl.-oz. (30-ml) serving: **Calories** 25, **Total fat** 1 g, **Saturated fat** 0 g, **Cholesterol** 0 mg, **Sodium** 80 mg, **Total carbohydrates** 4 g, **Protein** 0 g, **Claims**—low fat; low sodium; low calorie

PEANUT SAUCE   RECIPE 11.40

Yield: 28 fl. oz. (800 ml)

Garlic, chopped	1 tsp.	5 ml
Onion, small dice	6 oz.	180 g
Red pepper flakes, crushed	1 tsp.	5 ml
Kaffir lime leaves (optional)	4	4
Curry powder	2 tsp.	10 ml
Lemongrass, minced	1 oz.	30 g
Vegetable oil	1 fl. oz.	30 ml
Coconut milk	8 fl. oz.	250 ml
Cinnamon sticks	2	2
Bay leaves	4	4
Lime juice	1 fl. oz.	30 ml
Rice wine vinegar	4 fl. oz.	120 ml
Chicken stock	10 fl. oz.	300 ml
Peanut butter	10 oz.	300 g

1 Sauté the garlic, onion, red pepper flakes, lime leaves, curry powder and lemongrass in the vegetable oil for 5 minutes.

2 Add the remaining ingredients and simmer for 30 minutes. Stir often, as the sauce can burn easily. Serve warm.

Approximate values per 1-fl.-oz. (30-ml) serving: **Calories** 100, **Total fat** 8 g, **Saturated fat** 3 g, **Cholesterol** 0 mg, **Sodium** 115 mg, **Total carbohydrates** 5 g, **Protein** 3 g

RECIPE 11.41

Yield: 1 qt. (1 lt)

Assorted melons such as honeydew, cantaloupe, crenshaw	1 qt.	1 lt
Garlic, chopped	1 tsp.	5 ml
Brown sugar	2 Tbsp.	30 ml
Thai fish sauce	2 Tbsp.	30 ml
Serrano chiles, minced	1 Tbsp.	15 ml
Lime juice	2 fl. oz.	60 ml
Unsalted peanuts, roasted, chopped fine	4 Tbsp.	60 ml
Fresh mint	4 Tbsp.	60 ml

1 Cut the melons into small dice or shape into small balls using a parisienne scoop.

2 Combine remaining ingredients and toss with the melon pieces. Chill thoroughly. Serve with fish, shellfish or chicken.

Approximate values per 1-fl.-oz. (30-ml) serving: **Calories** 20, **Total fat** 0.5 g, **Saturated fat** 0 g, **Cholesterol** 0 mg, **Sodium** 70 mg, **Total carbohydrates** 4 g, **Protein** 0 g, **Vitamin C** 10%, **Claims**—low fat; low sodium; low calorie

RECIPE 11.42

THE BOULDER'S RESORT, Carefree, AZ

Former Corporate Executive Chef Charles Wiley

Yield: 1½ pt. (750 ml)

Red bell pepper, diced fine	2 oz.	60 g
Green bell pepper, diced fine	2 oz.	60 g
Small red onion, diced fine	2 oz.	60 g
Green onion, sliced fine	1	1
Garlic, roasted and puréed	1½ tsp.	8 ml
Fresh lemon juice	1 fl. oz.	30 ml
Serrano chile, minced	1	1
Cilantro, chopped	TT	TT
Plum tomatoes, seeded and diced	4	4
Avocado, diced	1	1
Salt and pepper	TT	TT

1 In a mixing bowl, combine the bell peppers, onions, garlic, lemon juice, chile and cilantro. Mix well.

2 Carefully fold in the tomatoes, then the avocado. Season to taste.

Approximate values per 1-fl.-oz. (30-ml) serving: **Calories** 15, **Total fat** 1.5 g, **Saturated fat** 0 g, **Cholesterol** 0 mg, **Sodium** 0 mg, **Total carbohydrates** 1 g, **Protein** 0 g, **Vitamin C** 15%, **Claims**—low fat; no cholesterol; low calorie

RECIPE 11.43

Yield: 2 qt. (2 lt)

Tomatillo	5 lb.	2 kg
Water	8 fl. oz.	250 ml
Jalapeños	3	3
Salt	1 Tbsp.	15 ml
Pepper	½ tsp.	2 ml
Garlic	2 Tbsp.	30 ml
Onion, chopped	4 oz.	120 g
Cilantro, chopped	2 oz.	60 g

1 Remove the husks from the tomatillos.
2 Combine the tomatillos with the water, jalapeños, salt, pepper, garlic and onion. Bring to a boil and simmer until tender, approximately 20 minutes.
3 Chop all ingredients in a food chopper or purée them in a blender for a smoother sauce.
4 Add the cilantro and adjust the seasonings. The sauce may be served warm or cold.

Approximate values per 1-fl.-oz. (30-ml) serving: **Calories** 20, **Total fat** 0 g, **Saturated fat** 0 g, **Cholesterol** 0 mg, **Sodium** 120 mg, **Total carbohydrates** 3 g, **Protein** 1 g, **Claims**—fat free; low sodium; low calorie

APPLE HORSERADISH SAUCE

RECIPE 11.44

Yield: 1 pt. (500 ml)

Granny Smith apples	4	4
Cider vinegar	2 fl. oz.	60 ml
Fresh horseradish, grated	2 oz.	60 g
Paprika	1 tsp.	5 ml
White wine	1 fl. oz.	30 ml

1 Grate the apples and moisten them with vinegar.
2 Add the horseradish and paprika.
3 Thin to the desired consistency with the wine.

Approximate values per 1-fl.-oz. (30-ml) serving: **Calories** 25, **Total fat** 0 g, **Saturated fat** 0 g, **Cholesterol** 0 mg, **Sodium** 0 mg, **Total carbohydrates** 6 g, **Protein** 0 g, **Claims**—fat free; no sodium; low calorie

MIGNONETTE SAUCE

RECIPE 11.45

Yield: 1 pt. (500 ml)

White pepper	2 tsp.	10 ml
Red wine vinegar	16 fl. oz.	500 ml
Shallot, minced	4 oz.	120 g
Salt	TT	TT

1 Combine all ingredients.

Approximate values per 1-fl.-oz. (30-ml) serving: **Calories** 5, **Total fat** 0 g, **Saturated fat** 0 g, **Cholesterol** 0 mg, **Sodium** 0.8 mg, **Total carbohydrates** 1 g, **Protein** 0 g, **Claims**—fat free; very low sodium; low calorie

NUOC CHAM
(VIETNAMESE DIPPING SAUCE)

RECIPE 11.46

Yield: 10 fl. oz. (300 ml)

Granulated sugar	5 Tbsp.	75 ml
Water	3 Tbsp.	50 ml
Fish sauce (nuoc mam)	5 Tbsp.	75 ml
Fresh lemon juice	4 fl. oz.	120 ml
Garlic clove, minced	1	1
Thai chile, seeded and minced	1	1
Shallot, minced	1	1

1 Whisk all the ingredients together in a nonreactive bowl and allow to stand for at least 30 minutes at room temperature before serving.

Approximate values per 1-fl.-oz. (30-ml) serving: **Calories** 0, **Total fat** 0 g, **Saturated fat** 0 g, **Cholesterol** 0 mg, **Sodium** 700 mg, **Total carbohydrates** 8 g, **Protein** 1 g, **Vitamin C** 20%, **Claims**—no calories; fat free; good source of Vitamin C

RECIPE 11.47   HERB OIL

STOUFFER STANFORD COURT HOTEL, San Francisco, CA

Former Executive Chef Ercolino Crugnale

Yield: 4 fl. oz. (120 ml)

Fresh parsley	2 oz.	60 g
Fresh tarragon	1 oz.	30 g
Fresh thyme	1 oz.	30 g
Olive oil	approx. 4 fl. oz.	approx. 120 ml

1 Blanch the herbs in hot water for 10 seconds. Cool and dry thoroughly.
2 Measure the volume of the herbs and put them in a blender. Add an equal volume of olive oil.
3 Purée and strain through a mesh strainer.

Approximate values per 1-fl.-oz. (30-ml) serving: **Calories** 110, **Total fat** 8 g, **Saturated fat** 1 g, **Cholesterol** 0 mg, **Sodium** 35 mg, **Total carbohydrates** 8 g, **Protein** 3 g, **Vitamin A** 20%, **Iron** 70%, **Claims**—no cholesterol; low sodium

---

RECIPE 11.48   PERSILLADE

Although not a liquid sauce, persillade (payr-se-yad) is a classic parsley topping used to finish a dish in much the same way as a sauce. Persillade adds flavor and texture to grilled or roasted meats, especially beef and lamb, or vegetables.

Yield: 1 lb. (450 g)

Garlic, minced	1 oz.	30 g
Fresh parsley, chopped	3 oz.	90 g
Fresh bread crumbs	6 oz.	180 g
Whole butter, melted	6 fl. oz.	180 ml

1 Combine the garlic, parsley and bread crumbs. Drizzle on the butter and toss to blend.
2 Sprinkle the persillade over cooked meats or vegetables as a topping, then place the dish under a broiler until lightly browned.

Approximate values per ½-oz. (15-g) serving: **Calories** 50, **Total fat** 4.5 g, **Saturated fat** 3 g, **Cholesterol** 10 mg, **Sodium** 30 mg, **Total carbohydrates** 3 g, **Protein** 1 g

A FIRST-RATE SOUP IS MORE CREATIVE THAN A SECOND-RATE PAINTING.

—Abraham Maslow, American psychologist
(1908–1970)

12

SOUPS

HERBSAINT, New Orleans, LA
Chef Donald Link

**AFTER STUDYING THIS
CHAPTER, YOU WILL BE
ABLE TO:**

▶ prepare a variety of clear and
  thick soups

▶ garnish and serve soups
  appropriately

The variety of ingredients, seasonings and garnishes that can be used for soups is virtually endless, provided you understand the basic procedures for making different kinds of soup. Great soups can be made from the finest and most expensive ingredients or from leftovers from the previous evening's dinner service and trimmings from the day's production. Although fresh ingredients are preferable, wise use of leftovers means that a daily soup special can be an economical, practical menu item.

This chapter extends to soups the skills and knowledge learned in Chapter 11, Stocks and Sauces. In Chapter 11, we discussed making stocks, thickening liquids, using a liaison and skimming impurities, techniques that apply to soup making as well. Here we discuss techniques such as clarifying consommés and thickening soups with vegetable purées. This chapter also covers cream soups, cold soups and guidelines for garnishing and serving a variety of soups.

Most soups can be classified by cooking technique and appearance as either clear or thick.

Clear soups include **broths** made from meat, poultry, game, fish or vegetables as well as **consommés,** which are broths clarified to remove impurities.

Thick soups include cream soups and purée soups. The most common **cream soups** are those made from vegetables cooked in a liquid that is thickened with a starch and puréed; cream is then incorporated to add richness and flavor. **Purée soups** are generally made from starchy vegetables or legumes. After the main ingredient is simmered in a liquid, the mixture—or a portion of it—is puréed.

Some soups (notably **bisques** and **chowders** as well as **cold soups** such as gazpacho and fruit soup) are neither clear nor thick soups. Rather, they use special preparation methods or a combination of the methods mentioned before.

A soup's quality is determined by its flavor, appearance and texture. A good soup should be full-flavored, with no off or sour tastes. Flavors from each of the soup's ingredients should blend and complement, with no one flavor overpowering another. Consommés should be crystal clear. The vegetables in vegetable soups should be brightly colored, not gray. Garnishes should be attractive and uniform in size and shape. The soup's texture should be very precise. If it is supposed to be smooth, then it should be very smooth and lump-free. If the soft and crisp textures of certain ingredients are supposed to contrast, the soup should not be overcooked, as this causes all the ingredients to become mushy and soft.

Garnishing is an important consideration when preparing soups. When applied to soups, the word *garnish* has two meanings. The first is the one more typically associated with the word. It refers to foods added to the soup as decoration—for example, a broccoli floret floated on a bowl of cream of broccoli soup. The second refers to foods that may serve not only as decorations but also as critical components of the final product—for example, noodles in a bowl of chicken noodle soup. In this context, the noodles are not ingredients

ESCOFFIER'S CLASSIFICATION OF SOUPS

In his 1903 culinary treatise *Le Guide culinaire,* Auguste Escoffier recognized many more categories of soups than we do today. They include the following:

> *Clear soups,* which are always "clear consommés with a slight garnish in keeping with the nature of the consommé."
>
> *Purées,* which are made from starchy vegetables and are thickened with rice, potato or soft bread crumbs.
>
> *Cullises,* which use poultry, game or fish for a base and are thickened with rice, lentils, espagnole sauce or bread soaked in boiling salted water.
>
> *Bisques,* which use shellfish cooked with a mirepoix as a base and are thickened with rice.

> *Veloutés,* which use velouté sauce as a base and are finished with a liaison of egg yolks and cream.
>
> *Cream soups,* which use béchamel sauce as a base and are finished with heavy cream.
>
> *Special soups,* which are those that do not follow the procedures for veloutés or creams.
>
> *Vegetable soups,* which are usually paysanne or peasant-type and "do not demand very great precision in the apportionment of the vegetables of which they are composed, but they need great care and attention, notwithstanding."

> *Foreign soups,* "which have a foreign origin whose use, although it may not be general, is yet sufficiently common."

Because of changes in consumer health consciousness and kitchen operations, many of the distinctions between Escoffier's classic soups have now become blurred and, in some cases, eliminated. As discussed in this chapter, for example, clear consommés and vegetable soups are now made with stocks or broths; most cream soups use velouté as a base and are finished with milk or cream rather than a liaison. But not everything has changed: The procedures for making purées and bisques are essentially the same today as they were when Escoffier haunted the great kitchens of Europe.

because they are not used to make the chicken soup. Rather, they are added to chicken soup to create a different dish. These additional items are still referred to as garnishes, however.

▶ CLEAR SOUPS

All clear soups start as stock or broth. Broths may be served as finished items, used as the base for other soups or refined (clarified) into consommés.

BROTHS

The techniques for making stocks discussed in Chapter 11 are identical to those used for making broths. Like stocks, broths are prepared by simmering flavoring ingredients in a liquid for a long time. Broths and stocks differ, however, in two ways. First, broths are made with meat instead of just bones. Second, broths (often with a garnish) can be served as finished dishes, while stocks are generally used to prepare other items.

Broths are made from meat, poultry, fish or vegetables cooked in a liquid. An especially full-flavored broth results when a stock and not just water is used as the liquid. Cuts of meat from the shank, neck or shoulder result in more flavorful broths, as will the flesh of mature poultry. Proper temperature, skimming and straining help produce well-flavored, clear broths.

▶ PROCEDURE FOR PREPARING BROTHS

1 Truss or cut the main ingredient.

2 Brown the meat; brown or sweat the mirepoix or vegetables as necessary.

3 Place the main ingredient and mirepoix or vegetables in an appropriate stockpot and add enough cold water or stock to cover. Add a bouquet garni or sachet d'épices if desired.

4 Bring the liquid slowly to a boil; reduce to a simmer and cook, skimming occasionally, until the main ingredient is tender and the flavor is fully developed.

5 Carefully strain the broth through a china cap lined with damp cheesecloth; try to disturb the flavoring ingredients as little as possible in order to preserve the broth's clarity.

6 Cool and store following the procedures for cooling stocks. Or bring to a boil, garnish as desired and hold for service.

RECIPE 12.1 BEEF BROTH

Yield: 8 qt. (8 lt)

Beef shank, neck or shoulder cut in 2-in. (5-cm) thick pieces	12 lb.	5.5 kg
Vegetable oil	8 fl. oz.	250 ml
Water or beef stock, cold	2 gal.	8 lt
Mirepoix	2 lb.	900 g
Turnips, medium dice	8 oz.	250 g
Leeks, medium dice	8 oz.	250 g
Tomato, seeded and diced	8 oz.	250 g
Sachet:		
Bay leaf	1	1
Dried thyme	1/2 tsp.	2 ml
Peppercorns, crushed	1/2 tsp.	2 ml
Parsley stems	8	8
Garlic cloves, crushed	2	2
Salt	TT	TT

1 Brown the meat in 4 fluid ounces (120 milliliters) of oil, then place it in a stockpot. Add the stock or water and bring to a simmer. Simmer gently for 2 hours, skimming the surface as necessary.

2 After the meat has simmered for 2 hours, caramelize the mirepoix in the remaining oil and add it to the liquid. Add the turnips, leeks, tomato and sachet.

3 Simmer until full flavor has developed, approximately 1 hour. Skim the surface as necessary.

4 Carefully strain the broth through cheesecloth and season to taste. Cool and refrigerate.

Approximate values per 6-fl.-oz. (180-ml) serving: **Calories** 70, **Total fat** 6 g, **Saturated fat** 1 g, **Cholesterol** 2 mg, **Sodium** 630 mg, **Total carbohydrates** 2 g, **Protein** 2 g

BROTH-BASED SOUPS

Broths are often used as bases for such familiar soups as vegetable, chicken noodle and beef barley.

Transforming a broth into a broth-based vegetable soup, for example, is quite simple. Although a broth may be served with a vegetable (or meat) garnish, a broth-based vegetable soup is a soup in which the vegetables (and meats) are cooked directly in the broth, adding flavor, body and texture to the finished product. Any number of vegetables can be used to make a vegetable soup; it could be a single vegetable as in onion soup or a dozen different vegetables for a hearty minestrone.

When making broth-based vegetable soups, each ingredient must be added at the proper time so that all ingredients are cooked when the soup is finished. The ingredients must cook long enough to add their flavors and soften sufficiently but not so long that they lose their identity and become too soft or mushy.

Because broth-based vegetable soups are made by simmering ingredients directly in the broth, they are generally not as clear as plain broths. But appearances are still important. So, when cutting ingredients for the soup, pay particular attention so that the pieces are uniform and visually appealing. Small dice, julienne, batonnet or paysanne cuts are recommended.

▶ PROCEDURE FOR PREPARING BROTH-BASED VEGETABLE SOUPS

1 Sweat long-cooking vegetables in butter or fat.

2 Add the appropriate stock or broth and bring to a simmer.

3 Add seasonings such as bay leaves, dried thyme, crushed peppercorns, parsley stems and garlic, in a sachet, allowing enough time for the seasonings to fully flavor the soup.

4 Add additional ingredients according to their cooking times.

5 Simmer the soup to blend all the flavors.

6 If the soup is not going to be served immediately, cool and refrigerate it.

7 Just before service, add any garnishes that were prepared separately or do not require cooking.

HEARTY VEGETABLE BEEF SOUP

RECIPE 12.2

Yield: 5 qt. (5 lt)

Butter or beef fat	6 oz.	170 g
Mirepoix, small dice	3 lb.	1.5 kg
Turnip, small dice	8 oz.	250 g
Garlic cloves, chopped	2	2
Beef broth or stock	4 qt.	4 lt
Beef, small dice	1 lb.	450 g
Sachet:		
Bay leaf	1	1
Dried thyme	½ tsp.	2 ml
Peppercorns, crushed	½ tsp.	2 ml
Parsley stems	8	8
Tomato **concassée**	12 oz.	350 g
Corn kernels, fresh, frozen or canned	12 oz.	350 g
Salt and pepper	TT	TT

1 Sweating the vegetables.

1 In a soup pot, sweat the mirepoix and turnip in the butter or fat until tender.

2 Add the garlic and sauté lightly.

3 Add the beef broth or stock and the diced beef; bring to a simmer. Add the sachet. Skim or degrease as necessary.

4 Simmer until the beef and vegetables are tender, approximately 1 hour.

5 Add the tomato concassée and corn; simmer for 10 minutes. Season to taste with salt and pepper.

6 Cool and refrigerate or hold for service.

Variations: A wide variety of vegetables can be added or substituted in this recipe. If leeks, rutabagas, parsnips or cabbage are used, they should be sweated to bring out their flavors before the liquid is added. Potatoes, fresh beans, summer squash and other vegetables that cook more quickly should be added according to their cooking times. Rice, barley and pasta garnishes should be cooked separately and added just before service.

2 The finished vegetable beef soup.

▶ **concassée** peeled, seeded and diced tomato

Approximate values per 6-fl.-oz. (180-ml) serving: **Calories** 170, **Total fat** 10 g, **Saturated fat** 5 g, **Cholesterol** 30 mg, **Sodium** 600 mg, **Total carbohydrates** 12 g, **Protein** 7 g, **Vitamin A** 20%

CONSOMMÉS

A consommé is a stock or broth that has been clarified to remove impurities so that it is crystal clear. Traditionally, all clear broths were referred to as consommés; a clear broth further refined using the process described later was referred to as a double consommé. The term *double consommé* is still used occasionally to describe any strongly flavored consommé.

Well-prepared consommés should be rich in the flavor of the main ingredient. Beef and game consommés should be dark in color; consommés made from poultry should have a golden to light amber color. They should have substantial body as a result of their high gelatin content, and all consommés should be perfectly clear with no trace of fat.

Because a consommé is a refined broth, it is absolutely essential that the broth or stock used be of the highest quality. Although the clarification process adds some flavor to the consommé, the finished consommé will be only as good as the stock or broth from which it was made.

THE CLARIFICATION PROCESS

To make a consommé, you clarify a stock or broth. The stock or broth to be clarified must be cold and grease-free. To clarify, the cold degreased stock or broth is combined with a mixture known as a **clearmeat** or **clarification.** A clearmeat is a mixture of egg whites; ground meat, poultry or fish; mirepoix, herbs and spices; and an acidic product, usually tomatoes, lemon juice or wine. (An **oignon brûlée,** also known as an *onion brûlée*, is also often added to help flavor and color the consommé.)

The stock or broth and clearmeat are then slowly brought to a simmer. As the albumen in the egg whites and meat begins to coagulate, it traps impurities suspended in the liquid. As coagulation continues, the albumen-containing items combine with the other clearmeat ingredients and rise to the liquid's surface, forming a **raft.** As the mixture simmers, the raft ingredients release their flavors, further enriching the consommé.

After simmering, the consommé is carefully strained through several layers of cheesecloth to remove any trace of impurities. It is then completely degreased, either by cooling and refrigerating, then removing the solidified fat, or by carefully ladling the fat from the surface. The result is a rich, flavorful, crystal-clear consommé.

▶ **oignon brûlée** French for "burnt onion," made by charring onion halves; used to flavor and color stocks and sauces

▶ PROCEDURE FOR PREPARING CONSOMMÉS

1 In a suitable stockpot (one with a spigot makes it much easier to strain the consommé when it is finished), combine the ground meat, lightly beaten egg white and other clearmeat ingredients.

2 Add the cold stock or broth and stir to combine with the clearmeat ingredients.

3 Over medium heat, slowly bring the mixture to a simmer, stirring occasionally.

4 As the raft forms, make a hole in its center so that the liquid can bubble through, cooking the raft completely and extracting as much flavor as possible from the raft ingredients.

5 Simmer the consommé until full flavor develops, approximately 1 to 1½ hours.

6 Carefully strain the consommé through several layers of cheesecloth and degrease completely.

7 If the consommé will not be used immediately, it should be cooled and refrigerated, following the procedures for cooling stocks discussed in Chapter 11. When the consommé is completely cold, remove any remaining fat that solidifies on its surface.

8 If, after reheating the consommé, small dots of fat appear on the surface, they can be removed by blotting with a small piece of paper towel.

BEEF CONSOMMÉ

Yield: 4 qt. (4 lt)

Egg whites	10	10
Ground beef, lean, preferably shank, neck or shoulder	2 lb.	1 kg
Mirepoix	1 lb.	450 g
Tomato, seeded and diced	12 oz.	340 g
Beef broth or stock, cold	5 qt.	5 lt
Onions brûlée	2	2
Sachet:		
Bay leaves	2	2
Dried thyme	½ tsp.	2 ml
Peppercorns, crushed	½ tsp.	2 ml
Parsley stems	8	8
Cloves, whole	2	2
Salt	TT	TT

1 Combining the ingredients for the clearmeat.

1 Whip the egg whites until slightly frothy.
2 Combine the egg whites, beef, mirepoix and tomato in an appropriate stockpot.
3 Add the cold beef broth or stock; mix well and add the onions brûlée and sachet.
4 Bring the mixture to a simmer over moderate heat, stirring occasionally. Stop stirring when the raft begins to form.
5 Break a hole in the center of the raft to allow the consommé to bubble through.
6 Simmer until full flavor develops, approximately 1½ hours.
7 Strain through several layers of cheesecloth, degrease and adjust the seasonings. Cool and refrigerate or hold for service.

Approximate values per 6-fl.-oz. (180-ml) serving: **Calories** 210, **Total fat** 10 g, **Saturated fat** 3.5 g, **Cholesterol** 40 mg, **Sodium** 870 mg, **Total carbohydrates** 14 g, **Protein** 15 g, **Vitamin A** 20%, **Vitamin C** 10%

2 Making a hole in the raft to allow the liquid to bubble through.

Note: Guidelines for garnishing consommés as well as some classic garnishes are listed on page 263.

CORRECTING A POORLY CLARIFIED CONSOMMÉ

A clarification may fail for a variety of reasons. For example, if the consommé is allowed to boil or if it is stirred after the raft has formed, a cloudy consommé can result. If the consommé is insufficiently clear, a second clarification can be performed using the following procedure. This second clarification should be performed only once, however, and only if absolutely necessary, because the eggs not only remove impurities but also some of the consommé's flavor and richness.

3 Degreasing the consommé with a paper towel.

1 Thoroughly chill and degrease the consommé.
2 Lightly beat four egg whites per gallon (4 liters) of consommé and combine with the cold consommé.
3 Slowly bring the consommé to a simmer, stirring occasionally. Stop stirring when the egg whites begin to coagulate.
4 When the egg whites are completely coagulated, carefully strain the consommé.

4 The finished consommé.

Table 12.1		SOUPS, THEIR THICKENING AGENTS AND FINISHES	
CATEGORY	**TYPE**	**THICKENING AGENT OR METHOD**	**FINISH**
Clear soups	Broths	None	Assorted garnishes
	Consommés	None	Assorted garnishes
Thick soups	Cream soups	Roux and/or puréeing	Assorted garnishes, cream or béchamel sauce
	Purée soups	Puréeing	Assorted garnishes; cream is optional
Other soups	Bisques	Roux or rice and puréeing	Garnish of main ingredient cream and/or butter
	Chowders	Roux	Cream
Cold soups	Cooked cold soups	Roux, arrowroot, cornstarch, puréeing, sour cream, yogurt	Assorted garnishes, cream, crème fraîche or sour cream
	Uncooked cold soups	Puréeing	Assorted garnishes, cream, crème fraîche or sour cream

▶ THICK SOUPS

There are two kinds of thick soups: cream soups and purée soups. In general, cream soups are thickened with a roux or other starch, while purée soups rely on a purée of the main ingredient for thickening. But in certain ways the two soups are very similar: Some purée soups are finished with cream or partially thickened with a roux or other starch.

CREAM SOUPS

Most cream soups are made by simmering the main flavoring ingredient (for example, broccoli for cream of broccoli soup) in a white stock or thin velouté sauce to which seasonings have been added. The mixture is then puréed and strained. After the consistency has been adjusted, the soup is finished by adding cream. In classic cuisine, thin béchamel sauce is often used as the base for cream soups and can be substituted for velouté in many cream soup recipes, if desired.

▶ **béchamel** (bay-shah-mell) a leading sauce made by thickening milk with a white roux and adding seasonings

Both hard vegetables (for example, celery and squash) and soft or leafy vegetables (for example, spinach, corn, broccoli and asparagus) are used for cream soups. Hard vegetables are generally sweated in butter without browning before the liquid is added. Soft and leafy vegetables are generally added to the soup after the liquid is brought to a boil. Because cream soups are puréed, it is important to cook the flavoring ingredients until they are soft and can be passed through a food mill easily.

All cream soups are finished with milk or cream. Using milk thins the soup while adding richness; using the same amount of cream adds much more richness without the same thinning effect. Cold milk and cream curdle easily if added directly to a hot or acidic soup.

To prevent curdling:

1 Never add cold milk or cream to hot soup. Bring the milk or cream to a simmer before adding it to the soup. Or, temper the milk or cream by gradually adding some hot soup to it and then incorporating the warmed mixture into the rest of the soup.

2 Add the milk or cream to the soup just before service, if possible.

3 Do not boil the soup after the milk or cream has been added.

▶ **cream sauce** a sauce made by adding cream to a béchamel sauce

4 Use béchamel or cream sauce instead of milk or cream to finish cream soups because the presence of roux or other starch helps prevent curdling.

▶ PROCEDURE FOR PREPARING CREAM SOUPS

1 In a soup pot, sweat hard vegetables such as squash, onions, carrots and celery in oil or butter without browning.

2 In order to thicken the soup:
   a. add flour and cook to make a blond roux, then add the cooking liquid (that is, the stock), or
   b. add the stock to the vegetables, bring the stock to a simmer and add a blond roux that was prepared separately, or
   c. add a thin velouté or béchamel sauce (which contain roux) to the vegetables.

3 Bring to a boil and reduce to a simmer.

4 Add any soft vegetables such as broccoli or asparagus, and a sachet or bouquet garni as desired.

5 Simmer the soup, skimming occasionally, until the vegetables are very tender.

6 Purée the soup by passing it through a food mill, blender, food processor or vertical cutter/mixer (VCM). Strain through a china cap if desired. If the soup is too thick, adjust the consistency by adding hot white stock.

7 Finish the soup by adding hot milk or cream or a thin béchamel or cream sauce. Adjust the seasonings and serve.

CREAM OF BROCCOLI SOUP   RECIPE 12.4

Yield: 6 qt. (6 lt)

Whole butter	3 oz.	90 g
Onions, medium dice	12 oz.	340 g
Celery, medium dice	3 oz.	90 g
Broccoli, chopped	3 lb.	1.4 kg
Chicken velouté sauce, hot	4 qt.	4 lt
Chicken stock, hot	approx. 2 qt.	approx. 2 lt
Heavy cream, hot	24 fl. oz.	700 ml
Salt and white pepper	TT	TT
Broccoli florets, blanched	8 oz.	250 g

1 Sweat the onions, celery and broccoli in the butter, without browning, until they are nearly tender.

2 Add the velouté sauce. Bring to a simmer and cook until the vegetables are tender, approximately 15 minutes. Skim the surface periodically.

3 Purée the soup, then strain it through a china cap.

4 Return the soup to the stove and thin it to the correct consistency with the hot chicken stock.

5 Bring the soup to a simmer and add the hot cream. Season to taste with salt and white pepper.

6 Garnish with blanched broccoli florets just before service.

Variations: To make cream of asparagus, cauliflower, corn, pea or spinach soup, substitute an equal amount of the chosen vegetable for the broccoli. If using fresh spinach, precook the leaves slightly before proceeding with the recipe.

Approximate values per 6-fl.-oz. (180-ml) serving: **Calories** 140, **Total fat** 12 g, **Saturated fat** 7 g, **Cholesterol** 40 mg, **Sodium** 340 mg, **Total carbohydrates** 5 g, **Protein** 4 g, **Vitamin A** 20%, **Vitamin C** 70%

1 Adding the velouté sauce.

2 Puréeing the soup through a food mill.

3 Garnishing the finished soup.

PURÉE SOUPS

Purée soups are hearty soups made by cooking starchy vegetables or legumes in a stock or broth, then puréeing all or a portion of them to thicken the soup. Purée soups are similar to cream soups in that they both consist of a main ingredient that is first cooked in a liquid, then puréed. The primary difference is that unlike cream soups, which are thickened with starch, purée soups generally do not use additional starch for thickening. Rather, purée soups depend on the starch content of the main ingredient for thickening. Also, purée soups are generally coarser than cream soups and are typically not strained after puréeing. When finishing purée soups with cream, follow the guidelines discussed previously for adding cream to cream soups.

Purée soups can be made with dried or fresh beans such as peas, lentils and navy beans, or with any number of vegetables, including cauliflower, celery root, turnips and potatoes. Diced potatoes or rice are often used to help thicken vegetable purée soups.

▶ PROCEDURE FOR PREPARING PURÉE SOUPS

1 Sweat the mirepoix in butter without browning.
2 Add the cooking liquid.
3 Add the main ingredients and a sachet or bouquet garni.
4 Bring to a boil, reduce to a simmer and cook until all the ingredients are soft enough to purée easily. Remove and discard the sachet or bouquet garni.
5 Reserve a portion of the liquid to adjust the soup's consistency. Purée the rest of the soup by passing it through a food mill, food processor, blender or VCM.
6 Add enough of the reserved liquid to bring the soup to the correct consistency. If the soup is still too thick, add hot stock as needed.
7 Return the soup to a simmer and adjust the seasonings.
8 Add hot cream to the soup if desired.

Table 12.2	CREAM AND PURÉE SOUPS	
	CREAM SOUPS	**PURÉE SOUPS**
Technique	Cook principal ingredient in stock or velouté sauce	Cook principal ingredient in stock or water
Thickener	Roux or roux-thickened sauce	Purée of starchy ingredients
Texture	Strained; very smooth and rich	Not strained; slightly coarse and grainy

PURÉE OF SPLIT PEA SOUP

RECIPE 12.5

Yield: 4 qt. (4 lt)

Bacon, diced	3 oz.	90 g
Mirepoix, medium dice	1 lb.	450 g
Garlic cloves, chopped	2	2
Chicken stock	3 qt.	3 lt
Split peas, washed and sorted	1 lb.	450 g
Ham hocks or meaty ham bones	1½ lb.	650 g
Sachet:		
Bay leaves	2	2
Dried thyme	½ tsp.	2 ml
Peppercorns, crushed	½ tsp.	2 ml
Salt and pepper	TT	TT
Croutons, sautéed in butter	as needed for garnish	

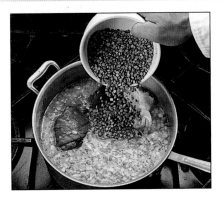

1 Adding peas to the stockpot.

1 In a stockpot, **render** the bacon by cooking it slowly and allowing it to release its fat; sweat the mirepoix and garlic in the fat without browning them.

2 Add the chicken stock, peas, ham hocks or bones and sachet. Bring to a boil, reduce to a simmer and cook until the peas are soft, approximately 1 to 1½ hours.

3 Remove the sachet and ham hocks or bones. Pass the soup through a food mill and return it to the stockpot.

4 Remove the meat from the hocks or bones. Cut the meat into medium dice and add it to the soup.

5 Bring the soup to a simmer and, if necessary, adjust the consistency by adding hot chicken stock. Adjust the seasonings with salt and pepper and serve, garnished with croutons.

2 Puréeing the split pea soup.

Variations: White beans, yellow peas and other dried beans can be soaked overnight in water and used instead of split peas.

Approximate values per 6-fl.-oz. (180-ml) serving: **Calories** 110, **Total fat** 4 g, **Saturated fat** 1.5 g, **Cholesterol** 20 mg, **Sodium** 870 mg, **Total carbohydrates** 6 g, **Protein** 11 g

ADJUSTING THE CONSISTENCY OF THICK SOUPS

Cream and purée soups tend to thicken when made in advance and refrigerated. To dilute a portion being reheated, add hot stock, broth, water or milk to the hot soup as needed.

If the soup is too thin, additional roux, beurre manié or cornstarch mixed with cool stock can be used to thicken it. If additional starch is added to thicken the soup, it should be used sparingly and the soup should be simmered a few minutes to cook out the starchy flavor. A liaison of egg yolks and heavy cream can be used to thicken cream soups when added richness is also desired. Remember, the soup must not boil after the liaison is added or it may curdle.

3 Garnishing the finished soup.

▶ **render** to melt and clarify fat

▶ OTHER SOUPS

Several popular types of soup do not fit the descriptions of, or follow the procedures for, either clear or thick soups. Soups such as bisques and chowders as well as many cold soups use special methods or a combination of the methods used for clear and thick soups.

BISQUES

Traditional bisques are shellfish soups thickened with cooked rice. Today, bisques are prepared using a combination of the cream and purée soup procedures. They are generally made from shrimp, lobster or crayfish and are thickened with a roux instead of rice for better stability and consistency.

Much of a bisque's flavor comes from crustacean shells, which are simmered in the cooking liquid, puréed (along with the mirepoix), returned to the cooking liquid and strained after further cooking. Puréeing the shells and returning them to the soup also adds the thickness and grainy texture associated with bisques.

Bisques are enriched with cream, following the procedures for cream soups, and can be finished with butter for additional richness. The garnish should be diced flesh from the appropriate shellfish.

▶ PROCEDURE FOR PREPARING BISQUES

1 Caramelize the mirepoix and main flavoring ingredient in fat.
2 Add a tomato product and deglaze with wine.
3 Add the cooking liquid (stock or velouté sauce).
4 Incorporate roux if needed.
5 Simmer, skimming as needed.
6 Strain the soup, reserving the solids and liquid. Purée the solids in a food mill or processor and return them to the liquid. Return to a simmer.
7 Strain the soup through a fine chinois or a china cap lined with cheesecloth.
8 Return the soup to a simmer and finish with hot cream.

To add even more richness to the bisque, monté au beurre with whole butter or a compound butter such as shrimp or lobster butter just before the soup is served. Also, if desired, add 3 ounces (90 milliliters) of sherry to each gallon (4 liters) of soup just before service.

RECIPE 12.6 **SHRIMP BISQUE**

Yield: 4 qt. (4 lt)

Clarified butter	3 fl. oz.	90 ml
Mirepoix, small dice	1 lb.	450 g
Shrimp shells and/or lobster or crayfish shells and bodies	2 lb.	1 kg
Garlic cloves, chopped	2	2
Tomato paste	2 oz.	60 g
Brandy	4 fl. oz.	120 ml
White wine	12 fl. oz.	350 ml
Fish velouté (made with shrimp stock)	4 qt.	4 lt
Sachet:		
Bay leaf	1	1
Dried thyme	½ tsp.	2 ml
Peppercorns, crushed	½ tsp.	2 ml
Parsley stems	8	8
Heavy cream, hot	1 pt.	500 ml
Salt and white pepper	TT	TT
Cayenne pepper	TT	TT
Shrimp, peeled and deveined	1 lb.	450 g

1 Caramelize the mirepoix and shrimp shells in the butter.
2 Add the garlic and tomato paste and sauté lightly.
3 Add the brandy and flambé.

4 Add the white wine. Deglaze and reduce the liquid by half.

5 Add the velouté and sachet and simmer for approximately 1 hour, skimming occasionally.

6 Strain, discarding the sachet and reserving the liquid and solids. Purée the solids and return them to the liquid. Return to a simmer and cook for 10 minutes.

7 Strain the bisque through a fine chinois or china cap lined with cheesecloth.

8 Return the bisque to a simmer and add the hot cream.

9 Season to taste with salt, white pepper and cayenne pepper.

10 Cook the shrimp and slice or dice them as desired. Garnish each portion of soup with cooked shrimp.

Approximate values per 4-fl.-oz. (120-ml) serving: **Calories** 110, **Total fat** 10 g, **Saturated fat** 6 g, **Cholesterol** 60 mg, **Sodium** 160 mg, **Total carbohydrates** 2 g, **Protein** 4 g, **Vitamin A** 10%

CHOWDERS

Although chowders are usually associated with the eastern United States where fish and clams are plentiful, they are of French origin. Undoubtedly the word chowder is derived from the Breton phrase *faire chaudière,* which means to make a fish stew in a caldron. The procedure was probably brought to Nova Scotia by French settlers and later introduced to New England.

Chowders are hearty soups with chunks of the main ingredients (including, virtually always, diced potatoes) and garnishes. With some exceptions (notably, Manhattan clam chowder), chowders contain milk or cream. Although there are thin chowders, most chowders are thickened with roux. The procedures for making chowders are similar to those for making cream soups except that chowders are not puréed and strained before the cream is added.

▶ PROCEDURE FOR PREPARING CHOWDERS

1 Render finely diced salt pork over medium heat.

2 Sweat mirepoix in the rendered pork.

3 Add flour to make a roux.

4 Add the liquid.

5 Add the seasoning and flavoring ingredients according to their cooking times.

6 Simmer, skimming as needed.

7 Add milk or cream.

NEW ENGLAND–STYLE CLAM CHOWDER   RECIPE 12.7

Yield: 3 qt. (3 lt)

Canned clams with juice*	2 qt.	2 lt
Water or fish stock	approx. 1½ qt.	approx. 1.5 lt
Potatoes, small dice	1 lb. 4 oz.	600 g
Salt pork, small dice	8 oz.	250 g
Onions, small dice	1 lb.	500 g
Celery, small dice	8 oz.	250 g
Flour	4 oz.	120 g
Milk	1 qt.	1 lt
Heavy cream	8 fl. oz.	250 ml
Salt and pepper	TT	TT
Tabasco sauce	TT	TT
Worcestershire sauce	TT	TT
Fresh thyme	TT	TT

1 Drain the clams, reserving both the clams and their liquid. Add enough water or stock so that the total liquid equals 2 quarts (2 liters).

2 Simmer the potatoes in the clam liquid until nearly cooked through. Strain and reserve the potatoes and the liquid.

3 Render the salt pork. Add the onions and celery to the rendered fat and cook until tender but not brown.

4 Add the flour and cook to make a blond roux.

5 Add the clam liquid to the roux, whisking away any lumps.

6 Simmer for 30 minutes, skimming as necessary.

7 Bring the milk and cream to a boil and add to the soup.

8 Add the clams and potatoes, and season to taste with salt, pepper, Tabasco sauce, Worcestershire sauce and thyme.

9 Garnish each serving with fresh herbs as desired.

*If using fresh clams for the chowder, wash and steam approximately $\frac{1}{2}$ bushel of chowder clams in a small amount of water to yield $1\frac{1}{4}$ quarts (1.25 liters) of clam meat. Chop the clams. Strain the liquid through several layers of cheesecloth to remove any sand that may be present. Add enough water or stock so that the total liquid is 2 quarts (2 liters). Continue with the recipe, starting at step 2.

Approximate values per 6-fl.-oz. (180-ml) serving: **Calories** 250, **Total fat** 15 g, **Saturated fat** 7 g, **Cholesterol** 45 mg, **Sodium** 930 mg, **Total carbohydrates** 17 g, **Protein** 11 g, **Vitamin A** 10%, **Vitamin C** 10%, **Calcium** 15%

COLD SOUPS

Cold soups can be as simple as a chilled version of a cream soup or as creative as a cold fruit soup blended with yogurt. Other than the fact that they are cold, cold soups are difficult to classify because many of them use unique or combination preparation methods. Regardless, they are divided here into two categories: cold soups that require cooking and those that do not.

COOKED COLD SOUPS

Many cold soups are simply a chilled version of a hot soup. For example, consommé madrilène and consommé portugaise are prepared hot and served cold. Vichyssoise is a cold version of puréed potato-leek soup. When serving a hot soup cold, there are several considerations:

1 If the soup is to be creamed, add the cream at the last minute. Although curdling is not as much of a problem as it is with hot soups, adding the cream at the last minute helps extend the soup's shelf life.

2 Cold soups should have a thinner consistency than hot soups. To achieve the proper consistency, use less starch if starch is used as the thickener, or use a higher ratio of liquid to main ingredient if the soup is thickened by puréeing. Consistency should be checked and adjusted at service time.

3 Cold dulls the sense of taste, so cold soups require more seasoning than hot ones. Taste the soup just before service and adjust the seasonings as needed.

4 Always serve cold soups as cold as possible using chilled bowls.

SAFETY ALERT

COOKED COLD SOUP

Cooked cold soups, especially those made with potatoes, beans, dairy products or other high-protein foods, are potentially hazardous foods and must be chilled quickly and held at or below 40°F (4°C). Because these soups will not be reheated for service, cross-contamination is also a concern. Keep the soup covered and store above any raw meat, poultry or seafood in the cooler.

VICHYSSOISE (COLD POTATO-LEEK SOUP)

RECIPE 12.8

Yield: 4 qt. (4 lt) **Method:** Purée

Leeks, white part only	2 lb.	1 kg
Whole butter	8 oz.	250 g
Potatoes, large dice	2 lb.	1 kg
Chicken stock	3½ qt.	3½ lt
Salt and white pepper	TT	TT
Heavy cream	24 fl. oz.	700 ml
Chives, snipped	as needed for garnish	
Fried sweet potato frizzles	as needed for garnish	

1 Split the leeks lengthwise and wash well to remove all sand and grit. Slice them thinly.

2 Sweat the leeks in the butter without browning them.

3 Add the diced potatoes and chicken stock, season with salt and white pepper and bring to a simmer.

4 Simmer until the leeks and potatoes are very tender, approximately 45 minutes.

5 Purée the soup in a food processor, blender or food mill; strain through a fine sieve.

6 Chill the soup well.

7 At service time, incorporate the heavy cream and adjust the seasonings. Serve in chilled bowls, garnished with snipped chives and sweet potato frizzles.

Approximate values per 6-fl.-oz. (180-ml) serving: **Calories** 300, **Total fat** 22 g, **Saturated fat** 13 g, **Cholesterol** 70 mg, **Sodium** 660 mg, **Total carbohydrates** 19 g, **Protein** 6 g, **Vitamin A** 20%, **Vitamin C** 20%

Many cooked cold soups use fruit juice (typically apple, grape or orange) as a base and are thickened with cornstarch or arrowroot as well as with puréed fruit. For additional flavor, wine is sometimes used in lieu of a portion of the fruit juice. Cinnamon, ginger and other spices that complement fruit are commonly added, as is lemon or lime juice, which adds acidity as well as flavor. Crème fraîche, yogurt or sour cream can be used as an ingredient or garnish to add richness.

FRESH PEACH AND YOGURT SOUP

RECIPE 12.9

Yield: 2 qt. (2 lt) **Method:** Purée

Fresh peaches	4 lb.	1.8 kg
Dry white wine	24 fl. oz.	700 ml
Honey	4 oz.	120 g
Lemon juice	2 fl. oz.	60 ml
Cinnamon, ground	¼ tsp.	1 ml
Plain nonfat yogurt	8 oz.	225 g
Heavy cream	TT	TT
Pistachios, chopped fine	as needed for garnish	

1 Pit and coarsely chop the peaches without peeling. Place in a nonreactive saucepan. Add the wine, honey and lemon juice. Cover and simmer for 30 minutes.

2 Purée the peach mixture in a blender. Strain and chill.

1 Simmering the peaches.

2 Straining the peach pureé.

3 The finished soup.

3 Stir in the cinnamon, yogurt and heavy cream.
4 Chill thoroughly. Serve in chilled bowls, garnished with finely chopped pistachio nuts.

Approximate values per 6-fl.-oz. (180-ml) serving: **Calories** 140, **Total fat** 0 g, **Saturated fat** 0 g, **Cholesterol** 0 mg, **Sodium** 20 mg, **Total carbohydrates** 32 g, **Protein** 3 g, **Vitamin A** 10%, **Vitamin C** 25%, **Claims**—fat free; very low sodium; good source of fiber

UNCOOKED COLD SOUPS

Some cold soups are not cooked at all. Rather, they rely only on puréed fruits or vegetables for thickness, body and flavor. Cold stock is sometimes used to adjust the soup's consistency. Dairy products such as cream, sour cream or crème fraîche are sometimes added to enrich and flavor the soup.

RECIPE 12.10   GAZPACHO

Yield: 4 qt. (4 lt)   **Method:** Uncooked

Tomato, peeled and diced	2 lb. 8 oz.	1.2 kg
Onion, medium dice	8 oz.	250 g
Green bell pepper, medium dice	1	1
Red bell pepper, medium dice	1	1
Cucumber, peeled, seeded, medium dice	1 lb.	500 g
Garlic, minced	1 oz.	30 g
Red wine vinegar	2 fl. oz.	60 ml
Lemon juice	2 fl. oz.	60 ml
Olive oil	4 fl. oz.	120 ml
Salt and pepper	TT	TT
Cayenne pepper	TT	TT
Fresh bread crumbs (optional)	3 oz.	90 g
Tomato juice	3 qt.	3 lt
White stock	as needed	as needed
Garnish:		
Tomato, peeled, seeded, small dice	8 oz.	250 g
Red bell pepper, small dice	4 oz.	120 g
Green bell pepper, small dice	4 oz.	120 g
Yellow bell pepper, small dice	4 oz.	120 g
Cucumber, peeled, seeded, small dice	3 oz.	90 g
Green onion, sliced fine	2 oz.	60 g
Fresh basil	as needed for garnish	

1 Combine and purée all ingredients except the tomato juice, stock and garnish in a VCM, food processor or blender.
2 Stir in the tomato juice.
3 Adjust the consistency with the stock.
4 Stir in the vegetable garnishes and adjust the seasonings.
5 Serve in chilled cups or bowls garnished with fresh basil.

Approximate values per 6-fl.-oz. (180-ml) serving: **Calories** 70, **Total fat** 0.5 g, **Saturated fat** 0 g, **Cholesterol** 0 mg, **Sodium** 600 mg, **Total carbohydrates** 14 g, **Protein** 3 g, **Vitamin A** 15%, **Vitamin C** 70%, **Claims**—low fat; no cholesterol

▶ GARNISHING SOUPS

Garnishes can range from a simple sprinkle of chopped parsley on a bowl of cream soup to tiny profiteroles stuffed with foie gras adorning a crystal-clear bowl of consommé. Some soups are so full of attractive, flavorful and colorful foods that are integral parts of the soup (for example, vegetables and chicken in chicken vegetable soup) that no additional garnishes are necessary. In others, the garnish determines the type of soup. For example, a beef broth garnished with cooked barley and diced beef becomes beef barley soup.

GUIDELINES FOR GARNISHING SOUPS

Although some soups (particularly consommés) have traditional garnishes, many soups depend on the chef's imagination and the kitchen's inventory for the finishing garnish. The only rules are as follows:

1 The garnish should be attractive.
2 The meats and vegetables used should be neatly cut into an appropriate and uniform shape and size. This is particularly important when garnishing a clear soup such as a consommé, as the consommé's clarity highlights the precise (or imprecise) cuts.
3 The garnish's texture and flavor should complement the soup.
4 Starches and vegetables used as garnishes should be cooked separately, reheated and placed in the soup bowl before the hot soup is added. If they are cooked in the soup, they may cloud or thicken the soup or alter its flavor, texture and seasoning.
5 Garnishes should be cooked just until done; meat and poultry should be tender but not falling apart, vegetables should be firm but not mushy, and pasta and rice should maintain their identity. These types of garnishes are usually held on the side and added to the hot soup at the last minute to prevent overcooking.

GARNISHING SUGGESTIONS

Some garnishes are used to add texture, as well as flavor and visual interest, to soups. Items such as crunchy croutons or oyster crackers, or crispy crumbled bacon on a cream soup, or diced meat in a clear broth soup add texture variety that makes the final product more appealing.

▶ Clear soups—any combination of julienne cuts of the same meat, poultry, fish or vegetable that provides the dominant flavor in the stock or broth; vegetables (cut uniformly into any shape), pasta (flat, small tortellini or tiny ravioli), gnocchi, quenelles, barley, spaetzle, white or wild rice, croutons, crepes, tortillas or won tons.

CLASSIC CONSOMMÉS

Many classic consommés are known by their garnishes:

Consommé brunoise—blanched or sautéed brunoise of turnip, leek, celery and onion.

Consommé julienne—blanched or sautéed julienne of carrot, turnip, leek, celery, cabbage and onion.

Consommé paysanne—blanched or sautéed paysanne of leek, turnip, carrot, celery and potato.

Consommé bouquetière—assorted blanched vegetables.

Consommé madrilène—tomatoes or tomato juice; served hot or cold.

Consommé royale—cooked custard cut into tiny shapes.

Angel hair consommé—cooked angel hair (vermicelli) pasta.

Consommé with profiteroles—tiny profiteroles (pâte à choux rounds) stuffed with foie gras.

▶ Cream soups, hot or cold—toasted slivered almonds, sour cream or crème fraîche, croutons, grated cheese or puff pastry fleurons; cream vegetable soups are usually garnished with slices or florets of the main ingredient.

▶ Purée soups—julienne cuts of poultry or ham, sliced sausage, croutons, grated cheese, bacon bits.

▶ Any soup—finely chopped fresh herbs, snipped chives, edible flowers, parsley or watercress.

▶ SOUP SERVICE

PREPARING SOUPS IN ADVANCE

Most soups can be made ahead of time and reheated as needed for service. To preserve freshness and quality, small batches of soup should be heated as needed throughout the meal service.

Clear soups are quite easy to reheat because there is little danger of scorching. If garnishes are already added to a clear soup, care should be taken not to overcook the garnishes when reheating the soup. All traces of fat should be removed from a consommé's surface before reheating.

Thick soups present more of a challenge. To increase shelf life and reduce the risk of spoilage, cool and refrigerate a thick soup when it is still a base (that is, before it is finished with milk or cream). Just before service, carefully reheat the soup base using a heavy-gauge pot over low heat. Stir often to prevent scorching. Then finish the soup (following the guidelines noted earlier) with boiling milk or cream, a light béchamel sauce or a liaison and adjust the seasonings. Always taste the soup after reheating and adjust the seasonings as needed.

TEMPERATURES

The rule is simple: Serve hot soup hot and cold soup cold. Hot clear soups should be served near boiling; 210°F (99°C) is ideal. Hot cream soups should be served at slightly lower temperatures; 190°F–200°F (88°C–93°C) is acceptable. Cold soups should be served at a temperature of 40°F (4°C) or below, and are sometimes presented in special serving pieces surrounded by ice.

CONCLUSION

Soup, often served as the first course, may determine the success or failure of an entire meal. Although a wide variety of ingredients can be used to make both clear and thick soups, including trimmings and leftovers, poor-quality ingredients make poor-quality soups. By using, adapting and combining the basic techniques described in this chapter with different ingredients, you can create an infinite number of new and appetizing hot or cold soups. But exercise good judgment when combining flavors and techniques; they should blend well and complement each other. Moreover, any garnishes that are added should contribute to the appearance and character of the finished soup. And remember, always serve hot soups hot and cold soups cold.

1 What are the differences between a stock and a broth?

2 What are the differences between a beef consommé and a beef-based broth? How are they similar?

3 What are the differences between a cream soup and a purée soup? How are they similar?

4 Create a recipe for veal consommé.

5 Discuss several techniques for serving soup. What can be done to ensure that soups are served at the correct temperature?

6 Explain how and why soups are garnished. Why is it sometimes said that the noodles in a chicken noodle soup are actually a garnish?

RECIPE 12.11   CHICKEN AND SAUSAGE GUMBO

Note: This dish appears in the chapter opening photograph.

CHEF DONALD LINK

Inspired by his grandfather, Chef Donald Link began cooking at a very young age. By age 15, he was working in a professional kitchen washing dishes, and soon thereafter he began cooking professionally. In 1993, after working for several years in various restaurants in Louisiana, Chef Link moved to San Francisco. He worked for a year at the wildly popular Cha Cha Cha and then attended the California Culinary Academy.

In 1995, he was an extern at Susan Spicer's Bayona Restaurant in New Orleans, Louisiana, eventually continuing on to become sous chef there. In 1997, he returned to San Francisco to open Jardinière with Traci Des Jardin. He then became executive chef at San Francisco's Elite Café, where he received rave reviews and appeared on local cooking shows.

Chef Link recently teamed with his mentor, Susan Spicer, to open Herbsaint Bar and Restaurant in New Orleans' French Quarter. Herbsaint (the name refers to an anise-flavored liqueur made in New Orleans) serves contemporary French-American cuisine in an upscale casual atmosphere.

HERBSAINT BAR AND RESTAURANT, New Orleans, LA
Chef Donald Link

Gumbo, a thick, spicy stew, is traditional fare in the delta region of the American South. Gumbo is usually made with poultry, fish, shellfish or sausage and is thickened with dark roux. Okra or filé powder (ground sassafras leaves) may also be added for thickening. Filé powder is sometimes added at the time of service for additional flavor. Gumbo is traditionally served over white rice.

Yield: 5 qt. (4.8 lt)

Cayenne pepper	1 Tbsp.	15 ml
Paprika	1 Tbsp.	15 ml
White pepper	1 Tbsp.	15 ml
Black pepper	1 Tbsp.	15 ml
Chicken, boneless, skinless, cut in 1-in. (2.5-cm) pieces	4 lb.	1.8 kg
Salt	3 Tbsp.	45 ml
Flour	20 oz.	600 g
Vegetable oil	28 fl. oz.	840 ml
Onions, medium dice	1 pt.	450 ml
Celery, medium dice	1 pt.	450 ml
Green bell pepper, medium dice	1 pt.	450 ml
Garlic, chopped	2 Tbsp.	30 ml
Filé powder	2 Tbsp.	30 ml
Bay leaves	4	4
Chicken stock	4 qt.	4 lt
Andouille sausage, sliced, cut in half circles	2 lb.	900 g
Okra	1 lb.	450 g
Long-grain white rice, cooked	3 c.	710 ml
Green onion tops, sliced	1 pt.	450 ml

1. Combine the cayenne pepper, paprika, white pepper and black pepper. Season the chicken with 1 tablespoon (15 milliliters) of salt and 1 tablespoon (15 milliliters) of the pepper mix. Dust the chicken with some of the flour. Pan-fry the chicken in 8 fluid ounces (240 milliliters) of the vegetable oil until well browned. Remove the chicken from the pan and reserve.

2. Strain the oil used to brown the chicken in order to remove burnt particles. Return the strained oil to the pan. Add 16 fluid ounces (450 milliliters) of fresh vegetable oil. Over medium heat, add the remaining flour while stirring with a whisk to make a roux. Cook the roux very slowly over medium heat, stirring often, until it becomes a copper-brown color, approximately 45 minutes to 1 hour.

3. Add the onions, celery, bell pepper, garlic, filé powder, bay leaves and the remaining salt and pepper mix. Cook for 5 minutes. Add the chicken stock and bring to a simmer. Skim the fat from the surface and cook for approximately 1½ hours, skimming occasionally.

4 When the strong roux flavor fades, add the reserved chicken and andouille. Cook the gumbo for 1 more hour, skimming regularly.

5 Sauté the okra in the remaining 4 fluid ounces (120 milliliters) of vegetable oil, drain and add to the gumbo. Adjust the seasonings with the salt, pepper, cayenne, filé powder, hot sauce or other seasonings as desired.

6 Serve each portion of gumbo with 1 to 2 tablespoons (15 to 30 milliliters) of simmered rice (page 701) and garnish with sliced green onion tops.

Approximate values per 8-fl.-oz. (240-ml) serving: **Calories** 750, **Total fat** 52 g, **Saturated fat** 11 g, **Cholesterol** 100 mg, **Sodium** 2240 mg, **Total carbohydrates** 36 g, **Protein** 35 g, **Vitamin A** 15%, **Vitamin C** 40%, **Iron** 20%

WILD MUSHROOM AND VEAL SOUP

RECIPE 12.12

Yield: 1 qt. (1 lt)   **Method:** Broth

Garlic, minced	2 tsp.	10 ml
Olive oil	2 fl. oz.	60 ml
Assorted wild mushrooms, such as		
shiitake, oyster, cèpes and morels	8 oz.	250 g
Brown veal stock	24 fl. oz.	700 ml
Fresh parsley, minced	2 Tbsp.	30 ml
Fresh mint, minced	4 Tbsp.	60 ml
Salt and pepper	TT	TT
French bread croutons	as needed for garnish	
Fresh parsley, chopped fine	as needed for garnish	

1 Briefly sauté the garlic in the olive oil. Add the mushrooms and cook until they are tender and any liquid given off has evaporated.

2 Add the veal stock, parsley and mint; simmer for 15 minutes. Season to taste.

3 Place one crouton in each soup bowl. Ladle in the soup and garnish with the finely chopped parsley.

Approximate values per 8-fl.-oz. (240-ml) serving: **Calories** 100, **Total fat** 7 g, **Saturated fat** 1 g, **Cholesterol** 0 mg, **Sodium** 460 mg, **Total carbohydrates** 8 g, **Protein** 3 g, **Vitamin A** 90%, **Vitamin C** 15%.

CHICKEN SOUP WITH MATZO BALLS

RECIPE 12.13

Yield: 2 gal. (8 lt)   **Method:** Broth

Chicken pieces	8–10 lb.	4–4.4 kg
Chicken stock	10 qt.	10 lt
Mirepoix	1 lb.	500 g
Sachet:		
Bay leaf	1	1
Dried thyme	½ tsp.	2 ml
Peppercorns, crushed	½ tsp.	2 ml
Parsley stems	10	10
Salt and pepper	TT	TT
Fresh parsley, chopped	as needed for garnish	
Matzo Balls (recipe follows)		

1 Simmer the chicken in the stock for 2 hours, skimming as necessary.

2 Add the mirepoix and sachet. Simmer for another hour.

3 Strain and degrease the broth. Adjust seasonings.

4 Bring to a boil at service time. Portion into heated bowls, garnish with chopped parsley and one or two matzo balls.

MATZO BALLS

Yield: 48 Balls

Eggs	4	4
Water	2 fl. oz.	60 ml
Chicken fat or butter, softened	2 oz.	60 g
Matzo meal	4 oz.	120 g
Salt and white pepper	TT	TT

1 Beat the eggs with the water. Stir in the fat.

2 Add matzo meal, salt and white pepper. The batter should be as thick as mashed potatoes.

3 Chill for at least 1 hour.

4 Bring 2 quarts of water to a gentle boil. Using a #70 portion scoop, shape the batter into balls. Carefully drop each ball into the hot water. Cover and simmer until fully cooked, approximately 30 minutes. Remove the matzo balls from the water and serve in hot chicken soup.

Approximate values per 6-fl.-oz. (180-ml) serving with 2 matzo balls: **Calories** 60, **Total fat** 3 g, **Saturated fat** 1 g, **Cholesterol** 25 mg, **Sodium** 800 mg, **Total carbohydrates** 3 g, **Protein** 6 g, **Claims**–low fat

RECIPE 12.14

FRENCH ONION SOUP

Yield: 4 qt. (4 lt)   **Method:** Broth

Yellow onions, sliced thin	10 lb.	4.4 kg
Clarified butter	8 fl. oz.	250 ml
Beef stock	4 qt.	4 lt
Chicken stock	4 qt.	4 lt
Fresh thyme	½ oz.	15 g
Salt and pepper	TT	TT
Sherry	8 fl. oz.	250 ml
Toasted French bread slices	as needed for garnish	
Gruyère cheese, grated	as needed for garnish	

1 Sauté the onions in the butter over low heat. Carefully caramelize them thoroughly without burning.

2 Deglaze the pan with 8 ounces (250 milliliters) of the beef stock. Cook au sec. Repeat this process until the onions are a very dark, even brown.

3 Add the remaining beef stock and the chicken stock and thyme.

4 Bring to a simmer and cook 20 minutes to develop flavor. Adjust the seasonings and add the sherry.

5 Serve in warm bowls. Top each portion with a slice of toasted French bread and a thick layer of cheese. Place under the broiler or salamander until the cheese is melted and lightly browned.

Approximate values per 6-fl.-oz. (180-ml) serving: **Calories** 280, **Total fat** 12 g, **Saturated fat** 6 g, **Cholesterol** 25 mg, **Sodium** 1370 mg, **Total carbohydrates** 34 g, **Protein** 9 g, **Vitamin A** 25%, **Vitamin C** 20%

1 Caramelize the onions thoroughly.

2 Sprinkle grated cheese on top of each serving of soup.

3 The finished soup.

SOUTHEAST ASIAN CONSOMMÉ WITH LEMONGRASS

RECIPE 12.15

CONNECTICUT CULINARY INSTITUTE, **Farmington, CT**
Chef Jamie Roraback

Yield: 2 qt. (2 lt)   **Method:** Consommé

Egg whites	6	6
Ground chicken, duck or lean pork	1 lb.	450 g
Mirepoix, medium dice	8 oz.	225 g
Fresh lime juice	1 Tbsp.	15 ml
White chicken, duck or pork stock, cold	2½ qt.	2.5 lt
Sachet:		
Bay leaf	1	1
Dried thyme	¼ tsp.	2 ml
Peppercorns, crushed	¼ tsp.	2 ml
Parsley stems	4	4
Star anise	2	2
Fresh ginger, chopped coarse	2 Tbsp.	30 ml
Lime zest	2 tsp.	10 ml
Lemongrass, chopped	3 Tbsp.	45 ml
Shiitake mushroom stems	3 Tbsp.	45 ml
Thai chile peppers, chopped	2	2
Cilantro stems	4	4
Soy sauce	TT	TT
Salt and white pepper	TT	TT
Sugar	TT	TT
Garnish:		
Rice noodles	8 oz.	225 g
Snow peas	4 oz.	120 g
Carrots, lozenge cut	4 oz.	120 g
Shiitake mushroom caps, thinly sliced	2 oz.	60 g
Cilantro leaves	3 Tbsp.	45 ml
Fresh mint leaves, chiffonade	1 Tbsp.	15 ml
Fresh basil leaves, chiffonade	2 Tbsp.	30 ml

1 Whip the egg whites until slightly frothy.

2 Combine the egg whites, ground meat, mirepoix and lime juice in an appropriate stockpot and stir well.

3 Add the cold stock, mix well and add the sachet.

4 Bring the mixture to a simmer over moderate heat, stirring occasionally.

5 Break a hole in the center of the raft and allow the consommé to bubble through. Simmer until full flavor develops, approximately 1½ hours.

6 Strain the consommé through several layers of damp cheesecloth or a coffee filter, degrease and adjust the seasonings with soy sauce, salt, white pepper and sugar to taste.

7 Rehydrate the rice noodles in hot water, cool in an ice bath, drain and hold for service. Pull the strings from the snow peas, cut them on the bias, blanch, chill in an ice bath, drain and hold them for service. Blanch the carrots, chill them in an ice bath and hold them for service.

8 For each serving, heat a small portion of noodles, snow peas, carrots and mushroom caps by immersing them in boiling water for a few seconds, then place them in soup bowls. Ladle the hot consommé over the vegetables and add fresh herbs to taste.

Approximate values per 8-fl.-oz. (240-ml) serving: **Calories** 130, **Total fat** 1 g, **Saturated fat** 0 g, **Cholesterol** 0 mg, **Sodium** 870 mg, **Total carbohydrates** 27 g, **Protein** 3 g, **Vitamin A** 70%, **Vitamin C** 15%, **Claims**—low fat; no saturated fat; no cholesterol; high in vitamin A; source of vitamin C

RECIPE 12.16   JAVIER'S REDFISH SOPA

PESCE RESTAURANT, HOUSTON, TX
Chef Mark Holley

Yield: 6 Servings   **Method:** Broth

Fresh corn	4 ears	4 ears
Grapeseed oil	2 Tbsp.	30 ml
Red bell pepper, small dice	4 Tbsp.	60 ml
Poblano chile, small dice	4 Tbsp.	60 ml
Yellow onion, small dice	4 Tbsp.	60 ml
Redfish Sopa Base (recipe follows)	3 pt.	1.5 lt
Redfish, medium dice	1 lb.	450 g
Kosher salt	TT	TT
Black pepper	TT	TT
Limes	3	3
Fresh cilantro, minced	1 Tbsp.	15 ml
Fresh thyme, minced	½ tsp.	2 ml
Fresh oregano, minced	½ tsp.	2 ml
Avocado, medium dice	1	1
Corn tortillas, cut into strips and fried	6	6

1 Cut the corn kernels from the cobs.

2 Heat the oil in a small saucepan. Sauté the bell pepper, poblano, corn kernels and onion for 1 to 2 minutes.

3 Add the redfish sopa base and bring to a boil. Reduce to a simmer, add the redfish and continue to simmer for 2 minutes. Season with salt and pepper.

4 Ladle the soup into serving bowls. Squeeze the juice of half a lime over each bowl of soup. Sprinkle with the fresh herbs and top with the diced avocado and fried tortilla strips.

Approximate values per serving: **Calories** 680, **Total fat** 33 g, **Saturated fat** 5 g, **Cholesterol** 40 mg, **Sodium** 5140 mg, **Total carbohydrates** 56 g, **Protein** 44 g, **Vitamin A** 50%, **Vitamin C** 200%, **Calcium** 20%, **Iron** 25%

REDFISH SOPA BASE

Yield: 3 pt. (1.4 lt)

Fresh corn	4 ears	4 ears
Grapeseed oil	2 Tbsp.	30 ml
Garlic, chopped	1 Tbsp.	15 ml
Yellow onion, chopped	1 c.	240 ml
Green bell pepper, chopped	1 c.	240 ml
Poblano chile, chopped	½ c.	120 ml
Celery, chopped	1 c.	240 ml
Shellfish stock	1½ gal.	6 lt
Bouquet garni	1	1
Masa harina	½ c.	120 ml
Water	4 fl. oz.	120 ml
Chilli powder	2 Tbsp.	30 ml
Cumin	1 Tbsp.	15 ml
Serrano chiles, chopped	3	3
Kosher salt	3 Tbsp.	45 ml
Black pepper	2 tsp.	10 ml

1 Cut the corn kernels from the cobs. Reserve the corn and the cobs.

2 Heat the oil in a small stockpot. Add the garlic, onions, bell peppers, poblanos and celery. Cook, stirring occasionally, until lightly caramelized, approximately 8 to 10 minutes.

3 Add the shellfish stock, corn cobs and bouquet garni. Bring to a boil and reduce by half. Remove and discard the corn cobs.

4 Make a slurry with the masa harina and water. Add to the stock while whisking to prevent lumps. Stir in the chilli powder and cumin.

5 Add the serrano chiles, corn kernels, salt and pepper. Simmer for 5 minutes,
  remove from the heat and purée the base in a blender. Chill and reserve.

Approximate values per 8-fl.-oz. (240-ml) serving: **Calories** 340, **Total fat** 14 g, **Saturated fat**
2.5 g, **Cholesterol** 10 mg, **Sodium** 5020 mg, **Total carbohydrates** 27 g, **Protein** 26 g, **Vitamin A**
35%, **Vitamin C** 140%, **Iron** 15%

PHO BO (HANOI BEEF AND NOODLE SOUP)   RECIPE 12.17

*Pho is the ubiquitous Vietnamese soup; it is widely eaten for breakfast and ap-
pears at meals throughout the day and into the evening. Beef (bo) is the most
typical version, especially in the North. Each vendor has his or her own methods for flavoring and enriching the broth, but all allow the customer to season
and garnish their own bowls to taste with an assortment of chilies, fish sauces,
fresh herbs and condiments. Pho is a perfect example of the Vietnamese belief
that diners should be participants in preparing their food. Such rituals reinforce respect for the food and the friends with whom we share it.*

Yield: 1 qt. (1 lt)   **Method:** Broth

Oxtails or beef bones	4 lb.	2 kg
Water	as needed	as needed
Onion	1	1
Ginger, 3-in. (7.5-cm) piece	1	1
Salt	TT	TT
Fish sauce	3 fl. oz.	90 ml
Sachet:		
Star anise, whole	8	8
Cloves	5	5
Cinnamon stick	1	1
Bay leaves	3	3
Garnishes:		
Onions, sliced thin	as needed	as needed
Mung beans	as needed	as needed
Fresh herbs: mint, cilantro, basil	as needed	as needed
Lime wedges	as needed	as needed
Fish sauce	as needed	as needed
Fresh chiles, minced	as needed	as needed
Chile sauce	as needed	as needed
Rice vermicelli, cooked	1 lb.	450 g
Beef tenderloin, raw, sliced thin	6 oz.	180 g

1 Place the oxtails in a stockpot and add enough water to cover them by approximately 4 inches (10 centimeters). Bring it to a boil and then reduce to a
  simmer, skimming the surface as necessary.

2 Halve and char the onion for an onion brûlée. Split the ginger lengthwise and
  char its surface. Add the onion brûlée, charred ginger, salt, fish sauce and sachet to the stockpot.

3 Simmer the broth for 4 to 5 hours. Remove the sachet and strain the broth
  through a chinois. Adjust the seasonings and maintain the broth at a simmer.

4 Put the garnishes in bowls or trays and place them on each table.

5 Reheat the vermicelli by dropping them into boiling water for a few seconds.
  Divide the reheated vermicelli noodles into six warm bowls. Place several

pieces of raw beef tenderloin on top of each portion of vermicelli. Pour very hot broth into each bowl.

6 Serve the hot broth to the diners, allowing them to garnish their portions with onions, mung beans, herbs, lime wedges, fish sauce, chiles and chile sauce as desired.

Approximate values per 8-fl.-oz. (240-ml) serving: **Calories** 360, **Total fat** 7 g, **Saturated fat** 3 g, **Cholesterol** 20 mg, **Sodium** 640 mg, **Total carbohydrates** 63 g, **Protein** 9 g

---

RECIPE 12.18   MINESTRONE

Minestrone is a rich vegetable soup of Italian heritage. Northern Italian versions are made with beef stock, butter, rice and ribbon-shaped pasta. Southern Italian versions, such as the one given here, contain tomatoes, garlic, olive oil and tube-shaped pasta. The vegetables should be fresh and varied. Substitute or change those listed as necessary to reflect the season.

Yield: 2 gal. (8 lt)		**Method:** Broth
Dry white beans	1 lb.	450 g
Olive oil	2 Tbsp.	30 ml
Onions, diced	10 oz.	300 g
Garlic cloves, minced	2	2
Celery, diced	1 lb.	450 g
Carrots, diced	12 oz.	340 g
Zucchini, diced	1 lb.	450 g
Green beans, cut in ½-inch (1.25-cm) pieces	10 oz.	300 g
Cabbage, diced	1 lb.	450 g
Vegetable stock	5 qt.	5 lt
Tomato concassée	1 lb.	450 g
Tomato paste, low-sodium	12 oz.	340 g
Fresh oregano, chopped	1 Tbsp.	15 ml
Fresh basil, chopped	2 Tbsp.	30 ml
Fresh chervil, chopped	1 Tbsp.	15 ml
Fresh parsley, chopped	2 Tbsp.	30 ml
Salt and pepper	TT	TT
Elbow macaroni, cooked	4 oz.	120 g
Parmesan, grated	as needed for garnish	

1 Soak the beans in cold water overnight, then drain.
2 Cover the beans with water and simmer until tender, about 40 minutes. Reserve the beans.
3 Sauté the onions in the oil. Add the garlic, celery and carrots and cook for 3 minutes.
4 Add the zucchini, green beans and cabbage, one type at a time, cooking each briefly.
5 Add the stock, tomato concassée and tomato paste. Cover and simmer for 2½ to 3 hours.
6 Stir in the chopped herbs and season to taste with salt and pepper.
7 Add the drained beans and cooked macaroni.
8 Bring the soup to a simmer and simmer 15 minutes. Serve in warm bowls, garnished with Parmesan.

Approximate values per 6-fl.-oz. (180-ml) serving: **Calories** 70, **Total fat** 1.5 g, **Saturated fat** 0 g, **Cholesterol** 1 mg, **Sodium** 530 mg, **Total carbohydrates** 10 g, **Protein** 3 g, **Vitamin A** 20%, **Vitamin C** 20%, **Claims**—low fat

POSOLE

NEWBURY COLLEGE, Brookline, MA
Senior Instructor Scott Doughty

Yield: 3 qt. (3 lt)   **Method:** Broth

Pork shoulder	3 lb.	1.4 kg
Chicken stock	1 qt.	1 lt
Hominy, canned	56 oz.	1.5 kg
Onions, medium dice	1½ lb.	680 g
Garlic, chopped	1½ Tbsp.	23 ml
Fresh oregano, chopped	1½ tsp.	8 ml
Salt	1 tsp.	5 ml
Black pepper	¼ tsp.	2 ml
Cayenne pepper	¼ tsp.	2 ml
Chicken, 2½–3 lb. (1.1–1.3 kg)	1	1
Olive oil	as needed	as needed
Chilli powder	2 Tbsp.	30 ml
Canned diced tomatoes, drained	8 oz.	225 g
Anaheim chiles, medium dice	¾ c.	180 ml
Fresh cilantro, chopped	½ c.	120 ml
Garnishes:		
Limes	2	2
Corn tortillas	6	6
Vegetable oil	as needed	as needed
Romaine lettuce, chiffonade	8 oz.	225 g
Cider vinegar	2 Tbsp.	30 ml
Onions, small dice	8 oz.	225 g

1 Trim the fat from the pork shoulder and cut the meat into medium dice. Place the meat in a heavy saucepot with the chicken stock. Add more stock if necessary to just cover the meat. Bring to a simmer. Skim the scum from the surface.

2 Drain the hominy and soak it in cold water until needed.

3 After the pork has simmered for 2 minutes, add one-third of the onions, half of the garlic, the oregano, salt, black pepper and cayenne pepper. Simmer for 1 hour.

4 Bone and skin the chicken. Cut the meat into medium dice and refrigerate until needed.

5 Sweat the remaining two-thirds of the onions in a sauté pan in a little olive oil until soft. Add the remaining garlic and cook an additional 2 minutes. Add the raw chicken and cook until it loses its raw look. Mix in the chilli powder, tomatoes, Anaheim chiles and drained hominy. Cook until the flavors have blended. Add the mixture to the pork in the saucepot.

6 Simmer until the chicken is cooked. Add the cilantro. Adjust the consistency of the posole with chicken stock, if necessary.

7 For service, cut the limes into wedges. Cut the tortillas in half, then cut them crosswise into thin strips and fry them in hot oil until crisp. Toss the romaine lettuce with the cider vinegar. Garnish each bowl with romaine lettuce, diced onions, fried tortilla strips and a lime wedge.

Approximate values per 8-fl.-oz (240-ml) serving: **Calories** 550, **Total fat** 27 g, **Saturated fat** 8 g, **Cholesterol** 130 mg, **Sodium** 900 mg, **Total carbohydrates** 37 g, **Protein** 40 g, **Vitamin A** 30%, **Vitamin C** 7%, **Calcium** 10%, **Iron** 20%

RECIPE 12.20

THE SCHOOL OF CULINARY ARTS AT KENDALL COLLEGE,
EVANSTON, IL

Chef Mike Artlip, CEC, CCE

Yield: 5 gal. (19 lt)   **Method:** Cream

Mirepoix, small dice	5 lb.	2.4 kg
Olive oil	4 fl. oz.	120 ml
Whole butter	4 oz.	120 g
Salt and pepper	TT	TT
Tomato juice, canned	46 fl. oz.	1.4 lt
Water	10 qt.	9.5 lt
Tomatoes, crushed, #10 can	1	1
Sachet:		
Parsley stems	½ oz.	15 g
Black peppercorns, crushed	20	20
Bay leaves	5	5
Fresh thyme	10 sprigs	10 sprigs
Worcestershire sauce	2 fl. oz.	60 ml
Fresh thyme, chopped	as needed	as needed
Heavy cream, scalded	3 qt.	3 lt

1 Sweat the mirepoix in the oil and butter without caramelizing. Season with salt and pepper.

2 Deglaze the pan with the tomato juice. Add the water and crushed tomatoes. Add the sachet, bring to a boil, reduce to a low simmer and cook for 40 minutes.

3 Adjust the seasonings with the Worcestershire sauce, thyme, salt and pepper. Continue simmering for 20 minutes.

4 Remove the sachet and purée the soup with an immersion blender until smooth. Strain the scalded cream through a china cap and add it to the soup. Simmer for 10 minutes; adjust the seasonings and serve.

Approximate values per 8-fl.-oz. (240-ml) serving: **Calories** 160, **Total fat** 16 g, **Saturated fat** 9 g, **Cholesterol** 50 mg, **Sodium** 115 mg, **Total carbohydrates** 5 g, **Protein** 1 g, **Vitamin A** 60%, **Vitamin C** 10%

RECIPE 12.21

Yield: 40 fl. oz. (1.2 lt)   **Method:** Cream

Onion, chopped	2 oz.	60 g
Assorted fresh wild mushrooms such as		
shiitake, oysters and morels, chopped	8 oz.	225 g
Butter	4 oz.	120 g
Flour	4 Tbsp.	60 ml
Salt	1 tsp.	3 ml
Black pepper	TT	TT
Dried thyme	1 tsp.	3 ml
Chicken stock	8 fl. oz.	225 ml
Milk	24 fl. oz.	680 ml
Marsala	2 fl. oz.	60 ml
Lemon juice	1 Tbsp.	15 ml

1 Sauté the onion and mushrooms in the butter over medium heat. Cook until they are tender and any liquid given off has evaporated.

2 Blend in the flour, salt, pepper and thyme. Gradually stir in the chicken stock, then the milk.

3 Cook until the soup thickens slightly, but do not allow it to boil. Stir in the marsala and the lemon juice.

4 Purée half of the soup (including half of the mushrooms) and then stir it back into the remaining soup. Or, use an immersion blender to blend the soup in the pot, stopping when approximately half of the mushrooms have been puréed. Leave approximately half of the mushroom pieces intact for texture. Add more stock if necessary to achieve the desired consistency. Adjust the seasonings and serve.

Note: If fresh wild mushrooms are not available, substitute 1 ounce (30 grams) of dried wild mushrooms and 4 ounces (120 grams) of fresh button mushrooms. To prepare the dried mushrooms, remove and discard the stems, then soak them in the marsala and 2 fluid ounces (60 milliliters) of water for at least 1 hour. Add any remaining soaking liquid to the soup.

Variation: *Cream of Chicken*—Reduce the quantity of mushrooms to 4 ounces (120 grams). Add 6 ounces (180 grams) of shredded, cooked chicken after the mushrooms are lightly puréed.

Approximate values per 8-fl.-oz. (240-ml) serving: **Calories** 310, **Total fat** 24 g, **Saturated fat** 15 g, **Cholesterol** 70 mg, **Sodium** 680 mg, **Total carbohydrates** 16 g, **Protein** 7 g, **Vitamin A** 20%, **Calcium** 20%

CHEDDAR AND LEEK SOUP   RECIPE 12.22

Yield: 2 qt. (2 lt)   **Method:** Cream

Whole butter	1 oz.	30 g
Mirepoix, chopped fine	8 oz.	250 g
Leeks, chopped fine	8 oz.	250 g
Flour	2 oz.	60 g
Chicken stock	1½ qt.	1.5 lt
Sachet:		
Bay leaf	1	1
Dried thyme	¼ tsp.	1 ml
Peppercorns, crushed	¼ tsp.	1 ml
Dry white wine or flat beer	4 fl. oz.	120 ml
Half-and-half	4 fl. oz.	120 ml
Cheddar cheese, grated	1 lb.	500 g
Salt	TT	TT
Cayenne pepper	TT	TT
Fresh parsley, chopped	as needed for garnish	
Croutons	as needed for garnish	

1 Sweat the mirepoix and leeks in the butter until tender.

2 Stir in the flour and cook to make a blond roux.

3 Add the stock and sachet and bring to a boil. Add the wine or beer, half-and-half and cheese. Simmer for 1 hour.

4 Strain; adjust seasonings with salt and cayenne pepper. Thin with additional warm half-and-half, if necessary.

5 Serve in warm bowls, garnished with parsley and croutons.

Approximate values per 6-fl.-oz. (180-ml) serving: **Calories** 250, **Total fat** 18 g, **Saturated fat** 11 g, **Cholesterol** 55 mg, **Sodium** 730 mg, **Total carbohydrates** 8 g, **Protein** 14 g, **Vitamin A** 15%, **Calcium** 35%

RECIPE 12.23

MULLIGATAWNY SOUP

NASHVILLE STATE TECH CULINARY, NASHVILLE, TN

Chef Ken Morlino, CEC

Yield: 1 qt. (1 lt) **Method:** Cream

Ingredient		
Unsalted butter	2 Tbsp.	30 ml
Mirepoix	12 oz.	360 g
Flour	2 Tbsp.	30 ml
Curry powder	2 tsp.	10 ml
Chicken stock	1 qt.	1 lt
Chicken meat, cooked, diced	½ c.	120 ml
Green apple, diced	¼ c.	60 ml
Mushrooms, sliced	½ c.	120 ml
Milk, warm	4 fl. oz.	120 ml
Salt and white pepper	TT	TT

1 In a saucepot, heat the butter over medium heat, add the mirepoix and sauté for 5 minutes.
2 Add the flour and curry powder and cook to form a blond roux.
3 Add the chicken stock. Bring to a simmer and cook for 15 minutes.
4 Add the chicken, apple and mushrooms and cook for 15 more minutes.
5 Finish with the warm milk and season with salt and white pepper.

Approximate values per 8-fl.-oz (240-ml) serving: **Calories** 180, **Total fat** 10 g, **Saturated fat** 5 g, **Cholesterol** 35 mg, **Sodium** 740 mg, **Total carbohydrates** 14 g, **Protein** 8 g, **Vitamin A** 130%, **Vitamin C** 10%

RECIPE 12.24

SOUTHWESTERN BLACK BEAN SOUP

Yield: 4 qt. (4 lt) **Method:** Purée

Ingredient		
Dried black beans, soaked	1 lb.	500 g
Vegetable stock or water	5 qt.	5 lt
Sachet:		
Bay leaves	2	2
Dried thyme	½ tsp.	2 ml
Peppercorns, cracked	10	10
Canola oil	1 Tbsp.	15 ml
Onions, diced	4 oz.	120 g
Garlic cloves, minced	2	2
Anaheim chile, diced	1 oz.	30 g
Jalapeño or serrano chile, minced	1 Tbsp.	15 ml
Cumin, ground	1 tsp.	5 ml
Coriander, ground	1 tsp.	5 ml
Dried oregano	1 tsp.	5 ml
Salt and pepper	TT	TT
Lime wedges	as needed for garnish	
Fresh cilantro, chopped	as needed for garnish	

1 Combine the beans and stock or water and bring to a simmer. Add the sachet.
2 Sauté the onions, garlic and chile in the oil. Add to the saucepot.
3 Stir in the cumin, coriander and oregano.
4 Simmer the soup, uncovered, approximately 2–3 hours. The beans should be very soft, just beginning to fall apart. Add additional water or stock if necessary.

5 Purée about half of the soup, then stir it back into the remaining soup. Season to taste with salt and pepper.

6 Serve in warmed bowls garnished with lime wedges and chopped cilantro.

Approximate values per 6-fl.-oz. (180-ml) serving: **Calories** 70, **Total fat** 2 g, **Saturated fat** 0 g, **Cholesterol** 0 mg, **Sodium** 1010 mg, **Total carbohydrates** 9 g, **Protein** 4 g, **Claims**–low fat; no saturated fat; no cholesterol

ROASTED POBLANO CHILE AND CORN SOUP

RECIPE 12.25

CONNECTICUT CULINARY INSTITUTE, FARMINGTON, CT
Chef Jamie Roraback

Yield: 4 qt. (4 lt.) **Method:** Purée

Lime	1	1
Sour cream	1 pt.	500 ml
Vegetable oil	3 fl. oz.	90 ml
Poblano chiles	12	12
Fresh corn, with husks	8 ears	8 ears
Onions, medium dice	1 qt.	1 lt
Carrots, medium dice	1 qt.	1 lt
Garlic cloves, peeled	8	8
Chicken or vegetable stock	2 qt.	2 lt
Heavy cream	1 qt.	1 lt
Salt and pepper	TT	TT
Poblano chile, julienne	as needed for garnish	
Corn kernels, cooked	as needed for garnish	
Fried tortilla strips	as needed for garnish	

1 Squeeze the juice from the lime and combine it with the sour cream. Cover and refrigerate for at least one hour.

2 Using a total of 1 fluid ounce (30 milliliters) of the vegetable oil, rub the chiles with oil and place on a sheet pan. Roast the chiles at 450°F (230°C) until well blistered, approximately 10 to 15 minutes. Remove them from the oven and cool. Peel the chiles, remove the seeds and veins, then coarsely chop them.

3 Roast the ears of corn in their husks at 450°F (230°C) for 10 to 15 minutes. Allow the ears to cool, then shuck them and cut the kernels from the cob.

4 Heat a sauté pan on the stove top until very hot. Toss the onions, carrots and garlic cloves in the remaining vegetable oil. Drop the vegetables into the hot pan and allow them to char. Stir occasionally to char them evenly. Transfer the charred vegetables to a heavy soup pot.

5 Add the roasted peppers and corn kernels to the pot. Add enough stock to cover the ingredients, then bring to a boil and reduce to a simmer. Simmer until the ingredients are tender, approximately 30 minutes. Purée the soup in a blender or food processor and strain if desired. Return the soup to the same pot, add the heavy cream and reduce to the desired consistency. Season to taste with salt and pepper.

6 Serve the soup garnished with julienne of poblano chile, corn kernels, fried tortilla strips and the lime-flavored sour cream.

Approximate values per 8-fl.-oz (240-ml) serving: **Calories** 430, **Total fat** 35 g, **Saturated fat** 18 g, **Cholesterol** 95 mg, **Sodium** 410 mg, **Total carbohydrates** 27 g, **Protein** 6 g, **Vitamin A** 250%, **Vitamin C** 15%, **Calcium** 10%, **Iron** 10%

RECIPE 12.26

ROASTED VEGETABLE SOUP

Yield: 2 qt. (2 lt)　　　　　　　　　　**Method:** Purée

Onions, chopped coarse	1 lb.	450 g
Zucchini, chopped coarse	1 lb.	450 g
Yellow squash, chopped coarse	1 lb.	450 g
Red bell pepper, chopped coarse	6 oz.	180 g
Yellow bell pepper, chopped coarse	6 oz.	180 g
Green bell pepper, chopped coarse	6 oz.	180 g
Roma tomatoes, chopped coarse	8 oz.	250 g
Asparagus spears, chopped coarse	8 oz.	250 g
Olive oil	4 fl. oz.	120 ml
Salt	1 Tbsp.	15 ml
Black pepper	1 tsp.	5 ml
Dried thyme	1 tsp.	5 ml
Chicken stock	2 qt.	2 lt
Roasted garlic purée	2 oz.	60 g

1 Combine the chopped vegetables with the olive oil, salt, pepper and thyme. Toss to coat the vegetables evenly with the oil and seasonings.

2 Spread the vegetables on a sheet pan and roast in a 450°F (230°C) oven until they are well browned.

3 Remove the vegetables from the oven and place them in a saucepot. Add the chicken stock and roasted garlic purée. Bring to a boil, reduce to a simmer and cook until all of the vegetables are very tender, approximately 30 minutes.

4 Purée the soup in batches in a blender or food processor. Strain through a coarse china cap or pass through a food mill. Season to taste with salt and pepper.

5 Serve the soup garnished with chopped parsley and toasted baguette slices.

Approximate values per 8-fl.-oz. (240-ml) serving: **Calories** 210, **Total fat** 15 g, **Saturated fat** 2 g, **Cholesterol** 0 mg, **Sodium** 1570 mg, **Total carbohydrates** 19 g, **Protein** 5 g, **Vitamin A** 40%, **Vitamin C** 200%, **Iron** 10%

RECIPE 12.27

CALLALOO WITH CRAB

NEWBURY COLLEGE, BROOKLINE, MA
Senior Instructor Scott Doughty

Yield: 2 qt. (2 lt)　　　　　　　　　　**Method:** Purée

Callaloo or spinach	1 lb.	450 g
Olive oil	2 Tbsp.	30 ml
Onions, small dice	1 lb.	450 g
Green onions, chopped fine	6 oz.	180 g
Garlic cloves, minced	2	2
Coconut milk	1 qt.	1 lt
Milk	1 pt.	450 ml
Fresh pumpkin, peeled, seeded, small dice	1 lb.	450 g
Salt	½ tsp.	3 ml
Black pepper	¼ tsp	1 ml
Crab meat	1 lb.	450 g

1 Wash the callaloo or spinach. Remove the stems and tough ribs and chop coarsely.

2 Heat the oil in a rondeau and sweat the onions. Add the green onions and garlic and sweat for 2 more minutes. Add the callaloo or spinach, coconut milk, milk, pumpkin, salt and pepper. Bring the soup to a boil and reduce to a simmer. Cook for 30 minutes.

3 Purée half of the soup in a blender, food processor or food mill. Return it to the pot with the remaining soup.

4 Pick over the crab meat to remove any bits of shell and add the meat to the soup. Adjust the seasonings and serve.

Approximate values per 8-fl.-oz (240-ml) serving: **Calories** 410, **Total fat** 31 g, **Saturated fat** 23 g, **Cholesterol** 65 mg, **Sodium** 370 mg, **Total carbohydrates** 19 g, **Protein** 19 g, **Vitamin A** 50%, **Vitamin C** 70%, **Calcium** 30%, **Iron** 35%

ROASTED CORN CHOWDER   RECIPE 12.28

Yield: 1 qt. (1 lt)   **Method:** Purée

Corn, unshucked	10 ears	10 ears
Milk, warm	3 pt.	1500 ml
Salt pork, small dice	4 oz.	120 g
Celery, small dice	5 oz.	150 g
Onions, small dice	10 oz.	300 g
Garlic cloves, minced	4	4
Flour	2 oz.	60 g
Chicken stock	1 qt.	1 lt
Potatoes, peeled, medium dice	12 oz.	350 g
Cream, warm	4 fl. oz.	120 ml
Worcestershire sauce	1 Tbsp.	15 ml
Fresh thyme	1 tsp.	5 ml
Nutmeg, ground	TT	TT
Salt and white pepper	TT	TT

1 Roast the ears of corn, in their husks, in a 400°F (204°C) oven for 45 minutes. Cool, shuck the corn and cut off the kernels. Purée half the corn kernels in a blender, adding a small amount of milk if necessary.

2 Render the salt pork. Add the celery, onions and garlic and sauté lightly.

3 Stir in the flour and cook to make a blond roux.

4 Add the chicken stock and remaining milk and bring to a simmer.

5 Add the potatoes, the puréed corn and the remaining corn kernels. Simmer for 10 minutes.

6 Add the cream; adjust the seasonings with Worcestershire sauce, thyme, nutmeg, salt and white pepper and simmer for 5 minutes.

7 Serve in warm bowls.

Approximate values per 8-fl.-oz (240-ml) serving: **Calories** 370, **Total fat** 21 g, **Saturated fat** 10 g, **Cholesterol** 55 mg, **Sodium** 520 mg, **Total carbohydrates** 38 g, **Protein** 13 g, **Vitamin A** 15%, **Vitamin C** 20%, **Calcium** 30%, **Claim**—good source of fiber, vitamin A, vitamin C, calcium

RECIPE 12.29

THE BROWN PALACE HOTEL, Denver, CO

Executive Chef Mark Black

Yield: 10 Servings		**Method:** Purée
Fresh artichokes	20	20
Kosher salt	2 Tbsp.	30 ml
Lemons, sliced	3	3
Olive oil	2 fl. oz.	60 ml
Celery, small dice	½ c.	120 ml
Leeks, small dice	½ c.	120 ml
White onions, small dice	1 c.	240 ml
Shallots, small dice	½ c.	120 ml
Garlic, minced	1 Tbsp.	15 ml
Bay leaf	1	1
Vegetable stock	1 qt.	1 lt
Salt and pepper	TT	TT
Truffles, sliced	5 oz.	150 g
Opal Basil Oil (recipe follows)	as needed	as needed

1 Simmer the artichokes in salted lemon water until tender. Remove them from the water and cool in an ice bath. Peel away the leaves. Remove the hearts and bottoms and dice them.

2 In a soup pot, heat the olive oil and add the celery, leeks, onions, shallots and garlic and sauté until tender.

3 Add the diced artichokes, bay leaf and stock and simmer for approximately 45 minutes.

4 Remove from the heat, remove the bay leaf, purée the soup in a blender and strain through a chinois.

5 Adjust the seasonings with salt and pepper and adjust the consistency with additional stock if necessary.

6 Pour the soup into hot soup bowls. Garnish with sliced truffles and Opal Basil Oil and serve.

Approximate values per serving, without oil: **Calories** 190, **Total fat** 6 g, **Saturated fat** 1 g, **Cholesterol** 0 mg, **Sodium** 580 mg, **Total carbohydrates** 32 g, **Protein** 10 g, **Vitamin A** 15%, **Vitamin C** 45%, **Calcium** 10%, **Iron** 20%

OPAL BASIL OIL

Yield: 4 fl. oz. (120 ml)		
Fresh opal basil leaves, large	6	6
Extra virgin olive oil	4 fl. oz.	120 ml

1 With a small wand blender, blend the basil and olive oil. Hold for 24 hours and then strain through cheesecloth.

Approximate values per fluid ounce (30 ml): **Calories** 250, **Total fat** 28 g, **Saturated fat** 4 g, **Cholesterol** 0 mg, **Sodium** 0 mg, **Total carbohydrates** 0 g, **Protein** 0 g

CHILLED BEET AND BUTTERMILK SOUP

RECIPE 12.30

BISHOP'S RESTAURANT, VANCOUVER, BC
Chefs Michael Allemeier and Dennis Green

Yield: 4 Servings   **Method:** Purée

Beets, large	4	4
Red onion, sliced	1	1
Red wine vinegar	2 Tbsp.	30 ml
Sugar	2 Tbsp.	30 ml
Buttermilk	1 pt.	500 ml
Salt and pepper	TT	TT
Chives, chopped	2 Tbsp.	30 ml
Sour cream or crème fraîche	2 Tbsp.	30 ml

1 In a medium saucepan, combine beets, onion, vinegar and sugar with enough water to cover. Bring to a boil, reduce heat and simmer until tender, about 30 minutes. Strain, reserving liquid for later use.

2 Purée beets using a blender or food processor, adding enough of the reserved liquid to facilitate a smooth purée.

3 When cooled to room temperature, stir in the buttermilk and season to taste with salt and pepper. If the soup is too thick, dilute it with some of the reserved cooking liquid. Chill thoroughly.

4 Garnish with chopped chives and a quenelle of sour cream or crème fraîche.

Approximate values per 6-fl.-oz. (180-ml) serving: **Calories** 120, **Total fat** 3 g, **Saturated fat** 1.5 g, **Cholesterol** 7 mg, **Sodium** 170 mg, **Total carbohydrates** 19 g, **Protein** 5 g, **Vitamin C** 10%

CHILLED CHERRY SOUP

RECIPE 12.31

Yield: 4 qt. (4 lt)   **Method:** Purée

Cherries, pitted	5 lb.	2.25 kg
Apple juice	approx. 2 qt.	approx. 2 lt
Sachet:		
Cinnamon sticks	2	2
Cloves, whole	4	4
Honey	6 oz.	170 g
Cornstarch	1 oz.	30 g
Lemon juice	TT	TT
Dry champagne or sparkling wine	8 fl. oz.	250 ml
Crème fraîche	as needed for garnish	
Toasted slivered almonds	as needed for garnish	

1 Combine the cherries, apple juice, sachet and honey. Bring to a simmer and cook for 30 minutes. Remove the sachet.

2 Dilute the cornstarch with a small amount of cold apple juice. Add it to the soup for thickening. Simmer the soup for 10 minutes to cook out the starchy flavor.

3 Purée the soup in a food processor or blender and strain if desired; chill thoroughly.

4 At service, adjust the seasoning with lemon juice. Stir in chilled champagne or sparkling wine and serve garnished with crème fraîche and toasted, slivered almonds.

Approximate values per 6-fl.-oz. (229-ml) serving: **Calories** 150, **Total fat** 0 g, **Saturated fat** 0 g, **Cholesterol** 0 mg, **Sodium** 0 mg, **Total carbohydrates** 34 g, **Protein** 1 g, **Vitamin C** 15%, **Claims—** fat free; no sodium; good source of fiber

RECIPE 12.32

RESTAURANT KEVIN TAYLOR, Denver, CO
Chef Kevin Taylor

Yield: 6 Servings   **Method:** Purée

Vichyssoise:		
Yukon Gold potatoes	6	6
Half-and-half	1 qt.	1 lt
Cayenne pepper	1 tsp.	5 ml
Saffron	½ tsp.	3 ml
Hot pepper sauce	1 tsp.	5 ml
Worcestershire sauce	1 tsp.	5 ml
Salt and white pepper	TT	TT
Potato salad:		
Yukon Gold potato, cooked, small dice	1	1
Red onion, minced	2 Tbsp.	30 ml
Fresh chervil, chopped	¼ tsp.	1 ml
Chives, chopped	¼ tsp.	1 ml
Crème frâiche	2 Tbsp.	30 ml
Salt and pepper	TT	TT
Leek vinaigrette:		
Leek	1	1
Olive oil	2 Tbsp.	30 ml
Black pepper	¼ tsp.	1 ml
Fresh herbs, assorted, chopped	1 tsp.	5 ml
Brown sugar	1 tsp.	5 ml
Champagne vinegar	3 Tbsp.	45 ml
Salt	1 tsp.	5 ml
Lemon juice	1 tsp.	5 ml
Fresh herb sprigs	as needed for garnish	

1 To prepare the soup, simmer the unpeeled potatoes in salted water until very tender. Drain the potatoes and pass through a ricer. Place the riced potatoes in a medium saucepot with the half-and-half, cayenne pepper and saffron. Simmer for 10 minutes and strain through a fine china cap. Place the strained soup in a medium saucepot and simmer for 3 to 5 minutes. Add the hot pepper sauce, Worcestershire sauce, salt and white pepper to taste. Thin with additional half-and-half if necessary. Cool in an ice bath.

2 To prepare the potato salad, combine the diced potato, onion, chervil, chives, and crème frâiche in a small mixing bowl and season with salt and pepper.

3 To prepare the vinaigrette, cut the leek into ¼-inch (6-millimeter) slices, wash well and blanch in boiling salted water for 30 seconds. In a small mixing bowl, combine the leek, olive oil, pepper, herbs, brown sugar, champagne vinegar, salt and lemon juice. Mix the ingredients and let stand for 2 hours before serving.

4 Ladle 8 fluid ounces (240 milliliters) of the chilled soup into each chilled soup bowl. Place a small amount of potato salad in the center and cover with the leek vinaigrette. Garnish with fresh herbs and serve.

Approximate values per 8-fl.-oz. (240-ml) serving: **Calories** 420, **Total fat** 22 g, **Saturated fat** 12 g, **Cholesterol** 80 mg, **Sodium** 500 mg, **Total carbohydrates** 41 g, **Protein** 9 g, **Vitamin C** 25%, **Calcium** 20%

COOKING IS AT ONCE ONE OF THE SIMPLEST AND MOST GRATIFYING OF THE ARTS, BUT TO COOK WELL ONE MUST LOVE AND RESPECT FOOD.
—*Craig Claiborne, American food critic (1920–2000)*

PRINCIPLES OF MEAT COOKERY

▶ **primal cuts** the primary divisions of muscle, bone and connective tissue produced by the initial butchering of the carcass

▶ **subprimal cuts** the basic cuts produced from each primal

▶ **fabricated cuts** individual portions cut from a subprimal

▶ **marbling** whitish streaks of inter- and intramuscular fat

▶ **subcutaneous fat** also known as exterior fat; the fat layer between the hide and muscles

▶ **collagen** a protein found in connective tissue, it is converted into gelatin when cooked with moisture

▶ **elastin** a protein found in connective tissues, particularly ligaments and tendons; it often appears as the white or silver covering on meats known as silverskin

Meats—beef, veal, lamb and pork—often consume the largest portion of your food purchasing dollar. In this chapter, we discuss how to protect your investment. You will learn how to determine the quality of meat, how to purchase meat in the form that best suits your needs and how to store it. We also discuss several of the dry-heat, moist-heat and combination cooking methods introduced in Chapter 10, Principles of Cooking, and how they can best be used so that a finished meat item is appealing to both the eye and palate. Although each of the cooking methods is illustrated with a single beef, veal, lamb or pork recipe, the analysis is intended to apply to all meats.

In Chapters 14 through 17, you will learn about the specific cuts of beef, veal, lamb and pork typically used in food service operations, as well as some basic butchering procedures. Recipes using these cuts and applying the various cooking methods are included at the end of each of those chapters.

▶ MUSCLE COMPOSITION

The carcasses of cattle, sheep, hogs and furred game animals consist mainly of edible lean muscular tissue, fat, connective tissue and bones. They are divided into large cuts called **primals.** Primal cuts are rarely cooked; rather, they are usually reduced to **subprimal cuts,** which in turn, can be cooked as is or used to produce **fabricated cuts.** For example, the beef primal known as a short loin can be divided into subprimals, including the strip loin. The strip loin can be fabricated into other cuts, including New York steaks. The primals, subprimals and fabricated cuts of beef, veal, lamb and pork are discussed in Chapters 14 through 17, respectively; game is discussed in Chapter 19.

Muscle tissue gives meat its characteristic appearance; the amount of connective tissue determines the meat's tenderness. Muscle tissue is approximately 72 percent water, 20 percent protein, 7 percent fat and 1 percent minerals. A single muscle is composed of many bundles of muscle cells or fibers held together by connective tissue. See Figures 13.1 and 13.2. The thickness of the cells, the size of the cell bundles and the connective tissues holding them together form the grain of the meat and determine the meat's texture. When the fiber bundles are small, the meat has a fine grain and texture. Grain also refers to the direction in which the muscle fibers travel. When an animal fattens, some of the water and proteins in the lean muscle tissue are replaced with fat, which appears as **marbling.** Marbling adds tenderness and flavor to meat and is a principal factor in determining meat quality.

Connective tissue forms the walls of the long muscle cells and binds them into bundles. It surrounds the muscle as a membrane and also appears as the tendons and ligaments that attach the muscles to the bone. Most connective tissue consists of either **collagen** or **elastin.** Collagen breaks down into gelatin and water when cooked using moist heat. Elastin, on the other hand, will not break down under normal cooking conditions. Because elastin remains stringy and tough, tendons and ligaments should be trimmed away before meat is cooked.

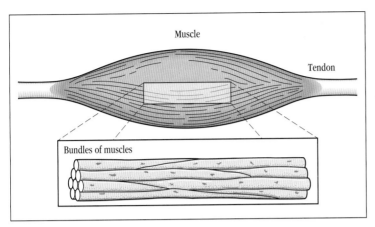

FIGURE 13.1 ▶ Muscle tissue

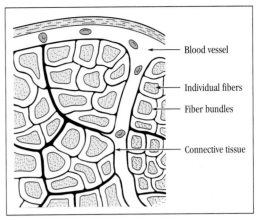

FIGURE 13.2 ▶ Crosscut of a bundle of muscle fibers

Connective tissue develops primarily in the frequently used muscles. Therefore, cuts of meat from the shoulder (also known as the chuck), which the animal uses constantly, tend to be tougher than those from the back (also known as the loin), which are used less frequently. As an animal ages, the collagen present within the muscles becomes more resistant to breaking down through moist-heat cooking. Therefore, the meat of an older animal tends to be tougher than that of a younger one. Generally, the tougher the meat, the more flavorful it is, however.

▶ **butcher** to slaughter and/or dress or fabricate animals for consumption

▶ **dress** to trim or otherwise prepare an animal carcass for consumption

▶ **fabricate** to cut a larger portion of raw meat (for example, a primal or subprimal), poultry or fish into smaller portions

▶ **carve** to cut cooked meat or poultry into portions

▶ INSPECTION AND GRADING OF MEATS

INSPECTION

All meat produced for public consumption in the United States is subject to USDA inspection. Inspections ensure that products are processed under strict sanitary guidelines and are wholesome and fit for human consumption. Inspections do not indicate a meat's quality or tenderness, however. Whole carcasses of beef, pork, lamb and veal are labeled with a round stamp identifying the slaughterhouse. See Figure 13.3. The stamp shown in Figure 13.4 is used for fabricated or processed meats and is found on either the product or its packaging.

FIGURE 13.3 ▶ USDA inspection stamp for whole carcasses

DOMESTICATION OF ANIMALS

Early humans were hunter-gatherers, dependent on what their immediate environment offered for food. As "opportunistic" meat eaters, they ate meat when they could obtain it.

Anthropologists believe that the cultivation of grains and the birth of agriculture, which took place sometime around 9000 B.C., led directly to the domestication of animals. Sheep and goats were attracted to the fields of grain, and dogs and pigs to the garbage heaps of the new communities. Rather than allow these animals to interfere with food production, people tamed them, thus providing a steadier supply of meat. The first animals to be domesticated were most likely sheep, soon followed by goats. These animals—ruminants—can digest cellulose (humans cannot), so they could feed on stalks instead of valuable grains. Dogs and pigs, which prefer the same foods as humans, were tamed later, once there were more certain food supplies. Cattle were the most recently domesticated food animal, probably coming under control between 6100 and 5800 B.C.

FIGURE 13.4 ▶ USDA inspection stamp for fabricated or processed meats

FIGURE 13.5 ▶ Quality grade stamp for USDA prime

FIGURE 13.6 ▶ USDA yield grade stamp

GRADING

USDA grading provides a voluntary, uniform system by which producers, distributors and consumers can measure differences in the quality of meats and make price-quality comparisons. There are two parts to this grading system: quality grades and yield grades.

Quality grades, established in 1927, are a guide to the eating qualities of meat: its tenderness, juiciness and flavor. Based on an animal's age and the meat's color, texture and degree of marbling, the USDA quality grades are:

▶ Beef—USDA Prime, Choice, Select, Standard, Commercial, Utility, Cutter and Canner
▶ Veal—USDA Prime, Choice, Good, Standard, Utility
▶ Lamb—USDA Prime, Choice, Good, Utility
▶ Pork—USDA No. 1, No. 2, No. 3, Utility

USDA Prime meats are produced in limited quantities for use in the finest restaurants, hotels and gourmet markets. They are well marbled and have thick coverings of firm fat. See Figure 13.5.

USDA Choice meat is the most commonly used grade in quality food service operations and retail markets. Choice meat is well marbled (but with less fat than Prime) and will produce a tender and juicy product.

Although lacking the flavor and tenderness of the higher grades, beef graded USDA Select or USDA Standard, and lamb and veal graded USDA Good, are also used in food service operations and retail outlets. The term *no roll* refers to beef that has not been grade-stamped (rolled) by a USDA inspector. Much of the beef sold in the United States, especially at retail, is no roll, but would have been USDA Select if graded.

The lower grades of beef, lamb and veal are usually used for processed, ground or manufactured items such as meat patties or canned meat products.

Yield grades, established in 1965, measure the amount of usable meat (as opposed to fat and bones) on a carcass and provide a uniform method of identifying cuttability differences among carcasses. Yield grades apply only to beef and lamb and appear in a shield similar to that used for the quality grade stamp. The shields are numbered from 1 to 5, with number 1 representing the greatest yield and number 5 the smallest. See Figure 13.6. Beef and lamb can be graded for either quality or yield or both.

Grading is a voluntary program. Many processors, purveyors and retailers (especially pork and veal producers) develop and use their own labeling systems to provide quality assurance information. These private systems do not necessarily apply the USDA's standards. In fact, some pork inspection programs actually apply more stringent quality standards.

▶ AGING MEATS

When animals are slaughtered, their muscles are soft and flabby. Within 6 to 24 hours, rigor mortis sets in, causing the muscles to contract and stiffen. Rigor mortis dissipates within 48 to 72 hours under refrigerated conditions. All meats should be allowed to rest, or age, long enough for rigor mortis to dissipate completely. Meats that have not been aged long enough for rigor mortis to dissipate, or that have been frozen during this period, are known as "green meats." They will be very tough and flavorless when cooked.

Typically, initial aging takes place while the meat is being transported from the slaughterhouse to the supplier or food service operation. Beef and lamb are sometimes aged for longer periods to increase their tenderness and flavor characteristics. Pork is not aged further because its high fat content turns rancid easily, and veal does not have enough fat to protect it during an extended aging period.

WET AGING

Today, most preportioned or precut meats are packaged and shipped in vacuum-sealed plastic packages (sometimes known generically by the manufacturer's trade name, Cryovac). Wet aging is the process of storing vacuum-packaged meats under refrigeration for up to six weeks. This allows natural enzymes and microorganisms time to break down connective tissue, which tenderizes and flavors the meat. As this chemical process takes place, the meat develops an unpleasant odor that is released when the package is opened; the odor dissipates in a few minutes.

Wet-Aged New York Strip

DRY AGING

Dry aging is the process of storing fresh meats in an environment of controlled temperature, humidity and air flow for up to six weeks. This allows enzymes and microorganisms to break down connective tissues. Dry aging is actually the beginning of the natural decomposition process. Dry-aged meats can lose from 5 to 20 percent of their weight through moisture evaporation. They can also develop mold, which adds flavor but must be trimmed off later. Moisture loss combined with additional trimming can substantially increase the cost of dry-aged meats. Dry-aged meats are generally available only through smaller distributors and specialty butchers.

Dry-Aged Beef Short Loin

▶ PURCHASING AND STORING MEATS

Several factors determine the cuts of meat your food service operation should use:

1 Menu: The menu identifies the types of cooking methods used. If meats are to be broiled, grilled, roasted, sautéed or fried, more tender cuts should be used. If they are to be stewed or braised, flavorful cuts with more connective tissue can be used.

2 Menu price: Cost constraints may prevent an operation from using the best-quality meats available. Generally, the more tender the meat, the more expensive it is. But the most expensive cuts are not always the best choice for a particular cooking method. For example, a beef tenderloin is one of the most expensive cuts of beef. Although excellent grilled, it will not necessarily produce a better braised dish than the tougher, fattier brisket.

3 Quality: Often, several cuts or grades of meat can be used for a specific dish, so each food service operation should develop its own quality specifications.

PURCHASING MEATS

Once you have identified the cuts of meat your operation needs, you must determine the forms in which they will be bought. Meats are purchased in a variety of forms: as large as an entire carcass that must be further fabricated or as small as an individual cut (known as **portion control** or **P.C.**) ready to cook and serve. You should consider the following when deciding how to purchase meats:

1 Employee skills: Do your employees have the skills necessary to reduce large pieces of meat to the desired cuts?

2 Menu: Can you use the variety of bones, meat and trimmings that result from fabricating large cuts into individual portions?

▶ **vacuum packaging** a food preservation method in which fresh or cooked food is placed in an airtight container (usually plastic). Virtually all air is removed from the container through a vacuum process, and the container is then sealed.

A TENDER HISTORY

In *Food in History,* Reay Tannahill suggests that prehistoric hunters developed weapons and stealth tactics in order to kill their quarry without alerting it to danger and provoking fright, fight or flight. She notes that muscle tissues from animals that die placidly contain glycogen. At death, glycogen breaks down into various substances, including lactic acid, a natural preservative. Animals experiencing fright, fight or flight just before death, however, use up their glycogen. Tannahill theorizes that prehistoric hunters recognized and responded to what science much later confirmed: Meat from animals that die peacefully is sweeter and more tender.

NO, IT DOESN'T GLOW

Fresh and frozen beef, lamb, pork and poultry can be irradiated in order to control the presence of microorganisms, such as *E. coli* and *Salmonella,* which can cause food-borne illnesses. Although the permitted dose of ionizing radiation kills significant numbers of insects, pathogenic bacteria and parasites on and in the meat, it does not make food radioactive or compromise the food's nutritional values. Nor does radiation noticeably alter a food's flavor, texture or appearance.

The FDA requires that any packaged food subjected to radiation for preservation be labeled "treated with radiation" or "treated by irradiation" and display the radura symbol shown here.

▶ **freezer burn** the surface dehydration and discoloration of food that results from moisture loss at below-freezing temperatures

FIGURE 13.7 ▶ **Quality grades of beef—no roll (top), Choice and Prime (bottom)**

3 Storage: Do you have ample refrigeration and freezer space so that you can be flexible in the way you purchase your meats?

4 Cost: Considering labor costs and trim usage, is it more economical to buy larger cuts of meat or P.C. units?

IMPS/NAMP

The USDA publishes Institutional Meat Purchasing Specifications (IMPS) describing products customarily purchased in the food service industry. IMPS identifications are illustrated and described in *The Meat Buyers Guide,* published by the National Association of Meat Purveyors (NAMP). The IMPS/NAMP system is a widely accepted and useful tool in preventing miscommunications between purchasers and purveyors. Meats are indexed by a numerical system: Beef cuts are designated by the 100 series, lamb by the 200 series, veal by the 300 series, pork by the 400 series, and portion cuts by the 1000 series. Commonly used cuts of beef, veal, lamb and pork and their IMPS numbers, as well as applicable cooking methods and serving suggestions, are discussed in Chapters 14 through 17.

STORING MEATS

Meat products are highly perishable and potentially hazardous foods, so temperature control is the most important thing to remember when storing meats. Fresh meats should be stored at temperatures between 30°F and 35°F (−1°C and 2°C). Vacuum-packed meats should be left in their packaging until they are needed. Under proper refrigeration, vacuum-packed meats with unbroken seals have a shelf life of three to four weeks. If the seal is broken, shelf life is reduced to only a few days. Meats that are not vacuum packed should be loosely wrapped or wrapped in air-permeable paper. Do not wrap meats tightly in plastic wrap, as this creates a good breeding ground for bacteria and will significantly shorten a meat's shelf life. Store meats on trays and away from other foods to prevent cross-contamination.

When freezing meats, the faster the better. Slow freezing produces large ice crystals that tend to rupture the muscle tissues, allowing water and nutrients to drip out when the meat is thawed. Most commercially packaged meats are frozen by blast freezing, which quickly cools by blasting −40°F (−40°C) air across the meat. Most food service facilities, however, use a slower and more conventional method known as still-air freezing. Still-air freezing is the common practice of placing meat in a standard freezer at about 0°F (−18°C) until it is frozen.

The ideal temperature for maintaining frozen meat is −50°F (−45°C). Frozen meat should not be maintained at any temperature warmer than 0°F (−18°C). Moisture- and vaporproof packaging will help prevent **freezer burn.** The length of frozen storage life varies with the species and type of meat. As a general rule, properly handled meats can be frozen for six months. Frozen meats should be thawed at refrigerator temperatures, not at room temperature or in warm water.

▶ PREPARING MEATS

Certain procedures are often applied to meats before cooking to add flavor and/or moisture. These include marinating and rubs, discussed in Chapter 9, Mise en Place, and barding and larding.

BARDING

Barding is the process of covering the surface of meat or poultry with thin slices of pork fatback and tying them in place with butcher's twine. Barded meat or poultry is usually roasted. As the item cooks, the fatback continuously bastes it, adding flavor and moisture. A drawback to barding is that the fatback prevents the meat or poultry from developing the crusty exterior associated with roasting.

LARDING

Larding is the process of inserting small strips of pork fat into meat with a larding needle. Larded meat is usually cooked by braising. During cooking, the added fat contributes moisture and flavor. Although once popular, larding is rarely used today because advances in selective breeding produce consistently tender, well-marbled meat.

Barding a Pheasant

▶ APPLYING VARIOUS COOKING METHODS

In Chapter 10, Principles of Cooking, you learned the basic techniques for broiling, grilling, roasting, sautéing, pan-frying, deep-frying, poaching, simmering, braising and stewing. In Chapters 14 through 17, you will learn more about applying these cooking methods to beef, veal, lamb and pork. Here we apply these methods to meat cookery in general.

DRY-HEAT COOKING METHODS

Dry-heat cooking methods subject food directly to the heat of a flame (broiling and grilling), hot air (roasting) or heated fat (sautéing and pan-frying). These cooking methods firm proteins without breaking down connective tissue. They are not recommended for tougher cuts or those high in connective tissue.

Larding Meat

BROILING AND GRILLING

The broiling or grilling process adds flavor; additional flavors are derived from the seasonings. The broiler or grill should brown the meat, keeping the interior juicy. The grill should leave appetizing crosshatch marks on the meat's surface. To serve a good-quality broiled or grilled product, you must start with good-quality meat.

Selecting Meats to Broil or Grill
Only the most tender cuts should be broiled or grilled because direct heat does not tenderize. Fat adds flavor as the meat cooks, so the meat should be well marbled. Some external fat is also beneficial. Too much fat, however, will cause the broiler or grill to flare up, burning or discoloring the meat and adding objectionable flavors. Connective tissue toughens when meat is broiled or grilled, so trim away as much of it as possible.

Seasoning Meats to Be Broiled or Grilled
Meats that have not been marinated should be well seasoned with salt and pepper just before being placed on the broiler or grill. If they are preseasoned and allowed to rest, the salt will dissolve and draw out moisture, making it difficult to brown the meat properly. Some chefs feel so strongly about this that they season broiled or grilled meats only after they are cooked. Pork and veal, which have a tendency to dry out when cooked, should be basted with seasoned butter or oil during cooking to help keep them moist. Meats can be glazed or basted with barbecue sauce as they cook.

Cooking Temperatures
Red meats should be cooked at sufficiently high temperatures to caramelize their surface, making them more attractive and flavorful. At the same time, the broiler or grill cannot be too hot, or the meat's exterior will burn before the interior is cooked.

FIGURE 13.8 ▶ Degrees of doneness. Meat cooked rare, medium rare, medium and medium well

Because veal and pork are normally cooked to higher internal temperatures than beef and lamb, they should be cooked at slightly lower temperatures so that their exteriors are not overcooked when their interiors are cooked properly. The exterior of white meats should be a deep golden color when finished.

Degrees of Doneness

Consumers request and expect meats to be properly cooked to specific degrees of doneness. It is your responsibility to understand and comply with these requests. Meats can be cooked very rare (or bleu), rare, medium rare, medium, medium well or well done. Figure 13.8 shows the proper color for these different degrees of doneness. This guide can be used for red meats cooked by any method.

Larger cuts of meat, such as a châteaubriand or thick chops, are often started on the broiler or grill to develop color and flavor and then finished to temperature in the oven to ensure complete, even cooking.

Determining Doneness

Broiling or grilling meat to the proper degree of doneness is an art. Larger pieces of meat will take longer to cook than smaller ones, but how quickly a piece of meat cooks is determined by many other factors: the temperature of the broiler or grill, the temperature of the piece of meat when placed on the broiler or grill, the type of meat and the thickness of the cut. Because of these variables, timing alone is not a useful tool in determining doneness.

The most reliable method of determining doneness of a small piece of meat is by pressing the piece of meat with a finger and gauging the amount of resistance it yields. Very rare (bleu) meat will offer almost no resistance and feel almost the same as raw meat. Meat cooked rare will feel spongy and offer slight resistance to pressure. Meat cooked medium will feel slightly firm and springy to the touch. Meat cooked well done will feel quite firm and spring back quickly when pressed. See Table 13.1.

Accompaniments to Broiled and Grilled Meats

Because a broiler or grill cannot be deglazed to form the base for a sauce, compound butters or sauces such as béarnaise are often served with broiled or grilled meats. Brown sauces such as bordelaise, chasseur, périgueux or brown mushroom sauce also complement many broiled or grilled items. Additional sauce suggestions are found in Table 11.5.

Table 13.1   DETERMINING DONENESS OF BROILED AND GRILLED ITEMS

DEGREES OF DONENESS	COLOR	DEGREE OF RESISTANCE	IDEAL TEMPERATURE
Very rare (bleu)	Very red and raw-looking center (the center is cool to the touch)	Almost no resistance	115°F–120°F 46°C–49°C
Rare	Large deep red center	Spongy; very slight resistance	125°F–130°F 52°C–54°C
Medium rare	Bright red center	Some resistance, slightly springy	130°F–140°F 54°C–60°C
Medium	Rosy pink to red center	Slightly firm; springy	140°F–150°F 60°C–66°C
Medium well	Very little pink at the center, almost brown throughout	Firm; springy	155°F–165°F 68°C–74°C
Well done	No red	Quite firm; springs back quickly when pressed	Not recommended

▶ PROCEDURE FOR BROILING OR GRILLING MEATS

1 Heat the broiler or grill.

2 Use a wire brush to remove any charred or burnt particles that may be stuck to the broiler or grill grate. The grate can be wiped with a lightly oiled towel to remove any remaining particles and to help season it.

3 Prepare the item to be broiled or grilled by trimming off any excess fat and connective tissue and marinating or seasoning it as desired. The meat may be brushed lightly with oil to help protect it and keep it from sticking to the grate.

4 Place the item in the broiler or on the grill. Following the example in Chapter 10, turn the meat to produce the attractive crosshatch marks associated with grilling. Use tongs to turn or flip the meat without piercing the surface (this prevents valuable juices from escaping).

5 Cook the meat to the desired doneness while developing the proper surface color. To do so, adjust the position of the meat on the broiler or grill, or adjust the distance between the grate and heat source.

GRILLED LAMB CHOPS WITH HERB BUTTER   RECIPE 13.1

Yield: 2 Servings   **Method:** Grilling

Lamb chops, loin or rib, approx. 1 in. (2.5 cm) thick	6	6
Salt and pepper	TT	TT
Oil	as needed	as needed
Herb butter	6 thin slices or 6 small rosettes	

1 Preheat the grill for 15 minutes.

2 Season the lamb chops with salt and pepper; brush with oil.

3 Place the lamb chops on the grill, turning as necessary to produce the proper crosshatching. Cook to the desired doneness.

4 Remove the lamb chops from the grill and place a slice or rosette of herb butter on each chop.

5 Serve immediately as the herb butter melts. The plate can be placed under the broiler for a few seconds to help melt the herb butter.

Approximate values per 6.5-oz. (195-g) serving: **Calories** 623, **Total fat** 50 g, **Saturated fat** 27 g, **Cholesterol** 224 mg, **Sodium** 1186 mg, **Total carbohydrates** 0 g, **Protein** 42 g, **Vitamin A** 40%

1 Brushing the lamb chops with oil.

2 Placing the lamb chops on the grill.

3 Rotating the lamb chops 90 degrees to create crosshatch marks.

4 Turning the chops over to finish them on the other side.

ROASTING

Properly roasted meats should be tender, juicy and evenly cooked to the appropriate degree of doneness. They should have a pleasant appearance when whole as well as when sliced and plated.

Selecting Meats to Roast

Because roasting is a dry-heat cooking method and will not tenderize the finished product, meats that are to be roasted should be tender and well marbled. They are usually cut from the rib, loin or leg sections.

Seasoning Meats to Be Roasted

Seasonings are especially important with smaller roasts and roasts with little or no fat covering. With these roasts, some of the seasonings penetrate the meat while the remainder help create the highly seasoned crust associated with a good roast. A large roast with heavy fat covering (for example, a steamship round or prime rib) does not benefit from being seasoned on the surface because the seasonings will not penetrate the fat layer, which is trimmed away before service.

When practical, a roast with excess fat should be trimmed, leaving just a thin fat layer so that the roast bastes itself while cooking. A lean roast can be barded or larded before cooking to add richness and moisture. Lamb legs are sometimes studded with garlic cloves by piercing the meat with a paring knife and then pressing slivers of raw garlic into the holes.

A roast is sometimes cooked on a bed of mirepoix, or mirepoix is added to the roasting pan as the roast cooks. The mirepoix raises the roast off the bottom of the roasting pan, preventing the bottom from overcooking. This mirepoix, however, does not add any flavor to the roast. Rather, it combines with the drippings to add flavor to the jus, sauce or gravy that is made with them.

Cooking Temperatures

Small roasts such as a rack of lamb or a beef tenderloin should be cooked at high temperatures, 375°F–450°F (191°C–232°C) so that they develop good color during their short cooking times.

Traditionally, large roasts were started at high temperatures to sear the meat and seal in the juices; they were then finished at lower temperatures. Studies have shown, however, that searing does not seal in juices and that roasts cooked at constant, low temperatures provide a better yield with less shrinkage than roasts that have been seared. Temperatures between 275°F and 325°F (135°C and 163°C) are ideal for large roasts. These temperatures will produce a large, evenly cooked pink center portion.

Determining Doneness

The doneness of **small roasts** such as a rack of lamb is determined in much the same way as broiled or grilled meats. With experience, the chef develops a sense of timing as well as a feel for gauging the amount of resistance by touching the meat. These techniques, however, are not infallible, especially with large roasts.

Although timing is useful as a general guide for determining doneness, there are too many variables for it to be relied upon exclusively. With this caution in mind, Table 13.2 lists general cooking times for roasted meats.

The best way to determine the doneness of a **large roast** is to use an instant-read thermometer, as shown in Figure 13.9. The thermometer is inserted into the center or thickest part of the roast and away from any bones. The proper finished temperatures for roasted meats are listed in Table 13.2.

Carryover Cooking and Resting

Cooking does not stop the moment a roast is removed from the oven. Through conduction, the heat applied to the outside of the roast continues to penetrate,

FIGURE 13.9 ▶ Proper placement of an instant-read thermometer

Table 13.2   DETERMINING DONENESS OF ROASTS

DEGREE OF DONENESS	IDEAL INTERNAL TEMPERATURE AFTER CARRYOVER	MINUTES PER POUND*
Very rare	125°F–130°F 52°C–54°C	12–15
Rare	130°F–140°F 54°C–60°C	15–18
Medium	140°F–150°F 60°C–66°C	18–20
Well done	150°F–165°F 66°C–74°C	20–25

*Assumes meat was at room temperature before roasting and cooked at a constant 325°F (163°C).

cooking the center for several more minutes. Indeed, the internal temperature of a small roast can rise by as much as 5°F–10°F (3°C–6°C) after being removed from the oven. With a larger roast, such as a 50-pound steamship round, it can rise by as much as 20°F (11°C). Therefore, remove roasted meats before they reach the desired degree of doneness, and allow **carryover cooking** to complete the cooking process. The temperatures listed in Table 13.2 are internal temperatures after allowing for carryover cooking.

As meat cooks, its juices flow toward the center. If the roast is carved immediately after it is removed from the oven, its juices would run from the meat, causing it to lose its color and become dry. Letting the meat rest before slicing allows the juices to redistribute themselves evenly throughout the roast so that the roast will retain more juices when carved. Small roasts, such as a rack of lamb, need to rest only 5 to 10 minutes; larger roasts such as a steamship round of beef require as much as an hour.

▶ **carryover cooking** the cooking that occurs after a food is removed from a heat source; it is accomplished by the residual heat remaining in the food

Accompaniments to Roasted Meats

Roasts may be served with a sauce based on their natural juices (called *au jus*), as described in the recipe for Roast Prime Rib of Beef au Jus, page 296, or with a pan gravy made with drippings from the roast. Additional sauce suggestions are found in Table 11.5.

▶ PROCEDURE FOR ROASTING MEATS

1 Trim excess fat, tendons and silverskin from the meat. Leave only a thin fat covering, if possible, so that the roast bastes itself as it cooks.

2 Season the roast as appropriate and place it in a roasting pan. The roast may be placed on a bed of mirepoix or on a rack.

3 Roast the meat, uncovered, at the desired temperature (the larger the roast, the lower the temperature), usually 275°F–425°F (135°C–220°C).

4 If a jus or pan gravy is desired and a mirepoix was not added at the start of cooking, it may be added 30 to 45 minutes before the roast is done, thus allowing it to caramelize while the roast finishes cooking.

5 Cook to the desired temperature.

6 Remove the roast from the oven, allowing carryover cooking to raise the internal temperature to the desired degree of doneness. Allow the roast to rest before slicing or carving it. As the roast rests, prepare the jus, sauce or pan gravy.

RECIPE 13.2   ROAST PRIME RIB OF BEEF AU JUS

Yield: 18 Boneless Servings, 8 oz. (250 g) each   **Method:** Roasting

Oven-ready rib roast, IMPS #109, approx. 16 lb. (7.5 kg)	1	1
Salt and pepper	TT	TT
Garlic, chopped	TT	TT
Mirepoix	1 lb.	500 g
Brown stock	2 qt.	2 lt

1 Pull back the netting, fold back the fat cap and season the roast well with the salt, pepper and chopped garlic. Replace the fat cap and netting; place the roast in an appropriate-sized roasting pan. Roast at 300°F–325°F (160°C–165°C).

2 Add the mirepoix to the pan approximately 45 minutes before the roast is finished cooking. Continue cooking until the internal temperature reaches 125°F (52°C), approximately 3 to 4 hours. Carryover cooking will raise the internal temperature of the roast to approximately 138°F (59°C).

3 Remove the roast from the pan and allow it to rest in a warm place for 30 minutes.

4 Drain the excess fat from the roasting pan, reserving the mirepoix and any drippings in the roasting pan.

5 Caramelize the mirepoix on the stove top; allow the liquids to evaporate, leaving only brown drippings in the pan.

6 Deglaze the pan with brown stock. Stir to loosen all the drippings.

7 Simmer the jus, reducing it slightly and allowing the mirepoix to release its flavor; season with salt and pepper if necessary.

8 Strain the jus through a china cap lined with cheesecloth. Skim any remaining fat from the surface with a ladle.

9 Remove the netting from the roast. Trim and slice the roast as described on page 297 and serve with approximately 1 to 2 ounces (30 to 60 milliliters) jus per person.

1 Draining off the excess fat.

2 Caramelizing the mirepoix.

Approximate values per 9-oz. (270-g) serving: **Calories** 951, **Total fat** 79 g, **Saturated fat** 32 g, **Cholesterol** 214 mg, **Sodium** 278 mg, **Total carbohydrates** 1 g, **Protein** 56 g, **Iron** 40%

3 Deglazing the pan with brown stock.

4 Simmering the jus, reducing it slightly and allowing the mirepoix to release its flavors.

5 Straining the jus through a china cap and cheesecloth.

Carving Roasts

All the efforts that went into selecting and cooking a perfect roast will be wasted if the roast is not carved properly. Roasts are always carved against the grain; carving it with the grain produces long stringy, tough slices. Cutting across the muscle fibers produces a more attractive and tender portion. Portions may be cut in a single thick slice, as with Roast Prime Rib of Beef, or in many thin slices. The following photographs illustrate several different carving procedures.

▶ CARVING PRIME RIB

1 Removing the netting, cap fat and chine bones.

2 Trimming the excess fat from the eye muscle.

3 Slicing the rib in long, smooth strokes, the first cut (end cut) without a rib bone, the second cut with a rib bone, the third without, and so on.

▶ CARVING PRIME RIB ON THE SLICER

1 When producing large quantities of prime rib, it is often more practical to slice it on a slicing machine. Following the steps illustrated above, remove the netting, cap fat and chine bone; trim excess fat from the eye muscle. Then use a long slicer and completely remove the rib eye from the rib bones, being careful to stay as close as possible to the bones to avoid wasting any meat.

2 After placing the rib on the slicing machine, set the machine to the desired thickness. The blade will have to be adjusted often because a roast's thickness fluctuates.

▶ CARVING A STEAMSHIP ROUND OF BEEF

1 After setting the roast on the cutting board with the exposed femur bone (large end of the roast) down and the tibia (shank bone) or "handle" up, trim the excess exterior fat to expose the lean meat.

2 Begin slicing with a horizontal cut toward the shank bone, then make vertical cuts to release the slices of beef.

3 Keeping the exposed surface as level as possible, continue carving, turning the roast as necessary to access all sides.

▶ CARVING A LEG OF LAMB

1 Holding the shank bone firmly, cut toward the bone.

2 Cutting parallel to the shank bone to remove the slices.

3 Rotating the leg as needed to access the meat on all sides.

SAUTÉING

Sautéing is a dry-heat cooking method in which heat is conducted by a small amount of fat. Sautéed meats should be tender (a reflection of the quality of the raw product) and of good color (determined by proper cooking temperatures) and have a good overall flavor. Any accompanying sauce should be well seasoned and complement the meat without overpowering it.

Selecting Meats to Sauté

As with broiling, grilling and roasting, you should use tender meats of the highest quality in order to produce good results when sautéing. The cuts should be uniform in size and shape in order to promote even cooking.

Seasoning Meats to Be Sautéed

The sauces that almost always accompany sautéed meats provide much of the seasoning. The meat, however, can be marinated or simply seasoned with salt and pepper. If marinated, the meat must be patted dry before cooking to ensure proper browning. Some meats are dusted with flour before cooking to seal in juices and promote even browning.

Determining Doneness

As with broiled and grilled meats, the doneness of sautéed meats is determined by touch and timing. Red meats should be well browned; veal and pork should be somewhat lighter.

Accompaniments to Sautéed Meats

Sauces served with sautéed meats are usually made directly in the sauté pan, using the **fond.** They often incorporate a previously thickened sauce. Sauce suggestions for sautéed meats are found in Table 11.5.

▶ PROCEDURE FOR SAUTÉING MEATS

1 Heat a sauté pan and add enough oil or clarified butter to just cover the bottom. The pan should be large enough to hold the meat in a single layer. A pan that is too large may cause the fat or meat to burn.

2 Cut the meat into **cutlets, scallops, émincés, medallions, mignonettes, noisettes, chops** or small even-sized pieces. Season the meat and dredge in flour if desired.

3 Add the meat to the sauté pan in a single layer. Do not crowd the pan.

4 Adjust the temperature so that the meat's exterior browns properly without burning and the interior cooks. The heat should be high enough to complete the cooking process before the meat begins to stew in its own juices.

5 Small items may be tossed using the sauté pan's sloped sides to flip them back on top of themselves. Do not toss the meat more than necessary,

▶ **fond** (1) French for stock or base; (2) the concentrated juices, drippings and bits of food left in pans after foods are roasted or sautéed; it is used to flavor sauces made directly in the pans in which the foods were cooked

▶ **cutlet** a relatively thick, boneless slice of meat

▶ **scallop** a thin, boneless slice of meat

▶ **émincé** a small, thin, boneless piece of meat

▶ **paillarde** a scallop of meat pounded until thin, usually grilled

▶ **medallion** a small, round, relatively thick slice of meat

▶ **mignonette** a medallion

▶ **noisette** a small, usually round, portion of meat cut from the rib

▶ **chop** a cut of meat, including part of the rib

however. The pan should remain in contact with the heat source as much as possible to maintain proper temperatures. Larger items should be turned using tongs or a kitchen fork. Avoid burns by not splashing hot fat.

6 Larger items can be finished in an oven. Either place the sauté pan in the oven or transfer the meat to another pan. The latter procedure allows a sauce to be made in the original pan as the meat continues to cook.

▶ PROCEDURE FOR PREPARING A SAUCE IN THE SAUTÉ PAN

1 If a sauce is to be made in the pan, hold the meat in a warm spot while preparing the sauce. When the meat is removed from the pan, leave a small amount of fat as well as the fond. If there is excessive fat, degrease the pan, leaving just enough to cover its bottom. Add ingredients such as garlic, shallots and mushrooms that will be used as garnishes and sauce flavorings; sauté them.

2 Deglaze the pan with wine or stock. Scrape the pan, loosening the fond and allowing it to dissolve in the liquid. Reduce the deglazing liquid by approximately three-quarters.

3 Add jus lié or stock to the pan. Cook and reduce the sauce to the desired consistency.

4 Add any ingredients that do not require cooking, such as herbs and spices. Adjust the seasonings with salt and pepper.

5 For service, the meat may be returned to the pan for a moment to reheat it and coat it with the finished sauce. The meat should remain in the sauce just long enough to reheat. Do not attempt to cook the meat in the sauce.

SAUTÉED VEAL SCALLOPS WITH WHITE WINE LEMON SAUCE

RECIPE 13.3

Yield: 6 Servings	**Method:** Sautéing	
Veal scallops, 3 oz. (90 g) each	12	12
Clarified butter	2 fl. oz.	60 ml
Flour	4 oz.	120 g
Salt and pepper	TT	TT
Shallots, chopped	2 Tbsp.	30 ml
White wine	6 fl. oz.	180 ml
Lemon juice	2 fl. oz.	60 ml
Brown veal stock	4 fl. oz.	120 ml
Unsalted butter	2 oz.	60 g
Lemon wedges	12	12

1 Adding the veal scallops to the pan. Note the relationship of scallops to pan size.

1 Pound the scallops to a uniform thickness, as described in Chapter 15, Veal.

2 Heat a sauté pan and add the clarified butter.

3 Dredge the scallops in flour seasoned with salt and pepper and add to the pan in a single layer. Sauté on each side for 1–2 minutes. As the first scallops are done, remove them to a warm platter and sauté the remaining scallops.

4 Add the chopped shallots to the pan and sauté.

5 Deglaze the pan with the white wine and lemon juice.

6 Add the brown veal stock and reduce by half.

7 Swirl in the butter (monté au beurre).

8 Adjust the seasonings with salt and pepper.

9 Serve two scallops per person with approximately 1 ounce (30 milliliters) of sauce. Garnish with lemon wedges.

2 Adding the chopped shallots to the pan and sautéing them.

Approximate values per 8-oz. (240-g) serving: **Calories** 537, **Total fat** 28 g, **Saturated fat** 13 g, **Cholesterol** 208 mg, **Sodium** 325 mg, **Total carbohydrates** 17 g, **Protein** 47 g, **Vitamin A** 22%

3 Deglazing the pan with white wine and lemon juice.

4 Adding the brown veal stock and reducing by half.

5 Swirling in the butter and adjusting the seasonings.

PAN-FRYING

Pan-frying uses more fat than sautéing to conduct heat. Pan-fried meats should be tender (a reflection of the quality of the raw product) and of good color (determined by proper cooking temperatures) and have a good overall flavor. Meats to be pan-fried are usually breaded. In addition to providing flavor, breading seals the meat. The breading should be free from breaks, thus preventing the fat from coming into direct contact with the meat or collecting in a pocket formed between the meat and the breading. Pan-fried items should be golden in color, and the breading should not be soggy.

Selecting Meats to Pan-Fry

As with other dry-heat cooking methods, tender meats of high quality should be used because the meat will not be tenderized by the cooking process. Meats that are pan-fried are often cut into cutlets or scallops.

Seasoning Meats to Be Pan-Fried

Pan-fried meats are usually seasoned lightly with salt and pepper either by applying them directly to the meat or by adding them to the flour and bread crumbs used in the breading procedure.

Determining Doneness

The most accurate way to determine the doneness of a pan-fried item is by timing. The touch method is difficult to use because of the large amounts of hot fat. It also may not be as accurate as with broiled or grilled meats because pan-fried meats are often quite thin. The thinness of the meat also means that thermometer readings may not be accurate.

Accompaniments to Pan-Fried Meats

Any sauce served with pan-fried meats is usually made separately because there is no fond created during the pan-frying process. Sauce suggestions are listed in Table 11.5.

▶ PROCEDURE FOR PAN-FRYING MEATS

1 Slice and pound the meat into scallops, as described in Chapter 15, Veal.

2 Bread the meat using the standard breading procedure detailed in Chapter 9, Mise en Place.

3 Heat a moderate amount of fat or oil in a heavy pan. The temperature should be slightly lower than that used to sauté so that the breading will be nicely browned when the item is fully cooked.

4 Place the meat in the pan, being careful not to splash the hot fat. The fat should come one-third to halfway up the side of the meat. Fry until brown. Turn and brown the other side. Ideally, pan-fried meats should be fully cooked when they are well browned on both sides.

5 Remove the meat from the pan; drain it on absorbent paper before serving.

BREADED VEAL CUTLETS

Yield: 10 Servings **Method:** Pan-frying

Veal cutlets, 4 oz. (120 g) each	10	10
Salt and pepper	TT	TT
Flour	as needed for breading	
Eggs	as needed for breading	
Milk	as needed for breading	
Bread crumbs	as needed for breading	
Vegetable oil	as needed	as needed
Whole butter	6 oz.	180 g
Lemon wedges	20	20

1 Using a mallet, pound the cutlets to an even thickness, approximately ¼ inch (6 millimeters).

2 Season the cutlets with salt and pepper.

3 Bread the cutlets using the standard breading procedure described in Chapter 9, Mise en Place.

4 Heat a heavy pan to moderate heat; add approximately ⅛ inch (3 millimeters) of oil.

5 Add the cutlets in a single layer. Do not crowd the pan. Brown on one side, then the other. Total cooking time should be approximately 4 minutes.

6 Remove the cutlets and drain on absorbent paper.

7 Melt the butter in a small pan until it foams.

8 Place one cutlet on each plate and pour approximately ½ ounce (15 milliliters) butter over each portion. Garnish with lemon wedges.

Approximate values per 5-oz. (150-g) serving: **Calories** 501, **Total fat** 37 g, **Saturated fat** 17 g, **Cholesterol** 193 mg, **Sodium** 338 mg, **Total carbohydrates** 5 g, **Protein** 36 g, **Vitamin A** 17%

1 Adding the breaded cutlets to the hot pan. Note the amount of oil in the pan.

2 Turning the cutlets to brown on the second side.

3 Melting the butter in a separate pan until it foams.

4 Pouring the butter over the cutlet.

DEEP-FRYING

Deep-frying quickly cooks foods submerged in hot fat. It does not have a tenderizing effect. As even the choicest cuts of meat can always benefit from some tenderizing, deep-frying is not usually used for beef, veal, lamb or pork. There are exceptions, however. For example, commercially available frozen breaded meat cutlets are sometimes deep-fried, and some Asian dishes require deep-frying small pieces of beef or pork before finishing the meat in a sauce. (See Crispy Sweet and Sour Pork, page 402.)

MOIST-HEAT COOKING METHODS

Moist-heat cooking methods subject food to heat and moisture. Moist heat is often, but not always, used to tenderize tougher cuts of meat through long, slow cooking. Simmering is the only moist-heat cooking method discussed here, as it is the only one frequently used with meat.

SIMMERING

Simmering is usually associated with specific tougher cuts of meat that need to be tenderized through long, slow, moist cooking. Quality simmered meats have good flavor and texture. The flavor is determined by the cooking liquid; the texture is a result of proper cooking temperatures and time.

Selecting Meats to Simmer

Meats such as fresh or corned beef brisket, fresh or cured hams and tongue are often simmered. Beef briskets and tongues, pork butts and hams are often simmered whole.

Seasoning Meats to Be Simmered

If the meat to be simmered was cured by either smoking (as with cured hams, ham hocks and smoked pork butt) or pickling (as with corned beef and pickled tongue), the cooking liquid will not be used to make a sauce and should not be seasoned. Indeed, simmering cured meats helps leach out some of the excess salt, making the finished dish more palatable.

Cooking Temperatures

Moist-heat cooking methods generally use lower temperatures than dry-heat cooking methods. Meats are normally simmered at temperatures between 180°F and 200°F (82°C and 93°C). In some food service operations, meats such as hams and corned beef are cooked at temperatures as low as 150°F (66°C) for up to 12 hours. Although lower cooking temperatures result in less shrinkage and a more tender finished product, cooking times can be increased to the point that very low cooking temperatures may not be practical.

Determining Doneness

Simmered meats are always cooked well done, which is determined by tenderness. The size and quality of the raw product determines the cooking time. Undercooked meats will be tough and chewy. Overcooked meats will be stringy and may fall apart.

To test large cuts of meat for doneness, a kitchen fork should be easily inserted into the meat and the meat should slide off the fork. Smaller pieces of meat should be tender to the bite or easily cut with a table fork.

Accompaniments to Simmered Meats

Simmered meats are often served with boiled or steamed vegetables, as in the case of corned beef and cabbage. Pickled meats are usually served with mustard or horseradish sauce on the side.

▶ PROCEDURE FOR SIMMERING MEATS

1 Cut, trim or tie the meat according to the recipe.
2 Bring an adequate amount of liquid to a boil. There should be enough liquid to cover the meat completely. Too much liquid will leach off much of the meat's flavor; too little will leave a portion of the meat exposed, preventing it from cooking. Because the dish's final flavor is determined by the flavor of the liquid, use plenty of mirepoix, flavorings and seasonings.
3 When simmering smoked or cured items, start them in cold water. This helps draw off some of the strong smoked or pickled flavors.

4 Add the meat to the liquid.

5 Reduce the heat to the desired temperature and cook until the meat is tender. Do not allow the cooking liquid to boil. Boiling results in a tough or overcooked and stringy product. If the simmered meat is to be served cold, a moister and juicier product can be achieved by removing the pot from the stove before the meat is fully cooked. The meat and the liquid can be cooled in a water bath like that for a stock, as described in Chapter 11, Stocks and Sauces. This allows the residual heat in the cooking liquid to finish cooking the meat.

NEW ENGLAND BOILED DINNER

RECIPE 13.5

Yield: 12 Servings, 6 oz. (180 g) each   **Method:** Simmering

Corned beef brisket, 8 lb. (6.5 kg)	1	1
White stock	as needed	as needed
Sachet:		
Bay leaves	2	2
Dried thyme	½ tsp.	2 ml
Peppercorns, cracked	½ tsp.	2 ml
Parsley stems	10	10
Mustard seeds	1 Tbsp.	15 ml
Cinnamon sticks	2	2
Allspice berries	4	4
Baby red beets	24	24
Baby turnips	24	24
Baby carrots	24	24
Brussels sprouts	24	24
Pearl onions	24	24
Red Bliss potatoes	24	24

1 Placing the corned beef and sachet in an appropriate pot and covering with stock.

1 Place the beef in a pot and add enough stock to cover it. Add the sachet, bring to a boil and reduce to a simmer.

2 Simmer until the beef is tender, approximately 3 hours. Remove the beef and hold in a hotel pan in a small amount of the cooking liquid.

3 Peel or prepare the vegetables and potatoes as needed and cook separately in a portion of the cooking liquid.

4 Carve the beef and serve with two of each of the vegetables and horseradish sauce (page 214).

Approximate values per serving: **Calories** 1067, **Total fat** 58 g, **Saturated fat** 19 g, **Cholesterol** 296 mg, **Sodium** 3844 mg, **Total carbohydrates** 73 g, **Protein** 64 g, **Vitamin A** 27%, **Vitamin C** 200%, **Iron** 66%

2 Presenting the carved beef with the vegetable garnish.

COMBINATION COOKING METHODS

Braising and stewing are referred to as combination cooking methods because both dry heat and moist heat are used to achieve the desired results.

BRAISING

Braised meats are first browned and then cooked in a liquid that serves as a sauce for the meat. A well-prepared braised dish has the rich flavor of the meat in the sauce and the moisture and flavor of the sauce in the meat. It should be almost fork tender but not falling apart. The meat should have an attractive color from the initial browning and final glazing.

Selecting Meats to Braise

Braising can be used for tender cuts (such as those from the loin or rib) or tougher cuts (such as those from the chuck or shank). Any meat to be braised should be well marbled with an ample fat content in order to produce a moist finished product.

If tender cuts such as veal chops or pork chops are braised, the finished dish has a uniquely different flavor and texture than if the meats were cooked by a dry-heat method. Tender cuts require shorter cooking times than tougher cuts because lengthy cooking is not needed to break down connective tissue.

More often, braising is used with tougher cuts that are tenderized by the long, moist cooking process. Cuts from the chuck and shank are popular choices, as they are very flavorful and contain relatively large amounts of collagen, which adds richness to the finished product.

Large pieces of meat can be braised, then carved like a roast. Portion control cuts and diced meats can also be braised.

Seasoning Meats to Be Braised

The seasoning and overall flavor of a braised dish is largely a function of the quality of the cooking liquid and the mirepoix, herbs, spices and other ingredients that season the meat as it cooks. However, braised meats can be marinated before they are cooked to tenderize them and add flavor. The marinade is then sometimes incorporated into the braising liquid. Salt and pepper may be added to the flour if the meat is dredged before it is browned, or the meat may be seasoned directly (although the salt may draw out moisture and inhibit browning).

A standard sachet and a tomato product are usually added at the start of cooking. The tomato product adds flavor and color to the finished sauce as well as acid to tenderize the meat during the cooking process. Final seasoning should not take place until cooking is complete and the sauce will not be reduced further.

Cooking Temperatures

Braised meats are always browned before simmering. As a general rule, smaller cuts are floured before browning; larger cuts are not. Flouring seals the meat, promotes even browning and adds body to the sauce that accompanies the meat. Whether floured or not, the meat is browned in fat. After browning, white meats should be golden to amber in color; red meats should be dark brown. Do not brown the meat too quickly at too high a temperature since it is important to develop a well-caramelized surface. The caramelized surface adds color and flavor to the final product.

The meat and the braising liquid are brought to a boil over direct heat. The temperature is then reduced below boiling, and the pot is covered. Cooking can be finished in the oven or on the stove top. The oven provides gentle, even heat without the risk of scorching. If braising is finished on the stove top, proper temperatures must be maintained carefully throughout the cooking process, and great care must be taken to prevent scorching or burning. Lower temperatures and longer cooking times result in more even cooking and thorough penetration of the cooking liquid, providing a more flavorful final product.

Finishing Braised Meats

Near the end of the cooking process, the lid may be removed from oven-braised meats. Finishing braised meats without a cover serves two purposes. First, the meat can be glazed by basting it often. (As the basting liquid evaporates, the meat is browned and a strongly flavored glaze is formed.) Second, removing the lid allows the cooking liquid to reduce, thickening it and concentrating its flavors for use as a sauce.

Determining Doneness

Braised meats are done when they are tender. A fork inserted into the meat should meet little resistance. Properly braised meats should remain intact and not fall apart when handled gently.

Braised meats that fall apart or are stringy are overcooked. If the finished product is tough, it was probably undercooked or cooked at too high a temperature. If the entire dish lacks flavor, the meat may not have been properly browned or the cooking liquid may have been poorly seasoned.

Accompaniments to Braised Meats

Large braised items are often served like roasts. They are carved against the grain in thin slices and served with their sauce. Vegetables can be cooked with the braised meat, cooked separately and added when the main item has finished cooking or added at service. If the vegetables are cooked with the main item, they should be added at intervals based on their individual cooking times to prevent overcooking.

▶ PROCEDURE FOR BRAISING MEATS

The liquid used for braising is usually thickened in one of three ways:

1 With a roux added at the start of the cooking process; the roux thickens the sauce as the meat cooks.
2 Prethickened before the meat is added.
3 Thickened after the meat is cooked either by puréeing the mirepoix or by using roux, arrowroot or cornstarch.

The procedure for braising meats includes variations for whichever thickening method is selected.

1 Heat a small amount of oil in a heavy pan.
2 Dredge the meat to be braised in seasoned flour, if desired, and add it to the oil.
3 Brown the meat well on all sides and remove from the pan.
4 Add a mirepoix to the pan and caramelize it well. If using roux, it should be added at this time.
5 Add the appropriate stock or sauce so that when the meat is returned to the pan the liquid comes approximately one-third of the way up the side of the meat.
6 Add aromatics and seasonings.
7 Return the meat to the sauce. Tightly cover the pot and bring it to a simmer. Cook slowly either on the stove top or by placing the covered pot directly in an oven at 250°F–300°F (120°C–150°C).
8 Cook the item, basting or turning it often so that all sides of the meat benefit from the moisture and flavor of the sauce.
9 When the meat is done, remove it from the pan and hold it in a warm place while the sauce is finished.
10 The sauce may be reduced on the stove top to intensify its flavors. If the meat was braised in a stock, the stock may be thickened using a roux, arrowroot or cornstarch. Strain the sauce or, if desired, purée the mirepoix and other ingredients and return them to the sauce. Adjust the sauce's consistency as desired.

RECIPE 13.6   AUNT RUTHIE'S POT ROAST

1 Browning the brisket.

2 Sautéing the onions and garlic.

3 Basting the brisket. Note the proper amount of cooking liquid.

Yield: 12 Servings, 6 oz. (180 g) meat and 4 oz. (120 g.) sauce

Method: Braising

Vegetable oil	3 fl. oz.	90 ml
Beef brisket	6 lb.	2.7 kg
Onions, thinly sliced	3 lb.	1.4 kg
Garlic, minced	2 Tbsp.	30 ml
Brown veal stock	1 qt.	1 lt
Tomato sauce	1 pt.	450 ml
Brown sugar	4 oz.	120 g
Paprika	1 tsp.	5 ml
Dry mustard	2 tsp.	10 ml
Lemon juice	8 fl. oz.	250 ml
Ketchup	8 oz.	250 g
Red wine vinegar	8 fl. oz.	250 ml
Worcestershire sauce	2 fl. oz.	60 ml
Salt and pepper	TT	TT

1 Heat the oil in a large skillet. Add the beef and brown thoroughly. Remove and reserve the brisket.
2 Add the onions and garlic to the pan and sauté.
3 Add the stock and tomato sauce to the pan.
4 Return the brisket to the pan, cover tightly and bring to a boil. Braise at 325°F (160°C) for 1½ hours, basting or turning the brisket often.
5 Combine the remaining ingredients and add to the pan.
6 Continue cooking and basting the brisket until tender, approximately 1 hour.
7 Remove the brisket, degrease the sauce and adjust its consistency and seasonings. Do not strain the sauce.
8 Slice the brisket against the grain and serve with the sauce.

Approximate values per serving: **Calories** 803, **Total fat** 52 g, **Saturated fat** 16 g, **Cholesterol** 224 mg, **Sodium** 3290 mg, **Total carbohydrates** 40 g, **Protein** 46 g, **Vitamin A** 25%, **Vitamin C** 100%

STEWING

Stewing, like braising, is a combination cooking method. In many ways, the procedures for stewing are identical to those for braising, although stewing is usually associated with smaller or bite-sized pieces of meat.

There are two main types of stews: brown stews and white stews.

When making **brown stews,** the meat is first browned in fat; then a cooking liquid is added. The initial browning adds flavor and color to the finished product. The same characteristics apply to a good brown stew that apply to a good braised dish: It should be fork tender and have an attractive color and a rich flavor.

There are two types of **white stews: fricassees,** in which the meat is first cooked in a small amount of fat without coloring, then combined with a cooking liquid; and **blanquettes,** in which the meat is first blanched, then rinsed and added to a cooking liquid. A white stew should have the same flavor and texture characteristics as a brown stew, but should be white or ivory in color.

Selecting Meats to Stew

Stewing uses moist heat to tenderize meat just as braising does; therefore, many of the same cuts can be used. Meats that are to be stewed should be trimmed of excess fat and connective tissue and cut into 1- to 2-inch (2.5- to 5-cm) cubes.

STEW TERMINOLOGY

Ragoût (ra-GOO)–A general term that refers to white or brown stews in which the meat is cooked by dry heat before a liquid is added. In French, ragoût means "to bring back the appetite."

Fricassee (FRIHK-uh-see)–A white ragoût usually made from white meat or small game, seared without browning and garnished with small onions and mushrooms.

Navarin (nah-veh-rahng)–A brown ragoût generally made with turnips, other root vegetables, onions, peas and lamb.

Blanquette (blahn-KEHT)–A white stew in which the meat is first blanched, then added to a stock or sauce to complete the cooking and tenderizing process. Blanquettes are finished with a liaison of egg yolks and heavy cream.

Chili con carne–A ragoût of ground or diced meat cooked with onions, chile peppers, cumin and other spices. Despite the objections of purists, chili sometimes contains beans.

Goulash–A Hungarian beef stew made with onions and paprika and garnished with potatoes.

Seasoning Meats to Be Stewed

Stews, like braised meats, get much of their flavor from their cooking liquid. A stew's seasoning and overall flavor is a direct result of the quality of the cooking liquid and the vegetables, herbs, spices and other ingredients added during cooking.

Cooking Temperatures

Meats for brown stews are first cooked at high temperatures over direct heat until well browned. Meats for fricassees are first sautéed at low temperatures so that they do not develop color.

Once the cooking liquid has been added and the moist-heat cooking process has begun, do not allow the stew to boil. Stews benefit from low-temperature cooking. If practical, stews can be covered and finished in the oven.

Determining Doneness

Stewed meats are done when they are fork tender. Test them by removing a piece of meat to a plate and cutting it with a fork. Any vegetables that are cooked with the meat should be added at the proper times so that they and the meat are completely cooked at the same time.

Accompaniments to Stewed Meats

Stews are often complete meals in themselves, containing meat, vegetables and potatoes in one dish. Stews that do not contain a starch are often served with pasta or rice.

▶ PROCEDURE FOR STEWING MEATS—BROWN STEWS

Red meats, lamb and game are used in brown stews. The procedure for making a brown stew is very similar to braising.

1 Trim the meat of excess fat and silverskin and cut into 1- to 2-inch (2.5- to 5-cm) pieces.

2 Dredge the meat in flour if desired. Heat an appropriate-sized pan and add enough oil to cover the bottom. Cook the meat in the oil, browning it well on all sides. Onions and garlic can be added at this time and browned.

3 Add flour to the meat and fat and cook to make a brown roux.

4 Gradually add the liquid to the roux, stirring to prevent lumps. Bring the stew to a boil and reduce to a simmer.

5 Add a tomato product and a sachet or a bouquet garni. Cover and place in the oven or continue to simmer on the stove top until the meat is tender. Add other ingredients such as vegetables or potatoes at the proper time so that they will be done when the meat is tender.

6 When the meat is tender, remove the sachet or bouquet garni. The meat may be strained out and the sauce thickened with roux, cornstarch or arrowroot or reduced to concentrate its flavors.

7 If not added during the cooking process, vegetables and other garnishes may be cooked separately and added to the finished stew.

RECIPE 13.7　　　　　　　BROWN BEEF STEW

1 Browning the beef.

2 Sautéing the garlic and onions until slightly browned.

3 Adding the flour and making a roux.

Yield: 8 Servings, 8-oz. (240-g) each		**Method:** Stewing
Oil	2 fl. oz.	60 ml
Beef chuck or shank, trimmed and cut into 1½-in. (3.5-cm) cubes	4 lb. 8 oz.	2 kg
Salt	2 tsp.	10 ml
Black pepper	½ tsp.	2 ml
Onions, small dice	10 oz.	300 g
Garlic, chopped	1 tsp.	5 ml
Flour	1½ oz.	45 g
Red wine	8 fl. oz.	250 ml
Brown stock	1 qt.	1 lt
Tomato purée	4 oz.	120 g
Sachet:		
Bay leaves	2	2
Dried thyme	½ tsp.	2 ml
Peppercorns, crushed	½ tsp.	2 ml
Parsley stems	10	10

1 Heat a heavy pot until very hot and add the oil.
2 Season the beef with salt and pepper and add it to the pot, browning it well on all sides. Do not overcrowd the pot. If necessary, cook the beef in several batches.
3 Add the onions and garlic and sauté until the onions are slightly browned.
4 Add the flour and stir to make a roux. Brown the roux lightly.
5 Add the red wine and brown stock slowly, stirring to prevent lumps.
6 Add the tomato purée and the sachet.
7 Bring to a simmer and cook until the beef is tender, approximately 1½ to 2 hours.
8 If desired, remove the cooked beef from the sauce and strain the sauce. Return the beef to the sauce.
9 Degrease the stew by skimming off the fat.

Variation: Vegetables such as turnips, carrots, celery and pearl onions can be cooked separately and added to the stew as garnish.

Approximate values per 8-oz. (240-g) serving: **Calories** 590, **Total fat** 32 g, **Saturated fat** 11 g, **Cholesterol** 185 mg, **Sodium** 710 mg, **Total carbohydrates** 15 g, **Protein** 58 g, **Vitamin A** 45%, **Iron** 40%

4 Adding the red wine and beef stock.

5 Adding the tomato pureé and sachet.

6 Degreasing the stew.

▶ PROCEDURE FOR STEWING MEATS—BRAISED WHITE STEWS (FRICASSEES)

The procedure for making fricassees is similar to the procedure for brown stews. The primary difference is that the meat is sautéed but not allowed to brown. The braised white stew (fricassee) procedure outlined here is the basis for Veal Fricassee, page 357.

1 Trim the meat of excess fat and silverskin and cut into 1- to 2-inch (2.5- to 5-cm) pieces.
2 Heat an appropriate-sized pan and add enough oil to cover the bottom. Add the meat (and often an onion) to the pan and cook without browning.
3 Sprinkle the meat (and onion) with flour and cook to make a blond roux.
4 Gradually add the liquid, stirring to prevent lumps. Bring the stew to a boil and reduce to a simmer.
5 Add a bouquet garni and seasonings. Cover the stew and place in the oven or continue to simmer on the stove top, being careful not to burn or scorch the stew.
6 Continue to cook until the meat is tender. If the sauce is too thin, remove the meat from the sauce and hold the meat in a warm place. Reduce the sauce to the proper consistency on the stove top or thicken it by adding a small amount of blond roux, cornstarch or arrowroot.

▶ PROCEDURE FOR STEWING MEATS—SIMMERED WHITE STEWS (BLANQUETTES)

Unlike fricassees, blanquettes contain meat that was blanched, not sautéed. (Because the meat is cooked only by moist heat and never by dry heat, the blanquette cooking process is not a true combination cooking method; nevertheless, because of its striking similarities to stewing, it is included here.) The most common blanquette is made with veal and is known as blanquette de veau, but any white meat or lamb can be prepared in this manner using a variety of garnishes. The simmered white stew (blanquette) procedure outlined here is the basis for Blanquette of Lamb, page 380.

1 Trim the meat of excess fat and silverskin and cut into 1- to 2-inch (2.5- to 5-cm) pieces.
2 Blanch the cubed meat by placing the meat in an appropriate pot, covering with cool water, adding salt, and bringing it rapidly to a boil. Drain the water. Rinse the meat to remove any impurities.
3 Return the meat to the pot and add enough stock to cover. Add a bouquet garni, salt and pepper. Simmer until the meat is tender, approximately 1 to 1½ hours.
4 Strain the meat from the stock. Discard the bouquet garni. Bring the stock to a boil, thicken it with a blond roux and simmer for 15 minutes.
5 Return the meat to the thickened stock. Add a liaison of cream and egg yolks to enrich and thicken the stew. Heat the stew to a simmer. Do not boil or the egg yolks will curdle.
6 If any vegetables are to be added, they should be cooked separately and added to the thickened stock with the meat.
7 Adjust the seasonings with a few drops of lemon juice, nutmeg or salt and pepper as needed.

CONCLUSION

Because meat may account for the largest portion of your food-cost dollar, it should be purchased carefully, stored properly and fabricated appropriately. The various cuts and flavors of meat (beef, veal, lamb and pork) can be successfully broiled, grilled, roasted, sautéed, pan-fried, simmered, braised or stewed, provided you follow a few simple procedures and learn which cuts respond best to the various cooking methods.

QUESTIONS FOR DISCUSSION

1 Explain the difference between primals, subprimals and fabricated cuts of meat. Why is it important to be skilled in meat fabrication?

2 What is connective tissue composed of, and where is it found? What happens to connective tissue at normal cooking temperatures?

3 Discuss the government's role in regulating the marketing and sale of meat.

4 At what temperature should fresh meat be stored? At what temperature should frozen meat be stored?

5 Would it be better to grill or braise a piece of meat that contains a great deal of connective tissue? Explain your answer.

6 List three ways to improve the cooking qualities of lean meats. What techniques can be used to compensate for the lack of fat?

7 Describe the similarities between sautéing meats and pan-frying them. Describe the differences.

8 Describe the similarities between braising meats and stewing them. Describe the differences.

BEEF IS THE SOUL OF COOKING.
—*Marie-Antoin Carême, French chef
(1784–1833)*

BEEF

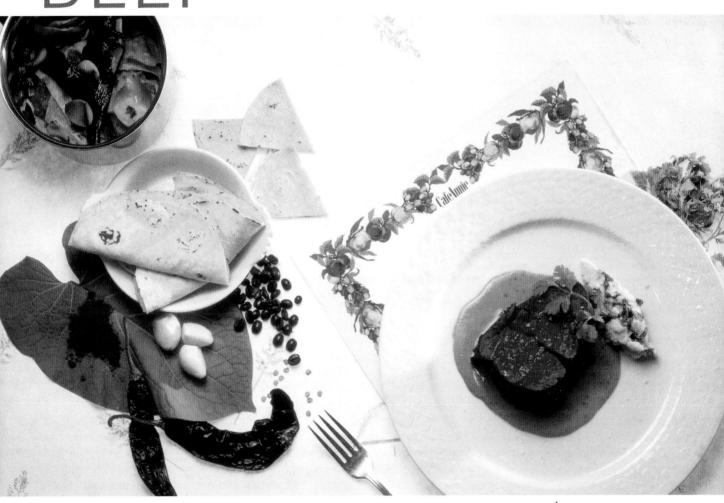

CAFÉ ANNIE, Houston, TX
Chef-Owner Robert Del Grande
Executive Chef Ben Berryhill

AFTER STUDYING THIS
CHAPTER, YOU WILL BE
ABLE TO:

▶ identify the primal, subprimal
and fabricated cuts of beef

▶ perform basic butchering
procedures

▶ apply appropriate cooking
methods to several common
cuts of beef

Beef is the meat of domesticated cattle. Most of the beef Americans eat comes from steers, which are male cattle castrated as calves and specifically raised for beef. Although Americans are consuming less beef today than we once did, we still consume far more beef than any other meat. The beef we are eating is leaner than that of years past thanks to advances in animal husbandry and closer trimming of exterior fat.

▶ PRIMAL AND SUBPRIMAL CUTS OF BEEF

After the steer is slaughtered, it is cut into four pieces (called quarters) for easy handling. This is done by first splitting the carcass down the backbone into two bilateral halves. Each half is divided into the forequarter (the front portion) and the hindquarter (the rear portion) by cutting along the natural curvature between the 12th and 13th ribs. The quartered carcass is then further reduced into the primal cuts and the subprimal and fabricated cuts.

The primal cuts of beef are the chuck, brisket and shank, rib, short plate, short loin, sirloin, flank and round. Figure 14.1 shows the relationship between a steer's bone structure and the primal cuts. It is important to know the location of bones when cutting or working with meats. This makes meat fabrication and carving easier and aids in identifying cuts. Figure 14.2 shows the primal cuts of beef and their location on the carcass. An entire beef carcass can range in weight from 500 to more than 800 pounds (225 to 360 kg).

FOREQUARTER

CHUCK

The primal chuck is the animal's shoulder; it accounts for approximately 28 percent of carcass weight. It contains a portion of the backbone, five rib bones and portions of the blade and arm bones.

Because an animal constantly uses its shoulder muscles, chuck contains a high percentage of connective tissue and is quite tough. This tough cut of beef, however, is one of the most flavorful.

The primal chuck is used less frequently than other primal cuts in food service operations. If cooked whole, the chuck is difficult to cut or carve because of the large number of bones and relatively small muscle groups that travel in different directions.

The primal chuck produces several fabricated cuts: cross rib pot roast, chuck short ribs, cubed or tenderized steaks, stew meat and ground chuck. Because the meat is less tender, the fabricated cuts usually benefit from moist-heat cooking or combination cooking methods such as stewing and braising.

BRISKET AND SHANK

The brisket and shank are located beneath the primal chuck on the front half of the carcass. Together, they form a single primal that accounts for approximately 8 percent of carcass weight. This primal consists of the steer's breast (the brisket), which contains the ribs and breast bone, and its arm (the foreshank), which contains only the shank bone.

The ribs and breast bone are always removed from the brisket before cooking. The boneless brisket is very tough and contains a substantial percentage of fat, both intermuscular and subcutaneous. It is well suited for moist-heat and

▶ **boxed beef** industry terminology for primal and subprimal cuts of beef that are vacuum-sealed and packed into cardboard boxes for shipping from the packing plant to retailers and food service operations

▶ **certified angus beef** a brand created in 1978 to distinguish the highest-quality beef produced from descendants of the black, hornless Angus cattle of Scotland. The meat must meet American Angus Association standards for yield, marbling and age, and be graded as high choice or prime.

▶ **Kobe beef** an exclusive type of beef traditionally produced in Kobe, Japan. Wagyu cattle are fed a special diet, which includes beer to stimulate the animal's appetite during summer months. The animals are massaged with sake to relieve stress and muscle stiffness in the belief that calm, contented cattle produce better-quality meat. This special treatment produces meat that is extraordinarily tender and full-flavored, and extraordinarily expensive. Kobe Beef America introduced Wagyu cattle to the United States in 1976. KBA's cattle are raised without hormones and the meat is dry-aged for 21 days prior to sale.

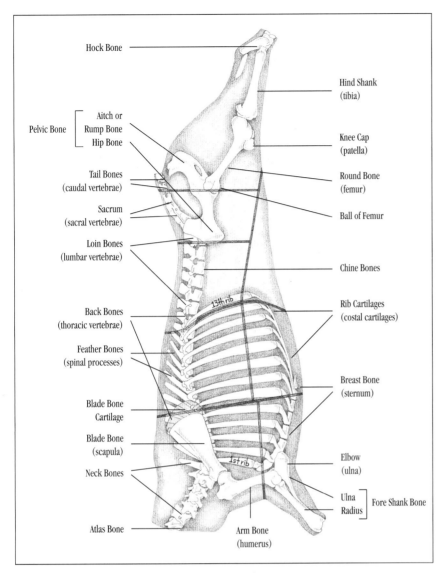

FIGURE 14.1 ▶ The skeletal structure of a steer

A COW BY ANY OTHER NAME...

Cattle is the collective name for all domesticated oxen (genus *Bos*). Cattle are classified as

Bulls—male cattle, usually not raised to be eaten.

Calves—young cows or bulls prized for their meat.

Cows—female cattle after their first calving, raised in this country principally for milk and calf production. In France, cows are used for beef when they are no longer needed for milk.

Heifers—young cows or cows before their first calving. Heifer meat and organs are becoming increasingly popular as a food source.

Stags—male cattle castrated after maturity, principally used for dog food.

Steers—male cattle castrated prior to maturity and principally raised for beef.

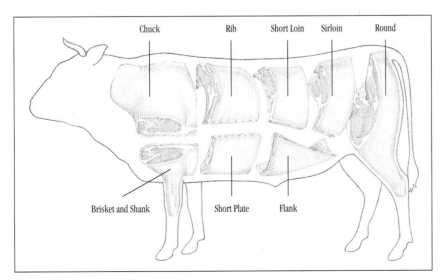

FIGURE 14.2 ▶ The primal cuts of beef

combination cooking methods such as simmering or braising. It is often pickled or corned to produce corned beef brisket, or cured and peppered to make pastrami.

Beef foreshanks are very flavorful and high in collagen. Because collagen converts to gelatin when cooked using moist heat, foreshanks are excellent for making soups and stocks. Ground shank meat is often used to help clarify and flavor consommés because of its rich flavor and high collagen content.

RIB

The primal beef rib accounts for approximately 10 percent of carcass weight. It consists of ribs 6 through 12 as well as a portion of the backbone.

This primal is best known for yielding roast prime rib of beef. Prime rib is not named after the quality grade USDA Prime. Rather, its name reflects the fact that it constitutes the majority of the primal cut. The eye meat of the rib (the center muscle portion) is not a well-exercised muscle and therefore is quite tender. It also contains large amounts of marbling compared to the rest of the carcass and produces rich, full-flavored roasts and steaks. Although roasting the eye muscle on the rib bones produces a moister roast, the eye meat can be removed to produce a boneless rib eye roast or cut into rib eye steaks. The rib bones that are separated from the rib eye meat are quite meaty and flavorful and can be served as barbecued beef ribs. The ends of the rib bones that are trimmed off the primal rib to produce the rib roast are known as beef short ribs. They are meaty and are often served as braised beef short ribs.

Oven-Ready Rib Roast

Beef Rib Eye Roll

SHORT PLATE

The short plate is located directly below the primal rib on a side of beef; it accounts for approximately 9 percent of the overall weight of the carcass. The short plate contains rib bones and cartilage and produces the short ribs and skirt steak.

Short ribs are meaty, yet high in connective tissue, and are best when braised. Skirt steak is often marinated and grilled as fajitas. Other, less meaty portions of the short plate are trimmed and ground.

Skirt Steak

HINDQUARTER

SHORT LOIN

The short loin is the anterior (front) portion of the beef loin. It is located just behind the rib and becomes the first primal cut of the hindquarter when the side of beef is divided into a forequarter and hindquarter. It accounts for approximately 8 percent of carcass weight.

The short loin contains a single rib, the 13th, and a portion of the backbone. With careful butchering, this small primal can yield several subprimal and fabricated cuts, all of which are among the most tender, popular and expensive cuts of beef.

Porterhouse Steak

The loin eye muscle, a continuation of the rib eye muscle, runs along the top of the T-shaped bones that form the backbone. Beneath the loin eye muscle on the other side of the backbone is the tenderloin, the most tender cut of all.

When the short loin is cut in cross sections with the bone in, it produces—starting with the rib end of the short loin—club steaks (which do not contain any tenderloin), T-bone steaks (which contain only a small portion of tenderloin) and porterhouse steaks (which are cut from the sirloin end of the short loin and contain a large portion of tenderloin).

Strip Loin

The whole tenderloin can also be removed and cut into châteaubriand, filet mignon and tournedos. A portion of the tenderloin is located in the sirloin portion of the loin. When the entire beef loin is divided into the primal short loin and primal sirloin, the large end of the tenderloin (the butt tenderloin) is separated from the remainder of the tenderloin and remains in the sirloin; the smaller end of the tenderloin (the short tenderloin) remains in the short loin. If the tenderloin is to be kept whole, it must be removed before the short loin and sirloin are separated. The loin eye meat can be removed from the bones, producing a boneless strip loin, which is very tender and can be roasted or cut into boneless strip steaks.

SIRLOIN

The sirloin is located in the hindquarter, between the short loin and the round. It accounts for approximately 7 percent of carcass weight and contains part of the backbone as well as a portion of the hip bone.

The sirloin produces bone-in or boneless roasts and steaks that are flavorful and tender. With the exception of the tenderloin portion, however, these subprimals and fabricated cuts are not as tender as those from the strip loin. Cuts from the sirloin are cooked using dry-heat methods such as broiling, grilling or roasting.

Tenderloin

Top Sirloin Butt

FLANK

The flank is located directly beneath the loin, posterior to (behind) the short plate. It accounts for approximately 6 percent of carcass weight. The flank contains no bones.

Although quite flavorful, it is a less tender cut with a good deal of fat and connective tissue. Flank meat is usually trimmed and ground, with the exception of the flank steak or London broil. The flank also contains a small piece of meat known as the hanging tenderloin. Although not actually part of the tenderloin, it is very tender and can be cooked using any method.

Flank Steak

ROUND

The primal round is very large, weighing as much as 200 pounds (90 kg) and accounting for approximately 24 percent of carcass weight. It is the hind leg of the animal and contains the round, aitch, shank and tail bones.

Meat from the round is flavorful and fairly tender. The round yields a wide variety of subprimal and fabricated cuts: the top round, outside round, eye round (the outside round and the eye round together are called the bottom round), knuckle and shank. See Figure 14.3. Steaks cut from the round are less tender, but because they have large muscles and limited intermuscular fat, the top round and knuckle make good roasts. The bottom round is best when braised. The hindshank is prepared in the same fashion as the foreshank.

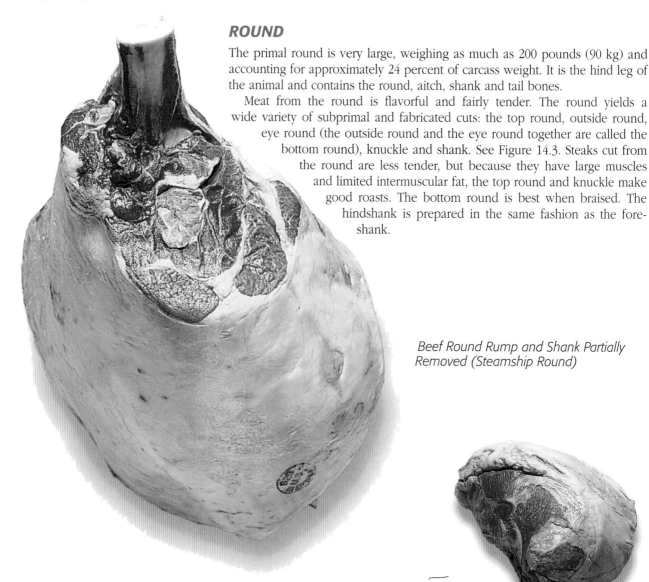

Beef Round Rump and Shank Partially Removed (Steamship Round)

Top (or Inside) Round

BEEF: FROM COLUMBUS TO CATTLE DRIVES

Although cattle have been domesticated for several thousand years, they have been in the New World only since 1493, when Columbus brought them along on his second expedition to the West Indies. During the succeeding decades, the Spanish brought cattle to Florida and Texas, where they thrived in the dry, hot climates.

The New World's desire for beef steadily grew from the 1500s to the early 1800s. By the mid-1800s, America's demand for beef outpaced the supply available from local family farms, and so cattle ranching was born. Based principally in the Southwest and West, ranchers used the open range to support large cattle herds. Texas longhorns, descended from the original Spanish cattle stock, were the animal of choice. Prized for the quality of their meat, longhorns are hardy animals that live off the range and demand little care. They grow rapidly on forage such as mesquite beans, prickly pear, weeds, shrubs and buffalo grass. Ranchers brought the cattle from the range to slaughterhouses near consumer markets or to places like Kansas City with rail links to the populous East Coast.

The open range, so vital to the 19th-century cattle industry, began to disappear rapidly after the signing of the Homestead Act of 1862. Squabbles with sheep ranchers further eroded the range land available for the great cattle herds to roam. And, as the railroads expanded westward, the cattle drives shortened and the economies of scale that supported cattle ranching began to dwindle. Although there are still many large cattle ranches, by the early 20th century, great cattle drives had become nothing more than fodder for Hollywood.

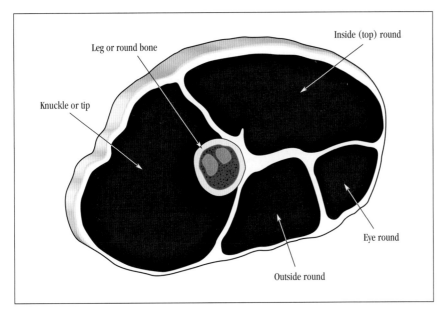

FIGURE 14.3 ▶ Cross cut of muscles in a whole round

ORGAN MEATS

Several organ meats are used in food service operations. This group of products is known as **offal.** It includes the heart, kidney, tongue, tripe (stomach lining) and oxtail. Offal benefit from moist-heat cooking and are often used in soup, stew or braised dishes.

▶ **offal** (OFF-uhl) also called variety meats; edible entrails (for example, the heart, kidneys, liver, sweetbreads and tongue) and extremities (for example, oxtail and pig's feet) of an animal

▶ BUTCHERING PROCEDURES

Although many food service operations buy their beef previously cut and portioned, it is still important for a cook to be able to fabricate cuts of beef and perform basic butchering tasks.

▶ PROCEDURE FOR CUTTING A NEW YORK STEAK
FROM A BONELESS STRIP LOIN

1 Square up the strip loin by trimming off the lip so it extends 1 to 2 inches (2.5 to 5 centimeters) from the eye muscle.

2 Turn the strip over and trim off any fat or connective tissue.

3 Turn the strip back over and trim the fat covering to a uniform thickness of ¼ inch (6 millimeters).

4 Cut the steaks to the thickness or weight desired.

5 The eye meat of steaks located on the sirloin end of the strip is divided by a strip of connective tissue. Steaks cut from this area are called vein steaks and are inferior to steaks cut from the rib end of the strip.

▶ PROCEDURE FOR TRIMMING A FULL BEEF TENDERLOIN AND CUTTING IT INTO CHÂTEAUBRIAND, FILET MIGNON AND TENDER TIPS

1 Cut and pull the excess fat from the entire tenderloin to expose the meat.

2 Remove the chain muscle from the side of the tenderloin. (Although it contains much connective tissue, the chain muscle may be trimmed and the meat used as tenderloin trimmings in various dishes.)

3 Trim away all of the fat and silverskin. Do so by loosening a small piece of silverskin, then, holding the loosened silverskin tightly with one hand, cut it away in long strips, angling the knife up toward the silverskin slightly so that only the silverskin is removed and no meat is wasted.

4 Cut the tenderloin as desired into (left to right) tips, châteaubriand, filet mignon, tournedo tips, and tenderloin tips.

▶ PROCEDURE FOR BUTTERFLYING MEATS

Many cuts of boneless meats such as tenderloin steaks and boneless pork chops can be butterflied to create a thinner cut that has a greater surface area and cooks more quickly.

1 Make the first cut nearly all the way through the meat, keeping it attached by leaving approximately ¼ inch (6 millimeters) uncut.

2 Make a second cut, this time cutting all the way through, completely removing the steak from the tenderloin.

FIFTEEN SECONDS OF FLAME—A STEAK'S OWN STORY

Every cook knows that when you cook a good steak, you have to make painful compromises. You learn to blast it at high temperatures because you need more than 300°F to produce a crust with those rich, caramelized flavors that form like magic from the meat's natural sugars and amino acids. (Scientists call this process the Maillard reaction, named for the French physician who, almost a century ago, was the first to investigate similar reactions between proteins and sugars in the human body.) But you don't want the steak's interior to go much above 135°F because that's the temperature at which it stays juicy. Above that, the strands of proteins in the muscle fibers contract so much that they start to squeeze out their juices. Renowned food science author Harold McGee shocked the cooking world in 1984 when he used these principles to demonstrate that searing meat at high heat does precisely the opposite of "sealing in" those juices—it starts to dry them out.

So what usually happens when you throw your steak on the fire? You end up with a great Maillard crust, a juicy rare or rosy center—and then there's a dry, chewy "gray zone" in between.

McGee had a hunch that computers could figure out a satisfactory solution. He figured some Silicon Valley scientists could modify some mathematical simulation software to study how heat moves through meat. They could. McGee ran hundreds of simulations, in effect asking the computer: What's the best way to get the heat to diffuse through the meat so it cooks as fast and evenly as possible?

The computer told them that chefs are cooking their steaks, well, wrong. The computer simulation shows that when you throw a steak on the fire and just let it sit there, sizzling away, and then you flip the meat only once before you serve it, you're messing with the heat diffusion. There's such a huge difference between the temperatures on the side that's facing the fire and the side that's turned away that the heat inside your steak fluxes all over the place. (This applies only to beef.)

"But," McGee says, "the computer model shows that if you keep flipping the meat as you cook it, the heat diffuses through the meat much more evenly, so it cooks much more evenly. Our study suggests that the optimum flipping time is every 15 seconds."

Every 15 seconds? "Maybe that's a little extreme; it might be inconvenient," McGee says, laughing. "The computer model shows that flipping the meat every 30 seconds will work almost as well." And another recent study, at Lawrence Livermore National Laboratory, shows that frequent flipping makes steaks more healthful, too: It reduces the amount of carcinogenic compounds that can be generated when you cook over high heat by as much as 75 percent.

DANIEL ZWERDLING,
Senior Correspondent with
National Public Radio
This sidebar originally appeared
in *Gourmet Magazine*.

Table 14.1 USING COMMON CUTS OF BEEF

PRIMAL	SUBPRIMAL OR FABRICATED CUT	IMPS	COOKING METHODS	SERVING SUGGESTIONS
Chuck	Chuck roll tied	116A	Combination (braise; stew)	Pot roast; beef stew
	Stew meat	135A	Combination (stew)	Beef stew
	Ground beef	136	Dry heat (broil or grill; roast) Combination (braise; stew)	Hamburgers; meatloaf Chili con carne; beef stews
Brisket and shank	Brisket	120	Moist heat (simmer) Combination (braise)	Corned beef; New England boiled dinner Pot roast
	Shank	117	Combination (braise)	Shredded beef for tamales or hash
Rib	Oven-ready rib roast	109	Dry heat (roast)	Roast prime rib
	Rib eye roll	112	Dry heat (roast)	Roast prime rib
Short plate	Skirt steak	121D	Dry heat (broil or grill)	Steak; fajitas
	Short ribs	123A	Combination (braise)	Braised short ribs
Short loin	Porterhouse or T-bone steaks	173, 174	Dry heat (broil or grill)	Steaks
	Strip loin	180	Dry heat (broil or grill; roast; sauté)	New York steak; minute steak; entrecôtes bordelaise
	Tenderloin	189	Dry heat (broil or grill; roast)	Tournedos Rossini; beef Wellington
Flank	Flank steak	193	Dry heat (broil or grill) Combination (braise)	London broil Braised stuffed flank steak
Round	Steamship round	160	Dry heat (roast)	Roast beef
	Top (inside) round	168	Dry heat (roast) Combination (braise)	Roast beef Braised beef roulade

CONCLUSION

Antonin Carême once said that "beef is the soul of cooking." It is also the most popular meat consumed in the United States and undoubtedly will play an important role on almost any menu. Beef's assertive flavor stands up well to most any sauce and seasonings.

Prefabricated products are readily available. But performing some basic fabrication procedures in your own kitchen saves money and allows you to cut the meat to your exact specifications. Each primal and subprimal cut has its own distinct characteristics. The primal rib, short loin and sirloin produce the most popular and most expensive cuts of beef. Once the beef is properly fabricated, choose the appropriate dry-heat, moist-heat or combination cooking method for that cut.

QUESTIONS FOR DISCUSSION

1 List each beef primal cut and describe its location on the carcass. For each primal cut, identify two subprimal or fabricated cuts taken from it.

2 Would it be better to use the chuck for grilling or stewing? Explain your answer.

3 Which fabricated cuts contain a portion of the tenderloin? What cooking methods are best suited for these cuts? Explain your answer.

4 Most steaks are cut from the hindquarter. What popular steak is cut from the forequarter, and why is it tender when other cuts from the forequarter are relatively tough?

5 Visit the National Cattleman's Beef Association Web site to learn more. Does cooking method affect the fat and cholesterol content of a beef steak? How has consumer demand for beef products changed over the past year?

6 Locate one or two restaurants in your area that participate in the Certified Angus Beef program.

FILET OF BEEF WITH COFFEE BEANS

Note: This dish appears in the chapter opening photograph.

CAFÉ ANNIE, HOUSTON, TX
Chef-Owner Robert Del Grande
Executive Chef Ben Berryhill

Yield: 6 Servings   **Method:** Roasting

Beef tenderloin	1	1
Kosher salt	1 tsp.	5 ml
Black pepper	1 tsp.	5 ml
Virgin olive oil	2 Tbsp.	30 ml
Coffee beans, ground very fine	2 Tbsp.	30 ml
Cocoa powder	1 Tbsp.	15 ml
Cinnamon, ground	1/8 tsp.	0.5 ml
Pasilla chile broth:		
Whole butter	1/2 oz.	15 g
White onions, roughly chopped	8 oz.	240 g
Garlic cloves, whole, peeled	6	6
Pasilla chiles, stemmed, seeded,		
torn into large pieces	1/2 oz.	15 g
White corn tortilla, shredded	3/4 oz.	22 g
Chicken stock	20 fl. oz.	575 ml
Heavy cream	2 fl. oz.	60 ml
Kosher salt	1 tsp.	5 ml
Brown sugar	1 tsp.	5 ml
Creamy white grits with bitter greens:		
Water	1 qt.	1 lt
Salt	1 1/2 tsp.	8 ml
White grits, coarse	1 1/4 c.	300 ml
Yellow onions, minced	6 oz.	180 g
Garlic cloves, minced	2	2
Whole butter	1/2 oz.	15 g
Arugula (or other bitter greens),		
roughly chopped	4 oz.	120 g
Cilantro sprigs	as needed for garnish	

CHEF ROBERT DEL GRANDE

In 1981, armed with his freshly minted Ph.D. in biochemistry from the University of California at Riverside, Robert Del Grande followed Mimi Kinsman (now Mimi Del Grande) to Houston, where Mimi was visiting her sister and brother-in-law, Candice and Lonnie Schiller. There, he began experimenting in the kitchen of the Schiller's restaurant, Café Annie. Robert remained in Houston and soon became the executive chef of Café Annie.

Café Annie is a fine dining restaurant serving innovative regional cuisine. Under Chef Robert's guidance, Café Annie has won virtually every culinary award: the James Beard, Fine Dining Hall of Fame, DiRoNA and Gourmet magazine's Best of City, among others. Chef Robert has cooked with Julia Child and for President Bush at the economic summit, and has been featured in many national and regional magazines. He has contributed indelibly to what has come to be known as "Southwestern Cuisine."

The Del Grandes and the Schillers also own and operate Café Express, an innovative chain of sophisticated cafes offering "Good Food Fast," and Taco Milagro, which offers patrons Chef Robert's vision of Mexican cuisine.

1 Trim the beef tenderloin, removing all silverskin. Cut a 2- to 2-pound-8-ounce (0.9- to 1.1-kilogram) piece from the large (butt) end of the tenderloin. Tie this filet with butchers twine at 1/2-inch (1.2-centimeter) intervals. Rub the filet with salt and pepper, then rub it with the oil.

2 Stir together the ground coffee, cocoa powder and cinnamon. Spread the mixture on a work surface and roll the filet in it in order to coat the beef evenly. Allow the beef to marinate for approximately 30 minutes.

3 To prepare the pasilla chile broth, heat a medium saucepan over medium-high heat. Add the butter and sauté the onions and garlic until browned. Add the pasilla chiles and tortilla pieces and sauté until golden brown.

4 Add the chicken stock and bring to a boil. Reduce to a simmer, cover loosely and cook for 10 minutes. Remove from the heat and cool. Purée the sauce in a blender until smooth and strain through a china cap. Add the cream, salt

and brown sugar and stir to combine. The sauce should not be very thick; thin it with additional chicken stock or water if necessary. Hold for service.

5 To prepare the grits and greens, bring the water to a boil in a heavy-bottomed saucepot. Add the salt and stir in the grits. Cover the pot and simmer gently, stirring every 2 to 3 minutes until the water is absorbed and the grits are tender, approximately 20 minutes.

6 In a separate pan, sauté the onions and garlic in the butter until the onions are translucent. Add the greens, sauté just until wilted, then remove from the pan.

7 Place the filet on a rack in a roasting pan. Roast the filet at 400°F (200°C) for 10 minutes. Lower the heat to 250°F (120°C) and cook the beef to the desired doneness, approximately 20 minutes for medium rare. Remove from the oven, remove the twine and allow to rest before carving.

8 To serve, stir the greens into the grits. Spoon grits into the center of each plate. Ladle a portion of the pasilla sauce around the grits. Slice the filet to the desired thickness and serve one thick slice or several thin slices fanned on each plate. Garnish with cilantro sprigs.

Approximate values per serving: **Calories** 560, **Total fat** 26 g, **Saturated fat** 10 g, **Cholesterol** 130 mg, **Sodium** 1740 mg, **Total carbohydrates** 41 g, **Protein** 41 g, **Vitamin A** 30%, **Vitamin C** 15%, **Iron** 40%

RECIPE 14.2   MARINATED LONDON BROIL

Yield: 6 Servings, 5–8 oz. (150–250 g) each		**Method:** Grilling
Marinade:		
Olive oil	4 fl. oz.	120 ml
Balsamic vinegar	4 fl. oz.	120 ml
Fresh rosemary, chopped	2 Tbsp.	30 ml
Garlic, minced	2 oz.	60 g
Black pepper	1 tsp.	5 ml
Beef flank steak, 2–3 lb. (1–1½ kg)	1	1

1 Combine the marinade ingredients in a hotel pan.

2 Add the flank steak to the marinade and coat completely. Allow the meat to marinate for at least 4 hours.

3 Grill the steak rare to medium rare. If cooked further, the meat will become extremely tough.

4 Carve into ¼-inch- (6-millimeter-) thick slices, cutting diagonally across the grain.

Approximate values per 8-oz. (240-g) serving: **Calories** 470, **Total fat** 23 g, **Saturated fat** 10 g, **Cholesterol** 152 mg, **Sodium** 188 mg, **Total carbohydrates** 0 g, **Protein** 61 g, **Iron** 40%

RECIPE 14.3   FILET STANLEY

BRENNAN'S RESTAURANT, NEW ORLEANS, LA
Chef Michael Roussel

Yield: 8 Servings		**Method:** Grilling
Beef filets, 8 oz. (225 g) each, halved horizontally	8	8
Salt and pepper	TT	TT
Butter	4 oz.	120 g
Bananas, sliced in half lengthwise	8	8
Holland rusks	16	16
Horseradish Cream Sauce (page 235)	4 fl. oz.	120 ml
Brennan's Red-Wine and Mushroom Sauce (page 233)	1 pt.	450 ml

1 Sprinkle the beef filets with salt and pepper and grill until done as desired.

2 In a large skillet, melt the butter and sauté the bananas until tender and lightly browned, approximately 4 minutes per side.

3 To serve, arrange two Holland rusks each in the center of eight warm plates. Arrange a slice of banana on either side of the rusks near the edge of the plate. Spoon Horseradish Cream Sauce between the bananas and the rusks.

4 Place a piece of cooked filet on each rusk and top with Red-Wine and Mushroom Sauce.

Approximate values per serving: **Calories** 840, **Total fat** 46 g, **Saturated fat** 23 g, **Cholesterol** 235 mg, **Sodium** 380 mg, **Total carbohydrates** 53 g, **Protein** 54 g, **Vitamin A** 70%, **Vitamin C** 40%, **Iron** 45%

CHÂTEAUBRIAND　　　　　　　　　　　　　　　　RECIPE 14.4

CHEF LELAND ATKINSON, WASHINGTON, DC

French chefs of the late 19th century began referring to the classic filet de boeuf *(a very thick steak cut from the best part of the filet) as Châteaubriand in reference to the 19th century statesman and author of the same name. The dish is traditionally served with béarnaise sauce, a bouquetière of vegetables and château potatoes.*

Yield: 2 Servings　　　　　　　　　　**Method:** Roasting

Beef filet, cut from the large (head) end of the tenderloin, 16–24 oz. (500–750 g)	1	1
Salt and pepper	TT	TT
Clarified butter	as needed	as needed

1 Tie the beef with butcher's twine and season with salt and pepper.

2 Sauté the beef in clarified butter until it is well browned.

3 Transfer the beef to a 450°F (230°C) oven and roast until done, approximately 10–12 minutes for rare (internal temperature of 125°F/52°C), or 15–18 minutes for medium (140°F/60°C).

4 Remove the beef from the oven and allow it to rest for at least 5 minutes before carving.

5 At service time, slice the beef evenly on a slight diagonal bias.

Approximate values per 10-oz. (300-g) serving: **Calories** 705, **Total fat** 40 g, **Saturated fat** 18 g, **Cholesterol** 270 mg, **Sodium** 1350 mg, **Total carbohydrates** 1 g, **Protein** 80 g, **Vitamin A** 13%, **Iron** 66%

BEEF WELLINGTON　　　　　　　　　　　　　　RECIPE 14.5

Yield: 10 Servings　　　　　　　　　　**Method:** Roasting

Beef tenderloin, trimmed, 4 to 4 lb. 8 oz. (1.8 to 2 kg)	1	1
Salt and pepper	TT	TT
Vegetable oil	as needed	as needed
Pâté de foie gras	8 oz.	240 g
Truffle peelings, chopped fine	1 oz.	30 g
Puff pastry (page 1010)	2 lb.	1 kg
Egg wash	as needed	as needed
Madeira sauce (page 217)	20 fl. oz.	600 ml

1 Trim 3 to 4 inches (7.5 to 10 centimeters) of the tail from the tenderloin. (The small tail portion can be used for some other preparation.) Season the tenderloin with salt and pepper and sear in a small amount of vegetable oil in a large rondeau. Remove from the pan and cool.

2 Spread the surface of the tenderloin with the pâté de foie gras. Sprinkle the truffles over the pâté.

3 Roll the puff pastry dough into a rectangle approximately 3/16 inch (5 millimeters) thick and large enough to wrap around the entire tenderloin.

4 Turn the tenderloin over and place it lengthwise, pâté side down, in the center of the pastry. Fold the ends over and wrap the pastry around the tenderloin, sealing it with egg wash and trimming off any excess.

5 Transfer the Wellington to a baking sheet, placing the seam side down. Brush the surface with egg wash.

6 Bake the Wellington in a 350°F (180°C) oven until the center reaches 125°F–130°F (52°C–54°C), approximately 40 minutes. Do not overcook; the crust holds in steam and heat, thus enhancing the effects of carryover cooking.

7 Carve the Wellington tableside or on a buffet with Madeira sauce served on the side.

Variation: Individual Wellingtons can be made by cutting the tenderloin into 4- to 5-ounce (120- to 150-gram) filet mignons, using smaller pieces of puff pastry and reducing the cooking time to approximately 20 minutes.

Approximate values per serving: **Calories** 720, **Total fat** 44 g, **Saturated fat** 14 g, **Cholesterol** 160 mg, **Sodium** 700 mg, **Total carbohydrates** 29 g, **Protein** 48 g, **Vitamin A** 15%, **Iron** 40%

RECIPE 14.6   HOME-STYLE MEATLOAF

Yield: 16 Servings, 8 oz. (250 g) each   **Method:** Baking

Onions, small dice	1 lb.	450 g
Celery, small dice	8 oz.	250 g
Garlic, chopped	2 Tbsp.	30 ml
Vegetable oil	2 fl. oz.	60 ml
Fresh bread crumbs	6 oz.	180 g
Tomato juice	1 pt.	450 ml
Ground beef	4 lb.	1.8 kg
Ground pork	4 lb.	1.8 kg
Eggs, beaten	4	4
Salt	4 tsp.	20 ml
Black pepper	1 Tbsp.	15 ml
Parsley, chopped	4 Tbsp.	60 ml
Worcestershire sauce	3 Tbsp.	45 ml
Ketchup	as needed	as needed

1 Sauté the onions, celery and garlic in the oil until tender. Remove from the heat and cool.

2 Combine all the ingredients except the ketchup and mix well.

3 Form into loaves of the desired size and place in loaf pans.

4 Brush the top of each loaf with ketchup as desired. Bake at 350°F (180°C) until the meatloaf reaches an internal temperature of 165°F (74°C), approximately 40 minutes for a 9-inch × 5-inch (22-centimeter × 12-centimeter) loaf pan.

5 Allow the loaves to rest for 15 minutes before slicing. Cut slices of the desired thickness and serve with a tomato or mushroom sauce.

Approximate values per serving: **Calories** 590, **Total fat** 38 g, **Saturated fat** 13 g, **Cholesterol** 255 mg, **Sodium** 920 mg, **Total carbohydrates** 11 g, **Protein** 48 g, **Vitamin C** 20%, **Iron** 25%

SALISBURY STEAK

RECIPE 14.7

THE SCHOOL OF CULINARY ARTS AT KENDALL COLLEGE, EVANSTON, IL
Chef Mike Artlip, CEC, CCE

Yield: 40 Servings, 5 oz. (150 g) each   **Method:** Baking

Mirepoix, minced	5 lb. 4 oz.	2.5 kg
Olive oil	7 fl. oz.	210 ml
Dried thyme	1 tsp.	5 ml
Dried marjoram	5 tsp.	25 ml
Black pepper	1½ tsp.	8 ml
Salt	TT	TT
Cornflake crumbs	10½ oz.	315 g
Eggs, beaten	7	7
Worcestershire sauce	4 tsp.	20 ml
Milk	5 fl. oz.	150 ml
Ground beef	13 lb. 4 oz.	6.3 kg
Mushroom sauce (page 217)	as needed	as needed

1 Sauté the mirepoix in the olive oil until tender. Add the thyme, marjoram, pepper and salt. Remove from the pan, cool, and refrigerate until cold.
2 Combine the mirepoix with the cornflake crumbs, eggs, Worcestershire sauce and milk and mix well.
3 Add the beef, adjust the seasonings and mix well.
4 Make a small patty and cook it. Taste it to check the seasonings and adjust them if necessary.
5 Scale 40 5-ounce (150-gram) portions of the mixture. Alternatively, use a slightly rounded #8 scoop to portion the mixture. Form each portion into a flattened football-shaped patty and place on a baking sheet.
6 Bake the Salisbury steaks at 325°F (160°C) until done, approximately 10 to 15 minutes. Serve with mushroom sauce.

Approximate values per serving, without sauce: **Calories** 410, **Total fat** 25 g, **Saturated fat** 9 g, **Cholesterol** 135 mg, **Sodium** 180 mg, **Total carbohydrates** 12 g, **Protein** 32 g, **Vitamin A** 90%, **Vitamin C** 16%, **Calcium, Iron** 30%

TOURNEDOS ROSSINI

RECIPE 14.8

Yield: 4 Servings   **Method:** Sautéing

Tournedos, 3 oz. (90 g) each	8	8
Clarified butter	as needed	as needed
Croutons, cut to the size of the tournedos	8	8
Foie gras, 1-oz. (30-g) slices	8	8
Truffle slices	8	8
Madeira	4 fl. oz.	120 ml
Demi-glace	8 fl. oz.	250 ml
Salt and pepper	TT	TT

1. Sauté the tournedos in clarified butter to the desired doneness. Place each tournedo on top of a crouton. Top each with a slice of foie gras, then a slice of truffle. Hold in a warm place.

2. Degrease the pan. Deglaze the pan with the Madeira and add the demi-glace.

3. Reduce the sauce to the desired consistency and adjust the seasonings.

4. Warm the tournedos briefly under a broiler or in the oven. Pour the sauce around the tournedos. Garnish with watercress, sautéed asparagus and château potatoes.

Approximate values per serving: **Calories** 652, **Total fat** 29 g, **Saturated fat** 13 g, **Cholesterol** 460 mg, **Sodium** 860 mg, **Total carbohydrates** 36 g, **Protein** 60 g, **Vitamin A** 682%, **Iron** 164%

RECIPE 14.9

MINUTE STEAK DIJONAISE

Yield: 2 Servings   **Method:** Sautéing

Sirloin steaks, trimmed, 6 oz. (170 g)	2	2
Dijon mustard	1 oz.	30 g
Onions, small dice	2 oz.	60 g
Clarified butter	1 fl. oz.	30 ml
Heavy cream	3 fl. oz.	90 ml
Whole butter	1 oz.	30 g
Salt and pepper	TT	TT

1. Pound the steaks to a ¼-inch (6-millimeter) thickness.

2. Cover one side of each sirloin first with 1½ teaspoons (8 milliliters) of the mustard and then half of the onion, pressing the onion firmly into the steak.

3. Sauté the steaks in the clarified butter, presentation (onion) side down first. Remove and hold in a warm place.

4. Degrease the pan. Add the cream and reduce by half. Add the rest of the Dijon mustard.

5. Monté au beurre. Adjust the seasonings and serve the steaks with the sauce.

Approximate values per serving: **Calories** 671, **Total fat** 45 g, **Saturated fat** 23 g, **Cholesterol** 255 mg, **Sodium** 2050 mg, **Total carbohydrates** 6 g, **Protein** 60 g, **Vitamin A** 36%, **Iron** 44%

RECIPE 14.10

BEEF STROGANOFF

Yield: 8 Servings, 8 oz. (250 g) each   **Method:** Sautéing

Tenderloin tips, émincé	2 lb.	1 kg
Clarified butter	3 Tbsp.	45 ml
Onions, medium dice	4 oz.	120 g
Mushrooms, halved	1 lb.	450 g
Demi-glace	10 fl. oz.	300 ml
Heavy cream	10 fl. oz.	300 ml
Sour cream	8 oz.	250 g
Dijon mustard	1 Tbsp.	15 ml
Fresh dill, chopped	1 Tbsp.	15 ml
Fresh parsley, chopped	1 Tbsp.	15 ml
Salt and pepper	TT	TT
Egg noodles, cooked	24 oz.	700 g

1 Sauté the tenderloin tips in the butter, searing on all sides. Remove the meat and set aside.

2 Add the onions to the pan and sauté lightly. Add the mushrooms and sauté until dry.

3 Add the demi-glace. Bring to a boil, reduce to a simmer and cook for 10 minutes.

4 Add the cream, sour cream, mustard and any meat juices that accumulated while holding the meat.

5 Return the meat to the sauce to reheat. Stir in the dill and parsley. Adjust the seasonings and serve over hot egg noodles.

Approximate values per serving: **Calories** 635, **Total fat** 39 g, **Saturated fat** 20 g, **Cholesterol** 201 mg, **Sodium** 510 mg, **Total carbohydrates** 32 g, **Protein** 40 g, **Vitamin A** 41%, **Iron** 46%, **Calcium** 11%

ENTRECÔTES BORDELAISE
RECIPE 14.11

Yield: 4 Servings	**Method:** Sautéing	
Beef marrow	4 oz.	120 g
Entrecôtes, 14 oz. (400 g) each	2	2
Salt and pepper	TT	TT
Clarified butter	2 fl. oz.	60 ml
Shallots, chopped	2 Tbsp.	30 ml
Red wine	8 fl. oz.	250 ml
Demi-glace	12 fl. oz.	340 ml
Whole butter	1 oz.	30 g

1 Slice the marrow into rounds and poach in salt water for 3 minutes. Drain the marrow and set it aside.

2 Season the steaks and sauté them in the clarified butter to the desired doneness. Finish in the oven if desired. Remove to a platter and hold in a warm place.

3 Sauté the shallots in the same pan.

4 Deglaze the pan with the wine and reduce by half. Add the demi-glace; simmer for 5 minutes.

5 Monté au beurre.

6 Add the marrow to the sauce. Adjust the seasonings and serve the steaks with the sauce.

Approximate values per serving: **Calories** 610, **Total fat** 35 g, **Saturated fat** 17 g, **Cholesterol** 200 mg, **Sodium** 810 mg, **Total carbohydrates** 5 g, **Protein** 57 g, **Vitamin A** 21%, **Iron** 44%

PEPPER STEAK
RECIPE 14.12

Yield: 2 Servings	**Method:** Sautéing	
Boneless strip steaks, approx. 8 oz. (250 g) each	2	2
Salt	TT	TT
Peppercorns, cracked	3 Tbsp.	45 ml
Clarified butter	1 fl. oz.	30 ml
Cognac	2 fl. oz.	60 ml
Heavy cream	4 fl. oz.	120 ml
Whole butter	2 oz.	60 g

1 Season the steaks with salt. Spread the peppercorns in a hotel pan and press the steaks into them, lightly coating each side.

2 Sauté the steaks in the clarified butter over high heat for 2 to 3 minutes on each side.

1 Press the steaks into the peppercorns.

2 Flambé the cognac on the steaks.

3 Pour the finished sauce over each steak.

3 Remove the pan from the heat. Pour the cognac over the steaks, return the pan to the heat and flambé. When the flames subside, remove the steaks from the pan and keep them warm on a plate.

4 Add the cream to the pan. Bring to a boil and reduce for 2 minutes over high heat; monté au beurre. Pour this sauce over the steaks and serve immediately.

Approximate values per serving: **Calories** 950, **Total fat** 73 g, **Saturated fat** 42 g, **Cholesterol** 300 mg, **Sodium** 1525 mg, **Total carbohydrates** 8 g, **Protein** 51 g, **Vitamin A** 72%, **Iron** 46%, **Calcium** 13%

RECIPE 14.13   BEEF FAJITAS

Yield: 6 Servings   **Method:** Grilling/Sautéing

Marinade:		
Garlic cloves	4	4
Salt	1 ½ tsp.	8 ml
Black pepper, ground coarse	1 ½ tsp.	8 ml
Cumin	1 ½ tsp.	8 ml
Onion powder	1 ½ tsp.	8 ml
Chilli powder	1 ½ tsp.	8 ml
Skirt steak	2 lb.	900 g
Vegetable oil	2 Tbsp.	30 ml
Bell peppers, mixed, red, yellow and green, sliced thin	3	3
Onion, sliced thin	1	1
Garlic cloves, chopped	2	2
Cilantro sprigs	as needed for garnish	

1 Make the marinade by chopping and mashing the garlic into a paste. In a bowl, combine the garlic paste with the remaining marinade ingredients.

2 Trim the fat from the skirt steak. Cut the steak into two or three pieces if necessary. Add the steaks to the marinade, turning them several times to coat all sides. Cover the steak and marinate in the refrigerator for at least 1 hour or overnight.

3 Grill the steak on a hot grill to the desired doneness. Remove the steak and allow it to rest for 10 minutes.

4 Add the oil to a heavy sauté pan, heat the pan until very hot and sauté the peppers, onion and garlic just until they begin to soften.

5 Slice the steak against the grain into thin slices. Arrange the steak and pepper mixture on very hot cast-iron platters and garnish with the cilantro. The platters should be sizzling as they are presented to the table.

6 Serve the fajitas accompanied by warm flour or corn tortillas, fresh salsa, sour cream, and guacamole.

Approximate values per serving: **Calories** 630, **Total fat** 24 g, **Saturated fat** 7 g, **Cholesterol** 80 mg, **Sodium** 700 mg, **Total carbohydrates** 61 g, **Protein** 41 g, **Vitamin A** 25%, **Vitamin C** 170%, **Iron** 35%, **Claims**—good source of fiber, vitamins A and C and iron

SWISS STEAK

RECIPE 14.14

Yield: 10 Servings   **Method:** Braising

Beef bottom round steaks, 6 oz. (180 g) each	10	10
Flour	as needed for dredging	
Salt and pepper	TT	TT
Oil	2 fl. oz.	60 ml
Onions, small dice	1 lb.	450 g
Garlic cloves, crushed	3	3
Celery, diced	8 oz.	250 g
Flour	4 oz.	120 g
Brown stock	5 pt.	2.2 lt
Tomato purée	6 oz.	180 g
Sachet:		
Bay leaves	2	2
Dried thyme	1/2 tsp.	2 ml
Peppercorns, crushed	1/2 tsp.	2 ml
Parsley stems	8	8

1 Dredge the steaks in flour seasoned with salt and pepper.

2 Heat the oil in a roasting pan and brown the steaks well on both sides. Remove the steaks.

3 Add the onions, garlic and celery; sauté until tender.

4 Add the flour and cook to a brown roux.

5 Gradually add the brown stock, whisking until the sauce is thickened and smooth. Add the tomato purée and sachet.

6 Return the steaks to the braising pan, cover and cook in a 300°F (150°C) oven until tender, approximately 2 hours.

7 Remove the steaks from the sauce. Discard the sachet. Strain the sauce and adjust the seasonings. Serve the steaks with the sauce.

Approximate values per serving: **Calories** 601, **Total fat** 26 g, **Saturated fat** 7 g, **Cholesterol** 170 mg, **Sodium** 390 mg, **Total carbohydrates** 30 g, **Protein** 61 g, **Vitamin A** 49%, **Vitamin C** 12%, **Iron** 52%

RECIPE 14.15   BRAISED SHORT RIBS OF BEEF

Yield: 8 Servings, 8 oz. (230 g) each   **Method:** Braising

Flour	4 oz.	120 g
Salt	1 Tbsp.	15 ml
Black pepper	1 tsp.	5 ml
Dried rosemary	½ tsp.	2 ml
Short ribs of beef, cut in 2-in. (5-cm) portions	6 lb.	2.7 kg
Vegetable oil	1 fl. oz.	30 ml
Onions, chopped	6 oz.	170 g
Celery, chopped	4 oz.	120 g
Brown beef stock	24 fl. oz.	700 ml
Roux	as needed	as needed
Salt and pepper	TT	TT

1 Combine the flour, salt, pepper and rosemary. Dredge the ribs in the seasoned flour.

2 Heat the oil in a heavy brazier and brown the ribs well. Remove and hold in a warm place.

3 Add the onions and celery to the brazier and sauté lightly.

4 Return the ribs to the pan, add the stock and cook in a 300°F (150°C) oven until done, approximately 2½ hours.

5 Remove the ribs from the liquid and skim off the excess fat.

6 Bring the liquid to a boil on the stove top; thicken it with roux to the desired consistency and simmer for 15 minutes. Strain the sauce and adjust the seasonings. Return the ribs to the sauce and simmer for 5 minutes.

Approximate values per serving: **Calories** 1150, **Total fat** 70 g, **Saturated fat** 27 g, **Cholesterol** 320 mg, **Sodium** 1154 mg, **Total carbohydrates** 18 g, **Protein** 110 g, **Vitamin A** 18%, **Iron** 85%

RECIPE 14.16   HUNGARIAN GOULASH

Yield: 10 Servings, 8 oz. (250 g) each   **Method:** Stewing

Onions, medium dice	2 lb.	900 g
Lard or vegetable oil	2 fl. oz.	60 ml
Hungarian paprika	4 Tbsp.	60 ml
Garlic, chopped	1 Tbsp.	15 ml
Caraway seeds	½ tsp.	2 ml
Salt	TT	TT
Black pepper	½ tsp.	2 ml
White stock	1 qt.	1 lt
Tomato paste	4 oz.	120 g
Beef stew meat, cut in 1½-in. (4-cm) cubes	5 lb.	2.2 kg

1 Sauté the onions in the lard or oil, browning lightly.

2 Add the paprika, garlic, caraway seeds, salt and pepper; mix well.

3 Add the white stock and tomato paste. Bring to a boil, then reduce to a simmer.

4 Add the meat and continue simmering until the meat is very tender, approximately 1½ hours. Adjust the seasonings and serve.

Approximate values per 12-oz. (360-g) serving: **Calories** 645, **Total fat** 32 g, **Saturated fat** 12 g, **Cholesterol** 235 mg, **Sodium** 910 mg, **Total carbohydrates** 13 g, **Protein** 73 g, **Vitamin A** 28%, **Vitamin C** 20%, **Iron** 63%

BEEF BOURGUIGNON

Yield: 10 Servings, 8 oz. (250 g) each   **Method:** Stewing

Marinade:		
Garlic cloves, crushed	3	3
Onions, sliced	3	3
Carrots, sliced	2	2
Parsley stems	10	10
Bouquet garni:		
Carrot stick, 4 in. (10 cm)	1	1
Leek, split, 4-in. (10-cm) piece	1	1
Fresh thyme	1 sprig	1 sprig
Bay leaf	1	1
Peppercorns, crushed	10	10
Salt	TT	TT
Dry red wine, preferably Burgundy	26 fl. oz.	750 ml
Beef chuck, cubed for stew	4 lb.	1.8 kg
Vegetable oil	2 fl. oz.	60 ml
Flour	2 Tbsp.	30 ml
Tomato paste	1 Tbsp.	15 ml
Tomatoes, quartered	4	4
Brown stock	1 pt.	450 ml
Mushrooms, quartered	1 lb.	450 g
Unsalted butter	1½ oz.	45 g
Pearl onions, boiled and peeled	30	30
Salt and pepper	TT	TT

1 Combine the garlic, onions, carrots, parsley, bouquet garni, peppercorns, salt and wine to make a marinade.

2 Marinate the meat for several hours under refrigeration.

3 Remove and drain the meat. Reserve the marinade.

4 Dry the beef and sauté it in the oil until well browned. Do this in several batches if necessary.

5 Return all the meat to the pot. Sprinkle with flour and cook to make a blond roux.

6 Stir in the tomato paste and cook for 5 minutes.

7 Add the reserved marinade, tomatoes and brown stock. Cook in a 350°F (180°C) oven until the meat is tender, approximately 2½ hours.

8 Remove the meat from the sauce. Strain the sauce through a china cap, pressing to extract all the liquid. Discard the solids. Return the liquid and the beef to the pot.

9 Sauté the mushrooms in the butter and add them to the meat and sauce. Add the pearl onions and adjust the seasonings. Simmer for 10 minutes to blend the flavors.

Approximate values per serving: **Calories** 315, **Total fat** 15 g, **Saturated fat** 6.5 g, **Cholesterol** 97 mg, **Sodium** 640 mg, **Total carbohydrates** 8 g, **Protein** 30 g, **Vitamin A** 27%, **Vitamin C** 13%, **Iron** 26%

CHILI CON CARNE

Yield: 5 qt. (5 lt)   **Method:** Stewing

Onions, medium dice	1 lb.	450 g
Vegetable oil	1 Tbsp.	15 ml
Garlic, chopped	2 oz.	60 g

Continued

Ground beef	2 lb. 8 oz.	1.2 kg
Tomatoes, crushed	3 lb.	1.5 kg
Tomatoes, diced	4 lb.	1.8 kg
Brown stock	1 qt.	1 lt
Chilli powder	1 oz.	30 g
Cumin	2 tsp.	10 ml
Bay leaves	4	4
Worcestershire sauce	3 Tbsp.	45 ml
Green chiles, diced	8 oz.	250 g
Salt and pepper	TT	TT

1 Sauté the onions in the oil until tender. Add the garlic and sauté for 1 minute.

2 Add the beef and brown, stirring occasionally. Drain off the excess fat.

3 Add the remaining ingredients, bring to a simmer, cover and cook for 1 hour.

4 Remove the bay leaves and adjust the seasonings.

Variation: *Chili with Beans*—Before the final adjustment of seasonings, stir in 12 ounces (340 grams) of dried red kidney beans that have been soaked, simmered until tender and drained.

Approximate values per 1½-c. (360-ml) serving: **Calories** 290, **Total fat** 13 g, **Saturated fat** 5 g, **Cholesterol** 55 mg, **Sodium** 690 mg, **Total carbohydrates** 23 g, **Protein** 22 g, **Vitamin A** 80%, **Vitamin C** 50%, **Calcium** 10%, **Iron** 25%, **Claims**—good source of fiber, vitamins A and C, iron and calcium

---

RECIPE 14.19 **TEXAS CHILI AND BEANS**

NEWBURY COLLEGE, Brookline, MA
Senior Instructor Scott Doughty

Yield: 1 gal. (4 lt) **Method:** Stewing

Vegetable oil or lard	3 fl. oz.	90 ml
Beef stew meat, medium dice	4 lb.	1.8 kg
Onions, medium dice	1 lb.	450 g
Garlic cloves, chopped	10	10
Chicken stock	2 qt.	2 lt
Tomato sauce, canned	1 pt.	450 ml
Anaheim chile, small dice	10 oz.	300 g
Salt	¾ tsp.	4 ml
Black pepper	½ tsp.	3 ml
Chilli powder	5 Tbsp.	75 ml
Cayenne pepper	½ tsp.	3 ml
Dried oregano	½ tsp.	3 ml
Cumin, ground	4 tsp.	20 ml
Masa harina or cornmeal	½ c.	120 ml
Pinto Beans (recipe follows)	as needed	as needed

1 Heat a rondeau over medium heat and add the oil. Add the meat, onions and garlic. Cook, stirring, until the meat has lost its raw look and is cooking in its own juices.

2 Add 1 quart (1 liter) of the chicken stock, the tomato sauce, Anaheim chiles, salt, black pepper, chilli powder, cayenne pepper, oregano and cumin. Simmer the chili for 2 hours, skimming the fat and scum occasionally.

3 Make a slurry with the masa harina and 8 fluid ounces (240 milliliters) of cold chicken stock. Stir the slurry into the chili. Continue to cook until the meat is very tender, stirring occasionally to prevent it from scorching. Adjust the sea-

soning with salt, black pepper, chilli powder, cayenne pepper, oregano or ground cumin to taste. Thin the chili with additional chicken stock if desired.

4 Cooked pinto beans can be added to the chili or served separately.

Approximate values per 8-fl.-oz. (240-ml) serving: **Calories** 270, **Total fat** 14 g, **Saturated fat** 4 g, **Cholesterol** 70 mg, **Sodium** 710 mg, **Total carbohydrates** 12 g, **Protein** 24 g, **Vitamin A** 25%, **Vitamin C** 90%, **Iron** 20%

PINTO BEANS

Yield: 1 qt. (2 lt)

Pinto beans, dry	1 lb.	450 g
Water, cold	as needed	as needed
Jalapeño pepper	1	1
Onions, minced	6 oz.	180 g
Salt	1 1/2 tsp.	8 ml

1 Soak the pinto beans in water for several hours and then drain them. Put them in a saucepan and add enough cold water to cover them thoroughly. Pierce the jalapeño several times with a paring knife and add it to the beans. Bring the beans to a boil, add the onions, cover and reduce to a simmer.

2 Adding enough water to keep the beans barely covered, allow the beans to simmer until they are tender but not mushy, approximately 45 minutes. When the beans are nearly done, allow the liquid to reduce slightly and thicken into a sauce.

3 Season the beans to taste with salt and discard the jalapeño.

Approximate values per 4-fl.-oz. (120-ml) serving: **Calories** 190, **Total fat** 0.5 g, **Saturated fat** 0, **Cholesterol** 0, **Sodium** 440 mg, **Total carbohydrates** 36 g, **Protein** 11 g, **Iron** 20%, **Claims**—low fat, no saturated fat, no cholesterol, high in fiber, high in iron

CARPACCIO

RECIPE 14.20

Yield: 8 Servings

Beef tenderloin, trimmed of all silverskin and fat	1 lb.	450 g
Mayonnaise, fresh	8 oz.	250 g
Dijon mustard	1 Tbsp.	15 ml
Salt and pepper	TT	TT
Onions, sliced thin	4 oz.	120 g
Capers, chopped	4 tsp.	20 ml
Cracked black pepper	TT	TT
Olive oil	3 Tbsp.	45 ml

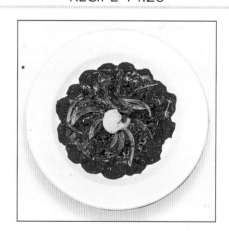

1 Place the tenderloin in the freezer until nearly frozen.

2 Combine the fresh mayonnaise with the mustard. Season with salt and pepper.

3 Slice the nearly frozen tenderloin on an electric slicer very thin, almost transparent. On a very cold plate, arrange one slightly overlapping layer of thin slices of beef.

4 Sprinkle each plate of beef with 1/2 teaspoon (2.5 milliliters) of capers, a generous amount of cracked black pepper, salt and 1/2 ounce (15 grams) of sliced onions. Drizzle with 1 teaspoon (5 milliliters) of the olive oil and spoon 1/2 ounce (15 grams) of the mayonnaise in the center of each plate. Serve very cold.

Approximate values per 4-oz. (120-g) serving: **Calories** 360, **Total fat** 33 g, **Saturated fat** 7 g, **Cholesterol** 70 mg, **Sodium** 250 mg, **Total carbohydrates** 1 g, **Protein** 16 g

Happy and successful cooking doesn't rely only on know-how; it comes from the heart, makes great demands on the palate and needs enthusiasm and a deep love of food to bring it to life.

—*Georges Blanc, French chef in* Ma Cuisine des Saisons, 1984

VEAL

BROWN PALACE, Denver, CO
Mark Black, Executive Chef

AFTER STUDYING THIS
CHAPTER, YOU WILL BE
ABLE TO:

▶ identify the primal, subprimal
and fabricated cuts of veal

▶ perform basic butchering
procedures

▶ apply appropriate cooking
methods to several common
cuts of veal

Veal is the meat of young, usually male, calves that are by-products of the dairy industry. Dairy cows must calve before they begin to give milk. Calves that aren't used in the dairy herds are used in today's veal industry. Although veal may come from any calf under the age of nine months, most comes from calves slaughtered when they are 8 to 16 weeks old. Veal is lighter in color than beef, has a more delicate flavor and is generally more tender. Young veal has a firm texture, light pink color and very little fat. As soon as a calf starts eating solid food, the iron in the food begins to turn the young animal's meat red. Meat from calves slaughtered when they are older than five months is called calf. It tends to be a deeper red, with some marbling and external fat.

Veal's mild flavor and low fat content makes it a popular meat, especially among those looking for an alternative to beef. Its delicate flavor is complemented by both classic and modern sauces.

▶ PRIMAL AND SUBPRIMAL CUTS OF VEAL

After slaughter, the calf carcass can be split down the backbone into two bilateral halves or, more typically, cut along the natural curvature between the 11th and 12th ribs into a foresaddle (front portion) and a hindsaddle (rear portion). The veal carcass yields five primal cuts: three from the foresaddle (the shoulder, foreshank and breast, and rib), and two from the hindsaddle (the loin and leg). The veal shoulder, rib and loin primals contain both bilateral portions; that is, a veal loin contains both sides of the animal's loin.

Figure 15.1 shows the relationship between the calf's bone structure and the primal cuts. As with all meats, it is important to know the location of bones when cutting or working with veal. This makes meat fabrication and carving easier and aids in identifying cuts. Figure 15.2 shows the primal cuts of veal and their location. A veal carcass weighs in a range of 60 to 245 pounds (27 to 110 kg).

FORESADDLE

SHOULDER

Similar to the beef shoulder or chuck, the veal shoulder accounts for 21 percent of the carcass weight. It contains four rib bones (as opposed to five in the beef chuck) and portions of the backbone, blade and arm bones.

The backbone, blade and arm bones are sometimes removed and the meat roasted or stuffed and roasted. Although shoulder chops and steaks can be fabricated, they are inferior to the chops cut from more tender areas such as the loin or rib. Often the shoulder meat is ground or cubed for stew. Because of the relatively large amount of connective tissue it contains, meat from the shoulder is best braised or stewed.

FORESHANK AND BREAST

The foreshank and breast are located beneath the shoulder and rib sections on the front half of the carcass. They are considered one primal cut. Combined, they account for approximately 16 percent of the carcass weight. This primal

FORMULA-FED VEAL VERSUS FREE-RANGE VEAL

Most veal produced today is known as formula-fed veal. Formula-fed calves are fed only nutrient-rich liquids; they are tethered in pens only slightly larger than their bodies in order to restrict their movements. Preventing the calves from eating grasses and other foods containing iron keeps their flesh white; restricting movement keeps their muscles from toughening. In recent years, controversy and allegations of cruelty have arisen concerning these methods.

An alternative to formula-fed veal is free-range veal. Free-range veal is produced from calves that are allowed to roam freely and eat grasses and other natural foods. Because they consume feed containing iron, their flesh is a reddish pink and has a substantially different flavor than meat from formula-fed calves of the same age.

Opinions differ on which has the better flavor. Some chefs prefer the consistently mild,

sweet taste of formula-fed veal. Others prefer the more substantial flavor of free-range veal. The two are interchangeable in recipes. Cost, however, may be the ultimate deciding factor when determining which to use. Free-range veal is more expensive than formula-fed veal because of its limited production.

contains rib bones and rib cartilage, breast bones and shank bones. Because the calf is slaughtered young, many of the breast bones are cartilaginous rather than bony.

This cartilage, as well as the ample fat and connective tissue also present in the breast, breaks down during long moist cooking, thus making the flavorful breast a good choice for braising. Veal breast can also be cubed for stews such as veal fricassee and veal blanquette, rolled and stuffed, or trimmed and ground.

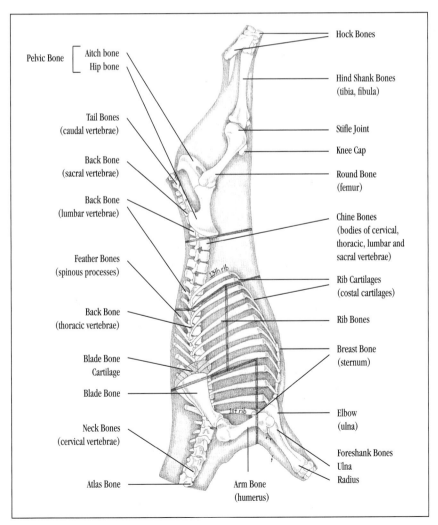

FIGURE 15.1 ▶ The skeletal structure of a calf

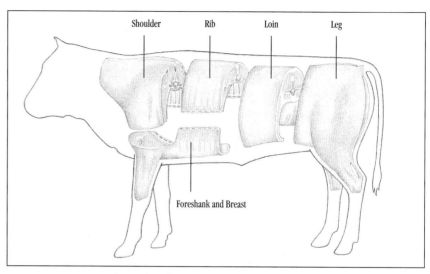

FIGURE 15.2 ▶ **The primal cuts of veal**

The foreshank is also very flavorful but tough. It can be braised whole or sliced perpendicular to the shank bone and braised to produce osso buco.

RIB

The double rib, also known as a veal hotel rack, is a very tender, relatively small cut accounting for approximately 9 percent of the carcass weight. It is very popular and very expensive. The double rack consists of two racks, each with seven rib bones and a portion of the backbone. Veal racks can be roasted either whole or split into two sides. Veal racks can be boned out; each side produces a veal rib eye and a small piece of tenderloin known as the short tenderloin, both of which make excellent roasts. More often, veal racks are trimmed and cut into chops, which can also be bone-in or boneless, to be grilled, sautéed or braised.

HINDSADDLE

LOIN

The veal loin is posterior to the primal rib, contains two ribs (numbers 12 and 13) and accounts for approximately 10 percent of the carcass weight. The loin consists of the loin eye muscle on top of the rib bones and the tenderloin under them.

The veal loin eye is very tender, and the tenderloin is, without a doubt, the most tender cut of veal. If the primal veal loin is separated from the primal leg before the tenderloin is removed, the tenderloin will be cut into two pieces. The small portion (short tenderloin) remains in the primal loin, and the large portion (butt tenderloin) remains in the sirloin portion of the primal leg. The tenderloin is sometimes removed and cut into medallions. The veal

Veal Hotel Rack, Split

Veal Loin

Loin Chops

Boneless Strip Loin

loin is often cut into chops, bone-in or boneless. It is usually cooked using dry-heat methods such as broiling, grilling, roasting or sautéing.

LEG

The primal veal leg consists of both the sirloin and the leg. Together, they account for approximately 42 percent of the carcass weight. The primal leg is separated from the loin by a cut perpendicular to the backbone immediately anterior to the hip bone, and it contains portions of the backbone, tail bone, hip bone, aitch bone, round bone and hind shank.

Veal Leg

Although it is tender enough to be roasted whole, the veal leg is typically fabricated into cutlets and scallops. To fabricate these cuts, the leg is first broken down into its major muscles: the top round, eye round, knuckle, sirloin, bottom round (which includes the sirloin) and butt tenderloin. Each of these muscles can be reduced to scallops by trimming all fat and visible connective tissue and slicing against the grain to the desired thickness. The scallops then should be pounded carefully to tenderize them further and to prevent them from curling when cooked.

The hindshank is somewhat meatier than the foreshank, but both are prepared and cooked in the same manner.

Because the veal carcass is small enough to be handled easily, it is sometimes purchased in forms larger than the primal cuts described earlier. Depending on employee skill, available equipment and storage space and an ability to utilize fully all the cuts and trimmings that fabricating meat produces, you may want to purchase veal in one of the following forms:

Top Round

▶ *Foresaddle:* The anterior (front) portion of the carcass after it is severed from the hindsaddle by a cut following the natural curvature between the 11th and 12th ribs. It contains the primal shoulder, foreshank and breast, and rib.

▶ *Hindsaddle:* The posterior portion of the carcass after it is severed from the foresaddle. It contains the primal loin and leg.

▶ *Back:* The trimmed rib and loin sections in one piece. The back is particularly useful when producing large quantities of veal chops.

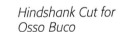

Hindshank Cut for Osso Buco

▶ *Veal side:* One bilateral half of the carcass, produced by cutting lengthwise through the backbone.

ORGAN MEATS

Several calf organ meats are used in food service operations.

Sweetbreads

SWEETBREADS

Sweetbreads are the thymus glands of veal (Fr. *ris de veau*) and lamb (*ris d'agneau*). As an animal ages, its thymus gland shrinks; therefore, sweetbreads are not available from older cattle or sheep. Veal sweetbreads are much more popular than lamb sweetbreads in this country. Good-quality sweetbreads should be plump and firm, with the exterior membrane intact. Delicately flavored and tender, they can be prepared by almost any cooking method.

CALVES' LIVER

Calves' liver is much more popular than beef liver because of its tenderness and mild flavor. Good-quality calves' liver should be firm and moist, with a

Calves' Liver

shiny appearance and without any off-odor. It is most often sliced and sautéed or broiled and served with a sauce.

KIDNEYS

Kidneys are more popular in other parts of the world than in the United States. Good-quality kidneys should be plump, firm and encased in a shiny membrane. Properly prepared kidneys have a rich flavor and firm texture; they are best prepared by moist-heat cooking methods and are sometimes used in stew or kidney pie.

Kidneys

▶ BUTCHERING PROCEDURES

Many food service operations purchase veal in primal or other large cuts and fabricate it in-house to their own specifications. There are several important veal fabrication and butchering techniques you should master.

▶ PROCEDURE FOR BONING A LEG OF VEAL

1 Remove the shank by cutting through the knee joint. Remove the excess fat and flank meat.

2 Remove the butt tenderloin from the inside of the pelvic bone.

3 Remove the pelvic bone by carefully cutting around the bone, separating it from the meat. Continue until the bone is completely freed from the meat.

4 With the inside of the leg up, remove the top round by cutting along the natural seam.

5 Remove the shank meat. (It is the round piece of meat lying between the eye round and the bone, on the shank end of the leg.)

6 Remove the round bone and the knuckle together by cutting around the bone and through the natural seams separating the knuckle from the other muscles. Separate the knuckle meat from the bone.

7 Remove the sirloin.

8 Remove the eye round from the bottom round.

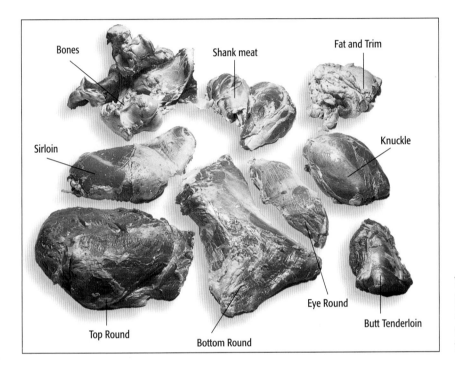

Bones

Shank meat

Fat and Trim

Knuckle

Sirloin

Eye Round

Butt Tenderloin

Top Round

Bottom Round

The completely boned-out veal leg, producing a top round, eye round, knuckle, shank meat, butt tenderloin, sirloin, bottom round bones and trimmings.

► PROCEDURE FOR CUTTING AND POUNDING SCALLOPS

1 Veal scallops are cut from relatively large pieces of veal (here, a portion of the top round). All fat and silverskin must be trimmed. Going against the grain, cut slices approximately ¼ inch (3 millimeters) thick; cut on the bias to produce larger pieces.

2 Place the scallops between two pieces of plastic wrap and pound lightly with a spreading motion to flatten and tenderize the meat. Be careful not to tear or pound holes in the meat.

▶ PROCEDURE FOR CUTTING ÉMINCÉ

1 Émincé is cut from relatively small, lean pieces of meat. Here veal is cut across the grain into small, thin slices.

▶ PROCEDURE FOR BONING A VEAL LOIN AND CUTTING IT INTO BONELESS VEAL CHOPS

1 Remove the tenderloin in a single piece from the inside of the loin by following the vertebrae and cutting completely around the tenderloin.

2 From the backbone side, cut along the natural curve of the backbone, separating the loin meat from the backbone.

3 Trim any excess fat from the loin, and trim the flank to create a 3-inch (7.5-centimeter) lip. Tightly roll up the loin with the flank on the outside.

4 Tie the loin, using the procedure described next, at 1-inch (2.5-centimeter) intervals. Cut between the pieces of twine for individual boneless loin chops.

▶ PROCEDURE FOR TYING MEATS

Here we apply the tying procedure to a boneless veal loin; the same procedure can be used on any type of meat.

1 Cut a piece of string long enough to wrap completely around the loin. Holding one end between the thumb and forefinger, pass the other end around it and across the strings. Loop the loose end of the string around your finger.

2 Wrap the string around itself and pass the loose end back through the hole.

3 Pull to tighten the knot. Adjust the string so it is snug against the meat.

4 Loop one end of the string around your thumb and forefinger. Reach through with your thumb and forefinger and pull the other string back through the loop. Pull both strings to tighten the knot, thus preventing the first knot from loosening. Trim the ends of the strings.

5 Continue in this fashion until the entire loin is tied. The strings should be tied at even intervals, just snug enough to hold the shape of the loin; they should not dig into or cut the meat.

▶ PROCEDURE FOR CLEANING AND PRESSING SWEETBREADS

Before fabrication, you should submerge the sweetbreads in cold milk or water, cover, and place them in the refrigerator overnight in order to soak out any blood. Then blanch them in a court bouillon for 20 minutes.

1 Remove the sweetbreads from the poaching liquid and allow them to cool.

2 Using your hands, pull off any sinew or membranes that may be present on the surface of the sweetbreads.

3 Wrap the sweetbreads in cheesecloth.

4 Tie the ends with butcher's twine.

5 Place the wrapped sweetbreads in a half hotel pan or similar container.

6 Place another half hotel pan on top of the sweetbreads; place a weight in the pan to press the sweetbreads. Pressing sweetbreads in this manner improves their texture.

▶ PROCEDURE FOR CLEANING CALVES' LIVER

1 Trim the large sinew and outer membrane from the bottom of the liver.

2 Turn the liver over and peel the membrane off with your hands.

3 The liver can be cut into thick or thin slices a needed.

▶ PROCEDURE FOR CLEANING VEAL KIDNEYS

1 Split the kidneys lengthwise, exposing the fat and sinew.

2 With a sharp knife, trim away the fat and kidney is now ready for cooking.

Table 15.1   USING COMMON CUTS OF VEAL

PRIMAL	SUBPRIMAL OR FABRICATED CUT	IMPS	COOKING METHODS	SERVING SUGGESTIONS
Shoulder	Cubed veal	1395	Combination (stew)	Blanquette or fricassee
	Ground veal	1396	Dry heat (broil or grill) Combination (braise)	Veal patties Stuffing; meatballs
Foreshank and breast	Foreshank	312	Combination (braise)	Osso buco
	Breast	313	Combination (braise)	Stuffed veal breast
Rib	Hotel rack	306	Dry heat (broil or grill; roast)	Grilled veal chop; roast veal with porcini mushrooms
	Rib chops	1306	Dry heat (broil or grill) Combination (braise)	Grilled veal chop Braised veal chop with risotto
	Rib eye	307	Dry heat (broil or grill; roast)	Broiled veal rib eye with chipotle sauce; roasted veal rib eye marchand de vin
			Combination (braise)	Braised rib eye
Loin	Veal loin	331	Dry heat (broil or grill; roast; sauté)	Roasted veal loin with wild mushrooms; sautéed veal medallions with green peppercorn sauce
	Loin chops	1332	Dry heat (broil or grill; sauté)	Broiled or sautéed veal chops with mushroom sauce
			Combination (braise)	Braised veal chops lyonnaise
	Boneless strip loin	344	Dry heat (broil or grill; roast; sauté)	Roasted veal loin sauce poulette
	Veal tenderloin	346	Dry heat (broil or grill; roast; sauté)	Grilled tenderloin; roasted tenderloin; sautéed tenderloin with garlic and herbs
Leg	Leg	334	Dry heat (roast; sauté) Combination (stew)	Veal scallopini Blanquette
	Top round	349A	Dry heat (roast; sauté)	Veal marsala
	Bottom round	NA	Dry heat (sauté) Combination (braise)	Sautéed scallops with Calvados Stuffed veal scallops
	Hindshank	337	Moist heat (simmer) Combination (braise)	Veal broth Osso buco
Offal	Sweetbreads	715	Dry heat (pan-fry; sauté)	Sautéed sweetbreads beurre noisette
			Combination (braise)	Braised sweetbreads Madeira
	Calves' liver	704	Dry heat (broil or grill; sauté)	Broiled or sautéed calves' liver with onion and bacon
	Kidneys	NA	Combination (braise)	Kidney pie

Although veal may not be as popular as beef or pork, it is versatile and easy to cook and adds variety to menus. Veal is much more delicately flavored than beef, with a finer texture and lighter color. Its flavor blends well with a variety of sauces and other ingredients without overpowering them. Veal can be cooked by almost any dry-heat, moist-heat or combination cooking method.

Veal quality varies greatly among purveyors. Purchase only from reputable companies to be sure you are receiving a consistently high-quality product. Because veal carcasses are relatively small, they are sometimes purchased as primal cuts for your further fabrication.

CONCLUSION

1 Compare the appearance and flavor of beef and veal.

2 What are the differences between milk-fed veal and free-range veal?

3 Describe two differences between a beef carcass and a veal carcass.

4 List each veal primal and describe its location on the carcass. For each primal, identify two subprimals or fabricated cuts taken from it.

5 Would it be better to use a veal loin for grilling or braising? Explain your answer.

6 What are veal sweetbreads? Describe how sweetbreads should be prepared for cooking.

7 Certain groups oppose the use of milk-fed or formula-fed veal, saying that the animals are treated in an inhumane manner. What are these organizations? Are their arguments valid? What are the alternatives?

GRILLED VEAL CHOP WITH WILD MUSHROOM RAGOÛT

RECIPE 15.1

Note: This dish appears in the chapter opening photograph.

THE BROWN PALACE HOTEL, DENVER, CO
Executive Chef Mark Black

Yield: 8 Servings   **Method:** Grilling

Veal chops, frenched, 8 oz. (240 g) ea.	8	8
Olive oil	4 oz.	120 g
Salt and pepper	TT	TT
Wild Mushroom Ragoût (recipe follows)	as needed	as needed

1 Brush the veal chops with olive oil and season with salt and pepper. Grill over a hot grill to the desired doneness.

2 Arrange each chop with side dishes as desired, top with Wild Mushroom Ragoût.

Approximate values per serving: **Calories** 580, **Total fat** 26 g, **Saturated fat** 5 g, **Cholesterol** 125 mg, **Sodium** 620 mg, **Total carbohydrates** 13 g, **Protein** 64 g, **Vitamin C** 15%, **Iron** 15%

WILD MUSHROOM RAGOÛT

Yield: 8 Servings

Bacon, diced	3 oz.	90 g
Garlic, minced	1 Tbsp.	15 ml
Shallots, minced	1 Tbsp.	15 ml
Leeks, julienne	1 c.	240 ml
Pearl onions, peeled	1 pt.	450 ml
Fresh thyme, chopped	1 Tbsp.	15 ml
Wild mushrooms, mixed	12 oz.	350 g
White wine	1 pt.	450 ml
Veal demi-glace	1 qt.	1 lt
Plum tomatoes, concassée	4	4
Salt and pepper	TT	TT

1 Render the bacon in a saucepot. Add the garlic, shallots, leeks, onions and thyme and sauté until tender.

2 Add the mushrooms and sauté for 5 minutes. Deglaze with the white wine and simmer for 10 to 15 minutes.

3 Add the demi-glace and reduce to the desired consistency, approximately 15 minutes.

4 Add the tomato concassée, adjust the seasonings and hold for service.

Approximate values per serving: **Calories** 240, **Total fat** 2.5 g, **Saturated fat** 1 g, **Cholesterol** 5 mg, **Sodium** 540 mg, **Total carbohydrates** 13 g, **Protein** 32 g, **Vitamin C** 15%

CHEF MARK BLACK

Mark Black is a graduate of the Culinary Institute of America in Hyde Park, New York. A longtime veteran of Quorum Hotels & Resorts, Chef Black returned to the company's flagship hotel, Denver's Brown Palace, in 1998. As this century-old hotel's executive chef, he oversees its entire culinary operation—its catering department as well as its four restaurants, including the Palace Arms, Denver's only four-star restaurant. On behalf of the Palace Arms, Chef Black was invited to cook at the prestigious James Beard House in New York in March 2001, where he participated in the "History is Hot" dinner.

Chef Black has also been the executive chef at Quorum's Mesa Pavilion Hilton in Mesa, Arizona, and has held positions at the Sheraton Miramar in Santa Monica, California, the Hyatt Regency in Hilton Head, South Carolina, and the Hyatt Regency in Beaver Creek, Colorado. He began his career at the Celestial Restaurant in Cincinnati, Ohio.

ROSEMARY-ROASTED VEAL CHOPS WITH PORCINI MUSHROOMS

THE FOUR SEASONS, NEW YORK, NY

Chef Christian Albin

Yield: 4 Servings		**Method:** Roasting
Veal chops, 12–14 oz. (350–400 g) each	4	4
Salt and pepper	TT	TT
Fresh rosemary	4 sprigs	4 sprigs
Flour	as needed for dredging	
Paprika	TT	TT
Clarified butter	4 fl. oz.	120 ml
White wine	4 fl. oz.	120 ml
Brown veal stock	1 pt.	450 ml
Unsalted butter	2 oz.	60 g

1 Season the veal chops with salt and pepper. Press a rosemary sprig onto one side of each chop. Mix the flour and paprika and dredge the chops (both sides) in this mixture.

2 Heat the clarified butter in a sauté pan. Place the chops in the pan, rosemary side down. Roast in a preheated 375°F (190°C) oven for 7 minutes. Turn the chops carefully to keep the rosemary sprigs intact. Roast for 5 to 6 minutes more. Remove the chops and keep warm.

3 To make the sauce, degrease the pan and deglaze with the white wine. Add the veal stock and any juices that have accumulated under the chops. Simmer to reduce to 8 fluid ounces (250 milliliters). Monté au beurre, strain and adjust the seasonings.

4 Serve the chops with grilled porcini mushrooms, roasted shallots and roasted red and yellow bell peppers.

Approximate values per serving: **Calories** 1138, **Total fat** 67 g, **Saturated fat** 31 g, **Cholesterol** 519 mg, **Sodium** 828 mg, **Total carbohydrates** 9 g, **Protein** 117 g, **Vitamin A** 50%, **Iron** 33%, **Calcium** 19%

VEAL KEBABS

Yield: 4 Servings		**Method:** Grilling
Onion	1	1
Green bell pepper	1	1
Boneless veal leg, cut in 1-in. (2.5-cm) cubes	2 lb.	1 kg
Marinade:		
Olive oil	4 fl. oz.	120 ml
White wine	2 fl. oz.	60 ml
Lemon juice	2 fl. oz.	60 ml
Assorted fresh herbs such as parsley, tarragon, sage and dill, chopped	2 Tbsp.	30 ml
Salt and pepper	TT	TT

1 Cut the onion and bell pepper into 1-inch (2.5-centimeter) chunks.

2 Prepare the kebabs by threading the veal, onions and bell peppers onto each of four skewers, alternating the items.

3 Prepare the marinade by combining the oil, wine, lemon juice, herbs, salt and pepper.

4 Marinate the skewers, refrigerated, for 3 hours.

5 Drain the kebabs; season with salt and pepper and grill to the desired doneness.

Approximate values per serving: **Calories** 650, **Total fat** 40 g, **Saturated fat** 8 g, **Cholesterol** 234 mg, **Sodium** 691 mg, **Total carbohydrates** 6 g, **Protein** 64 g, **Vitamin C** 35%, **Iron** 20%

ROAST VEAL LOIN   RECIPE 15.4

Yield: 6 Servings, 6 oz. (180 g) each   **Method:** Roasting

Boneless veal loin roast, 3 lb. (1.5 kg)	1	1
Salt and pepper	TT	TT
Onions, chopped medium	2	2
Carrots, chopped medium	2	2
Garlic cloves, chopped	4	4
Fresh thyme	3 sprigs	3 sprigs
Bay leaves	2	2
Jus lié	1 pt.	500 ml

1 Tie the veal loin roast with butcher's twine.

2 Season the meat with salt and pepper and place it in a roasting pan. Scatter the onions, carrots, garlic, thyme and bay leaves around it.

3 Roast at 425°F (220°C) for approximately 45 minutes.

4 Remove the meat from the roasting pan and cut away the twine. Hold in a warm place for service.

5 Deglaze the roasting pan with the jus lié. Strain the vegetables and liquid through a chinois into a small saucepan. Discard the solids.

6 Bring the sauce to a boil and skim as much fat as possible from the surface. Season with salt and pepper. Spoon a portion of the sauce over the veal; serve the remainder on the side.

Approximate values per serving: **Calories** 526, **Total fat** 31 g, **Saturated fat** 12 g, **Cholesterol** 209 mg, **Sodium** 509 mg, **Total carbohydrates** 6 g, **Protein** 54 g, **Vitamin A** 47%, **Iron** 16%

SAUTÉED VEAL SCALLOPS WITH CALVADOS   RECIPE 15.5

Yield: 6 Servings   **Method:** Sautéing

Mushrooms, sliced	12 oz.	340 g
Clarified butter	4 fl. oz.	120 ml
Golden Delicious apples	3	3
Veal scallops, pounded, 6 oz. (170 g) each	6	6
Salt and pepper	TT	TT
Shallots, minced	2	2
Calvados	2 fl. oz.	60 ml
Crème fraîche	8 fl. oz.	250 ml
Fresh parsley, chopped	1 Tbsp.	15 ml

1 Sauté the mushrooms in a portion of the clarified butter until dry. Remove and reserve.

2 Peel and core the apples. Cut each into 12 wedges.

3 Sauté the apple wedges in a portion of the clarified butter until slightly browned and tender. Remove and reserve.

4 Season the veal scallops with salt and pepper. Sauté in the remaining clarified butter. (This may be done in two or three batches.) Remove and reserve.

5 Add the shallots to the pan and sauté without browning.

6 Deglaze with the Calvados. Flambé the Calvados.

7 Add the sautéed mushrooms and crème fraîche. Bring to a boil and reduce until it thickens slightly.

8 Return the scallops to the pan to reheat. Serve each scallop with sauce, garnished with six apple slices and chopped parsley.

Approximate values per serving: **Calories** 650, **Total fat** 41 g, **Saturated fat** 21 g, **Cholesterol** 295 mg, **Sodium** 710 mg, **Total carbohydrates** 14 g, **Protein** 56 g, **Vitamin A** 30%

RECIPE 15.6

VEAL MARSALA

Yield: 6 Servings, 7 oz. (210 g) each

Method: Sautéing

Veal scallops, pounded, 3 oz. (90 g) each	12	12
Salt and pepper	TT	TT
Flour	as needed for dredging	
Clarified butter	2 fl. oz.	60 ml
Olive oil	2 fl. oz.	60 ml
Dry marsala	6 fl. oz.	180 ml
Brown veal stock	4 fl. oz.	120 ml
Whole butter	1½ oz.	45 g

1 Season the scallops with salt and pepper. Dredge the scallops in flour and sauté them in a mixture of the clarified butter and oil, a few at a time, until all are cooked.

2 Remove the scallops and set aside. Degrease the pan and deglaze with marsala. Add the stock and reduce until it begins to thicken.

3 Return the scallops to the sauce to reheat. Remove the scallops to plates or a serving platter.

4 Reduce the sauce until it becomes syrupy; adjust the seasonings. Monté au beurre and spoon the sauce over the veal.

Approximate values per 7-oz. (210-g) serving: **Calories** 430, **Total fat** 28 g, **Saturated fat** 12 g, **Cholesterol** 165 mg, **Sodium** 650 mg, **Total carbohydrates** 9 g, **Protein** 36 g, **Vitamin A** 15%

RECIPE 15.7

SAUTÉED CALVES' LIVER WITH ONIONS

Yield: 10 Servings

Method: Sautéing

Onion, julienne	1 lb. 8 oz.	700 g
Clarified butter	3 fl. oz.	90 ml
Salt and pepper	TT	TT
White wine	8 fl. oz.	250 ml
Fresh parsley, chopped	1 Tbsp.	15 ml
Calves' liver, 6-oz. (180-g) slices	10	10
Flour	as needed for dredging	

1 Sauté the onions in 1 fluid ounce (30 milliliters) of clarified butter until golden brown. Season with salt and pepper.

2 Add the white wine, cover and braise until the onions are tender, approximately 10 minutes. Stir in the chopped parsley.

3 Dredge the liver in flour seasoned with salt and pepper.

4 In a separate pan, sauté the liver in the remaining clarified butter until done. The liver should be slightly pink in the middle.

5 Serve the liver with a portion of the onions and their cooking liquid.

Approximate values per 6-oz. (180-g) serving: **Calories** 270, **Total fat** 9 g, **Saturated fat** 3 g, **Cholesterol** 535 mg, **Sodium** 520 mg, **Total carbohydrates** 16 g, **Protein** 30 g, **Vitamin A** 1190%, **Vitamin C** 50%

VEAL CORDON BLEU   RECIPE 15.8

THE ART INSTITUTE OF WASHINGTON, ARLINGTON, VA
Chef John Harrison

Yield: 4 Servings	**Method:** Deep-frying	
Veal cutlets, 4 oz. (120 g) each	4	4
Salt and white pepper	TT	TT
Parsley, chopped	4 tsp.	20 ml
Ham slices, 1 oz. (30 g) each	4	4
Swiss cheese slices, 1 oz. (30 g) each	4	4
All-purpose flour	as needed	as needed
Egg wash	as needed	as needed
Bread crumbs	as needed	as needed

1 Place the veal cutlets on a film-covered cutting board and cover them with a layer of film wrap. Using a meat mallet, gently pound the cutlets to an even thickness of approximately ¼ inch (6 millimeters). Remove the film wrap.

2 Season the cutlets with salt and white pepper and sprinkle them with the chopped parsley.

3 Place one slice of ham and one slice of cheese on each cutlet. If the slices are larger than the cutlet, cut the slices in half and layer them on the cutlet.

4 Begin rolling the veal cutlet. Fold the ends toward the center to close the ends of the roll and finish rolling. Refrigerate the veal rolls for 15 minutes.

5 Bread the veal rolls using the standard breading procedure and refrigerate for an additional 15 minutes.

6 Using the basket method, deep-fry the rolls at 325°F (160°C) until fully cooked, approximately 8 minutes. Serve the veal cordon bleu with a flavored hollandaise or a béarnaise sauce.

Variation: Turkey Cordon Bleu—Substitute 4-ounce (120-gram) turkey breast cutlets for the veal.

Approximate values per serving: **Calories** 470, **Total fat** 34 g, **Saturated fat** 13 g, **Cholesterol** 140 g, **Sodium** 500 mg, **Total carbohydrates** 1 g, **Protein** 40 g, **Calcium** 30%

VEAL POJARSKI   RECIPE 15.9

NEWBURY COLLEGE, BROOKLINE, MA
Senior Instructor Scott Doughty

Yield: 6 Servings	**Method:** Pan-frying	
Lean veal	2 lb.	900 g
Nutmeg	¼ tsp.	1 ml
Salt	½ tsp.	3 ml
Black pepper	¼ tsp.	1 ml
Heavy cream, cold	1 pt.	480 ml
Fresh bread crumbs	1 qt.	1 lt
Clarified butter	as needed	as needed
Chasseur sauce (page 217)	as needed	as needed

1 Remove any gristle or thick fat from the veal. Pass it through a grinder with the large die once, and then once with the fine die. Spread the veal on a half-sheet pan and chill thoroughly.

2 When the veal is thoroughly chilled, transfer it to a well-chilled bowl. Add the nutmeg, salt, pepper and cream. Blend well. Then blend in ¾ cup (180 milliliters) of the bread crumbs.

3 Working quickly, divide the mixture into 6 portions and shape them into patties approximately 1 inch (2.5 centimeters) thick. Roll the patties in the remaining bread crumbs; chill until ready to cook.

4 Heat two large sauté pans and add a thin film of clarified butter to each one. Place half of the patties into each pan and cook until they are golden brown, approximately 5 minutes. Turn them over carefully and continue cooking until done, approximately 5 more minutes. Serve with Chasseur sauce.

Approximate values per serving: **Calories** 560, **Total fat** 38 g, **Saturated fat** 21 g, **Cholesterol** 235 mg, **Sodium** 470 mg, **Total carbohydrates** 17 g, **Protein** 38 g, **Vitamin A** 25%, **Calcium** 10%, **Iron** 10%

RECIPE 15.10

VEAL MARENGO

Yield: 6 Servings, 10 oz. (300 g) each   **Method:** Braising

Lean boneless veal, cut in 2-in. (5-cm) cubes	2 lb. 8 oz.	1.1 kg
Salt and pepper	TT	TT
Flour	as needed for dredging	
Vegetable oil	1½ fl. oz.	45 ml
Clarified butter	3 fl. oz.	90 ml
Onion, sliced fine	12 oz.	350 g
Carrot, sliced fine	10 oz.	300 g
Garlic cloves, crushed	2	2
Tomato paste	1 oz.	30 g
Flour	2 Tbsp.	30 ml
Dry white wine	6 fl. oz.	170 ml
Brown veal stock	1 pt.	450 ml
Bouquet garni:		
Carrot stick, 4 in. (10 cm)	1	1
Leek, split, 4-in. (10-cm) piece	1	1
Fresh thyme	1 sprig	1 sprig
Bay leaf	1	1
Mushrooms, washed and quartered	8 oz.	250 g
Tomato, diced	1 lb.	500 g
Pearl onions, boiled and peeled	24	24

1 Season the veal cubes with salt and pepper and dredge in flour.

2 Sauté the veal in 1 fluid ounce (30 milliliters) of oil and 1 fluid ounce (30 milliliters) of clarified butter, browning well on all sides. Remove the meat and set aside.

3 Add 1½ fluid ounces (45 milliliters) of butter and sauté the onions, carrots and garlic without coloring. Stir in the tomato paste and return the veal to the pan. Sprinkle with the 2 tablespoons (30 milliliters) of flour and cook to make a blond roux.

4 Add the wine, stock and bouquet garni to the pan; bring to a boil. Cover and braise until the meat is tender, approximately 1½ hours.

5 Sauté the mushrooms until dry in the remaining oil and butter without browning. Add the tomato to the pan and sauté over high heat for 3 minutes. Season with salt and pepper. Remove from the heat and reserve.

6 When the veal is tender, remove it from the pan with a slotted spoon and set aside. Strain the sauce.

7 Return the veal to the sauce along with the mushrooms, tomato and pearl onions. Bring to a boil and simmer for 5 minutes. Adjust the seasonings.

Approximate values per 10-oz. (300-g) serving: **Calories** 340, **Total fat** 16 g, **Saturated fat** 6 g, **Cholesterol** 125 mg, **Sodium** 490 mg, **Total carbohydrates** 15 g, **Protein** 32 g, **Vitamin A** 70%, **Vitamin C** 25%

SWEETBREADS GRENOBLE   RECIPE 15.11

Yield: 8 Servings   **Method:** Sautéing

Sweetbreads, blanched and pressed	8	8
Salt and pepper	TT	TT
Flour	as needed for dredging	
Clarified butter	2 fl. oz.	60 ml
Dry white wine	2 fl. oz.	60 ml
Whole butter	4 oz.	120 g
Capers	½ c.	250 ml
Lemons, cut into segments, membranes removed	3	3
Veal demi-glace	2 fl. oz.	60 ml

1 Slice the sweetbreads and season with salt and pepper. Dust each piece lightly with flour.

2 Heat the clarified butter in a large sauté pan; add the sweetbreads and cook on each side for 1 to 2 minutes, until golden brown. Transfer the sweetbreads to a roasting pan and bake in a 375°F (190°C) oven for 5 minutes.

3 Deglaze the sauté pan with the wine. Add the whole butter, capers and lemon segments and cook over high heat for 1 to 2 minutes. Add the demi-glace and cook until thoroughly heated, approximately 1 more minute.

4 Arrange the sweetbreads on plates and top with the sauce.

Approximate values per serving: **Calories** 345, **Total fat** 22 g, **Saturated fat** 13 g, **Cholesterol** 512 mg, **Sodium** 461 mg, **Total carbohydrates** 4 g, **Protein** 33 g, **Vitamin A** 14%, **Vitamin C** 51%

OSSO BUCO   RECIPE 15.12

CHEF LELAND ATKINSON, WASHINGTON, DC

Yield: 4 Servings   **Method:** Braising

Veal shank, cut in 1-in. (2.5-cm) pieces	8–12 pieces	8–12 pieces
Salt and pepper	TT	TT
Flour	4 oz.	120 g
Olive oil	as needed	as needed
Garlic clove, minced	1	1
Carrot, diced	4 oz.	120 g
Lemon zest, grated	1 Tbsp.	15 ml
White wine	8 fl. oz.	250 ml
Brown veal stock	1 qt.	1 lt
Tomato purée	2 Tbsp.	30 ml
Gremolada:		
Garlic clove, chopped fine	1	1
Lemon zest	1 Tbsp.	15 ml
Fresh Italian parsley, chopped	1 Tbsp.	15 ml

1 Season the veal with salt and pepper and dredge the pieces in flour. Sauté them in olive oil until brown on both sides.

2 Add the garlic and carrot and sauté briefly.

3 Add the lemon zest, wine, stock and tomato purée. Bring to a boil and reduce to a simmer. Braise on the stove top or in a 325°F (160°C) oven until the meat is tender but not falling from the bone, approximately 40 to 60 minutes.

4 Remove the cover and reduce the sauce until thick. Adjust the seasonings.

5 At service time, transfer the meat to a serving platter and ladle the sauce over it. Combine the gremolada ingredients and sprinkle over the meat and sauce.

Approximate values per serving: **Calories** 350, **Total fat** 12 g, **Saturated fat** 2 g, **Cholesterol** 55 mg, **Sodium** 1500 mg, **Total carbohydrates** 41 g, **Protein** 20 g, **Vitamin A** 80%, **Vitamin C** 20%, **Iron** 20%

RECIPE 15.13   STUFFED BREAST OF VEAL

Yield: 12 Servings, 8 oz. (240 g) each		**Method:** Braising
Stuffing:		
Onion, small dice	8 oz.	250 g
Garlic, chopped	2 tsp.	10 ml
Whole butter	1 oz.	30 g
Ground veal	1 lb.	450 g
Fresh bread crumbs	4 oz.	120 g
Nutmeg	TT	TT
Salt and pepper	TT	TT
Eggs, beaten	2	2
Mushrooms, sliced	1 lb.	450 g
Clarified butter	2 fl. oz.	60 ml
Spinach leaves, stemmed and washed	4 oz.	120 g
Veal breast, approx. 8 lb. (3.6 kg)	1	1
Mirepoix, large dice	1 lb.	450 g
White wine	8 fl. oz.	250 ml
Brown veal stock	3 pt.	1.5 lt
Garlic, chopped	1 tsp.	5 ml
Bouquet garni:		
Carrot stick, 4 in. (10 cm)	1	1
Leek, split, 4-in. (10-cm) piece	1	1
Fresh thyme	1 sprig	1 sprig
Bay leaves	2	2

1 To make the stuffing, sauté the onion and garlic in the butter until tender. Cool. Combine with the remaining stuffing ingredients and mix well.

2 Sauté the mushroom in 1 fluid ounce (30 milliliters) of the clarified butter and cool.

3 Blanch the spinach and cool.

4 Bone the veal breast. Reserve the bones.

5 Butterfly the veal breast and open it into a large rectangular shape.

6 Spread the stuffing over the breast; leave a 1-inch (2.5-centimeter) border around the edges.

7 Open the spinach leaves and carefully lay them on top of the stuffing. Sprinkle the mushrooms on top of the spinach leaves.

8 Roll the breast up in a cylindrical shape so that the spinach leaves form a spiral in the center. Tie with butcher's twine.

9 Brown the breast in the remaining clarified butter.

10 Remove the breast and pour off all but 1 fluid ounce (30 milliliters) of the grease. Add the mirepoix to the pan and sauté.

11 Add the reserved veal bones and place the veal breast on top of the bones.

12 Add the wine, stock, garlic and bouquet garni.

13 Cover and braise the breast until tender, approximately 2½ hours.

14 Remove the breast from the pan and remove the twine. Skim any fat from the sauce.

15 Reduce the sauce and, if desired, thicken it slightly with a small amount of roux or beurre manié. Strain it through a fine chinois and adjust the seasonings.

16 Slice the veal breast and serve with the sauce.

Approximate values per serving: **Calories** 750, **Total fat** 30 g, **Saturated fat** 11 g, **Cholesterol** 445 mg, **Sodium** 660 mg, **Total carbohydrates** 11 g, **Protein** 109 g, **Vitamin A** 15%, **Iron** 30%

VEAL FRICASSEE

RECIPE 15.14

Yield: 16 Servings, 8 oz. (240 g) each   **Method:** Stewing

Veal stew meat, cut in 2-in. (5-cm) cubes	8 lb.	3.5 kg
Salt and white pepper	TT	TT
Whole butter	6 oz.	180 g
Onion, small dice	12 oz.	350 g
Garlic, chopped	1 tsp.	5 ml
Flour	6 oz.	180 g
White wine	4 fl. oz.	120 ml
White stock	3 qt.	3 lt
Bouquet garni:		
Carrot stick, 4 in. (10 cm)	1	1
Leek, split, 4-in. (10-cm) piece	1	1
Fresh thyme	1 sprig	1 sprig
Bay leaf	1	1
Heavy cream, hot	1 pt.	450 ml

1 Season the veal with salt and pepper and sauté in the butter without browning, approximately 2 minutes.

2 Add the onions and garlic and sauté without coloring, approximately 2 minutes.

3 Add the flour and cook to make a blond roux, approximately 3 minutes.

4 Add the wine and stock, stir well to remove any lumps of roux and bring to a boil. Add the bouquet garni, cover and braise until the veal is tender, approximately 30 minutes.

5 Remove the veal from the sauce and reserve. Strain the sauce through a fine chinois and return it to the pan. Degrease the sauce.

6 Add the heavy cream to the sauce. Reduce slightly to thicken if necessary. Return the veal to the sauce and adjust the seasonings.

7 Serve the fricassee with rice pilaf.

Approximate values per 8-oz. (240-g) serving: **Calories** 340, **Total fat** 18 g, **Saturated fat** 8 g, **Cholesterol** 165 mg, **Sodium** 540 mg, **Total carbohydrates** 6 g, **Protein** 40 g, **Vitamin A** 10%

I LIKE A COOK WHO SMILES OUT LOUD WHEN HE TASTES HIS OWN WORK. LET GOD WORRY ABOUT YOUR MODESTY, I WANT TO SEE YOUR ENTHUSIASM.

—Robert Farrer Capon

16

LAMB

BISHOP'S RESTAURANT, Vancouver, BC
Painting by Alexandria Dikeakos, Vancouver, BC

L amb is the meat of sheep slaughtered when they are less than one year old. Meat from sheep slaughtered after that age is called mutton. Spring lamb is young lamb that has not been fed grass or grains. Because lamb is slaughtered at an early age, it is quite tender and can be prepared by almost any cooking method.

Lamb has a strong and distinctive flavor. It goes well with boldly flavored sauces and accompaniments.

▶ PRIMAL AND SUBPRIMAL CUTS OF LAMB

After the young sheep is slaughtered, it is usually reduced to the primal cuts: shoulder, breast, rack, loin and leg. Like some veal primals, lamb primals are crosscut sections and contain both bilateral halves (for example, the primal leg contains both hind legs). Lamb primals are not classified into a forequarter and hindquarter like beef, or a foresaddle and hindsaddle like veal.

Figure 16.1 shows the relationship between the lamb's bone structure and the primal cuts. As with all meats, it is important to know the location of bones when cutting or working with lamb. This makes meat fabrication and carving easier and aids in identifying cuts. Figure 16.2 shows the primal cuts of lamb and their location on the carcass. A lamb carcass generally weighs between 41 and 75 pounds (20 and 35 kg).

SHOULDER

The primal lamb shoulder is a relatively large cut accounting for 36 percent of the carcass weight. The lamb shoulder contains four rib bones and the arm, blade and neck bones as well as many small, tough muscles whose grains travel in different directions.

All these bones and muscle groups make it nearly impossible to cook and carve a whole shoulder. Although the shoulder may be cut into chops, or boned and then roasted or braised, with or without stuffing, it is more commonly diced for stew or ground for patties.

BREAST

The primal lamb breast contains the breast and foreshank portions of the carcass. Together they account for approximately 17 percent of the carcass weight and contain the rib, breast and shank bones. The primal breast is located beneath the primal rack and contains the rib tips, which are cut off to produce the rack. When separated from the rest of the breast, these small ribs are called Denver ribs and can be substituted for pork ribs where desired.

Although the breast is not used extensively in food service operations, it can be stuffed and braised, either bone-in or boneless. Lamb foreshanks are quite meaty and may be braised and served as an entrée, used for broths, or ground.

RACK

The primal lamb rack is also known as the hotel rack. It is located between the primal shoulder and loin. Containing eight ribs and portions of the backbone, it accounts for approximately 8 percent of the carcass weight.

The rack is valued for its tender rib eye muscle. The hotel rack is usually split in half and trimmed so that each set of ribs can be easily cut into chops. The

▶ **frenching** a method of trimming racks or individual chops of meat, especially lamb, in which the excess fat is cut away leaving the eye muscle intact; all meat and connective tissue are removed from the rib bone

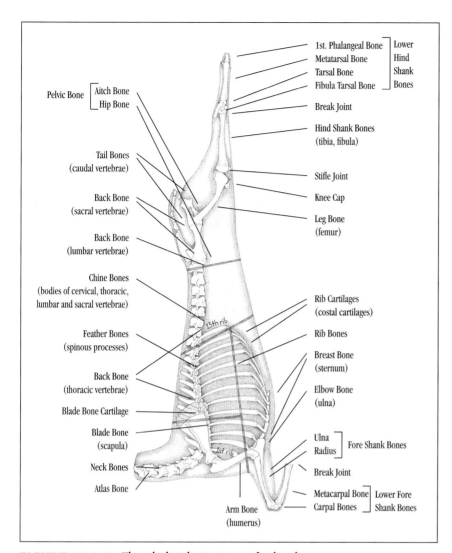

Pelvic Bone ⎡ Aitch Bone
⎣ Hip Bone

1st. Phalangeal Bone ⎤ Lower
Metatarsal Bone | Hind
Tarsal Bone | Shank
Fibula Tarsal Bone ⎦ Bones

Break Joint

Hind Shank Bones
(tibia, fibula)

Tail Bones
(caudal vertebrae)

Back Bone
(sacral vertebrae)

Stifle Joint

Knee Cap

Back Bone
(lumbar vertebrae)

Leg Bone
(femur)

Chine Bones
(bodies of cervical, thoracic,
lumbar and sacral vertebrae)

Rib Cartilages
(costal cartilages)

Rib Bones

13th rib

Feather Bones
(spinous processes)

Breast Bone
(sternum)

Back Bone
(thoracic vertebrae)

Elbow Bone
(ulna)

Blade Bone Cartilage

Blade Bone
(scapula)

Ulna ⎤
Radius ⎦ Fore Shank Bones

1st rib

Neck Bones

Break Joint

Atlas Bone

Metacarpal Bone ⎤ Lower Fore
Carpal Bones ⎦ Shank Bones

Arm Bone
(humerus)

FIGURE 16.1 ▶ The skeletal structure of a lamb

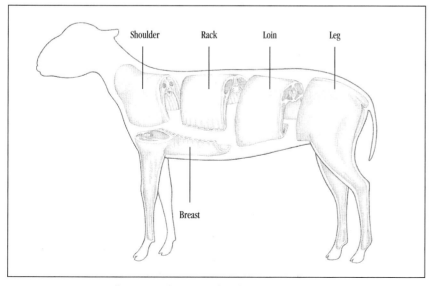

Shoulder   Rack   Loin   Leg

Breast

FIGURE 16.2 ▶ The primal cuts of lamb

IMPERIALIST, COLONIALIST AND REVOLUTIONARY SHEEP

Columbus brought sheep to the New World on his second voyage in 1493. The Spanish soon established breeding centers in the Caribbean islands, then in Mexico and Panama. In 1565, people and livestock, including sheep, settled in St. Augustine, Florida.

During the 16th and 17th centuries, the Spanish established missions in Texas, New Mexico, Arizona and California in order to bridge their Florida and Mexico settlements. They brought sheep with them as an easily cared-for source of food and wool.

Sheep raising was not as easily established in the British colonies along the eastern seaboard. Many of the sheep brought with the early colonists were consumed for food during the harsh winters. More and more sheep had to be imported in order to satisfy the colonists' competing demands for food and clothing. By the mid-17th century, however, sheep were flourishing in the New England colonies and supplying an abundance of meat and wool.

In an attempt to maintain control of the wool trade, the British restricted the export of

sheep to the American colonies and forbade the import of colonial wool and woolens. Retaliating against these restrictive trade practices, the colonists passed laws forbidding the use of sheep for food in order to preserve the flocks for wool. This protectionist scheme helped assure a strong supply of materials for the domestic woolen industry that flourished after the Revolutionary War.

Frenched Lamb Rack

Lamb Rack

split racks can then be grilled, broiled or roasted as racks or cut into single or double rib chops before cooking.

LOIN

The loin is located between the primal rib and leg. It contains rib number 13 and portions of the backbone as well as the loin eye muscle, tenderloin and flank. It accounts for approximately 13 percent of the carcass weight.

Except for the flank, the loin meat is very tender and is invariably cooked using a dry-heat method such as broiling, grilling or roasting. The loin may be boned to produce boneless roasts or chops or cut into chops with the bone in. The loin eye may be removed and cut into medallions or noisettes.

*Lamb Loin
Trimmed*

LEG

The primal leg is a large section accounting for approximately 34 percent of the carcass weight. It is the posterior portion of the carcass, separated from the loin by a straight cut anterior to the hip bone cartilage. As with veal, the cut of meat that would be the sirloin on a beef carcass is separated from the lamb loin by this cut and becomes part of the primal leg. The lamb leg contains several bones: the backbone, tail, hip, aitch, round and shank bones.

Lamb Leg

The primal leg is rarely used as is. More often, it is split into two legs and partially or fully boned. Lamb legs are quite tender—the sirloin end more so than the shank end—and are well suited to a variety of cooking methods. A bone-in leg is often roasted for buffet service or braised with vegetables or beans for a hearty dish. Steaks can also be cut from the bone-in leg, with the sirloin end producing the most tender cuts. A boneless leg can be tied and roasted, with or without stuffing, or trimmed and cut into scallops. The shank end can be diced for stew or ground for patties.

Because lamb carcasses are so easily handled, purveyors often sell them whole or cut in a variety of ways to better meet their customers' needs. As well as whole carcass, primal and fabricated cuts, lamb can be purchased in the following forms:

Boned, Rolled and Tied Leg of Lamb

▶ *Foresaddle:* The anterior (front) portion of the carcass after it is severed from the hindsaddle by a cut following the natural curvature between the 12th and 13th ribs. It contains the primal shoulder, breast and foreshank and rack.

▶ *Hindsaddle:* The posterior portion of the carcass after it is severed from the foresaddle. It contains the primal loin and leg together with the kidneys.

▶ *Back:* The trimmed rack and loin sections in one piece. The back is particularly useful when producing large quantities of lamb chops.

▶ *Bracelet:* The primal hotel rack with the connecting breast sections.

Domestic (left) and New Zealand Lamb Chops

▶ BUTCHERING PROCEDURES

Lamb is unique among the common meat animals in that it is small enough to be handled easily in its carcass form. Thus, food service operations sometimes purchase lamb whole and fabricate the desired cuts themselves. This is practical if the operation has the necessary employee skills, equipment and storage space, as well as a need for all the various cuts and trimmings that butchering a whole carcass produces. A few important lamb fabrication and butchering techniques follow.

▶ PROCEDURE FOR FRENCHING A RACK OF LAMB

1 With a meat saw, trim the ribs to approximately 3 inches (7.5 centimeters), measuring from the rib eye on each side of the rack.

2 Turn the rack over and cut down both sides of the feather bones, completely separating the meat from the bone.

3 Turn the rack back over. Using a meat saw, cut between the ribs and the chine bone at a 45-degree angle, exposing the lean meat between the ribs and the vertebral junctures.

4 By pulling and cutting along the natural seam, remove the thick layers of fat and the meat between them from the rack's surface.

5 Make an even cut through the fat, perpendicular to the ribs, 1 inch (25 centimeters) from the rib eye. Trim away all meat and fat from the rib ends. The ribs should be completely clean.

6 Trim away the fat covering. Leave either a thin layer to protect the meat during cooking or trim the fat away completely to produce a very lean rack. The rack can also be cut into chops.

▶ PROCEDURE FOR TRIMMING AND BONING A LAMB LEG FOR ROASTING OR GRILLING

1 With the tip of the knife, trim around the pelvic bone; stay close to the bone to avoid wasting any meat. Cut the sinew inside the socket and remove the bone.

2 Trim away most of the exterior fat.

3 Cut off the shank portion completely and scrape the bone clean. This makes a handle to hold while carving the lamb.

4 Fold the flap of the sirloin over on top of the ball of the leg bone and tie with butcher's twine. This helps the leg cook evenly.

▶ PROCEDURE FOR BONING A LAMB LOIN FOR ROASTING

1 Start with a trimmed lamb loin (double). With the skin side up, trim the thin layer of connective tissue called the fell from the loin's surface.

2 Turn the loin over and trim the fat from around the tenderloins.

3 Starting in the middle of the backbone, cut between the tenderloin and the vertebrae, separating them but leaving the tenderloin attached to the flank. Continue until you reach the end of the vertebrae. Repeat on the other side.

4 Slide the knife under the vertebrae and the rib and cut back all the way to the backbone, separating the eye muscle from the vertebrae.

5 Pull the backbone out with your hands, keeping the loins intact.

6 Turn the loins over and trim the surface fat to ¼ inch (6 millimeters).

7 Roll the flank flaps under from each side.

8 Tie the roast with butcher's twine at even intervals.

▶ PROCEDURE FOR CUTTING LAMB NOISETTES FROM A LOIN

1 Removing the loin eye muscle by cutting down along the backbone and along the vertebrae. Trim the eye muscle, leaving a thin layer of fat if desired.

2 Cut the eye meat into noisettes of the desired thickness.

Table 16.1 USING COMMON CUTS OF LAMB

PRIMAL	SUBPRIMAL OR FABRICATED CUT	IMPS	COOKING METHODS	SERVING SUGGESTIONS
Shoulder	Shoulder lamb chop	1207	Dry heat (broil or grill)	Broiled or grilled lamb chops
	Diced lamb	1295	Combination (stew)	Lamb stew; lamb curry
	Ground lamb	1296	Dry heat (broil or grill; sauté)	Patties
Breast	Breast	209	Combination (braise)	Lamb breast stuffed with mushrooms
Hotel Rack	Lamb rack	204	Dry heat (broil or grill; roast; sauté)	Roast rack of lamb with garlic and rosemary
	Frenched lamb rack	204C	Dry heat (broil or grill; roast; sauté)	Broiled lamb with mustard and hazelnut crust
Loin	Lamb loin trimmed	232	Dry heat (broil or grill; roast; sauté)	Noisettes of lamb with roasted garlic sauce
	Loin chops	1232	Dry heat (broil or grill; sauté)	Broiled loin chops with herb butter
Leg	Lamb leg	233A	Dry heat (broil or grill; roast)	Kebabs; roast leg of lamb
	Boned rolled tied leg of lamb	233B	Dry heat (roast)	Roast leg of lamb

CONCLUSION

Even though lamb accounts for a small percentage of the meat consumed in this country, many people who do not prepare lamb at home will order it at a restaurant. Because lamb is slaughtered under the age of one year, its meat is tender and it can be prepared by almost any cooking method. Its strong, distinctive flavor allows you to offer bold, robust sauces and accompaniments that might mask the flavors of other meats.

QUESTIONS FOR DISCUSSION

1 Describe the basic differences between a lamb carcass and a beef carcass.
2 List each lamb primal and describe its location on the carcass. Identify two subprimals or fabricated cuts taken from each primal.
3 Which cooking methods are most appropriate for a breast of lamb? Explain your answer.
4 Describe the procedure for preparing a frenched rack of lamb from a primal hotel rack.
5 What is the best way to purchase lamb for a food service operation that cuts its own meat and uses large quantities of lamb chops? Explain your answer.

ROAST RACK OF LAMB WITH MINT AND CELERIAC SAUCE

RECIPE 16.1

Note: This dish appears in the chapter opening photograph.

BISHOP'S RESTAURANT, Vancouver, BC
Chefs Michael Allemeier and Dennis Green

Yield: 4 Servings   **Method:** Roasting

Lamb racks, cleaned and frenched, 2 lb. (1 kg) each	2	2
Salt and pepper	TT	TT
Fresh white bread cubes, crusts removed	1 pt.	500 ml
Fresh mint, chopped	2 Tbsp.	30 ml
Fresh parsley, chopped	2 Tbsp.	30 ml
Fresh chives, chopped	2 Tbsp.	30 ml
Dijon mustard	2 Tbsp.	30 ml
Potato and Celeriac Purée (recipe follows)	as needed	as needed
Mint and Celeriac Sauce (recipe follows)	as needed	as needed
Fresh mint sprigs	2	2

1 Season the lamb racks with salt and pepper and sear on both sides.

2 Transfer the lamb to a roasting pan and roast in a 400°F (200°C) oven until medium rare, approximately 15 to 20 minutes.

3 Meanwhile, combine the bread cubes and the herbs in a food processor and process until well blended. Set aside.

4 Remove the lamb from the roasting pan and smear with the mustard. Coat the racks with the bread crumb mixture.

5 Allow the lamb to rest for 10 minutes before carving.

6 Serve with Potato and Celeriac Purée and Mint and Celeriac Sauce. Garnish with fresh mint.

Approximate values per serving: **Calories** 1240, **Total fat** 64 g, **Saturated fat** 22 g, **Cholesterol** 400 mg, **Sodium** 880 mg, **Total carbohydrates** 40 g, **Protein** 126 g, **Iron** 70%

POTATO AND CELERIAC PURÉE

Yield: 8 Servings, 4 oz. (120 g) each

Potatoes, peeled and cut into pieces	1 lb. 8 oz.	750 g
Celeriac (celery root), peeled and cut into 1-inch (2.5-cm) pieces	8 oz.	250 g
Heavy cream	8 fl. oz.	250 ml
Whole butter	2 Tbsp.	30 ml
Salt and pepper	TT	TT

1 Combine the potatoes and celeriac in a saucepan and cover with water. Bring to a boil, reduce the heat, and simmer until tender, approximately 30 minutes.

2 Strain. Mash the potatoes and celeriac using a food mill or potato ricer.

BISHOP'S RESTAURANT, VANCOUVER, BC

Bishop's Restaurant is a small but very special place, widely considered one of Vancouver's finest restaurants. Its founder and owner, John Bishop, was born in Wales and developed his love of cooking as a child. After studying at a hotel school, he worked as a chef at various venues throughout Great Britain. In 1972 he moved to Vancouver, where he became head chef and later maitre d' at Umberto's. His namesake restaurant opened in 1985.

John Bishop's goal is to present perfect, understated, delicious food; for him, quality and freshness of ingredients are of the utmost importance. He calls his style of cuisine *international new food:* a creative style of cooking grounded in European traditions. The cooking methods are still roasting, grilling, poaching and steaming—and the preparation techniques are still classic. The plate presentations, like the restaurant dining room, are clean, simple and completely unpretentious. As Mr. Bishop says, "We're not reinventing the wheel, but we do stay away from fussy and ridiculously complicated. Who needs it when you have flavorful fresh ingredients to start with?"

Chefs Dennis Green of British Columbia and Michael Allemeier of South Africa have led Bishop's kitchen over the years, while John Bishop focuses his energies on the front of the house, where he is known as an unswerving perfectionist and the consummate host.

3. Heat the cream and the butter just to a boil. Add to the hot potato mixture. Using an electric mixer fitted with the whip attachment, whip the purée until fluffy. Season to taste with salt and pepper.

Approximate values per 4-oz. (120-g) serving: **Calories** 225, **Total fat** 14 g, **Saturated fat** 9 g, **Cholesterol** 50 mg, **Sodium** 125 mg, **Total carbohydrates** 22 g, **Protein** 3 g, **Vitamin A** 15%, **Vitamin C** 22%

MINT AND CELERIAC SAUCE

Yield: 1 pt. (500 ml)

Whole butter	2 Tbsp.	30 ml
Shallots, chopped fine	4 oz.	120 g
Garlic cloves, minced	2	2
Celeriac (celery root), peeled and chopped	4 oz.	120 g
Red wine vinegar	2 fl. oz.	60 ml
Port	4 fl. oz.	120 ml
Fresh mint, chopped	½ c.	120 ml
Demi-glace	1 pt.	500 ml

1 Melt the butter in a saucepan. Add the shallots, garlic and celeriac and sauté until tender, but not brown.
2 Add the vinegar and reduce au sec.
3 Add the port and mint and reduce by half.
4 Add the demi-glace and simmer for 30 minutes. Strain and keep warm for service. The sauce can be made up to one day in advance and refrigerated, then reheated as needed.

Approximate values per 2-fl.-oz. (60-ml) serving: **Calories** 70, **Total fat** 6 g, **Saturated fat** 4 g, **Cholesterol** 15 mg, **Sodium** 90 mg, **Total carbohydrates** 2 g, **Vitamin A** 8%, Claims—low sodium; no sugar

RECIPE 16.2

GRILLED RACK OF LAMB WITH ROSEMARY AND SPICY BELL PEPPER JELLY

VINCENT ON CAMELBACK, PHOENIX, AZ
Chef Vincent Guerithault

Yield: 8 Servings		**Method:** Grilling
Red bell peppers	2	2
Yellow bell peppers	2	2
Red serrano chiles	8	8
Sugar	8 oz.	250 g
Lamb racks, frenched, 9 oz. (270 g) each	4	4
Salt and pepper	TT	TT
Dried rosemary sprigs*	8	8

1 To make the pepper jelly, julienne the bell peppers and chiles. Mix with the sugar and refrigerate overnight.
2 At service time, cook the pepper mixture (along with the liquid formed while refrigerated) over low heat for approximately 10 to 15 minutes. Cool and keep the pepper jelly at room temperature.
3 Cut each lamb rack in half. Season with salt and pepper.
4 Grill the lamb over mesquite to the desired temperature.

5 Cut the racks into chops and plate the lamb and pepper jelly. Garnish each plate with a dried rosemary sprig and flame. When the rosemary flames, blow it out at once and serve immediately so that the essence of rosemary is fresh.

*To dry rosemary, place fresh rosemary sprigs in a 350°F (180°C) oven for approximately 10 minutes.

Approximate values per 9-oz. (270-g) serving: **Calories** 430, **Total fat** 17 g, **Saturated fat** 6 g, **Cholesterol** 110 mg, **Sodium** 400 mg, **Total carbohydrates** 34 g, **Protein** 35 g, **Vitamin A** 45%, **Vitamin C** 280%, **Iron** 20%

SHISH KEBAB   RECIPE 16.3

Yield: 10 Servings   **Method:** Grilling or Broiling

Marinade:

Onion, small dice	12 oz.	350 g
Garlic, chopped	1 oz.	30 g
Lemon juice	4 fl. oz.	120 ml
Salt	2 tsp.	10 ml
Black pepper	1 tsp.	5 ml
Fresh oregano, chopped	2 tsp.	10 ml
Olive oil	8 fl. oz.	250 ml
Cumin, ground	2 tsp.	10 ml
Coriander, ground	1 Tbsp.	15 ml
Fresh mint, chopped	2 tsp.	10 ml
Lamb leg or shoulder, boneless, trimmed and cut in 2-in. (5-cm) cubes	5 lb.	2.2 kg

1 Combine the marinade ingredients and add the lamb. Marinate for 2 hours.
2 Place three to four cubes of lamb on each of 10 skewers. Grill or broil to the desired doneness. Serve with rice pilaf.

Approximate values per 7.5-oz. (225-g) serving: **Calories** 410, **Total fat** 17 g, **Saturated fat** 6 g, **Cholesterol** 205 mg, **Sodium** 170 mg, **Total carbohydrates** 0 g, **Protein** 64 g, **Iron** 30%

LAMB PATTIES WITH MINT   RECIPE 16.4

Yield: 6 Servings, 6 oz. (180 g) each   **Method:** Grilling or Broiling

Ground lamb	1 lb. 12 oz.	800 g
Fresh bread crumbs	2 oz.	60 g
Egg, beaten	1	1
Onion, minced	3 oz.	90 g
Garlic cloves, crushed	2	2
Fresh mint, chopped	3 Tbsp.	45 ml
Salt and pepper	TT	TT

1 Place the lamb in a bowl and mix in the bread crumbs, egg, onions, garlic and mint. Add salt and pepper to taste and mix well. Form the mixture into six patties.
2 Grill or broil the patties until browned on both sides. Garnish with extra mint if desired.

Approximate values per 6-oz. (180-g) serving: **Calories** 430, **Total fat** 28 g, **Saturated fat** 11 g, **Cholesterol** 165 mg, **Sodium** 590 mg, **Total carbohydrates** 9 g, **Protein** 35 g, **Iron** 20%

RECIPE 16.5

BROILED LAMB KIDNEYS

Yield: 10 Servings   **Method:** Broiling

Lamb kidneys	20	20
Bacon fat	2 oz.	60 g
Salt and pepper	TT	TT
Grain mustard	16 oz.	480 g

1 Split the lamb kidneys lengthwise; remove the fat and gristle.
2 Arrange the kidney halves on skewers, four halves per skewer.
3 Brush the kidneys with bacon fat, season with salt and pepper and broil, turning once halfway through cooking, until well browned but still pink in the center, approximately 6 to 8 minutes.
4 Serve four halves per portion with 1½ ounces (45 grams) of grain mustard each.

Approximate values per 7-oz. (210-g) serving: **Calories** 320, **Total fat** 15 g, **Saturated fat** 4.5 g, **Cholesterol** 965 mg, **Sodium** 1080 mg, **Total carbohydrates** 4 g, **Protein** 43 g, **Vitamin A** 25%, **Vitamin C** 35%, **Iron** 120%

RECIPE 16.6

RACK OF LAMB WITH MUSTARD AND HAZELNUTS

Yield: 4 Servings   **Method:** Roasting

Lamb racks, frenched, 2 lb.–2 lb. 8 oz. (0.9–1.1 kg) each	2	2
Salt and pepper	TT	TT
Olive oil	2 fl. oz.	60 ml
Dijon mustard	2 oz.	60 g
Fresh bread crumbs	1 oz.	30 g
Hazelnuts, chopped fine	2 oz.	60 g
Molasses	2 Tbsp.	30 ml

1 Season the racks with salt and pepper and brown well in the olive oil.
2 Spread the mustard over the surface of the racks.
3 Combine the bread crumbs, nuts and molasses and press this mixture into the mustard to form a crust.

1 Spreading mustard over the rack.

2 Pressing the breadcrumb mixture into the mustard.

3 Slicing the cooked rack into chops.

4 Roast the racks at 375°F (190°C) until medium rare, approximately 30 minutes.

5 Allow the racks to rest 15 minutes. Carve into chops and serve with marchand de vin sauce made with lamb jus lié (page 217).

Approximate values per serving: **Calories** 700, **Total fat** 43 g, **Saturated fat** 10 g, **Cholesterol** 195 mg, **Sodium** 880 mg, **Total carbohydrates** 14 g, **Protein** 64 g, **Iron** 35%

ROAST LOIN OF COLORADO LAMB RECIPE 16.7

THE BROWN PALACE HOTEL, DENVER, CO
Executive Chef Mark Black

Yield: 8 Servings	**Method:** Roasting	
Lamb loins, boneless, trimmed	4	4
Salt and pepper	TT	TT
Vegetable oil	as needed	as needed
Goat Cheese and Potato Custard		
(recipe follows)	8 servings	8 servings
Thyme Merlot Sauce (recipe follows)	as needed	as needed

1 Season the lamb loins with salt and pepper. Sear the lamb in hot oil in a sauté pan. Transfer the pan to a 325°F (160°C) oven and roast to medium rare, approximately 15 minutes. Remove from the oven and allow to rest for 15 minutes before slicing.

2 Unmold one custard on each serving plate. Ladle a portion of sauce in front of the custard. Slice and fan half of a lamb loin attractively on each plate. Garnish as desired and serve.

Approximate values per serving, with sauce and custard: **Calories** 530, **Total fat** 26 g, **Saturated fat** 12 g, **Cholesterol** 325 mg, **Sodium** 480 mg, **Total carbohydrates** 11 g, **Protein** 57 g, **Vitamin A** 50%, **Vitamin C** 10%, **Calcium** 10%, **Iron** 30%

GOAT CHEESE AND POTATO CUSTARD

Yield: 8 Servings	**Method:** Baking	
Whole butter	1 oz.	30 g
Russet potatoes, 90 ct., peeled,		
medium dice	2	2
Salt and white pepper	TT	TT
Eggs	6	6
Milk	4 fl. oz.	120 ml
Nutmeg, ground	TT	TT
Goat cheese	4 oz.	120 g
Fresh chives, sliced	2 Tbsp.	30 ml

1 Melt the butter and toss the diced potatoes in the butter. Spread the potatoes on a sheet pan, season with salt and white pepper and roast at 375°F (190°C) until tender, approximately 25 minutes.

2 Whisk together the eggs and milk. Season the mixture with salt, white pepper and a little nutmeg.

3 Crumble the goat cheese over the potatoes and sprinkle with the chives. Divide the potato mixture among eight buttered, 4-fluid-ounce (120-milliliter) soufflé dishes. Divide the custard among the soufflé dishes. Bake the custards at 300°F (150°C) until set, approximately 40 minutes. Remove from the oven and hold for service.

Approximate values per serving: **Calories** 160, **Total fat** 10 g, **Saturated fat** 5 g, **Cholesterol** 175 mg, **Sodium** 110 mg, **Total carbohydrates** 8 g, **Protein** 9 g, **Vitamin A** 10%

THYME MERLOT SAUCE

Yield: 12 fl. oz. (360 ml)　　　　　　**Method:** Reduction

Garlic, minced	¼ tsp.	2 ml
Shallots, minced	1 tsp.	5 ml
Clarified butter	1 Tbsp.	15 ml
Merlot wine	6 fl. oz.	180 ml
Bay leaf	1	1
Fresh thyme, chopped	1 tsp.	5 ml
Lamb stock	20 fl. oz.	600 ml
Salt and pepper	TT	TT

1　Sauté the garlic and shallots in the clarified butter until translucent. Add the wine, bay leaf and thyme and reduce by half. Add the stock and reduce by half again. Strain and season to taste. Hold for service.

Approximate values per 1-fl. oz. (30-ml) serving: **Calories** 25, **Total fat** 1 g, **Saturated fat** 0.5 g, **Cholesterol** 5 mg, **Sodium** 135 mg, **Total carbohydrates** 2 g, **Protein** 0 g, **Vitamin A** 25%

RECIPE 16.8　　　　　　## ROAST LEG OF LAMB WITH JALAPEÑO

VINCENT ON CAMELBACK, Phoenix, AZ
Chef Vincent Guerithault

Yield: 12 Servings, 5–6 oz. (150–180 g) each　　　　**Method:** Roasting

Leg of lamb, 6–8 lb. (2.7–3.6 kg)	1	1
Jalapeño peppers	6	6
Olive oil	1 Tbsp.	15 ml
Dixon (or Chimayo) chile powder	2 Tbsp.	30 ml
Salt and pepper	TT	TT
Garlic heads	12	12
Fresh thyme	1 sprig	1 sprig
Fresh rosemary	1 sprig	1 sprig
Water	8 fl. oz.	250 ml
Chicken glaze	2 oz.	60 g

1　Trim the leg, removing most of the fat; leave the bone intact.
2　Roast the jalapeños over an open flame. When they are blackened, remove the skin and cut each pepper in half. Make 12 slits in the lamb and slide one half jalapeño pepper into each slit.
3　Brush the lamb with olive oil and dust with the Dixon or Chimayo chile powder, salt and pepper.
4　Sauté the lamb over a high flame or grill, turning frequently.
5　When the lamb is golden in color, transfer it to a roasting pan. Surround the lamb with the garlic heads, thyme and rosemary. Roast at 400°F (200°C) for 45 minutes, turning the leg three or four times. When the lamb is done, remove it and the garlic from the pan and set aside.
6　To make the sauce, add the water and chicken glaze to the pan and bring to a boil. Simmer 5 minutes and strain.
7　Serve each lamb portion with one head of garlic . (Cut off the bottom of each garlic head before serving.) Top each serving with 1 tablespoon (15 milliliters) of sauce.

Approximate values per serving: **Calories** 540, **Total fat** 26 g, **Saturated fat** 9 g, **Cholesterol** 245 mg, **Sodium** 530 mg, **Total carbohydrates** 1 g, **Protein** 75 g, **Iron** 35%

STUFFED LEG OF LAMB

RECIPE 16.9

Yield: 12 Servings, 5–6 oz. (150–180 g) each

Method: Roasting

Bacon, fine dice	3 oz.	90 g
Fennel bulb, fine dice	1	1
Garlic cloves, chopped fine	2	2
Wild mushrooms such as shiitake, chanterelles or porcini, chopped	12 oz.	340 g
Parsley, chopped	2 Tbsp.	30 ml
Fresh thyme	½ tsp.	2 ml
Fresh rosemary	½ tsp.	2 ml
Salt and pepper	TT	TT
Dry white wine	8 fl. oz.	250 ml
Fresh bread crumbs	3 oz.	90 g
Leg of lamb, 6–8 lb. (2.7–3.6 kg)	1	1
Mirepoix	1 lb.	500 g

1 To make the stuffing, sauté the bacon until crisp. Add the fennel and sauté lightly.

2 Add the garlic and sauté. Add the mushrooms, parsley, thyme, rosemary, salt and pepper and sauté for an additional 2 minutes.

3 Deglaze with white wine and reduce by three-quarters. Remove from the heat.

4 Stir in the bread crumbs.

5 Completely bone out the leg, following the natural seams in the meat. Cut off the shank meat for use in another recipe. Fill the cavity left by the bone with stuffing.

6 Season the lamb with salt and pepper. Close the leg around the stuffing and seal the opening by tying with butcher's twine.

7 Place the stuffed leg in a roasting pan on a bed of mirepoix.

8 Roast at 375°F (190°C) until medium rare, approximately 1 hour. Serve au jus or with a pan gravy.

Approximate values per serving: **Calories** 540, **Total fat** 20 g, **Saturated fat** 7 g, **Cholesterol** 230 mg, **Sodium** 630 mg, **Total carbohydrates** 12 g, **Protein** 78 g, **Iron** 35%

LEG OF LAMB WITH CARAMELIZED BUTTERNUT SQUASH, CRISPY POLENTA AND ROSEMARY JUS

RECIPE 16.10

PRIMITIVO WINE BAR, Colorado Springs, CO

John Broening, Executive Chef

Yield: 8 Servings

Method: Roasting

Leg of lamb, boneless, trimmed well	1	1
Marinade:		
Olive oil	4 fl. oz.	120 ml
Fresh rosemary, chopped	1 Tbsp.	15 ml
Garlic, chopped	2 tsp.	10 ml
Dried lavender	1 tsp.	5 ml
Fennel seeds, toasted	1 Tbsp.	15 ml
Black peppercorns, cracked, toasted	1 Tbsp.	15 ml

Continued

Rosemary jus:

Lamb scraps, diced	4 oz.	120 g
Whole butter	4 tsp.	20 ml
Shallots, chopped	1 Tbsp.	15 ml
Brandy	2 Tbsp.	30 ml
Red wine	6 fl. oz.	180 ml
Brown veal stock	1 pt.	450 ml
Chicken stock	1 pt.	450 ml
Tomato paste	2 Tbsp.	30 ml
Fresh rosemary	2 sprigs	2 sprigs
Salt and pepper	TT	TT
Olive oil	2 Tbsp.	30 ml
Whole butter	1 oz.	30 g
Fresh spinach, stemmed	4 oz.	120 g
Salt and pepper	TT	TT
Crispy Polenta (recipe follows)	24 oz.	700 g
Caramelized Butternut Squash (recipe follows)	8 oz.	240 g
Oven-dried tomato halves	16	16

1 Cut the leg of lamb into eight servings. Combine the marinade ingredients and marinate the lamb for at least 4 hours.

2 To prepare the jus, brown the lamb scraps in 1 teaspoon (5 milliliters) of butter. Pour off the excess fat. Reduce the heat and sweat the shallots for 2 minutes. Add the brandy and flambé. Add the red wine and reduce by three-quarters. Add both stocks and the tomato paste and reduce by half, skimming carefully. Turn off the heat, add the rosemary sprigs and infuse for 5 minutes. Strain the sauce through a chinois. Monté au beurre with the remaining butter and adjust the seasonings.

3 Season the lamb with salt and pepper and sauté in olive oil until brown. Roast the lamb at 350°F (180°C) for approximately 5 minutes. Remove from the oven and allow it to rest for 10 minutes.

4 Heat the butter in a sauté pan until noisette. Add the spinach and toss until it wilts. Season with salt and pepper and hold in a warm place.

5 Slice the lamb and arrange on eight warm plates. Ladle the jus around the lamb. Add 3 ounces (90 grams) of warm Crispy Polenta and 1 ounce (30 grams) of Caramelized Butternut Squash. Garnish with the spinach and the oven-dried tomato halves.

Approximate values per serving: **Calories** 620, **Total fat** 31 g, **Saturated fat** 10 g, **Cholesterol** 230 mg, **Sodium** 520 mg, **Total carbohydrates** 6 g, **Protein** 71 g, **Vitamin A** 60%, **Vitamin C** 15%, **Iron** 35%

CRISPY POLENTA

Yield: 24 oz. (700 g)

Water	1 qt.	1 lt
Salt	1 Tbsp.	15 ml
Polenta	6 oz.	180 g
Whole butter	2 oz.	60 g
Parmesan, grated	4 Tbsp.	60 ml
Black pepper	½ tsp.	3 ml
Nutmeg, ground	¼ tsp.	1 ml
Flour	as needed	as needed

1 In a heavy-bottomed pot, bring the water and salt to a boil. Slowly whisk in the polenta, stirring constantly. Reduce the heat to a simmer. Cook the polenta, stirring frequently, until it pulls away from the sides of the pot, approximately 20 minutes.

2 Whisk in the butter, Parmesan, pepper and nutmeg. Turn onto a buttered sheet pan covered with parchment paper. Refrigerate until cold.

3 Cut the polenta into large dice. Toss the pieces in flour and, using the basket method, deep-fry at 325°F (160°C) until crisp. Hold for service.

Approximate values per 3-oz. (90-g) serving: **Calories** 130, **Total fat** 7 g, **Saturated fat** 4 g, **Cholesterol** 20 mg, **Sodium** 60 mg, **Total carbohydrates** 14 g, **Protein** 3 g

CARAMELIZED BUTTERNUT SQUASH

Yield: 8 oz. (240 g)

Butternut squash, large dice	8 oz.	225 g
Olive oil	2 Tbsp.	30 ml
Salt and pepper	TT	TT
Brown sugar	2 Tbsp.	30 ml

1 Combine the ingredients in a stainless steel bowl and stir gently. Spread the squash evenly on a sheet pan and roast at 325°F (160°C) until lightly browned, approximately 20 minutes.

Approximate values per 1-oz. (30-g) serving: **Calories** 70, **Total fat** 3.5 g, **Saturated fat** 0 g, **Cholesterol** 0 mg, **Sodium** 0 mg, **Total carbohydrates** 10 g, **Protein** 1 g, **Vitamin A** 90%, **Vitamin C** 20%

HONEY-MUSTARD DENVER RIBS   RECIPE 16.11

Yield: 14 lb. (6.2 kg)	**Method:** Roasting	
Lamb ribs, trimmed	20 lb.	9 kg
Salt	4 oz.	120 g
Black pepper	2 oz.	60 g
Honey	4 lb.	1.8 kg
Dijon mustard	3 lb.	1.4 kg
Lemon juice	1 pt.	450 ml

1 Rub the ribs with salt and pepper.

2 Place the ribs on a rack and roast at 375°F (190°C) for 30 minutes.

3 Combine the honey, mustard and lemon juice.

4 Baste the ribs generously with the honey-mustard mixture. Roast an additional 30 minutes, basting every 10 minutes.

Approximate values per 8-oz. (240-g) serving: **Calories** 1020, **Total fat** 47 g, **Saturated fat** 16 g, **Cholesterol** 285 mg, **Sodium** 2110 mg, **Total carbohydrates** 61 g, **Protein** 88 g, **Vitamin C** 15%, **Iron** 35%

RECIPE 16.12

SAUTÉED LAMB LOIN WITH STUFFED RÖSTI POTATOES AND CHERRY CONFIT

RECIPE 16.12

CHEF LELAND ATKINSON, Washington, DC

Yield: 6 Servings, 5 oz. (150 g) each   **Method:** Sautéing

Idaho potatoes, large	2	2
Parmesan, grated	5 oz.	150 g
Salt and pepper	TT	TT
Clarified butter	as needed	as needed
Goat cheese	6 oz.	180 g
Black pepper, freshly ground	TT	TT
Fresh rosemary, chopped	1 tsp.	5 ml
Fresh chives, chopped	1 tsp.	5 ml
Lamb, eye of loin, trimmed, 2 lb. 4 oz. (1 kg)	1	1
Clarified butter	2 fl. oz.	60 ml
Port	4 fl. oz.	120 ml
Lamb jus lié	12 fl. oz.	350 ml
Whole butter	1 oz.	30 g
Cherry Confit (page 821)	as needed	as needed

1. Peel and julienne the potatoes.
2. Combine the potatoes with the Parmesan, salt and pepper.
3. Heat the clarified butter in an 8-inch (20-centimeter) nonstick pan. Add the potato mixture and pack it tightly with the back of a spoon. Cook over moderate heat until the potatoes begin to brown.
4. Flip the rösti potatoes and place the pan in a 350°F (180°C) oven. Flipping once, cook until the potatoes are crisp and evenly browned on the outside and soft in the center, approximately 20 minutes on each side.
5. Transfer the rösti potatoes to a wire cooling rack to rest.
6. Slice the rösti horizontally into two round halves. Spread the bottom half with the room-temperature goat cheese. Grind black pepper over the cheese, sprinkle the herbs evenly over the surface and carefully replace the top.
7. Season the lamb and sauté it in 2 fluid ounces (60 milliliters) of clarified butter, turning frequently, until the desired doneness is achieved, approximately 8 to 12 minutes.
8. Remove the lamb and allow it to rest before slicing.
9. Deglaze the pan with the port and add the lamb jus lié. Reduce by half and monté au beurre.
10. At service time, ladle the sauce onto six warm plates, slice the lamb and arrange over the sauce. Cut the rösti into wedges and arrange on the plate. Spoon Cherry Confit around the lamb and serve at once.

Approximate values per serving: **Calories** 660, **Total fat** 39 g, **Saturated fat** 21 g, **Cholesterol** 215 mg, **Sodium** 1260 mg, **Total carbohydrates** 12 g, **Protein** 64 g, **Vitamin A** 60%, **Calcium** 45%

RECIPE 16.13

NOISETTES OF LAMB WITH GARLIC SAUCE

Yield: 4 Servings   **Method:** Sautéing

Lamb noisettes, 2–3 oz. (60–90 g) each	8	8
Salt and pepper	TT	TT
Fresh thyme	1 tsp.	5 ml

Garlic heads	3	3
Fresh rosemary	1 sprig	1 sprig
Olive oil	2 fl. oz.	60 ml
Red wine	4 fl. oz.	120 ml
Jus lié	1 pt.	450 ml

1 Season the noisettes with salt, pepper and thyme.

2 Break the garlic into cloves. Cook the cloves with the rosemary in 1 fluid ounce (30 milliliters) of oil over low heat until they are very soft, approximately 10 minutes.

3 Deglaze with the wine. Add the jus lié; simmer and reduce by half.

4 Strain the sauce through a china cap, pushing to extract some of the garlic. Return the sauce to the saucepan and adjust the consistency and seasonings.

5 Sauté the noisettes to the desired degree of doneness in the remaining oil; serve with the sauce.

Approximate values per 5.5-oz. (165-g) serving: **Calories** 370, **Total fat** 26 g, **Saturated fat** 6 g, **Cholesterol** 105 mg, **Sodium** 660 mg, **Total carbohydrates** 1 g, **Protein** 32 g

CHIAPPETTI'S LAMB SHANK WITH LENTILS AND COUNTRY VEGETABLES

RECIPE 16.14

CHEF STEVEN CHIAPPETTI, Chicago, IL

Yield: 2 Servings   **Method:** Braising

Vegetable oil	as needed	as needed
Lamb shanks, approx. 1 lb. 8 oz. (720 g) each	2	2
Onions, diced	4 oz.	120 g
Carrots, sliced	4 oz.	120 g
Celery, diced	4 oz.	120 g
Bay leaves	2	2
Lamb stock	1 qt.	1 lt
Soy sauce	4 fl. oz.	120 ml
Molasses	5½ oz.	165 g
Lentils, soaked	8 oz.	250 g
Salt and pepper	TT	TT

1 Heat a small amount of oil in a sauté pan. Sear the lamb shanks.

2 Add the onions, carrots, celery and bay leaves to the pan. Then add the lamb stock, soy sauce and molasses to the pan and dissolve the fond with the liquid.

3 Place the pan with the lamb shanks and vegetables in a 400°F (200°C) oven and cook, uncovered, for 1½ hours.

4 Frequently baste the lamb with the molasses-soy broth.

5 Add the lentils and cook for another hour. Season to taste with salt and pepper.

6 Serve the lamb shanks, vegetables and lentils on a large platter.

Approximate values per serving: **Calories** 1660, **Total fat** 45 g, **Saturated fat** 16 g, **Cholesterol** 710 mg, **Sodium** 6300 mg, **Total carbohydrates** 92 g, **Protein** 222 g, **Vitamin A** 90%, **Calcium** 35%, **Iron** 130%

RECIPE 16.15   IRISH LAMB STEW

Yield: 12 Servings, 8 oz. (250 g) each   **Method:** Stewing

Lamb shoulder, 1½-in. (4-cm) cubes	4 lb.	1.8 kg
White stock	3 pt.	1.5 lt
Sachet:		
Bay leaf	1	1
Dried thyme	½ tsp.	2 ml
Peppercorns, crushed	½ tsp.	2 ml
Parsley stems	10	10
Garlic cloves, crushed	4	4
Onion, sliced	1 lb.	450 g
Leek, sliced	8 oz.	225 g
Potato, peeled, large dice	1 lb. 8 oz.	700 g
Salt and white pepper	TT	TT
Carrots, tournéed or batonnet	20	20
Turnips, tournéed or batonnet	20	20
Potatoes, tournéed or batonnet	20	20
Pearl onions, peeled	20	20
Fresh parsley, chopped	1 Tbsp.	15 ml

1 Combine the lamb, stock, sachet, onions, leeks and diced potatoes. Season with salt and white pepper. Bring to a simmer and skim the surface. Simmer the stew on the stove top or cover and cook in the oven at 350°F (180°C) until the lamb is tender, approximately 1 hour.

2 Degrease the stew; remove and discard the sachet.

3 Remove the pieces of diced potato and puré them in a food mill or ricer. Use the potato purée to thicken the stew to the desired consistency.

4 Simmer the stew for 10 minutes to blend the flavors.

5 Cook the tournéed or batonnet vegetables and potatoes and pearl onions separately. At service, heat the vegetable garnishes and add to each portion of stew.

6 Garnish with chopped parsley and serve.

Approximate values per 8-oz. (240-g) serving: **Calories** 560, **Total fat** 26 g, **Saturated fat** 10 g, **Cholesterol** 175 mg, **Sodium** 840 mg, **Total carbohydrates** 26 g, **Protein** 54 g, **Vitamin A** 80%, **Iron** 30%

RECIPE 16.16   WINTER LAMB STEW

PENNSYLVANIA COLLEGE OF TECHNOLOGY, WILLIAMSPORT, PA

Chef Mary G. Trometter, Assistant Professor

Yield: 4 qt. (4 lt)   **Method:** Stewing

Wide egg noodles	24 oz.	675 g
Vegetable oil	2 Tbsp.	30 ml
Lamb leg, boneless, 6 lb. (2.7 kg)	1	1
Salt	2 tsp.	10 ml
Peppercorns, crushed	2 tsp.	10 ml
Worcestershire sauce	7½ fl. oz.	225 ml
Flour	12 oz.	350 g
Fresh sage, chopped	1 Tbsp.	15 ml
Vegetable oil	6 fl. oz.	180 ml
Lamb or beef stock	20 fl. oz.	600 ml
Mild barbecue sauce	10 fl. oz.	300 ml

Steak sauce	5 fl. oz.	150 ml
Celery, medium dice	9 oz.	260 g
Carrot, medium dice	8 oz.	240 g
Cabbage, coarsely chopped	6 oz.	180 g
Parsnips, small dice	8 oz.	240 g
Canned tomatoes, seeded and diced	15 oz.	425 g
Collard greens, chopped	2 oz.	60 g
Clarified butter	1 fl. oz.	30 ml
Kosher salt	TT	TT
Black pepper	TT	TT
Pearl onions, glazed	6 oz.	180 g
Fresh parsley, minced	2 oz.	60 g

1 Boil the pasta al dente. Drain, chill in an ice bath, drain again, toss in 2 tablespoons (30 milliliters) of vegetable oil and reserve for service.

2 Trim the lamb of excess fat. Dice the lamb into stew meat–sized cubes and place in a stainless steel bowl. Combine the salt, crushed peppercorns and 2½ fluid ounces (75 milliliters) of the Worcestershire sauce and pour over the lamb cubes. Massage the marinade into the lamb to coat well. Cover and refrigerate for 20 to 30 minutes.

3 Season the flour with the sage. Heat some of the oil in a heavy pan. Dredge the lamb cubes in the seasoned flour and, working with small batches, sear the lamb in the hot oil. Add more oil as needed. Remove the browned lamb from the pan as it is done and reserve.

4 Deglaze the pan with the stock. Add the barbecue sauce, steak sauce and remaining Worcestershire sauce to the pot and stir to blend.

5 Add the celery, carrots, cabbage, parsnips and tomatoes and stir to combine. Return the seared lamb to the pot. Cover the pot and simmer until the lamb is tender.

6 Reheat the noodles in boiling water.

7 Sauté the collard greens in the clarified butter and season them with kosher salt and pepper. Drain the noodles and toss them with the collard greens. Place a portion of the noodles and greens on a plate and ladle the stew on top. Garnish with the glazed onions and minced parsley.

Approximate values per 8-fl.-oz. (240-ml) serving: **Calories** 600, **Total fat** 24 g, **Saturated fat** 6 g, **Cholesterol** 145 mg, **Sodium** 940 mg, **Total carbohydrates** 52 g, **Protein** 43 g, **Vitamin A** 110%, **Vitamin C** 36%, **Calcium** 10%, **Iron** 35%

LAMB IN INDIAN COCONUT CURRY SAUCE

RECIPE 16.17

Yield: 3 pt. (1.4 lt) **Method:** Stewing

Salt	1 Tbsp.	15 ml
Cumin, ground	2 Tbsp.	30 ml
Coriander, ground	2 Tbsp.	30 ml
Turmeric, ground	2 Tbsp.	30 ml
Cayenne pepper	1 tsp.	5 ml
Garam masala	2½ Tbsp.	40 ml
Black pepper	1 tsp.	5 ml
Lamb leg, 3 lb. (1.3 kg)	1	1
Ginger, 4-in. (10-cm) piece	1	1
Garlic cloves	8	8

Continued

Water	8 fl. oz.	240 ml
Vegetable oil	3 fl. oz.	90 ml
Onions, chopped fine	4 oz.	120 g
Tomatoes, peeled and chopped fine	8 oz.	240 g
Coconut milk	24 fl. oz.	700 ml

1 Combine the salt, cumin, coriander, turmeric, cayenne, garam masala and black pepper.

2 Trim the lamb leg and then cut it into 1-inch (2.5-centimeter) pieces. Place the lamb in a stainless steel bowl and season it with approximately half of the spice mix. Marinate, refrigerated, for at least 1 hour or overnight.

3 Chop the ginger to a paste, place the paste in a double layer of cheesecloth and squeeze out as much juice as possible. Reserve the juice and discard the pulp.

4 Purée the garlic in a blender or food processor with the water and ginger juice until fairly smooth.

5 Heat the oil in a heavy-bottomed pot and add the lamb. Brown the lamb on all sides and then remove it from the pot.

6 Sauté the onions in the same pot until lightly caramelized and then add the garlic-ginger purée. Cook until all of the liquid has evaporated and only oil remains. Add the remaining spice mix and cook for approximately 20 seconds.

7 Add the tomatoes, reduce the heat and continue cooking for 3 to 4 minutes. Add the coconut milk a little at a time, incorporating it into the sauce each time before adding more. Return the lamb to the pan and simmer for 30 minutes or until the lamb is tender. Serve with steamed rice and naan.

Approximate values per ½-c. (120-ml) serving: **Calories** 440, **Total fat** 36 g, **Saturated fat** 19 g, **Cholesterol** 75 mg, **Sodium** 660 mg, **Total carbohydrates** 7 g, **Protein** 23 g, **Vitamin C** 10%, **Iron** 30%

RECIPE 16.18   BLANQUETTE OF LAMB

Yield: 10 Servings, 8 oz. (240 g) each   **Method:** Stewing

White beans, dried	1 lb.	500 g
Onion piquet	2	2
Bouquet garni, for each:	2	2
Carrot stick, 4 in. (10 cm)	1	1
Leek, split, 4-in. (10-cm) piece	1	1
Fresh thyme	1 sprig	1 sprig
Bay leaf	1	1
Lamb leg or shoulder, cut in 1½-inch (4-cm) cubes	4 lb.	1.8 kg
White stock	1½ qt.	1½ lt
Sachet:		
Bay leaf	1	1
Dried thyme	½ tsp.	2 ml
Peppercorns, crushed	½ tsp.	2 ml
Parsley stems	10	10
Garlic cloves, crushed	4	4
Salt	TT	TT
Blond roux	2 oz.	60 g
Heavy cream	10 fl. oz.	300 ml
Dijon mustard	3 Tbsp.	45 ml
Egg yolks	4	4

1 Simmering the lamb.

2 Whisking the roux into the reduced cooking liquid.

3 Whisking a liaison into the sauce.

1 Soak the beans in cold water for 12 hours. Drain, then add enough fresh water to cover the beans by 2–4 inches (5–10 centimeters).

2 Add one onion piquet and one bouquet garni and cook until the beans are tender, approximately 1½ hours. Remove and discard the onion piquet and bouquet garni.

3 Blanch the lamb cubes in boiling salted water.

4 Place the blanched lamb in a pot. Add the stock and the second onion piquet, the second bouquet garni, the sachet and salt. Simmer until the meat is tender, approximately 1½ hours.

5 Remove the meat from the liquid and reserve. Reduce the cooking liquid to 1 quart (1 liter). Incorporate the roux.

6 Combine the heavy cream, mustard and egg yolks and add to the reduced stock as a liaison.

7 Return the lamb to the sauce and adjust the seasonings. Heat the sauce and meat thoroughly but do not allow it to boil. Serve the blanquette with the cooked beans.

4 Adding the lamb to the sauce.

Approximate values per 8-oz. (240-g) serving: **Calories** 710, **Total fat** 43 g, **Saturated fat** 19 g, **Cholesterol** 315 mg, **Sodium** 740 mg, **Total carbohydrates** 14 g, **Protein** 67 g, **Vitamin A** 15%, **Iron** 40%

LAMB NAVARIN

RECIPE 16.19

Yield: 10 Servings, 10 oz. (300 g) each	**Method:** Stewing	
Olive oil	3 Tbsp.	45 ml
Lean lamb shoulder, large dice	3 lb.	1.5 kg
Sugar	1 Tbsp.	15 ml
Salt and pepper	TT	TT
Flour	3 Tbsp.	45 ml
White stock	1 qt.	1 lt
White wine	4 fl. oz.	120 ml
Tomato concassée	8 oz.	250 g
Bouquet garni:		
Carrot stick, 4 in. (10 cm)	1	1
Leek, split, 4-in. (10-cm) piece	1	1
Fresh thyme	1 sprig	1 sprig
Bay leaf	1	1

Continued

Potato, peeled, medium dice	1 lb. 8 oz.	650 g
Carrot, medium dice	1 lb.	450 g
White turnip, peeled, medium dice	1 lb.	450 g
Pearl onions, peeled	12	12
Fresh green peas	6 oz.	180 g

1 In a braiser, brown the meat in the olive oil.

2 Sprinkle the meat with the sugar and season with salt and pepper.

3 Add the flour and cook to make a blond roux.

4 Add the stock and wine. Add the tomatoes and bouquet garni; bring to a boil. Cover and cook in the oven at 375°F (190°C) until the meat is almost tender, approximately 1 to 1½ hours.

5 Remove the meat and hold it in a warm place. Strain the sauce and skim off any excess fat.

6 Combine the sauce, meat, potatoes, carrots, turnips and onions. Cover and cook until the vegetables are almost tender, approximately 25 minutes.

7 Add the peas and cook for 10 minutes more.

Approximate values per 10-oz. (300-g) serving: **Calories** 450, **Total fat** 16 g, **Saturated fat** 5 g, **Cholesterol** 145 mg, **Sodium** 480 mg, **Total carbohydrates** 27 g, **Protein** 50 g, **Vitamin A** 110%, **Vitamin C** 35%

BUT I WILL PLACE THIS CAREFULLY FED PIG
WITHIN THE CRACKLING OVEN; AND, I PRAY,
WHAT NICER DISH CAN E'ER BE GIVEN TO MAN.
—*Aeschylus, ancient Greek poet*
  (c. 525–456 B.C.E.)

17

PORK

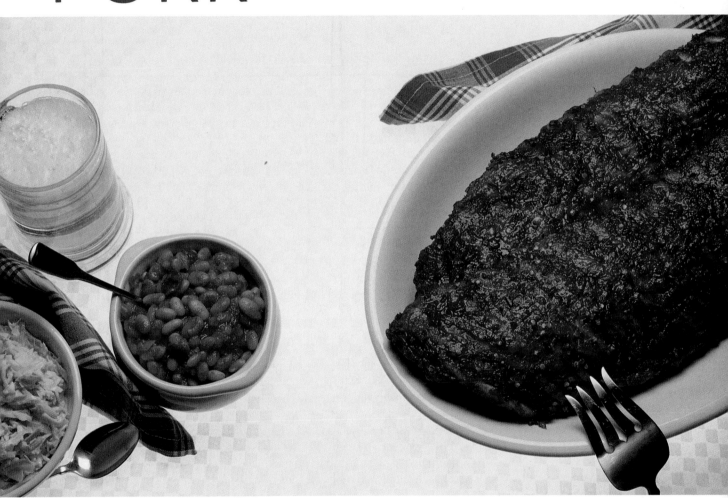

FABULOUS FOOD CATERING,
Phoenix, AZ

**AFTER STUDYING THIS
CHAPTER, YOU WILL BE
ABLE TO:**

▶ identify the primal, subprimal
and fabricated cuts of pork

▶ perform basic butchering
procedures

▶ apply appropriate cooking
methods to several common
cuts of pork

Pork is the meat of hogs, usually butchered before they are one year old. With the exception of beef, Americans consume more pork than any other meat. The pork we eat is leaner and healthier than it once was because of advances in animal husbandry.

Since hogs are butchered at a young age, their meat is generally very tender with a delicate flavor. It is well suited to a variety of cooking methods. More than two-thirds of the pork marketed in the United States is cured to produce products such as smoked hams and smoked bacon. Cured pork products are discussed in Chapter 27, Charcuterie.

▶ PRIMAL AND SUBPRIMAL CUTS OF PORK

After a hog is slaughtered, it is generally split down the backbone, dividing the carcass into bilateral halves. Like the beef carcass, each side of the hog carcass is then further broken down into the primal cuts: shoulder, Boston butt, belly, loin and fresh ham.

Hogs are bred specifically to produce long loins; the loin contains the highest-quality meat and is the most expensive cut of pork. Pork is unique in that the ribs and loin are considered a single primal. They are not separated into two different primals, as are the ribs and loin of beef, veal and lamb.

Figure 17.1 shows the relationship between the hog's bone structure and the primal cuts. As with all meats, it is important to know the location of bones when cutting or working with pork. This makes meat fabrication and carving easier and aids in identifying cuts. Figure 17.2 shows the primal cuts of pork and their location on the carcass. A hog carcass generally weighs in a range of 120 to 210 pounds (55 to 110 kg).

SHOULDER

The primal shoulder, known as the picnic ham, is the lower portion of the hog's foreleg; it accounts for approximately 20 percent of the carcass weight. The shoulder contains the arm and shank bones and has a relatively high ratio of bone to lean meat.

Because all pork comes from hogs slaughtered at a young age, the shoulder is tender enough to be cooked by any method. It is, however, one of the least tender cuts of pork. It is available smoked or fresh. The shoulder is fairly inexpensive and, when purchased fresh, it can be cut into shoulder butt steaks or boned and cut into smaller pieces for sautéing or stewing. Whole pork shoulder is the cut preferred by many barbecue pit masters throughout the American South.

The foreshank is called the shoulder hock and is almost always smoked. Shoulder hocks are often simmered for long periods in soups, stews and braised dishes to add flavor and richness.

BOSTON BUTT

The primal Boston butt is a square cut located just above the primal pork shoulder. It accounts for approximately 7 percent of the carcass weight.

The Boston butt is very meaty and tender, with a good percentage of fat to lean meat. Containing only a small portion of the blade bone, the Boston butt is a good choice when a recipe calls for a solid piece of lean pork. The

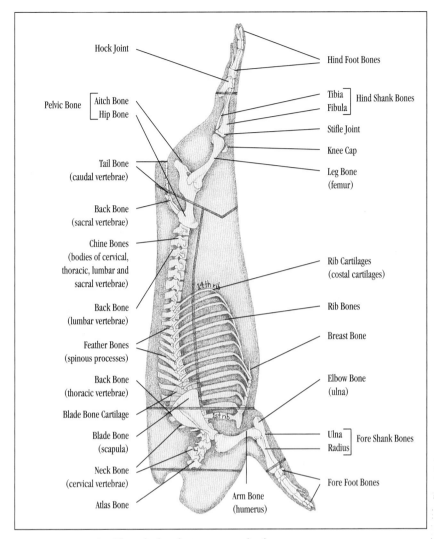

Hock Joint

Hind Foot Bones

Pelvic Bone

Aitch Bone
Hip Bone

Tibia
Fibula } Hind Shank Bones

Stifle Joint

Knee Cap

Tail Bone
(caudal vertebrae)

Leg Bone
(femur)

Back Bone
(sacral vertebrae)

Chine Bones
(bodies of cervical,
thoracic, lumbar and
sacral vertebrae)

14th rib

Rib Cartilages
(costal cartilages)

Back Bone
(lumbar vertebrae)

Rib Bones

Feather Bones
(spinous processes)

Breast Bone

Back Bone
(thoracic vertebrae)

Elbow Bone
(ulna)

Blade Bone Cartilage

1st rib

Blade Bone
(scapula)

Ulna
Radius } Fore Shank Bones

Neck Bone
(cervical vertebrae)

Fore Foot Bones

Atlas Bone

Arm Bone
(humerus)

FIGURE 17.1 ▶ The skeletal structure of a hog

HOGS: A SOURCE FOR SLOGANS

Hogs were first brought to Florida by Spanish explorers in 1539, and they thrived in this heavenly new environment. The British shipped hogs to the colonies, and as early as 1639, Virginia's colonists were supplying England with ham and bacon. During colonial days, pork was packed in barrels for shipment, giving rise to the term "meat packing." During the War of 1812, the U.S. government shipped pork to American soldiers in barrels stamped with the letters "US" and the name of the meat packer, Sam Wilson. The soldiers referred to the meat as "Uncle Sam's meat," thus giving birth to the national government's nickname, Uncle Sam.

Boston Butt

Loin

Fresh Ham

Shoulder

Belly

FIGURE 17.2 ▶ The primal cuts of pork

Boston Butt

fresh Boston butt is sometimes cut into steaks or chops to be broiled or sautéed. When the Boston butt is smoked, it is usually boneless and called a cottage ham.

BELLY

The primal pork belly is located below the loin. Accounting for approximately 16 percent of the carcass weight, it is very fatty with only streaks of lean meat. It contains the spareribs, which are always separated from the rest of the belly before cooking.

Spareribs usually are sold fresh but can also be smoked. Typically, they are simmered and then grilled or baked while being basted with a spicy barbecue sauce. The remainder of the pork belly is nearly always cured and smoked to produce bacon.

Pork Spareribs

LOIN

The loin is cut from directly behind the Boston butt and includes the entire rib section as well as the loin and a portion of the sirloin area. The primal loin accounts for approximately 20 percent of the carcass weight. It contains a portion of the blade bone on the shoulder end, a portion of the hip bone on the ham end, all the ribs and most of the backbone.

The primal pork loin is the only primal cut of pork not typically smoked or cured. Most of the loin is a single, very tender eye muscle. It is quite lean but contains enough intramuscular and subcutaneous fat to make it an excellent choice for a moist-heat cooking method such as braising. Or it can be prepared with dry-heat cooking methods such as roasting or sautéing. The loin also contains the pork tenderloin, located on the inside of the rib bones on the sirloin end of the loin. The tenderloin is the most tender cut of pork; it is very versatile and can be trimmed, cut into medallions and sautéed, or the whole tenderloin can be roasted or braised. The most popular cut from the loin is the pork chop. Chops can be cut from the entire loin, the choicest being center-cut chops from the primal loin after the blade bone and

Pork Loin

Pork Tenderloin

Pork Backribs

Pork Loin Chops

sirloin portions at the front and rear of the loin are removed. The pork loin can be purchased boneless or boned and tied as a roast. A boneless pork loin is smoked to produce Canadian bacon. The rib bones, when trimmed from the loin, can be served as barbecued pork back ribs.

Although not actually part of the primal loin, fatback is the thick layer of fat—sometimes more than an inch (2.5 centimeters) thick—between the skin and the lean eye muscle. It has a variety of uses in the kitchen, especially in the preparation of charcuterie items.

FRESH HAM

The primal fresh ham is the hog's hind leg. It is a rather large cut accounting for approximately 24 percent of the carcass weight. The ham contains the aitch, leg and hind shank bones. Fresh ham, like the legs of other meat animals, contains large muscles with relatively small amounts of connective tissue.

Like many other cuts of pork, hams are often cured and smoked. But fresh hams also produce great roasts and can be prepared using almost any cooking method. When cured and smoked, hams are available in a variety of styles; they can be purchased bone-in, shankless or boneless, partially or fully cooked. Fully cooked hams are also available canned. There is a specific ham for nearly every use and desired degree of convenience. The shank portion of the ham is called the ham hock. It is used in the same manner as the shoulder hock.

Fresh Ham

▶ BUTCHERING PROCEDURES

Other than suckling pigs (which are very young, very small whole pigs used for roasting or barbecuing whole), pork products generally are not purchased in forms larger than the primal cuts described earlier. There are a few important pork fabrication and butchering techniques that you should master, however.

▶ PROCEDURE FOR BONING A PORK LOIN

1 Starting on the sirloin end of a full pork loin, remove the tenderloin in one piece by making smooth cuts against the inside of the rib bones. Pull gently on the tenderloin as you cut.

2 Turn the loin over and cut between the ribs and the eye meat. Continue separating the meat from the bones, following the contours of the bones, until the loin is completely separated from the bones.

3 Trim around the blade bone on the shoulder end of the loin and remove it.

The fully boned loin will consist of (from left to right) cartilage, the tenderloin, boneless loin and loin bones.

▶ PROCEDURE FOR TYING A BONELESS PORK ROAST
   WITH THE HALF-HITCH METHOD

1 Wrap the loose end of the string around the pork loin and tie it with a double knot.

2 Make a loop and slide it down over the roast to approximately 1 inch (2.5 centimeters) from the first knot.

3 Make another loop and slide it down. Continue in this fashion until the whole roast has been tied.

4 Turn the roast over and cut the string, leaving enough to wrap lenghwise around the roast to the original knot.

5 Wrap the string around the end of the roast, then around the string that formed the last loop. Continue in this fashion for the length of the roast, pulling the string tight after wrapping it around each loop.

6 Turn the roast back over. Wrap the string around the front end of the roast and secure it to the first loop at the point where you tied the first knot.

7 The finished roast. Note the even intervals at which the strings are tied. They should be just snug enough to hold the shape of the roast; they should not dig in or cut the meat.

▶ PROCEDURE FOR CUTTING A CHOP FROM A PORK LOIN

Center-cut pork chop can be cut from the center portion of a bone-in pork loin without the aid of a saw by using a boning knife and a heavy cleaver. Trim the excess fat from the loin, leaving a ¼-inch (6-millimeter) layer to protect the meat during cooking.

1 Cut through the meat with the knife.

2 Use the cleaver to chop through the chine bone.

3 To produce a cleaner chop, trim the meat from the end of the rib bone. Then, with the boning knife, separate the loin meat from the chine bones and separate the chine bone from the rib with the cleaver.

▶ PROCEDURE FOR CUTTING A POCKET IN A PORK CHOP

To make a pocket in a pork chop for stuffing, start with a thick chop or a double rib chop. Cut the pocket deep enough to hold ample stuffing, but be careful not to puncture either surface of the chop.

1 Use the tip of a boning knife to cut a pocket.

Table 17.1	USING COMMON CUTS OF PORK			
PRIMAL	**SUBPRIMAL OR FABRICATED CUT**	**IMPS**	**COOKING METHODS**	**SERVING SUGGESTIONS**
Shoulder	Picnic shoulder	405	Dry heat (roast or bake)	Smoked picnic shoulder
Boston butt	Boston butt	406	Dry heat (broil or grill; sauté) Moist heat (simmer)	Broiled Boston butt steaks Choucroute
Belly	Bacon	539	Dry heat (sauté) Moist heat (simmer) Combination (braise)	Breakfast meat Seasoning Seasoning
	Spareribs	416A	Combination (steam then grill)	Barbecued spareribs
Loin	Pork loin	410	Dry heat (roast) Combination (braise)	Roast pork Braised pork chops
	Pork tenderloin	415	Dry heat (broil or grill; sauté; roast)	Roast pork tenderloin
	Pork back ribs	422	Combination (steam then grill)	Barbecued back ribs
	Pork loin chops	1410	Dry heat (broil or grill) Combination (braise)	Broiled loin chop with mushroom sauce Braised loin chop with leeks and fennel
Fresh ham	Fresh ham	401A	Dry heat (roast)	Roast pork with apricots and almonds

▶ PROCEDURE FOR TRIMMING A PORK TENDERLOIN

As with a beef tenderloin, the pork tenderloin must be trimmed of all fat and silverskin. Follow the procedures outlined in Chapter 14, Beef, for trimming a beef tenderloin.

1 Use a boning knife to remove the silverskin from a pork tenderloin.

CONCLUSION

Pork can be enjoyed cured, processed or fresh. The mild flavor of fresh pork blends well with many different seasonings, making it a popular menu item. It is naturally tender and can be prepared by almost any dry-heat, moist-heat or combination cooking method. Properly fabricated and prepared, it can be a nutritious meat.

1 List each pork primal, and describe its location on the carcass. Identify two subprimals or fabricated cuts taken from each primal.

2 What is unique about the primal pork loin as compared to the beef or veal loin?

3 Are fatback and bacon taken from the same primal? How are they different?

4 What is the only primal cut of pork that is not typically smoked or cured? How is it best cooked? Explain your answer.

5 What is the World Pork Expo? How is such an event useful for chefs and restauranteurs?

RECIPE 17.1

CAROLINA BARBECUED RIBS

CHEF ALAN "SKIP" HAUSE

Now owner and executive chef of his own catering company—Fabulous Food, Inc.—in Phoenix, Arizona, Chef Alan "Skip" Hause began studying culinary arts in high school, graduating from the Dutchess County Board of Cooperative Educational Services Technical High School in 1977. He continued his education at the Culinary Institute of America in Hyde Park, New York, graduating with an AOS degree in 1979.

After interning with a large hotel in Atlanta, Chef Hause headed west. In Phoenix he worked his way up the culinary ladder in independent restaurants, eventually becoming executive chef of a large full-service catering and special-event company, a position he held for 15 years. In 1995, he and his charming wife, Chantal, opened their own company, specializing in social and corporate catering. He is co-author of this textbook.

As Chef Hause tells students and externs, "Use your time in school to learn the *hows* and *whys* of cooking. Learn the principles now; learn recipes later. Your chefs and instructors possess a wealth of information and experience. Draw information from them and learn from their experiences."

NOTE: This dish appears in the chapter opening photograph.

Yield: 6 Servings, approx. 4 ribs each   **Method:** Roasting

Salt and pepper	TT	TT
Crushed red pepper flakes	1 Tbsp.	15 ml
Pork back ribs, 3–4 lb.		
(1.3–1.8 kg) slab	2	2
White vinegar	1 pt.	450 ml
Sauce:		
Onion, chopped coarse	5 oz.	150 g
Garlic cloves	3	3
Green bell pepper, chopped coarse	4 oz.	120 g
Plum tomatoes, canned	1 pt.	450 ml
Red Devil hot sauce	8 fl. oz.	225 ml
Brown sugar	10 oz.	300 g
Lemon juice	2 fl. oz.	60 ml

1 Combine the salt, pepper and red pepper flakes. Rub this mixture over both sides of the ribs, coating them well.

2 Place the ribs in a nonreactive pan and add the vinegar. Cover and refrigerate several hours or overnight.

3 Uncover the ribs, turn them presentation side down and bake in a 375°F (190°C) oven for 1½ hours.

4 Remove the ribs from the liquid and place on a clean sheet pan, turning them so that the presentation side is up. Increase the oven temperature to 400°F (200°C) and bake for an additional 30 minutes.

5 Prepare the sauce by puréeing the onions, garlic, bell peppers and tomatoes in a food processor or blender. Pour this mixture into a nonreactive saucepan and add the remaining sauce ingredients.

6 Simmer the sauce over low heat until it thickens, approximately 15 to 20 minutes.

7 Brush the ribs with the sauce and serve additional sauce on the side. Serve with Creamy Coleslaw, page 782, and Baked Beans, page 664.

Approximate values per serving: **Calories** 1410, **Total fat** 68 g, **Saturated fat** 23 g, **Cholesterol** 315 mg, **Sodium** 1280 mg, **Total carbohydrates** 65 g, **Protein** 134 g, **Vitamin A** 20%, **Vitamin C** 120%, **Iron** 35%

BEER-MARINATED PORK TENDERLOIN

Yield: 6 Servings, 6 oz. (180 g) each	**Method:** Grilling	
Pork tenderloins, approx. 14 oz. (400 g) each	3	3
Marinade:		
Light soy sauce	4 fl. oz.	120 ml
Beer, room temperature	12 fl. oz.	360 ml
Light brown sugar	2 oz.	60 g
Fresh ginger, grated	1½ Tbsp.	22 ml

1 Clean the tenderloins, removing all visible fat and silverskin.

2 Combine the marinade ingredients, stirring until the sugar dissolves.

3 Place the tenderloins in a hotel pan and cover with the marinade. Cover the pan and refrigerate for 2 to 6 hours.

4 Remove the tenderloins from the marinade and grill over medium-hot coals, turning as needed.

5 Allow the cooked tenderloins to rest for 5 minutes, then slice thinly on the bias.

Approximate values per serving: **Calories** 592, **Total fat** 42 g, **Saturated fat** 16 g, **Cholesterol** 143 mg, **Sodium** 762 mg, **Total carbohydrates** 13 g, **Protein** 35 g, **Iron** 13%

PORK CHIMICHURRI KABOBS

Chimichurri is a thick, fresh herb sauce from Argentina, where it is traditionally served as an accompaniment to grilled meats. In this recipe it is used as both a marinade and a sauce.

Yield: 8 Servings of pork, 1 pt. (470 ml) sauce	**Method:** Grilling	
Chimichurri sauce		
Garlic cloves, peeled	8	8
Onions, chopped	4 oz.	120 g
Fresh lemon juice	3 Tbsp.	50 ml
Dried oregano, crushed	2 Tbsp.	30 ml
Fresh parsley	1 bunch	1 bunch
Olive oil	6 fl. oz.	180 ml
Sherry wine vinegar	2 fl. oz.	60 ml
Salt	1 tsp.	5 ml
Red pepper flakes	½ tsp.	3 ml
Black pepper	½ tsp.	3 ml
Pork loin, trimmed	2 lb.	1.8 kg

1 Combine the sauce ingredients in a food processor fitted with the metal blade and pulse until the ingredients are thoroughly blended, but not puréed. The mixture should be slightly coarse.

2 Cut the pork into ¾-inch (2-centimeter) cubes and place them in a nonreactive pan. Add approximately three-quarters of the chimichurri sauce and stir thoroughly. Cover and refrigerate for 4 to 6 hours. Reserve the remaining sauce to serve with the kabobs.

3 Remove the pork from the marinade, discarding any marinade left in the pan. Arrange the pork on eight skewers. Cook on a hot grill, turning as necessary to cook thoroughly and brown evenly. Serve with black beans and rice and the reserved chimichurri sauce.

Variations: Use boneless, skinless chicken or cubes of lamb shoulder meat in place of the pork.

Approximate values per serving with ½ Tbsp. (7 ml) sauce: **Calories** 200, **Total fat** 11 g, **Saturated fat** 3.5 g, **Cholesterol** 70 mg, **Sodium** 85 mg, **Total carbohydrates** 1 g, **Protein** 25 g

RECIPE 17.4

**THE SCHOOL OF CULINARY ARTS
AT KENDALL COLLEGE, EVANSTON, IL**
Chef Mike Artlip, CEC, CCE

Yield: 25–30 Servings   **Method:** Roasting

Fresh ham, approx. 22 lb. (10 kg)	1	1
Garlic heads, minced	3	3
Dried oregano	½ oz.	15 g
Adobo seasoning	TT	TT
Salt and pepper	TT	TT
Mojo criollo	10 fl. oz.	300 ml

▶ **adobo seasoning** a commercial spice blend; although several brands are available, most include dried chiles, Mexican oregano, cumin, black pepper, garlic powder and onion powder

▶ **mojo criollo** a citrus and herb marinade used in Latino cuisines; bottled brands are available in Hispanic markets

1 Using a skewer or meat fork, poke holes over the entire surface of the ham approximately 1 to 2 inches (2.5 to 5 centimeters) deep.
2 Combine the garlic, oregano, adobo seasoning, salt and pepper and rub the ham with the mixture, being sure to push the garlic and seasonings into the holes. Pour the mojo criollo over the ham. Marinate the ham under refrigeration for 24 hours.
3 Remove the ham from the marinade and place on a rack in a roasting pan. Roast at 325°F (160°C) until the center reaches 155°F (68°C), approximately 4 hours.
4 Allow the ham to rest for 30 minutes before carving.

Approximate values per serving: **Calories** 550, **Total fat** 31 g, **Saturated fat** 11 g, **Cholesterol** 205 mg, **Sodium** 135 mg, **Total carbohydrates** 2 g, **Protein** 62 g, **Vitamin C** 10%, **Iron** 15%

RECIPE 17.5

Yield: 16 Servings, 6 oz. (180 g) each   **Method:** Baking

Ham, fully cooked, bone in,		
12–14 lb. (5.4–6.3 kg)	1	1
Brown sugar	6 oz.	180 g
Cloves, ground	½ tsp.	2 ml
Crushed pineapple, with juice	16 oz.	500 g
Bourbon	8 fl. oz.	250 ml
Orange marmalade	8 oz.	250 g

1 Peel the skin from the ham and trim the exterior fat to an even thickness of ¼ inch (6 millimeters).
2 Combine the sugar and cloves and pat this mixture evenly over the top of the ham. Roast the coated ham at 350°F (180°C) for 30 minutes.
3 Combine the pineapple, bourbon and marmalade in a saucepan over medium heat. Do not allow the bourbon to flame.
4 Pour the sauce over the ham and cook until done, basting frequently, approximately 3 hours.
5 Remove the ham from the roasting pan. Keep it warm and allow it to rest for 30 minutes before carving.

Approximate values per 6-oz. (180-g) serving: **Calories** 610, **Total fat** 19 g, **Saturated fat** 6 g, **Cholesterol** 185 mg, **Sodium** 4520 mg, **Total carbohydrates** 24 g, **Protein** 85 g, **Iron** 20%

CHINESE BARBECUED SPARERIBS

RECIPE 17.6

Yield: approx. 24 ribs

Method: Roasting

Sparerib racks, 2 lb. 8 oz. (1.1 kg) each	2	2
Garlic cloves, crushed	2	2
Tomato ketchup	2 Tbsp.	30 ml
Soy sauce	2 Tbsp.	30 ml
Hoisin sauce	2 Tbsp.	30 ml
Red wine	2 Tbsp.	30 ml
Fresh ginger, grated	1 Tbsp.	15 ml
Honey	1 Tbsp.	15 ml

1 Cut the spareribs into individual ribs and arrange them on a rack in a baking pan. Roast for 45 minutes at 300°F (150°C).

2 Combine the remaining ingredients into a sauce. Brush the spareribs lightly with the sauce. Roast for 30 minutes more.

3 Turn the spareribs and brush with more sauce. Roast until the ribs are well browned, approximately 30 minutes.

Approximate values per rib: **Calories** 181, **Total fat** 11 g, **Saturated fat** 4 g, **Cholesterol** 49 mg, **Sodium** 118 mg, **Total carbohydrates** 1 g, **Protein** 21 g, **Iron** 4%

PORK LOIN WITH PRUNES

RECIPE 17.7

Yield: 6 Servings, 6 oz. (180 g) each

Method: Roasting

Boneless pork loin roast, 3 lb. (1.5 kg)	1	1
Salt and pepper	TT	TT
Prunes, pitted	1 lb. 8 oz.	750 g
Carrot, chopped coarse	3 oz.	90 g
Onion, chopped coarse	6 oz.	180 g
Vegetable oil	1 Tbsp.	15 ml
Clarified butter	1 Tbsp.	15 ml
Fresh rosemary	1 tsp.	5 ml
Fresh thyme	1 tsp.	5 ml
Bay leaf, crushed	1	1
Garlic cloves	2	2
Apple juice	8 fl. oz.	250 ml
White stock	8 fl. oz.	250 ml
Sugar	2 oz.	60 g
Vinegar	2 fl. oz.	60 ml

1 Butterflying the pork loin.

2 Rolling the pork loin around the filling.

3 The cooked loin sliced for service.

1 Trim and butterfly the pork loin; reserve the trimmings. (To butterfly the loin, slice it partway through the center and open it like a book, then flatten it into a rectangular shape.) Season with salt and pepper.

2 Reserve 12 prunes and arrange the remaining prunes along the length of the loin. Roll up the loin and tie with butcher's twine.

3 Brown the pork roll and pork trimmings, carrots and onions in the oil and butter.

4 Add the herbs and garlic and roast the pork on the bed of trimmings and vegetables at 350°F (180°C), basting frequently with the fat that accumulates in the pan, until done, approximately 45 to 60 minutes.

5 Poach the reserved prunes in the apple juice until plump; set aside.

6 Remove the roast from the pan and keep it warm. Degrease the pan and deglaze with the white stock. Simmer for 15 minutes, then strain.

7 Combine the sugar and vinegar in a saucepan. Bring to a boil and cook without stirring until the mixture turns a caramel color. Immediately remove from the heat and add the juices from the roasting pan. When the sputtering stops, return the pan to the heat and skim any fat from the surface; keep the sauce warm over low heat.

8 Drain the prunes. Remove the twine from the roast. Slice and serve the meat with the sauce and poached prunes.

Approximate values per serving: **Calories** 850, **Total fat** 16 g, **Saturated fat** 5 g, **Cholesterol** 185 mg, **Sodium** 530 mg, **Total carbohydrates** 110 g, **Protein** 66 g, **Vitamin A** 45%, **Vitamin C** 15%, **Iron** 30%

RECIPE 17.8 ROASTED PORK LOIN WITH PEANUT SAUCE

NEWBURY COLLEGE, BROOKLINE, MA

Senior Instructor Scott Doughty

Yield: 6–8 Servings   **Method:** Roasting

Pork loin, center cut, bone in, 5 lb. (2.2 kg)	1	1
Salt	3/4 tsp.	4 ml
Black pepper	1 1/2 tsp.	8 ml
Fresh ginger, peeled, chopped	1 Tbsp.	15 ml
Mirepoix	1 1/2 c.	360 ml
Chicken or pork stock	6 fl. oz.	180 ml
Peanut Sauce (recipe follows)	as needed	as needed

1 Bone the pork loin and trim the excess fat from the surface, leaving a 1/8-inch (3-millimeter) layer. Reserve some of the fat for the sauce. Rub all of the surfaces of the meat with the salt, pepper and ginger. Tie the roast in several places.

2 Distribute the mirepoix in a roasting pan and place the tied pork loin on it. Place the roasting pan in a preheated 450°F (230°C) oven. Reduce the oven to 325°F (160°C) and roast the loin until it reaches 150°F (66°C) in the center, approximately 50 minutes. Carryover cooking will continue to cook the roast after it is removed from the oven.

3 Transfer the roast to a warm place and allow it to rest for at least 10 minutes. Remove the strings.

4 If meat juices remain in the pan, heat the pan over medium heat until they reduce to form a fond. Do not allow it to burn. Pour off the fat. Deglaze the pan with the stock and reduce by half. Strain and reserve the liquid for the Peanut Sauce.

5 Slice the pork loin into thin slices and serve with Peanut Sauce.

Approximate values per serving with 1 fl. oz. (30 ml) sauce: **Calories** 560, **Total fat** 36 g, **Saturated fat** 12 g, **Cholesterol** 160 mg, **Sodium** 650 mg, **Total carbohydrates** 5 g, **Protein** 52 g, **Vitamin A** 40%, **Iron** 15%

PEANUT SAUCE

Yield: 20 fl. oz. (550 ml)

Pork fat	6 oz.	180 g
Garlic, minced	1 tsp.	5 ml
Cayenne pepper	½ tsp.	2 ml
Cider vinegar	1 Tbsp.	15 ml
Soy sauce	1 Tbsp.	15 ml
Chicken stock	1 pt.	480 ml
Salt	1 tsp.	5 ml
Deglazing liquid from the pork roast	3 fl. oz.	90 ml
Peanut butter	4 oz.	120 g
Cornstarch	2 Tbsp.	30 ml
Water, cold	4 fl. oz.	120 g

1 Cook the trimmed pork fat in a saucepan to render 1 fluid ounce (30 milliliters) of rendered fat. Discard the remaining fat.

2 Sauté the garlic and cayenne pepper in the rendered fat without browning.

3 Combine the cider vinegar, soy sauce, chicken stock, salt and the deglazing liquid from the pork roast. Add it to the garlic. Stir in the peanut butter until it blends.

4 Combine the cornstarch and water. Stir this slurry into the sauce. Return the sauce to a simmer. Do not allow it to boil or it will curdle. Hold in a warm spot for service.

Approximate values per 1-fl.-oz. (30-ml) serving: **Calories** 50, **Total fat** 4 g, **Saturated fat** 1 g, **Cholesterol** 0 mg, **Sodium** 260 mg, **Total carbohydrates** 2 g, **Protein** 2 g

SAUTÉED PORK MEDALLIONS WITH RED PEPPER AND CITRUS

RECIPE 17.9

Yield: 8 Servings, 6 oz. (180 g) each   **Method:** Sautéing

Pork loin, boneless, 3 lb. (1.4 kg)	1	1
Salt and pepper	TT	TT
Olive oil	6 fl. oz.	180 ml
Orange juice	6 fl. oz.	180 ml
Lemon juice	2 Tbsp.	30 ml
Green onions, sliced	4 oz.	120 g
Oranges	4	4
Flour	as needed for dredging	
Red bell pepper, julienne	12 oz.	350 g
Grand Marnier	4 fl. oz.	120 ml
Demi-glace	1 pt.	450 ml

1 Season the pork with salt and pepper and marinate overnight in 4 fluid ounces (120 milliliters) of the olive oil, 4 fluid ounces (120 milliliters) of the orange juice, 1 tablespoon (15 milliliters) of the lemon juice and 2 ounces (60 grams) of the green onions.

2 Zest the oranges. Blanch and refresh the zest. Peel and section the oranges.

3 Cut the pork into 3-ounce (90-gram) medallions and pound lightly.

4 Dredge the medallions in flour seasoned with salt and pepper.

5 Sauté the medallions in the remaining olive oil until done, approximately 5 minutes. Remove from the pan and reserve.

6 Add the bell peppers and remaining green onions to the pan and sauté lightly.

7 Remove the pan from the flame and deglaze with Grand Marnier.

8 Add the demi-glace, orange zest, and remaining orange and lemon juices. Adjust the seasonings.

9 Serve two medallions of pork per portion with sauce. Garnish with the orange sections.

Approximate values per 6-oz. (180-g) serving: **Calories** 275, **Total fat** 15 g, **Saturated fat** 3 g, **Cholesterol** 68 mg, **Sodium** 195 mg, **Total carbohydrates** 11 g, **Protein** 25 g, **Vitamin C** 60%

RECIPE 17.10   JAMBALAYA

THE SCHOOL OF CULINARY ARTS
AT KENDALL COLLEGE, Evanston, IL
Chef Mike Artlip, CEC, CCE

Yield: 40 Servings

Andouille or smoked sausage, medium dice	2 lb. 8 oz.	1.2 kg
Tasso ham, medium dice (optional)	1 lb. 4 oz.	600 g
Garlic, chopped	4 oz.	120 g
Onion, medium dice	1 lb. 4 oz.	600 g
Green bell pepper, medium dice	12 oz.	360 g
Red bell pepper, medium dice	4 oz.	120 g
Celery, medium dice	12 oz.	360 g
Green onions, chopped	1 bunch	1 bunch
Olive oil	as needed	as needed
Cajun spice mix (page 541)	TT	TT
Long-grain white rice	1 lb. 8 oz.	720 g
Tomatoes, diced, canned	7 c.	1.7 lt
Chicken stock	20 fl. oz.	600 ml
Shrimp, peeled, deveined	2 lb. 8 oz.	1.2 kg
Salt and pepper	TT	TT

1 In a large rondeau, sauté the andouille and tasso to render their fat. Remove the meat and reserve. Add the garlic, onions, bell peppers, celery and green onions to the fat and sauté. If there is not enough fat, add a small amount of olive oil.

2 As the vegetables soften, season them with a little Cajun spice mix.

3 Add the rice and toss until all the rice is coated with the fat. Add the tomatoes and their liquid and stir to combine.

4 Add the stock, shrimp, reserved andouille and tasso and bring to a simmer.

5 Cook at a low simmer until the rice is done, approximately 15 minutes, checking the seasoning periodically. Add more Cajun spice mix, salt and pepper as necessary. There will be little to no liquid left in the pan when the rice is done.

Variation: *Vegetarian Jambalaya*—Substitute assorted cooked beans and vegetables for the shrimp, andouille and tasso and use vegetable stock instead of chicken stock.

Approximate values per serving: **Calories** 210, **Total fat** 9 g, **Saturated fat** 3 g, **Cholesterol** 65 mg, **Sodium** 390 mg, **Total carbohydrates** 20 g, **Protein** 12 g, **Vitamin C** 30%, **Iron** 10%

MIE GORENG
(INDONESIAN FRIED NOODLES WITH PORK)

Yield: 3 lb. (1.3 kg) **Method:** Stir-frying

Rice vermicelli	10 oz.	280 g
Pork loin, boneless, trimmed	1 lb.	450 g
Peanut oil	2 Tbsp.	30 ml
Red pepper flakes	1/2 tsp.	3 ml
Napa cabbage, chopped	3 c.	700 ml
Celery, sliced	1/2 c.	120 ml
Green onions, thinly sliced	2	2
Dried shrimp paste (optional)	1/2 tsp.	2 ml
Garlic cloves, chopped	2	2
Fresh ginger, grated	1 tsp.	5 ml
Soy sauce	4 Tbsp.	60 ml

1 Break the vermicelli into thirds. Cook in rapidly boiling water until al dente. Drain and rinse with cold water.

2 Cut the pork into 1/4-inch (6-centimeter) strips. Heat a wok or large sauté pan; add 1 tablespoon (15 milliliters) of the oil. Stir-fry the pork with the red pepper flakes until cooked through, approximately 2 to 3 minutes. Remove the pork from the pan and set aside.

3 Add the remaining oil to the pan and stir-fry the cabbage, celery and green onions until they are slightly wilted. Add the shrimp paste, garlic and ginger. Then add the noodles along with the soy sauce. Return the meat to the pan and cook briefly, just until the meat is thoroughly reheated. Serve immediately.

Approximate values per 8-oz. (240-g serving): **Calories** 360, **Total fat** 11 g, **Saturated fat** 3 g, **Cholesterol** 45 mg, **Sodium** 730 mg, **Total carbohydrates** 40 g, **Protein** 24 g, **Iron** 20%

NATAING
(CAMBODIAN-STYLE RED PORK)

Yield: 4 Servings, 1/2 cup (120 ml) each **Method:** Sautéing

Vegetable oil	2 Tbsp.	30 ml
Ground pork	8 oz.	225 g
New Mexico chile, ground	1 Tbsp.	15 ml
Cayenne pepper	1/2 tsp.	2 ml
Garlic cloves, sliced very thin	6	6
Shallot, sliced very thin	1	1
Granulated sugar	3 Tbsp.	45 ml
Coconut milk, unsweetened	8 fl. oz.	240 ml
Fish sauce	1 Tbsp.	15 ml
Peanuts, chopped	2 oz.	60 g
Cilantro sprigs	as needed for garnish	

1 In a sauté pan, heat the oil and sauté the pork with the ground chiles and cayenne until the meat is brown.

2 Add the garlic and shallots and sauté until soft.

3 Add the sugar, coconut milk and fish sauce. Cook for approximately 10 minutes or until the pork is fully cooked and the flavors are well blended. Add the peanuts.

4 Garnish with the cilantro sprigs and serve warm with rice.

Approximate values per 1/2-c. (120-ml) serving: **Calories** 430, **Total fat** 35 g, **Saturated fat** 16 g, **Cholesterol** 40 mg, **Sodium** 410 mg, **Total carbohydrates** 17 g, **Protein** 16 g, **Vitamin A** 15%, **Iron** 15%

RECIPE 17.13

CRISPY SWEET AND SOUR PORK

**THE SCHOOL OF CULINARY ARTS
AT KENDALL COLLEGE, EVANSTON, IL**

Chef Mike Artlip, CEC, CCE

Yield: 40 Servings   **Method:** Deep-frying

Marinade:		
Chinese rice wine	3½ fl. oz.	100 ml
Salt	1 tsp.	5 ml
Cornstarch	3 Tbsp.	45 ml
White pepper	1 tsp.	5 ml
Garlic, minced	1½ Tbsp.	23 ml
Fresh ginger, minced	1 Tbsp.	15 ml
Sesame oil	1½ Tbsp.	23 ml
Soy sauce	1½ Tbsp.	23 ml
Eggs, beaten	6	6
Pork butt, lean, 2-in. (5-cm) dice	5 lb.	2.4 kg
Cornstarch	6 oz.	180 g
Green bell peppers, large dice	7	7
Tomatoes, chopped into 2-in. (5-cm) pieces	6 lb.	2.8 kg
Sauce:		
Cornstarch	10 oz.	300 g
Water, cold	40 fl. oz.	1.2 lt
Garlic heads, minced	5	5
Vegetable oil	1 fl. oz.	30 ml
Granulated sugar	32 oz.	900 g
Ketchup	1½ c.	360 ml
Soy sauce	3 fl. oz.	90 ml
Cider vinegar	22 fl. oz.	660 ml
Pineapple chunks, #10 can, drained, juice reserved	½ can	½ can

1 Combine the ingredients for the marinade. Add the diced pork and marinate for 30 minutes.

2 Add the cornstarch to the pork and mix well. The mixture should look like a batter. Add more cornstarch if the mixture is too thin. Allow the mixture to rest until it becomes sticky, approximately 15 minutes.

3 Using the swimming method, deep-fry the pork cubes until fully cooked, dark brown and crisp, approximately 2 to 3 minutes. Stir with a spider to prevent the pieces from sticking together while deep-frying. Drain well and reserve.

4 Steam the bell peppers until they begin to soften slightly. Add the tomatoes to the steamer and cook until they begin to soften. Remove the vegetables from the steamer and reserve.

5 To make the sauce, combine the cornstarch and water to form a slurry. Sauté the garlic in the vegetable oil without browning. Add the remaining sauce ingredients and the reserved pineapple juice and bring to a simmer. Thicken the sauce with the slurry, using just enough of the slurry to achieve the desired consistency.

6 Add the bell pepper and tomato mixture and the pineapple chunks. Bring the sauce to a simmer. Reheat the pork in a hot oven and add to the sauce immediately before service. Serve with white rice.

Approximate values per serving: **Calories** 300, **Total fat** 6 g, **Saturated fat** 2 g, **Cholesterol** 70 mg, **Sodium** 420 mg, **Total carbohydrates** 47 g, **Protein** 14 g, **Vitamin A** 15%, **Vitamin C** 60%, **Iron** 10%, **Claims**—supplies vitamin A and iron, high in vitamin C

STUFFED PORK CHOPS   RECIPE 17.14

Yield: 10 Servings   **Method:** Braising

Thick-cut pork chops, approx. 8 oz. (250 g) each	10	10
Celery, small dice	4 oz.	120 g
Onion, small dice	6 oz.	180 g
Whole butter, melted	6 oz.	180 g
Fresh bread cubes, ½ in. (1.2 cm)	8 oz.	250 g
Parsley, chopped	1 Tbsp.	15 ml
Salt and pepper	TT	TT
White stock	approx. 8 fl. oz.	approx. 250 ml
Olive oil	2 fl. oz.	60 ml
Demi-glace	1 qt.	1 lt

1 Cut pockets in the chops.

2 Sauté the celery and onions in 2 ounces (60 grams) of butter until tender.

3 Combine the celery, onions and remaining butter with the bread cubes, parsley, salt and pepper. Add enough stock to moisten the dressing.

4 Stuff the mixture into each of the pork chops. Seal the pockets with toothpicks and tie with butcher's twine.

5 In a braiser, brown the stuffed chops well on each side in the olive oil.

6 Add the demi-glace. Bring to a simmer, cover and place in a 325°F (160°C) oven. Cook until tender, approximately 45 minutes.

7 Remove the chops from the pan. Degrease the sauce and reduce to the desired consistency. Strain the sauce and adjust the seasonings.

Approximate values per 10-oz. (300-g) serving: **Calories** 650, **Total fat** 38 g, **Saturated fat** 16 g, **Cholesterol** 225 mg, **Sodium** 390 mg, **Total carbohydrates** 5 g, **Protein** 70 g, **Vitamin A** 15%, **Iron** 15%

1 Stuffing the pork chops.

2 Closing the stuffed chops with toothpicks.

3 The finished chops.

RECIPE 17.15

CHOUCROUTE

Yield: 12 Servings—4 oz. (120 g) sauerkraut, 1 sausage and 7 oz. (200 g) pork each

Method: Braising

Bacon, medium dice	8 oz.	250 g
Onion, medium dice	12 oz.	340 g
Garlic, chopped fine	1½ oz.	45 g
Granny Smith apples, medium dice	8 oz.	250 g
Sauerkraut	2 lb. 8 oz.	1 kg
Dry white wine	4 fl. oz.	120 ml
White wine vinegar	4 fl. oz.	120 ml
Chicken stock	1 pt.	500 ml
Sachet:		
Juniper berries	6	6
Bay leaves	3	3
Cloves	2	2
Caraway seeds	1 tsp.	5 ml
Boneless pork butt, 4 lb. (1.8 kg)	1	1
Smoked pork loin	2 lb.	1 kg
Red potatoes, peeled and quartered	3 lb.	1.4 kg
Bratwurst	12 links	12 links
Salt and pepper	TT	TT

1 Render the bacon.

2 Sauté the onions, garlic and apples in the bacon fat without browning.

3 Rinse the sauerkraut and squeeze out the liquid. Add the sauerkraut to the pan.

4 Stir in the wine, vinegar, stock and sachet.

5 Place the pork butt on the sauerkraut. Cover and braise in a 325°F (160°C) oven for 1 hour.

6 Add the smoked pork loin and potatoes and braise an additional 30 minutes.

7 Add the bratwurst and braise until all the meats are tender and the potatoes are done, approximately 30 minutes. Remove and discard the sachet. Season to taste with salt and pepper.

8 Carve the meats and serve with a portion of the sauerkraut and potatoes.

Approximate values per serving: **Calories** 940, **Total fat** 50 g, **Saturated fat** 18 g, **Cholesterol** 255 mg, **Sodium** 1910 mg, **Total carbohydrates** 33 g, **Protein** 90 g, **Vitamin C** 35%, **Iron** 30%

RECIPE 17.16

CASSOULET

CHEF LELAND ATKINSON, WASHINGTON, DC

Yield: 8 Servings—8 oz. (250 g) pork stew, 1½ oz. (45 g) sausage and 1 piece of duck each

Method: Stewing

White beans	1 lb.	450 g
White stock	2 qt.	2 lt
Smoked ham, large dice	8 oz.	250 g
Bouquet garni:		
Carrot stick, 4 in. (10 cm)	1	1
Leek, split, 4-in. (10-cm) piece	1	1
Fresh thyme	1 sprig	1 sprig
Bay leaf	1	1
Lamb or other sausage	1 lb.	450 g
Onion, medium dice	6 oz.	180 g

Garlic, chopped	½ oz.	15 g
Pork butt, cut in 2-in. (5-cm) cubes	1 lb. 8 oz.	700 g
Salt and pepper	TT	TT
Olive oil	1 fl. oz.	30 ml
Mirepoix	8 oz.	250 g
White wine	6 fl. oz.	180 ml
Tomato concassée	1 lb.	450 g
Demi-glace	1 pt.	450 ml
Brown stock	8 fl. oz.	250 ml
Sachet:		
Bay leaf	1	1
Dried thyme	½ tsp.	2 ml
Peppercorns, cracked	½ tsp.	2 ml
Parsley stems	8	8
Garlic cloves, crushed	2	2
Duck Confit (page 461)	8 pieces	8 pieces

1 To make the bean stew, soak the white beans overnight in water. Drain and combine with the white stock, ham and bouquet garni. Bring to a simmer and cook for 30 minutes. Add the sausage, onions and garlic; simmer until the beans are tender.

2 Remove and reserve the sausage.

3 Drain the beans, reserving both the beans and the cooking liquid. Reduce the cooking liquid by half and combine with the beans.

4 To make the meat stew, season the pork with salt and pepper and brown it in the olive oil. Remove and reserve the meat.

5 Add the mirepoix to the pan and sauté. Deglaze with the white wine and add the tomato concassée, demi-glace, brown stock and sachet. Cover and simmer the pork until tender, approximately 45 minutes.

6 Remove the meat from the sauce and reserve. Discard the sachet. Reduce the sauce until thick; return the meat to the sauce.

7 To serve, scrape the excess fat from the Duck Confit. Place the duck in a roasting pan and roast at 350°F (180°C) until the meat is hot and the skin is crisp, approximately 20 minutes.

8 Place a portion of hot beans in a soup plate. Place a portion of the Duck Confit in the plate. Arrange a portion of the meat stew on top of the beans and around the duck.

9 Slice the sausage and add it to the plate. Garnish with fresh herbs.

Approximate values per serving: **Calories** 630, **Total fat** 37 g, **Saturated fat** 12 g, **Cholesterol** 130 mg, **Sodium** 2360 mg, **Total carbohydrates** 23 g, **Protein** 53 g, **Vitamin** C 25%, **Iron** 30%

THE FACT IS THAT IT TAKES MORE THAN INGREDIENTS AND TECHNIQUE TO COOK A GOOD MEAL. A GOOD COOK PUTS SOMETHING OF HIMSELF INTO THE PREPARATION—HE COOKS WITH ENJOYMENT, ANTICIPATION, SPONTANEITY, AND HE IS WILLING TO EXPERIMENT.

—Pearl Bailey, American entertainer
  (1918–1990) in Pearl's Kitchen, 1973

18

POULTRY

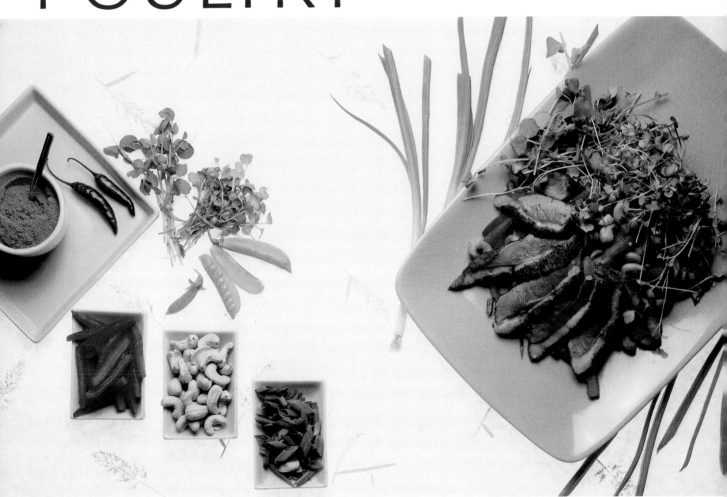

SENCHA, Colorado Springs, CO
Brent Beavers, Executive Chef

Poultry is the collective term for domesticated birds bred for eating. They include chickens, ducks, geese, guineas, pigeons and turkeys. (Game birds such as pheasant, quail and partridge are described in Chapter 19, Game; farm-raised ratites—ostrich, emu and rhea—are discussed here.) Poultry is generally the least expensive and most versatile of all main-dish foods. It can be cooked by almost any method, and its mild flavor goes well with a wide variety of sauces and accompaniments.

In this chapter, we discuss the different kinds and classes of poultry and how to choose those that best suit your needs. You will learn how to store poultry properly to prevent food-borne illnesses and spoilage, how to butcher birds to produce the specific cuts you need and how to apply a variety of cooking methods properly.

Many of the cooking methods discussed here have been applied previously to meats. Although there are similarities with these methods, there are also many distinct differences. As you study this chapter, review the corresponding cooking methods for meats and note the similarities and differences.

▶ MUSCLE COMPOSITION

The muscle tissue of poultry is similar to that of mammals in that it contains approximately 72 percent water, 20 percent protein, 7 percent fat and 1 percent minerals; it consists of bundles of muscle cells or fibers held together by connective tissue. Unlike red meat, poultry does not contain the intramuscular fat known as marbling. Instead, a bird stores fat in its skin, its abdominal cavity and the fat pad near its tail. Poultry fat is softer and has a lower melting point than other animal fats. It is easily rendered during cooking.

As with red meats, poultry muscles that are used more often tend to be tougher than those used less frequently. Also, the muscles of an older bird tend to be tougher than those of a younger one. Because the majority of poultry is marketed at a young age, however, it is generally very tender.

The breast and wing flesh of chickens and turkeys is lighter in color than the flesh of their thighs and legs. This color difference is due to a higher concentration of the protein myoglobin in the thigh and leg muscles. Myoglobin is the protein that stores oxygen for the muscle tissues to use. More-active muscles require more myoglobin and tend to be darker than less-active ones. Because chickens and turkeys generally do not fly, their breast and wing muscles contain little myoglobin and are therefore a light color. Birds that do fly have only dark meat. Dark meat also contains more fat and connective tissue than light meat, and its cooking time is longer.

Skin color may vary from white to golden yellow, depending on what the bird was fed. Such color differences are not an indication of overall quality.

▶ IDENTIFYING POULTRY

The USDA recognizes six categories or **kinds** of poultry: chicken, duck, goose, guinea, pigeon and turkey. Each poultry kind is divided into **classes** based predominantly on the bird's age and tenderness. The sex of young birds is not

Table 18.1 USDA CHICKEN CLASSES

CLASS	DESCRIPTION	AGE	WEIGHT	COOKING METHOD
Game hen	Young or immature progeny of Cornish chickens or of a Cornish chicken and a White Rock chicken; very flavorful	5–6 weeks	2 lb. (1 kg) or less	Split and broil or grill; roast
Broiler/fryer	Young with soft, smooth-textured skin; relatively lean; flexible breastbone	13 weeks	3 lb. 8 oz. (1.5 kg) or less	Any cooking method; very versatile
Roaster	Young with tender meat and smooth-textured skin; breastbone is less flexible than broiler's	3–5 months	3 lb. 8 oz.–5 lb. (1.5–2 kg)	Any cooking method
Capon	Surgically castrated male; tender meat with soft, smooth-textured skin; bred for well-flavored meat; contains a high proportion of light to dark meat and a relatively high fat content	Under 8 months	6–10 lb. (2.5–4.5 kg)	Roast
Hen/stewing	Mature female; flavorful but less tender meat; non-flexible breastbone	Over 10 months	2 lb. 8 oz.–8 lb. (1–3.5 kg)	Stew or braise

significant for culinary purposes. It does matter, however, with older birds: Older male birds are tough and stringy and have less flavor than older female birds. Tables 18.1 through 18.6 list identifying characteristics and suggested cooking methods for each of the various kinds and classes of poultry.

CHICKEN

Chicken (Fr. *poulet*) is the most popular and widely eaten poultry in the world. It contains both light and dark meat and has relatively little fat. A young, tender chicken can be cooked by almost any method; an older bird is best stewed or braised. Chicken is extremely versatile and may be seasoned, stuffed, basted or garnished with almost anything. Chicken is inexpensive and readily available, fresh or frozen, in a variety of forms.

The French *poulet de Bresse* is a special category of chicken, frequently touted as the world's finest. The only certified-origin chicken in the world, it is a blue-legged variety raised near the village of Bresse in southeastern Burgundy. These are free-range birds fed a special diet of milk products plus sweet corn and other grains. An identifying leg band is attached to each young chick, and authentic birds will be sold with the banded leg attached. They are available in the United States, at a premium price, from specialty food importers.

Rock Cornish Game Hen

Chicken Broiler/Fryer

Capon

Table 18.2   USDA DUCK CLASSES

CLASS	DESCRIPTION	AGE	WEIGHT	COOKING METHOD
Broiler/fryer	Young bird with tender meat; a soft bill and windpipe	8 weeks or less	3 lb. 8 oz.–4 lb. (1.5–1.8 kg)	Roast at high temperature
Roaster	Young bird with tender meat; rich flavor; easily dented wind-pipe	16 weeks or less	4–6 lb. (1.8–2.5 kg)	Roast
Mature	Old, bird with tough flesh; hard bill and windpipe	6 months or older	4–6 lb. (1.8–2.5 kg)	Braise

DUCK

▶ **duckling** a duck slaughtered before it is eight weeks old

▶ **magret** (may-gray) a duck breast, traditionally taken from the ducks that produce foie gras; It is usually served boneless but with the skin intact

The duck (Fr. *canard*) used most often in commercial food service operations is a roaster **duckling.** It contains only dark meat and large amounts of fat. In order to make the fatty skin palatable, it is important to render as much fat as possible. Duck has a high percentage of bone and fat to meat; for example, a 4-pound duck will serve only two people, while a 4-pound roasting chicken will serve four people.

Roaster Duckling

GOOSE

A goose (Fr. *oie*) contains only dark meat and has very fatty skin. It is usually roasted at high temperatures to render the fat. Roasted goose is popular at holidays and is often served with an acidic fruit-based sauce to offset the fattiness.

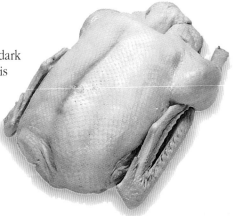

Young Goose

Table 18.3   USDA GOOSE CLASSES

CLASS	DESCRIPTION	AGE	WEIGHT	COOKING METHOD
Young	Rich, tender dark meat with large amounts of fat; easily dented windpipe	6 month or less	6–12 lb. (2.5–5.5 kg)	Roast at high temperature, accompany with acidic sauces
Mature	Tough flesh and hard windpipe	Over 6 months	10–16 lb. (4.5–7 kg)	Braise or stew

Table 18.4 **USDA GUINEA CLASSES**

CLASS	DESCRIPTION	AGE	WEIGHT	COOKING METHOD
Young	Tender meat; flexible breastbone	3 months	12 oz.–1 lb. 8 oz. (0.3–0.7 kg)	Bard and roast; sauté
Mature	Tough flesh; hard breastone	Over 3 months	1–2 lb (0.5–1 kg)	Braise or stew

GUINEA

A guinea or guinea fowl (Fr. *pintade*) is the domesticated descendant of a game bird. It has both light and dark meat and a flavor similar to pheasant. Guinea is tender enough to sauté. Because it contains little fat, a guinea is usually barded prior to roasting. Guinea, which is relatively expensive, is not as popular here as it is in Europe.

Young Guinea

PIGEON

Squab

The young pigeon (Fr. *pigeon*) used in commercial food service operations is referred to as **squab.** Its meat is dark, tender and well suited for broiling, sautéing or roasting. Squab has very little fat and benefits from barding.

TURKEY

Turkey (Fr. *dinde*) is the second most popular category of poultry in the United States. It has both light and dark meat and a relatively small amount of fat. Younger turkey is economical and can be prepared in almost any manner.

RATITES

Ratites are a family of flightless birds with small wings and flat breastbones. They include the **ostrich** (which is native to Africa), the **emu** (native to Australia) and the **rhea** (native to South America). Ratite meat, which is classified as red meat, even though it is poultry flesh, is a dark, cherry-red color with a flavor similar to beef, but a little sweeter, and a soft texture. It is low in fat and calories. Most ratite meat is from birds slaughtered at 10 to 13 months of age. It

Turkey

Table 18.5 **USDA PIGEON CLASSES**

CLASS	DESCRIPTION	AGE	WEIGHT	COOKING METHOD
Squab	Immature pigeon; very tender, dark flesh and a small amount of fat	4 weeks	12 oz.–1 lb. 8 oz. (0.3–0.7 kg)	Broil, roast or sauté
Pigeon	Mature bird; coarse skin and tough flesh	Over 4 weeks	1–2 lb (0.5–1 kg)	Braise or stew

Table 18.6   **USDA TURKEY CLASSES**

CLASS	DESCRIPTION	AGE	WEIGHT	COOKING METHOD
Fryer/roaster	Immature bird of either sex (males are called toms); tender meat with smooth skin; flexible breastbone	16 weeks or less	4–9 lb. (2–4 kg)	Roast or cut into scallops and sauté or pan-fry
Young	Tender meat with smooth skin; less-flexible breastbone	8 months or less	8–22 lb. (3.5–10 kg)	Roast or stew
Yearling	Fully matured bird; reasonably tender meat and slightly coarse skin	15 months or less	10–30 lb. (4.5–13 kg)	Roast or stew
Mature	Older bird with coarse skin and tough flesh	15 months or older	10–30 lb. (4.5–13 kg)	Stew, ground or used in processed products

Ostrich Fan

is generally cut from the back (which contains the very tender tenderloin), the thigh (also known as the fan) and the leg, and is available as steaks, filets, medallions, roasts, cubes or ground.

Ratite meat is often prepared like veal. The more tender cuts, such as those from the back or thigh, can be marinated and then cooked by dry-heat cooking methods, especially broiling and grilling, roasting and pan-frying. Because it has little fat, care must be taken to avoid overcooking, and these products are usually served medium rare to medium. Tougher cuts, such as those from the leg, are best ground or prepared with combination cooking methods.

LIVERS, GIZZARDS, HEARTS AND NECKS

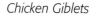

Chicken Giblets

Livers, gizzards, hearts and necks are commonly referred to as **giblets.** Although most poultry kinds are sold with giblets, chickens can be purchased with or without them, depending on your needs.

Giblets can be used in a variety of ways. Gizzards (a bird's second stomach), hearts and necks are often used to make giblet gravy. Gizzards are sometimes trimmed and deep-fried; hearts are sometimes served sautéed and creamed. Necks are very flavorful and can be added to stocks for flavor and richness. Livers, hearts and gizzards are not added to stocks, however, because of their strong flavors.

Chicken livers are often used in pâtés, sautéed or broiled with onions and served as an entrée.

A TURKEY BY ANY OTHER NAME . . .

In *Food in History,* Reay Tannahill explains why we call a turkey a turkey and not a peru. Turkeys were known as *uexolotl* to 16th-century native Central Americans. They were first brought to Europe by returning Spanish explorers early in the 1500s. Turkish merchants visiting Seville, Spain, on their journeys to and from the eastern Mediterranean brought these exotic birds to England, where the English dubbed them "turkie-cocks." This was eventually shortened to "turkeys." The Turks called these birds "hindi," suggesting that they believed the birds originated in India (as opposed to the Indies). This was a belief shared by the French, who called the bird *coq d'Inde,* which was later corrupted to *dinde* or *dindon.* The Germans followed suit, calling the bird *indianische Henn,* as did the Italians, who called it *galle d'India.* Meanwhile, in India, the bird was called a *peru*—which was a little closer to the geographical mark.

FOIE GRAS

Foie gras is the enlarged liver of a duck or goose. Considered a delicacy since Roman times, it is now produced in many parts of the world, including the United States. Foie gras is produced by methodically fattening the birds by force-feeding them specially prepared corn while limiting their activity. Fresh foie gras consists of two lobes that must be separated, split and deveined. Good foie gras will be smooth, round and putty-colored. It should not be yellow or grainy. Goose foie gras is lighter in color and more delicate in flavor than that of duck. Duck foie gras has a deeper, winy flavor and is more frequently used than goose foie gras. Fresh foie gras can be grilled, roasted, sautéed or made into pâtés or terrines. No matter which cooking method is used, care must be taken not to overcook the liver. Foie gras is so high in fat that overcooking will result in the liver actually melting away. Most foie gras used in this country is pasteurized or canned. Canned foie gras may consist of solid liver or small pieces of liver compacted to form a block. Canned foie gras mousse is also available. Truffles are a natural accompaniment to foie gras and are used in many canned preparations.

Duck Foie Gras

► NUTRITION

Poultry is an economical source of high-quality protein. Poultry's nutritional values are similar to other meats, except that chicken and turkey breast meat is lower in fat and higher in niacin than other lean meats. Generally, dark meat contains more niacin and riboflavin than white meat.

► INSPECTION AND GRADING OF POULTRY

INSPECTION

All poultry produced for public consumption in the United States is subject to USDA inspection. Inspections ensure that products are processed under strict sanitary guidelines and are wholesome and fit for human consumption. Inspections do not indicate a product's quality or tenderness. The round inspection stamp illustrated in Figure 18.1 can be found either on a tag attached to the wing or included in the package labeling.

GRADING

Grading poultry is voluntary but virtually universal. Birds are graded according to their overall quality, with the grade (USDA A, B or C) shown on a shield-shaped tag affixed to the bird or on a processed product's packaging. See Figure 18.2.

According to the USDA, Grade A poultry is free from deformities, with thick flesh and a well-developed fat layer; free of pinfeathers, cuts or tears and broken bones; free from discoloration and, if it is frozen, free from defects that occur during handling or storage. Nearly all poultry used in wholesale and retail outlets is Grade A. Grade B and C birds are used primarily for processed poultry products.

Quality grades have no bearing on the product's tenderness or flavor. A bird's tenderness is usually indicated by its class (for example, a "young turkey" is younger and more tender than a yearling). Its grade (USDA A, B or C) within each class is determined by its overall quality.

FIGURE 18.1 ► USDA inspection stamp for poultry

Grade Mark

FIGURE 18.2 ► Grade stamp for USDA Grade A poultry

FREE-RANGE CHICKENS

Chicken has become increasingly popular in recent years, in part because it is inexpensive, versatile and considered healthier than meat. Indeed, more than 100 million chickens are processed weekly in this country. To meet an ever-increasing demand, chickens are raised indoors in huge chicken houses that may contain as many as 20,000 birds. They are fed a specially formulated mixture composed primarily of corn and soybean meal. Animal protein, vitamins, minerals and small amounts of antibiotics are added to produce quick-growing, healthy birds.

Many consumers feel that chickens raised this way do not have the flavor of chickens that are allowed to move freely and forage for food. Some consumers are concerned about the residual effects of the vitamins, minerals and antibiotics added to the chicken feed. To meet the demand for chickens raised the "old-fashioned way," some farmers raise (and many fine establishments offer) free-range chickens.

Although the USDA has not standardized regulations for free-range chicken, generally the term *free-range* applies to birds that are allowed unlimited access to the area outside the chicken house. Often they are raised without antibiotics, fed a vegetarian diet (no animal fat or by-products), processed without the use of preservatives and raised under more humane growing methods than conventionally grown birds. Most free-range chickens are marketed at 9–10 weeks old and weigh 4½ to 5 pounds (2 to 2½ kilograms)–considerably more mature and heavier than conventional broilers. They are generally sold with heads and feet intact and are more expensive than conventionally raised chickens.

Many consumers (in both the dining room and the kitchen) feel that free-range chicken is superior in flavor and quality. Others find no perceptible differences. As a consumer, you will have to decide whether any difference is worth the added expense.

▶ PURCHASING AND STORING POULTRY

PURCHASING POULTRY

Poultry can be purchased in many forms: fresh or frozen, whole or cut up, bone-in or boneless, portion controlled (P.C.), individually quick-frozen (IQF) or ground. Chicken and turkey are also widely used in prepared and convenience items and are available fully cooked and vacuum-wrapped or boned and canned. Although purchasing poultry in a ready-to-use form is convenient, it is not always necessary; poultry products are easy to fabricate and portion. Whole fresh poultry is also less expensive than precut or frozen products.

As with meats, you should consider your menu, labor costs, storage facilities and employee skills when deciding whether to purchase whole fresh poultry or some other form.

STORING POULTRY

Poultry is a potentially hazardous food. It is highly perishable and particularly susceptible to contamination by salmonella bacteria. It is critical that poultry be stored at the correct temperatures.

Fresh chickens and other small birds can be stored on ice or at 32°F–34°F (0°C–2°C) for up to two days; larger birds can be stored up to four days at these temperatures. Frozen poultry should be kept at 0°F (−18°C) or below (the colder the better) and can be held for up to six months. It should be thawed gradually under refrigeration, allowing two days for chickens and as long as four days for larger birds. Never attempt to cook poultry that is still partially frozen; it will be impossible to cook the product evenly, and the areas that were still frozen may not reach the temperatures necessary to destroy harmful bacteria. Never partially cook poultry one day and finish cooking it later; bacteria are more likely to grow under such conditions.

SANITATION AND CROSS-CONTAMINATION

Review the information in Chapter 2, Food Safety and Sanitation, before butchering any poultry. Be sure that all work surfaces, cutting boards, knives, hands and other equipment used to prepare poultry products are clean and sanitary. Be careful that juices and trimmings from poultry do not come in contact with other foods. Anything coming in contact with raw poultry should be cleaned and sanitized before it comes in contact with any other food. Cooked foods should never be placed in containers that were used to hold the raw product. Kitchen towels that are used to handle poultry or clean up after butchering should be sanitized before being reused to prevent cross-contamination.

▶ BUTCHERING PROCEDURES

Poultry is easier to butcher than meats and is often processed on-site. You should be able to perform the following commonly encountered procedures. Because the different kinds of poultry are similar in structure, these procedures apply to a variety of birds.

▶ PROCEDURE FOR CUTTING A BIRD IN HALF

Often the first step in preparing poultry is to cut the bird in half. Broiler and fryer chickens are often split to make two portions. This procedure removes the backbone and breast bone (also known as the keel bone) for a neat finished product.

1 Square up the bird by placing it on its back and pressing on the legs and breast to create a more uniform appearance.

2 Place the bird on its breast and hold the tail tightly with the thumb and forefinger of one hand. Using a rigid boning knife and in a single swift movement, cut alongside the backbone from the bird's tail to head.

3 Lay the bird flat on the cutting board and remove the backbone by cutting through the ribs connecting it to the breast.

4 Bend the bird back, breaking the breast bone free.

5 Run your fingers along the bone to separate the breast meat from it; pull the bone completely free. Be sure to remove the flexible cartilage completely.

6 Cut through the skin to separate the bird into two halves. The halves are ready to be cooked; for a more attractive presentation, follow Steps 7 and 8.

7 Trim off the wing tips and the ends of the leg bone.

8 Make a slit in the skin below the leg and tuck the leg bone into the slit.

▶ PROCEDURE FOR CUTTING A BIRD INTO PIECES

This is one of the most common butchering procedures. It is also very simple once you understand the bird's structure and are able to find each of its joints.

1 Remove the leg by pulling the leg and thigh away from the breast and cutting through the skin and flesh toward the thigh joint.

2 Cut down to the thigh joint, twist the leg to break the joint and cut the thigh and leg from the carcass. Be careful to trim around the oyster meat (the tender morsel of meat located next to the backbone); leave it attached to the thigh. Repeat with the other leg.

3 To split the breast, follow Steps 2 through 6 for cutting a bird in half. Cut the breast into two halves.

4 The bird is now cut into four quarters.

5 To cut the bird into six pieces, separate the thigh from the leg by making a cut guided by the line of fat on the inside of the thigh and leg.

6 To cut the bird into eight pieces, separate the wing from the breast by cutting the joint, or split the breast, leaving a portion of the breast meat attached to the wing.

▶ PROCEDURE FOR PREPARING A BONELESS BREAST

A boneless chicken breast is one of the most versatile and popular poultry cuts. It can be broiled, grilled, baked, sautéed, pan-fried or poached. Boneless turkey breast can be roasted or sliced and sautéed as a substitute for veal. The skin can be removed or left intact.

1 Remove the keel bone from the bone-in breast, following Steps 4, 5 and 6 for cutting a bird in half.

2 With the chicken breast lying skin side down, separate the rib bones, wing and wishbone from the breast. Leave the two tender pieces of meat known as the tenderloins attached to the breast. Repeat the procedure on the other side, being sure to remove the small wishbone pieces from the front of the breast.

3 The skin may be left intact or removed to produce a skinless boneless breast.

▶ PROCEDURE FOR PREPARING A SUPRÊME OR AIRLINE BREAST

A chicken suprême or airline breast is half of a boneless chicken breast with the first wing bone attached. The tip of the wing bone is removed, yielding a neat and attractive portion that can be prepared by a variety of cooking methods. The skin can be left on or removed.

1 Remove the legs from a chicken following Steps 1 and 2 for cutting a bird into pieces. Place the bird on its back. Locate the wishbone, trim around it and remove it.

2 Cut along one side of the breast bone, separating the meat from the bone.

3 Following the natural curvature of the ribs, continue cutting to remove the meat from the bones.

4 When you reach the wing joint, cut through the joint, keeping the wing attached to the breast portion. Cut the breast free from the carcass.

5 Make a cut on the back of the joint between the first and second wing bones.

6 Break the joint and pull the meat and skin back to expose a clean bone. Trim the wing bone.

7 The suprême can be prepared skin-on or skinless.

▶ PROCEDURE FOR BONING A CHICKEN LEG AND THIGH

Chicken breasts are usually more popular than legs and thighs. There are, however, uses for boneless, skinless leg and thigh meat; they can be stuffed or used for ballotines, for example.

1 Carefully cut through the skin, meat and tendons at the base of the leg. Be sure to cut through completely to the bone.

2 Pull the skin off the leg with your hands, then break the joint between the leg and thigh. Twist and pull out the leg bone.

3 Working from the inside of the thigh bone, separating it from the meat.

4 Cut around the cartilage at the joint between the leg and thigh and remove the thigh bone and cartilage.

▶ MARINATING POULTRY

Most poultry is quite mild in flavor, so a marinade is often used to add flavor and moisture, especially to poultry that will be broiled or grilled. Barbecued chicken is a simple and popular example of marinated poultry. Other poultry marinades can be a mixture of white wine or lemon juice, oil, salt, pepper, herbs and spices, such as that given in Recipe 18.1.

WHITE WINE MARINADE   RECIPE 18.1

Yield: 1 qt. (1 lt)

Garlic, minced	2 tsp.	10 ml
Onion, small dice	5 oz.	150 g
Dry white wine	24 fl. oz.	750 ml
Bay leaves	2	2
Dried thyme	2 tsp.	10 ml
White pepper	1 tsp.	5 ml
Salt	1 Tbsp.	15 ml
Lemon juice	1 fl. oz.	30 ml
Vegetable oil	4 fl. oz.	120 ml

1 Combine all ingredients.

Approximate values per 1-fl.-oz. (30-ml) serving: **Calories** 35, **Total fat** 3.5 g, **Saturated fat** 0 g, **Cholesterol** 0 mg, **Sodium** 220 mg, **Total carbohydrates** 1 g, **Protein** 0 g, Claims—no saturated fat; no cholesterol; no sugar; low calorie

Poultry absorbs flavors quickly, so if pieces are left too long in an acidic marinade, they may take on undesirable flavors. Two hours is often sufficient, with smaller pieces requiring less time in the marinade than larger ones.

If the marinade contains oil, drain the poultry well to avoid flare-up when the item is placed on the broiler or grill. Use a clean kitchen towel or a paper towel to wipe excess moisture from the poultry's surface so that it browns more easily. The marinade can be used to baste the item during cooking, but leftover marinade should not be served uncooked or reused because of the danger of bacterial contamination from the raw poultry.

▶ APPLYING VARIOUS COOKING METHODS

The principles of cooking discussed in Chapter 10 and applied to meats in earlier chapters also apply to poultry. Dry-heat methods are appropriate for young, tender birds. Moist-heat methods should be used with older, less tender products.

DRY-HEAT COOKING METHODS

Cooking poultry with dry-heat methods—broiling and grilling, roasting, sautéing, pan-frying and deep-frying—presents some unique challenges. Large birds such as turkeys benefit from low-heat cooking but are better when served with the crispy skin gained through higher temperatures. Duck and goose skins contain a great deal of fat that must be rendered during the cooking process. Small birds such as squab must be cooked at sufficiently high temperatures to crisp their skins but can be easily overcooked. Boneless chicken breasts, particularly flavorful and popular when broiled or grilled, are easily overcooked and become dry because they do not contain bones to help retain moisture during cooking. Proper application of the following dry-heat cooking methods will help meet these challenges and ensure a good-quality finished product.

BROILING AND GRILLING

Broiled and grilled poultry should have a well-browned surface and can show crosshatched grill marks. It should be moist, tender and juicy throughout. It may be seasoned to enhance its natural flavors or marinated or basted with any number of flavored butters or sauces.

Selecting Poultry to Broil or Grill

Smaller birds such as Cornish hens, chickens and squab are especially well suited for broiling or grilling. Whole birds should be split or cut into smaller pieces before cooking; their joints may be broken so that they lie flat. Quail and other small birds can be skewered before being broiled to help them cook evenly and retain their shape. Be especially careful when cooking breast portions or boneless pieces; the direct heat of the broiler or grill can overcook the item very quickly.

Seasoning Poultry to Be Broiled or Grilled

Poultry is fairly neutral in flavor and responds well to marinating. Poultry may also be basted periodically during the cooking process with flavored butter, oil or barbecue sauce. At the very least, broiled or grilled poultry should be well seasoned with salt and pepper just before cooking.

Determining Doneness

With the exception of duck breasts and squab, which are sometimes left pink, broiled or grilled poultry is always cooked well done. This makes the poultry particularly susceptible to becoming dry and tough because it contains little fat and is cooked at very high temperatures. Particular care must be taken to ensure that the item does not become overcooked.

Four methods are used to determine the doneness of broiled or grilled poultry:

1 *Touch*—When the item is done, it will have a firm texture, resist pressure and spring back quickly when pressed with a finger.

2 *Temperature*—Use an instant-read thermometer to determine the item's internal temperature. This may be difficult, however, because of the item's size and the heat from the broiler or grill. Insert the thermometer in the thickest part of the item away from any bones. It should read 165°F–170°F (74°C–77°C) at the coolest point.

3 *Looseness of the joints*—When bone-in poultry is done, the leg will begin to move freely in its socket.

4 *Color of the juices*—Poultry is done when its juices run clear or show just a trace of pink. This degree of doneness is known in French as *à point*.

Accompaniments to Broiled and Grilled Poultry

If the item was basted with an herb butter, it can be served with additional butter; if the item was basted with barbecue sauce, it should be served with the same sauce. Be careful, however, that any marinade or sauce that came in contact with the raw poultry is not served unless it is cooked thoroughly to destroy harmful bacteria. Additional sauce suggestions are found in Table 11.5.

Broiled or grilled poultry is very versatile and goes well with almost any side dish. Seasoned and grilled vegetables are a natural accompaniment, and deep-fried potatoes are commonly served.

▶ PROCEDURE FOR BROILING OR GRILLING POULTRY

As with meats, broiled or grilled poultry can be prepared by placing it directly on the grate. Poultry is also often broiled using a rotisserie.

1 Heat the broiler or grill.

2 Use a wire brush to remove any charred or burnt particles that may be stuck to the broiler or grill grate. The grate can be wiped with a lightly oiled towel to remove any remaining particles and help season it.

3 Prepare the item to be broiled or grilled by marinating or seasoning as desired; it may be brushed lightly with oil to keep it from sticking to the grate.

4 Place the item on the grate, presentation side (skin side) down. Following the example in Chapter 10, turn the item to produce the attractive crosshatch marks associated with grilling. Baste the item often. Use tongs to turn or flip the item without piercing the surface so that juices do not escape.

5 Develop the proper surface color while cooking the item until it is done *à point*. To do so, adjust the position of the item on the broiler or grill, or adjust the distance between the grate and heat source. Large pieces and bone-in pieces that are difficult to cook completely on the broiler or grill can be finished in the oven.

A commonly used procedure to cook a large volume of poultry is to place the seasoned items in a broiler pan or other shallow pan and then place the pan directly under the broiler. Baste the items periodically, turning them once when they are halfway done. Items begun this way can be easily finished by transferring the entire pan to the oven.

GRILLED CHICKEN BREAST WITH RED PEPPER BUTTER

RECIPE 18.2

Yield: 4 Servings   **Method:** Grilling

Chicken breast, boneless, skinless	2	2
Salt and pepper	TT	TT
Garlic, chopped	1 tsp.	1 tsp.
Vegetable oil	1 Tbsp.	15 ml
Red pepper butter (page 224)	2 oz.	60 g

1 Trim any excess fat from the breasts. Split each breast into two pieces by removing the small piece of cartilage that joins the halves.

2 Season the breasts with the salt, pepper and garlic. Coat the breasts on all sides with the vegetable oil.

3 Heat and prepare the grill.

4 Grill the chicken breasts until done, turning them to produce attractive crosshatch markings.

5 Remove the chicken from the grill and place on a plate for service. Place a ½-ounce (15-gram) slice of red pepper butter on top of each breast. If necessary, place the plate under a broiler or salamander for a few seconds so that the butter begins to melt.

Approximate values per serving: **Calories** 240, **Total fat** 14 g, **Saturated fat** 6 g, **Cholesterol** 95 mg, **Sodium** 60 mg, **Total carbohydrates** 1 g, **Protein** 28 g, **Vitamin A** 10%, **Vitamin C** 15%

1 Season the chicken breasts.

2 Place the chicken on the grill at a 45° angle to the grates.

3 Using tongs, turn the chicken to cook the other side.

4 The cooked chicken is topped with red pepper butter.

ROASTING

Properly roasted (or baked) poultry is attractively browned on the surface and tender and juicy throughout. Proper cooking temperatures ensure a crisp exterior and juicy interior. Most roasted poultry is cooked until the juices run clear. Squab and duck breasts are exceptions; they are often served medium rare or pink.

Selecting Poultry to Roast

Almost every kind of poultry is suitable for roasting, but younger birds produce a more tender finished product. Because of variations in fat content, different kinds of poultry require different roasting temperatures and procedures.

▶ PROCEDURE FOR TRUSSING POULTRY

Trussing is tying a bird into a more compact shape with thread or butcher's twine. Trussing allows the bird to cook more evenly, helps the bird retain moisture and improves the appearance of the finished product. There are many methods for trussing poultry, some of which require a special tool called a trussing needle. Here we show a simple method using butcher's twine.

Seasoning Poultry to Be Roasted

Although the mild flavor of most poultry is enhanced by a wide variety of herbs and spices, roasted poultry is often only lightly seasoned with salt and pepper. Poultry that is roasted at high temperatures should never be seasoned with herbs on its surface because the high cooking temperatures will burn them. If herbs or additional spices are used, they should be stuffed into the cavity. A mirepoix or a bouquet garni may also be added to the cavity for additional flavor. The cavities of dark-meated birds such as ducks and geese are often stuffed with fresh or dried fruits.

1 Square up the bird by pressing it firmly with both hands. Tuck the first joint of the wing behind the back or trim off the first and second joints as shown.

2 Cut a piece of butcher's twine approximately three times the bird's length. With the breast up and the neck toward you, pass the twine under the bird approximately 1 inch (2.5 centimeters) in front of the tail.

3 Bring the twine up around the legs and cross the ends, creating an X between the legs. Pass the ends of the twine below the legs.

4 Pull the ends of the twine tightly across the leg and thigh joints and across the wings if the first and second joints are trimmed off, or just above the wings if they are intact.

5 Pull the string tight and tie it securely just above the neck.

6 Two examples of properly trussed birds: one with the wings intact and one with the first and second wing joints removed.

Barding Poultry to Be Roasted

Guineas, squabs or any skinless birds without an adequate fat covering to protect them from drying out during roasting can be barded. Bard the bird by covering its entire surface with thin slices of fatback, securing them with butcher's twine. See page 290.

Cooking Temperatures

Small birds such as squab and Cornish game hens should be roasted at the relatively high temperatures of 375°F–400°F (190°C–200°C). These temperatures help produce crisp, well-colored skins without overcooking the flesh. Chickens are best roasted at temperatures between 350°F and 375°F (180°C and 190°C). This temperature range allows the skin to crisp and the flesh to cook without causing the bird to stew in its own juices. Large birds such as capons and turkeys are started at high temperatures of 400°F–425°F (200°C–220°C) to brown the skin, then finished at lower temperatures of 275°F–325°F (135°C–160°C) to promote even cooking and produce a moister product. Ducks and geese, which are very high in fat, must be roasted at the high temperatures of 375°F–425°F (190°C–220°C) to render as much fat from the skin as possible. Duck and goose skins are often pricked before roasting so that the rendered fat can escape; this helps create a crispy skin.

Basting Roasted Poultry

With the exception of fatty birds such as ducks and geese, all poultry items should be basted while they roast in order to help retain moisture. To baste a bird, spoon or ladle the fat that collects in the bottom of the roasting pan over the bird at 15-to-20-minute intervals. Lean birds that are not barded will not produce enough fat for basting and may be brushed with butter in the same manner.

Determining Doneness

Four methods are used to determine the doneness of roasted poultry. It is best to use a combination of these methods.

1 *Temperature*—Test the internal temperature of the bird with an instant-read thermometer. The thermometer should be inserted in the bird's thigh, which is the last part to become fully cooked. It should not touch the bone and should read 165°F–170°F (74°C–77°C) at the coolest point. This method works best with large birds such as capons and turkeys. Large birds are subject to some degree of carryover cooking. This is not as much of a concern with poultry as it is with meat because large birds are always cooked well done.

2 *Looseness of the joints*—The thigh and leg will begin to move freely in their sockets when the bird is done.

3 *Color of juices*—This method is used with birds that are not stuffed. Use a kitchen fork to tilt the bird, allowing some of the juices that have collected in the cavity to run out. Clear juices indicate that the bird is done. If the juices are cloudy or pink, the bird is undercooked.

4 *Time*—Because there are so many variables, timing alone is less reliable than other methods. It is useful, however, for planning production when large quantities are roasted and as a general guideline when used with other methods. Table 18.7 gives some general timing guidelines for roasting several kinds of poultry.

Accompaniments to Roasted Poultry

▶ **dressing** another name for a bread stuffing used with poultry

The most common accompaniments to roasted poultry are bread stuffing and gravy. Large birds, such as capons and turkeys, produce adequate drippings for making sauce or pan gravy. Small birds, such as squab and Cornish game hens, are often stuffed with wild rice or other ingredients and served with a sauce that is made separately.

Ducks and geese are complemented by stuffings containing rice, fruits, berries and nuts. They are very fatty, and if stuffed, they should be roasted on a rack or mirepoix bed to ensure that the fat that collects in the pan during roasting does not penetrate the cavity, making the stuffing greasy. Ducks and geese are often served with a citrus- or fruit-based sauce. Its high acid content complements these rich, fatty birds.

Table 18.7 ROASTING TEMPERATURES AND TIMES

POULTRY KIND OR CLASS	COOKING TEMPERATURES		MINUTES PER LB (500 g)
Capons	350–375°F	180–190°C	18–20 min.
Chickens	375–400°F	190–200°C	15–18 min.
Ducks and geese	375–425°F	190–220°C	12–15 min.
Game hens	375–400°F	190–210°C	45–60 min. total
Guineas	375–400°F	190–200°C	18–20 min.
Squab	400°F	200°C	30–40 min. total
Turkeys (large)	325°F	160°C	12–15 min.

▶ PROCEDURE FOR STUFFING POULTRY

Small birds such as Cornish game hens, small chickens and squab can be stuffed successfully. Stuffing larger birds, especially for volume production, is impractical and can be dangerous for the following reasons:

1 Stuffing is a good bacterial breeding ground, and because it is difficult to control temperatures inside a stuffed bird, there is a risk of food-borne illness.

2 Stuffing poultry is labor intensive.

3 Stuffed poultry must be cooked longer to cook the stuffing properly; this may cause the meat to be overcooked, becoming dry and tough.

When stuffing any bird, use the following guidelines:

1 Always be aware of temperatures when mixing the raw ingredients. All ingredients should be cold when they are mixed together, and the mixture's temperature should never be allowed to rise above 45°F (7°C).

2 Stuff the raw bird as close to roasting time as possible.

3 The neck and main body cavities should be loosely stuffed. The stuffing will expand during cooking.

4 After the cavities are filled, their openings should be secured with skewers and butcher's twine or by trussing.

5 After cooking, remove the stuffing from the bird and store separately.

▶ PROCEDURE FOR ROASTING POULTRY

1 Season, bard, stuff and/or truss the bird as desired.

2 Place the bird in a roasting pan. It may be placed on a rack or a bed of mirepoix in order to prevent scorching and promote even cooking.

3 Roast uncovered, basting every 15 minutes.

4 Allow the bird to rest before carving to allow even distribution of juices. As the bird rests, prepare the pan gravy or sauce.

ROAST TURKEY WITH CHESTNUT DRESSING AND GIBLET GRAVY

RECIPE 18.3

Yield: 16 Servings, 4 oz. (120 g) turkey, 3 oz. (90 g) dressing and 4 oz. (120 ml) gravy each

Method: Roasting

Young turkey, 12–15 lb. (5.5–6.5 kg) with giblets	1	1
Salt and pepper	TT	TT
Mirepoix	20 oz.	600 g
Onion, small dice	8 oz.	225 g
Celery, small dice	6 oz.	180 g
Whole butter	4 oz.	120 g
Dried bread cubes	2 lb.	1 kg
Eggs, beaten	2	2
Fresh parsley, chopped	1 Tbsp.	15 ml
Chicken stock	2¼ qt.	2 lt
Chestnuts, cooked and peeled, chopped coarse	8 oz.	225 g
All-purpose flour	3 oz.	90 g

1 Placing the trussed turkey in the roasting pan.

2 Adding the mirepoix to the roasting pan.

3 Tossing the dressing ingedients together.

4 Browning the mirepoix.

5 Deglazing the roasting pan.

6 Transferring the mirepoix and stock to a saucepot.

7 Straining the gravy through a china cap and cheesecloth.

1 Remove the giblets from the turkey's cavity and set aside. Season the turkey inside and out with salt and pepper. Truss the turkey.

2 Place the turkey in a roasting pan. Roast at 400°F (200°C) for 30 minutes. Reduce the temperature to 325°F (160°C) and continue cooking the turkey to an internal temperature of 160°F (71°C), approximately 2½ to 3 hours. Baste the turkey often during cooking. Approximately 45 minutes before the turkey is done, add the mirepoix to the roasting pan. If the turkey begins to overbrown, cover it loosely with aluminum foil.

3 To make the dressing, sauté the onions and celery in the butter until tender.

4 In a large bowl, toss together the bread cubes, salt, pepper, eggs, parsley, sautéed onions and celery, 4 ounces (120 milliliters) of chicken stock and the chestnuts.

5 Place the dressing in a buttered hotel pan and cover with aluminum foil or buttered parchment paper. Bake at 350°F (180°C) until done, approximately 45 minutes.

6 As the turkey roasts, simmer the giblets (neck, heart and gizzard) in 1 quart (1 liter) of the chicken stock until tender, approximately 1½ hours.

7 When the turkey is done, remove it from the roasting pan and set it aside to rest. Degrease the roasting pan, reserving 3 ounces (90 grams) of the fat to make a roux.

8 Place the roasting pan on the stove top and brown the mirepoix.

9 Deglaze the pan with a small amount of chicken stock. Transfer the mirepoix and stock to a saucepot, and add the remaining stock and the broth from the giblets. Bring to a simmer and degrease.

10 Make a blond roux with the reserved fat and the flour. Add the roux to the liquid, whisking well to prevent lumps. Simmer 15 minutes. Strain the gravy through a china cap lined with cheesecloth.

11 Remove the meat from the turkey neck. Trim the gizzard. Finely chop the neck meat, heart and gizzard and add to the gravy. Adjust the seasonings.

12 Carve the turkey and serve with a portion of chestnut dressing and giblet gravy.

Approximate values per serving: **Calories** 720, **Total fat** 23 g, **Saturated fat** 9 g, **Cholesterol** 250 mg, **Sodium** 700 mg, **Total carbohydrates** 41 g, **Protein** 87 g, **Vitamin A** 6%, **Iron** 40%

Carving Roasted Poultry

Poultry can be carved in the kitchen, at tableside or on a buffet in a variety of manners. The carving methods described next produce slices of both light and dark meat.

▶ PROCEDURE FOR CARVING A TURKEY, CAPON OR OTHER LARGE BIRD

1 After roasting, allow the turkey to stand for 20 minutes so that the juices can redistribute themselves. Holding the turkey firmly with a carving fork, pry a leg outward and locate the joint. Remove the leg and thigh in one piece by cutting through the joint with the tip of a knife.

2 Repeat the procedure on the other side. Once both legs and thighs have been removed, slice the meat from the thigh by holding the leg firmly with one hand and slicing parallel to the bone.

3 Separate the thigh from the leg bone by cutting through the joint. Slice the meat from the leg by cutting parallel to the bone.

4 Cut along the backbone, following the natural curvature of the bones separating the breast meat from the ribs.

5 Remove an entire half breast and slice it on the cutting board as shown. Cut on an angle to produce larger slices.

6 Alternatively, the breast can be carved on the bird. Make a horizontal cut just above the wing in toward the rib bones.

7 Slice the breast meat as shown.

▶ PROCEDURE FOR CARVING A CHICKEN OR OTHER SMALL BIRD

1 After allowing the roasted chicken to rest for 15 minutes so that the juices can redistribute themselves, cut through the skin between the leg and breast.

2 Use a kitchen fork to pry the leg and thigh away from the breast. Locate the thigh's ball joint and cut through it with the knife tip, separating it completely from the rest of the chicken. Be sure to cut around the delicate oyster meat, leaving it attached to the thigh.

3 With the knife tip, cut through the skin and meat on one side of the breast bone. Cut and pull the meat away from the bones with the knife.

4 Cut through the wing joint, separating the breast meat and wing from the carcass. Repeat this procedure on the other side of the bird.

5 The chicken is now quartered.

6 To cut it into eight pieces, separate the wings from the breasts and the thighs from the legs.

POÊLÉING

Poêléing (pwah-lay-ing) is a cooking method similar to both roasting and braising. The item is cooked in the oven in a covered pot so that it cooks in its own juices and steam. Although this is a moist-heat cooking technique (because the item steams in its own juices), it is used only for tender cuts, not those that need long, slow braising. The cooking time is usually shorter than that needed for dry roasting.

The item to be poêléed can first be browned in hot fat and then laid on a bed of matignon, covered and cooked in the oven. If the item was not first browned in hot fat, it can later be browned by removing the lid toward the end of cooking. Doneness is determined using the same techniques as those used for roasting.

Vegetables to be served with the dish can be added to the poêlé as it cooks or cooked separately and plated with the finished item.

The sauce for a poêlé is made from the flavorful cooking juices left in the pan. They are mixed with a liquid (stock, jus lie or demi-glace) and finished using the same techniques as those for a braised dish. The matignon can be left in the finished sauce or strained out.

▶ PROCEDURE FOR POÊLÉING POULTRY

1 Sear the main item in hot butter or oil, if desired.

2 Place the main item on a bed of matignon. Add vegetables or other ingredients as called for in the recipe.

3 Cover and cook in the oven until done. Baste periodically with pan juices or with additional butter.

4 If the main item was not first browned in hot fat, it can be browned by removing the lid toward the end of the cooking period, if desired.

5 Remove the main item when done.

6 To make a sauce, add a liquid to the matignon and cooking juices in the pan and reduce. Remove the matignon if desired and add flavorings as directed in the recipe.

POÊLÉ OF CHICKEN WITH PEARL ONIONS AND MUSHROOMS

RECIPE 18.4

Yield: 4 Servings   **Method:** Poêléing

Chickens, 2 lb. 8 oz.–3 lb. (1–1.4 kg) each	2	2
Salt and pepper	TT	TT
Fresh herbs, assorted stems and sprigs	2 oz.	60 g
Butter, clarified	4 fl. oz.	120 ml
Matignon:		
Slab bacon or smoked ham, small dice	3 oz.	90 g
Onion, small dice	6 oz.	180 g
Celery, small dice	3 oz.	90 g
Carrot, small dice	3 oz.	90 g
Garlic, chopped	2 tsp.	10 ml
Pearl onions, blanched and peeled	4 oz.	120 g
Button mushrooms, stemmed	8 oz.	240 g
White wine	4 fl. oz.	120 ml
Demi-glace	2 pt.	1 lt
Tomato concassée	4 oz.	120 g
Fresh herbs, assorted, chopped	2 tsp.	10 ml

1 Place the chicken on the matignon.

2 Baste the chicken with fat from the pan during cooking.

3 Carefully remove the cooked chicken from the pan.

4 The plated poêlé of chicken.

1 Season the chicken cavities with salt and pepper and stuff them with the herb stems and sprigs. Truss the birds and season the outside with salt and pepper.

2 Heat half the butter in a roasting pan that is just large enough to hold the birds without crowding. Sauté the bacon until most of the fat is rendered. Add the diced onions, celery and carrots and sauté until they begin to brown. Add the garlic and cook for 1 more minute.

3 Place the trussed chickens on top of the matignon. Baste them with the remaining butter. Cover the roasting pan with its lid and place in a 325°F (160°C) oven until done, approximately 1½ hours, basting the chickens with fat from the pan every 20 minutes. Remove the lid for the last 30 minutes of cooking to allow the chickens to brown lightly.

4 Remove the chickens from the pan and allow them to rest in a warm place. Place the roasting pan on the stove top. Remove a small amount of the accumulated fat from the roasting pan to a sauté pan and sauté the onions and mushrooms in the sauté pan until nearly tender.

5 Bring the liquid in the roasting pan to a boil; remove any excess fat or scum with a ladle. Add the white wine and reduce by half. Add the demi-glace and bring to a simmer. Adjust the thickness of the sauce. If desired, strain the sauce. Add the onions, mushrooms, tomato concassée and chopped herbs to the sauce. Bring to a simmer and adjust the seasonings.

6 Carve the chickens and serve them with a portion of the sauce and vegetables.

Approximate values per serving: **Calories** 1670, **Total fat** 106 g, **Saturated fat** 39 g, **Cholesterol** 475 mg, **Sodium** 2110 mg, **Total carbohydrates** 48 g, **Protein** 129 g, **Vitamin A** 170%, **Vitamin C** 50%, **Calcium** 10%, **Iron** 45%

SAUTÉING

Sautéed poultry should be tender and juicy, its flavor developed by proper browning. Additional flavors come from a sauce made by deglazing the pan, usually with wine, and adding garnishes, seasonings and liquids. Stir-frying is a popular method of sautéing poultry; boneless pieces are cut into strips and quickly cooked with assorted vegetables and seasonings.

Selecting Poultry to Sauté

Most poultry is quite tender and well suited for sautéing. Although small birds such as squab can be sautéed bone-in, large pieces and bone-in cuts from larger birds should not be sautéed. Boneless breasts, suprêmes, scallops and cutlets are the most common and practical cuts for sautéing. Because they are high in fat, boneless duck breasts can be sautéed without additional fat.

Seasoning Poultry to Be Sautéed

Poultry has a delicate flavor that is enhanced by a wide variety of herbs, spices, condiments and marinades. Flavor combinations are limited only by your imagination. When poultry items are dusted with flour before sautéing, the seasonings may first be added to the flour.

Cooking Temperatures

The sauté pan and the cooking fat must be hot before the poultry is added. The temperature at which the poultry is then sautéed is determined by its thickness and the desired color of the finished product. A thin, boneless slice requires relatively high temperatures so that its surface is browned before the center is overcooked. A thicker cut such as a suprême requires lower temperatures so that neither its surface nor the fond are burned before the item is fully cooked. Adjust the temperature throughout the cooking process in order to achieve the desired results, never letting the pan become too cool.

If the pan is overcrowded or otherwise allowed to cool, the poultry will cook in its own juices and absorb oil from the pan, resulting in a poor-quality product.

Determining Doneness

Thin cuts of poultry cook very quickly, so timing is a useful tool; it is less useful with thicker cuts. Experienced cooks can tell the doneness of an item by judging the temperature of the sauté pan and the color of the item being cooked.

A more practical method is to press the item with your finger and judge the resistance. Very undercooked poultry will offer little resistance and feel mushy. Slightly underdone poultry will feel spongy and will not spring back when your finger is removed. Properly cooked poultry will feel firm to the touch and will spring back when your finger is removed. Overcooked poultry will feel very firm, almost hard, and will spring back quickly when your finger is removed.

Accompaniments to Sautéed Poultry

Sautéed poultry is usually served with a sauce made directly in the pan in which the item was cooked. The sauce uses the fond for added flavor. A wide variety of ingredients, including garlic, onions, shallots, mushrooms and tomatoes, are commonly added to the pan as well as wine and stock. Table 11.5 suggests several sauces for sautéed poultry.

Sautéed items are often served with a starch such as pasta, rice or potatoes.

▶ PROCEDURE FOR SAUTÉING POULTRY

1 Heat a sauté pan and add enough fat or oil to just cover the bottom.
2 Add the poultry item, presentation side down, and cook until browned.
3 Turn the item, using tongs or by tossing the item back upon itself using the pan's sloped sides.
4 Larger items can be finished in an oven. Either place the sauté pan in the oven or transfer the poultry to another pan. The latter procedure allows a sauce to be made in the original pan as the poultry cooks in the oven. Hold smaller pieces that are thoroughly cooked in a warm place so that the pan can be used for making the sauce.

▶ PROCEDURE FOR PREPARING A SAUCE IN THE SAUTÉ PAN

1 Pour off any excess fat or oil from the sauté pan, leaving enough to sauté the sauce ingredients.
2 Add ingredients such as garlic, shallots and mushrooms that will be used as garnishes and sauce flavorings; sauté them.
3 Deglaze the pan with wine, stock or other liquids. Scrape the pan, loosening the fond and allowing it to dissolve in the liquid. Reduce the liquid.

4 Add any ingredients that do not require long cooking times such as herbs and spices. Adjust the sauce's consistency and seasonings.

5 For service, the poultry can be returned to the pan for a moment to reheat it and to coat it with the sauce. The poultry should remain in the sauce just long enough to reheat. Do not attempt to cook the poultry in the sauce.

6 Serve the poultry with the accompanying sauce.

CHICKEN SAUTÉ WITH ONIONS, GARLIC AND BASIL

RECIPE 18.5

1 Sautéing the breasts in butter.

2 The fond left in the pan after sautéing the chicken.

3 Sautéing the onions and garlic.

Yield: 6 Servings, 5-oz. (150-g) each | | **Method:** Sautéing

Chicken breasts, boneless, skinless, approx. 8 oz. (250 g) each	3	3
Salt and pepper	TT	TT
Flour	as needed for dredging	
Clarified butter	1 fl. oz.	30 ml
Onion, small dice	2 oz.	60 g
Garlic cloves, chopped	6	6
Dry white wine	4 fl. oz.	120 ml
Lemon juice	1 Tbsp.	15 ml
Tomato concassée	6 oz.	180 g
Chicken stock	4 fl. oz.	120 ml
Fresh basil leaves, chiffonade	6	6

1 Split the chicken breasts and remove the cartilage connecting the two halves.

2 Season the chicken with salt and pepper; dredge in flour.

3 Sauté the breasts in the butter, browning them and cooking *à point.* Hold in a warm place.

4 Add the onions and garlic to the fond and butter in the pan; sauté until the onions are translucent.

5 Deglaze the pan with the white wine and lemon juice.

6 Add the tomato concassée and chicken stock. Sauté to combine the flavors; reduce the sauce to the desired consistency.

7 Add the basil to the sauce and return the chicken breasts for reheating. Adjust the seasonings and serve one half breast per portion with a portion of the sauce.

Approximate values per 5-oz. (150-g) serving: **Calories** 230, **Total fat** 8 g, **Saturated fat** 3.5 g, **Cholesterol** 90 mg, **Sodium** 580 mg, **Total carbohydrates** 9 g, **Protein** 30 g, **Vitamin C** 10%, **Iron** 10%

4 Deglazing the pan with white wine and lemon juice.

5 Adding the tomatoes and chicken stock and sautéing to combine the flavors.

6 Returning the chicken to the pan to reheat.

PAN-FRYING

Pan-fried poultry should be juicy. Its coating or batter should be crispy, golden brown, not excessively oily and free from any breaks that allow fat to penetrate. Both the poultry and the coating should be well seasoned.

Selecting Poultry to Pan-Fry

The most common pan-fried poultry is fried chicken. Young tender birds cut into small pieces produce the best results. Other cuts commonly pan-fried are boneless portions such as chicken breasts and turkey scallops.

Seasoning Poultry to Be Pan-Fried

Pan-fried poultry is usually floured, breaded or battered before cooking. (Breadings and batters are discussed in Chapter 9, Mise en Place.) Typically, the seasonings are added to the flour, breading or batter before the poultry is coated. Seasonings can be a blend of any number of dried herbs and spices. But often only salt and pepper are required because the poultry will be served with a sauce or other accompaniments for additional flavors.

Cooking Temperatures

The fat should always be hot before the poultry is added. The temperature at which it is cooked is determined by the length of time required to cook it thoroughly. Pan-frying generally requires slightly lower temperatures than those used for sautéing. Within this range, thinner items require higher temperatures to produce good color in a relatively short time. Thicker items and those containing bones require lower cooking temperatures and longer cooking times.

Determining Doneness

Even the largest pan-fried items may be too small to be accurately tested with an instant-read thermometer, and using the touch method can be difficult and dangerous because of the amount of fat used in pan-frying. So timing and experience are the best tools to determine doneness. Thin scallops cook very quickly, so it is relatively easy to judge their doneness. On the other hand, fried chicken can take as long as 30–45 minutes to cook, requiring skill and experience to determine doneness.

Accompaniments to Pan-Fried Poultry

Because pan-frying does not produce fond or drippings that can be used to make a sauce, pan-fried poultry is usually served with lemon wedges, a vegetable garnish or a separately made sauce. Fried chicken is an exception; it is sometimes served with a country gravy made by degreasing the pan, making a roux with a portion of the fat and adding milk and seasonings.

▶ PROCEDURE FOR PAN-FRYING POULTRY

1 Heat enough fat in a heavy sauté pan to cover the item to be cooked one quarter to halfway up its side. The fat should be at approximately 325°F (163°C).

2 Add the floured, breaded or battered item to the hot fat, being careful not to splash. The fat must be hot enough to sizzle and bubble when the item is added.

3 Turn the item when the first side is the proper color; it should be half cooked at this point. Larger items may need to be turned more than once to brown them properly on all sides.

4 Remove the browned poultry from the pan and drain it on absorbent paper.

RECIPE 18.6   *PAN-FRIED CHICKEN WITH PAN GRAVY*

1 Dipping the chicken pieces in the buttermilk.

2 Dredging the chicken in the flour mixture.

3 Adding the chicken to the oil. The bubbling fat indicates the proper cooking temperature.

Yield: 8 Servings, 2-pieces each   **Method:** Pan-Frying

Frying chickens, 2 lb. 8 oz.–3 lb. (1.1–1.4 kg) each, cut in 8 pieces	2	2
Salt and pepper	TT	TT
Garlic powder	2 tsp.	10 ml
Onion powder	2 tsp.	10 ml
Dried oregano	1 tsp.	5 ml
Dried basil	1 tsp.	5 ml
Flour	9½ oz.	270 g
Buttermilk	8 fl. oz.	250 ml
Oil	as needed	as needed
Onion, small dice	4 oz.	120 g
Half-and-half or chicken stock	1½ pt.	750 ml

1 Season the chicken with salt and pepper.
2 Add the herbs and spices to 8 ounces (250 grams) of the flour.
3 Dip the chicken pieces in the buttermilk.
4 Dredge the chicken in the seasoned flour.
5 Pan-fry the chicken in oil until done, approximately 40 minutes, turning so that it cooks evenly. Reduce the heat as necessary to prevent the chicken from becoming too dark. Or remove the chicken when well browned, drain it and finish cooking it in the oven.
6 To make the pan gravy, pour off all but 3 tablespoons (45 milliliters) of oil from the pan, carefully reserving the fond.
7 Add the diced onions and sauté until translucent.
8 Add 1½ ounces (45 grams) of flour and cook to make a blond roux.
9 Whisk in the liquid and simmer approximately 15 minutes.
10 Strain through cheesecloth and adjust the seasonings.
11 Serve 2 pieces of chicken per person with 4 fluid ounces (120 milliliters) of gravy.

Approximate values per 2-piece serving (6-7 ounces), before frying: **Calories** 650, **Total fat** 31 g, **Saturated fat** 12 g, **Cholesterol** 190 mg, **Sodium** 190 mg, **Total carbohydrates** 32 g, **Protein** 57 g, **Fiber** 1 g, **Vitamin A** 15%, **Vitamin C** 4%, **Calcium** 15%, **Iron** 20%,

4 Turning the chicken so that it cooks evenly.

5 Sautéing the diced onions until translucent.

6 Adding the liquid to the roux.

DEEP-FRYING

Young, tender poultry are an excellent and popular choice for deep-frying. The pieces should be golden brown on the outside and moist and tender on the inside. They should be neither greasy nor tough. Chopped cooked poultry can also be mixed with a heavy béchamel or velouté sauce and seasonings, breaded and deep-fried as croquettes, which are discussed in Chapter 20, Fish and Shellfish.

Selecting and Seasoning Poultry to Be Deep-Fried

Portioned chickens and whole small birds, such as Rock Cornish game hen, are best for deep-frying. Although they can be marinated or seasoned directly, it is more common to season the batter or breading that will coat them. Additional flavors come from the sauces and accompaniments served with the deep-fried poultry. Lemon wedges, sweet and sour sauce or tangy barbecue sauces are popular accompaniments to deep-fried poultry.

▶ PROCEDURE FOR DEEP-FRYING POULTRY

1 Cut, trim or otherwise prepare the poultry to be deep-fried. Season and bread or batter it, as desired.

2 Heat the fat to the desired temperature, usually around 350°F (177°C). Breaded or battered poultry cooks quickly and the fat must be hot enough to cook the food's interior without burning its surface.

3 Carefully place the poultry in the hot fat using the basket method.

4 Deep-fry the food until done. It should have a crispy, golden brown surface.

5 Remove the deep-fried poultry from the fat and hold it over the fat, allowing the excess fat to drain. Transfer the food to a hotel pan either lined with absorbent paper or fitted with a rack. Season with salt, if desired.

6 If the deep-fried poultry is to be held for later service, place it under a heat lamp.

SPICY FRIED CHICKEN TENDERS WITH CHIPOTLE DIPPING SAUCE

RECIPE 18.7

Yield: 4 Servings　　　　　　**Method:** Deep-Frying

Chicken tenders (or tenderloins), tendons removed	24	24
Seasoned flour:		
Flour	8 oz.	450 g
Chilli powder	3 Tbsp.	45 ml
Paprika	3 Tbsp.	45 ml
Granulated garlic	2 Tbsp.	30 ml
Black pepper	2 tsp.	10 ml
Cayenne pepper	1 Tbsp.	15 ml
Dried thyme	1 Tbsp.	15 ml
Dried oregano	1 Tbsp.	15 ml
Salt	3 Tbsp.	45 ml
Egg wash:		
Eggs	4	4
Milk	4 Tbsp.	120 ml
Bread crumbs	as needed	as needed
Sauce:		
Barbecue Sauce (page 241)	8 fl. oz.	240 ml
Chipotle peppers, canned, puréed	1 Tbsp.	15 ml
Honey	1 oz.	60 g

1　Lightly pound the chicken pieces to an even thickness.

2　Combine the ingredients for the seasoned flour.

3　Beat the eggs and milk.

4 Bread the chicken tenders using the standard breading procedure, placing each fully breaded piece on a parchment-lined sheet pan. Refrigerate until ready to cook.

5 Place the sauce ingredients in a small saucepan and simmer until the flavors blend, approximately 5 minutes.

6 Using the basket method, deep-fry the chicken pieces at 325°F (160°C) until done, approximately 4 minutes. Drain and serve with the warm sauce.

Approximate values per serving: **Calories** 380, **Total fat** 12 g, **Saturated fat** 2.5 g, **Cholesterol** 160 mg, **Sodium** 2680 mg, **Total carbohydrates** 33 g, **Protein** 34 g, **Vitamin A** 60%, **Vitamin C** 15%, **Iron** 25%

MOIST-HEAT COOKING METHODS

The moist-heat cooking methods most often used with poultry are poaching and simmering. Poaching is used to cook tender birds for short periods. Simmering is used to cook older, tougher birds for longer periods in order to tenderize them. Poaching and simmering are similar procedures, the principal differences being the temperature of the cooking liquid and the length of cooking time.

POACHING AND SIMMERING

Poached or simmered poultry should be moist, tender and delicately flavored. Although the poultry is cooked in water, overcooking will cause it to become dry and tough. During cooking, some of the poultry's flavor is transferred to the cooking liquid, which can be used to make a sauce for the finished product.

Selecting Poultry to Poach or Simmer

Young birds are best suited for poaching; boneless chicken pieces are the most commonly used parts. Older, tougher birds are usually simmered. Duck and geese are rarely poached or simmered because of their high fat content.

Seasoning Poultry to Be Poached or Simmered

When poaching poultry, it is especially important to use a well-seasoned and highly flavored liquid in order to infuse as much flavor as possible into the item being cooked. Either strong stock with a sachet or a mixture of stock or water and white wine with a bouquet garni or onion piquet produces good results. The poultry should be completely covered with liquid so that it cooks evenly. However, if too much liquid is used and it is not strongly flavored, flavors may be leached out of the poultry, resulting in a bland finished product.

Poultry is often simmered in water instead of stock. A sachet and a generous mirepoix should be added to help flavor it. Typically, simmering birds results in a strong broth that may be used to complete the recipe or reserved for other uses.

Cooking Temperatures

For best results, poultry should be poached at low temperatures, between 160°F and 175°F (71°C–79°C). Cooking poultry to the proper doneness at these temperatures produces a product that is moist and tender.

Simmering is done at slightly higher temperatures, between 185°F (85°C) and the boiling point. When simmering, do not allow the liquid to boil, as this may result in a dry, tough and stringy finished product.

Determining Doneness

Poached poultry, whether whole or boneless, is cooked just until done. An instant-read thermometer inserted in the thigh or thicker part of the bird should read 165°F (74°C). Any juices that run from the bird should be clear or show only a trace of pink.

Simmered poultry is usually cooked for longer periods to allow the moist heat to tenderize the meat. A chicken that weighs 3 pounds 8 ounces (1.5 kilograms), for example, may take 2½ hours to cook.

Accompaniments to Poached and Simmered Poultry

Poached or simmered poultry can be served hot or cold. The meat from these birds can be served cold in salads, served hot in casseroles or used in any dish that calls for cooked poultry.

Poached items are typically served with a flavored mayonnaise or a sauce made from the reduced poaching liquid, such as sauce suprême. Poultry is also often poached as a means of producing a low-calorie dish. If so, a vegetable coulis makes a good sauce, or the poultry can be served with a portion of its cooking liquid and a vegetable garnish.

Simmered poultry to be served cold will be moister and more flavorful if it is cooled in its cooking liquid. To do so, remove the pot containing the bird and the cooking liquid from the heat when the bird is still slightly undercooked. Cool the meat and broth in a water bath following the procedures in Chapter 11, Stocks and Sauces. Once cooled, remove the meat and wipe off any congealed broth before proceeding with the recipe.

▶ PROCEDURE FOR POACHING OR SIMMERING POULTRY

1 Cut or truss the item to be cooked as directed in the recipe.

2 Prepare the cooking liquid and bring it to a simmer. Submerge the poultry in the cooking liquid, or arrange the items to be poached in an appropriate pan and add the poaching liquid to the pan.

3 Poach or simmer the item to the desired doneness in the oven or on the stove top. Maintain the proper cooking temperature throughout the process.

4 Remove the poultry and hold it for service in a portion of the cooking liquid or, using an ice bath, cool the item in its cooking liquid.

5 The cooking liquid may be used to prepare an accompanying sauce or reserved for use in other dishes.

POACHED BREAST OF CHICKEN WITH TARRAGON SAUCE

RECIPE 18.8

Yield: 8 Servings, 4 oz. (120 g) each	**Method:** Poaching	
Chicken breasts, boneless, skinless, approx. 8 oz. (250 g) each	4	4
Whole butter	1½ oz.	45 g
Salt and white pepper	TT	TT
White wine	4 fl. oz.	120 ml
Chicken stock	1 pt.	450 ml
Bay leaf	1	1
Dried thyme	¼ tsp.	1 ml
Dried tarragon	1 tsp.	5 ml
Flour	1 oz.	30 g
Heavy cream	4 fl. oz.	120 ml
Fresh tarragon sprigs	as needed for garnish	

1 Trim any rib meat and fat from the breasts. Cut the breasts into two pieces, removing the strip of cartilage that joins the halves.

2 Select a pan that will just hold the breasts when they are placed close together. Rub the pan with approximately ½ ounce (15 grams) of butter.

3 Season the chicken breasts with salt and white pepper, and arrange them in the buttered pan, presentation side up.

1 Arranging the breasts in an appropriate pan.

2 Adding the white wine, chicken stock and seasonings to the pan.

3 Covering the breasts with a piece of buttered parchment paper.

4 Adding the cream to the thickened sauce.

5 Plating the poached chicken breast.

4 Add the white wine, stock, bay leaf, thyme and dried tarragon.

5 Cut and butter a piece of parchment paper and cover the chicken breasts.

6 Bring the liquid to a simmer and reduce the temperature to poach the chicken.

7 Make a blond roux with 1 ounce (30 grams) of butter and the flour; set aside to cool.

8 When the breasts are done, remove them from the liquid. Thicken the liquid with the roux. Add the cream. Simmer and reduce to the desired consistency.

9 Strain the sauce through cheesecloth and adjust the seasonings.

10 Serve each half breast nappéd with approximately 2 fluid ounces (60 milliliters) of sauce; garnish each portion with a sprig of fresh tarragon.

Approximate values per 4-oz. (115-g) serving: **Calories** 250, **Total fat** 13 g, **Saturated fat** 7 g, **Cholesterol** 105 mg, **Sodium** 590 mg, **Total carbohydrates** 4 g, **Protein** 29 g, **Vitamin A** 10%

COMBINATION COOKING METHODS

Braising and stewing use both dry and moist heat to produce a moist, flavorful product. The principal difference between braising and stewing when applied to meats is the size of the cut being cooked: Large cuts of meat are braised; smaller ones are stewed. Because most poultry is relatively small, this distinction does not readily apply in poultry cookery; therefore, the two cooking methods are discussed together here.

BRAISING AND STEWING

Braised or stewed poultry should be moist and fork tender. The poultry is always served with the liquid in which it was cooked. Ducks and geese are braised or stewed in much the same way as red meats. Chicken cacciatore, coq au vin and chicken fricassee are examples of braised or stewed chicken dishes.

Selecting Poultry to Braise or Stew

Braising and stewing, being slow, moist cooking processes, are often thought of as a means to tenderize tough meats. Although they can be used to tenderize older, tougher birds, these cooking methods are more often selected as a means of adding moisture and flavor to poultry that is inherently tender, such as young ducks and chickens. Typically, the birds are disjointed and cooked bone-in, just until done, so that they retain their juiciness.

Seasoning Poultry to Be Braised or Stewed

Braised or stewed items obtain much of their flavor from the cooking liquid and other ingredients added during the cooking process. The main item and the cooking liquid should be well seasoned. If other seasonings such as an onion piquet, sachet, bouquet garni or dried herbs and spices are required, they should be added at the beginning of the cooking process rather than at the end. This allows the flavors to blend and penetrate the larger pieces of poultry. If the poultry is dredged in flour prior to browning, seasonings may be added directly to the flour. As with all dishes using combination cooking methods, the finished dish should have the flavor of the poultry in the sauce and the moisture and flavor of the sauce in the poultry.

Cooking Temperatures

Some recipes, such as chicken cacciatore and coq au vin, require the main item to be thoroughly browned during the initial stages; others, such as chicken fricassee, do not. In either case, after the liquid is added, it is important to maintain a slow simmer rather than a rapid boil. This can be done on the stove top or in the oven. Low temperatures control the cooking and produce a tender, juicy finished product.

Determining Doneness

Tenderness is the key to determining doneness. It can be determined by inserting a kitchen fork into the poultry. There should be little resistance, and the poultry should freely fall off the fork. The pieces should retain their shape, however; if they fall apart, they are overdone. Small boneless pieces can be tested by cutting into them with a fork.

Accompaniments to Braised or Stewed Poultry

All braises and stews are cooked in a liquid that results in a sauce or broth served as part of the finished dish. Rice, pasta or boiled potatoes are natural accompaniments to almost any braised or stewed dish, as are boiled vegetables.

▶ PROCEDURE FOR BRAISING OR STEWING POULTRY

1 Sear the main item in butter or oil, developing color as desired.
2 Add vegetables and other ingredients as called for in the recipe and sauté.
3 Add flour or roux if used.
4 Add the appropriate liquid.
5 Cover and simmer on the stove top or in the oven until done.
6 Add seasonings and garnishes at the appropriate times during the cooking process.
7 Finish the dish by adding cream or a liaison to the sauce or by adjusting its consistency. Adjust the seasonings.
8 Serve a portion of the poultry with the sauce and appropriate garnish.

RECIPE 18.9

Yield: 8 Servings, 2 pieces each   **Method:** Braising

Frying chickens, 2 lb. 8 oz.–3 lb. (1.1–1.4 kg) each, cut into 8 pieces	2	2
Salt and white pepper	TT	TT
Clarified butter	3 fl. oz.	90 ml
Onion, medium dice	10 oz.	300 g
Flour	3 oz.	90 g
Dry white wine	8 fl. oz.	250 ml
Chicken stock	1 qt.	1 lt
Sachet:		
Bay leaf	1	1
Dried thyme	½ tsp.	2 ml
Peppercorns, cracked	½ tsp.	2 ml
Parsley stems	8	8
Garlic clove, crushed	1	1
Heavy cream	8 fl. oz.	250 ml
Nutmeg	TT	TT

1 Sautéing the chicken and onions in butter.

2 Sprinkling the flour over the chicken.

3 Deglazing the pan with white wine.

1 Season the chicken with salt and white pepper.

2 Sauté the chicken in the butter without browning. Add the onions and continue to sauté until they translucent.

3 Sprinkle the flour over the chicken and onions and stir to make a roux. Cook the roux for 2 minutes without browning.

4 Deglaze the pan with the white wine. Add the chicken stock and sachet; season with salt. Cover and simmer until done, approximately 30 to 45 minutes.

5 Remove the chicken from the pan and hold in a warm place. Strain the sauce through cheesecloth and return it to a clean pan.

6 Add the cream and bring the sauce to a simmer. Add the nutmeg and adjust the seasonings. Return the chicken to the sauce to reheat it for service.

Approximate values per 8-oz. (240-g) serving: **Calories** 700, **Total fat** 20 g, **Saturated fat** 12 g, **Cholesterol** 60 mg, **Sodium** 7950 mg, **Total carbohydrates** 113 g, **Protein** 15 g, **Vitamin A** 20%

4 Removing the chicken from the pot.

5 Straining the sauce through cheesecloth.

6 Returning the chicken to the sauce to reheat it for service.

The renowned French gastronome and author Jean-Anthelme Brillat-Savarin (1755–1826) once observed that "poultry is for the cook what canvas is for the painter." He meant, of course, that poultry, including chicken, duck, goose, guinea, pigeon and turkey, are wonderfully versatile foods that can be cooked by almost any method and with almost any seasonings, and can be served with many accompaniments and garnishes.

CONCLUSION

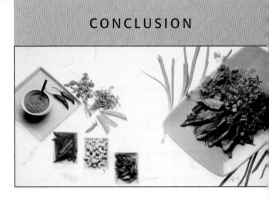

QUESTIONS FOR DISCUSSION

1 List the six categories or kinds of poultry recognized by the USDA. How are these categories then divided into classes?

2 How should fresh poultry be stored? Discuss several procedures that should be followed carefully when working with poultry to prevent cross-contamination.

3 What is a suprême? Describe the step-by-step procedure for preparing a chicken suprême.

4 What is trussing? Why is this technique used with poultry?

5 Which poultry items are best suited for broiling or grilling? Explain your answer.

6 Describe the characteristics of properly roasted poultry. Which classes of poultry are recommended for roasting?

7 What is foie gras? Why must you be extremely careful when cooking foie gras?

RECIPE 18.10

KOLANTA DUCK SALAD

Note: This dish appears in the Chapter Opening photograph.

CHEF BRENT BEAVERS

Like so many of today's successful chefs, Brent Beavers began his food service career in a dish room. After an early job as a dishwasher/prep cook at The Painted Lady, Chef Beavers apprenticed for two years under Chef Christine Adrian of La Petite Maison in Colorado Springs, Colorado. After working in a variety of restaurants, he is now executive chef at Sencha in Colorado Springs, Colorado. Sencha's success has earned him two invitations to cook for James Beard Foundation dinners.

In addition to his work behind the line, Chef Beavers is also currently pursuing a college degree in anthropology. His advice for students is to just "keep it simple. Don't hide the flavors of the food you are creating."

SENCHA, COLORADO SPRINGS, CO
Chef Brent Beavers

Yield: 6 Servings   **Method:** Grilling

Turmeric, ground	1 c.	240 ml
Black pepper	1 Tbsp.	15 ml
Kosher salt	1 Tbsp.	15 ml
Cumin, ground	1 Tbsp.	15 ml
Duck breasts, boneless, skin on	6	6
Cashews, roasted	1 lb.	450 g
Thai chiles	7	7
Fresh tomato juice	1 pt.	450 ml
Tomato, slivered	3 lb.	1.4 kg
Green onions, sliced	4 oz.	120 g
Salt and pepper	TT	TT
Pea shoots	3 oz.	90 g
English sprout mix	3 oz.	90 g

1 Stir together the turmeric, pepper, salt and cumin. Score the skin of the duck breasts and rub the breasts generously with the spice mix. Place on a parchment-lined sheet pan and refrigerate for a minimum of 3 hours.

2 Combine the cashews, Thai chiles and tomato juice and let stand for 5 minutes to allow the flavors to blend.

3 Grill the duck breasts to medium rare over low heat, rendering as much fat from the skin side as possible. Remove from the grill and hold in a warm place.

4 Combine the tomato and green onions in a stainless steel bowl. Add the cashew and tomato juice mixture and season with salt and pepper. Toss and allow to marinate for 5 minutes. Drain off the excess liquid and reserve.

5 Place the tomato salad mixture on plates. Slice the duck breasts on the bias and fan on top of the salad.

6 Add the pea shoots and sprouts to the plates and drizzle with 1 tablespoon (15 milliliters) of the reserved marinade liquid.

Approximate values per serving: **Calories** 850, **Total fat** 53 g, **Saturated fat** 11 g, **Cholesterol** 165 mg, **Sodium** 2070 mg, **Total carbohydrates** 57 g, **Protein** 48 g, **Vitamin A** 45%, **Vitamin C** 220%, **Calcium** 15%, **Iron** 100%

APRICOT AND BOURBON GRILLED CHICKEN

PENNSYLVANIA COLLEGE OF TECHNOLOGY, WILLIAMSPORT, PA
Chef Mary G. Trometter, Assistant Professor

Yield: 4 Servings   **Method:** Grilling

Marinade:		
Dijon mustard	¼ c.	60 ml
Dark brown sugar	¼ c.	60 ml
Soy sauce	2 Tbsp.	30 ml
Bourbon	2 Tbsp.	30 ml
Worcestershire sauce	1 tsp.	5 ml
Chicken breasts, boneless, skinless	2	2
Basting sauce:		
Apricot preserves	¼ c.	60 ml
White wine vinegar	2 Tbsp.	30 ml
Worcestershire sauce	2 tsp.	10 ml
Dijon mustard	2 tsp.	10 ml
Honey	2 tsp.	10 ml
Red pepper flakes, crushed	¼ tsp.	2 ml
Almonds, sliced, toasted	as needed for garnish	

1 Combine the marinade ingredients and transfer to a shallow, stainless steel pan.

2 Split each chicken breast into two halves by removing the cartilage that divides the halves. Place the chicken in the marinade and turn several times to coat it well. Cover the pan with plastic wrap and refrigerate for 1 to 3 hours.

3 Combine the basting sauce ingredients in a small saucepan and simmer for 10 minutes to blend the flavors. Strain if desired and refrigerate until needed.

4 Remove the chicken from the marinade and place on a preheated grill. Grill for approximately 2 minutes, brush with the basting sauce, turn and brush with more basting sauce. Continue to baste frequently and grill until done. Garnish with toasted almonds at service time.

Approximate values per serving: **Calories** 280, **Total fat** 2.5 g, **Saturated fat** 0.5 g, **Cholesterol** 100 mg, **Sodium** 440 mg, **Total carbohydrates** 22 g, **Protein** 40 g, **Vitamin C** 10%, **Iron** 10%, **Claims**—low fat; low saturated fat; source of vitamin C and iron

MURGH KEBAB (CHICKEN KEBAB)

Yield: 6 Servings   **Method:** Grilling

Chicken breasts, boneless, skinless	2 lb.	1 kg
Saffron	½ tsp.	3 ml
Water, hot	2 Tbsp.	30 ml
Garlic, crushed	1 tsp.	5 ml
Vegetable oil	1 Tbsp.	15 ml
Salt	1 tsp.	5 ml
Coriander, ground	2 tsp.	10 ml
Yogurt	2 Tbsp.	30 ml

1 Cut the chicken breasts into 2-inch (5-centimeter) pieces.

2 In a stainless steel bowl, stir the saffron into the hot water and allow it to steep for 5 minutes. Add the garlic, vegetable oil, salt, coriander and yogurt to the bowl. Stir to combine the ingredients.

3 Add the chicken pieces and marinate, in the refrigerator, for 4 hours.

4 Skewer the chicken pieces onto bamboo or stainless steel skewers. Grill until done, approximately 10 to 15 minutes. Serve the chicken kebabs with grilled vegetables and rice.

Approximate values per serving: **Calories** 200, **Total fat** 6 g, **Saturated fat** 1.5 g, **Cholesterol** 90 mg, **Sodium** 460 mg, **Total carbohydrates** 1 g, **Protein** 34 g

---

RECIPE 18.13

CHICKEN YAKITORI

Yield: 8 Servings	**Method:** Grilling	
Soy sauce	8 fl. oz.	250 ml
Sake	8 fl. oz.	250 ml
Granulated sugar	2 oz.	60 g
Chicken breasts, boneless	2 lb.	1 kg
Cornstarch	1 Tbsp.	15 ml
Sesame seeds	1 Tbsp.	15 ml

1 Combine the soy sauce, sake and sugar. Reserve 8 fluid ounces (250 milliliters) of the mixture.

2 Brush the chicken with a portion of the reserved soy sauce mixture and grill over hot charcoal until done, basting regularly.

3 To make the sauce, combine 2 ounces (60 milliliters) of the soy sauce mixture with the cornstarch. Bring the remainder to a boil in a small saucepan and stir in the cornstarch slurry. Stirring constantly, continue boiling until the sauce thickens. Simmer 1 minute.

4 Serve with short-grain white rice and garnish with sesame seeds.

Approximate values per 6-oz. (180-g) serving: **Calories** 240, **Total fat** 4.5 g, **Saturated fat** 1 g, **Cholesterol** 95 mg, **Sodium** 1700 mg, **Total carbohydrates** 12 g, **Protein** 37 g

---

PAN-ROASTED SONOMA FREE-RANGE CHICKEN WITH FINGERLING POTATOES AND HERB JUS

RECIPE 18.14

HERBSAINT BAR AND RESTAURANT, NEW ORLEANS, LA
Chef Donald Link

Yield: 4 Servings	**Method:** Sautéing	
Free-range chicken	1	1
Onion, small, chopped	1	1
Celery, chopped	1 c.	240 ml
Carrot, chopped	1	1
Fresh rosemary	1 sprig	1 sprig
Fresh thyme	1 sprig	1 sprig
Garlic cloves	4	4
Chicken stock, cold	4 qt.	4 lt
Fingerling potatoes	2 lb.	1 kg
Olive oil	3 fl. oz.	90 ml
Salt and pepper	TT	TT
Fresh rosemary, chopped	1 tsp.	5 ml
Fresh herbs, assorted, chopped	2 tsp.	10 ml
Whole butter	½ oz.	15 g

1 Cut the chicken into two skin-on airline breasts and two skin-on boneless leg and thigh portions, reserving the carcass and bones.

2 Roast the chicken bones at 400°F (200°C) until brown. Put the bones in a saucepot with the onion, celery, carrot, rosemary, thyme and garlic and cover with cold chicken stock. Bring to a boil, reduce to a simmer and cook for 3 to 4 hours. Strain the stock into a small saucepot. Bring to a boil and reduce by two-thirds or until the flavor becomes strong and the stock begins to thicken.

3 Toss the potatoes in 1 fluid ounce (30 milliliters) of the olive oil, salt, pepper and rosemary. Roast at 400°F (200°C) until done, approximately 15 minutes.

4 Heat a large sauté pan over high heat and add the remaining olive oil. Season the chicken with salt and pepper. Place the chicken in the pan, skin side down, and cook without turning until the skin is crisp. Transfer the pan to a 400°F (200°C) oven and roast until the chicken is done, approximately 7 minutes.

5 Add the chopped herbs to the reduced stock and swirl in the butter. Serve one piece of chicken accompanied by fingerling potatoes. Spoon the sauce around the chicken.

Approximate values per serving: **Calories** 980, **Total fat** 58 g, **Saturated fat** 14 g, **Cholesterol** 195 mg, **Sodium** 2930 mg, **Total carbohydrates** 51 g, **Protein** 64 g, **Vitamin** C 40%, **Iron** 35%

ROAST CORNISH GAME HEN WITH WILD RICE STUFFING

RECIPE 18.15

Yield: 6 Servings   **Method:** Roasting

Onion, fine dice	3 oz.	90 g
Mushrooms, chopped	6 oz.	180 g
Whole butter, melted	6 oz.	180 g
Wild rice, cooked	1½ c.	350 ml
Dried thyme, crushed	½ tsp.	2 ml
Dried marjoram, crushed	½ tsp.	2 ml
Salt and pepper	TT	TT
Rock Cornish game hens	6	6

1 Sauté the onions and mushrooms in 2 ounces (60 grams) of the melted butter until tender. Cool.

2 Stir in the rice and herbs and season to taste with salt and pepper.

3 Stuff the cavity of each hen loosely with the rice mixture. Truss and place in a roasting pan.

1 Loosely stuff each hen with some of the wild rice mixture.

2 Truss the hens.

3 The game hens plated for service.

4 Brush the hens with the remaining butter and season with salt and pepper. Roast at 400°F (200°C) for 15 minutes.

5 Reduce the oven temperature to 300°F (150°C) and roast until the juices run clear, approximately 30 minutes. Baste two or three times with melted butter.

6 Serve the hens with a pan gravy or a sauce made separately, such as mushroom sauce.

Approximate values per 14-oz. (420-g) serving: **Calories** 970, **Total fat** 65 g, **Saturated fat** 26 g, **Cholesterol** 330 mg, **Sodium** 1580 mg, **Total carbohydrates** 12 g, **Protein** 86 g, **Vitamin A** 35%, **Iron** 25%

RECIPE 18.16

CHICKEN BREAST SAUTÉ WITH ROASTED RED PEPPER SAUCE

NASHVILLE STATE TECH CULINARY, NASHVILLE, TN
Chef Ken Morlino, CEC

Yield: 4 Servings   **Method:** Sautéing

Olive oil	2 Tbsp.	30 ml
Chicken breasts, boneless, skinless, 6–8 oz. (180–225 g) each	4	4
Salt and pepper	TT	TT
Flour	as needed for dredging	
Onion, medium dice	1 oz.	30 g
Garlic cloves, minced	2	2
White wine	2 fl. oz.	60 ml
Chicken stock	4 fl. oz.	120 ml
Roma tomato concassée	8 fl. oz.	240 ml
Red bell pepper, roasted, seeded, medium dice	1	1
Mushrooms, sliced	2 oz.	60 g
Unsalted butter	2 Tbsp.	30 ml
Heavy cream	6 fl. oz.	180 ml
Green onions, sliced	2 Tbsp.	30 ml
Parmesan	as needed	as needed

1 Heat the olive oil in a sauté pan. Season the chicken breasts with salt and pepper and dredge them in the flour. Sear the chicken breasts in the hot oil. Remove the chicken from the sauté pan and hold on a plate in a warm spot.

2 Add the onions and garlic to the hot oil and sauté for 2 minutes. Deglaze the pan with the white wine and then add the chicken stock, tomato concassée and bell pepper. Bring to a simmer and reduce the liquid by half.

3 In a separate pan, sauté the mushrooms in the butter and keep warm.

4 Warm the cream slightly and add it to the sauce. Simmer the sauce until it starts to thicken. Return the chicken breasts and the juice that has accumulated on the plate to the pan and simmer until the chicken is done, approximately 2 minutes. Season the sauce with salt and pepper.

5 Serve garnished with the sautéed mushrooms and green onions. Sprinkle with Parmesan.

Note: If a smoother sauce is desired, purée the sauce before adding the chicken.

Approximate values per serving: **Calories** 480, **Total fat** 29 g, **Saturated fat** 16 g, **Cholesterol** 185 mg, **Sodium** 210 mg, **Total carbohydrates** 8 g, **Protein** 42 g, **Vitamin A** 60%, **Vitamin C** 110%, **Iron** 10%

CHICKEN STUFFED WITH SPINACH AND RICOTTA CHEESE IN SAFFRON SAUCE

RECIPE 18.17

CHEF LELAND ATKINSON, WASHINGTON, DC

Yield: 4 Servings   **Method:** Sautéing

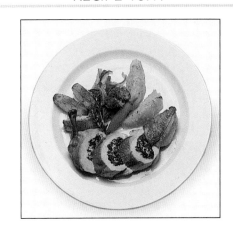

Spinach, stemmed	1 lb.	450 g
Ricotta	4 oz.	120 g
Egg whites, lightly beaten	2	2
Salt and pepper	TT	TT
Airline chicken breasts, skin on, 9 oz. (250 g) each	4	4
Clarified butter	2 Tbsp.	30 ml
White wine	1 pt.	450 ml
Saffron	1 pinch	1 pinch
Chicken velouté	8 fl. oz.	250 ml
Heavy cream, hot	2 fl. oz.	60 ml

1 Blanch, refresh and drain the spinach. Squeeze it tightly to remove as much moisture as possible, then chop it finely.

2 To make the stuffing, combine the ricotta, egg whites and spinach in a mixing bowl; season to taste.

3 Place the chicken breasts on a cutting board, skin side down. Using a boning knife, carefully make a pocket that runs the length of each breast.

4 Put the stuffing in a pastry bag and pipe the stuffing into each pocket. Do not overfill the chicken breasts because the stuffing expands as it cooks.

5 Sauté the chicken in the clarified butter until well browned. Transfer the chicken to a sheet pan and finish in a 350°F (180°C) oven, approximately 10 to 12 minutes.

6 Deglaze the sauté pan with the white wine.

7 Add the saffron, bring to a boil and reduce by half.

8 Add the velouté and the cream. Adjust the seasonings and consistency; strain.

9 Ladle the sauce onto four warm plates. Slice and then arrange the chicken in the sauce; garnish as desired.

Approximate values per 17-oz. (510-g) serving: **Calories** 880, **Total fat** 40 g, **Saturated fat** 16 g, **Cholesterol** 265 mg, **Sodium** 3190 mg, **Total carbohydrates** 42 g, **Protein** 88 g, **Vitamin A** 110%, **Vitamin C** 25%, **Iron** 30%

CHICKEN LAZONE

RECIPE 18.18

BRENNAN'S RESTAURANT, NEW ORLEANS, LA
Chef Michael Roussel

Yield: 4 Servings   **Method:** Sautéing

Salt	1 tsp.	5 ml
Chilli powder	1½ tsp.	8 ml
Onion powder	1½ tsp.	8 ml
Garlic powder	2 tsp.	10 ml
Chicken breasts, boneless, skinless	4	4
Whole butter	2 oz.	60 g
Heavy cream	4 fl. oz.	120 ml
Egg noodles, cooked	as needed	as needed
Fresh parsley, chopped	as needed for garnish	

1 Combine the seasonings in a bowl and coat the chicken breasts with the mixture.

2 Melt 1 ounce (30 grams) of the butter in a sauté pan, then cook the chicken breasts over medium heat, turning once, until done, approximately 7 to 8 minutes. Remove the chicken from the pan and hold in a warm oven.

3 Pour the cream into the pan and lower the heat. Simmer for several minutes, stirring, until the sauce thickens. Whisk in the remaining butter.

4 For service, arrange the chicken breasts over the egg noodles. Top with the cream sauce and garnish with the chopped parsley.

Approximate values per serving: **Calories** 360, **Total fat** 26 g, **Saturated fat** 15 g, **Cholesterol** 145 mg, **Sodium** 660 mg, **Total carbohydrates** 3 g, **Protein** 29 g, **Vitamin A** 25%

RECIPE 18.19

ROMAN-STYLE FREE-RANGE CHICKEN

CHEF ODETTE FADA, New York, NY

Yield: 4 Servings   **Method:** Sautéing

Free-range chicken breast halves, suprême cut	4	4
Extra virgin olive oil	2 Tbsp.	30 ml
Salt	TT	TT
Vegetable or chicken broth	8 fl. oz.	225 ml
Garlic cloves, chopped fine	4	4
Anchovy fillets in oil, chopped fine	3	3
Fresh rosemary, chopped fine	TT	TT
White wine vinegar	2 Tbsp.	30 ml

1 Sauté the chicken breasts in the olive oil, skin side down. Season with salt.

2 Cook until the chicken begins to brown, then turn it and cook for an additional 2 minutes.

3 Add the broth and reduce by two-thirds, approximately 5 minutes.

4 Combine the garlic, anchovies, rosemary and vinegar.

5 When the chicken is done, add the vinegar mixture to the cooking liquid.

6 Remove the chicken from the heat, slice each breast in six pieces and arrange on a hot plate. Pour the sauce over the sliced chicken.

Approximate values per 7.5-oz. (225-g) serving: **Calories** 360, **Total fat** 19 g, **Saturated fat** 4.5 g, **Cholesterol** 125 mg, **Sodium** 820 mg, **Total carbohydrates** 3 g, **Protein** 46 g, **Vitamin A** 15%

RECIPE 18.20

SAUTÉED CHICKEN WITH KENTUCKY BOURBON

Yield: 1 Serving   **Method:** Sautéing

Chicken breast, boneless, skinless	1	1
Salt and pepper	TT	TT
Flour	as needed for dredging	
Olive oil	as needed	as needed
Garlic, minced	1/2 tsp.	2 ml
Shallots, chopped	1 tsp.	5 ml

Spinach	1 oz.	30 g
Kentucky bourbon	1 Tbsp.	15 ml
Chicken stock	1 fl. oz.	30 ml
Heavy cream	2 fl. oz.	60 ml

1 Season the chicken breast with salt and pepper and dredge it in flour. Sauté in olive oil until done and remove from the pan.

2 Add the garlic and shallots to the pan and sauté until tender. Add the spinach and sauté until wilted.

3 Add the bourbon and flame. Then add the chicken stock and cream and reduce until slightly thickened.

4 Return the chicken to the sauce to reheat.

5 Pour the spinach and sauce on a plate and arrange the chicken on top.

Approximate values per 9-oz. (270-g) serving: **Calories** 670, **Total fat** 42 g, **Saturated fat** 17 g, **Cholesterol** 230 mg, **Sodium** 2590 mg, **Total carbohydrates** 15 g, **Protein** 58 g, **Vitamin A** 50%, **Iron** 20%

SPICED CHICKEN CUTLETS

RECIPE 18.21

NEWBURY COLLEGE, BROOKLINE, MA
Senior Instructor Scott Doughty

Yield: 8 Servings

Method: Sautéing

Chicken breast, boneless, skinless	3 lb.	1.3 kg
Flour	as needed for dredging	
Salt and pepper	TT	TT
Clarified butter or ghee	3 fl. oz.	100 ml
Ginger, minced	1 Tbsp.	15 ml
Garlic cloves, minced	6	6
Onion, minced	1	1
Mustard seeds	2 tsp.	10 ml
Yogurt	12 oz.	350 g
Cumin, ground	½ tsp.	3 ml
Coriander, ground	½ tsp.	3 ml
Fresh lime juice	2 tsp.	10 ml
Cilantro, chopped	3 Tbsp.	45 ml

1 Cut each chicken breast in half. Pound each half until the cutlets are approximately ¼ inch (6 millimeters) thick.

2 Season the flour with salt and pepper.

3 Heat 2 fluid ounces (60 milliliters) of the butter or ghee in a large sauté pan. Dredge the chicken cutlets in the flour and sauté them for a few minutes on each side until lightly brown. Remove the chicken from the pan and hold.

4 In the same pan, melt the remaining butter or ghee; add the ginger, garlic, onion and mustard seeds and sauté until the mustard seeds begin to pop.

5 Reduce the heat; add the yogurt, cumin, coriander and lime juice and mix well. Bring to a simmer and adjust the seasonings.

6 Return the cutlets to the pan just long enough to reheat them. Serve the cutlets garnished with chopped cilantro and accompanied by saffron rice seasoned with cinnamon.

Approximate values per serving: **Calories** 300, **Total fat** 14 g, **Saturated fat** 7 g, **Cholesterol** 120 mg, **Sodium** 115 mg, **Total carbohydrates** 6 g, **Protein** 37 g, **Calcium** 10%

RECIPE 18.22

CHICKEN AND SNOW PEAS IN BLACK BEAN SAUCE

Yield: 4 Servings   **Method:** Stir-frying

Chicken breast, boneless, skinless	2 lb.	1 kg
Egg white	1	1
Chinese rice wine	6 fl. oz.	180 ml
Cornstarch	2 Tbsp.	30 ml
Soy sauce	2 fl. oz.	60 ml
Granulated sugar	2 tsp.	10 ml
Onions, small	2	2
Peanut oil	4 fl. oz.	120 ml
Garlic, minced	1 Tbsp.	15 ml
Fresh ginger, minced	2 tsp.	10 ml
Fermented black beans, mashed	3 Tbsp.	45 ml
Snow peas, fresh	4 oz.	120 g

1 Slice the chicken into thin strips, approximately 1½ inches by ¼ inch (4 centimeters by 0.6 centimeters).

2 Combine the egg white, one-third of the wine and 1 tablespoon (15 milliliters) of the cornstarch. Add the chicken and refrigerate for 2 hours.

3 For the sauce, mix the soy sauce, sugar and the remaining wine and cornstarch.

4 Quarter the onions and separate the layers.

5 Stir-fry the chicken in 3 ounces (90 milliliters) of the oil. Remove and set aside.

6 If necessary, add all the remaining oil and stir-fry the garlic and ginger for 30 seconds. Add the onions and mashed beans and stir-fry for 30 seconds. Add the snow peas and cook for 1 minute.

7 Return the chicken to the wok, add the sauce mixture and stir-fry until hot and the sauce has thickened.

8 Serve immediately with short-grain white rice.

Variation: Add 2 ounces (60 grams) sliced mushrooms and reduce the amount of snow peas by half.

Approximate values per serving: **Calories** 750, **Total fat** 46 g, **Saturated fat** 10 g, **Cholesterol** 190 mg, **Sodium** 1050 mg, **Total carbohydrates** 14 g, **Protein** 71 g, **Vitamin C** 25%

RECIPE 18.23

CHICKEN KIEV

THE ART INSTITUTE OF WASHINGTON, ARLINGTON, VA
Chef John Harrison

Yield: 4 Servings   **Method:** Deep-frying

Chicken breasts, boneless, skinless, 5 oz. (140 g) each	4	4
Salt and pepper	TT	TT
Unsalted butter	4 oz.	120 g
Chives, chopped	2 Tbsp.	30 ml
All-purpose flour	as needed	as needed
Egg wash	as needed	as needed
Bread crumbs, dry	as needed	as needed

1 Place the chicken breasts on a film-covered cutting board. Cover them with a layer of film wrap. Using a meat mallet, gently pound the breasts to an even thickness of approximately ⅓ inch (8 millimeters). Do not make any holes in the chicken. Remove the film wrap from the top of the chicken.

2 Season the chicken with salt and pepper. Cut the unsalted butter into four 1-ounce (30-gram), 3-inch- (7.5-centimeter-) long pieces. Place one piece of butter on the long edge of each pounded breast. Spread the chopped chives evenly over the butter.

3 Beginning with the butter-and-chive edge, roll each breast until the butter is covered. Fold the ends of the breast toward the center and continue rolling. Cover and refrigerate the chicken breasts for 15 minutes.

4 Bread the stuffed chicken breasts using the standard breading procedure and refrigerate them for another 15 minutes.

5 Gently place the chicken breasts in a deep-fryer basket and deep-fry at 325°F (160°C) until golden brown and fully cooked, approximately 10 minutes.

6 Gently remove the chicken from the basket to prevent the butter from leaking out. Serve immediately garnished with lemon slices.

Variations: Substitute other herbs such as tarragon, basil, dill or cilantro for the chives, or substitute a compound butter for the butter and herbs in the recipe.

Approximate values per serving: **Calories** 420, **Total fat** 32 g, **Saturated fat** 16 g, **Cholesterol** 145 mg, **Sodium** 95 mg, **Total carbohydrates** 0, **Protein** 33 g, **Vitamin A** 20%

CHICKEN AND MUSHROOM CRÊPES WITH SAUCE MORNAY

RECIPE 18.24

PENNSYLVANIA COLLEGE OF TECHNOLOGY, WILLIAMSPORT, PA
Chef Mary G. Trometter, Assistant Professor

Yield: 6 Crêpes　　　　　　　　　　**Method:** Poaching

Chicken stock	1 pt.	450 ml
Salt	TT	TT
Chicken, boneless, skinless	1 lb.	450 g
Mushrooms, sliced	5 oz.	150 g
Clarified butter	1 Tbsp.	15 ml
Fresh thyme, tarragon, and parsley, minced	1 Tbsp.	15 ml
Black pepper	TT	TT
Savory crêpes (page 602)	6	6
Mornay sauce (page 213)	1 pt.	450 ml
Paprika	as needed for garnish	

1 Bring the chicken stock to a simmer and season with the salt.

2 Poach the chicken in the stock until done. Remove the chicken from the stock, reserving the stock. Allow the chicken to cool slightly and then cut it into medium dice.

3 Sauté the mushrooms in the clarified butter with the herbs until the mushrooms are tender. Season the mixture with salt and pepper. Combine the chicken with the mushrooms and refrigerate until cold.

4 Divide the chicken and mushrooms into six portions. Spoon one portion of the mixture into the center of each crêpe. Roll the crêpe around the mixture and place in a buttered baking dish, seam side down.

5 Heat the Mornay sauce over medium heat; thin with a portion of the reserved poaching liquid if necessary. Spoon the sauce over the crêpes. Garnish with a light sprinkle of paprika if desired. Bake at 350°F (180°C) until hot and lightly brown, approximately 20 minutes.

Approximate values per crêpe: **Calories** 420, **Total fat** 27 g, **Saturated fat** 15 g, **Cholesterol** 185 mg, **Sodium** 960 mg, **Total carbohydrates** 23 g, **Protein** 25 g, **Vitamin A** 15%, **Calcium** 15%

RECIPE 18.25

CHICKEN CURRY

Yield: 4 Servings		**Method:** Simmering
Onions, small dice	8 oz.	250 g
Garlic, crushed	2 tsp.	10 ml
Ghee or clarified butter	2 Tbsp.	30 ml
Wet masala:		
Fresh ginger, fine dice	2 oz.	60 g
Turmeric	1½ tsp.	8 ml
Coriander seeds, ground	1½ tsp.	8 ml
Cumin seeds, ground	1 tsp.	5 ml
Cayenne pepper	1 tsp.	5 ml
Fenugreek, ground	½ tsp.	3 ml
Coconut milk	20 fl. oz.	575 ml
Roasting chicken, 3 lb. (1.3 kg), cut into 8 pieces	1	1
Salt	1 tsp.	5 ml
Green chiles, slit lengthwise	3	3
Lemon juice	1 fl. oz.	30 ml

1 Stir-fry the onions and garlic in the ghee until the onions are golden brown.
2 To make the wet masala, mix the ginger, turmeric, coriander, cumin, cayenne pepper and fenugreek; add just enough of the coconut milk to form a paste.
3 Add the wet masala to the onions and stir-fry for 8 minutes.
4 Add the chicken pieces and cook, turning them frequently, for 6 to 8 minutes.
5 Add the remaining coconut milk, salt and chiles. Bring to a boil, cover and reduce to a simmer. Cook until the chicken is done, approximately 45 minutes.
6 Just before service, stir in the lemon juice and adjust the seasonings. Serve with Saffron Rice (page 729) and a chutney.

Approximate values per serving: **Calories** 1130, **Total fat** 64 g, **Saturated fat** 39 g, **Cholesterol** 285 mg, **Sodium** 1070 mg, **Total carbohydrates** 32 g, **Protein** 107 g, **Vitamin C** 25%, **Iron** 70%

RECIPE 18.26

THAI GREEN CURRY WITH CHICKEN AND EGGPLANT

Yield: 5 lb. (2.2 kg)		**Method:** Simmering
Thai or Japanese eggplant, medium dice	1 pt.	470 ml
Peanut oil	2 fl. oz.	60 ml
Green Curry Paste (recipe follows)	20 fl. oz.	600 ml
Coconut milk	1 qt.	1 lt
Chicken breast, boneless, skinless	2 lb.	900 g
Fish sauce	4 fl. oz.	120 ml

Granulated sugar	6 Tbsp.	90 ml
Coconut cream	8 fl. oz.	240 ml
Fresh Kaffir lime leaves	12	12
Fresh basil leaves	½ c.	120 ml

1 Sweat the eggplant in 1 fluid ounce (30 milliliters) of the peanut oil until tender. Remove from the heat and reserve.

2 Sauté the Green Curry Paste in the remaining peanut oil. Slowly stir in the coconut milk. Bring to a boil and simmer until slightly thickened.

3 Add the chicken, eggplant, fish sauce and sugar. Simmer until the chicken is cooked, approximately 5 minutes.

4 Stir in the coconut cream. Stir in the lime leaves and basil. Serve with steamed rice.

Approximate values per 8-oz. (240-g) serving: **Calories** 460, **Total fat** 33 g, **Saturated fat** 23 g, **Cholesterol** 55 mg, **Sodium** 1190 mg, **Total carbohydrates** 19 g, **Protein** 25 g, **Vitamin A** 25%, **Vitamin C** 150%, **Iron** 25%, **Claims**—good source of fiber, vitamin A and C

GREEN CURRY PASTE

Yield: 20 fl. oz (600 ml)

Jalapeño peppers	10	10
Thai chiles	5	5
Cilantro stems, chopped	½ c.	120 ml
Garlic cloves	8	8
Shallots, chopped	4 Tbsp.	60 ml
Lemon grass, chopped	4 Tbsp.	60 ml
Fresh galangal slices	5	5
Cumin	1 tsp.	5 ml
Shrimp paste	1 tsp.	5 ml

1 Combine all the ingredients in a blender and process until smooth.

COQ AU VIN

RECIPE 18.27

Yield: 8 Servings, 2 pieces each   **Method:** Braising

Chickens, 2 lb. 8 oz.–3 lb. (1.1–1.4 kg) each	2	2
Flour	as needed for dredging	
Salt and pepper	TT	TT
Clarified butter	2 fl. oz.	60 ml
Brandy	4 fl. oz.	120 ml
Bouquet garni:		
Carrot stick, 4 in. (10 cm)	1	1
Leek, split, 4-in. (10-cm) piece	1	1
Fresh thyme	1 sprig	1 sprig
Bay leaf	1	1
Garlic cloves, peeled and crushed	6	6
Red wine	24 fl. oz.	700 ml
Chicken stock	8 fl. oz.	250 ml
Bacon **lardons**	4 oz.	120 g
Pearl onions, peeled	18	18
Mushrooms, medium, quartered	10	10
Beurre manié	as needed	as needed
Large triangular croutons	8	8

▶ **lardons** diced, blanced, fried bacon

1 Cut each chicken into eight pieces and dredge in flour seasoned with salt and pepper.

2 Heat the clarified butter in a braising pan; brown the chicken.

3 Add the brandy and ignite. When the flame dies, add the bouquet garni, garlic, red wine and chicken stock. Bring to a boil, then reduce to a simmer.

4 Cover the pan and simmer until the chicken is tender, approximately 40 minutes.

5 In a separate pan, sauté the bacon until the fat begins to render. Add the onions and sauté until they begin to brown. Cook the bacon and onions covered, over low heat, until the onions are tender. Add the mushroom and cook them until tender.

6 Remove the chicken from the pan and adjust the sauce's consistency with the beurre manié. Strain the sauce through a china cap and adjust the seasonings.

7 Spoon the bacon, onions and mushrooms onto a serving platter, place the chicken over them and ladle the sauce over the finished dish. Serve with triangular croutons.

Approximate values per 12-oz. (360-g) serving: **Calories** 860, **Total fat** 51 g, **Saturated fat** 17 g, **Cholesterol** 330 mg, **Sodium** 910 mg, **Total carbohydrates** 17 g, **Protein** 83 g, **Vitamin A** 60%, **Iron** 35%

RECIPE 18.28   CHICKEN CACCIATORE

Yield: 8 Servings, 2 pieces each   **Method:** Braising

Frying chickens, 2 lb. 8 oz.–3 lb. (1.1–1.4 kg) each	2	2
Flour	2 oz.	60 g
Salt and pepper	TT	TT
Olive oil	2 fl. oz.	60 ml
Onion, medium dice	4 oz.	120 g
Garlic cloves, chopped	3	3
Mushrooms, sliced	8 oz.	250 g
Dried thyme	¼ tsp.	1 ml
White wine	2 fl. oz.	60 ml
Brandy	1 fl. oz.	30 ml
Demi-glace	1 pt.	450 ml
Tomato concassée	12 oz.	340 g

1 Cut each chicken into eight pieces and dredge in flour seasoned with salt and pepper.

2 Heat the oil in a heavy braizer and brown the chicken well. Remove the chicken from the pan. Degrease the pan, leaving 1 tablespoon (15 milliliters) of fat.

3 Add the onions and garlic and sauté lightly. Add the mushrooms and thyme and continue sautéing until the mushrooms are tender.

4 Deglaze the pan with the white wine and brandy. Add the demi-glace and tomato concassée.

5 Return the chicken to the pan and season with salt and pepper. Cover and cook until the chicken is done, approximately 30 minutes.

6 Serve two pieces of chicken with a portion of sauce.

Approximate values per 13-oz. (390-g) serving: **Calories** 650, **Total fat** 29 g, **Saturated fat** 7 g, **Cholesterol** 235 mg, **Sodium** 500 mg, **Total carbohydrates** 11 g, **Protein** 86 g, **Vitamin A** 10%, **Iron** 25%

CHICKEN WITH 40 CLOVES OF GARLIC   RECIPE 18.29

Yield: 4 Servings, 2 pieces each   **Method:** Braising

Chicken, 2 lb. 8 oz. (1.1 kg), cut in 8 pieces	1	1
Dry white wine	26 fl. oz.	750 ml
Flour	as needed for dredging	
Salt and pepper	TT	TT
Olive oil	2 Tbsp.	30 ml
Garlic cloves, unpeeled	40	40
Fresh thyme	4 sprigs	4 sprigs
Fresh rosemary	1 sprig	1 sprig
French bread croutons	8	8
Fresh parsley, chopped	as needed for garnish	

1 Marinate the chicken pieces in the white wine for 1 to 2 hours under refrigeration. Remove and pat dry.

2 Dredge the chicken in flour and season lightly with salt and pepper. Sauté the chicken in the olive oil.

3 Remove the chicken from the pan and sauté the garlic until it begins to brown. Place the chicken on top of the garlic in a single layer. Add the wine marinade and herbs and cover.

4 Braise in a 325°F (160°C) oven until tender, approximately 45 minutes.

5 Remove the chicken and garlic from the pan and reserve. Remove and discard the herbs. Place the pan on the stove top and reduce the sauce until slightly thick. Season with salt and pepper.

6 Serve two pieces of chicken and several of the garlic cloves resting on two French bread croutons. Top with a portion of the sauce and garnish with chopped parsley.

Approximate values per 12.5-oz. (375-g) serving: **Calories** 600, **Total fat** 18 g, **Saturated fat** 4 g, **Cholesterol** 240 mg, **Sodium** 820 mg, **Total carbohydrates** 20 g, **Protein** 91 g, **Vitamin C** 15%, **Iron** 25%

LOUISIANA CHICKEN   RECIPE 18.30

NEWBURY COLLEGE, Brookline, MA
Senior Instructor Scott Doughty

Yield: 8 Servings   **Method:** Braising

Chickens, 3 lb. (1.3 kg) each	2	2
Onions, small dice	2	2
Celery, small dice	2	2
Green bell peppers, small dice	2	2
Clarified butter	2 fl. oz.	60 ml
Garlic cloves, minced	3	3
Tomatoes, canned, diced (with liquid)	1 qt.	1 lt
Black olives, pitted, quartered	12	12
Cayenne pepper	½ tsp.	2 ml
Fresh thyme	1½ tsp.	8 ml
Fresh oregano, chopped	1½ tsp.	8 ml
Salt and pepper	TT	TT
Bay leaves	2	2
Parsley, minced	2 Tbsp.	30 ml
Olive oil	4 fl. oz.	120 ml
Flour	1 oz.	30 g
White wine	12 fl. oz.	350 ml

1 Quarter the chickens.

2 Cook the onions, celery and bell peppers in the butter for 5 minutes without browning. Add the garlic and cook for 3 minutes. Add the tomatoes with their juice, the olives, cayenne pepper, thyme, oregano, 1 teaspoon (5 milliliters) of salt, ½ teaspoon (3 milliliters) of black pepper, the bay leaves and parsley. Cover and simmer gently for 25 minutes.

3 Heat the oil in a brazier. Season the chicken with salt and pepper. Cook the chicken, skin side down, until golden brown. Transfer the chicken to a 2-inch-(5-centimeter-) deep hotel pan, skin side up. Pour off and discard all but 1 fluid ounce (30 milliliters) of the fat from the brazier.

4 Add the flour to the brazier and cook to make a brown roux. Stir in the wine and simmer until thickened. Add the tomato mixture. Return to a simmer and ladle the sauce over the chicken. Bake at 375°F (190°C) until the chicken reaches an internal temperature of 160°F (71°C), approximately 25 minutes.

Approximate values per serving: **Calories** 560, **Total fat** 30 g, **Saturated fat** 10 g, **Cholesterol** 160 mg, **Sodium** 330 mg, **Total carbohydrates** 14 g, **Protein** 51 g, **Vitamin A** 30%, **Vitamin C** 80%, **Iron** 20%

RECIPE 18.31   COUNTRY BRAISED CHICKEN

NEWBURY COLLEGE, Brookline, MA
Senior Instructor Scott Doughty

Yield: 8 Servings   **Method:** Braising

Flour	6 oz.	180 g
Salt	1 Tbsp.	15 ml
Black pepper	1 tsp.	5 ml
Paprika	1 tsp.	5 ml
Cayenne pepper	1 tsp.	5 ml
Chickens, cut into 8 pieces	2	2
Whole butter	1 oz.	30 g
Vegetable oil	1 fl. oz.	30 ml
Tomatoes	2 lb.	1 kg
Onions, small dice	3	3
Green bell peppers, chopped	4	4
Garlic cloves, chopped	3	3
Curry powder	1 Tbsp.	15 ml
Mace	1 tsp.	5 ml
Chicken stock	as needed	as needed
Almonds, toasted	2 oz.	60 g

1 Combine the flour, salt, pepper, paprika and cayenne pepper. Dredge the chicken in the seasoned flour.

2 Pan-fry the chicken in the butter and oil, skin side down, until evenly browned. Turn and cook on the other side for 30 seconds. Remove the chicken and hold.

3 Prepare tomato concassée. Sweat the onions and bell peppers with the garlic, curry powder and mace in a sauté pan. Add the tomato concassée.

4 Place the browned chicken on top of the vegetables, cover and braise to an internal temperature of 165°F (74°C), approximately 25 minutes. Remove the chicken pieces as they are done, beginning with the breast pieces. Continue cooking until all of the chicken is done.

5 Degrease the sauce if necessary, and adjust its consistency with the chicken stock. Then adjust the seasonings and pour the sauce into a serving pan. Place the chicken on top of the sauce and garnish with the toasted almonds. Serve with steamed rice on the side.

Approximate values per serving: **Calories** 340, **Total fat** 23 g, **Saturated fat** 6 g, **Cholesterol** 30 mg, **Sodium** 470 mg, **Total carbohydrates** 24 g, **Protein** 11 g, **Vitamin A** 30%, **Vitamin C** 130%, **Iron** 15%

BRAISED CHICKEN WITH APPLE CIDER AND CASHEW BUTTER

RECIPE 18.32

CHEF LELAND ATKINSON, Washington, DC

Yield: 8 Servings   **Method:** Braising

Shallots, minced	2 oz.	60 g
Clarified butter	2½ fl. oz.	75 ml
Calvados	12 fl. oz.	375 ml
Fresh thyme, chopped	2 tsp.	10 ml
Cashews	3 oz.	90 g
Honey	1 Tbsp.	15 ml
Unsalted butter	1 lb.	450 g
Salt and pepper	TT	TT
Chickens, 3 lb. 8 oz. (1.6 kg) each, quartered	2	2
Flour	as needed for dredging	
Mirepoix	12 oz.	350 g
Garlic head, cut in half	1	1
Apple cider	1 pt.	450 ml
Cider vinegar	1 Tbsp.	15 ml
Chicken stock	3 pt.	1350 ml
Bay leaves	2	2
Fresh thyme	1 sprig	1 sprig
Blond roux	as needed	as needed

1 To make the cashew butter, lightly sauté the shallots in 1 tablespoon (15 milliliters) of the clarified butter. Add 4 ounces (120 milliliters) of the Calvados and the chopped thyme and reduce au sec. Remove from the heat and cool.

2 Place the cashews in a food processor and process to a medium-fine consistency. Add the cooled shallots, honey and unsalted butter. Season with salt and pepper and process well.

3 Season the chicken with salt and pepper and dredge in flour.

4 Brown the chicken evenly in the remaining clarified butter.

5 Remove the chicken. Add the mirepoix and garlic to the pan; sauté for 1 minute.

6 Add the remaining Calvados, cider and vinegar; reduce by half.

7 Return the chicken to the pan and add the chicken stock and herbs. Cover and braise until done, approximately 15 minutes. Remove the chicken from the pan. (The breasts and wings will cook more quickly and must be removed before the thigh and leg pieces.)

8 Reduce the stock by half. Use the roux to thicken to a light consistency.

9 Strain the sauce, monté au beurre with the cashew butter and season to taste with salt and pepper. Ladle the sauce over the chicken and serve at once.

Approximate values per 17-oz. (510-g) serving: **Calories** 1265, **Total fat** 73 g, **Saturated fat** 38 g, **Cholesterol** 480 mg, **Sodium** 1220 mg, **Total carbohydrates** 22 g, **Protein** 130 g, **Vitamin A** 60%

RECIPE 18.33   CHICKEN POT PIE

Yield: 15 Servings, 10 oz. (280 g) each

Whole butter	1 oz.	30 g
White mushrooms, quartered	8 oz.	240 g
Salt and pepper	TT	TT
Red potatoes, medium dice	6 oz.	180 g
Carrots, medium dice	6 oz.	180 g
Pearl onions	6 oz.	180 g
Peas	6 oz.	180 g
Corn kernels	6 oz.	180 g
Chicken velouté sauce	3 pt.	1.5 lt
Heavy cream	8 fl. oz.	240 ml
Chicken, cooked, large dice	2 lb. 8 oz.	1.2 kg
Flaky pie dough or puff pastry	as needed	as needed
Egg wash	as needed	as needed

1 Heat the butter in a small sauté pan and sauté the mushrooms. Season with salt and pepper.

2 Blanch or steam the potatoes, carrots, onions, peas and corn separately until tender.

3 Bring the velouté to a simmer. Add the cream and simmer for 5 minutes.

4 Add the chicken, potatoes and vegetables to the sauce, season with salt and pepper and ladle into a shallow half-size hotel pan.

5 Brush the edges of the pan with egg wash and cover the pan with the pie dough or puff pastry. Egg wash the top of the dough or pastry and make one or two small slices in the top of the dough to allow steam to escape as the pie cooks. Bake at 400°F (200°C) until the top is well browned, approximately 15 minutes.

Variation: *Turkey Pot Pie*—Substitute an equal amount of turkey for the chicken.

Approximate values per serving, without crust: **Calories** 330, **Total fat** 18 g, **Saturated fat** 9 g, **Cholesterol** 110 mg, **Sodium** 530 mg, **Total carbohydrates** 16 g, **Protein** 27 g, **Vitamin A** 70%

RECIPE 18.34   DUCK BREAST WITH RED RICE, CHARD AND APRICOT MUSTARD

PRIMITIVO WINE BAR, COLORADO SPRINGS, CO
John Broening, Executive Chef

Yield: 8 Servings   **Method:** Sautéing

Duck breasts, skin on	8	8
Salt and pepper	TT	TT
Chard leaves, torn	3 oz.	90 g
Whole butter	4 oz.	120 g

Chicken stock	1 pt.	450 ml
Red Rice, cooked (recipe follows)	2 qt.	2 lt
Parsley, chopped	3 Tbsp.	45 ml
Apricot Mustard (recipe follows)	1 c.	240 ml
Almonds, sliced, toasted	1 oz.	30 g

1 Score the skin of the duck breasts in a crosshatch pattern with a sharp knife. Season with salt and pepper and place the breasts skin side down in a rondeau. Without turning the breasts, cook them over low heat, rendering the fat from their skin, until the skin is golden brown and crisp, approximately 15 minutes. Turn the duck breasts in the pan and turn off the heat. Allow them to rest in the pan for 30 seconds. Then remove the breasts from the pan and allow them to rest in a warm place for 10 minutes.

2 Sauté the chard in 2 ounces (60 grams) of the butter until it wilts. Season with salt and pepper.

3 Bring the chicken stock to a boil. Add the cooked Red Rice and season with salt and pepper. Vigorously beat in the remaining butter and parsley and heat over moderate heat until the rice is hot, approximately 1 minute.

4 Slice the duck breasts and arrange on eight warm plates. Garnish with the wilted chard, brush the breasts with the Apricot Mustard, sprinkle with almonds and serve with Red Rice on the side.

Approximate values per serving: **Calories** 640, **Total fat** 20 g, **Saturated fat** 10 g, **Cholesterol** 40 mg, **Sodium** 2740 mg, **Total carbohydrates** 103 g, **Protein** 12 g, **Vitamin A** 35%, **Vitamin C** 10%, **Iron** 15%

RED RICE

Yield: 2 qt. (2 lt)

Whole butter	1 Tbsp.	15 ml
Shallots, minced	4 Tbsp.	60 ml
Red rice	1 lb.	450 g
Chicken stock	2 qt.	2 lt
Bay leaves	2	2
Salt	2 tsp.	10 ml

▶ **red rice** an unmilled short- or long-grain rice from the Himalayas; it has a russet-colored bran and an earthy, nutty flavor

1 In a heavy-bottomed pot, melt the butter and sweat the shallots, without coloring, for approximately 10 minutes. Add the rice and stir to coat.

2 Add the chicken stock, bay leaves and salt and bring to a boil. Cover, reduce the heat to a simmer and cook until the liquid is absorbed, approximately 20 minutes.

3 Spread the cooked rice on a sheet pan, remove the bay leaves and refrigerate.

Approximate values per ½-c. (120-ml) serving: **Calories** 115, **Total fat** 1.5 g, **Saturated fat** 0.5 g, **Cholesterol** 2.5 mg, **Sodium** 635 mg, **Total carbohydrates** 23 g, **Protein** 2.5 g

APRICOT MUSTARD

Yield: 3½ c. (830 ml)

Dry mustard	½ c.	120 ml
Water, cold	4 fl. oz.	120 ml
Granulated sugar	8 oz.	240 g
Rice vinegar	8 fl. oz.	240 ml
Salt	⅛ tsp.	0.5 ml
Fresh ginger, minced	1 Tbsp.	15 ml
Dried apricots, chopped	1 c.	240 ml
Fresh lemon juice	1 Tbsp.	15 ml

1 Whisk together the dry mustard and water and allow the mixture to rest for 1 hour.

2 In a heavy-bottomed pot, bring the sugar, vinegar, salt and ginger to a boil. Add the apricots and simmer until the apricots are soft, approximately 15 minutes. Add the mustard mixture and simmer for 5 minutes.

3 Transfer the sauce to a blender. Add the lemon juice and blend until smooth. Adjust the consistency with water, if necessary.

Approximate values per 1-Tbsp. (15-ml) serving: **Calories** 30, **Total fat** 0, **Saturated fat** 0, **Cholesterol** 0, **Sodium** 5 mg, **Total carbohydrates** 6 g, **Protein** 0, **Claims**—low calorie; fat free; low sodium

RECIPE 18.35

WARM DUCK BREAST SALAD WITH ASIAN SPICES AND HAZELNUT VINAIGRETTE

FETZER VINEYARD, HOPLAND, CA

Culinary Director, John Ash

Yield: 4 Servings		**Method:** Sautéing
Whole boneless duck breasts,		
12 oz. (350 g) each	2	2
Marinade:		
Garlic, minced	1 tsp.	5 ml
Green onions, minced	2 Tbsp.	30 ml
Oyster sauce	2 tsp.	10 ml
Light soy sauce	1 tsp.	5 ml
Rice wine or dry sherry	1 tsp.	5 ml
Sugar	1 tsp.	5 ml
Five-spice powder	½ tsp.	3 ml
Hazelnut vinaigrette:		
Garlic, minced	1 Tbsp.	15 ml
Hazelnut oil	3 fl. oz.	90 ml
Walnut or light olive oil	3 fl. oz.	90 ml
Chives, minced	1 Tbsp.	15 ml
Balsamic vinegar	2 Tbsp.	30 ml
Light soy sauce	1 tsp.	5 ml
Sugar	¼ tsp.	1 ml
Mixed baby greens	4–6 oz.	120–180 g
Hazelnuts, toasted, skinned		
and chopped coarse	2 oz.	60 g

1 Trim the excess fat from the duck breasts and separate the breasts into halves.

2 Combine the marinade ingredients. Thoroughly coat the duck with the marinade and marinate for at least 2 hours.

3 Combine the hazelnut vinaigrette ingredients at least 2 hours before service so that the flavors will develop.

4 Wipe the marinade from the breasts and sauté them, skin side down first, in a dry sauté pan until medium rare, approximately 2½ minutes per side. Do not overcook.

5 Arrange a mixture of baby greens on four plates. Slice the breasts on the diagonal and arrange on the plates with the greens. Drizzle the hazelnut vinaigrette over the greens, sprinkle with hazelnuts and serve.

Approximate values per 9-oz. (270-g) serving: **Calories** 820, **Total fat** 68 g, **Saturated fat** 10 g, **Cholesterol** 230 mg, **Sodium** 240 mg, **Total carbohydrates** 7 g, **Protein** 44 g, **Vitamin C** 20%, **Iron** 35%

DUCK CONFIT   RECIPE 18.36

Yield: 4 Servings

Duck, 4 lb. (1.8 kg), cut into 4 pieces	1	1
Kosher salt	2 Tbsp.	30 ml
Black pepper, cracked	1 tsp.	5 ml
Bay leaves	4	4
Fresh thyme	6 sprigs	6 sprigs
Garlic cloves, crushed	6	6
Duck or goose fat, melted	2 lb.	900 g

1 Rub the duck with the salt. Place it skin side down in a roasting pan just large enough to hold the pieces in one layer; season with the pepper, crumbled bay leaves, thyme and garlic. Cover and refrigerate overnight.

2 Bake the duck at 325°F (160°C) until brown, approximately 15 to 20 minutes. Add enough melted duck or goose fat to cover the pieces completely.

3 Cover the pan and cook in a 300°F (150°C) oven until the duck is very tender, approximately 2 hours.

4 Remove the duck from the fat and place in a deep hotel pan. Ladle enough of the cooking fat over the pieces to cover them completely. Be careful not to add any of the cooking juices.

5 Cover the pan and refrigerate for 2 days to allow the flavors to mellow.

6 To serve, remove the duck from the fat and scrape off the excess fat. Bake at 350°F (180°C) until the skin is crisp and the meat is hot, approximately 30 minutes.

Approximate values per serving: **Calories** 670, **Total fat** 16 g, **Saturated fat** 4.5 g, **Cholesterol** 700 mg, **Sodium** 3960 mg, **Total carbohydrates** 6 g, **Protein** 125 g, **Vitamin C** 25%, **Iron** 130%

1 Season the duck.

2 After the duck browns, cover it with melted fat and return it to the oven.

3 Remove the duck from the congealed fat, scraping off the excess.

RECIPE 18.37

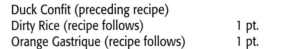

DUCK CONFIT WITH DIRTY RICE AND ORANGE GASTRIQUE

HERBSAINT BAR AND RESTAURANT, New Orleans, LA
Chef Donald Link

Yield: 4 Servings

Duck Confit (preceding recipe)		
Dirty Rice (recipe follows)	1 pt.	450 ml
Orange Gastrique (recipe follows)	1 pt.	450 ml

1 Prepare Duck Confit as described in the preceding recipe.
2 Reheat the duck pieces in a convection oven for service. Arrange the duck over a mound of Dirty Rice surrounded by Orange Gastrique. Garnish with fresh herbs.

DIRTY RICE

Yield: 3 c. (700 ml)

Vegetable oil	1 Tbsp.	15 ml
Chicken livers, chopped	½ c.	120 ml
Pork or beef, chopped	½ oz.	120 g
Onion, small dice	2 oz.	60 g
Garlic, minced	1 tsp.	5 ml
Salt and pepper	as needed	as needed
Cayenne pepper	as needed	as needed
Paprika	as needed	as needed
Chicken stock	4 fl. oz.	120 ml
Long-grain white rice, cooked	1 pt.	450 ml
Green onions, sliced	4 Tbsp.	60 ml
Parsley, chopped	4 Tbsp.	60 ml

1 Heat the oil in a heavy-bottomed saucepan until smoking. Add the livers and the pork or beef and sauté until well browned.
2 Add the onions, garlic and spices and continue to cook and brown the mixture. Deglaze with a little chicken stock and continue to cook until all the ingredients are well browned.
3 Add the remaining chicken stock, the cooked rice, green onions and parsley. Stir and cook until the rice is hot and then serve.

Approximate values per 4-fl. oz. (120-ml) serving: **Calories** 170, **Total fat** 6 g, **Saturated fat** 2 g, **Cholesterol** 95 mg, **Sodium** 90 mg, **Total carbohydrates** 17 g, **Protein** 9 g, **Vitamin A** 80%, **Vitamin C** 20%, **Iron** 15%

ORANGE GASTRIQUE

Yield: 1 pt. (450 ml)

Granulated sugar	8 oz.	240 ml
Water	4 fl. oz.	120 ml
Orange zest	2 Tbsp.	30 ml
Orange juice	1 pt.	450 ml
Star anise	2	2
Brown stock	2 qt.	2 lt
Honey	3 Tbsp.	45 ml
Whole butter	1 Tbsp.	15 ml

1 Combine the sugar and water and cook over medium heat until lightly caramelized.

2 Add the zest, juice and star anise and stir together until the sugar is dissolved and the sauce is smooth. Add the stock and reduce until the sauce thickens and coats the back of a spoon.

3 Stir in the honey and monté au beurre.

Approximate values per 1-fl. oz. (30-ml) serving: **Calories** 100, **Total fat** 1 g, **Saturated fat** 0.5 g, **Cholesterol** 0 mg, **Sodium** 320 mg, **Total carbohydrates** 24 g, **Protein** 1 g, **Vitamin A** 60%, **Vitamin C** 30%

DUCK À L'ORANGE

CHEF LELAND ATKINSON, WASHINGTON, DC

Yield: 4 Servings	**Method:** Roasting	
Duckling, 5–6 lb. (2.2–2.8 kg)	1	1
Salt and pepper	TT	TT
Duck or chicken stock	8 fl. oz.	250 ml
Sugar	1 Tbsp.	15 ml
Champagne vinegar	1 Tbsp.	15 ml
Brandy	2 Tbsp.	30 ml
Orange juice	12 fl. oz.	350 ml
Lemon juice	from 1 lemon	from 1 lemon
Whole butter	1 tsp.	5 ml
Orange zest, julienne	4 Tbsp.	60 ml
Oranges, peeled and sectioned	4	4

1 Prick the duck with a fork and season well with salt and pepper.

2 Roast the duck at 400°F (200°C) for 15 minutes. Reduce the heat to 350°F (180°C) and cook until done, approximately 45 to 60 minutes. Remove the duck from the roasting pan and hold in a warm place.

3 Degrease the roasting pan. Place the pan on the stove top and deglaze with the stock.

4 Melt the sugar and vinegar together in a saucepan and lightly caramelize the mixture.

5 Remove the caramelized sugar from the stove top and add the brandy.

6 Add the stock, pan drippings and juices to the pan of sugar and reduce until the sauce is slightly thickened, approximately 10 minutes. Monté au beurre. Strain and degrease the sauce.

7 Blanch the orange zest in boiling water.

8 Place the duck on a warm serving platter. Arrange the orange sections around it. Sprinkle the zest over the duck. Pour the sauce over the duck and serve additional sauce on the side.

Approximate values per 28-oz. (840-g) serving: **Calories** 1810, **Total fat** 147 g, **Saturated fat** 54 g, **Cholesterol** 475 mg, **Sodium** 1050 mg, **Total carbohydrates** 30 g, **Protein** 91 g, **Vitamin A** 60%, **Vitamin C** 190%, **Iron** 50%

ROAST GOOSE WITH CABBAGE AND APPLES

Yield: 8 Servings, 6 oz. (180 g) each	**Method:** Roasting	
Goose, approx. 12 lb. (6 kg)	1	1
Salt and pepper	TT	TT
Caraway seeds	1 Tbsp.	15 ml
Onion, large dice	6 oz.	180 g

Continued

Carrot, large dice	3 oz.	90 g
Celery, large dice	3 oz.	90 g
Green cabbage, shredded	1 lb.	450 g
Potatoe, large dice	3 lb.	1.4 kg
Tart apple, cored and diced	1 lb.	450 g
Apple cider	1 qt.	1 lt

1 Remove the giblets from the goose; remove the fat from its cavity. Rinse the goose and pat dry. Sprinkle its interior and exterior with salt, pepper and caraway seeds. Truss the goose and place it breast side up on a rack in a roasting pan.
2 Roast in a 425°F (220°C) oven for 30 minutes. Prick the skin all over with a fork to release fat.
3 Reduce the oven temperature to 350°F (180°C) and continue roasting for another 45 minutes. Baste the bird occasionally with the fat accumulating in the pan.
4 Meanwhile, combine the vegetables and apple, and season with salt and pepper.
5 After roasting for a total of 1¼ hours, remove the goose from the pan and drain off all but 3 tablespoons (45 milliliters) of fat. Place the vegetable mixture in the roasting pan and toss to coat with the fat.
6 Place the goose on top of the vegetable mixture and pour the apple cider over all. Return to the oven and continue roasting until done, approximately 1½ hours.
7 Remove the bird from the roasting pan and allow it to rest for 20 to 30 minutes before carving. Serve with the cooked vegetable and apple mixture.

Approximate values per serving: **Calories** 1230, **Total fat** 62 g, **Saturated fat** 18 g, **Cholesterol** 205 mg, **Sodium** 670 mg, **Total carbohydrates** 101 g, **Protein** 66 g, **Vitamin A** 35%, **Vitamin C** 60%, **Iron** 60%

RECIPE 18.40   GRILLED SQUAB WITH BASIL BUTTER

1 Marinating the squab in white wine marinade.

2 Drying the squab.

Yield: 4 Servings

Squab, whole	4	4
Fresh basil leaves	16	16
White Wine Marinade (page 419)	1 pt.	450 ml
Basil butter	6 oz.	180 g

1 Remove the backbone and breast bone from each squab. The birds will lie flat and remain in one piece.
2 Make a slit below each leg and tuck the leg bone into the slit.
3 Carefully slide two basil leaves under the skin over each breast to cover the meat.
4 Marinate the squab in the White Wine Marinade for 1 to 2 hours.
5 Heat and prepare the grill.
6 Remove the squab from the marinade and pat dry.
7 Melt approximately 4 ounces (120 grams) of the basil butter, leaving enough for eight thin slices to be served with the finished dish.
8 Brush the squab with basil butter and place it skin side down on the grill. Grill the squab, turning once and basting periodically with the melted basil butter. Finish in the oven if necessary.
9 Serve the squab with a slice of basil butter melting over each breast.

Approximate values per serving: **Calories** 690, **Total fat** 50 g, **Saturated fat** 26 g, **Cholesterol** 260 mg, **Sodium** 1070 mg, **Total carbohydrates** 0 g, **Protein** 60 g, **Vitamin A** 40%

3 Brushing the squab with the melted basil butter.

4 Grilling the squab.

5 Serving the squab with a slice of basil butter.

SQUAB SALAD WITH MELON

RECIPE 18.41

CHEF ODETTE FADA, NEW YORK, NY

Yield: 6 Servings   **Method:** Sautéing

Squab	3	3
Salt and pepper	TT	TT
Extra virgin olive oil	as needed	as needed
Dry black currants	2 Tbsp.	30 ml
Tahitian squash, thin slices	18	18
Mâche lettuce, small bunches	6	6

1 Bone the squab breasts and remove the thighs and legs. Season with salt and pepper and sauté the breasts and thighs in olive oil until done, approximately 10 to 15 minutes.

2 Place the currants in a bowl and cover with hot water.

3 Cook the squash slices in boiling water for 40 seconds. Cut the slices in half and arrange them on each of six plates as fans opening toward the plate's border.

4 On the other side of each plate, arrange some mâche lettuce; season with salt and pepper.

5 Slice the breasts; arrange the meat with the legs on the squash. Keep the plates in a warm place.

6 Drain the currants and sauté in 2 tablespoons (30 milliliters) of olive oil. Sprinkle the currants around the plates and serve.

Approximate values per serving: **Calories** 230, **Total fat** 10 g, **Saturated fat** 2.5 g, **Cholesterol** 85 mg, **Sodium** 460 mg, **Total carbohydrates** 3 g, **Protein** 31 g, **Vitamin A** 20%, **Vitamin C** 30%

TURKEY BURGER

RECIPE 18.42

Yield: 4 Servings   **Method:** Grilling

Fresh ginger, minced	2 tsp.	10 ml
Garlic, chopped	1 tsp.	5 ml
Sesame oil	1 tsp.	5 ml
White mushrooms, chopped	4 oz.	120 g
Green onion, chopped fine	1	1
Ground turkey	20 oz.	600 g
Salt	½ tsp.	3 ml
Black pepper	¼ tsp.	1 ml

Continued

Glaze:		
Soy sauce	4 tsp.	20 ml
Sesame oil	2 tsp.	10 ml
Fresh ginger, minced	½ tsp.	3 ml
Garlic, chopped	1 tsp.	5 ml
Soft bagels, flat bread or other		
bread as desired	4 pieces	4 pieces
Sesame seeds	4 tsp.	20 ml
Lettuce and tomato	as need for garnish	

1 Sauté the ginger and garlic in the sesame oil for one minute. Add the mushrooms and green onion and sauté approximately one minute longer. Do not fully cook the mushrooms; allow them to retain most of their liquid in order to add moisture to the finished burgers. Remove the mushroom mixture from the heat, spread on a sheet pan and refrigerate until cold.

2 Combine the cold mushroom mixture with the ground turkey, salt and pepper and mix well. Form the mixture into four patties.

3 Stir the glaze ingredients together.

4 Oil the grate of a hot grill. Brush the burgers with the glaze and grill to the desired doneness, basting occasionally with the glaze.

5 Serve each burger open-faced on a toasted bagel or warm flatbread. Sprinkle with sesame seeds and serve accompanied by lettuce leaves, tomato slices or other garnishes as desired.

Approximate values per serving: **Calories** 370, **Total fat** 17 g, **Saturated fat** 4 g, **Cholesterol** 110 mg, **Sodium** 960 mg, **Total carbohydrates** 22 g, **Protein** 30 g, **Iron** 20%

RECIPE 18.43 — TURKEY MEATLOAF

Yield: 8 Servings, 7 oz. (210 g) each **Method:** Baking

Onion, small dice	8 oz.	450 g
Celery, small dice	3 oz.	90 g
Olive oil	2 Tbsp.	30 ml
Garlic cloves, minced	3	3
Dried thyme	2 tsp.	10 ml
Dried sage	1 tsp.	5 ml
Salt	1 tsp.	5 ml
Black pepper, freshly ground	½ tsp.	3 ml
Ground turkey	2½ lb.	1.1 kg
Wheat bran	2 oz.	60 g
Ketchup	2 oz.	60 g
Worcestershire sauce	1 Tbsp.	15 ml
Italian parsley, chopped fine	½ c.	120 ml
Egg whites, beaten	2	2

1 Sauté the onions and celery in olive oil until translucent but not brown. Add the garlic, herbs, salt and pepper and sauté for 2 minutes. Remove from the pan and cool.

2 Place the turkey in a bowl and add the bran, ketchup, Worcestershire sauce, parsley and egg whites and mix well. Stir in the cooled onion mixture and adjust the seasonings.

3 Spray a 9-inch × 5-inch × 3-inch (22.5-centimeter × 12.5-centimeter × 7.5-centimeter) loaf pan with nonstick cooking spray and fill the pan with the turkey mixture.

4 Bake the loaf at 350°F (180°C) to an internal temperature of 160°F (71°C), approximately 1 hour 20 minutes.

5 Allow the meatloaf to cool in the pan for 15 minutes. Remove from the pan, slice and serve.

Variations: The turkey meatloaf mixture can be formed into meatballs of the desired size, browned in a sauté pan, finished in the oven and used in place of traditional meatballs in any recipe.

Approximate values per serving: **Calories** 290, **Total fat** 16 g, **Saturated fat** 3.5 g, **Cholesterol** 110 mg, **Sodium** 560 mg, **Total carbohydrates** 11 g, **Protein** 27 g, **Vitamin C** 15%, **Iron** 20%

TURKEY SCALLOPINE WITH CAPERS AND LEMON

RECIPE 18.44

Yield: 4 Servings   **Method:** Sautéing

Turkey breast, cut into ⅛-in. (3-mm) scallopines, 3 oz. (90 g) each	8	8
Salt and white pepper	TT	TT
Flour	as needed for dredging	
Clarified butter	2 fl. oz.	60 ml
Dry white wine	4 fl. oz.	120 ml
Fresh lemon juice	2 fl. oz.	60 ml
Capers	3 Tbsp.	45 ml

1 Gently pound each turkey slice with a meat mallet. Season with salt and white pepper and dredge in flour.

2 Sauté the turkey in the clarified butter until golden brown. Remove and hold in a warm place.

3 Deglaze the pan with the wine, then add the lemon juice and capers. Return the turkey to the pan to coat with the sauce and reheat.

4 Serve two slices with a portion of the sauce.

Approximate values per 6-oz. (180-g) serving: **Calories** 390, **Total fat** 13 g, **Saturated fat** 8 g, **Cholesterol** 180 mg, **Sodium** 910 mg, **Total carbohydrates** 13 g, **Protein** 56 g, **Vitamin A** 10%

TURKEY TONNATO (TURKEY IN TUNA SAUCE)

RECIPE 18.45

Yield: 10 Servings

Turkey breast, skin on, 3–4 lb. (1.4–1.8 kg)	1	1
Garlic cloves, slivered	4	4
Chicken stock	2 qt.	2 lt
White wine, dry	1 pt.	450 ml
Mirepoix	2 lb.	1 kg
Sachet:		
Bay leaves	2	2
Fresh thyme	1 sprig	1 sprig
Italian parsley	6 sprigs	6 sprigs
Black peppercorns, whole	10	10

Continued

Sauce:

Extra virgin olive oil	6 fl. oz.	180 ml
Egg yolk	1	1
Tuna, canned in oil	6 oz.	180 g
Garlic clove	1	1
Anchovy fillets, rinsed, diced	3	3
Fresh lemon juice	2 Tbsp.	30 ml
Heavy cream	2 fl. oz.	60 ml
Salt	TT	TT
White pepper, freshly ground	TT	TT
Capers, rinsed, dried	3 Tbsp.	45 ml
Italian parsley, chopped fine	as needed for garnish	
Black olives	as needed for garnish	
Capers	as needed for garnish	
Black pepper, cracked	as needed for garnish	

1 Make several 1-inch-(5-centimeter-) deep incisions in the turkey breast. Insert a sliver of garlic into each incision.

2 Place the turkey breast in a stockpot. Add the stock, wine, mirepoix and sachet. Add more stock to cover the turkey if necessary. Bring to a boil, reduce the heat and poach the turkey for 1½ hours or until nearly done. Remove the pot from the stove and allow the turkey to cool in liquid. Strain 8 fluid ounces (240 milliliters) of the stock and reserve it for the sauce.

3 To prepare the sauce, purée the olive oil, egg yolk, tuna, garlic, anchovies and lemon juice in a blender. Transfer the purée to a bowl. Stir in the cream and then gradually stir in the reserved turkey stock a little at a time until the sauce is the consistency of heavy cream. You may not need all of the stock. Season with salt and white pepper, then stir in the caper.

4 Remove the turkey from the stock. Remove and discard the skin. Slice the breast into very thin slices. Spread a thin layer of tuna sauce in a shallow hotel pan. Arrange overlapping slices of turkey on the sauce. Pour a small amount remaining sauce over the turkey slices and smooth with a spatula. Cover and refrigerate overnight.

5 To serve, arrange the slices of turkey on a serving platter. Drizzle the sauce over the turkey and garnish with chopped parsley, black olives, capers and cracked black pepper.

Approximate values per serving: **Calories** 420, **Total fat** 25 g, **Saturated fat** 5 g, **Cholesterol** 155 mg, **Sodium** 340 mg, **Total carbohydrates** 1 g, **Protein** 46 g, **Iron** 15%

RECIPE 18.46   **SPICED OSTRICH TENDERLOIN**

Yield: 2 Servings   **Method:** Broiling

Cumin seeds	1 Tbsp.	15 ml
Fennel seeds	1 Tbsp.	15 ml
Black peppercorns	2 tsp.	10 ml
White peppercorns	2 tsp.	10 ml
Garlic cloves, minced	2	2
Ostrich tenderloins, 4 oz. (120 g) each	2	2
Olive oil	1 Tbsp.	15 ml
Salt	TT	TT

1 Grind the cumin, fennel and peppercorns together in a spice grinder. Combine the ground spices with the garlic.

2 Brush the tenderloins with the olive oil, coat with the spice mixture and season lightly with salt.

3 Cook the ostrich under a broiler to the desired degree of doneness.

4 Remove from the broiler and slice into thin pieces for service.

Approximate values per 4-oz. (120-g) serving: **Calories** 169, **Total fat** 5 g, **Saturated fat** 1 g, **Cholesterol** 91 mg, **Sodium** 106 mg, **Total carbohydrates** 5 g, **Protein** 27 g, **Iron** 46%

GRILLED OSTRICH TENDERLOIN WITH TAGARISHI YAMS AND WESTERN SLOPE CHERRY GLAZE

RECIPE 18.47

SENCHA, COLORADO SPRINGS, CO
Chef Brent Beavers

Yield: 1 Serving **Method:** Grilling

Ostrich tenderloin	6 oz.	180 g
Salt and pepper	TT	TT
Vegetable oil	as needed	as needed
Whole butter	1 Tbsp.	15 ml
Fresh spinach, cleaned	1 oz.	30 g
Tagarishi Yams (recipe follows)	6 oz.	180 g
Western Slope Cherry Glaze (recipe follows)	2 fl. oz.	60 ml

1 Season the ostrich with salt and pepper. Brush with oil and grill until medium rare, approximately 3 to 6 minutes.

2 Heat the butter in a sauté pan until noisette. Add the spinach and toss until it wilts. Season with salt and pepper and hold in a warm place.

3 Mound the Yams on a serving plate. Slice the ostrich against the grain and on the bias in ¼-inch- (6-millimeter-) thick slices. Fan the slices on the serving plate. Arrange the cooked spinach over the potatoes. Ladle the Cherry Glaze on and in front of the ostrich slices and serve.

Approximate values per serving: **Calories** 650, **Total fat** 27 g, **Saturated fat** 15 g, **Cholesterol** 200 mg, **Sodium** 570 mg, **Total carbohydrates** 60 g, **Protein** 41 g, **Vitamin A** 45%, **Vitamin C** 45%, **Calcium** 10%, **Iron** 60%

TAGARISHI YAMS

Yield: 5 lb. (2.2 kg)

Cuban yams, peeled and quartered	5 lb.	2.2 kg
Whole butter	8 oz.	240 g
Heavy cream	1 pt.	450 ml
Tagarishi	1 Tbsp.	15 ml
Salt	2 tsp.	10 ml
Black pepper, ground	TT	TT

▶ **tagarishi** a Japanese spice available at Asian markets

1 Simmer the yams in salted water until tender. Drain well. Place the yams, butter, cream and tagarishi in the bowl of a mixer fitted with a paddle. Mix on low until the mixture reaches the desired consistency. Do not overmix. Adjust the seasonings with salt and pepper.

Approximate values per 4-oz. (120-g) serving: **Calories** 240, **Total fat** 18 g, **Saturated fat** 11 g, **Cholesterol** 55 mg, **Sodium** 260 mg, **Total carbohydrates** 19 g, **Protein** 2 g, **Vitamin A** 15%

WESTERN SLOPE CHERRY GLAZE

Yield: 2 qt. (2 lt)

Fresh cherries, pitted	2 lb.	1 kg
Port wine	1 pt.	450 ml
Oranges	2	2
Simple syrup	2 pt.	900 ml
Chicken stock	2 pt.	900 ml

1 Combine the cherries and port in a saucepot. Bring to a boil and reduce au sec.

2 Zest and squeeze the juice from the oranges.

3 Add the zest, orange juice, simple syrup and stock to the cherries and reduce to the consistency of a thin glaze.

Approximate values per 1-fl.-oz. (30-ml) serving: **Calories** 80, **Total fat** 0 g, **Saturated fat** 0 g, **Cholesterol** 0 mg, **Sodium** 60 mg, **Total carbohydrates** 18 mg, **Protein** 0 g, **Claims**–fat free

RECIPE 18.48

SAUTÉED CHICKEN LIVERS

Yield: 4 Appetizer Servings, 4 oz. (120 g) each   **Method:** Sautéing

Chicken livers, trimmed	1 lb.	450 g
Salt and pepper	TT	TT
Flour	as needed for dredging	
Vegetable oil	1 fl. oz.	30 ml
Shallots, minced	2 Tbsp.	60 ml
Raspberry vinegar	4 fl. oz.	120 ml
Raspberry jam	2 Tbsp.	60 ml
French bread croutons	4	4
Watercress	as needed for garnish	

1 Rinse the livers and pat dry. Season with salt and pepper and dredge in flour.

2 Sauté the livers in the oil until just barely pink, approximately 3 to 4 minutes. Remove the livers from the pan and hold in a warm place.

3 Using the fat remaining in the pan, sauté the shallots until tender. Deglaze with the vinegar.

4 Add the jam. Simmer until thickened. Return the livers to the pan and toss to coat with the sauce.

5 Serve on warm plates with French bread croutons; garnish with watercress.

Approximate values per 4-oz. (120-g) serving: **Calories** 330, **Total fat** 14 g, **Saturated fat** 3 g, **Cholesterol** 715 mg, **Sodium** 660 mg, **Total carbohydrates** 22 g, **Protein** 30 g, **Vitamin A** 560%, **Iron** 60%

TORCHON OF FOIE GRAS WITH APPLE
AND DUCK GELÉES

RECIPE 18.49

Torchon (tour-shahn) is French for a cloth or towel, such as a dishcloth. The term is sometimes used to refer to dishes in which the item has been shaped into a cylinder by being wrapped in a cloth or towel.

Yield: 10 Servings		**Method:** Poaching
Foie gras, A grade	1	1
Cognac	1 Tbsp.	15 ml
Salt	1½ tsp.	8 ml
Allspice	½ tsp.	3 ml
Fennel, ground	½ tsp.	3 ml
Black pepper, ground	TT	TT
Juniper berries, chopped	2	2
Rich duck stock, clear	as needed	as needed
Apple Gelée (recipe follows)	as needed	as needed

1 Immerse the foie gras in ice water for 2 to 3 hours. Then remove it from the ice water and hold at room temperature for approximately 30 minutes to allow it to soften slightly. Bisect the lobes of the foie gras and carefully remove all evident veins.

2 Place the foie gras pieces in a hotel pan without letting them overlap. Season them with the cognac, salt, allspice, fennel, pepper and juniper berries.

3 Lay a 12-inch × 12-inch (30-centimeter × 30-centimeter) piece of plastic wrap on a work surface. Divide the foie gras in half and place half of it on the plastic wrap and roll into a tight cylinder. Repeat with the other half. Refrigerate both rolls overnight.

4 Remove the foie gras from the refrigerator and hold at room temperature for 30 minutes. Lay a 12-inch × 12-inch (30-centimeter × 30-centimeter) piece of cheesecloth on a work surface. Remove one roll of foie gras from the plastic and transfer it to the cheesecloth. Roll the foie gras very tightly in the cheesecloth, twist the ends of the cloth very tightly and tie with kitchen twine. Then tie the roll at two even intervals to prevent the foie gras from becoming misshapen during cooking. Repeat with the second foie gras roll.

5 Prepare an ice bath large enough to hold the rolls. Heat 4 quarts (4 liters) of water in a wide shallow pot to 185°F (85°C). Working with one roll at a time, poach the rolls for 1 minute and transfer them directly to the ice bath. Chill the foie gras in the ice bath for 15 minutes.

6 Remove the foie gras rolls from the ice water, wrap them in absorbent kitchen towels and hang in the refrigerator for 12 to 24 hours.

7 To make the duck gelée, reduce the duck stock to 1 to 2 cups (250 to 500 milliliters) of liquid. (The greater the gelatin content, the less reduction is necessary.) Pour into a shallow pan and refrigerate. The finished duck gelée should be gelled and firm enough to hold its shape when plated.

8 To serve, remove the towel and the cheesecloth from the foie gras. Using a hot knife, smooth the sides of the foie gras torchon and cut slices of the desired thickness. Serve with toasted bread, the Apple Gelée and the duck gelée.

Approximate values per serving: **Calories** 110, **Total fat** 3.5 g, **Saturated fat** 1.5 g, **Cholesterol** 410 mg, **Sodium** 460 mg, **Total carbohydrates** 5 g, **Protein** 13 g, **Vitamin A** 490%, **Iron** 130%

APPLE GELÉE

Yield: 12 fl. oz. (350 ml)

Star anise	⅛ tsp.	0.5 ml
Apple juice, pure	3 pt.	1.5 lt
Salt	TT	TT
Green apple	½	½
Lemon juice	1 tsp.	5 ml
Gelatin sheets	4	4

1 Add the star anise to the apple juice. Bring the juice to a boil and reduce by half. Season with salt.

2 Cut the apple brunoise and toss with the lemon juice.

3 Soak the gelatin sheets in cold water for approximately 5 minutes. Squeeze out the water and dissolve them in the hot apple juice.

4 Pour the mixture into a shallow pan. Cool over an ice bath. When the mixture begins to set, stir in the brunoise apple so that the apple pieces become suspended in the gelée and are evenly dispersed. Refrigerate until firm.

Approximate values per 1-fl. oz. (30-ml serving): **Calories** 10, **Total fat** 0 g, **Saturated fat** 0 g, **Cholesterol** 0 mg, **Sodium** 10 mg, **Total carbohydrates** 15 g, **Protein** 2 g, **Claims**—fat free, low sodium

SAUTÉED FOIE GRAS ON WILD MUSHROOM DUXELLES WITH TOASTED BRIOCHE

RECIPE 18.50

CHEF LELAND ATKINSON, WASHINGTON, DC

Yield: 4 Servings	**Method:** Sautéing	
Fresh foie gras, A grade	1 lb.	450 g
Wild mushrooms	1 lb.	450 g
Shallots, chopped	2 Tbsp.	30 ml
Garlic, chopped	1 tsp.	5 ml
Whole butter	1 Tbsp.	15 ml
Tomato paste	1 tsp.	5 ml
Brandy	1 Tbsp.	15 ml
Fresh thyme	1 tsp.	5 ml
Salt and pepper	TT	TT
Madeira sauce (page 217)	8 fl. oz.	250 ml
Brioche (page 987)	8 slices	8 slices

1 Allow the foie gras to come to near room temperature. With a sharp knife, scrape the thin membrane from the outside of the liver. Gently pull the pieces apart. Gently pull out any visible veins. Slice the liver on a slight bias into slices approximately 1 inch (2.5 centimeters) thick. Cover and chill until service.

2 To make the duxelles, clean and chop the wild mushrooms.

3 Sauté the shallots and garlic in the butter.

4 Add the mushrooms and cook until they first release their moisture and then begin to dry, approximately 5 minutes.

5 Add the tomato paste and brandy and cook until dry, stirring often.

6 Add the thyme and adjust the seasonings with salt and pepper. Remove the duxelles from the heat.

7 Quickly sauté the foie gras in a hot dry pan until it is browned on both sides but still bright pink in the middle, approximately 2 minutes.

8 Portion the duxelles onto four warm serving plates. Ladle the Madeira sauce around the duxelles. Blot the foie gras on a dry towel and arrange it over the top of the duxelles. Serve with toasted brioche.

Approximate values per serving: **Calories** 1160, **Total fat** 75 g, **Saturated fat** 23 g, **Cholesterol** 330 mg, **Sodium** 1450 mg, **Total carbohydrates** 92 g, **Protein** 30 g, **Vitamin A** 150%, **Iron** 60%

FRIED FROG LEGS IN FINES HERBES BUTTER

RECIPE 18.51

HERBSAINT BAR AND RESTAURANT, New Orleans, LA
Chef Donald Link

Yield: 24 Legs   **Method:** Deep-Frying

Fines herbes butter:		
Unsalted butter, soft	8 oz.	240 g
Parsley, chopped	1 Tbsp.	15 ml
Fresh tarragon, chopped	1 tsp.	5 ml
Fresh chervil, chopped	1 tsp.	5 ml
Chives, sliced	1 tsp.	5 ml
Garlic, minced	½ tsp.	3 ml
Cayenne pepper	½ tsp.	3 ml
Salt	1 tsp.	5 ml
Frog leg pairs, cut in half	12	12
Salt and pepper	TT	TT
Flour	1 lb.	900 ml
Buttermilk	8 fl. oz.	240 ml

1 Combine all the ingredients for the fines herbes butter and mix well.

2 Pat the frog legs dry and season them with salt and pepper. Dredge the frog legs in flour, dip them in buttermilk, drain and dredge in flour again.

3 Deep-fry the frog legs until golden brown and done, approximately 5 to 7 minutes. Drain, place in a stainless steel bowl and coat generously with the fines herbes butter.

4 Arrange the legs attractively on a plate, garnish as desired and serve hot.

Approximate values per leg: **Calories** 170, **Total fat** 10 g, **Saturated fat** 5 g, **Cholesterol** 35 mg, **Sodium** 125 mg, **Total carbohydrates** 15 g, **Protein** 6 g

FROGS

Frogs are amphibians that can be prepared like poultry or fish. Their texture and flavor are similar to those of chicken. Most of the frogs used in food service operations are farm-raised, so their meat is quite tender. Typically, only the legs are eaten. They are sold frozen, in pairs, attached by a small portion of backbone.

ONE CAN NEVER KNOW TOO MUCH; THE MORE ONE
LEARNS, THE MORE ONE SEES THE NEED TO LEARN
MORE AND THAT STUDY AS WELL AS BROADENING
THE MIND OF THE CRAFTSMAN PROVIDES AN EASY
WAY OF PERFECTING YOURSELF IN THE PRACTICE OF
YOUR ART.

—*Auguste Escoffier, French chef (1846–1935)*

19

GAME

THE SANCTUARY AT CAMELBACK, Paradise Valley, AZ
Charles Wiley, Executive Chef of Elements

AFTER STUDYING THIS
CHAPTER, YOU WILL BE
ABLE TO:

▶ identify a variety of game

▶ understand game inspection
practices

▶ purchase game appropriate for
your needs

▶ store game properly

▶ prepare game for cooking

▶ apply various cooking methods
to game

Game (Fr. *gibier*) are animals hunted for sport or food. Traditionally, game supplies depended upon the season and the hunter's success. But game's increasing popularity in food service operations has led to farm-raising and animal husbandry techniques. As a result, pheasant, quail, deer, rabbit and other animals, although still considered game, are now farm- or ranch-raised and commercially available throughout the year.

The life of game creatures is reflected in their flesh's appearance, aroma, flavor and texture. Generally, game flesh has a dark color and a strong but not unpleasant aroma. It has a robust flavor and less fat than other meats or poultry and is more compact, becoming quite tough in older animals.

Selecting the best cooking methods for game depends on the animal's age and the particular cut of flesh. Younger animals will, of course, be more tender than older ones. Flesh from the loin or less-used muscles will also be tender and therefore can be prepared with dry-heat cooking methods. Flesh from much-used muscles, such as the leg and shoulder, will be tougher and should be prepared with combination cooking methods. Less-tender cuts can also be used in sausages, pâtés and forcemeats, as discussed in Chapter 27, Charcuterie.

▶ IDENTIFYING GAME

FURRED OR GROUND GAME

Furred game includes large animals such as deer, moose, bear, wild boar and elk as well as smaller animals such as rabbit, squirrel, raccoon and opossum. Although each of these animals (and many others) is hunted for sport and food, only a few species are widely available to food service operations.

Although venison, boar and elk may seem unusual to many Americans, even rarer meats are available to the daring diner. Zebra, bear, wildebeest and other "big game" animals are sometimes available through exotic game purveyors. Most often these meats are grilled, roasted or stewed.

Reptiles, particularly rattlesnake and alligator, are now also being raised on farms to meet increased demand. Reptiles are usually braised, or sliced and deep-fried. They have a mild flavor with a texture similar to lobster.

Large game animals are rarely sold whole or in primal portions. Instead, the meat is available precut into subprimals or portions. So, except for those that are used for rabbits, this chapter does not provide butchering techniques.

ANTELOPE

The blackbuck antelope, about half the size of a large deer, is ranch-raised in the United States. Although it has almost no body fat, the meat retains a high amount of moisture. The meat is fine-grained, with a flavor that is only slightly stronger than deer meat (venison). It should be butchered and cooked in a manner similar to venison.

BISON (AMERICAN BUFFALO)

Once found in huge herds roaming the plains states, bison or buffalo were hunted into near-extinction during the 19th century. Buffalo now live on reservations or ranches, where they are raised like beef cattle. Their meat is juicy and flavorful and may be prepared in the same manner as lean beef.

Buffalo Steak

DEER

The deer family includes elk, moose, reindeer, red-tailed deer, white-tailed deer (Fr. *chevreuil*) and mule deer. Meat from any of these animals is known as **venison** (Fr. *venaisan*). Farm-raised venison, particularly from the Scottish red deer bred in New Zealand and the United States, is commercially available all year. Axis deer, a species originally from India and Nepal, provides some of the finest-quality venison. Like cattle, axis deer graze on grass, so their meat is especially mild and tender. Venison is typically dark red with a mild aroma. It is leaner than other meats, having almost no intramuscular fat or marbling.

▶ **venison** flesh from any member of the deer family, including antelope, elk, moose, reindeer, red-tailed deer, white-tailed deer, mule deer and axis deer

The most popular commercial venison cuts are the loin, leg and rack. The loin is tender enough to roast, sauté or grill to medium rare. It can be left attached along the backbone to form a cut known as the saddle. The leg is often marinated in red wine and prepared with combination cooking methods. Other cuts can also be stewed or braised or used in sausages and pâtés. Butchering procedures for venison are similar to those for lamb discussed in Chapter 16.

RABBIT

Rabbits (Fr. *lapin*) are small burrowing animals that have long been raised for food. Rabbit has mild, lean and relatively tender flesh. Its flavor and texture are similar to chicken. Ranch-raised rabbit is available all year, either whole or cut, fresh or frozen. The average weight of a whole dressed rabbit is 2 pounds 8 ounces to 3 pounds (1.2 to 1.4 kilograms). Young rabbit can be roasted, pan-fried, stewed or braised and is popular in rustic "country-style" dishes, especially casseroles and pâtés.

Venison Saddle

MEAT OF THE FUTURE: BEEFALO

Beefalo is produced by cross-breeding a bison with a domestic beef animal. To be a registered full-blooded beefalo, the animal has to be three-eighths bison and five-eighths domestic beef. The five-eighths domestic beef portion is not restricted to any breed; it is often a combination of two or more breeds such as Hereford, Angus or Charolais. In 1985, the USDA approved a special label for beefalo; it is labeled either "Beef from Beefalo" or "Beefalo Beef."

Beefalo looks and tastes much like modern beef. The animal itself is hard to distinguish from any other beef animal. Beefalo meat is tender because the animals gain weight faster and go to market at younger ages. The meat is slightly sweeter in taste than beef.

Beefalo is lower in cholesterol than beef, fish or chicken and lower in calories and fat than beef. It offers a great alternative to beef for the diet- and health-conscious guest. The

per-pound cost of beefalo may be slightly higher than beef cuts, but its low amount of interior and exterior fat gives it a higher yield with a price per usable pound comparable to beef.

Because of beefalo's finer fiber and low fat content, it cooks in one-third to one-half the time of beef and should be cooked to either rare or medium rare.

JAMES J. MUTH, MBA, CFBE,
Chef Instructor, Grand Rapids Community College

▶ PROCEDURE FOR BUTCHERING A RABBIT

1 Place the rabbit on its back. Remove the hind legs by cutting close to the backbone and through the joint on each side. Each thigh and leg can be separated by cutting through the joint.

2 Remove the forelegs by cutting beneath the shoulder blades.

3 Cut through the breast bone and spread open the rib cage. Using a boning knife, separate the flesh from the rib bones and remove the bones.

4 Cut through the backbone to divide the loin into the desired number of pieces.

5 The cut-up rabbit: hind legs, thighs, loin in three pieces, forelegs.

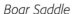

Boar Saddle

WILD BOAR

A close relative of the domesticated hog, wild boar (Fr. *sanglier*) is leaner, with a stronger flavor. Though plentiful in Europe and parts of America, wild boar is available only during autumn. A limited supply of farm- or ranch-raised boar is available all year, however.

Baby boar (under six months old) is considered a delicacy, but mature animals (one to two years old) have the best flavor. The meat is most often roasted, and may be used in sausages or terrines. Boar can often be substituted in recipes for venison or pork.

FEATHERED OR WINGED GAME

Feathered game includes upland birds such as wild turkeys, pheasants, quails, doves and woodcocks; songbirds such as larks; and waterfowl such as wild geese and ducks. Wild birds cannot be sold in the United States. An ever-increasing number of these birds are being farm-raised to meet consumer demand, however.

Table 19.1   USING FURRED GAME

ANIMAL	COMMONLY PURCHASED CUTS	COOKING METHODS	SUGGESTED USE
Antelope	Purchased and prepared in the same manner as deer		
Bison	Purchased and prepared in the same manner as lean beef		
Deer	Loin	Dry heat (roast; sauté; grill)	Sautéed medallions; whole roast loin; grilled steaks
	Leg	Combination (braise; stew)	Marinate and braise; pot roast with cranberries; chili; sausage; forcemeat
	Rack	Dry heat (roast; grill)	Grilled chops
Rabbit	Full carcass	Dry heat (sauté; pan-fry; roast; grill) Combination (braise; stew)	Pan-fried rabbit with cream gravy Braised rabbit with mushrooms
Wild Boar	Loin Chops	Dry heat (roast) Combination (braise)	Roast loin with mustard crust Marinate and braise; stew with red wine and sour cream; sausage; forcemeat

Game birds are available whole or precut into pieces, fresh or frozen. Butchering techniques will not be shown in this chapter as they are the same as those for domesticated poultry discussed in Chapter 18.

Because game birds tend to have less fat than other poultry, they are often barded with fat and cooked to medium rare. If cooked well done, they become dry and stringy.

PARTRIDGE

The Hungarian and chukar partridges (Fr. *perdrix*) of Europe were introduced into the United States and Canada during the 19th century. Now found principally in the prairie and western mountain states, partridges are widely raised on game preserves and farms, producing a good commercial supply.

The flavor of partridge is less delicate than that of pheasant, and the meat tends to be tougher. Partridge may be roasted or cut into pieces and sautéed or braised. Each bird weighs about 1 pound (450 grams) dressed.

Chukar Partridge

PHEASANT

The most popular of game birds, the pheasant (Fr. *faisan*) was introduced into Europe from Asia during the Middle Ages. Its mild flavor is excellent for roasting, stewing or braising. The hen is smaller and more tender than the cock. Stock made from the carcass is often used for consommé or sauce.

Farm-raised birds are available fresh or frozen. A dressed bird weighs about 1 pound 8 ounces to 2 pounds 4 ounces (680 grams to 1 kilogram) and serves two people.

Pheasant

QUAIL

The quail (Fr. *caille*) is a migratory game bird related to the pheasant. The more popular European and Californian species are farm-raised and available all year.

Quail are very small, with only about 1 to 2 ounces (30 to 60 grams) of breast meat each. Quail may be grilled (especially on skewers), roasted, broiled or sautéed and are often boned and served whole with a stuffing of forcemeat or rice. Because they are so lean, roasted quail benefit from barding.

Quail

WILD GAME—DELICIOUS, NUTRITIOUS AND AVAILABLE

Wild game is now widely available for use in restaurants and at home. The best of wild game provides a safe, delicious and nutritious dining experience.

In almost all states, our native game animals are protected from harvesting for commercial purposes. It is a violation of state wildlife laws to kill and sell the meat from native species such as the whitetail deer, mule deer, pronghorn antelope, etc. These laws were written when only native game was present in America. Since then, a growing number of non-native species of deer and antelope have been introduced to ranches in America, and this has made it possible to harvest deer and antelope legally for meat production.

Oddly enough, however, meats such as antelope, venison, rabbit, and most other game meats are not subject to inspection under federal and most state meat inspection regulations. This is not because the authorities do not believe the meat should be inspected. When the meat inspection laws were written, these meats were not legally available and therefore were not included in the Federal Meat Act. County and city health codes, however, do re-

quire that any meat served to the public must be from "an approved source" which is interpreted as "inspected." Therefore, any game meat served in a restaurant should be certified as inspected by either state or federal meat inspection authorities.

Game meat is available from farmed (domesticated) deer and from free-ranging (ranched) deer and antelope. Most farmed deer are taken to a fixed conventional slaughterhouse where they are slaughtered and processed in the same way as cattle, sheep and goats. Ranched deer can be properly harvested only by an elaborate procedure that involves taking a mobile slaughter facility and meat inspector to the field, where the animals are killed by shooting them with a high-powered rifle under the supervision of the meat inspector. The carcass is then processed inside the mobile facility to avoid any contamination of the meat. This field harvesting eliminates any stress that might occur in transport of farmed deer to the slaughterhouse.

Farmed deer tend to be relatively more uniform in size and flavor. Free-ranging deer and antelope produce meat of more complex flavor

due to the variety of their diet. The difference is somewhat like the difference in cultivated mushrooms and wild mushrooms, or pen-raised chickens compared with free-range chickens. Meat from free-range animals is more expensive due to higher labor and inspection costs.

Meat from both deer and antelope can be legally labeled "venison." All venison is relatively lean when compared with conventional red meats and requires special attention when cooking to avoid drying out the meat and toughening it. Tender cuts should be cooked as little as possible (rare to medium rare) to retain the maximum amount of moisture. Quick sautéing, grilling or roasting to retain a medium rare center is most satisfactory for tender cuts such as the loin, tenderloin, and leg.

Braising is the most effective method for cooking the less tender cuts such as the shoulder, ribs and shanks. Beef broth and red wine are good liquids for braising. The toughest cut of meat will be very satisfactorily tenderized if braised for a sufficient period of time (which may be as long as two or three hours). When properly cooked, these cuts can surpass the more tender cuts in flavor.

MIKE HUGHES,
Broken Arrow Ranch, Ingram, Texas

▶ NUTRITION

Even ranch-raised game animals live in the wild and are generally more active and less well fed than domesticated animals. This lifestyle produces animals whose meat has less fat than that of domesticated animals. Most game is also lower in cholesterol and has approximately one-third fewer calories than beef. Game is also generally high in protein and minerals.

▶ INSPECTION OF GAME

The USDA and most states restrict the sale of wild game. Truly wild game can be served only by those who hunt and share their kill.

DOMESTIC GAME

Unlike meat and poultry from domesticated animals, game is not graded for quality. Farm- or ranch-raised game is subject only to voluntary inspections for wholesomeness. Generally, however, game is processed under the same federal inspection requirements as domesticated meats and poultry. State regulations vary and are constantly being expanded and improved in response to consumer demands.

HOW TO HANG GAME

The following information may be useful if you find yourself with a need to hang freshly killed game. Most game should be eviscerated (drawn or gutted) as soon as possible, then suspended by either the hind legs or the head in a dry, well-ventilated place. Because the fur or feathers help prevent bacterial contamination, they should be left intact during hanging; game should be skinned or plucked just before butchering. The length of time necessary for hanging depends on the species and age of the animal. Two days may be sufficient for a rabbit, while up to three weeks may be necessary for a deer or boar. Hanging is generally complete when the first whiff of odor is detected (although traditionalists prefer pheasant to be hung until extremely ripe).

IMPORTED GAME

Only USDA-approved countries are permitted to export game to the United States. Upon arrival in this country, game shipments are subject to USDA spot inspections.

▶ PURCHASING AND STORING GAME

PURCHASING GAME

Furred game meats are available fresh or frozen. Game birds are available cleaned and boned, fresh or frozen. Use the same criteria to determine the freshness of game as you would any other meat or poultry: The flesh should be firm, without slime or an off-odor.

Fresh game is sometimes **hung** before cooking to allow the meat to mature or age. During hanging, carbohydrates (glycogen) stored in muscle tissues are converted to lactic acid. This process tenderizes the flesh and strengthens its flavor. But hanging is not necessary, especially if you object to "gamy" flavors. Commercially sold game is generally fully aged and ready to use when delivered. It does not need, nor will it benefit from, hanging.

STORING GAME

As with any fresh or frozen meat, game should be well wrapped and stored under refrigeration at temperatures below 40°F (4°C). Because the flesh is generally dry and lean, frozen game should be used within four months. Thaw frozen game slowly under refrigeration to prevent moisture loss.

▶ MARINATING FURRED GAME

Tradition calls for marinating game, particularly furred game, in strong mixtures of red wine, herbs and spices. Commercially raised game does not necessarily have to be marinated. Modern animal husbandry techniques used at game ranches assure the chef of receiving meat from young, tender animals. Farm-raised game animals also have a naturally milder flavor than their truly wild cousins.

For those preferring the flavors imparted by traditional marinades, the following red wine marinade is included. After the meat is removed, the marinade may be added to the cooking liquid or reduced and used in a sauce. Do not serve uncooked marinade.

RECIPE 19.1

RED-WINE MARINADE FOR GAME

Yield: 1½ qt. (1.5 lt)

Carrot, chopped fine	2 oz.	60 g
Onion, chopped fine	2 oz.	60 g
Garlic, minced	1 Tbsp.	15 ml
Dried thyme	1 tsp.	5 ml
Bay leaves	2	2
Juniper berries, whole	2 tsp.	10 ml
Peppercorns, whole	1 Tbsp.	15 ml
Sage, ground	½ tsp.	2 ml
Red wine	1 qt.	1 lt
Red wine vinegar	4 fl. oz.	120 ml

1 Combine all ingredients.

2 Place the meat in the marinade and marinate for the desired time. Tender, farm-raised game may need only 30 minutes; older, wild animals may need 1 to 2 days.

Approximate values per 1-fl.-oz. (30-ml) serving: **Calories** 5, **Total fat** 0 g, **Saturated fat** 0 g, **Cholesterol** 0 mg, **Sodium** 0 mg, **Total carbohydrates** 1 g, **Protein** 0 g, **Vitamin A** 6%, **Claims—** fat free; no saturated fat; no cholesterol; no sodium; low calorie

CONCLUSION

Game is becoming increasingly popular because of consumer desires for leaner, healthier meats. Only farm-raised game can be used in food service operations. Luckily, many popular game items are now farm-raised, government-inspected and readily available. Generally, game flesh has a dark color, a strong but not unpleasant aroma and a robust flavor. You should butcher, prepare and cook game according to the comparable guidelines for other meats and poultry.

QUESTIONS FOR DISCUSSION

1 Explain the differences between truly wild game and ranch-raised game.

2 What is hanging? Is it necessary for modern food service operations to hang game?

3 Which cuts of furred game are best suited to dry-heat cooking methods? Which are best for combination cooking methods?

4 Can game birds be purchased whole? How are they fabricated?

5 What degree of doneness is best suited for game birds? Explain your answer.

6 Texas is home to several large game ranches. Explore their Internet sites to learn more about the operation of game ranches and the varieties of venison available.

ACHIOTE-BASTED RACK OF VENISON WITH SMOKED CORN PUDDING

RECIPE 19.2

Note: This dish appears in the chapter opening photograph.

THE BOULDER'S RESORT, CAREFREE, AZ
Former Corporate Executive Chef Charles Wiley

CHEF CHARLES WILEY

During high school he was a weekend dishwasher; today Chef Charles "Chuck" Wiley is the executive chef of Elements at The Sanctuary on Camelback, Paradise Valley, Arizona. Along the way he attended Anchorage Community College for a course in baking and pastries and was executive chef for The Boulder's Resort in Carefree, Arizona. In 1992, he received a scholarship to the School for American Chefs, directed by Madeline Kamman at Beringer Vineyards in California, and in 2000 he was inducted into the Arizona Culinary Hall of Fame.

His advice for those beginning a career in the culinary arts is to "try to be the very best you can be each day; don't play games and treat people the way you would like to be treated."

Yield: 4 Servings   **Method:** Grilling

Venison chops, 6 oz. (180 g) each	4	4
Achiote Paste (recipe follows)	½ c.	120 ml
Kosher salt	TT	TT
Black pepper	TT	TT
Olive oil	1 tsp.	5 ml
Shiitake mushroom caps	8	8
Haricot vert, blanched and shocked	24	24
Roma tomatoes, quartered	2	2
Smoked Corn Pudding (recipe follows)	2 c.	500 ml
Barley Risotto (recipe follows)	4 servings	4 servings
Venison Red-Wine Jus (recipe follows)	4 fl. oz.	120 ml

1. Prepare a mesquite or gas grill. Brush the chops with Achiote Paste and season with salt and pepper. Grill to medium rare, brushing with additional Achiote Paste. Remove the chops from the grill, cover loosely and keep warm.

2. Heat the oil in a small sauté pan and add the mushrooms. Cook for 2 to 3 minutes over medium heat. Add the haricot vert and tomatoes; season with salt and pepper. Cook for an additional 2 to 3 minutes; remove from the heat.

3. Spoon ½ cup (120 milliliters) of the Smoked Corn Pudding in the center of a warm dinner plate. Spoon one-quarter of the haricot vert mixture on top of the pudding. Cut each chop in thirds and arrange the pieces around the pudding. Top with Barley Risotto and pour 1 fluid ounce (30 milliliters) of Venison Red-Wine Jus around the venison. Serve immediately.

Approximate values per serving: **Calories** 930, **Total fat** 37 g, **Saturated fat** 17 g, **Cholesterol** 370 mg, **Sodium** 1660 mg, **Total carbohydrates** 87 g, **Protein** 63 g, **Vitamin A** 100%, **Vitamin C** 60%, **Iron** 60%

ACHIOTE PASTE

Yield: ½ c. (120 ml)

Ancho chiles	3	3
Garlic clove	1	1
Allspice	¼ tsp.	1 ml
Cumin seeds, toasted and ground	½ tsp.	3 ml
Annatto seeds	1 tsp.	5 ml
Olive oil	1 tsp.	5 ml
White wine vinegar	2 Tbsp.	30 ml
Orange juice	2 fl. oz.	60 ml
Kosher salt	½ tsp.	3 ml

1 Toast the ancho chiles in a skillet over medium heat for 2 minutes, or until they release some oil and have a toasted aroma. Let cool slightly, then core, seed and tear into strips.

2 Place the ancho strips in a blender with the remaining ingredients and purée until smooth.

Approximate values per 3-Tbsp. (45-ml) serving: **Calories** 25, **Total fat** 1.5 g, **Saturated fat** 0 g, **Cholesterol** 0 mg, **Sodium** 200 mg, **Total carbohydrates** 3 g, **Protein** 0 g

SMOKED CORN PUDDING

Yield: 2 c. (500 ml)

Whole butter	3 Tbsp.	45 ml
Milk	1 pt.	500 ml
Yellow cornmeal	½ c.	120 ml
Kosher salt	TT	TT
Black pepper	TT	TT
Corn, lightly smoked, kernels removed	2 ears	2 ears
Onion, chopped	3 Tbsp.	45 ml
Eggs, separated	3	3

1 Coat an 8-inch- (20-centimeter-) square pan with 1 tablespoon (15 milliliters) of butter.

2 In a medium saucepan, bring the milk to a boil. Lower the heat and gradually whisk in the cornmeal. Cook over low heat for 10 minutes, stirring with a wooden spoon.

3 Add the salt, pepper, corn, onions and remaining butter; cook for an additional 3 minutes. Remove from the heat and add the egg yolks one at a time, beating well with a wooden spoon after each addition.

4 Add a pinch of salt to the egg whites and beat with a fine whisk until stiff. Fold the whipped egg whites into the cornmeal mixture, one half at a time. Pour into the buttered pan and bake at 350°F (180°C) until golden brown, approximately 30 minutes.

Approximate values per ½-c. (120-ml) serving: **Calories** 340, **Total fat** 18 g, **Saturated fat** 9 g, **Cholesterol** 200 mg, **Sodium** 200 mg, **Total carbohydrates** 31 g, **Protein** 12 g, **Vitamin A** 20%, **Calcium** 15%

BARLEY RISOTTO

Yield: 4 Servings

Barley	½ c.	120 ml
Water	1 pt.	500 ml
Whole butter	½ oz.	15 g
Garlic cloves, chopped	4	4
Chicken stock	8 fl. oz.	250 ml
Green onions or chives, sliced	3 Tbsp.	45 ml
Asiago cheese, grated	¼ c.	60 ml
Kosher salt	TT	TT
Black pepper	TT	TT

1 Cook the barley in the water until barely done; strain.

2 Melt the butter in a large saucepan over medium heat. Add the garlic and cook until fragrant, approximately 2 minutes. Add the barley and, stirring with a wooden spoon, completely coat the barley with the butter.

3 Increase the heat and add 4 fluid ounces (125 milliliters) of the chicken stock. Stir until all the stock is absorbed, then add the remaining stock. Cook until almost all the stock is absorbed and remove from heat.

4 Stir in the green onions and cheese, and season to taste with salt and pepper.

Approximate values per serving: **Calories** 180, **Total fat** 9 g, **Saturated fat** 5 g, **Cholesterol** 25 mg, **Sodium** 280 mg, **Total carbohydrates** 20 g, **Protein** 5 g, **Vitamin A** 10%, **Claims**—no sugar; good source of fiber

VENISON RED-WINE JUS

Yield: 1 pt. (500 ml)

Bacon, chopped	2 Tbsp.	30 ml
Shallots, chopped	2	2
Carrot, chopped	3 oz.	90 g
Garlic, chopped	2 tsp.	10 ml
Celery stalk, chopped	1	1
Onion, chopped	2 oz.	60 g
Red wine	1 pt.	500 ml
Venison or venison/veal stock	1 qt.	1 lt

1 In a medium saucepan, render the bacon over low heat. Add the shallots, carrots, garlic, celery and onions; cook until tender.

2 Add the red wine and reduce to a glaze.

3 Add the stock and reduce by two-thirds. Pass through a fine strainer and check the consistency. Return to the saucepan and reduce further if necessary.

Approximate values per 1-fl.-oz. (30-ml) serving: **Calories** 30, **Total fat** 1 g, **Saturated fat** 0 g, **Cholesterol** 1.5 mg, **Sodium** 228 mg, **Total carbohydrates** 5 g, **Protein** 1 g, **Vitamin A** 15%, **Claims**—low fat; low cholesterol

MARINATED LOIN OF VENISON ROASTED WITH MUSTARD

RECIPE 19.3

FETZER VINEYARDS, HOPLAND, CA
Culinary Director, John Ash

Yield: 8 to 10 Servings, 6–8 oz. (180–250 g) each   **Method:** Roasting

Marinade:

Carrots, medium	3	3
Yellow onion, large	1	1
Shallots, whole	3	3
Garlic cloves	3	3
Olive oil	2 Tbsp.	30 ml
Hearty red wine	40 fl. oz.	1.2 lt
Red wine vinegar	4 fl. oz.	120 ml
Bay leaves	4	4
Parsley stalks	6	6
Juniper berries, whole	16	16
Sea salt	2 tsp.	10 ml
Peppercorns	12	12

Continued

Mustard coating:		
Garlic cloves	3	3
Green onions, chopped	2 oz.	60 g
Chardonnay	3 fl. oz.	90 ml
Fresh sage	1 tsp.	5 ml
Fresh thyme	1 tsp.	5 ml
Dijon mustard	1 c.	250 ml
Olive oil	2 fl. oz.	60 ml
Sea salt	1 tsp.	5 ml
Venison loin, 5 lb. (2.2 kg), well-trimmed	1	1

1 For the marinade, coarsely chop the vegetables and garlic and sauté them in the oil until lightly browned.

2 Add the wine, vinegar and remaining marinade ingredients and bring to a boil.

3 Reduce the heat and simmer for 10 minutes. Cool before using.

4 For the mustard coating, place all of the ingredients in a food processor or blender and quickly process until smooth. The mixture should be very thick. Cover and refrigerate.

5 In a nonreactive pan, pour the cooled marinade over the loin and marinate, covered, in the refrigerator for up to 24 hours. Turn occasionally.

6 Remove the meat from the marinade, pat dry and quickly sear the meat in a hot sauté pan or on the grill.

7 Place the loin in a roasting pan and coat well with the mustard coating. Roast at 450°F (230°C) for 5 minutes; then reduce the heat to 375°F (190°C) and roast for an additional 10–15 minutes, until the meat is medium rare.

8 Serve on warm plates with Creamy Polenta with Wild Mushrooms (page 724).

Approximate values per 8-oz. (240-g) serving: **Calories** 340, **Total fat** 13 g, **Saturated fat** 3 g, **Cholesterol** 190 mg, **Sodium** 460 mg, **Total carbohydrates** 4 g, **Protein** 53 g, **Iron** 50%

RECIPE 19.4

CHILLI-RUBBED VENISON WITH CARAMELIZED BERRY SAUCE

CAFÉ ALLEGRE, ORLANDO, FL
Chef Kevin Fonzo

Yield: 4 Servings   **Method:** Sautéing

Chilli powder	2 Tbsp.	30 ml
Salt	1 tsp.	5 ml
Black pepper	1 tsp.	5 ml
Venison leg, 5-oz. (150-g) portions	4	4
Olive oil	1 Tbsp.	15 ml
Mashed potatoes	as needed	as needed
Caramelized Berry Sauce (recipe follows)	8 fl. oz.	250 ml

1 In a small bowl, combine the chilli powder, salt and pepper to make a dry rub. Rub the venison with this mixture until well coated.

2 Heat the olive oil in a medium-sized sauté pan. Cook the venison to medium rare, making sure to brown all sides of the meat.

3 Remove the venison from the pan and allow it to rest for 1 minute, then slice into medallions.

4 Mound the mashed potatoes into the center of each plate. Arrange the venison in a fan around the potatoes. Ladle on the Caramelized Berry Sauce and garnish as desired.

Approximate values per serving: **Calories** 330, **Total fat** 13 g, **Saturated fat** 4 g, **Cholesterol** 116 mg, **Sodium** 1654 mg, **Total carbohydrates** 10 g, **Protein** 43 g, **Vitamin A** 26%, **Vitamin C** 14%, **Iron** 51%

CARAMELIZED BERRY SAUCE

Yield: 2 qt. (2 lt)

Granulated sugar	6 oz.	180 g
Water	4 fl. oz.	120 ml
Strawberries, sliced	1 c.	250 ml
Raspberries	1½ pt.	750 ml
Blackberries	1 pt.	500 ml
Blueberries	1 c.	250 ml
Veal stock	1 gal.	4 lt.

1 Combine the sugar and water in a large saucepot. Bring to a boil and cook to a rich, golden brown.

2 Add all the berries to the caramelized sugar. Cook for 1 minute.

3 Add the veal stock and bring to a boil. Lower the heat to a simmer and reduce by half. Strain the sauce through a fine chinois and keep warm for service.

Approximate values per 2-fl.-oz. (60-ml) serving: **Calories** 39, **Total fat** 0 g, **Saturated fat** 0 g, **Cholesterol** 0 mg, **Sodium** 580 mg, **Total carbohydrates** 9 g, **Protein** 1 g, **Vitamin** C 13%

VENISON MEDALLIONS GRAND VENEUR   RECIPE 19.5

Yield: 2 Servings   **Method:** Sautéing

Venison medallions, 3 oz. (90 g) each	4	4
Salt and pepper	TT	TT
Clarified butter	1 fl. oz.	30 ml
White wine	1 fl. oz.	30 ml
Poivrade sauce (page 217)	6 fl. oz.	180 ml
Red currant jelly	2 tsp.	10 ml
Heavy cream	1 fl. oz.	30 ml

1 Season the medallions with salt and pepper, and sauté in the clarified butter to the desired doneness. Remove and reserve.

2 Degrease the pan and deglaze with the white wine.

3 Add the poivrade sauce and bring to a simmer. Stir in the currant jelly, add the cream and adjust the seasonings.

4 Return the medallions to the sauce to reheat. Serve two medallions per person with a portion of the sauce.

Approximate values per 6-oz. (180-g) serving: **Calories** 410, **Total fat** 21 g, **Saturated fat** 12 g, **Cholesterol** 195 mg, **Sodium** 1250 mg, **Total carbohydrates** 15 g, **Protein** 39 g, **Vitamin A** 15%

RECIPE 19.6

CITRUS AND JUNIPER ELK LOIN WITH PARSNIP PURÉE AND PORT REDUCTION

RECIPE 19.6

THE BROWN PALACE HOTEL, DENVER, CO
William Dexter, Executive Sous Chef

Yield: 8 Servings   **Method:** Roasting

Marinade:		
Fresh orange juice	8 fl. oz.	240 ml
Fresh grapefruit juice	8 fl. oz.	240 ml
Fresh lemon juice	2 fl. oz.	60 ml
Fresh lime juice	1 fl. oz.	30 ml
Canola oil	6 fl. oz.	180 ml
Gin	1 fl. oz.	30 ml
Black peppercorns, cracked	1 Tbsp.	15 ml
Juniper berries, cracked	12	12
Elk loin, silverskin removed	1	1
Port wine	1½ pt.	700 ml
Glace de viande	2 fl. oz.	60 ml
Salt and pepper	TT	TT
Vegetable oil	as needed	as needed
Fresh herbs, chopped fine	2 Tbsp.	30 ml
Parsnip Purée (page 658)	3 lb.	1.4 kg

1 Combine all of the marinade ingredients and submerge the elk loin in the marinade for 24 hours.

2 In a small saucepot, reduce the port wine to 6 fluid ounces (180 milliliters). Add the glace de viande and simmer for 5 minutes. Adjust the seasonings and hold for service.

3 Remove the elk loin from the marinade. Pat dry and season with salt and pepper. Sear the loin in a hot sauté pan with a small amount of vegetable oil. Roast the loin in a 350°F (180°C) oven to an internal temperature of 120°F (49°C), approximately 10 minutes. Allow the loin to rest for 15 minutes before slicing.

4 Stir the herbs into the Parsnip Purée. Pipe a mound of Parsnip Purée into the center of each serving plate. Fan slices of the elk loin over the parsnips and spoon the sauce over the elk. Garnish as desired.

Approximate values per serving: **Calories** 700, **Total fat** 20 g, **Saturated fat** 9 g, **Cholesterol** 160 g, **Sodium** 390 mg, **Total carbohydrates** 45 g, **Protein** 57 g, **Vitamin C** 15%, **Iron** 35%

RECIPE 19.7

BRAISED ANTELOPE IN SOUR CREAM

Yield: 8 Servings, 6–8 oz. (180–250 g) each   **Method:** Braising

Salt pork	3 oz.	90 g
Bottom round of antelope, 4–5 lb. (2–2.5 kg)	1	1
Onion, small dice	12 oz.	350 g
Garlic cloves, sliced	2	2
Carrot, sliced	8 oz.	250 g
Red wine	24 fl. oz.	700 ml
Veal or game stock	3 pt.	1.5 lt
Bay leaves	2	2
Fresh rosemary, chopped	1 tsp.	5 ml

Fresh thyme	½ tsp.	2 ml
Juniper berries, crushed	10	10
Tomato paste	2 Tbsp.	30 ml
Clarified butter	2 Tbsp.	30 ml
Flour	2 Tbsp.	30 ml
Sour cream	1 pt.	500 ml
Salt and pepper	TT	TT

1 Render the salt pork. Brown the antelope meat well in the fat.

2 Add the onions, garlic and carrots; sauté until the vegetables are tender.

3 Add the red wine, stock, herbs, juniper berries and tomato paste. Braise in a 325°F (160°C) oven until the meat is tender, approximately 1½ to 2 hours.

4 Remove the meat from the pan and hold in a warm place. If necessary, make a blond roux with the butter and flour and use it to thicken the sauce. Bring to a simmer, then strain the sauce.

5 Add the sour cream, heat the sauce thoroughly and season to taste with salt and pepper. Slice the meat thinly and top with sauce for service.

Approximate values per 8-oz. (240-g) serving: **Calories** 580, **Total fat** 21 g, **Saturated fat** 11 g, **Cholesterol** 320 mg, **Sodium** 1110 mg, **Total carbohydrates** 24 g, **Protein** 72 g, **Vitamin A** 80%

VENISON AND BLACK BEAN CHILI   RECIPE 19.8

Yield: 4 qt. (4 lt)   **Method:** Braising

Dried black beans	1 lb.	450 g
Water	2 qt.	2 lt
Venison round, trimmed, medium dice	3 lb.	1.3 kg
Peanut oil	3 fl. oz.	90 ml
Garlic cloves, minced	6	6
Onion, small dice	1 lb. 8 oz.	680 g
Jalapeños, seeded and chopped fine	3	3
Masa harina (corn flour)	2 oz.	60 g
Chilli powder	1 oz.	30 g
Cayenne pepper	1 tsp.	5 ml
Cumin, ground	3 Tbsp.	45 ml
Peeled tomatoes, canned	1 lb. 8 oz.	680 g
Veal stock	1 qt.	1 lt
Salt and pepper	TT	TT
Tabasco sauce	TT	TT

1 Soak the beans in water overnight. Drain and simmer in 2 quarts (2 liters) of water until tender, approximately 30 to 40 minutes.

2 Sauté the venison in the oil until brown. Remove and reserve.

3 Sauté the garlic, onions and jalapeños in the same pan until tender. Add the masa harina, chilli powder, cayenne and cumin. Cook for 5 minutes.

4 Add the tomatoes, stock and reserved meat. Cover and braise on the stove top or in a 325°F (160°C) oven for 30 to 40 minutes.

5 Add the beans and cook for an additional 15 minutes. Season to taste with salt, pepper and Tabasco sauce. Thin with additional stock if necessary.

Approximate values per 8-oz. (240-g) serving: **Calories** 320, **Total fat** 9 g, **Saturated fat** 2 g, **Cholesterol** 70 mg, **Sodium** 510 mg, **Total carbohydrates** 31 g, **Protein** 28 g, **Vitamin A** 15%, **Iron** 30%

RECIPE 19.9   GRILLED BUFFALO STEAK

Yield: 1 Serving   **Method:** Grilling

Buffalo strip loin steak, 8 oz. (250 g)	1	1
Salt and pepper	TT	TT
Oil	1 Tbsp.	15 ml

1 Season the steak well with salt and pepper.
2 Brush with oil and grill to the desired degree of doneness.
3 Serve the steak with a full-flavored sauce such as a bordelaise (page 217) or poivrade sauce (page 217).

Approximate values per serving, without sauce: **Calories** 400, **Total fat** 18 g, **Saturated fat** 3 g, **Cholesterol** 140 mg, **Sodium** 1290 mg, **Total carbohydrates** 1 g, **Protein** 61 g, **Iron** 30%

RECIPE 19.10   BRAISED RABBIT WITH CAVATELLI PASTA

FETZER VINEYARDS, HOPLAND, CA
Culinary Director, John Ash

Yield: 4 Servings   **Method:** Braising

Rabbit, 4 lb. (1.8 kg), cut into quarters	1	1
Salt and pepper	TT	TT
Olive oil	2 fl. oz.	60 ml
Chanterelle or shiitake mushrooms, stemmed and sliced	8 oz.	250 g
Yellow onion, sliced	6 oz.	180 g
Garlic, slivered	3 Tbsp.	45 ml
Carrot, small dice	3 oz.	90 g
Celery, sliced thin	3 oz.	90 g
Sun-dried tomatoes, sliced	1 pt.	500 ml
Zinfandel wine	1 pt.	500 ml
Tomato concassée	1 pt.	500 ml
Fresh thyme	1 tsp.	5 ml
Fresh sage, minced	1 tsp.	5 ml
Rabbit or chicken stock	1 qt.	1 lt
Parsley, chopped fine	4 Tbsp.	60 ml
Fresh basil, chopped	4 Tbsp.	60 ml
Cavatelli, cooked, hot	24 oz.	700 g
Fresh basil sprigs	as needed for garnish	
Asiago, Parmesan or Dry Jack cheese, shaved	as needed for garnish	

1 Season the rabbit pieces with salt and pepper.
2 In a large saucepan, heat the oil and quickly brown the rabbit. Remove and reserve.
3 Add the mushrooms, onions, garlic, carrots and celery and sauté until very lightly browned.
4 Return the rabbit to the pan and add the sun-dried tomatoes, wine, tomato concassée, thyme, sage and stock. Cover and simmer until the rabbit is tender and begins to pull away from the bones, approximately 45 to 50 minutes.

5 Remove the rabbit, separate the meat from the bones, discard the bones, and cut the meat into bite-sized pieces.

6 Strain the sauce, reserving the vegetables, and return the sauce to the saucepan. Bring to a boil and cook over high heat to reduce and thicken slightly, approximately 8 to 10 minutes.

7 Adjust the seasonings. Add the reserved meat and vegetables and heat. Stir in the parsley and basil just before serving.

8 Toss the hot pasta with the rabbit sauce. Garnish with basil sprigs and cheese.

Approximate values per serving: **Calories** 1270, **Total fat** 47 g, **Saturated fat** 11 g, **Cholesterol** 285 mg, **Sodium** 2220 mg, **Total carbohydrates** 90 g, **Protein** 122 g, **Vitamin A** 60%, **Iron** 100%

BRAISED RABBIT

RECIPE 19.11

MISSISSIPPI UNIVERSITY FOR WOMEN, COLUMBUS, MS
Chef Jim Fitzgerald, Ph.D., CCP

Yield: 4 Servings

Method: Braising

Rabbit, 2–3 lb. (1–1.5 kg)	1	1
Oil or clarified butter	8 fl. oz.	240 ml
Yellow onion, diced	1	1
Garlic clove, minced	1	1
Celery stalks, diced	2	2
Carrot, grated	1/4 c.	60 ml
Cloves, ground	1/8 tsp.	1 ml
Cayenne pepper	1/8 tsp.	1 ml
Port wine	4 fl. oz.	120 ml
Chorizo sausages, sliced	4 oz.	120 g
Unsweetened chocolate, chopped	1 oz.	30 g
All-purpose flour	2 oz.	60 g
Veal or chicken stock	2 pt.	1 lt
Salt and pepper	TT	TT

1 Cut the rabbit into seven pieces. In a rondeau, brown the rabbit in the oil or clarified butter. Remove from the pan and reserve.

2 In the same pan, brown the onions and then add the garlic and cook for 1 minute. Add the celery, carrot, cloves and cayenne and cook for 2 more minutes.

3 Deglaze the pan with the wine and reduce au sec. Add the chorizo and chocolate, stirring well to prevent the chocolate from scorching.

4 Sprinkle the flour into the pan and cook to make a roux.

5 Whisk in 1 pint (450 milliliters) of the stock and cook until it thickens.

6 Add the remaining stock and the rabbit and bring to a simmer. Cover and place in a 325°F (160°C) oven and braise, basting the rabbit pieces with the braising liquid as needed, until fork tender, approximately 45 minutes.

Approximate values per 11-oz. (330-g) serving: **Calories** 610, **Total fat** 46 g, **Saturated fat** 9 g, **Cholesterol** 85 mg, **Sodium** 560 mg, **Total carbohydrates** 14 g, **Protein** 31 g, **Vitamin A** 25%, **Iron** 15%

RECIPE 19.12

ROAST PHEASANT WITH COGNAC AND APPLES

Yield: 2 Servings **Method:** Roasting

Pheasant	1	1
Salt and pepper	TT	TT
Fatback	as needed	as needed
Mirepoix	12 oz.	350 g
Tart apples	2	2
Whole butter	1 oz.	30 g
Cognac	3 fl. oz.	90 ml
Crème fraîche	4 fl. oz.	120 ml

1 Season the pheasant with salt and pepper. Bard the body with the fatback.

2 Roast on a bed of mirepoix at 350°F (180°C) until done, approximately 1½ hours.

3 Peel, core and slice each apple into eight pieces. Sauté the apples in the butter just until tender.

4 When the pheasant is done, remove it from the pan and reserve in a warm place. Deglaze the pan with the cognac, add the crème fraîche and bring to a simmer. Strain the sauce and adjust the seasonings.

5 Serve one half pheasant per person, accompanied by the sliced apples and sauce.

Approximate values per serving: **Calories** 630, **Total fat** 40 g, **Saturated fat** 23 g, **Cholesterol** 220 mg, **Sodium** 1360 mg, **Total carbohydrates** 21 g, **Protein** 46 g, **Vitamin A** 45%

RECIPE 19.13

PHEASANT ROASTED WITH CINNAMON AND BACON WITH RED CHILE PECAN SAUCE

CAFÉ ANNIE, HOUSTON, TX
Chef-Owner Robert Del Grande
Executive Chef Ben Berryhill

Yield: 4 Servings **Method:** Roasting

Pheasants, whole	2	2
Spice rub:		
Cinnamon, ground	2 tsp.	10 ml
Ancho chile powder	2 tsp.	10 ml
Sea salt	2 tsp.	10 ml
Black peppercorns, cracked	2 tsp.	10 ml
Whole butter, melted	1 oz.	30 g
Rich pheasant stock:		
Bacon slices, chopped	2	2
Whole butter	½ oz.	15 g
Onion, small, chopped	1	1
Carrot, small, chopped	1	1
Celery stalk, chopped	1	1
Garlic cloves	6	6
Bay leaf, whole	1	1
Chicken stock	1 qt.	1 lt
Red chile pecan sauce:		
Pecan pieces, toasted	3 oz.	90 g
Rich pheasant stock	12 fl. oz.	350 ml
Cascabel chiles, lightly toasted,		
stemmed and seeded	3	3

Heavy cream	2 fl. oz.	60 ml
Salt and pepper	TT	TT
Glaze:		
Maple syrup	2 Tbsp.	30 ml
Cinnamon, ground	½ tsp.	2 ml
Balsamic vinegar	2 Tbsp.	30 ml
Whole butter, melted	1 oz.	30 g
Applewood-smoked bacon		
slices, cooked crisp	4	4
Watercress sprigs	as needed for garnish	

1 Wash, dry and truss the pheasants. Combine the ingredients for the spice rub. Brush the birds with the melted butter and rub with the spice rub.

2 Roast the birds at 300°F (150°C) for 30 minutes. Remove the birds from the oven and detach the legs and thighs from the birds. Return the legs and thighs to the oven to roast until done, approximately 15 more minutes. Remove the breasts from the carcass, leaving the wings intact. Cut the carcass into several pieces and reserve. Arrange the breasts and legs on seperate broiler platters or pans and hold for service.

3 To prepare the stock, sauté the bacon in the butter. Add the remaining vegetables and the garlic and sauté until browned. Add the pheasant bones and sauté lightly. Add the bay leaf and chicken stock. Bring to a boil, reduce to a simmer and skim off any impurities that rise to the surface. Simmer for 45 minutes, strain and then reduce to 1½ cups (350 milliliters).

4 To make the red chile pecan sauce, combine all of the ingredients except the cream in a small saucepan and bring to a boil. Reduce to a simmer and cook for 30 minutes. Transfer the mixture to a blender and purée until smooth. Return the sauce to the saucepan and add the heavy cream. Bring the sauce to a simmer, adjust the seasonings and hold for service.

5 To make the glaze, combine all of the ingredients and mix well. Brush the pheasant pieces with the glaze. Broil the pheasant until the skin is very crisp. Transfer the breast pieces to a 300°F (150°C) oven and cook until done.

6 To serve, spoon a portion of the red chile pecan sauce on the plate. Slice the pheasant breast and arrange a sliced breast and a leg/thigh on each dinner plate. Garnish the plates with slices of crisp bacon and sprigs of watercress. Serve additional sauce on the side.

Approximate values per serving: **Calories** 1300, **Total fat** 86 g, **Saturated fat** 29 g, **Cholesterol** 365 mg, **Sodium** 2430 mg, **Total carbohydrates** 26 g, **Protein** 104 g, **Vitamin A** 170%, **Vitamin C** 45%, **Calcium** 15%, **Iron** 45%

GRILLED QUAIL WITH BALSAMIC HONEY GLAZE

RECIPE 19.14

SENCHA, COLORADO SPRINGS, CO
Chef Brent Beavers

Yield: 6 Servings   **Method:** Grilling

Quail, semiboneless	12	12
Salt and pepper	TT	TT
Vegetable oil	as needed	as needed
Cooked greens	6 oz.	180 g
Smoked Bacon and Black Quinoa Pilaf		
(recipe follows)	6 c.	700 ml
Balsamic Honey Glaze (recipe follows)	as needed	as needed

1 Season the quail with salt and pepper and brush with the oil. Grill the quail on a hot, well-seasoned grill until they are medium, approximately 6 minutes.

2 Arrange a portion of the greens on each serving plate. Mound the pilaf on the plate and place two quail on each plate, breast side up. Brush the quail with the Balsamic Honey Glaze and serve.

Approximate values per serving: **Calories** 780, **Total fat** 35 g, **Saturated fat** 10 g, **Cholesterol** 175 mg, **Sodium** 400 mg, **Total carbohydrates** 60 g, **Protein** 56 g, **Vitamin A** 140%, **Vitamin C** 90%, **Calcium** 10%, **Iron** 70%

SMOKED BACON AND BLACK QUINOA PILAF

Yield: 4 qt. (4 lt) **Method:** Pilaf

Bacon slices	10	10
Onion, small dice	6 oz.	180 g
Carrot, peeled, small dice	8 oz.	240 g
Red bell pepper, small dice	8 oz.	240 g
Basmati rice	3 c.	700 ml
Black quinoa	3 c.	700 ml
Water	5 pt.	2.2 lt
Salt and pepper	TT	TT
Sugar peas, shelled, cooked	8 oz.	240 g
Green onions, sliced	1 oz.	30 g

1 Dice the bacon and cook in a medium saucepan until crisp. Remove the bacon and reserve.

2 Add the onions, carrots and bell peppers to the bacon grease and sauté for 2 minutes. Add the rice and quinoa and sauté until the rice becomes translucent and is completely coated with the bacon grease.

3 Add the water, bring to a boil, season with salt and pepper, cover and cook over low heat for approximately 20 minutes or until the liquid is absorbed and the grains are tender. Remove from the heat and fluff with a fork. Add the reserved bacon, peas and green onions. Hold for service.

Approximate values per 4-fl.-oz. (120-ml) serving: **Calories** 180, **Total fat** 4 g, **Saturated fat** 1 g, **Cholesterol** 5 mg, **Sodium** 100 mg, **Total carbohydrates** 29 g, **Protein** 6 g, **Vitamin A** 50%, **Vitamin C** 30%, **Iron** 10%

BALSAMIC HONEY GLAZE

Yield: 3 c. (700 ml)

Balsamic vinegar	1 qt.	950 ml
Honey	1 lb.	450 g
Black pepper	1 tsp.	5 ml

1 Combine all ingredients in a small saucepot. Simmer and reduce until it reachs a syruplike consistency.

Approximate values per 1-fl.-oz. (30-ml) serving: **Calories** 80, **Total fat** 0 g, **Saturated fat** 0 g, **Cholesterol** 0 mg, **Sodium** 10 mg, **Total carbohydrates** 22 g, **Protein** 0 g

IN THE HANDS OF AN ABLE COOK, FISH CAN BECOME AN INEXHAUSTIBLE SOURCE OF PERPETUAL DELIGHT.

—Jean-Anthelme Brillat-Savarin (1755–1826)

20

FISH
AND SHELLFISH

PESCE RESTAURANT, Houston, TX
Chef Mark Holley

AFTER STUDYING THIS
CHAPTER, YOU WILL BE
ABLE TO:

▶ understand the structure and
  composition of fish and
  shellfish

▶ identify a variety of fish and
  shellfish

▶ purchase fish and shellfish
  appropriate for your needs

▶ store fish and shellfish properly

▶ prepare fish and shellfish for
  cooking

▶ apply various cooking methods
  to fish and shellfish

Fish are aquatic vertebrates with fins for swimming and gills for breathing. Of the more than thirty thousand species known, most live in the seas and oceans; freshwater species are far less numerous. Shellfish are aquatic invertebrates with shells or carapaces. They are found in both fresh and salt water.

Always an important food source, fish and shellfish have become increasingly popular in recent years, due in part to demands from health-conscious consumers. Because of increased demand and improved preservation and transportation techniques, good-quality fish and shellfish, once found only along seacoasts and lakes, are now readily available to almost every food service operation.

Many fish and shellfish species are very expensive; all are highly perishable. Because their cooking times are generally shorter and their flavors more delicate than meat or poultry, special attention must be given to fish and shellfish to prevent spoilage and to produce high-quality finished products.

In this chapter, you will learn how to identify a large assortment of fish and shellfish as well as how to properly purchase and store them, fabricate or prepare them for cooking and cook them by a variety of dry-heat and moist-heat cooking methods. This chapter presents many of the cooking methods applied to meats and poultry in the previous chapters. Review the corresponding procedures for meats and poultry, and note the similarities and differences.

▶ STRUCTURE AND MUSCLE COMPOSITION

The fish and shellfish used in food service operations can be divided into three categories: fish, mollusks and crustaceans.

Fish (Fr. *poisson*) include both fresh- and saltwater varieties. They have fins and an internal skeleton of bone and cartilage. Based upon shape and skeletal structure, fish can be divided into two groups: round fish and flatfish. **Round fish** swim in a vertical position and have eyes on both sides of their heads. Their bodies may be truly round, oval or compressed. **Flatfish** have asymmetrical, compressed bodies, swim in a horizontal position and have both eyes on top of their heads. Flatfish are bottom dwellers; most are found in deep ocean waters around the world. The skin on top of their bodies is dark, to camouflage them from predators, and can change color according to their surroundings. Their scales are small, and their dorsal and anal fins run the length of their bodies.

Mollusks (Fr. *mollusque*) are shellfish characterized by soft, unsegmented bodies with no internal skeleton. Most mollusks have hard outer shells. Single-shelled mollusks such as abalone are known as **univalves.** Those with two shells, such as clams, oysters and mussels, are known as **bivalves.** Squid and octopus, which are known as **cephalopods,** do not have a hard outer shell. Rather, they have a single thin internal shell called a *pen* or *cuttlebone.*

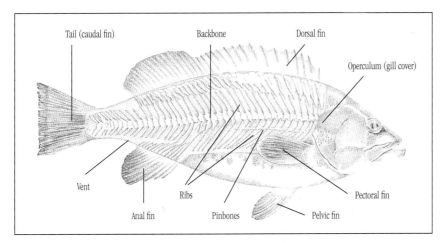

FIGURE 20.1 ▷ Bone structure of a round fish

SEAFOOD

Seafood means different things to different people. For some, the term applies only to shellfish or to shellfish and other small edible marine creatures. For others, it is limited to saltwater shellfish or to saltwater shellfish and fish. For yet others, it refers to all fish and shellfish, both freshwater and saltwater. Because of the term's vagueness, it is not used here.

Crustaceans (Fr. *crustacé*) are also shellfish. They have a hard outer skeleton or shell and jointed appendages. Crustaceans include lobsters, crabs and shrimp.

The flesh of fish and shellfish consists primarily of water, protein, fat and minerals. Fish flesh is composed of short muscle fibers separated by delicate sheets of connective tissue. Fish, as well as most shellfish, are naturally tender, so the purpose of cooking is to firm proteins and enhance flavor. The absence of the oxygen-carrying protein myoglobin makes fish flesh very light or white in color. (The orange color of salmon and some trout comes from pigments found in their food.) Compared to meats, fish do not contain large amounts of intermuscular fat. But the amount of fat a fish does contain affects the way it responds to cooking. Fish containing a relatively large amount of fat, such as salmon and mackerel, are known as fatty or oily fish. Fish such as cod and haddock contain very little fat and are referred to as lean fish. Shellfish are also very lean.

▷ IDENTIFYING FISH AND SHELLFISH

Identifying fish and shellfish properly can be difficult because of the vast number of similar-appearing fish and shellfish that are separate species within each family. Adding confusion are the various colloquial names given to the same fish or the same name given to different fish in different localities. Fish with an

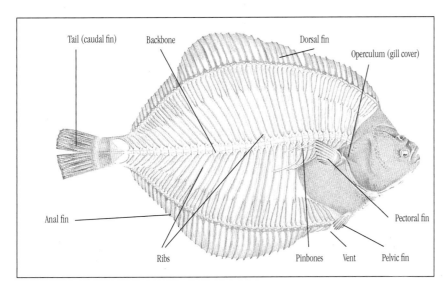

FIGURE 20.2 ▷ Bone structure of a flatfish

unappealing name may also be given a catchier name or the name of a similar but more popular item for marketing purposes. Moreover, some species are referred to by a foreign name, especially on menus.

The FDA publishes a list of approved market names for food fish in *The Seafood List: FDA Guide to Acceptable Market Names for Food Fish Sold in Interstate Commerce 2001,* available from the U.S. Government Printing Office, Washington, D.C. Deviations from this list are strongly discouraged but difficult to enforce. We attempt to use the most common names for each item, whether they are zoologically accurate or not.

FISH

ROUND FISH

Bass (Fr. *bar*) commonly refers to a number of unrelated spiny-finned fish. The better-known freshwater bass varieties (largemouth, smallmouth, redeye and black) are actually members of the sunfish family. They are lean and delicate but, as game, not commercially available in the United States. The saltwater bass varieties (black sea bass and striped bass) are popular commercial items.

Black sea bass are sometimes referred to as rock sea bass. They have a lean, firm white flesh with a mild flavor and flaky texture. They usually weigh from 1½ to 3 pounds (720 to 1360 grams) and are most prevalent in the Atlantic Ocean between New York and North Carolina. Black sea bass can be prepared by almost any cooking method and are often served whole in Chinese and Italian cuisines.

Black Sea Bass

Striped bass, often erroneously referred to as rockfish, are **anadromous.** True striped bass cannot be marketed because pollution and overfishing have damaged the supply. A hybrid of striped bass and either white bass or white perch is **aquafarmed** for commercial use, however. It is this hybrid that food service operations receive as striped bass. Whole fish weigh from 1 to 5 pounds (450 grams to 2.2 kilograms). Striped bass have a rich, sweet flavor and firm texture. They can be steamed, baked, poached or broiled.

Striped Bass

Catfish are scaleless freshwater fish common in southern lakes and rivers and now aquafarmed extensively. Aquafarm raising eliminates the "muddy" flavor once associated with catfish and ensures a year-round supply. The flesh is pure white with a moderate fat content; a mild, sweet flavor; and a firm texture. Channel catfish are the most important commercially. They usually weigh from 1½ to 5 pounds (720 grams to 2.2 kilograms). The smaller of these fish are known as **fiddlers;** they are often deep-fried and served whole. Catfish may be prepared by almost any cooking method, but are especially well suited to frying. Note that other species are often imported to the United States under the generic name *catfish.* Only products labeled "U.S. Farm-Raised Catfish" provide the consistent high quality and flavor that consumers have come to expect, however.

The **cod** (Fr. *cabillaud*) family includes Atlantic and Pacific cod as well as pollock, haddock, whiting and hake. Cod have a mild, delicate flavor and lean, firm white flesh that flakes apart easily. Cod can be prepared by most cooking methods, although grilling is not recommended because the flesh is too flaky.

Atlantic cod are the best-selling fish in America. They are

▶ **anadromous** a fish that migrates from a saltwater habitat to spawn in fresh water

▶ **aquafarming** also known as aquaculture, the business, science and practice of raising large quantities of fish and shellfish in tanks, ponds or ocean pens

Catfish

Atlantic Cod

SURIMI

Surimi is made from a highly processed fish paste colored, flavored and shaped to resemble shrimp, lobster, crab or other shellfish. Most surimi is based on Alaskan pollock, but some blends include varying amounts of real crab, shrimp or other items. Available chilled or frozen, surimi is already fully cooked and ready to add to salads, pasta, sauces or other dishes. Surimi is very low in fat and relatively high in protein. Because of processing techniques, however, it has more sodium and fewer vitamins and minerals than the real fish or shellfish it replaces. Americans now comsume more than 100 million pounds of surimi each year, and its popularity continues to grow. The FDA requires that all surimi products be labeled "imitation."

available fresh, whole or drawn, or cut into fillets or steaks. They are also available frozen and are often used for precooked or prebreaded sticks or portions. Smoked cod and dried salt cod (Sp. *bacalao*) are also available. Although cod may reach 200 pounds (90 kilograms), most market cod weigh 10 pounds (4.4 kilograms) or less. **Scrod** is a marketing term for cod or haddock weighing less than 2½ pounds (1.1 kilograms) or less than 20 inches (50 centimeters) in length.

Haddock, the second most commercially important fish, look like thin, small Atlantic cod and weigh about 2 to 5 pounds (900 grams to 2.3 kilograms). They have a stronger flavor and more delicate texture than Atlantic cod.

Pacific cod, also known as gray cod, are found in the northern Pacific Ocean and are not as abundant as their Atlantic cousins. Pacific cod are most often available frozen; they should be labeled "true cod" to distinguish them from rock cod and black cod, which are unrelated.

Pollock, also known as Boston bluefish or blue cod, are plentiful in the northern Atlantic and Pacific Oceans. Their flesh is gray-pink when raw, turning white when cooked. Pollock are often frozen at sea, then reprocessed into surimi. They can also be salted or smoked.

Pollock

Eels (Fr. *anguille*) are long, snakelike freshwater fish with dorsal and anal fins running the length of their bodies. (The conger eel is from a different family and has little culinary significance.) American and European eels are available live, whole, gutted or as fillets. Eels have a high fat content and firm flesh; they are sweet and mildly flavored. Their tough skin should be removed before cooking. Eels may be steamed, baked, fried or used in stews. Baby eels are a springtime delicacy, especially in Spain, where they are pan-fried in olive oil and garlic with hot red peppers. Smoked eels are also available.

Eel

The **grouper** family includes almost four hundred varieties found in temperate waters worldwide. The more common Atlantic Ocean varieties are the yellowfin grouper, black grouper, red grouper and gag; the Pacific Ocean varieties are the sea bass (also known as jewfish and different from the black sea bass) and spotted cabrilla. Although some species can reach 800 pounds or more, most commercial varieties are sold in the 5- to 20-pound (2.2- to 8.8-kilogram) range. They have lean white flesh with a mild to sweet flavor and very firm texture. Their skin, which is tough and strongly flavored, is generally removed before cooking. Grouper fillets may be baked, deep-fried, broiled or grilled.

Grouper

Herring (Fr. *hareng*) are long, silvery-blue fish found in both the northern Atlantic and Pacific Oceans. Their strongly flavored flesh has a moderate

Sardines

to high fat content. Whole herring weigh up to 8 ounces (225 grams). Fresh herring may be butterflied or filleted and roasted, broiled or grilled. But because herring are very soft and tend to spoil quickly, they are rarely available fresh. More often, they are smoked (and known as kippers) or cured in brine.

Very young, small herring are known as **sardines** (Fr. *sardine*). They have fatty, oily flesh with a flaky texture. Sardines are usually sold canned, whole or as skinned and boned fillets, or fried or smoked and packed in oil or sauce. Sardines are used primarily for sandwiches and salads.

John Dory, also known as St. Peter's fish, have a distinctive round, black spot with a yellow halo on each side of the body. Their flesh is white, firm and finely flaked. They may be filleted and prepared like flounder and are a classic bouillabaisse ingredient.

John Dory

Mackerel (Fr. *maquereau*) of culinary importance include king and Spanish mackerel as well as tuna and wahoo, which are discussed separately later. The species known as Atlantic and Pacific mackerel are not generally used for food because of their small size and high fat content. Mackerel flesh has a high fat content, gray to pink coloring, a mild flavor and flaky texture. The flesh becomes firm and off-white when cooked. Mackerel are best broiled, grilled, smoked or baked.

Mackerel

Mahi-mahi is the more commonly used name for dolphin or dolphinfish; this Hawaiian name is used to distinguish them from the marine mammal of the same name. (Dolphins and porpoises are marine mammals.) Also known by their Spanish name, *dorado,* mahi-mahi are brilliantly colored fish found in tropical seas. Mahi-mahi weigh about 15 pounds (6.6 kilograms) and are sold whole or as fillets. Their flesh is off-white to pink, lean and firm with a sweet flavor. Dolphinfish can be broiled, grilled or baked. The meat may become dry when cooked, however, so a sauce or marinade is recommended.

Mahi-Mahi

Monkfish are also known as angler fish, goosefish, rape and lotte. These extraordinarily ugly fish are rarely seen whole, for the large head is usually discarded before reaching market. Only the tail is edible; it is available in fillets, fresh or frozen. The scaleless skin must be removed. The flesh is lean, pearly white and very firm. Its texture and flavor have earned monkfish the nickname of "poor man's lobster." Monkfish absorb flavors easily and are baked, steamed, fried, grilled or broiled. They are also used for stews and soups.

Monkfish Tail

Orange roughy are caught in the South Pacific off the coasts of New Zealand and Australia. They have bright orange skin and firm, pearly-white flesh with a low fat content and extremely bland flavor. Orange roughy are almost always marketed as skinless, boneless frozen fillets, averaging 6 to 8 ounces (140 to 225 grams) each. Widely available year-round, they can be broiled, steamed, grilled or prepared in the same manner as cod.

Orange Roughy

Red Snapper

Red snapper is also known as the American or northern red snapper. Although there are many members of the snapper family, only one is the true red snapper. Red-skinned rockfish are often mislabeled as the more popular red snapper or Pacific snapper, a practice that is currently legal only in California. True red snapper have lean, pink flesh that becomes white when cooked; it is sweet-flavored and flaky. They are sold whole or as fillets with the skin left on for identification. Red snapper may reach 35 pounds, but most are marketed at only 4 to 6 pounds (1.8 to 2.7 kilograms) or as 1- to 3-pound (450-gram to 1.3-kilogram) fillets. Red snapper can be prepared using almost any cooking method. The head and bones are excellent for stock.

Salmon (Fr. *saumon*) flourish in both the northern Atlantic and Pacific Oceans, returning to the freshwater rivers and streams of their birth to spawn. Salmon flesh gets its distinctive pink-red color from fat-soluble carotenoids found in the crustaceans on which they feed.

Atlantic salmon is the most important commercially, accounting for one-quarter of all salmon produced worldwide. Extensive aquafarms in Norway, Canada and Scotland produce a steady supply of Atlantic salmon. For marketing purposes, the fish's point of origin is often added to the name (for example, Norwegian, Scottish or Shetland Atlantic salmon). Atlantic salmon have a rich pink color and moist flesh. Their average weight is from 4 to 12 pounds (1.8 to 5.4 kilograms). Wild Atlantic salmon are almost never available.

Atlantic Salmon

Chinook or **king salmon** from the Pacific are also highly desirable. They average from 5 to 30 pounds (2.2 to 13.2 kilograms) and have red-orange flesh with a high fat content and rich flavor. Like other salmon, their flesh separates into large flakes when cooked. Chinooks are often marketed by the name of the river from which they are harvested (for example, Columbia, Yukon or Copper Chinook salmon). They are distinguished by the black interior of their mouth.

Chinook or King Salmon

Coho or **silver salmon** have a pinkish flesh and are available fresh or frozen, wild or from aquafarms. Wild coho average from 3 to 12 pounds (1.3 to 5.4 kilograms), while aquafarmed coho are much smaller, usually less than 1 pound (450 grams).

Mini Coho Salmon

Other varieties, such as chum, sockeye, red, blueback and pink salmon, are usually canned but may be available fresh or frozen.

Salmon can be prepared by many cooking methods: broiling, grilling, poaching, steaming or baking. Frying is not recommended, however, because of their high fat content. Salmon fillets are often cured or smoked. **Gravlax** is salmon that has been cured for one to three days with salt, sugar and dill. **Lox** is salmon that has been cured in a salted brine and then, typically, cold-smoked. **Nova** is used in the eastern United States to refer to a less-salty, cold-smoked salmon.

Sea bream is the name given to a large family of fish found in the Mediterranean (gilt-head bream), the Caribbean (porgy), the Atlantic (black sea bream) and the Indo-Pacific (emperor and snapper). Because the marketing term *bream* is applied to so many different fish, it is difficult to generalize about their characteristics. Some have very few bones, others have quite a few; some have a rich flavor, others are very mild; some weigh up to 20 pounds (9.6 kilograms), others rarely exceed 5 pounds (kilograms). Black sea bream, for example, is a good pan fish, reaching only 35 cm in length and weighing less than 6 pounds (2.9 kilograms). Their flesh is firm, mild and low in fat. Also marketed as Thai snapper, they are good for baking, grilling or frying.

Black Sea Bream

Sharks provide delicious eating, despite their less-than-appealing appearance and vicious reputation. Mako and blue sharks are the most desirable, with mako often being sold as swordfish. Sand shark, sharpnose, blacktip, angel and thresher are also available commercially. Most sharks have lean flesh with a mild flavor and firm texture. The flesh is white

Blacktip Shark

with tinges of pink or red when raw, turning off-white when cooked. Makos weigh from 30 to 250 pounds (13.5 To 112.5 kilograms); other species may reach as much as 1000 pounds (450 kilograms). All sharks have cartilaginous skeletons and no bones; therefore, they are not actually fish, but rather marine invertebrates. Sharks are usually cut into loins or wheels, then into steaks or cubes. They can be broiled, grilled, baked or fried. An ammonia smell indicates that the shark was not properly treated when caught. Do not buy or eat it.

Swordfish take their name from the long, swordlike bill extending from their upper jaw. These popular fish average about 250 pounds (112.5 kilograms). Their flesh is lean and sweet with a very firm, meatlike texture; it may be gray, pink or off-white when raw, becoming white when cooked. Swordfish are most often available cut into wheels or portioned into steaks perfect for grilling or broiling.

Swordfish Wheel

Tilapia is the name given to several species of freshwater, aquafarm-raised fish bred worldwide. They grow quickly in warm water, reaching about 3 pounds (1.3 kilograms); they are available whole or filleted, fresh or frozen. The flesh is similar to catfish—lean, white and sweet, with a firm texture. Tilapia are sometimes marketed as cherry snapper or sunshine snapper, even though they are not members of the snapper family.

Tilapia

Trout (Fr. *truite*) are members of the salmon family. Most of the freshwater trout commercially available are aquafarm-raised rainbow trout, although brown trout and brook trout are also being aquafarmed. Some trout species spend part of their lives at sea, returning to fresh water to spawn. On the West Coast, these are called salmon trout or steelhead. Trout have a low to moderate fat content, a flaky texture and a delicate flavor that can be easily overwhelmed by strong sauces. The flesh may be white, orange or pink. Trout are usually marketed at 8 to 10 ounces (225 to 280 grams) each, just right for an individual portion. Lake trout, sometimes known as char, are not aquafarmed and have little commercial value because of their extremely high fat content. Trout can be baked, pan-fried, smoked or steamed.

Red Mountain Trout

Rainbow Trout

Tuna (Fr. *thon*) varieties include the bluefin, yellowfin, bonito, bigeye and blackfin. Ahi is the popular market name for either yellowfin or bigeye tuna. All are members of the mackerel family and are found in tropical and subtropical waters around the world. Tuna are large fish, weighing up to several hundred pounds each. Bluefin, the finest and most desirable for sashimi, are becoming very scarce because of overfishing. Regular canned tuna is usually prepared from yellowfin or skipjack; canned white tuna is prepared from albacore, also known as longfin tuna. Pacific tuna that is frozen at sea to preserve its freshness is referred to as clipper fish. Any of these species may be found fresh or frozen, however. Tuna is usually cut into four boneless loins for market. The loins are then cut into steaks, cubes or chunks. The flesh has a low to moderate fat content (a higher fat content is preferred for sashimi) and a deep red color. The dark, reddish-brown muscle that runs along the lateral line is very fatty and can be removed. Tuna flesh turns light gray when cooked and is very firm, with a mild flavor. Tuna work well for grilling or broiling and may be marinated or brushed with seasoned oil during cooking. Tuna are often prepared medium rare to prevent dryness.

Yellowfin Tuna

Table 20.1 FLOUNDER (A.K.A. SOLE)	
ATLANTIC OCEAN	**PACIFIC OCEAN**
Blackback/Winter flounder/Lemon sole	Arrowtooth
Fluke/Summer flounder	Petrale sole
Starry flounder	Rex sole
Yellowtail flounder	English sole
Windowpane flounder	Rock sole
Gray sole/Witch flounder	Sand sole
	Yellowfin sole
	Domestic Dover sole/Pacific flounder
	Butter sole

Wahoo, also known as ono, are found throughout tropical and subtropical waters, but are particularly associated with Hawaii (*ono* even means "good to eat" in Hawaiian). They are actually a type of mackerel and are cooked like any other mackerel.

Wahoo

Whitefish species inhabit the freshwater lakes and streams of North America. Lake whitefish, the most important commercially, are related to salmon. They are marketed at up to 7 pounds (3.2 kilograms) and are available whole or filleted. The flesh is firm and white, with a moderate amount of fat and a sweet flavor. Whitefish may be baked, broiled, grilled or smoked and are often used in processed fish products.

FLATFISH

Flounder (Fr. *flet*) have lean, firm flesh that is pearly or pinkish-white with a sweet, mild flavor. Although they are easily boned, most are deheaded and gutted at sea and sold as fresh or frozen fillets. These fillets are very thin and can dry out or spoil easily, so extra care should be taken in handling, preparing and storing them. Recipes that preserve moisture work best with flounder; poaching, steaming or frying are recommended. Many types of flounder are marketed as sole, perhaps in an attempt to cash in on the popularity of true sole. The FDA permits this practice.

English sole are actually flounder caught off the West Coast of the United States. They are usually marketed simply as "fillet of sole." They are a plentiful species of fair to average quality.

Petrale sole, another West Coast flounder, are generally considered the finest of the domestic "soles." They are most often available as fillets, which tend to be thicker and firmer than other sole fillets.

Domestic Dover sole are also Pacific flounder. They are not as delicate or flavorful as other species of sole or flounder. Moreover, they are often afflicted with a parasite that causes their

TRASH FISH

Ocean pout are considered a "trash fish," or fish that fishermen throw away because there is little or no consumer demand and therefore no market value.

Long ago, lobster were considered trash and good for nothing but chicken feed. More recently, monkfish was a trash fish in the U.S., and now we can't get enough. Obscure species are often trash fish until someone somewhere tastes them and realizes that they offer some incredible flavors and textures.

Searobins, dogfish, skate, and whiting are still considered trash fish in America, though they are gradually becoming more popular and will someday be readily available at fish markets.

from *The Great American Seafood Cookbook* by SUSAN HERRMANN LOOMIS

Lemon Sole

Alaskan Halibut

True Dover Sole

Turbot

Abalone

flesh to have a slimy, gelatinous texture. Domestic Dover sole are not recommended if other sole or flounder are available.

Lemon sole are the most abundant and popular East Coast flounder. They are also known as blackback or winter flounder (during the winter, they migrate close to shore from the deeper, colder waters). They average 2 pounds (900 grams) in weight.

Halibut are among the largest flatfish; they often weigh up to 300 pounds (135 kilograms). The FDA recognizes only two halibut species: Atlantic (eastern) and Pacific (northern, Alaskan, western) halibut. Both have lean, firm flesh that is snow-white with a sweet, mild flavor. California halibut, which are actually flounder, are similar in taste and texture but average only 12 pounds (5.4 kilograms) each. Halibut may be cut into boneless steaks or skewered on brochettes. The flesh, which dries out easily, can be poached, baked, grilled or broiled and is good with a variety of sauces.

Sole (Fr. *sole*) are probably the most flavorful and finely textured flatfish. Indeed, because of the connotations of quality associated with the name, "sole" is widely used for many species that are not members of the sole *Soleidae* family. Even though the FDA allows many species of flatfish to be called "sole" for marketing purposes, no true sole is commercially harvested in American waters. Any flatfish harvested in American waters and marketed as sole is actually flounder.

True **Dover sole**, a staple of classic cuisine, are a lean fish with pearly-white flesh and a delicate flavor that can stand up to a variety of sauces and seasonings. They are a member of the *Soleidae* family and come only from the waters off the coasts of England, Africa and Europe. They are imported into this country as fresh whole fish or fresh or frozen fillets.

Turbot are a Pacific flatfish of no great culinary distinction. In Europe, however, the species known as turbot (Fr. *turbot*) are large diamond-shaped fish highly prized for their delicate flavor and firm, white flesh. They are also marketed as brill.

MOLLUSKS

UNIVALVES

Univalves are mollusks with a single shell in which the soft-bodied animal resides. They are actually marine snails with a single foot, used to attach the creature to fixed objects such as rocks.

Abalone have brownish-gray, ear-shaped shells. They are harvested in California, but California law does not permit canning abalone or shipping it out of state. Some frozen abalone is available from Mexico; canned abalone is imported from Japan. Abalone are lean with a sweet, delicate flavor similar to that of clams. They are too tough to eat unless tenderized with a mallet or rolling pin. They may then be eaten raw or prepared seviche-style. Great care must be taken when grilling or sautéing abalone, as the meat becomes very tough when overcooked.

Conch are found in warm waters off the Florida Keys and in the Caribbean. The beautiful peachy-pink shell of the queen conch is prized by beachcombers. Conch meat is lean, smooth and very firm with a sweet-smoky flavor and chewy texture. It can be sliced and pounded to tenderize it, eaten raw with lime juice or slow-cooked whole.

BIVALVES

Bivalves are mollusks with two bilateral shells attached by a central hinge.

Clams (Fr. *clovisses*) are harvested along both the East and West Coasts, with Atlantic clams being more significant commercially. Atlantic Coast clams include hard-shell, soft-shell and surf clams. Clams are available all year, either live in the shell or fresh-shucked (meat removed from the shell). Canned clams, whether minced, chopped or whole, are also available.

Atlantic hard-shell clams or **quahogs** have hard, blue-gray shells. Their chewy meat is not as sweet as other clam meat. Quahogs have different names, depending upon their size. **Littlenecks** are generally under 2 inches (5 centimeters) across the shell and usually are served on the half shell or steamed. They are the most expensive clams. **Cherrystones** are generally under 3 inches (7.5 centimeters) across the shell and are sometimes eaten raw but are more often cooked. **Topnecks** are usually cooked and are often served as stuffed clams. **Chowders,** the largest quahogs, are always eaten cooked, especially minced for chowder or soup.

Littlenecks
Cherrystones

Topnecks

Soft-shell clams, also known as Ipswich, steamer and long-necked clams, have thin, brittle shells that do not completely close because of the clam's protruding black-tipped siphon. Their meat is tender and sweet. They are sometimes fried but are more often served steamed.

Surf clams are deep-water clams that reach sizes of 8 inches (20 centimeters) across. They are most often cut into strips for frying or are minced, chopped, processed and canned.

Pacific clams are generally too tough to eat raw. The most common is the **Manila clam,** which was introduced along the Pacific coast during the 1930s. Resembling a quahog with a ridged shell, it can be served steamed or on the half shell. **Geoducks** are the largest Pacific clam, sometimes weighing up to 10 pounds (4.5 kilograms) each. They look like huge soft-shell clams with a large, protruding siphon. Their tender, rich bodies and briny flavor are popular in Asian cuisines.

Cockles are small bivalves, about 1 inch (2.5 centimeters) long, with ridged shells. They are more popular in Europe than the United States and are sometimes used in dishes such as paella and fish soups or stews.

Mussels (Fr. *moule*) are found in waters worldwide. They are excellent steamed in wine or seasoned broth and can be fried or used in soups or pasta dishes.

Cockles

Blue mussels are the most common edible mussel. They are found in the wild along the Atlantic Coast and are aquafarmed on both coasts. Their meat is plump and sweet with a firm, muscular texture. The orangish-yellow meat of cultivated mussels tends to be much larger than that of wild mussels and therefore worth the added cost. Blue mussels are sold live in the shell and average from 10 to 20 per pound. Although available all year, the best-quality blue mussels are harvested during the winter months.

SNAILS

Although snails (more politely known by their French name, escargots) are univalve land animals, they share many characteristics with their marine cousins. They can be poached in court bouillon or removed from their shells and boiled or baked briefly with a seasoned butter or sauce. They should be firm but tender; overcooking makes snails tough and chewy. The most popular varieties are the large white Burgundy snail and the small garden variety called petit gris. Fresh snails are available from snail ranches through speciality suppliers. The great majority of snails, however, are purchased canned; most canned snails are produced in France or Taiwan.

Soft-Shell Clams

Manila Clams

Blue Mussels

Greenshell Mussels

Greenshell (or greenlip) **mussels** from New Zealand and Thailand are much larger than blue mussels, averaging 8 to 12 mussels per pound. Their shells are paler gray, with a distinctive bright-green edge.

Oysters (Fr. *huitre*) have a rough gray shell. Their soft, gray, briny flesh can be eaten raw directly from the shell. They can also be steamed or baked in the shell or shucked and fried, sautéed or added to stews or chowders. Most oysters available in the United States are commercially grown and sold either live in the shell or shucked. There are four main domestic species.

Atlantic oysters, also called American or Eastern oysters, have darker, flatter shells than other oysters.

European flat oysters are often incorrectly called Belon (true Belon oysters live only in the Belon river of France); they are very round and flat and look like giant brownish-green Olympias.

Olympias are the only oysters native to the Pacific Coast; they are tiny (about the size of a 50-cent coin).

Gulf Oysters

Olympia Oysters

Pacific oysters, also called Japanese oysters, are aquafarmed along the Pacific Coast; they have curly, thick striated shells and silvery-gray to gold to almost-white meat. Although it may seem as though there are hundreds of oyster species on the market, only two are commercially significant: the Atlantic oyster and the Pacific oyster. These two species yield dozens of different varieties, however, depending on their origin. For example, Atlantic oysters may be referred to as bluepoints, Chesapeake Bay, Florida Gulf, Long Island and so on, while Pacific oysters include Penn Cove Select, Westcott Bay, Hamma-Hamma, Kumamoto and Portuguese, among others. An oyster's flavor reflects the minerals, nutrients and salts in its water and mud bed, so a Bristol from Maine and an Apalachicola from Florida will taste very different, even though they are the same Atlantic species.

Scallops contain an edible white adductor muscle that holds together the fan-shaped shells. Because they die quickly, they are almost always shucked and cleaned on-board ship. The sea scallop and the bay scallop, both cold-water varieties, and the calico scallop, a warm-water variety, are the most important commercially. Sea scallops are the largest, with an average count of 20–30 per pound. Larger sea scallops are also available. Bay scallops average 70–90 per pound; calico scallops average 70–110 per pound. Fresh or frozen shucked, cleaned scallops are the most common market form, but live scallops in the shell and shucked scallops with roe attached (very popular in Europe) are also available. Scallops are sweet, with a tender texture. Raw scallops should be a translucent ivory color and nonsymmetrically round and should feel springy. They can be steamed, broiled, grilled, fried, sautéed or baked. When overcooked, however, scallops quickly become chewy and dry. Only extremely fresh scallops should be eaten raw.

European Flat Oysters

Bluepoint Oysters

Hamma-Hamma Oysters

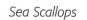

Sea Scallops

CEPHALOPODS

Cephalopods are marine mollusks with distinct heads, well-developed eyes, a number of arms that attach to the head near the mouth and a saclike fin-bearing mantle. They do not have an outer shell; instead, there is a thin internal shell called a *pen* or *cuttlebone.*

Octopus is generally quite tough and requires mechanical tenderization or long, moist-heat cooking to make it palatable. Most octopus is imported from Portugal, though fresh ones are available on the East Coast during the winter. Octopus is sold by the pound, fresh or frozen, usually whole. Octopus skin is gray when raw, turning purple when cooked. The interior flesh is white, lean, firm and flavorful.

Octopus

Squid, known by their Italian name, *calamari,* are becoming increasingly popular in the United States. Similar to octopuses but much smaller, they are harvested along both American coasts and elsewhere around the world (the finest are the East Coast loligo or winter squid). They range in size from an average of 8–10 per pound to the giant South American squid, which is sold as tenderized steaks. The squid's tentacles, mantle (body tube) and fins are edible. Squid meat is white to ivory in color, turning darker with age. It is moderately lean, slightly sweet, firm and tender, but it toughens quickly if overcooked. Squid are available either fresh or frozen and packed in blocks.

Squid

CRUSTACEANS

Crustaceans are found in both fresh and salt water. They have a hard outer shell and jointed appendages, and they breathe through gills.

Crayfish (Fr. *écrevisse*), generally called *crayfish* in the North and *crawfish* or *crawdad* in the South, are freshwater creatures that look like miniature lobsters. They are harvested from the wild or aqua-farmed in Louisiana and the Pacific Northwest. They are from 3½ to 7 inches (8 to 17.5 centimeters) in length when marketed and may be purchased live or precooked and frozen. The lean meat, found mostly in the tail, is sweet and tender. Crayfish can be boiled whole and served hot or cold. The tail meat can be deep-fried or used in soups, bisque or sauces. Crayfish are a staple of Cajun cuisine, often used in gumbo, étouffée and jambalaya. Whole crayfish become brilliant red when cooked and may be used as a garnish.

Crayfish

Crabs (Fr. *crabe*) are found along the North American coast in great numbers and are shipped throughout the world in fresh, frozen and canned forms. Crab meat varies in flavor and texture and can be used in a range of prepared dishes, from chowders to curries to casseroles. Crabs purchased live should last up to five days; dead crabs should not be used.

King crabs are very large crabs (usually around 10 pounds or 4.4 kilograms) caught in the very cold waters of the northern Pacific. Their meat is very sweet and snow-white. King crabs are always sold frozen, usually in the shell. In-shell forms include sections or clusters, legs and claws or split legs. The meat is also available in "fancy" packs of whole leg and body meat, or shredded and minced pieces.

King Crab Legs

Dungeness Crab

Soft-Shell Crabs

Stone Crab Claws

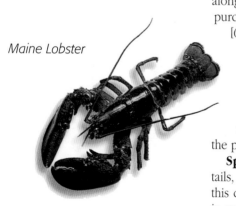

Maine Lobster

Blue Crab

Snow Crab Legs

Dungeness crabs are found along the West Coast. They weigh 1½ to 4 pounds (680 grams to 1.8 kilograms), and have delicate, sweet meat. They are sold live, precooked and frozen, or as picked meat, usually in 5-pound (2.2-kilogram) vacuum-packed cans.

Blue crabs are found along the entire eastern seaboard and account for approximately 50 percent of the total weight of all crab species harvested in the United States. Their meat is rich and sweet. Blue crabs are available as hard-shell or soft-shell. Hard-shell crabs are sold live, precooked and frozen, or as picked meat. Soft-shell crabs are those harvested within six hours after molting and are available live (generally only from May 15 to September 15) or frozen. They are often steamed and served whole. Soft-shells can be sautéed, fried, broiled or added to soups or stews. Blue crabs are sold by size, with an average diameter of 4–7 inches (10–18 centimeters).

Snow or **spider crabs** are an abundant species, most often used as a substitute for the scarcer and more expensive king crab. They are harvested from Alaskan waters and along the eastern coast of Canada. Snow crab is sold precooked, usually frozen. The meat can be used in soups, salads, omelets or other prepared dishes. Legs are often served cold as an appetizer.

Stone crabs are generally available only as cooked claws, either fresh or frozen (the claws cannot be frozen raw because the meat sticks to the shell). In stone-crab fishery, only the claw is harvested. After the claw is removed, the crab is returned to the water where, in approximately 18 months, it regenerates a new claw. Claws average 2½ to 5½ ounces (75 to 155 grams) each. The meat is firm, with a sweet flavor similar to lobster. Cracked claws are served hot or cold, usually with cocktail sauce, lemon butter or other accompaniments.

Lobsters have brown to blue-black outer shells and firm, white meat with a rich, sweet flavor. Lobster shells turn red when cooked. They are usually poached, steamed, simmered, baked or grilled, and can be served hot or cold. Picked meat can be used in prepared dishes, soups or sautés. Lobsters must be kept alive until just before cooking. Dead lobsters should not be eaten. The Maine, also known as American or clawed lobster, and the spiny lobster are the most commonly marketed species.

Maine lobsters have edible meat in both their tails and claws; they are considered superior in flavor to all other lobsters. They come from the cold waters along the northeast coast and are most often sold live. Maine lobsters may be purchased by weight (for example, 1¼ pounds [525 grams], 1½ pounds [650 grams] or 2 pounds [900 grams] each), or as chix (that is, a lobster weighing less than 1 pound [450 grams]). Maine lobsters may also be purchased as culls (lobsters with only one claw) or bullets (lobsters with no claws). They are available frozen or as cooked, picked meat.

Figure 20.3 shows a cross-section of a Maine lobster and identifies the stomach, tomalley (the olive-green liver) and coral (the roe). The stomach is not eaten; the tomalley and coral are very flavorful and are often used in the preparation of sauces and other items.

Spiny lobsters have very small claws and are valuable only for their meaty tails, which are notched with short spines. Nearly all spiny lobsters marketed in this country are sold as frozen tails, often identified as rock lobster. Harvested in many parts of the world, those found off Florida and Brazil and in the

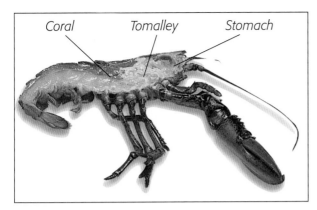

FIGURE 20.3

Caribbean are marketed as warm-water tails; those found off South Africa, Australia and New Zealand are called cold-water tails. Cold-water spiny tails are considered superior to their warm-water cousins.

Slipper lobster, lobsterette and **squat lobster** are all clawless species found in tropical, subtropical and temperate waters worldwide. Although popular in some countries, their flavor is inferior to both Maine and spiny lobsters. **Langoustine** are small North Atlantic lobsters.

Shrimp (Fr. *crevette*) are found worldwide and are widely popular. Gulf whites, pinks, browns and black tigers are just a few of the dozens of shrimp varieties used in food service operations. Although fresh, head-on shrimp are available, the most common form is raw, head-off (also called green headless) shrimp with the shell on. Most shrimp are deheaded and frozen at sea to preserve freshness. Shrimp are available in many forms: raw, peeled and deveined; cooked, peeled and deveined; and individually-quick frozen, as well as in a variety of processed, breaded or canned products. Shrimp are graded by size, which can range from 400 per pound (titi) to 8 per pound (extra-colossal), and are sold in counts per pound. For example, shrimp marketed as "21–26 count" means that there is an average of 21 to 26 shrimp per pound; shrimp marketed as "U-10" means that there are fewer than 10 shrimp per pound.

Prawn is often used interchangeably with the word *shrimp* in English-speaking countries. Although it is perhaps more accurate to refer to freshwater species as prawns and saltwater species as shrimp, in commercial practice, prawn refers to any large shrimp. Equally confusing, *scampi* is the Italian name for the Dublin Bay prawn (which is actually a species of miniature lobster), but in the United States *scampi* refers to shrimp sautéed in garlic butter.

Tiger Shrimp

Shrimp

Green Headless Shrimp

Prawn

▶ NUTRITION

Fish and shellfish are low in calories, fat and sodium, and are high in protein and vitamins A, B and D. Fish and shellfish are also high in minerals, especially calcium (particularly in canned fish with edible bones), phosphorus, potassium and iron (especially mollusks). Fish are high in a group of polyunsaturated fatty acids called omega-3, which may help combat high blood cholesterol levels and aid in preventing some heart disease. Shellfish are not as high in cholesterol as was once thought. Crustaceans are higher in cholesterol than mollusks, but both have considerably lower levels than red meat or eggs.

The cooking methods used for fish and shellfish also contribute to their healthfulness. The most commonly used cooking methods—broiling, grilling, poaching and steaming—add little or no fat.

FIGURE 20.4 ▶ PUFI mark and statements

FIGURE 20.5 ▶ Product inspection stamp

FIGURE 20.6 ▶ Grade A stamp

▶ INSPECTION AND GRADING OF FISH AND SHELLFISH

INSPECTION

Unlike mandatory meat and poultry inspections, fish and shellfish inspections are voluntary. They are performed in a fee-for-service program supervised by the United States Department of Commerce (USDC).

Type 1 inspection services cover plant, product and processing methods from the raw material to the final product. The "Packed Under Federal Inspection" (PUFI) mark or statement shown in Figure 20.4 can be used on product labels processed under Type 1 inspection services. It signifies that the product is safe and wholesome, is properly labeled, has reasonably good flavor and odor, and was produced under inspection in an official establishment.

Type 2 inspection services are usually performed in a warehouse, processing plant or cold storage facility on specific product lots. See Figure 20.5. A lot inspection determines whether the product complies with purchase agreement criteria (usually defined in a spec sheet) such as condition, weight, labeling and packaging integrity.

Type 3 inspection services are for sanitation only. Fishing vessels or plants that meet the requirements are recognized as official establishments and are included in the *USDC Approved List of Fish Establishments and Products*. The list is available to governmental and institutional purchasing agents as well as to retail and restaurant buyers.

GRADING

Only fish processed under Type 1 inspection services are eligible for grading. Each type of fish has its own grading criteria, but because of the great variety of fish and shellfish, the USDC has been able to set grading criteria for only the most common types.

The grades assigned to fish are A, B or C. Grade A products are top quality and must have good flavor and odor and be practically free of physical blemishes or defects. The great majority of fresh and frozen fish and shellfish consumed in restaurants is Grade A. See Figure 20.6. Grade B indicates good quality; Grade C indicates fairly good quality. Grade B and C products are most often canned or processed.

▶ PURCHASING AND STORING FISH AND SHELLFISH

DETERMINING FRESHNESS

Because fish and shellfish are highly perishable, an inspection stamp does not necessarily ensure top quality. A few hours at the wrong temperature or a couple of days in the refrigerator can turn high-quality fish or shellfish into garbage. It is important that you be able to determine for yourself the freshness and quality of the fish and shellfish you purchase or use. Freshness should be checked before purchasing and again just before cooking.

Freshness can be determined by the following criteria:

1 *Smell*—This is by far the easiest way to determine freshness. Fresh fish should have a slight sea smell or no odor at all. Any off-odors or ammonia odors are a sure sign of aged or improperly handled fish.

2 *Eyes*—The eyes should be clear and full. Sunken eyes mean that the fish is drying out and is probably not fresh.

3 *Gills*—The gills should be intact and bright red. Brown gills are a sign of age.

4 *Texture*—Generally, the flesh of fresh fish should be firm. Mushy flesh or flesh that does not spring back when pressed with a finger is a sign of poor quality or age.

5 *Fins and scales*—Fins and scales should be moist and full without excessive drying on the outer edges. Dry fins or scales are a sign of age; damaged fins or scales may be a sign of mishandling.

6 *Appearance*—Fish cuts should be moist and glistening, without bruises or dark spots. Edges should not be brown or dry.

7 *Movement*—Shellfish should be purchased live and should show movement. Lobsters and other crustaceans should be active. Clams, mussels and oysters that are partially opened should snap shut when tapped with a finger. (Exceptions are geoduck, razor and steamer clams whose siphons protrude, preventing the shell from closing completely.) Ones that do not close are dead and should not be used. Avoid mollusks with broken shells or heavy shells that might be filled with mud or sand.

PURCHASING FISH AND SHELLFISH

Fish are available from wholesalers in a variety of market forms:

▸ **Whole** or **round**—as caught, intact.

▸ **Drawn**—viscera (internal organs) are removed; most whole fish are purchased this way.

▸ **Dressed**—viscera, gills, fins and scales are removed.

▸ **Pan-dressed**—viscera and gills are removed; fish is scaled and fins and tail are trimmed. The head is usually removed, although small fish, such as trout, may be pan-dressed with the head still attached. Pan-dressed fish are then pan-fried.

▸ **Butterflied**—a pan-dressed fish, boned and opened flat like a book. The two sides remain attached by the back or belly skin.

▸ **Fillet**—the side of a fish removed intact, boneless or semi-boneless, with or without skin.

▸ **Steak**—a cross-section slice, with a small section of backbone attached; usually prepared from large round fish.

▸ **Wheel or center-cut**—used for swordfish and sharks, which are cut into large boneless pieces from which steaks are then cut.

You should purchase fish in the market forms most practical for your operation. Although fish fabrication is a relatively simple chore requiring little specialized equipment, before you decide to cut your own fish, you should consider the following:

1 The food service operation's ability to utilize the bones and trim that cutting whole fish produces

2 The employees' ability to fabricate fillets, steaks or portions as needed

3 The storage facilities

4 The product's intended use

Most shellfish can be purchased live in the shell, shucked (the meat removed from the shell) or processed. Both live and shucked shellfish are usually purchased by counts (that is, the number per volume). For example, standard live Eastern oysters are packed 200–250 (the count) per bushel (the unit of volume); standard Eastern oyster meats are packed 350 per gallon. Crustaceans are sometimes packed by size based on the number of pieces per pound; for example, crab legs or shrimp are often sold in counts per pound. Crustaceans are also sold either by grades based on size (whole crabs) or by weight (lobsters).

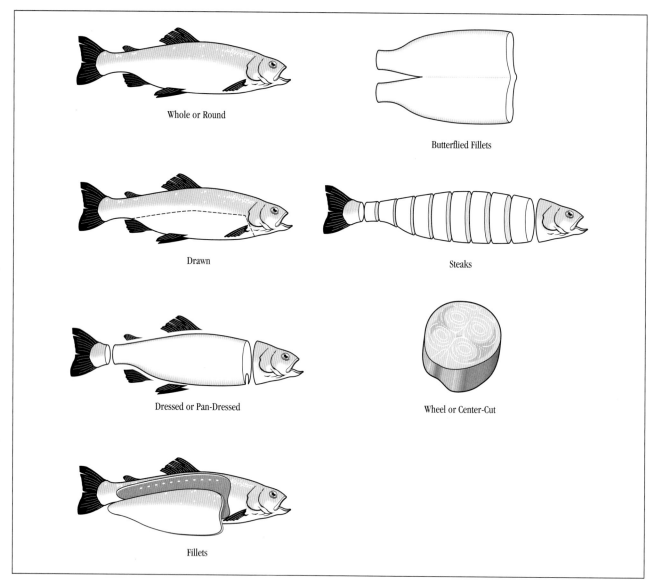

Whole or Round

Butterflied Fillets

Drawn

Steaks

Dressed or Pan-Dressed

Wheel or Center-Cut

Fillets

FIGURE 20.7 ▶ Market forms

STORING FISH AND SHELLFISH

The most important concern when storing fish and shellfish is temperature. All fresh fish should be stored at temperatures between 30°F and 34°F (−1°C to 1°C). Fish stored in a refrigerator at 40°F (4°C) will have approximately half the shelf life of fish stored at 32°F (0°C).

Most fish are shipped on ice and should be stored on ice in the refrigerator as soon as possible after receipt. Whole fish should be layered directly in crushed or shaved ice in a perforated pan so that the melted ice water drains away. If crushed or shaved ice is not available, cubed ice may be used provided it is put in plastic bags and gently placed on top of the fish to prevent bruising and denting. Fabricated and portioned fish may be wrapped in moisture-proof packaging before icing to prevent the ice and water from damaging the exposed flesh. Fish stored on ice should be drained and re-iced daily.

Fresh scallops, fish fillets that are purchased in plastic trays and oyster and clam meats should be set on or packed in ice. Do not let the scallops, fillets or meats come in direct contact with the ice.

Clams, mussels and oysters should be stored at 40°F (4°C), at high humidity and left in the boxes or net bags in which they were shipped. Under ideal con-

Whole fish properly stored in a perforated pan and covered with crushed ice.

ditions, shellfish can be kept alive for up to one week. Never store live shellfish in plastic bags and do not ice them.

If a saltwater tank is not available, live lobsters, crabs and other crustaceans should be kept in boxes with seaweed or damp newspaper to keep them moist. Most crustaceans circulate salt water over their gills; icing them or placing them in fresh water will kill them. Lobsters and crabs will live for several days under ideal conditions.

Like most frozen foods, frozen fish should be kept at temperatures of 0°F (−18°C) or colder. Colder temperatures greatly increase shelf life. Frozen fish should be thawed in the refrigerator; once thawed, they should be treated like fresh fish.

► FABRICATING PROCEDURES

As discussed, fish and shellfish can be purchased in many forms. Here we demonstrate several procedures for cutting, cleaning and otherwise fabricating or preparing fish and shellfish for cooking and serving.

► PROCEDURE FOR SCALING FISH

This procedure is used to remove the scales from fish that will be cooked with the skin on.

Place the fish on a work surface or in a large sink. Grip the fish by the tail and, working from the tail toward the head, scrape the scales off with a fish scaler or the back of a knife. Be careful not to damage the flesh by pushing too hard. Turn the fish over and remove the scales from the other side. Rinse the fish under cool water.

► PROCEDURE FOR PAN-DRESSING FLATFISH

1 Place the scaled fish on a cutting board and remove the head by making a V-shaped cut around it with a chef's knife. Pull the head away and remove the viscera.

2 Rinse the fish under cold water, removing all traces of blood and viscera from the cavity.

3 Using a pair of kitchen shears, trim off the tail and all of the fins.

▶ PROCEDURE FOR FILLETING ROUND FISH

Round fish produce two fillets, one from either side.

2 Turn the knife toward the tail; using smooth strokes, cut from head to tail, parallel to the backbone. The knife should bump against the backbone so that no flesh is wasted; you will feel the knife cutting through the small pin bones. Cut the fillet completely free from the bones. Repeat on the other side.

1 Using a chef's knife, cut down to the backbone just behind the gills. Do not remove the head.

3 Trim the rib bones from the fillet with a flexible boning knife.

4 The finished fillet.

▶ PROCEDURE FOR FILLETING FLATFISH

Flatfish produce four fillets: two large bilateral fillets from the top and two smaller bilateral fillets from the bottom. If the fish fillets are going to be cooked with the skin on, the fish should be scaled before cooking (it is easier to scale the fish before it is filleted). If the skin is going to be removed before cooking, it is not necessary to scale the fish.

1 With the dark side of the fish facing up, cut along the backbone from head to tail with the tip of a flexible boning knife.

2 Turn the knife and, using smooth strokes, cut between the flesh and the rib bones, keeping the flexible blade against the bone. Cut the fillet completely free from the fish. Remove the second fillet, following the same procedure.

3 Turn the fish over and remove the fillets from the bottom half of the fish, following the same procedure.

▶ PROCEDURE FOR SKINNING DOVER SOLE

Dover sole is unique in that its skin can be pulled from the whole fish with a simple procedure. The flesh of other small flatfish such as flounder, petrale sole and other types of domestic sole is more delicate; pulling the skin away from the whole fish could damage the flesh. These fish should be skinned after they are filleted.

Make a shallow cut in the flesh perpendicular to the length of the fish, just in front of the tail and with the knife angled toward the head of the fish. Using a clean towel, grip the skin and pull it toward the head of the fish. The skin should come off cleanly, in one piece, leaving the flesh intact.

▶ PROCEDURE FOR SKINNING FISH FILLETS

Here we use a salmon fillet to demonstrate the procedure for skinning fish fillets. Use the same procedure to skin all types of fish fillets.

Place the fillet on a cutting board with the skin side down. Starting at the tail, use a meat slicer or a chef's knife to cut between the flesh and skin. Angle the knife down toward the skin, grip the skin tightly with one hand and use a sawing motion to cut the skin cleanly away from the flesh.

▶ PROCEDURE FOR PULLING PIN BONES FROM SALMON FILLETS

Round fish fillets contain a row of intramuscular bones running the length of the fillet. Known as pin bones, they are usually cut out with a knife to produce boneless fillets. In the case of salmon, they can be removed with salmon tweezers or small needle-nose pliers.

Place the fillet (either skinless or not) on the cutting board, skin side down. Starting at the front or head end of the fillet, use your fingertips to locate the bones and use the pliers to pull them out one by one.

▶ PROCEDURE FOR CUTTING TRANCHES

A **tranche** is a slice cut from fillets of large flat or round fish. Usually cut on an angle, tranches look large and increase plate coverage.

Place the fillet on the cutting board, skin side down. Using a slicer or chef's knife, cut slices of the desired weight. The tranche can be cut to the desired size by adjusting the angle of the knife. The greater the angle, the greater the surface area of the tranche.

▶ PROCEDURE FOR CUTTING STEAKS FROM SALMON AND SIMILARLY SIZED ROUND FISH

Steaks are produced from salmon and similarly sized round fish by simply making crosscuts of the whole fish. First scale, gut and remove the fins from the fish. Then:

Using a chef's knife, cut through the fish, slicing steaks of the desired thickness. The steaks will contain some bones that are not necessarily removed.

▶ PROCEDURE FOR PEELING AND DEVEINING SHRIMP

Peeling and deveining shrimp is a simple procedure done in most commercial kitchens. The tail portion of the shell is often left on the peeled shrimp to give it an attractive appearance or make it easier to eat. This procedure can be used on both cooked and uncooked shrimp.

1 Grip the shrimp's tail between your thumb and forefinger. Use your other thumb and forefinger to grip the legs and the edge of the shell.

2 Pull the legs and shell away from the flesh, leaving the tail and first joint of the shell in place if desired.

3 Place the shrimp on a cutting board and use a paring knife to make a shallow cut down the back of the shrimp, exposing the digestive tract or "vein."

4 Pull out the vein while rinsing the shrimp under cold water.

▶ PROCEDURE FOR BUTTERFLYING SHRIMP

Butterflying raw shrimp improves their appearance and increases their surface area for even cooking. To butterfly shrimp, first peel them using the procedure outlined earlier. Then:

Instead of making a shallow cut to expose the vein, make a deeper cut that nearly slices the shrimp into two bilateral halves. Pull out the vein while rinsing the shrimp under cold water.

▶ PROCEDURE FOR PREPARING LIVE LOBSTERS FOR BROILING

A whole lobster can be cooked by plunging it into boiling water or court bouillon. If the lobster is to be broiled, it must be split lengthwise before cooking.

1 Place the live lobster on its back on a cutting board and pierce its head with the point of a chef's knife. Then, in one smooth stroke, bring the knife down and cut through the body and tail without splitting it completely in half.

2 Use your hands to crack the lobster's back so that it lies flat. Crack the claws with the back of a chef's knife.

3 Cut through the tail and curl each half of the tail to the side. Remove and discard the stomach. The tomalley (the olive-green liver) and, if present, the coral (the roe) can be removed and saved for a sauce or other preparation.

▶ PROCEDURE FOR PREPARING LIVE LOBSTERS FOR SAUTÉING

A whole lobster may also be cut into smaller pieces for sautéing or other preparations.

1 Using the point of a chef's knife, pierce the lobster's head.

2 Cut off the claws and arms.

3 Cut the tail into cross-sections.

4 Split the head and thorax in half. The tomalley and coral (if present) can be removed and saved for further use. The head and legs may be added to the recipe for flavor, but there is very little meat in them and they are typically discarded.

5 Crack the claws with a firm blow, using the back of a chef's knife.

▶ PROCEDURE FOR REMOVING COOKED LOBSTER MEAT
   FROM THE SHELL

Many recipes call for cooked lobster meat. Cook the lobster by plunging it into a boiling court bouillon and simmering for 6–8 minutes per pound. Remove the lobster and allow it to cool until it can be easily handled. Then:

1 Pull the claws and large legs away from the body. Break the claw away from the leg. Split the legs with a chef's knife and remove the meat, using your fingers or a pick.

2 Carefully crack the claw with a mallet or the back of a chef's knife without damaging the meat. Pull out the claw meat in one piece.

3 Pull the lobster's tail away from its body and use kitchen shears to trim away the soft membrane on the underside of the tail.

4 Pull the meat out of the shell in one piece.

▶ PROCEDURE FOR OPENING CLAMS

Opening raw clams efficiently requires practice. Like all mollusks, clams should be cleaned under cold running water with a brush to remove all mud, silt and sand that may be stuck to their shells. A knife may be more easily inserted into a clam if the clam is washed and allowed to relax in the refrigerator for at least one hour before it is opened.

1 Hold the clam firmly in a folded towel in the palm of your hand; the notch in the edge of the shell should be toward your thumb. With the fingers of the same hand, squeeze and pull the blade of the clam knife between the clamshells. Do not push on the knife handle with your other hand; you will not be able to control the knife if it slips and you can cut yourself.

2 Pull the knife between the shells until it cuts the muscle. Twist the knife to pry the shells apart. Slide the knife tip along the top shell and cut through the muscle. Twist the top shell, breaking it free at the hinge; discard it.

3 Use the knife tip to release the clam from the bottom shell.

▶ PROCEDURE FOR OPENING OYSTERS

1 Clean the oyster by brushing it under running water.

2 Hold the cleaned oyster firmly in a folded towel in the palm of your hand. Insert the tip of an oyster knife in the hinge and use a twisting motion to pop the hinge apart. Do not use too much forward pressure on the knife; it can slip and you could stab yourself.

3 Slide the knife along the top of the shell to release the oyster from the shell. Discard the top shell.

4 Use the knife tip to release the oyster from the bottom shell.

▶ PROCEDURE FOR CLEANING AND DEBEARDING MUSSELS

Mussels are not normally eaten raw. Before cooking, a clump of dark threads called the beard must be removed. Because this could kill the mussel, cleaning and debearding must be done as close to cooking time as possible.

1 Clean the mussel with a brush under cold running water to remove sand and grit.

2 Pull the beard away from the mussel with your fingers or a small pair of pliers.

▶ APPLYING VARIOUS COOKING METHODS

Fish and shellfish can be prepared by the dry-heat cooking methods of broiling and grilling, roasting (baking), sautéing, pan-frying and deep-frying, as well as the moist-heat cooking methods of steaming, poaching and simmering.

DETERMINING DONENESS

Unlike most meats and poultry, nearly all fish and shellfish are inherently tender and should be cooked just until done. Indeed, overcooking is the most common mistake made when preparing fish and shellfish. The Canadian Department of Fisheries recommends that all fish be cooked 10 minutes for every inch (2.5 centimeters) of thickness, regardless of cooking method. Although this may be a good general policy, variables such as the type and the form of fish and the exact cooking method used suggest that one or more of the following methods of determining doneness are more appropriate for professional food service operations:

1 *Translucent flesh becomes opaque*—The raw flesh of most fish and shellfish appears somewhat translucent. As the proteins coagulate during cooking, the flesh becomes opaque.

2 *Flesh becomes firm*—The flesh of most fish and shellfish firms as it cooks. Doneness can be tested by judging the resistance of the flesh when pressed with a finger. Raw or undercooked fish or shellfish will be mushy and soft. As it cooks, the flesh offers more resistance and springs back quickly.

3 *Flesh separates from the bones easily*—The flesh of raw fish remains firmly attached to the bones. As the fish cooks, the flesh and bones separate easily.

4 *Flesh begins to flake*—Fish flesh consists of short muscle fibers separated by thin connective tissue. As the fish cooks, the connective tissue breaks down and the groups of muscle fibers begin to flake, that is, separate from one another. Fish is done when the flesh begins to flake. If the flesh flakes easily, the fish will be overdone and dry.

Remember, fish and shellfish are subject to carryover cooking. Because they cook quickly and at low temperatures, it is better to undercook fish and shellfish and allow carryover cooking or residual heat to finish the cooking process.

DRY-HEAT COOKING METHODS

Dry-heat cooking methods are those that do not require additional moisture at any time during the cooking process. The dry-heat cooking methods used with fish and shellfish are broiling and grilling, roasting (usually referred to as baking when used with fish and shellfish), sautéing, pan-frying and deep-frying.

BROILING AND GRILLING

After brushing with oil or butter, fish can be grilled directly on the grate or placed on a heated platter under the broiler. Broiled or grilled fish should have a lightly charred surface and a slightly smoky flavor as a result of the intense radiant heat of the broiler or grill. The interior should be moist and juicy. Broiled or grilled shellfish meat should be moist and tender with only slight coloration from the grill or broiler.

Selecting Fish and Shellfish to Broil or Grill

Nearly all types of fish and shellfish can be successfully broiled or grilled. Salmon, trout, swordfish and other oily fish are especially well suited to grilling, as are lean fish such as bass and snapper. Fillets of lean flatfish with delicate textures, such as flounder and sole, are better broiled. They should be placed on a preheated broiling (sizzler) platter before being placed under the broiler.

Oysters and clams are often broiled on the half shell with flavored butters, bread crumbs or other garnishes and served sizzling hot. Squid can be stuffed, secured with a toothpick and broiled or grilled. Brushed with butter, split lobsters, king crabs and snow crabs are often broiled or grilled. Whole lobsters can be split and broiled or grilled, or their tails can be removed, split and cooked separately. Large crab legs can also be split and broiled or grilled. Shrimp and scallops are often broiled in flavored butters or grilled on skewers for easy handling.

Seasoning Fish and Shellfish to Be Broiled or Grilled

All fish should be brushed lightly with butter or oil before being placed on the grill or under the broiler. The butter or oil prevents sticking and helps leaner fish retain moisture. For most fish, a simple seasoning of salt and pepper suffices. But most fish do respond well to marinades, especially those made with white wine and lemon juice. Because most fish are delicately flavored, they should be marinated for only a brief time. (Even marinated fish should be brushed with butter or oil before cooking.) Herbs should be avoided because they will burn from the intense heat of the broiler or grill.

Clams, oysters and other shellfish that are stuffed or cooked with butters, vegetables, bacon or other accompaniments or garnishes gain flavor from these ingredients. Be careful, however, not to overpower the delicate flavors of the shellfish by adding too many strong flavorings.

Lemon wedges are the traditional accompaniment to broiled or grilled fish and shellfish. But they can be served with sauces made separately. Butter sauces such as a beurre blanc are popular, as their richness complements the lean fish. Vegetable coulis are a good choice for a healthier, lower-fat accompaniment. Additional sauce suggestions are found in Table 11.5. If the item is cooked on a broiler platter with a seasoned butter, it is often served with that butter.

Almost any side dish goes well with broiled or grilled fish or shellfish. Fried or boiled potatoes, pasta and rice are all good choices. Grilled vegetables are a natural choice.

▶ PROCEDURE FOR BROILING OR GRILLING FISH AND SHELLFISH

All fish is delicate and must be carefully handled to achieve an attractive finished product. When broiling whole fish or fillets with their skin still on, score the skin by making several diagonal slashes approximately ¼ inch (6 millimeters) deep at even intervals. This prevents the fish from curling during cooking, promotes even cooking and creates a more attractive finished product. Be especially careful not to overcook the item. It should be served as hot as possible as soon as it is removed from the broiler or grill.

1 Heat the broiler or grill.
2 Use a wire brush to remove any charred or burnt particles that may be stuck to the broiler or grill grate. The grate can be wiped with a lightly oiled towel to remove any remaining particles and help season it.
3 Prepare the item to be broiled or grilled. For example, cut the fish into steaks or tranches of even thickness; split the lobster; peel and/or skewer the shrimp. Season or marinate the item as desired. Brush the item with oil or butter.
4 Place the item on a grill, presentation side down. If using a broiler, place the item directly on the grate or on a preheated broiler platter. Tender fish are usually broiled presentation side up on a broiler platter.
5 If practical, turn the item to produce the attractive crosshatch marks associated with grilling that are discussed in Chapter 10, Principles of Cooking. Items less than ½ inch (12 millimeters) thick cooked on a preheated broiler platter do not have to be turned over.
6 Cook the item to the desired doneness and serve immediately.

RECIPE 20.1

1 Scoring the fish skin.

Yield: 1 Serving   **Method:** Broiling

Black sea bass fillet, skin on, approx. 8 oz. (225 g)	1	1
Salt and pepper	TT	TT
Whole butter, melted	as needed	as needed
Leek, julienne	1	1
Lemon juice	2 tsp.	10 ml
Herb butter (page 223)	2 slices	2 slices

1 Score the skin of the fillet with three diagonal cuts approximately ¼ inch (6 millimeters) deep.
2 Season the fillet with salt and pepper and brush with melted butter.

3 Place the fillet on a preheated broiler platter, skin side up, and place under the broiler.

4 Blanch the leek in boiling water until nearly tender.

5 Drain the leek and sauté in 1 tablespoon (15 milliliters) of whole butter until tender. Add the lemon juice; season with salt and pepper.

6 Remove the fish from the broiler when done. Top with the herb butter and serve on a bed of sautéed leeks.

Approximate values per serving: **Calories** 260, **Total fat** 15 g, **Saturated fat** 8 g, **Cholesterol** 80 mg, **Sodium** 790 mg, **Total carbohydrates** 11 g, **Protein** 21 g, **Vitamin A** 15%, **Vitamin C** 15%

BAKING

The terms *baking* and *roasting* are used interchangeably when applied to fish and shellfish. One disadvantage of baking fish is that the short baking time does not allow the surface of the fish to caramelize. To help correct this problem, fish can be browned in a sauté pan with a small amount of oil to achieve the added flavor and appearance of a browned surface, and then finished in an oven.

Selecting Fish and Shellfish to Bake

Fatty fish produce the best baked fish. Fish fillets and steaks are the best market forms to bake, as they cook quickly and evenly and are easily portioned. Although lean fish can be baked, it tends to become dry, and must be basted often.

Seasoning Fish and Shellfish to Be Baked

The most popular seasonings for baked fish are lemon, butter, salt and pepper. Fish can also be marinated before baking for added flavor. But baked fish usually depend on the accompanying sauce for much of their flavor.

Shellfish are often stuffed or mixed with other ingredients before baking. For example, raw oysters on the half shell can be topped with spinach, watercress and Pernod (oysters Rockefeller) and baked. Shrimp are often butterflied, stuffed and baked; lobsters are split, stuffed and baked. Many food service operations remove clams from their shells; mix them with bread crumbs, seasonings or other ingredients; refill the shells and bake the mixture.

Accompaniments to Baked Fish and Shellfish

Baked fish is often served with a flavorful sauce such as a creole sauce (page 218) or a beurre blanc (page 222). Additional sauce suggestions are found in Table 11.5. Almost any type of rice, pasta or potato is a good accompaniment, as is any variety of sautéed vegetable.

▶ PROCEDURE FOR BAKING FISH AND SHELLFISH

1 Portion the fish or shellfish and arrange on a well-oiled or buttered pan, presentation side up.

2 Season as desired and brush the surface of the fish or shellfish generously with melted butter; add garnishes or flavorings as desired or directed in the recipe.

3 Place the pan in a preheated oven at approximately 400°F (200°C).

4 Baste periodically during the cooking process (more often if the fish is lean). Remove from the oven when the fish is slightly underdone.

2 Placing the fish on a broiler platter, under the broiler.

3 Serving the fish on a bed of sautéed leeks.

RECIPE 20.2   BAKED RED SNAPPER

Yield: 4 Servings   **Method:** Baking

Red snapper fillets, 8 oz. (250 g) each	4	4
Salt and white pepper	TT	TT
Whole butter, melted	2 oz.	60 g
Mint leaves, chopped	1 Tbsp.	15 ml
Garlic, minced	1 tsp.	5 ml
Tomato concassée	4 oz.	120 g
White wine	2 fl. oz.	60 ml
Lemon juice	2 fl. oz.	60 ml

1 Brushing the fillets with butter.

1 Place the snapper on a buttered baking pan. Season the fillets with salt and white pepper; brush with butter.

2 Combine the mint, garlic and tomato concassée, and spoon on top of each portion of the fish.

3 Add the white wine and lemon juice to the pan.

4 Bake at 400°F (200°C), basting once halfway through the cooking process, until done, approximately 15 minutes.

Approximate values per serving: **Calories** 600, **Total fat** 16 g, **Saturated fat** 8 g, **Cholesterol** 140 mg, **Sodium** 850 mg, **Total carbohydrates** 55 g, **Protein** 60 g, **Vitamin A** 25%, **Vitamin C** 35%

2 Topping each portion with mint and tomato concassée.

SAUTÉING

Sautéing is a very popular cooking method for fish and shellfish. It lightly caramelizes the food's surface, giving it additional flavor. Typically, other ingredients such as garlic, onions, vegetables, wine and lemon juice are added to the fond to make a sauce.

Selecting Fish and Shellfish to Sauté

Both fatty and lean fish may be sautéed. Flatfish are sometimes dressed and sautéed whole, as are small round fish such as trout. Larger fish such as salmon can be cut into steaks or filleted and cut into tranches. The portions should be relatively uniform in size and thickness and fairly thin to promote even cooking. Although clams, mussels and oysters are not often sautéed, scallops and crustaceans are popular sauté items.

Seasoning Fish and Shellfish to Be Sautéed

Many types of fish—especially sole, flounder and other delicate, lean fish fillets—are often dredged in plain or seasoned flour before sautéing. Seasoned butter is used to sauté some items, such as scampi-style shrimp. These items derive their flavor from the butter; additional seasonings should not be necessary.

3 The finished fish.

Cooking Temperatures

The sauté pan and cooking fat must be hot before the fish or shellfish are added. Do not add too much fish or shellfish to the pan at one time, or the pan and fat will cool, letting the foods simmer in their own juices. Thin slices and small pieces of fish and shellfish require a short cooking time, so use high temperatures in order to caramelize their surfaces without overcooking. Large, thick pieces of fish or shellfish being cooked in the shell may require slightly lower cooking temperatures to ensure that they are cooked without overbrowning their surfaces.

Accompaniments to Sautéed Fish and Shellfish

Sautéed fish and shellfish are nearly always served with a sauce made directly in the sauté pan. This sauce may be as simple as browned butter (beurre noisette) or a complicated sauce flavored with the fond. In some cases, seasoned butter is used to sauté the fish or shellfish and the butter is then served with the main item. See Table 11.5 for additional sauce suggestions.

Mildly flavored rice and pasta are good choices to serve with sautéed fish or shellfish.

▶ PROCEDURE FOR SAUTÉING FISH AND SHELLFISH

1 Cut or portion the fish or shellfish.

2 Season the item and dredge in seasoned flour if desired.

3 Heat a suitable sauté pan over moderate heat; add enough oil or clarified butter to cover the bottom to a depth of about ⅛ inch (3 millimeters).

4 Add the fish or shellfish to the pan (fish should be placed presentation side down); cook until done, turning once halfway through the cooking process. Add other foods as called for in the recipe.

5 Remove the fish or shellfish. If a sauce is to be made in the sauté pan, follow the procedures discussed in Chapter 18, Poultry.

SAUTÉED HALIBUT WITH THREE-COLOR PEPPERS AND SPANISH OLIVES

RECIPE 20.3

Yield: 4 Servings   **Method:** Sautéing

Halibut fillets, 6 oz. (170 g) each	4	4
Salt and pepper	TT	TT
Olive oil	2 fl. oz.	60 ml
Onions, sliced	3 oz.	90 g
Garlic, minced	2 tsp.	10 ml
Green bell pepper, julienne	3 oz.	90 g
Red bell pepper, julienne	3 oz.	90 g
Yellow bell pepper, julienne	3 oz.	90 g
Tomato concassée	8 oz.	250 g
Spanish olives, pitted and quartered	2 oz.	60 g
Fresh thyme, chopped	2 tsp.	10 ml
Lemon juice	2 fl. oz.	60 ml
Fish stock	2 fl. oz.	60 ml

1 Season the fillets with salt and pepper.

2 Heat a sauté pan and add the olive oil.

3 Sauté the halibut, turning once. Remove and reserve in a warm place.

4 Add the onions and garlic to the same pan and sauté for approximately 1 minute. Add the bell peppers and sauté for 1 to 2 minutes more.

5 Add the tomato concassée, olives and thyme; sauté briefly.

Continued

1 Sautéing the halibut fillets.

2 Sautéing the onions, garlic and peppers.

3 Adding the fish stock.

4 Returning the fish to the pan to reheat.

6 Add the lemon juice and deglaze the pan. Add the fish stock, simmer for 2 minutes to blend the flavors and adjust the seasonings.

7 Return the fish to the pan to reheat. Serve each fish fillet on a bed of vegetables with sauce and an appropriate garnish.

Approximate values per serving: **Calories** 420, **Total fat** 21 g, **Saturated fat** 3 g, **Cholesterol** 70 mg, **Sodium** 870 mg, **Total carbohydrates** 10 g, **Protein** 47 g, **Vitamin A** 15%, **Vitamin C** 110%

PAN-FRYING

Pan-frying is very similar to sautéing, but it uses more fat to cook the main item. Pan-fried fish is always coated with flour, batter or breading to help seal the surface and prevent the flesh from coming in direct contact with the cooking fat. Properly prepared pan-fried fish and shellfish should be moist and tender with a crisp surface. If battered or breaded, the coating should be intact with no breaks.

Selecting Fish and Shellfish to Pan-Fry
Both fatty and lean fish may be pan-fried. Trout and other small fish are ideal for pan-frying, as are portioned fillets of lean fish such as halibut. Pan-fried fish and shellfish should be uniform in size and relatively thin so that they cook quickly and evenly.

Seasoning Fish and Shellfish to Be Pan-Fried
Although fish and shellfish can be marinated or seasoned directly, it is more common to season the flour, batter or breading that will coat them. Batters, for example, can contain cheese, and breadings can contain nuts and other ingredients to add different flavors to the fish or shellfish. Review the battering and breading procedures discussed in Chapter 9, Mise en Place. Additional seasonings come from sauces and other accompaniments served with the pan-fried fish or shellfish.

Cooking Temperatures
The fat should always be hot before the fish or shellfish are added. Breaded or battered fish fillets cook very quickly, and the fat should be hot enough to brown the coating without overcooking the interior. Whole pan-fried fish take longer to cook and therefore require a slightly lower cooking temperature so that the surface does not become too dark before the interior is cooked.

Accompaniments to Pan-Fried Fish and Shellfish
Lemon wedges are the classic accompaniment to pan-fried fish and shellfish. Sauces that accompany pan-fried items are made separately. Mayonnaise-based sauces such as tartar sauce (page 770) and rémoulade sauce are especially popular; rich wine-based sauces should be avoided. Vegetable coulis, such as tomato, also complement many pan-fried items. Additional sauce suggestions are found in Table 11.5.

▶ PROCEDURE FOR PAN-FRYING FISH AND SHELLFISH

1 Heat enough clarified butter or oil in a heavy sauté pan so that it will come one-third to halfway up the side of the item. The fat should be at a temperature between 325°F and 350°F (163°C and 177°C).

2 Add the floured, breaded or battered item to the pan, being careful not to splash the hot fat. Cook until done, turning once halfway through the cooking process.

3 Remove the food and drain on absorbent paper.

4 Serve it promptly with an appropriate sauce.

BLUE CRAB CAKES

RECIPE 20.4

Yield: 15 Cakes, 2 oz. (60 g) each   **Method:** Pan-Frying

Blue crab meat	1 lb.	450 g
Heavy cream	6 fl. oz.	180 ml
Red bell pepper, small dice	2 oz.	60 g
Green bell pepper, small dice	2 oz.	60 g
Clarified butter	as needed	as needed
Green onions, sliced	1 bunch	1 bunch
Fresh bread crumbs	6 oz.	180 g
Salt and pepper	TT	TT
Dijon mustard	1 Tbsp.	15 ml
Worcestershire sauce	TT	TT
Tabasco sauce	TT	TT
Egg, slightly beaten	1	1

1 Mixing all ingredients for the crab cakes.

1 Carefully pick through the crab meat, removing any pieces of shell. Keep the lumps of crab meat as large as possible.

2 Place the cream in a saucepan and bring to a boil. Reduce by approximately one-half. Chill the cream well.

3 Sauté the bell peppers in a small amount of clarified butter until tender.

4 Combine the crab meat, reduced cream, bell peppers, green onions and approximately 3 ounces (90 grams) of the bread crumbs along with the salt, pepper, Dijon mustard, Worcestershire sauce, Tabasco sauce and egg. Mix to combine all ingredients, trying to keep the lumps of crab meat intact.

5 Using a mold, form the crab mixture into cakes of the desired size.

6 Place the remaining bread crumbs in an appropriately sized hotel pan. Place the crab cakes, a few at a time, in the hotel pan and cover with the bread crumbs. To help them adhere, press the crumbs lightly into the cakes.

7 Heat a sauté pan over moderate heat and add enough clarified butter to cover the bottom approximately ¼ inch (6 millimeters) deep.

8 Add the crab cakes to the pan and cook until done, turning once when the first side is nicely browned. Remove and drain on absorbent paper.

Approximate values per 2-oz. (60-g) cake serving: **Calories** 130, **Total fat** 6 g, **Saturated fat** 3.5 g, **Cholesterol** 60 mg, **Sodium** 650 mg, **Total carbohydrates** 9 g, **Protein** 10 g, **Vitamin C** 15%

2 Forming the crab cakes.

3 Pan-frying the crab cakes.

DEEP-FRYING

Deep-frying is the process of cooking foods by submerging them in hot fat. Typically, fish or shellfish are breaded or battered before deep-frying. Alternatively, they can be formed into croquettes or fritters. Properly deep-fried fish and shellfish should be moist and tender, not greasy or tough. Their coating should be crispy and golden brown.

Selecting Fish and Shellfish to Deep-Fry

Whole small fish and fillets of lean fish such as catfish or halibut are excellent for deep-frying. The fillets should be of uniform size and relatively thin so that they cook quickly and evenly. Fatty fish, such as salmon, are ideal for croquettes. Peeled shrimp and shucked mollusks, especially clams and oysters, can be breaded, battered or formed into fritters and deep-fried. Deep-fried breaded or battered sliced squid or octopus served with a dipping sauce makes an excellent hors d'oeuvre.

Seasoning Fish and Shellfish to Be Deep-Fried

Typically, seasonings used for deep-fried fish or shellfish are added to the breading or batter, although salt and pepper should be added after frying. Additional flavors come from sauces or accompaniments.

Accompaniments to Deep-Fried Fish and Shellfish

As with pan-fried fish and shellfish, lemon wedges and mayonnaise-based sauces such as tartar sauce and rémoulade sauce are popular accompaniments to deep-fried fish and shellfish. Spicy tomato- or soy-based dipping sauces are also excellent choices. Traditional English fish and chips is served with malt vinegar.

▶ PROCEDURE FOR DEEP-FRYING FISH AND SHELLFISH

1 Shuck, peel, cut, trim or otherwise prepare the fish or shellfish to be deep-fried. Season, bread or batter it, as desired.

2 Heat the fat to the desired temperature, usually around 350°F (177°C). Breaded or battered fish or shellfish cook quickly and the fat must be hot enough to cook the food's interior without burning its surface.

3 Carefully place the food in the hot fat using either the basket method or swimming method.

4 Deep-fry the fish or shellfish until done. Doneness is usually determined by color, timing or sampling.

5 Remove the deep-fried food from the fat and hold it over the fryer, allowing the excess fat to drain off. Transfer the food to a hotel pan either lined with absorbent paper or fitted with a rack. Season with salt, if desired.

6 If the deep-fried fish or shellfish is to be held for later service, place it under a heat lamp.

DEEP-FRIED CATFISH FILLETS WITH TARTAR SAUCE

RECIPE 20.5

Yield: 8 Servings

Catfish fillets, cut into uniform-sized pieces	3 lb.	1.5 kg
Salt and pepper	TT	TT
Flour	as needed for breading	
Egg wash	as needed for breading	
White cornmeal	as needed for breading	
Tartar Sauce (page 770)	12 fl. oz.	360 ml

1 Flouring the seasoned fish fillets.

2 Passing the floured fillets through the egg wash.

3 Coating the fillets with white cornmeal.

4 Deep-frying the fillets using the basket method.

1 Season the fillets with salt and pepper.
2 Bread the fillets using the standard breading procedure described in Chapter 9, Mise en Place.
3 Using the basket method, deep-fry the fillets until done. Drain well and serve with the Tartar Sauce.

Approximate values per 8-oz. (240-g) serving: **Calories** 600, **Total fat** 46 g, **Saturated fat** 10 g, **Cholesterol** 160 mg, **Sodium** 910 mg, **Total carbohydrates** 16 g, **Protein** 31 g, **Iron** 15%

MOIST-HEAT COOKING METHODS

Fish and shellfish lend themselves well to moist-heat cooking methods, especially steaming, poaching and simmering. Steaming best preserves the food's natural flavors and cooks without adding fat. Poaching is also popular, especially for fish. Poached fish can be served hot or cold, whole or as steaks, fillets or portions. Boiling, which is actually simmering, is most often associated with crustaceans.

STEAMING

Steaming is a very natural way to cook fish and shellfish without adding fats. Fish are steamed by suspending them over a small amount of boiling liquid in a covered pan. The steam trapped in the pan gently cooks the food while preserving its natural flavors and most nutrients. The liquid used to steam fish and shellfish can be water or a court bouillon with herbs, spices, aromatics or wine added to infuse the item with additional flavors. Mussels and clams can be steamed by placing them directly in a pan, adding a small amount of wine or other liquid and covering them. Their shells will hold them above the liquid as they cook. Fish and shellfish can also be steamed by wrapping them in parchment paper together with herbs, vegetables, butters or sauces as accompaniments and baking them in a hot oven. This method of steaming is called **en papillote.**

Steamed fish and shellfish should be moist and tender. They should have clean and delicate flavors. Any accompaniments or sauces should complement the main item without masking its flavor. Fish and shellfish cooked en papillote should be served piping hot so that the aromatic steam trapped by the paper escapes as the paper is cut open tableside.

Selecting Fish and Shellfish to Steam

Mollusks (for example, clams and mussels), fatty fish (for example, salmon and sea bass) and lean fish (for example, sole) all produce good results when steamed. The portions should be of uniform thickness and no more than 1 inch (2.5 centimeters) thick to promote even cooking.

Seasoning Fish and Shellfish to Be Steamed

Steamed fish and shellfish rely heavily on their natural flavors and often require very little seasoning. Nevertheless, salt, pepper, herbs and spices can be applied directly to the raw food before steaming. Flavored liquids used to steam fish and shellfish will contribute additional flavors. If the liquid is served with the fish or shellfish as a broth or used to make a sauce to accompany the item, it is especially important that the liquid be well seasoned. Lemons, limes and other fruits or vegetables can also be cooked with the fish or shellfish to add flavors. Clams and mussels often do not require additional salt, as the liquor released when they open during cooking is sufficiently salty.

Accompaniments to Steamed Fish and Shellfish

Steamed fish and shellfish are popular partly because they are low in fat. In keeping with this perception, a low or nonfat sauce or a simple squeeze of lemon and steamed fresh vegetables are good accompaniments. If fat is not a concern, then an emulsified butter sauce such as beurre blanc (page 222) or hollandaise (page 219) may be a good choice. Table 11.5 lists several sauce suggestions.

Classic New England steamed clams are served with a portion of the steaming liquid; steamed mussels are served with a sauce that is created from the wine and other ingredients used to steam them.

▶ PROCEDURE FOR STEAMING FISH AND SHELLFISH

1 Portion the fish to an appropriate size. Clean the shellfish.

2 Prepare the cooking liquid. Add seasoning and flavoring ingredients as desired and bring to a boil.

3 Place the fish or shellfish in the steamer on a rack or in a perforated pan and cover tightly.

4 Steam the fish or shellfish until done.

5 Serve the fish or shellfish immediately with the steaming liquid or an appropriate sauce.

RECIPE 20.6

STEAMED SALMON WITH LEMON AND OLIVE OIL

Yield: 1 Serving   **Method:** Steaming

Lemon zest, blanched	1 Tbsp.	15 ml
Lemon juice	2 Tbsp.	30 ml
Salt and pepper	TT	TT
Virgin olive oil	2 Tbsp.	30 ml
White wine	8 fl. oz.	250 ml
Bay leaf	1	1
Leeks, chopped	2 oz.	60 g
Fresh thyme	1 sprig	1 sprig
Peppercorns, cracked	1 tsp.	5 ml
Salmon tranche or steak, approx. 6 oz. (180 g)	1	1

1 To make the dressing, combine the lemon zest, lemon juice, salt and pepper. Whisk in the olive oil.

2 Combine the wine, bay leaf, leeks, thyme and peppercorns in the bottom of a steamer.

3 Season the salmon with salt and pepper and place it in the steamer basket.

4 Cover the steamer and bring the liquid to a boil. Cook the fish until done, approximately 4 to 6 minutes.

5 Plate the salmon and spoon the dressing over it.

Approximate values per serving: **Calories** 620, **Total fat** 40 g, **Saturated fat** 6 g, **Cholesterol** 95 mg, **Sodium** 700 mg, **Total carbohydrates** 16 g, **Protein** 48 g, **Vitamin C** 50%

1 Placing the fish in the steamer.

2 Spooning the dressing over the fish.

RED SNAPPER EN PAPILLOTE

RECIPE 20.7

Yield: 6 Servings   **Method:** Steaming

Clarified butter	as needed	as needed
Leek, julienne	3 oz.	90 g
Fennel bulb, julienne	4 oz.	120 g
Carrots, julienne	3 oz.	90 g
Celery, julienne	3 oz.	90 g
Red bell pepper, julienne	3 oz.	90 g
Red snapper fillets, skin on, 6 oz. (180 g) each	6	6
Salt and pepper	TT	TT
Basil Butter (page 223)	9 oz.	270 g

1 Cut six heart-shaped pieces of parchment paper large enough to contain one portion of the fish and vegetables when folded in half.

2 Brush each piece of parchment paper with clarified butter.

3 Toss the vegetables together. Place one-sixth of the vegetables on half of each piece of the buttered parchment paper.

4 Place one portion of red snapper on each portion of vegetables, skin side up; season with salt and pepper.

5 Top each portion of fish with 1½ ounces (45 grams) of basil butter.

6 Fold each piece of paper over and crimp the edges to seal it.

7 Place the envelopes (papillotes) on sheet pans and bake in a preheated oven at 450°F (230°C) for 8 to 10 minutes.

8 When baked, the parchment paper should puff up and brown. Remove from the oven and serve immediately. The envelope should be carefully cut open tableside to allow the aromatic steam to escape.

Approximate values per serving: **Calories** 380, **Total fat** 19 g, **Saturated fat** 11 g, **Cholesterol** 125 mg, **Sodium** 680 mg, **Total carbohydrates** 6 g, **Protein** 46 g, **Vitamin A** 50%, **Vitamin C** 30%

1 Cutting heart-shaped pieces of parchment paper.

2 Placing the vegetables, red snapper and compound butter on the buttered parchment paper.

3 Crimping the edge of the parchment paper to seal it.

4 The finished papillotes.

POACHING

Poaching is a versatile and popular method for cooking fish. Shellfish are rarely poached, however. The exception is squid, which can be quickly poached and chilled for use in salads and other preparations.

There are two distinct poaching methods.

The first is the **submersion method,** in which the fish is completely covered with a liquid, usually a court bouillon, fish stock or fish fumet. It is cooked until just done. The poached fish is then served (either hot or cold) with a sauce sometimes made from a portion of the cooking liquid but more often made separately. Whole fish (wrapped in cheesecloth to preserve its shape during cooking), tranches and steaks can all be cooked by submersion poaching.

The second method, called **shallow poaching,** combines poaching and steaming to achieve the desired results. The main item, usually a fillet, tranche or steak, is placed on a bed of aromatic vegetables in enough liquid to come approximately halfway up its sides. The liquid, called a **cuisson,** is brought to a simmer on the stove top. The pan is then covered with a piece of buttered parchment paper or a lid, and cooking is completed either on the stove top or in the oven. Shallow-poached fish is usually served with a sauce made with the reduced cooking liquid. (Sometimes the main item is sautéed lightly before the cooking liquid is added. If so, the cooking method is more accurately braising, as both dry- and moist-heat cooking methods are used.)

Selecting Fish to Poach

Lean white fish such as turbot, bass and sole are excellent for poaching. Some fatty fish such as salmon and trout are also excellent choices.

Seasoning Fish to Be Poached

Fish poached by either submersion or shallow poaching gain all of their seasonings from the liquid in which they are cooked and the sauce with which they are served. Therefore, it is very important to use a properly prepared court bouillon, fish fumet or a good-quality fish stock well seasoned with vegetables such as shallots, onions or carrots as well as ample herbs, spices and other seasonings. Many poached fish recipes call for wine. When using wine either in the cooking liquid or sauce, be sure to choose a wine of good quality. Most fish are very delicately flavored, and using poor-quality wine might ruin an otherwise excellent dish. Citrus, especially lemon, is always a popular seasoning; lemon juice or zest may be added to the poaching liquid, the sauce or the finished dish.

Accompaniments to Poached Fish

Poached fish cooked by submersion go well with rich sauces like hollandaise and beurre blanc. If fat is a concern, a better choice may be a vegetable coulis (for example, broccoli or red pepper). Cold poached fish are commonly served with mayonnaise-based sauces such as sauce vert or rémoulade. Shallow-poached fish are served with sauces such as a white wine sauce or beurre blanc made from a reduction of the liquids in which the fish were poached. See Table 11.5 for additional sauce suggestions.

Poached fish are often served with rice or pasta and steamed or boiled vegetables.

▶ PROCEDURE FOR SUBMERSION POACHING

1 Prepare the cooking liquid. Whole fish should be started in a cold liquid; gradually increasing the liquid's temperature helps preserve the appearance of the fish. Portioned fish should be started in a simmering liquid to preserve their flavor and more accurately estimate cooking time.

2 Use a rack to lower the fish into the cooking liquid. Be sure the fish is completely submerged.

3 Poach the fish at 175°F–185°F (79°C–85°C) until done.

4 Remove the fish from the poaching liquid, moisten with a portion of the liquid and hold in a warm place for service. Or remove the fish from the poaching liquid, cover it to prevent drying and allow it to cool, then refrigerate.

5 Serve the poached fish with an appropriate sauce.

WHOLE POACHED SALMON

RECIPE 20.8

Yield: 18–20 Servings   **Method:** Submersion poaching

Salmon, drawn, 4–5 lb. (1.8–2.2 kg)	1	1
Court bouillon (Page 205)	as needed	as needed

1. Place the fish on a lightly oiled rack or screen and secure with butcher's twine.
2. Place the rack or screen in a pot and cover with cold court bouillon.
3. Bring the court bouillon to a simmer over moderate heat. Reduce the heat and poach the fish at 175°F–180°F (79°C–85°C) until done, approximately 30 to 45 minutes.
4. If the fish is to be served hot, remove it from the court bouillon, draining well, and serve immediately with an appropriate garnish. If it is to be served cold, remove it from the court bouillon, draining well, cool and refrigerate for several hours before decorating and garnishing as desired.

Approximate values per 4-oz. (120-g) serving: **Calories** 114, **Total fat** 3 g, **Saturated fat** 1 g, **Cholesterol** 29 mg, **Sodium** 80 mg, **Total carbohydrates** 0 g, **Protein** 22 g, **Calcium** 6%

1 Arranging the whole fish on a rack.

2 Preparing the court bouillon.

3 Removing and draining the fish.

▶ PROCEDURE FOR SHALLOW POACHING

1. Butter a sauteuse and add aromatic vegetables as directed in the recipe.
2. Add the fish to the pan.
3. Add the cooking liquid to the pan.
4. Cover the pan with buttered parchment paper or a lid.
5. Bring the liquid to a simmer and cook the fish on the stove top or in the oven until done.
6. Remove the fish from the pan, moisten with a portion of the liquid and hold in a warm place for service.
7. Reduce the cuisson and finish the sauce as directed in the recipe.
8. Serve the poached fish with the sauce.

FILLETS OF SOLE BONNE FEMME

RECIPE 20.9

Yield: 2 Servings   **Method:** Shallow poaching

Sole fillets, approx. 2½ oz. (75 g) each	4	4
Salt and pepper	TT	TT
Whole butter	2 tsp.	10 ml
Shallots, minced	1 tsp.	5 ml

Continued

1 Arranging the sole on the bed of shallots and mushrooms.

2 Covering the fish with buttered parchment paper after the liquid is added.

3 Adding the velouté to the cuisson.

Mushrooms, sliced	4 oz.	120 g
White wine	3 fl. oz.	90 ml
Fish stock	4 fl. oz.	120 ml
Fish velouté	4 fl. oz.	120 ml
Lemon juice	TT	TT
Parsley, chopped	1 tsp.	5 ml

1 Season the sole with salt and pepper.

2 Melt the butter in a sauté pan. Add the shallots and mushrooms and arrange the sole fillets over them. Add the wine and fish stock.

3 Bring the liquid to a simmer. Cover the fish with buttered parchment paper and cook on the stove top or in a 350°F (180°C) oven until done, approximately 5 to 8 minutes.

4 Remove the sole and reserve in a warm place.

5 Reduce the cuisson until approximately 1 fluid ounce (30 milliliters) remains. Add the velouté. Add lemon juice to taste and adjust the seasonings. Serve the sauce with the fish, sprinkled with chopped parsley.

Approximate values per serving: **Calories** 440, **Total fat** 14 g, **Saturated fat** 5 g, **Cholesterol** 120 mg, **Sodium** 3750 mg, **Total carbohydrates** 27 g, **Protein** 42 g

SIMMERING

"Boiled" lobster, crab and shrimp are not actually boiled; rather, they are cooked whole in their shells by simmering. Although they are not as delicate as some fish, these crustaceans can become tough and are easily overcooked if the cooking liquid is allowed to boil.

Selecting Shellfish to Simmer

Lobsters, crabs and shrimp are commonly cooked by simmering. Their hard shells protect their delicate flesh during the cooking process.

Seasoning Shellfish to Be Simmered

The shellfish being simmered are not seasoned. Rather, they gain flavor by being cooked in a seasoned or flavored liquid, typically salted water or court bouillon. A sachet of pickling spice or Old Bay seasoning is sometimes used for additional flavor.

Determining Doneness

Timing is the best method for determining the doneness of simmered shellfish. This varies depending on the size of the shellfish and how quickly the liquid returns to a simmer after the shellfish is added. Shrimp cook in as little as 3–5 minutes; crabs cook in 5–10 minutes; and it can take as little as 6–8 minutes for a 1-pound (450-gram) lobster to cook and 15–20 minutes for a 2½-pound (1.1-kilogram) lobster.

Accompaniments to Simmered Shellfish

The standard accompaniments to simmered shellfish are lemon wedges and melted butter. If the shellfish is being eaten cold, the traditional sauce is a tomato-based cocktail sauce. Nearly any type of vegetable or starch goes well with simmered shellfish, the most common being fresh corn on the cob and boiled potatoes.

▶ PROCEDURE FOR SIMMERING OR BOILING SHELLFISH

1 Bring court bouillon or water to a boil.

2 Add the shellfish to the liquid. Bring the liquid back to a boil and reduce to a simmer. (Whenever an item is added to boiling water, it lowers the water's temperature. The greater the amount of water, however, the faster it

will return to a boil. So, to accelerate the time within which the water returns to a boil after the shellfish is added, use as much water as possible.)

3 Cook until done.

4 Remove the shellfish from the liquid and serve immediately, or cool by dropping them in ice water if they are to be eaten cold.

BOILED LOBSTER

RECIPE 20.10

Yield: 1 Serving

Lobster, 1 lb. 8 oz. (650 g)	1	1
Boiling salted water	4 gal.	16 lt
Lemon wedges	4	4
Whole butter, melted	2 oz.	60 g

1 Drop the lobster into the boiling water. Bring the water back to a boil, reduce to a simmer and cook the lobster until done, approximately 12 minutes.

2 Remove the lobster from the pot, drain and serve immediately with lemon wedges and melted butter on the side.

3 If the lobster is to be eaten cold, drop it in a sink of ice water to stop the cooking process. When cool enough to handle, remove the meat from the shell following the procedures discussed earlier.

Approximate values per 1-lb. (450-g) serving: **Calories** 650, **Total fat** 26 g, **Saturated fat** 15 g, **Cholesterol** 390 mg, **Sodium** 1960 mg, **Total carbohydrates** 11 g, **Protein** 93 g, **Vitamin A** 35%, **Vitamin C** 45%

COMBINATION COOKING METHODS

Combination cooking methods are used with meats, game and poultry in part to tenderize them. Because fish and shellfish are inherently tender, they do not necessarily benefit from such procedures. As noted in the section on shallow poaching, fish can, on occasion, be lightly sautéed or browned and then poached. Although this procedure is a combination cooking method, it is used to enhance flavors and not to tenderize the product.

You may encounter fish or shellfish recipes with the word *braised* or *stew* in the title. Note, however, that these recipes rarely follow the traditional combination cooking methods discussed in this book.

In part because of consumers' increased health awareness, more and more food service operations are expanding their selections of fish and shellfish. Their task is aided by the tremendous variety of high-quality fish and shellfish now available. A variety of dry-heat and moist-heat cooking methods can be used with these products, and a variety of sauces and accompaniments can be served with them. Regardless of how they are served, care and attention are required in order to select, store and avoid overcooking fish and shellfish.

CONCLUSION

1 Discuss six techniques for determining the freshness of fish and shellfish.

2 What are the physical differences between a flatfish and a round fish? How do fabrication techniques vary for these fish?

3 List four market forms for fish, and discuss several factors that may determine the form most appropriate for an operation to purchase.

4 List the three categories of mollusks, and give an example of a commonly used food from each category.

5 Discuss four methods for determining the doneness of fish or shellfish. Why is it important not to overcook fish and shellfish?

6 Explain the differences between shallow poaching and submersion poaching. Why is poaching a commonly used method for preparing fish and shellfish?

7 Why are combination cooking methods rarely used with fish and shellfish? Why is boiling rarely used?

WHOLE ROASTED RED SNAPPER   RECIPE 20.11

Note: This dish appears in the chapter opening photograph.

PESCE RESTAURANT, HOUSTON, TX
Chef Mark Holley

Yield: 2 Servings   **Method:** Roasting

Whole red snapper, black sea bass		
or **red fish**, approx. 3 lb. (1.4 kg)	1	1
Kosher salt	TT	TT
Black pepper	TT	TT
Fresh rosemary	1 sprig	1 sprig
Fresh oregano	1 sprig	1 sprig
Fresh tarragon	1 sprig	1 sprig
Herb baste:		
Fresh lemon juice	2 fl. oz.	60 ml
Extra virgin olive oil	4 fl. oz.	120 ml
Fresh herbs, assorted, chopped	3 Tbsp.	45 ml
Italian parsley	as needed	as needed
Fresh thyme	as needed	as needed
Lemon crown	1	1
Pesce's Salsa Verde (recipe follows)	4 fl. oz.	120 ml
Provençale Sauce (recipe follows)	4 fl. oz.	120 ml

1 Scale the fish. Cut out the gills and remove the fins if desired. Score the flesh of the fish by cutting on the bias behind the gills, in the middle of the fish and in front of the tail. Season the cavity of the fish with salt and pepper and stuff with the rosemary, oregano and tarragon sprigs.

2 Combine the herb baste ingredients and brush the entire outer surface of the fish with the baste. Season the outside of the fish with salt and pepper. Be sure to season the scored openings.

3 Place the fish on an oiled roasting pan and roast at 500°F (260°C) until done, approximately 20 to 25 minutes.

4 Remove the herbs from the cavity and transfer the fish to a serving pan. Place the Italian parsley and thyme attractively in the cavity of the fish. Garnish with a lemon crown and serve with Pesce's Salsa Verde and Provençale Sauce.

Approximate values per serving: **Calories** 1130, **Total fat** 88 g, **Saturated fat** 12 g, **Cholesterol** 125 mg, **Sodium** 640 mg, **Total carbohydrates** 12 g, **Protein** 72 g, **Vitamin A** 40%, **Vitamin C** 90%, **Calcium** 15%, **Iron** 15%

PESCE'S SALSA VERDE

Yield: 1 qt. (1 lt)

Fresh Italian parsley	2 oz.	60 g
Fresh cilantro	4 oz.	120 g
Fresh mint	½ oz.	15 g
Fresh basil	½ oz.	15 g
Shallots, chopped	2 oz.	60 g

Continued

CHEF MARK HOLLEY

Chef Mark Holley is executive chef of Pesce, which is considered one of Houston's best restaurants and is particularly known for its innovative offerings of fresh fish and shellfish. Before joining Pesce, Chef Holley worked for the Brennan family of restaurants, including positions as garde-manger of Commander's Palace and chef de cuisine of Brennan's Houston. Chef Holley is well respected for pursuing excellence from his restaurant's team of culinary professionals and for his friendly, easygoing manner with customers.

In his spare time, Chef Holley has earned a bachelor's degree in hotel and restaurant management. He did not attend a culinary school and advises aspiring chefs to work for a time in the industry before attending a culinary program.

▶ **red fish** a name applied to various species of fish around the world. In the United States, it generally refers to a member of the drum family found in the Southern Atlantic and the Gulf of Mexico. It has a reddish-bronze skin; firm, ivory flesh with a mild flavor and a typical market weight of 2–8 lb. (0.9–3.6 kg), and is also known as channel bass, red drum and red bass.

Garlic, chopped	3 Tbsp.	45 ml
Serrano chile, chopped	1 Tbsp.	15 ml
Chile flakes	½ tsp.	3 ml
Fresh lemon juice	5 fl. oz.	150 ml
Fresh lime juice	2 fl. oz.	60 ml
Fish sauce	2 fl. oz.	60 ml
Extra virgin olive oil	1 pt.	450 ml

1 Place the herbs, shallots, garlic, serrano and chile flakes in a food processor and process to a paste.

2 With the machine running, add the lemon and lime juices. Add the fish sauce and slowly add the olive oil. Refrigerate.

Approximate values per 2-Tbsp. (30-ml) serving: **Calories** 130, **Total fat** 14 g, **Saturated fat** 2 g, **Cholesterol** 0 mg, **Sodium** 180 mg, **Total carbohydrates** 2 g, **Protein** 0 g, **Vitamin C** 10%

PROVENÇAL SAUCE

Yield: 2 qt. (2 lt)

Yellow onion, julienne	1 c.	240 ml
Olive oil	2 fl. oz.	60 ml
Garlic, sliced very thin	½ c.	120 ml
White wine	4 fl. oz.	120 ml
Tomato purée	1 qt.	1 lt
Tomato concassée, medium dice	1 qt.	1 lt
Red bell pepper, roasted, julienne	½ c.	120 ml
Yellow bell pepper, roasted, julienne	½ c.	120 ml
Green bell pepper, roasted, julienne	½ c.	120 ml
Black olives, pitted	½ c.	120 ml
Green olives, pitted	½ c.	120 ml
Tomato paste	3 Tbsp.	45 ml
Shrimp stock	12 fl. oz.	350 ml
Fresh basil, chiffonade	¼ c.	60 ml
Salt and pepper	TT	TT

1 Sauté the onions in the olive oil until transparent. Add the garlic and sauté without browning for 2 minutes.

2 Add the wine and deglaze. Add the tomato purée and the tomato concassée, bring to a simmer and cook for 5 minutes.

3 Add the bell peppers, olives, tomato paste and stock. Bring to a simmer and cook until the flavors are blended and it reaches the proper consistency, approximately 30 minutes. Add the basil and season with salt and pepper.

Approximate values per 1-fl.-oz. (30-ml) serving: **Calories** 25, **Total fat** 1 g, **Saturated fat** 0, **Cholesterol** 0, **Sodium** 35 mg, **Total carbohydrates** 3 g, **Protein** 1 g, **Vitamin C** 10%

RECIPE 20.12   CAJUN-GRILLED TROUT WITH APPLE SALSA

Yield: 1 Serving   **Method:** Grilling

Trout, dressed, head and fins removed	1	1
Clarified butter or vegetable oil	as needed	as needed
Cajun Spice Mix (recipe follows)	TT	TT
Apple Salsa (recipe follows)	4 Tbsp.	60 ml
Lemon wedge	1	1
Fresh herb sprig	1	1

1 Brush both sides of the trout lightly with clarified butter or vegetable oil. Season the flesh side of the trout generously with the Cajun Spice Mix.

2 Grill the trout on a hot, well seasoned grill. Place the flesh side down first, turn to produce crosshatch marks and then turn the trout over to cook briefly on the second side. The trout will cook very quickly. Be careful not to overcook it.

3 Serve the trout with Apple Salsa. Garnish with the lemon wedge and fresh herb sprig.

Approximate values per serving: **Calories** 310, **Total fat** 9 g, **Saturated fat** 2.5 g, **Cholesterol** 195 mg, **Sodium** 150 mg, **Total carbohydrates** 16 g, **Protein** 40 g

CAJUN SPICE MIX

Yield: 6 oz. (180 g)

Salt	1 oz.	30 g
Garlic powder	1 oz.	30 g
White pepper	½ oz.	15 g
Oregano, dried, ground	⅓ oz.	10 g
Onion powder	1 oz.	30 g
Black pepper	½ oz.	15 g
Cayenne pepper	¼ oz.	7 g
Thyme, dried, ground	⅓ oz.	10 g
Paprika	1 oz.	30 g

1 Combine all ingredients and mix well.

Approximate values per ½-oz. (15-g) serving: **Calories** 35, **Total fat** 0.5 g, **Saturated fat** 0 g, **Cholesterol** 0 mg, **Sodium** 920 mg, **Total carbohydrates** 8 g, **Protein** 1 g, **Vitamin A** 35%, **Iron** 15%

APPLE SALSA

Yield: 3 c. (710 ml)

Granny Smith apples, small dice	4	4
Orange zest, chopped	1 tsp.	5 ml
Lemon zest, chopped	1 tsp.	5 ml
Lime zest, chopped	1 tsp.	5 ml
Water	2 fl. oz.	60 ml
Jalapeños, minced	1 tsp.	5 ml
Cilantro, chopped	4 Tbsp.	60 ml
Green onions, sliced thin	6	6
Cranberry sauce, jellied, canned	1 c.	240 ml
Salt and pepper	TT	TT

1 Combine the ingredients and chill.

Approximate values per 2 Tbsp. (60-ml) serving: **Calories** 30, **Total fat** 0 g, **Saturated fat** 0 g, **Cholesterol** 0 mg, **Sodium** 0 mg, **Total carbohydrates** 8 g, **Protein** 0 g, **Claims**—low calorie, fat free, no cholesterol, no sodium

TERIYAKI SALMON WITH PINEAPPLE PAPAYA SALSA

RECIPE 20.13

Yield: 4 Servings   **Method:** Grilling

Marinade:		
Soy sauce	8 fl. oz.	250 ml
Garlic, crushed	1 tsp.	5 ml

Continued

Ginger, minced	1 tsp.	5 ml
Brown sugar	2 oz.	60 g
Sake	4 fl. oz.	120 ml
Salmon, tranches, 4 oz. (120 g) each	4	4
Vegetable oil	as needed	as needed
Pineapple Papaya Salsa (page 819)	1 pt.	450 ml

1 To make the marinade, combine the soy sauce, garlic, ginger, brown sugar and sake.

2 Marinate the salmon tranches in the marinade for 15 minutes.

3 Remove the salmon tranches from the marinade and pat dry. Brush them with vegetable oil and broil or grill until done.

4 Serve the salmon on a bed of warmed Pineapple Papaya Salsa.

Approximate values per serving: **Calories** 330, **Total fat** 9 g, **Saturated fat** 2 g, **Cholesterol** 65 mg, **Sodium** 3770 mg, **Total carbohydrates** 28 g, **Protein** 35 g, **Vitamin C** 60%

RECIPE 20.14   ACAPULCO CATFISH GRILL

Yield: 12 Servings   **Method:** Grilling

Frozen U.S. farm-raised catfish fillets or strips	3 lb.	1.3 kg
Lime juice	2 fl. oz.	60 ml
Olive oil	2 Tbsp.	30 ml
Acapulco Spice Blend (recipe follows)	4 Tbsp.	60 ml

1 Place the frozen catfish in a hotel pan, cover and thaw under refrigeration.

2 Combine the lime juice and oil and brush over the surface of each catfish fillet. Sprinkle all surfaces of each fillet with 1 teaspoon (5 milliliters) of Acapulco Spice Blend. Let stand 15 to 20 minutes, covered and refrigerated.

3 Heat the grill and cook the fillets 2 to 3 minutes on one side. Turn and continue cooking another 2 to 3 minutes.

Approximate values per 4-oz. (120-g) serving: **Calories** 180, **Total fat** 11 g, **Saturated fat** 2.5 g, **Cholesterol** 55 mg, **Sodium** 65 mg, **Total carbohydrates** 2 g, **Protein** 18 g, **Iron** 10%

ACAPULCO SPICE BLEND

Yield: 1½ c. (360 ml)

Cumin seeds	1 c.	240 ml
Dried oregano	½ c.	120 ml
Garlic, granulated	¼ c.	60 ml
Chilli powder	2 Tbsp.	30 ml
Black pepper, coarsely ground	2 Tbsp.	30 ml
Red pepper, ground	1 tsp.	5 ml
Salt	TT	TT

1 Toast the cumin seeds. Allow them to cool, then grind in a spice grinder.

2 Combine all ingredients. Cover and store in a cool, dry place.

GRILLED SWORDFISH WITH TRUFFLE MASHED POTATOES AND CANNELLINI BEAN RELISH

RECIPE 20.15

PESCE RESTAURANT, HOUSTON, TX
Chef Jonathan Long

Yield: 4 Servings   **Method:** Grilling

Red beets	as needed	as needed
Lotus root	as needed	as needed
Salt and pepper	TT	TT
Swordfish steaks, 6 oz. (180 g) ea.	4	4
Grapeseed oil	as needed	as needed
Truffle Mashed Potatoes		
(recipe follows)	16 oz.	450 g
Parsley sprigs	as needed	as needed
Cannellini Bean Relish (recipe follows)	12 oz.	350 g

1 Slice the red beets and lotus root into thin slices on an electric slicer. Using the swimming method, deep-fry the vegetables at approximately 325°F (163°C) until crisp. Remove from the fryer, drain on paper towels and season with salt.

2 Season the swordfish steaks with salt and pepper, brush them with grapeseed oil and grill to medium doneness.

3 Using a stainless steel ring, form a circle of Truffle Mashed Potatoes in the center of each plate.

4 Place a swordfish portion on top of the potatoes. Top the swordfish with the fried beets and lotus root and a sprig of parsley. Spoon the Cannellini Bean Relish around the plate and serve.

Approximate values per serving: **Calories** 450, **Total fat** 24 g, **Saturated fat** 7 g, **Cholesterol** 60 mg, **Sodium** 230 mg, **Total carbohydrates** 32 g, **Protein** 30 g, **Vitamin A** 10%, **Vitamin C** 30%, **Iron** 20%

TRUFFLE MASHED POTATOES

Yield: 2½ lb. (1.1 kg)

Russet potatoes, peeled, large dice	2 lb.	900 g
Whole butter, melted	2 oz.	60 g
Milk, scalded	6 fl. oz.	180 ml
Truffle oil	2 tsp.	10 ml
Salt and pepper	TT	TT

1 Simmer the potatoes in salted water until tender. Drain well.

2 Whip the potatoes on high speed for 30 seconds. Scrape down the bowl and whip for an additional 30 seconds eliminating all lumps. Add the butter and milk and mix well on low speed. Add the truffle oil and season with salt and pepper.

Approximate values per ½-c. (120-ml) serving: **Calories** 130, **Total fat** 6 g, **Saturated fat** 3.5 g, **Cholesterol** 15 mg, **Sodium** 15 mg, **Total carbohydrates** 17 g, **Protein** 2 g, **Vitamin C** 10%

CANNELLINI BEAN RELISH

Yield: 1½ lb. (680 g)

White beans, cooked	3 c.	700 ml
Cherry tomatoes, quartered	½ c.	120 ml
Green olives, pitted, sliced thin	¼ c.	60 ml
Black olives, pitted, sliced thin	¼ c.	60 ml
Red bell pepper, roasted, small dice	¼ c.	60 ml
Green bell pepper, roasted, small dice	¼ c.	60 ml
Fresh basil, chopped	1 Tbsp.	15 ml
Fresh parsley, chopped	1 Tbsp.	15 ml
Capers	1 Tbsp.	15 ml
Extra virgin olive oil	4 fl. oz.	120 ml
Sherry wine vinegar	2 Tbsp.	30 ml
Rice vinegar	2 Tbsp.	30 ml
Balsamic vinegar	1 Tbsp.	15 ml
Salt and pepper	TT	TT
Garlic oil:		
Extra virgin olive oil	2 Tbsp.	30 ml
Garlic, minced	1 Tbsp.	15 ml

1 Combine all of the ingredients except the garlic oil and gently toss together.

2 To make the garlic oil, heat the olive oil in a small pan. Add the garlic and sauté until it is lightly browned.

3 Pour the hot garlic oil over the salad and toss to combine.

Approximate values per 3-oz. (90-g) serving: **Calories** 150, **Total fat** 10.5 g, **Saturated fat** 0 g, **Cholesterol** 0 mg, **Sodium** 90 mg, **Total carbohydrates** 12 g, **Protein** 3 g, **Vitamin C** 12%, **Iron** 12%

RECIPE 20.16

OVEN-FRIED PECAN CATFISH

Yield: 12 Servings   **Method:** Baking

Dijon mustard	8 fl. oz.	240 ml
Milk	6 fl. oz.	180 ml
Pecans, ground	14 oz.	420 g
U.S. farm-raised catfish fillets	12	12

1 Mix the Dijon mustard and milk in a shallow dish. Spread the pecans out on a piece of parchment paper.

2 Dip each fillet into the mustard mixture, then roll in the ground pecans. Coat each fillet thoroughly, shaking off any excess. Place the fillets on a lightly oiled baking sheet.

3 Bake at 450°F (230°C) until the catfish flakes easily when tested with a fork, approximately 10 to 12 minutes.

Variation: *Tropical Oven-Fried Catfish*—Combine 4 fluid ounces (120 milliliters) of low-fat buttermilk with 1 teaspoon (5 milliliters) each of black pepper, salt and ginger, and ⅛ teaspoon (1 milliliter) of cinnamon. Crush 9 ounces (270 grams) of cornflakes into crumbs. Bread 12 catfish fillets using the standard breading procedure. Cover and refrigerate for at least 30 minutes to set the coating, and then bake as directed above.

Approximate values per serving: **Calories** 410, **Total fat** 31 g, **Saturated fat** 4.5 g, **Cholesterol** 75 mg, **Sodium** 600 mg, **Total carbohydrates** 6 g, **Protein** 29 g, **Iron** 10%

ROASTED SALMON

NEWBURY COLLEGE, Brookline, MA
Senior Instructor Scott Doughty

Yield: 6 Servings **Method:** Baking

Salmon fillet, 2½ lb. (1.1 kg)	1	1
Seasoning blend:		
Caraway seeds	1 tsp.	5 ml
Cumin seeds	1 tsp.	5 ml
Black mustard seeds	1 Tbsp.	15 ml
Dried oregano	2 Tbsp.	30 ml
Dried thyme	2 Tbsp.	30 ml
Dried basil	2 Tbsp.	30 ml
Dried tarragon	2 Tbsp.	30 ml
Dried rosemary	1 Tbsp.	15 ml
Salt	2 tsp.	10 ml
Allspice, ground	2 tsp.	10 ml
Coriander seeds, ground	1 tsp.	5 ml
Cardamom, ground	1 tsp.	5 ml
Paprika	¼ C.	60 ml
Black pepper	1 tsp.	5 ml
White pepper	1 tsp.	5 ml
Cayenne pepper	½ tsp.	2 ml
Egg whites, beaten	2	2
Olive oil	as needed	as needed
Tomato Butter Sauce with Thyme (page 240)	1 pt.	480 ml
Lemon wedges	as needed for garnish	
Fresh Italian parsley	as needed for garnish	

1 Remove the pin bones and skin from the salmon fillet. Cut away the dark flesh. Cut the fillet into six tranches. Place them in a holding pan, boned side down. Cover and refrigerate.

2 Combine the caraway, cumin and mustard seeds and grind them in a spice grinder until nearly a powder. Add the oregano, thyme, basil, tarragon and rosemary and grind all to a powder. In a bowl, combine them with the salt, allspice, coriander, cardamom and paprika and the black, white and cayenne peppers.

3 Preheat the oven to 450°F (230°C). Place several sizzle platters in the oven.

4 Put the egg whites into a small, shallow hotel pan. Put the herb and spice mixture into a separate shallow pan.

5 Dip a piece of salmon, skinned side up, into the egg whites, coating only one side of the salmon. Immediately dredge the dipped side into the herb and spice mixture. Repeat with the remaining pieces of salmon.

6 Place one of the hot sizzle platters on a burner over medium neat. Brush it with a thin film of olive oil and place a few of the salmon fillets on it, coated side down. Place the fish in the oven and repeat with the remaining platters and salmon fillets.

7 Monitor the salmon and remove the platters when the salmon is still slightly undercooked. Invert them and place the tranches in a hotel pan or onto plates. Ladle the Tomato Butter Sauce with Thyme into the pan between the fillets or onto the plate around the fillets. Garnish with the lemon wedges and Italian parsley, or as desired, and serve.

Approximate values per serving: **Calories** 670, **Total fat** 48 g, **Saturated fat** 17 g, **Cholesterol** 165 mg, **Sodium** 840 mg, **Total carbohydrates** 16 g, **Protein** 42 g, **Vitamin A** 80%, **Vitamin C** 90%, **Calcium** 15%, **Iron** 30%

RECIPE 20.18

PISTACHIO-CRUSTED SALMON WITH GINGERED DAL AND CILANTRO CHUTNEY

PRIMITIVO WINE BAR, Colorado Springs, CO

John Broening, Executive Chef

Yield: 8 Servings   **Method:** Roasting

Salmon fillets, 5 oz. (150 g) ea.	8	8
Canola oil	4 Tbsp.	60 ml
Salt and pepper	TT	TT
Tamarind Glaze (recipe follows)	as needed	as needed
Pistachios, lightly toasted, crushed	4 oz.	120 g
Whole butter	2 oz.	60 g
Spinach, stemmed and cleaned	1 lb.	450 g
Gingered Dal, warm (recipe follows)	as needed	as needed
Tomato Syrup (page 232)	as needed	as needed
Cilantro Chutney (recipe follows)	as needed	as needed
Cilantro leaves	24	24
Mint leaves	24	24

1 Brush each salmon fillet with oil, season with salt and pepper and place on a sheet pan. Brush the fillets with Tamarind Glaze and then press the pistachios onto the presentation side of each fillet. Roast in a 350°F (180°C) oven for approximately 10 minutes.

2 In a large wok, or in several smaller sauté pans, brown the butter and then sauté the spinach until it wilts. Season with salt and pepper and hold for service.

3 Mound spinach in the center of each of eight warm plates. Arrange three quenelles of Gingered Dal around the spinach. Place the fish on top of the spinach, then arrange the Tomato Syrup and Cilantro Chutney around the fish. Garnish with the fresh herbs.

Approximate values per serving: **Calories** 460, **Total fat** 34 g, **Saturated fat** 8 g, **Cholesterol** 100 mg, **Sodium** 130 mg, **Total carbohydrates** 6 g, **Protein** 33 g, **Vitamin A** 90%, **Vitamin C** 40%, **Calcium** 10%, **Iron** 15%

TAMARIND GLAZE

Yield: 1 pt. (450 ml)

Tamarind paste	1 c.	240 ml
Brown sugar	1 c.	240 ml
Fresh ginger, minced	1 Tbsp.	15 ml

1 Combine the ingredients and simmer until thick. Strain through a china cap.

Approximate values per 1-fl.-oz.(30-ml) serving: **Calories** 70, **Total fat** 0 g, **Saturated fat** 0 g, **Cholesterol** 0 mg, **Sodium** 10 mg, **Total carbohydrates** 18 g, **Protein** 0 g

GINGERED DAL

Yield: 1 qt. (1 lt)

Yellow lentils (dal)	1 pt.	450 ml
Water	1 qt.	1 lt.
Yukon Gold potatoes, peeled, large dice	2	2
Fresh ginger, 1-in. (2.5-cm) piece, cut in 3 slices	1	1
Salt	TT	TT
Whole butter	6 oz.	180 g

Onion, small dice	1	1
Cumin seeds	1 Tbsp.	15 ml
Black mustard seeds	2 Tbsp.	30 ml
Fresh lemon juice	2 Tbsp.	30 ml

1 Bring the lentils, water, potatoes, ginger and salt to a boil. Cover and simmer until the lentils are tender and the water is absorbed, approximately 1 hour.

2 In a large sauté pan, melt the butter and add the onion, cumin and mustard seeds. Cook until the butter is slightly brown. Transfer to a large mixing bowl. Add the lentil mixture and mash with a wooden spoon. Season with salt and pepper and add the lemon juice. Hold warm for service.

Approximate values per 4-fl.-oz.(120-ml) serving: **Calories** 370, **Total fat** 19 g, **Saturated fat** 11 g, **Cholesterol** 45 mg, **Sodium** 10 mg, **Total carbohydrates** 38 g, **Protein** 14 g, **Vitamin A** 15%, **Vitamin C** 10%, **Iron** 30%

CILANTRO CHUTNEY

Yield: 12 fl. oz. (350 ml)

Cilantro, leaves and small stems	3 bunches	3 bunches
Jalapeños, seeded	3	3
Fresh ginger, chopped	2 Tbsp.	30 ml
Honey	2 Tbsp.	30 ml
Garlic, chopped	2 tsp.	10 ml
Canola oil	1 Tbsp.	15 ml
Cumin seeds, toasted	2 tsp.	10 ml
Almonds, toasted	3 Tbsp.	45 ml
Fresh lime juice	1 Tbsp.	15 ml
Salt and pepper	TT	TT

1 Place all ingredients in a blender and blend to a pestolike consistency.

Approximate values per 1-fl.-oz. (30-ml) serving: **Calories** 45, **Total fat** 2.5 g, **Saturated fat** 0 g, **Cholesterol** 0 mg, **Sodium** 15 mg, **Total carbohydrates** 6 g, **Protein** 1 g, **Vitamin A** 35%, **Vitamin C** 40%

PEPPERCORN-CRUSTED YELLOWFIN TUNA WITH SAFFRON AND FAVA BEAN RISOTTO

RECIPE 20.19

PESCE RESTAURANT, Houston, TX
Chef Mark Holley

Yield: 4 Servings		**Method:** Searing/Baking
Olive oil	as needed	as needed
Yellowfin tuna fillets, 6 oz. (180 g) ea.	4	4
Dijon mustard	as needed	as needed
Black peppercorns, crushed	as needed	as needed
Saffron and Fava Bean Risotto (recipe follows)	12 oz.	350 g
Herb oil (page 244, made with chives)	as needed	as needed
Balsamic vinegar, reduced to a syrup	as needed	as needed
Micro greens	½ c.	120 ml
Truffle Vinaigrette (recipe follows)	2 Tbsp.	30 ml

1 Heat the olive oil in a sauté pan. Brush the tuna with the Dijon mustard and sprinkle evenly with the crushed peppercorns to form a crust.

2 Sear the tuna for 1 minute on each side and finish in a 350°F (180°C) oven until medium rare, approximately 3 minutes. Remove from the oven and allow to rest.

3 Place 3 ounces (90 grams) of Saffron and Fava Bean Risotto in the center of each of four plates. Drizzle chive oil and the balsamic vinegar reduction around the risotto. Slice the tuna fillets in half and place on top of the risotto.

4 Toss the micro greens in the Truffle Vinaigrette and mound on top of the tuna.

Approximate values per serving: **Calories** 300, **Total fat** 9 g, **Saturated fat** 2 g, **Cholesterol** 80 mg, **Sodium** 140 mg, **Total carbohydrates** 9 g, **Protein** 42 g

SAFFRON AND FAVA BEAN RISOTTO

Yield: 2 qt. (2 lt)

Shrimp stock	3 pt.	1.4 lt
Saffron threads	1 tsp.	5 ml
Olive oil	4 Tbsp.	60 ml
Unsalted butter	2 oz.	60 g
Yellow onions, small dice	1 oz.	30 g
Arborio rice	1 pt.	450 ml
Kosher salt	TT	TT
Black pepper	TT	TT
Oyster mushrooms	4 oz.	120 g
Fava beans, blanched	½ c.	120 ml
Parmesan, grated	2 Tbsp.	30 ml

1 Bring the shrimp stock to a simmer and add the saffron threads.

2 Heat half of the olive oil and half of the butter in a heavy saucepan and sauté the onions until they are golden. Add the rice and stir to coat it with the oil and butter.

3 Over medium high heat, add 4 fluid ounces (120 milliliters) of the shrimp stock to the rice. Stir and cook until the liquid is absorbed. Add another portion of stock, stir and cook until the liquid is absorbed. Continue adding stock, one portion at a time, stirring often, until the rice is creamy but still firm in the center. The process will take approximately 20 minutes.

4 In a separate pan, sauté the mushrooms in the remaining olive oil until tender. Season with salt and pepper.

5 Fold the mushrooms, fava beans, Parmesan and remaining butter into the risotto and season with salt and pepper. Serve immediately.

Approximate values per 8-fl.-oz. (240-ml) serving: **Calories** 330, **Total fat** 15 g, **Saturated fat** 5 g, **Cholesterol** 20 mg, **Sodium** 320 mg, **Total carbohydrates** 38 g, **Protein** 10 g

TRUFFLE VINAIGRETTE

Yield: 20 fl. oz. (600 ml)

Fresh truffles, chopped	¼ c.	60 ml
Truffle oil	4 fl. oz.	120 ml
Extra virgin olive oil	8 fl. oz.	240 ml
Shallots, minced	1 Tbsp.	15 ml
Dijon mustard	2 Tbsp.	30 ml
Chives, sliced	2 tsp.	10 ml
Honey (optional)	1 Tbsp.	15 ml
Rice wine vinegar	2 fl. oz.	60 ml
Sherry vinegar	2 fl. oz.	60 ml
Salt and pepper	TT	TT

1 Whisk all of the ingredients together.

Approximate values per 1-fl.-oz. (30-ml) serving: **Calories** 150, **Total fat** 17 g, **Saturated fat** 2.5 g, **Cholesterol** 0 mg, **Sodium** 40 mg, **Total carbohydrates** 1 g, **Protein** 0 g

CHA CA
(HANOI-STYLE FISH WITH DILL)

RECIPE 20.20

Yield: 4 Servings
Method: Sautéing / Stir-frying

Marinade:		
Fresh ginger, 1-in. (2.5-cm) piece, peeled and chopped	1	1
Fresh Thai or serrano chiles	2	2
Granulated sugar	1 Tbsp.	15 ml
Nuoc mam (fish sauce)	2 Tbsp.	30 ml
Turmeric, ground	4 Tbsp.	60 ml
Water	4 Tbsp.	60 ml
Fresh lemon juice	2 Tbsp.	30 ml
Catfish fillets	1 lb.	450 g
Vegetable oil	2 fl. oz.	60 ml
Shallot, thinly sliced	1	1
Garlic cloves, thinly sliced	2	2
Fresh dill	6 oz.	180 g
Green onions, chopped	4	4
Rice vermicelli, cooked	as needed	as needed
Peanuts, chopped	4 Tbsp.	60 ml
Nuoc cham (page 243)	as needed	as needed

1 Prepare the marinade by grinding the ginger, chiles and sugar into a paste. Add the remaining marinade ingredients and stir until dissolved.

2 Cut the catfish into 1-inch (2.5-centimeter) pieces. Toss the catfish in the marinade. Cover and refrigerate for 1 hour.

3 Heat a sauté pan or wok and add the oil. Sauté the shallot and garlic until translucent, but not brown. Add the fish and any remaining marinade to the hot pan and cook, stirring carefully until the fish is almost done, approximately 2 minutes.

4 Cut the dill into 1½-inch (3.75-centimeter) pieces. Add half of the dill and half of the green onions to the fish and cook until they wilt.

5 Arrange the remaining dill and green onions on a warm serving platter. Pour the fish and wilted herbs on top.

6 Reheat the vermicelli by dropping it in boiling water for a few seconds. Drain well.

7 Serve the sautéed fish and herbs with individual bowls of rice vermicelli. Each diner then places some of the herbs and fish on top of the noodles, adds a sprinkle of chopped peanuts and drizzles with nuoc cham.

Approximate values per serving: **Calories** 320, **Total fat** 23 g, **Saturated fat** 4 g, **Cholesterol** 55 mg, **Sodium** 770 mg, **Total carbohydrates** 6 g, **Protein** 19 g, **Vitamin A** 30%, **Vitamin C** 60%, **Iron** 10%

RED SNAPPER VERACRUZ

RECIPE 20.21

Yield: 4 Servings
Method: Sautéing

Red snapper fillets, skinless, 6 oz. (170 g) each	4	4
Salt and pepper	TT	TT
Flour	as needed for dredging	
Olive oil	2 fl. oz.	60 ml
Onion, medium dice	6 oz.	180 g
Garlic cloves, minced	4	4

Continued

Lemon juice	1 fl. oz.	30 ml
Fish or chicken stock	8 fl. oz.	250 ml
Jalapeño, seeded, small dice	1	1
Tomato concassée	1 lb. 8 oz.	650 g
Pimento-stuffed green olives, quartered	20	20
Sugar	1 tsp.	5 ml
Cinnamon stick	1	1
Dried thyme	½ tsp.	2 ml
Dried marjoram	½ tsp.	2 ml
Capers	2 Tbsp.	30 ml
Fresh cilantro	as needed for garnish	

1 Season the fillets with salt and pepper and dredge in flour. Sauté the fillets in olive oil until done. Remove and reserve in a warm place.

2 Add the onion and garlic to the pan and sauté until tender. Deglaze the pan with the lemon juice and add the stock, jalapeño, tomato concassée, olives, sugar, cinnamon stick, thyme and marjoram.

3 Simmer 10 minutes. Remove the cinnamon stick and add the capers. Season to taste.

4 Return the fish to the pan to reheat. Serve on warm plates garnished with fresh cilantro.

Variations: Substitute bass or halibut fillets for the red snapper.

Approximate values per serving: **Calories** 570, **Total fat** 22 g, **Saturated fat** 3 g, **Cholesterol** 80 mg, **Sodium** 1820 mg, **Total carbohydrates** 41 g, **Protein** 51 g, **Vitamin C** 70%

RECIPE 20.22   TROUT NANCY

BRENNAN'S RESTAURANT, New Orleans, LA
Chef Michael Roussel

Yield: 8 Servings   **Method:** Sautéing

Trout fillets	8	8
Salt and pepper	TT	TT
Flour	as needed for dredging	
Whole butter	4 oz.	120 g
Lump crab meat, picked	1½ lb.	750 g
Capers	½ c.	120 ml
Brennan's Lemon Butter Sauce (page 238)	12 fl. oz.	360 ml
Fresh parsley, chopped	4 Tbsp.	60 ml

1 Season the trout on both sides with salt and pepper, then dredge in flour.

2 Melt the butter in a large sauté pan. Cook the trout over medium heat until flaky, approximately 4 minutes per side. Remove the trout from the pan and hold in a warm oven for service.

3 Heat the crab meat and the capers briefly in the same sauté pan.

4 For service, place each trout fillet on a warm plate and top with the crab meat and capers. Spoon sauce over the fish, garnish with parsley and serve.

Approximate values per serving: **Calories** 630, **Total fat** 52 g, **Saturated fat** 30 g, **Cholesterol** 255 mg, **Sodium** 560 mg, **Total carbohydrates** 5 g, **Protein** 35 g, **Vitamin A** 40%, **Vitamin C** 15%, **Calcium** 15%

MACADAMIA NUT–CRUSTED HALIBUT WITH RED ONION, TOMATO AND BALSAMIC SALSA

RECIPE 20.23

NEWBURY COLLEGE, Brookline, MA

Senior Instructor Scott Doughty

Yield: 4 Servings   **Method:** Sautéing

Macadamia nuts	4 oz.	120 g
Flour	8 oz.	240 g
Halibut fillet	2 lb.	900 g
Salt and pepper	TT	TT
Egg, slightly beaten	1	1
Olive oil	as needed	as needed
Red Onion, Tomato and Balsamic Vinegar Salsa (recipe follows)	1 pt.	480 ml
Herb sprigs	as needed for garnish	

1 Place the nuts on a half sheet pan and toast them lightly in the oven. Combine the toasted nuts with 4 ounces (120 grams) of flour in a food processor. Process until the nuts are chopped finely, but not pulverized.

2 Cut the halibut into four portions.

3 Season the fillets with salt and pepper and then bread them using the standard breading procedure described in Chapter 9, Mise en Place. The nut-flour mixture is the final coating.

4 Heat a sautoir and add a thin film of olive oil. Place the breaded fillets in the oil, leaving some space between each fillet so that they will cook properly. Sauté the fillets until they are a deep golden brown and crusty, then turn them over and cook until the fish is medium rare to medium. Remove the fillets from the pan. Residual heat will complete the cooking.

5 Spoon some of the salsa onto a serving platter and place the fillets on top of the salsa. Spoon a small dollop of salsa on each fillet and place a small herb sprig next to it. Serve the remaining salsa on the side.

Approximate values per serving: **Calories** 740, **Total fat** 42 g, **Saturated fat** 6 g, **Cholesterol** 125 mg, **Sodium** 300 mg, **Total carbohydrates** 36 g, **Protein** 55 g, **Vitamin A** 25%, **Vitamin C** 40%, **Calcium** 15%, **Iron** 30%

RED ONION, TOMATO AND BALSAMIC SALSA

Yield: 8 Servings

Red onion, small dice	1	1
Tomatoes concassée, medium dice	8	8
Balsamic vinegar	2 fl. oz.	60 ml
Olive oil	2 fl. oz.	60 ml
Salt	½ tsp.	3 ml
Cayenne pepper	⅛ tsp.	1 ml

1 Combine all of the ingredients in a bowl. Cover and chill until ready to serve.

Approximate values per serving: **Calories** 100, **Total fat** 7 g, **Saturated fat** 1 g, **Cholesterol** 0 mg, **Sodium** 160 mg, **Total carbohydrates** 8 g, **Protein** 1 g, **Vitamin A** 15%, **Vitamin C** 40%

RECIPE 20.24

FLYING FISH, SEATTLE, WA
Chef-Owner Christine Keff

Yield: 6 Servings   **Method:** Sautéing

Swordfish steaks	6	6
Black peppercorns, crushed	1 Tbsp.	15 ml
Fresh lime juice	2 fl. oz.	60 ml
Soy sauce	2 fl. oz.	60 ml
Risotto Cakes (recipe follows)	6	6

1 Coat the swordfish steaks evenly with the crushed peppercorns.

2 Heat a wok or cast-iron skillet over high heat until very hot. Place the steaks in the hot pan and cook for 1 minute per side.

3 Combine the lime juice and soy sauce. Deglaze the fish with the soy mixture and cook just until the liquid evaporates. Turn the fish frequently to coat it with the sauce.

4 Serve with Risotto Cakes and steamed bok choy.

Approximate values per serving: **Calories** 145, **Total fat** 4 g, **Saturated fat** 1 g, **Cholesterol** 42 mg, **Sodium** 784 mg, **Total carbohydrates** 3 g, **Protein** 22 g, **Claims**—low saturated fat

RISOTTO CAKES

Yield: 6 Servings

Soybean oil	8 fl. oz.	250 ml
Garlic cloves, minced	2	2
Onion, chopped	2 oz.	60 g
Salt	1 tsp.	5 ml
Black pepper	1 tsp.	5 ml
Arborio rice	1 pt.	500 ml
Chicken stock, simmering	1 qt.	1 lt
Water, hot	as needed	as needed
Parmesan, grated	2 Tbsp.	60 ml
Flour, seasoned with salt and pepper	as needed for breading	
Egg, beaten	1	1
Panko (Japanese bread crumbs)	½ c.	120 ml

1 Heat 1 tablespoon (15 milliliters) of the oil in a deep sauté pan. Add the garlic, onion and ½ teaspoon (3 milliliters) each of salt and pepper. Cook over medium heat until the onion is translucent.

2 Add the rice and sauté for 1 to 2 minutes, being careful not to burn the rice.

3 Reduce the heat to medium low and add ¼ cup (120 milliliters) of the chicken stock. Cook for approximately 15 minutes, stirring frequently and adding the remaining stock slowly as needed. If additional liquid is needed for the rice to be fully cooked and tender, add hot water.

4 Add the Parmesan and season with salt and pepper.

5 Press the risotto into an even layer on a lightly greased baking sheet. Cool completely in the refrigerator.

6 Cut out six cakes, using a cookie cutter or knife. Bread the cakes with seasoned flour, egg wash and panko, using the standard breading procedure described in Chapter 9, Mise En Place.

7 Heat the remaining soybean oil in a deep sauté pan to 340°F (171°C). Cook the cakes on both sides until golden brown.

Approximate values per serving: **Calories** 507, **Total fat** 39 g, **Saturated fat** 6 g, **Cholesterol** 37 mg, **Sodium** 639 mg, **Total carbohydrates** 30 g, **Protein** 9 g

SESAME SWORDFISH

RECIPE 20.25

Yield: 1 Serving   **Method:** Sautéing

Leeks, julienne	4 oz.	120 g
Swordfish steak, 6 oz. (170 g)	1	1
Sesame oil	1 fl. oz.	30 ml
Sesame seeds	1 fl. oz.	30 g
Fish stock	2 fl. oz.	60 ml
Tamari sauce	1 Tbsp.	15 ml

1 Deep-fry the leeks at 280°F (138°C) until golden brown. Drain well.
2 Brush both sides of the fish with sesame oil. Coat both sides of the fish with the sesame seeds, pressing to make a solid, even coating.
3 In a very hot pan, sauté the fish in the remaining oil. Turn the fish and finish cooking it in a 375°F (190°C) oven.
4 Remove the fish from the pan and hold on a warm plate. Deglaze the pan with the fish stock. Add the tamari sauce and heat thoroughly.
5 Place the fish on a bed of fried leeks, then pour the sauce over the fish and serve immediately.

Variations: Substitute a tuna or shark steak for the swordfish steak.

Approximate values per serving: **Calories** 780, **Total fat** 52 g, **Saturated fat** 9 g, **Cholesterol** 85 mg, **Sodium** 1410 mg, **Total carbohydrates** 24 g, **Protein** 53 g, **Vitamin C** 25%, **Calcium** 35%

SPECKLED TROUT BENESTANTE

RECIPE 20.26

PESCE RESTAURANT, HOUSTON, TX
Chef Mark Holley

Yield: 4 Servings   **Method:** Sautéing

Speckled trout fillets, boneless, skin on, 6 oz. (180 g) each	8	8
Salt and pepper	TT	TT
Flour	as needed for dredging	
Grapeseed oil	as needed for sautéing	
Vegetable oil	1 Tbsp.	15 ml
Onion, julienne	¼ c.	60 ml
Celery root, julienne	¼ c.	60 ml
Orzo pasta, cooked	2 pt.	900 ml
Heavy cream	6 fl. oz.	180 ml
Swiss chard, chiffonade	¼ c.	60 ml
Tomato concassée, julienne	¼ c.	60 ml
Parmesan, grated	2 Tbsp.	30 ml
Fresh herbs, assorted, chopped	1 Tbsp.	15 ml
Salt and pepper	TT	TT

Continued

Chicken or fish stock	as needed	as needed
Shiitake mushrooms, trimmed	1 ½ oz.	45 g
Oyster mushrooms, trimmed	1 ½ oz.	45 g
Artichokes, cooked, quartered	3	3
Jumbo lump crab meat	6 oz.	180 g
Beurre Blanc (page 222)	8 fl. oz.	240 ml
Fresh lemon juice	2 tsp.	10 ml
Fresh chervil, chopped	1 Tbsp.	15 ml
Chervil sprigs	4	4

1 Season the trout with salt and pepper and dredge in flour. Sauté in the grape-seed oil until done. Remove and hold in a warm place.

2 Heat the vegetable oil in a clean sauté pan and sauté the onion for 1 minute. Add the celery root and sauté for 30 seconds.

3 Add the orzo pasta and heavy cream. Cook until the cream has been reduced by half.

4 Add the Swiss chard and tomato concassée, return to a simmer and cook until thick and creamy, approximately 2 minutes.

5 Fold in the Parmesan and fresh herbs and season with salt and pepper. Thin the sauce with a small amount of chicken or fish stock if it becomes too thick.

6 In a separate pan, sauté the mushrooms in a small amount of vegetable oil for approximately 3 minutes. Add the artichokes and crab meat and gently sauté. Be careful not to break up the lumps of crab meat.

7 Mix the Beurre Blanc with the lemon juice and chopped chervil and ladle 2 fluid ounces (60 milliliters) of the sauce onto each of four plates. Place a portion of pasta in the center of each plate. Top the pasta with two trout fillets and arrange the mushroom, artichoke and crab mixture around the fish. Garnish with a sprig of chervil.

Approximate values per serving: **Calories** 1420, **Total fat** 90 g, **Saturated fat** 45 g, **Cholesterol** 420 mg, **Sodium** 1110 mg, **Total carbohydrates** 55 g, **Protein** 92 g, **Vitamin A** 40%, **Vitamin C** 45%, **Calcium** 40%, **Iron** 30%

SEARED TUNA WITH JASMINE RICE AND WASABI PONZU

RECIPE 20.27

RESTAURANT KEVIN TAYLOR, Denver, CO
Chef Kevin Taylor

Yield: 4 Servings

Soy sauce	2 fl. oz.	60 ml
Chicken stock	2 fl. oz.	60 ml
Fresh lemon juice	2 fl. oz.	60 ml
Olive oil	2 fl. oz.	60 ml
Wasabi powder	2 Tbsp.	30 ml
Vegetable oil	2 Tbsp.	30 ml
Tuna portions, sushi grade, 4 oz. (120 g) each	4	4
Jasmine rice, freshly cooked	1 pt.	450 ml

1 Combine the soy sauce, chicken stock, lemon juice and olive oil in a medium saucepot and bring to a simmer. In a small bowl combine the wasabi powder with just enough water to make a paste. Combine the wasabi paste with the soy sauce mixture and hold in a warm spot.

2 Heat the vegetable oil in a sauté pan over high heat. Place the tuna in the pan and sear on all sides. Remove the tuna and drain well on a towel.

3 Place a large spoonful of rice in the middle of each of four serving bowls. Slice the rare tuna and fan 5 to 7 slices around each bowl of rice. Spoon 2–3 fluid ounces (60–90 milliliters) of the ponzu sauce over the tuna. Garnish with additional wasabi paste and herbs or baby greens as desired.

Approximate values per serving: **Calories** 420, **Total fat** 22 g, **Saturated fat** 3 g, **Cholesterol** 50 mg, **Sodium** 1110 mg, **Total carbohydrates** 26 g, **Protein** 30 g, **Vitamin C** 20%, **Iron** 10%

PAN-SEARED SEA BASS WITH BEET VINAIGRETTE

RECIPE 20.28

STOUFFER STANFORD COURT HOTEL, San Francisco, CA
Former Chef Ercolino Crugnale

Yield: 10 Servings   **Method:** Sautéing

Chilean sea bass, diamond-cut fillets, 3 oz. (90 g) each	20	20
Salt and pepper	TT	TT
Olive oil	as needed	as needed
Shiitake mushrooms, sliced	10 oz.	300 g
Zucchini, julienne	10 oz.	300 g
Yellow squash, julienne	10 oz.	300 g
Red bell pepper, julienne	5 oz.	150 g
Chicken stock	10 fl. oz.	300 ml
Beet Vinaigrette (recipe follows)	3 fl. oz.	90 ml
Potatoes, peeled, julienne and deep-fried crisp	20 oz.	600 g

1 Season the fish on both sides. Sauté in olive oil until fully cooked.

2 Meanwhile, sauté the shiitake mushrooms in olive oil for 30 seconds. Add the zucchini, squash and bell pepper.

3 Deglaze the pan with chicken stock and adjust the seasonings.

4 To serve, pool the Beet Vinaigrette onto 10 warm plates. For an interesting effect, drizzle the sauce drop by drop into the middle of the plate from a height of 3 feet (1 meter), then pool the remaining sauce on the plate. Place the vegetables in the center with the fried potatoes on top. Arrange the fish on the vegetables.

Approximate values per serving: **Calories** 430, **Total fat** 15 g, **Saturated fat** 4 g, **Cholesterol** 90 mg, **Sodium** 610 mg, **Total carbohydrates** 29 g, **Protein** 44 g, **Vitamin A** 10%, **Vitamin C** 30%

BEET VINAIGRETTE

Yield: 1 qt. (1 lt)

Beet juice	3 pt.	1.5 lt
Fresh horseradish, grated	3 Tbsp.	45 ml
Shallot, minced	2 Tbsp.	30 ml
Garlic, minced	1 Tbsp.	15 ml
Fresh thyme	1 bunch	1 bunch
Black peppercorns	10	10
Apple cider vinegar	8 fl. oz.	250 ml
White wine	4 fl. oz.	120 ml
Poultry demi-glace	4 fl. oz.	120 ml
Cornstarch	2 Tbsp.	30 ml
Water	2 Tbsp.	30 ml
Salt	TT	TT

1 Combine the beet juice, horseradish, shallot, garlic, thyme and black pepper-corns. Reduce to 1½ pints (700 milliliters).
2 Add the vinegar, white wine and demi-glace; simmer for 20 minutes.
3 Combine the cornstarch and water until smooth. Whisk the slurry into the sauce and bring to a boil. Strain through a fine-mesh china cap and season to taste.

Approximate values per 1-fl.-oz. (30-ml) serving: **Calories** 20, **Total fat** 0 g, **Saturated fat** 0 g, **Cholesterol** 0 mg, **Sodium** 100 mg, **Total carbohydrates** 4 g, **Protein** 1 g, **Claims**—fat free; low sodium; low calorie

RECIPE 20.29 — PAN-FRIED TROUT WITH TOASTED GARLIC

Yield: 1 Serving   **Method:** Pan-frying

Trout, pan-dressed	1	1
Salt and pepper	TT	TT
Flour	as needed for dredging	
Clarified butter	1 fl. oz.	30 ml
Whole butter	1 Tbsp.	15 ml
Garlic cloves, sliced thin	2	2
Lemon juice	1 fl. oz.	30 ml
Fresh parsley, chopped	½ tsp.	3 ml

1 Season the trout with salt and pepper; dredge in flour.
2 Pan-fry the trout in the clarified butter until lightly browned and cooked through. Remove and reserve.
3 Degrease the pan, add the whole butter and cook until it begins to brown.
4 Add the garlic and sauté a few seconds, until the garlic begins to brown.
5 Add the lemon juice and parsley and swirl to combine with the butter.
6 Top the fish with the sauce and serve.

Approximate values per serving: **Calories** 650, **Total fat** 47 g, **Saturated fat** 23 g, **Cholesterol** 165 mg, **Sodium** 1600 mg, **Total carbohydrates** 28 g, **Protein** 28 g, **Vitamin A** 45%, **Vitamin C** 30%

RECIPE 20.30 — SALMON CROQUETTES

Croquettes are made from cooked meats, poultry, vegetables, fish, shellfish or potatoes, usually bound with a heavy béchamel or velouté sauce and seasoned. They are shaped into cones or patties, then breaded and deep-fried.

Yield: 12 Croquettes   **Method:** Deep-frying

Onion, small dice	2 oz.	60 g
Whole butter	3 oz.	90 g
Flour	3 oz.	90 g
Milk	8 fl. oz.	250 ml
Salmon, poached and flaked	1 lb.	450 g
Fresh dill, chopped	TT	TT
Salt and pepper	TT	TT
Lemon juice	1 Tbsp.	15 ml
Flour	as needed for breading	
Egg wash	as needed for breading	
Fine bread crumbs	as needed for breading	

1 Sauté the onion in the butter until translucent.
2 Add the flour and cook to make a white roux.

3 Add the milk to make a heavy béchamel sauce. Cook the sauce until very thick, approximately 5 minutes.

4 Remove the sauce from the heat and transfer it to a mixing bowl. Add the flaked salmon. Season with dill, salt, pepper and lemon juice and mix well.

5 Spread the mixture in a hotel pan, cover and refrigerate until cold.

6 Portion the mixture using a #20 portion scoop. Form each portion into a cone shape. Bread the croquettes using the standard breading procedure described in Chapter 9, Mise en Place.

7 Using the basket method, deep-fry the breaded croquettes until done.

Approximate values per croquette: **Calories** 140, **Total fat** 9 g, **Saturated fat** 4.5 g, **Cholesterol** 40 mg, **Sodium** 470 mg, **Total carbohydrates** 7 g, **Protein** 9 g, **Vitamin A** 8%, **Calcium** 10%

1 Portioning the croquette mixture with a portion scoop.

2 Forming the mixture into cone shapes.

3 Deep-frying the breaded corquettes using the basket method.

WHOLE SIZZLING CATFISH WITH GINGER AND PONZU SAUCE

RECIPE 20.31

CHINOIS ON MAIN, SANTA MONICA, CA
Chef Wolfgang Puck

Yield: 4 Servings   **Method:** Deep-frying

Catfish, cleaned, 3 lb. (1.3 kg)	1	1
Salt and pepper	TT	TT
Fresh ginger, ¼-inch (6-millimeters) slices, blanched	6	6
Peanut oil	as needed	as needed
Lemon juice	as needed	as needed
Ponzu sauce:		
Soy sauce	4 fl. oz.	120 ml
Mirin	4 fl. oz.	120 ml
Rice vinegar	4 fl. oz.	120 ml
Lemon juice	4 fl. oz.	120 ml
Fresh wood ear mushrooms	as needed for garnish	
Fresh cilantro	as needed for garnish	
Green onions	as needed for garnish	

1 Season the catfish with salt and pepper. Make three 2-inch (5-centimeter) incisions on each side of the fish and stuff each incision with blanched ginger.

2 Using the basket method, deep-fry the catfish in peanut oil, being careful to submerge the entire fish. Cook until golden-colored and crispy.

3 Squeeze fresh lemon juice over the top of the fish.

4 Combine the ponzu sauce ingredients.

5 Serve the whole catfish on a platter garnished with wood ear mushrooms, cilantro and green onions. Serve the ponzu sauce on the side.

Approximate values per serving: **Calories** 970, **Total fat** 50 g, **Saturated fat** 12 g, **Cholesterol** 305 mg, **Sodium** 2710 mg, **Total carbohydrates** 60 g, **Protein** 70 g, **Vitamin C** 25%, **Calcium** 20%, **Iron** 40%

POACHED HALIBUT WITH LOBSTER SAUCE, CHANTERELLES, CORN AND FAVA BEANS

RECIPE 20.32

PRIMITIVO WINE BAR, COLORADO SPRINGS, CO

John Broening, Executive Chef

Yield: 6 Servings		**Method:** Shallow poaching
Lobsters, 1 lb. 12 oz. (800 g) ea.	3	3
Court bouillon (page 205)	2 gal.	8 lt
Whole butter	5 oz.	150 g
Halibut fillets, 5 oz. (150 g) ea.	6	6
Salt and pepper	TT	TT
Chanterelle mushrooms	1 c.	240 ml
Lobster Stock (recipe follows)	1 qt.	1 lt
Red potatoes, cooked, medium dice	1 c.	240 ml
Corn kernels, cooked	½ c.	120 ml
Fava beans, cooked	½ c.	120 ml
Fresh lemon juice	2 Tbsp.	30 ml
Fresh basil leaves	12	12

1 Kill the lobsters by slicing between the eyes with the point of a chef's knife. Remove the tails, arms and claws. Reserve the uncooked shells for the stock. Simmer the lobster tails, arms and claws in the court bouillon. Cook the tails and arms for approximately 6 minutes and the claws slightly longer. Remove the meat from the shells, keeping the tail meat and claw meat intact. Cut each tail in half lengthwise.

2 Heat 1 ounce (30 grams) of butter in each of two sauté pans. Season the halibut with salt and pepper. Sauté three fillets in each pan for approximately 20 seconds without browning.

3 In a third pan, sauté the mushrooms in 1 ounce (30 grams) of the remaining butter until tender. Season with salt and pepper.

4 Add half of the lobster stock, mushrooms, potatoes and corn to each pan of halibut and bring to a simmer. Place the halibut in a 300°F (150°C) oven until done, approximately 8 to 10 minutes. Remove the halibut and hold in a warm place.

5 Add half of the fava beans, lobster meat, lemon juice and basil to each pan. Swirl half of the remaining butter into each pan and remove from the heat. Adjust the seasonings.

6 Divide the halibut among six heated soup plates and top with the vegetables.

Approximate values per serving: **Calories** 500, **Total fat** 25 g, **Saturated fat** 13 g, **Cholesterol** 170 mg, **Sodium** 550 mg, **Total carbohydrates** 17 g, **Protein** 52 g, **Vitamin A** 20%, **Vitamin C** 10%, **Calcium** 15%, **Iron** 15%

LOBSTER STOCK

Yield: 1 qt. (1 lt)		
Whole butter	1 oz.	30 g
Onion, minced	1	1

Leek, minced	1	1
Fennel bulb, minced	½	½
Carrot, minced	½	½
Brandy	2 fl. oz.	60 ml
Uncooked lobster shells, reserved from main recipe	as needed	as needed
White wine	8 fl. oz.	240 ml
Tomato juice	24 fl. oz.	700 ml
Water	24 fl. oz.	700 ml
Bay leaves	2	2
Cayenne pepper	1 pinch	1 pinch

1 Melt the butter in a saucepot. Sweat the onion, leek, fennel and carrot until soft, approximately 10 minutes. Flambé with the brandy and add the lobster shells. Add the white wine and reduce by half.

2 Add the tomato juice, water, bay leaves and cayenne pepper. Bring to a boil, skim and simmer for 1 hour. Strain and cool.

POACHED ORANGE ROUGHY FILLETS WITH WHITE WINE, TOMATO AND BASIL CREAM

RECIPE 20.33

CONNECTICUT CULINARY INSTITUTE, FARMINGTON, CT

Chef Jamie Roraback

Yield: 1 Serving **Method:** Shallow poaching

Whole butter, softened	2 tsp.	10 ml
Shallot, minced	1 Tbsp.	15 ml
Orange roughy fillets, 4 oz. (120 g) each	2	2
Salt and white pepper	TT	TT
White wine	4 fl. oz.	120 ml
Fish stock	4 fl. oz.	120 ml
Heavy cream (optional)	2 fl. oz.	60 ml
Tomato concassée	2 Tbsp.	30 ml
Fresh basil, chopped	1 Tbsp.	15 ml

1 Rub the bottom of an 8-inch (20-centimeter) sauté pan with the softened butter. Sprinkle the shallot into the pan.

2 Season the orange roughy fillets with salt and white pepper. Place the fillets in the sauté pan, presentation side up.

3 Add enough of the white wine and fish stock so that the liquid just covers the fish. Cover the pan and heat the poaching liquid to approximately 185°F (85°C). Do not let it boil. Poach the fillets until slightly underdone, approximately 3 to 4 minutes.

4 Remove the fish from the pan to a warm plate, cover and hold in a warm place.

5 Bring the poaching liquid to a boil and reduce until approximately 2 fluid ounces (60 milliliters) remain. If desired, add the heavy cream and reduce until the sauce is slightly thickened, approximately 1 minute. Add the tomato concassée and basil and cook only until they are warm. Adjust the seasonings with salt and white pepper. Plate the fish fillets and serve the sauce over the fish.

Approximate values per serving: **Calories** 340, **Total fat** 10 g, **Saturated fat** 5 g, **Cholesterol** 65 mg, **Sodium** 340 mg, **Total carbohydrates** 4 g, **Protein** 37 g, **Vitamin A** 15%, **Vitamin C** 10%, **Calcium** 10%

PAUPIETTES OF SOLE WITH MOUSSELINE OF SHRIMP

RECIPE 20.34

Yield: 6 Servings   **Method:** Poaching

Raw shrimp meat	12 oz.	360 g
Egg white	1	1
Heavy cream	6 fl. oz.	180 ml
Salt and white pepper	TT	TT
Lemon sole fillets, skinless,		
4 oz. (120 g) each	12	12
Whole butter	as needed	as needed
Shallot, chopped	2 oz.	60 g
Parsley stems, chopped	6	6
White vermouth	6 fl. oz.	180 ml
Shrimp stock	12 fl. oz.	360 ml
Beurre manié	approx. 1½ oz.	approx. 45 g

1 To make the mousseline, purée the shrimp meat in a food processor. Add the egg white and pulse to incorporate. Slowly add 2 fluid ounces (60 milliliters) of the cream to the shrimp while pulsing the processor. Season the mousseline with salt and white pepper.

2 Place the sole fillets, skin side up, on a cutting board and cover with plastic wrap. Then flatten the fillets slightly with a mallet.

3 Spread each fillet with a portion of the mousseline. Roll up the fillets, starting with the thickest part and finishing with the tail portion.

4 Butter a sauteuse and sprinkle with the chopped shallot and parsley stems. Place the sole **paupiettes** in the sauteuse and add the vermouth and shrimp stock. Bring the liquid to a boil, cover with a piece of buttered parchment paper and place in a 350°F (180°C) oven. Poach until nearly done.

5 Remove the sole from the sauteuse and reserve in a warm place.

6 Return the sauteuse to the heat and reduce the cuisson slightly. Thicken the cuisson to the desired consistency with the beurre manié. Add the remaining cream, bring the sauce to a boil and strain through a fine chinois. Adjust the seasonings.

7 Serve two paupiettes per portion on a pool of sauce.

▶ **paupiette** a thin slice of meat or fish that is rolled around a filling of finely ground meat or vegetables, then fried, baked or braised in wine or stock

Approximate values per serving: **Calories** 450, **Total fat** 18 g, **Saturated fat** 9 g, **Cholesterol** 310 mg, **Sodium** 970 mg, **Total carbohydrates** 4 g, **Protein** 69 g, **Vitamin A** 35%

1 Using a mallet to flatten a fillet slightly.

2 Spreading the fillet with the mousseline.

3 Rolling the paupiettes.

CHILLED POACHED SALMON ROULADE WITH THAI NOODLE SALAD AND SOY MOLASSES VINAIGRETTE

RECIPE 20.35

CHEF LELAND ATKINSON, WASHINGTON, DC

Yield: 5 Servings   **Method:** Poaching

Red bell pepper, julienne	6 oz.	180 g
Yellow bell pepper, julienne	6 oz.	180 g
Onions, julienne	5 oz.	150 g
Olive oil	1 fl. oz.	30 ml
Salmon fillet, skin off, pin bones removed, approx. 2 lb. (1 kg)	1	1
Salt and pepper	TT	TT
Fresh cilantro, chopped	2 bunches	2 bunches
Thai Noodle Salad (recipe follows)	as needed	as needed
Soy Molasses Vinaigrette (recipe follows)	as needed	as needed

1 Quickly sauté the bell peppers and onions in the olive oil; drain and cool.

2 Trim the fat and dark flesh from the skin side of the fillet. Carefully butterfly the fillet, cover it with plastic wrap and pound gently.

3 Place the salmon, skin side up, on a rectangular piece of plastic wrap that extends at least 3 inches (7.5 centimeters) beyond each end of the fillet.

4 Season the fish with salt and pepper; sprinkle the cilantro over it. Distribute the cooled onions and peppers over the cilantro, leaving at least a 2-inch (5-centimeter) edge of salmon uncovered on all sides.

5 Roll the salmon and onion-pepper mixture into a tight pinwheel and firmly knot the ends of the plastic wrap.

6 Tightly roll the fish in aluminum foil, twisting the ends to form a tight cylinder.

7 Poach or steam the fish until it reaches an internal temperature of 110°F (43°C). Remove from the poaching liquid and chill.

8 At service time, unwrap the chilled salmon and carefully slice it. Arrange the sliced salmon on plates with the Thai Noodle Salad. Pour 3 fluid ounces (90 milliliters) of the Soy Molasses Vinaigrette around the salmon at the last moment.

Approximate values per serving: **Calories** 430, **Total fat** 20 g, **Saturated fat** 4 g, **Cholesterol** 105 mg, **Sodium** 850 mg, **Total carbohydrates** 11 g, **Protein** 51 g, **Vitamin C** 150%

THAI NOODLE SALAD

Yield: 5 Servings

Cellophane noodles	3.4 oz.	100 g
Fresh cilantro, chopped	2 bunches	2 bunches
Oyster sauce	2 Tbsp.	30 ml
Sesame oil	1 Tbsp.	15 ml
Garlic, minced	½ Tbsp.	8 ml
Soy sauce	2 Tbsp.	30 ml
Red pepper, crushed	1 pinch	1 pinch

1 Pour boiling water over the noodles and allow them to steep until they are al dente, approximately 5 minutes. Refresh in cold water. Drain well.

2 Toss the noodles with the other ingredients. Adjust the seasonings to taste.

Approximate values per serving: **Calories** 100, **Total fat** 3 g, **Saturated fat** 0 g, **Cholesterol** 0 mg, **Sodium** 540 mg, **Total carbohydrates** 18 g, **Protein** 0 g, **Claims**—low fat

SOY MOLASSES VINAIGRETTE

Yield: 1 pt. (450 ml)

Molasses	4 fl. oz.	120 ml
Rice vinegar	2 fl. oz.	60 ml
Soy sauce	8 fl. oz.	250 ml
Fresh ginger, chopped coarse	1 tsp.	5 ml
Olive oil	as needed	as needed

1 Combine the molasses, rice vinegar, soy sauce and fresh ginger in a saucepan. Bring to a boil and remove from the heat immediately. Allow the mixture to rest, undisturbed, for 1 hour.

2 Strain and chill the molasses mixture. Add the olive oil at service time.

Approximate values per 1-fl.-oz. (30-ml) serving: **Calories** 35, **Total fat** 1 g, **Saturated fat** 0 g, **Cholesterol** 0 mg, **Sodium** 820 mg, **Total carbohydrates** 6 g, **Protein** 1 g, **Claims—**low fat; low calorie

STEAMED BLACK BASS WITH SANSHO PEPPER

RECIPE 20.36

THE FOUR SEASONS, New York, NY
Chef Christian Albin

Yield: 6 Servings		**Method:** Steaming
Black bass fillets, skin on, approx.		
5 oz. (150 g) each	6	6
Leek, large, cut into strips	1	1
Sansho pepper and sea salt	TT	TT
Vinaigrette:		
Lime	1	1
Lemon	1	1
Olive oil	3 Tbsp.	45 ml
Pommery mustard	1 tsp.	5 ml
Salt and pepper	TT	TT

1 Lightly score the fish skin, then place the fillets, skin side up, and the leeks in a steamer basket. Season with sansho pepper and sea salt. Steam for approximately 5 minutes.

2 To make the vinaigrette, zest and juice the lime and lemon. Blanch the zests in water. Drain and mix the zests and juices with the olive oil and Pommery mustard; season to taste with salt and pepper.

3 Plate the fish fillets and garnish with the leeks. Drizzle the vinaigrette over the fish and leeks.

Approximate values per serving: **Calories** 220, **Total fat** 7 g, **Saturated fat** 1.5 g, **Cholesterol** 125 mg, **Sodium** 530 mg, **Total carbohydrates** 5 g, **Protein** 35 g, **Vitamin C** 20%

RECIPE 20.37

STUFFED STRIPED BASS CARTOCCIO

PESCE RESTAURANT, Houston, TX
Chef Mark Holley

Yield: 1 Serving		**Method:** Steaming en papillote
Fennel bulb, shaved	½ c.	120 ml
Tomato concassée	¼ c.	60 ml
Leek, julienne	¼ c.	60 ml

Shrimp, 26–30 count, peeled, deveined	8	8
Jumbo lump crab meat	3 oz.	90 g
Panko (Japanese bread crumbs)	2 Tbsp.	30 ml
Kosher salt	½ tsp.	3 ml
Black peppercorns, crushed	⅛ tsp.	1 ml
Vinaigrette:		
Extra virgin olive oil	2 Tbsp.	30 ml
Truffle oil	2 Tbsp.	30 ml
Sherry wine vinegar	2 Tbsp.	30 ml
Fresh lemon juice	3 Tbsp.	45 ml
Dijon mustard	2 tsp.	10 ml
Fresh herbs, assorted, chopped	2 tsp.	10 ml
Unsalted butter	2 tsp.	10 ml
Striped bass fillet, 8 oz. (240 g)	1	1
Salt and pepper	TT	TT

1. In a small bowl, combine the fennel, tomato concassée, leek, shrimp, crab meat, panko, kosher salt and crushed peppercorns. Toss the ingredients together gently without breaking up the lumps of crab meat.

2. In a separate bowl, combine the vinaigrette ingredients. Add three-quarters of the vinaigrette to the vegetable, shrimp and crab meat mixture and toss to coat.

3. Place a 17½-inch- (45-centimeter-) square piece of aluminum foil on a work surface. Rub the foil with the butter, leaving a 2-inch (5-centimeter) border unbuttered.

4. Season the fish generously with salt and pepper and position on one side of the piece of foil. Place the shellfish mixture on top of the fish. Drizzle the remaining vinaigrette over the top.

5. Seal the foil by folding it corner to corner to form a large triangle. Crimp the edges of the foil to seal it tightly. Place the foil package on a sheet pan and bake at 375°F (190°C) until done, approximately 15 minutes depending on the thickness of the fish.

6. Place the foil package on a serving plate. Carefully cut the foil along the sealed edge and fold it back to expose the fish. Serve immediately while the fragrant steam is still escaping from the package.

Approximate values per serving: **Calories** 1030, **Total fat** 71 g, **Saturated fat** 14 g, **Cholesterol** 350 mg, **Sodium** 1960 mg, **Total carbohydrates** 29 g, **Protein** 71 g, **Vitamin A** 20%, **Vitamin C** 70%, **Calcium** 20%, **Iron** 30%

BRAISED SHARK WITH LEMON PESTO

RECIPE 20.38

MISSISSIPPI UNIVERSITY FOR WOMEN, COLUMBUS, MS
Chef Jim Fitzgerald, Ph.D., CCP

Yield: 4 Servings   **Method:** Braising

Olive oil	2 Tbsp.	30 ml
Unsalted butter	2 Tbsp.	30 ml
Shark steaks, skinless, 6 oz. (180 g) each	4	4
Flour	as needed for dredging	
Yellow onion, chopped	1	1
Red bell pepper, diced	1	1
Bay leaf	1	1
Basil leaves, minced	10	10

Continued

Garlic, minced	1 tsp.	5 ml
Tomato, fresh or canned, chopped	1 c.	240 ml
Dry white wine	4 fl. oz	120 ml
Salt and pepper	TT	TT
Lemon Pesto (recipe follows)	as needed	as needed

1 Heat the olive oil and butter in a large rondeau.
2 Lightly dredge the fish in flour and dust off any excess. Brown the fish in the rondeau on both sides, remove from the pan and reserve.
3 Add the onion and bell pepper to the rondeau and cook until the onion is translucent. Add the bay leaf, basil and garlic. Cook for 1 minute. Add the tomato and wine and bring to simmer. Cook for 2 minutes.
4 Return the fish to the pan; season with salt and pepper and cover. Braise in a 375°F (190°C) oven until the steaks are done, approximately 6 to 8 minutes. Serve with a portion of the cooking liquid and drizzle with Lemon Pesto.

Approximate values per serving: **Calories** 410, **Total fat** 21 g, **Saturated fat** 6 g, **Cholesterol** 100 mg, **Sodium** 140 mg, **Total carbohydrates** 14 g, **Protein** 38 g, **Vitamin A** 50%, **Vitamin C** 110%, **Iron** 15%

LEMON PESTO

Yield: 1 pt. (500 ml)

Lemons	4	4
Garlic cloves	5	5
Fresh basil	2 c.	450 ml
Parsley, chopped	1½ c.	350 ml
Salt	2 tsp.	10 ml
Extra virgin olive oil	10 fl. oz.	300 ml

1 Zest the lemons. Combine the zest, garlic, basil, parsley and salt in a food processor fitted with the metal blade. Process until minced.
2 With the motor running, drizzle in the olive oil to form a sauce.

Approximate values per 1-fl.-oz. (30-ml) serving: **Calories** 150, **Total fat** 17 g, **Saturated fat** 2.5 g, **Cholesterol** 0 mg, **Sodium** 290 mg, **Total carbohydrates** 1 g, **Protein** 0 g, **Vitamin A** 10%, **Vitamin C** 20%

ESCOLAR WITH EGGPLANT AND CARROT PURÉES AND TOMATO, OLIVE AND PRESERVED LEMON SAUCE

RECIPE 20.39

PRIMITIVO WINE BAR, COLORADO SPRINGS, CO
John Broening, Executive Chef

Yield: 4 Servings   **Method:** Braising

Whole butter	2 oz.	60 g
Escolar fillets, 4 oz. (120 g) each	4	4
Salt and white pepper	TT	TT
Fish stock	1 pt.	450 ml
Spinach, stemmed	4 oz.	120 g
Fresh lemon juice	as needed	as needed
Eggplant Purée (recipe follows)	as needed	as needed
Carrot Purée (recipe follows)	as needed	as needed
Tomato, Olive and Preserved Lemon Sauce (recipe follows)	as needed	as needed

| Cilantro sprigs | as needed for garnish |
| Black and white sesame seeds, toasted | as needed for garnish |

1 Heat 1 ounce (30 grams) of butter in a sauté pan. Season the fish with salt and white pepper and sauté for 30 seconds. Turn the fillets, add the fish stock and bring to a boil. Place the pan in a 350°F (180°C) oven until the fish is done, approximately 10 minutes. Remove the fish and hold in a warm place.

2 Melt 1 ounce (30 grams) of butter in a sauté pan and cook until noisette. Add the spinach and toss until it wilts. Season the spinach with salt and white pepper and a little lemon juice. Hold for service.

3 On each of four warm plates, place one quenelle of Eggplant Purée and one quenelle of Carrot Purée. Top with the sautéed spinach, the Tomato, Olive and Preserved Lemon Sauce and a fillet. Garnish with cilantro sprigs and sesame seeds.

Note: Escolar is a very oily fish from South America with white, flaky flesh. Halibut or sea bass may be substituted.

Approximate values per serving: **Calories** 370, **Total fat** 28 g, **Saturated fat** 13 g, **Cholesterol** 95 mg, **Sodium** 270 mg, **Total carbohydrates** 12 g, **Protein** 19 g, **Vitamin A** 300%, **Vitamin C** 25%, **Iron** 10%

EGGPLANT PURÉE

Yield: 1 pt. (450 ml)

Japanese eggplants	4	4
Olive oil	4 fl. oz.	120 ml
Salt and pepper	TT	TT
Cumin, toasted	1 tsp.	5 ml
Parsley, chopped	2 Tbsp.	30 ml

1 Cut the eggplants in half lengthwise and score the flesh with a paring knife. Toss with half of the oil. Season with salt and pepper and roast, cut side down, in a 300°F (150°C) oven until soft, approximately 20 to 30 minutes. Remove and cool.

2 Scrape the eggplant flesh from the skins and discard the skins. Mix the flesh with the remaining ingredients. Hold warm for service.

Approximate values per 1-fl.-oz. (30-ml) serving: **Calories** 80, **Total fat** 7 g, **Saturated fat** 1 g, **Cholesterol** 0 mg, **Sodium** 0 mg, **Total carbohydrates** 4 g, **Protein** 1 g

CARROT PURÉE

Yield: 1 pt. (450 ml)

Carrots, large dice	1 lb.	450 g
Harissa	1 Tbsp.	15 ml
Cumin, toasted	1 tsp.	5 ml
Honey	2 Tbsp.	30 ml
Whole butter	3 oz.	90 g
Salt and pepper	TT	TT

1 Boil the carrots in salted water until very tender. Drain well and purée in a food processor with the remaining ingredients. Hold warm for service.

Approximate values per 1-fl.-oz. (30-ml) serving: **Calories** 60, **Total fat** 4.5 g, **Saturated fat** 2.5 g, **Cholesterol** 10 mg, **Sodium** 10 mg, **Total carbohydrates** 5 g, **Protein** 0 g, **Vitamin A** 160%

TOMATO, OLIVE AND PRESERVED LEMON SAUCE

Yield: 1 qt. (1 lt)

Lemons	3	3
Water	1 qt.	1 lt
Granulated sugar	8 oz.	240 g
Salt	as needed	as needed
Chile flakes	1/8 tsp.	1 ml
Onion, medium dice	1	1
Carrot, medium dice	1/2	1/2
Whole butter	1 1/2 oz.	45 g
Garlic, minced	1 tsp.	5 ml
Fresh ginger, minced	1 tsp.	5 ml
Tomato concassée	3 c.	700 ml
Fish stock	8 fl. oz.	240 ml
Cumin, toasted	1 tsp.	5 ml
Honey	2 Tbsp.	30 ml
Harissa	1 Tbsp.	15 ml
Niçoise olives, pitted	16	16
Black pepper	TT	TT
Fresh cilantro, chopped	2 Tbsp.	30 ml

1 Slice the lemons thinly and remove all seeds. Combine the lemon slices with the water, sugar, salt and chile flakes. Bring the mixture to a boil and simmer for 15 minutes. Cool the preserved lemons in the liquid until ready to use.

2 Sweat the onion and carrot in the butter until tender, approximately 20 minutes. Add the garlic and ginger and sweat for 1 minute. Add the tomato concassée, fish stock, cumin, honey, harissa, olives and 3 tablespoons (45 milliliters) of chopped preserved lemons and simmer for 10 minutes. Season to taste with salt and black pepper. Add the cilantro.

Approximate values per 1-fl.-oz. (30-ml) serving: **Calories** 25, **Total fat** 1.5 g, **Saturated fat** 0.5 g, **Cholesterol** 5 mg, **Sodium** 40 mg, **Total carbohydrates** 4 g, **Protein** 0 g, **Vitamin A** 10%, **Claims**—low calorie, low fat, low sodium, source of Vitamin A

RECIPE 20.40

GRILLED SHRIMP

NEWBURY COLLEGE, BROOKLINE, MA
Senior Instructor Scott Doughty

Yield: 6 Servings		**Method:** Grilling
Fresh rosemary	2 sprigs	2 sprigs
Shrimp, 16–20 count, peeled and deveined	2 lb.	900 g
Salt and black pepper	TT	TT
Olive oil	as needed	as needed

1 Strip the rosemary leaves from the stems and chop the leaves.

2 Season the shrimp with salt. Coat the shrimp with pepper as desired.

3 Toss the shrimp with the rosemary and a small amount of olive oil until the shrimp are lightly and evenly coated with oil and the rosemary is evenly distributed. Allow the shrimp to marinate for 2 hours.

4 Preheat the grill. Arrange the shrimp on the grill and cook until the shrimp are cooked one-third of the way through and have attractive grill marks, approximately 1 to 2 minutes. Turn them and repeat. Remove the shrimp from

the grill when they are still slightly underdone in the middle, residual heat will continue cooking them. Do not overcook the shrimp or they will be tough and dry.

Approximate values per serving: **Calories** 200, **Total fat** 7 g, **Saturated fat** 1 g, **Cholesterol** 230 mg, **Sodium** 220 mg, **Total carbohydrates** 1 g, **Protein** 31 g, **Iron** 20%

LOBSTER THERMIDOR

RECIPE 20.41

THE ART INSTITUTE OF WASHINGTON, ARLINGTON, VA

Chef John Harrison

Yield: 4 Servings **Method:** Sautéing/Baking

Whole butter	3 oz.	90 g
Shallots, fine dice	3 oz.	90 g
Mushrooms, quartered	1 pt.	470 ml
Salt and pepper	TT	TT
Lobster or shellfish stock	8 fl. oz.	240 ml
Heavy cream	1 pt.	470 ml
Brandy	3 fl. oz.	90 ml
Dry sherry	3 fl. oz.	90 ml
Worcestershire sauce	½ tsp.	2 ml
Cayenne pepper or hot sauce	½ tsp.	2 ml
Lobster meat, cooked, medium dice	24 oz.	670 g
Fresh bread crumbs	¾ c.	180 ml
Fresh parsley, chopped	1 Tbsp.	15 ml
Lobster body shells or pastry shells	4	4
Parmesan, grated	4 Tbsp.	60 ml
Pimentos, julienne	as needed	as needed

1 Heat a heavy sautoir. Add the butter and the shallots and cook until the shallots are translucent. Add the mushrooms and cook until they soften. Season the mixture with salt and pepper.

2 Add the stock and heavy cream. Bring to a boil and reduce by half. Stir in the brandy, sherry, Worcestershire sauce and cayenne pepper. Return to a boil and cook for 1 minute.

3 In a separate bowl, mix together the lobster, bread crumbs and parsley. Gently combine the lobster mixture with the mushrooms and sauce. Adjust the seasonings with salt and pepper.

4 Fill four lobster body shells or pastry shells with the lobster mixture. Sprinkle with Parmesan and bake at 350°F (180°C) until hot, approximately 10 to 15 minutes. Garnish with the pimentos and serve.

Approximate values per serving: **Calories** 880, **Total fat** 65 g, **Saturated fat** 40 g, **Cholesterol** 340 mg, **Sodium** 960 mg, **Total carbohydrates** 16 g, **Protein** 44 g, **Vitamin A** 60%, **Calcium** 30%, **Iron** 10%

CLAMS CASINO

RECIPE 20.42

Yield: 36 Clams **Method:** Baking

Bacon slices, diced	4	4
Onion, minced	1 oz.	30 g
Red bell pepper, minced	1 oz.	30 g

Continued

Green bell pepper, minced	1 oz.	30 g
Whole butter	6 oz.	180 g
Lemon juice	1 Tbsp.	15 ml
Worcestershire sauce	2 tsp.	10 ml
Tabasco sauce	TT	TT
Clams, scrubbed	36	36
Fresh bread crumbs	2 oz.	60 g

1 Fry the bacon until well done. Drain the fat, reserving 2 tablespoons (30 milliliters).

2 Sauté the onion and bell peppers in the bacon fat until tender; remove from the heat and cool.

3 Combine 4 ounces (120 grams) of the butter, lemon juice, Worcestershire sauce, Tabasco sauce, bacon pieces and sautéed vegetables and chill.

4 Open the clams, leaving the meat in the bottom shell. Top each clam with 1 teaspoon (5 milliliters) of the seasoned butter.

5 Melt 2 ounces (60 grams) of butter in a sauté pan and toss the bread crumbs in the butter. Top each clam with a portion of the bread crumbs.

6 Bake at 400°F (200°C) until light brown and bubbling, approximately 10 minutes. Serve immediately.

Approximate values per clam: **Calories** 45, **Total fat** 4 g, **Saturated fat** 2.5 g, **Cholesterol** 10 mg, **Sodium** 65 mg, **Total carbohydrates** 1 g, **Protein** 0 g

---

RECIPE 20.43   **OYSTERS ROCKEFELLER**

Yield: 36 Oysters   **Method:** Baking

Unsalted butter	8 oz.	250 g
Fresh parsley, chopped	1 oz.	30 g
Celery, chopped	2 oz.	60 g
Fennel bulb, chopped	2 oz.	60 g
Shallots, chopped	2 oz.	60 g
Garlic, chopped	1 tsp.	5 ml
Watercress, chopped	4 oz.	120 g
Pernod	2 fl. oz.	60 ml
Fresh bread crumbs	2 oz.	60 g
Salt and pepper	TT	TT
Oysters, on the half shell	36	36
Rock salt	as needed	as needed

1 Heat the butter in a sauté pan. Add the parsley, celery, fennel, shallots and garlic and cook for 5 minutes.

2 Add the watercress and cook for 1 minute.

3 Add the Pernod and bread crumbs; season with salt and pepper.

4 Transfer the mixture to a food processor and purée.

5 Top each oyster with approximately 2 teaspoons (10 milliliters) of the vegetable mixture; it should coat the oyster's entire surface.

6 Bake the oysters on a bed of rock salt at 450°F (230°C) until the mixture bubbles, approximately 6 to 7 minutes.

Approximate values per oyster: **Calories** 170, **Total fat** 9 g, **Saturated fat** 4.5 g, **Cholesterol** 105 mg, **Sodium** 450 mg, **Total carbohydrates** 9 g, **Protein** 13 g, **Vitamin A** 15%, **Iron** 60%

CRAB MEAT FLAN WITH RED PEPPER COULIS AND CHIVES

THE WHITE HOUSE, Washington, DC
Executive Sous Chef John Moeller

Yield: 6 Servings   **Method:** Baking

Lump crab meat	8 oz.	250 g
Fresh chives, chopped	1 bunch	1 bunch
Salt and white pepper	TT	TT
Eggs	5	5
Heavy cream	1 pt.	500 ml
Sherry	1 fl. oz.	30 ml
Whole butter, melted	as needed	as needed
Beurre Blanc (page 222)	18 fl. oz.	560 ml
Red Pepper Coulis (page 225)	3 fl. oz.	90 ml
Fresh chive stems	12	12
Caviar or lumpfish roe	as needed for garnish	

1 Clean the crab meat and toss with the chopped chives. Season with salt and white pepper.

2 Beat the eggs together lightly and add the cream. Add the sherry and the crab meat mixture. Adjust the seasonings.

3 Coat six ramekins with melted butter and fill with the flan mixture. Place the ramekins in a water bath and bake at 350°F (180°C) until set, approximately 45 to 50 minutes.

4 Pool the Beurre Blanc on six serving plates. Unmold the flans and place in the center of each plate. Decorate the plates with the Red Pepper Coulis and garnish with the chive stems and caviar.

Approximate values per serving: **Calories** 460, **Total fat** 43 g, **Saturated fat** 25 g, **Cholesterol** 350 mg, **Sodium** 750 mg, **Total carbohydrates** 4 g, **Protein** 14 g, **Vitamin A** 50%, **Vitamin C** 15%

SCALLOPS AND SHRIMP SAMBUCA

SCOTTSDALE COMMUNITY COLLEGE, Scottsdale, AZ

Yield: 1 Serving, 9 oz. (270 g)   **Method:** Sautéing

Fennel bulb, julienne	1 oz.	30 g
Carrot, julienne	1 oz.	30 g
Celery, julienne	1 oz.	30 g
Shrimp, U-10, butterflied	3	3
Whole butter	1 Tbsp.	15 ml
Bay scallops	3 oz.	90 g
Salt and white pepper	TT	TT
Sambuca	1 fl. oz.	30 ml
Heavy cream	3 fl. oz.	90 ml
Puff pastry fleurons	2	2
Fresh dill	1 sprig	1 sprig

1 Blanch the fennel, carrot and celery. Refresh in cold water, drain and reserve.

2 Sauté the shrimp in the butter over high heat for 1 minute. Add the scallops and sauté for 30 more seconds. Season the shellfish with salt and white pepper, remove and reserve in a warm place.

3 Deglaze the pan with Sambuca. Add the cream. Boil and reduce until the sauce thickens. Add the vegetables, scallops and shrimp to the pan and simmer until the shellfish is done, approximately 2 minutes. Adjust the seasonings.

4 Serve the vegetables and shellfish mounded on a warm plate, garnished with the fleurons and dill.

Approximate values per 9-oz. (270-g) serving: **Calories** 1350, **Total fat** 58 g, **Saturated fat** 31 g, **Cholesterol** 695 mg, **Sodium** 3370 mg, **Total carbohydrates** 117 g, **Protein** 90 g, **Vitamin A** 120%, **Calcium** 70%, **Iron** 140%

SEARED DIVER SCALLOP WITH CHANTERELLES, POTATO GAUFRETTES AND BLOOD ORANGE CREAM

RECIPE 20.46

RESTAURANT KEVIN TAYLOR, Denver, CO
Chef Kevin Taylor

Yield: 4 Servings   **Method:** Sautéing

Russet potato	1	1
Blood oranges	5	5
Heavy cream	2 fl. oz.	60 ml
Unsalted butter	4 oz.	120 g
Salt and pepper	TT	TT
Granulated sugar	as needed	as needed
Diver scallops, U-8	4	4
Canola oil	as needed	as needed
Fresh chanterelle mushrooms, trimmed	1 pt.	450 ml
Olive oil	as needed	as needed

▶ **diver scallops** scallops that are harvested from the ocean by divers who hand-pick each one; diver scallops tend to be less gritty than those harvested by dragging, and hand-harvesting is more ecologically friendly

1 Peel the potato and trim into a cylinder shape. Using a mandoline and the ridged cutting blade, cut thin slices of potato, turning the potato 60 to 90 degrees between each slice and adjusting the thickness of the slices until a waffle pattern (gaufrette) is produced. Using the swimming method, deep-fry the potato slices at 325°F (163°C) until crisp and lightly browned. Drain on a paper towel.

2 Juice the blood oranges. Strain the juice. Place the juice in a small saucepot and reduce by two-thirds. Add the heavy cream and reduce this mixture by one-third. Reduce the heat and slowly whisk in the butter to form a sauce. Season with salt and pepper. If the sauce is too tart, adjust the flavor with a small amount of sugar. Hold the sauce in a warm place.

3 Season the scallops with salt and pepper. In a medium sauté pan over high heat, sear the scallops in a little canola oil until browned on one side. Turn the scallops and place the pan in a 400°F (200°C) oven until cooked to the desired doneness, approximately 3 to 5 minutes.

4 Sauté the chanterelles in a small amount of olive oil until tender. Season with salt and pepper.

5 Place a portion of the blood orange sauce in the bottom of each of four small soup plates. Place a portion of the chanterelles in the middle of each bowl on top of the sauce. Place a seared scallop on top of the chanterelles and garnish each plate with two or three gaufrette potatoes.

Approximate values per serving: **Calories** 350, **Total fat** 32 g, **Saturated fat** 18 g, **Cholesterol** 85 mg, **Sodium** 35 mg, **Total carbohydrates** 13 g, **Protein** 5 g, **Vitamin A** 25%, **Vitamin C** 60%

SHRIMP WITH OLIVE OIL AND GARLIC

RECIPE 20.47

Yield: 4 Servings   **Method:** Sautéing

Garlic, chopped	4 Tbsp.	60 ml
Extra virgin olive oil	4 fl. oz.	120 ml
Shrimp, 26–30 count, in shell	2 lb. 4 oz.	1 kg
Coarse sea salt	1 Tbsp.	15 ml
Lemon juice	2 Tbsp.	30 ml

1 Sauté the garlic in the olive oil until translucent.

2 Add the shrimp and salt. Toss to coat the shrimp with the oil and cook just until the shrimp are pink, approximately 5 minutes. Add the lemon juice.

3 Arrange the shrimp on warm serving plates; top with the oil, garlic and lemon juice left in the pan. Serve immediately.

Approximate values per serving: **Calories** 530, **Total fat** 31 g, **Saturated fat** 4.5 g, **Cholesterol** 555 mg, **Sodium** 2380 mg, **Total carbohydrates** 2 g, **Protein** 60 g, **Vitamin A** 20%, **Vitamin C** 20%, **Iron** 50%

SHRIMP CURRY WITH MANGO

RECIPE 20.48

CONNECTICUT CULINARY INSTITUTE, FARMINGTON, CT
Chef Jamie Roraback

Yield: 4 Servings   **Method:** Sautéing

Clarified butter or ghee	2 Tbsp.	30 ml
Shrimp, 16–20 count, peeled and deveined	12	12
Onion, thinly sliced	1 c.	240 ml
Fresh ginger, minced	1 Tbsp.	15 ml
Jalapeño, seeded and minced	1 Tbsp.	15 ml
Curry powder	2 Tbsp.	30 ml
Chicken stock	8 fl. oz.	240 ml
Cornstarch	2 Tbsp.	30 ml
Water	1 Tbsp.	15 ml
Coconut milk	4 fl. oz.	120 ml
Fresh mango, diced	4 oz.	120 g
Cilantro, chopped coarse	1 Tbsp.	15 ml
Salt and pepper	TT	TT
Granulated sugar	TT	TT

1 Heat the clarified butter or ghee in a sauté pan. Add the shrimp and sauté until just cooked. Remove the shrimp from the pan and reserve.

2 In the same pan, sauté the onion for approximately 3 minutes or until wilted and slightly golden on the edges. Add the ginger, jalapeño and curry powder and sauté for 1 minute. Add the chicken stock, scraping up any bits stuck to the bottom of the pan.

3 Combine the cornstarch and water to make a slurry. Bring the stock mixture to a boil, then whisk a small amount of the slurry into the liquid. Continue adding slurry slowly until the sauce is the desired thickness.

4 Add the coconut milk, mango, cilantro and shrimp to the pan. Season to taste with salt, pepper and sugar and simmer to combine the flavors, approximately 1 minute. Serve the curry with steamed basmati rice.

Approximate values per serving: **Calories** 190, **Total fat** 13 g, **Saturated fat** 10 g, **Cholesterol** 45 mg, **Sodium** 210 mg, **Total carbohydrates** 14 g, **Protein** 5 g, **Vitamin A** 25%, **Vitamin C** 15%, **Iron** 15%

RECIPE 20.49 LOBSTER À L'AMÉRICAINE

Yield: 4 Servings, 4–5 oz. (120–130 g)
of lobster and 4 oz. (120 g) of sauce each   **Method:** Sautéing

Lobsters, 1 lb. 12 oz. (750 g) each	2	2
Clarified butter	2 fl. oz.	60 ml
Shallots, chopped	1 oz.	30 g
Garlic, chopped	1 tsp.	5 ml
Brandy	4 fl. oz.	120 ml
Dry white wine	8 fl. oz.	250 ml
Fish stock	16 fl. oz.	450 ml
Tomato concassée	8 oz.	250 g
Sachet:		
Bay leaf	1	1
Dry thyme	1/2 tsp.	2 ml
Peppercorns, cracked	1/2 tsp.	2 ml
Parsley stems	6	6
Cayenne	TT	TT
Heavy cream, hot	8 fl. oz.	250 ml
Beurre manié	as needed	as needed
Whole butter, softened	2 oz.	60 g
Salt and pepper	TT	TT

1 Cut the lobster for sautéing. Reserve the tomalley and coral if present.
2 Heat the clarified butter and sauté the lobster pieces for 30 seconds.
3 Add the shallots and garlic to the pan and sauté for 30 seconds more.
4 Remove the pan from the stove and add the brandy. Return the pan to the flame, ignite the brandy and allow it to burn for a few seconds. Add the white wine, fish stock, tomato concassée, sachet and cayenne.
5 Simmer for 5 minutes. Remove the lobster from the sauce. Remove the meat from the shells and reserve. Return the shells to the sauce.
6 Add the cream to the sauce. Bring to a boil and reduce by half.
7 Strain the sauce. Return to a simmer and thicken with beurre manié if needed.
8 Combine the whole butter with the reserved tomalley and coral and blend well. Monté au beurre with the tomalley and coral butter. Adjust the seasonings and serve the sauce over the lobster meat.

Approximate values per serving: **Calories** 780, **Total fat** 47 g, **Saturated fat** 28 g, **Cholesterol** 410 mg, **Sodium** 2340 mg, **Total carbohydrates** 9 g, **Protein** 80 g, **Vitamin A** 70%, **Calcium** 30%

RECIPE 20.50 FRESHWATER SHRIMP WRAPPED IN POTATO

CHEF STEVEN CHIAPPETTI, CHICAGO, IL

Yield: 2 Servings   **Method:** Pan-frying

Freshwater shrimp, jumbo	2	2
Potato, large	1	1
Garlic clove, minced	1	1
Spinach, cleaned	1 bunch	1 bunch
Soy sauce	2 Tbsp.	30 ml
Brown sugar	1 Tbsp.	15 ml
Wasabi powder	4 Tbsp.	60 ml

| Water, warm | 1 Tbsp. | 15 ml |
| Corn oil | 2 fl. oz. | 60 ml |

1 Clean the shrimp, leaving the tail attached. Cut the potato into thin threads and wrap the threads tightly around the shrimp, covering them completely.

2 In a sauté pan, cook the garlic until golden brown. Add the spinach and cook until tender.

3 In a small pan, mix the soy sauce with the brown sugar, place on the stove and reduce by half.

4 Blend the wasabi powder with the warm water until smooth.

5 Place the corn oil in a shallow pan and heat. When the oil is hot, carefully place the shrimp in the oil and cook until golden brown.

6 Arrange the sautéed spinach in a tight circle on each plate and drizzle with the wasabi.

7 Drench the shrimp in the soy sauce reduction and place on top of the spinach.

Approximate values per serving: **Calories** 490, **Total fat** 28 g, **Saturated fat** 4 g, **Cholesterol** 165 mg, **Sodium** 1250 mg, **Total carbohydrates** 36 g, **Protein** 22 g, **Vitamin A** 25%, **Vitamin C** 45%, **Iron** 30%

THAI CRAB CAKE

RECIPE 20.51

FLYING FISH, SEATTLE, WA
Chef-Owner Christine Keff

Yield: 4 Servings

Crab meat	2 c.	500 ml
Panko (Japanese bread crumbs)	2 c.	500 ml
Lemongrass Mayonnaise (recipe follows)	1 c.	250 ml
Green onions, chopped fine	4	4
Fresh basil, chopped fine	2 Tbsp.	30 ml
Fresh cilantro, chopped fine	2 Tbsp.	30 ml
Fresh mint, chopped fine	2 Tbsp.	30 ml
Fish sauce	TT	TT
Clarified butter	as needed	as needed
Mixed baby greens	as needed for garnish	
Orange supremes	as needed for garnish	
Lemongrass Mayonnaise	as needed for garnish	

1 Gently stir together the crab meat, panko, Lemongrass Mayonnaise, green onions, herbs and fish sauce. Divide into four portions and form into cakes.

2 Heat a little clarified butter and then sauté each cake for 3 minutes on each side over medium heat, until golden brown.

3 Serve on a plate garnished with baby greens, orange supremes and additional Lemongrass Mayonnaise.

Approximate values per 6-oz. (180-g) serving: **Calories** 544, **Total fat** 31 g, **Saturated fat** 6 g, **Cholesterol** 124 mg, **Sodium** 1006 mg, **Total carbohydrates** 45 g, **Protein** 21 g

LEMONGRASS MAYONNAISE

Yield: 1 pt. (450 ml)

Egg yolks	2	2
Rice wine vinegar	1½ Tbsp.	23 ml
Mirin	1 Tbsp.	15 ml

Continued

Soy sauce	1 tsp.	5 ml
Fish sauce	1 tsp.	5 ml
Lemongrass Oil (recipe follows)	10 fl. oz.	300 ml

1 Place all the ingredients except the Lemongrass Oil into a food processor or blender and process for 30 seconds or until well blended.
2 With the processor running, drizzle in the oil to form an emulsion.

Approximate values per 1-fl.-oz. (30-ml) serving: **Calories** 146, **Total fat** 15 g, **Saturated fat** 3 g, **Cholesterol** 33 mg, **Sodium** 113 mg, **Total carbohydrates** 2 g, **Protein** 1 g

LEMONGRASS OIL

Yield: 10 fl. oz. (300 ml)

Fresh ginger, peeled, sliced thin	¼ c.	60 ml
Lemongrass, chopped	¼ c.	60 ml
Peanut oil	10 fl. oz.	300 ml

1 Place all the ingredients in a small saucepan and bring to a simmer over low heat. Simmer for 5 minutes.
2 Remove from the heat and allow the flavored oil to stand overnight at room temperature. Strain before using.

Approximate values per 1-fl.-oz. (30-ml) serving: **Calories** 186, **Total fat** 21 g, **Saturated fat** 4 g, **Cholesterol** 0 mg, **Sodium** 0 g, **Total carbohydrates** 1 g, **Protein** 0 g

JUMBO LUMP BLUE CRAB AND LANGOUSTINE CAKE WITH RHUBARB PRESERVES AND CITRUS VANILLA SAUCE

RECIPE 20.52

RESTAURANT KEVIN TAYLOR, Denver, CO
Chef Kevin Taylor

Yield: 4 Servings **Method:** Sautéing

Olive oil	2 tsp.	10 ml
Garlic, chopped	1 tsp.	5 ml
Langoustine meat or baby shrimp, raw, peeled and deveined	4 oz.	120 g
Scallops	4 oz.	120 g
Egg whites	1	1
Green onions, minced	6	6
Serrano chile, minced	1	1
Fresh cilantro, chopped	2 Tbsp.	30 ml
Dry bread crumbs	4 Tbsp.	60 ml
Fresh lime juice	2 tsp.	10 ml
Lump blue crab meat	8 oz.	240 g
Heavy cream	2 fl. oz.	60 ml
Salt and pepper	TT	TT
Vegetable oil	as needed	as needed
Citrus-Vanilla Sauce (recipe follows)	10 fl. oz.	300 ml
Rhubarb Preserves (recipe follows)	6 oz.	180 g
Fresh cilantro leaves	as needed for garnish	

1 Heat a small sauté pan and add the olive oil and garlic. Add the langoustine or shrimp and cook until done, approximately 1 minute. Remove the shellfish from the pan and chill thoroughly.

2 Combine the scallops and egg whites in the bowl of a food processor and process until emulsified and stiff.

3 Place the scallop mixture in a mixing bowl and add the green onions, chile, chopped cilantro, bread crumbs, lime juice, crab meat and chilled langoustine or shrimp. Whip the cream to soft peaks, then slowly fold it into the scallop mixture. Season the mixture with salt and pepper, form into cakes and refrigerate.

4 Sauté the crab cakes on one side in a small amount of vegetable oil. Turn the cakes and place the pan in a 350°F (160°C) oven to cook for approximately 5 to 7 minutes. Remove the cakes from the pan and drain on paper towels.

5 Ladle a portion of the Citrus-Vanilla Sauce on each of four warm plates and then place a crab cake in the middle of each plate. Spoon the Rhubarb Preserves on top of each cake, garnish with cilantro leaves and serve.

Approximate values per serving: **Calories** 760, **Total fat** 61 g, **Saturated fat** 36 g, **Cholesterol** 260 mg, **Sodium** 350 mg, **Total carbohydrates** 27 g, **Protein** 25 g, **Vitamin A** 50%, **Vitamin C** 80%, **Calcium** 15%, **Iron** 10%

CITRUS-VANILLA SAUCE

Yield: 10 fl. oz. (300 ml)

Oranges	2	2
Lemon	1	1
Lime	1	1
Vanilla bean, split	1	1
Heavy cream	2 fl. oz.	60 ml
Unsalted butter	8 oz.	240 g
Salt	TT	TT

1 Squeeze the juice from the oranges, lemon and lime. In a medium saucepot, combine the citrus juices with the vanilla bean. Bring to a simmer and reduce by two-thirds. Add the cream to the mixture and reduce by two-thirds. Lower the heat and slowly whisk in the butter to form a beurre blanc sauce. Season with salt, strain the sauce and reserve in a warm place.

Approximate values per 1-fl.-oz. (30-ml) serving: **Calories** 190, **Total fat** 21 g, **Saturated fat** 13 g, **Cholesterol** 60 mg, **Sodium** 5 mg, **Total carbohydrates** 3 g, **Protein** 0 g, **Vitamin A** 15%, **Vitamin C** 20%

RHUBARB PRESERVES

Yield: 6 oz. (180 g)

Rhubarb, chopped	4 oz.	120 g
Granulated sugar	3 Tbsp.	45 ml
Port wine	2 fl. oz.	60 ml
Water	8 fl. oz.	240 ml

1 In a small saucepot, combine all ingredients. Simmer for 25 minutes and purée in a food processor. Cool before serving.

Approximate values per 1-oz. (30-g) serving: **Calories** 45, **Total fat** 0 g, **Saturated fat** 0 g, **Cholesterol** 0 mg, **Sodium** 0 mg, **Total carbohydrates** 8 g, **Protein** 0 g

RECIPE 20.53

FRIED OYSTERS WITH HERBED CRÈME FRAÎCHE

Yield: 4 Appetizer Servings   **Method:** Deep-frying

Leeks, julienne	3	3
Oysters, scrubbed	24	24
Flour	4 oz.	120 g
Eggs	2	2
Egg yolks	2	2
Fresh bread crumbs	8 oz.	240 g
Sauce:		
Cornichons, chopped fine	1 Tbsp.	15 ml
Capers, chopped fine	2 Tbsp.	30 ml
Dijon mustard	1 tsp.	5 ml
Paprika	½ tsp.	2 ml
Parsley, minced	2 Tbsp.	30 ml
Crème fraîche	4 fl. oz.	120 ml

1 Deep-fry the leeks at 280°F (138°C) until golden brown. Drain and set aside.

2 Open the oysters. Strain and reserve the liquor.

3 Poach the oysters in the liquor for 30 seconds. Drain, reserving the liquid. Cool the liquid and oysters separately.

4 Bread the oysters using the standard breading procedure described in Chapter 9, Mise en Place.

5 Deep-fry the oysters at 375°F (190°C) until browned, approximately 1 minute.

6 Prepare the sauce by combining all the sauce ingredients except the crème fraîche. Whip the crème fraîche until stiff. Fold in the cornichon mixture. Chill until service.

7 Serve the oysters on a nest of leeks with the sauce.

Approximate values per serving: **Calories** 1220, **Total fat** 44 g, **Saturated fat** 17 g, **Cholesterol** 785 mg, **Sodium** 2870 mg, **Total carbohydrates** 118 g, **Protein** 89 g, **Vitamin A** 50%, **Vitamin C** 70%, **Iron** 380%

RECIPE 20.54

SPICY CALAMARI SALAD

THE BAMBOO CLUB, PHOENIX, AZ

Yield: 4 Servings, 6 oz. (180 g) each   **Method:** Deep-frying

Marinade:		
Lemon juice	4 fl. oz.	120 ml
Red wine vinegar	1 pt.	450 ml
Garlic powder	1 Tbsp.	15 ml
Squid, cleaned and cut into rings	1 lb.	450 g
Red bell pepper, sliced thin	3 oz.	90 g
Green bell pepper, sliced thin	3 oz.	90 g
Oyster mushrooms, sliced	12 oz.	350 g
Whole butter	1 Tbsp.	15 ml
Garlic, chopped	1 Tbsp.	15 ml
Oyster sauce	4 Tbsp.	60 ml
Chile flakes	TT	TT
Flour	6 oz.	180 g
Baking powder	1½ Tbsp.	22 ml
Cornstarch	1½ Tbsp.	22 ml
Boston lettuce, torn into small pieces	8 oz.	250 g
Fresh cilantro or Italian parsley	as needed for garnish	

1 Combine the marinade ingredients. Marinate the squid in the marinade for three days.

2 Sauté the bell peppers and mushrooms in the butter. Add the garlic, oyster sauce and chile flakes. Set aside.

3 Drain the squid, pressing out as much liquid as possible. Combine the flour, baking powder and cornstarch; toss with the squid until well coated.

4 Deep-fry the squid at 350°F (177°C) until crispy and golden brown. Drain and toss with the peppers and mushrooms. Serve on a bed of lettuce, garnished with cilantro or Italian parsley.

Approximate values per 6-oz. (180-g) serving: **Calories** 450, **Total fat** 13 g, **Saturated fat** 4 g, **Cholesterol** 305 mg, **Sodium** 720 mg, **Total carbohydrates** 55 g, **Protein** 29 g, **Vitamin A** 20%, **Vitamin C** 100%, **Calcium** 35%

SOFT-SHELL CRAB PO' BOY SANDWICH   RECIPE 20.55

CAFÉ ALLEGRE, ORLANDO, FL
Chef Kevin Fonzo

Yield: 6 Sandwiches

Soft-shell crabs, cleaned	6	6
Salt and pepper	TT	TT
Flour	as needed for breading	
Egg wash	as needed for breading	
Blue cornmeal	as needed for breading	
Creole Rémoulade Sauce (page 771)	1½ pt.	720 ml
Lettuce, shredded	3 pt.	480 ml
Mini-baguettes, sliced in half and toasted	6	6
Tomato slices	18	18

1 Season the crabs with salt and pepper. Bread each crab using the standard breading procedure described in Chapter 9, Mise en Place.

2 Using the basket method, deep-fry the crabs until done.

3 Spread the Creole Rémoulade Sauce evenly over the baguettes.

4 Divide the shredded lettuce over the bottoms of the baguettes, then top with the tomato slices, crab and the tops of the baguettes. Serve with sautéed potatoes or potato salad.

Approximate values per sandwich: **Calories** 530, **Total fat** 21 g, **Saturated fat** 5 g, **Cholesterol** 45 mg, **Sodium** 1440 mg, **Total carbohydrates** 66 g, **Protein** 18 g, **Vitamin A** 20%, **Vitamin C** 50%

SHRIMP POACHED IN ORANGE JUICE, GINGER AND SAUTERNE   RECIPE 20.56

FROM *ALLEN SUSSER'S NEW WORLD CUISINE AND COOKERY* BY ALLEN SUSSER, NORTH MIAMI BEACH, FL

Yield: 4 Servings	**Method:** Poaching	
Jumbo shrimp, raw	16	16
Orange juice, fresh squeezed	1 pt.	500 ml
Fresh ginger, julienne	2 Tbsp.	30 ml
Sauterne	4 fl. oz.	120 ml
Shallots, julienne	1 pt.	500 ml
Carrots, julienne	1 pt.	500 ml

Continued

Kosher salt	1 tsp.	5 ml
Black pepper	1 tsp.	5 ml

1 Peel, clean and butterfly the shrimp.
2 Place all the ingredients in a low-sided pan with a lid and slowly warm over low heat to just about a simmer. Cover the pan and poach the shrimp for 3 to 4 minutes. The shrimp should be rosy pink and firm to the touch.
3 Remove from the heat and serve the shrimp with the vegetables and broth.

Approximate values per serving: **Calories** 410, **Total fat** 4 g, **Saturated fat** 1 g, **Cholesterol** 665 mg, **Sodium** 1360 mg, **Total carbohydrates** 21 g, **Protein** 73 g, **Vitamin A** 190%, **Vitamin C** 130%, **Iron** 60%

RECIPE 20.57

CHILLED SHELLFISH PLATTER

THE FOUR SEASONS, New York, NY
Chef Christian Albin

Yield: 2 Appetizer Servings   **Method:** Boiled/Raw

Lobster, boiled	1	1
Oysters	4	4
Shrimp, U-10, boiled and peeled, tails intact	4	4
Lump crab meat	3 oz.	90 g
Carrots	as needed for garnish	
Celery	as needed for garnish	
Scallions	2	2
Baby fennel bulb, split and blanched	1	1
Red oak leaf lettuce	as needed for garnish	

1 Remove the tail from the lobster. Remove the meat from the tail in one piece and cut it in half lengthwise.
2 Clean and open the oysters, leaving the oyster meat on the half-shell.
3 Mound crushed ice on a large serving platter. Position the lobster head and body in the center of the ice. Place the pieces of lobster tail around the lobster body. Arrange the remaining shellfish over the ice, using the carrots, celery, scallions, fennel and red oak leaf lettuce as garnish.

Approximate values per serving: **Calories** 490, **Total fat** 4.5 g, **Saturated fat** 1 g, **Cholesterol** 325 mg, **Sodium** 1780 mg, **Total carbohydrates** 26 g, **Protein** 85 g, **Vitamin A** 320%, **Vitamin C** 60%

RECIPE 20.58

STEAMED SCALLOPS WITH GINGER, BASIL AND ORANGE

VINCENT ON CAMELBACK, Phoenix, AZ
Chef Vincent Guerithault

Yield: 1 Serving   **Method:** Steaming

Oranges	2	2
Lime	1	1
Flour tortilla, 8 in. (20 cm)	1	1
Scallops, large	3	3
Ginger, grated	1 tsp.	5 ml
Carrot, julienne	2 oz.	60 g
Celery, julienne	1 oz.	30 g
Tomato, small dice	2 Tbsp.	30 ml
Fresh basil, chopped	1 Tbsp.	15 ml

Olive oil	1 Tbsp.	15 ml
Salt and pepper	TT	TT
White wine	8 fl. oz.	250 ml
Shallot, chopped	1 tsp.	5 ml

1 Zest the oranges and then cut them in ½-inch (1.2-centimeter) slices. Peel the lime and cut it into ¼-inch (6-millimeter) slices.

2 Line a small bamboo steamer with the flour tortilla.

3 Place the scallops on top of the tortilla. Add the orange zest, ginger, carrot, celery, tomato, basil, olive oil, two slices of lime and a dash of salt and pepper. Cover.

4 Place the white wine, chopped shallot, orange slices and remaining lime slices in the bottom of the steamer pan. Steam the scallops over the seasoned wine until done, approximately 5 minutes.

Approximate values per serving: **Calories** 540, **Total fat** 18 g, **Saturated fat** 2.5 g, **Cholesterol** 45 mg, **Sodium** 1660 mg, **Total carbohydrates** 67 g, **Protein** 27 g, **Vitamin A** 120%, **Vitamin C** 270%, **Iron** 40%

STEAMED MUSSELS WITH LEEKS AND CARROTS

RECIPE 20.59

CHEF LELAND ATKINSON, WASHINGTON, DC

Yield: 2 Servings   **Method:** Steaming

Mussels, debearded and scrubbed	2 lb.	900 g
Dry white wine	8 fl. oz.	250 ml
Garlic, chopped	1 oz.	30 g
Black pepper	½ tsp.	2 ml
Fresh thyme	4 sprigs	4 sprigs
Bay leaves	2	2
Leek, julienne	2 oz.	60 g
Carrot, julienne	2 oz.	60 g
Whole butter	4 oz.	120 g
Fresh parsley, chopped	1 Tbsp.	15 ml

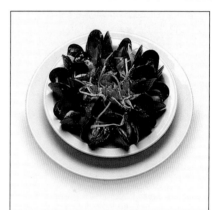

1 Combine the mussels, wine, garlic, pepper, thyme, bay leaves, leeks and carrots in a large sautoir.

2 Cover the pan and bring to a boil. Steam until the mussels open.

3 Remove the mussels and arrange them in two large soup plates.

4 Reduce the cooking liquid by half, monté au beurre and pour the sauce over the mussels. The carrots and leeks should remain on top of the mussels as garnish.

5 Sprinkle with chopped parsley and serve with French bread.

Approximate values per serving: **Calories** 1220, **Total fat** 67 g, **Saturated fat** 33 g, **Cholesterol** 375 mg, **Sodium** 2170 mg, **Total carbohydrates** 44 g, **Protein** 110 g, **Vitamin A** 140%, **Vitamin C** 120%, **Iron** 200%

PAELLA

RECIPE 20.60

CHEF LELAND ATKINSON, WASHINGTON, DC

Yield: 4 Servings   **Method:** Steaming

Chicken thighs	4	4
Salt and pepper	TT	TT
Olive oil	2 fl. oz.	60 ml
Onion, medium dice	2 oz.	60 g

Continued

Garlic, chopped	1 Tbsp.	15 ml
Red bell pepper, medium dice	2 oz.	60 g
Green bell pepper, medium dice	2 oz.	60 g
Long-grain rice	12 oz.	350 g
Saffron	1 pinch	1 pinch
Chicken stock, well seasoned, hot	26 fl. oz.	750 ml
Chorizo, cooked, sliced	4 oz.	120 g
Clams, scrubbed	12	12
Cockles, scrubbed	12	12
Shrimp, 16–20 count	12	12
Lobster, cut up	1	1
Mussels, debearded and scrubbed	12	12

1 Season the chicken with salt and pepper. Pan-fry it in the olive oil, browning it well. Cook until done, approximately 20 minutes. Remove the chicken and reserve.

2 Add the onion, garlic and bell peppers to the pan and sauté until tender.

3 Add the rice and sauté until it turns translucent.

4 Add the saffron to the chicken stock. Stir the chicken stock into the rice and bring to a boil.

5 Add the chorizo, clams and cockles to the pan. Cover and place in a 375°F (190°C) oven for 20 minutes.

6 Add the shrimp, lobster and cooked chicken to the pan. Cover and cook for an additional 15 minutes.

7 Add the mussels to the pan and cook until the shrimp and lobster are done, the chicken is hot and all the shellfish are opened, approximately 5 minutes.

Approximate values per serving: **Calories** 930, **Total fat** 41 g, **Saturated fat** 10 g, **Cholesterol** 650 mg, **Sodium** 2050 mg, **Total carbohydrates** 31 g, **Protein** 110 g, **Vitamin A** 25%, **Vitamin C** 60%, **Iron** 70%

RECIPE 20.61   SEAFOOD FRICASSEE

PESCE RESTAURANT, HOUSTON, TX
Chef Mark Holley

Yield: 1 Serving

Barramundi fillet, 6 oz. (180 g)	1	1
Sea scallops, U-10	2	2
Salt and pepper	TT	TT
Olive oil	as needed	as needed
Shallot, minced	1 tsp.	5 ml
Greenlip mussels, cleaned	3	3
White wine	2 fl. oz.	60 ml
Champagne Cream Sauce (recipe follows)	2 fl. oz.	60 ml
Champagne grapes	1 Tbsp.	15 ml
Chives, sliced	¼ tsp.	2 ml
Asparagus spears, trimmed, steamed, hot	3	3
Roasted red bell pepper strips, hot	1 oz.	1 oz.
Leek, julienne, fried	as needed for garnish	

1 Season the barramundi and sea scallops with salt and pepper. Heat a small amount of olive oil in a sauté pan, add the fish and scallops and sear over high heat. Remove the fish and scallops from the pan and reserve.

2 In the same sauté pan, sauté the shallot and mussels briefly and deglaze with the wine. Add the Champagne Cream Sauce and simmer until the mussels are open and the sauce has thickened slightly. Add the grapes and chives.

3 Place the fish and scallops in a 350°F (180°C) oven for approximately 5 minutes to reheat.

4 Season the asparagus spears and bell pepper with salt and pepper and arrange them at the top of the plate. Remove the fish and scallops from the oven and place the fish in the center of the plate. Arrange the scallops and mussels around the fish. Spoon or pour the sauce around the fish and garnish with the fried leek.

Approximate values per serving: **Calories** 740, **Total fat** 49 g, **Saturated fat** 29 g, **Cholesterol** 250 mg, **Sodium** 630 mg, **Total carbohydrates** 14 g, **Protein** 42 g, **Vitamin A** 70%, **Vitamin C** 100%, **Calcium** 15%, **Iron** 20%

CHAMPAGNE CREAM SAUCE

Yield: 1 pt. (450 ml)

Unsalted butter	1 tsp.	5 ml
Yellow onion, medium dice	½ c.	120 ml
Bay leaves	2	2
Chardonnay	8 fl. oz.	240 ml
Champagne	8 fl. oz.	240 ml
Crab, whole, dressed, crushed	1 lb.	450 g
Heavy cream	1 qt.	1 lt
Kosher salt	1 tsp.	5 ml
Black pepper	¼ tsp.	2 ml
Sour cream	1 Tbsp.	15 ml

1 Heat the butter in a small saucepan over medium heat. Add the onion and bay leaves and sauté until the onion is translucent, approximately 3 minutes.

2 Add the wine, champagne and crab and reduce by half. Add the heavy cream and reduce by half, or until the sauce is thick enough to coat the back of a spoon. Add the salt and pepper.

3 Strain the sauce through a china cap, pressing well to remove all liquid from the shells, and then add the sour cream.

4 Blend the sauce with a few pulses of an immersion blender just enough to froth the sauce. Hold for service.

Approximate values per 1-fl.-oz. (30-ml) serving: **Calories** 230, **Total fat** 22 g, **Saturated fat** 14 g, **Cholesterol** 85 mg, **Sodium** 170 mg, **Total carbohydrates** 2 g, **Protein** 1 g, **Vitamin A** 20%

CREOLE SEAFOOD STEW

RECIPE 20.62

PESCE RESTAURANT, HOUSTON, TX
Chef Mark Holley

Yield: 1 Serving

Extra virgin olive oil	1 fl. oz.	30 ml
Shrimp, U-12, head on	2	2
Creole Spice Mix (recipe follows)	1 tsp.	5 ml
Seafood Boudin (recipe follows)	1 link	1 link
Garlic, sliced thin	1 tsp.	5 ml
Mussels	4	4
Sea scallops	4	4

Continued

Littleneck clams	3	3
White wine	5 fl. oz.	150 ml
Fresh herbs, assorted, chopped	1 tsp.	5 ml
Saffron Tomato Broth (recipe follows)	10 fl. oz.	300 ml
Shrimp stock	as needed	as needed
Pepper Garnish (recipe follows)	2 Tbsp.	30 ml

1 Heat the oil in a sauté pan. Season the shrimp with 1 teaspoon (5 milliliters) of the Creole spice mix. Sauté the shrimp and the Seafood Boudin for 1 minute.

2 Add the garlic, mussels, scallops and clams and sauté for 30 seconds. Add the white wine, herbs and Saffron Tomato Broth and bring to a boil. Add enough shrimp stock to create the desired amount of liquid in the finished product. Reduce the heat and simmer for 3 minutes.

3 Ladle the stew into a bowl, arranging the shellfish attractively. Garnish with the Pepper Garnish and serve.

Approximate values per serving, without broth: **Calories** 620, **Total fat** 35 g, **Saturated fat** 5 g, **Cholesterol** 115 mg, **Sodium** 1630 mg, **Total carbohydrates** 12 g, **Protein** 40 g, **Vitamin A** 20%, **Vitamin C** 70%, **Calcium** 10%, **Iron** 60%

CREOLE SPICE MIX

Yield: 17 oz. (510 g)

Kosher salt	8 oz.	240 g
Granulated garlic	2 oz.	60 g
Black pepper	2 oz.	60 g
Cayenne pepper	1/2 oz.	15 g
Granulated onion	1 1/4 oz.	37 g
Paprika	2 1/2 oz.	75 g
Thyme, dried	1/2 oz.	15 g
Oregano, dried	1/2 oz.	15 g

1 Combine all of the ingredients for the Creole spice mix and stir together.

Approximate values per ounce (30 g): **Calories** 45, **Total fat** 1 g, **Saturated fat** 0 g, **Cholesterol** 0 mg, **Sodium** 5250 mg, **Total carbohydrates** 10 g, **Protein** 2 g, **Vitamin A** 50%, **Vitamin C** 10%, **Iron** 20%

SEAFOOD BOUDIN

Yield: 4 lb. (1.8 kg)

Firm white fish (snapper, grouper, flounder)	1 lb.	450 g
Shrimp, 36–42 count, peeled and deveined	2 lb.	900 g
Heavy cream, cold	2 fl. oz.	60 ml
Shallots, minced	2 Tbsp.	30 ml
Garlic, minced	1 Tbsp.	15 ml
Fresh herbs, assorted, chopped	1 Tbsp.	15 ml
Hot sauce	2 Tbsp.	30 ml
Worcestershire sauce	2 Tbsp.	30 ml
Egg white, whipped	1	1
Chile flakes	1 tsp.	5 ml
Creole Spice Mix	1 Tbsp.	15 ml
Wild rice, cooked, cold	1/4 c.	60 ml
White rice, cooked, cold	1 c.	240 ml
Green onion, sliced fine	1/2 c.	120 ml
Fresh parsley, chopped fine	1/4 c.	60 ml

Kosher salt	1 Tbsp.	15 ml
Black pepper	¼ tsp.	1 ml
Garnish:		
Lump crab meat, fresh	8 oz.	240 g
Shrimp, peeled and deveined	8 oz.	240 g

1 Chill a grinder attachment fitted with a ⅛-inch (3-millimeter) plate. Chill the white fish and shrimp well. Grind the fish and shrimp into a stainless steel bowl.

2 Place the bowl over an ice bath and stir in the cream. Fold in the remaining ingredients, except the garnish, until thoroughly mixed. Gently fold in the garnish.

3 Stuff the mixture into prepared casings and twist into 2-inch (5-centimeter) links. Poach the boudin in water to an internal temperature of 145°F (63°C). Cool in ice water. Remove from the ice water, pat dry, cover and refrigerate.

Approximate values per 2-oz. (60-g) link: **Calories** 50, **Total fat** 1 g, **Saturated fat** 0.5 g, **Cholesterol** 40 mg, **Sodium** 330 mg, **Total carbohydrates** 2 g, **Protein** 7 g, **Claims**—low fat, no saturated fat

SAFFRON TOMATO BROTH

Yield: 2 qt. (2 lt)

Onion, large dice	1 pt.	450 ml
Carrot, large dice	1 pt.	450 ml
Celery, large dice	1 pt.	450 ml
Fennel bulb, chopped	1 pt.	450 ml
Olive oil	4 fl. oz.	120 ml
Garlic cloves	12	12
Shrimp shells	1 lb. 8 oz.	700 g
Lobster shells	1 lb. 8 oz.	700 g
Crab shells	1 lb. 8 oz.	700 g
Tomato purée	1 c.	240 ml
Roma tomatoes, halved	12	12
White wine	3 pt.	1.5 lt
Water	2½ gal.	9 lt
Pernod	8 fl. oz.	240 ml
Fresh thyme	6 sprigs	6 sprigs
Fresh oregano	6 sprigs	6 sprigs
Bay leaves	6	6
Saffron threads	1 Tbsp.	15 ml

1 Sauté the onion, carrot, celery and fennel in the oil until caramelized. Add the garlic and continue to sauté for 1 minute.

2 Add the shrimp, lobster and crab shells and cook for 2 minutes. Add the tomato purée and tomatoes and cook for 10 minutes.

3 Add the wine, water, Pernod, thyme, oregano and bay leaves and simmer for 1 to 1½ hours. Strain the stock, return to the pot, add the saffron and reduce by one-quarter.

PEPPER GARNISH

Yield: 1 c. (240 ml)

Red bell pepper, fine julienne	¼ c.	60 ml
Yellow bell pepper, fine julienne	¼ c.	60 ml
Poblano pepper, fine julienne	¼ c.	60 ml
Leek, fine julienne	¼ c.	60 ml
Extra virgin olive oil	1 Tbsp.	15 ml
Salt	¼ tsp.	1 ml
Black pepper	¼ tsp.	1 ml
Fresh herbs, assorted, chopped	1 tsp.	5 ml

1 Sauté the peppers and leek in the olive oil until slightly wilted, approximately 1 minute. Season with the salt, pepper and chopped herbs. Cool and reserve.

Approximate values per tablespoon (15 ml): **Calories** 10, **Total fat** 1 g, **Saturated fat** 0 g, **Cholesterol** 0 mg, **Sodium** 35 mg, **Total carbohydrates** 1 g, **Protein** 0 g, **Vitamin C** 20%

RECIPE 20.63   CRAWFISH ÉTOUFFÉE

Yield: 4 Servings

Corn oil	4 fl. oz.	120 ml
Flour	4 oz.	120 g
Onion, large, chopped fine	1	1
Celery stalk, chopped fine	1	1
Green bell pepper, chopped	½	½
Garlic cloves, minced	3	3
Shrimp broth or clam juice	1¼ pt.	600 ml
Lemon juice	1 Tbsp.	15 ml
Crawfish fat (optional)	2 oz.	60 g
Salt	1 tsp.	5 ml
Black pepper	½ tsp.	3 ml
Cayenne pepper	½ tsp.	3 ml
Dried thyme	½ tsp.	3 ml
Bay leaf	1	1
Louisiana hot sauce	1 Tbsp.	15 ml
Crawfish tails, frozen	1 lb.	450 g
Green onions, sliced	2	2
White rice, cooked	1 qt.	1 lt.

1 Heat the oil in a large sauté pan. Whisk in the flour and cook, stirring constantly, to make a medium dark roux.
2 Add the onion, celery, bell pepper and garlic and sauté over medium low heat until the vegetables are tender, approximately 10 minutes.
3 Slowly add the shrimp broth or clam juice and bring to a boil. Reduce the heat to a simmer and add the lemon juice, crawfish fat, salt, and black pepper, cayenne and herbs. Simmer for 15 minutes to thicken.
4 Add the hot sauce and the crawfish tails and simmer for approximately 10 minutes. Add the green onions and adjust the seasonings. Serve over cooked rice.

Approximate values per serving: **Calories** 880, **Total fat** 32 g, **Saturated fat** 4 g, **Cholesterol** 130 mg, **Sodium** 1190 mg, **Total carbohydrates** 107 g, **Protein** 40 g, **Vitamin A** 300%, **Vitamin C** 480%, **Calcium** 45%, **Iron** 90%

RECIPE 20.64   SEVICHE

In a seviche, the fish and shellfish are "cooked" by the acids in the citrus juice. Although a variety of fish or shellfish may be used, it is extremely important that the products be absolutely fresh. Use a nonreactive container such as stainless steel or plastic for mixing or storing the seviche. Aluminum and other metals may react with the acids in the lime juice, giving the food a metallic flavor.

Yield: 3 lb. (1.4 kg)

Raw scallops and/or shrimp	1 lb.	450 g
Raw firm white fish	1 lb.	450 g
Fresh lime juice	8 fl. oz.	240 ml
Serrano chiles, minced	4	4

Red onion, fine dice	6 oz.	180 g
Fresh cilantro, minced	4 Tbsp.	60 ml
Olive oil	2 Tbsp.	30 ml
Tomato concassée	8 oz.	250 g
Garlic, chopped	2 tsp.	10 ml
Salt and pepper	TT	TT

1　Chop the scallops, shrimp and fish coarsely but evenly. Place in a nonreactive container and add the lime juice. Cover and marinate in the refrigerator for 4 hours. The fish should turn opaque and become firm.

2　Toss in the remaining ingredients and season to taste with salt and pepper. Chill thoroughly and serve as a salad or with tortilla chips.

3　If the seviche is going to be held for more than 2 hours, drain the liquid and refrigerate separately. The reserved liquid can then be tossed with the other ingredients at service time.

Approximate values per 4-oz. (120-g) serving: **Calories** 120, **Total fat** 4.5 g, **Saturated fat** 0.5 g, **Cholesterol** 30 mg, **Sodium** 250 mg, **Total carbohydrates** 5 g, **Protein** 13 g, **Vitamin A** 10%, **Vitamin C** 20%, **Claims**—low saturated fat

I HAD AN EXCELLENT REPAST—THE BEST REPAST
POSSIBLE—WHICH CONSISTED SIMPLY OF BOILED
EGGS AND BREAD AND BUTTER. IT WAS THE QUALITY
OF THESE SIMPLE INGREDIENTS THAT MADE THE
OCCASION MEMORABLE. THE EGGS WERE SO GOOD
THAT I AM ASHAMED TO SAY HOW MANY OF THEM I
CONSUMED. . . . IT MIGHT SEEM THAT AN EGG
WHICH HAS SUCCEEDED IN BEING FRESH HAS DONE
ALL THAT CAN BE REASONABLY EXPECTED OF IT.

—Henry James, American novelist (1843–1916)

21

EGGS AND BREAKFAST

CAFÉ ALLEGRE, Orlando, FL
Executive Chef Kevin Fonzo

AFTER STUDYING THIS CHAPTER, YOU WILL BE ABLE TO:

▶ understand the composition of eggs

▶ purchase and store eggs properly

▶ apply various cooking methods to eggs

▶ prepare pancakes and other griddlecakes

▶ offer customers a variety of breakfast foods

Nature designed eggs as the food source for developing chicks. Eggs, particularly chicken eggs, are also an excellent food for humans because of their high protein content, low cost and ready availability. They are extremely versatile and are used throughout the kitchen, either served alone or as ingredients in a prepared dish. Eggs are used to provide texture, flavor, structure, moisture and nutrition in everything from soups and sauces to breads and pastries.

Egg dishes are, of course, most often associated with the meals breakfast and brunch. But food service operations must offer a variety of breakfast options to appeal to a wide range of consumers.

Breakfast cookery is often one of the first line positions a new cook will be offered. This important duty requires speed, timing and precision and can help an apprentice or beginning cook develop organized, efficient work habits.

This chapter discusses cooking methods used for eggs as well as breakfast meats, griddlecakes, crêpes and cereals. Other foods typically served at breakfast, such as coffee, tea, fruit and cheese, are discussed elsewhere in this text.

▶ EGGS

COMPOSITION

The primary parts of an egg are the shell, yolk and albumen. See Figure 21.1.

The **shell,** composed of calcium carbonate, is the outermost covering of the egg. It prevents microbes from entering and moisture from escaping, and also protects the egg during handling and transport. The breed of the hen determines shell color; for chickens, it can range from bright white to brown. Shell color has no effect on quality, flavor or nutrition.

The yolk is the yellow portion of the egg. It constitutes just over one-third of the egg and contains three-fourths of the calories, most of the minerals and vitamins and all the fat. The yolk also contains lecithin, the compound responsible for emulsification in products such as hollandaise sauce and mayonnaise. Egg yolk solidifies (coagulates) at temperatures between 149°F and 158°F (65°C and 70°C). Although the color of a yolk may vary depending on the hen's feed, color does not affect quality or nutritional content.

The **albumen** is the clear portion of the egg and is often referred to as the **egg white.** It constitutes about two-thirds of the egg and contains more than half of the protein and riboflavin. Egg white coagulates, becoming firm and opaque, at temperatures between 144°F and 149°F (62°C and 65°C).

An often-misunderstood portion of the egg is the **chalazae cords.** These thick, twisted strands of egg white anchor the yolk in place. They are neither imperfections nor embryos. The more prominent the chalazae, the fresher the egg. Chalazae do not interfere with cooking or with whipping egg whites.

Eggs are sold in Jumbo, Extra Large, Large, Medium, Small and Peewee sizes, as determined by weight per dozen. See Figure 21.2. Food service operations generally use Large eggs, which weigh 24 ounces per dozen. Other sizes are based on plus or minus 3 ounces per dozen; Medium eggs weigh 21 ounces per dozen while Extra Large eggs weigh 27 ounces per dozen.

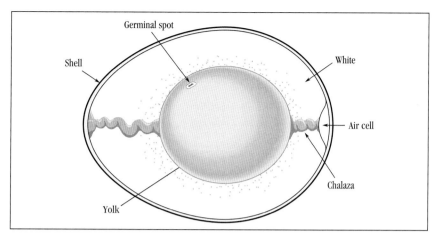

FIGURE 21.1 ▶ An egg

GRADING

Eggs are graded by the USDA or a state agency following USDA guidelines. The grade AA, A or B is given to an egg based upon interior and exterior quality, not size. The qualities for each grade are described in Table 21.1. Grade has no effect on nutritional values.

STORAGE

Improper handling quickly diminishes egg quality. Eggs should be stored at temperatures below 40°F (4°C) and at a relative humidity of 70 to 80 percent. Eggs will age more during one day at room temperature than they will during one week under proper refrigeration. As eggs age, the white becomes thinner and the yolk becomes flatter. Although this will change the appearance of poached or fried eggs, age has little effect on nutrition or behavior during cooking procedures. Older eggs, however, should be used for hard-cooking, as the shells are easier to remove than those on fresh eggs.

Cartons of fresh, uncooked eggs will keep for at least four to five weeks beyond the pack date if properly refrigerated. Hard-cooked eggs left in their shells and refrigerated should be used within one week.

Store eggs away from strongly flavored foods to reduce odor absorption. Rotate egg stock to maintain freshness. Do not use dirty, cracked or broken eggs, as they may contain bacteria or other contaminants. Frozen eggs should be thawed in the refrigerator and used only in dishes that will be thoroughly cooked, such as baked products.

SANITATION

Eggs are a potentially hazardous food. Rich in protein, they are an excellent breeding ground for bacteria. *Salmonella* is of particular concern with eggs and egg products because the bacteria are commonly found in a chicken's intestinal

NOT JUST CHICKENS

When most people refer to an "egg," they mean a chicken's egg. But other eggs are sometimes used in the kitchen:

Bantam egg: the egg from a breed of small chicken; it is about half the size of a regular chicken egg and has the same characteristics.

Duck egg: an egg with an off-white shell and a richer flavor and higher fat content than a chicken's egg; when it is boiled, the white turns bluish and the yolk turns red-orange.

Goose egg: a white-shelled egg that is four to five times larger than a chicken egg; it also has a somewhat richer flavor.

Guinea fowl egg: an egg with an ivory shell flecked with brown; its flavor is more delicate than that of a chicken egg.

Gull egg: an egg whose shell is covered with light to dark brown blotches; it comes in various small sizes and has a slightly fishy flavor.

Ostrich egg: an egg that is twenty times as large as a chicken egg, and has a thick, and ivory-colored shell.

Partridge egg: a small egg with a white, buff or olive shell; it has a mild flavor.

Quail egg: a small egg with a speckled brown shell; it has a rich flavor.

Turkey egg: a large egg with a brown shell; it has a delicate flavor.

Turtle egg: a reptile's egg with a soft shell that is buff or speckled; it has a mild, rich flavor.

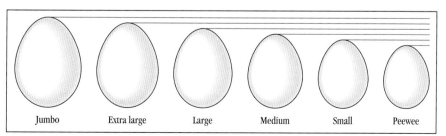

| Jumbo | Extra large | Large | Medium | Small | Peewee |

FIGURE 21.2 ▶ Egg sizes

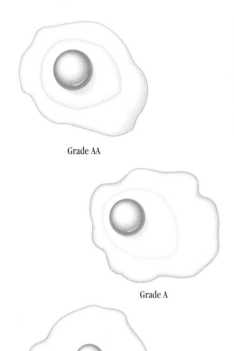

Grade AA

Grade A

Grade B

Table 21.1 **EGG GRADES**

	GRADE AA	GRADE A	GRADE B
Spread*	Remains compact	Spreads slightly	Spreads over wide area
Albumen	Clear, thick and firm; prominent chalazae	Clear and reasonably firm; prominent chalazae	Clear; weak or watery
Yolk	Firm; centered; stands round and high; free from defects	Firm; stands fairly high; practically free from defects	Enlarged and flattened; may show slight defects
Shell	Clean; of normal shape; unbroken		Slight stains permissible; abnormal shape; unbroken
Use	Any use, especially frying, poaching and cooking in shell		Baking, scrambling, used in bulk egg products

*Spread refers to the appearance of the egg when first broken onto a flat surface.

▶ **pasteurization** the process of heating something to a certain temperature for a specific period in order to destroy pathogenic bacteria

tract. Although shells are cleaned at packinghouses, some bacteria may remain. Therefore, to prevent contamination, it is best to avoid mixing a shell with the liquid egg.

Inadequately cooking or improperly storing eggs may lead to food-borne illnesses. USDA guidelines indicate that **pasteurization** is achieved when the whole egg stays at a temperature of 140°F (60°C) for 3½ minutes. Hold egg dishes below 40°F (4°C) or above 145°F (63°C). Never leave an egg dish at room temperature for more than one hour, including preparation and service time. Never reuse a container after it has held raw eggs without thoroughly cleaning and sanitizing it.

EGG PRODUCTS

Food service operations often want the convenience of buying eggs out of the shell in the exact form needed: whole eggs, yolks only or whites only. These processed items are called egg products and are subject to strict pasteurization standards and USDA inspections. Egg products can be frozen, refrigerated or dried. Precooked, preportioned and blended egg products are also available.

EGG SUBSTITUTES

Concerns about the cholesterol content of eggs have increased the popularity of egg substitutes. There are two general types of substitutes. The first is a complete substitute made from soy or milk proteins. It should not be used in recipes where eggs are required for thickening. The second substitute contains real albumen, but the egg yolk has been replaced with vegetable or milk products. Egg substitutes have a different flavor from real eggs, but may be useful for people on a restricted diet.

NUTRITION

Eggs contain vitamins A, D, E and K and the B-complex vitamins. They are rich in minerals and do not contain as much cholesterol as was once feared. In fact, the American Heart Association now suggests that it is acceptable to consume up to four egg yolks per week as part of a balanced diet.

▶ WHIPPED EGG WHITES

Egg whites are often whipped into a foam that is then incorporated into cakes, custards, soufflés, pancakes and other products. The air beaten into the egg foam gives products lightness and assists with leavening.

▶ PROCEDURE FOR WHIPPING EGG WHITES

1 Use fresh egg whites that are completely free of egg yolk and other impurities. Warm the egg whites to room temperature before whipping; this helps a better foam to form.

2 Use a clean bowl and whisk. Even a tiny amount of fat can prevent the egg whites from foaming properly.

3 Whip the whites until very foamy, then add salt or cream of tartar as directed.

4 Continue whipping until soft peaks form, then gradually add granulated sugar as directed.

5 Whip until stiff peaks form. Properly whipped egg whites should be moist and shiny; overwhipping will make the egg whites appear dry and spongy or curdled.

6 Use the whipped egg whites immediately. If liquid begins to separate from the whipped egg whites, discard them; they cannot be rewhipped successfully.

1 Egg whites whipped to soft peaks.

▶ APPLYING VARIOUS COOKING METHODS

No other food is as popular for breakfast, or as versatile, as the egg. Eggs can be cooked by almost any method and served with a wide array of seasonings, accompaniments and garnishes. Whatever cooking method is selected, be sure to prepare the eggs carefully: Overcooked eggs and those cooked at too high a temperature will be tough and rubbery. Undercooked eggs may transmit pathogenic bacteria and pose a risk of food-borne illness.

The following cooking methods are those most often used for egg-based dishes. They include dry-heat cooking methods (baking, sautéing and pan-frying) and moist-heat cooking methods (in-shell cooking and poaching).

2 Egg whites whipped to stiff peaks.

▶ DRY-HEAT COOKING METHODS

BAKING

SHIRRED EGGS

Baked eggs, also referred to as shirred eggs, are normally prepared in individual ramekins or baking dishes. The ramekins can be lined or partially filled with ingredients such as bread, ham, creamed spinach or artichokes. The eggs are often topped with grated cheese, fresh herbs or a sauce. When properly cooked, the egg whites should be set while the yolks are soft and creamy.

3 Spongy, overwhipped egg whites.

▶ PROCEDURE FOR PREPARING SHIRRED EGGS

1 Coat each ramekin with melted butter. Add flavoring ingredients as desired.

2 Break one or two eggs into each ramekin. Do not break the yolks. Season with salt and pepper.

3 Bake the eggs until the white is firm, approximately 12–15 minutes. Approximately 3–5 minutes before the eggs are done, add cream or top the eggs with grated cheese, diced ham, fresh herbs or other ingredients as desired.

RECIPE 21.1

1 Adding the eggs to the ramekin on top of the ham.

2 The finished shirred eggs with ham.

Yield: 1 Serving		**Method:** Baking
Whole butter, melted	as needed	as needed
Baked ham, sliced thin	½ oz.	15 g
Eggs	2	2
Salt and pepper	TT	TT
Heavy cream, hot	1 Tbsp.	15 ml
Swiss cheese, grated	1 Tbsp.	15 ml

1 Brush the interior of a 6-ounce (180-milliliter) ramekin with melted butter. Line the ramekin with the ham.

2 Break the eggs into a cup and pour them carefully into the ramekin on top of the ham. Season with salt and pepper.

3 Bake at 325°F (160°C) until the eggs begin to set, approximately 8 to 10 minutes. Remove from the oven, then add the cream and grated cheese. Return to the oven until the eggs are cooked and the cheese is melted. Serve immediately.

Approximate values per serving: **Calories** 280, **Total fat** 22 g, **Saturated fat** 10 g, **Cholesterol** 470 mg, **Sodium** 300 mg, **Total carbohydrates** 2 g, **Protein** 17 g, **Vitamin A** 30%

QUICHE

Quiche is a classic breakfast and brunch entrée. It consists of an egg custard (eggs, cream or milk and seasonings) and fillings baked in a crust.

The filling usually includes at least one type of cheese and can also include any number of other ingredients such as cooked, diced meats (for example, sausage, crumbled bacon, ham, fish or shellfish) or blanched vegetables (for example, mushrooms, sautéed onions, asparagus or broccoli). The flavor and texture of these ingredients should complement one another without overpowering the delicate egg custard. Quiche is a good way of using leftovers, but the ingredients should still be fresh and of good quality.

The crust may be made with whole wheat flour, cornmeal or other grains for added flavor and texture. A recipe for quiche dough is given on page 1024.

▶ PROCEDURE FOR PREPARING QUICHE

1 Prepare and bake a pie shell.

2 Prepare the garnishes and flavoring ingredients and add them to the pie shell.

3 Prepare a custard and add it to the pie shell. Ratios of eggs to milk or heavy cream vary depending on the specific recipe, but 6–8 eggs to 1 quart (1 liter) of liquid is usually sufficient to bind the custard.

4 Bake the quiche until set; allow it to cool slightly before cutting.

RECIPE 21.2

Yield: 1 Quiche, 10 in. (25 cm)		**Method:** Baking
Bacon, diced and cooked	4 oz.	120 g
Swiss or Gruyère cheese, shredded	2 oz.	60 g
Pie shell, 10-in. (25-cm) diameter, baked	1	1
Eggs	4	4
Milk	1 pt.	450 ml
Heavy cream	4 fl. oz.	120 ml
Salt and pepper	TT	TT
Nutmeg	TT	TT

1 Place the bacon and shredded cheese in the baked pie shell.

2 To make the custard, combine the eggs, milk and cream, and season with salt, pepper and nutmeg.

3 Pour the custard over the bacon and cheese and bake at 350°F (180°C) until the custard is cooked, approximately 1 hour.

Approximate values per ⅛-quiche serving: **Calories** 330, **Total fat** 25 g, **Saturated fat** 11 g, **Cholesterol** 105 mg, **Sodium** 420 mg, **Total carbohydrates** 14 g, **Protein** 12 g, **Vitamin A** 10%, **Calcium** 15%

SAUTÉING

SCRAMBLED EGGS

Scrambled eggs are eggs whisked with seasonings and then sautéed. They are stirred nearly constantly during cooking. The finished eggs should be light and fluffy with a tender, creamy texture. A small amount of milk or cream may be added to the eggs to provide a more delicate finished product. Overcooking or cooking at too high a temperature causes the eggs to become tough and rubbery.

Scrambled eggs are often flavored by sautéing other foods (for example, onions, mushrooms or diced ham) in the pan before adding the eggs or by adding other foods (for example, grated cheeses or herbs) to the eggs just before cooking is complete. Suggested additions include finely diced bell peppers, onions, mushrooms, zucchini or tomatoes; cottage cheese or any variety of shredded firm cheese; crumbled bacon; diced ham, turkey or beef; bits of smoked salmon, cooked shrimp or cooked sausage; and fresh herbs.

Scrambled eggs can also be prepared using only egg whites. Because all of an egg's fat is stored in the yolk, no-yolk scrambled egg dishes are lower in fat, cholesterol and calories. Water or nonfat milk can be used in place of whole milk or cream to further reduce the fat and calorie content of the finished dish. Remember that egg whites coagulate at a lower temperature than yolks, so adjust the cooking time and temperature accordingly.

▶ PROCEDURE FOR PREPARING SCRAMBLED EGGS

1 Break the eggs into a mixing bowl. Season lightly with salt and pepper. Add 1 scant tablespoon (12 milliliters) of milk or cream per egg and whisk everything together.

2 Heat a sauté pan, add clarified butter or oil and heat until the fat begins to sizzle.

3 Sauté any additional ingredients in the hot fat.

4 Pour the eggs into the pan all at once. As the eggs begin to set, slowly stir the mixture with a spatula. Lift cooked portions to allow uncooked egg to flow underneath.

5 Sprinkle on additional ingredients such as cheese or herbs.

6 Cook just until the eggs are set, but still shiny and moist. Remove from the pan and serve immediately.

1 Stirring the scrambled eggs.

2 The properly cooked eggs.

SCRAMBLED EGGS

RECIPE 21.3

Yield: 6 Servings, 4 oz. (120 g) each   **Method:** Sautéing

Eggs	12	12
Heavy cream	2 fl. oz.	60 ml
Salt and pepper	TT	TT
Clarified butter	2 fl. oz.	60 ml

1 Combine the eggs, cream, salt and pepper in a mixing bowl. Whisk until well blended.

2 Heat the clarified butter in a sauté pan.

3 Pour the egg mixture into the hot pan and cook, stirring frequently, until set, approximately 2 minutes. The eggs should be set, but still shiny and moist.

Approximate values per 4-oz. (120-g) serving: **Calories** 250, **Total fat** 21 g, **Saturated fat** 10 g, **Cholesterol** 460 mg, **Sodium** 210 mg, **Total carbohydrates** 1 g, **Protein** 13 g, **Vitamin A** 30%

OMELETS

Omelets are needlessly intimidating egg creations that begin as scrambled eggs. They are usually prepared as individual servings using two or three eggs. The cooked eggs are either folded around or filled with a warm savory mixture.

The filling may contain vegetables, cheeses and/or meats. Any filling ingredient that needs cooking should be cooked before being added to the omelet. Because the eggs cook relatively quickly, raw fillings would not be cooked properly until the eggs were overcooked.

▶ PROCEDURE FOR PREPARING FOLDED OMELETS

1 Fully cook any meats and blanch or otherwise cook any vegetables that will be incorporated into the omelet.

2 Heat an omelet pan over moderately high heat and add clarified butter.

3 Whisk the eggs together in a small bowl. Season with salt and pepper if desired.

4 Pour the eggs into the pan and stir until they begin to set, approximately 10 seconds.

5 Pull cooked egg from the sides of the pan toward the center, allowing raw egg to run underneath. Continue doing so for 20 to 30 seconds.

6 Spoon any fillings on top of the eggs or add any other garnishes.

7 When cooked as desired, flip one side of the omelet toward the center with a spatula or a shake of the pan. Slide the omelet onto the serving plate so that it lands folded in thirds with the seam underneath.

8 Spoon any sauce or additional filling on top, garnish as desired, and serve immediately.

RECIPE 21.4   SHRIMP AND AVOCADO OMELET

1 Lifting the edge of the eggs to allow them to cook evenly.

Yield: 1 Serving   **Method:** Sautéing

Shrimp, peeled, deveined and cut into pieces	3 oz.	90 g
Green onions, sliced	1 Tbsp.	15 ml
Clarified butter	1 fl. oz.	30 ml
Eggs	3	3
Salt and pepper	TT	TT
Avocado, peeled and diced	¼	¼
Fresh cilantro, chopped	2 tsp.	10 ml

1 Sauté the shrimp and onions in half of the butter for 1 minute. Remove from the heat and set aside.

2 Heat an omelet pan and add the remaining butter.

3 Whisk the eggs together in a small bowl, season with salt and pepper and pour into the omelet pan.

4 Stir the eggs as they cook. Stop when they begin to set. Lift the edges as the omelet cooks to allow the raw eggs to run underneath.

2 Adding the filling to the eggs.

3 Folding the eggs.

4 Rolling the omelet onto the plate.

5 When the eggs are nearly set, add the shrimp filling, avocado and cilantro. Fold the front of the eggs over and roll the omelet onto a plate.

Approximate values per serving: **Calories** 590, **Total fat** 47 g, **Saturated fat** 19 g, **Cholesterol** 865 mg, **Sodium** 620 mg, **Total carbohydrates** 4 g, **Protein** 39 g, **Vitamin A** 60%, **Vitamin C** 20%, **Iron** 30%

French-style omelets are similar, but the eggs are cooked without a filling, then tightly rolled onto a plate for service. A cut is made into the finished omelet and the filling is spooned in.

▶ PROCEDURE FOR PREPARING FRENCH-STYLE OMELETS

1 Heat an omelet pan over moderately high heat and add clarified butter.

2 Whisk the eggs together in a small bowl. Season with salt and pepper if desired.

3 Pour the eggs into the pan and stir until they begin to set, approximately 10 seconds.

4 Pull cooked egg from the sides of the pan toward the center, allowing raw egg to run underneath. Continue doing so for 20–30 seconds.

5 When cooked as desired, flip one side of the omelet toward the center with a spatula or a shake of the pan. Roll the omelet onto the serving plate so that it lands with the seam underneath.

1 Rolling the omelet onto the serving plate.

2 Using a paring knife to cut into the center of the omelet.

3 Spooning in the filling.

4 The finished omelet.

FRITTATAS

Frittatas are essentially open-faced omelets of Spanish-Italian heritage. They may be cooked in small pans as individual portions or in large pans, then cut into wedges for service. A relatively large amount of hearty ingredients are mixed directly into the eggs. The eggs are first cooked on the stove top, then the pan is transferred to an oven or placed under a salamander or broiler to finish cooking.

▶ PROCEDURE FOR PREPARING FRITTATAS

1 Fully cook any meats and blanch or otherwise prepare any vegetables that will be incorporated into the frittata.

2 Heat a sauté pan and add clarified butter.

3 Whisk the eggs, flavorings and any other ingredients together; pour into the pan.

4 Stir gently until the eggs begin to set. Gently lift cooked egg at the edge of the frittata so that raw egg can run underneath. Continue cooking until the eggs are almost set.

5 Place the pan in a hot oven or underneath a salamander or broiler to finish cooking and lightly brown the top.

6 Slide the finished frittata out of the pan onto a serving platter.

RECIPE 21.5	GARDEN FRITTATA

Yield: 1 Serving		**Method:** Sautéing
Chicken breast meat, boneless, skinless	2 oz.	60 g
Garlic, chopped	1 tsp.	5 ml
Cumin	TT	TT
Salt and pepper	TT	TT
Mushrooms, sliced	1 oz.	30 g
Unsalted butter	1 Tbsp.	15 g
Jalapeño, seeded, minced	1 tsp.	5 ml
Red bell pepper, roasted, seeded, peeled, julienne	1 oz.	30 g
Green onions, sliced	1 oz.	30 g
Fresh cilantro	2 tsp.	10 ml
Eggs, beaten	3	3
Monterey Jack or Cheddar cheese, shredded	1 oz.	30 g

1 Rub the chicken breast with the garlic, cumin, salt and pepper. Grill or broil the chicken until done. Allow it to rest briefly, then cut it into strips.

2 In a well-seasoned 9-inch (22-centimeter) sauté pan, sauté the mushrooms in the butter until tender. Add the jalapeño and sauté for 30 seconds. Add the chicken, bell pepper, green onions and cilantro and sauté until hot.

3 Add the eggs and season with salt and pepper. Cook the mixture, stirring and lifting the eggs to help them cook evenly, until they begin to set.

4 Sprinkle the cheese over the eggs and place under a salamander or broiler to melt the cheese and finish cooking the eggs. Slide the frittata onto a plate or cut into wedges for smaller portions.

Approximate values per serving: **Calories** 590, **Total fat** 39 g, **Saturated fat** 18 g, **Cholesterol** 755 mg, **Sodium** 400 mg, **Total carbohydrates** 8 g, **Protein** 51 g, **Vitamin A** 60%, **Vitamin C** 90%, **Calcium** 35%, **Iron** 20%, **Claims**—good source of fiber, vitamins A and C, calcium and iron

PAN-FRYING

Pan-fried eggs are commonly referred to as **sunny side up** or **over easy, over medium** or **over hard.** These are visibly different products produced with proper timing and technique. Very fresh eggs are best for pan-frying, as the yolk holds its shape better and the white spreads less.

Sunny-side-up eggs are not turned during cooking; their yellow yolks remain visible. They should be cooked over medium-low heat long enough to firm the whites and partially firm the yolks: approximately 4 minutes if cooked on a 250°F (120°C) cooking surface.

For "over" eggs, the egg is partially cooked on one side, then gently flipped and cooked on the other side until done. The egg white should be firm, and its edges should not be brown. The yolk should never be broken regardless of the degree of doneness. Not only is a broken yolk unattractive, but the spilled yolk will coagulate on contact with the hot pan, making it difficult to serve.

For over-easy eggs, the yolk should remain very runny; on a 250°F (120°C) cooking surface, the egg should cook for about 3 minutes on the first side and 2 minutes on the other. Over-medium eggs should be cooked slightly longer, until the yolk is partially set. For over-hard eggs, the yolk should be completely cooked.

▶ PROCEDURE FOR PAN-FRYING EGGS

1 Select a sauté pan just large enough to accommodate the number of eggs being cooked. (An 8-inch-diameter [20-centimeter] pan is appropriate for up to three eggs.)

2 Add a small amount of clarified butter and heat until the fat just begins to sizzle.

3 Carefully break the eggs into the pan.

4 Continue cooking over medium-low heat until the eggs reach the appropriate degree of firmness. Sunny-side-up eggs are not flipped during cooking; "over" eggs are flipped once during cooking.

5 When done, gently flip the "over" eggs once again so that the first side is up, then gently slide the cooked eggs out of the pan onto the serving plate. Serve immediately.

Basted eggs are a variation of sunny-side-up eggs. Basted eggs are cooked over low heat with the hot butter from the pan spooned over them as they cook. Another version of basted eggs is made by adding 1–2 teaspoons (5–10 milliliters) of water to the sauté pan and then covering the pan. The steam cooks the top of the eggs.

▶ MOIST-HEAT COOKING METHODS

IN-SHELL COOKING (SIMMERING)

The difference between **soft-cooked eggs** (also called **soft-boiled**) and **hard-cooked eggs** (also called **hard-boiled**) is time. Both styles refer to eggs cooked in their shell in hot water. Despite the word *boiled* in their names, eggs cooked in the shell should never be boiled. Boiling toughens eggs and causes discoloration. Instead, the eggs should be simmered. Soft-cooked eggs are usually simmered for 3 to 5 minutes; hard-cooked eggs may be simmered for as long as 12 to 15 minutes.

Sometimes it is difficult to remove the shell from very fresh eggs. Eggs that are a few days old are better for cooking in the shell.

▶ PROCEDURE FOR PREPARING SOFT-COOKED EGGS

1 Fill a saucepan or stockpot with sufficient water to cover the eggs. Bring the water to a simmer.

2 Carefully lower each egg into the simmering water. Simmer uncovered for 3 to 5 minutes, depending on the firmness desired.

1 Pouring the eggs into the sauté pan.

2 Flipping the eggs.

3 Sliding the eggs onto a plate for service.

3 Lift each egg out of the water with a slotted spoon or spider. Crack the large end of the shell carefully and serve immediately.

▶ PROCEDURE FOR PREPARING HARD-COOKED EGGS

1 Repeat steps 1 and 2 for soft-cooked eggs, simmering the eggs for 12 to 15 minutes.

2 Lift each egg out of the water with a slotted spoon or spider and place in an ice bath. When the eggs are cool enough to handle, peel them and use as desired or cover and refrigerate for up to 5 days.

POACHING

Eggs that are to be poached should always be very fresh. They should also be kept very cold until used, as cold egg whites stay together better when dropped into hot water. Poached eggs should be soft and moist; the whites should be firm enough to encase the yolk completely, but the yolk should still be runny.

Some chefs add salt to the poaching water for flavor; others believe that the salt causes the egg whites to separate. To help the egg whites cling together, add 2 tablespoons (30 milliliters) of white vinegar per quart (liter) of water.

▶ PROCEDURE FOR POACHING EGGS

1 Fill a saucepan or stockpot with at least 3 inches (7.5 centimeters) of water. Add salt and vinegar if desired. Bring the water to a simmer and hold at a temperature of approximately 200°F (90°C).

2 One at a time, crack the eggs into a small ramekin or cup. If a piece of shell falls into the egg, it should be removed; if the yolk breaks, the egg can be set aside for some other use.

3 Gently slide each egg into the simmering water and cook for 3–5 minutes.

4 Lift the poached egg out of the water with a slotted spoon. Trim any ragged edges with a paring knife. Serve immediately.

For quantity service, eggs can be poached in advance and held for up to one day. To do so, cook the eggs as described. As each egg is removed from the hot water, set it in a hotel pan filled with ice water to stop the cooking process. The eggs can then be stored in the ice water until needed. For banquet-style service, all the eggs can be reheated at once by placing the entire pan on the stove top. Or the eggs can be reheated one or two at a time by placing them in a pan of barely simmering water until they are hot.

RECIPE 21.6	POACHED EGGS

Yield: 1 Serving		**Method:** Poaching
Water	as needed	as needed
Salt	1 tsp.	5 ml
Vinegar	2 Tbsp.	30 ml
Eggs	2	2

1 Bring the water to a simmer; add the salt and vinegar.

2 Crack one egg into a cup and carefully add it to the water. Repeat with the other egg.

3 Cook the eggs to the desired doneness, approximately 3 to 5 minutes. Remove them from the water with a slotted spoon and serve as desired or carefully lower them into ice water and refrigerate for later use.

Approximate values per 3½-oz. (105-g) serving: **Calories** 140, **Total fat** 10 g, **Saturated fat** 3 g, **Cholesterol** 425 mg, **Sodium** 280 mg, **Total carbohydrates** 1 g, **Protein** 12 g, **Vitamin A** 20%

1 Adding an egg to a pot of simmering water.

2 Lowering the eggs into ice water to cool them for future use.

▶ BREAKFAST & BRUNCH

Breakfast is often an on-the-go, rushed experience; hence the popularity of breakfast sandwiches, jumbo muffins and disposable coffee cups. Brunch, on the other hand, is a leisurely experience, combining breakfast and lunch into a social occasion. Brunch menus include traditional breakfast foods along with almost anything else. Unlike breakfast, brunch is often accompanied by champagne or other alcoholic beverages and concludes with a pastry or dessert.

Food service operations must offer a variety of breakfast options to appeal to a wide range of consumers. Hotels and resorts may offer a complimentary continental-style breakfast of coffee, juice and sweet rolls; a full-service à la carte dining room; a room service menu and a casual snack bar. The grand hotel Sunday and holiday brunch buffet is an American institution for celebrations and special occasions.

Office, retail and commercial complexes are peppered with small shops selling coffee, muffins, bagels and sweet rolls. Coffeehouses offering a variety of coffee blends and drinks, pastries, breads and quiche are also popular. Even fast-food facilities have expanded their menus and hours of operation to meet the needs of early-morning diners.

The foods served at breakfast include most of the foods served at other times during the day. A diner's perceptions of the proper breakfast depends on his or her cultural, ethnic, economic and geographic background as well as sleep patterns and work schedule.

Breakfast menus typically include the following items:

▶ Coffee, tea or other hot beverages

▶ Fruits or fruit juices

▶ Eggs

▶ Breads, including sweet breads

▶ Cereals and grains

▶ Potatoes

▶ Pancakes, waffles and French toast

▶ Meats or fish

▶ Dairy products, including milk, cheese and yogurt

Although few people could sit down to a breakfast including all of these components even occasionally, most food service operations find it necessary to offer some items from each category in order to meet their customers' expectations.

BREAKFAST MEATS

At other meals, meat is typically the principal food, but at breakfast it is usually an accompaniment. Breakfast meats tend to be spicy or highly flavored. A hearty breakfast menu may include a small beef steak (usually sirloin and often pan-fried) or pork chop. Corned beef, roast beef or roast turkey can be diced or shredded, then sautéed with potatoes and other ingredients for a breakfast hash. Fish, particularly smoked products, are also served at breakfast.

But the most popular breakfast meats are bacon (including Canadian-style bacon), ham and sausages. They are all discussed in Chapter 27, Charcuterie. Bacon can be cooked on a flat griddle or in a heavy skillet or baked on a sheet pan. Regardless of the method used, the cooked bacon should be drained on absorbent paper towels to remove excess fat. Canadian-style bacon is very lean and requires little cooking, although slices are usually sautéed briefly before serving. The round slices may be served like ham and are essential for eggs Benedict. A ham steak is simply a thick slice ideal for breakfast. Fully cooked ham only needs to be heated briefly on a griddle or in a sauté pan before service. The most popular breakfast sausages are made from uncured, uncooked meats. They can be mild to spicy, slightly sweet or strongly seasoned with sage. Recipes for country-style and other sausages are at the end of Chapter 27. Breakfast sausage is available in bulk, links or preformed patties. Link sausage is often partially cooked by steam, then browned by sautéing at service time. It should be drained on absorbent paper towels to remove excess fat before service.

GRIDDLECAKES

Pancakes and waffles are types of griddlecakes or griddle breads. They are usually leavened with baking soda or baking powder and are quickly cooked on a very hot griddle or waffle iron with very little fat. Griddlecakes should be more than just an excuse for eating butter and maple syrup, however. They should have a rich flavor and a light, tender, moist interior.

Pancake and waffle batters may be flavored with tangy buckwheat flour, fruits, whole grains or nuts. Both pancakes and waffles are usually served with plain or flavored butter and fruit compote or syrup. Waffles must be cooked in a special waffle iron, which gives the cakes a distinctive gridlike pattern and a crisp texture. Electric waffle irons are available with square, round and even heart-shaped grids. The grids should be seasoned well, then never washed. (Follow the manufacturer's directions for seasoning.) Belgian waffles are especially light and crisp because of the incorporation of whipped egg whites and/or yeast. They are often made in a waffle iron with extra deep grids and are served for breakfast or as a dessert, topped with fresh fruit, whipped cream or ice cream.

▶ PROCEDURE FOR MAKING PANCAKES

1 Prepare the batter.
2 Heat a flat griddle or large sauté pan over moderately high heat. Add clarified butter.
3 Portion the pancake batter onto the hot griddle using a portion scoop, ladle or adjustable batter dispenser. Pour the portioned batter in one spot; it should spread into an even circle. Drop the batter so that no two pancakes will touch after the batter spreads.
4 Cook until bubbles appear on the surface, and the bottom of the cake is set and golden brown. Flip the pancake using an offset spatula.
5 Cook the pancake until the second side is golden brown. Avoid flipping the pancake more than once as this causes it to deflate.

BUTTERMILK PANCAKES

Yield: 24 Pancakes

Flour	1 lb.	450 g
Granulated sugar	2 Tbsp.	30 ml
Baking powder	1 Tbsp.	15 ml
Salt	1½ tsp.	7 ml
Buttermilk	1½ pt.	750 ml
Unsalted butter, melted	2 oz.	60 g
Eggs, beaten	3	3
Clarified butter	as needed	as needed

1 Sift the flour, sugar, baking powder and salt together.
2 Combine the buttermilk, melted butter and eggs and add them to the dry ingredients. Mix just until the ingredients are combined.
3 If the griddle is not well seasoned, coat it lightly with clarified butter. Once its temperature reaches 375°F (190°C), drop the batter onto it in 2-fluid-ounce (60-milliliter) portions using a ladle, portion scoop or batter portioner.
4 When bubbles appear on the pancake's surface and the bottom is browned, flip the pancake to finish cooking.

Variations: *Blueberry Pancakes*—Gently stir 1 pint (450 milliliters) of fresh or frozen blueberries into the batter. If using frozen berries, drain them thoroughly then pat dry with paper towels before adding them to the batter. Serve with blueberry syrup or compote.

Apple-Pecan Pancakes—Gently fold 4 ounces (120 grams) of chopped cooked apples, ¼ teaspoon (2 milliliters) of cinnamon and 1 ounce (30 grams) of finely chopped pecans into the batter.

Approximate values per pancake: **Calories** 120, **Total fat** 4 g, **Saturated fat** 2.5 g, **Cholesterol** 35 mg, **Sodium** 250 mg, **Total carbohydrates** 17 g, **Protein** 4 g

CRÊPES

Crêpes are thin, delicate, unleavened pancakes. They are made with a very liquid egg batter cooked in a small, very hot sauté pan or crêpe pan. Crêpe batter can be flavored with buckwheat flour, cornmeal or other grains. Crêpes are not eaten as is, but are usually filled and garnished with sautéed fruits, scrambled eggs, cheese or vegetables. Crêpes can be prepared in advance, then filled and reheated in the oven.

Blintzes are crêpes that are cooked on only one side, then filled with cheese, browned in butter and served with sour cream, fruit compote or preserves. A recipe for cheese blintzes is provided at the end of this chapter.

▶ PROCEDURE FOR PREPARING CRÊPES

1 Prepare the batter.
2 Heat a well-seasoned crêpe pan or small sauté pan over moderately high heat. Add a small amount of clarified butter.
3 Ladle a small amount of batter into the pan. Tilt the pan so that the batter spreads and coats the bottom evenly.

4 Cook until the crêpe is set and the bottom begins to brown, approximately 1 minute. Flip the crêpe over with a quick flick of the wrist or by lifting it carefully with a spatula.

5 Cook the crêpe for an additional 30 seconds. Slide the finished crêpe from the pan. Crêpes can be stacked between layers of parchment paper for storage.

RECIPE 21.8 — CRÊPES

Yield: 30 Crêpes, 6 in. (15 cm) each

Whole eggs	6	6
Egg yolks	6	6
Water	12 fl. oz.	350 ml
Milk	18 fl. oz.	550 ml
Granulated sugar	6 oz.	180 g
Salt	1 tsp.	5 ml
Flour	14 oz.	420 g
Unsalted butter, melted	5 oz.	150 g
Clarified butter	as needed	as needed

1 Whisk together the eggs, egg yolks, water and milk. Add the sugar, salt and flour; whisk together. Stir in the melted butter. Cover and set aside to rest for at least 1 hour before cooking.

2 Heat a small sauté or crêpe pan; brush lightly with clarified butter. Pour in 1–1½ fluid ounces (30–45 milliliters) of batter; swirl to coat the bottom of the pan evenly.

3 Cook the crêpe until set and light brown, approximately 30 seconds. Flip it over and cook a few seconds longer. Remove from the pan.

4 Cooked crêpes may be used immediately or covered and held briefly in a warm oven. Crêpes can also be wrapped well in plastic wrap and refrigerated for 2–3 days or frozen for several weeks.

Variation: *Savory Crêpes*—Reduce the sugar to 1 tablespoon (15 milliliters.). Substitute up to 5 ounces (150 grams) of buckwheat flour or whole wheat flour for an equal amount of the all-purpose flour if desired.

Approximate values per 2-oz. (60-g) serving: **Calories** 140, **Total fat** 7 g, **Saturated fat** 3.5 g, **Cholesterol** 95 mg, **Sodium** 100 mg, **Total carbohydrates** 17 g, **Protein** 4 g

1 Coating the bottom of the pan evenly with the batter.

2 Flipping the crêpe. Notice the proper light brown color.

CEREALS AND GRAINS

Oats, rice, corn and wheat are perhaps the most widely eaten breakfast foods. Processed breakfast cereals are ready-to-eat products made from these grains. Most consumers now think of breakfast cereal as a cold food, but not so long ago only hot grains were breakfast staples. Oatmeal served as a hot porridge is still popular, especially with toppings such as cream, brown sugar, fresh or dried fruit or fruit preserves. Grits, made from ground corn, are another grain product served hot at breakfast. Grits may be topped with butter and presented as a starch side dish or served in a bowl as a porridge with cream and brown sugar. Oats and oatmeal, grits and other grains are discussed in Chapter 23, Potatoes, Grains and Pasta.

Ready-to-eat (cold) cereal is usually topped with milk or light cream and sugar. Fresh or dried fruits may be added. Many products are enriched or fortified with vitamins and minerals to compensate for the nutrients lost during processing. Creative cooks can avoid overly sweet, artificially flavored commercial products by making their own ready-to-eat breakfast cereals such as **muesli** or granola, a toasted blend of whole grains, nuts and dried fruits. The results are less expensive, more nutritious and far more interesting.

▶ **muesli** (MYOOS-lee) a breakfast cereal made from raw or toasted cereal grains, dried fruits, nuts and dried milk solids and usually eaten with milk or yogurt; sometimes known as granola

CRUNCHY GRANOLA   RECIPE 21.9

Yield: 3 qt. (3 lt)

Brown sugar	8 oz.	250 g
Water, hot	4 fl. oz.	120 ml
Canola oil	6 fl. oz.	180 ml
Old-fashioned oats	18 oz.	500 g
Wheat germ	4 oz.	120 g
Coconut, shredded	2½ oz.	75 g
Salt (optional)	1 Tbsp.	15 ml
Whole-wheat flour	2 oz.	60 g
Amaranth flour	2 oz.	60 g
Unbleached all-purpose flour	2 oz.	60 g
Yellow cornmeal	2 oz.	60 g
Pecans, chopped	4 oz.	120 g

1 Dissolve the brown sugar in the hot water. Add the oil.

2 Combine the dry ingredients in a large bowl. Mix thoroughly by hand.

3 Add the brown-sugar-and-oil mixture to the dry ingredients; toss to combine.

4 Spread out the granola in a thin layer on a sheet pan. Bake at 200°F (90°C) until crisp, approximately 1½ to 2 hours. Toss lightly with a metal spatula every 30 minutes.

5 Let the baked granola cool completely at room temperature, then store in an airtight container. Chopped dried fruits, additional nuts or fresh fruits can be added at service time.

Approximate values per ¼-cup (30-g) serving: **Calories** 140, **Total fat** 7 g, **Saturated fat** 1 g, **Cholesterol** 0 mg, **Sodium** 5 mg, **Total carbohydrates** 17 g, **Protein** 3 g

FROM HEALTH FOOD TO SUGAR SNACK

The century-old, multibillion-dollar-a-year American breakfast cereal industry, unlike any other in the world, is rooted in health foods. During the 1890s, Dr. John Harvey Kellogg directed a sanitarium in Battle Creek, Michigan. Among the healthful foods prescribed for his patients was his special mixture of whole grains called "granula." John, along with his brother Will, next created and began marketing wheat flakes as a nutritious breakfast food. They were not an immediate success, however; people found a cold breakfast unappealing. Undeterred, Will continued toying with cold cereals,

eventually creating flakes made from toasted corn and malt. Thanks to a massive advertising campaign, the American public finally embraced corn flakes and a financial empire was born.

Charles W. Post was a patient of Dr. Kellogg's Battle Creek Sanitarium in 1891. He adopted the principles of healthful eating espoused by the Kellogg brothers and soon opened his own spa, complete with a factory producing his "Post Toasties" and "grape-nuts." He promoted them as a cure for appendicitis, consumption and malaria.

Soon Battle Creek became a boomtown, home to more than 40 breakfast cereal companies. Unfortunately for the consumer, not all manufacturers—then and now—were as concerned about health as John, Will and C. W. The addition of sugar, sometimes totaling more than half the cereal's weight, makes some of today's breakfast products more sugary than candy bars. Even some of the granola cereals touted as healthier alternatives to other breakfast cereals and snacks contain 20 percent sugar or more. But at least they no longer claim to cure malaria.

CONCLUSION

Eggs are found in practically every kitchen and served as the principal ingredient or incorporated into various dishes. How to select, handle and cook them well are basic skills all student chefs must master. They must also master the skills needed to prepare breakfast items. Breakfast is an important meal for consumers and food service operations alike. Breakfast menus may offer a variety of items, including fruits, cereals, eggs, pancakes and cured meats, or they can be devoted to one or two specialty items such as coffee and cinnamon rolls. Whatever is served should be prepared and served with care.

QUESTIONS FOR DISCUSSION

1 Explain the difference between an omelet and a frittata.
2 Describe four different types of pan-fried eggs, and explain how each is prepared.
3 What is the difference between a soft-cooked egg and a hard-cooked egg? Why are these eggs simmered instead of boiled?
4 Explain the differences between a typical breakfast and a typical brunch. Create a sample menu for each of these meals.
5 List three types of griddlecakes and explain how they are prepared.

SOUTHWESTERN SCRAMBLED EGGS WITH GREEN CHILE AND CHORIZO

RECIPE 21.10

Note: This dish appears in the chapter opening photograph.

CAFÉ ALLEGRE, ORLANDO, FL
Executive Chef Kevin Fonzo

Yield: 4 Servings

Eggs	10	10
Milk	8 fl. oz.	250 ml
Salt and pepper	TT	TT
Olive oil	1 Tbsp.	15 ml
Chorizo, cooked	4 oz.	120 g
Green chiles, canned, chopped	¼ c.	60 ml
Tomatoes, chopped	½ c.	120 ml
Pepperjack cheese, shredded	¼ c.	60 ml
Green onions, chopped	¼ c.	60 ml
Avocado, sliced	1	1
Flour tortilla, heated on a grill and cut into thin wedges	1	1

1 Whisk the eggs and milk together in a mixing bowl. Season with salt and pepper and set aside.

2 Heat a large sauté pan and add the olive oil. Add the chorizo and cook until heated thoroughly. Add the chiles and tomatoes and cook for 2 minutes.

3 Add the eggs to the sauté pan and cook over low heat, stirring vigorously and constantly with a rubber spatula.

4 When the eggs begin to set, add the cheese and green onions. Cook until the cheese melts.

5 Serve immediately, garnished with slices of avocado and tortilla.

Approximate values per serving: **Calories** 525, **Total fat** 39 g, **Saturated fat** 12 g, **Cholesterol** 570 mg, **Sodium** 648 mg, **Total carbohydrates** 15 g, **Protein** 28 g, **Vitamin A** 28%, **Vitamin C** 53%, **Calcium** 20%, **Iron** 19%

CHEF KEVIN FONZO

While in high school, Kevin Fonzo worked as a line cook in an old inn in upstate New York. He went on to study at the Culinary Institute of America in Hyde Park, New York. After graduating in 1986, he worked in restaurants in New York and Hilton Head, South Carolina, as well as at *Ciboulette* and *Phoenix Brewing Company* in Atlanta, Georgia. He is now the chef and owner of *Café Allegre*, one of Orlando's finest restaurants.

Chef Fonzo has cooked for numerous charity events. He often gives cooking classes and his writings have appeared in several cooking journals. Chef Fonzo believes that "cooking is not just a job. The separation from chef to cook is all in the heart; it becomes a lifestyle."

GREEK-STYLE SCRAMBLED EGGS

RECIPE 21.11

Yield: 6 Servings, 5 oz. (150 g) each

Eggs	12	12
Heavy cream	2 fl. oz.	60 ml
Salt and pepper	TT	TT
Onion, diced fine	2 oz.	60 g
Clarified butter	3 fl. oz.	90 ml
Spinach, chiffonade	2 oz.	60 g
Feta, crumbled	4 oz.	120 g
Greek olives, pitted and chopped	3 Tbsp.	45 ml

1 Combine the eggs, cream, salt and pepper in a mixing bowl. Whisk until well blended.

2 Sauté the onion in the butter until translucent but not brown.

3 Pour the egg mixture into the pan and cook, stirring frequently, until half cooked, approximately 1 minute.

4 Add the spinach to the eggs and continue cooking. Just before the eggs are fully cooked, sprinkle on the feta.

5 Spoon the cooked egg mixture onto serving plates and garnish with the olives. Serve immediately.

Approximate values per 5-oz. (160-g) serving: **Calories** 290, **Total fat** 23 g, **Saturated fat** 11 g, **Cholesterol** 465 mg, **Sodium** 380 mg, **Total carbohydrates** 4 g, **Protein** 16 g, **Vitamin A** 30%, **Calcium** 15%, **Iron** 10%

RECIPE 21.12 — ROLLED SOUFFLÉ

NEWBURY COLLEGE, BROOKLINE, MA
Senior Instructor Scott Doughty

Yield: 22 Slices, 1 oz. (30 g) each

Whole butter	as needed	as needed
Flour	1 Tbsp.	15 ml
Milk, cold	8 fl. oz.	225 ml
Eggs, separated	6	6
Parmesan, grated	4 oz.	120 g
Duxelles (page 667)	12 oz.	350 g
Aurora sauce (page 214)	1 qt.	950 ml
Watercress	1 bunch	1 bunch
Parsley, chopped	2 Tbsp.	30 ml

1 Brush a half sheet pan with butter and line it with parchment paper.

2 Heat 1 tablespoon (15 milliliters) of butter in a small saucepan. Add the flour and cook to make a blond roux. Slowly add the cold milk to the roux to form a paste. Bring slowly to a simmer and continue to cook for 10 minutes, stirring constantly. Transfer the sauce to a stainless steel bowl.

3 Beat the egg yolks into the sauce. In a separate bowl, beat the egg whites with a balloon whisk until stiff, shiny peaks form. Stir approximately 1/3 of the whites into the sauce and yolk mixture. Gently fold in another 1/3 of the whites and repeat with the last 1/3 of the whites. Fold in the Parmesan.

4 Spread the mixture onto the prepared half sheet pan. Bake at 350°F (180°C) until done, approximately 15 minutes. Keep the oven door closed during cooking.

5 Heat the duxelles. Remove the soufflé from the oven and separate it from the edges of the pan with a paring knife. Turn the soufflé out onto a clean surface. Spread the duxelles over the entire surface of the soufflé. Roll it up jelly-roll fashion. Be sure the paper does not get rolled up with the soufflé. Trim the ends from the soufflé to make it attractive.

6 For buffet service, slice three or four pieces from the soufflé and place the remaining soufflé on a platter. Pour Aurora sauce over it, allowing the sauce to run attractively onto the platter. Arrange the reserved slices at one end of the soufflé and garnish with watercress and chopped parsley. Serve the remaining Aurora sauce on the side.

Approximate values per slice: **Calories** 130, **Total fat** 10 g, **Saturated fat** 6 g, **Cholesterol** 105 mg, **Sodium** 350 mg, **Total carbohydrates** 4 g, **Protein** 6 g

EGGS BENEDICT

Yield: 1 Serving

English muffin, split	1	1
Canadian bacon slices, ¼ in. (6 mm) thick	2	2
Salt	TT	TT
Vinegar	2 Tbsp.	30 ml
Eggs	2	2
Hollandaise (page 219)	4 fl. oz.	120 ml
Truffle slices or black olive halves	2	2

1 Toast the English muffin.
2 Sauté or griddle the bacon slices until hot.
3 Bring 1 quart (1 liter) of water to a boil and add the salt and vinegar.
4 Add the eggs and poach until done.
5 Place the muffins on a plate and top with the bacon slices. Place an egg on each slice of bacon and cover with the hollandaise sauce.
6 Garnish each egg with a truffle slice or black olive half and serve.

Variations: *Poached Eggs Sardou*—Poached eggs and creamed spinach on an artichoke bottom with hollandaise sauce.

Poached Eggs Princess Style—Poached eggs on an English muffin with asparagus tips and hollandaise sauce.

Approximate values per serving: **Calories** 970, **Total fat** 69 g, **Saturated fat** 33 g, **Cholesterol** 610 mg, **Sodium** 2480 mg, **Total carbohydrates** 53 g, **Protein** 33 g, **Vitamin A** 80%, **Iron** 25%

CRABCAKES BENEDICT

CAFÉ ALLEGRE, ORLANDO, FL
Chef Kevin Fonzo

Yield: 6 Servings

English muffins, split and toasted	6	6
Crab Cakes (page 529)	12	12
Eggs, poached	12	12
Tomato Chile Hollandaise (recipe follows)	12 fl. oz.	360 ml

1 Place an open English muffin on each plate. Top each muffin half with a Crab Cake, a poached egg and 2 fluid ounces (60 milliliters) of Tomato Chile Hollandaise sauce.
2 Serve with gaufrette potatoes and fresh fruit.

Approximate values per serving: **Calories** 715, **Total fat** 43 g, **Saturated fat** 20 g, **Cholesterol** 539 mg, **Sodium** 2620 mg, **Total carbohydrates** 53 g, **Protein** 32 g, **Vitamin A** 48%, **Vitamin C** 15%, **Calcium** 35%, **Iron** 27%

TOMATO CHILE HOLLANDAISE

Yield: 1 qt. (1 lt)

Hollandaise (page 219)	1 qt.	1 lt
Chilli powder	1 Tbsp.	15 ml
Tomato paste	1 Tbsp.	15 ml

1 Stir the chilli powder and tomato paste into the Hollandaise Sauce.

Approximate values per 4-fl. oz. (120-ml) serving: **Calories** 129, **Total fat** 11 g, **Saturated fat** 6 g, **Cholesterol** 26 mg, **Sodium** 830 mg, **Total carbohydrates** 8 g, **Protein** 3 g, **Vitamin A** 15%

RECIPE 21.15 — EGGS HUSSARDE

BRENNAN'S RESTAURANT, NEW ORLEANS, LA
Chef Michael Roussel

Yield: 4 Servings   **Method:** Poaching

Whole butter	2 Tbsp.	30 ml
Canadian bacon or ham slices	8	8
Holland rusks	8	8
Marchand de vin (page 217)	1 pt.	500 ml
Poached eggs	8	8
Hollandaise (page 219)	1 pt.	500 ml

1 Melt the butter in a large sauté pan and warm the Canadian bacon or ham over low heat.

2 Arrange 2 Holland rusks on each plate and cover with the slices of warm bacon or ham. Spoon marchand de vin over the meat, then top with a poached egg.

3 Ladle hollandaise over the eggs and serve.

Approximate values per serving: **Calories** 1230, **Total fat** 105 g, **Saturated fat** 60 g, **Cholesterol** 875 mg, **Sodium** 2170 mg, **Total carbohydrates** 28 g, **Protein** 34 g, **Vitamin A** 90%, **Vitamin C** 25%, **Calcium** 10%, **Iron** 25%

RECIPE 21.16 — OYSTERS BENEDICT

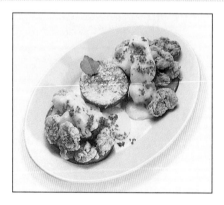

BRENNAN'S RESTAURANT, NEW ORLEANS, LA
Chef Michael Roussel

Yield: 4 Servings   **Method:** Deep-frying

Corn flour	3 c.	360 ml
Salt	½ tsp.	3 ml
Black pepper	½ tsp.	3 ml
Cayenne pepper	¼ tsp.	1 ml
Oysters, shucked	48	48
Vegetable oil	as needed	as needed
Whole butter	2 Tbsp.	30 ml
Canadian bacon or smoked ham slices	8	8
Hollandaise (page 219)	1 pt.	500 ml

1 Blend the corn flour with the salt, black pepper and cayenne in a shallow pan. Dredge the oysters in the seasoned corn flour until well coated.

2 Heat the oil in a deep-fat fryer to 375°F (191°C). Using the basket method, deep-fry the oysters until golden brown, approximately 3 minutes. Drain on absorbent paper towels.

3 Melt the butter in a large sauté pan and sauté the Canadian bacon or ham just until warmed. Arrange two slices each on four serving plates. Mound six fried oysters over each piece of bacon or ham and top with hollandaise.

Approximate values per serving: **Calories** 1780, **Total fat** 122 g, **Saturated fat** 58 g, **Cholesterol** 940 mg, **Sodium** 3720 mg, **Total carbohydrates** 72 g, **Protein** 90 g, **Vitamin A** 40%, **Vitamin C** 60%, **Calcium** 50%, **Iron** 400%

BUCKWHEAT CRÊPES WITH SAUSAGE AND APPLE STUFFING

RECIPE 21.17

THE CONYERS HOUSE, SPERRYVILLE, VA

Yield: 8 Servings

All-purpose flour	3 oz.	90 g
Buckwheat flour	1 oz.	30 g
Eggs	2	2
Salt	¼ tsp.	1 ml
Milk	4 fl. oz.	120 ml
Water	6 fl. oz.	180 ml
Unsalted butter, melted	1 oz.	30 g
Vegetable oil	as needed	as needed
Pork sausage, bulk	1 lb.	450 g
Unsalted butter	2 oz.	60 g
Apples, medium, peeled, cored and diced	6	6
Cinnamon, ground	1 tsp.	5 ml
Apple cider	4 fl. oz.	120 ml
Sour cream	8 oz.	250 g
Fresh sage	2 Tbsp.	30 ml

1 To make the crêpes, mix the flours together in a medium bowl. Add the eggs and salt. Stir to make a thick batter.

2 Whisk in the milk, then add the water a little at a time. Whisk in the melted butter. Set the batter aside to rest for 20 minutes.

3 Heat a crêpe pan and coat it lightly with oil. Pour 1½ fluid ounces (45 milliliters) of batter into the pan, lifting and tilting to coat the pan evenly.

4 Brown the crêpe lightly on one side, cooking until the surface is firm. Remove from the pan and hold in a warm oven until ready to fill and serve. Repeat this process until all the crêpes are made.

5 To make the filling, crumble the sausage into a sauté pan; cook over medium-high heat until fully cooked. Remove the sausage from the pan with a slotted spoon and place in a mesh strainer to drain excess fat.

6 Pour off all but 1 tablespoon (15 milliliters) of fat. Add the butter to the pan and melt over medium heat. Add the diced apples and sauté until soft.

7 Sprinkle the cinnamon over the apples and pour in the apple cider. Cook until the cider is reduced by half.

8 Return the drained sausage to the pan. Add the sour cream and sage. Mix well and heat thoroughly.

9 To assemble, spoon a portion of the filling onto each crêpe. Roll the crêpe around the filling and serve immediately.

Approximate values per 6-oz. (180-g) serving: **Calories** 240, **Total fat** 11 g, **Saturated fat** 6 g, **Cholesterol** 75 mg, **Sodium** 140 mg, **Total carbohydrates** 29 g, **Protein** 5 g, **Vitamin A** 10%, **Claims**—good source of fiber

RECIPE 21.18

STRAWBERRY CRÊPES FITZGERALD

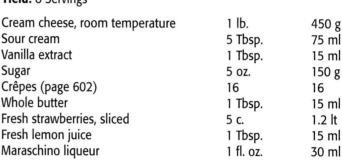

BRENNAN'S RESTAURANT, NEW ORLEANS, LA
Chef Michael Roussel

Yield: 8 Servings

Cream cheese, room temperature	1 lb.	450 g
Sour cream	5 Tbsp.	75 ml
Vanilla extract	1 Tbsp.	15 ml
Sugar	5 oz.	150 g
Crêpes (page 602)	16	16
Whole butter	1 Tbsp.	15 ml
Fresh strawberries, sliced	5 c.	1.2 lt
Fresh lemon juice	1 Tbsp.	15 ml
Maraschino liqueur	1 fl. oz.	30 ml

1 Combine the cream cheese, sour cream, vanilla and 1 ounce (30 grams) of the sugar in a mixing bowl and beat until smooth.

2 Place 3 tablespoons (45 milliliters) of the filling on one end of each crêpe; roll the crêpes around the filling and then refrigerate them while preparing the topping.

3 To make the topping, heat the butter and the remaining 4 ounces (120 grams) of sugar in a large saucepan. Cook over medium heat, stirring until the sugar dissolves. Add the strawberries and lemon juice.

4 Bring the mixture to a boil, then reduce the heat and simmer until the liquid thickens, approximately 10 to 12 minutes. Add the maraschino liqueur and flambé.

5 To serve, place 2 crêpes on each plate and spoon approximately 6 fluid ounces (180 milliliters) of warm strawberry topping over the crêpes.

Approximate values per serving: **Calories** 630, **Total fat** 37 g, **Saturated fat** 22 g, **Cholesterol** 260 mg, **Sodium** 380 mg, **Total carbohydrates** 65 g, **Protein** 13 g, **Vitamin A** 20%, **Vitamin C** 100%

RECIPE 21.19

CHEESE BLINTZES

Yield: 16 Blintzes

Eggs	3	3
Milk	8 fl. oz.	250 ml
Vegetable oil	1 fl. oz.	30 ml
Salt	½ tsp.	2 ml
Flour	4 oz.	120 g
Clarified butter	as needed	as needed
Ricotta	12 oz.	350 g
Egg yolk	1	1
Salt	¼ tsp.	1 ml
Lemon juice	1 tsp.	5 ml
Vanilla extract	1 tsp.	5 ml
Whole butter	2 oz.	60 g

1 To make the batter, whisk together the eggs, milk and oil. Add the salt. Stir in the flour and mix until smooth. Allow the batter to rest for 30 minutes.

2 Heat a crêpe pan and add a small amount of clarified butter.

3 Pour 1 fluid ounce (30 milliliters) of the batter into the pan. Tip the pan so that the batter coats the entire surface in a thin layer.

4 Cook the pancake until browned on the bottom. Remove it from the pan.

5 To make the filling, drain the ricotta in a china cap. Combine the egg yolk, salt, lemon juice and vanilla extract with the cheese and mix well.

6 To assemble, place a pancake on the work surface with the cooked side down. Place 1 ounce (30 grams) of the filling in the center of the pancake. Fold the opposite ends in and then roll up to form a small package.

7 Sauté each blintz in butter until hot. Serve with sour cream or fruit compote as desired.

Approximate values per 2-oz. (60-g) serving: **Calories** 110, **Total fat** 7 g, **Saturated fat** 3.5 g, **Cholesterol** 65 mg, **Sodium** 170 mg, **Total carbohydrates** 7 g, **Protein** 5 g

WAFFLES
RECIPE 21.20

Yield: 20 Waffles

All-purpose flour	18 oz.	570 g
Salt	2 tsp.	10 ml
Baking powder	3 Tbsp.	45 ml
Granulated sugar	2 oz.	60 g
Eggs	4	4
Milk, warm	24 fl. oz.	710 ml
Unsalted butter, melted	5 oz.	140 g
Vanilla extract	2 tsp.	10 ml

1 Mix the dry ingredients together in a large bowl.

2 Whisk the eggs together in a separate bowl; add the milk, butter and vanilla extract.

3 Pour the liquid mixture into the dry ingredients, stirring to blend. Keep refrigerated until ready to use. Batter may be made up to one day in advance.

4 Cook in a preheated waffle iron according to the manufacturer's directions. Serve waffles immediately with your choice of toppings.

Variation: *Pecan Waffles*—Sprinkle 1 Tbsp. (15 ml) of chopped pecans over the batter as soon as it is poured onto the waffle iron. Substitute 1 tsp. (5 ml) of pecan flavoring for the vanilla extract if desired.

Approximate values per waffle: **Calories** 190, **Total fat** 8 g, **Saturated fat** 4.5 g, **Cholesterol** 65 mg, **Sodium** 480 mg, **Total carbohydrates** 25 g, **Protein** 5 g, **Calcium** 20%

DUTCH BABY PANCAKE
RECIPE 21.21

Dutch baby pancakes are a cross between a soufflé, a crêpe and a pancake. Because only the edges rise during baking, the center can be filled with sautéed apples, pears or peaches just before service. The plain pancake is also delicious sprinkled with powdered sugar and fresh lemon juice.

Yield: 1 Pancake, 10 in. (25 cm)

Flour	5 oz.	140 g
Milk	8 fl. oz.	250 ml
Eggs	3	3
Granulated sugar	3 Tbsp.	45 ml
Salt	¼ tsp.	1 ml
Vanilla extract	1 tsp.	5 ml
Whole butter	1 Tbsp.	15 ml
Powdered sugar	as needed	as needed
Fresh lemon juice	from ½ lemon	from ½ lemon

1 Place the flour in a large mixing bowl. In a separate container blend the milk, eggs, granulated sugar, salt and vanilla. Whisk the egg mixture into the flour, beating until well blended and smooth.

2 Place the butter in a heavy 10-inch (25-centimeter) skillet and put the skillet into a hot oven. When the pan is hot and the butter melted but not burned, remove the pan from the oven and immediately pour in the batter. Return the pan to a 425°F (220°C) oven and bake until puffed, dry and lightly browned, approximately 25 minutes.

3 Dust with powdered sugar and sprinkle with lemon juice and serve immediately.

Approximate values per ¼-pancake serving: **Calories** 290, **Total fat** 9 g, **Saturated fat** 4.5 g, **Cholesterol** 175 mg, **Sodium** 220 mg, **Total carbohydrates** 40 g, **Protein** 10 g, **Calcium** 10%, **Iron** 10%

RECIPE 21.22

CINNAMON FRENCH TOAST

French toast begins with slices of day-old bread. (It is known in France as pain perdu, *meaning "lost bread," probably because it provided a way to use bread that would otherwise have been discarded.) French bread, sourdough bread, raisin bread, challah, whole-wheat bread and even stale croissants can be used. The bread is dipped into a batter of eggs, sugar, milk or cream and flavorings, then sautéed in butter and served very hot. It may be topped with powdered sugar, fresh fruit, fruit compote or maple syrup as desired.*

Yield: 6 Servings

Eggs, beaten	10	10
Heavy cream	4 fl. oz.	120 ml
Salt	TT	TT
Cinnamon, ground	TT	TT
Thick-sliced bread such as sourdough, cinnamon, banana or brioche	12 slices	12 slices
Unsalted butter	as needed	as needed
Powdered sugar	as needed	as needed

1 Whisk together the eggs, cream, salt and cinnamon.

2 Place the egg mixture in a shallow pan. Place the slices of bread in the egg mixture and let soak for 2 to 3 minutes, turning them over after the first minute or so.

3 Cook the slices of French toast in a lightly buttered, preheated sauté pan or griddle set at 350°F (180°C) until well browned. Turn the slices and cook on the second side until done.

4 Cut each slice of bread into two triangles.

5 Arrange four triangles on each plate and dust with powdered sugar.

Approximate values per 5-oz. (150-g) serving: **Calories** 320, **Total fat** 17 g, **Saturated fat** 7 g, **Cholesterol** 380 mg, **Sodium** 420 mg, **Total carbohydrates** 28 g, **Protein** 15 g, **Vitamin A** 25%, **Iron** 15%

CUISINE IS WHEN THINGS TASTE LIKE THEMSELVES.

—*Curnonsky (Maurice Edmond Sailland), French writer (1872–1956)*

22

VEGETABLES

GREENS, San Francisco, CA
Chef Annie Somerville

AFTER STUDYING THIS CHAPTER, YOU WILL BE ABLE TO:

▶ identify a variety of vegetables

▶ purchase vegetables appropriate for your needs

▶ store vegetables properly

▶ understand how vegetables are preserved

▶ prepare vegetables for cooking or service

▶ apply various cooking methods to vegetables

Long overcooked and underrated, vegetables are enjoying a welcomed surge in popularity. Gone are the days when a chef included vegetables as an afterthought to the "meat and potatoes" of the meal. Now, properly prepared fresh vegetables are used to add flavor, color and variety to almost any meal. Many restaurants are featuring vegetarian entrées, an extensive selection of vegetable side dishes or an entire vegetarian menu. This trend reflects the demands of more knowledgeable and health-conscious consumers as well as the increased availability of high-quality fresh produce.

In this chapter, we identify many of the vegetables typically used by food service operations. (Potatoes, although they are vegetables, are discussed in Chapter 23, Potatoes, Grains and Pasta, while salad greens are discussed in Chapter 24, Salads and Salad Dressings.) Here we also discuss how fresh and preserved vegetables are purchased, stored and prepared for service or cooking. Many of the cooking methods analyzed in Chapter 10, Principles of Cooking, are then applied to vegetables.

The term **vegetable** refers to any herbaceous plant that can be partially or wholly eaten. An herbaceous plant has little or no woody tissue. The portions we consume include the leaves, stems, roots, tubers, seeds and flowers. Vegetables contain more starch and less sugar than fruits. Therefore vegetables tend to be savory, not sweet. Also unlike fruits, vegetables are most often eaten cooked, not raw.

▶ IDENTIFYING VEGETABLES

This book presents fruits and vegetables according to the ways most people view them and use them, rather than by rigid botanical classifications. Although produce such as tomatoes, peppers and eggplants are botanically fruits, they are prepared and served like vegetables and are included here under the category we call "fruit-vegetables." Potatoes, although botanically vegetables, are discussed with other starches in Chapter 23, Potatoes, Grains and Pasta.

We divide vegetables into nine categories based upon either botanical relationship or edible part: cabbages, fruit-vegetables, gourds and squashes, greens, mushrooms and truffles, onions, pods and seeds, roots and tubers, and stalks. A vegetable may have several names, varying from region to region or on a purveyor's whim. The names given here follow generally accepted custom and usage.

CABBAGES

The *Brassica* or cabbage family includes a wide range of vegetables used for their heads, flowers or leaves. They are generally quick-growing, cool-weather crops. Many are ancient plants with unknown origins. They are inexpensive, readily available and easy to prepare.

BOK CHOY

Bok choy, also known as pok choy, is a white-stemmed variety of southern Chinese cabbage. The relatively tightly packed leaves are dark green, with long white ribs attached at a bulbous stem. The stalks are crisp and mild with a flavor similar to romaine lettuce. Although bok choy may be eaten raw, it is most often stir-fried or used in soups.

Choose heads with bright white stalks and dark green leaves; avoid those with brown, moist spots. Fresh bok choy is available all year. Jars of pickled and fermented bok choy (known as Korean kim chee) are also available.

BROCCOLI

Broccoli, a type of flower, has a thick central stalk with grayish-green leaves topped with one or more heads of green florets. Broccoli may be eaten raw or steamed, microwaved or sautéed and served warm or cold. Broccoli stalks are extremely firm and benefit from blanching. Stems are often slow-cooked for soups. Generally, broccoli leaves are not eaten.

Choose firm stalks with compact clusters of tightly closed dark green florets. Avoid stalks with yellow flowers. Broccoli is available all year.

Bok Choy

▶ PROCEDURE FOR CUTTING BROCCOLI SPEARS

Cut off the thick, woody portion of the stalk, then cut the florets and stems into spears.

Broccoli

BRUSSELS SPROUTS

Brussels sprouts (Fr. *choux de Bruxelles*) were first cultivated around 1700. The plant produces numerous small heads arranged in neat rows along a thick stalk. The tender young sprouts are similar to baby cabbages and are usually steamed or roasted. Brussels sprouts have a strong, nutty flavor that blends well with game, ham, duck or rich meats.

Choose small, firm sprouts that are compact and heavy. The best size is ¾ to 1½ inches (2 to 4 centimeters) in diameter. They should be bright green and free of blemishes. Their peak season is from September through February.

Brussels Sprouts

CAULIFLOWER

Cauliflower (Fr. *chou-fleur*) is the king of the cabbage family. Each stalk produces one flower or head surrounded by large green leaves. The head, composed of creamy white florets, can be cooked whole or cut into separate florets for steaming, blanching or stir-frying.

Choose firm, compact heads. Any attached leaves should be bright green and crisp. A yellow color or spreading florets indicate that the vegetable is overly mature. Cauliflower is available all year, especially from the late fall through the spring.

Cauliflower

▶ PROCEDURE FOR CUTTING CAULIFLOWER FLORETS

1 Cut off the stem and leaves.

2 Cut the florets off of the core.

HEAD CABBAGES (GREEN AND RED)

Cabbage (Fr. *chou*) has been a staple of northern European cuisine for centuries. The familiar green cabbage has a large, firm, round head with tightly packed pale green leaves. Flat and cone-shaped heads are also available. Red (or purple) cabbage is a different strain and may be tougher than green cabbage. Cabbage can be eaten raw (as in coleslaw) or used in soups or stews; it can be braised, steamed or stir-fried. The large, waxy leaves can also be steamed until soft, then wrapped around a filling of seasoned meat.

Choose firm heads without dried cores. Cabbages are available all year.

Green and Red Cabbages

KALE

Kale has large ruffled, curly or bumpy leaves. Its rather bitter flavor goes well with rich meats such as game, pork or ham. Kale is typically boiled, stuffed or used in soups.

Choose leaves that are crisp, with a grayish-green color. Kale is available all year; its peak season is during the winter months.

Ornamental Kale

Ornamental or flowering kale, sometimes marketed as "savoy," is edible, but its pink, purple, yellow or white-and-green variegated leaves are best used for decoration and garnish.

Kale

KOHLRABI

Although it looks rather like a round root, kohlrabi is actually a bulbous stem vegetable created by crossbreeding cabbages and turnips. Both the leaves (which are attached directly to the bulbous stem) and the roots are generally removed before

Kohlrabi

sale. Depending on the variety, the skin may be light green, purple or green with a hint of red. The interior flesh is white, with a sweet flavor similar to turnips. (Kohlrabi can be substituted for turnip in many recipes.) Younger plants are milder and more tender than large, mature ones. The outer skin must be removed from mature stems; young stems need only to be well scrubbed before cooking. Kohlrabi can be eaten raw, or it can be cooked (whole, sliced or diced) with moist-heat cooking methods such as boiling and steaming. Kohlrabi may also be hollowed out and stuffed with meat or vegetable mixtures.

Choose small, tender stems with fresh, green leaves. Peak season for kohlrabi is from June through September.

NAPA CABBAGE

Napa cabbage, also known as Chinese cabbage, is widely used in Asian cuisines. It has a stout, elongated head with relatively tightly packed, firm, pale green leaves. It is moister and more tender than common green and red cabbages, with a milder, more delicate flavor. Napa cabbage may be eaten raw but is particularly well suited for stir-frying or steaming.

Choose heads with crisp leaves that are free of blemishes. Napa cabbage is available fresh all year.

Napa Cabbage

SAVOY

Savoy cabbage has curly or ruffled leaves, often in variegated shades of green and purple. (The term *savoyed* is used to refer to any vegetable with bumpy, wavy or wrinkled leaves.) Savoy cabbage tends to be milder and more tender than regular cabbages and can be substituted for them, cooked or uncooked. Savoy leaves also make an attractive garnish.

Choose heads that are loose or tight, depending on the variety, with tender, unblemished leaves. Peak season is from August through the spring.

Savoy

FRUIT-VEGETABLES

Botanists classify avocados, eggplants, peppers and tomatoes as fruits because they develop from the ovary of flowering plants and contain one or more seeds. Chefs, however, prepare and serve them like vegetables; therefore they are discussed here.

AVOCADOS

Avocados include several varieties of pear-shaped fruits with rich, high-fat flesh. This light golden-green flesh surrounds a large, inedible, oval-shaped seed (pit). Some varieties have smooth, green skin; others have pebbly, almost black skin. Avocados should be used at their peak of ripeness, a condition that lasts only briefly. Firm avocados lack the desired flavor and creamy texture. Ripe avocados should be soft to the touch but not mushy. Ripe Haas avocados have almost-black skins; the skins of the other varieties remain green when ripe. Firm avocados can be left at room temperature to ripen, then refrigerated for one or two days. Avocados are most often used raw to garnish salads, mashed or puréed for sauces, sliced for sandwiches or diced for omelets. Avocado halves are popular containers for chilled meat, fish, shellfish or poultry salads. Because avocado flesh turns brown very quickly once cut, dip avocado halves or slices in lemon juice and keep unused portions tightly covered with plastic wrap.

Avocados

Choose avocados that are free of blemishes or moist spots. The flesh should be free of dark spots or streaks. Available all year, the peak season for Haas avocados is April through October; for Fuertes avocados, it is November through April.

▶ PROCEDURE FOR CUTTING AND PITTING AVOCADOS

1 Cut the avocado in half lengthwise. Separate the two halves with a twisting motion.

2 Insert a chef's knife into the pit and twist to remove.

3 Scoop the flesh out of the skin with a large spoon.

EGGPLANT: TO SALT OR NOT TO SALT?

Eggplants are filled with cells that contain water and are surrounded by tiny air pockets. The presence of heat will squeeze the air out of the pockets. If the eggplant has not been salted, oil is then free to seep into these pockets and the eggplant becomes soggy when fried.

But when salt is sprinkled on an eggplant, it draws the water out of the cells. The cells then collapse, which in turn makes the air pockets collapse. As a result, no oil can seep into the tiny pockets during the frying process.

–DANIEL ZWERDLING, senior correspondent with National Public Radio. This sidebar originally appeared in *Gourmet.*

EGGPLANTS

Two types of eggplants (Fr. *aubergine*) are commonly available: Asian and western. Asian varieties are either round or long and thin, with skin colors ranging from creamy white to deep purple. Western eggplants, which are more common in the United States, tend to be shaped like a plump pear with a shiny lavender to purple-black skin. Both types have a dense, khaki-colored flesh with a rather bland flavor that absorbs other flavors well during cooking. Eggplants can be grilled, baked, steamed, fried or sautéed. They are commonly used in Mediterranean and East Indian cuisines (especially in vegetarian dishes), but also appear in European and North American dishes. The skin may be left intact or removed before or after cooking, as desired. Sliced eggplants may be salted and left to drain for 30 minutes to remove moisture and bitterness before cooking.

Western Eggplant

Choose plump, heavy eggplants with a smooth, shiny skin that is not blemished or wrinkled. Asian varieties tend to be softer than western. Eggplants are available all year; their peak season is during the late summer.

Japanese Eggplant

Asian Eggplants

PEPPERS

Members of the *Capsicum* family are native to the New World. When "discovered" by Christopher Columbus, he called them "peppers" because of their sometimes fiery flavor. These peppers, which include sweet peppers and hot peppers (chiles), are unrelated to peppercorns, the Asian spice for which Columbus was actually searching. Interestingly, New World peppers were readily accepted in Indian and Asian cuisines, in which they are now considered staples.

Fresh peppers are found in a wide range of colors—green, red, yellow, orange, purple or white—as well as shapes, from tiny teardrops to cones to spheres. They have dense flesh and a hollow central cavity. The flesh is lined with placental ribs (the white internal veins), to which tiny yellowish-white seeds are attached. A core of seeds is also attached to the stem end of each pepper.

Chile peppers get their heat from capsaicin, which is found not in the flesh or seeds, but in the placental ribs. Thus a pepper's heat can be greatly reduced by carefully removing the ribs and attached seeds. Generally, the smaller the chile, the hotter it is. The amount of heat varies from variety to variety, however, and even from one pepper to another depending on growing conditions. Hot, dry conditions result in hotter peppers than do cool, moist conditions. A pepper's heat can be measured by Scoville Heat Units, a subjective rating in which the sweet bell pepper usually rates 0 units, the jalapeño rates from 2500 to 5000 units, the tabasco rates from 30,000 to 50,000 units and the habanero rates a whopping 100,000 to 300,000 units.

When selecting peppers, choose those that are plump and brilliantly colored with smooth, unblemished skins. Avoid wrinkled, pitted or blistered peppers. A bright green stem indicates freshness.

Green Bell Pepper

Sweet Peppers

Common sweet peppers, known as bell peppers, are thick-walled fruits available in green, red, yellow, purple, orange and other colors. They are heart-shaped or boxy, with a short stem and crisp flesh. Their flavor is warm, sweet (red peppers tend to be the sweetest) and relatively mild. Raw bell peppers may be sliced or diced and used in salads or sandwiches. Bell peppers can also be stuffed and baked, grilled, fried, sautéed or puréed for soups, sauces or condiments. Green bell peppers are available all year; other colors are more readily available during the summer and fall.

Red and Yellow Bell Peppers

▶ PROCEDURE FOR CUTTING PEPPERS JULIENNE

1 Trim off the ends of the pepper; cut away the seeds and core.

2 Cut away the pale ribs, trimming the flesh to the desired thickness.

3 Slice the flesh in julienne.

A PEPPER BY ANY OTHER NAME

The popularity of southwestern cuisine, hot condiments and salsas has brought with it a new appreciation and respect for chiles. Diners, and chefs, may find the names given to the various chiles confusing, however. Most chiles can be used either fresh or dried; drying changes not only the pepper's flavor, but also its name. Regional variations in chile names also add to the confusion. Several of the more frequently encountered chiles are listed here according to the names most commonly used for both their fresh and dried forms:

Fresh (*Fresca*)	Dried (*Seco*)
Anaheim	Mild Red or California
Ancho	Ancho or Pastilla
Chilaca	Pastilla or Negro
Jalapeño	Chipotle (smoked)
Mirasol	Guajillo
New Mexico Green	New Mexico Red
New Mexico Red	Chile Colorado
Pimento	Paprika
Poblano	Mulato

Hot Peppers

Hot peppers, also known as chiles, are also members of the *Capsicum* family. Although a chile's most characteristic attribute is its pungency, each chile actually has a distinctive flavor, from mild and rich to spicy and sweet to fiery hot.

Chiles are commonly used in Asian, Indian, Mexican and Latin American cuisines. The larger (and milder) of the hot peppers, such as Anaheim and poblano, can be stuffed and baked or sautéed as a side dish. Most chiles, however, are used to add flavor and seasoning to sauces and other dishes.

Fresh chiles are available all year and are also available canned in a variety of processed forms such as whole or diced, roasted, pickled or marinated.

(clockwise from bottom left) Red and Green Serrano, Green and Red Jalapeño, Yellow Hot, Poblano and Anaheim Chiles

Habanero

▶ PROCEDURE FOR CORING JALAPEÑOS

Cut the jalapeño in half lengthwise. Push the core and seeds out with your thumb. You can avoid burning your fingers by wearing rubber gloves when working with hot chiles.

Dried chiles are widely used in Mexican, Central American and southwestern cuisines. They can be ground to create a powdered spice called chilli or soaked in a liquid, and then puréed for sauces or condiments. Drying radically alters the flavor of chiles, making them stronger and more pungent. Just as one type of fresh chile cannot be substituted for another without altering a dish's flavor, so too dried chiles cannot be substituted without flavor changes.

Choose dried chiles that are clean and unbroken, with some flexibility. Avoid any with white spots or a stale aroma.

Dried Chiles: (top to bottom) California, Ancho, De Árbol

▶ PROCEDURE FOR ROASTING PEPPERS

1 Roast the pepper over an open flame until completely charred.

2 Place the pepper in a plastic bag to sweat for a few minutes, then remove the burnt skin and rinse under running water.

TOMATILLOS

Tomatillos, also known as Mexican or husk tomatoes, grow on small, weedy bushes. They are bright green, about the size of a small tomato, and are covered with a thin, papery husk. They have a tart, lemony flavor and crisp, moist flesh. Although they are an important ingredient in southwestern and northern Mexican cuisines, tomatillos may not be readily available in other areas. Tomatillos can be used raw in salads, puréed for salsa or cooked in soups, stews or vegetable dishes.

Choose tomatillos whose husks are split but still look fresh. The skin should be plump, shiny and slightly sticky. They are available all year; their peak season is during the summer and fall.

Tomatillos

TOMATOES

Tomatoes (Fr. *tomate* or *pomme d'amour*; It. *pomodoro*) are available in a wide variety of colors and shapes. They vary from green (unripe) to golden yellow to ruby red; from tiny spheres (currant tomatoes) to huge, squat ovals (beefsteak). Some, such as the plum tomato, have lots of meaty flesh with only a few seeds; others, such as the slicing tomato, have lots of seeds and juice, but only a few meaty membranes. All tomatoes have a similar flavor, but the levels of sweetness and acidity vary depending on the species, growing conditions and ripeness at harvest.

(clockwise from lower right) Pear, Cherry, Plum and Beefsteak Tomatoes

Because tomatoes are highly perishable, they are usually harvested when mature but still green (unripe), then shipped to wholesalers who ripen them in temperature- and humidity-controlled rooms. The effect on flavor and texture is unfortunate.

Tomatoes are used widely in salads, soups, sauces and baked dishes. They are most often eaten raw, but can be grilled, pickled, pan-fried, roasted or sautéed as a side dish.

Choose fresh tomatoes that are plump with a smooth, shiny skin. The color should be uniform and true for the variety. Tomatoes are available all year; most varieties have a summer peak season. Many canned tomato products are also available (for example, purée, paste, sauce or stewed whole). Sun-dried and air-dried tomatoes are available in crumbs, pieces, slivers or halves, dry or packed in oil. The dry-pack version can be soaked in oil or steeped in hot water to soften before use.

Sun-Dried Tomatoes

THREE TREASURES OF THE NEW WORLD

In lieu of many spices, golden treasures and precious gems, early Spanish explorers returned to Spain with items of much greater significance: tomatoes, potatoes and corn. Unfortunately for those who financed the voyagers, the value of this produce was not immediately appreciated.

The Spanish and the Italians hailed the tomato (whose name comes from the Aztec name *tomatl*) as an aphrodisiac–perhaps because of its resemblance to the human heart–when it arrived from the New World during the 16th century. But even though tomatoes soon became part of Spanish and Italian cuisines, most other Europeans, New World colonists and, later, Americans considered tomatoes poisonous. (There is some truth to this notion: tomato vines and leaves contain tomatine, an alkaloid that can cause health problems.) Thus for many years and in many societies, only the adventurous ate tomatoes.

The potato, first delivered to Europe from its native Peru by Francisco Pizarro in the 16th century, did not win wide acceptance in haute cuisine until Antoine-Augustin Parmentier (1737–1813), a French army pharmacist, induced King Louis XVI of France (who reigned from 1775 to 1793) to try one. The king and his courtiers liked them so much they even began wearing potato blossom boutonnières. Parmentier was ultimately honored for his starchy contribution to French cuisine by having several potato dishes named for him, such as *potage Parmentier* (potato soup). Not only did Parmentier lobby for the acceptance of the potato as a food fit for a king, he also prophesied that the potato would make starvation impossible. Potatoes ultimately did become a staple of many diets. But, sadly, the converse of Parmentier's prophecy came true during the Irish potato famine of 1846–1848, when a terrible blight destroyed the potato crop. Nearly 1.5 million people died, and an equal number emigrated to the United States. They brought with them a cuisine that incorporated potatoes; thus an appreciation of the common potato was reintroduced to its native land.

When returning from his second voyage to the New World, Columbus took corn with him. Called *mahiz* or *maize* by West Indian natives, corn had been a staple of Central American diets for at least 5000 years. Although Europeans did not actively shun corn as they did tomatoes and potatoes, corn never really caught on in most of Europe. (As with another famous New World import, corn's origin was mistakenly attributed by the British, Dutch, Germans and Russians to Turkey. They called corn "Turkish wheat"; the Turks simply called it "foreign grain.") Grown for human consumption mostly in Italy, Spain and southwestern France, corn was and still is usually eaten ground and boiled as polenta. But despite an unenthusiastic European reception, corn's popularity quickly spread well beyond Europe: Within 50 years of Columbus's journey, corn was being cultivated in lands as distant from the New World as China, India and sub-Saharan Africa.

▶ PROCEDURE FOR PREPARING TOMATO CONCASSÉE

1 With a paring knife, mark an X on the bottom of the tomato just deep enough to penetrate the skin.

2 Blanch the tomato in boiling water for 20 seconds; refresh in ice water.

3 Using a paring knife, cut out the core and peel the tomato.

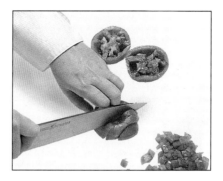

4 Cut the tomato in half horizontally and squeeze out the seeds and juice.

5 Chop or dice the tomato as desired for the recipe.

GOURDS AND SQUASHES

The *Cucurbitaceae* or gourd family includes almost 750 species; its members are found in warm regions worldwide. Gourds are characterized by large, complex root systems with quick-growing, trailing vines and large leaves. Their flowers are often attractive and edible. Although some members of the gourd family originated in Africa, chayotes and most squashes are native to the Americas.

CHAYOTES

The chayote, also known as the merliton or vegetable pear, is a food staple throughout Central America. The vine bears slightly lumpy, pear-shaped fruits with a smooth, light green skin and a paler green flesh. There is a single white, edible seed in the center. Chayotes are starchy and very bland and are usually combined with more flavorful ingredients. They may be eaten raw, but their flavor and texture benefit from roasting, steaming, sautéing or grilling.

Chayotes

Choose chayotes that have well-colored skin with few ridges. Avoid those with very soft spots or bruises. Their peak season is the late fall and winter.

CUCUMBERS

Cucumbers can be divided into two categories: pickling and slicing. The two types are not interchangeable. Pickling cucumbers include the cornichon, dill and gherkin. They are recognizable by their sharp black or white spines and are quite bitter when raw. Slicing cucumbers include the burpless, the seedless English (or hothouse), the lemon (which is round and yellow) and the common green market cucumber. Most have relatively thin skins and may be marketed with a wax coating to prevent moisture loss and improve appearance. Waxed skins should be peeled. All cucumbers are valued for their refreshing cool taste and astringency. Slicing cucumbers are usually served raw, in salads or mixed with yogurt and dill or mint as a side dish, especially for spicy dishes. Pickling cucumbers are generally served pickled, with no further processing.

(from left to right) Pickling, Green and Hothouse Cucumbers

Choose cucumbers that are firm but not hard. Avoid those that are limp or yellowed or have soft spots. The common varieties are available all year, although peak season is from April through October.

Acorn

Spaghetti

Butternut

Banana

SQUASHES

Squashes are the fleshy fruits of a large number of plants in the gourd family. Many varieties are available in a range of colors, shapes and sizes. Squashes can be classified as winter or summer based on their peak season and skin type. All squashes have a center cavity filled with many seeds, although in winter varieties the cavity is more pronounced. Squash blossoms are also edible: They may be added to salads raw, dipped in batter and deep-fried or filled with cheese or meat and baked.

Choose squashes with unbroken skins and good color for the variety. Avoid any squash with soft, moist spots.

Winter Squashes

Winter squashes include the acorn, banana, butternut, Hubbard, pumpkin and spaghetti varieties. They have hard skins (shells) and seeds, neither of which is generally eaten. The flesh, which may be removed from the shell before or after cooking, tends to be sweeter and more strongly flavored than that of summer squash. Winter squashes are rarely used raw; they can be baked, steamed or sautéed. Most winter squashes can also be puréed for soups or pie fillings. Their peak season is October through March.

Pumpkin

Summer Squashes

Summer squashes include the pattypan, yellow crookneck and zucchini varieties. They have soft edible skins and seeds that are generally not removed before cooking. Most summer squashes may be eaten raw, but are also suitable for grilling, sautéing, steaming or baking. Although summer squashes are now available all year, their peak season is April through September.

Zucchini

Yellow Crookneck

GREENS

The term *greens* refers to a variety of leafy green vegetables that may be served raw, but are usually cooked. Greens have long been used in the cuisines of India, Asia and the Mediterranean and are an important part of regional cuisine in the southern United States. Most have strong, spicy flavors. The milder varieties of greens that are almost always eaten raw include the lettuces discussed in Chapter 24, Salads and Salad Dressings.

Greens have an extremely high water content, which means that cooking causes drastic shrinkage. As a general rule, allow 8 ounces (250 grams) per portion before cooking.

Choose young, tender greens with good color and no limpness. Avoid greens with dry-looking stems or yellow leaves. Most greens are available fresh all year, especially from November through June. The more popular greens are also available canned or frozen.

Collard Greens

COLLARDS

Collard greens, often simply referred to as collards, are a type of cabbage with loose, leafy heads of bright green leaves. Collards have a sharp, tangy flavor and look like a cross between mustard greens and kale. Considered a staple ingredient in poverty cooking of the American South, collards are typically slow-simmered with ham hocks or bacon until very tender, then served with their cooking liquid. Collards are high in iron and vitamins A and C and are best if picked young or after the first frost of autumn.

MUSTARD

Mustard, a member of the cabbage family, was brought to America by early European immigrants. Mustard has large, dark green leaves with frilly edges. It is known for its assertive, bitter flavor. Mustard greens can be served raw in salads or used as garnish. They can also be cooked, often with white wine, vinegar and herbs.

Choose crisp, bright green leaves without discoloration.

Mustard

SORREL

Sorrel is an abundant and rather ordinary wild member of the buckwheat family. Its tartness and sour flavor are used in soups and sauces and to accent other vegetables. It is particularly good with fatty fish or rich meats. Sorrel leaves naturally become the texture of a purée after only a few minutes of moist-heat cooking.

Choose leaves that are fully formed, with no yellow blemishes.

Sorrel

SPINACH

Spinach (Fr. *épinard*) is a versatile green that grows rapidly in cool climates. It has smooth, bright green leaves attached to thin stems. Spinach may be eaten raw in salads, cooked by almost any moist-heat method, microwaved or sautéed. It can be used in stuffings, baked or creamed dishes, soups or stews. Spinach grows in sandy soil and must be rinsed repeatedly in cold water to remove all traces of grit from the leaves. It bruises easily and should be handled gently during washing. Stems and large midribs should be removed.

Spinach

Choose bunches with crisp, tender, deep green leaves; avoid yellow leaves or those with blemishes.

SWISS CHARD

Chard—the reference to "Swiss" is inexplicable—is a type of beet that does not produce a tuberous root. It is used for its wide, flat, dark green leaves. Chard can be steamed, sautéed or used in soups. Its tart, spinachlike flavor blends well with sweet ingredients such as fruit.

Choose leaves that are crisp, with some curliness or savoying. Ribs should be an unblemished white or red.

Swiss Chard

TURNIP GREENS

The leaves of the turnip root have a pleasantly bitter flavor, similar to peppery mustard greens. The dark green leaves are long, slender and deeply indented. Turnip greens are best eaten steamed, sautéed, baked or microwaved.

Turnip Greens

Portabella

MUSHROOMS AND TRUFFLES

MUSHROOMS

Mushrooms (Fr. *champignon;* It. *funghi*) are members of a broad category of plants known as fungi. (Fungi have no seeds, stems or flowers; they reproduce through spores.) Mushrooms have a stalk with an umbrellalike top. Although not actually a vegetable, mushrooms are used and served in much the same manner as vegetables.

Several types of cultivated mushroom are available. They include the common (or white), shiitake, crimini (also known as the Italian brown), straw, enokidake (also called enoki) and cloud ear (also known as wood ear or Chinese black). Button mushrooms are the smallest, most immature form of the common mushroom. The largest cultivated mushroom is the portabella, which is actually an overgrown crimini; it can grow up to 6 inches (15 centimeters) in diameter.

Black Trumpet   *Clam Shell*

Hen of the Woods

Many wild mushrooms are gathered and sold by specialty purveyors. Because wild mushroom spores are spread around the world by air currents, the same item may be found in several areas, each with a different common name. Wild mushrooms have a stronger earthy or nutty flavor than cultivated mushrooms, and should generally be cooked before eating.

Pom Pom Blanc

Shiitake

Porcini (cèpe or cep)   *Morel*

White

Mushrooms, whether cultivated or gathered from the wild, are available fresh, canned or dried. Because mushrooms are composed of up to 80 percent water, dried products are often the most economical, even though they may cost hundreds of dollars per pound. Dried mushrooms can be stored in a cool, dry place for months. When needed, they are rehydrated by soaking in warm water until soft, approximately 10–20 minutes.

Enokidake

SAFETY ALERT

MUSHROOM SAFETY

Some mushrooms are deadly; others can cause severe illness. Picking edible mushrooms in the wild is not simply a process of comparing specimens with photographs or illustrations in a guidebook. So, do not gather mushrooms from the wild unless you are accompanied by a well-trained, experienced mycologist or guide. Always purchase wild mushrooms from reputable purveyors.

Oyster

Choose fresh mushrooms that are clean, without soft or moist spots or blemishes. Fresh cultivated mushrooms are generally available all year; fresh wild mushrooms are available seasonally, usually during the summer and fall. Cultivated mushrooms with exposed gills (the ridges on the underside of the umbrellalike top) are old and should be avoided. Fresh mushrooms can be refrigerated in an open container for up to five days. Normally, it is not necessary to peel mushrooms; if they are dirty, they should be quickly rinsed (not soaked) in cool water just before use.

TRUFFLES

Truffles are actually tubers that grow near the roots of oak or beech trees. They can be cultivated only to the extent that oak groves are planted to encourage truffle growth. The two principal varieties are the Périgord (black) and the Piedmontese (white). Fresh truffles are gathered in the fall and are rarely marketed outside their locale. Truffles, especially white ones, have a strong aroma and flavor, requiring only a small amount to add their special flavor to soups, sauces, pasta and other items. Black truffles are often used as a garnish or to flavor pâtés, terrines or egg dishes. Because fresh imported truffles can cost several hundred dollars per pound, most kitchens purchase truffles canned, dried or processed.

Black Truffles

▶ PROCEDURE FOR FLUTING MUSHROOMS

Use the sharp edge of a straight paring knife to cut thin curves into the mushroom cap. Fluted mushrooms may be baked or poached, then used as garnish.

ONIONS

Onions are strongly flavored, aromatic members of the lily family. Most have edible grasslike or tubular leaves. Almost every culture incorporates them into its cuisine as a vegetable and for flavoring.

BULB ONIONS

Common or bulb onions (Fr. *oignons*) may be white, yellow (Bermuda or Spanish) or red (purple). Medium-sized yellow and white onions are the most strongly flavored. Larger onions tend to be sweeter and milder. Widely used as a flavoring ingredient, onions are indispensable in mirepoix. Onions are also prepared as a side dish by deep-frying, roasting, grilling, steaming or boiling.

Pearl onions are small, about ½ inch (1.25 centimeters) in diameter, with yellow or white skins. They have a mild flavor and can be grilled, boiled, roasted or sautéed whole as a side dish, or used in soups or stews.

Red Onion

Yellow Onion

Pearl Onions

Shallots

Walla-Walla Sweet Onions

White Onions

Sweet onion varieties include the Vidalia, Maui, Walla-Walla, Texas 1015 SuperSweet and OSO Sweet. These bulb onions have a higher water content, more sugar and less sulfuric compounds than other onions. They are best for eating raw, making them good choices for sandwiches, salads, hamburgers and the like. Cooking destroys much of their perceived sweetness and special flavor. Each sweet onion variety is available for a brief period from January through August. All have a very short shelf life and should not be stored more than a few weeks.

Choose onions that are firm and dry and feel heavy. The outer skins should be dry and brittle. Avoid onions that have begun to sprout. Store onions in a cool, dry, well-ventilated area. Do not refrigerate onions until they are cut. With the exception of sweet onions, most varieties are available all year.

GARLIC

Garlic

Garlic (Fr. *ail;* Sp. *ajo*) is also used in almost all the world's cuisines. A head of garlic is composed of many small cloves. Each clove is wrapped in a thin husk or peel; the entire head is encased in several thin layers of papery husk. Of the three hundred or so types of garlic known, only three are commercially significant. The most common is pure white, with a sharp flavor. A Mexican variety is pale pink and more strongly flavored. Elephant garlic is apple-sized and particularly mild. Although whole bulbs can be baked or roasted, garlic is most often separated into cloves, peeled, sliced, minced or crushed and used to flavor a wide variety of dishes. When using garlic, remember that the more finely the cloves are crushed, the stronger the flavor will be. Cooking reduces garlic's pungency; the longer it is cooked, the milder it becomes.

Choose firm, dry bulbs with tightly closed cloves and smooth skins. Avoid bulbs with green sprouts. Store fresh garlic in a cool, well-ventilated place; do not refrigerate. Fresh garlic is available all year. Jars of processed and pickled garlic products are also available.

LEEKS

Leeks (Fr. *poireaux*) look like large, overgrown scallions with a fat white tip and wide green leaves. Their flavor is sweeter and stronger than scallions, but milder than common bulb onions.

Leeks must be carefully washed to remove the sandy soil that gets between the leaves. Leeks can be baked, braised or grilled as a side dish, or used to season stocks, soups or sauces.

Choose leeks that are firm, with stiff roots and stems. Avoid those with dry leaves, soft spots or browning. Leeks are available all year.

Leeks

▶ PROCEDURE FOR CLEANING LEEKS

1 Trim the root end from the leek.

2 Cut away the dark green top and slice the white portion in half lengthwise.

3 Rinse the leek thoroughly under running water to remove soil.

SCALLIONS

Scallions, also known as green onions or bunch onions, are the immature green stalks of bulb onions. The leaves are bright green with either a long and slender or slightly bulbous white base. Green onions are used in stir-fries and as a flavoring in other dishes. The green tops can also be sliced in small rings and used as a garnish.

Choose scallions with bright green tops and clean white bulbs. Avoid those with limp or slimy leaves. Scallions are available all year; their peak season is the summer.

Scallions

SHALLOTS

Shallots (Fr. *échalotes*) are shaped like small bulb onions with one flat side. When peeled, a shallot separates into multiple cloves, similar to garlic. They have a mild, yet rich and complex flavor. Shallots are the basis of many classic sauces and meat preparations; they can also be sautéed or baked as a side dish.

Choose shallots that are plump and well shaped. Avoid those that appear dry or have sprouted. Store shallots in a cool, dry, unrefrigerated place. Shallots are available all year.

Shallots

PODS AND SEEDS

Pod and seed vegetables include corn, legumes and okra. They are grouped together here because the parts consumed are all the seeds of their respective plants. In some cases, only the seeds are eaten; in others, the pod containing the seeds is eaten as well. Seeds are generally higher in protein and carbohydrates (starch and fiber) than other vegetables.

CORN

Sweet corn (Fr. *maïs*; Sp. *maíz*) is actually a grain, a type of grass. Corn kernels, like peas, are plant seeds. (Dried corn products are discussed in Chapter 23, Potatoes, Grains and Pasta.) The kernels, which may be white or yellow, are attached to a woody, inedible cob. The cob is encased by strands of hair-like fibers called silks and covered in layers of thin leaves called husks. Shuck the ears (remove the silks and husks) prior to cooking; although the husks may be left on for roasting or grilling. Shucked ears can be grilled, boiled, microwaved or steamed. The kernels can be cut off of the cob before or after cooking. Corn on the cob is available fresh or frozen; corn kernels are available canned or frozen.

Yellow and White Corn

Choose freshly picked ears with firm, small kernels. Avoid those with mold or decay at the tip of the cob or brownish silks. Summer is the peak season for fresh corn.

▶ PROCEDURE FOR CUTTING KERNELS OFF EARS OF CORN

Hold the cob upright and use a chef's knife to slice off the kernels.

LEGUMES

Beans (Fr. *haricots;* It. *fagiolio*) and peas (Fr. *pois*) are members of the legume family, a large group of vegetables with double-seamed pods containing a single row of seeds. Of the hundreds of known varieties of beans, some are used for their edible pods, others for shelling fresh and some only for their dried seeds. Dried beans are actually several varieties of seeds or peas left in the pod until mature, then shelled and dried.

Fresh Beans

Green Beans

Beans used for their edible pods, commonly referred to as green beans, string beans, runner beans or snap beans, are picked when immature. Except for the stem, the entire pod can be eaten. This category includes the American green bean, the yellow wax bean and the French haricot vert, a long, slender pod with an intense flavor and tender texture. If there are any strings along the pod's seams, they should be pulled off before cooking. Beans may be left whole, cut lengthwise into thin slivers (referred to as French cut) or cut crosswise on the diagonal.

Shelling beans are those grown primarily for the edible seeds inside the pod. Common examples are flageolets, lima beans and fava (broad) beans. Their tough pods are not usually eaten.

Haricots Verts

All beans can be prepared by steaming, microwaving or sautéing. They can be added to soups or stews, and they blend well with a variety of flavors, from coconut milk to garlic and olive oil. Cooked beans can be chilled and served as a salad or crudité.

Choose beans that have a bright color without brown or soft spots. Large pods may be tough or bitter. The peak season for fresh beans is from April through December. Most bean varieties are available frozen or canned, including pickled and seasoned products.

Dried Beans

Anthropologists report that for thousands of years, cultures worldwide have preserved some members of the legume family by drying. Common dried beans include kidney beans, pinto beans, chickpeas, lentils, black beans, black-eyed peas and split green peas. Shape is the clearest distinction among these products: Beans are oval or kidney-shaped; lentils are small, flat disks; peas are round.

Black-Eyed Peas

Black Beans

Beans and peas destined for drying are left on the vine until they are fully matured and just beginning to dry. They are then harvested, shelled and quickly

Lentils

dried with warm air currents. Some dried legumes are sold split, which means the skin is removed, causing the seed's two halves to separate.

Most dried beans need to be soaked in water before cooking. Soaking softens and rehydrates the beans, thus reducing cooking time. Lentils and split peas generally do not require soaking, however, and will cook faster than beans. After soaking, beans are most often simmered or baked in a liquid until soft and tender. One type may be substituted for another in most recipes, although variations in color, starch content and flavor should be considered.

Dried beans and peas are available in bulk or in 1 pound (450 gram) poly-bags. They should be stored in a cool, dry place, but not refrigerated. Many of these beans are also available fully cooked, then canned or frozen. Some dried beans may be fermented or processed into flour, oil or bean curd.

▶ PROCEDURE FOR SOAKING DRIED BEANS

1 Pick through the dried beans and remove any grit, pebbles or debris.

2 Place the beans in a bowl and cover with cold water; remove any skins or other items that float to the surface.

3 Drain the beans in a colander, then rinse under cold running water.

4 Return the beans to a bowl and cover with fresh cold water. Allow approximately 3 cups (750 milliliters) of water for each cup of beans.

5 Soak the beans in the cold water for the time specified in the recipe, usually several hours or overnight. Drain through a colander, discarding the water.

▶ PROCEDURE FOR QUICK-SOAKING DRIED BEANS

The soaking procedure can be accelerated by the following technique:

1 Rinse and pick through the beans.

2 Place the beans in a saucepan and add enough cool water to cover them by 2 inches (5 centimeters).

3 Bring to a boil and simmer for 2 minutes.

4 Remove from the heat, cover and soak for 1 hour.

5 Drain and discard the soaking liquid. Proceed with the recipe.

Fresh Shelling Peas

Of the shelling peas that are prepared fresh, the most common are green garden peas (English peas) and the French petit pois. Because they lose flavor rapidly after harvest, most shelling peas are sold frozen or canned. Shelling peas have a delicate, sweet flavor best presented by simply steaming until tender but still al dente. Peas may also be braised with rich meats such as ham or used in soups. Cooked peas are attractive in salads or as garnish.

Choose small fresh pea pods that are plump and moist. Peak season is April and May.

Fresh green **soy beans** (**soya**) (Japan: *edamame*) are becoming a popular shelling pea in the United States. When picked before maturity, soybeans have a light green, fuzzy pod and a tender, sweet pea. Fresh green soybeans are delicious steamed in the pod, then chilled, popped open and eaten out of hand as a snack. Often served in sushi restaurants or with other Asian cuisines, they are extremely high in protein, fiber and phytochemicals. When allowed to mature and then prepared like other dried beans, however, soybeans become extremely tough, hard to digest and bitter. Mature soybeans are best used for processing into oil, tofu, sauce and other foodstuffs.

Red Kidney Beans

Pinto Beans

Great Northern Beans

Fresh Shelling Peas

Soy Beans

Snow Peas

Edible Pea Pods

Snow peas, also known as Chinese pea pods, are a common variety of edible pea pod. They are flat and have only a few very small green peas. Snow peas have a string along their seams that can be removed by holding the leafy stem and pulling from end to end. The pods can be eaten raw, lightly blanched or steamed, or stir-fried.

Another variety of edible pea pod is the sugar snap pea, a cross between the garden pea and snow pea, which was developed during the late 1970s. They are plump, juicy pods filled with small, tender peas. The entire pod is eaten; do not shell the peas before cooking.

Choose pea pods that are firm, bright green and crisp. Avoid those with brown spots or a shriveled appearance. Pea pods are available all year; their peak season is in March and April.

OKRA

Okra

Okra, a common ingredient in African and Arab cuisines, was brought to the United States by slaves and French settlers. It is now integral to Creole, Cajun, southern and southwestern cuisines. Its mild flavor is similar to asparagus. Okra is not eaten raw; it is best pickled, boiled, steamed, or deep-fried. Okra develops a gelatinous texture when cooked for long periods, so it is used to thicken gumbos and stews. To avoid the slimy texture some find objectionable, do not wash okra until ready to cook, then trim the stem end only. Cook okra in stainless steel because other metals cause discoloration.

Choose small to medium pods (1½ to 2 inches; 3.75 to 5 centimeters) that are deep green, without soft spots. Pale spears with stiff tips tend to be tough. Okra's peak season is from June through September. Frozen okra is widely available.

ROOTS AND TUBERS

Taproots (more commonly referred to as roots) are single roots that extend deep into the soil to supply the above-ground plant with nutrients. Tubers are fat underground stems. Most roots and tubers can be used interchangeably. All store well at cool temperatures, without refrigeration. Potatoes, the most popular tuber, are discussed in Chapter 23, Potatoes, Grains and Pasta.

BEETS

Although records suggest that they were first eaten in ancient Greece, beets are most often associated with the colder northern climates, where they grow for most of the year. Beets can be boiled, then peeled and used in salads, soups or baked dishes.

Choose small to medium-sized beets that are firm, with smooth skins. Avoid those with hairy root tips, as they may be tough. Beets are available all year; their peak season is March to October.

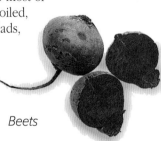

Beets

CARROTS

Carrots (Fr. *carotte*), among the most versatile of vegetables, are large taproots. Although several kinds exist, the Imperator is the most common. It is long and pointed, with a medium to dark orange color. It has a mild, sweet flavor. Carrots

Carrots

TOFU

Tofu or bean curd (Fr. *fromage de soja*) is a staple of Japanese and Chinese cuisines and is gaining acceptance in American kitchens because of its high nutritional value, low cost and flavor adaptability. Tofu is made by processing soybeans into "milk," which is then coagulated (nowadays with calcium sulfate). The curds are then placed in a perforated mold lined with cloth and pressed with a weight to remove the liquid. The result is a soft, creamy-white substance similar to cheese. Tofu is easy to digest and very high in protein, with very little fat and sodium and no cholesterol.

Tofu is an ancient foodstuff, probably created in China during the 2nd century A.D. It was introduced to Japan by Buddhist priests during the 8th century and was "discovered" by Western travelers during the 17th century. Today, Japanese tofu is said to be the finest, perhaps because of the superiority of the soybeans grown in the Yamato region, near the city of Kyoto. Japanese cuisine values the natural flavor and texture of tofu and uses it in a tremendous variety of ways. Chinese cuisine uses it as an additive, not as a principal ingredient.

Tofu may be eaten fresh; added to soup, broth or noodle dishes; tossed in cold salads; grilled, deep-fried or sautéed. Its flavor is

Silken Tofu

bland, but it readily absorbs flavors from other ingredients.

Two types of tofu are widely available: cotton and silken. Cotton tofu is the most common. Its texture is firm, with an irregular surface caused by the weave of the cotton fabric in which it is wrapped for pressing. Silken tofu has a silky-smooth appearance and texture, and a somewhat more delicate flavor. Unlike cotton tofu, the water has not been pressed out of silken tofu. Consequently, silken tofu should not be cooked at high temperatures or for a long time, as it falls apart easily. The use of either type in most recipes is simply a matter of personal preference.

Fresh tofu is usually packaged in water. It should be refrigerated and kept in water until used. If the water is drained and changed daily, the tofu should last for one week.

can be cut into a variety of shapes and eaten raw, used for a mirepoix or prepared by moist-heat cooking methods, grilling, microwaving or roasting. They are also grated and used in baked goods, particularly cakes and muffins.

Choose firm carrots that are smooth and well shaped, with a bright orange color. If the tops are still attached, they should be fresh-looking and bright green. Carrots are available all year.

CELERY ROOT

Celery root, also known as celeriac, is a large, round root, long popular in northern European cuisines. It is a different plant from stalk celery, and its stalks and leaves are not eaten. Celery root has a knobby brown exterior; a creamy white, crunchy flesh and a mild, celerylike flavor. Its thick outer skin must be peeled away; the flesh is then cut as desired. Often eaten raw, celery root can be baked, steamed or boiled. It is used in soups, stews or salads and goes well with game and rich meats. Raw celery root may be placed in acidulated water to prevent browning.

Choose small to medium-sized roots that are firm and relatively clean, with a pungent smell. Their peak season is October through April.

Celery Root

JERUSALEM ARTICHOKE

Despite their name, Jerusalem artichokes are actually tubers from a variety of sunflower unrelated to artichokes. Consequently, growers are now marketing these vegetables as *sunchokes.* Their lumpy brown skin is usually peeled away (even though it is edible) to reveal a crisp, white interior with a slightly nutty flavor. They may be eaten raw, chopped or grated into salads, or boiled or steamed for a side dish or soup.

Sunchokes

Jicama

JICAMA

Jicama is actually a legume that grows underground as a tuber. It is becoming increasingly popular because of its sweet, moist flavor; crisp texture; low calorie content and long shelf life. After its thick brown skin is cut away, the crisp, moist white flesh can be cut as desired. Jicama is often eaten raw in salads, with salsa or as a crudité. It is also used in stir-fried dishes.

Choose firm, well-shaped jicamas that are free of blemishes. Size is not an indication of quality or maturity. They are available all year; their peak season is January through May.

PARSNIPS

Parsnips (Fr. *panais*) are taproots that look and taste like white carrots and have the texture of sweet potatoes. Parsnips should be 5 to 10 inches (12.5 to 25 centimeters) in length, with smooth skins and tapering tips. Parsnips, peeled like carrots, can be eaten raw or cooked by almost any method. When steamed until very soft, they can be mashed like potatoes.

Choose small to medium-sized parsnips that are firm, smooth and well shaped; avoid large, woody ones. Parsnips are available all year; their peak season is December through April.

Parsnips

RADISHES

Red Radishes

Daikon

Radishes (Fr. *radis*) are used for their peppery flavor and crisp texture. Radishes are available in many colors, including white, black and all shades of red; most have a creamy to pure white interior. Asian radishes, known as daikons, produce roots 2 to 4 inches (5 to 10 centimeters) in diameter and 6 to 20 inches (15 to 20 centimeters) long. Radishes can be steamed or stir-fried, but most often are eaten raw, in salads or used as garnish. Radish leaves can be used in salads or cooked as greens.

Choose radishes that are firm, not limp. Their interior should be neither dry nor hollow. Radishes are available all year.

RUTABAGAS

Rutabagas

Rutabagas are a root vegetable and a member of the cabbage family. Their skin is purple to yellow, and they have yellow flesh with a distinctive starchy, cabbagelike flavor. Rutabagas and turnips are similar in flavor and texture when cooked and may be used interchangeably. Rutabaga leaves are not eaten. Rutabagas should be peeled with a vegetable peeler or chef's knife, then cut into quarters, slices or cubes. They are often baked, boiled and then puréed, or sliced and sautéed. They are especially flavorful when seasoned with caraway seeds, dill or lemon juice.

Choose small to medium-sized rutabagas that are smooth and firm and feel heavy. Their peak season is January through March.

TURNIPS

Also a root vegetable from the cabbage family, turnips have white skin with a rosy-red or purple blush and a white interior. Their flavor, similar to that of a radish, can be rather hot. Turnips should be peeled, then diced, sliced or julienned for cooking. They may be baked or cooked with moist-heat cooking methods, and are often puréed like potatoes.

Choose small to medium-sized turnips that have smooth skin and feel heavy. They should be firm, not rubbery or limp. Any attached leaves should be bright green and tender. Spring is their peak season.

Turnips

WATER CHESTNUTS

Water chestnuts are the tuber of an Asian plant that thrives in water. The brownish-black skin is peeled away to reveal a moist, crisp, white interior, which can be eaten raw or cooked. When cooked, water chestnuts retain their crunchy texture, making them a popular addition to stir-fried dishes. They are also used in salads and casseroles or wrapped in bacon for rumaki hors d'oeuvre.

Fresh Water Chestnuts

STALKS

Stalk vegetables are plant stems with a high percentage of **cellulose** fiber. These vegetables should be picked while still young and tender. Tough fibers should be trimmed before cooking.

▶ **cellulose** a complex carbohydrate found in the cell wall of plants; it is edible but indigestible by humans

ARTICHOKES

Artichokes (Fr. *artichaut*) are the immature flowers of a thistle plant introduced to America by Italian and Spanish settlers. Young, tender globe artichokes can be cooked whole, but more mature plants need to have the fuzzy center (known as the choke) removed first. Whole artichokes can be simmered, steamed or microwaved; they are often served with lemon juice, garlic butter or hollandaise sauce. The heart may be cooked separately, then served in salads, puréed as a filling or served as a side dish. Artichoke hearts and leafless artichoke bottoms are both available canned.

Choose fresh artichokes with tight, compact heads that feel heavy. Their color should be solid green to gray-green. Brown spots on the surface caused by frost are harmless. Artichokes' peak season is March through May.

Artichokes

▶ PROCEDURE FOR PREPARING FRESH ARTICHOKES

1 Using kitchen shears or scissors, trim the barbs from the large outer leaves of the artichoke.

2 With a chef's knife, cut away the stem and the top of the artichoke. Steam or boil the artichoke as desired.

Use a sharp knife to peel away the tough outer skin from large asparagus spears.

ASPARAGUS

Asparagus (Fr. *asperges*), a member of the lily family, has bright green spears with a ruffle of tiny leaves at the tip. Larger spears tend to be tough and woody, but can be used in soups or for purée. Asparagus is eaten raw or steamed briefly, stir-fried, microwaved or grilled. Fresh spring asparagus is excellent with nothing more than lemon juice or clarified butter; asparagus with hollandaise sauce is a classic preparation.

Asparagus

Choose firm, plump spears with tightly closed tips and a bright green color running the full length of the spear. Asparagus should be stored refrigerated at 40°F (4°C), upright in ½ inch (1.25 centimeters) of water or with the ends wrapped in moist paper toweling. The stalks should not be washed until just before use. Canned and frozen asparagus are also available. Peak season is March through June.

A European variety of white asparagus is sometimes available fresh, or readily available canned. It has a milder flavor and soft, tender texture. It is produced by covering the stalks with soil as they grow; this prevents sunlight from reaching the plant and retards the development of chlorophyll.

Fresh Bamboo Shoots

BAMBOO SHOOTS

Stripped of their tough brown outer skins, the tender young shoots of certain varieties of bamboo are edible. They make excellent additions to stir-fried dishes or can be served like asparagus. Although fresh shoots are available in Asia, canned peeled shoots packed in brine or water are more common in the United States. Canned shoots should be rinsed well before use.

CELERY

Once a medicinal herb, stalk celery (Fr. *céleri*) is now a common sight in kitchens worldwide. Stalk celery is pale green with stringy curved stalks. Often eaten raw in salads or as a snack, it can be braised or steamed as a side dish. Celery is also a mirepoix component.

Choose stalks that are crisp, without any sign of dryness. Celery is available all year.

Celery

FENNEL

Fennel (Fr. *fenouil*) is a Mediterranean favorite used for thousands of years as a vegetable (the bulb), an herb (the leaves) and a spice (the seeds). The bulb (often incorrectly referred to as sweet anise) has short, tight, overlapping celerylike stalks with

Fennel

feathery leaves. The flavor is similar to anise or licorice, becoming milder when cooked. Fennel bulbs may be eaten raw or grilled, steamed, sautéed, baked or microwaved.

Choose a fairly large, bright white bulb on which the cut edges appear fresh, without dryness or browning. The bulb should be compact, not spreading. Fresh fennel's peak season is September through May.

HEARTS OF PALM

Hearts of palm are the tender interiors of stems from cabbage palm trees. They are ivory-colored and slender, with a delicate flavor similar to asparagus. Fresh hearts of palm are sometimes available in Florida (where they are grown); canned ones are widely available everywhere. Hearts of palm are generally used uncooked in salads or marinated in herb vinaigrette.

Hearts of Palm

NOPALES

The pads of a prickly pear cactus can be prepared as a vegetable known as nopales. Cactus pads have a flavor similar to green bell peppers. Their texture tends to be rather gelatinous or mucilaginous, making them good for stews or sauces. To prepare fresh nopales, hold the pad with tongs and cut off the thorns and "eyes" with a sharp knife or vegetable peeler. Trim off the edge all the way around. Slice the pad into julienne strips or cubes. The pieces can be boiled or steamed and served hot, or chilled and added to salads. Nopales can also be sautéed with onions, peppers and seasonings for a side dish or added to southwestern-style casseroles.

Nopales

Some cultivated varieties have thin, thornless pads. Choose pads that are stiff and heavy without blemishes. They should not be dry or soggy. Fresh cactus pads are available all year, with peak season in the late spring. Canned and pickled nopales are also available.

BABY VEGETABLES

Many fine restaurants serve baby vegetables: tiny turnips, finger-length squash, miniature carrots and petite heads of cauliflower. First cultivated in Europe but now widely available throughout the United States, baby vegetables include both hybrids bred to be true miniatures as well as regular varieties that are picked before maturity. Baby vegetables are often marketed with blossoms or greens still attached. They tend to be easily bruised and are highly perishable. Many baby vegetables can be eaten raw, but they are usually left whole, then steamed or lightly sautéed and attractively presented as an accompaniment to meat, fish or poultry entrées.

Baby Zucchini with Blossoms

Chiogghi Beets

Baby Yellow Squash with Blossoms

Baby Globe Carrots

ANCIENT PLANTS AND ANCIENT WAYS VANISH

Since the days of Columbus, half of all native American crop varieties have become extinct. If this trend continues, several hundred more will become extinct in our lifetimes. Similarly, ancient farming practices have all but been abandoned. As late as the 1920s, the Tohono O'odham Indians of Arizona still used traditional methods to cultivate more than 10,000 acres without pumping groundwater. Today, only a few scattered floodwater fields remain.

When species disappear we lose an irreplaceable source of genetic diversity—a source of extraordinary genes that could someday improve modern hybrid crops. When native desert crops vanish, so does the ancient tradition of native agriculture, which has selected these crops over millennia to thrive in extreme temperatures, in alkaline soils without millions of gallons of precious water and without expensive, ecologically destructive chemicals.

Today, six highly bred species—wheat, rice, corn, sorghum, potatoes and cassava—supply most of the world's nutrition. As food crops become more and more homogeneous, they often lose their natural ability to tolerate pests, disease and drought. In the past, farmers grew thousands of food crop varieties. These traditional crop varieties contain a storehouse of genetic diversity that enables them to flourish in the most difficult environments. This broad spectrum of genetic variability is a cushion against natural predators and diseases. Wild chiles from the Sierra Madre, for example, are highly disease resistant. Their virus-tolerant genes have been bred into commercial varieties of bell pepper and jalapeños.

Native Seeds/SEARCH, one of the country's first regional seed banks, was founded to keep ancient desert plants and traditional farming methods from disappearing forever. Since 1983 we've ridden mules into remote areas and made more than 1200 collections of desert-adapted crops and wild relatives. We've gathered the seeds of chapalote (a brown popcorn), blue indigo (used for dyes), tepary (a heat- and drought-tolerant bean), teosinte (a wild relative of corn), wild chiles and other plants. These seeds are available to researchers, gardeners, farmers and seed banks. Seeds are offered free to Native Americans.

Each loss of biological and cultural diversity alters and damages the balance of life on earth, often in ways we do not understand. Each loss of leaf, stem and flower diminishes our earth's richness and beauty in ways we often don't appreciate until they're gone.

—DR. GARY PAUL NABHAN, Native Seeds/SEARCH, Tucson, AZ

▶ NUTRITION

Most vegetables are more than 80 percent water; the remaining portions consist of carbohydrates (primarily starches) and small amounts of protein and fat. The relative lack of protein and fat makes most vegetables especially low in calories.

Much of a vegetable's physical structure is provided by generally indigestible substances such as cellulose and lignin, also known as fiber. This fiber produces the characteristic stringy, crisp or fibrous textures associated with vegetables.

BACK TO BASICS

Great strides in agriculture have been made during the past two centuries. Pesticides, fungicides and herbicides now eliminate or control pests that once would have devoured, ruined or choked crops. Chemical fertilizers increase yields of many of the world's staples. But not everyone has greeted these developments with open arms.

During the past few decades, scientific and medical investigators have documented, or at least suggested, health risks associated with certain synthetic pesticides, fertilizers and other products. These findings have led to a renewed interest in a now multibillion-dollar-a-year back-to-the-basics approach to farming: organic farming. Specialty farms, orchards and even wineries now offer organically grown products (or, in the case of wineries, wines made from or-

ganically grown grapes). These products come with few, if any, intentional additives and should be free of any incidental additives. Proponents argue that these products are better for you and better for the health of the farm workers.

The U.S. Department of Agriculture regulates the production and labeling of organically

grown foods. It requires that any natural food labeled "100 percent organic" must contain only organic ingredients—that is, those grown and manufactured without the use of added hormones, pesticides, synthetic fertilizers, and so on; soil cannot have been treated with unapproved synthetics for three years for a crop to be called organic. To be labeled organic or to display the USDA organic seal, processed foods must contain at least 95 percent organic ingredients by weight. Processed foods with 70 to 95 percent organic ingredients may be labeled "made with organic ingredients"; processed foods with less than 70 percent organic ingredients may list those ingredients on the information panel but may not use the term *organic* anywhere on the front of the package.

TO BE OR NOT TO BE: VEGETARIAN

In the not-too-distant past, vegetarianism was linked with aging hippies, musty health food stores and the religiously observant. Not any more. Now most supermarkets stock vegetarian burgers, soy cheeses, tofu and rice milk, while national chains of modern, upscale groceries cater specifically to vegetarian and health-conscious shoppers. Even fast-food restaurants now offer foods such as vegetarian submarine sandwiches and soy-filled tacos.

So, just how many vegetarians are there in the United States? The Vegetarian Resource Group has tried to answer this question. In a 2000 poll, it asked adult respondents, "Which of the following foods, if any, [do] you never eat? Meat, Poultry, Fish/Seafood, Dairy Prod-ucts, Eggs, Honey." Approximately 2.5 percent of the sample population responded that they did not eat meat, poultry or fish, while a total of 4.5 percent indicated they did not eat red meat. In fact, only 72 percent indicated that they eat items from all of the listed food groups. When the same question was asked in 1994 and again in 1997, only about 1 percent indicated that they were vegetarian (defined as those who never eat meat, poultry or fish).

Adults aren't the only vegetarians. According to another Vegetarian Resource Group poll in 2000, 2 percent of children ages 6 to 17 responded that they never eat meat, fish or poultry, while 6 percent don't eat red meat.

Significantly, nonvegetarians also enjoy meatless dishes from time to time. According to a 1999 poll, approximately 57 percent of U.S. adults say they "sometimes, often or always" order a vegetarian entrée when dining out.

This growing demand for vegetarian food clearly has an impact on restaurants and institutional food service operations. When more than half of the population sometimes orders vegetarian cuisine, it is no longer sufficient to offer a one-dish-fits-all vegetarian entrée. As with nonvegetarian dishes, flavor, freshness, quality and variety will keep customers satisfied and eager to return.

Vegetables are also a good source of vitamins and minerals. Care must be taken during preparation to preserve their nutritional content, however. Once peeled or cut, vegetables lose nutrients to the air, or to any liquid in which they are allowed to soak. Vitamins are concentrated just under the skin, so peel vegetables thinly, if at all.

► PURCHASING AND STORING FRESH VEGETABLES

Fresh vegetables should be selected according to seasonal availability. Using a vegetable at the peak of its season has several advantages: Price is at its lowest, selection is at its greatest and the vegetable's color, flavor and texture are at their best.

GRADING

The USDA has a voluntary grading system for fresh vegetables traded on wholesale markets. The system is based on appearance, condition and other factors affecting waste or eating quality. Grades for all vegetables include, in descending order of quality, U.S. Extra Fancy, U.S. Fancy, U.S. Extra No. 1 and U.S. No. 1. There are also grades that apply only to specific vegetables, for example, U.S. No. 1 Boilers for onions.

Consumer or retail grading is currently required only for potatoes, carrots and onions. It uses alphabetical listings, with Grade A being the finest.

PURCHASING

Fresh vegetables are sold by weight or count. They are packed in cartons referred to as cases, lugs, bushels, flats or crates. The weight or count packed in each of these containers varies depending on the size and type of vegetable as well as the packer. For example, celery is packed in 55-pound cartons containing 18–48 heads depending on the size of each head.

► **demi-vegetarian** a term sometimes used to describe people who eat little or no meat but may eat fish

► **fruitarian** someone who eats only plant foods such as fruits, grains and nuts that can be harvested without killing the plant

► **lacto-ovovegetarian or ovo-lactovegetarian** a vegetarian who also eats dairy products and eggs; theirs is probably the most typical vegetarian diet

► **lactovegetarian** a vegetarian who eats dairy products but not eggs

► **ovovegetarian** a vegetarian who eats eggs but not dairy products

► **vegan—(VEE-gun)** a vegetarian who does not eat dairy products, eggs, honey or any other animal product; vegans usually also avoid wearing and using animal products such as fur, leather or wool

► **vegetarian** a person who does not eat any meat, poultry, game, fish, shellfish or animal by-products such as gelatin or animal fats; may not eat dairy products and eggs

Some of the more common fresh vegetables (for example, onions, carrots, celery and lettuces) can be purchased from wholesalers trimmed, cleaned and cut according to your specifications. Although the unit price will be higher for diced onions than for whole onions, for example, the savings in time, labor, yield loss and storage space can be substantial. Processed vegetables may suffer a loss of nutrients, moisture and flavor, however.

RIPENING

Although vegetables do not ripen in the same manner as fruits, they do continue to breathe (respire) after harvesting. The faster the respiration rate, the faster the produce ages or decays. This decay results in wilted leaves and dry, tough or woody stems and stalks. Respiration rates vary according to the vegetable variety, its maturity at harvest and its storage conditions after harvest.

Ripening proceeds more rapidly in the presence of ethylene gas. Ethylene gas is emitted naturally by fruits and vegetables and can be used to encourage further ripening in some produce, especially fruit-vegetables such as tomatoes. Items harvested and shipped when mature but green (unripe) can be exposed to ethylene gas to induce color development (ripening) just before sale.

STORING

Some fresh vegetables are best stored at cool temperatures, between 40°F and 60°F (4°C and 16°C), ideally in a separate produce refrigerator. These include winter squash, potatoes, onions, shallots and garlic. If a produce refrigerator is not available, store these vegetables at room temperature in a dry area with good ventilation. Do not store them in a refrigerator set at conventional temperatures. Colder temperatures convert the starches in these vegetables to sugars, changing their texture and flavor.

Most other vegetables benefit from cold storage at temperatures between 34°F and 40°F (2°C and 4°C) with relatively high levels of humidity. Greens and other delicate vegetables should be stored away from apples, tomatoes, bananas and melons, as the latter give off a great deal of ethylene gas.

▶ PURCHASING AND STORING PRESERVED VEGETABLES

Preservation techniques are designed to extend the shelf life of vegetables. These methods include irradiation, canning, freezing and drying. Except for drying, these techniques do not substantially change the vegetable's texture or flavor. Canning and freezing can also be used to preserve cooked vegetables.

IRRADIATED VEGETABLES

The irradiation process uses ionizing radiation (usually gamma rays of cobalt 60 or cesium 137) to sterilize foods. When foods are subjected to radiation, parasites, insects and bacteria are destroyed, ripening is slowed and sprouting is prevented. Irradiation works without a noticeable increase in temperature; consequently, the flavor and texture of fresh foods are not affected. Some nutrients, however, may be destroyed. Irradiated vegetables do not need to be sprayed with post-harvest pesticides, and they have an extended shelf life.

The FDA classifies irradiation as a food additive. Although not yet approved for all foods, grains, fruits and vegetables may be treated with low-dose radiation. Irradiated foods must be labeled "Treated with radiation" or "Treated by irradiation." The symbol shown in Figure 22.1 may also be used.

Irradiated produce is purchased, stored and used like fresh produce.

FIGURE 22.1 ▶ Irradiation symbol

CANNED VEGETABLES

Canned vegetables are the backbone of menu planning for many food service operations. In commercial canning, raw vegetables are cleaned and placed in a sealed container, then subjected to high temperatures for a specific period. Heating destroys the microorganisms that cause spoilage, and the sealed environment created by the can eliminates oxidation and retards decomposition. But the heat required by the canning process also softens the texture of most vegetables and alters their nutritional content; many vitamins and minerals may be lost through the canning process. Green vegetables may also suffer color loss, becoming a drab olive hue.

Canned vegetables are graded by the USDA as U.S. Grade A or Fancy, U.S. Grade B or Extra-Select, and U.S. Grade C or Standard. U.S. Grade A vegetables must be top quality, tender and free of blemishes. U.S. Grade C vegetables may lack uniformity or flavor, but can be used in casseroles or soups if cost is a concern.

Combinations of vegetables as well as vegetables with seasonings and sauces are available canned. For example, corn kernels are available canned in water, in seasonings and sauces, combined with other vegetables or creamed. Canned vegetables are easy to serve because they are essentially fully cooked during the canning process.

Canned vegetables are purchased in cases of standard-sized cans (see Appendix II). Canned vegetables can be stored almost indefinitely at room temperature. Once a can is opened, any unused contents should be transferred to an appropriate storage container and refrigerated. Cans with bulges should be discarded immediately, without opening.

FROZEN VEGETABLES

Frozen vegetables are almost as convenient to use as canned. However, they often require some cooking, and expensive freezer space is necessary if an inventory is to be maintained. Regardless, freezing is a highly effective method for preserving vegetables. It severely inhibits the growth of microorganisms that cause spoilage without destroying many nutrients. Generally, green vegetables retain their color, although the appearance and texture of most vegetables may be somewhat altered because of their high water content: Ice crystals form from the water in the cells and burst the cells' walls.

Some vegetables are available individually quick-frozen (IQF). This method employs blasts of cold air, refrigerated plates, liquid nitrogen, liquid air or other techniques to chill the vegetables quickly. Speeding the freezing process can greatly reduce the formation of ice crystals.

Combinations of vegetables as well as vegetables with seasonings and sauces are available frozen. Some frozen vegetables are raw when frozen; others are blanched before freezing so that final cooking time is reduced. Many others are fully cooked before freezing and need only to be thawed or heated for service. Frozen vegetables generally do not need to be thawed before being heated. Once thawed or cooked, they should be stored in the refrigerator and reheated in the same manner as fresh vegetables. Do not refreeze previously frozen vegetables.

Frozen vegetables are graded in the same manner as canned vegetables. They are usually packed in cases containing 1- to 2-pound (450-gram to 1.8-kilogram) boxes or bags. All frozen vegetables should be sealed in moistureproof wrapping and kept at a constant temperature of 0°F (−18°C) or below. Temperature fluctuations can draw moisture from the vegetables, causing poor texture and flavor loss. Adequate packaging also prevents freezer burn, an irreversible change in the color, texture and flavor of frozen foods.

▶ **miso** (ME-so) a thick paste made by salting and fermenting soybeans and rice or barley; generally used as a flavoring

▶ **seitan** (SAY-tan) a form of wheat gluten; it has a firm, chewy texture and a bland flavor; traditionally simmered in a broth of soy sauce or tamari with ginger, garlic and kombu (seaweed)

▶ **tempeh** (TEHM-pay) fermented whole soybeans mixed with a grain such as rice or millet; it has a chewy consistency and a yeasty, nutty flavor

▶ **tofu** also known as bean curd; it is created from soymilk using a method similar to the way animal milk is separated into curds and whey in the production of cheese. See page 635.

▶ **TSP** (Textured soy protein) also known as textured soy flour; defatted soy protein compressed into granules or chunks; usually sold dried and rehydrated before cooking; used as a meat extender and in commercially produced meat replacements

DRIED VEGETABLES

Except for beans, peas, peppers, mushrooms and tomatoes, few vegetables are commonly preserved by drying. Unlike other preservation methods, drying dramatically alters flavor, texture and appearance. The loss of moisture concentrates flavors and sugars and greatly extends shelf life.

▶ APPLYING VARIOUS COOKING METHODS

Vegetables are cooked in order to break down their cellulose and gelatinize their starches. Cooking gives vegetables a pleasant flavor; creates a softer, more tender texture and makes them more digestible. Ideally, most vegetables should be cooked as briefly as possible in order to preserve their flavor, nutrients and texture. Unfortunately, sometimes you must choose between emphasizing appearance and maintaining nutrition because cooking methods that preserve color and texture often remove nutrients.

ACID/ALKALI REACTIONS

The acid or alkali content of the cooking liquid affects the texture and color of many vegetables. This is of greater concern with moist-heat cooking methods, but it is also a consideration with dry-heat cooking methods, as they often call for blanched or parboiled vegetables.

TEXTURE

The acidity or alkalinity of the vegetable's cooking liquid influences the finished product's texture. If an acid such as lemon juice, vinegar or wine is added to the liquid for flavoring, the vegetable will resist softening and will require a longer cooking time. On the other hand, an alkaline cooking medium will quickly soften the vegetable's texture and may cause it to become mushy. Alkalinity also causes nutrient loss (especially thiamin) and may impart a bitter flavor. Alkalinity can be caused by tap water, detergent residue on utensils or the addition of baking soda (a base) to the cooking liquid. (You could add, for example, ⅛ teaspoon [0.6 milliliter] of baking soda per cup [225 milliliters] of beans to speed the softening of dried beans.)

COLOR

The acidity or alkalinity of the liquid also affects the plant's pigments, causing both desirable and undesirable color changes. There are three principal pigment categories: chlorophyll, carotenoid and flavonoid. A plant's unique color is the result of a combination of these pigments. Chlorophyll pigments predominate in green vegetables such as spinach, green beans and broccoli. Carotenoid pigments predominate in orange and yellow vegetables such as carrots, tomatoes, red peppers and winter squashes. Flavonoid pigments predominate in red, purple and white vegetables such as red cabbage, beets and cauliflower.

Initially, as vegetables are cooked, their original colors intensify. Exposure to heat makes pigments, especially chlorophyll, appear brighter. Exposure to acids and bases affects both chlorophyll and flavonoid pigments. Acids will gradually turn green vegetables an olive-drab color, while a slight alkalinity promotes chlorophyll retention. The opposite occurs with vegetables containing flavonoids: They retain desirable colors in a slightly acidic environment while losing colors in an alkaline one. (Carotenoids are not affected by either acidity or alkalinity.) Color changes alone do not affect flavor, but the altered appearance can make the product so visually unappealing as to become inedible.

Colors also change as the naturally occurring acids in vegetables are released during cooking. If the cooking pan is kept covered, the acids can concentrate, creating richer flavonoid pigments but destroying chlorophyll pigments.

this one's right

1 Spinach cooked with an acid (left) and an alkali.

2 Cauliflower cooked with an acid (left) and an alkali.

3 Red cabbage cooked with an acid (left) and an alkali.

all backwards

Thus, if color is the one and only concern, vegetables with a high amount of chlorophyll should be cooked in an alkaline liquid, and vegetables with a high amount of flavonoids should be cooked in an acidic liquid. But remember, the improvement in color usually comes at the expense of texture and nutrients.

GUIDELINES FOR VEGETABLE COOKERY

The following general guidelines for vegetable cookery should be considered regardless of the cooking method used:

1 Vegetables should be carefully cut into uniform shapes and sizes to promote even cooking and provide an attractive finished product.

2 Cook vegetables for as short a time as possible to preserve texture, color and nutrients.

3 Cook vegetables as close to service time as possible. Holding vegetables in a steam table continues to cook them.

4 When necessary, vegetables may be blanched in advance, refreshed in ice water and refrigerated. They can then be reheated as needed.

5 White and red vegetables (those with flavonoid pigments) may be cooked with a small amount of acid such as lemon juice, vinegar or white wine to help retain their color.

6 When preparing an assortment of vegetables, cook each type separately, then combine them. Otherwise, some items would become overcooked in the time required to properly cook others.

Table 22.1 **ACID/ALKALI REACTIONS**

VEGETABLE	PIGMENT FAMILY	EFFECT OF ACID ON:		EFFECT OF ALKALI ON:*		
		COLOR	TEXTURE	COLOR	TEXTURE	COOK COVERED?
Spinach, broccoli	chlorophyll	drab olive green	firm	bright green	mushy	no
Carrots, rutabagas	caroteniod	no change	firm	no change	mushy	no difference
Cauliflower	flavonoid	white	firm	yellow	mushy	yes
Red cabbage	~~flavonoid~~ *anthocyanins*	red	firm	blue	mushy	yes

* Alkalinity always causes a loss of thiamin and other nutrients.

DETERMINING DONENESS

There are so many types of vegetables, with such varied responses to cooking, that no one standard for doneness is appropriate. Each item should be evaluated on a recipe-by-recipe basis. Generally, however, most cooked vegetables are done when they are just tender when pierced with a fork or the tip of a paring knife. Leafy vegetables should be wilted but still have a bright color.

You can avoid overcooking vegetables by remembering that some carryover cooking will occur through the residual heat contained in the foods. Always rely on subjective tests—sight, feel, taste and aroma—rather than the clock.

DRY-HEAT COOKING METHODS
BROILING AND GRILLING

Broiling and grilling use high heat to cook vegetables quickly. This preserves their nutritional content and natural flavors. The radiant heat of the broiler or grill caramelizes the vegetables, creating a pleasant flavor that is not generally achieved when vegetables are cooked by other methods.

Selecting and Preparing Vegetables to Broil or Grill

Broiling is often used to cook soft vegetables such as tomatoes or items that might not rest easily on a grill rack. Broiling is also used to warm and brown items just before service. If necessary, the vegetables can be basted to prevent them from drying out under the broiler's direct heat. Sometimes a cooked vegetable is napped with sauce or clarified butter and placed briefly under the broiler as a finishing touch at service time.

A large range of vegetables can be grilled. Carrots, peppers, squashes, eggplants and similar vegetables should be cut into broad, thin slices. They can then be placed on the grill in the same manner as a portion of meat or fish to create attractive crosshatchings. (See Chapter 10, Principles of Cooking.) Smaller vegetables such as mushrooms, cherry tomatoes and pearl onions can be threaded onto skewers for easy handling.

Seasoning Vegetables to Be Broiled or Grilled

Vegetables contain little fat and therefore benefit greatly from added fat when being broiled or grilled. The added fat can be a brushing of clarified butter or a marinade such as one made from olive oil and herbs. Some vegetables may be brushed with butter and coated with bread crumbs or Parmesan before broiling.

▶ PROCEDURE FOR BROILING OR GRILLING VEGETABLES

1 Heat the grill or broiler.
2 Use a wire brush to remove any charred or burnt particles that may be stuck to the broiler or grill grate. The grate may be wiped with a lightly oiled towel to remove any remaining particles and help season it.
3 Prepare the vegetables to be broiled or grilled by cutting them into appropriate shapes and sizes, then seasoning, marinating or otherwise preparing them as desired or directed in the recipe.
4 Place the vegetables on the broiler grate, broiler platter or grill grate and cook to the desired doneness while developing the proper surface color.

GRILLED VEGETABLE SKEWERS   RECIPE 22.1

Grilling skewers of marinated vegetables.

Yield: 12 Skewers	**Method:** Grilling	
Marinade:		
Rice wine vinegar	4 fl. oz.	120 ml
Vegetable oil	8 fl. oz.	250 ml
Garlic, chopped	1 oz.	30 g
Dried thyme	2 tsp.	10 ml
Salt	1 Tbsp.	15 ml
Black pepper	½ tsp.	2 ml
Zucchini	6 oz.	180 g
Yellow squash	6 oz.	180 g
Broccoli florets, large	12	12
Cauliflower florets, large	12	12
Onion, large dice	24 pieces	24 pieces
Red bell pepper, large dice	12 pieces	12 pieces
Mushroom caps, medium	12	12

1 Combine all the marinade ingredients and set aside.

2 Cut the zucchini and yellow squash into ½-inch- (1.2-centimeter-) thick semi-circles.

3 Blanch and refresh the zucchini, yellow squash, broccoli florets, cauliflower florets, onions and red bell peppers as discussed later, under Moist-Heat Cooking Methods.

4 Drain the vegetables well and combine them with the marinade. Add the mushroom caps to the marinade. Marinate the vegetables for 30 to 45 minutes, remove and drain well.

5 Skewer the vegetables by alternating them on 6-inch (10-centimeter) bamboo skewers.

6 Place the vegetable skewers on a hot grill and cook until done, turning as needed. The vegetables should brown and char lightly during cooking. Serve hot.

Approximate values per serving: **Calories** 60, **Total fat** 2.5 g, **Saturated fat** 0 g, **Cholesterol** 0 mg, **Sodium** 610 mg, **Total carbohydrates** 8 g, **Protein** 2 g, **Vitamin C** 90%, **Claims**—low fat; no cholesterol; good source of fiber

ROASTING AND BAKING

The terms *roasting* and *baking* are used interchangeably when referring to vegetables. Roasting or baking is used to bring out the natural sweetness of many vegetables while preserving their nutritional values. The procedures are basically the same as those for roasting meats.

Selecting and Preparing Vegetables to Roast or Bake

Hearty vegetables such as winter squash and eggplant are especially well suited for roasting or baking. Vegetables such as onions, carrots and turnips are sometimes cooked alongside roasting meats or poultry. The vegetables add flavor to the finished roast and accompanying sauce, and the fats and juices released from the cooking roast add flavor to the vegetables.

Vegetables can be baked whole or cut into uniform-sized pieces. Squash, for example, is usually cut into large pieces. Vegetables may be peeled or left unpeeled, depending on the desired finished product.

Seasoning Vegetables to Be Roasted or Baked

Vegetables may be seasoned with salt and pepper and rubbed with butter or oil before baking, or they may be seasoned afterward with a wide variety of herbs and spices. Some vegetables, such as winter squashes and sweet potatoes, may be seasoned with brown sugar or honey as well.

▶ PROCEDURE FOR ROASTING OR BAKING VEGETABLES

1 Wash the vegetables. Peel, cut and prepare them as desired or directed in the recipe.
2 Season the vegetables and rub with oil or butter if desired.
3 Place the vegetables in a baking dish and bake in a preheated oven until done.

RECIPE 22.2   **BAKED BUTTERNUT SQUASH**

Yield: 4 Servings, 4 oz. (120 g) each   **Method:** Baking

Butternut squash, medium dice	1 lb.	450 g
Salt and pepper	TT	TT
Cinnamon	¼ tsp.	1 ml
Cardamom, ground	⅛ tsp.	0.5 ml
Brown sugar	2 Tbsp.	30 ml
Lemon juice	2 Tbsp.	30 ml
Whole butter, melted	2 oz.	60 g

1 Place the squash in a buttered pan. Season with salt, pepper, cinnamon, cardamom and brown sugar.
2 Drizzle the lemon juice and butter over the top of the squash.
3 Bake, uncovered, in a 350°F (180°C) oven until tender, approximately 50 minutes.

Approximate values per 4-oz. (120-g) serving: **Calories** 190, **Total fat** 12 g, **Saturated fat** 7 g, **Cholesterol** 30 mg, **Sodium** 700 mg, **Total carbohydrates** 20 g, **Protein** 1 g, **Vitamin A** 90%, **Vitamin C** 35%

SAUTÉING

Sautéed vegetables should be brightly colored and slightly crisp when done and show little moisture loss. When sautéing vegetables, all preparation must be complete before cooking begins because timing is important and cooking progresses rapidly. Have all vegetables, herbs, spices, seasonings and sauces ready before you begin.

Selecting and Preparing Vegetables to Sauté

A wide variety of vegetables can be sautéed. Whatever vegetables are used, they should be cut into uniform-sized pieces to ensure even cooking.

Quick-cooking vegetables such as summer squashes, onions, greens, stalks, fruit-vegetables and mushrooms can be sautéed without any preparation except washing and cutting. Other vegetables such as Brussels sprouts, green beans, winter squashes, broccoli, cauliflower and most root vegetables are usually first blanched or otherwise partially cooked by baking, steaming or simmering. They are then sautéed to reheat and finish. Carrots, squash and other vegetables are sometimes finished by sautéing in butter and then adding a small amount of honey or maple syrup to glaze them. Some cooked vegetables are reheated by simply sautéing them in a small amount of stock or sauce.

Seasoning Vegetables to Be Sautéed

Sautéed vegetables can be seasoned with a great variety of herbs and spices. Seasonings should be added toward the end of the cooking process after all other ingredients have been incorporated in order to accurately evaluate the flavor of the finished dish.

Because sautéing vegetables uses slightly lower temperatures than sautéing meats and poultry, usually whole butter can be used instead of clarified butter. For additional flavors, fats such as bacon fat, olive oil, nut oils or sesame oil can be used in place of butter.

▶ PROCEDURE FOR SAUTÉING VEGETABLES

1 Wash and cut the vegetables into uniform shapes and sizes.

2 Heat a sauté pan and add enough fat to just cover the bottom. The pan should be large enough to hold the vegetables without overcrowding.

3 When preparing an assortment of vegetables, add the ingredients according to their cooking times (first add the vegetables that take the longest to cook). Plan carefully so that all vegetables will be done at the same time. Do not overcrowd the pan; maintain high enough heat so that the vegetables do not cook in their own juices.

4 Toss the vegetables using the sloped sides of the sauté pan or wok to flip them back on top of themselves. Do not toss more than necessary. The pan should remain in contact with the heat source as much as possible to maintain proper temperatures.

5 Add any sauces or vegetables with high water content, such as tomatoes, last.

6 Season the vegetables as desired with herbs or spices, or add ingredients for a glaze.

STIR-FRIED ASPARAGUS WITH SHIITAKE MUSHROOMS

RECIPE 22.3

Yield: 4 Servings, 4 oz. (120 g) each	**Method:** Sautéing	
Asparagus	1 lb.	450 g
Shiitake mushrooms, fresh	6 oz.	180 g
Vegetable oil	1 Tbsp.	15 ml
Sesame oil	1 Tbsp.	15 ml
Garlic, chopped	2 tsp.	10 ml
Oyster sauce	4 fl. oz.	120 ml
Crushed red chiles, optional	TT	TT

1 Wash the asparagus, trim the ends and slice on the bias into 1- to 2-inch (2.5- to 5-centimeter) pieces.

2 Wash the mushrooms, trim off the stems and slice the caps into ½-inch (1.2-centimeter) thick slices.

3 Heat the oils in a wok or sauté pan.

4 Add the garlic and stir-fry for a few seconds.

5 Add the mushrooms and asparagus and stir-fry for 1 minute.

6 Add the oyster sauce and crushed red chiles (if used) and continue to stir-fry until the asparagus is nearly tender, approximately 3 minutes.

Approximate values per 4-oz. (120-g) serving: **Calories** 140, **Total fat** 8 g, **Saturated fat** 1 g, **Cholesterol** 10 mg, **Sodium** 1130 mg, **Total carbohydrates** 13 g, **Protein** 5 g, **Vitamin C** 50%

PAN-FRYING

Pan-frying is not as popular as other techniques for cooking vegetables. Green tomatoes, however, are sometimes seasoned, floured and pan-fried; eggplant slices are seasoned, floured, pan-fried and used for eggplant parmesan. When pan-frying vegetables, follow the procedures outlined in Chapter 10, Principles of Cooking.

DEEP-FRYING

Deep-frying is a popular method of preparing vegetables such as potatoes, squashes and mushrooms. They can be served as hors d'oeuvre, appetizers or accompaniments to a main dish. Vegetables can also be grated or chopped and incorporated into fritters or croquettes. Any deep-fried item should have a crisp, golden exterior with a tender, nongreasy center.

Selecting and Seasoning Vegetables to Be Deep-Fried

Except for potatoes (which are discussed in Chapter 23, Potatoes, Grains and Pasta), most vegetables are breaded or battered before deep-frying. Slow-cooking vegetables such as broccoli and cauliflower should be blanched in boiling water before breading or battering. Blanching speeds cooking and allows the interior to cook completely before the surface burns.

Although vegetables that will be deep-fried can be marinated or seasoned directly, it is more common to season the batter or breading that will coat them. Additional flavors come from the sauces and accompaniments served with the deep-fried vegetables. Creamy herb dressings, spicy tomato or soy-based dipping sauces are popular accompaniments.

▶ PROCEDURE FOR DEEP-FRYING VEGETABLES

1 Slice, trim or otherwise prepare the vegetables to be deep-fried. Blanch them if necessary. Season and bread or batter them, as desired.

2 Heat the fat to the desired temperature, usually between 325°F and 350°F (160°C and 180°C). Breaded or battered vegetables cook quickly and the fat must be hot enough to cook the food's interior without burning its surface.

3 Carefully place the vegetables in the hot fat using either the basket method or swimming method as appropriate.

4 Deep-fry the vegetables until done. They should have a crispy, golden brown surface.

5 Remove the deep-fried vegetables from the fat and hold them over the fryer, allowing the excess fat to drain off. Transfer the food to a hotel pan either lined with absorbent paper or fitted with a rack. Season with salt, if desired.

6 If the deep-fried vegetables are to be held for later service, place them under a heat lamp.

RECIPE 22.4   **BEER-BATTERED ONION RINGS**

Yield: 1 qt. (1 lt) of batter, enough for approx. 4 lb. (1.8 kg) of rings   **Method:** Deep-frying

Flour	10 oz.	300 g
Baking powder	2 tsp.	10 ml
Salt	2 tsp.	10 ml
White pepper	1/4 tsp.	1 ml
Egg	1	1
Beer	1 pt.	450 ml
Onions, whole	4 lb.	1.8 kg
Flour	as needed for dredging	

1 Sift the dry ingredients together.

2 Beat the egg in a separate bowl. Add the beer to the beaten egg.

3 Add the egg-and-beer mixture to the dry ingredients; mix until smooth.

4 Peel the onions and cut in 1/2-inch- (1.2-centimeter-) thick slices.

1 Dredging the onion rings in flour.

2 Dipping the floured rings in batter.

5 Break the slices into rings and dredge in flour.

6 Dip the rings in the batter a few at a time. Using the swimming method, deep-fry at 375°F (191°C) until done. Drain on absorbent paper, season with additional salt and white pepper and serve hot.

Approximate values per 1-oz. (30-g) serving: **Calories** 230, **Total fat** 10 g, **Saturated fat** 2.5 g, **Cholesterol** 5 mg, **Sodium** 460 mg, **Total carbohydrates** 31 g, **Protein** 4 g

3 Frying the onion rings using the swimming method.

MOIST-HEAT COOKING METHODS
BLANCHING AND PARBOILING

Blanching and parboiling are variations on boiling; the difference between them is the length of cooking time. Blanched and parboiled vegetables are often finished by other cooking methods such as sautéing.

Blanching is the partial cooking of foods in a large amount of boiling water for a very short time, usually only a few seconds. Besides preparing vegetables for further cooking, blanching is used to remove strong or bitter flavors, soften firm foods, set colors or loosen skins for peeling. Kale, chard, snow peas and tomatoes are examples of vegetables that are sometimes blanched for purposes other than preparation for further cooking.

Parboiling is the same as blanching, but the cooking time is longer, usually several minutes. Parboiling is used to soften vegetables and shorten final cooking times. Parboiling is commonly used for preparing root vegetables, cauliflower, broccoli and winter squashes.

BOILING

Vegetables are often boiled. Boiled vegetables can be served as is, or they can be further prepared by quickly sautéing with other ingredients, puréeing or mashing. Boiled vegetables are also chilled, then used in salads.

Starchy root vegetables are generally not boiled but rather simmered slowly so that the heat penetrates to their interiors and cooks them evenly. Green vegetables should be boiled quickly in a large amount of water in order to retain their color and flavor.

Refreshing

Unless the boiled, blanched or parboiled vegetables will be eaten immediately, they must be quickly chilled in ice water after they are removed from the cooking liquid. This prevents further cooking and preserves (sets) their colors. This process is known as **refreshing** or **shocking** the vegetables. The vegetables are removed from the ice water as soon as they are cold. Never soak or hold the vegetables in the water longer than necessary, or valuable nutrients and flavor will be leached away.

▶ PROCEDURE FOR REFRESHING VEGETABLES

1 Blanch, parboil or boil the vegetables to the desired doneness.

2 Remove the vegetables from the cooking liquid and submerge them in ice water just until they are cold.

Selecting and Preparing Vegetables to Boil

Nearly any type of vegetable can be boiled. Carrots, cabbages, green beans, turnips and red beets are just a few of the most common ones. Vegetables can be large or small, but they should be uniform in size to ensure even cooking. Some vegetables are cooked whole and require only washing before boiling. Others must be washed, peeled and trimmed or cut into smaller or more manageable sizes.

Seasoning Vegetables to Be Boiled

Often vegetables are boiled in nothing more than salted water. Lemon juice, citrus zest, wine and other acidic ingredients are sometimes added to white and red vegetables; if so, they should be added to the liquid before the vegetables. Herbs and spices in a sachet or a bouquet garni are often used to add flavor to boiled vegetables and should be added according to the recipe.

After boiling, vegetables are sometimes finished with herbs, spices, butter, cream or sauces.

▶ PROCEDURE FOR BOILING VEGETABLES

1 Wash, peel, trim and cut the vegetables into uniform shapes and sizes.

2 Bring an adequate amount of water, stock, court bouillon or other liquid to a boil. The liquid should cover the vegetables, and they should be able to move around freely without overcrowding.

3 Add seasonings if desired or directed in the recipe.

4 Add the vegetables to the boiling liquid. If more than one vegetable is to be cooked and they have different cooking times, they should be cooked separately to ensure that all are cooked to the proper doneness. The pot may be covered if cooking white, red or yellow vegetables. Do not cover the pot when boiling green vegetables.

5 Cook the vegetables to the desired doneness.

6 Remove the vegetables from the water with a slotted spoon or a spider or drain through a colander.

7 Refresh the vegetables in ice water, drain and refrigerate until needed, or finish the hot boiled vegetables as desired and serve immediately.

BRUSSELS SPROUTS IN PECAN BUTTER

RECIPE 22.5

Yield: 6 Servings, 3 oz. (90 g)   **Method:** Boiling

Brussels sprouts	1 lb.	450 g
Whole butter	2 oz.	60 g
Pecans, chopped	4 oz.	120 g
Salt and pepper	TT	TT

1 Trim the Brussels sprouts and mark an X in the bottom of each with a paring knife to promote even cooking.

2 Boil the sprouts in salted water until tender, approximately 10 minutes.

3 Drain and hold the sprouts in a warm place.

4 Heat the butter in a sauté pan until noisette. Add the pecans and toss to brown them.

5 Add the Brussels sprouts and toss to reheat and blend flavors. Adjust the seasonings and serve.

Approximate values per 3-oz. (90-g) serving: **Calories** 240, **Total fat** 21 g, **Saturated fat** 6 g, **Cholesterol** 20 mg, **Sodium** 480 mg, **Total carbohydrates** 10 g, **Protein** 4 g, **Vitamin A** 15%, **Vitamin C** 80%

1 Marking an X in the bottom of each Brussels sprout.

2 Boiling the Brussels sprouts in the appropriate amount of water.

3 Tossing the Brussels sprouts with the butter.

▶ PROCEDURE FOR COOKING DRIED BEANS

Dried beans are best rehydrated by soaking as discussed earlier and then cooking in a boiling (actually simmering) liquid. After rehydration and cooking, the beans can be served or further cooked in baked, sautéed or puréed dishes.

1 After soaking, place the drained beans in a heavy saucepan and cover with cold water or stock. Allow approximately three times as much liquid as there are beans. Add flavoring ingredients as directed in the recipe, but do not add acids or salt until the beans have reached the desired tenderness. Acids and salt cause the exterior of beans to toughen and resist any further efforts at tenderizing.

2 Slowly bring the liquid to a boil. Boil uncovered for 10 minutes or as directed in the recipe. Use a ladle to remove any scum that rises to the surface.

3 Cover and reduce the heat. Allow the mixture to simmer until the beans are tender. Whole beans generally require 1 to 2½ hours, lentils 20 to 35 minutes and split peas 30 to 60 minutes. Add additional hot liquid if necessary. Do not stir the beans during cooking.

4 Drain the cooked beans through a colander.

RECIPE 22.6

Yield: 3 pt. (1.5 lt)

White beans	1 pt.	450 ml
Water	as needed	as needed
Carrots, small dice	4 oz.	120 g
Celery, small dice	2 oz.	60 g
Leeks, sliced, blanched	2 oz.	60 g
Dressing:		
Red wine vinegar	3 Tbsp.	45 ml
Fresh lemon juice	2 tsp.	10 ml
Dijon mustard	1/2 oz.	15 g
Shallots, minced	1 Tbsp.	15 ml
Olive oil	6 fl. oz.	180 ml
Salt and pepper	TT	TT
Green onions, minced	2	2
Parsley, chopped	1 Tbsp.	15 ml
Fresh thyme, chopped	1 Tbsp.	15 ml

1 Draining the beans.

1 Pick through the beans to remove any grit, pebbles or debris. Place the beans in a bowl of water and remove any skins or other items that float to the top. Drain and rinse the beans. Place the beans in a clean bowl and soak them for at least 1 hour or overnight.

2 Drain the beans and place them in a saucepot with 6 cups (1.5 liters) of water. Bring to a boil, reduce to a simmer and cook until the beans are tender, approximately 1 hour. Drain the beans, spread on a sheet pan, cool and refrigerate.

3 Blanch and refresh the carrots, celery and leeks. Drain and chill.

4 To make the dressing, combine the vinegar, lemon juice and mustard. Add the shallots and whisk in the olive oil a little bit at a time. Season with salt and pepper.

5 Toss the beans with the blanched vegetables, green onions, parsley and thyme. Add the dressing and toss together. Adjust the seasonings and serve chilled.

2 Blanching the vegetables.

Approximate values per 1/2-cup (120-ml) serving: **Calories** 250, **Total fat** 15 g, **Saturated fat** 2 g, **Cholesterol** 0 mg, **Sodium** 40 mg, **Total carbohydrates** 23 g, **Protein** 8 g, **Vitamin A** 50%, **Calcium** 10%, **Iron** 20%

3 Tossing the salad ingredients together.

STEAMING

Vegetables can be steamed in a convection steamer or by placing them in a basket or on a rack and suspending them over boiling liquid in a wok, saucepan or hotel pan. Vegetables can also be pan-steamed by cooking them in a covered pan with a small amount of liquid; most of the cooking is done by steam because only a small portion of the food is submerged in the liquid. Steamed vegetables can be eaten plain, partially cooked and sautéed lightly to finish, incorporated into casseroles or puréed. If they are not served immediately, they must be refreshed and refrigerated until used.

Properly steamed vegetables should be moist and tender. They generally retain their shape better than boiled vegetables. Vegetables cook very rapidly in steam, and overcooking is a common mistake.

Selecting and Preparing Vegetables to Steam

Nearly any vegetable that can be boiled can also be steamed successfully. All vegetables should be washed, peeled and trimmed if appropriate and cut into uniform-sized pieces. Pan-steaming is appropriate for vegetables that are small

4 The finished salad ready for buffet service.

or cut into fairly small pieces such as peas and beans or broccoli and cauliflower florets.

Seasoning Vegetables to Be Steamed

Steaming produces vegetables with clean, natural flavors. Foods cooked in convection steamers can be seasoned with herbs and spices; convection steamers use plain water to produce steam, so the foods being cooked do not gain flavor from the cooking liquid. Vegetables steamed over liquids or pan-steamed in small amounts of liquids can be flavored by using stocks or court bouillon as the cooking liquid. Herbs, spices and aromatic vegetables can be added to any liquid for additional flavor.

▶ PROCEDURE FOR STEAMING VEGETABLES

1 Wash, peel, trim and cut the vegetables into uniform shapes and sizes.

2 If a convection steamer is not being used, prepare a steaming liquid and bring it to a boil in a covered pan or double boiler.

3 Place the vegetables in a perforated pan in a single layer; do not crowd the pan. Place the pan over the boiling liquid or add the vegetables to the liquid.

4 Cover the pan and cook to the desired doneness.

5 Remove the vegetables from the steamer and serve, or refresh and refrigerate until needed.

BROCCOLI ALMONDINE

RECIPE 22.7

Yield: 6 Servings, 6 oz. (180 g) each	**Method:** Steaming	
Broccoli, fresh	2 lb.	1 kg
Salt and pepper	TT	TT
Whole butter	2 oz.	60 g
Almonds, sliced	1 oz.	30 g
Garlic clove, minced	1	1
Lemon juice	2 fl. oz.	60 ml

1 Cut the broccoli into uniform spears. Rinse and sprinkle lightly with salt and pepper.

2 Place the broccoli in a single layer in a perforated hotel pan and cook in a convection steamer until tender but slightly crisp, approximately 3 minutes.

3 Melt the butter in a sauté pan. Add the almonds and garlic and cook just until the nuts are lightly browned.

4 Arrange the broccoli on plates for service and sprinkle with the lemon juice. Drizzle the almonds and butter over the broccoli and serve immediately.

Approximate values per 6-oz. (180-g) serving: **Calories** 160, **Total fat** 10 g, **Saturated fat** 5 g, **Cholesterol** 20 mg, **Sodium** 500 g, **Total carbohydrates** 10 g, **Protein** 6 g, **Vitamin A** 35%, **Vitamin C** 110%

1 Placing the broccoli spears in a perforated pan.

2 Drizzling the browned almonds and butter over the broccoli.

COMBINATION COOKING METHODS

BRAISING AND STEWING

Braised and stewed vegetables are cooked slowly in a small amount of liquid. The liquid, including any given off by the vegetables, is reduced to a light sauce, becoming part of the finished product. Generally, a braised dish is prepared with only one vegetable; a stew is a mixture of several vegetables. The main ingredients are sometimes browned in fat before the liquid is added in order to enhance flavor and color.

Both braises and stews can be exceptionally flavorful because they are served with all of their cooking liquid. (Boiled vegetables lose some of their flavor to the cooking liquid.) Braised and stewed vegetables generally can be held hot for service longer than vegetables prepared by other cooking methods.

Selecting and Preparing Vegetables to Braise or Stew

Various lettuces, especially romaine and Boston, are often braised. Cabbages, Belgium endive, leeks and many other vegetables are also commonly braised. Stews may contain a wide variety of vegetables such as summer squashes, eggplant, onions, peppers, tomatoes, carrots, celery and garlic. Leafy green vegetables and winter squashes are less commonly braised or stewed.

The vegetables should be washed and peeled or trimmed if appropriate. Vegetables to be braised may be left whole, cut into uniform pieces or shredded, as desired. Lettuces are usually cut into halves or quarters; cabbage is usually shredded.

Seasoning Vegetables to Be Braised or Stewed

Both braises and stews usually include flavoring ingredients such as garlic, herbs, bacon or mirepoix. The liquid may consist of water, wine, stock or tomato juice. Vegetables can even be braised in butter and sugar or honey to create a glazed dish.

Both braises and stews can be seasoned with a variety of herbs and spices. Add the seasonings before covering the pot to finish the cooking process. Strongly flavored vegetables such as celery root and turnips are usually parboiled first in order to reduce their strong presence.

▶ PROCEDURE FOR BRAISING AND STEWING VEGETABLES

1 Wash, peel, trim and cut the vegetables.

2 Sauté or sweat the flavoring ingredients in fat to release their flavors. Or sauté or sweat the main ingredients in fat.

3 For a braise, add the main ingredient in a single layer. For a stew, add the ingredients according to their cooking times or as directed in the recipe.

4 Add the cooking liquid; it should partially cover the vegetables. Bring the liquid to a boil, reduce to a simmer, cover and cook in the oven or on the stove top until done.

5 If desired, remove the main ingredients from the pan and reduce the sauce or thicken it with beurre manié, cornstarch or arrowroot. Then return the main ingredients to the sauce.

RECIPE 22.8   **BRAISED CELERY WITH BASIL**

Yield: 12 Servings, 3 oz. (90 g) each	**Method:** Braising	
Celery heads	3	3
Onions, small dice	8 oz.	250 g
Garlic, minced	2 tsp.	10 ml
Whole butter	2 oz.	60 g
Olive oil	1 fl. oz.	30 ml
Fresh thyme	1 tsp.	5 ml
Fresh basil leaves, chiffonade	20	20
Dry white wine	8 fl. oz.	250 ml
Chicken stock	1 pt.	500 ml
Salt and pepper	TT	TT

1 Trim the outer ribs from the celery heads, leaving only the tender hearts. Trim the heads to 6-inch (15-centimeter) lengths. Trim the root slightly, leaving each head together. Cut each head lengthwise into quarters.

2 Sauté the onions and garlic in the butter and olive oil, without coloring, until tender. Add the celery quarters to the pan and sauté, turning occasionally.

3 Add the thyme, basil, wine and chicken stock. Bring to a boil, reduce to a simmer, cover and braise in the oven at 350°F (180°C) until tender, approximately 1 hour.

4 Remove the celery and reserve. Reduce the cooking liquid on the stove top until it thickens. Adjust the liquid's seasonings and return the celery to the pan to reheat. Serve the celery with a portion of the sauce.

Approximate values per 3-oz. (90-g) serving: **Calories** 60, **Total fat** 4.5 g, **Saturated fat** 1.5 g, **Cholesterol** 5 mg, **Sodium** 170 mg, **Total carbohydrates** 2 g, **Protein** 1 g

1 Trimming and cutting the celery.

2 Adding the liquid to the celery.

3 Reducing the sauce.

MICROWAVING

Fresh vegetables are among the few foods that can be consistently well prepared in a microwave oven. Often microwave cooking can be accomplished without any additional liquid, thus preserving nutrients. With microwaving, colors and flavors stay true, and textures remain crisp.

Microwave cooking is actually a form of steaming. As explained in Chapter 10, Principles of Cooking, microwaves agitate water molecules, thus creating steam. The water may be the moisture found naturally in the food or may be added specifically to create the steam.

Cooking time depends on the type of microwave oven as well as on the freshness, moisture content, maturity and quantity of vegetables being prepared.

Selecting and Preparing Vegetables to Microwave

Any vegetable that can be steamed successfully can be microwaved with good results. Because typical microwave ovens are relatively small, they are impractical for producing large quantities of food. They are most useful for reheating small portions of vegetables that have been blanched or partially cooked using another cooking method.

Seasoning Vegetables to Be Microwaved

Microwaving, like steaming, brings out the natural flavors of food. Herbs and spices can be added to the vegetables before they are microwaved. Or, after microwaving, the vegetables can be tossed with butter, herbs and spices or combined with a sauce.

▶ PROCEDURE FOR MICROWAVING VEGETABLES

1 Wash, peel, trim and cut the vegetables into uniform shapes and sizes.

2 Place the vegetables in a steamer designed for microwave use or arrange the vegetables in a microwavable dish. Cover the vegetables with the lid or plastic wrap. If using plastic wrap, it should be punctured to allow some steam to escape during cooking.

3 Cook the vegetables to the desired doneness, allowing for some carryover cooking, or reheat the previously cooked vegetables until hot. Stir or turn the vegetables as necessary to promote even cooking.

4 Serve the vegetables or refresh and refrigerate until needed.

PURÉEING

Puréeing is a technique often used with vegetables. Cooked vegetable purées can be served as is, or they can be used as an ingredient in other preparations such as pumpkin pie, mashed potatoes or vegetable soufflés. Purées can also be bound with eggs, seasoned and used to make vegetable timbales and terrines.

Puréed vegetables are generally first cooked by baking, boiling, steaming or microwaving. White, red and yellow vegetables should be cooked until quite soft. They are more easily puréed when hot or warm; this also helps ensure a smooth finished purée. For most preparations, green vegetables must be refreshed after cooking and puréed while cold, or they will overcook and become discolored.

Seasoning Vegetables to Be Puréed

Vegetables for purées can be seasoned before they are puréed following the guidelines for the cooking procedure used. They can also be seasoned after they are puréed with a wide variety of ingredients such as herbs or spices, cheese, honey or brown sugar.

Finishing Puréed Vegetables

Purées can be finished with stocks, sauces, butter or cream to add richness and flavor. First purée the main ingredient, then add additional liquids to obtain the desired consistency.

▶ PROCEDURE FOR PURÉEING VEGETABLES

1 Cook the vegetables. White, red and yellow vegetables should be cooked until very soft. Green vegetables should be cooked until tender but not overcooked to the point of being discolored.

2 Purée the vegetables in a VCM, food processor or blender or by passing them through a food mill.

3 Season or finish the puréed vegetables as desired or directed in the recipe, or use them in another recipe.

RECIPE 22.9 | **PARSNIP PURÉE**

Yield: 2 qt. (2 lt)	**Method:** Boiling/Puréeing	
Parsnips	4 lb.	1.8 kg
Russet potatoes	1 lb. 8 oz.	650 g
Heavy cream, hot	8 fl. oz.	250 ml
Whole butter, melted	4 oz.	120 g
Salt and white pepper	TT	TT

1 Peel the parsnips and potatoes, and cut into large pieces of approximately the same size.

2 Boil the vegetables separately in salted water until tender.

3 Drain the vegetables well. Purée them together through a food mill.

1 Passing the parsnips and potatoes through a food mill.

2 The finished Parsnip Purée.

4 Add the cream and butter and mix to combine. Adjust the consistency by adding cream as desired. Season the mixture with salt and white pepper and serve hot.

Variations: *Turnip Purée*—Substitute turnips for the parsnips. *Winter Squash Purée*—Select approximately 6½ pounds (3 kilograms) of winter squash (e.g. acorn, butternut, pumpkin) and cut them in halves or quarters. Scoop out the seeds, then roast the squash, cut side down, in a 375°F (190°C) oven until tender. Scoop the flesh from the shells and substitute it for the parsnips.

Approximate values per ½-c. (120-ml) serving: **Calories** 240, **Total fat** 12 g, **Saturated fat** 7 g, **Cholesterol** 35 mg, **Sodium** 220 mg, **Total carbohydrates** 31 g, **Protein** 3 g, **Vitamin A** 10%, **Vitamin C** 35%

CONCLUSION

Vegetables are an essential part of the human diet. They provide the body with vitamins, minerals and fiber and appeal to the appetite with flavor, color and texture. Increasing market availability of fresh, high-quality vegetables as well as new hybrids gives you an ever-increasing variety of vegetables from which to choose. Vegetables are a relatively inexpensive food that can be prepared in limitless ways. They can be served as an entire meal or as an accompaniment to or part of a wide variety of other dishes. And when cooking vegetables, remember what James Beard (1903–1985), the great American food consultant, culinary educator and writer once said: "No vegetable exists which is not better slightly undercooked."

QUESTIONS FOR DISCUSSION

1 Explain how the season affects the price, quality and availability of vegetables.

2 List and describe three processing techniques commonly used to extend the shelf life of vegetables.

3 What special concerns exist regarding the storage of fresh vegetables? Explain why some vegetables should not be refrigerated.

4 Why is it important to cut vegetables into a uniform size before cooking?

5 Discuss several techniques used for determining the doneness of vegetables. Is carryover cooking a concern when preparing vegetables? Explain your answer.

6 Discuss the role of acid in a cooking liquid used for preparing vegetables. Which vegetables, if any, benefit from an acidic cooking environment?

7 Describe the necessary mise en place and procedure for refreshing vegetables.

8 Locate information on farmer's markets in your area. What are the advantages and disadvantages of purchasing vegetables from a local grower?

9 Many people are very concerned about the use of genetically modified organisms (GMO) and bioengineered products in the foods they eat. What is the federal government's position on these foodstuffs? What organizations are working to prohibit the use of GMOs? Why? Do you agree or disagree with their arguments?

SUMMER VEGETABLES
WITH TARRAGON AÏOLI

RECIPE 22.10

Note: This dish appears in the chapter opening photograph.

GREENS, SAN FRANCISCO, CA
Chef Annie Somerville

Yield: 6 Servings   **Method:** Boiling

Baby artichokes	6	6
Carrots	8 oz.	250 g
Yellow or green zucchini	1 lb.	500 g
Sunburst squash	1 lb.	500 g
Blue lake green beans	8 oz.	250 g
Yellow wax beans	8 oz.	250 g
Broccoli florets	1 lb.	500 g
Cauliflower florets	1 lb.	500 g
Red radishes	1 bunch	1 bunch
Cherry tomatoes	½ pt.	250 ml
Niçoise or Gaeta olives	8 oz.	250 g
Tarragon Aïoli (recipe follows)	8 oz.	250 g

1 Trim the artichokes. Steam or boil them until tender; refresh.
2 Cut the carrots, zucchini and squash as desired. Snip the ends from the beans. Parboil the vegetables (except the radishes, tomatoes and olives), one variety at a time, in salted water until nearly tender but still crisp. Refresh each and drain well.
3 Wash the radishes. Trim the root end but leave the green tops attached.
4 Wash the cherry tomatoes and remove the stems.
5 Loosely arrange the vegetables on a platter, leaving room for the aïoli unless it is to be served separately in a small bowl.

TARRAGON AÏOLI

Yield: ½ pt. (250 ml)

Egg yolk, large	1	1
Fresh lemon juice	1 Tbsp.	15 ml
Light olive oil	8 fl. oz.	250 ml
Garlic clove, chopped	1	1
Champagne vinegar	1 tsp.	5 ml
Fresh tarragon, chopped	2 tsp.	10 ml
Salt	TT	TT

1 Whisk the yolk and ½ teaspoon (3 milliliters) of lemon juice together until smooth.
2 Whisk in the oil, very slowly at first, until the aïoli begins to emulsify. Add a few drops of lemon juice as necessary to thin the sauce. Continue until all the oil and lemon juice have been incorporated.
3 Season with the garlic, vinegar, tarragon and salt. If the aïoli is too thick, thin it with a little warm water.

Approximate values per serving: **Calories** 470, **Total fat** 35 g, **Saturated fat** 5 g, **Cholesterol** 30 mg, **Sodium** 770 mg, **Total carbohydrates** 29 g, **Protein** 8 g, **Vitamin A** 120%, **Vitamin C** 150%

CHEF ANNIE SOMERVILLE

The inspiration for Greens, one of the fore-most vegetarian restaurants in America, was the renowned vegetarian kitchen at the Tassajara Zen Mountain Center in Carmel Valley, California, where Chef Annie Somerville also received her culinary foundation. Opened in San Francisco in 1979, Greens features creative vegetarian cuisine using the finest seasonal organic produce and other high-quality ingredients. It maintains a close relationship with its purveyors, especially the Zen Center's Green Gulch Farm and Star Route Farms in Bolinas.

At Greens, Chef Somerville creates a new menu daily, sometimes drawing from a repertoire of dishes, many of which are influenced by the cuisines of the Mediterranean, Mexico and the American Southwest. She tries to create dishes that balance and contrast colors, flavors and textures and have simple yet stylish presentations. Chef Somerville notes that "We keep changing and evolving, noting what other cooks are doing around the world, but always keeping the focus on what is seasonal."

RECIPE 22.11

BROILED TOMATO

RUTH'S CHRIS STEAK HOUSE, PHOENIX, AZ

Yield: 1 Serving		**Method:** Broiling
Tomato, large	1	1
Granulated sugar	2 tsp.	10 ml
Whole butter, melted	1 oz.	30 g
Fresh parsley, chopped	1 Tbsp.	15 ml

1 Core and halve the tomato.
2 Sprinkle sugar on top of each half. Place on a broiler platter and broil until tender.
3 Drizzle with butter and garnish with parsley.

Approximate values per serving: **Calories** 170, **Total fat** 12 g, **Saturated fat** 7 g, **Cholesterol** 30 mg, **Sodium** 130 mg, **Total carbohydrates** 14 g, **Protein** 1 g, **Vitamin A** 20%, **Vitamin C** 40%

RECIPE 22.12

GRILLED PORTABELLA MUSHROOMS

Yield: 3 Servings, 4 oz. (120 g) each		**Method:** Grilling
Portabella mushrooms caps	1 lb.	500 g
Olive oil	1 Tbsp.	15 ml
Garlic, chopped	1 tsp.	5 ml
Salt and pepper	TT	TT
Fresh thyme	1 tsp.	5 ml

1 Wipe the mushroom caps clean with a damp towel.
2 Combine the olive oil and garlic and brush the mixture on the mushroom caps.
3 Season the mushrooms with salt, pepper and thyme.
4 Grill or broil the mushrooms until tender, approximately 8 minutes, depending on the size of the caps.

Approximately values per 4-oz. (120-g) serving: **Calories** 140, **Total fat** 10 g, **Saturated fat** 1.5 g, **Cholesterol** 0 mg, **Sodium** 790 mg, **Total carbohydrates** 8 g, **Protein** 6 g, **Claims**—no cholesterol; high fiber

RECIPE 22.13

GRILLED BABY SQUASH WITH HONEY CARDAMOM BUTTER

SENCHA, COLORADO SPRINGS, CO

Chef Brent Beavers

Yield: 6 Servings		**Method:** Grilling
Baby pattypan squash, yellow, green and white	30	30
Vegetable oil	as needed	as needed
Black pepper	TT	TT
Honey Cardamom Butter (recipe follows)	6 oz.	180 g

1 If some of the squash are large, cut them in halves or quarters so they will cook uniformly.
2 Brush the squash with oil and season them with pepper.

3 Drain any excess oil from the squash, then cook on a hot grill until they begin to brown and are tender, approximately 6 to 8 minutes.

4 Remove from the grill and arrange on hot plates. Top each serving of squash with 1 to 2 tablespoons (15 to 30 milliliters) of Honey Cardamom Butter.

Approximate values per serving: **Calories** 230, **Total fat** 23 g, **Saturated fat** 14 g, **Cholesterol** 60 mg, **Sodium** 150 mg, **Total carbohydrates** 6 g, **Protein** 3 g, **Vitamin A** 25%, **Vitamin C** 45%

HONEY CARDAMOM BUTTER

Yield: 1 lb. (450 g)

Whole butter	1 lb.	450 g
Cardamom	2 Tbsp.	30 ml
Kosher salt	1 tsp.	5 ml
Black pepper	1 tsp.	5 ml
Honey	2 fl. oz.	60 ml

1 In a sauté pan, heat the butter until it begins to brown. Add the cardamom, salt and pepper. Remove from the heat and add the honey.

2 Cool the mixture at room temperature until it begins to solidify. Transfer to the bowl of a small mixer and whip until it emulsifies. Transfer to a piece of parchment paper or plastic and form into a log. Refrigerate until ready to use.

Approximate values per 1-oz. (30-g) serving: **Calories** 220, **Total fat** 23 g, **Saturated fat** 14 g, **Cholesterol** 60 mg, **Sodium** 150 mg, **Total carbohydrates** 4 g, **Protein** 0, **Vitamin A** 15%

ARIZONA BAKED CORN   RECIPE 22.14

NEWBURY COLLEGE, Brookline, MA
Senior Instructor Scott Doughty

Yield: 8 Servings   **Method:** Baking

Onions, minced	1 pt.	450 ml
Vegetable oil	1 fl. oz.	30 ml
Celery, minced	2 Tbsp.	30 ml
Chilli powder	5 Tbsp.	75 ml
Chipotle peppers, canned, seeded and minced	5 tsp.	25 ml
Tomato sauce, canned	6 fl. oz.	180 ml
Chicken stock, hot	8 fl. oz.	225 ml
Fresh corn kernels	3 lb.	1.4 kg
Salt	¾ tsp.	4 ml
Monterey Jack, grated	4 oz.	120 g

1 Sweat the onions in the vegetable oil for 8 minutes without browning. Add the celery and cook for an additional 2 minutes.

2 Stir in the chilli powder, chipotle peppers, tomato sauce, stock, corn and salt.

3 Pour the mixture into a buttered 2-inch- (5-centimeter-) deep one-third-size hotel pan. Cover and bake at 350°F (180°C) for 1 hour 15 minutes. Uncover, spread the grated cheese over the top and return to the oven until the cheese melts and begins to brown.

Approximate values per serving: **Calories** 310, **Total fat** 11 g, **Saturated fat** 3.5 g, **Cholesterol** 15 mg, **Sodium** 600 mg, **Total carbohydrates** 51 g, **Protein** 11 g, **Vitamin A** 40%, **Vitamin C** 35%, **Calcium** 15%, **Iron** 10%, **Claims**—high in vitamins A and C; source of calcium and iron

RECIPE 22.15

BAKED BEANS

Note: This dish appears in the Chapter 17 opening photograph.

Yield: 1½ qt. (1.5 lt)   **Method:** Baking

Great Northern beans, soaked	1 lb.	450 g
Onions, small dice	4 oz.	120 g
Anaheim chile, small dice	1 oz.	30 g
Molasses	3 oz.	90 g
Brown sugar	3 oz.	90 g
Catsup	8 oz.	250 g
Prepared mustard	2 Tbsp.	30 ml
Cider vinegar	1 Tbsp.	15 ml
Worcestershire sauce	2 Tbsp.	30 ml
Tabasco sauce	TT	TT
Salt and pepper	TT	TT

1 Simmer the beans in water until almost tender, approximately 45 minutes. Drain well.
2 Combine the remaining ingredients, blending well.
3 Add the sauce to the beans, tossing to coat thoroughly. Adjust the seasonings.
4 Place the beans in a hotel pan or a 2-quart (2-liter) baking dish. Cover and bake in a 350°F (180°C) oven until the beans are completely tender, approximately 30 to 40 minutes.

Approximate values per 3-oz. (90-g) serving: **Calories** 120, **Total fat** 0 g, **Saturated fat** 0 g, **Cholesterol** 0 mg, **Sodium** 490 mg, **Total carbohydrates** 26 g, **Protein** 4 g, **Vitamin C** 15%, **Claims**—fat free; good source of fiber

RECIPE 22.16

GARLIC TIMBALES

Yield: 8 Timbales, 2 oz. (60 ml) each   **Method:** Baking

Garlic cloves, peeled	10	10
Milk	3 fl. oz.	90 ml
Heavy cream	8 fl. oz.	250 ml
Eggs	2	2
Dried thyme	1 tsp.	5 ml
Salt and pepper	TT	TT

1 Butter eight small ramekins or timbales.
2 Place the garlic in a small saucepan, add enough water to cover and bring to a boil. Drain. Repeat this blanching procedure two more times.
3 Place the garlic in a blender with the milk and blend. Add the cream, eggs and thyme; blend until smooth. Season with salt and pepper.
4 Divide the custard among the timbales and place in a water bath. Bake for 30 to 45 minutes at 325°F (160°C).
5 Run a paring knife around the rim and unmold onto the serving plate.

Variations: *Broccoli or Cauliflower Timbales*—Place 1 ounce (30 grams) of blanched broccoli or cauliflower in each buttered timbale before adding the garlic custard mixture.

Approximate values per 2-oz. (60-g) serving: **Calories** 130, **Total fat** 12 g, **Saturated fat** 7 g, **Cholesterol** 95 mg, **Sodium** 320 mg, **Total carbohydrates** 3 g, **Protein** 3 g, **Vitamin A** 15%

MUSHROOM AND MANCHEGO TIMBALES

RECIPE 22.17

Yield: 12 Timbales, 2½ fl. oz. (70 ml) each   **Method:** Sautéing/Baking

Whole butter	1 oz.	30 g
Shallots, minced	4	4
Mushrooms, chopped fine	4 oz.	120 g
Heavy cream	10 fl. oz.	300 ml
Large eggs	3	3
Salt	½ tsp.	3 ml
Paprika	¼ tsp.	1 ml
Nutmeg	⅛ tsp.	0.5 ml
Spanish Manchego cheese, grated	2 c.	470 ml

1 Melt the butter in a sauté pan and cook the shallots and mushrooms until tender and just beginning to brown, approximately 5 minutes.

2 Beat together the cream, eggs, salt, paprika and nutmeg in a large bowl. Stir in the cheese and the sautéed mushrooms and shallots.

3 Coat 12 small ramekins with clarified butter. Spoon the custard into the ramekins.

4 Place the ramekins in a baking pan and place on the shelf of a preheated 325°F (160°C) oven. Pour hot water into the baking pan so that the water reaches halfway up the sides of the ramekins. Bake for 30 minutes or until a knife inserted in the custard comes out clean.

5 Allow the custards to sit for approximately 5 minutes, then unmold and serve warm.

6 The timbales can be made in advance and then reheated by covering the ramekins with aluminum foil and returning them to a hot water bath for approximately 10 minutes.

Approximate values per timbale: **Calories** 200, **Total fat** 19 g, **Saturated fat** 11 g, **Cholesterol** 110 mg, **Sodium** 240 mg, **Total carbohydrates** 2 g, **Protein** 7 g, **Vitamin A** 15%, **Calcium** 15%

ROASTED TOMATO, ONION AND GOAT CHEESE FRITTATINI

RECIPE 22.18

Yield: 24 Servings   **Method:** Baking

Roma tomatoes	4	4
Salt and pepper	TT	TT
Extra virgin olive oil	4 Tbsp.	60 ml
Vegetable shortening	as needed	as needed
Red onion, finely diced	½	½
Eggs	5	5
Milk	2 fl. oz.	60 ml
Parmesan, grated	3 Tbsp.	45 ml
Fresh basil leaves, chopped	1 Tbsp.	15 ml
Goat cheese, crumbled	2 oz.	60 g

1 Quarter the tomatoes and squeeze out the excess juice. Toss the tomatoes with salt, pepper and a small amount of the olive oil. Spread them on a sheet pan and roast in a 350°F (180°C) oven for 20 minutes. Allow the tomatoes to cool, then chop coarsely.

2 Brush 24 muffin cups well with the vegetable shortening.

3 Heat the remaining olive oil in a small sauté pan. Add the onion and cook until translucent but not brown. Remove from the heat and cool to room temperature.

4 In a medium bowl, beat the eggs. Beat in the milk, then add the parmesan, onion, chopped basil, goat cheese and tomatoes. Season with salt and pepper and stir well.

5 Fill the prepared muffin tins one-third full with the mixture. Bake at 350°F (180°C) until the frittatini are golden and feel firm to the touch. Cool slightly, carefully unmold and serve warm.

6 As a first course, serve one frittatini per person garnished with fresh basil leaves and accompanied by approximately ¼ cup (60 milliliters) of dressed mesclun salad. Serve two per person for a main course, or present the frittatini on a decorative serving platter for a buffet.

Approximate values per frittatini: **Calories** 50, **Total fat** 4 g, **Saturated fat** 1 g, **Cholesterol** 45 mg, **Sodium** 40 mg, **Total carbohydrates** 1 g, **Protein** 2 g

---

RECIPE 22.19   STUFFED CUBANELLE PEPPERS

SOUTHERN NEW HAMPSHIRE UNIVERSITY, MANCHESTER, NH

John C. Knorr

Yield: 12 Peppers		**Method:** Blanching/Baking
Cubanelle peppers	12	12
Chicken breasts, boneless, skinless	24 oz.	680 g
Salt and pepper	TT	TT
Vegetable oil	2 tsp.	10 ml
Cream cheese, soft	12 oz.	340 g
Salsa	2½ pt.	1.2 lt
Monterey Jack, shredded	12 oz.	340 g

1 Cut ½ inch (1.5 centimeters) from the top of each pepper and reserve the tops. Remove the membranes and seeds from the body and blanch in boiling water for 30 seconds. Remove from the water, drain and cool.

2 Season the chicken breasts with salt and pepper. Brush them with vegetable oil and grill until done. Cool the chicken and slice into thin strips.

3 Combine the chicken, cream cheese and 1¼ cups (300 milliliters) of the salsa in a small mixer. Season with salt and pepper and mix well but do not purée.

4 Fill the peppers with the chicken mixture and replace the tops. Place the peppers in a baking dish and cover with the remaining salsa and shredded cheese. Bake the peppers at 375°F (190°C) until hot, approximately 30 minutes.

Note: If Cubanelle peppers are not available, fresh de agua, pimento (*chile pimiento*) or small poblano chiles can be substituted.

Approximate values per serving: **Calories** 320, **Total fat** 21 g, **Saturated fat** 12 g, **Cholesterol** 90 mg, **Sodium** 730 mg, **Total carbohydrates** 12 g, **Protein** 23 g, **Vitamin A** 35%, **Vitamin C** 140%, **Calcium** 30%, **Iron** 15%

SCALLOPED EGGPLANT

RECIPE 22.20

NEWBURY COLLEGE, Brookline, MA
Senior Instructor Scott Doughty

Yield: 8 Servings   **Method:** Sautéing/Baking

Green bell peppers, small dice	2 oz.	60 g
Onions, small dice	2 oz.	60 g
Butter	2 oz.	60 g
Eggplants, peeled, medium dice	2	2
Tomato concassée	2 lb.	900 g
Salt	1½ tsp.	8 ml
Black pepper	¼ tsp.	2 ml
Fresh bread crumbs, crustless	6 oz.	180 g
Clarified butter	1 fl. oz.	30 ml

1 Sauté the bell peppers and onions in the butter until slightly browned. Add the eggplant, tomatoes concassée, salt and pepper. Cook gently for 10 minutes. Transfer to a 2-inch- (5-centimeter-) deep one-third-size hotel pan.

2 Combine the bread crumbs with the clarified butter and spread over the top of the eggplant.

3 Bake at 375°F (190°C) until the eggplant is tender and the bread crumbs are browned, approximately 30 to 40 minutes.

Approximate values per serving: **Calories** 190, **Total fat** 10 g, **Saturated fat** 6 g, **Cholesterol** 25 mg, **Sodium** 560 mg, **Total carbohydrates** 24 g, **Protein** 4 g, **Vitamin A** 25%, **Vitamin C** 50%

DUXELLES

RECIPE 22.21

Yield: 12 oz. (350 g)   **Method:** Sautéing

Mushrooms	1 lb.	500 g
Shallots, minced	2 Tbsp.	30 ml
Garlic, chopped	1 tsp.	5 ml
Whole butter	1 Tbsp.	15 ml
Salt and pepper	TT	TT
Fresh parsley, chopped	1 Tbsp.	15 ml

1 Sautéing the mushrooms and shallots.

2 The finished duxelles.

1 Chop the mushrooms very finely.

2 Sauté the shallots and garlic in the butter until tender. Add the mushrooms and sauté until dry.

3 Season with salt and pepper and add the parsley. Cool and then use the duxelles as a stuffing for vegetables or as a flavoring ingredient in other recipes.

Approximate values per 1-oz. (30-g) serving: **Calories** 20, **Total fat** 1 g, **Saturated fat** 0.5 g, **Cholesterol** 5 mg, **Sodium** 210 mg, **Total carbohydrates** 2 g, **Protein** 1 g, **Claims**—low fat; low cholesterol; low calorie

---

RECIPE 22.22

MAPLE-GLAZED CARROTS

Yield: 16 Servings, 4 oz. (120 g) each   **Method:** Sautéing

Carrots	4 lb.	1.8 kg
Whole butter	4 oz.	120 g
Salt and pepper	TT	TT
Maple syrup	4 fl. oz.	120 ml
Fresh parsley, chopped	2 Tbsp.	30 ml

1 Peel the carrots and cut into a shape such as oblique, tourné or rondelle.

2 Parboil the carrots in salt water and refresh. The carrots should be very firm.

3 Sauté the carrots in the butter until nearly tender.

4 Season with salt and pepper, and add the maple syrup. Cook briefly, tossing the carrots so that they are coated with the maple syrup. Garnish with the parsley.

Approximate values per 4-oz. (120-g) serving: **Calories** 120, **Total fat** 6 g, **Saturated fat** 3.5 g, **Cholesterol** 15 mg, **Sodium** 260 mg, **Total carbohydrates** 16 g, **Protein** 1 g, **Vitamin A** 220%, **Vitamin C** 15%

RECIPE 22.23

CREAMED CORN WITH BASIL

Yield: 10 Servings, 4 oz. (120 g) each   **Method:** Sautéing

Corn	12 ears	12 ears
Onion, small dice	4 oz.	120 g
Whole butter	2 oz.	60 g
Heavy cream	8 fl. oz.	250 ml
Fresh basil leaves, chopped	2 Tbsp.	30 ml
Salt and white pepper	TT	TT

1 Cut the kernels from the ears.

2 Sauté the onion in the butter without browning.

3 Add the corn and sauté until hot.

4 Add the cream. Bring to a boil and reduce slightly. Add the basil and season with salt and white pepper.

Approximate values per 4-oz. (120-g) serving: **Calories** 210, **Total fat** 14 g, **Saturated fat** 8 g, **Cholesterol** 45 mg, **Sodium** 290 mg, **Total carbohydrates** 19 g, **Protein** 3 g, **Vitamin A** 15%

1 Sautéing the onions and garlic.

2 Adding the peppers, eggplant and zucchini.

3 The finished ratatouille.

RATATOUILLE

RECIPE 22.24

Yield: 16 Servings, 4 oz. (120 g) each   **Method:** Sautéing

Onion, medium dice	12 oz.	360 g
Garlic, chopped	1 Tbsp.	15 ml
Olive oil	4 fl. oz.	120 ml
Green bell pepper, medium dice	6 oz.	180 g
Red bell pepper, medium dice	6 oz.	180 g
Eggplant, medium dice	12 oz.	360 g
Zucchini, medium dice	8 oz.	250 g
Tomato concassée	24 oz.	620 g
Fresh basil leaves, chiffonade	1 oz.	30 g
Salt	1 oz.	30 g
Black pepper	TT	TT

1   Sauté the onion and garlic in the olive oil.
2   Add the bell peppers, eggplant and zucchini and sauté until tender, approximately 10 minutes.
3   Add the tomato concassée, basil and seasonings. Sauté for 5 minutes. Adjust the seasonings.

Approximate values per 4-oz. (120-g) serving: **Calories** 90, **Total fat** 7 g, **Saturated fat** 1 g, **Cholesterol** 0 mg, **Sodium** 690 mg, **Total carbohydrates** 6 g, **Protein** 1 g, **Vitamin C** 35%, **Claims**—low saturated fat; no cholesterol

BEET AND CORN SALAD

RECIPE 22.25

PRIMITIVO WINE BAR, COLORADO SPRINGS, CO
John Broening, Executive Chef

Yield: 8 Servings   **Method:** Boiling

Dressing:		
Fresh lime juice	2 fl. oz.	60 ml
Granulated sugar	2 tsp.	10 ml
Salt and pepper	TT	TT
Extra virgin olive oil	4 fl. oz.	120 ml
Corn oil	4 fl. oz.	120 ml

Continued

Beets, small, red, gold or candy stripe	1 lb.	450 g
Salt	TT	TT
Ears of corn, silk removed	6	6
Green onion, minced	1	1
Fresh cilantro leaves	¼ c.	60 ml
Goat cheese, crumbled	4 oz.	120 g
Black pepper	TT	TT
Arugula	1 bunch	1 bunch

1 To make the dressing, whisk together the lime juice, sugar, salt and pepper. Slowly whisk in the oils to emulsify.

2 Boil the beets in salted water until tender, approximately 15 minutes. Drain, cool, peel, dice and reserve.

3 Boil the ears of corn in salted water until tender, approximately 3 minutes. Drain, cool, cut the kernels from the cobs and reserve.

4 In a stainless steel bowl, mix together the beets, corn, green onion, cilantro and goat cheese. Toss with the dressing and adjust the seasoning with salt and pepper. Garnish with the arugula and serve.

Approximate values per serving: **Calories** 370, **Total fat** 31 g, **Saturated fat** 6 g, **Cholesterol** 5 mg, **Sodium** 110 mg, **Total carbohydrates** 21 g, **Protein** 6 g, **Vitamin A** 15%, **Vitamin C** 20%

RECIPE 22.26   **PEAS WITH FENNEL AND BACON**

Yield: 1 lb. 8 oz. (680 g)   **Method:** Sautéing/Simmering

Olive oil	4 Tbsp.	60 ml
Garlic clove, minced	1	1
Onion, small dice	4 oz.	120 g
Fennel bulb, small dice	6 oz.	180 g
Bacon, blanched, small dice	4 oz.	120 g
Peas, fresh or frozen	1½ lb.	700 g
Salt and pepper	TT	TT
Chicken stock	4 fl. oz.	120 ml

1 Heat the olive oil in a medium sauté pan. Add the garlic, onion and fennel. Sauté until the vegetables are soft. Add the bacon and sauté for 3 minutes. Add the peas and mix well. Season with salt and pepper.

2 Add the chicken stock and cook over low heat until almost no liquid remains and the peas are tender. Adjust the seasonings and serve hot.

Approximate values per 4-oz. (120-g) serving: **Calories** 220, **Total fat** 12 g, **Saturated fat** 2.5 g, **Cholesterol** 5 mg, **Sodium** 8 mg, **Total carbohydrates** 20 g, **Protein** 8 g, **Vitamin A** 15%, **Vitamin C** 35%, **Iron** 10%

RECIPE 22.27   **WOK VEGETABLES**

FLYING FISH, Seattle, WA
Chef-Owner Christine Keff

Yield: 6 Servings   **Method:** Sautéing

Green cabbage	½ head	½ head
Zucchini	1	1
Yellow squash	1	1
Peanut oil	1 Tbsp.	15 ml
Fresh ginger, 1-in. (2.5-cm) piece, peeled and chopped fine	1	1
Garlic cloves, chopped fine	2	2

Fresh cilantro, chopped coarse	2 oz.	60 g
Peanuts, roasted, unsalted, chopped	2 Tbsp.	30 ml
Sesame oil	1 Tbsp.	15 ml
Sesame seeds	1 tsp.	5 ml
Soy sauce	2 Tbsp.	30 ml
Fresh lime juice	2 Tbsp.	30 ml
Mirin	2 Tbsp.	30 ml
Rice wine vinegar	2 Tbsp.	30 ml
Salt and pepper	TT	TT

1 Core the cabbage and cut into a rough julienne.
2 Grate the outside of the zucchini and the yellow squash, discarding the inner seeds.
3 Heat the peanut oil in a wok or large skillet over high heat. Add the ginger, garlic, cabbage, squashes, cilantro, peanuts, sesame oil and sesame seeds. Cook, tossing frequently, until the vegetables begin to wilt.
4 Deglaze the pan with soy sauce, lime juice, mirin and vinegar. Season to taste with salt and pepper.

Approximate values per 6-oz. (180-g) serving: **Calories** 114, **Total fat** 7 g, **Saturated fat** 1 g, **Cholesterol** 0 mg, **Sodium** 443 mg, **Total carbohydrates** 12 g, **Protein** 3 g, **Claims**–low saturated fat no cholesterol good source of fiber

STIR-FRIED SNOW PEAS

RECIPE 22.28

Yield: 6 Servings, 3 oz. (90 g) each   **Method:** Sautéing

Snow peas	1 lb.	500 g
Garlic, chopped	2 tsp.	10 ml
Vegetable oil	2 fl. oz.	60 ml
Sesame oil	1 tsp.	5 ml
Water chestnuts, sliced	4 oz.	120 g
Salt	TT	TT

1 Snap the snow peas and remove the strings.
2 Blanch the snow peas and refresh.
3 Stir-fry the garlic in the vegetable and sesame oils for 10 seconds. Add the water chestnuts.
4 Add the snow peas and stir-fry until tender, approximately 1 minute. Season to taste with salt.

Approximate values per 3-oz. (90-g) serving: **Calories** 130, **Total fat** 10 g, **Saturated fat** 1.5 g, **Cholesterol** 0 mg, **Sodium** 0 mg, **Total carbohydrates** 8 g, **Protein** 2 g, **Vitamin C** 80%

SPICED BEAN CURD

RECIPE 22.29

Yield: 4 Servings, 4 fl. oz. (120 ml) each   **Method:** Sautéing

Soy sauce, dark	2 Tbsp.	30 ml
Rice wine	1 Tbsp.	15 ml
Peanut butter	1 oz.	30 g
Brown sugar	1 tsp.	5 ml
Asian-style hot sauce	1 tsp.	5 ml
Bean curd (tofu), firm	1 lb.	450 g
Sesame oil	2 fl. oz.	60 ml

Continued

Fresh ginger, minced	1 Tbsp.	15 ml
Garlic, finely minced	1 Tbsp.	15 ml
Bean sprouts, washed and drained	1 pt.	450 ml
Green onions, sliced	3	3
Peanuts, chopped	3 Tbsp.	50 ml

1 In a small bowl combine the soy sauce, rice wine, peanut butter, brown sugar and hot sauce. Mix well and set aside.

2 Cut the bean curd into medium dice. Heat a wok or sauté pan, add the sesame oil and the bean curd and stir-fry until the curd begins to brown, approximately 5 minutes. Gently remove the bean curd from the wok or sauté pan and hold in a warm place.

3 In the same pan, stir-fry the ginger and garlic until they start to brown. Add the soy sauce and rice wine mixture to the pan.

4 Return the bean curd to the pan. Add the bean sprouts and green onions and stir-fry just long enough to coat everything with the sauce. Garnish with peanuts and serve.

Approximate values per serving: **Calories** 320, **Total fat** 26 g, **Saturated fat** 4 g, **Cholesterol** 0 mg, **Sodium** 560 mg, **Total carbohydrates** 12 g, **Protein** 15 g, **Vitamin C** 15%, **Calcium** 20%, **Iron** 15%, **Claims**—good source of fiber, vitamin C, calcium and iron

RECIPE 22.30

PAN-FRIED EGGPLANT WITH TOMATO SAUCE

NEWBURY COLLEGE, BROOKLINE, MA

Senior Instructor Scott Doughty

Yield: 8 Servings　　　　　　　　　**Method:** Pan-frying

Eggplant, large	1	1
Tomato sauce	1 pt.	450 ml
Flour	4 oz.	120 g
Salt	as needed	as needed
White pepper	1 tsp.	5 ml
Egg wash	1 c.	240 ml
Fresh bread crumbs, crustless	8 oz.	240 g
Vegetable oil	as needed	as needed

1 Trim the ends from the eggplant. Remove strips of peel, lengthwise, with a chef's knife, leaving narrow strips of peel between the cuts. Cut into round slices 1/4 inch (6 millimeters) thick.

2 Warm the tomato sauce.

3 Season the flour with salt and add the white pepper. Using the standard breading procedure described in Chapter 9, Mise en Place, bread the eggplant slices (finishing with the bread crumbs) and arrange them in a single layer on a sheet pan. Separate the layers with parchment.

4 Heat two sautoirs and add a 1/4-inch (6-millimeter) layer of oil in each. When the oil is hot, pan-fry the eggplant slices until golden brown, then turn and cook until tender. Remove and drain on a rack. Repeat until all the slices are cooked, adding more oil as necessary.

5 Arrange the slices on a large serving platter and ladle the tomato sauce attractively over the eggplant.

Approximate values per serving: **Calories** 220, **Total fat** 10 g, **Saturated fat** 1.5 g, **Cholesterol** 55 mg, **Sodium** 530 mg, **Total carbohydrates** 29 g, **Protein** 6 g, **Vitamin A** 15%, **Vitamin C** 15%, **Iron** 10%

TEMPURA VEGETABLES
WITH DIPPING SAUCE

RECIPE 22.31

Yield: 1 qt. (1 lt) of batter,
enough for 4 lb. (1.8 kg) of vegetables   **Method:** Deep-frying

Dipping sauce:		
Mirin	2 fl. oz.	60 ml
Soy sauce	4 fl. oz.	120 ml
Rice wine vinegar	2 fl. oz.	60 ml
Lemon juice	1 Tbsp.	15 ml
Wasabi powder	1 tsp.	5 ml
Tempura batter:		
Eggs	2	2
Sparkling water, cold	1 pt.	500 ml
Flour	10 oz.	300 g
Sweet potato, approx. 8 oz. (250 g)	1	1
Broccoli florets	8 oz.	250 g
Mushrooms, small, whole	1 lb.	450 g
Zucchini, batonnet	8 oz.	250 g

1 Combine all of the dipping sauce ingredients. Set aside.

2 To prepare the batter, beat the eggs and add the cold water.

3 Add the flour to the egg-and-water mixture and mix until the flour is incorporated. There should still be small lumps in the batter. Overmixing develops gluten, which is undesirable.

4 Peel the sweet potato and cut it into ¼-inch- (6-millimeter-) thick slices. If the potato is large, cut each slice in half to make semicircles.

5 Blanch the broccoli florets briefly in boiling water. Drain and pat dry with paper towels.

6 Drop the vegetables in the batter a few at a time. Remove them from the batter one at a time and drop them into the deep-fryer using the swimming method. Cook until done. Remove and drain.

7 Arrange the tempura vegetables on a serving platter. Serve the dipping sauce on the side.

Approximate values per 4-oz. (120-g) serving: **Calories** 240, **Total fat** 15 g, **Saturated fat** 2.5 g, **Cholesterol** 25 mg, **Sodium** 530 mg, **Total carbohydrates** 22 g, **Protein** 5 g, **Vitamin A** 50%, **Vitamin C** 30%, **Iron** 10%

1 Mixing the tempura batter.

2 Battering the vegetables.

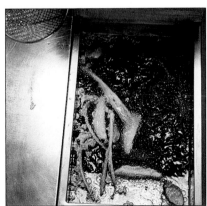

3 Frying the vegetables using the swimming method.

4 Arranging the tempura vegetables for service.

RECIPE 22.32

TUNA-STUFFED CHILE RELLENO WITH SALSA AND TEQUILA MOLE

▶**Cojita (ko-HEE-ta)** an aged, hard, salty Mexican cow's-milk cheese; similar to feta, although not soaked in brine

SENCHA, Colorado Springs, CO
Chef Brent Beavers

Yield: 5 Servings		**Method:** Pan-frying
Poblano chiles	5	5
Fresh tuna, small dice	20 oz.	550 g
Monterey Jack, shredded	10 oz.	300 g
Eggs, separated	7	7
Vegetable oil	as needed	as needed
Flour	as needed for dredging	
Salt and pepper	TT	TT
Rice, cooked	3¾ c.	830 ml
Rellenos Salsa (recipe follows)	1 qt.	1 lt
Cojita	3 oz.	90 g
Tequila Mole (recipe follows)	as needed	as needed

1 Roast the poblanos, then slit them from top to bottom and remove the seeds, keeping the skin intact.
2 Stuff each chile with 4 ounces (120 grams) of tuna and 2 ounces (60 grams) of cheese.
3 Whip the egg whites to soft peaks. Whip the yolks and fold the yolks into the whites until well mixed.
4 Pour vegetable oil into a large heavy saucepan to a depth of ¾ inch (2 centimeters) and heat.
5 Season the flour with salt and pepper. Roll the chiles in the flour and gently dip them into the egg mixture. Immediately fry them until they are golden brown, approximately 6 to 7 minutes.
6 Plate each chile on a mound of rice topped with Rellenos Salsa and crumbled cojita. Using a squirt bottle, add the Tequila Mole.

Approximate values per serving, with salsa: **Calories** 830, **Total fat** 40 g, **Saturated fat** 18 g, **Cholesterol** 415 mg, **Sodium** 1150 mg, **Total carbohydrates** 49 g, **Protein** 72 g, **Vitamin A** 190%, **Vitamin C** 160%, **Calcium** 80%, **Iron** 45%

RELLENOS SALSA

Yield: 1 qt. (1 lt)

Tomatoes	2 lb. 8 oz.	1.1 kg
Onion, peeled, large dice	1	1
Jalapeños	5 oz.	150 g
Garlic cloves	4	4
Fresh basil, chopped	½ c.	120 ml
Fresh tomato juice	1 pt.	450 ml
Salt and pepper	TT	TT

1 Place the tomatoes, onion, jalapeños and garlic in a saucepot and add enough water to cover. Bring to a boil and cook until the onion is tender, approximately 5 minutes.
2 Drain the vegetables. Peel the tomatoes and discard the skin. Remove the stems from the jalapeños and discard. Purée the vegetables in a food processor until very smooth.

3 Return the purée to a saucepan, add the basil and tomato juice and bring to a boil. Season with salt and pepper and hold for service.

Approximate values per ounce (30 g): **Calories** 15, **Total fat** 0 g, **Saturated fat** 0 g, **Cholesterol** 0 mg, **Sodium** 60 mg, **Total carbohydrates** 3 g, **Protein** 1 g, **Vitamin C** 25%

TEQUILA MOLE

Yield: 3 pt. (1.4 lt)

Garlic cloves	3 oz.	90 g
Onions, chopped	2 lb.	900 g
Poblano chiles, chopped	2 lb. 8 oz.	1.1 kg
Olive oil	2 fl. oz.	60 ml
Tequila	2 Tbsp.	30 ml
Chocolate syrup	4 fl. oz.	120 ml
Cocoa powder	2 oz.	60 g
Five-spice powder	3 Tbsp.	45 ml

1 Sweat the garlic, onions and poblanos in the oil until tender. Add the tequila and cook for 1 minute. Add the chocolate syrup and cocoa and mix well. Add the five-spice powder and remove from the heat.

2 Purée in a food processor or blender until very smooth, thinning with a little water if necessary.

Approximate values per ounce (30 g): **Calories** 45, **Total fat** 1.5 g, **Saturated fat** 0 g, **Cholesterol** 0 mg, **Sodium** 0 mg, **Total carbohydrates** 8 g, **Protein** 1 g, **Vitamin C** 100%

SWISS CHARD WITH LEMON AND PINE NUTS

RECIPE 22.33

Yield: 8 Servings, 3-oz. (90 g) each   **Method:** Simmering

Swiss chard, trimmed, stems and leaves separated	2 lb.	1 kg
Water	1 pt.	500 ml
Lemon juice	2 fl. oz.	60 ml
Extra virgin olive oil	2 fl. oz.	60 ml
Salt and pepper	TT	TT
Pine nuts, toasted and chopped	2 oz.	60 g

1 Cut the chard into 1- to 2-inch (2.5- to 5-centimeter) strips on a diagonal.

2 Combine the chard, water and 1 ounce (30 grams) of lemon juice in a nonreactive pan. Simmer until tender, stirring frequently, approximately 10 to 15 minutes.

3 Drain. Toss with the remaining lemon juice and the olive oil. Season with salt and pepper and arrange on plates. Garnish with the pine nuts.

Approximate values per 3-oz. (90-g) serving: **Calories** 220, **Total fat** 12 g, **Saturated fat** 1.5 g, **Cholesterol** 0 mg, **Sodium** 1020 mg, **Total carbohydrates** 19 g, **Protein** 8 g, **Vitamin A** 130%, **Vitamin C** 130%, **Iron** 50%, **Claims**—no cholesterol; high fiber

RECIPE 22.34

COLLARD GREENS

JOLIET JUNIOR COLLEGE, Joliet, IL
Keith G. Vonhoff, CCE, CEPC, CHA, CHE, FMP, CCP

Yield: 8 Servings		**Method:** Simmering
Ham hocks, smoked	6	6
Chile flakes	½ tsp.	3 ml
Water	as needed	as needed
Collard greens	4 lb.	1.8 kg
Green onions, small dice	2	2
Brown sugar	2 tsp.	10 ml
Cider vinegar	2 fl. oz.	60 ml
Salt and pepper	TT	TT

1 In a medium saucepot, combine the ham hocks and chile flakes. Cover with 1 inch (2.5 centimeters) of water, bring to a boil, reduce to a simmer and cook until the hocks are tender, approximately 1 hour. Remove the hocks from the pot, reserving the cooking liquid, which is known as pot liquor.

2 Wash, trim and cut the collard greens. Add them to the pot liquor and simmer until tender, approximately 45 minutes to 1 hour.

3 Add the green onions, sugar and vinegar to the greens. Bring to a simmer and reduce the liquid until it coats the collard greens. Season to taste with salt and pepper.

4 Remove the meat from the ham hocks and cut into a medium dice. Stir the diced ham into the greens and serve.

Approximate values per serving: **Calories** 200, **Total fat** 10 g, **Saturated fat** 3.5 g, **Cholesterol** 40 mg, **Sodium** 60 mg, **Total carbohydrates** 15 g, **Protein** 16 g, **Vitamin A** 170%, **Vitamin C** 80%, **Calcium** 30%, **Iron** 10%

RECIPE 22.35

CALABACITAS

Yield: 1 qt. (1 lt)		**Method:** Simmering
White onion, large, chopped coarse	1	1
Red bell pepper, seeded, chopped fine	½	½
Garlic cloves, minced	2	2
Corn oil	1 Tbsp.	15 ml
Corn kernels	8 oz.	250 g
Yellow squash, chopped	1 lb.	500 g
Zucchini, chopped	1 lb.	500 g
Anaheim chiles, roasted, peeled, seeded and diced	2	2
Water, hot	4 fl. oz.	120 ml
Cumin, ground	1 tsp.	5 ml
Salt and pepper	TT	TT

1 In a large, deep pan sauté the onion, bell pepper and garlic in the oil. Add the corn and cook until very lightly browned.

2 Add the squash, zucchini and chiles along with the water, cumin and seasonings. Cover, reduce the heat, and simmer until tender, approximately 15 minutes. Adjust the seasonings

Approximate values per ½-c. (120-ml) serving: **Calories** 70, **Total fat** 2.5 g, **Saturated fat** 0 g, **Cholesterol** 0 mg, **Sodium** 10 mg, **Total carbohydrates** 13 g, **Protein** 2 g, **Vitamin A** 15%, **Vitamin C** 80%, **Claims**—low fat, low sodium; no saturated fat; no cholesterol; good source of vitamins A and C

SPINACH AU GRATIN

RUTH'S CHRIS STEAK HOUSE, Phoenix, AZ

RECIPE 22.36

Yield: 8 Servings, 8 oz. (240 g) each

Method: Boiling/Broiling

Clarified butter	1 fl. oz.	30 ml
Flour	1 oz.	30 g
Half-and-half	1 pt.	450 ml
Frozen chopped spinach, thawed	2 lb. 8 oz.	2.4 kg
Salt and pepper	TT	TT
Cheddar cheese, shredded	1 lb. 8 oz.	700 g

1 Heat the butter in a saucepan. Add the flour and cook to make a blond roux.

2 Add the half-and-half, whisking to remove any lumps of roux. Bring to a simmer and cook for 15 minutes.

3 Drop the spinach into boiling salted water and cook for 2 minutes. Remove from the heat and drain well.

4 Combine the hot spinach with the cream sauce and adjust the seasonings.

5 Fill eight 10-ounce gratin dishes with the creamed spinach. Top each with 3 ounces (90 grams) of shredded Cheddar cheese and place under the broiler until the cheese is melted and browned and the spinach is very hot. Serve immediately.

Approximate values per 8-oz. (240-g) serving: **Calories** 510, **Total fat** 38 g, **Saturated fat** 24 g, **Cholesterol** 120 mg, **Sodium** 960 mg, **Total carbohydrates** 14 g, **Protein** 28 g, **Vitamin A** 140%, **Calcium** 90%

GLAZED PEARL ONIONS

RECIPE 22.37

Yield: 1 lb. (450 g)

Method: Boiling

Pearl onions, peeled	1 lb.	500 g
Whole butter	1½ oz.	45 g
Granulated sugar	1 Tbsp.	15 ml
Salt and pepper	TT	TT

1 Place the onions, butter and sugar in a sauté pan and add enough water to barely cover.

2 Boil the onions, allowing the water to evaporate. As the water evaporates, the butter-and-sugar mixture will begin to coat the onions. When the water is

1 Boiling the pearl onions.

2 Glazing the onions in butter and sugar.

nearly gone, test the doneness of the onions. If they are still firm, add a small amount of water and continue to boil until the onions are tender.

3 Sauté the onions in the butter-and-sugar mixture until they are glazed. Season to taste.

Variations: Vegetables such as carrots, turnips, zucchini and other squashes can also be glazed with this procedure. They should be cut into appropriate shapes such as a tourné and be large enough so that they glaze properly without overcooking. When preparing a mix of glazed vegetables, cook each type separately because each has a different cooking time.

Approximate values per 2-oz. (60-g) serving: **Calories** 70, **Total fat** 4.5 g, **Saturated fat** 2.5 g, **Cholesterol** 10 mg, **Sodium** 340 mg, **Total carbohydrates** 8 g, **Protein** 1 g

---

RECIPE 22.38

MIXED BEAN SALAD

Yield: 12 Servings, 3 oz. (90 g) each	**Method:** Steaming/Boiling	
Green beans, cut in ½-in. (1.2-cm) pieces	4 oz.	120 g
Dressing:		
White wine vinegar	2 fl. oz.	60 ml
Olive oil	3 fl. oz.	90 ml
Lemon juice	1 Tbsp.	15 ml
Lemon peel, grated	1 tsp.	5 ml
Garlic cloves, crushed	2	2
White wine	1 Tbsp.	15 ml
Dried red chile, chopped fine	1	1
Red kidney beans, soaked and cooked	8 oz.	250 g
Chickpeas, soaked and cooked	8 oz.	250 g
Lima or cannellini beans, soaked and cooked	8 oz.	250 g
Green onions, chopped	1 bunch	1 bunch
Salt and pepper	TT	TT

1 Steam the green beans until done but still crisp, approximately 3 to 4 minutes.
2 Combine the dressing ingredients.
3 Mix together all the drained beans and peas, and pour the dressing over them. Add the green onions, season with salt and pepper and toss to combine. Marinate for several hours before serving.

Approximate values per 3-oz. (90-g) serving: **Calories** 150, **Total fat** 8 g, **Saturated fat** 1 g, **Cholesterol** 0 mg, **Sodium** 210 mg, **Total carbohydrates** 14 g, **Protein** 5 g, **Iron** 10%, **Claims—** low saturated fat; no cholesterol; good source of fiber

---

RECIPE 22.39

BUTTERNUT SQUASH WITH BLACK BEANS

Yield: 24 oz. (680 g)	**Method:** Steaming	
Fresh butternut squash	10 oz.	300 g
Vegetable oil	1 Tbsp.	15 ml
Onions, chopped	3 oz.	90 g
Garlic cloves, minced	2	2

Sherry	2 fl. oz.	60 ml
Vegetable broth	2 fl. oz.	60 ml
Black beans, cooked	1 pt.	470 ml
Salt	½ tsp.	2 ml
Cumin, ground	½ tsp.	2 ml
Dried thyme	½ tsp.	2 ml
Green onions, sliced	3	3
Salt and pepper	TT	TT

1 Peel the squash and cut it into ½-inch (1.2-centimeter) cubes.

2 Heat the oil in a large sauté pan. Add the onions, garlic and squash and sauté until the onions are soft. Add the sherry and broth. Cover the pan loosely and simmer until the squash is tender, approximately 8 minutes.

3 Add the beans, salt, cumin and thyme and continue to simmer until the beans are thoroughly heated. Stir in the green onions and adjust the seasonings.

Approximate values per 4-oz. (120-g) serving: **Calories** 130, **Total fat** 3 g, **Saturated fat** 0 g, **Cholesterol** 0 mg, **Sodium** 240 mg, **Total carbohydrates** 21 g, **Protein** 6 g, **Vitamin A** 70%, **Vitamin C** 20%, **Iron** 10%, **Claims**—low fat; no saturated fat; no cholesterol; good source of fiber and vitamins A and C

RED BEANS AND RICE WITH ANDOUILLE

RECIPE 22.40

Yield: 10 Servings, 8 oz. (240 ml) of beans

Method: Simmering

Red kidney beans	1 lb.	450 g
Water	as needed	as needed
Spice mix:		
Bay leaves	5	5
Dried thyme	2 tsp.	10 ml
Dried oregano	2 tsp.	10 ml
Cayenne pepper	½ tsp.	3 ml
Black pepper	½ tsp.	3 ml
Water	1 gal.	4 lt
Smoked ham hocks	2	2
Celery, small dice	1 pt.	450 ml
Onions, small dice	1 pt.	450 ml
Green bell peppers, small dice	1 c.	225 ml
Garlic cloves	4	4
Andouille, sliced on the bias ¼ in.		
(6 mm) thick	1 lb.	450 g
Salt and pepper	TT	TT
Simmered Rice (page 701)	2 pt.	900 ml

1 Soak the beans in water overnight and drain.

2 Combine the spice mix ingredients and reserve.

3 In a heavy-bottomed saucepot, combine 1 gallon (4 liters) of water with the ham hocks, beans, celery, onions, bell peppers, garlic and spice mix. Bring to a boil, reduce to a simmer and cook for 1 hour.

4 Remove the ham hocks from the pot. Separate the meat from the bones and discard the skin, bones and cartilage. Cut the meat medium dice. Add the meat and the andouille slices to the pot and simmer, stirring often, until the beans are very tender and begin to break up, approximately 30 minutes. Add more water if necessary to prevent the beans from burning. Remove the bay leaves and adjust the seasonings.

Continued

5 To serve, mound a portion of the rice on a soup plate and ladle the red beans around it.

Approximate values per serving: **Calories** 430, **Total fat** 17 g, **Saturated fat** 6 g, **Cholesterol** 45 mg, **Sodium** 460 mg, **Total carbohydrates** 48 g, **Protein** 21 g, **Vitamin C** 30%, **Calcium** 10%, **Iron** 30%

SPINACH AND MUSHROOM CRÊPE WITH RED-WINE AND BROWN BUTTER SAUCE

RECIPE 22.41

HERBSAINT BAR AND RESTAURANT,
NEW ORLEANS, LA
Chef Donald Link

Yield: 10 Crêpes

Crêpes:		
Eggs	2	2
Flour	4 oz.	120 g
Milk	4 fl. oz.	120 ml
Whole butter, melted	2 oz.	60 g
Filling:		
Unsalted butter	1 tsp.	5 ml
Portabella mushrooms, medium dice	2	2
Salt	1/4 tsp.	1 ml
Black pepper	1/4 tsp.	1 ml
Garlic, minced	1/2 tsp.	3 ml
Spinach, stemmed	1/2 lb.	240 g
Red-Wine and Brown Butter Sauce:		
Granulated sugar	1 Tbsp.	15 ml
Red wine	1 pt.	450 ml
Whole butter	1 1/2 oz.	45 g

1 To make the crêpe batter, whisk the eggs together. Add the flour and whisk in the milk until smooth. Whisk in 1 tablespoon (15 milliliters) of melted butter. If the batter is too thick, adjust the consistency with water or additional milk.

2 Heat a 10-inch (25-centimeter) nonstick pan over moderate heat. Brush it with a portion of the remaining melted butter. Add 1 fluid ounce (30 milliliters) of batter to the pan. Swirl to cover the entire bottom of the pan with the batter. Cook the crêpe until lightly browned, turn and cook for a few seconds on the second side. Remove and reserve. Repeat with the remaining batter.

3 In a saucepot, melt the unsalted butter and sauté the mushrooms until soft. Season with salt and pepper, add the garlic and sauté for a few seconds. Add the spinach and cook until wilted. Remove from the pan. Season with salt and pepper.

4 Place a portion of the spinach mixture on each crêpe and roll the crêpes around the mixture (the browned side of the crêpe should be on the outside).

5 To make the sauce, combine the sugar and wine in a small saucepan and reduce by two-thirds. In a separate pan, heat the butter until it browns. Combine the wine reduction and the browned butter. The finished sauce will appear to have separated.

6 Serve one or two crêpes per person accompanied by roasted baby vegetables and drizzled with the Red-Wine and Brown Butter Sauce.

Approximate values per crêpe: **Calories** 190, **Total fat** 10 g, **Saturated fat** 6 g, **Cholesterol** 65 mg, **Sodium** 100 mg, **Total carbohydrates** 14 g, **Protein** 4 g, **Vitamin A** 40%, **Vitamin C** 10%, **Iron** 10%

FENNEL AND MUSHROOMS À LA GRECQUE

RECIPE 22.42

Yield: 18 Servings, 3 oz. (90 g) **Method:** Boiling

Mushrooms, small	1 lb.	500 g
Pearl onions, peeled	4 oz.	120 g
Olive oil	2 fl. oz.	60 ml
White wine	4 fl. oz.	120 ml
White stock	1 pt.	500 ml
Tomato concassée	12 oz.	360 g
Tomato paste	1 oz.	30 g
Lemon juice	1 fl. oz.	30 ml
Coriander, ground	1 tsp.	5 ml
Bouquet garni:		
Carrot stick, 4 in. (10 cm)	1	1
Leek, split, 4-in. (10-cm) piece	1	1
Fresh thyme sprig	1	1
Bay leaf	2	2
Salt and pepper	TT	TT
Fennel bulb, batonnet	1 lb.	500 g

1 Wash the mushrooms and trim the stems.

2 Sauté the onions in the olive oil, browning lightly. Add the white wine, stock, tomato concassée, tomato paste, lemon juice, coriander and bouquet garni. Season to taste with salt and pepper and bring to a boil.

3 Add the fennel and mushrooms and simmer for 15 minutes.

4 Remove from the heat and allow to cool to room temperature. Remove the bouquet garni. Adjust the seasonings and refrigerate. Serve chilled.

Approximate values per 3-oz. (90-g) serving: **Calories** 60, **Total fat** 3.5 g, **Saturated fat** 0 g, **Cholesterol** 0 mg, **Sodium** 240 mg, **Total carbohydrates** 5 g, **Protein** 2 g, **Vitamin C** 15%, **Claims**—no saturated fat; no cholesterol

BRAISED RED CABBAGE WITH APPLES

RECIPE 22.43

Yield: 16 Servings, 4 oz. (120 g) each **Method:** Braising

Red cabbage	3 lb.	1.4 kg
Bacon, medium dice	12 oz.	360 g
Onions, medium dice	8 oz.	250 g
Salt and pepper	TT	TT
Red wine	8 fl. oz.	250 ml
White stock	8 fl. oz.	250 ml
Cinnamon sticks	2	2
Apples, tart, cored and diced	12 oz.	360 g
Brown sugar	1 oz.	30 g
Cider vinegar	2 fl. oz.	60 ml

1 Shred the cabbage.

2 Render the bacon. Add the onions and sweat in the bacon fat until tender.

3 Add the cabbage and sauté for 5 minutes. Season with salt and pepper. Add the wine, stock and cinnamon sticks. Cover and braise until the cabbage is almost tender, approximately 20 minutes.

Continued

4 Add the apples, brown sugar and vinegar and mix well.

5 Cover and braise until the apples are tender, approximately 5 minutes. Remove the cinnamon sticks before service.

Approximate values per 4-oz. (120-g) serving: **Calories** 170, **Total fat** 11 g, **Saturated fat** 4 g, **Cholesterol** 20 mg, **Sodium** 540 mg, **Total carbohydrates** 11 g, **Protein** 8 g, **Vitamin C** 50%

RECIPE 22.44

BRAISED ROMAINE LETTUCE

Yield: 12 Servings, 5 oz. (150 g) each   **Method:** Braising

Romaine lettuce	3 heads	3 heads
Onions, small dice	8 oz.	250 g
Celery, small dice	8 oz.	250 g
Carrots, small dice	8 oz.	250 g
Bacon, small dice	8 oz.	250 g
Brown stock	24 fl. oz.	700 ml
Salt and pepper	TT	TT

1 Trim the lettuce heads. Blanch them in salted boiling water and refresh.

2 Combine the onions, celery, carrots, bacon and brown stock in a saucepot and simmer for 10 minutes.

3 Quarter the romaine heads and trim off most of the core, leaving just enough to hold the leaves together.

4 Pour the brown stock mixture into a hotel pan and arrange the lettuce portions in the pan. Season with salt and pepper.

5 Cover the pan and braise in a 350°F (180°C) oven for approximately 1 hour. Serve each portion with vegetables, bacon and a portion of the cooking liquid.

Approximate values per 5-oz. (150-g) serving: **Calories** 140, **Total fat** 10 g, **Saturated fat** 3.5 g, **Cholesterol** 15 mg, **Sodium** 340 mg, **Total carbohydrates** 6 g, **Protein** 7 g, **Vitamin A** 50%, **Vitamin C** 30%

RECIPE 22.45

BRAISED PUMPKIN

Yield: 1 pt.   **Method:** Braising

Vegetable oil	1 Tbsp.	15 ml
Pumpkin, fresh, large dice	1 pt.	475 ml
Vegetable stock	4 fl. oz.	120 ml
Soy sauce	1 Tbsp.	15 ml
Apple juice	1 Tbsp.	15 ml
Onions, chopped fine	6 oz.	180 g
White pepper	1/8 tsp.	0.5 ml
Salt	TT	TT
Green onions, sliced	4	4

1 In a sauté pan, heat the oil and sauté the pumpkin until lightly browned.

2 Add the stock, soy sauce, apple juice, onions and white pepper. Bring the mixture to a boil, cover and reduce the heat to a simmer.

3 Simmer the pumpkin for 10 to 12 minutes. Add salt to taste and garnish with the green onions.

Approximate values per 1/2-c. (120-ml) serving: **Calories** 70, **Total fat** 3.5 g, **Saturated fat** 0, **Cholesterol** 0, **Sodium** 380 mg, **Total carbohydrates** 8 g, **Protein** 2 g, **Vitamin A** 20%, **Vitamin C** 15%, **Claims**—no cholesterol, good source of vitamin A and C

ARTICHOKES STUFFED WITH ITALIAN SAUSAGE

RECIPE 22.46

Yield: 8 Servings   **Method:** Braising

Artichokes	8	8
Bulk sausage meat	1 lb.	500 g
Onions, chopped fine	1 lb.	500 g
Garlic, chopped fine	2 Tbsp.	30 ml
Cumin, ground	1 tsp.	5 ml
Fresh cilantro, chopped	4 oz.	120 g
Fresh thyme	2 tsp.	10 ml
Fresh bread crumbs	4 oz.	120 g
Tabasco sauce	TT	TT
Salt and pepper	TT	TT
Olive oil	2 fl. oz.	60 ml
Chicken stock	1 qt.	1 lt

1 Trim the stem and barbs from the artichokes. Using a tablespoon, scoop out the choke from the center of each artichoke.

2 Cook the sausage meat, breaking it up into small pieces. Pour off the fat. Add the onions and garlic and sauté until tender.

3 Add the cumin, cilantro, thyme and bread crumbs. Season with Tabasco sauce, salt and pepper.

4 Stuff the artichokes with the sausage mixture.

5 Place the artichokes in a braising pan and drizzle with olive oil. Add the chicken stock.

6 Bring the stock to a boil. Cover and braise until the artichokes are tender, approximately 1 hour.

Approximate values per serving: **Calories** 420, **Total fat** 26 g, **Saturated fat** 7 g, **Cholesterol** 45 mg, **Sodium** 1270 mg, **Total carbohydrates** 29 g, **Protein** 18 g, **Vitamin C** 30%, **Calcium** 15%, **Iron** 20%

COOKING SHOULD BE A CAREFULLY BALANCED
REFLECTION OF ALL THE GOOD THINGS OF THE EARTH.
—*Jean & Pierre Troisgros, French chefs*

POTATOES, GRAINS AND PASTA

23

RESTAURANT KEVIN TAYLOR, Denver, CO
Chef Kevin Taylor

**AFTER STUDYING THIS
CHAPTER, YOU WILL BE
ABLE TO:**

▶ identify a variety of potatoes

▶ apply various cooking methods
to potatoes

▶ identify a variety of grains

▶ apply various cooking methods
to grains

▶ identify pasta products

▶ make fresh pasta

▶ cook pasta

Potatoes, grains (corn, rice, wheat and others) and pastas are collectively known as starches. Some of these foods are vegetables; others are grasses. Pastas, of course, are prepared products made from grains. Starches are, for the most part, staple foods: foods that define a cuisine and give it substance. All are high in starchy carbohydrates, low in fat and commonly used as part of a well-balanced meal.

Today's chefs are rediscovering traditional and ethnic dishes that rely on grains seldom used in typical American food service operations. Pasta, made from a variety of grains in numerous shapes and flavors and accompanied by countless sauces and garnishes, now regularly appears on many menus alongside the ubiquitous potato prepared for many classic and modern dishes.

▶ POTATOES

Potatoes (Fr. *pommes de terre*) are one of the few vegetables native to the New World, probably originating in the South American Andes. Botanically, potatoes are succulent, nonwoody annual plants. The portion we consume is the tuber, the swollen fleshy part of the underground stem. Potatoes are hardy and easy to grow, making them inexpensive and widely available. Americans eat nearly 50 pounds of potatoes annually, making them one of the top 20 vegetables in the United States.

IDENTIFYING POTATOES

Discussed here are some of the more commonly used types of potatoes. Other varieties are regularly being developed or rediscovered and tested in the market place.

Choose potatoes that are heavy and very firm with clean skin and few eyes. Avoid those with many eyes, sprouts, green streaks, soft spots, cracks or cut edges. Most varieties are available all year. When ordering potatoes, note that size A is larger than size B, which must be between 1½ and 2¼ inches (3.75 and 5.5 centimeters) in diameter.

New potatoes are small, immature potatoes (of any variety) that are harvested before their starches develop. Although red potatoes can be "new," not all new potatoes are necessarily red-skinned. Conversely, not all red-skinned potatoes are new. True new potatoes are waxy with a high moisture content and a thin, delicate skin.

FINGERLINGS

Fingerling potatoes are typically heirloom varieties, related to the original potato varieties from the Andes. They are generally small, long and finger-shaped or oblong with good flavor. The Russian Banana looks like a small banana and has a firm texture and rich, buttery flavor. The red-streaked French Fingerling has a nutty flavor while the red Ruby Crescent has a strong, earthy flavor. All fingerling varieties tend to be low in starch and are good for roasting and in potato salads.

PURPLE POTATOES

Purple (or blue) potatoes have a deep purple skin. The flesh is bright purple, becoming lighter when cooked. They are mealy, with a flavor and texture similar to russets. The most common varieties are All Blue and Caribe, which were also quite popular in the mid-19th century.

RED POTATOES

Red potatoes have a thin red skin and crisp, white, waxy flesh, best suited to boiling or steaming. They do not have the dry, mealy texture that successful baking requires. Red potatoes are round, instead of long or oblong; popular varieties are Red Pontiac and Norland.

Fingerlings

Purple Potatoes

RUSSET (BURBANK) POTATOES

Russet potatoes, commonly referred to as Idaho potatoes, are the standard baking potato. They are long with rough, reddish-brown skin and mealy flesh. Russets are excellent baked and are the best potatoes for frying. They tend to fall apart when boiled. They are marketed in several size categories and should be purchased in the size most appropriate for their intended use.

Red Potatoes

Russet Potatoes

WHITE POTATOES

White potatoes are available in round or long varieties. They have a thin, tender skin with a tender, waxy yellow or white flesh. Round white potatoes are also referred to as chef or all-purpose potatoes. White potatoes are usually cooked with moist heat or used for sautéing. White Rose and Finnish Yellow (or Yellow Finn) are popular varieties.

Another variety of white potato known as the **Yukon Gold** is a medium-sized, slightly flattened, oval potato. They have a delicate pale yellow skin with shallow pink eyes. Their pale yellow flesh has a creamy texture and rich, buttery, nutty flavor. Yukon Gold potatoes are suitable for most cooking methods and will retain their yellow color when baked, boiled or fried. First bred by botanists in Canada, Yukon Golds are now grown throughout the United States. Other lesser-known gold-fleshed varieties include Michigold, Donna, Delta Gold, Banana and Saginaw Gold.

White Potatoes

Yukon Gold Potatoes

SWEET POTATOES

Sweet potatoes are from a different botanical family than ordinary potatoes, although they are also tubers that originated in the New World. Two types are commonly available. One has yellow flesh and a dry, mealy texture; it is known as a boniato, white or Cuban sweet potato. The other has a darker orange, moister flesh and is high in sugar; it is known as a red sweet potato. Both types have thick skins ranging in color from light tan to brownish red. (Sometimes dark-skinned sweet potatoes are erroneously labeled yams.) Sweet potatoes should be chosen according to the desired degree of sweetness. They are best suited for boiling, baking and puréeing, although the less sweet varieties can be deep-fried. The cooked flesh can also be used in breads, pies and puddings. Sweet potatoes are available canned, often in a spiced or sugary sauce.

Sweet Potatoes

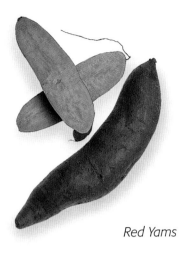

Red Yams

YAMS

Yams are a third type of tuber, botanically different from both sweet and common potatoes. Yams are less sweet than sweet potatoes, but they can be used interchangeably. The flesh of yams ranges from creamy white to deep red. Yams are Asian in origin and are now found in Africa, South America and the southern United States.

NUTRITION

Potatoes contain a high percentage of easily digested complex carbohydrates and little or no fat. They are also a good source for minerals and vitamins, especially vitamin B6, vitamin C and potassium.

PURCHASING AND STORING POTATOES

MEALY VERSUS WAXY

One of the most important considerations in selecting potatoes is choosing between the mealy and waxy varieties. You should understand the differences and purchase the type best suited to your needs.

Mealy potatoes (also known as starchy potatoes) have a high starch content and thick skin. They are best for baking and are often ordered from suppliers simply as "bakers." Their low sugar content also allows them to be deep-fried long enough to fully cook the interior without burning the exterior. Mealy potatoes tend to fall apart when boiled, making them a good choice for whipped or puréed potatoes.

Waxy potatoes have a low starch content and thin skin. They are best for boiling. They will not develop the desired fluffy texture when baked. They tend to become limp and soggy when deep-fried because of their high moisture content.

GRADING

Like other vegetables, potatoes are subject to the voluntary USDA grading system. Although U.S. Fancy is the highest grade, most potatoes sold on the wholesale market are U.S. No. 1. Potatoes sold on the retail market can also be graded as either U.S. Grade A or U.S. Grade B.

PURCHASING

Potatoes are usually packed in 50-pound cartons. Counts vary depending on average potato size. For example, in a 100-count carton, each potato would weigh an average of 8 ounces. Eighty-, 90- and 100-count cartons are the most common.

Table 23.1 **COMPARISON OF MEALY AND WAXY POTATOES**

	CONTENT OF:			BEST TO:			
	STARCH	MOISTURE	SUGAR	BAKE	BOIL	SAUTÉ	DEEP-FRY
Mealy: russet, white rose, purple	high	low	low	✓			✓
Waxy: red, new (red), Finnish yellow	low	high	high		✓	✓	

Generally, larger-sized potatoes (that is, smaller counts) are more expensive. Size does not affect quality, however, so the size selected should be determined by intended use.

STORING

Temperatures between 50°F and 65°F (10°C and 18°C) are best for storing potatoes. Do not store potatoes in the refrigerator. At temperatures below 40°F (4°C), potato starch turns to sugar, making the cooked product too sweet and increasing the risk that the potato will turn gray or streaky when cooked. Potatoes with a high sugar content also burn more easily when fried.

Potatoes should be stored in a dark room, as light promotes chlorophyll production, turning them green and bitter. A green patch indicates the possible presence of solanine, a toxin harmful if eaten in large amounts, and should be peeled away. Solanine is also present in the eyes and sprouts, and they, too, should be removed and discarded before cooking.

Under proper conditions, fresh baking or general-purpose potatoes should last for two months; new potatoes will keep for several weeks. Do not wash potatoes until ready to use, as washing promotes spoilage.

APPLYING VARIOUS COOKING METHODS

Potatoes have a relatively neutral flavor, making them a perfect accompaniment to many savory dishes. They can be prepared with almost any dry- or moist-heat cooking method: baking, sautéing, pan-frying, deep-frying, boiling or steaming. They can be combined with other ingredients in braises and stews. Potatoes are used in soups (vichyssoise), dumplings (gnocchi), breads, pancakes (latkes), puddings, salads and even vodka.

Many potato dishes, both classic and modern, employ more than one cooking method. For example, lorette potatoes require boiling and deep-frying; hash browns require parboiling, then sautéing. Even french fries are best when first blanched in hot oil before final deep frying.

DETERMINING DONENESS

Most potatoes are considered done when they are soft and tender or offer little resistance when pierced with a knife tip. Fried potatoes should have a crisp, golden-brown surface; the interior should be moist and tender.

ROASTING AND BAKING

Potatoes are often roasted with meat or poultry, becoming coated with the fat and drippings released from the main item as it cooks. Either mealy or waxy potatoes, peeled or unpeeled, can be roasted successfully.

Mealy potatoes such as russets are ideal for baking. The skin is left intact, although it may be pierced with a fork to allow steam to escape. A true baked potato should not be wrapped in foil or cooked in a microwave; this changes the cooking method to steaming and prevents a crisp skin from forming. A properly baked potato should be white and fluffy, not yellowish or soggy. Once baked, potatoes can be eaten plain (or with butter, sour cream and other garnishes) or used in other recipes.

▶ PROCEDURE FOR BAKING POTATOES

1 Scrub the potatoes well.

2 Using a fork, pierce the potato skins.

3 Rub the potatoes with oil and salt if desired. Do not wrap them in foil.

4 Bake the potatoes until done. A paring knife should penetrate them easily.

RECIPE 23.1

BAKED POTATOES

Yield: 8 Servings	**Method:** Baking	
Russet potatoes	8	8
Vegetable oil	3 Tbsp.	45 ml
Kosher salt	3 Tbsp.	45 ml

1 Scrub the potatoes well, but do not peel them. Pierce the skin of each potato to allow steam to escape.
2 Rub the potatoes with the oil, then sprinkle with kosher salt.
3 Place the potatoes on a rack over a sheet pan. Bake in a 400°F (200°C) oven until done, approximately 1 hour. The potatoes should yield to gentle pressure, and a paring knife inserted in the thickest part should meet little resistance.
4 Hold uncovered in a warm spot and serve within 1 hour.

Variation: *Twice-Baked Potatoes* (**Yield:** 16 Servings)—Cut baked potatoes in half lengthwise. Carefully scoop out the flesh, leaving the skins intact. Whip the potato flesh with 8 ounces (225 grams) sour cream, 2 ounces (60 grams) butter and 2 ounces (60 grams) cooked, crumbled bacon and then add salt and pepper to taste. Thin with hot milk if necessary. The mixture should be light and fluffy, not lumpy. Pile the filling back into the skins, mounding the tops. Brush the mounded potatoes with clarified butter and sprinkle with Parmesan. Arrange on a sheet pan and bake at 425°F (220°C) until thoroughly reheated and lightly browned.

Approximate values per 7.5-oz. (225-g) potato: **Calories** 270, **Total fat** 5 g, **Saturated fat** 0.5 g, **Cholesterol** 0 mg, **Sodium** 2630 mg, **Total carbohydrates** 51 g, **Protein** 5 g, **Vitamin C** 45%, **Claims**—low saturated fat; no cholesterol; good source of fiber

Baking en Casserole

Many classic potato dishes require baking either raw or parboiled potatoes with sauce, cheese, meat or other seasonings in a baking dish or casserole. Well-known examples include scalloped potatoes, which are baked in béchamel sauce, and potatoes au gratin, which are topped with cheese and baked. These dishes usually develop a crisp, brown crust, which is part of their appeal.

The casserole should hold its shape when cut; the potatoes should be tender, and the sauce should be smooth, not grainy.

Potato casseroles can be fully baked, then held loosely covered in a steam table for service. Portions can be reheated or browned briefly under a broiler or salamander at service time.

▶ PROCEDURE FOR BAKING POTATOES EN CASSEROLE

1 Prepare the potatoes by washing, peeling, slicing or partially cooking as desired or as directed in the recipe.
2 Add the potatoes to the baking pan in layers, alternating with the sauce, cream, cheese or other ingredients. Or combine the potatoes with the other ingredients and place in a buttered baking pan.
3 Bake the potatoes until done.

SAFETY ALERT

Cooked potato dishes, especially those with cream, butter or custard, are potentially hazardous foods. They must be held for service at 140°F (60°C) or higher. Be sure to reheat potato dishes to 165°F (74°C) or higher.

RECIPE 23.2

GRATIN DAUPHINOISE

Yield: 4–5 lb. (1.8–2.2 kg)	**Method:** Baking en casserole	
Russet potatoes	3 lb.	1.3 kg
Whole butter	as needed	as needed
Salt and white pepper	TT	TT
Nutmeg	¼ tsp.	2 ml

Gruyère, grated	8 oz.	250 g
Half-and-half	24 fl. oz.	700 ml
Egg yolks	3	3

1 Peel the potatoes and cut them into very thin slices.
2 Place a single layer of potatoes in a well-buttered, full-sized hotel pan.
3 Season with salt, white pepper and a small amount of nutmeg. Sprinkle on a thin layer of cheese.
4 Add another layer of potatoes, seasonings and cheese and repeat until all the potatoes and about three-quarters of the cheese are used.
5 Heat the half-and-half to a simmer. Whisk the egg yolks together in a bowl, then gradually add the hot half-and-half.
6 Pour the cream-and-egg mixture over the potatoes. Top with the remaining cheese.
7 Bake uncovered at 350°F (180°C) until the potatoes are tender and golden brown, approximately 50 to 60 minutes.

Approximate values per 4-oz. (120-g) serving: **Calories** 160, **Total fat** 8 g, **Saturated fat** 5 g, **Cholesterol** 55 mg, **Sodium** 160 mg, **Total carbohydrates** 15 g, **Protein** 6 g, **Vitamin C** 15%, **Calcium** 15%

1 Layering gratin potatoes.

2 Finished gratin potatoes.

SAUTÉING AND PAN-FRYING

Waxy potatoes, such as red- and white-skinned varieties, are best for sautéing or pan-frying. Often they are first parboiled or even fully cooked—a convenient way to use leftover boiled potatoes. They are then cooked in fat following the general procedures for sautéing and pan-frying discussed in Chapter 10, Principles of Cooking.

The fat can be clarified butter, oil, bacon fat or lard, depending on the desired flavor of the finished dish. The fat must be hot before the potatoes are added so that they will develop a crust without absorbing too much fat. Sautéed potatoes should have a crisp, well-browned crust and tender interior. They should be neither soggy nor greasy.

Potatoes can be sautéed or pan-fried by two methods: tossing and still-frying. The **tossing method** is used to cook relatively small pieces of potatoes in a small amount of fat. The potatoes are tossed using the pan's sloped sides so that they brown evenly on all sides. The **still-frying method** is used to create a disc-shaped potato product. The shredded or sliced potatoes are added to the pan, usually covering its bottom, and allowed to cook without stirring or flipping until they are well browned on the first side. The entire mass is then turned and cooked on the second side. When the potatoes are done, they can be cut into wedges for service.

▶ PROCEDURE FOR SAUTÉING AND PAN-FRYING POTATOES

1 Wash, trim, peel, cut and/or cook the potatoes as desired or as directed in the recipe.
2 Heat the pan, add the fat and heat the fat. Add the potatoes to the hot fat. Do not overcrowd the pan. Use enough fat to prevent the potatoes from sticking to the pan. Depending on the recipe, use either the tossing method or the still-frying method.
3 Add garnishes, seasonings and other ingredients as desired or as directed in the recipe.
4 Cook the potatoes until done.

RECIPE 23.3 LYONNAISE POTATOES

Yield: 8 Servings, 4 oz. (120 g) each   **Method:** Sautéing

Potatoes, waxy	2 lb.	1 kg
Onions, julienne	8 oz.	250 g
Clarified butter	4 fl. oz.	120 ml
Salt and pepper	TT	TT

1 Partially cook the potatoes by baking, boiling or steaming. Allow them to cool.
2 Peel and cut the potatoes into ¼-inch (½-centimeter-) thick slices.
3 Sauté the onions in half of the butter until tender. Remove the onions from the pan with a slotted spoon and set aside.
4 Add the remaining butter to the pan. Add the potatoes and sauté, tossing as needed, until well browned on all sides.
5 Return the onions to the pan and sauté to combine the flavors. Season to taste with salt and pepper.

Approximate values per 4-oz. (120-g) serving: **Calories** 170, **Total fat** 12 g, **Saturated fat** 7 g, **Cholesterol** 30 mg, **Sodium** 650 mg, **Total carbohydrates** 16 g, **Protein** 1 g, **Vitamin A** 10%

DEEP-FRYING

Potato chips and french fries (Fr. *pomme frites*) are extremely popular in a variety of shapes, sizes and seasonings. Although a wide range of shapes, sizes and preseasoned frozen products are available, fresh fried potatoes can be a delicious, economical menu item.

Top-quality russet potatoes are recommended for deep-frying. The peel may be removed or left attached. If peeled, the potatoes should be soaked in clear, cold water until ready to cut and cook. This keeps them crisp and white by leaching some of the starch that might otherwise make the potatoes gummy or cause smaller cuts to stick together when cooked.

Deep-fried potatoes are usually blanched in oil ranging in temperature from 250°F to 300°F (120°C to 150°C) until tender and translucent. They are then drained and held for service, at which time they are finished in hotter oil, usually at a temperature between 350°F and 375°F (180°C and 190°C).

Deep-frying is also used to finish cooking several classic potato dishes such as croquettes and dauphine, in which fully cooked potatoes are puréed, seasoned, shaped and fried.

Deep-fried potatoes should be drained on absorbent paper briefly and served immediately.

▶ PROCEDURE FOR DEEP-FRYING POTATOES

1 Wash, peel or trim the potatoes as desired.
2 Cut the potatoes into uniform-sized pieces.
3 Using the basket method, blanch the potatoes in deep fat at 250°F (121°C) for 2 to 3 minutes, depending on the size of the pieces.
4 Drain the potatoes and spread them out in a single layer on a baking sheet or in a hotel pan.
5 Just before service, submerge the potatoes in deep fat at 350°F–375°F (177°C–191°C), using the basket method.
6 Cook until golden brown. Remove from the fat, drain and serve immediately.

DEEP-FRIED POTATOES

RUTH'S CHRIS STEAK HOUSE, Phoenix, AZ

Yield: Varies   **Method:** Deep-frying

Idaho potatoes, 70 count	as needed	as needed
Hot fat	as needed	as needed
Salt and pepper	TT	TT
Parsley, chopped	as needed for garnish	

1 Cut each potato into the desired shape; for example:
    Cottage fries—circles ¼ inch (60 millimeters) thick
    Shoestring potatoes—long juliennes (allumettes)
    French fries—sticks ⅜ inch × ⅜ inch × 3 inches (1 centimeter × 1 centimeter × 7 centimeters)
    Steak fries—four large wedges

2 Using the basket method, deep-fry the potatoes in 250°F (120°C) fat until lightly browned, approximately 2 to 3 minutes. Remove and drain. Hold the partially cooked potatoes in a single layer on a baking sheet or in a hotel pan.

3 For service, deep-fry the partially cooked potatoes in 350°F (180°C) fat until golden in color and done. Season to taste with salt and pepper.

4 Garnish with parsley if desired.

Approximate values per 1-oz. (30-g) serving: **Calories** 90, **Total fat** 4.5 g, **Saturated fat** 1.5 g, **Cholesterol** 0 mg, **Sodium** 60 mg, **Total carbohydrates** 11 g, **Protein** 1 g

Cottage Fries

Shoestring Potatoes

French Fries

Steak Fries

MORE THAN A FRENCH FRY

Thanks to the genius of Carême, Escoffier and others, few vegetables have as extensive a classic repertoire as potatoes. Some of these dishes begin with the duchesse (duh-SHEES) potatoes mixture; in this regard, duchesse potatoes can be considered the mother of many classic potato preparations. For example,

Duchesse + Tomato concassée = Marquis

Duchesse + Chopped truffles + Almond coating + Deep-frying = Berny

Duchesse + Shaping + Breading + Deep-frying = Croquettes

Duchesse + Pâte à choux = Dauphine

Dauphine + Grated Parmesan + Piped shape + Deep-frying = Lorette

Other classic potato preparations not based on duchesse potatoes include the following:

Anna—thin potato slices are arranged in several circular layers in a round pan coated with clarified butter; additional butter is brushed on, and the potatoes are baked until crisp, then cut into wedges for service.

Boulangère—onions and potatoes are sautéed in butter, then transferred to a baking pan or added to a partially cooked roast in a roasting pan; stock is added, and the potatoes are cooked uncovered until done.

Château—tournéed potatoes are sautéed in clarified butter until golden and tender.

Parisienne—small spheres are cut from raw, peeled potatoes with a Parisienne scoop; they are seasoned and sautéed in clarified butter, then tossed with a meat glaze and garnished with chopped parsley.

Rösti—potatoes are shredded, seasoned and pan-fried in the shape of a pie, then cut into wedges for service.

BOILING

Waxy potatoes are best for all moist-heat cooking methods. Boiled potatoes (which are actually simmered) may be served as is or used in multistep preparations such as purées, salads, soups and baked casseroles. Potatoes are usually boiled in water, although stock may be used or milk added for flavor. Always begin cooking potatoes in cold liquid to ensure even cooking. Unlike other vegetables, potatoes should not be refreshed in cold water; it makes them soggy.

▶ PROCEDURE FOR BOILING POTATOES

1 Wash, peel or trim the potatoes as desired.

2 Cut the potatoes into uniform-sized pieces to promote even cooking. The pieces should not be too small, or they will absorb a large amount of water as they cook, making the final product soggy.

3 Add the potatoes to enough cool liquid to cover them by several inches. Bring to a boil, reduce to a simmer and cook until done. If a slightly firm finished product is desired, remove and drain the potatoes when they are slightly underdone and allow carryover cooking to finish cooking them.

4 Drain the potatoes in a colander and serve or use for further preparation.

RECIPE 23.5

MASHED POTATOES

Yield: 3 lb. 8 oz. (1.5 kg)   **Method:** Boiling

Potatoes, waxy	5 lb.	2.2 kg
Salt	1 Tbsp.	15 ml
Whole butter, melted, hot	4 oz.	120 g
Milk, hot	8 fl. oz.	240 ml
Salt	1 tsp.	5 ml
White pepper	$\frac{1}{4}$ tsp.	2 ml

1 Wash and peel the potatoes. Cut each potato into four to six uniform-sized pieces.

2 Place the potatoes in a pot, cover them with water and add 1 tablespoon (15 milliliters) of salt to the water. Bring the water to a boil, reduce to a simmer and cook until the potatoes are tender. Do not overcook the potatoes.

3 When the potatoes are cooked, drain them well in a colander. The potatoes must be very dry. Transfer them to the bowl of an electric mixer. Using the whip attachment, whip the potatoes for 30 to 45 seconds. Scrape the sides and bottom of the bowl and whip for another 15 seconds or until the potatoes are smooth and free of lumps. The potatoes must be smooth before adding any liquids or they will remain lumpy.

4 Add the melted butter, hot milk and seasonings. Whip on low speed to incorporate all of the ingredients. Scrape the sides and bottom of the bowl and whip again for several seconds. Adjust consistency and seasoning.

Variations: *Garlic Mashed Potatoes*—Sweat 1 ounce (30 grams) of chopped garlic in the melted butter for 5 to 10 minutes without browning. Strain the butter if desired. Add the hot garlic butter in place of the melted butter in the recipe.

Horseradish Mashed Potatoes—Add 1 ounce (30 grams) of freshly grated horseradish to the potatoes with the seasonings.

Approximate values per 4-oz. (120-g) serving: **Calories** 190, **Total fat** 7 g, **Saturated fat** 4.5 g, **Cholesterol** 20 mg, **Sodium** 350 mg, **Total carbohydrates** 29 g, **Protein** 3 g, **Vitamin C** 20%

▶ GRAINS

Botanically, grains are grasses that bear edible seeds. Corn, rice and wheat are the most significant. Both the fruit (that is, the seed or kernel) and the plant are called a grain.

Most grain kernels are protected by a **hull** or husk. All kernels are composed of three distinct parts: the **bran, endosperm** and **germ.** See Figure 23.1. The bran is the tough outer layer covering the endosperm. Bran is a good source of fiber and B-complex vitamins. The endosperm is the largest part of the kernel and is a source of protein and carbohydrates (starch). It is the part used primarily in milled products such as flour. The germ is the smallest portion of the grain and is the only part that contains fat. It is also rich in thiamin. The bran, endosperm and germ can be separated by milling.

IDENTIFYING GRAINS

This section presents information on corn, rice and wheat as well as several minor grains that are nutritionally significant and gaining popularity.

Some products are available in a stone-ground form. This means that the grains were ground with a stone mill rather than by the steel blades typically used for **cracking, grinding, hulling** and **pearling.** Stone grinders are gentler and more precise, so they are less likely to overgrind the grain. Stone-ground products will always be labeled as such and are usually more expensive than steel-ground ones.

CORN

Corn (Sp. *maíz;* It. *granturco*) is the only grain that is also eaten fresh as a vegetable. (Fresh corn is discussed in Chapter 22, Vegetables.) Its use as a dried grain dates back several thousand years in Central America and long preceded its use as a vegetable.

Cornmeal

Cornmeal is made by drying and grinding a special type of corn known as dent, which may be yellow, white or blue. Cornmeal is most often used in breads, as

▶ **cracking** a milling process in which grains are broken open

▶ **grinding** a milling process in which grains are reduced to a powder; the powder can be of differing degrees of fineness or coarseness

▶ **hulling** a milling process in which the hull or husk is removed from grains

▶ **pearling** a milling process in which all or part of the hull, bran and germ are removed from grains

Cornmeal

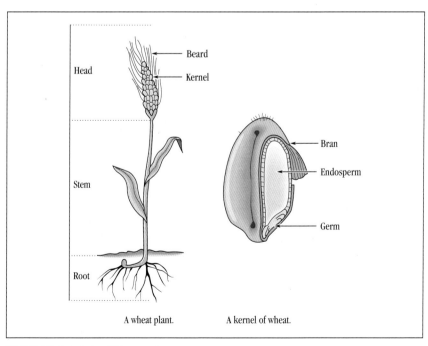

A wheat plant.   A kernel of wheat.

FIGURE 23.1 ▶ **Wheat**

a coating for fried foods or cooked as polenta or mush. Products made with cornmeal have a gritty texture and a sweet but starchy flavor.

Hominy

Hominy

Hominy, also known as posole or samp, is dried corn that has been soaked in hydrated lime or lye. This causes the kernels to swell, loosening the hulls. The hulls and germs are removed and the kernels dried. These white or yellow kernels resemble popcorn, but with a soft, chewy texture and smoky-sour flavor. Hominy is available dried or cooked and canned. It may be served as a side dish or used in stews or soups. **Masa harina,** a finely ground flour made from dried hominy, is used for making breads, tortillas, tamales and other Mexican and southwestern dishes.

Grits

Grits

Grits are traditionally made by grinding dried hominy. These tiny white granules may be used in baked dishes but are most often served as a hot breakfast cereal, usually topped with butter or cheese. Quick-cooking and instant grits are available.

RICE

Rice (Fr. *riz;* It. *riso;* Sp. *arroz*) is the starchy seed of a semiaquatic grass. Probably originating on the Indian subcontinent or in Southeast Asia, rice is used as a staple by more than half the world's population.

Rice can be incorporated into almost any cuisine, from Asian to Spanish to classic French. Its flavor adapts to the foods and seasonings with which the rice is cooked or served. Its texture adds an appealing chewiness to meat and poultry dishes, salads, breads and puddings. Rice is not limited to a side dish, but may be used in stews or curries; for stuffing vegetables or game birds and in puddings, salads, beverages (such as Mexican *horchata*) and breads.

Rice is divided into three types based on seed size: **long-grain, medium-grain** and **short-grain.** Long-grain rice is the most versatile and popular worldwide. The grains remain firm, fluffy and separate when cooked. (Long-grain rice can, however, become sticky if overcooked or stirred frequently during cooking.) Short-grain rice has more starch and becomes quite tender and sticky when cooked. Italian risotto, Japanese zushi and Spanish paella are all traditionally made with short-grain rice. The appearance and starch content of medium-grain rice falls somewhere in between. Medium-grain rice becomes sticky when cool, so it is best eaten freshly made and piping hot.

Long-grain, medium-grain and short-grain rice are available in different processed forms. All rice is originally brown. The grains can be left whole, with the bran attached, for **brown rice.** Or they can be pearled for the more familiar polished **white rice.** Both brown rice and white rice can be processed into converted rice and instant rice.

Converted rice is parboiled to remove the surface starch. This procedure also forces nutrients from the bran into the grain's endosperm. Therefore, converted rice retains more nutrients than regular milled white rice, although the flavor is the same. Converted rice is neither precooked nor instant; in fact, it cooks more slowly than regular milled white rice.

Instant or **quick-cooking rice** is widely available and useful if time is a concern. Instant rice is created by fully cooking and then flash-freezing milled rice. Unfortunately, this processing removes some of the nutrients and flavor.

Converted Rice

Arborio Rice

Arborio Rice

Arborio is a round, short-grain rice used primarily in Italian dishes such as risotto. It is very sticky, with a white color and mild flavor.

Basmati Rice

Basmati is one of the finest long-grain rices in the world. It grows in the Himalayan foothills and is preferred in Indian cuisine. It is highly aromatic, with a sweet, delicate flavor and a creamy yellow color. Basmati rice is usually aged to improve its aromatic qualities and should be washed well before cooking. **Jasmine rice** is another aromatic long-grain rice. Similar to basmati, it is grown in Thailand and used throughout Southeast Asia.

Basmati Rice

Brown Rice

Brown rice is the whole natural grain of rice. Only the husk has been removed. Brown rice has a nutty flavor; its chewy texture is caused by the high-fiber bran. Brown rice absorbs more water and takes longer to cook than white rice.

Sticky Rice

Sticky rice is a short-grain rice used in many Asian cuisines. The short grains are fat and round with a high starch content and a pearly white color. When cooked, the grains tend to clump together, forming a sticky mass. Sticky rice must be soaked for several hours before being cooked. Also known as glutinous rice or sweet rice, it can be ground into flour and used for dumplings and pastries. Japanese sake and mirin and Chinese shaoxing are made from fermented sticky rice, as is rice vinegar.

Brown Rice

Wild Rice

Wild rice is prepared in the same manner as traditional rice, although it is actually the seed of an unrelated reedlike aquatic plant. Wild rice has long, slender grains with a dark brown to black color. It has a nuttier flavor and chewier texture than traditional rice. Three grades are available: giant (the best quality, with very long grains); fancy (a medium-sized grain, suitable for most purposes); and select (a short grain, suitable for soups, pancakes or baked goods). Cultivated in California, Idaho and Washington, it is generally served with game, used as a stuffing for poultry or combined with regular rice for a side dish. Wild rice is expensive, but small quantities are usually sufficient.

Wild Rice

Wild Pecan Rice

Wild pecan rice is neither wild nor made with pecans. It is a unique long-grain rice grown only in the bayou country of southern Louisiana. Wild pecan rice has a nutty flavor and exceptionally rich aroma.

Wild Pecan Rice

Guidelines for Cooking Rice

Rice may be rinsed before cooking to remove dirt and debris, but doing so also removes some of its nutrients. It is not necessary to rinse most American-grown rice, which is generally clean and free of insects. Rice may also be soaked before cooking. Soaking softens the grains, removes some starch and speeds cooking.

The standard ratio for cooking rice is 2 parts liquid to 1 part rice. The actual ratio varies, however, depending on the type of rice. Guidelines for cooking rice are found in Table 23.2.

WHEAT

Wheat (Fr. *blé*) is most often milled into the wide range of flours discussed in Chapter 29, Principles of the Bakeshop. But wheat and products derived from it are also used as starchy side dishes or ingredients in soups, salads, ground meat dishes and breads. These products include cracked wheat, bulgur and couscous. When cooked, they are slightly chewy with a mild flavor. All should be fluffy; none should be soggy or sticky.

Wheat germ and *wheat bran* are widely available and highly touted for their nutritional values. Bran and germ are not generally used plain, but may be added to bread or other cooked dishes.

> **SAFETY ALERT**
>
> Once cooked, rice is highly perishable. Because of its neutral pH and high protein content, cooked rice is a potentially hazardous food. To avoid the risk of food-borne illnesses, be sure to hold hot rice at 140°F (60°C) or higher. Leftover rice must be quickly cooled and stored at 40°F (4°C) or below. Leftover rice must be reheated to 165°F (74°C) or higher.

Table 23.2		GUIDELINES FOR COOKING RICE		
TYPE OF RICE	RATIO RICE: WATER (BY VOLUME)	PREPARATION	COOKING TIME (SIMMERING)	YIELD FROM 1 CUP RAW RICE
Arborio	1:2.5–3	Do not rinse or soak	15–20 min.	2½–3 c.
Basmati	1:1.75	Rinse well; soak	15 min.	3 c.
Brown, long-grain	1:2.5	Do not rinse; may soak	45–50 min.	3–4 c.
Converted	1:2.5	Do not rinse	20–25 min.	3–4 c.
White, long-grain (regular milled)	1:2	Do not rinse	15 min.	3 c.
Wild	1:3	Rinse	35–60 min., depending on grade	3–4 c.

Cracked Wheat

Cracked wheat is the whole wheat kernel (known as a **berry**) broken into varying degrees of coarseness. It is not precooked, and the kernel's white interior should be visible. The bran and germ are still intact, so cracked wheat has a great deal of fiber but a short shelf life. Whole wheat berries must be soaked for several hours before cooking. Cracked wheat can be fully cooked by long, gentle simmering.

Bulgur

Bulgur

Bulgur is a wheat berry that has had the bran removed; it is then steam-cooked, dried and ground into varying degrees of coarseness. Bulgur has a nutlike flavor and texture; it is a uniform golden-brown color (uncooked cracked wheat is not) and requires less cooking time than cracked wheat. Generally, cracked wheat and bulgur cannot be substituted for one another in recipes.

Bulgur needs only to be soaked in water, then drained, for use in salads, or briefly cooked when used in stews or pilafs. Bulgur is good with grilled meats and as an alternative to rice in stuffings and other dishes. The fine grind is most often used in packaged mixes such as tabouli; the medium grind is most often available in bulk.

Couscous

▶ **durum wheat** a species of very hard wheat with a particularly high amount of protein; it is used to make couscous or milled into semolina, which is used for making pasta

Couscous is made by removing the bran and germ from **durum wheat** berries. The endosperm is then steamed, pressed to form tiny pellets and dried. Couscous is available in varying degrees of coarseness; medium-fine is the most popular. Couscous is prepared by steaming over water or stock in a pot called a couscousière. Couscous, traditionally served with North African stews, can be used or served like rice.

Couscous

OTHER GRAINS

Barley

Barley

Barley is one of the oldest culinary grains, used by humans since prehistoric times. Barley is extremely hardy, growing in climates from the tropics to the near-Arctic. Although much of the barley crop is used to make beer or feed animals, some does find its way into soups, stews and stuffings. The most common type is pearled to produce a small, round white nugget of endosperm. It has a sweet, earthy flavor similar to oats, and goes well with onions, garlic and strong herbs. Barley's texture ranges from chewy to soft, depending on the amount of water in which it is cooked. Its starchiness can be used to thicken soups or stews.

Buckwheat/Kasha

Buckwheat is not a type of wheat; it is not even a grain. Rather, it is the fruit of a plant distantly related to rhubarb. Buckwheat is included here, however, because it is prepared and served in the same manner as grains.

The whole buckwheat kernel is known as a **groat.** The product most often sold as buckwheat is actually kasha, which is a hulled, roasted buckwheat groat. Kasha is reddish brown with a strong, nutty, almost scorched flavor. It is available whole or ground to varying degrees of coarseness. Whole kasha remains in separate grains after cooking; the finer grinds become rather sticky. Kasha can be served as a side dish, usually combined with pasta or vegetables, or it can be chilled and used in salads.

Raw buckwheat groats are ground into flour typically used in pasta, blini and other pancakes. Buckwheat flour contains no gluten-forming proteins, and it tends to remain grainy, with a sandy texture. Therefore, it should not be substituted for all the wheat flour in breads or baked goods.

Buckwheat/Kasha

Millet

Millet is a high-protein cereal grain with a bland, slightly nutty flavor and a white color. Used principally as animal fodder in the United States, millet can be cooked and eaten like rice or toasted like buckwheat and cooked like kasha. It can also be ground for flour (when used for baking, it is best combined with wheat flour). Millet is usually sold hulled, as the husk is extremely hard.

Millet

Oats

After rice, oats are probably the most widely accepted whole-grain product in the American diet. Oats are consumed daily as a hot breakfast cereal (oatmeal) and are used in breads, muffins, cookies and other baked goods.

An oat groat is the whole oat kernel with only the husk removed. It contains both the bran and germ. *Steel-cut oats,* sometimes known as Irish oats, are groats that are toasted and then cut into small pieces with steel blades. *Rolled oats,* marketed as "old-fashioned oats," are groats that have been steamed, then rolled into flat flakes. *Quick-cooking oats* are simply rolled oats cut into smaller pieces to reduce cooking time. *Instant oats* are partially cooked and dried before rolling so that they need only to be rehydrated in boiling water. Rolled oats and quick-cooking oats can be used interchangeably, but instant oats should not be substituted in most recipes.

Oat bran is the outer covering of a hulled oat. It is available as a separate product, although rolled and cut oats do contain some oat bran.

The term *oatmeal* is commonly used to refer to both processed groats and the cooked porridge made from them. The processed groats known as oatmeal are a gray-white color with a starchy texture and sweet flavor. They cook into the soft, thick porridge with a robust flavor called oatmeal.

Oats

Quinoa

Quinoa (keen-wa) is native to the South American Andes and was a common food of the Incas, who referred to it as the "mother grain." Although not botanically a true grain, quinoa's tiny seeds are treated as such. The grains (seeds) are small, flattened spheres, approximately ¹⁄₁₆ inch (1.5 millimeters) in diameter, ringed with the germ. They become translucent when cooked and have a slightly smoky or sesamelike flavor. Several varieties of quinoa are available, ranging in color from dark brown to almost white. The larger whiter varieties are most common and are considered superior.

Quinoa seeds have a natural, bitter-tasting coating, which protects them from birds and insects. Consequently, they should be placed in a fine-meshed colander and rinsed well with cool water for several minutes before use. Quinoa can then be cooked like rice, and will absorb about twice its volume of water. For a nuttier taste, toast the grain in a hot dry pan for about 5 minutes before adding the liquid. Quinoa can also be eaten as a hot breakfast cereal, used in lieu of rice, as a thickener for soups or stews and in salads, casseroles, breads and

Quinoa

desserts. Quinoa flour, ground from whole seeds, has a delicate nutty flavor. A gluten-free product, it is suitable for anyone bothered by wheat allergies. Quinoa is marketed as the world's "supergrain" because the seeds form a complete protein (with all of the essential amino acids) and contain important vitamins and minerals as well as carbohydrates and fat. Quinoa should be kept in the refrigerator or freezer for long-term storage. The leaves of the quinoa plant are similar to spinach and can be eaten as a vegetable.

NUTRITION

Grains are an excellent source of vitamins, minerals, proteins and fiber. The amount of milling or refining and the method of preparation affect their nutritional values, however. Unrefined and less-refined grains are excellent sources of dietary fiber. Rice is also quite nutritious: It is low in sodium and calories and contains all the essential amino acids. Some grains, especially white rice and oats, are usually enriched with calcium, iron and B-complex vitamins.

PURCHASING AND STORING GRAINS

PURCHASING

When buying grains, look for fresh, plump ones with a bright, even color. Fresh grains should not be shriveled or crumbly; there should be no sour or musty odors.

Grains are sold by weight. They come in bags or boxes ranging from 1 to 100 pounds. Ten-, 25- and 50-pound units are usually available.

STORING

All grains should be stored in airtight containers placed in a dark, cool, dry place. Airtight containers prevent dust and insects from entering. Airtight containers and darkness also reduce nutrient loss caused by oxidation or light. Coolness inhibits insect infestation; dryness prevents mold.

Vacuum-sealed packages will last for extended periods. Whole grains, which contain the oily germ, can be refrigerated to prevent rancidity.

APPLYING VARIOUS COOKING METHODS

Three basic cooking methods are used to prepare grains: simmering, risotto and pilaf. Unlike simmered grains, those cooked by either the risotto or pilaf method are first coated with hot fat. The primary distinction between the pilaf and risotto methods is the manner in which the liquid is then added to the grains. See Figure 23.2. When grains are used in puddings, breads, stuffings and baked casseroles, they are almost always first fully cooked by one of these methods.

DETERMINING DONENESS

Most grains should be cooked until tender, although some recipes do require a chewier or more al dente product. Doneness can usually be determined by cooking time and the amount of liquid remaining in the pan. Some grains, such as wild rice, are fully cooked when they puff open.

In general, grains will be fully cooked when almost all the cooking liquid has been-absorbed. This is indicated by the appearance of tunnel-like holes be-

SIMMERING	=	Grain	⟶	Boiling liquid	⟶	Cover and simmer
RISOTTO	=	Sauté grain	⟶	Hot liquid added gradually	⟶	Stir constantly
PILAF	=	Sauté grain	⟶	All liquid added at once	⟶	Cover and simmer

FIGURE 23.2 ▶ Cooking methods

tween the grains. Grains can be cooked until almost all of the liquid is absorbed, then removed from the heat and left to stand, covered, for 5–10 minutes. This allows the cooked grains to absorb the remaining moisture without burning.

SIMMERING

The most commonly used method for preparing grains is simmering. To do so, simply stir the grains into a measured amount of boiling salted water in a saucepan on the stove top. When the liquid returns to a boil, lower the heat, cover, and simmer until the liquid is absorbed and the grains are tender. The grains are not stirred during cooking.

The grains can be flavored by using stock as the cooking liquid. Herbs and spices can also be added.

▶ PROCEDURE FOR SIMMERING GRAINS

1 Bring the cooking liquid to a boil.
2 Stir in the grains. Add herbs or spices as desired or as directed in the recipe.
3 Return the mixture to a boil, cover and reduce to a simmer.
4 Simmer the grains until tender and most of the liquid is absorbed.
5 Remove the grains from the heat.
6 Drain if appropriate or keep covered and allow the excess moisture to evaporate, approximately 5 minutes. Fluff the grains with a fork before service.

SIMMERED RICE

RECIPE 23.6

Yield: 1½ pt. (750 ml)   **Method:** Simmering

Water	1 pt.	500 ml
Salt	½ tsp.	2 ml
White rice	1 c.	250 ml

1 Bring the water and salt to a boil in a heavy saucepan. Slowly add the rice.
2 Cover the pan and reduce the heat so that the liquid simmers gently. Cook until the rice is tender and the water is absorbed, approximately 15 to 20 minutes.
3 Remove from the heat and transfer to a hotel pan. Do not cover. Allow any excess moisture to evaporate for approximately 5 minutes.
4 Fluff the rice and serve, or refrigerate for use in another recipe.

Approximate values per ½ c. (120-ml) serving: **Calories** 150, **Total fat** 0 g, **Saturated fat** 0 g, **Cholesterol** 0 mg, **Sodium** 192 mg, **Total carbohydrates** 34 g, **Protein** 3 g, **Iron** 8%, **Claims**–fat free, no sugar

RISOTTO METHOD

Risotto is a classic northern Italian rice dish in which the grains remain firm but merge with the cooking liquid to become a creamy, almost puddinglike dish. True risotto is made with a short-grain starchy rice such as Arborio, but the risotto method can also be used to cook other grains such as barley and oats.

The grains are not rinsed before cooking, as this removes the starches needed to achieve the desired consistency. The grains are coated, but not cooked, in a hot fat such as butter or oil. A hot liquid is then gradually added to the grains so that the mixture is kept at a constant simmer. The cooking liquid should be a rich, flavorful stock. Unlike simmering and the pilaf method, the risotto method requires frequent, sometimes constant, stirring.

When finished, the grains should be creamy and tender, but still al dente in the center. Grated cheese, heavy cream, cooked meat, poultry, fish, shellfish, herbs and vegetables can be added to create a flavorful side dish or a complete meal.

▶ PROCEDURE FOR PREPARING GRAINS BY THE RISOTTO METHOD

1 Bring the cooking liquid (usually a stock) to a simmer.
2 Heat the fat in a heavy saucepan over moderate heat. Add any onions, garlic or other flavoring ingredients and sauté for 1–2 minutes without browning.
3 Add the grains to the saucepan. Stir well to make sure the grains are well coated with fat. Do not allow the grains to brown.
4 Add any wine and cook until it is fully absorbed.
5 Begin to add the simmering stock, 4 fluid ounces (120 milliliters) at a time, stirring frequently. Wait until each portion of cooking liquid is almost fully absorbed before adding the next.
6 Test for doneness after the grains have cooked for approximately 18 to 20 minutes.
7 Remove the saucepan from the heat and stir in any butter, grated cheese, herbs or other flavoring ingredients as directed. Garnish as desired and serve immediately.

RECIPE 23.7 — RISOTTO MILANESE

Yield: 24 Serving, 4 oz. (120 g) each   **Method:** Risotto

Chicken stock	2½ qt.	2.5 lt
Whole butter	4 oz.	120 g
Onions, minced	5 oz.	150 g
Arborio rice	1 lb. 8 oz.	700 g
Dry white wine	8 fl. oz.	250 ml
Saffron threads, crushed	½ tsp.	2 ml
Parmesan, grated	4 oz.	120 g

1 Bring the chicken stock to a simmer.
2 Heat 3 ounces (90 grams) of the butter in a large, heavy saucepan. Add the onions and sauté until translucent.
3 Add the rice to the onions and butter. Stir well to coat the grains with butter, but do not allow the rice to brown. Add the wine and stir until it is completely absorbed.
4 Add the saffron. Add the simmering stock, 4 fluid ounces (120 milliliters) at a time, stirring frequently. Wait until the stock is absorbed before adding the next 4-fluid-ounce (120-milliliter) portion.
5 After approximately 18 to 20 minutes, all the stock should be incorporated and the rice should be tender. Remove from the heat and stir in the remaining 1 ounce (30 grams) of butter and the grated cheese. Serve immediately.

Variations: *Risotto with Radicchio* (al Radicchio)—Omit the saffron and Parmesan. Just before the risotto is fully cooked, stir in 4 fluid ounces (120 milliliters) of heavy cream and 3 ounces (90 grams) of finely chopped radicchio leaves.

1 Sautéing the rice and onions in butter.

2 Adding the stock gradually while stirring frequently.

3 Stirring in the butter and grated cheese.

Risotto with Four Cheeses (al Quattro Formaggi)—Omit the saffron. When the risotto is fully cooked, remove from the heat and stir in 2 ounces (60 grams) each of grated Parmesan, Gorgonzola, Fontina and mozzarella. Garnish with toasted pine nuts and chopped parsley.

Risotto with Smoked Salmon (al Salmone Affumicato)—Omit the butter, saffron and Parmesan. Sauté the onions in 3 fluid ounces (90 milliliters) of corn or safflower oil instead of butter. When the risotto is fully cooked, remove from the heat and stir in 8 fluid ounces (240 milliliters) half-and-half, 3 fluid ounces (90 milliliters) fresh lemon juice and 8 to 10 ounces (240–300 grams) good-quality smoked salmon. Garnish with chopped fresh parsley and dill. Serve with lemon wedges.

Approximate values per 4-oz. (120-g) serving: **Calories** 110, **Total fat** 6 g, **Saturated fat** 3.5 g, **Cholesterol** 15 mg, **Sodium** 470 mg, **Total carbohydrates** 9 g, **Protein** 5 g

PILAF METHOD

For the pilaf method, the raw grains are lightly sautéed in oil or butter, usually with onions or seasonings for additional flavor. Hot liquid, often a stock, is then added. The pan is covered and the mixture is left to simmer until the liquid is absorbed.

▶ PROCEDURE FOR PREPARING GRAINS BY THE PILAF METHOD

1 Bring the cooking liquid (either water or stock) to a boil.

2 Heat the fat in a heavy saucepan over moderate heat. Add any onions, garlic or other flavorings and sauté for 1 to 2 minutes without browning.

3 Add the grains to the saucepan. Stir well to make sure the grains are well coated with fat. Do not allow the grains to brown.

4 All at once, add the hot cooking liquid to the sautéed grains.

5 Return the liquid to a boil, reduce to a simmer and cover.

6 Allow the mixture to simmer, either in the oven or on the stove top, until the liquid is absorbed.

BULGUR PILAF

RECIPE 23.8

Yield: 8 Servings, 4 oz. (120 g) each   **Method:** Pilaf

Whole butter	2 oz.	60 g
Onions, fine dice	4 oz.	120 g
Bulgur	10 oz.	300 g
Bay leaf	1	1
Chicken stock, hot	1 qt.	1 lt
Salt and pepper	TT	TT

1 Melt the butter in a large, heavy saucepan over moderate heat. Add the onions and sauté until translucent.

2 Add the bulgur and bay leaf. Sauté until the grains are well coated with butter.

3 Add the hot stock and season to taste with salt and pepper. Reduce the heat until the liquid barely simmers.

4 Cover and continue cooking until all the liquid is absorbed and the grains are tender, approximately 18 to 20 minutes.

5 Fluff with a fork and adjust the seasonings before service.

Variation: *Barley Pilaf*—Substitute 2 cups (500 milliliters) of pearled barley for the bulgur. Cooking time may increase by 10 to 15 minutes.

Approximate values per 4-oz. (120-g) serving: **Calories** 110, **Total fat** 7 g, **Saturated fat** 4 g, **Cholesterol** 15 mg, **Sodium** 470 mg, **Total carbohydrates** 9 g, **Protein** 4 g

1 Sautéing the bulgur in butter.

2 Adding the hot stock to the bulgur.

3 Fluffing the finished bulgur.

▶ PASTA

Pasta is made from an unleavened dough of wheat flour mixed with a liquid. The liquid is usually egg and/or water. The flour can be from almost any grain: wheat, buckwheat, rice or a combination of grains. The dough can be colored and flavored with puréed vegetables, herbs or other ingredients, and it can be cut or **extruded** into a wide variety of shapes and sizes.

Pasta can be cooked fresh while the dough is still moist and pliable, or the dough can be allowed to dry completely before cooking. Pasta can be filled or sauced in an endless variety of ways. It can stand alone or be used in salads, desserts, soups or casseroles.

Pasta is widely used in the cuisines of Asia, North America and Europe. In Italy, pasta dishes are usually served as a separate course, referred to as the *minestre;* in other European countries, Asia and the United States, pasta dishes may be served as an appetizer, entrée or side dish.

▶ **extrusion** the process of forcing pasta dough through perforated plates to create various shapes; pasta dough that is not extruded must be rolled and cut

IDENTIFYING PASTAS

The better-known pastas are based on the Italian tradition of kneading wheat flour with water and eggs to form a smooth, resilient dough. This dough is then rolled very thin and cut into various shapes before being boiled in water or dried for longer storage.

Commercially prepared dried pasta products are usually made with semolina flour. Semolina flour, ground from hard durum wheat and available from specialty purveyors, has a rich cream color and produces a very smooth, durable dough. Semolina dough requires a great deal of kneading, however, and bread flour is an acceptable substitute when preparing fresh pasta by hand.

Asian pasta, generally known as noodles, is made from wheat, rice, bean or buckwheat flour. It is available fresh or dried from commercial purveyors and at specialty markets.

ITALIAN-STYLE PASTA

Although all Italian-style pasta is made from the same type of dough, the finest commercial pastas are those made with pure semolina flour, which gives the dough a rich, yellow color. Gray or streaked dough probably contains softer flours. Dried pasta should be very hard and break with a clean snap. The surface should be lightly pitted or dull. (A smooth or glossy surface will not hold or absorb sauces as well.)

Dried pasta, both domestic and imported, is available in a wide range of flavors and shapes. In addition to the traditional white (plain), green (spinach) and red (tomato) pastas, manufacturers are now offering flavor combinations such as lemon-peppercorn, whole wheat–basil, jalapeño–black bean and carrot-ginger. Small pieces of herbs or other flavorings are often visible in these products.

There are hundreds of recognized shapes of pasta, but only two or three dozen are generally available in the United States. When experimenting with unusual flavors and shapes, be sure to consider the taste and appearance of the final dish after the sauce and any garnishes are added.

Italian-style pasta can be divided into three groups based on the shape of the final product: ribbons, tubes and shapes. There is no consistent English nomenclature for these pastas; the Italian names are recognized and applied virtually worldwide. (A specific shape or size may be given different names in different regions of Italy, however. These distinctions are beyond the scope of this text.)

Ribbons

Pasta dough can be rolled very thin and cut into strips or ribbons of various widths. All ribbon shapes work well with tomato, fish and shellfish sauces. Thicker ribbons, such as spaghetti and fettuccine, are preferred with cream or cheese sauces. Sheets of fresh pasta dough can be filled and shaped to create

Semolina

▶ **macaroni** any dried pasta made with wheat flour and water; only in the United States does the term refer to elbow-shaped tubes

THE MACARONI MYTH

The popular myth holds that noodles were first invented in China and discovered there by the Venetian explorer Marco Polo during the 13th century. He introduced the food to Italy and from there the rest of Europe. Although there is little doubt that the Chinese were making noodles by the 1st century A.D., it is now equally clear that they were not alone.

Middle Eastern and Italian cooks were preparing macaroni long before Marco Polo's adventures. A clear reference to boiled noodles appears in the *Jerusalem Talmud* of the 5th century A.D. There, rabbis debate whether noodles violate Jewish dietary laws (they do, but only during Passover). Tenth-century Arabic writings refer to dried noodles purchased from vendors. Literary references establish that

dishes called lasagna, macaroni and ravioli were all well known (and costly) in Italy by the mid-13th century.

Pasta's current popularity dates from the 18th century, when mass production by machine began in Naples, Italy. English gentlemen on their "grand tours" of the European continent developed a fondness for pasta; the word *macaroni* became a synonym for a dandy or a vain young man. Macaroni arrived in America with English colonists, who preferred it with cream sauce and cheese or in a sweet custard. Domestic factories soon opened, and by the Civil War (1861–1865), macaroni was available to the working class. Pasta became a staple of the American middle-class diet following the wave of Italian immigrants in the late 19th century.

During the 1980s pasta became ubiquitous. Restaurants began serving it in ways previously unimagined. Corner grocery stores and local supermarkets began offering at least a dozen different shapes, often fresh and sometimes flavored. Dedicated cooks began to make pasta from scratch, though they sometimes tossed it with bottled sauce. Many also became interested in Asian noodles. Chinese, Japanese, Korean and Thai restaurants expanded their menu offerings to include traditional noodle dishes that were eagerly ordered by curious consumers. Pasta's popularity continues to grow as chefs discover the versatility of this inexpensive, nutritious food.

Spinach Fettuccine

Lasagna

Fettuccine

Spaghetti

Capellini

ravioli, cappelletti and tortellini. Filled pasta is usually served with a light cream- or tomato-based sauce that complements the filling's flavors.

Tubes

Cylindrical forms or tubes are made by extrusion. The hollow tubes can be curved or straight, fluted or smooth. Tubes are preferred for meat and vegetable sauces and are often used in baked casseroles.

Manicotti

Ziti

Rigatoni

Penne

Spira

Shapes

The extrusion process can also be used to shape pasta dough into forms. The curves and textures produced provide nooks and crevices that hold sauces well. Shaped pastas, such as conchiglie, farfalle and fusilli, are preferred with meat sauces and oil-based sauces such as pesto. Larger shaped pastas can be cooked, then stuffed with meat or cheese fillings and baked or served as a casserole.

Conchiglie

Farfalle

Fusilli

Rotelle

Orzo

ASIAN NOODLES

Asian noodles are not cut into the same wealth of shapes and sizes as Italian-style pasta, nor are they flavored or colored with vegetable purées, herbs or other ingredients.

Virtually all Asian noodles are ribbons—some thin, some thick—folded into bundles and packaged. Differences arise because of the flours used for the dough.

Most dried Asian noodles benefit by soaking in hot water for several minutes before further preparation. The water softens the noodle strands; the bundles separate, and the noodles cook more evenly.

WHEAT NOODLES

Wheat noodles, also known as egg noodles, are the most popular and most widely available of the Asian noodles. They are thin, flat noodles with a springy texture; they are available fresh or dried. Dried egg noodles can be deep-fried after boiling to create crisp golden noodles (chow mein) used primarily as a garnish.

Japanese wheat noodles, known as *somen* (if thick) and *udon* (if thin), may be round, square or flat. They are eaten in broth or with a dipping sauce.

RICE NOODLES

Rice noodles are thin dried noodles made with rice flour. They should be soaked in hot water before cooking and rinsed in cool running water after boiling to remove excess starch and prevent sticking. Rice noodles are often served in soups or sautéed.

Rice vermicelli, which has very fine strands, can be fried in hot oil without presoaking. In only a few seconds, the strands will turn white, puff up and become crunchy. Mounds of crunchy rice noodles can be used as a base for sautéed dishes or for presenting hors d'oeuvres.

BEAN STARCH NOODLES

Bean starch noodles are also known as spring rain noodles, bean threads, bean noodles or cellophane noodles. They are thin, transparent noodles made from mung beans. Dried bean noodles can be fried in the same manner as rice vermicelli. Otherwise, they must be soaked in hot water before using in soups, stir-fries or braised dishes.

BUCKWHEAT NOODLES

Buckwheat flour is used in the noodles of northern Japan and the Tokyo region, known as soba noodles. Soba noodles are available fresh or dried and do not need soaking before cooking. They are traditionally served in broth or with a dipping sauce, but may be substituted for Italian-style pasta if desired.

NUTRITION

Pastas are very low in fat and are an excellent source of vitamins, minerals, proteins and carbohydrates. Also, the processed products are sometimes enriched with additional nutrients.

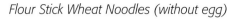

Flour Stick Wheat Noodles (without egg)

Fresh Wheat and Egg Noodles

Rice Vermicelli

Cellophane Noodles

Japanese Wheat Somen

DUMPLINGS

A **dumpling** is a small mound of dough cooked by steaming or simmering in a flavorful liquid. Dumplings are found in many cuisines: Italian gnocchi, Jewish matzo balls, German spaetzle, Chinese wontons, Belorussian pahmayne and Polish pierogi. Dumplings can be sweet or savory, plain or filled.

Plain or **drop dumplings** are made with a breadlike dough, often leavened with yeast or chemical leavening agents. They should be light and tender, but firm enough to hold their shape when cooked. Drop dumplings may be served with stews or broths, or coated with butter or sauce as an appetizer or side dish.

Filled dumplings are made by wrapping noodle dough around seasoned meat, vegetables, cheese or fruit. These parcels are then steamed, fried or baked and served as a snack food, appetizer or side dish. A recipe for deep-fried wontons is included in Chapter 28, Hors d'Oeuvre and Canapés.

PURCHASING AND STORING PASTA PRODUCTS

Pasta products are purchased by weight, either fresh or dried. Tubes and shapes are not generally available fresh. Dried products, by far the most common, are available in boxes or bags, usually in 1-, 10- and 20-pound units. They can be stored in a cool, dry place for several months. Fresh pasta can be stored in an airtight wrapping in the refrigerator for a few days or in the freezer for a few weeks.

PREPARING FRESH PASTA

MAKING FRESH PASTA

Fresh pasta is easy to make, requiring almost no special equipment and only a few staples. The basic form is the **sfoglia,** a thin, flat sheet of dough that is cut into ribbons, circles or squares.

Although pasta dough can be kneaded by hand, stretched and rolled with a rolling pin and cut with a chef's knife, pasta machines make these tasks easier. Pasta machines are either electric or manual. Some electric models mix and knead the dough, then extrude it through a cutting disk. An extrusion machine is most practical in a food service operation that regularly serves large quantities of pasta. The pasta machine more often encountered is operated manually with a hand crank. It has two rollers that knead, press and push the dough into a thin, uniform sheet. Adjacent cutting rollers slice the thin dough into various widths for fettuccine, spaghetti, capellini and the like.

RECIPE 23.9 **BASIC PASTA DOUGH**

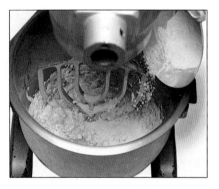

1 Adding flour to the mixing bowl and using the paddle until the mixture forms a soft dough.

2 The finished dough.

Yield: 4 lb. (1.8 kg)

Eggs	15	15
Olive oil	1 fl. oz.	30 ml
Salt	1 Tbsp.	15 ml
Bread flour*	2 lb. 8 oz.	1.1 kg

1 Place the eggs, oil and salt in a large mixer bowl. Use the paddle attachment to combine.
2 Add one-third of the flour and stir until the mixture begins to form a soft dough. Remove the paddle attachment and attach the dough hook.
3 Gradually add more flour until the dough is dry and cannot absorb any more flour.
4 Remove the dough from the mixer, wrap it well with plastic wrap and set it aside at room temperature for 20 to 30 minutes.
5 After the dough has rested, roll it into flat sheets by hand or with a pasta machine. Work with only a small portion at a time, keeping the remainder well covered to prevent it from drying out.
6 While the sheets of dough are pliable, cut them into the desired width with a chef's knife or pasta machine. Sheets can also be used for making ravioli, as illustrated next.

Variations: *Garlic-Herb*—Roast 1 head of garlic. Peel and purée the cloves and add to the eggs. Add up to 2 ounces (60 grams) of finely chopped assorted fresh herbs just before mixing is complete.

Spinach—Add 8 ounces (250 grams) of cooked, puréed and well-drained spinach to the eggs. Increase the amount of flour slightly if necessary.

Tomato—Add 4 ounces (120 grams) of tomato paste to the eggs; omit the salt. Increase the amount of flour slightly if necessary.

Chipotle—Purée 6 ounces (180 grams) of canned chipotle chiles in adobo sauce in a blender or food processor. Add the purée to the egg and oil mixture. Use additional flour, if necessary.

Approximate values per 1-oz. (30-g) serving: **Calories** 80, **Total fat** 2 g, **Saturated fat** 0.5 g, **Cholesterol** 50 mg, **Sodium** 125 mg, **Total carbohydrates** 13 g, **Protein** 3 g

*Semolina flour can be substituted for all or part of the bread flour in this recipe, although it makes a stronger dough that is more difficult to work with by hand.

▶ PROCEDURE FOR ROLLING AND CUTTING PASTA DOUGH

1 Work with a small portion of the dough. Leave the rest covered with plastic wrap to prevent it from drying out.

2 Flatten the dough with the heel of your hand.

3 Set the pasta machine rollers to their widest setting. Insert the dough and turn the handle with one hand while supporting the dough with the other hand. Pass the entire piece of dough through the rollers.

4 Dust the dough with flour, fold it in thirds and pass it through the pasta machine again.

5 Repeat the folding and rolling procedure until the dough is smooth. This may require four to six passes.

6 Tighten the rollers one or two marks, then pass the dough through the machine. Without folding it in thirds, pass the dough through the machine repeatedly, tightening the rollers one or two marks each time.

7 When the dough is thin enough to see your hand through it, but not so thin that it begins to tear, it is ready to use or cut into ribbons. This sheet is the *sfoglia*.

8 To cut the sfoglia into ribbons, gently feed a manageable length of dough through the desired cutting blades.

9 Lay out the pasta in a single layer on a sheet pan dusted with flour to dry. Layers of pasta ribbons can be separated with parchment paper.

1 Passing the entire piece of dough through the pasta machine.

2 Folding the dough in the thirds.

3 Passing the dough through the pasta machine to achieve the desired thinkness.

4 Using the pasta machine to cut the pasta into the desired width.

FILLING PASTA

Sheets of raw pasta dough can be filled or folded to create ravioli (squares), tortellini (round "hats" with a brim of dough), lunettes (circles of dough folded into half-moons), agnolotti (squares of dough folded into rectangles), cappelletti (squares of dough folded and shaped into rings) and other shapes. The filled pieces of dough are then cooked in boiling water using the procedure for cooking pasta ribbons discussed later. The filling can include almost anything— cheese, herbs, vegetables, fish, shellfish, meat or poultry. It can be uncooked or precooked. But any meat filling should be fully cooked before the pasta is assembled, as the time it takes for the dough to cook may not be sufficient to cook the filling.

Cannelloni is a different type of filled pasta: A large square of cooked dough is wrapped around a meat or cheese filling and baked. Popular lasagna dishes are similar. Lasagna are wide, flat sheets of pasta, that are cooked and then layered with cheese, tomato sauce and meat or vegetables as desired. The finished casserole is baked and cut into portions.

Some of the larger, commercially prepared pasta shapes such as large shells (conchigloni or rigate) or large tubes (manicotti) can be partially cooked in boiling water, then filled, sauced and baked as a casserole.

Asian noodle dough is also made into filled items such as dumplings, wontons, egg rolls (made with egg noodle dough) and spring rolls (made with rice paper). These items are usually steamed, pan-fried or deep-fried. When making filled pasta, consider the flavors and textures of the filling, dough and sauce. Each should complement the others.

▶ PROCEDURE FOR PREPARING RAVIOLI

1 Prepare a basic pasta dough of the desired flavor.

2 Prepare and chill the desired filling.

3 Roll out two thin sheets of dough between the rollers of a pasta machine. Gently lay the dough flat on the work surface.

4 Using a piping bag or a small portion scoop, place small mounds of filling on one of the dough pieces. Space the fillings evenly, allowing approximately 2 inches (5 centimeters) between each mound.

5 Brush the exposed areas of dough with water.

6 Gently place the second sheet of dough over the mounds and press firmly around each mound to remove air pockets and seal the dough.

7 Cut between the mounds with a chef's knife, pastry wheel or circular cutter.

1 Piping the filling onto the dough.

2 Pressing around the mounds of filling to seal the dough and remove any air pockets.

3 Cutting around the mounds with a circular cutter.

COOKING METHOD

DETERMINING DONENESS

Italian-style pastas are properly cooked when they are **al dente,** firm but tender. Cooking times vary depending on the shape and quantity of pasta, the amount of water used, the hardness of the water and even the altitude. Fresh pasta cooks rapidly, sometimes in seconds. Noodles and dried pasta may require several minutes.

Although package or recipe directions offer some guidance, the only way to accurately test doneness is to bite into a piece. When the pasta is slightly firmer than desired, remove it from the stove and drain. It will continue to cook through residual heat.

Unlike Italian pasta, Asian noodles are not served al dente. Rather, they are either boiled until very soft or stir-fried until very crisp.

BOILING

All Italian-style pasta and most Asian noodles are cooked by just one method: boiling. The secret to boiling pasta successfully is to use ample water. Allow 1 gallon (4 liters) of water for each pound (450 grams) of pasta.

Use a saucepan or stockpot large enough to allow the pasta to move freely in the boiling water; otherwise, the starch released by the dough will make the pasta gummy and sticky. The water should be brought to a rapid boil, then all the pasta should be added at once.

Salt should be added to the water. Pasta absorbs water and salt during cooking. Adding salt to the pasta after it is cooked will not provide the same seasoning effect.

Chefs disagree on whether to add oil to the cooking water. Purists argue against adding oil, on the theory that it makes the dough absorb water unevenly. Others think oil should be added to reduce surface foam. Another theory is that oil keeps the pasta from sticking, although this works only when added to cooked, drained pasta.

Asian noodles may be prepared by boiling until fully cooked, or they may be parboiled and then stir-fried with other ingredients to finish cooking.

▶ PROCEDURE FOR COOKING PASTA TO ORDER

1 Bring the appropriate amount of water to a boil over high heat.
2 Add oil to the water if desired.
3 Add the pasta and salt to the rapidly boiling water.
4 Stir the pasta to prevent it from sticking together. Bring the water back to a boil and cook until the pasta is done.
5 When the pasta is properly cooked, immediately drain it through a colander. A small amount of oil may be gently tossed into the pasta if desired to prevent it from sticking together.
6 Serve hot pasta immediately, or refresh it in cold water for later use in salads or other dishes. (Do not rinse pasta that is to be served hot.)

▶ PROCEDURE FOR COOKING DRIED PASTA IN ADVANCE

Fresh pasta is so delicate and cooks so rapidly (sometimes in as little as 15 seconds) that it should be cooked to order. Dried pasta, however, can be cooked in advance for quantity service.

1 Follow the preceding directions for cooking pasta, but stop the cooking process when the pasta is about two-thirds done.
2 Drain the pasta, rinse it lightly and toss it in a small amount of oil.

▶ **al dente** (al DEN-tay) Italian for "to the tooth"; used to describe a food, usually pasta, that is cooked only until it gives a slight resistance when one bites into it

3 Divide the pasta into appropriate-sized portions. Individual portions can be wrapped in plastic or laid on a sheet pan and covered. Refrigerate until needed.

4 When needed, place a portion in a china cap and immerse in boiling water to reheat. Drain, add sauce and serve immediately.

ACCOMPANIMENTS TO PASTA

Pasta is widely accepted by consumers and easily incorporated in a variety of cuisines—from Italian and Chinese to Eastern European and spa. It is used in broths; as a bed for stews, fish, shellfish, poultry or meat or tossed with sauce. Today's creative chefs are constantly developing nontraditional but delicious ways of serving pasta.

Pasta and Broths

Small shapes can be cooked in the broth with which they are served, or cooked separately, then added to the hot liquid at service time. Soups such as cappelletti in brodo and chicken noodle are examples of these techniques.

Pasta Sauces

There are hundreds of Italian pasta sauces as well as sauces for Italian-style pasta, but most can be divided into six categories: ragus, seafood sauces, vegetable sauces, cream sauces, garlic-oil sauces and uncooked sauces. Recipes for a selection of pasta sauces are included in Chapter 11, Stocks and Sauces.

Although there are no firm rules governing the combinations of sauces and pasta, Table 23.3 offers some of the more common combinations.

Table 23.3 COMBINING SAUCES, PASTA AND GARNISHES

SAUCE	DESCRIPTION	PASTA SHAPE	GARNISH
Ragu	Braised dishes used as sauce; flavorings, meat or poultry are browned, then a tomato product and stock, wine, water, milk or cream added	Ribbons, tubes, shapes, filled	Grated cheese
Seafood	White seafood sauces are flavored with herbs and made with white wine or stock; red seafood sauces are tomato-based	Ribbons (fettuccine and capellini)	Fish or shellfish
Vegetable	Includes both traditional sauces made with tomatoes and stock, flavored with garlic and red pepper, and modern sauces such as primavera	Ribbons, tubes, filled	Meatballs, sausage, grated cheese
Cream	Uses milk or cream and sometimes roux; usually cheese is added	Thick ribbons (spaghetti and fettuccine), filled	Ham, peas, sausage, mushrooms, smoked salmon, nuts, grated cheese
Garlic-Oil	(It. *aglio-olio*) Olive oil flavored with garlic and herbs; can be hot or cold, cooked or uncooked (pesto is an uncooked, cold sauce)	Ribbons, shapes, filled	Grated cheese (if uncooked or cold), herbs
Uncooked	A variety of dressings and garnishes such as fresh tomatoes, basil and olive oil; or olive oil, lemon juice, parsley, basil and hot red pepper flakes; capers, anchovies, olives, fresh herbs, fresh vegetables, flavored oils and cubed cheeses can also be used	Ribbons, shapes	Cubed or grated cheese, fresh vegetables, herbs

Most meals would seem incomplete without a starch. The most popular starches are potatoes, grains (especially rice) and pasta. All are low in fat and a good source of energy. Most can be prepared with several dry- and moist-heat cooking methods, and all can be sauced, seasoned or flavored in limitless ways.

1 Explain the differences between mealy and waxy potatoes. Give two examples of each.

2 Describe the two methods of sautéing or pan-frying potatoes.

3 Explain why duchesse potatoes are regarded as the "mother" of many classic potato dishes. Name and describe two such dishes.

4 All grains are composed of three parts. Name and describe each of these parts.

5 Describe and compare the three general cooking methods used to prepare grains.

6 Name the three categories of Italian-style pasta shapes and give an example of each.

7 Why is it necessary to use ample water when cooking pasta? Should pasta be cooked in salted water? Should oil be added to the cooking water? Explain your answers.

8 Discuss the differences between cooking fresh pasta and cooking dried, factory-produced pasta.

9 Different names are given to Italian pasta shapes from one region of Italy to another. Research the various regional Italian cuisines to determine other names for some of the pastas shown on pages 705–707.

10 Each of the types of sauce listed in Table 23.3 comes from a specific region of Italy. Which region is most closely associated with each type of sauce? Why?

OPEN RAVIOLI OF LOBSTER AND CORN WITH ENGLISH PEAS, ASPARAGUS AND AN HERB EMULSION

RECIPE 23.10

CHEF KEVIN TAYLOR

A native of Colorado, Chef Kevin Taylor is known for his creative, unpretentious approach to American cuisine. He has been cooking for more than 20 years and has owned restaurants in Denver and Boulder, Colorado, for more than a decade, including Restaurant Kevin Taylor, which opened in 1998 in Denver's historic Teatro Hotel.

Chef Taylor began cooking during high school, then apprenticed at a Denver country club where he learned classic French techniques from the club's European chefs. He moved on to become sous chef of Denver's Cherry Hills Country Club, and then, in 1987 at age 25, he opened his first restaurant, Zenith American Grill, which featured creative combinations of the freshest ingredients, many of them locally grown and organically raised. Chef Taylor's other operations include Jou Jou Bistro, Palattes and Dandelion Restaurant.

Cited as a rising star by national magazines and a guest chef at the James Beard House in New York City, Chef Taylor notes that he is "not interested in food that looks good, but has no flavor." In his restaurants, "flavor is paramount."

RESTAURANT KEVIN TAYLOR, DENVER, CO
Chef Kevin Taylor

Note: This dish appears in the chapter opening photograph.

Yield: 4 Servings

Semolina	4 oz.	120 g
Flour	4 oz.	120 g
Fresh herbs, minced (dill, chives, parsley)	3 Tbsp.	45 ml
Water, cold	as needed	as needed
Riesling wine	1 pt.	450 ml
Heavy cream	2 fl. oz.	60 ml
Unsalted butter	5 oz.	150 g
Lobsters, cooked, meat removed from shells	2	2
Asparagus, 1-in. (2.5-cm) pieces, cooked	¼ c.	60 ml
Corn kernels, cooked	¼ c.	60 ml
English peas, cooked	¼ c.	60 ml
Olive oil	as needed	as needed
Salt and pepper	TT	TT
Herb sprigs	as needed for garnish	

1 In a small mixing bowl or electric mixer, combine the semolina, flour and 1 tablespoon (15 milliliters) of the minced herbs. Slowly add enough cold water, mixing constantly, to form a ball. Knead the dough until it reaches the correct consistency. Use a pasta machine to roll the dough into sheets the thickness of a penny. Cut the sheets into eight rounds approximately 3½ inches (8.5 centimeters) in diameter. Dust the rounds with semolina and set aside.

2 In a small saucepot over high heat, reduce the wine by two-thirds. Add the heavy cream and reduce by two-thirds again. When the liquid begins to thicken, reduce the heat and whisk in the butter, a little at a time. Hold the sauce in a warm place.

3 Split the two lobster tail meat portions in half, creating four halves. Sauté the asparagus, corn and peas and the lobster tail, claw and body meat in olive oil for 30 seconds or until hot. Season to taste with salt and pepper.

4 Boil the pasta circles in salted water for 1 minute. Place one pasta round in the bottom of each of four soup plates. Divide the vegetable and lobster body meat mixture between the four pasta rounds. Place one half lobster tail meat portion on top of the vegetable mixture. Place the other pasta rounds over the mixture and lay a claw meat portion on top of each ravioli.

5 Place the butter sauce in a small mixing bowl, add the remaining minced herbs and blend with a small hand mixer. Season with salt and pepper and pour the herbed emulsion around the pasta. Garnish with fresh herbs.

Approximate values per serving: **Calories** 680, **Total fat** 36 g, **Saturated fat** 22 g, **Cholesterol** 170 mg, **Sodium** 240 mg, **Total carbohydrates** 49 g, **Protein** 23 g, **Vitamin A** 30%, **Vitamin C** 10%, **Iron** 20%

GRILLED POTATO SALAD

GREENS, San Francisco, CA
Chef Annie Somerville

Yield: 4 Servings   **Method:** Baking/Grilling

New potatoes	2 lb.	1 kg
Light olive oil	as needed	as needed
Salt and pepper	TT	TT
Cherry tomatoes, sweet one hundreds or pear cherry tomatoes	4 oz.	120 g
Red and yellow bell peppers, roasted, seeded and cut into strips	1 lb.	500 g
Basil Vinaigrette (recipe follows)		
Champagne vinegar	as needed	as needed
Frisée or salad greens (optional)	4 oz.	120 g
Niçoise or Gaeta olives	12	12

1 Toss the potatoes with the olive oil in a baking dish; sprinkle with a few pinches of salt and pepper.

2 Cover the potatoes and place in a 400°F (200°C) oven. Cook until tender, approximately 35 to 40 minutes. Set aside to cool.

3 Cut the cooled potatoes in halves or quarters if they are large. Thread onto skewers for grilling. (Skewers are not necessary if the grill grating is close together.) Grill the potatoes, cut side down, until they are golden and crisp with defined grill marks.

4 Cut the tomatoes in half or leave whole if small.

5 To assemble the salad, slide the grilled potatoes from the skewers and toss with the bell peppers, cherry tomatoes and Basil Vinaigrette. Adjust the seasoning, if necessary, with a splash of champagne vinegar and salt and pepper.

6 Loosely arrange the greens on plates or a platter, spoon the potatoes and other vegetables over the greens and garnish with the olives.

Approximate values per serving: **Calories** 350, **Total fat** 22 g, **Saturated fat** 3 g, **Cholesterol** 0 mg, **Sodium** 1420 mg, **Total carbohydrates** 33 g, **Protein** 4 g, **Vitamin C** 170%, **Calcium** 15%, **Iron** 10%

BASIL VINAIGRETTE

Yield: 4 fl. oz. (120 ml)

Champagne vinegar	1 fl. oz.	30 ml
Extra virgin olive oil	3 fl. oz.	90 ml
Fresh basil leaves	½ c.	120 ml
Salt	½ tsp.	3 ml
Garlic clove, chopped	1	1

1 Combine the ingredients in a blender or food processor until smooth.

Approximate values per 1-fl.-oz. (30-ml) serving: **Calories** 200, **Total fat** 21 g, **Saturated fat** 3 g, **Cholesterol** 0 mg, **Sodium** 290 mg, **Total carbohydrates** 1 g, **Protein** 0 g

RECIPE 23.12

GRILLED SWEET POTATOES WITH POBLANO CHILES AND ONIONS

CAFÉ ANNIE, HOUSTON, TX
Chef-Owner Robert Del Grande
Executive Chef Ben Berryhill

Yield: 8 Servings   **Method:** Grilling

Sweet potatoes, large	3	3
Vegetable oil	1 Tbsp.	15 ml
Barbecue Spice (recipe follows)	1 c.	240 ml
Poblano chiles	12 oz.	360 g
Yellow onions	8 oz.	240 g
Butter, melted	2 oz.	60 g
Salt	TT	TT
Mopping Sauce (recipe follows)	¾ c.	180 ml
Mexican queso blanco (cheese), grated	4 oz.	120 g

1 Rub the whole sweet potatoes with vegetable oil. Generously coat the sweet potatoes with Barbecue Spice.

2 Bake the sweet potatoes at 350°F (180°C) for approximately 40 minutes or until they are nearly done but still undercooked and firm in the middle. Remove from the oven and cool.

3 Char and peel the poblano chiles. Remove and discard the stems and seeds. Cut into ¼-inch (6-millimeter) slices. Peel the onions and cut them into ¼-inch (6-millimeter) slices. Separate the slices into rings. Combine the chile strips and the onion rings and sauté in 1 tablespoon (15 milliliters) of melted butter. Season to taste with salt.

4 Peel the sweet potatoes and cut them into long wedges. Liberally brush the wedges with the Mopping Sauce and season generously with the Barbecue Spice. Grill the wedges, being careful not to burn them. They should be evenly caramelized and fork tender when done. Season them with salt and brush them with the remaining melted butter.

5 Arrange the sweet potato wedges on a plate with a portion of the chiles and onions. Sprinkle with cheese and serve immediately.

Approximate values per serving: **Calories** 320, **Total fat** 17 g, **Saturated fat** 6 g, **Cholesterol** 20 mg, **Sodium** 120 mg, **Total carbohydrates** 40 g, **Protein** 5 g, **Vitamin A** 360%, **Vitamin C** 100%, **Calcium** 15%, **Iron** 20%, **Claims**—good source of fiber, vitamin A, vitamin C, calcium, iron

BARBECUE SPICE

Yield: 1 c. (240 ml)

Ancho chile powder	¼ c.	60 ml
Paprika	¼ c.	60 ml
Garlic powder	1 Tbsp.	15 ml
Cumin, ground, toasted	1 Tbsp.	15 ml
Coriander, ground, toasted	1 Tbsp.	15 ml
Dried oregano	1 Tbsp.	15 ml
Brown sugar	1 Tbsp.	15 ml
Granulated sugar	1 Tbsp.	15 ml

1 Combine all ingredients and mix well.

Approximate values per 2 Tbsp. (30 ml): **Calories** 45, **Total fat** 1.5 mg, **Saturated fat** 0 g, **Cholesterol** 0 mg, **Sodium** 40 mg, **Total carbohydrates** 9 g, **Protein** 1 g, **Vitamin A** 70%, **Vitamin C** 8%, **Calcium** 4%, **Iron** 10%

MOPPING SAUCE

Yield: ¾ c. (180 ml)

Peanut oil	2 fl. oz.	60 ml
Molasses	2 Tbsp.	30 ml
Brown sugar	2 Tbsp.	30 ml
Dijon mustard	1 Tbsp.	15 ml
Red wine vinegar	1 Tbsp.	15 ml
Balsamic vinegar	1 Tbsp.	15 ml
Maple syrup	1 Tbsp.	15 ml

1 Combine all ingredients and mix well.

Approximate values per 1-oz (30-g) serving: **Calories** 130, **Total fat** 9 g, **Saturated fat** 1.5 g, **Cholesterol** 0 mg, **Sodium** 70 mg, **Total carbohydrates** 12 g, **Protein** 0 g

 ## ROASTED FINGERLING POTATOES RECIPE 23.13

Yield: 4 Servings, 4 oz. (120 g) each   **Method:** Roasting

Fingerling potatoes, assorted	1 lb.	450 g
Fresh lemon juice	from 2 lemons	from 2 lemons
Italian herb blend	1 Tbsp.	15 ml
Salt	1 tsp.	5 ml
Black pepper	⅛ tsp.	1 ml
Olive oil	3 Tbsp.	45 ml

1 Cut the potatoes in halves or quarters and place in a bowl. Add the lemon juice, seasonings and oil and then toss to coat the potatoes thoroughly.

2 Place the seasoned potatoes in a shallow baking pan and roast at 425°F (220°C). Stir or turn the potatoes two or three times during cooking to promote even browning. Cook until the potatoes are tender, approximately 30 minutes.

Approximate values per serving: **Calories** 200, **Total fat** 10 g, **Saturated fat** 1.5 g, **Cholesterol** 0 mg, **Sodium** 590 mg, **Total carbohydrates** 27 g, **Protein** 2 g, **Vitamin C** 45%, **Iron** 10%, **Claim**—good source of fiber, vitamin C and iron

 ## CANDIED SWEET POTATOES RECIPE 23.14

Yield: 6 Servings, 4 oz. (120 g) each   **Method:** Baking

Sweet potatoes	2 lb.	1 kg
Brown sugar	5 oz.	150 g
Water	2 fl. oz.	60 ml
Whole butter	2 oz.	60 g
Vanilla extract	1 tsp.	5 ml

1 Wash the sweet potatoes and cut as necessary to promote even cooking.

2 Bake the sweet potatoes on a sheet pan at 350°F (180°C) until cooked but still firm, approximately 30 minutes.

3 Combine the brown sugar, water and butter and bring to a boil. Add the vanilla and remove from the heat.

4 Peel the potatoes and slice or cut as desired. Arrange the potatoes in a baking dish and pour the sugar mixture over them.

5 Sprinkle the potatoes with additional brown sugar if desired and bake for 20 minutes, basting occasionally with the sugar mixture.

Approximate values per 4-oz. (120-g) serving: **Calories** 320, **Total fat** 8 g, **Saturated fat** 5 g, **Cholesterol** 20 mg, **Sodium** 105 mg, **Total carbohydrates** 60 g, **Protein** 3 g, **Vitamin A** 340%, **Vitamin C** 60%

RECIPE 23.15 SCALLOPED POTATOES

Yield: 1 Pan, 9 in × 12 in.
(22 cm × 30 cm) **Method:** Baking

Potatoes, russet	5 lb.	2.2 kg
Béchamel (page 212)	36 fl. oz.	1 lt
Salt and white pepper	TT	TT
Nutmeg	TT	TT
Whole butter	as needed	as needed

1 Peel the potatoes and hold them in water to prevent browning. Pour the béchamel into a stainless steel bowl. Slice the potatoes thinly (a mandoline works well for this purpose) directly into the béchamel. Stir occasionally so that the sauce coats the potatoes.
2 Season as desired with the salt, white pepper and nutmeg.
3 Layer the potatoes and sauce in a buttered half-size hotel pan. Pour any remaining sauce over the top of the potatoes.
4 Bake covered at 350°F (180°C) for approximately 30 minutes. Uncover and bake until the potatoes are cooked and brown on top, approximately 20 to 30 minutes.

Approximate values per 4-oz. (120-g) serving: **Calories** 210, **Total fat** 8 g, **Saturated fat** 4.5 g, **Cholesterol** 20 mg, **Sodium** 730 mg, **Total carbohydrates** 33 g, **Protein** 3 g, **Vitamin C** 20%, **Claims**—good source of fiber and vitamin C

1 Layering the potatoes in a hotel pan.

2 Pouring the remaining cream sauce over the potatoes.

3 The finished scalloped potatoes.

RECIPE 23.16 SPICY SWEET POTATO AND CHESTNUT GRATIN

THE BOULDERS RESORT, CAREFREE, AZ
Former Corporate Executive Chef Charles Wiley

Yield: 6 Servings **Method:** Baking

Vegetable spray	as needed	as needed
Skim milk	8 fl. oz.	250 ml
Maple syrup	4 fl. oz.	120 ml
Garlic cloves, chopped	3	3
Ancho chiles	2	2
Sweet potatoes, large	2	2
Kosher salt and pepper	TT	TT
Leeks, white part only, sliced thin	3	3

Roasted chestnuts, chopped coarse	½ c.	120 ml
Aged Monterey Jack, grated	½ c.	120 ml
Chives, snipped	as needed	as needed

1 Lightly spray an ovenproof casserole dish with vegetable spray.

2 In a small saucepan, heat the milk and maple syrup. Remove from the heat, add the garlic and chiles and let steep for 30 minutes. Purée in a blender.

3 Peel and thinly slice the sweet potatoes. Lay one-third of the potato slices in one layer in the casserole dish, overlapping slightly. Season with salt and pepper.

4 Ladle one-third of the milk mixture over the potatoes.

5 Sprinkle with one-third of the leeks and one-third of the chestnuts. Then top with one-third of the cheese.

6 Repeat the layering process two more times.

7 Cover with foil and bake at 350°F (180°C) for 40 minutes. Uncover and bake until brown and bubbly, approximately 20 minutes.

8 Let sit for 20 minutes. Sprinkle with the snipped chives. Cut into squares or circles, or simply spoon out of the casserole dish for service.

Approximate values per 6-oz. (180-g) serving: **Calories** 170, **Total fat** 4 g, **Saturated fat** 2 g, **Cholesterol** 10 mg, **Sodium** 135 mg, **Total carbohydrates** 29 g, **Protein** 5 g, **Vitamin A** 15%, **Vitamin C** 30%, **Claims**—low cholesterol; low sodium

DELMONICO POTATOES

RECIPE 23.17

SPOKANE COMMUNITY COLLEGE, Spokane, WA

Instructor Peter Tobin, CEC, CCE

Yield: 10 lb. (4.4 kg)   **Method:** Steaming/Baking

Potatoes, peeled, medium dice	6 lb.	2.7 kg
Green bell peppers, small dice	4	4
Pimentos, small dice	12 oz.	350 g
Béchamel (page 212)	3 pt.	1.4 lt
Salt and pepper	TT	TT
Nutmeg	TT	TT

1 Steam the potatoes until cooked through but firm, approximately 7 minutes. Spread them on sheet pans and refrigerate.

2 Blanch and chill the bell peppers.

3 Combine all ingredients in a large bowl. Mix carefully so as not to break up the potatoes.

4 Place the potatoes in a shallow full-size hotel pan, cover and bake at 350°F (180°C) until the internal temperature reaches at least 165°F (74°C).

Approximate values per 4-oz. (120-g) serving: **Calories** 100, **Total fat** 4 g, **Saturated fat** 2 g, **Cholesterol** 10 mg, **Sodium** 340 mg, **Total carbohydrates** 15 g, **Protein** 2 g, **Vitamin C** 35%

THYME AND SWISS CHEESE POTATOES

RECIPE 23.18

SAN JOAQUIN DELTA COLLEGE, Stockton, CA

Charlotte M. Britto, RD, FADA

Yield: 36 Servings   **Method:** Baking

Onions, sliced thin	2 lb.	900 g
Olive oil	4 Tbsp.	60 ml
Garlic cloves	20	20

Continued

Dried thyme	2 Tbsp.	30 ml
Heavy cream	3 qt.	3 lt
Potatoes	10 lb.	4.4 kg
Vegetable spray	as needed	as needed
Salt and white pepper	TT	TT
Swiss cheese, grated	1 lb.	450 g

1 Sauté the onions in the olive oil until translucent. Remove from the heat and reserve.

2 Simmer the garlic and thyme in the cream for 15 minutes.

3 Peel and thinly slice the potatoes.

4 Spray three shallow half-size hotel pans with vegetable spray. Layer the potatoes and onions in the pans, seasoning each layer with salt and white pepper.

5 Pour the hot cream over the potatoes and onions. Bake uncovered in a 350°F (180°C) oven for 12 minutes. Reduce the temperature to 300°F (150°C) and cook for approximately 20 minutes or until the potatoes are nearly tender.

6 Sprinkle the grated Swiss cheese on top of the potatoes and return to the oven just long enough to melt the cheese.

Approximate values per serving: **Calories** 440, **Total fat** 34 g, **Saturated fat** 21 g, **Cholesterol** 120 mg, **Sodium** 70 mg, **Total carbohydrates** 28 g, **Protein** 8 g, **Vitamin A** 25%, **Vitamin C** 20%, **Calcium** 20%

RECIPE 23.19 — POTATO PANCAKES

Yield: 12 Pancakes, 2½ oz. (75 g) each	**Method:** Pan-frying	
Potatoes, all-purpose	2 lb.	1 kg
Eggs, beaten	3	3
Onions, minced	4 oz.	120 g
Flour	2 oz.	60 g
Baking powder	1 Tbsp.	15 ml
Nutmeg	TT	TT
Salt and pepper	TT	TT
Vegetable oil	4 fl. oz.	120 ml

1 Peel and coarsely grate the potatoes.

2 Transfer the grated potatoes to a bowl and add the beaten eggs, onions, flour and baking powder. Season with nutmeg, salt and pepper. Blend well.

3 Heat the oil. Form the potato mixture into 12 uniform-sized pancakes and pan-fry them until tender, turning once when well browned on the first side. Remove them from the pan and drain well.

Approximate values per pancake: **Calories** 140, **Total fat** 6 g, **Saturated fat** 1 g, **Cholesterol** 55 mg, **Sodium** 140 mg, **Total carbohydrates** 18 g, **Protein** 3 g, **Vitamin C** 10%

RECIPE 23.20 — RÖSTI POTATOES

THE FOUR SEASONS, NEW YORK, NY
Chef Christian Albin

Yield: 6 Servings	**Method:** Pan-frying	
Potatoes, boiling, large	4	4
Bacon fat	2 oz.	60 g
Lard	2 oz.	60 g
Kosher salt and pepper	TT	TT
Whole butter	1 oz.	30 g

1 Partially cook the potatoes in salted water until almost done. Drain and cool the potatoes, then peel and coarsely grate them.

2 Heat the bacon fat and lard in a heavy, shallow 10-inch (25-centimeter) skillet with sloping sides until quite hot. Spread half the potatoes over the bottom of the pan; sprinkle with salt and pepper. Cover with the remaining potatoes and cook over medium-high heat until the bottom turns brown and crusty, approximately 10 minutes.

3 Turn the potatoes in one piece. This is easiest to do by placing a large plate over the pan and turning both together so that the potatoes fall onto the plate. Slip the turned-over potatoes off the plate back into the pan, browned side up. Cook until the bottom is browned.

4 Before serving, smooth the edges of the potatoes with a spatula. Sprinkle with salt and brush the edge of the pan with whole butter. It will melt and run into the potatoes.

Variation: *Cheddar Cheese Rösti Potatoes*—Make two thin cakes from the coarsely grated potatoes. Top one with a layer of 7 ounces (210 grams) sour cream, 2 ounces (60 grams) cubed sharp Cheddar cheese and 2 tablespoons (30 milliliters) chopped chives. Top with the other cake. Dot with 1 tablespoon (15 milliliters) whole butter and bake in a 400°F (200°C) oven for 15 minutes.

Approximate values per serving: **Calories** 290, **Total fat** 23 g, **Saturated fat** 10 g, **Cholesterol** 30 mg, **Sodium** 430 mg, **Total carbohydrates** 19 g, **Protein** 2 g, **Vitamin C** 20%

POTATO-GINGER PURÉE

RECIPE 23.21

STOUFFER STANFORD COURT HOTEL, San Francisco, CA

Former Executive Chef Ercolino Crugnale

Yield: 2 lb. (1 kg) **Method:** Boiling

Potatoes	1 lb. 8 oz.	650 g
Heavy cream	4 fl. oz.	120 ml
Fresh ginger, grated	1 Tbsp.	15 ml
Whole butter	8 oz.	250 g
Salt and pepper	TT	TT

1 Peel the potatoes and cut them into 1-inch (2.5-centimeter) pieces. Then boil them in salted water until tender. Drain and set aside.

2 While the potatoes cook, bring the cream to a boil, add the ginger and let steep for 15 minutes. Purée and strain through a fine chinois.

3 Purée the potatoes, then add the butter and ginger cream. Season to taste with salt and pepper. Adjust the consistency with additional hot cream as needed.

Approximate values per 4-oz. (120-g) serving: **Calories** 311, **Total fat** 29 g, **Saturated fat** 18 g, **Cholesterol** 81 mg, **Sodium** 426 mg, **Total carbohydrates** 12 g, **Protein** 2 g, **Vitamin A** 28%

HERBED MASHED POTATOES WITH WHITE SAUCE

RECIPE 23.22

NEWBURY COLLEGE, Brookline, MA

Senior Instructor Scott Doughty

Yield: 18 lb. (8.2 kg) **Method:** Simmering

Potatoes, waxy	14 lb.	6.4 kg
Sauce:		
Clarified butter	2 fl. oz.	60 ml
Flour	2 oz.	60 g

Continued

Milk	1 pt.	450 ml
Salt and black pepper	TT	TT
Milk, warm	24 fl. oz.	750 ml
Heavy cream, hot	8 fl. oz.	240 ml
Butter, melted	1 lb.	450 g
Salt and black pepper	TT	TT
Fresh herbs, assorted, chopped	3 oz.	90 g
Parmesan, grated	6 oz.	180 g

1 Simmer the potatoes in salted water until tender.

2 To prepare the sauce, first heat the clarified butter in a small saucepot. Add the flour and cook to a blond roux. Whisk in the milk and bring to a simmer, stirring often. Cook until thick enough to completely coat the back of a spoon. Season with salt and pepper.

3 When the potatoes are tender, drain them well and place them in a large mixer fitted with the whisk attachment. Whip until smooth, scraping down the bowl as necessary. Add the milk, cream and butter, and season with salt and pepper. Mix well and then stir in the chopped herbs.

4 Spread the potatoes into a 2-inch- (5-centimeter-) deep full-size hotel pan and spread the sauce over the top. Sprinkle with grated Parmesan. Bake at 375°F (190°C) until the potatoes are browned on top and have reached an internal temperature of 165°F (74°C), approximately 12 minutes.

Approximate values per 4-oz. (120-g) serving: **Calories** 150, **Total fat** 8 g, **Saturated fat** 5 g, **Cholesterol** 25 mg, **Sodium** 60 mg, **Total carbohydrates** 17 g, **Protein** 3 g, **Vitamin C** 20%

Note: Use a blend of at least four of the following fresh herbs: thyme, rosemary, oregano, marjoram, sage, parsley, basil, chives and tarragon.

RECIPE 23.23

DUCHESSE POTATOES

Yield: 2 lb. (1 kg)	**Method:** Boiling	
Potatoes	2 lb.	1 kg
Whole butter	1 oz.	30 g
Nutmeg	TT	TT
Salt and pepper	TT	TT
Eggs	1	1
Egg yolks	2	2
Clarified butter	as needed	as needed

1 Peel and quarter the potatoes. Then boil them in salted water until tender. Drain and immediately turn them out onto a sheet pan to allow the moisture to evaporate.

2 While still warm, press the potatoes through a grinder or food mill, or grind through a grinder's medium die. Blend in the butter and season to taste with nutmeg, salt and pepper.

3 Mix in the eggs and egg yolks, blending well.

4 Transfer the duchesse mixture to a piping bag fitted with a large star tip. Pipe single portion-sized spirals onto a parchment-lined sheet pan. Brush with clarified butter and bake at 375°F (190°C) until the edges are golden brown, approximately 8 to 10 minutes. Serve immediately.

Usage: Duchesse potatoes are often used to decorate platters used for buffets or tableside preparations or to present chateaubriand. To create borders and garnishes, the standard mixture for duchesse potatoes is forced through a piping bag while still very hot and relatively soft.

Variation: *Potato Croquettes*–Shape the duchesse mixture into pyramids. Coat the pyramids with bread crumbs using the standard breading procedure described in Chapter 9, Mise en Place. Using the basket method, deep-fry at 360°F (182°C) until golden brown.

Approximate values per 3-oz. (90-g) serving: **Calories** 120, **Total fat** 3.5 g, **Saturated fat** 2 g, **Cholesterol** 65 mg, **Sodium** 250 mg, **Total carbohydrates** 18 g, **Protein** 3 g, **Vitamin C** 20%

1 Passing boiled potatoes through a food mill.

2 Piping duchesse potatoes.

3 The finished duchesse potatoes.

 ## DAUPHINE POTATOES

RECIPE 23.24

Yield: 3 lb. (1.3 kg) **Method:** Boiling

Duchesse Potatoes (page 722)	2 lb.	900 g
Pâte à Choux (page 997)	20 oz.	600 g

1 Combine the Duchesse Potatoes with the Pâte à Choux while both mixtures are still warm.

2 Pipe the mixture into the desired shapes on pieces of parchment paper. Chill until ready to cook. At service, deep-fry the potatoes until golden brown, using the swimming method.

Variation: *Lorette*–Add 4 ounces (120 grams) of grated Parmesan in Step 2. Pipe the mixture into small crescents on pieces of parchment paper. Deep-fry by carefully sliding the pieces of paper into the fryer; remove the paper with tongs when the potatoes float loose.

Approximate values per 4-oz. (120-g) serving: **Calories** 270, **Total fat** 18 g, **Saturated fat** 8 g, **Cholesterol** 140 mg, **Sodium** 470 mg, **Total carbohydrates** 23 g, **Protein** 5 g, **Vitamin C** 15%

 ## POLENTA

RECIPE 23.25

Yield: 1 lb. 12 oz. (800 g) **Method:** Simmering

Shallots, chopped	2 tsp.	10 ml
Whole butter	as needed	as needed
Milk, white stock or water	1 qt.	950 ml
Cornmeal, yellow or white	6 oz.	180 g
Salt and pepper	TT	TT

1 Sauté the shallots in 1 tablespoon (15 milliliters) of butter for 30 seconds. Add the milk, stock or water and bring to a boil.

2 Slowly add the cornmeal while stirring constantly to prevent lumps, then simmer for 30 minutes. Season with salt and pepper.

3 Scrape the polenta into a buttered nonaluminum dish; spread to an even thickness with a spatula that has been dipped in water. Refrigerate the polenta until well chilled.

4 To serve, unmold the polenta and cut into shapes. Sauté or grill the polenta for service, or sprinkle with grated Parmesan and heat under a broiler or salamander.

Approximate values per 4-oz. (120-g) serving: **Calories** 160, **Total fat** 3.5 g, **Saturated fat** 2 g, **Cholesterol** 10 mg, **Sodium** 400 mg, **Total carbohydrates** 25 g, **Protein** 6 g, **Vitamin A** 10%, **Calcium** 15%

RECIPE 23.26

CREAMY POLENTA WITH WILD MUSHROOMS

FETZER VINEYARDS, HOPLAND, CA

Culinary Director, John Ash

Yield: 8 Servings   **Method:** Simmering

Yellow onions, chopped coarse	12 oz.	340 g
White mushrooms, chopped coarse	4 oz.	120 g
Garlic, chopped fine	2 Tbsp.	30 ml
Dried porcini or cèpe mushrooms, rinsed, soaked in water and chopped coarse	2 oz.	60 g
Olive oil	5 fl. oz.	150 ml
Fresh basil, chopped fine	4 tsp.	20 ml
Fresh oregano, chopped fine	1 tsp.	5 ml
Chicken or vegetable stock	2 qt.	2 lt
Coarse polenta	12 oz.	360 g
Salt and pepper	TT	TT
Heavy cream	1 pt.	450 ml
Aged Asiago or Fontina, grated fine	4 oz.	120 g
Fresh wild mushrooms	8–10	8–10
Fresh basil sprigs	as needed for garnish	

1 Sauté the onions, white mushrooms, garlic and porcini or cèpes in 4 fluid ounces (120 milliliters) of olive oil until lightly colored. Add the basil, oregano and stock; bring to a boil.

2 Slowly stir in the polenta. Simmer for 10 minutes, stirring regularly. The polenta should be thick and creamy. Add more stock if necessary. Adjust the seasonings and keep warm.

3 Just before serving, add the cream and cheese and stir vigorously.

4 Sauté the fresh wild mushrooms in the remaining olive oil until tender. Spoon the polenta onto warm plates and garnish with the wild mushrooms and a sprig of fresh basil.

Approximate values per 8-oz. (240-g) serving: **Calories** 550, **Total fat** 46 g, **Saturated fat** 19 g, **Cholesterol** 95 mg, **Sodium** 1090 mg, **Total carbohydrates** 21 g, **Protein** 13 g, **Vitamin A** 35%, **Vitamin C** 15%, **Calcium** 20%, **Iron** 15%

POLENTA NAPOLEON
AND SMOKED TOMATO COULIS

RECIPE 23.27

THE BROWN PALACE HOTEL, DENVER, CO
William Dexter, Executive Sous Chef

Yield: 6 Servings

Garlic, minced	1 Tbsp.	15 ml
Olive oil	4½ fl. oz.	135 ml
Vegetable stock	1 qt.	1 lt
Milk	5½ c.	1.1 lt
Butter	6 oz.	180 g
Cornmeal	1 lb.	450 g
Fresh herbs, chopped	3 Tbsp	45 ml
Parmesan, shredded	10 oz.	300 g
Salt and pepper	TT	TT
Zucchini, sliced lengthwise ¼ in. (6 mm) thick	2	2
Yellow squash, sliced lengthwise ¼ in. (6 mm) thick	2	2
Portabella mushroom caps, cleaned	6	6
Balsamic vinegar	8 fl. oz.	240 ml
Red bell peppers, roasted, peeled, seeded	6	6
Asparagus spears, trimmed and blanched	30	30
Morels, cut in half, washed	6	6
Fresh basil leaves	12	12
Smoked Tomato Coulis (recipe follows)	12 fl. oz.	360 ml

1 Sauté the garlic in 3 tablespoons (45 milliliters) of olive oil for 2 minutes. Add the stock, milk and butter and bring to a boil.

2 Slowly stir in the cornmeal to avoid lumping. Simmer for 15 minutes, add the herbs and 7 ounces (210 grams) of the Parmesan and season with salt and pepper. Oil a half sheet pan with 3 tablespoons (45 milliliters) of olive oil. Pour the polenta into the pan, level with a spatula, cover and refrigerate.

3 Toss the zucchini, yellow squash and portabella caps in a small amount of olive oil, season with salt and pepper and grill until tender.

4 Cut six circles out of the polenta with a 4-inch (10-centimeter) round cutter. Split each circle in half horizontally.

5 In a small saucepan, reduce the balsamic vinegar to a syrup.

6 Shingle the slices of grilled zucchini on a work surface and cut six 4-inch (10-centimeter) circles from them. Follow the same procedure with the yellow squash. Cut the portabella mushrooms and bell peppers into 4-inch (10-centimeter) circles. Place the vegetable rounds on a sheet pan.

7 Sauté the asparagus spears and morels in a small amount of olive oil and season with salt and pepper.

8 At service time, sauté the polenta disks in a small amount of olive oil until hot. Reheat the vegetable circles briefly in a hot oven. Place one of the polenta disks on each of six plates. Layer the vegetable circles alternately on the polenta base, sprinkling the remaining Parmesan between each layer. Top each stack with another polenta disk.

9 Serve each napoleon with Smoked Tomato Coulis and garnish with the asparagus spears, morels, fresh basil and balsamic syrup.

Approximate values per serving: **Calories** 870, **Total fat** 51 g, **Saturated fat** 21 g, **Cholesterol** 85 mg, **Sodium** 880 mg, **Total carbohydrates** 73 g, **Protein** 32 g, **Vitamin A** 190%, **Vitamin C** 430%, **Calcium** 80%, **Iron** 30%

SMOKED TOMATO COULIS

Yield: 12 fl. oz. (360 ml)

Tomatoes, peeled	3	3
Garlic, minced	1 tsp.	5 ml
Shallots, minced	1 Tbsp.	15 ml
Olive oil	3 Tbsp.	45 ml
White wine	6 fl. oz.	180 ml
Vegetable stock	12 fl. oz.	360 ml
Salt and pepper	TT	TT

1 Cut the tomatoes in half. Smoke them with apple wood chips at 200°F (90°C) for 1 hour.

2 In a medium saucepot, sauté the garlic and shallots in the olive oil until translucent. Deglaze with the white wine and reduce by half. Roughly chop the tomatoes and add them to the pot. Add the stock. Simmer for 25 minutes. Purée the sauce and strain through a fine chinois. Adjust the seasoning with salt and pepper.

Approximate values per 1-fl.-oz. (30-ml) serving: **Calories** 50, **Total fat** 3.5 g, **Saturated fat** 0, **Cholesterol** 0, **Sodium** 40 mg, **Total carbohydrates** 2 g, **Protein** 0 g, **Vitamin C** 10%

RECIPE 23.28

GRITS AND CHEDDAR SOUFFLÉ

Yield: 8 Servings   **Method:** Simmering/Baking

Grits	1 ½ c.	350 ml
Water	1 ½ pt.	700 ml
Milk	1 ½ pt.	700 ml
Unsalted butter	4 oz.	120 g
Salt	TT	TT
Tabasco sauce	½ tsp.	2 ml
Sharp Cheddar cheese, grated	8 oz.	240 g
Eggs, separated	6	6
Granulated sugar	2 tsp.	10 ml

1 Combine the grits, water, milk, butter and salt in a heavy saucepan. Bring to a simmer and cook, stirring constantly, until thick, approximately 5 to 10 minutes.

2 Remove from the heat and stir in the Tabasco sauce and 6 ounces (180 grams) of the cheese.

3 Whisk the egg yolks together, then stir them into the grits mixture.

4 Whip the egg whites to soft peaks, add the sugar and whip to stiff peaks. Fold the egg whites into the grits mixture.

5 Pour the soufflé into a well-buttered 2-quart (2 liter) casserole or soufflé dish. Top with the remaining 2 ounces (60 grams) of cheese. Bake at 350°F (180°C) until set and browned, approximately 30 minutes. Serve immediately.

Approximate values per serving: **Calories** 410, **Total fat** 25 g, **Saturated fat** 9 g, **Cholesterol** 215 mg, **Sodium** 640 mg, **Total carbohydrates** 32 g, **Protein** 16 g, **Vitamin A** 40%, **Calcium** 30%

TEXAS CORNBREAD DRESSING WITH VENISON SAUSAGE

RECIPE 23.29

CAFÉ ANNIE, Houston, TX
Chef-Owner Robert Del Grande
Executive Chef Ben Berryhill

Yield: 10 Servings   **Method:** Baking

Cornbread:		
All-purpose flour	1 pt.	450 ml
Yellow cornmeal	1 pt.	450 ml
Granulated sugar	4 Tbsp.	60 ml
Salt	1 Tbsp.	15 ml
Baking powder	1 Tbsp.	15 ml
Baking soda	½ tsp.	3 ml
Eggs	2	2
Buttermilk	20 fl. oz.	550 ml
Butter, melted	4 oz.	120 g
Yellow onions, small dice	2	2
Garlic cloves, minced	4	4
Celery stalks, diced	2	2
Carrots, small dice	2	2
Butter	2 oz.	60 g
Venison sausage (or smoked sausage), diced	1 lb.	450 g
Poblano chiles, charred, peeled and diced	4	4
Dried oregano	1 Tbsp.	15 ml
Salt	2 tsp.	10 ml
Black pepper, freshly ground	1 tsp.	5 ml
Chicken stock	8 fl. oz.	240 ml

1 To make the cornbread, combine the dry ingredients in a bowl and mix well. In a separate bowl, combine the eggs and buttermilk and blend until smooth. Add the egg mixture and the melted butter to the dry mixture and blend until just combined. Pour the batter into a lightly greased 9-inch × 13-inch (22-centimeter × 32-centimeter) baking dish and bake at 350°F (180°C) for approximately 35 minutes. Cool.

2 In a sauté pan over medium heat, sauté the onions, garlic, celery and carrots in the butter until tender. Add the sausage and cook through.

3 Crumble the cornbread and add it to the vegetable mixture. Add the poblanos, oregano, salt and pepper and stir gently to incorporate. Drizzle the chicken broth over the mixture and toss to combine. Transfer the dressing to a baking dish and bake at 350°F (180°C) for 30 to 40 minutes or until the top is lightly browned and the dressing is hot.

Approximate values per 8-oz. (240-g) serving: **Calories** 540, **Total fat** 29 g, **Saturated fat** 15 g, **Cholesterol** 110 mg, **Sodium** 1970 mg, **Total carbohydrates** 53 g, **Protein** 14 g, **Vitamin A** 100%, **Vitamin C** 50%, **Calcium** 20%, **Iron** 20%

RECIPE 23.30

BROWN RICE WITH SPICED PECANS

NEWBURY COLLEGE, Brookline, MA

Senior Instructor Scott Doughty

Yield: 10 Servings		**Method:** Simmering
Chicken stock, hot	2½ pt.	1.2 lt
Salt	1 tsp.	5 ml
Brown rice	1 pt.	480 ml
Green onions	3	3
Butter	4 oz.	120 g
Spiced Pecans (recipe follows)	1 c.	240 ml

1 Bring the stock to a boil. Add the salt and rice. Return to a boil, cover, reduce to a simmer and cook until the rice is tender, approximately 50 to 60 minutes.

2 Thinly slice the green onions on the diagonal. Then quickly sauté them in the butter. Add the green onions to the rice. Chop the Spiced Pecans and add them to the rice mixture. Stir to combine and hold for service.

Approximate values per serving: **Calories** 350, **Total fat** 24 g, **Saturated fat** 8 g, **Cholesterol** 30 mg, **Sodium** 720 mg, **Total carbohydrates** 32 g, **Protein** 5 g, **Claims**—good source of fiber

SPICED PECANS

Yield: 1 c. (240 ml)

Butter	1 Tbsp.	15 ml
Cayenne pepper	⅛ tsp.	1 ml
Cinnamon	⅛ tsp.	1 ml
Salt	½ tsp.	3 ml
Worcestershire sauce	1 Tbsp.	15 ml
Hot sauce	1–2 drops	1–2 drops
Pecan halves	6 oz.	180 g

1 Combine the butter, cayenne pepper, cinnamon, salt, Worcestershire sauce and hot sauce. Add the pecan halves and blend well.

2 Spread the nuts onto a sheet pan and bake at 300°F (150°C) for 10 minutes. Toss with a spatula and bake for an additional 5 to 10 minutes. Remove from the oven and cool.

Approximate values per 1-oz. (30-g) serving: **Calories** 160, **Total fat** 17 g, **Saturated fat** 2 g, **Cholesterol** 5 mg, **Sodium** 170 mg, **Total carbohydrates** 3 g, **Protein** 2 g

RECIPE 23.31

CLASSIC RICE PILAF

Yield: 3 lb. (1.4 kg)		**Method:** Pilaf
Butter	1 oz.	30 g
Olive oil	1 fl. oz.	30 ml
Onions, fine dice	3 oz.	90 g
Bay leaf	1	1
Long-grain rice	1 pt.	450 ml
Chicken stock, boiling	1 qt.	1 lt
Salt	TT	TT

1 Heat the butter and olive oil in a heavy sautoir or sauce pot.

2 Add the onions and bay leaf and sauté until the onions are tender, but not brown.

3 Add the rice and stir to coat it completely with the hot fat. Do not allow the rice to brown.

4 Pour in the boiling chicken stock and season with salt.

5 Cover the pot tightly and place it in a 350°F (180°C) oven. Bake until the liquid is absorbed and the rice is fluffy and tender, approximately 18 to 20 minutes.

6 Transfer the cooked rice to a hotel pan and fluff the rice with a fork. Remove the bay leaf and keep the rice hot for service.

Variation: *Spanish Rice*—Substitute 2 ounces (60 grams) bacon fat for the butter. Add 3 chopped garlic cloves and 1 tablespoon (15 milliliters) pure ground chilli powder with the diced onion. In Step 3, sauté the rice until it browns slightly. In place of the chicken stock, use half chicken stock and half chopped canned tomatoes with juice. Add 1 tablespoon (15 milliliters) chopped cilantro when adding the liquids.

Approximate values per 6-oz. (180-g) serving: **Calories** 130, **Total fat** 7 g, **Saturated fat** 3 g, **Cholesterol** 7.5 mg, **Sodium** 440 g, **Total carbohydrates** 12 g, **Protein** 4 g

SAFFRON RICE

RECIPE 23.32

Yield: 6 Servings **Method:** Pilaf

Basmati rice	1 pt.	450 ml
Saffron threads	1 tsp.	5 ml
Boiling water	1 qt.	1 lt
Ghee or clarified butter	3 fl. oz.	90 ml
Cinnamon sticks, 2 in. (5 cm) long	1	1
Cloves, whole	4	4
Onions, fine dice	5 oz.	150 g
Dark brown sugar	1 Tbsp.	15 ml
Salt	2 tsp.	10 ml
Cardamom seeds	1/4 tsp.	2 ml

1 Wash the rice and drain thoroughly.

2 Steep the saffron in 2 fluid ounces (60 milliliters) of the boiling water.

3 In a saucepan, heat the ghee, then add the cinnamon and cloves. Add the onions and stir-fry until they are soft and slightly brown.

4 Add the rice and stir until it is well coated with the ghee and the grains are a light golden color.

5 Stirring constantly, add the remaining boiling water, brown sugar, salt and cardamom seeds. Bring to a boil and reduce to a simmer.

6 Gently stir in the saffron and its water, cover and simmer until the rice has absorbed all the liquid.

7 Fluff with a fork and serve at once.

Approximate values per 4-oz. (120-g) serving: **Calories** 370, **Total fat** 16 g, **Saturated fat** 9 g, **Cholesterol** 35 mg, **Sodium** 780 mg, **Total carbohydrates** 51 g, **Protein** 4 g

PILAU
(INDIAN-STYLE RICE PILAF)

RECIPE 23.33

Yield: 2.2 lb. (1 kg) **Method:** Pilaf

Saffron	1/4 tsp.	2 ml
Water, hot	2 fl. oz.	60 ml
Ghee or clarified butter	2 fl. oz.	60 ml
Onion, chopped fine	1	1

Continued

Fresh ginger, minced	2 tsp.	10 ml
Cumin, ground	1 tsp.	5 ml
Coriander, ground	½ tsp.	2 ml
Turmeric, ground	½ tsp.	2 ml
Cinnamon, ground	½ tsp.	2 ml
Cloves, ground	¼ tsp.	1 ml
Red pepper, dried, crushed	¼ tsp.	1 ml
Black pepper	⅛ tsp.	1 ml
Long-grain rice	1 c.	225 ml
Chicken stock, hot	14 fl. oz.	400 ml
Raisins	3 oz.	90 g
Green peas, frozen	3 oz.	90 g
Slivered almonds or cashews, unsalted	2 oz.	60 g
Salt and pepper	TT	TT

1 Soak the saffron in the hot water for 30 minutes.

2 Heat the ghee or butter in a medium saucepot. Add the onion, ginger and all of the spices and sauté for 5 minutes. Add the rice and cook, stirring, until the rice is golden and all of the fat is absorbed.

3 Add the saffron water and chicken stock to the rice. Reduce the heat to a simmer, cover and cook until all of the liquid is absorbed and the rice is tender, approximately 15 to 20 minutes.

4 Add the raisins, peas and nuts. Let stand for 5 minutes, adjust the seasonings and serve.

Approximate values per 1-c. (240-ml) serving: **Calories** 400, **Total fat** 19 g, **Saturated fat** 8 g, **Cholesterol** 30 mg, **Sodium** 250 mg, **Total carbohydrates** 53 g, **Protein** 7 g, **Vitamin A** 10%, **Vitamin C** 10%, **Iron** 15%

RECIPE 23.34   THAI FRIED RICE

Yield: 8 Servings   **Method:** Stir-frying

Vegetable oil	4 fl. oz.	120 ml
Fresh ginger, grated	1 Tbsp.	15 ml
Garlic, mashed	3 Tbsp.	45 ml
Assorted vegetables, medium dice (carrots, peppers, mushrooms, etc.)	3 c.	710 ml
Long-grain white rice, cooked and thoroughly chilled	2 pt.	1 lt
Eggs, slightly beaten	6	6
Tomato concassée	1 pt.	450 ml
Hot chile paste	2 Tbsp.	30 ml
Fish sauce	6 Tbsp.	90 ml
Fresh lime juice	1 Tbsp.	15 ml
Fresh cilantro, chopped	as needed	as needed

1 Heat the oil in a wok or rondeau. Add the ginger and garlic and stir-fry until lightly browned. Remove from the pan.

2 Stir-fry the vegetables and remove from the pan.

3 Stir-fry the rice until warmed through.

4 Make a well in the center of the rice and pour in the eggs. Cook the eggs until almost set before mixing them into the rice.

5 Add the tomato concassée, garlic, ginger and vegetables. Mix in the chile paste, fish sauce and lime juice. Stir-fry to a temperature of 165°F (74°C). Garnish with chopped cilantro.

Variations: *Chinese-Style Fried Rice*—Omit the hot chile paste, fish sauce, and lime juice. Add ½ cup (120 ml) chopped green onions to the assorted vegetables. Season with 1 tablespoon (15 milliliters) sesame oil and 4–6 tablespoons (120–180 milliliters) soy sauce. Omit the cilantro garnish.

House-Special Fried Rice—Prepare Chinese-Style Fried Rice, but add 4 ounces (120 grams) diced, cooked pork; 2 ounces (60 grams) thinly sliced, cooked chicken and 2 ounces (60 grams) cooked shrimp in Step 5.

Approximate values per serving: **Calories** 310, **Total fat** 18 g, **Saturated fat** 3.5 g, **Cholesterol** 160 mg, **Sodium** 1100 mg, **Total carbohydrates** 30 g, **Protein** 9 g, **Vitamin A** 110%, **Vitamin C** 35%

WILD RICE AND CRANBERRY STUFFING   RECIPE 23.35

Yield: 5 pt. (2.5 lt)		**Method:** Simmering
Dried morels	1 oz.	30 g
Wild rice	12 oz.	340 g
Onions, minced	8 oz.	225 g
Butter or chicken fat	2 oz.	60 g
Chicken stock, hot	approx. 1 qt.	approx. 1 lt
Dried cranberries	6 oz.	180 g
Salt and pepper	TT	TT
Fresh parsley, chopped fine	4 Tbsp.	60 ml

1 Soak the dried morels overnight in lightly salted water. Drain, reserving the liquid. Rinse well, drain again and chop coarsely.

2 Rinse the wild rice well in cold water.

3 Sauté the onions in the butter or chicken fat until tender. Add the mushrooms and wild rice.

4 Strain the reserved liquid from the mushrooms through several layers of cheesecloth to remove all sand and grit. Add enough chicken stock so that the liquid totals 3 pints (1.5 liters). Add the stock mixture and cranberries to the rice. Cover and simmer until the rice is dry and fluffy, approximately 45 minutes.

5 Season to taste with salt and pepper and stir in the parsley. This rice may be served as a side dish or used for stuffing duck or game hens.

Approximate values per 4-oz. (120-g) serving: **Calories** 190, **Total fat** 6 g, **Saturated fat** 3 g, **Cholesterol** 10 mg, **Sodium** 380 mg, **Total carbohydrates** 28 g, **Protein** 7 g

HOPPIN' JOHN   RECIPE 23.36

Yield: 12 Servings		**Method:** Simmering
Dried black-eyed or field peas	1 lb.	450 g
Bacon slices, chopped	3	3
Onions, chopped	8 oz.	240 g
Chicken stock	as needed	as needed
Long-grain rice	2 c.	450 ml
Salt and pepper	TT	TT

1 Rinse, sort and soak the peas. Cook until tender, according to the procedures found on page 653. Drain the peas, reserving the cooking liquid.

2 Fry the bacon in a large sauté pan. Add the onions and cook until tender. Add 28 fluid ounces (840 milliliters) of the reserved cooking liquid from the peas. If there is not enough cooking liquid available, use chicken stock as necessary.

3 Stir in the rice and the cooked peas. Bring to a boil, reduce the heat, cover and simmer without stirring until the rice is cooked and the liquid is absorbed, approximately 20 minutes.

4 Season to taste with salt and pepper. Stir well before serving.

Approximate values per serving: **Calories** 270, **Total fat** 3 g, **Saturated fat** 1 g, **Cholesterol** 5 mg, **Sodium** 80 mg, **Total carbohydrates** 48 g, **Protein** 11 g, **Iron** 20%, **Claims**—low fat, low saturated fat, low cholesterol, good source of fiber and iron

---

RECIPE 23.37

BAKED BARLEY WITH MUSHROOMS

Yield: 5 pt. (2.4 lt)		**Method:** Simmering
Beef stock, hot	2 qt.	2 lt
Salt	2 tsp.	10 ml
Black pepper	½ tsp.	3 ml
Barley	1 lb.	450 g
Mushrooms	1 lb.	450 g
Green bell peppers, small dice	12 oz.	350 g
Onions, minced	4 oz.	120 g
Bacon fat or butter	1 oz.	30 g

1 Combine the stock, salt, pepper and barley. Bring to a simmer and continue cooking at a simmer.

2 Trim the stems from the mushrooms and slice the caps into ¼ inch (6-millimeter) slices.

3 Sauté the mushrooms, bell peppers and onions in the bacon fat or butter until the mushrooms begin to release their moisture.

4 Add the mushroom mixture to the stock and barley mixture. Pour into a baking pan and bake at 375°F (190°C), uncovered, for 1 hour, stirring occasionally. Cover and bake until the barley is tender and the liquid has been absorbed, approximately 30 minutes.

Approximate values per ½-c. (120-ml) serving: **Calories** 120, **Total fat** 2 g, **Saturated fat** 0.5 g, **Cholesterol** 0 mg, **Sodium** 490 mg, **Total carbohydrates** 22 g, **Protein** 4 g, **Vitamin A** 50%, **Vitamin C** 30%, **Claims**—good source of fiber, vitamin A and vitamin C

RECIPE 23.38

QUINOA

THE RITZ-CARLTON, CHICAGO, IL
Executive Chef George Bumbaris

Yield: 1 c. (250 ml)		**Method:** Pilaf
Onions, diced	½ c.	120 ml
Olive oil	1 Tbsp.	30 ml
Quinoa	½ c.	120 ml
Water or vegetable stock	1 c.	250 ml
Kosher salt and pepper	TT	TT

1 In a small saucepot, sauté the onions in the olive oil over medium heat.

2 Add the quinoa and allow it to brown slightly.

3 Add the water or stock and season with salt and pepper. Bring to a full simmer.

4 Remove from the stove and cover the pot. Allow the quinoa to steep until tender, approximately 8 minutes.

Approximate values per 1-c. (240-ml) serving: **Calories** 540, **Total fat** 21 g, **Saturated fat** 2.5 g, **Cholesterol** 0 mg, **Sodium** 2020 mg, **Total carbohydrates** 72 g, **Protein** 16 g, **Iron** 45%, **Claims**—no cholesterol; high fiber

ORZO AND HERB SALAD   RECIPE 23.39

Yield: 24 oz. (720 g)

Orzo	1 lb.	500 g
Extra virgin olive oil	3 Tbsp.	45 ml
Fresh or frozen green peas	8 oz.	225 g
Celery, small dice	4 oz.	120 g
Plum tomatoes, medium dice	12 oz.	340 g
Fresh oregano, chopped	½ oz.	14 g
Fresh chives, chopped	½ oz.	14 g
Fresh parsley, chopped	½ oz.	14 g
Garlic cloves, minced	3	3
Red wine vinegar	2 Tbsp.	30 ml
Fresh lemon juice	4 Tbsp.	60 ml
Salt and white pepper	TT	TT

1 Cook the orzo in lightly salted boiling water until al dente. Drain in a colander and rinse well with cold water. Remove the orzo to a large bowl and drizzle 1 tablespoon (15 milliliters) of olive oil around the orzo and toss well.

2 Cook the peas in slightly salted boiling water for 1 to 2 minutes, drain, and rinse with cold water. Toss the peas, celery, tomatoes and orzo together.

3 Combine the remaining olive oil with the herbs, garlic, vinegar, lemon juice, salt and white pepper. Pour over the salad and toss gently to combine. Serve chilled.

Approximate values per 4-oz. (120-g) serving: **Calories** 140, **Total fat** 3 g, **Saturated fat** 0 g, **Cholesterol** 0 mg, **Sodium** 10 mg, **Total carbohydrates** 25 g, **Protein** 5 g, **Vitamin C** 15%, **Claims**–low fat, no saturated fat, no cholesterol, low sodium

CREAMED ORZO AND LEEKS   RECIPE 23.40

SPOKANE COMMUNITY COLLEGE, Spokane, WA
Instructor Peter Tobin, CEC, CCE

Yield: 20 Servings

Orzo	1 lb.	500 g
Salt	as needed	as needed
Whole butter	2 oz.	60 g
Leeks, thinly sliced	8 oz.	225 g
Chicken stock	1 pt.	450 ml
Heavy cream	4 fl. oz.	120 ml
Black pepper	TT	TT
Nutmeg	TT	TT
Parmesan, grated	2 oz.	60 g

1 Cook the orzo in salted boiling water until al dente. Drain and hold.

2 Melt the butter in a rondeau. Add the leeks and cook over medium heat until wilted.

3 Add the chicken stock and reduce until approximately 4 fluid ounces (120 milliliters) of liquid remains.

4 Add the orzo and cream and cook until thoroughly heated. Season with salt, pepper and nutmeg. Fold in the Parmesan just before serving.

Approximate values per serving: **Calories** 140, **Total fat** 6 g, **Saturated fat** 3.5 g, **Cholesterol** 15 mg, **Sodium** 125 mg, **Total carbohydrates** 18 g, **Protein** 4 g

RECIPE 23.41

GOAT-CHEESE RAVIOLI IN HERBED CREAM SAUCE

Yield: 72 ravioli, 2 in. (5 cm) each, and 1½ pt. (750 ml) sauce

Fresh goat cheese	11 oz.	330 g
Cream cheese	8 oz.	250 g
Fresh parsley, chopped	3 Tbsp.	45 ml
Fresh basil, chopped fine	3 Tbsp.	45 ml
Fresh thyme, chopped fine	2 tsp.	10 ml
Black pepper	TT	TT
Basic Pasta Dough (page 708)	2 lb.	1 kg
Heavy cream	1 qt.	1 lt
Parmesan, grated	2 oz.	60 ml
Salt	TT	TT

1 To make the cheese filling, combine the goat and cream cheeses with the parsley, 2 tablespoons (30 milliliters) basil and 1 teaspoon (5 milliliters) thyme; season to taste with pepper.

2 Make ravioli using the cheese mixture and the pasta dough.

3 To make the sauce, combine the cream with the remaining herbs and bring to a boil. Reduce by one-third and add the Parmesan. Season with salt and pepper.

4 Boil the ravioli until done. Drain, toss gently with the sauce and serve.

Approximate values per 8-oz. (240-g) serving: **Calories** 580, **Total fat** 48 g, **Saturated fat** 30 g, **Cholesterol** 185 mg, **Sodium** 510 mg, **Total carbohydrates** 23 g, **Protein** 15 g, **Vitamin A** 60%, **Calcium** 25%

RECIPE 23.42

MUSHROOM RAVIOLI IN RICH CHICKEN BROTH

PRIMITIVO WINE BAR, COLORADO SPRINGS, CO

John Broening, Executive Chef

Yield: 8 Servings

Pasta:		
Flour	1 lb.	500 g
Salt	1 Tbsp.	15 ml
Eggs	4	4
Extra virgin olive oil	4 Tbsp.	60 ml
Water, cold	4 fl. oz.	120 ml
Filling:		
Shiitake mushrooms	4 oz.	120 g
Oyster mushrooms	4 oz.	120 g
Unsalted butter	3 Tbsp.	45 ml
Shallots, minced	2 Tbsp.	30 ml
Brandy	2 Tbsp.	30 ml
White wine	3 Tbsp.	45 ml
Heavy cream	8 fl. oz.	240 ml
Goat cheese	2 oz.	60 g
Parmesan, grated	½ c.	120 ml
Parsley, chopped	1 Tbsp.	15 ml
Salt and pepper	TT	TT

Broth:

Carrots	2	2
Chicken thighs, legs, wings and backs	3 lb.	1.4 kg
Onion, sliced	1	1
Celery sticks, sliced	2	2
Garlic cloves, crushed	2	2
Bay leaves	2	2
Peppercorns	10	10
Fresh thyme	6 sprigs	6 sprigs
Niçoise olives, pitted	24	24
Fresh sage, minced	1 Tbsp.	15 ml
Parmesan, shaved	as needed for garnish	

1 To make the pasta dough, combine the flour and salt in a small mixer with a dough hook. Add the eggs, olive oil and water and mix on slow speed. If necessary, add more water until a dough ball is formed. Knead on medium speed until the dough is smooth and elastic. Cover the dough and refrigerate for 1 hour.

2 To make the filling, stem and slice the shiitake and oyster mushrooms. Sauté the mushrooms in the butter until they are soft and the liquid has evaporated. Add the shallots and sweat for 30 seconds. Add the brandy and flambé. Add the white wine and cook au sec. Add the cream and reduce until it is incorporated. Cool the mixture and transfer it to a food processor. Add the goat cheese, Parmesan and parsley. Season the mixture with salt and pepper and pulse until it is finely ground. Cool completely before using. Form the pasta and filling into ravioli following the procedures on page 710.

3 To make the broth, peel the carrots and cut grooves in them with a channel knife. Slice them on the bias ½ inch (1.2 centimeters) thick. Combine the carrots with the rest of the ingredients in a saucepot, bring to a simmer and cook for 2 hours. Strain, reserving the carrot slices.

4 At service time, bring 3 pints (1.4 liters) of the broth to a simmer. Add the reserved carrots, olives and sage. Blanch the ravioli in salted boiling water and add them to the gently simmering broth. Adjust the seasoning and divide the broth and ravioli between eight bowls. Garnish with shaved Parmesan as desired.

Approximate values per serving: **Calories** 580, **Total fat** 32 g, **Saturated fat** 14 g, **Cholesterol** 165 mg, **Sodium** 1760 mg, **Total carbohydrates** 53 g, **Protein** 16 g, **Vitamin A** 20%, **Calcium** 15%, **Iron** 20%

FETTUCCINE ALFREDO

RECIPE 23.43

Yield: 4 Servings, 6 oz. (180 g) each

Fresh fettuccine	8 oz.	250 g
Whole butter	2 oz.	60 g
Heavy cream	12 fl. oz.	350 ml
Parmesan, grated	2 oz.	60 g
Salt and white pepper	TT	TT

1 Boil the pasta, keeping it slightly undercooked. Refresh and drain.

2 To make the sauce, combine the butter, cream and Parmesan in a sauté pan. Bring to a boil and reduce slightly.

3 Add the pasta to the pan and boil the sauce and pasta until the sauce is thick and the pasta is cooked. Adjust the seasonings and serve.

Approximate values per 6-oz. (180-g) serving: **Calories** 630, **Total fat** 49 g, **Saturated fat** 29 g, **Cholesterol** 170 mg, **Sodium** 1000 mg, **Total carbohydrates** 33 g, **Protein** 14 g, **Vitamin A** 50%, **Calcium** 25%

RECIPE 23.44

FETTUCCINE CARBONARA

JOLIET JUNIOR COLLEGE, JOLIET, IL

Keith G. Vonhoff, CCE, CEPC, CHA, CHE, FMP, CCP

Yield: 4 Servings

Whole butter	1 oz.	30 g
Pancetta, parcooked and chopped	3 oz.	90 g
Garlic cloves, minced	2	2
Fettuccine, cooked and drained	18 oz.	500 g
Heavy cream	10 fl. oz.	300 ml
Parmesan, grated	4 oz.	120 g
Salt	TT	TT
White pepper	1/8 tsp.	1 ml
Egg yolks	2	2

1 Melt the butter in a sauté pan. Add the parcooked pancetta and cook until crisp.
2 Add the garlic. Sauté but do not brown.
3 Add the fettuccine. Toss and heat completely.
4 Add the heavy cream and bring to a simmer. Add the Parmesan. Season to taste with salt and white pepper.
5 Add the egg yolks and quickly stir to incorporate the eggs and thicken the sauce. Do not allow the sauce to boil. Serve immediately.

Approximate values per serving: **Calories** 680, **Total fat** 49 g, **Saturated fat** 28 g, **Cholesterol** 300 mg, **Sodium** 770 mg, **Total carbohydrates** 35 g, **Protein** 26 g, **Vitamin A** 35%, **Calcium** 45%, **Iron** 15%

FETTUCCINE CON PESTO ALLA TRAPANESE

RECIPE 23.45

CHEF ODETTE FADA, NEW YORK, NY

Yield: 4 Servings, 8 oz. (250 g) each

Fresh fettuccine	1 lb.	500 g
Salt	TT	TT
Fresh basil leaves	1/2 oz.	15 g
Garlic cloves, chopped fine	4	4
Bread crumbs	2 Tbsp.	30 ml
Almonds, chopped	1 oz.	30 g
Extra virgin olive oil	approx. 3 fl. oz.	approx. 90 ml
Roma tomatoes	8 oz.	250 g

1 Boil the pasta in salted water until almost done.
2 Lightly sauté the basil, garlic, bread crumbs and almonds in the oil.
3 Peel, seed and cut the tomatoes julienne. Add them to the pan and sauté to blend the flavors.
4 Drain the pasta, add it to the pan and sauté for 1 minute over a low flame.
5 Add more olive oil and salt as needed.

Approximate values per 8-oz. (240-g) serving: **Calories** 590, **Total fat** 29 g, **Saturated fat** 3.5 g, **Cholesterol** 20 mg, **Sodium** 640 mg, **Total carbohydrates** 68 g, **Protein** 15 g, **Vitamin C** 20%, **Iron** 15%

PEPE PASTA WITH SHRIMP, TOMATO AND TARRAGON

THE RITZ-CARLTON, CHICAGO, IL
Executive Chef George Bumbaris

Yield: 4 Servings

Onion, sliced	2 oz.	60 g
Olive oil	2 Tbsp.	30 ml
Garlic, minced	1 tsp.	5 ml
Tomato concassée	8 oz.	250 g
Dry white wine	4 fl. oz.	120 ml
Fresh shrimp, peeled and deveined	16	16
Chicken or shrimp stock	24 fl. oz.	750 ml
Pepe pasta, dry	1 c.	250 ml
Fresh lime juice	2 Tbsp.	30 ml
Whole butter	1 Tbsp.	15 ml
Fresh chives, chopped fine	1 Tbsp.	15 ml
Fresh tarragon, chopped	½ tsp.	3 ml
Fresh Italian parsley, chopped	½ tsp.	3 ml

1 In a medium-sized saucepot over medium heat, sauté the onion in the olive oil. Add the garlic and cook for 1 minute.
2 Add the tomato concassée, then add the white wine. Simmer until the liquid is reduced au sec.
3 Add the shrimp and cook for 3 to 4 minutes.
4 In a separate saucepot, bring the stock to a boil. Add the pepe pasta and simmer until the pasta is tender, approximately 15 minutes.
5 Drain the pasta and toss in the lime juice, butter and herbs.
6 Gently stir in the tomato-and-shrimp mixture and serve immediately.

Approximate values per serving: **Calories** 550, **Total fat** 15 g, **Saturated fat** 4 g, **Cholesterol** 670 mg, **Sodium** 1380 mg, **Total carbohydrates** 25 g, **Protein** 79 g, **Vitamin A** 30%, **Vitamin C** 35%, **Iron** 70%

PENNE WITH ASPARAGUS AND TOMATOES

Yield: 5 lb. (2.2 kg)

Asparagus spears	12 oz.	375 g
Salt	TT	TT
Extra virgin olive oil	4 Tbsp.	60 ml
Onions, small dice	2 oz.	60 g
Garlic cloves, chopped	12	12
Italian plum tomatoes, canned, drained and chopped	5 c.	1.2 lt
Salt	1 Tbsp.	15 ml
Red pepper flakes	TT	TT
Penne pasta, dry	1 lb.	450 g
Fresh basil leaves, chopped	1 oz.	30 g
Parmesan, grated	as needed for garnish	

1 Cook the asparagus spears in boiling salted water and refresh in ice water. Drain and cut the spears on the bias into 1-inch (2.5-centimeter) pieces.

2 Heat the olive oil in a sauté the onions and garlic until translucent. Add the tomatoes, salt and pepper flakes. Increase the head and cook 5 minutes, stirring occasionally. Keep warm.

3 Boil the penne in salted water until al dente, then drain well. Stir the asparagus into the warm sauce. Toss the pasta with the sauce and the chopped basil. Serve with freshly grated Parmesan.

Approximate values per 4-oz (120-g) serving: **Calories** 130, **Total fat** 3 g, **Saturated fat** 0 g, **Cholesterol** 0 g, **Sodium** 460 mg, **Total carbohydrates** 21 g, **Protein** 4 g, **Vitamin C** 15%

RECIPE 23.48   **CAPPELLETTI IN BRODO**

Yield: 10 (450 ml) Servings,
1 pt. with 12 cappelletti each

Filling:		
Pork loin, roasted	6 oz.	180 g
Mortadella	4 oz.	120 g
Ricotta	6 oz.	180 g
Parmesan, finely grated	6 oz.	180 g
Egg	1	1
Nutmeg	TT	TT
Basic Pasta Dough (page 708)	1 lb. 8 oz.	750 g
Beef Broth (page 250)	5 qt.	5 lt
Parmesan, shredded	8 oz.	250 g
Fresh parsley, chopped fine	3 Tbsp.	45 ml

1 To prepare the cappelletti filling, place the meats and cheeses in a food processor fitted with the metal blade. Process until finely ground. Add the egg and season lightly with nutmeg. Process until blended but not puréed.

2 Work with one-quarter of the pasta dough at a time, keeping the rest covered to prevent it from drying out. Roll out a portion of the dough until it is very thin. Cut the dough into 2-inch (5-centimeter) squares using a fluted pasta wheel.

3 Place 1 teaspoon (5 milliliters) of filling in the center of each square. Fold the dough over the filling to form a rectangle, pinching the edges together to seal. Bring the ends of each rectangle together, overlapping them and pressing to seal.

4 Place the finished cappelletti on a paper-lined sheet pan. Leave them uncovered and turn them over once or twice so that they dry evenly. Continue working until all the filling is used. The cappelletti may be cooked immediately or refrigerated for later use.

5 Heat the Beef Broth to a gentle boil. Drop the cappelletti in and cook until tender, approximately 3 to 5 minutes.

6 Portion the broth and cappelletti into 10 warmed soup bowls and garnish with the shredded Parmesan and parsley.

Approximate values per serving: **Calories** 270, **Total fat** 17 g, **Saturated fat** 10 g, **Cholesterol** 75 mg, **Sodium** 920 mg, **Total carbohydrates** 3 g, **Protein** 27 g, **Calcium** 60%

RECIPE 23.49   **MACARONI AND CHEESE**

Yield: 24 Servings, 8 oz. (250 g) each

Elbow macaroni	2 lb.	1 kg
Salt	TT	TT
Cheese sauce (page 212)	2 qt.	2 lt
Worcestershire sauce	TT	TT

Tabasco sauce	TT	TT
Cheddar cheese, grated	2 lb.	1 kg
Whole butter	3 oz.	90 g
Bread crumbs	8 oz.	250 g

1 Cook the macaroni in salted water until done. Drain, refresh in cold water, drain and reserve.

2 Season the Cheddar sauce with the Worcestershire and Tabasco sauces. Mix the macaroni with the cheese sauce and the shredded cheese.

3 Butter a full-sized hotel pan using approximately 1 ounce (30 grams) of the whole butter. Pour the macaroni mixture into the pan.

4 Melt the remaining butter in a small sauté pan. Add the bread crumbs and toss to coat. Sprinkle the bread crumbs evely over the macaroni.

5 Bake uncovered at 350°F (180°C) until hot, approximately 30 minutes.

VARIATIONS: *Macaroni and Cheese with Ham and Tomato*—Stir 2 pounds (1 kilogram) each of diced cooked ham and tomato concassée into the macaroni and cheese before pouring it into the hotel pan.

Approximate values per 6-oz. (180-g) serving: **Calories** 490, **Total fat** 28 g, **Saturated fat** 17 g, **Cholesterol** 80 mg, **Sodium** 430 mg, **Total carbohydrates** 39 g, **Protein** 21 g, **Vitamin A** 20%, **Calcium** 45%, **Iron** 15%

BAKED ZITI WITH FRESH TOMATO SAUCE   RECIPE 23.50

Yield: 30 Servings

Eggs	6	6
Ricotta	4 lb.	1.8 kg
Fresh thyme, chopped	2 Tbsp.	30 ml
Fresh oregano, chopped	2 Tbsp.	30 ml
Fresh basil, chopped	2 Tbsp.	30 ml
Salt and pepper	TT	TT
Italian sausage links	3 lb.	1.4 kg
Ziti, cooked, refreshed and drained	4 lb.	1.8 kg
Parmesan, grated	8 oz.	250 g
Fresh Tomato Sauce for Pasta (page 235)	3 qt.	3 lt
Mozzarella, shredded	2 lb.	1 kg

1 Combine the eggs, ricotta, thyme, oregano, basil, salt and pepper. Mix well and refrigerate.

2 Place the sausage links in a 2-inch- (5-centimeter-) deep full-sized hotel pan; cook in a 350°F (180°C) oven for 20 minutes. Remove and drain the sausage. Slice the links into rounds and reserve.

3 Pour off the sausage fat, then place the ziti in the hotel pan. Top with an even coating of the cheese mixture, sausage slices and Parmesan.

4 Pour the Fresh Tomato Sauce for Pasta over the top layer and stir slightly to distribute the sauce.

5 Bake at 375°F (190°C) for 1 hour. Sprinkle the mozzarella evenly over the pasta and return to the oven for 10 minutes. Serve.

Note: Ziti may also be prepared in individual casseroles. Decrease baking time as necessary.

Approximate values per serving: **Calories** 450, **Total fat** 23 g, **Saturated fat** 10 g, **Cholesterol** 130 mg, **Sodium** 1290 mg, **Total carbohydrates** 27 g, **Protein** 35 g, **Vitamin A** 40%, **Calcium** 70%, **Iron** 15%

RECIPE 23.51

SPINACH AND RICOTTA LASAGNA
WITH BOLOGNESE SAUCE

Yield: 28 Servings, 8 oz. (250 g) each

Fresh spinach pasta dough, rolled into sheets	2 lb.	1 kg
Spinach, stemmed	2 lb.	1 kg
Whole butter	2 oz.	60 g
Ricotta	1 lb.	500 g
Parmesan, grated	6 oz.	180 g
Eggs	2	2
Salt and pepper	TT	TT
Bolognese Sauce (page 236)	3 qt.	3 lt
Béchamel (page 212)	1 qt.	1 lt

1 Cut the pasta dough into 4-inch (10-centimeter) strips. Boil in salted water until done and drain well.

2 Sauté the spinach in the butter. Drain well and cool.

3 Combine the spinach with the ricotta, 4 ounces (120 grams) of the Parmesan and the eggs. Season to taste with salt and pepper.

4 Ladle a small amount of the Bolognese Sauce into the bottom of a standard full-sized hotel pan. Cover the sauce with a layer of cooked pasta. Spread a thin layer of the spinach-and-cheese mixture on the pasta. Ladle a portion of the Béchamel over the spinach and spread in a thin even layer. Ladle a portion of the Bolognese Sauce over the Béchamel and spread in an even layer.

5 Add another layer of pasta and repeat the process until all the ingredients are used, finishing with a layer of Béchamel. Sprinkle the remaining Parmesan on top and bake covered at 350°F (180°C) until heated through, approximately 40 minutes. Uncover the lasagna for the last 15 minutes so that it browns.

Approximate values per 7-oz. (210-g) serving: **Calories** 270, **Total fat** 8 g, **Saturated fat** 3.5 g, **Cholesterol** 200 mg, **Sodium** 1110 mg, **Total carbohydrates** 12 g, **Protein** 37 g, **Vitamin A** 30%, **Vitamin C** 20%, **Calcium** 20%, **Iron** 40%

1 Layering the sauces, pasta and cheese mixture in a hotel pan.

2 Pouring a layer of béchamel over the lasagna.

3 The finished lasagna.

CHILLED CHINESE NOODLE SALAD

Yield: 8 Servings, 4 oz. (120 g) each

Dressing:

Dark soy sauce	2 Tbsp.	30 ml
White vinegar	2 Tbsp.	30 ml
Salt	1 tsp.	5 ml
Granulated sugar	1 Tbsp.	15 ml
Peanut oil	1 Tbsp.	15 ml
Sesame oil	1 Tbsp.	15 ml
Orange zest	1 tsp.	5 ml
Red chile flakes	1/2 tsp.	2 ml
Chinese egg noodles, fresh	8 oz.	250 g
Salt	TT	TT
Bean sprouts, blanched	8 oz.	250 g
Carrots, finely shredded	6 oz.	180 g
Daikon, finely shredded	3 oz.	90 g
Green onions, sliced	2 oz.	60 g
Black sesame seeds	1 Tbsp.	15 ml
Fresh cilantro leaves	as needed for garnish	

1 Combine the dressing ingredients and whisk thoroughly.
2 Cook the egg noodles in rapidly boiling salted water until tender, approximately 2 minutes. Drain and refresh; drain again.
3 Toss the noodles with the bean sprouts, carrots, daikon, green onions and sesame seeds. Add the dressing and toss gently until the noodles and vegetables are thoroughly coated.
4 Chill well. Serve mounds of this noodle salad as an appetizer or an accompaniment for grilled fish or chicken. Garnish with cilantro.

Approximate values per 4-oz. (120-g) serving: **Calories** 110, **Total fat** 4.5 g, **Saturated fat** 0.5 g, **Cholesterol** 10 mg, **Sodium** 570 mg, **Total carbohydrates** 14 g, **Protein** 3 g, **Vitamin A** 40%, **Claims**—low cholesterol; low saturated fat

SPAETZLE

Yield: 30 Servings, 3 oz. (90 g) each

Eggs	12	12
Water	1 qt.	1 lt
Flour	3 lb.	1.4 kg
Salt	2 tsp.	10 ml
Nutmeg	1/2 tsp.	2 ml
Whole butter	8 oz.	250 g
Salt and white pepper	TT	TT
Fresh parsley, chopped	as needed for garnish	

1 Whisk the eggs to blend. Add the water, flour, salt and nutmeg. Mix by hand until well blended; the batter should be a smooth, gooey paste. Cover and refrigerate the batter.

Forcing the spaetzle through a perforated hotel pan.

2 Place the batter in a spaetzle maker, perforated steam table pan or colander suspended over a large pot of boiling water. Work the batter through the colander's holes using a plastic bowl scraper or rubber spatula. The batter should drop into the boiling water. Lower the water temperature to a simmer.

3 Cook the dumplings in the simmering water until they float to the surface, approximately 3 to 4 minutes. Remove them with a skimmer and refresh in a bowl of ice water.

4 For service, sauté the dumplings in butter to heat through. Season with salt and white pepper; garnish with chopped parsley.

Approximate values per 3-oz. (90-g) serving: **Calories** 250, **Total fat** 9 g, **Saturated fat** 4.5 g, **Cholesterol** 100 mg, **Sodium** 250 mg, **Total carbohydrates** 35 g, **Protein** 7 g, **Vitamin A** 10%, **Iron** 15%

ACCORDING TO THE SPANISH PROVERB, FOUR PERSONS ARE WANTED FOR TO MAKE A GOOD SALAD: A SPENDTHRIFT FOR OIL, A MISER FOR VINEGAR, A COUNSELOR FOR SALT, AND A MADMAN TO STIR IT ALL UP.

—*Abraham Hayward, English writer*
  (1801–1884)

SALADS
AND SALAD
DRESSINGS

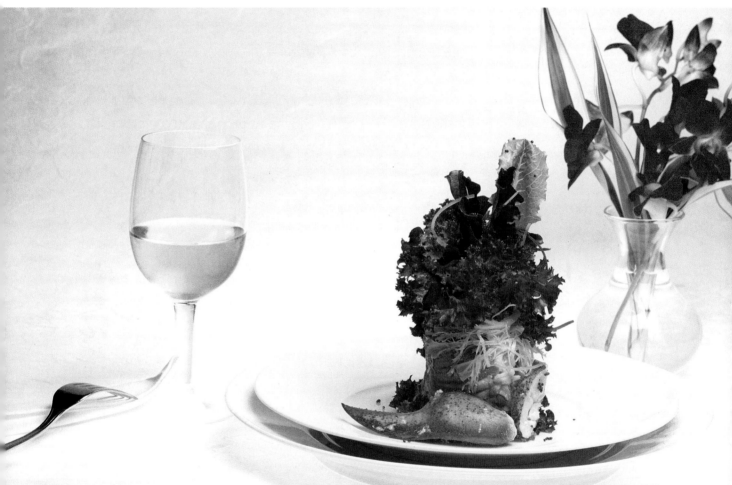

GOTHAM BAR & GRILL, New York, NY
Chef-Owner Alfred Portale

This chapter discusses all types of salads: the small plate of crisp iceberg lettuce with tomato wedges, cucumber slices and ranch dressing; the dinner plate of sautéed duck breast fanned across bright red grilled radicchio and toothy green arugula, sprayed with a vinaigrette dressing; the scoop of shredded chicken, mango chutney and seasonings, bound with mayonnaise; and the bowl of artichokes and mushrooms marinated in olive oil and lemon juice.

Each of these dishes fits the definition of a salad: a single food or a mix of different foods accompanied or bound by a dressing. A salad can contain meat, grains, fruits, nuts or cheese and absolutely no lettuce. It can be an appetizer, a second course served after the appetizer, an entrée (especially at lunch), a course following the entrée in the European manner or even dessert.

The color, texture and flavor of each salad ingredient should complement those of the others, and the dressing should complement all the ingredients. Harmony is critical to a salad's success—no matter what type of salad is being prepared.

This chapter opens with a section identifying greens commonly used in salads. A discussion of salad dressings follows. Finally, techniques for preparing green salads (both tossed and composed), bound salads, vegetable salads and fruit salads are discussed.

▶ SALAD GREENS

IDENTIFYING SALAD GREENS

Salad greens are not necessarily green: Some are red, yellow, white or brown. They are all, however, leafy vegetables. Many are members of the lettuce or chicory families.

LETTUCE

Lettuce (Fr. *laitue;* It. *lattuga*) has been consumed for nearly as long as people have kept records of what they and others ate. Archaeologists found that Persian royalty were served lettuce at their banquets more than 2500 years ago. Now grown and served worldwide, lettuces are members of the genus *Lactuca.* The most common types of lettuce are butterhead, crisp head, leaf and romaine.

Boston

Boston and bibb are two of the most popular butterhead lettuces. Their soft, pliable, pale green leaves have a buttery texture and flavor. Boston is larger and paler than bibb. Both Boston and bibb lettuce leaves form cups when separated from the heads; these cups make convenient bases for holding other foods on cold plates.

Iceberg

Iceberg lettuce is the most common of all lettuce varieties in the United States; it outsells all other varieties combined. Its tightly packed spherical head is composed of crisp, pale green leaves with a very mild flavor. Iceberg lettuce remains crisp for a relatively long time after being cut or prepared. Select heads that are firm but not hard and leaves that are free of burnt or rusty tips.

Boston

Iceberg

Leaf

Leaf lettuce grows in bunches. It has separate, ruffle-edged leaves branching from a stalk. Because it does not grow into a firm head, it is easily damaged during harvest and transport. Both red and green leaf lettuce have bright colors, mild flavors and tender leaves. Good-quality leaf lettuce should have nicely shaped leaves free of bruises, breaks or brown spots.

Romaine

Romaine lettuce, also known as **cos,** is a loosely packed head lettuce with elongated leaves and thick midribs. Its outer leaves are dark green and although they look coarse, they are crisp, tender and tasty without being bitter. The core leaves are paler and more tender but still crisp. Romaine has enough flavor to stand up to strongly flavored dressings such as the garlic and Parmesan cheese used in a Caesar salad. A good-quality head of romaine has dark green outer leaves that are free of blemishes or yellowing.

*Red and Green
Leaf Lettuces*

Baby Lettuces

Innovative chefs are always looking for new and different foods to add a twist or flair to their dishes. This has led to the popularity of baby lettuces and other specialty greens. Baby greens have similar but more subtle flavors than their mature versions. They are often less bitter and are always more tender and delicate. Because of their size and variety, they are perfect for composed salads. **Mesclun** is a mixture of several kinds of baby lettuces.

Romaine

Lola Rosa

Red Sails

Baby Green Bibb

Brune d'Hiver

Baby Red Oak Leaf

Baby Red Bibb

Pirate

Baby Red Romaine

Micro Greens

Belgian Endive

Curly Endive

Escarole

Radicchio

Arugula

Dandelion

Micro greens are even smaller than baby lettuces. They are the first true leaves of virtually any edible greens, such as lettuce, spinach, kale and so on. Micro greens are very fragile and must be handpicked and carefully packaged for delivery. Chefs enjoy using them as garnish, especially on entrée and appetizer plates.

Chicory

Chicories come in a variety of colors, shapes and sizes; most are slightly bitter. Chicories are quite hearty and can also be cooked, usually grilled or braised.

Belgian Endive

Belgian endive grows in small, tight heads with pointed leaves. It is actually the shoot of a chicory root. The small sturdy leaves are white at the base with yellow fringes and tips. (A purple-tipped variety is sometimes available.) Whole leaves can be separated, trimmed and filled with soft butters, cheeses or spreads and served as an hors d'oeuvre, or they can be used for composed salads. The leaves, cut or whole, can also be added to cold salads. Heads of Belgian endive are often braised or grilled and served with meat or poultry. As the name suggests, Belgian endive is imported from Belgium.

Curly Endive

In the United States, curly endive is often called by its family name, chicory, or its French name, frisée (free-ZAY). The dark green outer leaves are pointed, sturdy and slightly bitter. The yellow inner leaves are more tender and less bitter. Curly endive has a strong flavor that goes well with strong cheeses, game and citrus. It is often mixed with other greens to add texture and flavor.

Escarole

Escarole (es-kah-ROLE), sometimes called broadleaf endive, has thick leaves and a slightly bitter flavor. It has green outer leaves and pale green or yellow center leaves. Escarole is very sturdy and is often mixed with other greens for added texture. Its strong flavor stands up to full-flavored dressings and is a good accompaniment to grilled meats and poultry.

Radicchio

Radicchio (rah-DEE-kee-oh) resembles a small red cabbage. It retains its bright reddish color when cooked and is popular braised or grilled and served as a vegetable side dish. Because of its attractive color, radicchio is popular in cold salads, but it has a very bitter flavor and should be used sparingly and mixed with other greens in a tossed salad. The leaves form cups when separated and can be used to hold other ingredients when preparing composed salads. Radicchio is quite expensive and availability is sometimes limited.

OTHER SALAD GREENS AND INGREDIENTS

Leafy vegetables besides lettuce and chicory, as well as other ingredients, are used to add texture, flavor and color to salads. A partial listing follows.

Arugula

Arugula (ah-ROO-guh-lah), also known as rocket, is a member of the cabbage family. Arugula leaves are somewhat similar to broad dandelion leaves in size and shape. The best are 2 to 4 inches (5 to 10 centimeters) long. Arugula has a very strong, spicy, peppery flavor—so strong, in fact, that it is rarely served by itself. It is best when used to add zip to salads by combining it with other greens.

Dandelion

Dandelion grows as a weed throughout most of the United States. It has long, thin, toothed leaves with a prominent midrib. When purchasing dandelion for salads, look for small leaves; they are more tender and less bitter. Older, tougher leaves can be cooked and served as a vegetable.

Mâche

Mâche

Mâche (mahsh) or lamb's lettuce is very tender and very delicately flavored. Its small, curved, pale to dark green leaves have a slightly nutty flavor. Because its flavor is so delicate, mâche should be combined only with other delicately flavored greens such as Boston or bibb lettuce and dressed sparingly with a light vinaigrette dressing.

Sorrel

Sorrel, sometimes called sourgrass, has leaves similar to spinach in color and shape. Sorrel has a very tart, lemony flavor that goes well with fish and shellfish. It should be used sparingly and combined with other greens in a salad. Sorrel can also be made into soups, sauces and purées.

Sorrel

Spinach

Like sorrel, spinach can be cooked or used as a salad green. As a salad green, it is popularly served tossed with hot bacon dressing. Spinach is deep green with a rich flavor and tender texture. Good-quality spinach should be fairly crisp. Avoid wilted or yellowed bunches.

Spinach

Sprouts

Sprouts are not salad greens but are often used as such in salads and sandwiches. Sprouts are very young alfalfa, daikon or mustard plants. Alfalfa sprouts are very mild and sweet. Daikon and mustard sprouts are quite peppery.

Sprouts

Watercress

Watercress has tiny, dime-sized leaves and substantial stems. It has a peppery flavor and adds spice to a salad. Good-quality fresh watercress is dark green with no yellowing. To preserve its freshness, watercress must be kept very cold and moist. It is normally packed topped with ice. Individual leaves are plucked from the stems and rinsed just before service.

Watercress

Edible Flowers

Many specialty produce growers offer edible, pesticide-free blossoms. They are used for salads and as garnishes wherever a splash of color would be appreciated. Some flowers such as nasturtiums, calendulas and pansies are grown and picked specifically for eating. Others, such as yellow cucumber flowers and squash blossoms, are by-products of the vegetable industry.

Squash blossoms and other very large flowers should be cut in julienne strips before being added to salads. Pick petals from large and medium-sized flowers. Smaller whole flowers can be tossed in a salad or used as a garnish when composing a salad. Very small flowers or petals should be sprinkled on top of a salad so that they are not hidden by the greens.

Nasturtiums

Fresh Herbs

Basil, thyme, tarragon, oregano, dill, cilantro, marjoram, mint, sage, savory and even rosemary are used to add interesting flavors to otherwise ordinary salads. Because many herbs have strong flavors, use them sparingly so that the delicate flavors of the greens are not overpowered. Leafy herbs such as basil and sage can be cut chiffonade. Other herbs can be picked from their stems or chopped before being tossed with the salad greens. Flowering herbs such as chive blossoms are used like other edible

Calendulas

Pansies

flowers to add color, flavor and aroma. Refer to Chapter 7, Kitchen Staples, for more information on herbs.

NUTRITION

Salad greens are an especially healthful food. Greens contain virtually no fat and few calories and are high in vitamins A and C, iron and fiber. But when greens are garnished with meat and cheese and tossed with a dressing (many of which are oil based), fat and calories are added. In an attempt to maintain the healthful nature of greens, low-fat or fat-free dressings should be available to customers.

PURCHASING AND STORING SALAD GREENS

PURCHASING

Lettuces are grown in nearly every part of the United States; nearly all types are available year-round. Other important salad greens such as spinach are available all year; many of the specialty greens are seasonal.

Lettuce is generally packed in cases of 24 heads with varying weights. Other salad greens are packed in trays or boxes of various sizes and weights.

Because salad greens are simply washed and eaten, it is extremely important that they be as fresh and blemish-free as possible. Try to purchase salad greens daily. All greens should be fresh looking, with no yellowing. Heads should be heavy, with little or no damage to the outer leaves.

Many types of salad greens are available precut and prewashed. These greens are often vacuum-packed to increase shelf life, although delicate greens are sometimes loosely packaged in 5- to 10-pound (2- to 5-kilogram) boxes. Precut and prewashed greens are relatively expensive, but can reduce labor costs dramatically.

STORING

Although some types of salad greens are hearty enough to keep for a week or more under proper conditions, all salad greens are highly perishable. Generally, softer-leaved varieties such as Boston and bibb tend to perish more quickly than the crisper-leaved varieties such as iceberg and romaine.

Greens should be stored in their original protective cartons in a specifically designated refrigerator. Ideally, greens should be stored at temperatures between 34°F and 38°F (1°C and 3°C). (Most other vegetables should be stored at warmer temperatures of 40°F to 50°F [4°C to 10°C].) Greens should not be stored with tomatoes, apples or other fruits that emit ethylene gas, which causes greens to wilt and accelerates spoilage.

Do not wash greens until you need them, as excess water causes them to deteriorate quickly.

PREPARING SALAD GREENS

Unless salad greens are purchased precut and prewashed, they will need to undergo some preparation before service, principally tearing, cutting, washing and drying.

TEARING AND CUTTING

Some chefs want all salad greens torn by hand. Delicate greens such as butterhead and baby lettuces look nicer, and it is less likely they will be bruised if hand-torn. But often it is not practical to hand-tear all greens. It is perfectly acceptable to cut hardy greens with a knife.

▶ PROCEDURE FOR CUTTING ROMAINE LETTUCE

1 To cut romaine lettuce, trim the outer leaves and damaged tips with a chef's knife and split the head lengthwise.

2 Make one or two cuts along the length of the head, leaving the root intact, then cut across the width of the head.

3 Alternative method: Trim the outer leaves and damaged tips with a chef's knife. Pull the leaves from the core and cut the rib out of each leaf. The leaf can then be cut to the desired size.

▶ PROCEDURE FOR CORING ICEBERG LETTUCE

1 Loosen the core by gripping the head and smacking the core on the cutting board. (Do not use too much force or you may bruise the lettuce).

2 Remove the core and cut the lettuce as desired.

▶ PROCEDURE FOR REMOVING THE MIDRIB FROM SPINACH

Fold the leaf in half and pull off the stem and midrib. Only the tender leaf should remain.

SAFETY ALERT

HAND WASHING

Because salads are not cooked, it is especially important to be extra careful about proper hand washing when preparing them. Remember that many health departments require single-use gloves to be worn—and changed frequently—whenever working with products that will not be cooked before service.

WASHING

All lettuces and other salad greens should be washed before use. Even though they may look clean, greens may harbor hidden insects, sand, soil and pesticides. All greens should be washed after they are torn or cut. Whole heads can be washed by repeatedly dipping them in cold water and allowing them to drain. But washing whole heads is not recommended: It will not remove anything trapped near the head's center, and water trapped in the leaves can accelerate spoilage.

▶ PROCEDURE FOR WASHING SALAD GREENS

1 Fill a sink with very cold water. Place the cut or torn greens in the water.

2 Gently stir the water and greens with your hands and remove the greens. Do not allow the greens to soak. Using fresh water each time, repeat the procedure until no grit can be detected on the bottom of the sink after the greens are removed.

DRYING

Salad greens should be dried after washing. Wet greens do not stay as crisp as thoroughly dried ones. Also, wet greens tend to repel oil-based dressings and dilute their flavors. Greens may be dried by draining them well in a colander and blotting them with absorbent cloth or paper towels, or, preferably, they can be dried in a salad spinner, which uses centrifugal force to remove the water.

▶ PROCEDURE FOR DRYING GREENS

After washing the greens, place them in the basket of a salad spinner and spin for approximately 30 seconds.

▶ SALAD DRESSINGS

A dressing is a sauce for a salad. Just as sauces for hot foods should complement rather than mask the flavor of the principal food, the sauce (dressing) for a salad should complement rather than mask the flavors of the other ingredients. Although a great many ingredients can be used to make salad dressings, most are based on either a mixture of oil and vinegar, called a vinaigrette, or a mayonnaise or other emulsified product.

Vinaigrette-style dressings can be made without oil; creamy dressings similar to mayonnaise-based dressings can be made with sour cream, yogurt or buttermilk instead of mayonnaise. Nevertheless, for all practical purposes these dressings are still prepared like vinaigrettes and mayonnaise-based dressings and they are treated that way here.

VINAIGRETTE DRESSINGS

The simple vinaigrette, also known as basic **French dressing,** is a temporary emulsion of oil and vinegar seasoned with salt and pepper. The standard ratio is three parts oil to one part vinegar. The ratio can vary, however. When using strongly flavored oils, less than three parts oil to one part vinegar generally suffices. In some recipes, all or part of the vinegar is replaced with citrus juice, in which case, it may take more than one part vinegar and citrus juice to three parts oil to achieve the proper acidity level. The best way to determine the correct ratio of oil to vinegar is to taste the dressing, preferably on the food it will dress.

Oils and vinegars have unique flavors that can be mixed and matched to achieve the correct balance for a particular salad. Olive oil goes well with red wine vinegar; nut oils go well with balsamic or sherry vinegars. Neutral-flavored oils such as canola, corn or safflower can be mixed with a flavored vinegar.

Oil and vinegar repel each other and will separate almost immediately when mixed. They should be whisked together immediately before use.

OILS

Many types of oil can be used to make salad dressings. Light, neutral-flavored oils such as canola, corn, cottonseed, soybean and safflower are relatively low priced and used extensively for this purpose. Other oils can be used to add flavor. Olive oil is very popular; both mild-flavored pure olive oil and full-flavored extra virgin olive oil are used. Nut oils such as hazelnut and walnut are expensive, but they add unique and interesting flavors. Infused oils are also popular.

VINEGARS

Many different vinegars can be used to make salad dressings. Red wine vinegar is the most common because it is inexpensive and its flavor blends well with many foods. But other vinegars such as cider, balsamic and white wine are also used. Fruit-flavored vinegars (particularly raspberry) are extremely popular and widely available, as are herb- and garlic-flavored ones.

Flavored vinegars are easy to make. Fruit, herbs or garlic are added to a wine vinegar (either red or white) and left for several days for the flavors to blend. The vinegar is then strained off and used as desired.

Acidic juices such as lemon, orange and lime are sometimes substituted for all or part of the vinegar in a salad dressing.

OTHER FLAVORING INGREDIENTS

Herbs, spices, shallots, garlic, mustard and sugar are only a few of the many flavoring ingredients used to enhance a vinaigrette dressing. Items such as herbs, shallots and garlic should be minced or chopped before being added to the dressing. If dried herbs are used, the dressing should rest for at least 1 hour to allow the flavors to develop. Other ingredients may be added at any time.

▶ **French dressing** classically, a vinaigrette dressing made from oil, vinegar, salt and pepper; In the United States, the term also refers to a commercially prepared dressing that is creamy, tartly sweet and red-orange in color

▶ PROCEDURE FOR PREPARING A VINAIGRETTE

1 Choose an oil and vinegar that complement each other as well as the foods they will dress.

2 Combine the vinegar, seasonings and any other flavorings in a bowl.

3 Whisk in the oil.

4 Allow the finished dressing to rest a few hours at room temperature before using so that the flavors can blend.

5 Rewhisk immediately before use.

RECIPE 24.1

BASIC VINAIGRETTE DRESSING

Whisking together the vinaigrette dressing.

Yield: 1 qt. (1 lt)

Wine vinegar	8 fl. oz.	250 ml
Salt and pepper	TT	TT
Salad oil	24 fl. oz.	750 ml

1 Combine all ingredients and mix well. Store at room temperature.

Variations: *Dijon Vinaigrette*—Add 4 ounces (120 grams) of Dijon-style mustard to the vinegar and proceed with the recipe.

Herbed Vinaigrette—Add 2 tablespoons (30 milliliters) of fresh herbs or 1 tablespoon (15 milliliters) of dried herbs such as basil, tarragon, thyme, marjoram and chives to the vinaigrette.

Approximate values per 1-fl.-oz. (30-ml) serving: **Calories** 190, **Total fat** 22 g, **Saturated fat** 3 g, **Cholesterol** 0 mg, **Sodium** 75 mg, **Total carbohydrates** 0 g, **Protein** 0 g, **Claims**—no cholesterol; low sodium; no sugar

MAYONNAISE

Although most food service operations buy commercially made mayonnaise, every chef should know how it is made to more fully understand how to use it and why it reacts the way it does when used. Knowing how to make mayonnaise also allows you to create a mayonnaise with the exact flavorings you want.

Mayonnaise is an **emulsion.** An emulsion, or emulsified sauce, is formed when two liquids that would not ordinarily form a stable mixture are forced together and held in suspension. To make mayonnaise, oil is whisked together with a very small amount of vinegar. (It is the water in the vinegar that does not normally mix with oil.) As the oil and vinegar are whisked together, the oil breaks into microscopic droplets that are separated from each other by a thin barrier of vinegar. If left alone, the droplets would quickly regroup, forming a large puddle of oil and a small puddle of vinegar. To prevent the oil droplets from regrouping, an emulsifier is added. For mayonnaise, the emulsifier is lecithin, a protein found in egg yolks. (The acid in the vinegar also helps form the emulsion.) Lecithin has the unique ability to combine with both oil and water. It surrounds the oil droplets, preventing them from coming in contact with each other and regrouping.

The balance of vinegar, oil, lecithin and agitation (whipping) is crucial to achieve a proper emulsion. The higher the proportion of oil to vinegar, the thicker the sauce will be. The higher the proportion of vinegar to oil, the thinner the sauce will be. (For example, the emulsified vinaigrette dressing discussed on page 757 is a thin emulsion.)

There is a limit to how much oil each egg yolk can emulsify, however. One yolk contains enough lecithin to emulsify approximately 7 ounces (200 milli-

▶ **emulsion** a uniform mixture of two unmixable liquids; it is often temporary (for example, oil in water)

MAYONNAISE VS. SALAD DRESSING

Commercially prepared salad dressing is often used as a substitute for "real" mayonnaise. Although it may look, smell and spread like the real thing, salad dressing tends to be sweeter than mayonnaise. Salad dressing costs less than real mayonnaise because it is made without egg yolks, relying instead on chemical thickening agents. The cost is reduced further because the FDA requires salad dressing to contain only 30 percent oil, while mayonnaise must contain at least 65 percent oil.

liters) of oil. If more than that amount of oil per egg yolk is added, the sauce will break; that is, the oil and vinegar will separate, and the mayonnaise will become very thin.

INGREDIENTS

A neutral-flavored vegetable oil is most often used for a standard mayonnaise. Other oils are used to contribute their special flavors. For example, olive oil is used to make a special mayonnaise called *aïoli*.

Wine vinegar is used for a standard mayonnaise. Flavored vinegars such as tarragon vinegar are often used to create unique flavors.

Seasonings vary according to the intended use but typically include dry mustard, salt, pepper and lemon juice.

▶ PROCEDURE FOR PREPARING MAYONNAISE

1 Gather all ingredients and hold at room temperature. Room-temperature ingredients emulsify more easily than cold ones.

2 By hand or in an electric mixer or food processor, whip the egg yolks on high speed until frothy.

3 Add the seasonings to the yolks and whip to combine. Salt and other seasonings will dissolve or blend more easily when added at this point rather than to the finished mayonnaise.

4 Add a small amount of the liquid (for example, vinegar) from the recipe and whip to combine.

5 With the mixer on high or whisking vigorously by hand, begin to add the oil very slowly until an emulsion forms.

6 After the emulsion forms, the oil can be added a little more quickly but still in a slow, steady stream. The mayonnaise can now be whipped at a slightly slower speed.

7 The mayonnaise will become very thick as more oil is added. A small amount of liquid can be added if it becomes too thick. Alternate between oil and liquid two or three times until all the oil is added and the correct consistency is reached. Important: A large egg yolk has the ability to emulsify up to 7 fluid ounces (200 milliliters) of oil; adding more oil may cause the mayonnaise to break.

8 Adjust the seasonings and refrigerate immediately.

MAYONNAISE   RECIPE 24.2

Yield: 1 qt. (1 lt)

Egg yolks	4	4
Salt	1 tsp.	5 ml
White pepper	TT	TT
Dry mustard	1 tsp.	5 ml
Wine vinegar	3 Tbsp.	45 ml
Salad oil	28 fl. oz.	840 ml
Lemon juice	TT	TT

1 Place the egg yolks in the bowl of a mixer and whip on high speed until frothy.

2 Add the dry ingredients and half the vinegar to the yolks; whisk to combine.

3 Begin to add the oil a drop at a time until the mixture begins to thicken and an emulsion begins to form.

4 Add the remaining oil in a slow steady stream, thinning the mayonnaise occasionally by adding a little vinegar. Continue until all the oil and vinegar have been incorporated.

CONVENIENCE PRODUCTS

A great many prepared and dry-mix salad dressings are available. Although they vary greatly in quality, they can be very economical; they offer consistency, reduced labor costs and, sometimes, reduced food costs. Some of these products use stabilizers, artificial flavorings and colors; nearly all contain preservatives. When considering the advantages of prepared or dry-mix salad dressings, always keep quality in mind.

5 Adjust the seasonings and add lemon juice to taste.

6 Refrigerate until needed.

Approximate values per 1-fl.-oz. (30-ml) serving: **Calories** 230, **Total fat** 26 g, **Saturated fat** 3.5 g, **Cholesterol** 25 mg, **Sodium** 75 mg, **Total carbohydrates** 0 g, **Protein** 0 g

1 Whipping the egg yolks until frothy.

2 Adding the oil very slowly, allowing the emulsion to form.

3 The finished mayonnaise.

MAYONNAISE-BASED DRESSINGS

Mayonnaise-based salad dressings are salad dressings that use mayonnaise as a base, with other ingredients added for flavor, color and texture. These ingredients include dairy products (especially buttermilk and sour cream), vinegar, fruit juice, vegetables (either puréed or minced), tomato paste, garlic, onions, herbs, spices, condiments, capers, anchovies and boiled eggs. Recipes for several mayonnaise-based salad dressings appear at the end of this chapter.

EMULSIFIED VINAIGRETTE DRESSINGS

An emulsified vinaigrette is a standard vinaigrette dressing emulsified with whole eggs. An emulsified vinaigrette dressing is thinner and lighter than a mayonnaise-based dressing and heavier than a basic vinaigrette. Its flavor is similar to a basic vinaigrette, but it will not separate and it clings to greens quite easily.

▶ PROCEDURE FOR PREPARING AN EMULSIFIED VINAIGRETTE DRESSING

1 Gather all ingredients and hold at room temperature. Room-temperature ingredients emulsify more easily than cold ones.

2 Whip the eggs until frothy.

3 Add the dry ingredients and any flavorings such as garlic, shallots and herbs.

4 Add a small amount of the liquid from the recipe and whip to incorporate the ingredients.

5 With the mixer on high or whisking vigorously by hand, begin adding the oil very slowly until the emulsion forms.

6 After the emulsion is formed, the oil can be added a little more quickly, but still in a slow, steady stream.

7 Alternate between oil and liquid two or three times until all the oil is added. The dressing should be much thinner than mayonnaise. If it is too thick, it can be thinned with a little water, vinegar or lemon juice. Determine which to use by first tasting the dressing.

EMULSIFIED VINAIGRETTE DRESSING

RECIPE 24.3

Yield: 1 qt. (1 lt)

Eggs	2	2
Salt	1 Tbsp.	15 ml
White pepper	½ tsp.	2 ml
Paprika	1 Tbsp.	15 ml
Dry mustard	1 Tbsp.	15 ml
Granulated sugar	1 Tbsp.	15 ml
Herbes de Provence	1 Tbsp.	15 ml
Cayenne pepper	TT	TT
Wine vinegar or cider vinegar	4 fl. oz.	120 ml
Salad oil	24 fl. oz.	720 ml
Lemon juice	3 fl. oz.	90 ml

1 Place the eggs in the bowl of a mixer and whip at high speed until frothy.

2 Add the dry ingredients and approximately 1 fluid ounce (30 milliliters) of vinegar to the eggs; whip to combine.

3 While whipping at high speed, begin adding the oil very slowly until an emulsion forms.

4 Add the remaining oil in a slow, steady stream. Occasionally thin the dressing by adding a little vinegar and lemon juice. Continue until all the oil, vinegar and lemon juice have been incorporated.

5 Adjust the flavor and consistency.

6 Refrigerate until needed.

Approximate values per 1-fl.-oz. (30-ml) serving: **Calories** 200, **Total fat** 22 g, **Saturated fat** 3 g, **Cholesterol** 15 mg, **Sodium** 220 mg, **Total carbohydrates** 1 g, **Protein** 1 g

1 Whipping the whole eggs.

2 Adding the oil drop by drop to establish the emulsion.

3 The finished emulsified vinaigrette dressing.

▶ PREPARATION METHODS

There are two types of **green salads:** tossed and composed. The more informal **tossed salad** is prepared by placing the greens, garnishes and dressing in a large bowl and tossing to combine. A **composed salad** usually has a more elegant look. It is prepared by arranging each of the ingredients on plates in an artistic fashion.

Other types of salads include **bound salads,** which are cooked meats, poultry, fish, shellfish, pasta or potatoes bound with a dressing; **vegetable salads** and **fruit salads.**

GREEN SALADS

TOSSED SALADS

Tossed salads are made from leafy vegetables such as lettuce, spinach, watercress, arugula or dandelion greens. They may consist only of greens and dressing, or they can be garnished with fruits, vegetables, nuts or cheese. They can be dressed with many different types of dressings, from a light oil and vinegar to a hearty hot bacon. It is important that salad dressings be added at the last possible moment before service. Acidic dressings cause most greens to wilt and become soggy.

Matching Dressings and Salad Greens

There is a simple rule to follow when choosing dressings for salads: The more delicate the texture and flavor of the greens or other ingredients, the lighter and

Table 24.1	MATCHING DRESSINGS AND SALAD GREENS	
DRESSING	**GREENS**
Vinaigrette dressing made with vegetable oil and red wine vinegar	Any greens: iceberg, romaine, leaf lettuce, butterhead lettuce, escarole, curly endive, Belgian endive, radicchio, baby lettuces, sorrel, arugula, dandelion, micro greens
Vinaigrette dressing made with a nut oil and balsamic vinegar	Delicate greens; butterhead lettuce, bibb lettuce, Belgian endive, radicchio, baby lettuces, arugula, mâche, watercress, micro greens
Emulsified vinaigrette dressing	Any greens; romaine, leaf lettuce, butterhead lettuce, escarole, curly endive, Belgian endive, radicchio, baby lettuces, sorrel, arugula, watercress
Mayonnaise-based dressing such as blue cheese or green goddess	Hardy greens; iceberg, romaine, leaf lettuce, escarole, curly endive, sorrel, dandelion

more subtle the dressing should be. Vinaigrette-based dressings are much lighter than mayonnaise-based or similar dressings and should be used with butterhead lettuces, mâche or other delicate greens. Crisp head lettuce such as iceberg and hardy lettuce such as romaine can stand up to heavier, mayonnaise-based or similar dressings.

Salad Garnishes

It is impossible to make a complete list of the garnishes that can be combined with salad greens for a tossed salad. The following is a partial list:

▶ Vegetables—nearly any vegetable—raw, blanched or fully cooked—cut into appropriate sizes and uniform shapes.

▶ Fruits—citrus segments, apples or pears; dried fruits such as raisins, currants or apricots.

▶ Meats, poultry, fish and shellfish—cooked meats and poultry sliced or diced neatly and uniformly; poached, grilled or cured fish, diced or flaked; small, whole cooked shellfish such as shrimp and scallops; lobster or crab sliced, diced or chopped.

▶ Cheeses—grated hard cheeses such as Parmesan, Romano or Asiago; semihard cheeses such as Cheddar or Swiss, cut julienne or shredded.

▶ Nuts—nearly any are appropriate, roasted, candied or smoked.

▶ Croutons—assorted breads, seasoned in various ways and toasted.

▶ PROCEDURE FOR MAKING TOSSED SALADS

1 Select greens with various colors, textures and flavors.
2 Carefully cut or tear, wash and dry the greens.
3 Prepare the garnishes as directed or desired.
4 Prepare the dressing.
5 Combine the greens, garnishes and dressing by tossing them together, or toss the greens and garnishes and, using a spray bottle, spray the greens with the dressing.

MESCLUN SALAD WITH
RASPBERRY VINAIGRETTE

RECIPE 24.4

Yield: 6 Servings   **Method:** Tossed Salad

Baby lettuces, assorted	approx. 8 heads	approx. 8 heads
Mâche	4 oz.	120 g
Fresh herbs	2 Tbsp.	30 ml
Edible flowers	approx. 12	approx. 12
Raspberry Vinaigrette (page 765)	4 fl. oz.	120 ml

A simple mesclun salad.

1 Trim, wash and dry the baby lettuces and mâche.

2 Pick the fresh herbs from their stems. Leafy herbs such as basil may be cut chiffonade or left as whole leaves.

3 If desired, pick the petals from the edible flowers. Small flowers may be left whole.

4 Place the lettuces and mâche in a bowl and add the herbs. Ladle the Raspberry Vinaigrette over them and toss gently, using two spoons.

5 Transfer the salad to six cold plates. Some of the larger leaves may be used as liners if desired.

6 Garnish each salad with flowers or flower petals.

Approximate values per serving: **Calories** 150, **Total fat** 9 g, **Saturated fat** 1 g, **Cholesterol** 0 mg, **Sodium** 180 mg, **Total carbohydrates** 14 g, **Protein** 4 g, **Vitamin A** 35%, **Vitamin C** 120%

COMPOSED SALADS

Composed green salads usually use a green as a base and are built by artistically arranging other ingredients on the plate. There are usually four components: the base, body, garnish and dressing.

The **base** is usually a layer of salad greens that line the plate on which the salad will be served. Depending upon the desired effect, the leaves can be cup-shaped or flat.

The **body** is the main ingredient. It can be lettuce or other greens, or another salad made from cooked or blended ingredients, such as chicken salad or fruit.

The **garnish** is added to the salad for color, texture and flavor. It can be as substantial as a grilled, sliced duck breast or as simple as a sprinkling of chopped herbs; it can be warm or cold. The choice is unlimited, but whatever is used should always complement and balance the flavor of the body.

The **dressing** should complement rather than mask the other flavors in the salad. If the body already contains a dressing, such as a bound salad, additional dressing may not be necessary.

Composed green salads are usually dressed by ladling the dressing over the salad after it is plated. Alternatively, the individual ingredients can be dressed before they are arranged on the plate. A third method that may be limited by the intricacy of the salad but will save precious time during a busy period is to prepare individual salads on a sheet pan. Then, just before service, mist them with dressing using a spray bottle designated for this purpose; then transfer them to chilled plates using a spatula.

Transferring composed salads to chilled plates for service.

▶ PROCEDURE FOR MAKING COMPOSED SALADS

1 Gather all ingredients for the salad and wash, trim, cut, cook, chill or otherwise prepare them as necessary or as called for in the recipe.

2 Arrange all ingredients artistically on the plates, dressing each ingredient as desired or as directed in the recipe.

3 At service time, heat or cook any items that are being served hot and add them to the salad.

RECIPE 24.5   SALAD NIÇOISE

Yield: 6 Servings   **Method:** Composed

Red wine vinegar	4 fl. oz.	120 ml
Salt and pepper	TT	TT
Virgin olive oil	12 fl. oz.	360 ml
Fresh basil leaves, chiffonade	12	12
Chicory	1 head	1 head
Tomatoes	6	6
Cucumbers	1 lb. 8 oz	680 g
Green beans	12 oz.	340 g
Eggs, hard-boiled	6	6
Artichokes	6	6
Romaine lettuce, large leaves, washed	12	12
New potatoes, size B, boiled, quartered	12 oz.	360 g
Green bell peppers, batonnet	2	2
Tuna, fresh, grilled and chilled	1 lb. 8 oz.	680 g
Niçoise olives	4 oz.	120 g

1 Lining a cold salad plate with a base of lettuce leaves.

2 Arranging the remaining ingredients for the salad.

1 Make a vinaigrette dressing using the red wine vinegar, salt, pepper, olive oil and basil.
2 Wash and dry the chicory.
3 Core each tomato and cut into eight wedges.
4 Peel and slice the cucumbers.
5 Trim and cook the green beans al dente.
6 Peel the eggs and cut into wedges.
7 Cook the artichokes. Trim the outer leaves from each artichoke, leaving only the heart. Remove the choke from the heart and cut each heart into quarters.
8 Line each cold plate with two romaine lettuce leaves, then arrange the remaining ingredients artistically. Use the contrasting shapes, colors and textures to create an attractive presentation.
9 At service time, whisk the dressing to combine the ingredients and pour approximately 2½ ounces (75 milliliters) over each salad.

Approximate values per serving: **Calories** 890, **Total fat** 70 g, **Saturated fat** 11 g, **Cholesterol** 200 mg, **Sodium** 760 mg, **Total carbohydrates** 21 g, **Protein** 44 g, **Vitamin A** 130%, **Vitamin C** 60%, **Iron** 30%

BOUND SALADS

The creative chef can prepare a wide variety of salads by combining cooked meats, poultry, fish, shellfish, potatoes, pasta, grains and/or legumes with a dressing and garnishes. Although the combinations vary greatly, these salads are grouped here because their ingredients are all bound. That is, each salad consists of one or more ingredients held together in a cohesive mass. The binding agent can be either a vinaigrette or a mayonnaise-based or similar dressing. The ingredients should be evenly distributed throughout, and the degree of cohesiveness can range from tightly packed to flaky and easily separated.

The foods that can be used to produce bound salads are so varied that it is impossible to list them all. Generalizing preparation techniques is also very difficult. There are as many ways to prepare a bound salad as there are ingredients, dressings and garnishes.

Bound salads can be used as the body of a composed salad (for instance, a serving of egg salad on a bed of greens). Some are used in sandwiches but not ordinarily as side dishes—for example, tuna or chicken salad. Some are served as side dishes but not in sandwiches, for example, potato or pasta salad. Follow specific recipes and traditional uses for each salad until you are confident enough in your skills to let your imagination take over.

▶ GUIDELINES FOR MAKING BOUND SALADS

1 Preparing a salad from cooked foods is a good opportunity to use leftovers, but be sure they are fresh and of good quality. The finished salad can only be as good as each of its ingredients.

2 When making a bound salad, choose ingredients whose flavors blend well and complement each other.

3 Choose ingredients for color; a few colorful ingredients will turn a plain salad into a spectacular one.

4 To improve appearance, cut all ingredients the same size.

5 All ingredients should be cut into pieces that are small enough to be eaten easily with a fork.

6 Be sure all meats, poultry, fish and shellfish are properly cooked before using them. Improperly cooked foods can cause food-borne illness and spoilage.

7 Always chill cooked ingredients well before using them. Warm ingredients promote bacterial growth, especially in mayonnaise-based salads.

8 Always use dressings sparingly. They should enhance the flavors of the other salad ingredients, not mask them.

CHUTNEY CHICKEN SALAD   RECIPE 24.6

Yield: 8 lb. (3.6 kg)	**Method:** Bound	
Chicken meat, cooked	5 lb.	2.2 kg
Celery, small dice	8 oz.	250 g
Green onions, sliced	3 oz.	90 g
Mango chutney	12 oz.	340 g
Mayonnaise	1 lb.	500 g
Seedless grapes	12 oz.	340 g

Adding grapes to the chicken salad.

1 Remove any bones, skin and fat from the chicken and cut the meat into large dice.

2 Combine the chicken meat, celery, green onions, mango chutney and mayonnaise in a bowl; mix well.

3 Cut the grapes in half. Add them to the chicken mixture and toss gently to combine.

Approximate values per 4-oz. (120-g) serving: **Calories** 230, **Total fat** 14 g, **Saturated fat** 3 g, **Cholesterol** 70 mg, **Sodium** 135 mg, **Total carbohydrates** 4 g, **Protein** 22 g

VEGETABLE SALADS

Vegetable salads are made from cooked or raw vegetables or a combination of both. They can be served on buffets, as an appetizer or as a salad course. As with other salads, vegetable salads must successfully combine color, texture and flavor. Some vegetable salads such as coleslaw and carrot-raisin salad are made with mayonnaise. Most, however, are made by either marinating the vegetables or combining them in a vinaigrette dressing.

Almost any vegetable can be successfully marinated. The amount of time depends on the vegetables and the marinade, but several hours to overnight is usually sufficient for flavors to blend. Soft vegetables such as mushrooms, zucchini and cucumbers can be added directly to a cold marinade. Hard vegetables such as carrots and cauliflower should be blanched in salted water, refreshed, drained and then added to a cold marinade. Carrots, artichokes, mushrooms, cauliflower, zucchini, pearl onions and the like are sometimes simmered quickly in a marinade flavored with lemon juice and olive oil, and then served cold. This style is called **à la grecque.**

Many marinated salads will last several days under proper refrigeration. As the salads age in the marinade, they will change in appearance and texture. This may or may not be desirable. For example, mushrooms and artichokes become more flavorful, while green vegetables are discolored by the acids in the marinade. If marinated salads are prepared in advance, check their appearance as well as their seasonings carefully at service time.

▶ **à la grecque** (ah lah grehk) a preparation style in which vegetables are marinated in olive oil, lemon juice and herbs, then served cold

▶ PROCEDURE FOR PREPARING VEGETABLE SALADS

1 Gather and wash all vegetables.

2 Trim, cut, shred or otherwise prepare the vegetables as desired or as directed in the recipe.

3 Blanch or cook the vegetables if necessary.

4 Combine the vegetables with the marinade or dressing. Adjust the seasonings.

RECIPE 24.7

TOMATO AND ASPARAGUS SALAD WITH FRESH MOZZARELLA

Yield: 6 Servings

Asparagus	2 lb.	1 kg
Basic Vinaigrette Dressing (page 754)	1 pt.	500 ml
Tomatoes	6	6
Leaf lettuce	1 head	1 head
Fresh mozzarella	12 oz.	360 g
Fresh basil leaves, chiffonade	12	12

1 Trim the asparagus and blanch in salted water. Refresh, drain and marinate in 8 ounces (250 grams) of Basic Vinaigrette Dressing for approximately 15 minutes.

2 Core each tomato and cut into six wedges.

3 Clean the lettuce and separate the leaves.

4 Slice the mozzarella into 18 slices.

5 Arrange the tomatoes, cheese and asparagus on six plates using the lettuce as a base. Pour on the remaining dressing and garnish with the basil.

Approximate values per serving: **Calories** 410, **Total fat** 32 g, **Saturated fat** 9 g, **Cholesterol** 35 mg, **Sodium** 370 mg, **Total carbohydrates** 11 g, **Protein** 19 g, **Vitamin A** 20%, **Vitamin C** 110%, **Calcium** 40%

FRUIT SALADS

There are so many different fruits with beautiful bright colors and sweet delicious flavors that preparing fruit salads is easy work. Fruit salads are a refreshing addition to buffets and can be served as the first course of a lunch or dinner. A more elaborate fruit salad can be served as a light lunch.

Always prepare fruit salads as close to service time as possible. The flesh of many types of fruit becomes soft and translucent if cut long before service. Other fruits turn brown in a matter of minutes after cutting. Refer to Chapter 25, Fruits, for more information on this browning reaction and for information on specific fruits. Fruit salad recipes are found at the end of that chapter.

If a fruit salad is dressed at all, the dressing is usually sweet and made with honey or yogurt mixed with fruit juices or purées. Alternatively, Grand Marnier, crème de menthe or other liqueurs sprinkled over the salad can serve as a dressing. Fruit salads can be tossed or composed. Either should offer the diner a pleasing blend of colors, shapes, sizes, flavors and textures.

CONCLUSION

A salad can be a small part of a meal or the entire meal. There are many styles of salads, and a seemingly endless variety of foods can be used to prepare them. Salads are extremely popular, especially with those interested in lighter dining alternatives. You can tempt these diners by determining the appropriate style of the salads and skillfully combining the main ingredients and dressing to achieve a delicious and appealing balance of colors, textures and flavors.

QUESTIONS FOR DISCUSSION

1 Name several factors that will cause salad greens to wilt or deteriorate.
2 Describe the proper procedure for washing and drying lettuce.
3 Explain the difference between a vinaigrette and an emulsified vinaigrette dressing.
4 Describe the procedure for making mayonnaise. How can the flavor of a mayonnaise be altered?
5 Describe a typical bound salad. How does a bound salad differ from a dressed salad?
6 List five ways salads can be presented or offered on a menu.

RECIPE 24.8

SEAFOOD SALAD

Note: This dish appears in the chapter opening photograph.

GOTHAM BAR AND GRILL, New York, NY
Chef-Owner Alfred Portale

CHEF ALFRED PORTALE

Originally a jewelry designer, Chef Alfred Portale decided to switch careers and graduated from the Culinary Institute of America, Hyde Park, New York, in 1981 at the top of his class. He then spent three years apprenticing with such French culinary masters as Michel Guerard and the Troisgros brothers before returning to Manhattan to open the Gotham Bar & Grill in 1985.

Since then, Chef Portale has won the admiration and respect of the nation's toughest dining critics. The Gotham received four consecutive three-star reviews from *The New York Times,* and photographs of his signature towering presentations continue to grace international culinary journals. Chef Portale was named the Best Chef in New York in 1993, and the Gotham was nominated for Restaurant of the Year in 1994 at the James Beard Foundation awards. Chef Portale is the author of two award-winning cookbooks.

Chef Portale has become a familiar face at charities, benefits and festivals across the country. His favorite is the nationwide Citymeals-On-Wheels program, which raises money to feed the homeless and the elderly.

About his food, Alfred Portale says, "I work to offer dishes that are intensely flavored and accessible. Each plate should have a clarity that gives the customer the satisfaction of readily identifiable flavors. Plate design is also important to me, for I am looking to please on a number of levels. Most importantly though, at the Gotham we are working to understand the ways that people like to eat, things like time factors, degrees of elegance and nutritional concerns. In responding to these needs, we create an environment where each diner enjoys their meal in a rich and lively atmosphere."

Yield: 4 Servings

Lobster, 1 lb. 8 oz. (680 g)	1	1
Court bouillon	4 qt.	4 lt
Sea scallops	4 oz.	120 g
Squid, cleaned	3 oz.	90 g
Mussels, debearded	12	12
Avocado, ripe	1	1
Frisée	1 head	1 head
Baby red oak	1 head	1 head
Shallots, finely minced	2 Tbsp.	30 ml
Fresh basil, chopped	1 Tbsp.	15 ml
Fresh chives, finely minced	1 Tbsp.	15 ml
Fresh Italian parsley, chopped	1 Tbsp.	15 ml
Lemon Vinaigrette (recipe follows)	as needed	as needed
Salt and white pepper	TT	TT

1 Boil the lobster in the court bouillon, then chill it. Remove the meat from the shell and dice it.
2 Poach the sea scallops and squid in the same court bouillon. Cool and thinly slice them.
3 Steam the mussels in a portion of the court bouillon. Chill and remove the meat from the shells.
4 Peel, pit, quarter and thinly slice the avocado.
5 Wash and dry the greens.
6 Toss the shellfish with the shallots, herbs and a portion of the Lemon Vinaigrette. Dress the lettuces and avocado.
7 Season all with salt and white pepper. Arrange the lettuces, shellfish and fanned avocado on four plates.

Approximate values per serving: **Calories** 600, **Total fat** 34 g, **Saturated fat** 3.5 g, **Cholesterol** 230 mg, **Sodium** 1790 mg, **Total carbohydrates** 11 g, **Protein** 63 g, **Vitamin A** 30%, **Vitamin C** 50%, **Iron** 45%

LEMON VINAIGRETTE

Yield: 14 fl. oz. (400 ml)

Dijon-style mustard	1 tsp.	5 ml
Salt and white pepper	TT	TT
Red wine vinegar	1 fl. oz.	30 ml
Extra virgin olive oil	10 fl. oz.	300 ml
Lemon juice	2 fl. oz.	60 ml
Cayenne pepper	1/8 tsp.	1 ml

1 Whisk together the mustard, salt, white pepper and vinegar. Slowly whisk in the olive oil.

2 Adjust the acidity with the lemon juice and add a pinch of cayenne.

Approximate values per 1-fl.-oz. (30-ml) serving: **Calories** 180, **Total fat** 20 g, **Saturated fat** 2.5 g, **Cholesterol** 0 mg, **Sodium** 170 mg, **Total carbohydrates** 1 g, **Protein** 0 g, **Claims**—no cholesterol; no sugar

RASPBERRY VINAIGRETTE

RECIPE 24.9

Yield: 2 qt. (2 lt)

Red wine vinegar	8 fl. oz.	250 ml
Rice wine vinegar	8 fl. oz.	250 ml
Lemon juice	3 Tbsp.	45 ml
Dried thyme	1 Tbsp.	15 ml
Salt	1 Tbsp.	15 ml
Black pepper	1 Tbsp.	15 ml
Garlic, minced	1 Tbsp.	15 ml
Honey	4 oz.	120 g
Raspberry preserves, without seeds	8 oz.	250 g
Olive oil	12 fl. oz.	350 ml
Salad oil	1 pt.	450 ml

1 Whisk together the vinegars, lemon juice, thyme, salt, pepper and garlic.

2 Whisk in the honey and raspberry preserves.

3 Slowly whisk in the oils, emulsifying the dressing.

Approximate values per 1-fl.-oz. (30-ml) serving: **Calories** 130, **Total fat** 12 g, **Saturated fat** 1 g, **Cholesterol** 0 mg, **Sodium** 140 mg, **Total carbohydrates** 5 g, **Protein** 0 g, **Claims**—no cholesterol

FAT-FREE VINAIGRETTE

RECIPE 24.10

Yield: 8 fl. oz. (240 ml)

White wine vinegar	2 fl. oz.	60 ml
Dijon mustard	1 oz.	30 g
Fresh herbs, assorted, chopped	3 Tbsp.	45 ml
Shallots, roasted, chopped	4 oz.	120 g
Rich chicken stock	4 fl. oz.	120 ml
Salt and pepper	TT	TT

1 Place all of the ingredients in the bowl of a blender and blend well.

Variation: *Vegetarian Fat-Free Vinaigrette*—Use vegetable stock instead of chicken stock.

Approximate values per 1-fl.-oz. (30-ml) serving: **Calories** 20, **Total fat** 0 g, **Saturated fat** 0 g, **Cholesterol** 0 mg, **Sodium** 135 mg, **Total carbohydrates** 4 g, **Protein** 1 g, **Vitamin A** 15%, **Vitamin C** 25%, **Claims**—low calorie; fat free; high in vitamin C; source of vitamin A

RECIPE 24.11

BALSAMIC AND ROASTED GARLIC VINAIGRETTE

Yield: 1½ pt. (750 ml)

Garlic cloves	12	12
Balsamic vinegar	8 fl. oz.	250 ml
Dijon mustard	1 Tbsp.	15 ml
Olive oil	14 fl. oz.	420 ml
Salt and pepper	TT	TT

1 Roast the garlic in a 350°F (180°C) oven until soft, golden brown and fragrant. Peel the garlic cloves and mash them coarsely in a mixing bowl.
2 Add the vinegar and mustard, whisking to incorporate. Whisk in the olive oil and season with salt and pepper.

Approximate values per 1-fl.-oz. (30-ml) serving: **Calories** 150, **Total fat** 17 g, **Saturated fat** 2 g, **Cholesterol** 0 mg, **Sodium** 8 mg, **Total carbohydrates** 1 g, **Protein** 0 g, **Claims**—no cholesterol; low sodium

RECIPE 24.12

BLUE CHEESE VINAIGRETTE

NEWBURY COLLEGE, BROOKLINE, MA
Senior Instructor Scott Doughty

Yield: 20 fl. oz. (550 ml)

Blue cheese	8 oz.	225 g
Salt	1 tsp.	5 ml
Garlic, mashed	1 tsp.	5 ml
White wine vinegar	4 fl. oz.	120 ml
Black pepper	¼ tsp.	2 ml
Olive oil	12 fl. oz.	180 ml

1 Crumble the blue cheese and set aside 2 ounces (60 grams) of the chunks for garnish. Pass the remainder through a drum sieve or food mill fitted with a fine disk.
2 Combine the salt, garlic, vinegar and pepper. Add the olive oil in a slow steady stream, whisking constantly to incorporate. Gradually beat in the sieved blue cheese until smooth. Stir in the reserved blue cheese chunks.

Approximate values per 1-fl.-oz. (30-ml) serving: **Calories** 190, **Total fat** 19 g, **Saturated fat** 4.5 g, **Cholesterol** 10 mg, **Sodium** 270 mg, **Total carbohydrates** 1 g, **Protein** 2 g

RECIPE 24.13

CAESAR DRESSING

A traditional Caesar salad is made with romaine lettuce, croutons, Parmesan and a rich dressing flavored with garlic and anchovies. The dressing is sometimes prepared and tossed with the other ingredients tableside, but this food processor method is useful when larger quantities are needed.

Yield: 2 qt. (2 lt)   **Method:** Emulsion

Garlic, chopped	1 Tbsp.	15 ml
Eggs	2	2
Parmesan, grated	4 oz.	120 g
Balsamic vinegar	2 fl. oz.	60 ml
Red wine vinegar	2 fl. oz.	60 ml
Whole-grain mustard	1 Tbsp.	15 ml
Dijon-style mustard	1 Tbsp.	15 ml

Anchovy fillets	1 oz.	30 g
Salt	1 Tbsp.	15 ml
Black pepper	1 tsp.	5 ml
Vegetable oil	12 fl. oz.	340 ml
Olive oil	12 fl. oz.	340 ml

1 Combine the garlic, eggs, Parmesan, vinegars, mustards, anchovies, salt and pepper in the bowl of a food processor and process until smooth, approximately 1 minute.

2 With the machine running slowly, begin adding the oils to form an emulsion.

3 Continue until all the oil is incorporated.

Approximate values per 1-fl.-oz. (30-ml) serving: **Calories** 110, **Total fat** 11 g, **Saturated fat** 2 g, **Cholesterol** 10 mg, **Sodium** 170 mg, **Total carbohydrates** 0 g, **Protein** 1 g

MUSTARD DRESSING WITH GARLIC

RECIPE 24.14

NEWBURY COLLEGE, BROOKLINE, MA
Senior Instructor Scott Doughty

Yield: 1 pt. (450 ml)   **Method:** Temporary Emulsion

White wine vinegar	2 fl. oz.	60 ml
Salt	1/2 tsp.	3 ml
Black pepper	1/8 tsp.	1 ml
Garlic, mashed	1/4 tsp.	2 ml
Dijon mustard	2 Tbsp.	30 ml
Lemon juice	1/2 tsp.	3 ml
Olive oil	12 fl. oz.	180 ml

1 Combine everything except the olive oil in a bowl. Beat in the oil, by droplets at first, then in a thin stream.

Approximate values per 1-fl.-oz. (30-ml) serving: **Calories** 200, **Total fat** 21 g, **Saturated fat** 3 g, **Cholesterol** 0 mg, **Sodium** 125 mg, **Total carbohydrates** 3 g, **Protein** 0 g

POPPY SEED DRESSING

RECIPE 24.15

NEWBURY COLLEGE, BROOKLINE, MA
Senior Instructor Scott Doughty

Yield: 1 pt. (450 ml)   **Method:** Temporary Emulsion

Cider vinegar	8 fl. oz.	225 ml
Honey	6 fl. oz.	180 ml
Salt	3/4 tsp.	4 ml
Dry mustard	1 tsp.	5 ml
Celery leaves, minced	2 tsp.	10 ml
Green onion, white only, minced	1	1
Vegetable oil	8 fl. oz.	225 ml
Poppy seeds	1 1/2 Tbsp.	24 ml

1 Combine the vinegar, honey, salt, mustard, celery and green onion.

2 Beat in the oil, by droplets at first, then in a thin stream.

3 Add the poppy seeds and beat to distribute.

Note: For a creamier texture, make the dressing in a blender or food processor.

Approximate values per 1-fl.-oz. (30-ml) serving: **Calories** 180, **Total fat** 14 g, **Saturated fat** 1.5 g, **Cholesterol** 0 mg, **Sodium** 110 g, **Total carbohydrates** 14 g, **Protein** 0 g

RECIPE 24.16   SAUCE GRIBICHE

Gribiche is a cold mayonnaise-type sauce made with hard-cooked egg yolks instead of raw egg yolks. It is traditionally flavored with capers and herbs and is served with fish.

Yield: 1 qt. (1 lt)   **Method:** Temporary Emulsion

Hard-cooked egg yolks	4	4
Salt and pepper	TT	TT
Dijon-style mustard	1 Tbsp.	15 ml
Olive oil	1½ pt.	700 ml
White wine vinegar	3 fl. oz.	90 ml
Cornichons, chopped	1 oz.	30 g
Capers, chopped	1 Tbsp.	15 ml
Fresh mixed herbs such as parsley, chervil, tarragon or chives, chopped	1 oz.	30 g

1 Blend the egg yolks with the salt, pepper and mustard.

2 Very slowly, as if for mayonnaise, whisk in the olive oil. Occasionally, add a few drops of vinegar to thin the sauce.

3 Add the cornichons, capers and herbs; mix well. Adjust the seasonings and acidity with the remaining vinegar.

Approximate values per 1-fl.-oz. (30-ml) serving: **Calories** 190, **Total fat** 21 g, **Saturated fat** 3 g, **Cholesterol** 25 mg, **Sodium** 95 mg, **Total carbohydrates** 0 g, **Protein** 1 g

---

RECIPE 24.17   THOUSAND ISLAND DRESSING

Yield: 1 qt. (1 lt)   **Method:** Mayonnaise-Based

Red wine vinegar	1 Tbsp.	15 ml
Sugar	1 Tbsp.	15 ml
Mayonnaise	1 pt.	450 ml
Ketchup	8 oz.	250 g
Sweet pickle relish	6 oz.	180 g
Hard-cooked eggs, chopped	4	4
Fresh parsley, chopped	2 Tbsp.	30 ml
Green onions, chopped	1 bunch	1 bunch
Salt and pepper	TT	TT
Worcestershire sauce	TT	TT

1 Combine the vinegar and sugar; stir to dissolve the sugar.

2 Add the remaining ingredients and mix well.

3 Adjust the seasonings with the salt, pepper and Worcestershire sauce.

Approximate values per 1-fl.-oz. (30-ml) serving: **Calories** 120, **Total fat** 11 g, **Saturated fat** 2 g, **Cholesterol** 35 mg, **Sodium** 270 mg, **Total carbohydrates** 4 g, **Protein** 1 g

---

RECIPE 24.18   GREEN GODDESS DRESSING

Yield: 1 qt. (1 lt)   **Method:** Mayonnaise-Based

Fresh parsley	1 oz.	30 g
Mayonnaise	1 pt.	450 ml
Sour cream	12 oz.	360 g
Garlic, chopped	1 Tbsp.	15 ml

Anchovy fillets, minced	1 oz.	30 g
Fresh chives, chopped	1 oz.	30 g
Fresh tarragon, chopped	1 Tbsp.	15 ml
Lemon juice	1 fl. oz.	30 ml
Red wine vinegar	1 fl. oz.	30 ml
Salt and white pepper	TT	TT
Worcestershire sauce	TT	TT

1 Rinse and chop the parsley, but do not dry it or you will remove some of the chlorophyll.

2 Combine all the ingredients and mix well. Season to taste with salt, white pepper and Worcestershire sauce.

Approximate values per 1-fl.-oz. (30-ml) serving: **Calories** 80, **Total fat** 8 g, **Saturated fat** 2.5 g, **Cholesterol** 10 mg, **Sodium** 125 mg, **Total carbohydrates** 1 g, **Protein** 1 g

---

ROQUEFORT DRESSING

RECIPE 24.19

Yield: 1 qt. (1 lt) **Method:** Mayonnaise-Based

Mayonnaise	8 fl. oz.	250 ml
Red wine vinegar	1 fl. oz.	30 ml
Sour cream	8 fl. oz.	250 ml
Buttermilk	4 fl. oz.	120 ml
Garlic, chopped	1 tsp.	5 ml
Worcestershire sauce	1 tsp.	5 ml
Tabasco sauce	TT	TT
White pepper	TT	TT
Roquefort, crumbled	12 oz.	360 g

1 Combine all the ingredients except the Roquefort and mix well.

2 Add the crumbled Roquefort and combine.

Approximate values per 1-fl.-oz. (30-ml) serving: **Calories** 110, **Total fat** 10 g, **Saturated fat** 4 g, **Cholesterol** 20 mg, **Sodium** 240 mg, **Total carbohydrates** 1 g, **Protein** 3 g

---

LOW-FAT BLUE CHEESE DRESSING

RECIPE 24.20

Yield: 1 qt. (1 lt)

Nonfat yogurt	20 oz.	600 g
Low-fat buttermilk	6 fl. oz.	180 ml
Blue cheese, crumbled	4 oz.	120 g
White pepper	1/4 tsp.	1 ml
Worcestershire sauce	TT	TT
Dry mustard	1 tsp.	5 ml
Tabasco sauce	TT	TT

1 Combine all the ingredients in the bowl of a mixer or food processor and process until smooth.

Approximate values per 1-fl.-oz. (30-ml) serving: **Calories** 25, **Total fat** 1 g, **Saturated fat** 0.5 g, **Cholesterol** 5 mg, **Sodium** 65 mg, **Total carbohydrates** 2 g, **Protein** 2 g, **Claims**—low fat; low cholesterol; low sodium; low calorie

RECIPE 24.21

SUN-DRIED TOMATO AND BASIL AÏOLI

Aïoli (ay-OH-lee) is a mayonnaise made with garlic and olive oil, it comes from the Provence region of France and is often served with vegetables, fish and shellfish.

Yield: 1 qt. (1 lt)

Garlic cloves, mashed to a paste	4	4
Egg yolks	4	4
Lemon juice	2 Tbsp.	30 ml
Olive oil	1½ pt.	700 ml
Sun-dried tomatoes, packed in olive oil	4 oz.	120 g
Fresh basil, chopped	4 Tbsp.	60 ml
Salt	1 tsp.	5 ml
White pepper	½ tsp.	2 ml

1 Combine the garlic, egg yolks and a few drops of the lemon juice in a bowl and whip until frothy.

2 While whipping the egg yolk mixture, slowly add the olive oil until an emulsion begins to form. Continue adding the oil while whipping until all the oil is incorporated. A few drops of lemon juice may be added from time to time to thin the sauce.

3 Finely chop the sun-dried tomatoes. Add them, a portion of the olive oil in which they were packed, and the basil to the aïoli.

4 Season with salt, pepper and lemon juice.

Approximate values per 1-fl.-oz. (30-ml) serving: **Calories** 200, **Total fat** 21 g, **Saturated fat** 3 g, **Cholesterol** 25 mg, **Sodium** 80 mg, **Total carbohydrates** 3 g, **Protein** 1 g, **Vitamin A** 20%

RECIPE 24.22

TARTAR SAUCE

Yield: 1 pt. (500 ml)   **Method:** Mayonnaise-Based

Mayonnaise	1 pt.	500 ml
Capers, chopped	2 oz.	60 g
Sweet pickle relish	3 oz.	90 g
Onion, minced	2 Tbsp.	30 ml
Fresh parsley, minced	2 Tbsp.	30 ml
Lemon juice	1 Tbsp.	15 ml
Salt	TT	TT
Worcestershire sauce	TT	TT
Tabasco sauce	TT	TT

1 Stir all the ingredients together until well blended. Chill thoroughly before serving.

Approximate values per 1-fl. oz. (30-ml) serving: **Calories** 220, **Total fat** 23 g, **Saturated fat** 4 g, **Cholesterol** 20 mg, **Sodium** 420 mg, **Total carbohydrates** 2 g, **Protein** 0 g

RÉMOULADE SAUCE RECIPE 24.23

MISSISSIPPI UNIVERSITY FOR WOMEN, Columbus, MS

Chef Jim Fitzgerald, Ph.D., CCP

Yield: 1 pt. (470 ml) **Method:** Emulsion

Egg yolks	3	3
Salt	1/8 tsp.	1 ml
Lemon juice	1 Tbsp.	15 ml
Vegetable oil	12 fl. oz.	360 ml
Water, very hot	1 tsp.	5 ml
Salt and white pepper	TT	TT
Capers, drained and chopped	2 oz.	60 g
Cornichons, chopped	2 oz.	60 g
Chives, chopped	3 Tbsp.	45 ml
Dijon mustard	1 Tbsp.	15 ml
Anchovy fillets, chopped	3	3
Tabasco	TT	TT
Worcestershire sauce	1/2 tsp.	2 ml

1 Combine the egg yolks, salt and lemon juice in a mixing bowl or a food processor. While whisking, add the oil in drops to form an emulsion. When the mixture thickens, the remaining oil can be added in a slow, steady stream. Add the hot water and mix to lighten the mayonnaise's color.

2 Adjust the seasoning with salt, white pepper and additional lemon juice as necessary.

3 Stir in the remaining ingredients by hand. If the sauce is too thick, thin it with 1 tablespoon (15 milliliters) of red wine vinegar into which 1 teaspoon (5 milliliters) of sugar has been dissolved.

Variation: *Creole Rémoulade*—Omit the capers, cornichons and chives. In Step 3, add 1/2 cup (120 milliliters) finely chopped yellow onion, 3 ounces (90 grams) ketchup, 1 tablespoon (15 milliliters) minced garlic, 1/4 teaspoon (1 milliliter) cayenne pepper and 1/3 cup (85 milliliters) parsley, chopped fine.

Approximate values 1-fl.-oz. (30=ml) serving: **Calories** 200, **Total fat** 22 g, **Saturated fat** 3 g, **Cholesterol** 40 mg, **Sodium** 150 mg, **Total carbohydrates** 0 g, **Protein** 1 g

CUCUMBER-YOGURT SALAD
(KHIRA RAITA) RECIPE 24.24

Raita (RA-tah) are yogurt and vegetable salads typically served as condiments in Indian cuisine. Raita may be made with many types of vegetables, including eggplants, cooked potatoes, tomatoes and even bananas, and are meant as a cooling counterpoint to the spiciness of other dishes.

Yield: 1 qt. (1 lt)

Plain yogurt	1 pt.	500 ml
Cucumber, peeled and grated	12 oz.	360 g
Cumin	1 tsp.	5 ml
Salt and pepper	TT	TT
Sugar	1 Tbsp.	15 ml

Continued

Lime juice	1 Tbsp.	15 ml
Fresh cilantro, chopped	2 Tbsp.	30 ml
Jalapeño, minced	1 tsp.	5 ml
Paprika	as needed	as needed

1 Stir together all the ingredients except the paprika. Chill for several hours before service.

2 At service time, dust the top lightly with paprika.

Approximate values per 3-oz. (90-g) serving: **Calories** 40, **Total fat** 0 g, **Saturated fat** 0 g, **Cholesterol** 0 mg, **Sodium** 280 mg, **Total carbohydrates** 7 g, **Protein** 3 g, **Calcium** 10%, **Claims**—fat free; low calorie

CUCUMBER SUNOMONO (JAPANESE-STYLE CUCUMBER SALAD)

RECIPE 24.25

NEWBURY COLLEGE, Brookline, MA

Senior Instructor Scott Doughty

Yield: 10–12 Servings

Cucumbers, peeled, split and seeded	6	6
Salt	2½ tsp.	13 ml
Water chestnuts, whole	4 oz.	120 g
Green onions	1 bunch	1 bunch
Carrot	1	1
Fresh ginger, unpeeled	4 oz.	120 g
Rice wine vinegar	4 fl. oz.	120 ml
Sugar	2 tsp.	10 ml
Dark sesame oil	2 tsp.	10 ml
Sesame seeds	5 Tbsp.	75 ml
Soy sauce	as needed	as needed

1 Slice the cucumbers very thin with a knife or mandoline. Sprinkle 2 teaspoons (10 milliliters) of the salt evenly over them and mix well. Allow them to rest in a bowl for 20 to 30 minutes.

2 Very thinly slice the water chestnuts. Slice the green onions. Peel the carrot. Cut the carrot into 2-inch (5-centimeter) sections, cut each section lengthwise into very thin slices and cut each slice lengthwise into thin shreds. Cover and refrigerate the carrot shreds.

3 Rinse the cucumbers in several changes of cold water to remove the excess salt. Squeeze them in small batches in a clean towel to extract as much liquid as possible. Combine the cucumbers, chestnuts and green onions.

4 Mince and mash the ginger into a mushy consistency and squeeze it through several layers of cheesecloth to extract as much juice as possible. Discard the pulp. Mix 1 teaspoon (5 milliliters) of the juice with the vinegar, the remaining salt and the sugar. Beat in the sesame oil in a thin stream. Stir the dressing into the cucumber mixture and chill.

5 Toast the sesame seeds in a 325°F (160°C) oven until lightly browned.

6 To serve, place a portion of the marinated cucumbers on a plate and add some of the excess juice from the bowl. Garnish each salad with the carrot shreds and toasted sesame seeds. Serve soy sauce on the side.

Approximate values per serving: **Calories** 70, **Total fat** 3.5 g, **Saturated fat** 0 g, **Cholesterol** 0 mg, **Sodium** 170 g, **Total carbohydrates** 9 g, **Protein** 2 g, **Vitamin A** 40%

GARLIC CROUTONS

RECIPE 24.26

Yield: 1 lb. 4 oz. (550 g)

Whole butter	6 oz.	180 g
Garlic, chopped	1 Tbsp.	15 ml
French or sourdough bread cubes	1 lb. 8 oz.	700 g
Parmesan, grated	1 oz.	30 g
Dried basil	2 tsp.	10 ml
Dried oregano	2 tsp.	10 ml

1 Melt the butter in a small saucepan and add the garlic. Cook the garlic in the butter over low heat for 5 minutes.

2 Place the bread cubes in a bowl, then add the Parmesan and herbs.

3 Pour the garlic butter over the bread cubes and immediately toss to combine.

4 Spread the bread cubes on a sheet pan in a single layer and bake at 350°F (180°C). Stir the croutons occasionally and cook until dry and lightly browned, approximately 15 minutes.

Approximate values per 1-oz. (30-g) serving: **Calories** 200, **Total fat** 9 g, **Saturated fat** 5 g, **Cholesterol** 20 mg, **Sodium** 390 mg, **Total carbohydrates** 25 g, **Protein** 5 g, **Iron** 10%, **Calcium** 10%

CROUTONS

A crouton is simply a piece of bread that is toasted, sautéed or dried. Two types are often used.

The more familiar ones are small seasoned cubes of bread that are baked or toasted and sprinkled over soups or salads.

A more classic variety is made by sautéing slices of bread in clarified butter or olive oil until brown and crisp. The bread may be rough slices from a baguette, or shapes (such as hearts, diamonds or circles) cut from larger slices. Sautéed croutons have two advantages over the toasted variety: They stay crisp longer after coming in contact with moist foods, and they gain flavor from the butter or olive oil in which they are cooked. Sautéed croutons can be used to decorate the border of a serving dish, as a base for canapés, as a garnish for soups, as an accompaniment to spreads or caviar or as a base under some meat and game dishes.

ORGANIC MICROGREENS AND SPRING VEGETABLES WITH FRAGRANT HERB VINAIGRETTE AND DRY FARMER'S CHEESE

RECIPE 24.27

CAFÉ ANNIE, HOUSTON, TX
Chef-Owner Robert Del Grande
Executive Chef Ben Berryhill

Yield: 8 Servings of salad and
28 fl. oz. (850 ml) of dressing **Method:** Tossed

Lemon	1	1
Plum tomatoes, concassée	5	5
Shallot, minced	1	1
Garlic cloves, steamed and mashed	6	6
Serrano chile, seeded, minced	1	1
Champagne vinegar	2 Tbsp.	30 ml
Maple syrup	1 tsp.	5 ml
Virgin olive oil	4 fl. oz.	120 ml
Grapeseed oil	8 fl. oz.	240 ml
Fresh mint, chopped	¼ c.	60 ml
Fresh tarragon, chopped	¼ c.	60 ml
Salt	TT	TT
Assorted spring vegetables, blanched and chilled	3 c.	710 ml
Organic microgreens	8 oz.	225 g
Dry farmer's cheese	8 Tbsp.	120 ml

1 Juice the lemon.

2 Combine the tomato concassée, shallot, garlic, chile, vinegar, maple syrup and lemon juice in the bowl of a small mixer. Slowly whisk in the oils until thoroughly combined. Stir in the herbs and season with salt.

3 Toss the spring vegetables in a small amount of the dressing and season with salt.

4 For each salad, toss 1 ounce (30 grams) of the greens with a small amount of the dressing and arrange on a plate. Garnish with some of the seasoned spring vegetables and sprinkle each salad with 1 tablespoon (15 milliliters) of farmer's cheese.

Approximate values per serving with 1 fl. oz. (30 ml) of dressing: **Calories** 180, **Total fat** 16 g, **Saturated fat** 4.5 g, **Cholesterol** 15 mg, **Sodium** 100 mg, **Total carbohydrates** 6 g, **Protein** 4 g, **Vitamin A** 20%, **Vitamin C** 25%, **Calcium** 15%

SALAD OF SWEET AND BITTER GREENS WITH BALSAMIC MUSTARD VINAIGRETTE

RECIPE 24.28

PRIMITIVO WINE BAR, COLORADO SPRINGS, CO
John Broening, Executive Chef

Yield: 8 Servings   **Method:** Tossed

Focaccia or sourdough bread, day old, crust removed, small dice	4 oz.	120 g
Extra virgin olive oil	2 Tbsp.	30 ml
Salt and pepper	TT	TT
Fresh chives, minced	2 Tbsp.	30 ml
Fresh parsley, chopped	2 Tbsp.	30 ml
Fresh tarragon, chopped	2 Tbsp.	30 ml
Fresh chervil, chopped	2 Tbsp.	30 ml
Romaine lettuce, inner leaves, torn	2 heads	2 heads
Watercress, leaves with 1-in. (2.5-cm) stems	1 bunch	1 bunch
Radicchio leaves, torn	4	4
Shallots, minced	2 Tbsp.	30 ml
Cherry tomatoes, halved	2 c.	450 ml
Balsamic Mustard Vinaigrette (recipe follows)	6 fl. oz.	180 ml
Bibb lettuce, inner leaves	3 heads	3 heads

1 To make the croutons, toss the bread with the olive oil and season with salt and pepper. Spread on a sheet pan and bake at 300°F (150°C) for 15 minutes. Remove from the oven and cool.

2 Toss the chives, parsley, tarragon and chervil together.

3 Combine the croutons, herbs, romaine, watercress, radicchio, shallots, cherry tomatoes and Balsamic Mustard Vinaigrette in a mixing bowl. Season with salt and pepper and toss. Arrange the greens on eight chilled plates, using the bibb lettuce leaves as a base.

Approximate values per serving: **Calories** 230, **Total fat** 18 g, **Saturated fat** 2 g, **Cholesterol** 0 mg, **Sodium** 140 mg, **Total carbohydrates** 15 g, **Protein** 5 g, **Vitamin A** 90%, **Vitamin C** 80%, **Calcium** 10%, **Iron** 10%

BALSAMIC MUSTARD VINAIGRETTE

Yield: 6 fl. oz. (180 ml) **Method:** Temporary Emulsion

Balsamic vinegar	2 Tbsp.	30 ml
Dijon mustard	2 tsp.	10 ml
Shallots, minced	2 tsp.	10 ml
Salt and pepper	TT	TT
Extra virgin olive oil	4 Tbsp.	60 ml
Canola oil	4 Tbsp.	60 ml

1 In a stainless steel bowl, whisk together the vinegar, mustard, shallots, salt and pepper.
2 Combine the oils. Slowly whisk them into the vinegar and mustard mixture to form an emulsified dressing.

Approximate values per 1-fl.-oz. (30-g) serving: **Calories** 170, **Total fat** 18 g, **Saturated fat** 2 g, **Cholesterol** 0 mg, **Sodium** 45 mg, **Total carbohydrates** 1 g, **Protein** 0 g

WILTED SPINACH SALAD WITH ROASTED PEPPERS

RECIPE 24.29

GREENS, SAN FRANCISCO, CA
Chef Annie Somerville

Yield: 2 Large or 4 Small Servings **Method:** Tossed

Red or yellow bell pepper, medium	1	1
Extra virgin olive oil	3 fl. oz.	90 ml
Salt and pepper	TT	TT
Red onion, sliced thin	2 oz.	60 g
Baguette, thin slices for croutons	12	12
Spinach	1 lb.	450 g
Frisée or escarole	1 head	1 head
Balsamic vinegar	3 Tbsp.	45 ml
Garlic clove, chopped fine	1	1
Niçoise or Gaeta olives, pitted	10	10
Parmesan, grated	1 oz.	30 g

1 Roast and peel the bell pepper and cut into ¼-inch (6-millimeter) strips. Toss the pepper strips with ½ tablespoon (8 milliliters) of the olive oil and a few pinches of salt and pepper. Set aside to marinate.
2 Cover the onion slices with cold water to leach the strong onion flavor. Set aside.
3 Place the baguette slices on a baking sheet and brush them lightly with olive oil. Toast in a 375°F (190°C) oven until crisp and lightly browned, approximately 5 minutes.
4 Stem, wash and dry the spinach. Trim the stem end of the frisée or escarole and discard the tough outer leaves. Wash and dry.
5 Drain the onions. In a large bowl, combine the vinegar, garlic, ½ teaspoon (2 milliliters) of salt and a few pinches of pepper. Add the greens, onions, peppers and olives.
6 Heat the remaining olive oil in a small pan until it is very hot and just below the smoking point. Immediately pour it over the salad and toss with a pair of metal tongs to coat and wilt the leaves. Sprinkle on the Parmesan.
7 Add the croutons and serve immediately.

Approximate values per large serving: **Calories** 730, **Total fat** 52 g, **Saturated fat** 9 g, **Cholesterol** 10 mg, **Sodium** 1070 mg, **Total carbohydrates** 51 g, **Protein** 21 g, **Vitamin A** 480%, **Vitamin C** 330%, **Calcium** 60%, **Iron** 60%, **Claims**—high in fiber, high in vitamins A and C, calcium and iron

PINK GRAPEFRUIT AND AVOCADO SALAD

RECIPE 24.30

NEWBURY COLLEGE, Brookline, MA

Senior Instructor Scott Doughty

Yield: 12–16 Servings		**Method:** Composed
Bibb lettuce	3 heads	3 heads
Pink grapefruit	3	3
Avocados, ripe	4	4
Pecan halves	3 oz.	90 g
Clarified butter	1 Tbsp.	15 ml
Salt	¼ tsp.	2 ml
Chilli powder	2 tsp.	10 ml

1. Without tearing the lettuce leaves, gently remove them from the heads. Wash the lettuce leaves. Break off the tough part of the rib from the bottom of each leaf. Drain the leaves and then dry them. Refrigerate the cleaned leaves.
2. Peel the grapefruit, cut them into supremes and refrigerate.
3. Cut and pit the avocados, then slice them into wedges.
4. Lightly toast the pecans in a sauté pan with the butter, salt and chilli powder.
5. Arrange the larger leaves of lettuce on salad plates. Place the smaller leaves in the center of each plate, rounded sides up. Arrange the grapefruit and avocado around the lettuce mounds in an alternating fashion. Garnish with the toasted pecan halves. At service time, ladle a poppy seed dressing (page 767) or other dressing over each salad.

Approximate values per serving: **Calories** 160, **Total fat** 14 g, **Saturated fat** 2.5 g, **Cholesterol** 0 mg, **Sodium** 55 mg, **Total carbohydrates** 10 g, **Protein** 2 g, **Vitamin A** 20%, **Vitamin C** 45%

SALAD OF AHI TUNA SEARED WITH LAVENDER AND PEPPER WITH WHOLE-GRAIN MUSTARD SAUCE

RECIPE 24.31

FETZER VINEYARDS, Hopland, CA

Culinary Director, John Ash

Yield: 8 Servings		**Method:** Composed
Lavender-pepper coating:		
Coarse sea salt	1½ tsp.	7 ml
Whole black peppercorns	2 tsp.	10 ml
Whole fennel seeds	2 tsp.	10 ml
White peppercorns	1 tsp.	5 ml
Dried lavender flowers	1½ tsp.	7 ml
Ahi tuna, a solid 3-in.-(7.5-cm-) square piece, well trimmed	1 lb. 8 oz.	700 g

Olive oil	3 Tbsp.	45 ml
Mustard sauce:		
Whole-grain mustard	2 oz.	60 g
Olive oil	1 fl. oz.	30 ml
Mustard seeds, toasted	1 tsp.	5 ml
Rice wine vinegar	1 tsp.	5 ml
Sugar or honey	1 tsp.	5 ml
Baby greens	8 oz.	250 g
Edible flowers	as needed for garnish	

1 Using a mortar and pestle or a rolling pin, crush the lavender-pepper coating ingredients.

2 Lightly oil the tuna with 2 teaspoons (10 milliliters) of olive oil; coat it lightly and evenly with the lavender-pepper mixture. Heat the remaining oil in a skillet to just smoking and quickly sear the tuna on all sides. This should not take more than 2 minutes. Immediately chill the seared tuna.

3 Mix the mustard sauce ingredients. Set aside.

4 To serve, thinly slice the tuna into three or four medallions per serving. Arrange on a chilled plate with baby greens and a small dollop of the mustard sauce. Garnish with edible flowers.

Approximate values per serving: **Calories** 180, **Total fat** 10 g, **Saturated fat** 1.5 g, **Cholesterol** 35 mg, **Sodium** 570 mg, **Total carbohydrates** 3 g, **Protein** 20 g, **Vitamin C** 15%

VINE-RIPENED TOMATO SALAD

RECIPE 24.32

GREENS, San Francisco, CA
Chef Annie Somerville

Yield: 4 Servings   **Method:** Composed

Vine-ripened tomatoes	1 lb.	450 g
Cherry tomatoes	½ pt.	250 ml
Mixed baby greens	4 heads	4 heads
Salt and pepper	TT	TT
Cucumber, sliced on the bias	1	1
Extra virgin olive oil	3 Tbsp.	45 ml
Red wine vinegar	2 Tbsp.	30 ml

1 Core the vine-ripened tomatoes and cut into wedges or thick slices. Pluck the stems from the cherry tomatoes; leave whole if small or cut in half if large.

2 Wash the mixed baby greens and dry. Spread the greens on plates or a serving platter and arrange the vine-ripened tomatoes over them. Sprinkle the tomatoes with salt and pepper.

3 Garnish the tomatoes with cucumber slices.

4 Drizzle on the olive oil; follow with a light drizzle of vinegar.

5 Sprinkle the cherry tomatoes over the salad.

Approximate values per serving: **Calories** 190, **Total fat** 11 g, **Saturated fat** 1.5 g, **Cholesterol** 0 mg, **Sodium** 650 mg, **Total carbohydrates** 17 g, **Protein** 5 g, **Vitamin A** 35%, **Vitamin C** 140%, **Claims**—no cholesterol; good source of fiber

RECIPE 24.33

Yield: 25 Servings   **Method:** Composed

Fresh mozzarella	50 slices	50 slices
Tomatoes	50 slices	50 slices
Fresh basil leaves, chiffonade	4 Tbsp.	60 ml
Salt and pepper	TT	TT
Extra-virgin olive oil	3 Tbsp.	45 ml

1 Arrange the mozzarella and tomato slices in overlapping circles on a serving platter, alternating slices of cheese and tomato.
2 Sprinkle the basil, salt and pepper over the salad. Drizzle with the olive oil.

Approximate values per serving: **Calories** 190, **Total fat** 14 g, **Saturated fat** 8 g, **Cholesterol** 45 mg, **Sodium** 85 mg, **Total carbohydrates** 4 g, **Protein** 11 g, **Vitamin A** 15%, **Vitamin C** 20%, **Calcium** 35%

RECIPE 24.34

SMOKED MUSHROOM AND LENTIL SALAD WITH HOT BACON VINAIGRETTE

SENCHA, COLORADO SPRINGS, CO
Chef Brent Beavers

Yield: 8 Servings

Portabella mushrooms	8	8
Water	as needed	as needed
Salt and pepper	TT	TT
Red bell peppers, small dice	1 c.	240 ml
White onions, small dice	1 c.	240 ml
Fresh parsley, chopped	¼ c.	60 ml
Lentils, cooked	3 c.	700 ml
Spinach, stemmed and cleaned	1 lb.	450 g
Hot Bacon Vinaigrette (recipe follows)	as needed	as needed

1 Trim the stems from the mushrooms and scrape away the gills. Soak the caps in water for 1 minute. Remove the caps from the water and drain well. Season the mushrooms with salt and pepper. Smoke the mushroom caps in a stove top smoker for 5 minutes. Remove and cool.
2 Mix the bell peppers, onions and parsley with the lentils and season with salt and pepper.
3 Arrange the spinach on the plates. Sprinkle the lentil mixture over the spinach. Slice the mushroom caps on the bias and fan one cap over each salad.
4 Warm the Hot Bacon Vinaigrette in a small saucepan and dress the salads generously. Serve immediately.

Approximate values per serving, with vinaigrette: **Calories** 690, **Total fat** 59 g, **Saturated fat** 8 g, **Cholesterol** 5 mg, **Sodium** 460 mg, **Total carbohydrates** 26 g, **Protein** 12 g, **Vitamin A** 80%, **Vitamin C** 90%, **Iron** 25%

HOT BACON VINAIGRETTE

Yield: 8 Servings

Bacon slices	10	10
Corn oil	1 pt.	450 ml
Fresh basil, chopped	½ oz.	15 g

Fresh chives, sliced	½ oz.	15 g
Fresh marjoram, chopped	¼ oz.	7 g
Pear vinegar	8 fl. oz.	240 ml
Kosher salt	1 tsp.	5 ml
Black pepper	1 Tbsp.	15 ml

1 Dice the bacon. In a heavy saucepan, combine the bacon and the corn oil and cook until the bacon is crisp. Allow the bacon and oil to cool.

2 Whisk the herbs into the oil. Whisk in the pear vinegar and season with salt and pepper.

COBB SALAD
RECIPE 24.35

Yield: 8 Entrée Servings   **Method:** Composed

Romaine lettuce	8 oz.	250 g
Green leaf lettuce	4 oz.	120 g
Watercress	4 oz.	120 g
Avocados	4	4
Bacon slices	16	16
Roquefort cheese, crumbled	1 lb.	450 g
Turkey breast, roasted, julienne	1 lb.	450 g
Tomato concassée	1 lb.	450 g
Eggs, hard-cooked, chopped	4	4
Dijon mustard vinaigrette	24 oz.	700 ml

1 Tear, wash and dry the lettuces. Pick over and wash the watercress.

2 Pit and peel the avocados and cut into wedges.

3 Dice the bacon and cook in a sauté pan until crisp. Remove and drain well.

4 Toss the salad greens together and arrange the cheese, turkey, tomato concassée and eggs on top in an artistic fashion. Serve the vinaigrette on the side.

Approximate values per serving: **Calories** 1000, **Total fat** 84 g, **Saturated fat** 18 g, **Cholesterol** 215 mg, **Sodium** 1770 mg, **Total carbohydrates** 21 g, **Protein** 40 g, **Vitamin A** 45%, **Vitamin C** 60%, **Calcium** 45%, **Iron** 20%

GREEK SALAD
RECIPE 24.36

Yield: 3 lb. 8 oz. (1.6 kg)

Extra virgin olive oil	4 fl. oz.	120 ml
Lemon juice	2 fl. oz.	60 ml
Red wine vinegar	2 fl. oz.	60 ml
Garlic, minced	1 tsp.	10 ml
Fresh oregano, chopped	1 Tbsp.	30 ml
Cucumbers	2	2
Feta	12 oz.	350 g
Olives, Kalamata or other Greek variety	1 lb.	450 g
Fresh parsley, chopped	1 oz.	30 g
Green onions, sliced	1 bunch	1 bunch
Pepper	TT	TT
Romaine lettuce	1 head	1 head
Anchovy fillets	8	8
Tomatoes, cut into 6 wedges	3	3

1 To make the dressing, whisk together the olive oil, lemon juice, vinegar, garlic and oregano.
2 Peel the cucumbers and slice in half lengthwise. Remove the seeds and cut into batonnet.
3 Dice or crumble the feta into small pieces.
4 Combine the olives, cucumbers, chopped parsley and green onions in a bowl and add the dressing. Toss to combine and season to taste with pepper.
5 Line plates or a platter with the romaine lettuce leaves. Add the olive-cucumber mixture and sprinkle on the feta cheese. Garnish as desired with the anchovies and tomato wedges.

Approximate values per 6-oz. (180-g) serving: **Calories** 280, **Total fat** 24 g, **Saturated fat** 7 g, **Cholesterol** 35 mg, **Sodium** 900 mg, **Total carbohydrates** 9 g, **Protein** 7 g, **Vitamin A** 15%, **Vitamin C** 35%, **Calcium** 25%, **Iron** 15%

WARM LAMB SALAD WITH BOURBON VINAIGRETTE

RECIPE 24.37

Yield: 4 Servings   **Method:** Composed

Lamb loin, eye only	1	1
Salt and pepper	TT	TT
Olive oil	1 Tbsp.	15 ml
New potatoes	8	8
Green onions	4	4
Radicchio	2 heads	2 heads
Garlic cloves, chopped	2	2
Fresh rosemary, chopped	1/2 tsp.	2 ml
Whole butter	2 oz.	60 g
Bourbon	4 fl. oz.	120 ml
Balsamic vinegar	2 fl. oz.	60 ml
Mustard seeds	1 tsp.	5 ml
Orange supremes	24	24

1 Cut the lamb loin into four portions and tie each piece so that it retains its shape during cooking.
2 Season the lamb with salt and pepper. Sauté it in the olive oil to brown all sides. Transfer to a 350°F (180°C) oven and finish to medium rare.
3 Steam the potatoes until tender but still firm.
4 Cut the green onions on the bias.
5 Separate the radicchio leaves from the heads.
6 To make the dressing, sauté the garlic and rosemary in the butter without browning. Whisk in the bourbon, vinegar and mustard seeds, season with salt and pepper and keep hot.
7 Remove the twine and slice each portion of lamb into six slices. Slice the potatoes to the same thickness as the lamb.
8 Using the radicchio as the base, arrange the sliced potatoes, lamb and orange supremes on the plate. Sprinkle with the green onions. Drizzle the dressing over all the ingredients.

Approximate values per serving: **Calories** 300, **Total fat** 17 g, **Saturated fat** 8 g, **Cholesterol** 50 mg, **Sodium** 680 mg, **Total carbohydrates** 27 g, **Protein** 8 g, **Vitamin A** 10%, **Calcium** 10%

ASIAN CHICKEN SALAD

RECIPE 24.38

Yield: 3 lb. (1.4 kg)　　　　　　　**Method:** Bound

Rice vinegar	6 fl. oz.	180 ml
Soy sauce, reduced-sodium	4 fl. oz.	120 ml
Sugar	2 Tbsp.	30 ml
Fresh ginger, minced	3 Tbsp.	45 ml
White pepper	1 tsp.	5 ml
Chicken breast, boneless, skinless	1 lb. 8 oz.	680 g
Sesame oil	1 fl. oz.	30 ml
Snow peas	4 oz.	120 g
Carrot, julienne	4 oz.	120 g
Celery, julienne	4 oz.	120 g
Jicama, julienne	4 oz.	120 g
Fresh cilantro leaves	2 Tbsp.	30 ml

1 To make the dressing, combine the vinegar, soy sauce, sugar, ginger and white pepper. Set aside.

2 Cut the chicken breast into strips approximately ½ × ½ × 3 inches (1.2 × 1.2 × 8 centimeters). Stir-fry the chicken in the sesame oil until done. Remove from the pan, cool and refrigerate.

3 Blanch the vegetables in salted water. Refresh and drain well.

4 Combine the chicken with the vegetables and the dressing; add the cilantro. Toss and serve.

Approximate values per 4-oz. (120-g) serving: **Calories** 160, **Total fat** 4.5 g, **Saturated fat** 1 g, **Cholesterol** 50 mg, **Sodium** 740 mg, **Total carbohydrates** 10 g, **Protein** 19 g, **Vitamin A** 25%, **Vitamin C** 15%

NEW POTATO SALAD WITH MUSTARD AND DILL

RECIPE 24.39

Yield: 5 lb. (2.2 kg)　　　　　　　**Method:** Bound

New potatoes	4 lb.	1.8 kg
Mayonnaise	4 oz.	120 g
Sour cream	4 oz.	120 g
Garlic, chopped	1½ tsp.	7 ml
Salt	TT	TT
Black pepper	1½ tsp.	7 ml
Fresh dill, chopped	2 Tbsp.	30 ml
Dijon-style mustard	2 Tbsp.	30 ml
Green bell pepper, julienne	1	1
Red bell pepper, julienne	1	1
Red onion, julienne	6 oz.	180 g
Celery, julienne	4 oz.	120 g

1 Boil the potatoes in salted water until done but still firm. Chill well and cut into quarters.

2 Combine the mayonnaise, sour cream, garlic, salt, pepper, dill and mustard; mix well.

3 Combine all the ingredients and adjust the seasonings with salt and pepper.

Approximate values per 4-oz. (120-g) serving: **Calories** 110, **Total fat** 6 g, **Saturated fat** 1.5 g, **Cholesterol** 5 mg, **Sodium** 360 mg, **Total carbohydrates** 12 g, **Protein** 1 g, **Vitamin C** 25%

RECIPE 24.40 POTATO SALAD

Yield: 6 lb. 8 oz. (3 kg) **Method:** Bound

Potatoes, chef	4 lb.	1.8 kg
Eggs, hard-cooked	6	6
Celery, medium dice	8 oz.	250 g
Green onions, sliced	1 bunch	1 bunch
Radishes, chopped coarse	6 oz.	180 g
Mayonnaise	1 lb.	450 g
Dijon-style mustard	2 oz.	60 g
Fresh parsley, chopped	1 oz.	30 g
Salt and pepper	TT	TT

1 Boil the potatoes in salted water until nearly cooked. Drain the potatoes, spread them on a sheet pan and refrigerate until cold.
2 Peel the cold potatoes and cut into large dice.
3 Peel and chop the eggs.
4 Combine all the ingredients and adjust the seasonings with salt and pepper.

Approximate values per 4-oz. (120-g) serving: **Calories** 200, **Total fat** 16 g, **Saturated fat** 3 g, **Cholesterol** 65 mg, **Sodium** 390 mg, **Total carbohydrates** 11 g, **Protein** 3 g, **Vitamin C** 15%

RECIPE 24.41 CREAMY COLESLAW

Note: This dish appears in the Pork chapter opening photograph.

Yield: 2 lb. (1 kg) **Method:** Bound

Mayonnaise	8 oz.	250 g
Sour cream or crème fraîche	4 oz.	120 g
Sugar	1 oz.	30 g
Cider vinegar	1 fl. oz.	30 ml
Garlic clove, minced	1	1
Green cabbage, shredded	1 lb.	450 g
Red cabbage, shredded	8 oz.	250 g
Carrots, shredded	4 oz.	120 g
Salt and white pepper	TT	TT

1 Combine the mayonnaise, sour cream or crème fraîche, sugar, vinegar and garlic in a bowl; whisk together.
2 Add the shredded cabbages and carrots to the dressing and mix well. Season to taste with salt and pepper.

Approximate values per 4-oz. (120-g) serving: **Calories** 200, **Total fat** 19 g, **Saturated fat** 4.5 g, **Cholesterol** 20 mg, **Sodium** 340 mg, **Total carbohydrates** 8 g, **Protein** 1 g, **Vitamin A** 20%, **Vitamin C** 50%

RECIPE 24.42 COUSCOUS SALAD

Yield: 3 lb. (1.4 kg)

Couscous	6 oz.	180 g
Red bell pepper, medium dice	1	1
Green bell pepper, medium dice	1	1

Green onions, sliced on the bias	1 bunch	1 bunch
Cucumbers, peeled, seeded, medium dice	6 oz.	180 g
Black olives, pitted	4 oz.	120 g
Red onion, julienne	6 oz.	180 g
Dressing:		
Orange juice concentrate	3 fl. oz.	90 ml
Water	2 fl. oz.	60 ml
Rice vinegar	2 fl. oz.	60 ml
Garlic, chopped	1 tsp.	5 ml
Salt	1 tsp.	5 ml
Black pepper	1 tsp.	5 ml
Fresh oregano, chopped	2 tsp.	10 ml
Salad oil	3 fl. oz.	90 ml
Honey	2 Tbsp.	30 ml
Fresh thyme, chopped	2 tsp.	10 ml

1 Steam the couscous until tender; set aside to cool.
2 Combine the couscous with the vegetables.
3 Whisk together all the dressing ingredients.
4 Combine the salad ingredients with the dressing. Chill thoroughly before serving.

Approximate values per 3-oz. (90-g) serving: **Calories** 90, **Total fat** 6 g, **Saturated fat** 0.5 g, **Cholesterol** 0 mg, **Sodium** 200 mg, **Total carbohydrates** 7 g, **Protein** 1 g, **Vitamin C** 35%, **Claims**—low saturated fat; no cholesterol

TABOULI

RECIPE 24.43

Yield: 15 Servings, 3 oz. (90 g) each

Bulgur	10 oz.	300 g
Onions, brunoise	8 oz.	250 g
Green onions, sliced	2 oz.	60 g
Fresh parsley, chopped	6 oz.	180 g
Fresh mint, chopped	2 oz.	60 g
Olive oil	8 fl. oz.	250 ml
Lemon juice	8 fl. oz.	250 ml
Tomato concassée	1 lb.	500 g
Salt and pepper	TT	TT
Pine nuts, toasted	4 oz.	120 g

1 Place the bulgur in a bowl and cover with cold water. Soak the bulgur until tender, approximately 2 hours.
2 Drain the bulgur and squeeze out all the excess water.
3 Add the onions, green onions, parsley, mint, olive oil and lemon juice. Mix well.
4 Add the tomato concassée; mix to combine. Season with salt and pepper.
5 Garnish with the toasted pine nuts.

Approximate values per 4-oz. (120-g) serving: **Calories** 280, **Total fat** 21 g, **Saturated fat** 3 g, **Cholesterol** 0 mg, **Sodium** 280 mg, **Total carbohydrates** 17 g, **Protein** 5 g, **Vitamin A** 30%, **Vitamin C** 60%, **Iron** 70%, **Claims**—no cholesterol; good source of fiber

RECIPE 24.44

BREAD SALAD

Note: This dish appears in the sandwiches chapter opening photograph.

WILDFLOWER BREAD COMPANY, SCOTTSDALE, **AZ**

Yield: 20 Servings, 8 oz. (240 g) each

Crusty bread, cut into 1-in. (2.5-cm) cubes	1 gal.	4 lt
Tomatoes, diced	21 oz.	630 g
Fresh basil, chopped	2½ oz.	75 g
Fresh parsley, chopped	2½ oz.	75 g
Red bell peppers, diced	5 oz.	150 g
Mushrooms, marinated	5 oz.	150 g
Garlic, chopped	2 tsp.	10 ml
Garlic salt	TT	TT
Lemon pepper	TT	TT
Olive oil	5 oz.	150 ml
Red wine vinegar	3½ fl. oz.	105 ml
Fresh parsley, chopped	as needed for garnish	
Parmesan, grated	as needed for garnish	

1 Spread the bread cubes out on a sheet pan and allow them to dry at room temperature for 3 to 4 hours.

2 Mix the remaining ingredients (except the garnishes) together in a large bowl until everything is evenly distributed.

3 Toss the bread cubes into the salad and coat them well with the salad liquid.

4 Serve at room temperature, garnished with a light sprinkle of chopped parsley and grated Parmesan.

Approximate values per 8-oz. (240-g) serving: **Calories** 452, **Total fat** 10 g, **Saturated fat** 2 g, **Cholesterol** 1 mg, **Sodium** 1566 mg, **Total carbohydrates** 78 g, **Protein** 12 g, **Vitamin A** 31%, **Vitamin C** 40%, **Iron** 41%

TALKING OF PLEASURE, THIS MOMENT I WAS WRITING WITH ONE HAND, AND WITH THE OTHER HOLDING TO MY MOUTH A NECTARINE—HOW GOOD HOW FINE. IT WENT DOWN ALL PULPY, SLUSHY, OOZY, ALL ITS DELICIOUS EMBONPOINT MELTED DOWN MY THROAT LIKE A LARGE, BEATIFIED STRAWBERRY.

—*John Keats, English poet (1795–1821)*

25

FRUITS

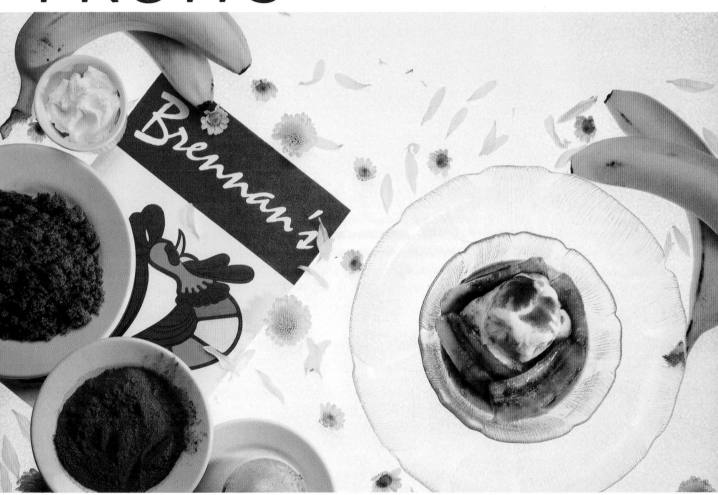

BRENNAN'S RESTAURANT, New Orleans, LA
Chef Michael Roussel

AFTER STUDYING THIS CHAPTER, YOU WILL BE ABLE TO:

▶ identify a variety of fruits

▶ purchase fruits appropriate for your needs

▶ store fruits properly

▶ understand how fruits are preserved

▶ prepare fruits for cooking or service

▶ apply various cooking methods to fruits

Botanically, a fruit is an organ that develops from the ovary of a flowering plant and contains one or more seeds. Culinarily, a fruit is the perfect snack food; the basis of a dessert, colorful sauce or soup or an accompaniment to meat, fish, shellfish or poultry. No food group offers a greater variety of colors, flavors and textures than fruit.

This chapter identifies many of the fruits typically used by food service operations. It then addresses general considerations in purchasing fresh and preserved fruits. A discussion follows about some of the cooking methods presented in Chapter 10, Principles of Cooking, as they apply to fruits. Recipes in which a fruit is the primary ingredient are presented at the chapter's end.

▶ IDENTIFYING FRUITS

This book presents fruits according to the ways most people view them and use them, rather than by rigid botanical classifications. Fruits are divided here into eight categories: berries, citrus, exotics, grapes, melons, pomes, stone fruits and tropicals, according to either their shape, seed structure or natural habitat. Botanically, tomatoes, beans, eggplant, capsicum peppers and other produce are fruits. But in ordinary thinking, they are not; they are vegetables and are discussed in Chapter 22, Vegetables.

A fruit may have several names, varying from region to region or on a purveyor's whim. Botanists are also constantly reclassifying items to fit new findings. The names given here follow generally accepted custom and usage.

BERRIES

Berries are small, juicy fruits that grow on vines and bushes worldwide. Berries are characterized by thin skins and many tiny seeds that are often so small they go unnoticed. Some of the fruits classified here as berries do not fit the botanical definition (for example, raspberries and strawberries), while fruits that are berries botanically (for example, bananas and grapes) are classified elsewhere.

Berries may be eaten plain or used in everything from beer to bread, soup to sorbet. They make especially fine jams and compotes.

Berries must be fully **ripened** on the vine, as they will not ripen further after harvesting. Select berries that are plump and fully colored. Avoid juice-stained containers and berries with whitish-gray or black spots of mold. All berries should be refrigerated and used promptly. Do not wash berries until you are ready to use them, as washing removes some of their aroma and softens them.

▶ ripe fully grown and developed; the fruit's flavor, texture and appearance are at their peak, and the fruit is ready to use as food

BLACKBERRIES

Blackberries are similar to raspberries, but are larger and shinier, with a deep purple to black color. Thorny blackberry vines are readily found in the wild; commercial production is limited. Their peak season is mid-June through August. Loganberries, Marionberries, olallie berries and boysenberries are blackberry hybrids.

BLUEBERRIES

Blueberries (Fr. *myrtilles*) are small and firm, with a true blue to almost black skin and a juicy, light gray-blue interior. Cultivated berries (high-bush varieties) tend to be larger than wild (low-bush) ones. Blueberries are native to North

America and are grown commercially from Maine to Oregon and along the Atlantic seaboard. Their peak season is short, from mid-June to mid-August.

CRANBERRIES

Cranberries, another native North American food, are tart, firm fruit with a mottled red skin. They grow on low vines in cultivated bogs (swamps) throughout Massachusetts, Wisconsin and New Jersey. Rarely eaten raw, they are made into sauce or relish or are used in breads, pies or pastries. Cranberries are readily available frozen or made into a jelly-type sauce and canned. Although color does not indicate ripeness, cranberries should be picked over before cooking to remove those that are soft or bruised. Their peak harvesting season is from Labor Day through October, leading to the association of cranberries with Thanksgiving dinner.

CURRANTS

Currants are tiny, tart fruits that grow on shrubs in grapelike clusters. The most common are a beautiful, almost translucent red, but black and golden (or white) varieties also exist. All varieties are used for jams, jellies and sauces, and black currants are made into a liqueur, crème de cassis. Although rarely grown in the United States, currants are very popular and widely available in Europe, with a peak season during the late summer. (The dried fruits called currants are not produced from these berries; they are a special variety of dried grapes.)

RASPBERRIES

Raspberries (Fr. *framboises*) are perhaps the most delicate of all fruits. They have a tart flavor and velvety texture. Red raspberries are the most common, with black, purple and golden berries available in some markets. When ripe, the berry pulls away easily from its white core, leaving the characteristic hollow center. Because they can be easily crushed and are susceptible to mold, most of the raspberries grown are marketed frozen. They grow on thorny vines in cool climates from Washington State to western New York and are imported from New Zealand and South America. The peak domestic season is from late May through November.

STRAWBERRIES

Strawberries (Fr. *fraises*) are brilliant red, heart-shaped fruits that grow on vines. The strawberry plant is actually a perennial herb, the berry's flesh is covered by tiny black seeds called achenes, which are the plant's true fruits. Select berries with a good red color and intact green leafy hull. (The hulls can be easily removed with a paring knife.) Avoid berries with soft or brown spots. Huge berries may be lovely to look at, but they often have hollow centers and little flavor or juice. Although strawberries are available to some extent all year, fresh California strawberries are at their peak from April through June.

The tiny wild or Alpine berries, known by their French name *fraises des bois,* have a particularly intense flavor and aroma. They are not widely available in the United States.

CITRUS (GENUS *CITRUS*)

Citrus fruits include lemons, limes, grapefruits, tangerines, kumquats, oranges and several hybrids. They are characterized by a thick rind, most of which is a bitter white pith (albedo) with a thin exterior layer of colored skin known as the **zest.** Their flesh is segmented and juicy. Citrus fruits are acidic, with a strong aroma; their flavors vary from bitter to tart to sweet.

Citrus fruits grow on trees and shrubs in tropical and subtropical climates worldwide. All citrus fruits are fully ripened on the tree and will not ripen further after harvesting. They should be refrigerated for longest storage.

Blackberries

Blueberries

Cranberries

White Currants

Red Currants

Raspberries

Strawberries

▶ **zest** the colored outer portion of the rind of citrus fruit; contains the oil that provides flavor and aroma

Select fruits that feel heavy and have thin, smooth skins. Avoid those with large blemishes or moist spots.

White Grapefruits

GRAPEFRUITS

Grapefruits (Fr. *pamplemousse*) are large and round with a yellow skin, thick rind and tart flesh. They are an 18th-century hybrid of the orange and pummelo (a large, coarse fruit used mostly in Middle and Far Eastern cuisines). Two varieties of grapefruit are widely available all year: white-fleshed and pink- or ruby-fleshed. White grapefruits produce the finest juice, although pink grapefruits are sweeter. Fresh grapefruits are best eaten raw or topped with brown sugar and lightly broiled.

Red Grapefruits

Kumquats

KUMQUATS

Kumquats are very small, oval-shaped, orange-colored fruits with a soft, sweet skin and slightly bitter flesh. They can be eaten whole, either raw or preserved in syrup, and may be used in jams and preserves.

Lemons

LEMONS

The most commonly used citrus fruits, lemons (Fr. *citrons*), are oval-shaped, bright yellow fruits available all year. Their strongly acidic flavor makes them unpleasant to eat raw but perfect for flavoring desserts and confections. Lemon juice is also widely used in sauces, especially for fish, shellfish and poultry. Lemon zest is candied or used as garnish.

Limes

LIMES

Limes (Fr. *limons*) are small fruits with thin skins ranging from yellow-green to dark green. Limes are too tart to eat raw and are often substituted for lemons in prepared dishes. They are also juiced or used in cocktails, curries or desserts. Lime zest can be grated and used to give color and flavor to a variety of dishes. Limes are available all year; their peak season is during the summer.

Navel Oranges

ORANGES

Oranges (Sp. *naranja*) are round fruits with a juicy, orange-colored flesh and a thin, orange skin. They can be either sweet or bitter.

Valencia oranges and navel oranges (a seedless variety) are the most popular sweet oranges. They can be juiced for beverages or sauces, and the flesh may be eaten raw, added to salads, cooked in desserts or used as a garnish. The zest may be grated or julienned for sauces or garnish. Sweet oranges are available all year; their peak season is from December to April. Blood oranges are also sweet but are small, with a rough, reddish skin. Their flesh is streaked with a blood-red color. Blood oranges are available primarily during the winter months and are eaten raw, juiced or used in salads or sauces. When selecting sweet oranges, look for fruits that feel plump and heavy, with unblemished skin. The color of the skin depends on weather conditions; a green rind does not affect the flavor of the flesh.

Valencia Oranges

Blood Oranges

Bitter oranges include the Seville and bergamot. They are used primarily for the essential oils found in their zest. Oil of bergamot gives Earl Grey tea its distinctive flavor; oil of Seville is essential to curaçao, Grand Marnier and orange flower water. Seville oranges are also used in marmalades and sauces for meats and poultry.

Tangerines

TANGERINES

Tangerines, sometimes referred to as mandarins, are small and dark orange. Their rind is loose and easily removed to reveal sweet, juicy, aromatic segments. Tangerines are most often eaten fresh and uncooked, but are available canned as mandarin oranges.

Tangelos are a hybrid of tangerines and grapefruits. They are the size of a medium orange; they have a bulbous stem end and few to no seeds.

▶ PROCEDURE FOR SEGMENTING CITRUS FRUITS

1 Citrus segments, known as *supremes,* are made by first carefully cutting off the entire peel (including the bitter white pith) in even slices.

2 Individual segments are then removed by gently cutting alongside each membrane.

▶ PROCEDURE FOR ZESTING CITRUS FRUITS

A five-hole zester is used to remove paper-thin strips of the colored rind.

▶ PROCEDURE FOR CUTTING CITRUS PEELS

Large strips of citrus zest may be used as a garnish or to flavor soups or sauces.

HYBRIDS AND VARIETIES

Several fruits are extremely responsive to selective breeding and crossbreeding and have been toyed with by botanists and growers since at least the time of ancient Rome. Two distinct products are recognized: hybrids and varieties. **Hybrids** result from crossbreeding fruits from different species that are genetically unalike. The result is a unique product. Citrus is particularly responsive to hybridization. **Varieties** result from breeding fruits of the same species that have different qualities or characteristics. Breeding two varieties of apples, for example, produces a third variety with the best qualities of both parents.

EXOTICS

Improved transportation has led to the increasing availability (although sporadic in some areas) of exotic or unusual fresh fruits such as figs, persimmons, pomegranates, prickly pears, rhubarb and star fruits. Other exotic fruits, such as breadfruit, durian, feijoa and loquat, are still available only on a limited basis from specialty purveyors and are not discussed here.

FIGS

Figs (Fr. *figues*) are the fruit of ficus trees. They are small, soft, pear-shaped fruits with an intensely sweet flavor and rich, moist texture made crunchy by a multitude of tiny seeds. Fresh figs can be sliced and served in salads or with cured meats such as prosciutto. They can also be baked, poached or used in jams, preserves or compotes.

Dark-skinned figs, known as Mission figs, are a variety planted at Pacific Coast missions during the 18th century. They have a thin skin and small seeds and are available fresh, canned or dried. The white-skinned figs grown commercially include the White Adriatic, used principally for drying and baking, and the all-purpose Kadota. The most important domestic variety, however, is the Calimyrna. These large figs have a rich yellow color and large nutty seeds. Fresh Calimyrna figs are the finest for eating out of hand; they are also available dried.

For the best flavor, figs should be fully ripened on the tree. Unfortunately, fully ripened figs are very delicate and difficult to transport. Most figs are in season from June through October; fresh Calimyrna figs are available only during June.

Calimyrna Figs

GOOSEBERRIES

Several varieties of gooseberry (Fr. *groseille maquereau*) are cultivated for culinary purposes. One well-known variety is the European gooseberry, a member of the currant family that grows on spiny bushes in cool, moist regions of the Northern Hemisphere. Its berries can be relatively large, like a small plum, but are usually less than 1 inch (2.5 centimeters) in diameter. The skin, which is firm and smooth or only slightly hairy, can be green, white (actually gray-green), yellow or red. The tart berries contain many tiny seeds. They are eaten fresh or used for jellies, preserves, tarts and other desserts or as a traditional accompaniment to rich or fatty dishes, such as goose and mackerel. North American gooseberry varieties are smaller, perfectly round, and pink to deep red at maturity. Although more prolific, these varietals lack flavor and are generally considered inferior to European gooseberries.

Cape gooseberries, also known as physalis, ground cherries and poha, are unrelated to European and American gooseberries. Native of Peru, they became popular during the 19th century along the African Cape of Good Hope, for which they are named. Australia and New Zealand are currently the largest producers. Cape gooseberries are covered with a paper-thin husk or calyx. About the size of a cherry, they have a waxy, bright orange skin and many tiny seeds. Their flavor is similar to coconut and oranges, but tarter. Cape gooseberries may be eaten raw, made into jam or used in desserts. Fresh, they make an especially striking garnish.

Cape Gooseberries

GUAVA

Guava (GWAH-vah) are a small, oval or pear-shaped fruit with a strong fragrance and a mild, slightly grainy flesh. They are excellent in jams and preserves, and guava juice is available plain or blended with other tropical fruit juices. Guava paste, a thick, sliceable gel, is a popular treat throughout Central America and the Caribbean. Guava will ripen if stored at room temperature and should be slightly soft and fully ripened for the best flavor.

Guava

LYCHEES

The lychee (LEE-chee), also spelled *litchi* or *leechee,* is the fruit of a large tree native to southern China and Southeast Asia. The fruits, which grow in clusters, are oval to round, red and about 1 inch (2.5 centimeters) in diameter. The tough outer skin encloses juicy, white, almost translucent flesh and one large seed. Neither the skin nor the seed are edible. The fruit travels well and is now cultivated in Florida and Hawaii, so supplies are relatively stable. Lychees are eaten fresh out of hand or juiced, and are widely available canned or dried. Fresh lychees are mild but sweet with a pleasant perfume.

Lychees

MANGOSTEENS

The mangosteen, another native of Southeast Asia, is cultivated in Java, Sumatra and the Philippines. Mangosteens (no relation to mangos) are the size of a small orange, with flattened ends. They have a thick, hard, deep reddish-purple rind with hard white petal-shaped protrusions at the stem end. The interior flesh is snow-white and segmented, looking something like a mandarin orange. The texture is juicy and delicate with a slightly astringent flavor. Because the fruit must ripen on the tree and keeps only a short time, it is rarely found fresh outside of local markets. Mangosteens are usually eaten fresh, although canned fruit and mangosteen juice is available.

Mangosteens

PERSIMMONS

Persimmons, sometimes referred to as kaki or Sharon fruits, are a bright orange, acorn-shaped fruit with a glossy skin and a large papery blossom. The flesh is bright orange and jellylike, with a mild but rich flavor similar to honey and plums. Persimmons should be peeled before use; any seeds should be discarded. Select bright orange fruits and refrigerate only after they are completely ripe. When ripe, persimmons will be very soft and the skin will have an almost translucent appearance.

Ripe persimmons are delicious eaten raw; halved and topped with cream or soft cheese or peeled, sliced and added to fruit salads. Persimmon bread, muffins, cakes and pies are also popular. Underripe persimmons are almost inedible, however. They are strongly tannic with a chalky or cottony texture.

Persimmons are tree fruits grown in subtropical areas worldwide, although the Asian varieties—now grown in California—are the most common. Fresh persimmons are available from October through January.

Persimmons

POMEGRANATES

An ancient fruit native to Persia (now Iran), pomegranates (POM-uh-gran-uhtz) have long been a subject of poetry and a symbol of fertility. Pomegranates are round, about the size of a large orange, with a pronounced calyx. The skin forms a hard shell with a pinkish-red color. The interior is filled with hundreds of small, red seeds (which are, botanically, the actual fruits) surrounded by juicy red pulp. An inedible yellow membrane separates the seeds into compartments. Pomegranates are sweet-sour, and the seeds are pleasantly crunchy. The bright red seeds make an attractive garnish. Pomegranate juice is a popular beverage in Mediterranean cuisines, and grenadine syrup is made from concentrated pomegranate juice.

Select heavy fruits that are not rock-hard, cracked or heavily bruised. Whole pomegranates can be refrigerated for several weeks. Pomegranates are available from September through December; their peak season is in October.

Pomegranates

PRICKLY PEARS

Prickly pear fruits, also known as cactus pears and barbary figs, are actually the berries of several varieties of cactus. They are barrel- or pear-shaped, about the size of a large egg. Their thick, firm skin is green or purple with small sharp

Prickly Pears

pins and nearly invisible stinging fibers. Their flesh is spongy, sweet and a brilliant pink-red, dotted with small black seeds. Prickly pears have the aroma of watermelon and the flavor of sugar-water.

Once peeled, prickly pears can be diced and eaten raw, or they can be puréed for making jams, sauces, custards or sorbets, to which they give a vivid pink color. Prickly pears are especially common in Mexican and southwestern cuisines.

Select fruits that are full-colored, heavy and tender, but not too soft. Avoid those with mushy or bruised spots. Ripe prickly pears can be refrigerated for a week or more. Prickly pears are grown in Mexico and several southwestern states and are available from September through December.

▶ PROCEDURE FOR PEELING PRICKLY PEARS

1 To avoid being stung by a prickly pear, hold it steady with a fork, then use a knife to cut off both ends.

2 Cut a lengthwise slit through the skin. Slip the tip of the knife into the cut and peel away the skin by holding it down while rolling the fruit away.

Rambutans

RAMBUTANS

Rambutans (ram-BOOT-enz), the fruit of a tree in the soapberry family, are closely related to lychees. Native to Malaysia, they are now cultivated throughout Southeast Asia. The bright-red, oval fruit is about the size of a small hen's egg, and is covered with long, soft spines, hence the name "hairy lychees." The interior has a white, lightly acidic pulp. Rambutans darken with age, so select brightly-colored fruit with soft, fleshy spines. Rambutans are eaten fresh and used in preserves and ice cream; they are also available canned.

Rhubarb

RHUBARB

Although botanically a vegetable, rhubarb (ROO-barb) is most often prepared as a fruit. It is a perennial plant that grows well in temperate and cold climates. Only the pinkish-red stems are edible; the leaves contain high amounts of oxalic acid, which is toxic.

Rhubarb stems are extremely acidic, requiring large amounts of sugar to create the desired sweet-sour taste. Cinnamon, ginger, orange and strawberry are particularly compatible with rhubarb. It is excellent for pies, cobblers, preserves or stewing. Young, tender stalks of rhubarb do not need to be peeled. When cooked, rhubarb becomes very soft and turns a beautiful light pink color.

Fresh rhubarb is sold as whole stalks, with the leaves removed. Select crisp, unblemished stalks. Rhubarb's peak season is during the early spring, from February through May. Frozen rhubarb pieces are readily available and are excellent for pies, tarts or jams.

STAR FRUITS

Star fruits, also known as carambola, are oval, up to 5 inches (12.5 centimeters) long, with five prominent ribs or wings running their length. A cross-section cut is shaped like a star. The edible skin is a waxy orange-yellow; it covers a dry, paler yellow flesh. Its flavor is similar to that of plums, sweet but bland. Star fruits do not need to be peeled or seeded. They are most often sliced and added to fruit salad or used as a garnish. Unripe fruits can be cooked in stews or chutneys.

Color and aroma are the best indicators of ripeness. The fruits should be a deep golden-yellow and there should be brown along the edge of the ribs. The aroma should be full and floral. Green fruits can be kept at room temperature to ripen, then refrigerated for up to two weeks. Star fruits are cultivated in Hawaii, Florida and California, though some are still imported from the Caribbean. Fresh fruits are available from August to February.

Star Fruits

GRAPES

Grapes (Fr. *raisins;* Sp. *uvas*) are the single largest fruit crop in the world, due, of course, to their use in wine making. This section, however, discusses only table grapes, those grown for eating. Grapes are berries that grow on vines in large clusters. California is the world's largest producer, with more than a dozen varieties grown for table use. Grapes are classified by color as white (which are actually green) or black (which are actually red). White grapes are generally blander than black ones, with a thinner skin and firmer flesh.

The grape's color and most of its flavor are found in the skin. Grapes are usually eaten raw, either alone or in fruit salads. They are also used as a garnish or accompaniment to desserts and cheeses. Dried grapes are known as raisins (Fr. *raisins sec*); usually made from Thompson Seedless or muscat grapes), currants (made from Black Corinth grapes and labeled Zante currants) or sultanas (made from sultana grapes).

Grapes are available all year because the many varieties have different harvesting schedules. Look for firm, unblemished fruits that are firmly attached to the stem. A surface bloom or dusty appearance is caused by yeasts and indicates recent harvesting. Wrinkled grapes or those with brown spots around the stem are past their prime. All grapes should be rinsed and drained prior to use.

Red Flame Grapes

RED FLAME GRAPES

Red Flame grapes are a seedless California hybrid, second only in importance to the Thompson Seedless. Red Flame grapes are large and round with a slightly tart flavor and variegated red color.

THOMPSON SEEDLESS GRAPES

The most commercially important table grapes are a variety known as Thompson Seedless, which are pale green with a crisp texture and sweet flavor. Their peak season is from June to November. Many are dried in the hot desert sun of California's San Joaquin Valley to produce dark raisins. For golden raisins, Thompson Seedless grapes are treated with sulfur dioxide to prevent browning, then dried mechanically.

Thompson Seedless Grapes

GRAPES INTO WINE

Virtually all the fine wine made in the world comes from varieties of a single grape species, *Vitis vinifera*. It is grown in the United States, Europe, South Africa, South America, the Middle East, Australia and wherever fine wine is made. The variety of grapes used in any given wine determines the wine's character, and most wine-producing countries carefully regulate the growing areas and production of grapes.

American wines are known by their varietal names, whereas European (especially French) wines are generally known by the vineyard's location. The major varietals of wine grapes and the wines in which they are used are listed here.

Grape Varietal	Wine
Pinot Noir	red Burgundy and champagne
Chardonnay	white Burgundy, Chablis and champagne
Syrah	Côte Rotie and Hermitage
Cabernet Sauvignon	Bordeaux and red Graves
Sauvignon Blanc	Sauterne, white Graves, fumé blanc and Sancerre
Merlot	Saint-Emilion and for blending with Cabernet Sauvignon
Zinfandel	red and white zinfandel (California claims a virtual monopoly)
Chenin Blanc	Vouvray

OTHER TABLE GRAPES

Of the table grapes containing seeds, the most important varieties are the Concord, Ribier and Emperor. They range from light red to deep black, and all three are in season during the autumn. Concord grapes, one of the few grape varieties native to the New World, are especially important for making juices and jellies.

Concord Grapes

MELONS

Like pumpkins and cucumbers, melons are members of the gourd family (*Cucurbitaceae*). The dozens of melon varieties can be divided into two general types: sweet (or dessert) melons and watermelons. Sweet melons have a tan, green or yellow netted or farrowed rind and dense, fragrant flesh. Watermelon has a thick, dark green rind surrounding crisp, watery flesh.

Melons are almost 90 percent water, so cooking destroys their texture, quickly turning the flesh to mush. Most are served simply sliced, perhaps with a bit of lemon or lime juice. Melons also blend well in fruit salads or with rich, cured meats such as prosciutto. Melons may be puréed and made into sorbet or chilled, uncooked soup.

Melons should be vine-ripened. A ripe melon should yield slightly and spring back when pressed at the blossom end (opposite the stem). It should also give off a strong aroma. Avoid melons that are very soft or feel damp at the stem end. Ripe melons may be stored in the refrigerator, although the flavor will be better at room temperature. Slightly underripe melons can be stored at room temperature to allow flavor and aroma to develop.

CANTALOUPES

American cantaloupes, which are actually muskmelons, are sweet melons with a thick, yellow-green netted rind, a sweet, moist, orange flesh and a strong aroma. (European cantaloupes, which are not generally available in this country, are more craggy and furrowed in appearance.)

As with all sweet melons, the many small seeds are found in a central cavity. Cantaloupes are excellent for eating alone and are especially good with ham or rich meats.

Avoid cantaloupes with the pronounced yellow color or moldy aroma that indicates overripeness. Mexican imports ensure a year-round supply, although their peak season is summer.

Cantaloupes

CASABA MELONS

Casaba Melons

The casaba melon is a teardrop-shaped sweet melon. It has a coarse, yellow skin and a thick, ridged rind; its flesh is creamy white to yellow. Casaba melons are used like cantaloupes. Casaba melons do not have an aroma, so selection must be based on a deep skin color and the absence of dark or moist patches. Their peak season is during September and October.

CRENSHAW MELONS

Crenshaw (or cranshaw) melons have a mottled, green-yellow ridged rind and orange-pink flesh. They are large pear-shaped sweet melons with a strong aroma. The flesh has a rich, spicy flavor and may be used like cantaloupe. Crenshaws are available from July through October; their peak season is during August and September.

Crenshaw Melons

HONEYDEW MELONS

Green Honeydews

Honeydew melons are large oval sweet melons with a smooth rind that ranges from white to pale green. Although the flesh is generally pale green, with a mild, sweet flavor, pink- or gold-fleshed honeydews are also available. Like casaba melons, honeydew melons have little to no aroma. They are available almost all year; their peak season is from June through October.

Gold Honeydews

SANTA CLAUS MELONS

Santa Claus or Christmas melons are large, elongated sweet melons with a green-and-yellow-striped, smooth rind. The flesh is creamy white or yellow and tastes like casaba. They are a winter variety, with peak availability during December, which explains the name.

Santa Claus Melons

Watermelon

WATERMELONS

Watermelons are large (up to 30 pounds or 13.5 kilograms) round or oval-shaped melons with a thick rind. The skin may be solid green, green-striped or mottled with white. The flesh is crisp and extremely juicy with small, hard, black seeds throughout. Seedless hybrids are available. Most watermelons have pink to red flesh, although golden-fleshed varieties are becoming more common.

Watermelons are of a different genus from the sweet melons described earlier. They are native to tropical Africa and are now grown commercially in Texas and several southern states.

Gold Watermelon

POMES

Pomes are tree fruits with thin skin and firm flesh surrounding a central core containing many small seeds called pips or carpels. Pomes include apples, pears and quince.

APPLES

Apples (Fr. *pommes*), perhaps the most common and commonly appreciated of all fruits, grow on trees in temperate zones worldwide. They are popular because of their convenience, flavor, variety and availability.

 Rome   *Red Delicious*

Apples can be eaten raw out of hand, or they can be used in a wide variety of cooked or baked dishes. They are equally useful in breads, desserts or vegetable dishes and go well with game, pork and poultry. Classic dishes prepared with apples are often referred to as *à la Normande*. Apple juice (cider) produces alcoholic and nonalcoholic beverages and cider vinegar.

Of the hundreds of known apple varieties, only 20 or so are commercially significant in the United States. Several varieties and their characteristics are noted in Table 25.1. Most have a moist, creamy white flesh with a thin skin of yellow, green or red. They range in flavor from very sweet to very tart, with an equally broad range of textures, from firm and crisp to soft and mealy.

Granny Smith *Golden Delicious*

 McIntosh

In Europe, apples are divided into distinct cooking and eating varieties. Cooking varieties are those that disintegrate to a purée when cooked.

American varieties are less rigidly classified. Nevertheless, not all apples are appropriate for all types of cooking. Those that retain their shape better during cooking are the best choices where slices or appearance are important. Varieties with a higher malic acid content break down easily, making them more appropriate for applesauce or juicing. Either type may be eaten out of hand, depending on personal preference.

Although not native to North America, apples are now grown commercially in 35 states, with Washington and New York leading in production. Apples are harvested when still sightly underripe, then stored in a controlled atmosphere (temperature and oxygen are greatly reduced) for extended periods until ready for sale. Modern storage techniques make fresh apples available all year, although their peak season is during the autumn.

Gala

When selecting apples, look for smooth, unbroken skins and firm fruits, without soft spots or bruises. Badly bruised or rotting apples should be

Table 25.1 APPLE VARIETIES

VARIETY	SKIN COLOR	FLAVOR	TEXTURE	PEAK SEASON	USE
Fiji	Yellow-green with red highlights	Sweet-spicy	Crisp	All year	Eating, in salads
Gala	Yellow-orange with red stripes	Sweet	Crisp	Aug.–March	Eating, in salads, sauce
Golden Delicious	Glossy, greenish-gold	Sweet	Semifirm	Sept.–Oct.	In tarts, with cheese, in salads
Granny Smith	Bright green	Tart	Firm and crisp	Oct.–Nov.	Eating, in tarts
Jonathan	Brilliant red	Tart to acidic	Tender	Sept.–Oct.	Eating, all-purpose
McIntosh	Red with green background	Tart to acidic	Soft	Fall	Applesauce, in closed pies
Pippin (Newton)	Greenish-yellow	Tart	Semifirm	Fall	In pies, eating, baking
Red Delicious	Deep red	Sweet but bland	Soft to mealy	Sept.–Oct.	Eating
Rome	Red	Sweet-tart	Firm	Oct.–Nov.	Baking, pies, sauces
Winesap	Dark red with yellow streaks	Tangy	Crisp	Oct.–Nov.	Cider, all-purpose

discarded immediately. They emit quantities of ethylene gas that speed spoilage of nearby fruits. (Remember the saying that "one bad apple spoils the barrel.") Store apples chilled for up to six weeks. Apple peels (the skin) may be eaten or removed as desired, but in either case, apples should be washed just prior to use to remove pesticides and any wax that was applied to improve appearance. Apple slices can be frozen (often with sugar or citric acid added to slow spoilage) or dried.

▶ PROCEDURE FOR CORING APPLES

1 Remove the core from a whole apple with an apple corer by inserting the corer from the stem end and pushing out the cylinder containing the core and seeds.

2 Alternatively, first cut an apple into quarters, then use a paring knife to cut away the core and seeds.

PEARS

Anjou

Pears (Fr. *poires*) are an ancient tree fruit grown in temperate areas throughout the world. Most of the pears marketed in the United States are grown in California, Washington and Oregon.

Although literally thousands of pear varieties have been identified, only a dozen or so are commercially significant. Several varieties and their characteristics are noted in Table 25.2. Pear varieties vary widely in size, color and flavor. They are most often eaten out of hand, but can be baked or poached. Pears are delicious with cheese, especially blue cheeses, and can be used in fruit salads, compotes or preserves.

Asian Pears

Bartlett

Asian pears, also known as Chinese pears or apple-pears, are of a different species than common pears. They have the moist, sweet flavor of a pear and the round shape and crisp texture of an apple. They are becoming increasingly popular in the United States, particularly those known as Twentieth Century or Nijisseiki.

Red d'Anjou

When selecting pears, look for fruits with smooth, unbroken skin and an intact stem. Pears will not ripen properly on the tree, so they are picked while still firm and should be allowed to soften before use. Underripe pears may be left at room temperature to ripen. A properly ripened pear should have a good fragrance and yield to gentle pressure at the stem end. Pears can be prepared or stored in the same ways as apples.

Bosc

QUINCE

Common quince (*kwence;* Fr. *coing*) resemble large, lumpy yellow pears. Their flesh is hard, with many pips or seeds, and they have a wonderful fragrance. Too astringent to eat raw, quince develop a sweet flavor and pink color when cooked with sugar. Quince are used in meat stews, jellies, marmalades and pies. They have a high **pectin** content and may be added to other fruit jams or preserves to encourage gelling.

Quince

▶ **pectin** a gelatin-like carbohydrate obtained from certain fruits; used to thicken jams and jellies

Table 25.2   PEAR VARIETIES

VARIETY	APPEARANCE	FLAVOR	TEXTURE	PEAK SEASON	USE
Anjou (Beurre d'Anjou)	Greenish-yellow skin; egg-shaped with short neck; red variety also available	Sweet and juicy	Firm, keeps well	Oct.–May	Eating, poaching, baking
Bartlett (Williams)	Thin yellow skin; bell-shaped; red variety also available	Very sweet, buttery, juicy	Tender	Aug.–Dec.	Eating, canning, in salads
Bosc	Golden-brown skin; long, tapered neck	Buttery	Dry, holds its shape well	Sept.–May	Poaching, baking
Comice	Yellow-green skin; large and chubby	Sweet, juicy	Smooth	Oct.–Feb.	Eating
Seckel	Tiny; brown to yellow skin	Spicy	Very firm, grainy	Aug.–Dec.	Poaching, pickling

Fresh quince, usually imported from South America or southeast Europe, are available from October through January. Select firm fruits with a good yellow color. Small blemishes may be cut away before cooking. Quince will keep for up to a month under refrigeration.

STONE FRUITS

Stone fruits, also known as drupes, include apricots, cherries, nectarines, peaches and plums. They are characterized by a thin skin, soft flesh and one woody stone or pit. Although most originated in China, the shrubs and trees producing stone fruits are now grown in temperate climates worldwide.

The domestic varieties of stone fruits are in season from late spring through summer. They tend to be fragile fruits, easily bruised and difficult to transport and have a short shelf life. Do not wash them until ready to use, as moisture can cause deterioration. Avoid ingesting the pits—most contain toxic acids. Stone fruits are excellent dried and are often used to make liqueurs and brandies.

APRICOTS

Apricots (Fr. *abricots*) are small, round stone fruits with a velvety skin that varies from deep yellow to vivid orange. Their juicy orange flesh surrounds a dark, almond-shaped pit. Apricots can be eaten out of hand, poached, stewed, baked or candied. They are often used in fruit compotes or savory sauces for meat or poultry, and are also popular in quick breads and fruit tarts or puréed for dessert sauces, jams, custards or mousses.

Apricots have a short season, peaking during June and July, and do not travel well. Select apricots that are well shaped, plump and fairly firm. Avoid ones that are greenish-yellow or mushy. Fresh apricots will last for several days under refrigeration, but the flavor is best at room temperature. If fresh fruits are unavailable, canned apricots are usually an acceptable substitute. Dried apricots and apricot juice (known as nectar) are readily available.

Apricots

CHERRIES

From the northern states, particularly Washington, Oregon, Michigan and New York, come the two most important types of cherry: the sweet cherry and the sour (or tart) cherry.

Sweet cherries (Fr. *cerises*) are round to heart-shaped, about 1 inch (2.5 centimeters) in diameter, with skin that ranges from yellow to deep red to nearly black. The flesh, which is sweet and juicy, may vary from yellow to dark red. The most common and popular sweet cherries are the dark red Bings. Yellow-red Royal Ann and Rainier cherries are also available in some areas.

Sweet cherries are often marketed fresh, made into maraschino cherries or candied for use in baked goods. Fresh sweet cherries have a very short season, peaking during June and July. Cherries will not ripen further after harvesting. Select fruits that are firm and plump with a green stem still attached. There should not be any brown spots around the stem. A dry or brown stem indicates that the cherry is less than fresh. Once the stem is removed, the cherry will deteriorate rapidly. Store fresh cherries in the refrigerator and do not wash them until ready to use.

Sour cherries are light to dark red and are so acidic they are rarely eaten uncooked. The most common sour cherries are the Montmorency and Morello. Most sour cherries are canned or frozen, or cooked with sugar and starch (usually cornstarch or tapioca) and sold as prepared pastry and pie fillings.

Both sweet and sour varieties are available dried.

Rainier Cherries

Bing Cherries

▶ PROCEDURE FOR PITTING CHERRIES

Remove the stem and place the cherry in the pitter with the indentation facing up. Squeeze the handles together to force out the pit.

PEACHES AND NECTARINES

Peaches (Fr. *pêches*) are moderate-sized, round fruits with a juicy, sweet flesh. Nectarines are a variety of peach, the main difference between the two being their skin. Peaches have a thin skin covered with fuzz, while nectarines have a thin, smooth skin. The flesh of either fruit ranges from white to pale orange. Although their flavors are somewhat different, they may be substituted for each other in most recipes.

Peaches and nectarines are excellent for eating out of hand or in dessert tarts or pastries. They are also used in jams, chutneys, preserves and savory relishes, having a particular affinity for Asian and Indian dishes. Although the skin is edible, peaches are generally peeled before being used. (Peaches are easily peeled if blanched first.)

Peaches and nectarines are either freestones or clingstones. With freestones, the flesh separates easily from the stone; freestone fruits are commonly eaten out of hand. The flesh of clingstones adheres firmly to the stone; they hold their shape better when cooked and are the type most often canned.

Select fruits with a good aroma; an overall creamy, yellow or yellow-orange color and an unwrinkled skin free of blemishes. Red patches are not an indication of ripeness; a green skin indicates that the fruit was picked too early and it will not ripen further. Peaches and nectarines will soften but do not become sweeter after harvesting.

The United States, especially California, is the world's largest producer of peaches and nectarines. Their peak season is through the summer months, with July and August producing the best crop. South American peaches are sometimes available from January to May. Canned and frozen peaches are readily available.

PLUMS

Plums (Fr. *prunes*) are round to oval-shaped fruits that grow on trees or bushes. Dozens of plum varieties are known, although only a few are commercially significant. Plums vary in size from very small to 3 inches (7.5 centimeters) in diameter. Their thin skin can be green, red, yellow or various shades of blue-purple.

Plums are excellent for eating out of hand. Plums can also be baked, poached or used in pies, cobblers or tarts; they are often used in jams or preserves, and fresh slices can be used in salads or compotes.

Fresh plums are widely available from June through October; their peak season is in August and September. When selecting plums, look for plump, smooth fruits with unblemished skin. Generally, they should yield to gentle pressure,

Peaches

Nectarines

Santa Rosa Plums

Damson Plums

although the green and yellow varieties remain quite firm. Avoid plums with moist, brown spots near the stem. Plums may be left at room temperature to ripen, then stored in the refrigerator. Prunes, discussed later, are produced by drying special plum varieties, usually the French Agen.

TROPICALS

Tropical fruits are native to the world's hot, tropical or subtropical regions. Most are now readily available throughout the United States thanks to rapid transportation and distribution methods. All can be eaten fresh, without cooking. Their flavors complement each other and go well with rich or spicy meat, fish and poultry dishes.

BANANAS

Common yellow bananas (Fr. *bananes*) are actually the berries of a large tropical herb. Grown in bunches called hands, they are about 7–9 inches (17.5–22.5 centimeters) long, with a sticky, soft, sweet flesh. Their inedible yellow skin is easily removed.

Properly ripened bananas are excellent eaten out of hand or used in salads. Lightly bruised or overripe fruits are best used for breads or muffins. Bananas blend well with other tropical fruits and citrus. Their unique flavor is also complemented by curry, cinnamon, ginger, honey and chocolate.

Common Yellow Bananas

Fresh bananas are available all year. Bananas are always harvested when still green, because the texture and flavor will be adversely affected if the fruits are allowed to turn yellow on the tree. Unripe bananas are hard, dry and starchy. Because bananas ripen after harvesting, it is acceptable to purchase green bananas if there is sufficient time for final ripening before use. Bananas should be left at room temperature to ripen. A properly ripened banana has a yellow peel with brown flecks. The tip should not have any remaining green coloring. As bananas continue to age, the peel darkens and the starches turn to sugar, giving the fruits a sweeter flavor. Avoid bananas that have large brown bruises or a gray cast (a sign of cold damage).

Plantains

Plantains, also referred to as cooking bananas, are larger but not as sweet as common bananas. They are frequently cooked as a starchy vegetable in tropical cuisines.

DATES

Dates (Fr. *datte*) are the fruit of the date palm tree, which has been cultivated since ancient times. Dates are about 1–2 inches (2.5–5 centimeters) long, with a paper-thin skin and a single grooved seed in the center. Most are golden to dark brown when ripe.

Although dates appear to be dried, they are actually fresh fruits. They have a sticky-sweet, almost candied texture and rich flavor. Dates provide flavor and moisture for breads, muffins, cookies and tarts. They can also be served with fresh or dried fruits, or stuffed with meat or cheese as an appetizer.

Medjool Dates

Pitted dates are readily available in several packaged forms: whole, chopped or extruded (for use in baking). Whole unpitted dates are available in bulk. Date juice is also available for use as a natural sweetener, especially in baked goods. Although packaged or processed dates are available all year, peak season for fresh domestic dates is from October through December. When selecting dates, look for those that are plump, glossy and moist.

KIWIS

Kiwis

Kiwis, sometimes known as kiwifruits or Chinese gooseberries, are small oval fruits, about the size of a large egg, with a thin, fuzzy brown skin. The flesh is bright green with a white core surrounded by hundreds of tiny black seeds.

Kiwis are sweet, but somewhat bland. They are best used raw, peeled and eaten out of hand or sliced for fruit salads or garnish. Although kiwis are not recommended for cooking because heat causes them to fall apart, they are a perfect addition to glazed fruit tarts and can be puréed for sorbets, sauces or mousses. Kiwis contain an enzyme similar to that in fresh pineapple and papaya, which has a tenderizing effect on meat and prevents gelling.

MANGOES

Mangoes

Mangoes (Fr. *mangue*) are oval or kidney-shaped fruits that normally weigh between 6 ounces and 1 pound (180 and 500 grams). Their skin is smooth and thin but tough, varying from yellow to orange-red, with patches of green, red or purple. As mangoes ripen, the green disappears. The juicy, bright orange flesh clings to a large, flat pit.

A mango's unique flavor is spicy-sweet, with an acidic tang. Mangoes can be puréed for use in drinks or sauces, or the flesh can be sliced or cubed for use in salads, pickles, chutneys or desserts. Mangoes go well with spicy foods such as curry and with barbecued meats.

Although Florida produces some mangoes, most of those available in the United States are from Mexico. Their peak season is from May through August. Select fruits with good color that are firm and free of blemishes. Ripe mangoes should have a good aroma, and should not be too soft or shriveled. Allow mangoes to ripen completely at room temperature, then refrigerate for up to one week.

FRIEDA AND THE KIWIFRUIT

How did a fuzzy brown unknown become a media darling and a hugely viable crop? The answer is, thanks to Frieda Caplan. In 1962 Frieda, founder of Frieda's, Inc., launched her historical worldwide promotion of kiwifruit. Acting on a suggestion that Chinese gooseberries, then grown only in New Zealand, might sell better under the name kiwifruit (the kiwi is the national bird of New Zealand), Frieda unleashed a produce giant. This story of the kiwifruit is studied throughout the world as one of the great successes in food marketing.

In 1980, after 18 years of Frieda's continual, creative, aggressive and expensive marketing, the kiwifruit became a North American star when nouvelle cuisine chefs prominently featured it in their mixes of strawberry, banana, melon and pineapples. Since that time, the question asked most commonly of Frieda's, Inc. is "What will be the next kiwifruit?"

The answer is that there will never be another kiwifruit. When the kiwifruit was accepted into the world's fruit vernacular, there was an unconditional paradigm shift. Today, new specialty produce does not have to go through the rigorous acceptance process inflicted on the kiwifruit. There can never be another kiwifruit because the marketing climate and consumer palate have shifted in a wonderful, irreversible way. Now when a new fruit like red bananas or yellow seedless watermelon comes onto the market, the consuming public does not react with fear and say "Bananas are supposed to be yellow" or "It really isn't watermelon if there aren't any seeds and it's not red." They respond with positive open minds (much the same as Frieda did when she purchased her first flat of kiwifruit in 1962) and a newfound knowledge that new foods will bring quality and variety, not discord, to their diets.

KAREN CAPLAN, Frieda's eldest daughter and President of Frieda's Inc.

▶ PROCEDURE FOR PITTING AND CUTTING MANGOES

1 Cut along each side of the pit to remove two sections.

2 Each section can then be cubed using the "hedgehog" technique: Make crosswise cuts through the flesh, just to the skin; press up on the skin side of the section, exposing the cubes.

3 The mango may be served like this, or the cubes can be cut off to use in salads or other dishes.

PAPAYAS

Papayas

The papaya (puh-PIE-yuh) is a greenish-yellow fruit shaped rather like a large pear and weighing 1–2 pounds (500–1000 grams). When halved, it resembles a melon. The flesh is golden to reddish-pink; its center cavity is filled with round, silver-black seeds resembling caviar. Ripe papayas can be eaten raw, with only a squirt of lemon or lime juice. They can also be puréed for sweet or spicy sauces, chilled soups or sorbets.

Papayas contain **papain,** which breaks down proteins, and therefore papayas are an excellent meat tenderizer. Meats can be marinated with papaya juice or slices before cooking. Papain, however, makes fresh papayas unsuitable for use in gelatins because it inhibits gelling. Unripe (green) papayas are often used in pickles or chutneys, and can be baked or stewed with meat or poultry.

▶ **papain** an enzyme found in papayas that breaks down proteins; used as the primary ingredient in many commercial meat tenderizers

Papaya seeds are edible, with a peppery flavor and slight crunch. They are occasionally used to garnish fruit salads or add flavor to fruit salsas and compotes.

Papayas are grown in tropical and subtropical areas worldwide. Although they are available year-round, their peak season is from April through June. Select papayas that are plump, with a smooth, unblemished skin. Color is a better determinant of ripeness than is softness: The greater the proportion of yellow to green skin color, the riper the fruit. Papayas may be held at room temperature until completely ripe, then refrigerated for up to one week.

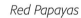

Red Papayas

PASSION FRUITS

Passion fruits (Fr. *granadillas*) have a firm, almost shell-like purple skin with orange-yellow pulp surrounding large, black, edible seeds. They are about the size and shape of large hen eggs, with a sweet, rich and unmistakable citrusy flavor. The pulp is used in custards, sauces and ice creams.

Passion Fruits

Select heavy fruits with dark, shriveled skin and a strong aroma. Allow them to ripen at room temperature, if necessary, then refrigerate. Passion fruits are now grown in New Zealand, Hawaii and California and should be available all year, although their peak season is in February and March. Bottles or frozen packs of purée are readily available and provide a strong, true flavor.

PINEAPPLES

Pineapples (Fr. *ananas*) are the fruit of a shrub with sharp spear-shaped leaves. Each fruit is covered with rough, brown eyes, giving it the appearance of a pine cone. The pale yellow flesh, which is sweet and very juicy, surrounds a cylindrical woody core that is edible but too tough for most uses. Most pineapples weigh approximately 2 pounds (1 kilogram), but dwarf varieties are also available.

Pineapples are excellent eaten raw, alone or in salads. Slices can be baked or grilled to accompany pork or ham. The cuisines of Southeast Asia incorporate pineapple into various curries, soups and stews. Pineapple juice is a popular beverage, often used in punch or cocktails. Canned or cooked pineapple can be added to gelatin mixtures, but avoid using fresh pineapple; an enzyme (bromelin) found in fresh pineapple breaks down gelatin.

Pineapples do not ripen after harvesting. They must be left on the stem until completely ripe, at which time they are extremely perishable. The vast majority of pineapples come from Hawaii. Fresh pineapples are available all year, with peak supplies in March through June. Select heavy fruits with a strong, sweet aroma and rich color. Avoid those with dried leaves or soft spots. Pineapples should be used as soon as possible after purchase. Pineapples are also available canned in slices, cubes or crushed, dried or candied.

▶ PROCEDURE FOR TRIMMING AND SLICING PINEAPPLES

1 Slice off the leaves and stem end. Stand the fruit upright and cut the peel off in vertical strips.

2 Cut the peeled fruit in quarters, then cut away the woody core.

3 The flesh can then be cut as desired.

▶ NUTRITION

Most fruits are quite nutritious. They have a high water content (usually 75 to 95 percent) and low protein and fat contents, all of which makes them low in calories. They are also an excellent source of fiber, and the sugar content of ripe fruits is a good source of energy. Some fruits, such as citrus, melons and strawberries, contain large amounts of vitamin C (which may be destroyed, however, by cooking or processing). Deep yellow and green fruits, such as apricots, mangoes and kiwis, are high in vitamin A; bananas, raisins and figs are a good source of potassium.

▶ PURCHASING FRESH FRUITS

Fresh fruits have not been subjected to any processing (such as canning, freezing or drying). Fresh fruits may be ripe or unripe, depending on their condition when harvested or the conditions under which they have been stored. In order to use fresh fruits to their best advantage, it is important to make careful purchasing decisions. The size of each piece of fruit, its grade or quality, its ripeness on delivery and its nutritional content may affect your ability to use the fruit in an appropriate and cost-effective manner.

GRADING

Fresh fruits traded on the wholesale market may be graded under the USDA's voluntary program. The grades, based on size and uniformity of shape, color and texture as well as the absence of defects, are U.S. Fancy, U.S. No. 1, U.S. No. 2 and U.S. No. 3. Most fruits purchased for food service operations are U.S. Fancy. Fruits with lower grades are suitable for processing into sauces, jams, jellies or preserves.

RIPENING

Several important changes take place in a fruit as it ripens. The fruit reaches its full size; its pulp or flesh becomes soft and tender; its color changes. In addition, the fruit's acid content declines, making it less tart, and its starch content converts into the sugars fructose and glucose, which provide the fruit's sweetness, flavor and aroma.

Unfortunately, these changes do not stop when the fruit reaches its peak of ripeness. Rather, they continue, deteriorating the fruit's texture and flavor and eventually causing spoilage.

Depending upon the species, fresh fruits can be purchased either fully ripened or unripened. Figs and pineapples, for example, ripen only on the plant and are harvested at or just before their peak of ripeness, then rushed to market. They should not be purchased unripened as they will never attain full flavor or texture after harvesting. On the other hand, some fruits, including bananas and pears, continue to ripen after harvesting and can be purchased unripened.

With most harvested fruits, the ripening time as well as the time during which the fruits remain at their peak of ripeness can be manipulated. For instance, ripening can be delayed by chilling. Chilling slows down the fruit's **respiration rate** (fruits, like animals, consume oxygen and expel carbon dioxide). The slower the respiration rate, the slower the conversion of starch to sugar. For quicker ripening, fruit can be stored at room temperature.

Ripening is also affected by ethylene gas, a colorless, odorless hydrocarbon gas. Ethylene gas is naturally emitted by ripening fruits and can be used to encourage further ripening in most fruits. Apples, tomatoes, melons and bananas

▶ **respiration rate** the speed with which the cells of a fruit use up oxygen and produce carbon dioxide during ripening give off the most ethylene and should be stored away from delicate fruits and vegetables, especially greens. Fruits that are picked and shipped unripened can be exposed to ethylene gas to induce ripening just before sale. Conversely, if you want to extend the life of ripe fruits a day or two, isolate them from other fruits and keep them well chilled.

Fresh fruits will not ripen further once they are cooked or processed. The cooking or processing method applied, however, may soften the fruits or add flavor.

PURCHASING

Fresh fruits are sold by weight or by count. They are packed in containers referred to as crates, bushels, cartons, cases, lugs or flats. The weight or count packed in each of these containers varies depending on the type of fruit, the purveyor and the state in which the fruits were packed. For example, Texas citrus is packed in cartons equal to $7/10$ of a bushel; Florida citrus is packed in cartons equal to $4/5$ of a bushel. Sometimes fruit size must be specified when ordering. A 30-pound case of lemons, for example, may contain 96, 112 or 144 individual lemons, depending on their size.

Some fresh fruits, especially melons, pineapples, peaches and berries, are available trimmed, cleaned, peeled or cut. Sugar and preservatives are sometimes added. They are sold in bulk containers, sometimes packed in water. These items offer a consistent product with a significant reduction in labor costs. The purchase price may be greater than that for fresh fruits, and flavor, freshness and nutritional qualities may suffer somewhat from the processing.

▶ PURCHASING AND STORING PRESERVED FRUITS

Preservation techniques are designed to extend the shelf life of fruits in essentially fresh form. These methods include irradiation, acidulation, canning, freezing and drying. Except for drying, these techniques do not substantially change the fruits' texture or flavor. Canning and freezing can also be used to preserve cooked fruits.

Preserves such as jellies and jams are cooked products and are discussed later in this chapter.

IRRADIATED FRUITS

As described in Chapter 22, Vegetables, some fruits can be subjected to ionizing radiation to destroy parasites, insects and bacteria. The treatment also slows ripening without a noticeable effect on the fruits' flavor and texture. Irradiated fruits must be labeled "treated with radiation," "treated by irradiation" or with the symbol shown in Figure 22.1.

ACIDULATION

Apples, pears, bananas, peaches and other fruits turn brown when cut. Although this browning is commonly attributed to exposure to oxygen, it is actually caused by the reaction of enzymes.

Enzymatic browning can be retarded by immersing cut fruits in an acidic solution such as lemon or orange juice. This simple technique is sometimes referred to as **acidulation.** Soaking fruits in water or lemon juice and water (called acidulated water) is not recommended. Unless a sufficient amount of salt or sugar is added to the water, the fruits will just become mushy. But if enough salt or sugar is added to retain texture, the flavor will be affected.

CANNED FRUITS

Almost any type of fruit can be canned successfully; pineapple and peaches are the largest sellers. In commercial canning, raw fruits are cleaned and placed in a sealed container, then subjected to high temperatures for a specific amount of time. Heating destroys the microorganisms that cause spoilage, and the sealed environment created by the can eliminates oxidation and retards decomposition. But the heat required by the canning process also softens the texture of most fruits. Canning has little or no effect on vitamins A, B, C and D because oxygen is not present during the heating process. Canning also has no practical effect on proteins, fats or carbohydrates.

In *solid pack* cans, little or no water is added. The only liquid is from the fruits' natural moisture. *Water pack* cans have water or fruit juice added, which must be taken into account when determining costs. *Syrup pack* cans have a sugar syrup—light, medium or heavy—added. The syrup should also be taken into account when determining food costs, and the additional sweetness should be considered when using syrup-packed fruits. Cooked fruit products such as pie fillings are also available canned.

Canned fruits are purchased in cases of standard-sized cans (see Appendix II). Once a can is opened, any unused contents should be transferred to an appropriate storage container and refrigerated. Cans with bulges should be discarded immediately, without opening.

FROZEN FRUITS

Freezing is a highly effective method for preserving fruits. It severely inhibits the growth of microorganisms that cause fruits to spoil. Freezing does not destroy nutrients, although the appearance or texture of most fruits can be affected because of their high water content. This occurs when ice crystals formed from the water in the cells burst the cells' walls.

Golden Raisins

Currants

Many fruits, especially berries and apple and pear slices, are now individually quick-frozen (IQF). This method employs blasts of cold air, refrigerated plates, liquid nitrogen, liquid air or other techniques to chill the produce quickly. Speeding the freezing process can greatly reduce the formation of ice crystals.

Fruits can be trimmed and sliced before freezing and are also available frozen in sugar syrup, which adds flavor and prevents browning. Berries are frozen whole, while stone fruits are usually peeled, pitted and sliced. Fruit purées are also available frozen.

Kiwis

Apricots

Frozen fruits are graded as U.S. Grade A (Fancy), U.S. Grade B (Choice or Extra Standard), or U.S. Grade C (Standard). The "U.S." indicates that a government inspector has graded the product, but packers may use grade names without an actual inspection if the contents meet the standards of the grade indicated.

IQF fruits can be purchased in bulk by the case. All frozen fruits should be sealed in moistureproof wrapping and kept at a constant temperature of 0°F (−18°C) or below. Temperature fluctuations can cause freezer burn.

Persimmons

Apples

DRIED FRUITS

Drying is the oldest known technique for preserving fruits, having been used for more than 5000 years. When ripe fruits are dried, they lose most of their moisture. This concentrates their flavors and sugars and dramatically extends shelf life. Although most fruits can be dried, plums (prunes), grapes (raisins, sultanas and currants), apricots and figs are the fruits most commonly dried. The drying method can

Pears

be as simple as leaving ripe fruits in the sun to dry naturally or the more cost-efficient technique of passing fruits through a compartment of hot, dry air to quickly extract moisture.

Dried fruits actually retain from 16 to 25 percent residual moisture, which leaves them moist and soft. They are often treated with sulfur dioxide to prevent browning (oxidation) and to extend shelf life. Dried fruits may be eaten out of hand; added to cereals or salads; baked in muffins, breads, pies or tarts; stewed for chutneys or compotes or used as a stuffing for roasted meats or poultry. Before use, dried fruits may be softened by steeping them for a short time in a hot liquid such as water, wine, rum, brandy or other liquor. Some dried fruits should be simmered in a small amount of water before use.

Store dried fruits in airtight containers to prevent further moisture loss; keep in a dry, cool area away from sunlight. Dried fruits may mold if exposed to both air and high humidity.

▶ JUICING

▶ **juice** the liquid extracted from any fruit or vegetable

▶ **nectar** the diluted, sweetened juice of peaches, apricots, guavas, black currants or other fruits, the juice of which would be too thick or too tart to drink straight

▶ **cider** mildly fermented apple juice; nonalcoholic apple juice may also be labeled cider

Fruit juice is used as a beverage, alone or mixed with other ingredients, and as the liquid ingredient in other preparations. Juice can be extracted from fruits (and some vegetables) in two ways: pressure and blending.

Pressure is used to extract juice from fruits such as citrus that have a high water content. Pressure is applied by hand-squeezing or with a manual or electric reamer. All reamers work on the same principle: A ribbed cone is pressed against the fruit to break down its flesh and release the juice. Always strain juices to remove seeds, pulp or fibrous pieces.

A blender or an electric juice extractor can be used to liquify less-juicy fruits and vegetables such as apples, carrots, tomatoes, beets and cabbage. The extractor pulverizes the fruit or vegetable, then separates and strains the liquid from the pulp with centrifugal force.

Interesting and delicious beverages can be made by combining the juice of one or more fruits or vegetables: pineapple with orange, apple with cranberry, strawberry with tangerine and papaya with orange. Color should be considered when creating mixed-juice beverages, however. Some combinations can cause rather odd color changes. Although yellow and orange juices are not a problem, those containing red and blue flavonoid pigments (such as Concord grapes, cherries, strawberries, raspberries and blueberries) can create some unappetizing colors. Adding an acid such as lemon juice helps retain the correct red and blue hues.

▶ APPLYING VARIOUS COOKING METHODS

Although most fruits are edible raw and typically served that way, some fruits can also be cooked. Commonly used cooking methods are broiling and grilling, baking, sautéing, deep-frying, poaching, simmering and preserving.

When cooking fruits, proper care and attention are critical. Even minimal cooking can render fruits overly soft or mushy. To combat this irreversible process, sugar can be added. When fruits are cooked with sugar, the sugar will be absorbed slowly into the cells, firming the fruits. Acids (notably lemon juice) also help fruits retain their structure. (Alkalis, such as baking soda, cause the cells to break down more quickly, reducing the fruits to mush.)

DETERMINING DONENESS

There are so many different fruits with such varied responses to cooking that no one standard for doneness is appropriate. Each item should be evaluated on a recipe-by-recipe basis. Generally, however, most cooked fruits are done when they are just tender when pierced with a fork or the tip of a paring knife. Simmered fruits, such as compotes, should be softer, cooked just to the point of disintegration.

You can avoid overcooking fruits by remembering that some carryover cooking will occur through the residual heat contained in the foods. Always rely on subjective tests—sight, feel, taste and aroma—rather than the clock.

DRY-HEAT COOKING METHODS

BROILING AND GRILLING

Fruits are usually broiled or grilled just long enough to caramelize sugars; cooking must be done quickly in order to avoid breaking down the fruits' structure. Good fruits to broil or grill are pineapples, apples, grapefruits, bananas, persimmons and peaches. The fruits may be cut into slices, chunks or halves as appropriate. A coating of sugar, honey or liqueur adds flavor, as do lemon juice, cinnamon and ginger.

When broiling fruits, use an oiled sheet pan or broiling platter. When grilling fruits, use a clean grill grate or thread the pieces onto skewers. Only thick fruit slices will need to be turned or rotated to heat fully. Broiled or grilled fruits can be served alone, as an accompaniment to meat, fish or poultry or as topping for ice creams or custards.

▶ PROCEDURE FOR BROILING OR GRILLING FRUITS

1 Select ripe fruits and peel, core or slice as necessary.

2 Top with sugar or honey to add flavor and aid caramelization.

3 Place the fruits on the broiler platter, sheet pan or grill grate.

4 Broil or grill at high temperatures, turning as necessary to heat the fruits thoroughly but quickly.

  BROILED GRAPEFRUIT   RECIPE 25.1

Yield: 8 Servings		**Method:** Broiling
Ruby grapefruits	4	4
Sweet sherry	2 Tbsp.	30 ml
Brown sugar	4 Tbsp.	60 ml

1 Cut each grapefruit in half (perpendicular to the segments), then section with a sharp knife, carefully removing any visible seeds.

2 Sprinkle the grapefruit halves with the sherry and sugar.

3 Arrange on a baking sheet and place under a preheated broiler. Cook briefly, only until well heated and the sugar caramelizes. Serve immediately.

Approximate values per serving: **Calories** 70, **Total fat** 0 g, **Saturated fat** 0 g, **Cholesterol** 0 mg, **Sodium** 0 mg, **Total carbohydrates** 16 g, **Protein** 1 g, **Vitamin C** 80%, **Claims**—fat free; no sodium

BAKING

After washing, peeling, coring or pitting, most pomes, stone fruits and tropicals can be baked to create hot, flavorful desserts. Fruits with sturdy skins, particularly apples and pears, are excellent for baking alone, as their skin (peel) holds in moisture and flavor. They can also be used as edible containers by filling the cavity left by coring with a variety of sweet or savory mixtures.

Combinations of fruits can also be baked successfully; try mixing fruits for a balance of sweetness and tartness (for example, strawberries with rhubarb or apples with plums).

Several baked desserts are simply fruits (fresh, frozen or canned) topped with a crust (called a *cobbler*), strudel (called a *crumple* or *crisp*) or batter (called a *buckle*). Fruits, sometimes poached first, can also be baked in a wrapper of puff pastry, flaky dough or phyllo dough to produce an elegant dessert.

▶ PROCEDURE FOR BAKING FRUITS

1 Select ripe but firm fruits and peel, core, pit or slice as necessary.
2 Add sugar or any flavorings.
3 Wrap the fruits in pastry dough if desired or directed in the recipe.
4 Place the fruits in a baking dish and bake uncovered in a moderate oven until tender or properly browned.

RECIPE 25.2 BAKED APPLES

Yield: 8 Servings **Method:** Baking

Apples, Red or Golden Delicious	8	8
Raisins	6 oz.	180 g
Orange zest	1½ Tbsp.	23 g
Brown sugar	4 oz.	120 g

1 Rinse and core each apple. The peels should be scored or partially removed to allow the pulp to expand without bursting the skin during baking.
2 Plump the raisins by soaking them in boiling water for 10 minutes. Drain the raisins thoroughly.
3 Combine the raisins, orange zest and brown sugar. Fill the cavity of each apple with this mixture.
4 Stand the apples in a shallow baking dish. Add enough water to measure about ½ inch (1.2 centimeters) deep.
5 Bake the apples at 375°F (190°C) for 15 minutes. Reduce the temperature to 300°F (150°C) and continue baking until the apples are tender but still hold their shape, approximately 1 hour. Occasionally, baste the apples with liquid from the baking dish.

Approximate values per apple: **Calories** 220, **Total fat** 0.5 g, **Saturated fat** 0 g, **Cholesterol** 0 mg, **Sodium** 10 mg, **Total carbohydrates** 52 g, **Protein** 1 g, **Vitamin C** 15%, **Claims**—low fat, no cholesterol, very low sodium, good source of fiber

SAUTÉING

Fruits develop a rich, syrupy flavor when sautéed briefly in butter, sugar and, if desired, spices or liqueur. Cherries, bananas, apples, pears and pineapples are good choices. They should be peeled, cored and seeded as necessary and cut into uniform-size pieces before sautéing.

For dessert, fruits are sautéed with sugar to create a caramelized glaze or syrup. The fruits and syrup can be used to fill crêpes or to top spongecakes or ice creams. Liquor may be added and the mixture flamed (flambéed) in front of diners, as with Bananas Foster (page 818).

For savory mixtures, onions, shallots or garlic are often added.

In both sweet and savory fruit sautés, the fat used should be the most appropriate for the finished product. Butter and bacon fat are typical choices.

▶ PROCEDURE FOR SAUTÉING FRUITS

1 Peel, pit and core the fruits as necessary and cut into uniform-size pieces.
2 Melt the fat in a hot sauté pan.

3 Add the fruit pieces and any flavoring ingredients. Do not crowd the pan, as this will cause the fruit to stew in its own juices.

4 Cook quickly over high heat.

SAVORY FRUIT

RECIPE 25.3

Yield: 1 pt. (500 ml)	**Method:** Sautéing	
Onions, fine dice	6 oz.	180 g
Whole butter or bacon fat	1 oz.	30 g
Apples (tart) or peaches, peeled	3	3
Apricots	3	3
Granulated sugar	4 oz.	120 g
Hot paprika	TT	TT
Salt and white pepper	TT	TT

1 Sweat the onions in the butter or bacon fat without browning.

2 Slice the apples or peaches and apricots into thin, even pieces. Add the apples to the onions and cook for 1–2 minutes. Add the apricots.

3 Sprinkle the sugar over the fruits and cook, uncovered, over medium heat until tender. Season with paprika, salt and white pepper.

4 Serve warm as an accompaniment to roast pork, game or other meat.

Approximate values per 1-oz. (30-g) serving: **Calories** 60, **Total fat** 1.5 g, **Saturated fat** 1 g, **Cholesterol** 5 mg, **Sodium** 50 mg, **Total carbohydrates** 12 g, **Protein** 0 g, Vitamin A 4%, **Claims**—low fat; low cholesterol; low sodium

DEEP-FRYING

Few fruits are suitable for deep-frying. Apples, bananas, pears, pineapples and firm peaches mixed in or coated with batter, however, produce fine results. These fruits should be peeled, cored, seeded and cut into evenly sized slices or chunks. They may also need to be dried with paper towels so that the batter or coating can adhere.

Fruit fritters are also a popular snack or dessert item. Fritters contain diced or chopped fish, shellfish, vegetables or fruits bound together with a thick batter and deep-fried. Because frying time is very short, the main ingredient is usually precooked. Fritters are spooned or dropped directly into the hot fat; they form a crust as they cook. Popular examples are clam fritters, corn fritters, artichoke fritters and apple fritters.

▶ PROCEDURE FOR DEEP-FRYING FRUIT—FRITTERS

1 Cut, chop and otherwise prepare the food to be made into fritters.

2 Precook any ingredients if necessary.

3 Prepare the batter as directed.

4 Scoop the fritters into deep fat at 350°F (180°C), using the swimming method.

5 Cook until done. The fritters should be golden brown on the outside and moist but set on the inside.

6 Remove the fritters from the fat and hold them over the fryer, allowing the excess fat to drain off. Transfer the food to a hotel pan either lined with absorbent paper or fitted with a rack. Serve hot.

7 If the fritters are to be held for later service, place them under a heat lamp.

RECIPE 25.4   **APPLE FRITTERS**

Yield: 100 Fritters, 2 in. (5 cm) each		**Method:** Deep-frying
Eggs, separated	6	6
Milk	1 pt.	500 ml
Flour	1 lb.	450 g
Baking powder	1 Tbsp.	15 ml
Salt	1 tsp.	5 ml
Sugar	2 oz.	60 g
Cinnamon, ground	½ tsp.	2 ml
Apples, peeled, cored, medium dice	1 lb. 8 oz.	700 g
Powdered sugar	as needed	as needed

1 Combine the egg yolks and milk.
2 Sift together the flour, baking powder, salt, sugar and cinnamon. Add the dry ingredients to the milk-and-egg mixture; mix until smooth.
3 Allow the batter to rest 1 hour.
4 Stir the apples into the batter.
5 Just before the fritters are to be cooked, whip the egg whites to soft peaks and fold into the batter.
6 Scoop the fritters into deep fat at 350°F (180°C), using the swimming method. Cook until done.
7 Dust with powdered sugar and serve hot.

Variation: *Banana Fritters*—Omit the cinnamon and apples. Add 3 tablespoons (45 milliliters) of finely grated orange zest, 4 fluid ounces (120 milliliters) of orange juice and 2 large bananas, peeled and diced (not puréed).

Approximate values per fritter: **Calories** 60, **Total fat** 4 g, **Saturated fat** 1 g, **Cholesterol** 15 mg, **Sodium** 5 mg, **Total carbohydrates** 6 g, **Protein** 1 g

1 Adding the dry ingredients to the liquids.

2 Folding the egg whites into the batter.

3 Dropping the fritters into the deep fat.

4 Dusting the fritters with powdered sugar.

MOIST-HEAT COOKING METHODS

POACHING

One of the more popular cooking methods for fruits is poaching. Poaching softens and tenderizes fruits and infuses them with additional flavors such as spices or wine. Poached fruits can be served hot or cold and used in tarts or pastries or as an accompaniment to meat or poultry dishes.

The poaching liquid can be water, wine, liquor or sugar syrup. (As noted earlier, sugar helps fruits keep their shape, although it takes longer to tenderize fruits poached in sugar syrup.) The low poaching temperature (185°F/85°C)

allows fruits to soften gradually. The agitation created at higher temperatures would damage them.

Cooked fruits should be allowed to cool in the flavored poaching liquid or syrup. Most poaching liquids can be used repeatedly. If they contain sufficient sugar, they can be reduced to a sauce or glaze to accompany the poached fruits.

▶ PROCEDURE FOR POACHING FRUITS

1 Peel, core and slice the fruits as necessary.

2 In a sufficiently deep, nonreactive saucepan, combine the poaching liquid (usually water or wine) with sugar, spices, citrus zest and other ingredients as desired or as directed in the recipe.

3 Submerge the fruits in the liquid. Place a circle of parchment paper over the fruits to help them stay submerged.

4 Place the saucepan on the stove top over a medium-high flame; bring to a boil.

5 As soon as the liquid boils, reduce the temperature. Simmer gently.

6 Poach until the fruits are tender enough for the tip of a small knife to be easily inserted. Cooking time depends on the type of fruit used, its ripeness and the cooking liquid.

7 Remove the saucepan from the stove top and allow the liquid and fruits to cool.

8 Remove the fruits from the liquid and then refrigerate. The liquid can be returned to the stove top and reduced until thick enough to use as a sauce or glaze or refrigerated for further use.

PEARS POACHED IN RED WINE

RECIPE 25.5

Yield: 8 Servings   **Method:** Poaching

Ripe pears, Anjou or Bartlett	8	8
Zinfandel wine	52 fl. oz.	1500 ml
Whole peppercorns	8–10	8–10
Vanilla bean	1	1
Granulated sugar	12 oz.	340 g
Fresh basil, chopped	1 oz.	30 g
Orange zest	from 1 orange	from 1 orange

1 Peel and core the pears, leaving the stems intact.

2 Combine the remaining ingredients in a large nonreactive saucepan. Arrange the pears in the liquid in a single layer.

3 Place the pears on the stove top over a medium-high flame. Bring to just below a boil, then immediately reduce the heat and allow the liquid to simmer gently. Cover with a round of parchment paper if necessary to keep the pears submerged.

4 Continue poaching the pears until tender, approximately 1 to 1½ hours. Remove the saucepan from the stove and allow the pears to cool in the liquid.

5 Remove the pears from the poaching liquid and return the liquid to the stove top. Reduce until the liquid is thick enough to coat the back of a spoon, then strain.

6 Serve the pears chilled or at room temperature in a pool of the reduced wine syrup.

Approximate values per 7-oz. (210-g) serving: **Calories** 410, **Total fat** 1.5 g, **Saturated fat** 0 g, **Cholesterol** 0 mg, **Sodium** 35 mg, **Total carbohydrates** 91 g, **Protein** 6 g, **Vitamin A** 40%, **Calcium** 90%, **Iron** 110%, **Claims**—low fat; no cholesterol; low sodium; high fiber

SIMMERING

Simmering techniques are used to make stewed fruits and compotes. Fresh, frozen, canned and dried fruits can be simmered or stewed. As with any moist-heat cooking method, simmering softens and tenderizes fruits. The liquid used can be water, wine or the juices naturally found in the fruits. Sugar, honey and spices may be added as desired. Stewed or simmered fruits can be served hot or cold, as a first course, a dessert or an accompaniment to meat or poultry dishes.

▶ PROCEDURE FOR SIMMERING FRUITS

1 Peel, core, pit and slice the fruits as necessary.
2 Bring the fruits and cooking liquid, if used, to a simmer. Cook until the fruit is tender.
3 Add sugar or other sweeteners as desired or as directed in the recipe.

RECIPE 25.6

DRIED FRUIT COMPOTE

Yield: 2 lb. (1 kg)   **Method:** Simmering

Dried apricots	5 oz.	150 g
Prunes, pitted	5 oz.	150 g
Dried pears or apples	5 oz.	150 g
Dried peaches	5 oz.	150 g
Water, hot	24 fl. oz.	720 ml
Cinnamon stick	1	1
Light corn syrup	12 fl. oz.	360 ml
Cointreau	2 fl. oz.	60 ml

1 Coarsely chop the fruits. Place the pieces in a nonreactive saucepan and add the water and cinnamon stick.
2 Bring the mixture to a simmer, cover and cook until tender, approximately 12–15 minutes.
3 Add the corn syrup and Cointreau. Simmer uncovered until thoroughly heated. Serve warm or refrigerate for longer storage.

Approximate values per 1-oz. (30-g) serving: **Calories** 60, **Total fat** 0 g, **Saturated fat** 0 g, **Cholesterol** 0 mg, **Sodium** 15 mg, **Total carbohydrates** 15 g, **Protein** 0 g, **Claims**—fat free; very low sodium

Apple Jelly   *Apricot Jam*

Orange Marmalade

▶ **concentrate** also known as a fruit paste or compound; a reduced fruit purée, without a gel structure, used as a flavoring

▶ **jam** a fruit gel made from fruit pulp and sugar

▶ **jelly** a fruit gel made from fruit juice and sugar

▶ **marmalade** a citrus jelly that also contains unpeeled slices of citrus fruit

▶ **preserve** a fruit gel that contains large pieces or whole fruits

PRESERVING

Fresh fruits can be preserved with sugar if the fruit and sugar mixture is concentrated by evaporation to the point that microbial spoilage cannot occur. The added sugar also retards the growth of, but does not destroy, microorganisms.

Pectin, a substance present in varying amounts in all fruits, can cause cooked fruits to form a semisolid mass known as a **gel.** Fruits that are visually unattractive but otherwise of high quality can be made into gels, which are more commonly known as **jams, jellies, marmalades** and **preserves.**

The essential ingredients of a fruit gel are fruit, pectin, acid (usually lemon juice) and sugar. They must be carefully combined in the correct ratio for the gel to form. For fruits with a low pectin content (such as strawberries) to form a gel, pectin must be added, either by adding a fruit with a high pectin content (for example, apples or quinces) or by adding packaged pectin.

Fruits, whether fresh, frozen, canned or dried, are one of the most versatile and popular of foods. Fruits can be used uncooked or incorporated into a soup, salad, bread, meat dish or dessert. When selecting fresh fruits, it is important to consider seasonal availability, storage conditions and ripeness. When using them, it is important that they be at their peak of ripeness for the best flavor, texture, aroma and appearance.

CONCLUSION

QUESTIONS FOR DISCUSSION

1 Define ripeness and explain why ripe fruits are most desirable. How does the ripening process affect the availability of some fruits?

2 Describe the proper storage conditions for most fruits. Which fruits emit ethylene gas, and why is this a consideration when storing fruits?

3 Explain why some apple varieties are preferred for cooking, while other varieties are preferred for eating. Which variety is generally preferred for making applesauce?

4 Which types of fruits are best for dry-heat cooking methods? Explain your answer. Why is sugar usually added when cooking any type of fruit?

5 List and describe three ways to prepare fruits for extended storage.

6 Research a tropical or exotic fruit that is not available in your local area. Where is this fruit originally from? How is it eaten or used in cooking? What challenges face producers and importers in bringing this fruit to market in the United States?

RECIPE 25.7

BANANAS FOSTER

Note: This dish appears in the chapter opening photograph.

BRENNAN'S RESTAURANT, NEW ORLEANS, LA
Chef Michael Roussel

BRENNAN'S RESTAURANT

After World War II, Owen Edward Brennan, then owner of the French Quarter's Old Absinthe House Saloon, became determined to have the best French and Creole restaurant in New Orleans. Many believe that he succeeded when, in 1946, he opened Brennan's Restaurant on Bourbon Street. This culinary Mecca served breakfast, lunch and dinner to Hollywood stars, national politicians, syndicated columnists and assorted celebrities. Owen's personal success was cut short by his sudden death in 1955, just before Brennan's Restaurant moved into a renovated mansion on Royal Street.

Still located at 417 Royal Street, Brennan's now features 12 elegantly decorated dining rooms with some 550 seats, and the mansion's former slave quarters houses an award-winning wine cellar. Owen's three sons—Pip, Jimmy and Ted—remain the sole owners and operators of their father's world-famous restaurant.

Owen Brennan is credited with popularizing the concept of a formal breakfast in a public restaurant through his "Breakfast at Brennan's" promotion. Not a traditional juice-and-toast meal, however, a typical Brennan's breakfast begins with a gin fizz and includes lamb chops with béarnaise, champagne, shrimp rémoulade, hot French bread, bread pudding and café diable. Through the years, Brennan's chefs have created and popularized some of this country's best known dishes: Eggs Hussarde, Oysters 2-2-2, Crêpes Fitzgerald (strawberry) and Bananas Foster.

Chef Paul Blangé was the ingenious creator of many of Brennan's signature dishes. Today, Chef Michael Roussel maintains Brennan's rich culinary traditions from the kitchen he has called home for 43 years.

Bananas Foster was created in 1951 by Brennan's chef Paul Blangé to promote New Orleans' role as the major port of entry for bananas arriving from Central and South America. The dish was named for Richard Foster, chairman of the New Orleans Crime Commission, a civic group working to clean up the French Quarter. Foster was a good friend to Owen Edward Brennan and a frequent customer at his restaurant. Today Brennan's flambés some 35,000 pounds of bananas each year for this world-famous dessert.

Yield: 4 Servings		**Method:** Sautéing
Whole butter	2 oz.	60 g
Brown sugar	8 oz.	225 g
Cinnamon, ground	½ tsp.	3 g
Banana liqueur	2 fl. oz.	60 ml
Bananas, cut into quarters	4	4
White rum	2 fl. oz.	60 ml
Vanilla ice cream	4 scoops	4 scoops

1 Combine the butter, sugar and cinnamon in a sauté or flambé pan. Cook over low heat, stirring until the sugar dissolves.

2 Stir in the banana liqueur, then place the bananas in the pan. When the bananas soften and begin to brown, carefully add the rum.

3 Continue to cook until the rum is hot, then tip the pan slightly to ignite the rum. When the flames subside, lift the bananas out of the pan and place 4 pieces over each portion of ice cream. Spoon the warm sauce over the ice cream and serve immediately.

Approximate values per serving: **Calories** 640, **Total fat** 23 g, **Saturated fat** 14 g, **Cholesterol** 70 mg, **Sodium** 65 mg, **Total carbohydrates** 103 g, **Protein** 4 g, **Vitamin A** 20%, **Vitamin C** 20%, **Calcium** 15%, **Iron** 10%, **Claims**—good source of fiber, vitamins A and C, calcium and iron

FIGS WITH BERRIES AND HONEY MOUSSE

RECIPE 25.8

GREENS, SAN FRANCISCO, CA
Chef Annie Somerville

Yield: 4 Servings

Raspberries or blackberries	1 pt.	450 ml
Fresh figs such as Black Mission, Kadota or Calmyrna	1 pt.	450 ml
Honey	6 oz.	180 g
Egg yolks	4	4
Salt	TT	TT
Heavy cream	1 pt.	450 ml
Fresh mint	as needed for garnish	

1 Pick through the berries, but do not rinse them because water will dilute their flavor.

2 Rinse the figs and cut them in half, leaving the stem attached.

3 To make the mousse, whisk the honey, yolks and salt together in a bowl over a pan of barely simmering water. Whisk the mixture continuously for 8 minutes. After 5 minutes, the mousse will begin to thicken and the texture will become creamy. Whisk vigorously until the mousse leaves thick ribbons on its surface when poured over itself. Set aside to cool. The texture of the cooled mousse will be stiff and sticky.

4 Whisk 2 tablespoons (30 milliliters) of cream into the mousse, working it until it loosens.

5 Whip the remaining cream until it is firm, fold it into the mousse until it is just incorporated, then whisk the two together. The texture will be light and creamy.

6 Loosely arrange the figs on a platter, sprinkle with the berries, garnish with mint and serve with the mousse.

Approximate values per serving: **Calories** 680, **Total fat** 47 g, **Saturated fat** 28 g, **Cholesterol** 370 mg, **Sodium** 200 mg, **Total carbohydrates** 57 g, **Protein** 6 g, **Vitamin A** 60%, **Vitamin C** 25%

PINEAPPLE PAPAYA SALSA

RECIPE 25.9

Yield: 2 qt. (2 lt)

Tomatoes	3	3
Fresh pineapple	1	1
Fresh papaya	1	1
Green onions, sliced	1 bunch	1 bunch
Fresh cilantro, chopped	1 bunch	1 bunch
Jalapeños, seeded, minced	2	2
Lemon juice	3 Tbsp.	45 ml
Garlic, chopped	1 tsp.	5 ml
Salt	2 tsp.	10 ml

1 Core and dice the tomatoes.

2 Peel and dice the pineapple.

3 Peel, seed and dice the papaya.

4 Combine all the ingredients and chill well.

Approximate values per 1-oz. (30-g) serving: **Calories** 25, **Total fat** 0 g, **Saturated fat** 0 g, **Cholesterol** 0 mg, **Sodium** 330 mg, **Total carbohydrates** 5 g, **Protein** 0 g, **Vitamin C** 45%, **Claims**—fat free; low calorie

RECIPE 25.10

TROPICAL FRUIT SALAD
WITH YOGURT DRESSING

Yield: 4 Small Salads

Mango, cut into ½-in. (1.2-cm) cubes	6 oz.	180 g
Pineapple, cut into ½-in. (1.2-cm) cubes	6 oz.	180 g
Papaya, cut into ½-in. (1.2-cm) cubes	4 oz.	120 g
Grapefruit segments	16	16
Pineapple or grapefruit juice	2 fl. oz.	60 ml
Plain nonfat yogurt	4 fl. oz.	120 ml
Honey	2 Tbsp.	30 ml
Fresh lime juice	1 Tbsp.	15 ml
Butterhead lettuce, large leaves, separated and cleaned	4	4
Kiwi, peeled and sliced	1	1
Poppy seeds	1 tsp.	5 ml

1 Mix the mango, pineapple, papaya and grapefruit together with the pineapple or grapefruit juice.

2 To make the dressing, whisk the yogurt, honey and lime juice together.

3 Line the plates with the butterhead lettuce. Arrange the kiwi slices and the fruit salad over the lettuce.

4 Drizzle the dressing over the fruits and top with poppy seeds.

Approximate values per 8-oz. (240-g) serving: **Calories** 170, **Total fat** 1 g, **Saturated fat** 0 g, **Cholesterol** 0 mg, **Sodium** 30 mg, **Total carbohydrates** 38 g, **Protein** 3 g, **Vitamin A** 20%, **Vitamin C** 150%, **Claims**—low fat; no cholesterol; very low sodium; good source of fiber

RECIPE 25.11

SWEET RICOTTA AND MASCARPONE
MOUSSE WITH FRESH BERRIES

Yield: 8 Servings

Whole-milk ricotta	24 oz	720 g
Mascarpone	12 oz.	360 g
Sugar	2 oz.	60 g
Orange zest	2 Tbsp.	30 ml
Vanilla extract	1 tsp.	5 ml
Heavy cream	1 pt.	450 ml
Powdered sugar	1 oz.	30 g
Fresh strawberries, cleaned, quartered	1 pt.	450 ml
Fresh raspberries	1 pt.	450 ml
Blackberries	1 pt.	450 ml
Fresh mint	8 sprigs	8 sprigs

1 Process the ricotta, mascarpone and sugar in the bowl of a food processor until smooth and creamy. Transfer to a mixing bowl. Stir the zest and vanilla into the ricotta.

2 Whip the heavy cream with the powdered sugar to stiff peaks.

3 Stir a small amount of the whipped cream into the ricotta mixture to lighten it. Add the remaining whipped cream and gently fold together until well combined.

4 Layer the mousse with the berries in eight large wine glasses. Garnish with berries and a mint sprig. Refrigerate up to 1 hour before serving.

Approximate values per serving: **Calories** 630, **Total fat** 53 g, **Saturated fat** 31 g, **Cholesterol** 180 mg, **Sodium** 120 mg, **Total carbohydrates** 27 g, **Protein** 15 g, **Vitamin A** 40%, **Vitamin C** 70%, **Calcium** 30%

GRATIN OF FRESH BERRIES
WITH CRÈME FRAÎCHE

RECIPE 25.12

Yield: 1 Serving

Assorted fresh berries, such as raspberries, blueberries and blackberries	4 oz.	120 g
Crème fraîche	2 fl. oz.	60 ml
Orange liqueur	1 tsp.	5 ml
Brown sugar	1 Tbsp.	15 ml

1 Arrange the berries in an even layer in a shallow, heatproof serving dish.

2 Stir the crème fraîche and orange liqueur together. Spoon this mixture over the berries.

3 Sprinkle the brown sugar over the crème. Place under a broiler or salamander just until the sugar melts. Serve immediately.

Approximate values per serving: **Calories** 210, **Total fat** 7 g, **Saturated fat** 4 g, **Cholesterol** 20 mg, **Sodium** 30 mg, **Total carbohydrates** 33 g, **Protein** 3 g, **Vitamin C** 40%, **Claims**—very low sodium; high fiber

GRILLED FRUIT KEBABS

RECIPE 25.13

Yield: 8 Skewers   **Method:** Grilling

Cantaloupe	½ melon	½ melon
Honeydew	¼ melon	¼ melon
Pineapple	½	½
Strawberries	8	8
Brown sugar	2 oz.	60 g
Lime juice	4 fl. oz.	120 ml
Cinnamon, ground	¼ tsp.	1 ml

1 Remove the rind and cut the melons and pineapple into 1-inch (2.5-centimeter) cubes. Hull the strawberries and leave whole.

2 To make the sugar glaze, combine the sugar, lime juice and cinnamon, stirring until the sugar dissolves.

3 Heat the grill and clean the grate thoroughly.

4 Thread the fruits onto kebab skewers, alternating colors for an attractive appearance.

5 Brush the fruits with the sugar glaze. Grill, rotating the skewers frequently to develop an evenly light brown surface.

6 Serve immediately as an appetizer, a garnish for ice cream or an accompaniment to rich meats such as pork or lamb.

Approximate values per skewer: **Calories** 70, **Total fat** 0 g, **Saturated fat** 0 g, **Cholesterol** 0 mg, **Sodium** 10 mg, **Total carbohydrates** 16 g, **Protein** 1 g, **Vitamin C** 50%, **Claims**—fat free; very low sodium

CHERRY CONFIT

RECIPE 25.14

Yield: 4 oz. (120 g)

Red onion, small dice	2 Tbsp.	30 ml
Whole butter	2 tsp.	10 ml

Continued

Dried cherries	3 oz.	90 g
Brandy	1 Tbsp.	15 ml
Port	1 Tbsp.	15 ml
Sherry vinegar	½ tsp.	3 ml

1 Sauté the onion in butter without coloring.
2 Add the cherries. Add the brandy and flambé.
3 Add the port and vinegar; cook until almost dry. Serve warm or at room temperature with charcuterie items or grilled or roasted meats.

Approximate values per 1-oz. (30-g) serving: **Calories** 35, **Total fat** 2 g, **Saturated fat** 1 g, **Cholesterol** 5 mg, **Sodium** 20 mg, **Total carbohydrates** 3 g, **Protein** 0 g, **Claims**—low fat; very low sodium; low calorie

---

RECIPE 25.15 **BRAISED RHUBARB**

Yield: 10 lb. (4.5 kg) **Method:** Braising

Tart green apples, peeled and cubed	2 lb. 8 oz.	1.1 kg
Rhubarb, IQF pieces	7 lb.	3.2 kg
Unsalted butter	4 oz.	120 g
Sweet white wine	8 fl. oz.	250 ml
Brown sugar	14 oz.	400 g
Vanilla extract	2 tsp.	10 ml
Cinnamon, ground	1 Tbsp.	15 ml
Nutmeg, ground	¼ tsp.	1 ml
Orange juice	2 fl. oz.	60 ml
Salt	½ tsp.	2 ml

1 Sauté the apples and rhubarb in the butter until they begin to soften.
2 Add the wine and reduce by half. Add the remaining ingredients. Simmer until the rhubarb is very tender.
3 Serve at room temperature in prebaked pastry cups, topped with crème chantilly, or serve warm over ice cream.

Approximate values per 1-oz. (30-g) serving: **Calories** 60, **Total fat** 2 g, **Saturated fat** 0.5 g, **Cholesterol** 0 mg, **Sodium** 25 mg, **Total carbohydrates** 11 g, **Protein** 0 g, **Claims**—low fat; no cholesterol; very low sodium

---

RECIPE 25.16 **BERRY COMPOTE**

Yield: 1 pt. (450 ml) **Method:** Simmering

Berries, fresh or frozen	1 pt.	500 ml
Granulated sugar	4 oz.	120 g
Oranges	2	2
Honey	3 fl. oz.	90 ml
Cinnamon stick	1	1
Brandy	3 Tbsp.	45 ml

1 Select an assortment of fresh or frozen berries—strawberries, blueberries, raspberries, blackberries and cherries can be used, depending on availability.
2 Place the fruits and sugar in a nonreactive saucepan. Add the juice from the two oranges. Bring to a simmer over low heat; cook until the fruits are soft but still intact.

3 Strain the mixture, saving both the fruits and the liquid. Return the liquid to the saucepan. Add the finely grated zest from one orange, the honey, cinnamon and brandy.

4 Bring to a boil and reduce until the mixture thickens enough to coat the back of a spoon. Remove from the heat and cool to room temperature.

5 Gently stir the reserved fruits into the sauce, cover and chill.

Approximate values per 1-oz. (30-g) serving: **Calories** 70, **Total fat** 0 g, **Saturated fat** 0 g, **Cholesterol** 0 mg, **Sodium** 0 mg, **Total carbohydrates** 16 g, **Protein** 0 g, **Vitamin C** 15%, **Claims**—fat free; no sodium

SUN-DRIED FRUIT COMPOTE WITH HONEY ICE CREAM

RECIPE 25.17

BISHOP'S RESTAURANT, Vancouver, BC
Chefs Michael Allemeier and Dennis Green

Yield: 6 Servings   **Method:** Boiling/Steeping

Zinfandel wine	12 fl. oz.	375 ml
Water	1 pt.	500 ml
Granulated sugar	12 oz.	375 g
Sundried fruits, such as apples, cherries and apricots, whole	2 c.	500 ml
Cinnamon stick	1	1
Cloves, whole	2	2
Nutmeg, ground	½ tsp.	3 ml
Vanilla bean	½	½
Black peppercorns	6	6
Fresh ginger, 1-in. (2.5-cm) piece, sliced	1	1
Honey Ice Cream (page 1120)		

1 In a nonreactive saucepan, combine the wine, water, and sugar. Bring to a boil, skim off any scum that forms, and add the fruit and spices.

2 Bring to a boil again, and remove from the heat.

3 Allow the compote to sit for several hours to allow the fruit to absorb some of the syrup.

4 To serve, warm the compote, and top each portion with a scoop of Honey Ice Cream.

Approximate values per 5-oz. (150-g) serving, without ice cream: **Calories** 290, **Total fat** 0 g, **Saturated fat** 0 g, **Cholesterol** 0 mg, **Sodium** 30 mg, **Total carbohydrates** 71 g, **Protein** 1 g, **Claims**—no fat; no cholesterol; very low sodium; good source of fiber

APPLESAUCE

RECIPE 25.18

Yield: 1 qt. (1 lt)   **Method:** Simmering

McIntosh apples	4 lb.	1.8 g
Cinnamon sticks	2	2
Granulated sugar	5 oz.	150 g
Lemon juice	1 Tbsp.	15 ml

1 Peel, core and quarter the apples. Place in a saucepan with just enough cold water to cover the bottom of the pan. Add the cinnamon sticks.

2 Bring to a simmer, cover and cook until the apples are tender, approximately 15 minutes.

3 Add the sugar and lemon juice. Simmer for 10 minutes.

4 Remove the cinnamon sticks and press the apples through a food mill.

Approximate values per 1-oz. (30-g) serving: **Calories** 50, **Total fat** 0 g, **Saturated fat** 0 g, **Cholesterol** 0 mg, **Sodium** 0 mg, **Total carbohydrates** 13 g, **Protein** 0 g, **Claims**—fat free; no sodium

FRESH CRANBERRY-ORANGE SAUCE

RECIPE 25.19

Yield: 3 qt. (3 lt)		**Method:** Simmering
Granulated sugar	1 lb.	450 g
Orange juice	4 fl. oz.	120 ml
Water	8 fl. oz.	225 ml
Fresh or frozen cranberries	1 lb. 8 oz.	700 g
Cinnamon stick	1	1
Orange liqueur	2 fl. oz.	60 ml
Orange zest, finely grated	2 Tbsp.	30 ml
Orange segments	20	20

1 Combine the sugar, juice and water in a nonreactive saucepan; bring to a boil.

2 Add the cranberries and cinnamon stick and simmer uncovered until the berries begin to burst, approximately 15 minutes. Skim off any foam that rises to the surface.

3 Add the orange liqueur and zest and simmer for another 5 minutes.

4 Remove from the heat and remove the cinnamon stick. Add the orange segments. Cool and refrigerate.

Variations: *Jalapeño-Cranberry Relish*—Omit the orange liqueur, zest and segments. Add 1 fresh jalapeño pepper, minced, and ½ cup (120 milliliters) of hot pepper jelly.

Approximate values per 1-oz. (30-g) serving: **Calories** 25, **Total fat** 0 g, **Saturated fat** 0 g, **Cholesterol** 0 mg, **Sodium** 0 mg, **Total carbohydrates** 6 g, **Protein** 0 g, **Claims**—fat free; no sodium; low calorie

MANGO CHUTNEY

RECIPE 25.20

Yield: 1½ qt. (1.5 lt)		**Method:** Simmering
Mangoes, peeled and diced	2 lb.	900 g
Onions, fine dice	4 oz.	120 g
Garlic cloves, minced	2	2
Cider vinegar	8 fl. oz.	250 ml
Dark brown sugar	8 oz.	250 g
Golden raisins	2½ oz.	75 g
Crystallized ginger	4 oz.	120 g
Salt	½ tsp.	2 ml
Cinnamon sticks	2	2
Red pepper flakes	½ tsp.	2 ml
Mustard seeds	½ tsp.	2 ml
Fresh ginger, minced	1 tsp.	5 ml
Lime juice	1 fl. oz.	30 ml

1 Combine the mangoes, onions, garlic, vinegar and sugar in a large, heavy saucepan. Cook until the sugar dissolves.

2 Stir in the raisins, crystallized ginger, salt and spices. Simmer until the onions and raisins are very soft, approximately 45 minutes. Skim foam from the surface as necessary.

3 Stir in the lime juice and adjust the seasonings.

4 Remove from the heat and cool uncovered. The chutney will thicken somewhat as it cools, but should be thinner than fruit preserves.

Approximate values per 1-oz. (30-g) serving: **Calories** 50, **Total fat** 0 g, **Saturated fat** 0 g, **Cholesterol** 0 mg, **Sodium** 30 mg, **Total carbohydrates** 12 g, **Protein** 0 g, **Vitamin C** 10%, **Claims—** fat free; very low sodium

THE GENTLE ART OF GASTRONOMY IS A FRIENDLY
ONE. IT HURDLES THE LANGUAGE BARRIER, MAKES
FRIENDS AMONG CIVILIZED PEOPLE, AND WARMS THE
HEART.

—Samuel Chamberlain, American author
   (1895–1975)

26

SANDWICHES

WILDFLOWER BREAD COMPANY, Scottsdale, AZ

AFTER STUDYING THIS
CHAPTER, YOU WILL BE
ABLE TO:

▶ select high-quality sandwich
   ingredients
▶ identify different types and
   styles of sandwiches
▶ prepare sandwiches to order

A sandwich is often the first meal a person learns to prepare. Even those who claim that they cannot cook often make delicious hot and cold sandwiches without considering it cooking. Mastering a grilled cheese sandwich or assembling the quintessential BLT may not require a degree in the culinary arts, but it does require the ability to select and use ingredients wisely.

Sandwiches, which are usually quick and easy to assemble, lend themselves well to a chef's creativity. Fancy sandwiches can become sensational menu additions in even the most formal restaurants, and amazing sandwiches can keep lunch customers visiting regularly. Sandwiches offer food service operations economical opportunities for using leftovers, and they offer customers, especially those with smaller budgets or appetites, meals to eat out of hand. Thus, the ability to correctly prepare hot and cold sandwiches to order is a fundamental skill in many food service operations.

▶ INGREDIENTS FOR SANDWICHES

Sandwiches are constructed from bread, a spread and one or more fillings. These components should be selected and combined carefully so that the finished sandwich is flavorful and visually appealing.

BREAD

Bread provides more than a convenient means for handling a sandwich. It holds or contains the spread and fillings and gives the sandwich its shape. Bread also adds flavor, texture, nutrition and color, and often determines the overall look of the finished product.

Health consciousness and consumer willingness to try new and unusual foods gives today's chefs the freedom to create sandwiches without relying on two slices of white bread. Virtually any bread can be used in sandwich making: rolls, biscuits, bagels, croissants, fruit and nut breads, whole-grain breads and savory breads as well as flatbreads such as naan, lavosh and tortillas; pocket breads such as pitas and flavorful breads such as focaccia and Swedish limpa.

Whatever bread is used and whether its flavor is mild or intense, the bread should complement the fillings and not overpower them. The bread should be fresh (although day-old bread is easier to slice and is excellent toasted) and its texture should be able to withstand moisture from the spread and fillings without becoming soggy or pasty. An overly hard or crusty bread, however, may make the sandwich difficult to eat.

SPREAD

A spread is used to add flavor, moisture and richness to the sandwich and, sometimes, it helps to hold or bind it together. Some spreads, especially plain or flavored butters, also act as a barrier to prevent the moisture in the filling from soaking into the bread.

There are three principal spreads: butter, mayonnaise, and vegetable purées.

HERO WORSHIP

Americans love sandwiches—not only the everyday classics, but larger-than-life regional masterpieces that go by colorful, often-interchangeable names: hoagies, submarines, heroes and so on. I've even heard them called "Dagwoods," after the Bumstead of comics fame who makes his monumental sandwiches in the middle of the night, invariably with a piece of Swiss cheese hanging over the side and an olive on a toothpick spear. They're "hoagies" in my native Philadelphia, supposedly after the Hog Island shipyard, where Italian workers ate big stuffed sandwiches during World War I. "Submarine" was coined in the next war, it is said, at a Connecticut submarine base. A sandwich is a "hero" when it's so huge it takes a hero to eat it—this from food journalist Clementine Paddleford, writing in the 1930s about New York's Manganaro's deli.

Call it what you like, and make what you like of it. Dagwood puts everything but the kitchen sink in his sandwich. Manganaro's still fills its version to the brim with Italian antipasti—meats, cheeses, peppers, lettuce and tomatoes. In my hometown, everything's optional but the Italian bread, lettuce, tomato, onion and salad oil. New Englanders eat something called a "grinder," a hero stuffed with hot meatballs, sausage and peppers, veal parmigiana or the like. These are aptly named and a real workout for the jaw! New Orleans has two big sandwiches: the round muffuletta, dressed in garlicky green-olive salad, and the warming po' boy, which is often soaked in gravy. Cuban immigrants press ham, roast pork, cheese and sweet pickles between slabs of French bread in a plancha, a kind of sandwich iron. But perhaps you have a better idea. Try it! Give it a jaunty title and who knows—perhaps both the recipe and its name will live on.

from SHEILA LUKINS USA COOKBOOK, by
Sheila Lukins,
Workman Publishing, 1997

BUTTER

One of the most common spreads, plain butter adds flavor and richness; it is also an excellent moisture barrier. Flavored or compound butters, discussed in Chapter 11, Stocks and Sauces, make excellent sandwich spreads, adding flavor dimensions to the finished product. For example, try caper butter on a Cajun-style blackened beef sandwich or a red chile honey butter on a smoked turkey sandwich. Any butter spread should be softened or whipped so that it will spread easily without tearing the bread.

MAYONNAISE

Perhaps the most popular sandwich spread, mayonnaise adds moisture, richness and flavor and complements most meat, poultry, fish, shellfish, vegetable, egg and cheese fillings. Like butter, mayonnaise can be made more exciting by adding flavoring ingredients. Condiments (for example, coarse-grained mustard or grated horseradish), herbs, spices and spice blends (for example, curry or chilli powder) and other ingredients such as sun-dried tomatoes and pesto sauce can be stirred into fresh or commercially prepared mayonnaise. Fresh mayonnaise can also be prepared with flavored oils, such as olive oil, walnut oil or chile oil. See Chapter 24, Salads and Salad Dressings, for recipes and additional information on mayonnaise.

VEGETABLE PURÉES

Puréed vegetables are often used as sandwich spreads; after all, lunch boxes everywhere would be incomplete without a purée of roasted peanuts (more commonly known as peanut butter) and fruit jelly. More sophisticated examples include black olive tapenade (page 911) for a sandwich of Italian meats and cheeses, or a well-seasoned chickpea purée with lemon and tahini paste for a vegetarian sandwich. Unlike butter, vegetable purées usually will not provide a moisture barrier between the bread and the fillings.

FILLING

The filling is the body of the sandwich, providing most of its flavor. A sandwich often contains more than one filling. For example, the filling in a Reuben sandwich is corned beef, cheese and sauerkraut, while in a BLT it is bacon, lettuce and tomato. Fillings for cold sandwiches must be precooked and properly chilled, although some hot sandwich fillings may be cooked to order.

When choosing fillings, be sure that the flavors complement each other. Their textures may be similar or contrasting. If an ingredient, such as lettuce, is supposed to be crisp, it should be very crisp, not limp. If an ingredient is supposed to be tender and moist, make sure it is so. Improperly prepared, poor-quality or mishandled filling ingredients can ruin an otherwise wonderful sandwich.

Popular fillings include the following:

BEEF

Although the classic hot beef sandwich is the hamburger, other hot or cold beef products are commonly used. For example, hot or cold small steaks, slices of larger cuts such as the tenderloin, thin slices of roast beef and so on, make excellent fillings. Also popular are hot or cold slices of cured beef products, including corned beef, pastrami and tongue as well as beef sausages such as salami, bologna and hot dogs.

PORK

Various ham and bacon products, served either hot or cold, are extremely popular. In addition, pork loin and tenderloin are light, white meats that adapt well to various flavor combinations and cooking methods. Barbecued pork, pork sausages and pork hot dogs are also popular.

POULTRY

Sliced turkey breast, either roasted or smoked, and processed turkey are often used in hot and cold sandwiches. Moreover, food substitutes such as turkey bologna, turkey pastrami, turkey hot dogs and turkey ham are becoming increasingly popular because they generally have a lower fat content than the beef or pork original. Boneless chicken breast, either sliced or whole, is also quite popular because it can be prepared by a variety of methods and complements a broad range of flavors.

FISH AND SHELLFISH

Although fried fish fillets are an old standard, grilled fish sandwiches are gaining in popularity. Canned fish products, particularly tuna and salmon, are also widely used. Often fish and shellfish, especially tuna, shrimp and crab, are used for mayonnaise-based bound salads. Sardines and anchovies are less popular than other fish, but are sometimes mixed into bound salads or arranged artistically on open-faced sandwiches.

VEGETABLES

Vegetables add texture, moisture, flavor and nutrition to most any sandwich. Fresh vegetables such as lettuce, onions and tomatoes are commonly used in combination with meat, cheese and other fillings. Celery or bell peppers add a nice crunchy texture to cheese or mayonnaise-based bound salad fillings. Vegetables, however, can stand on their own as sandwich fillings. Marinated, grilled vegetables can be used in hot or cold sandwiches, and a combination of sliced, fresh vegetables and a flavorful dressing wrapped in soft lavosh or a tortilla becomes a portable salad.

EGGS

Hard cooked eggs are most often used as an ingredient in a mayonnaise-based salad, where they are chopped and combined with pickle relish and seasonings. Hard-cooked eggs can also be sliced thin and used as an attractive garnish on open-faced sandwiches. Fried or scrambled eggs can be layered between pieces of bread or rolled in a tortilla for a breakfast sandwich.

CHEESE

Cheese is available in such a variety of textures, flavors, colors and styles that it is a welcome addition to nearly any sandwich. Sliced cheese can be used as a filling in hot or cold sandwiches, and melted cheese or a cheese sauce makes an excellent topping for hot open-faced sandwiches. Flavored cream cheese is also used as a spread or filling, particularly with bagels and fruit or nut breads.

BOUND SALADS

Protein salads bound with mayonnaise or salad dressing are popular sandwich fillings. Examples include chicken, tuna, egg and ham salads. Bound salads are discussed in Chapter 24, Salads and Salad Dressings.

▶ TYPES OF SANDWICHES

Sandwiches can be hot or cold, closed or open-faced, depending on the way in which the ingredients are assembled and presented.

HOT SANDWICHES

Hot closed sandwiches include those in which the filling ingredients are served hot, such as a hamburger or hot dog, and those where the entire sandwich is heated for service, such as a grilled cheese or Monte Cristo. Hot closed sandwiches can be categorized as basic, grilled or deep-fried.

Basic hot closed sandwiches are generally those in which the principal filling is served hot between two pieces of bread. These sandwiches may also include fillings that are not hot, such as tomato slices and lettuce leaves. Variations of the basic hot closed sandwich include tacos, quesadillas, burros (or burritos) and wraps, in which the hot and/or cold fillings are folded or wrapped in a tortilla or other supple flatbread.

▶ PROCEDURE FOR PREPARING WRAP SANDWICHES

1 The tortilla is topped with a spread or dressing.

2 Vegetables and meat, fish or poultry items are mounded across the tortilla.

3 The tortilla is rolled tightly around the filling.

Cooking grilled cheese sandwiches.

Grilled sandwiches are those in which the filling is placed between two pieces of bread, which are buttered on the outside and then browned on a griddle or in a sauté pan. The filling will be warmed during this procedure but will not cook. Therefore, fillings such as bacon or sliced meat should be fully cooked before the sandwich is assembled and grilled.

Deep-fried sandwiches are made by dipping a closed sandwich in egg batter or bread crumbs and then deep-frying it. The most common example is the Monte Cristo: white bread filled with sliced ham, Swiss cheese and Dijon mustard.

The hot open-faced turkey or steak sandwich proved long ago that sandwiches do not need to be eaten by hand. In the typical **hot open-faced sandwich,** bread (grilled, toasted or fresh) is placed on a serving plate, covered with hot meat or other filling and topped with an appropriate gravy, sauce or cheese. The completed dish is often browned under a broiler immediately before service. Condiments and garnishes are usually served on the side.

Perhaps the ultimate hot open-faced sandwich is the **pizza.** Bread dough is topped with sauce, cheese, meat and vegetables, then baked. Small personal-sized pizzas are a popular menu item in even upscale restaurants.

COLD SANDWICHES

Cold sandwiches are simply sandwiches that are eaten cold. They are made with raw ingredients that are not intended to be cooked, such as vegetables and cheese, or with meat, poultry, fish or shellfish that is precooked and then chilled before use as a filling. As with hot sandwiches, cold sandwiches may be closed or open-faced.

Cold closed sandwiches contain two or more pieces of bread with one or more fillings and one or more spreads. Cold closed sandwiches are usually eaten with the hands and come in three basic styles: basic, multidecker and tea.

Basic cold sandwiches are made with two pieces of bread or one split roll, one spread and one or more fillings. A tuna salad sandwich and an Italian-style submarine are both examples of basic cold closed sandwiches. A variation of the basic cold sandwich is a wrap with cold fillings—for example, an herb-flavored tortilla spread with peanut sauce and wrapped around spinach leaves, diced grilled chicken and cold cooked rice.

Multidecker cold sandwiches are made with three or more pieces of bread, one or more spreads and two or more fillings. The club sandwich, in which sliced turkey, bacon, lettuce and tomato are layered with three slices of toasted bread, is a classic example of a multidecker sandwich (See the recipe on page 848).

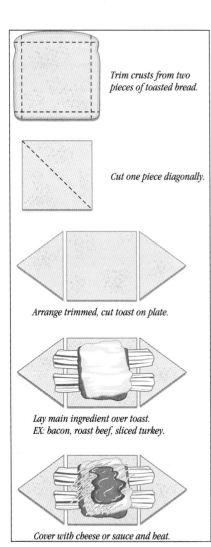

Trim crusts from two pieces of toasted bread.

Cut one piece diagonally.

Arrange trimmed, cut toast on plate.

Lay main ingredient over toast. EX: bacon, roast beef, sliced turkey.

Cover with cheese or sauce and heat.

FIGURE 26.1 ▶ **Arranging hot open-faced sandwiches**

▶ PROCEDURE FOR PREPARING COLD MULTIDECKER SANDWICHES

1 The first slice of toasted bread is spread with butter or mayonnaise, then topped with meat and vegetables.

2 The second slice of bread is added, then spread with mayonnaise.

3 A second layer of vegetables and meat is added.

4 The finished sandwich is cut into quarters for service.

HISTORY OF SANDWICHES

One of the earliest recorded references to foods eaten between two pieces of bread tells of Rabbi Hillel, a great Jewish teacher who lived sometime between 70 B.C. and 70 A.D. He created the Passover custom of eating haroseth (chopped nuts and apples) and mohror (bitter herbs) between two pieces of matzo (unleavened bread). This "sandwich" was intended to represent the mortar used by the Jews to build the Egyptians' pyramids and the bitter sadness of their internment away from the land of Israel.

The term *sandwich* came into use approximately 200 years ago. The Fourth Earl of Sandwich, Sir John Montague (1718–1792), is credited with popularizing the concept of eating meats and cheeses between two slices of bread. Apparently the Earl, not wanting to leave the gaming tables that he loved so much, would demand that his servants bring him meat and bread. He combined the two and ate them with one hand, allowing him a free hand to continue playing at the tables. Some historians argue that a more likely scenario is that, as the head of defense, the Earl was kept busy planning British strategy for the Revolutionary War underway in the American colonies. Whichever the case, the name stuck.

Sandwiches became more popular in the United States when soft white bread became common in the early 20th century. Today, sandwiches are found on breakfast, lunch and dinner menus and are served by every type of food service operation, from the most casual diner to the fanciest four-star dining room.

Open-faced sandwiches featuring smoked salmon (top), roast beef and shrimp (bottom) are attractively garnished with items that complement the principal ingredient.

Tea sandwiches are small, fancy constructions made with light, soft, trimmed breads and delicate fillings and spreads. They are usually cut or rolled into shapes such as diamonds, circles or pinwheels and served as a finger food at parties and receptions. The name derives from their service at afternoon tea.

Cold open-faced sandwiches are simply larger versions of canapés, which are discussed in Chapter 28, Hors d'Oeuvre and Canapés. The most popular style is the open-faced Norwegian sandwich known as **smørbrød.** As with canapés, much emphasis is placed on visual appeal. A single slice of bread is coated with a spread, then covered with thin slices of meat, poultry or fish, or a thin layer of a bound salad. Carefully cut and arranged garnishes such as hard-cooked eggs, fresh herbs, pickles, onions and radishes are used to complete the presentation. A simple version of an open-faced cold sandwich is a delicatessen classic—a bagel with lox and cream cheese.

▶ **smørbrød** (SMURR-brur) Norwegian cold open-faced sandwiches. Similarly, the Swedish term *smörgåsbord* (SMORE-guhs-bohrd) refers to a buffet or bread-and-butter table of salads, open-faced sandwiches, pickled or marinated fish, sliced meats and cheeses.

▶ SANDWICH MISE EN PLACE

Sandwiches are generally prepared to order, and their preparation usually requires a great deal of handwork. Therefore, the goal is to assemble all ingredients and equipment so that your motions will be as quick and efficient as possible at the time of final assembly. Because each menu and food service operation has its own requirements, there is no one correct station setup, but there are a few basic guidelines.

1 *Prepare ingredients.* All sandwich ingredients should be cooked, mixed, sliced and prepared ahead of service to facilitate quick, efficient assembly at service time. So, before service, slice the meats, cheeses and vegetables, clean and dry lettuce and other fresh vegetable ingredients, blend the flavored spreads, mix the bound salads, and so on.

FIGURE 26.2 ▶ A typical sandwich bar.

2 *Arrange and store ingredients.* Arrange all sandwich ingredients within easy reach of the work area. Cold items must be properly refrigerated at all times. A sandwich bar, similar to a steam table but with refrigerated compartments, is frequently used for this purpose. Under-counter refrigeration can be used for backup supplies and less frequently used ingredients. Sliced meats, cheeses and vegetables must be well covered to prevent dehydration or contamination. Many ingredients can be pre-portioned, either by weight or count, then wrapped in individual portions for storage.

3 *Select and arrange equipment.* The heavy equipment needed for making sandwiches can include preparation equipment such as meat slicers,

GREATEST HITS FROM THE SANDWICH COUNTER

Writing in his monumental *Le Guide culinaire* of 1903, Auguste Escoffier describes just two types of sandwiches: those "with two slices of buttered bread . . . covering a slice of ham or tongue, etc." and "the kind served at elaborate functions," which are much smaller, and in which the "sandwiched product (whatever this be)" is diced. Among his list of common sandwich ingredients are ham, beef, chicken, foie gras, caviar and watercress.

Today's cook must recognize a somewhat wider variety of sandwiches, however. And, as the following list shows, often a sandwich's popular name bears no connection to its ingredients.

BLT—Bacon, lettuce and tomato between two slices of toasted bread.

Club—Three slices of toasted bread usually layered with bacon, lettuce and tomato plus turkey or chicken. The sandwich, and

its name, most likely originated at the Saratoga Club during the 1890s.

Croque Monsieur—Ham and cheese sandwich dipped in beaten egg and grilled; made popular by bars and bistros throughout Paris.

Deli—Contains any of various meats commonly sold in a delicatessen, such as pastrami, corned beef, turkey, ham, roast beef and so on. Usually the meat is sliced very thin and piled very high between two slices of white or rye bread.

Fluffernutter—Peanut butter and marshmallow fluff spread on—what else?—white bread; popular during the 1960s.

French Dip—Thin slices of roast beef in a crusty French-bread roll served au jus.

Gyro—Well-seasoned rotisserie-roasted lamb, thinly sliced and served wrapped in pita bread with onions and cucumber-

yogurt dressing. A Greek-American creation, the gyro (YEAR-o) became popular at Greek lunch counters in New York City during the 1970s.

Patty Melt—Ground beef patty with grilled onions and cheese, grilled between two slices of buttered rye bread.

Po' Boy—French bread loaf split and filled with various ingredients, especially fried oysters or shrimp and rémoulade sauce. Created during the 1920s, it is New Orleans' version of a submarine sandwich.

Reuben—Corned beef, Swiss (Emmenthaler) cheese, sauerkraut and mustard or Thousand Island dressing grilled between two slices of rye bread. The Reuben was probably created during the early 1900s by Arnold Reuben, owner of New York City's Reuben's Restaurant.

griddles, grills, fryers and broilers as well as storage equipment such as refrigerated sandwich bars for cold ingredients and steam tables for hot ingredients. Even the simplest sandwich menu will require the use of basic hand tools such as spatulas, spreaders, portion scoops, knives and cutting boards. Be sure that the supply of such items is adequate to permit quick handwork and to avoid delays or cross-contamination.

▶ PRESENTING AND GARNISHING SANDWICHES

Sandwiches, especially cold closed sandwiches, are usually cut into halves, thirds or quarters for service. Cutting makes a sandwich easier for the customer to handle and allows for a more attractive presentation; the sandwich wedges can be arranged to add height to the plate and to expose the fillings' colors and textures. For sit-down service, hot closed sandwiches such as hamburgers are often presented open-faced. Condiments, such as mustard and mayonnaise, and garnishes, such as sliced tomatoes, onions, pickles and lettuce leaves, are served on the side or on one of the open bun halves. This tends to be a more attractive presentation, and it allows the customer to assemble and add ingredients to the sandwich as desired.

Although a sandwich can be a meal unto itself, it may be served with a salad or starch accompaniment. Potato chips or french-fried potatoes are, of course, standard fare, perhaps because they are also finger foods and they provide a crunchy texture. Bound salads, such as potato and macaroni, are also common starch accompaniments. Plated sandwiches have long been served with coleslaw, fruit salad or a small mixed green salad as side dishes. Even the standard soup-and-sandwich combo—half of a sandwich with a cup of soup—remains a popular lunch selection.

CONCLUSION

High-quality sandwiches are made from fresh, carefully prepared ingredients, presented in an appetizing and appealing manner. Flavors, colors and textures of the bread, spread and filling should be appropriate and complementary. Breads should be fresh, never stale, and appropriate for the finished sandwich. Spreads should be carefully chosen to add additional flavors and moisture to the sandwich but should not be used to cover or mask dry or poor-quality fillings or breads. Fillings provide the dominant flavor and are usually the source of the sandwich's name; they should be flavorful and properly prepared. The appearance of even the most basic sandwich can be improved by careful assembly and precise trimming and cutting.

QUESTIONS FOR DISCUSSION

1 List examples for each of the three primary sandwich components.
2 Explain the differences between a hot open-faced and a hot closed sandwich.
3 List several hand tools used in sandwich production, and explain the need for an ample supply of these tools.
4 Why is cross-contamination a concern when preparing sandwiches? What simple steps can be taken to avoid the spread of pathogenic microorganisms?

CHICKEN PESTO AND FETA SANDWICH   RECIPE 26.1

Note: This dish appears in the chapter opening photograph.

WILDFLOWER BREAD COMPANY, Scottsdale, AZ

Yield: 8 Sandwiches

Mushrooms, sliced thin	8 oz.	240 g
Balsamic vinaigrette	1 fl. oz.	30 ml
Red bell peppers, roasted	8 oz.	240 g
Tomatoes, medium	4	4
Chicken breasts, boneless, skinless, 4 oz. (120 g) each	8	8
Italian rolls	8	8
Pesto Sauce (page 237)	8 oz.	240 g
Feta	8 oz.	240 g

1 Marinate the mushrooms in the balsamic vinaigrette for at least 24 hours under refrigeration, stirring occasionally.

2 Slice the bell peppers into 1/4-inch- (6-millimeter-) wide strips.

3 Slice the tomatoes into 1/4-inch- (6-millimeter-) thick slices.

4 Trim any fat or rib meat from the chicken breasts and then grill until done.

5 To assemble each sandwich, slice one roll in half lengthwise. Spread 1 ounce (30 grams) of the Pesto Sauce on the bottom of the roll, then crumble 1 ounce (30 grams) of the feta on top of the Pesto Sauce, covering the entire surface. Place a chicken breast on top of the feta, then 1/2 ounce (15 grams) of the mushrooms on the chicken, then 1 ounce (30 grams) of the bell pepper strips on top of the mushrooms; finish with 3 tomato slices and the top of the roll. Insert two toothpicks, slice and serve.

Approximate values per sandwich: **Calories** 540, **Total fat** 20 g, **Saturated fat** 7 g, **Cholesterol** 135 mg, **Sodium** 830 mg, **Total carbohydrates** 39 g, **Protein** 51 g, **Vitamin A** 20%, **Vitamin C** 60%, **Calcium** 30%, **Iron** 25%

GROUPER SANDWICH WITH LEMON RÉMOULADE   RECIPE 26.2

CAFÉ ALLEGRE, Orlando, FL
Chef Kevin Fonzo

Yield: 6 Sandwiches

Olive oil	2 Tbsp.	30 ml
Grouper fillets, 5 oz. (150 g) each	6	6
Salt and pepper	TT	TT
Lemon Rémoulade (recipe follows)	6 Tbsp.	90 ml
Kaiser rolls, sliced, toasted	6	6
Mixed greens	3 c.	720 ml
Tomato slices	6	6

1 Heat the olive oil in a large sauté pan. Season the grouper fillets with salt and pepper and then sauté the fish until golden brown and cooked through.

2 To assemble each sandwich, spread 1 tablespoon (15 milliliters) of Lemon Rémoulade on the bottom half of the roll, then top with ½ cup (120 milliliters) of mixed greens, one tomato slice and one cooked fish fillet. Cover with the remaining half of the roll and serve.

Approximate values per serving: **Calories** 330, **Total fat** 8 g, **Saturated fat** 1 g, **Cholesterol** 40 mg, **Sodium** 380 mg, **Total carbohydrates** 36 g, **Protein** 28 g, **Vitamin A** 15%, **Vitamin C** 60%

LEMON RÉMOULADE

Yield: 20 fl. oz. (600 ml)

Mayonnaise	1 pt.	1 lt
Sweet pickle relish	3 oz.	90 g
Onion, chopped fine	2 Tbsp.	30 ml
Fresh parsley, chopped	2 Tbsp.	30 ml
Fresh lemon juice	2 Tbsp.	30 ml
Salt and black pepper	TT	TT
Worcestershire sauce	TT	TT
Tabasco sauce	TT	TT

1 Mix all the ingredients together until thoroughly blended.

Approximate values per 1-fl.-oz. (30-ml) serving: **Calories** 170, **Total fat** 18 g, **Saturated fat** 2.5 g, **Cholesterol** 15 mg, **Sodium** 160 mg, **Total carbohydrates** 2 g, **Protein** 0 g

RECIPE 26.3

HAMBURGER

Yield: 1 Sandwich

Ground round	4–6 oz.	120–180 g
Salt and pepper	TT	TT
Hamburger bun or other appropriate bread	1	1
Garnishes	as desired	as desired

1 Form the ground round into a patty, handling the beef as little as possible.
2 Season the patty with salt and pepper and broil or grill to the desired doneness, turning once. While the patty is cooking, toast the bun or bread if desired.
3 Remove the patty from the broiler or grill, place on one-half of the bun or one slice of bread and garnish the other with a lettuce leaf, a slice of onion, a slice of tomato and/or pickles. Serve with condiments such as ketchup and mustard.

Approximate values per sandwich: **Calories** 580, **Total fat** 32 g, **Saturated fat** 9 g, **Cholesterol** 99 mg, **Sodium** 355 mg, **Total carbohydrates** 40 g, **Protein** 29 g

Variations: Cheeseburger—Place one or two slices of American, Cheddar, Swiss or other cheese on the cooking patty approximately 1 minute before it is done.

Approximate values per sandwich: **Calories** 680, **Total fat** 42 g, **Saturated fat** 15 g, **Cholesterol** 130 mg, **Sodium** 520 mg, **Total carbohydrates** 42 g, **Protein** 36 g, **Calcium** 20%

Bacon Cheeseburger—Prepare a cheeseburger and place two slices of crisp bacon on top of the cheese when the patty is done.

Approximate values per sandwich: **Calories** 650, **Total fat** 39 g, **Saturated fat** 12 g, **Cholesterol** 110 mg, **Sodium** 560 mg, **Total carbohydrates** 41 g, **Protein** 33 g

Mushroom Burger—Sauté 2 ounces (60 grams) of sliced mushrooms in 1 to 2 teaspoons (5 to 10 milliliters) of butter or olive oil. Top the cooked hamburger or cheeseburger with the cooked mushrooms.

Approximate values per sandwich, without cheese: **Calories** 660, **Total fat** 37 g, **Saturated fat** 12 g, **Cholesterol** 110 mg, **Sodium** 400 mg, **Total carbohydrates** 48 g, **Protein** 33 g

California Burger—Prepare a hamburger or cheeseburger and serve on a whole-wheat bun accompanied by 2 ounces (60 grams) of guacamole, 1 ounce (30 grams) of alfalfa sprouts, two slices of ripe tomato and one thin slice of red onion.

Approximate values per sandwich, without cheese: **Calories** 690, **Total fat** 40 g, **Saturated fat** 9 g, **Cholesterol** 100 mg, **Sodium** 770 mg, **Total carbohydrates** 50 g, **Protein** 33 g, **Vitamin C** 20%

GRILLED RED SNAPPER BURGER WITH MANGO KETCHUP

RECIPE 26.4

FROM *ALLEN SUSSER'S NEW WORLD CUISINE AND COOKERY*
by Allen Susser, NORTH MIAMI BEACH, FL

Yield: 4 Sandwiches

Red snapper fillets, fresh	1 lb.	450 g
Egg whites	3	3
Kosher salt	1½ tsp.	7 ml
Cayenne pepper	¼ tsp.	1 ml
Thai fish sauce	1 Tbsp.	15 ml
Green onions, chopped	2 Tbsp.	30 ml
Fresh dill, chopped	1 tsp.	5 ml
Fresh bread crumbs	¼ c.	60 ml
Olive oil	2 Tbsp.	30 ml
French bread, quartered	1 loaf	1 loaf
Spinach, cleaned and dried	1 c.	225 ml
Mango Ketchup (recipe follows)	1 Tbsp.	15 ml

1 Chop the red snapper by hand or with a steel blade in a food processor. Place the chopped snapper in a large stainless steel bowl.
2 Add the egg whites, salt, cayenne, fish sauce, green onions and dill. Mix well.
3 Add enough bread crumbs to bind all the ingredients together.
4 Form into four burgers ½ inch (1.2 centimeters) thick and chill for approximately 30 minutes in the refrigerator.
5 Heat a grill or broiler until very hot. Drizzle a little olive oil over the burgers just before cooking. Grill or broil over high heat for about 1½ minutes on each side, being careful not to overcook the fish.
6 Serve the burgers immediately on the French bread with one-fourth of the spinach leaves and 1 tablespoon (15 milliliters) of Mango Ketchup on each.

Approximate values per sandwich: **Calories** 445, **Total fat** 11 g, **Saturated fat** 2 g, **Cholesterol** 55 mg, **Sodium** 1620 mg, **Total carbohydrates** 47 g, **Protein** 40 g, **Vitamin A** 50%, **Calcium** 20%

MANGO KETCHUP

Yield: 2 qt. (2 lt)

Mangoes, medium	5	5
Vinegar	3 Tbsp.	45 ml
Fresh ginger, chopped	1 Tbsp.	15 ml

Continued

Cinnamon, ground	1 dash	1 dash
Kosher salt	1 tsp.	5 ml
Granulated sugar	4 oz.	120 g
White wine	4 fl. oz.	120 ml
Allspice, ground	½ tsp.	2 ml
Cayenne pepper	½ tsp.	2 ml
Clove, whole	1	1

1 Peel and pit the mangoes. Purée the pulp in a food processor fitted with a stainless steel blade.

2 Add all the remaining ingredients and pulse together.

3 In a heavy-sided saucepan cook the mixture over low heat for 1 hour, until well reduced and thickened.

4 Remove from the heat and cool.

5 Strain through a fine sieve. Let set refrigerated for 24 hours.

Approximate values per 1-fl.-oz. (30-ml) serving: **Calories** 20, **Total fat** 0 g, **Saturated fat** 0 g, **Cholesterol** 0 mg, **Sodium** 35 mg, **Total carbohydrates** 5 g, **Protein** 0 g, **Vitamin A** 15%, **Claims**–low calorie; fat free

RECIPE 26.5   BLACKENED STEAK SANDWICH

Yield: 2 Sandwiches

New York strip steak, 10 oz. (280 g)	1	1
Blackened Steak Seasoning (recipe follows)	as needed	as needed
Clarified butter	1 fl. oz.	30 ml
Capers	1 Tbsp.	15 ml
Whole butter, softened	1 oz.	30 g
French bread, cut on the bias	2 slices	2 slices
Baby lettuce, cleaned	4 oz.	120 g
Roma tomatoes, sliced	2	2
Red onion, sliced	1 oz.	30 g

1 Heat a cast-iron skillet over high heat for 10 minutes. Pat the steak dry with a clean towel. Coat the steak in the Blackened Steak Seasoning.

2 Carefully place the steak into the hot pan and ladle ½ ounce (15 milliliters) of clarified butter over the steak. Be very careful, as the butter may flare up. There will be intense smoke and the steak will form a black crust. Cook the steak for approximately 2 minutes.

3 Turn the steak, ladle the remaining clarified butter over it and cook to the desired degree of doneness. Remove the steak from the pan and hold in a warm place.

4 Chop the capers and combine them with the softened butter. Spread each slice of bread with half of the caper butter.

5 Slice the steak on the bias.

6 To assemble each sandwich, place half of the warm steak on a slice of buttered bread and arrange half of the greens, tomatoes and onion attractively on the plate and serve.

Variation: To serve this sandwich cold, allow the steak to cool after cooking, then refrigerate it until completely cold. Proceed with the recipe.

Approximate values per sandwich: **Calories** 610, **Total fat** 38 g, **Saturated fat** 20 g, **Cholesterol** 180 mg, **Sodium** 650 mg, **Total carbohydrates** 21 g, **Protein** 44 g, **Vitamin A** 30%, **Vitamin C** 40%

BLACKENED STEAK SEASONING

Yield: 1½ oz. (45 g)

Paprika	1 Tbsp.	15 ml
Salt	2 tsp.	10 ml
Onion powder	1 tsp.	5 ml
Garlic powder	1 tsp.	5 ml
Cayenne pepper	1 tsp.	5 ml
White pepper	½ tsp.	3 ml
Black pepper	½ tsp.	3 ml
Dried thyme	½ tsp.	3 ml

1 Combine all ingredients and mix well.

PHILLY CHEESE STEAK SANDWICH   RECIPE 26.6

Yield: 1 Serving

Sub roll, 6 in. (15 cm)	1	1
Beef round, shaved thin	8 oz.	240 g
Vegetable oil	1 Tbsp.	15 ml
Salt and pepper	TT	TT
Provolone cheese slices	2	2

1 Split the sub roll in half lengthwise.

2 Sauté the shaved beef in the vegetable oil until done, approximately 1 minute. Season with salt and pepper.

3 Cut the cheese slices in half and line the bottom of the sub roll with two halves. Place the hot beef on top of the cheese and top with the remaining cheese. Place the top of the roll on the sandwich, cut in half and serve hot.

Variation: Sauté 2 ounces (60 grams) of sliced mushrooms, onions or red or green bell peppers in a small amount of vegetable oil and add them to the sandwich on top of the second layer of cheese.

Approximate values per sandwich: **Calories** 1110, **Total fat** 53 g, **Saturated fat** 19 g, **Cholesterol** 215 mg, **Sodium** 1510 mg, **Total carbohydrates** 69 g, **Protein** 85 g, **Vitamin A** 10%, **Calcium** 45%, **Iron** 60%

GRILLED BBQ PORTABELLA MUSHROOM
SANDWICH ON FOCACCIA   RECIPE 26.7

CAFÉ ALLEGRE, ORLANDO, FL
Chef Kevin Fonzo

Yield: 6 Sandwiches

Focaccia, cut into 6-in. (15-cm)		
squares	6	6
Portabella mushrooms	6	6
Barbecue Sauce (page 241)	2 fl. oz.	60 ml
Red bell peppers, roasted,		
peeled and julienne	2	2
Fresh basil leaves	30	30
Goat cheese, crumbled	6 Tbsp.	90 ml

1 Slice the focaccia squares horizontally and toast.
2 Brush the mushrooms with the Barbecue Sauce and grill until hot and tender.
3 To assemble each sandwich, place one mushroom on the bottom of a focaccia square and top with one-sixth of the bell pepper strips, five basil leaves and 1 tablespoon (15 milliliters) of goat cheese. Top with the remaining focaccia, cut in half and serve.

Approximate values per sandwich: **Calories** 330, **Total fat** 12 g, **Saturated fat** 3.5 g, **Cholesterol** 15 mg, **Sodium** 660 mg, **Total carbohydrates** 45 g, **Protein** 11 g, **Vitamin C** 80%, **Iron** 15%, **Claims**—good source of fiber

RECIPE 26.8

REUBEN SANDWICH

Yield: 1 Sandwich

Dark rye bread	2 slices	2 slices
Thousand Island dressing	2 Tbsp.	30 ml
Cooked corned beef, hot, sliced very thin	4 oz.	120 g
Sauerkraut, hot, drained well	2 oz.	60 g
Swiss (Emmenthaler) cheese	2 slices	2 slices
Whole butter, softened	as needed	as needed

1 Spread each slice of bread with approximately 1 tablespoon (15 milliliters) of Thousand Island dressing.
2 Place the hot corned beef, hot sauerkraut and cheese on one slice of bread. Top with the second slice of bread, keeping the dressing side inside the sandwich.
3 Butter the top slice of bread and place the sandwich on a hot griddle, butter side down. Carefully butter the second slice of bread.
4 Griddle the sandwich, turning once when the first side is well browned. The sandwich is done when both sides are well browned, the fillings are very hot and the cheese is melted.
5 Cut the sandwich in half diagonally and arrange as desired for service.

Approximate values per sandwich: **Calories** 560, **Total fat** 27 g, **Saturated fat** 10 g, **Cholesterol** 85 mg, **Sodium** 2150 mg, **Total carbohydrates** 39 g, **Protein** 40 g, **Vitamin A** 10%, **Vitamin C** 30%

SOUTHWESTERN GRILLED CHEESE SANDWICH WITH CHIPOTLE PURÉE AND AVOCADO

RECIPE 26.9

Yield: 1 Sandwich

Whole-grain bread	2 slices	2 slices
Monterey Jack with peppers	2 slices	2 slices
Chipotle Purée (recipe follows)	1 tsp.	5 ml
Crème fraîche	1 Tbsp.	15 ml
Avocado, sliced thin	2 oz.	60 g
Red onion, sliced thin	½ oz.	15 g
Fresh cilantro leaves	1 Tbsp.	15 ml
Whole butter, soft	1 oz.	30 g

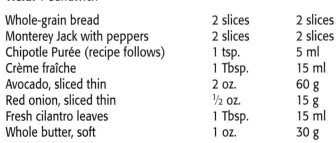

1 Top each slice of bread with a slice of cheese. Spread each slice with half of the Chipotle Purée and half of the crème fraîche.

2 Arrange the avocado slices, onion slices and cilantro leaves on one slice of the bread. Close the sandwich and press together lightly.

3 Butter the top slice of bread and place the sandwich, butter side down, on a hot griddle. Carefully butter the second slice of bread.

4 Griddle the sandwich, turning once when the first side is well browned. The sandwich is done when both sides are well browned and the cheese is melted.

5 Cut the sandwich in half diagonally and arrange as desired for service.

Approximate values per sandwich: **Calories** 730, **Total fat** 55 g, **Saturated fat** 28 g, **Cholesterol** 140 mg, **Sodium** 800 mg, **Total carbohydrates** 35 g, **Protein** 24 g, **Vitamin A** 45%, **Calcium** 60%

CHIPOTLE PURÉE

Yield: 8½ oz. (250 g)

Chipotle peppers in adobo sauce	7 oz.	200 g
Vegetable oil	1 fl. oz.	30 ml
Lime juice	from 1 lime	from 1 lime

1 Place all the ingredients in the bowl of a food processor and process until smooth.

Approximate values per 1-oz. (30-g) serving: **Calories** 35, **Total fat** 3 g, **Saturated fat** 0 g, **Cholesterol** 0 mg, **Sodium** 1290 mg, **Total carbohydrates** 1 g, **Protein** 0 g, **Vitamin C** 20%, **Claims**—low calories; low fat; high in vitamin C

MONTE CRISTO SANDWICH

RECIPE 26.10

Yield: 1 Sandwich

White bread	2 slices	2 slices
Whole butter, softened	as needed	as needed
Cooked turkey breast, sliced thin	1 oz.	30 g
Ham, sliced thin	1 oz.	30 g
Swiss (Emmenthaler) cheese	2 slices	2 slices
Egg	1	1
Milk	1 fl. oz.	30 ml

1 Spread one side of each slice of bread with butter.

2 Arrange the turkey breast, ham and cheese on top of the butter on one slice of bread.

3 Place the other slice of bread on top of the cheese, butter side against the cheese.

4 Beat the egg and milk together. Dip the sandwich in the egg batter and allow the batter to soak into the bread.

5 Using the swimming method, deep-fry the sandwich in oil at 375°F (190°C) until it is evenly browned. Remove from the oil and drain well. Cut the sandwich into four pieces and arrange as desired.

Approximate values per sandwich: **Calories** 630, **Total fat** 42 g, **Saturated fat** 24 g, **Cholesterol** 345 mg, **Sodium** 1050 mg, **Total carbohydrates** 27 g, **Protein** 35 g, **Vitamin A** 40%

RECIPE 26.11

FALAFEL

Yield: 12 Sandwiches

Chickpeas, dried	1 lb.	450 g
Garlic cloves, minced	6	6
Fresh Parsley, chopped	½ oz.	15 g
Chives, minced	½ oz.	15 g
Cumin, ground	1 Tbsp.	15 ml
Coriander, ground	2 tsp.	10 ml
Cayenne pepper	TT	TT
Eggs	3	3
Salt	TT	TT
Flour	5 oz.	150 g
Plain yogurt	6 oz.	180 g
Lemon juice	2 fl. oz.	60 ml
Pita bread	12	12
Iceberg lettuce, shredded	6 oz.	180 g
Tomatoes, diced	6 oz.	180 g

1 To make the falafel, soak the chickpeas following the procedures for dried beans outlined in Chapter 22, Vegetables. Drain the chickpeas, place them in a pot and cover with cool water. Simmer until tender, approximately 2 to 3 hours, remove from the heat and drain well.

2 Process the chickpeas in a food processor or a food chopper until coarsely chopped. Add the garlic, parsley, chives, cumin, coriander and cayenne and process for a few seconds.

3 Add the eggs, salt and flour and process briefly. Remove the falafel from the machine and chill in the refrigerator for 1 hour.

4 Combine the yogurt and lemon juice and mix well. Set aside.

5 Portion the falafel using a #50 scoop (there should be approximately 60 balls) and using the swimming method, deep-fry the balls at 375°F (190°C) until crisp and hot. Drain well and hold in a warm place.

6 To assemble each sandwich, cut a pita in half or open it to form a pocket and stuff with several balls of falafel and ½ ounce (15 grams) each of the shredded lettuce and diced tomatoes and then dress with the yogurt sauce. Arrange the sandwiches as desired and serve hot.

Approximate values per sandwich: **Calories** 290, **Total fat** 3 g, **Saturated fat** 0.5 g, **Cholesterol** 55 mg, **Sodium** 470 mg, **Total carbohydrates** 55 g, **Protein** 12 g, **Claims**—low fat; low saturated fat; good source of fiber

RECIPE 26.12

KENTUCKY HOT BROWN SANDWICH

Yield: 6 Sandwiches

Heavy cream, hot	6 fl. oz.	180 ml
Romano, grated	6 oz.	180 g
Velouté sauce, hot	1 qt.	1 lt
Dry sherry	1 fl. oz.	30 ml
White toast, crust removed	12 slices	12 slices
Turkey breast, sliced	1 lb. 8 oz.	720 g
Parmesan, grated	2 oz.	60 g
Tomato wedges	12	12
Bacon slices, lean, cooked crisp	12	12

1 To make the sauce, add the cream and the Romano to the velouté sauce and bring to a simmer. Simmer for 1 minute, then strain the sauce through a china cap. Stir in the sherry. Hold in a warm place for service.

2 Cut the toast diagonally into triangles.

3 To assemble each sandwich, arrange four toast triangles in a gratin dish and top with 4 ounces (120 grams) of turkey and 4 fluid ounces (120 milliliters) of sauce. Bake at 350°F (180°C) until brown, approximately 15 minutes.

4 Top each sandwich with Parmesan, two tomato wedges and two strips of bacon and serve very hot.

Approximate values per sandwich: **Calories** 720, **Total fat** 34 g, **Saturated fat** 17 g, **Cholesterol** 185 mg, **Sodium** 2180 mg, **Total carbohydrates** 45 g, **Protein** 59 g, **Vitamin A** 20%, **Calcium** 50%

ROAST BEEF AND BLUE CHEESE SANDWICH

RECIPE 26.13

WILDFLOWER BREAD COMPANY, SCOTTSDALE, AZ

Yield: 4 Sandwiches

Red bell peppers, roasted	8 oz.	240 g
Herb Mayonnaise (recipe follows)	8 Tbsp.	120 ml
White sourdough bread	8 slices	8 slices
Blue cheese, crumbled	6 oz.	180 g
Roast beef, rare, cold, sliced thin	1 lb.	440 g
Red onion, sliced thin	2 oz.	60 g
Tomato slices	12	12
Romaine lettuce	4 leaves	4 leaves

1 Slice the bell peppers into strips ¼ inch (6 millimeters) wide.

2 To assemble each sandwich, spread 2 tablespoons (30 milliliters) of Herb Mayonnaise on a slice of bread and top with 1½ ounces (45 grams) of blue cheese. Then place 4 ounces (120 grams) of the roast beef on top of the cheese and cover with ½ ounce (15 grams) of red onion, 2 ounces (60 grams) of bell pepper strips, three tomato slices, one leaf of romaine lettuce and a slice of bread.

Approximate values per sandwich: **Calories** 679, **Total fat** 42 g, **Saturated fat** 17 g, **Cholesterol** 105 mg, **Sodium** 1061 mg, **Total carbohydrates** 41 g, **Protein** 34 g, **Vitamin A** 73%, **Vitamin C** 170%, **Calcium** 30%, **Iron** 25%

HERB MAYONNAISE

Yield: 8 fl. oz. (240 ml)

Mayonnaise	8 fl. oz.	240 ml
Fresh basil, chopped	1 Tbsp.	15 ml
Fresh cilantro, chopped	1 tsp.	5 ml
Fresh parsley, chopped	1 tsp.	5 ml

1 Stir all the ingredients together until the herbs are evenly distributed throughout the mayonnaise. Chill until ready to use.

Approximate values per 1-fl.-oz. (30-ml) serving: **Calories** 200, **Total fat** 22 g, **Saturated fat** 3.5 g, **Cholesterol** 15 mg, **Sodium** 160 mg, **Total carbohydrates** 1 g, **Protein** 0 g

RECIPE 26.14

NEW ORLEANS-STYLE MUFFULETTA SANDWICH

Yield: 1 Sandwich, 4–6 Servings

Red bell pepper, roasted, chopped	1	1
Niçoise or Gaeta olives, pitted, chopped	4 oz.	120 g
Olives, green, pitted, chopped	4 oz.	120 g
Olive oil	4 fl. oz.	120 ml
Fresh Italian parsley, chopped	2 Tbsp.	30 ml
Anchovy fillets, mashed	2	2
Dried oregano	1 tsp.	5 ml
Lemon juice	1 Tbsp.	15 ml
Round Italian bread, 8-in. (18-cm) diameter	1	1
Arugula or curly endive, chiffonade	1½ oz.	45 g
Tomato concassée	6 oz.	180 g
Mortadella, sliced thin	6 oz.	180 g
Soppressata, sliced thin	4 oz.	120 g
Provolone or Fontina, sliced thin	4 oz.	120 g
Black pepper	TT	TT

1 To make the olive salad, combine the bell pepper, olives, olive oil, parsley, anchovies, oregano and lemon juice and marinate for several hours.

2 Cut the loaf of bread in half horizontally. Remove some of the soft interior of the bread to create a slight hollow area.

3 Drain the olive salad, reserving the oil. Brush the interior of the bread with the reserved oil, using it all.

4 Arrange the olive salad, greens, tomato concassée, mortadella, soppressata and cheese in layers on the bottom portion of the loaf of bread, finishing with a thick layer of olive salad. Season the layers with pepper as desired.

5 Place the top on the sandwich and wrap tightly with plastic wrap. Refrigerate the sandwich for several hours so that the layers will remain in place when the sandwich is cut.

6 Cut the sandwich into four to six wedges and arrange as desired for service.

Approximate values per sandwich: **Calories** 670, **Total fat** 57 g, **Saturated fat** 14 g, **Cholesterol** 60 mg, **Sodium** 2200 mg, **Total carbohydrates** 16 g, **Protein** 24 g, **Vitamin C** 80%, **Calcium** 30%

RECIPE 26.15

SOUTHWESTERN GRILLED CHICKEN WRAP

Yield: 12 Sandwiches

Chicken breast, boneless, skinless	3 lb.	1350 g
Salt and pepper	TT	TT
Avocados	3	3
Red bell peppers	2	2
Red onion	1	1
Tomatoes	2	2
Tortillas, 10 in. (24 cm)	12	12
Black Bean Spread (recipe follows)	3 lb.	1350 g
Black olives, sliced	1 c.	250 ml
Fresh cilantro, chopped	2 bunches	2 bunches
Cheddar, grated	1 lb. 8 oz.	750 g
Jalapeños, minced	2	2

1 Season the chicken breast with salt and pepper and grill or broil until done. Chill and cut into strips.

2 Peel the avocados and cut each into 12 slices. Clean the bell peppers and cut into strips. Slice the onion thinly. Dice the tomatoes.

3 To make each sandwich, place one tortilla on a cutting board and spread with approximately 4 ounces (120 grams) of Black Bean Spread.

4 Sprinkle $1/12$ of the bell peppers, onion, tomatoes, olives, cilantro, cheese and jalapeños over the bean spread.

5 Top with $1/12$ of the chicken and three slices of avocado.

6 Roll the tortilla around the ingredients tightly enough so that the sandwich will hold its shape. Cut the sandwich as desired for service.

Approximate values per sandwich: **Calories** 642, **Total fat** 37 g, **Saturated fat** 16 g, **Cholesterol** 118 mg, **Sodium** 695 mg, **Total carbohydrates** 37 g, **Protein** 41 g, **Vitamin A** 37%, **Vitamin C** 76%, **Calcium** 50%, **Iron** 22%

BLACK BEAN SPREAD

Yield: 3 lb. (1.3 kg)

Black beans, soaked and drained	1 lb. 8 oz.	680 g
Water	4 qt.	4 lt
Onions, diced	4 oz.	120 g
Tomatoes, diced	6 oz.	180 g
Fresh cilantro, chopped	2 Tbsp.	30 ml
Salt and pepper	TT	TT
Cumin, ground	1 tsp.	5 ml
Chilli powder	1 tsp.	5 ml

1 Combine the beans and the water, bring to a boil, reduce to a simmer and cook until tender, approximately 1 to $1\frac{1}{2}$ hours.

2 Add the remaining ingredients and simmer for 10 minutes.

3 Drain the beans, reserving the cooking liquid. Chill the beans and the liquid.

4 Purée the beans in a food processor, adding enough of the cooking liquid to make a soft, spreadable purée.

Approximate values per 2-oz. (60-g) serving: **Calories** 100, **Total fat** 0.5 g, **Saturated fat** 0 g, **Cholesterol** 0 mg, **Sodium** 51 mg, **Total carbohydrates** 37 g, **Protein** 12 g, **Claims**—low fat; no cholesterol; low sodium

VEGGIE WRAP

RECIPE 26.16

Yield: 1 Sandwich

Spinach-flavored tortilla	1	1
Garlic Yogurt Dressing (recipe follows)	2 Tbsp.	30 ml
Jasmine rice, cooked	3 oz.	90 g
Roma tomato, diced	2 Tbsp.	30 ml
Cucumber, julienne	1 oz.	30 g
Alfalfa sprouts	as needed	as needed
Broccoli florets, blanched	1 oz.	30 g
Red onion, sliced thin	1 oz.	30 g
Capers	1 Tbsp.	15 ml

1 Spread the tortilla with 1 tablespoon (15 milliliters) of the Garlic Yogurt Dressing.
2 Arrange the rice in a mound across the center of the tortilla. Top the rice with the vegetables and capers.
3 Drizzle the remaining Garlic Yogurt Dressing over the vegetables.
4 Using a piece of parchment paper as a wrapper, roll the tortilla tightly around the filling, then chill and serve.

Approximate values per sandwich: **Calories** 464, **Total fat** 3 g, **Saturated fat** 0.5 g, **Cholesterol** 0 g, **Sodium** 296 mg, **Total carbohydrates** 95 g, **Protein** 12 g, **Vitamin A** 12%, **Vitamin C** 45%, **Calcium** 14%, **Iron** 15%

GARLIC YOGURT DRESSING

Yield: 1 pt. (500 ml)

Plain nonfat yogurt	1 pt.	450 ml
Fresh parsley, minced	1 Tbsp.	15 ml
Garlic, minced	2 Tbsp.	30 ml
Dijon mustard	2 Tbsp.	30 ml
Black pepper	¼ tsp.	1 ml
Tabasco sauce	TT	TT

1 Combine all the ingredients and chill until ready to use.

Approximate values per 1 fl.-oz. (30-ml) serving: **Calories** 19, **Total fat** 0 g, **Saturated fat** 0 g, **Cholesterol** 1 mg, **Sodium** 46 mg, **Total carbohydrates** 3 g, **Protein** 2 g

RECIPE 26.17

CLUB SANDWICH

Yield: 1 Sandwich

Sliced bread, toasted	3 slices	3 slices
Mayonnaise	as needed	as needed
Lettuce leaves	2	2
Tomato slices	3	3
Bacon slices cooked crisp	3	3
Salt and pepper	TT	TT
Cooked turkey breast, sliced thin	3 oz.	90 g

1 Spread one side of each slice of bread with mayonnaise.
2 Arrange the lettuce, tomato and bacon on one slice of toast. Season with salt and pepper.
3 Place another slice of toast on top of the bacon.
4 Arrange the turkey breast on top of the second slice of toast.
5 Place the third slice of toast on top of the turkey breast, mayonnaise side down.
6 Place 4 frilled toothpicks in the sandwich, one on each side, approximately 1 inch (2.5 centimeters) in from the edge. Cut the sandwich diagonally into quarters and arrange as desired for service.

Approximate values per sandwich: **Calories** 530, **Total fat** 24 g, **Saturated fat** 6 g, **Cholesterol** 95 mg, **Sodium** 830 mg, **Total carbohydrates** 38 g, **Protein** 39 g, **Vitamin A** 4%, **Vitamin C** 10%

GRILLED SALMON CLUB
WITH CILANTRO AÏOLI

RECIPE 26.18

CAFÉ ALLEGRE, ORLANDO, FL
Chef Kevin Fonzo

Yield: 4 Sandwiches

Salmon fillets, 5 oz. (150 g) each	4	4
Salt and pepper	TT	TT
Olive oil	1 Tbsp.	15 ml
Wheat bread, toasted	12 slices	12 slices
Watercress	2 c.	500 ml
Red onion, cut in rings, ⅛-in.		
(3-mm) thick	8 rings	8 rings
Tomato, sliced thick	8 slices	8 slices
Cilantro Aïoli (recipe follows)	4 Tbsp.	60 ml

1 Season the salmon with salt and pepper and rub with the olive oil, then grill the salmon until medium rare.

2 To assemble each sandwich, top one slice of bread with ½ cup (120 milliliters) of watercress, then two red onion rings and two slices of tomato. Top with a second slice of bread.

3 Place one salmon fillet on the bread.

4 Spread the third slice of bread with 1 tablespoon (15 milliliters) of the Cilantro Aïoli and place on top of the salmon. Cut the sandwich and serve.

Approximate values per sandwich: **Calories** 471, **Total fat** 24 g, **Saturated fat** 3 g, **Cholesterol** 87 mg, **Sodium** 410 mg, **Total carbohydrates** 30 g, **Protein** 34 g, **Vitamin A** 27%, **Vitamin C** 36%, **Iron** 16%

CILANTRO AÏOLI

Yield: 1 qt. (2 lt)

Egg yolks	4	4
Salt	1 tsp.	5 ml
White pepper	TT	TT
Dijon mustard	1 tsp.	5 ml
White vinegar	3 Tbsp.	45 ml
Fresh cilantro, chopped	3 Tbsp.	45 ml
Lime juice	TT	TT
Salad oil	28 fl. oz.	840 ml

1 Combine all the ingredients except the oil in a blender. Process until thoroughly combined.

2 With the blender running, slowly pour the oil into the egg yolk mixture to form an emulsion.

Approximate values per 2-fl.-oz. (60-ml) serving: **Calories** 455, **Total fat** 51 g, **Saturated fat** 6 g, **Cholesterol** 53 mg, **Sodium** 140 mg, **Total carbohydrates** 0.5 g, **Protein** 0.8 g

RECIPE 26.19

EGGPLANT AND SUN-DRIED TOMATO PIZZA

GREENS, San Francisco, CA
Chef Annie Somerville

Yield: 1 Pizza 15 in. (37 cm) each, or
2 Pizzas, 9 in. (22 cm) each

Japanese eggplants	2	2
Extra virgin olive oil	2 fl. oz.	60 ml
Garlic, chopped	2 tsp.	10 ml
Salt and pepper	TT	TT
Pizza Dough (page 985)	1 lb.	450 g
Sun-dried tomatoes, packed in oil	5	5
Provolone, grated	4 oz.	120 g
Mozzarella, grated	2 oz.	60 g
Parmesan, grated	½ oz.	15 g
Fresh basil leaves, chiffonade	12	12

1 Slice the eggplants diagonally into ½-inch (1.2-centimeter) slices.

2 Toss the eggplants with 1 fluid ounce (30 grams) of olive oil and the garlic; season with salt and pepper.

3 Place the eggplant slices on a baking sheet and roast at 375°F (190°C) until soft in the center, approximately 15 to 20 minutes. Cool and slice into strips.

4 Preheat the oven to 500°F (260°C). Roll out the dough and place it on a lightly oiled pizza pan or well-floured wooden peel; brush it lightly with the remaining olive oil. Lay the eggplant and sun-dried tomatoes on top. Toss the Provolone and mozzarella together and sprinkle on the pizza.

5 Bake the pizza until the crust is golden and crisp, approximately 8 to 12 minutes. Remove from the oven and sprinkle with the Parmesan and basil.

Approximate values per 4-oz. (120-g) serving: **Calories** 420, **Total fat** 17 g, **Saturated fat** 5 g, **Cholesterol** 15 mg, **Sodium** 500 mg, **Total carbohydrates** 54 g, **Protein** 14 g, **Vitamin A** 100%, **Vitamin C** 30%

RECIPE 26.20

WHOLE WHEAT CALZONE WITH SPINACH AND FETA

SPOKANE COMMUNITY COLLEGE, Spokane, WA
Instructor Peter Tobin, CEC, CCE

Yield: 12 Servings

Crust:

Water, warm	1 pt.	450 ml
Granulated sugar	2 Tbsp.	30 ml
Yeast, dry	½ oz.	15 g
Whole-wheat flour	8 oz.	250 g
Bread flour	1 lb.	500 g
Olive oil	4 Tbsp.	60 ml
Salt	2 tsp.	10 ml

Filling:

Clarified butter	2 fl. oz.	60 ml
Onion, small dice	1	1
Frozen spinach, thawed, drained, chopped	24 oz.	675 g
Dried thyme	1 tsp.	5 ml

Cottage cheese	2 lb.	900 g
Feta	12 oz.	360 g
Nutmeg, ground	½ tsp.	2 ml
Salt	1 tsp.	5 ml
Pepper	1 tsp.	5 ml
Provolone or mozzarella, grated	1 c.	240 ml
Tomato sauce (page 235)	3 pt.	1.4 lt
Egg wash	4 fl. oz.	120 ml
Cornmeal	as needed	as needed

1 In a mixing bowl, combine the water and sugar and then add the yeast, flours, olive oil and salt. Using a dough hook, mix the dough on medium speed until it is smooth and elastic, approximately 10 minutes.

2 Place the dough in a lightly oiled bowl, cover with a towel and remove to a warm area to proof until the dough has doubled in volume, approximately 1 hour.

3 Heat the butter in a sauce pan. Add the onion and sauté lightly. Add the spinach and thyme and cook until heated through.

4 Transfer the spinach mixture to a bowl and stir in the cottage cheese, feta, nutmeg, salt, pepper and grated cheese. Spread the mixture on a sheet pan and refrigerate until completely cool.

5 To build the calzones, punch down the dough and divide into 12 equal pieces. Roll out each piece of dough into an 8-inch (20-centimeter) round. Spread the center of each round with 1 fluid ounce (30 milliliters) of Tomato sauce. Place 4–6 ounces (120–180 grams) of the spinach mixture in the middle of each round. Brush the edges of the dough with egg wash. Fold the dough in half around the filling, forming a half circle. Seal the edges with your fingers or the tines of a fork. Dust a sheet pan with cornmeal and place the calzones on the pan.

6 Brush the calzones with egg wash and bake at 425°F (220°C) until the crust is evenly browned and the filling is hot, approximately 7 to 10 minutes. Serve the calzones hot with Tomato Sauce on the side.

Approximate values per serving: **Calories** 660, **Total fat** 23 g, **Saturated fat** 11 g, **Cholesterol** 75 mg, **Sodium** 2300 mg, **Total carbohydrates** 78 g, **Protein** 37 g, **Vitamin A** 100%, **Vitamin C** 25%, **Calcium** 35%, **Iron** 30%

THERE ARE ONLY TWO QUESTIONS TO ASK ABOUT
FOOD. IS IT GOOD? AND IS IT AUTHENTIC? WE ARE
OPEN [TO] NEW IDEAS, BUT NOT IF IT MEANS
DESTROYING OUR HISTORY. AND FOOD IS HISTORY.

—*Giuliano Bugialli, quoted in* The New York
    Times, *May 9, 1984*

27

CHARCUTERIE

CHEF LELAND ATKINSON, Washington, D.C.

**AFTER STUDYING THIS
CHAPTER, YOU WILL BE
ABLE TO:**

▶ prepare a variety of forcemeats

▶ assemble and cook a variety of
  pâtés, terrines and sausages

▶ understand the proper methods
  for brining, curing and smoking
  meats and fish

▶ identify several cured pork
  products

Traditionally, charcuterie (shar-COO-turh-ree) was limited to the production of pork-based pâtés, terrines and galantines. Over the years, however, the term has come to include similar products made with game, poultry, fish, shellfish and even vegetables. Many of these are discussed here.

Charcuterie is an art and science in itself. This chapter is not intended to be a complete guide to the charcutier's art. Instead, we focus on procedures for making common charcuterie items that can be prepared easily in most kitchens. We also discuss the preparation of sausages as well as curing methods, including salt curing, brining and both cold and hot smoking. The chapter ends with information about several cured pork products.

▶ FORCEMEATS AND THEIR USES

A **forcemeat** is a preparation made from uncooked ground meats, poultry, fish or shellfish that is seasoned and then emulsified with fat. Forcemeats are the primary ingredient used to make pâtés, terrines, galantines and sausages.

The word *forcemeat* is derived from the French word *farce,* meaning "stuffing." Depending on the preparation method, a forcemeat can be very smooth and velvety, well-textured and coarse, or anything in between. Regardless of its intended use, it has a glossy appearance when raw and will slice cleanly when cooked. A properly emulsified forcemeat provides a rich flavor and a comforting texture on the palate.

Forcemeats are emulsified products. Emulsification is the process of binding two ingredients that ordinarily would not combine. (Emulsified sauces are discussed in Chapter 11, Stocks and Sauces; emulsified salad dressings are discussed in Chapter 24, Salads and Salad Dressings.) The proteins present in the meat, poultry, fish and shellfish combine easily with both fat and liquids. In forcemeats, these proteins act as a stabilizer that allows the fat and liquids, which ordinarily would not combine, to bind. When improperly emulsified forcemeats are cooked, they lose their fat, shrink and become dry and grainy. To ensure proper emulsification of a forcemeat:

1 The ratio of fat to other ingredients must be precise.
2 Temperatures must be maintained below 40°F (4°C).
3 The ingredients must be mixed properly.

FORCEMEAT INGREDIENTS

Forcemeats are usually meat, poultry, fish or shellfish combined with binders, seasonings and sometimes garnishes. Selections from each of these basic categories are used to make an array of forcemeats. All ingredients must be of the finest quality and added in just the right proportions.

MEATS

The **dominant meat** is the meat, poultry, fish or shellfish that gives the forcemeat its name and essential flavor. When preparing meats, poultry or fish for forcemeat, it is important to trim all silverskin, gristle and small bones so that the meat will be more easily ground and will produce a smoother finished product.

Many forcemeats contain some pork. Pork adds moisture and smoothness to the forcemeat. Without it, poultry-based forcemeats tend to be rubbery, while venison and other game-based forcemeats tend to be dry. The traditional ratio is one part pork to two parts dominant meat.

Many forcemeats also contain some liver. Pork liver is commonly used, as is chicken liver. Liver contributes flavor as well as binding to the forcemeat. For a finer texture, grind the livers and then force them through a drum sieve before incorporating them into the forcemeat.

FATS

Here, *fat* refers to a separate ingredient, not the fat in the dominant meat or pork, both of which should be quite lean in order to ensure the correct ratio of fat to meat. Usually pork fatback or heavy cream is used to add moisture and richness to the forcemeat. Because fat carries flavor, it also promotes the proper infusion of flavors and smoke.

BINDERS

There are two principal types of binders: panadas and eggs.

A **panada** (pah-nahd) is something other than fat that is added to a forcemeat to enhance smoothness (especially in fish mousselines, which tend to be slightly grainy in texture), to aid emulsification (especially in vegetable terrines, where the protein levels are insufficient to bind on their own) or both (for example, in liver mousses). It should not make up more than 20 percent of the forcemeat's total weight. Usually a panada is nothing more than crustless white bread soaked in milk or, more traditionally, a heavy béchamel or rice.

Eggs or egg whites are used as a primary binding agent in some styles of forcemeat. If used in forcemeats that have a large ratio of liver or liquids, they also add texture.

SEASONINGS

Forcemeats are seasoned with salt, curing salt, marinades and various herbs and spices.

Salt not only adds flavor to a forcemeat but also aids in the emulsification of the meat and fat. As with other foods, a forcemeat that lacks salt will taste flat.

Curing salt is a mixture of salt and sodium nitrite. Sodium nitrite controls spoilage by inhibiting bacterial growth. Equally important, curing salt preserves the rosy pink colors of some forcemeats that might otherwise oxidize to an unappetizing gray. Although currently regarded as substantially safer than the previously used potassium nitrate (saltpeter), some studies suggest that sodium nitrite is a carcinogen. For a typical consumer, however, the amount of sodium nitrite consumed from cured meats should not pose a substantial health threat.

Traditionally, ingredients for forcemeats were marinated for long periods, sometimes days, before grinding. The trend today is for a shorter marinating time so that the true flavors of the main ingredients shine through. Both classic and contemporary marinades include herbs, citrus zest, spices and liquors, all of which lend flavor, character and nuance to the forcemeat.

Pâté spice is a mixture of spices and dried herbs that can be premixed and used as needed.

PÂTÉ SPICE

RECIPE 27.1

Yield: 7²/₃ oz. (220 g)

Cloves	1 oz.	30 g
Dried ginger	1 oz.	30 g
Nutmeg	1 oz.	30 g

Continued

Paprika	1 oz.	30 g
Dried basil	⅔ oz.	20 g
Black pepper	⅔ oz.	20 g
White pepper	⅔ oz.	20 g
Bay leaf	⅓ oz.	10 g
Dried thyme	1 oz.	30 g
Dried marjoram	⅓ oz.	10 g

1 Grind all the ingredients in a spice grinder. Pass through a sieve to remove any large pieces.

Variation: This mixture can be used as is, or mix 1 ounce (30 grams) (or any amount desired) with 1 pound (450 grams) of salt. The salt-and-spice mixture can then be used to season forcemeats; ⅓ ounce (10 grams) per pound of forcemeat usually suffices for most pâtés.

Approximate values per 1-oz. (30-g) serving: **Calories** 20, **Total fat** 1 g, **Saturated fat** 0 g, **Cholesterol** 0 mg, **Sodium** 0 mg, **Total carbohydrates** 3 g, **Protein** 1 g, **Vitamin A** 6%

A forcemeat's seasoning and texture can be tested by cooking a small portion before the entire forcemeat is cooked. (Unlike sauces, stews and other dishes, you cannot taste and adjust a forcemeat's flavoring during the cooking process.) A small portion of a hearty forcemeat can be sautéed; a small portion of a more delicate forcemeat should be poached for 3–5 minutes. When cooked, the forcemeat should hold its shape and be slightly firm but not rubbery. If it is too firm, add a little cream.

GARNISHES

Forcemeat garnishes are meats, fat, vegetables or other foods added in limited quantities to provide contrasting flavors and textures and to improve appearance. The garnishes are usually diced, chopped or more coarsely ground than the dominant meat. Common garnishes include pistachio nuts, diced fatback, truffles or truffle peelings and diced ham or tongue.

EQUIPMENT FOR PREPARING FORCEMEATS

To properly prepare forcemeats, you should have a food chopper or food processor and a heavy-duty drum sieve with a metal band. You will also need a standard meat grinder or meat-grinding attachment with various-sized grinding dies.

An X-Blade and Assorted Dies for a Standard Grinder

PREPARING FORCEMEATS

The three common forcemeat preparations are **country-style, basic** and **mousseline.** Each can be produced easily in a typical food service operation. Other types of forcemeat preparations such as the emulsified mixture used to make hot dogs and bratwurst are not commonly encountered in food service operations and are not discussed here.

When preparing any forcemeat, certain guidelines must be followed:

1 Forcemeat preparations include raw meats, liver, eggs and dairy products. If improperly handled, these potentially hazardous foods create a good environment for the growth of microorganisms. To avoid the risk of foodborne illness, temperatures must be carefully controlled, and all cutting boards and food contact surfaces must be as sanitary as possible at all times.

2 To ensure a proper emulsification, the forcemeat must be kept cold— below 40°F (4°C)—at all times. Refrigerate all moist ingredients, and keep

forcemeats in progress in an ice bath. Chilling or freezing metal grinder and food processor parts helps keep the ingredients as cold as possible.

3 Cut all foods into convenient sizes that fit easily into grinder openings. Do not overstuff grinders or overfill food processors. When grinding items twice, always begin with a larger die, followed by a medium or small die. For exceptional smoothness, press the forcemeat through a sieve after grinding to remove any lumps or pieces of membrane.

COUNTRY-STYLE FORCEMEATS

A traditional country-style forcemeat is heavily seasoned with onions, garlic, pepper, juniper berries and bay leaves. It is the simplest of the forcemeats to prepare and yields the heartiest and most distinctive pâtés and sausages.

The dominant meat for a country-style forcemeat is usually ground once through the grinder's large die, then ground again through the medium die. This produces the characteristic coarse, country-style texture. As with most forcemeats, the dominant meat for a country-style forcemeat is usually marinated and seasoned prior to grinding and then mixed with some liver.

▶ PROCEDURE FOR PREPARING A COUNTRY-STYLE FORCEMEAT

1 Chill all ingredients and equipment thoroughly. Throughout preparation, they should remain at temperatures below 40°F (4°C).

2 Cut all meats into an appropriate size for grinding.

3 Marinate, under refrigeration, the dominant meat and pork with the desired herbs, spices and liquors.

4 If using liver, grind it and force it through a sieve.

5 Cut the fatback into an appropriate size and freeze.

6 Prepare an ice bath for the forcemeat. Then grind the dominant meat, pork and fat as directed in the recipe, usually once through the grinder's largest die and a second time through the medium die.

7 If using liver, eggs, panada or garnishes, fold them in by hand, remembering to keep the forcemeat over an ice bath at all times.

8 Cook a small portion of the forcemeat; adjust the seasonings and texture as appropriate.

9 Refrigerate the forcemeat until needed.

COUNTRY-STYLE FORCEMEAT   RECIPE 27.2

Yield: 5 lb. (2.2 kg)

Lean pork, diced	2 lb.	900 g
Pâté spice	2 Tbsp.	30 ml
Salt	1 Tbsp.	15 ml
Black pepper	TT	TT
Brandy	2 fl. oz.	60 ml
Pork liver, cleaned and diced	1 lb.	450 g
Fatback, diced	1 lb.	450 g
Onions, small dice	3 oz.	90 g
Garlic, minced	1 Tbsp.	15 ml
Fresh parsley, chopped	3 Tbsp.	45 ml
Eggs	6	6

1 Marinating the meat and fatback with herbs and spices.

1 Combine the diced pork with the pâté spice, salt, pepper and brandy; marinate under refrigeration for several hours.

2 Grind the liver and force it through a drum sieve. Reserve.

2 Forcing the ground liver through a sieve.

3 Grinding half of the meat a second time.

4 Incorporating the liver and eggs into the ground meat mixture over an ice bath to keep the forcemeat cold.

3 Grind the marinated pork and fatback through the grinder's large die.

4 Grind half of the pork and fatback a second time through the medium die along with the onions, garlic and parsley.

5 Working over an ice bath, combine the coarse and medium ground pork with the liver and eggs.

6 Cook and taste a small portion of the forcemeat and adjust the seasonings as necessary.

The forcemeat is now ready to use as desired in the preparation of pâtés, terrines, galantines and sausages.

Approximate values per 1-oz. (30-g) serving: **Calories** 90, **Total fat** 8 g, **Saturated fat** 3 g, **Cholesterol** 50 mg, **Sodium** 105 mg, **Total carbohydrates** 1 g, **Protein** 5 g, **Vitamin A** 30%

BASIC FORCEMEATS

Smoother and more refined than a country-style forcemeat, a basic forcemeat is probably the most versatile of all. It should be well seasoned, but the seasonings should not mask the dominant meat's flavor. Examples of basic forcemeats are those used in most game pâtés and terrines as well as traditional pâtés en croûte.

A basic forcemeat is made by grinding the meat and fat separately—the meat twice and the fat once. The fat is then worked into the meat, either by hand or in a food processor or chopper. A quicker method involves grinding the fat and meat together and then blending them in a food processor. Whichever method is used, some recipes call for the incorporation of crushed ice to minimize friction, reduce temperature and add moisture.

▶ PROCEDURE FOR PREPARING A BASIC FORCEMEAT

1 Chill all ingredients and equipment thoroughly. Throughout preparation, they should remain at temperatures below 40°F (4°C).

2 Cut all meats into an appropriate size for grinding.

3 Marinate, under refrigeration, the dominant meat and pork with the desired herbs, spices and liquors.

4 If using liver, grind it and force it through a sieve.

5 Cut the fatback into an appropriate size and freeze.

6 Grind the meats twice, once through the grinder's large die and then through the medium die; hold on an ice bath.

7 Grind the chilled or frozen fat once through the medium die and add it to the meat mixture.

8 Work the fat into the meat over an ice bath or in a well-chilled food processor or chopping machine.

9 Over an ice bath, add any required eggs, panada and/or garnishes and work them into the mixture.

10 Cook a small portion of the forcemeat in stock or water; adjust the seasonings and texture as appropriate.

11 Refrigerate the forcemeat until needed.

An alternative method for preparing a basic forcemeat replaces Steps 6 to 9 with the following procedures:

6a Grind the meats and fats together twice.

7a Place them in a food processor or chopper and blend until smooth.

8a Add any required eggs or panada while the machine is running and blend them in with the meat and fat.

9a Remove the forcemeat from the machine and, working over an ice bath, fold in any garnishes by hand.

Whichever method is used, a particularly warm kitchen or a lengthy running time in the food processor or chopping machine may necessitate the addition of small quantities of crushed ice to properly emulsify the forcemeat. Add the ice bit by bit while the machine is running.

BASIC FORCEMEAT   RECIPE 27.3

Yield: 4 lb. 8 oz. (2 kg)

Veal, diced	1 lb. 8 oz.	650 g
Lean pork, diced	1 lb. 8 oz.	650 g
Brandy	2 fl. oz.	60 ml
Pâté spice	2 tsp.	10 ml
Salt	1½ tsp.	7 ml
White pepper	TT	TT
Fatback, diced	1 lb. 8 oz.	650 g
Eggs	4	4
Ham, medium dice	4 oz.	120 g
Pistachio nuts	2 oz.	60 g
Black olives, chopped coarse	2 oz.	60 g

1 Combine the veal and pork with the brandy, pâté spice, salt and white pepper; marinate under refrigeration for several hours.

2 Grind the meats through the grinder's large die and again through the small die.

1 Grinding the meat through the chilled grinder.

2 Combining the fat with the meat in the food processor.

3 Adding the eggs to the meat.

4 Folding the garnishes into the forcemeat.

3 Grind the fatback through the grinder's small die.

4 Combine the meat and fat in the bowl of a food processor and blend until they are emulsified.

5 Work in the eggs until the forcemeat is smooth and well emulsified. Do not overprocess the forcemeat.

6 Fold in the ham, pistachio nuts and olives.

7 Cook a small portion of the forcemeat by poaching or sautéing it. Taste and adjust the seasonings as necessary.

The forcemeat is now ready to use as desired in the preparation of pâtés, terrines, galantines and sausages.

Approximate values per 1-oz. (30-g) serving: **Calories** 140, **Total fat** 12 g, **Saturated fat** 4.5 g, **Cholesterol** 45 mg, **Sodium** 80 mg, **Total carbohydrates** 1 g, **Protein** 7 g

MOUSSELINE FORCEMEATS

A properly made mousseline (moos-uh-LEEN) forcemeat is light, airy and delicately flavored. It is most often made with fish or shellfish but sometimes with veal, pork, feathered game or poultry. (A mousseline forcemeat is not the same as a mousse, which usually contains gelatin and is discussed later.)

A mousseline forcemeat is prepared by processing ground meats and cream in a food processor; often egg whites are added to lighten and enrich the mixture. The proportion of fish or dominant meat to eggs to cream is very important: too many egg whites, and the mousseline will be rubbery; too few, and it may not bind together. If too much cream is added, the mousseline will be too soft or will fall apart during cooking.

A mousseline forcemeat can be served hot or cold. It can be used to make fish sausages and a variety of timbales and terrines, or it can be used to make quenelles, which are discussed later. A shrimp mousseline is used with Paupiettes of Sole, page 560.

▶ PROCEDURE FOR PREPARING A MOUSSELINE FORCEMEAT

1 Chill all ingredients and equipment thoroughly. Throughout preparation, they should remain at temperatures below 40°F (4°C).

2 Cut all meats into an appropriate size for processing.

3 Grind the meat in a cold food processor until smooth. Do not overprocess.

4 Add eggs and pulse until just blended.

5 Add cream and seasonings in a steady stream while the machine is running. Stop the machine and scrape down the sides of the bowl once or twice during the processing. Do not run the machine any longer than necessary to achieve a smooth forcemeat.

6 If desired, pass the forcemeat through a drum sieve to remove any sinew or bits of bone.

7 Over an ice bath, fold in any garnishes by hand.

8 Poach a small amount of the mousseline in stock or water. Taste and adjust the seasonings and texture as necessary.

9 Refrigerate until ready for use.

MOUSSELINE FORCEMEAT   RECIPE 27.4

Yield: 4 lb. (1.8 kg)

Fish, scallops, skinless chicken breast or lean veal	2 lb.	900 g
Egg whites	4	4
Salt	1 Tbsp.	15 ml
White pepper	TT	TT
Nutmeg, ground	TT	TT
Cayenne pepper	TT	TT
Heavy cream	1 qt.	1 lt

1 Grind the dominant meat through a large die.

2 Process the meat in a food processor until smooth.

3 Add the egg whites one at a time and pulse the processor until they are incorporated.

4 Scrape down the sides of the processor's bowl and add the spices.

5 With the machine running, add the cream in a steady stream.

6 Scrape down the bowl again and process the mousseline until it is smooth and well mixed. Do not overprocess.

7 Remove the mousseline from the machine and hold in an ice bath. If additional smoothness is desired, force the mousseline through a drum sieve in small batches using a plastic scraper or rubber spatula.

8 Cook a small portion of the forcemeat by poaching it. Taste and adjust the seasonings and texture as necessary.

The forcemeat is now ready to cook as quenelles or use as desired in the preparation of pâtés, terrines, galantines and sausages.

Approximate values per 1-oz. (30-g) serving: **Calories** 80, **Total fat** 7 g, **Saturated fat** 4 g, **Cholesterol** 30 mg, **Sodium** 25 mg, **Total carbohydrates** 1 g, **Protein** 4 g, **Vitamin A** 8%

1 Processing the ground meat in a cold food processor just until smooth.

2 Adding the eggs and pulsing until blended.

3 Adding the cream in a steady stream while the machine runs.

4 Passing the forcemeat through a drum sieve to ensure a smooth finished product.

QUENELLES

Quenelles (kuh-NEHL) are small dumpling-shaped portions of a mousseline forcemeat poached in an appropriately flavored stock. Quenelles are a traditional garnish for many soups and a popular appetizer usually accompanied by a tomato coulis or a sauce based on a fish velouté. The technique used for making and poaching quenelles is also used for testing the seasoning and consistency of a mousseline forcemeat.

▶ PROCEDURE FOR PREPARING QUENELLES

1 Prepare a mousseline forcemeat.

2 Bring an appropriately flavored poaching liquid to a simmer.

3 Use two spoons to form the forcemeat into oblong-shaped dumplings. For small quenelles, use small spoons; for larger quenelles, use larger spoons.

4 Poach the quenelles until done. Test by breaking one in half to check the center's doneness.

5 Small soup-garnish-sized quenelles can be chilled in ice water, drained and held for service. Reheat them in a small amount of stock before garnishing the soup.

Forming the quenelles using two spoons and poaching until done.

▶ USING FORCEMEATS

Forcemeats are used as basic components in the preparation of other foods, including terrines, pâtés, galantines and sausages. Aspic jelly is also an important component of these products.

TERRINES, PÂTÉS AND GALANTINES

Traditionally, a **pâté** (pah-tay) was a fine savory meat filling wrapped in pastry, baked and served hot or cold. A **terrine** was considered more basic, consisting of coarsely ground and highly seasoned meats baked in an earthenware mold and always served cold. (The mold is also called a terrine, derived from the French word *terre,* meaning "earth.") Today, many types of pâtés are baked in loaf-type pans without a crust, which according to tradition would make them terrines, while pâtés baked in pastry are called **pâtés en croûte** (pah-tay awn croot). Thus, the terms *pâté* and *terrine* are now used almost interchangeably. **Galantines** (GAL-uhn-teen) are made from forcemeats of poultry, game or suckling pig wrapped in the skin of the bird or animal and poached in an appropriate stock. They are usually served cold. **Ballotines** (bahl-lo-teen) are similar, but generally use only deboned poultry legs and are served hot.

Terrines, pâtés and galantines are often made with forcemeats layered with garnishes to produce a decorative or mosaic effect when sliced. A wide variety of foods can be used as garnishes, including strips of ham, fatback or tongue; mushrooms or other vegetables; truffles and pistachio nuts. Garnishes should always be cooked before they are added to the pâté, terrine or galantine, or they will shrink during cooking, creating air pockets.

PÂTÉ PANS, MOLDS AND TERRINES

Pâté pans, molds and terrines come in a variety of shapes and sizes. Pâtés that are not baked in a crust can be prepared in standard metal loaf pans of any shape, although rectangular ones make portioning the cooked pâté much easier. For pâtés en croûte, the best pans are collapsible or hinged, thin-metaled ones. They make it easier to remove the pâté after baking. Collapsible and hinged pans come in various shapes and sizes, from small plain rectangles to large intricately fluted ovals. Traditional earthenware molds and terrines as well as ones made from enameled cast iron, metal, glass or even plastic are available. Most terrines are rectangular or oval in shape. Several of these pans are illustrated in Chapter 5, Tools and Equipment.

TERRINES

Terrines are forcemeats baked in a mold without a crust. The mold can be the traditional earthenware dish or some other appropriate metal, enameled cast iron or glass mold. Any type of forcemeat can be used to make a terrine. The terrine can be as simple as a baking dish filled with a forcemeat and baked until done. A more attractive terrine can be constructed by layering the forcemeat with garnishes to create a mosaic effect when sliced. A terrine can even be layered with different forcemeats—for example, a pink salmon mousseline layered with a white pike mousseline.

▶ PROCEDURE FOR PREPARING TERRINES

1 Prepare the desired forcemeat and garnishes and keep refrigerated until needed.

2 Line a mold with thin slices of fatback, blanched leafy vegetables or other appropriate liner. (Some chefs claim that the fatback keeps the terrine moist during cooking; most modern chefs do not agree but nevertheless use it for aesthetic purposes.) The lining should overlap slightly, completely covering the inside of the mold and extending over the edge of the mold by approximately 1 inch (2.5 centimeters). Alternatively, line the mold with plastic wrap.

3 Fill the terrine with the forcemeat and garnishes, being careful not to leave air pockets. Tap the mold several times on a solid work surface to remove any air pockets.

1 Lining a mold with thin slices of fatback.

2 Filling the terrine with the forcemeat and garnish.

3 Placing the herb-decorated terrine in a water bath.

4 Slicing the finished terrine.

4 Fold the liner or plastic wrap over the forcemeat and, if necessary, use additional pieces to completely cover its surface.

5 If desired, garnish the top of the terrine with herbs that were used in the preparation of the forcemeat.

6 Cover the terrine with its lid or aluminum foil and bake in a water bath in a 350°F (180°C) oven. Regulate the oven temperature so that the water stays between 170°F and 180°F (77°C and 82°C).

7 Cook the terrine to an internal temperature of 150°F (66°C) for meat-based forcemeats or 140°F (60°C) for fish- or vegetable-based forcemeats.

8 Remove the terrine from the oven and allow it to cool slightly. If desired, pour off any fat and liquid from around the terrine and cover it with cool liquid aspic jelly.

Several types of terrines are not made from traditional forcemeats; many others are not made from forcemeats at all. But all are nonetheless called terrines because they are molded or cooked in the earthenware mold called a terrine. These include liver (and foie gras) terrines, vegetable terrines, brawns or aspic terrines, mousses, rillettes and confits.

Liver terrines are popular and easy to make. Puréed poultry, pork or veal livers are mixed with eggs and a panada of cream and flour, then baked in a fatback-lined terrine. Although most livers purée easily in a food processor, a smoother finished product is achieved if the livers are forced through a drum sieve after or in lieu of puréeing them in the processor.

Foie gras terrines are made with the fattened geese or duck livers called foie gras. Foie gras is unique, even among other poultry livers, in that it consists almost entirely of fat. (See Chapter 18.) It requires special attention during cooking; if it is cooked improperly or too long, it turns into a puddle of very expensive fat.

Vegetable terrines, which have a relatively low fat content, are becoming increasingly popular. Beautiful vegetable terrines are made by lining a terrine with a blanched leafy vegetable such as spinach, then alternating layers of two or three separately prepared vegetable fillings to create contrasting colors and flavors. A different style of vegetable terrine is made by suspending brightly colored vegetables in a mousseline forcemeat to create a mosaic pattern when sliced.

Brawns or **aspic terrines** are made by simmering gelatinous cuts of meat (most notably, pigs' feet and head, including the tongue) in a rich stock with wine and flavorings. The stock is enriched with the gelatin and flavor from the meat, creating an unclarified aspic jelly. The meat is then pulled from the bone, diced and packed into the terrine mold. The stock is reduced to concentrate its gelatin content, strained through cheesecloth and poured over the meat in the terrine. After the terrine has set, it is removed from the mold and sliced for service. The finished product is a rustic and flavorful dish.

A more elegant-appearing brawn is made by lining a terrine mold with aspic jelly, arranging a layer of garnish (for example, sliced meats, vegetables or low-acid fruits) along the mold's bottom, adding aspic jelly to cover the garnish and repeating the procedure until the mold is full.

A **mousse** can be sweet or savory. Sweet mousses are described in Chapter 34, Custards, Creams, Frozen Desserts and Dessert Sauces. A savory mousse—which is not a mousseline forcemeat—is made from fully cooked meats, poultry, game, fish, shellfish or vegetables that are puréed and combined with a béchamel or other appropriate sauce, bound with gelatin and lightened with whipped cream. A mousse can be molded in a decorated, aspic-jelly-coated mold such as that described next, or it can be formed in molds lined with plastic wrap, which is peeled off after the mousse is unmolded. A small mousse can be served as an individual portion; a larger molded mousse can be displayed on a buffet.

ASPIC JELLY

Aspic jelly is a savory jelly produced by increasing the gelatin content of a strong stock and then clarifying the stock following the process for preparing consommé discussed in Chapter 12, Soups. Brown stock produces an amber aspic jelly; white stock produces a more lightly colored one.

Although gelatin is a natural ingredient present in all good meat or poultry stocks, its concentration level is not normally high enough to produce a firm aspic jelly. Additional gelatin is usually added to the stock in order to assist gelling (setting). This can be done in two ways. The first is to produce a stock with an extremely high gelatin content by using gelatinous meats and bones such as calves' feet, pigs' ears and pork skin; the second is to add plain gelatin to a

finished stock. An easier method of preparing aspic jelly is to add gelatin directly to a flavorful finished consommé.

Aspic jelly has many applications throughout the kitchen. In addition to adding flavor and shine, a coating of aspic jelly prevents displayed foods from drying out and inhibits the oxidation of sliced red meats. Aspic jelly is often lightly flavored with liquors such as Madeira and cut into decorative garnishes for both plated presentations and buffet displays. It is also used to bind savory mousses, glaze slices of pâté and coat molded mousses. Aspic jelly is funneled into cooked pâtés en croûte to fill the gaps created when the forcemeat shrinks during the cooking process. Aspic jelly is also the basis of aspic molds or terrines (often simply

called aspics), in which layers of cooked meats or vegetables are bound together and held in place by the aspic jelly. Many of these uses are discussed later.

The gelatin content of aspic jelly varies depending upon its intended use. Aspic jelly to be used only on a display can have a very high gelatin content for easier handling. Aspic jelly to be eaten should be fairly firm when cold, gelled at room temperature but tender enough to melt quickly in the mouth when eaten. To test the gelatin content of a liquid, pour a teaspoon (5 milliliters) onto a plate and refrigerate the plate for a few minutes. If the liquid does not gel firmly, additional gelatin can be softened in a small amount of cool liquid then added to the hot liquid.

▶ PROCEDURE FOR PREPARING ASPIC-JELLY-COATED CHILLED MOUSSES

A mold can be lined with aspic jelly, then decorated and filled with cold mousse. The aspic-jelly-coated mousse is then unmolded for an attractive presentation.

Rillettes and **confits** are actually preserved meats. Rillettes (ree-YEHT) are prepared by seasoning and slow-cooking pork or fatty poultry such as duck or goose in generous amounts of their own fat until the meat falls off the bone. The warm meat is mashed and combined with a portion of the cooking fat. The mixture is then packed into a crock or terrine, and rendered fat is strained over the top to seal it. Rillettes are eaten cold as a spread accompanied by bread or toast.

Confit (kohn-FEE) is prepared in a similar manner except that before cooking, the meat or poultry is often lightly salt-cured to draw out some moisture. The confit is then cooked until very tender but not falling apart. Confits are generally served hot. Like rillettes, confits can be preserved by sealing them with a layer of strained rendered fat. Properly prepared and sealed rillettes and confits will keep for several weeks under refrigeration.

Although it is sometimes incorrectly called chicken liver pâté, **chopped chicken liver** is prepared in a similar fashion to a rillette. Chopped chicken liver, however, will not have the keeping qualities of traditional rillettes or con-

Table 27.1	GELATIN CONCENTRATIONS	
TYPE OF GEL	**AMOUNT OF GELATIN PER GALLON (4 LT) OF WATER**	**TYPICAL USE**
Soft	2 oz. (60 g)	Cubed aspic jelly for edible garnishes
Firm	4 oz. (120 g)	Brushing slices of pâté or galantine; glazing edible centerpieces; molding terrines, aspics and brawns that will be sliced
Very firm	8 oz. or more (225 g or more)	Nonedible purposes such as coating nonedible centerpieces or trays for presentations

1 Set a metal mold in ice water and add 8 fluid ounces (250 milliliters) of cool liquid aspic jelly. Swirl the mold so the aspic jelly adheres to all sides. Pour out the excess aspic jelly. Repeat as needed to achieve the desired thickness; ¼ inch (6 millimeters) or less is usually sufficient.

2 Garnish the mold by dipping pieces of vegetable or other foods in the liquid aspic jelly and placing them carefully inside the aspic-jelly-coated mold. The mold can now be filled with a cold filling such as a mousse.

3 Refrigerate the mold until it is well chilled. Unmold the aspic by dipping the mold in warm water, then inverting and tapping the mold on a plate.

fits because it is not normally sealed in a crock or terrine with rendered fat. It should be eaten within a day or two of its preparation.

PÂTÉS EN CROÛTE

Considered by some to be the pinnacle of the charcutier's art, pâtés en croûte are forcemeats baked in a crust. The forcemeat can be country-style, basic or mousseline, but a basic forcemeat is most commonly used. Although pâtés en croûte can be baked without using a mold, a mold helps produce a more attractive finished product.

Pâté Dough (Pâte au Pâté)

The crust surrounding a baking forcemeat must be durable enough to withstand the long baking process and hold in the juices produced as the pâté bakes. Unfortunately, some of the more durable crusts are tough and unpleasant to eat.

The goal is to achieve a balance so that the crust will hold the juices of the baking pâté and still be relatively pleasant to the palate. Some pâtés, especially more delicate ones such as fish mousselines, can be wrapped in brioche dough (page 987).

RECIPE 27.5   PÂTÉ DOUGH

Yield: 1 lb. 8 oz. (680 g)

All-purpose flour	1 lb.	450 g
Shortening	7 oz.	200 g
Salt	1½ tsp.	7 ml
Water	5 fl. oz.	150 ml
Egg	1	1

1 Place the flour in the bowl of a mixer. Add the shortening and mix on low speed until smooth.

2 Combine the salt, water and egg; add them to the flour and shortening mixture.

3 Knead until smooth and refrigerate. The dough will be easier to work with if allowed to rest for at least 1 hour.

Approximate values per 1-oz. (30-g) serving: **Calories** 150, **Total fat** 9 g, **Saturated fat** 2 g, **Cholesterol** 10 mg, **Sodium** 100 mg, **Total carbohydrates** 15 g, **Protein** 2 g

▶ PROCEDURE FOR ASSEMBLING AND BAKING PÂTÉS EN CROÛTE

After preparing a forcemeat and pastry dough, all that remains is to assemble and bake the pâté en croûte. The amount of pastry dough and forcemeat needed is determined by the size of the mold or pan chosen.

1 Prepare the pâté dough and the forcemeat, keeping the forcemeat refrigerated until needed.

2 Roll out the dough into a rectangular shape ⅛ inch (3 millimeters) thick.

3 Using the pâté mold as a pattern, determine how much dough is needed to line its inside; allow enough dough along each side of the mold's length to cover the top when folded over. Mark the dough. Cut the dough slightly larger than the marked lines. Cut a second rectangular piece of dough that is slightly larger than the top of the mold; it will be used as a lid.

4 Lightly butter the inside of the mold.

5 Lightly dust the large rectangle of dough with flour, fold it over and transfer it to the mold.

6 Use your thumbs and a dough ball made from dough trimmings to form the dough neatly into the corners of the mold. Continue until the dough is of even thickness on all sides and in the corners.

7 Trim the dough, leaving ¾ inch (2 centimeters) on the ends and enough dough to cover the top along the sides.

8 Line the dough-covered mold with thin slices of fatback or ham, allowing ¾ inch (2 centimeters) extra around the top of the mold, or as directed in the recipe. This layer helps protect the pastry crust from coming in contact with the moist forcemeat, which would make it soggy.

9 Fill the lined mold with the forcemeat to ½ inch (1.2 centimeters) below the top of the mold, pressing it well into the corners to avoid air pockets. Layer and garnish as appropriate.

1 Cutting the dough into a large rectangle.

2 Pressing the dough into the mold with a floured dough ball.

3 Lining the dough-covered mold with thin slices of fatback.

4 Filling the lined mold with the forcemeat and garnish.

5 Placing the top on the pâté.

6 Pouring aspic jelly into the steam hole of the baked pâté through an aluminum foil chimney.

7 Slicing the pâté with a thin-bladed knife.

10 Fold the fatback or ham over the top of the forcemeat, using additional pieces if necessary to cover its entire surface. Fold the pastry over the forcemeat.

11 Brush the exposed surface of the pastry with egg wash; carefully cap with the top piece of dough. Press any overlapping dough down inside the sides of the mold with a small spatula.

12 Using round cutters, cut one or two holes in the top to allow steam to escape during cooking. Egg-wash the surface. Place a doughnut-shaped piece of dough around each of the holes. Egg-wash any decorations.

13 Bake the pâté in a preheated 450°F (230°C) oven for 15 minutes. Then cover the surface of the pâté with aluminum foil. Reduce the heat to 350°F (180°C) and continue baking until the internal temperature reaches 150°F (66°C) for meat pâtés or 140°F (60°C) for fish and vegetable pâtés.

14 Allow the pâté to cool for at least 1 hour or overnight. Using a funnel, pour cool liquid aspic jelly through the holes to fill the space created when the pâté shrank during cooking. Allow the pâté en croûte to cool overnight before slicing.

▶ PROCEDURE FOR GLAZING PÂTÉ SLICES WITH ASPIC JELLY

Slices of chilled terrines, pâtés en croûte or gallantines (discussed next) may be garnished and coated with aspic to preserve their color, prevent drying and create a more attractive presentation.

1 Cool the clarified aspic jelly by slowly stirring it over an ice bath.

2 Brush or spoon the aspic jelly over slices of chilled pâté arranged on a cooling rack. Repeat the process until the coating reaches the desired thickness.

GALANTINES

A classic galantine is a boned chicken stuffed with a chicken-based forcemeat to resemble its original shape and then poached. Today, galantines are still most often prepared from whole ducks or chickens, but they can also be made from game, veal, fish or shellfish. When appropriate, the forcemeat is stuffed in the skin, which has been removed in one piece, sometimes with flesh still attached. When the skin is not available, or in the case of fish and shellfish where there is no skin, the galantine is made by forming the forcemeat into a cylindrical shape and wrapping it in cheesecloth, or plastic wrap and foil, before poaching. Galantines are always served cold and are often displayed on buffets, sliced and glazed with aspic jelly.

A ballotine is similar to a galantine. It is made by removing the bones from a poultry leg, filling the cavity with an appropriate forcemeat and poaching or braising the leg with vegetables. Ballotines are often served hot with a sauce made from the cooking liquid.

▶ PROCEDURE FOR PREPARING A POULTRY GALANTINE

1 Bone the chicken by cutting through the skin along the length of the backbone and then following the natural curvature of the carcass. Keep all the meat attached to the skin. Remove the legs and wings by cutting through the joints when you reach them; leave the legs and wings attached to the skin. Then cut off the wings. Bone the thighs and legs, leaving the skin and meat attached to the rest of the bird. Trim the skin to form a large rectangle.

2 Prepare a forcemeat using the meat from the skinned bird or any other appropriate meat. Reserve a portion of the meat as garnish if desired. Prepare any other garnishes. Refrigerate the forcemeat and garnishes until needed.

3 Spread out the skin and meat on plastic wrap or several layers of cheesecloth with the skin side down and the flesh up.

4 Remove the chicken tenderloins and pull the tendon out of each. Butterfly the breasts and tenderloins and cover the entire skin with a thin layer of meat.

5 Arrange the forcemeat and garnishes in a cylindrical shape across the center of the skin.

6 Using the plastic or cheesecloth to assist the process, tightly roll the skin around the forcemeat and garnishes to form a tight cylinder.

7 Tie the ends of the cheesecloth with butcher's twine and secure the galantine at even intervals using strips of cheesecloth. If plastic wrap was used, wrap the galantine with heavy-duty aluminum foil.

1 Butterflying the breasts and tenderloins and placing a thin layer of meat over the skin.

2 Arranging the forcemeat and garnishes in a cylindrical shape across the center of the skin.

3 Using plastic wrap to roll the galantine into a tight cylinder.

4 Securing the galantine with heavy-duty aluminum foil.

5 Slicing the finished product.

8 Poach the galantine in water (or a full-flavored stock if wrapped in cheesecloth) to an internal temperature of 150°F (66°C) for meat-based forcemeats or 140°F (60°C) for fish- or vegetable-based forcemeats.

9 Cool the galantine in its cooking liquid until it can be handled. Remove the cheesecloth or plastic wrap and aluminum foil and rewrap the galantine in clean cheesecloth or plastic wrap. Refrigerate overnight before decorating or slicing.

SAUSAGES

Sausages are forcemeats stuffed into casings. For centuries, sausages consisted of ground meat, usually pork, and seasonings. Today, sausages are made not only from pork, but also from game, beef, veal, poultry, fish, shellfish and even vegetables.

There are three main types of sausages:

1 **Fresh sausages** include breakfast sausage links and Italian sausages. They are made with fresh ingredients that have not been cured or smoked.

2 **Smoked** and **cooked sausages** are made with raw meat products treated with chemicals, usually the preservative sodium nitrite. Examples are kielbasa, bologna and hot dogs.

3 **Dried** or **hard sausages** are made with cured meats, then air-dried under controlled conditions. Dried sausages may or may not be smoked or cooked. Dried or hard sausages include salami, pepperoni and soppressata.

Smoked and cooked sausages and dried or hard sausages are rarely prepared in typical food service operations. Rather, they are produced by specialty shops and will not be discussed here. We do, however, discuss the ingredients and procedures for a variety of fresh sausages that can be prepared in almost any kitchen.

SAUSAGE COMPONENTS

Sausage Meats

Sausage meats are forcemeats with particular characteristics and flavorings. Coarse Italian and lamb sausages, for example, are simply a country-style forcemeat without liver and with different seasonings, stuffed into casings and formed into links. Hot dogs, bratwurst and other fine-textured sausages are variations of basic forcemeats stuffed into casings and formed into links.

Sausage Casings

Although sausage mixtures can be cooked without casings, most sausages are stuffed into casings before cooking. Two types of sausage casings are commonly used in food service operations:

1 **Natural casings** are portions of hog, sheep or cattle intestines. Their diameters are measured in millimeters, and they come in several sizes depending upon the animal or portion of the intestine used. Sheep casings are considered the finest-quality small casings. Both hog and sheep casings are used to make hot dogs and many types of pork sausage. Beef casings are quite large and are used to make sausages such as ring bologna and Polish sausage. Most natural casings are purchased in salt packs. In order to rid them of salt and impurities, the casings must be carefully rinsed in warm water and allowed to soak in cool water for at least 1 hour or overnight before use.

2 **Collagen casings** are manufactured from collagen extracted from cattle hides. They are generally inferior to natural casings in taste and texture, but they do have advantages: Collagen casings do not require any washing or soaking prior to use, and they are uniform in size.

PREPARING SAUSAGES

Equipment for Making Sausages

Sausage-stuffing machines are best if you engage in large-scale sausage production. Otherwise, all you need is a grinder with a sausage nozzle. Nozzles are available in several sizes to accommodate the various casing sizes.

Sausage Nozzles

▶ PROCEDURE FOR PREPARING SAUSAGES

1 Prepare a forcemeat.

2 Thoroughly chill all parts of the sausage stuffer that will come in contact with the forcemeat.

3 Rinse and soak the casings if using natural ones. Cut the casings into 4- to 6-foot (1.2- to 1.8-meter) lengths.

4 Put the sausage in the sausage stuffer.

5 Slide the entire casing over the nozzle of the sausage stuffer. Tie the end in a knot and pierce with a skewer to prevent an air pocket.

6 Support and guide the casing off the end of the nozzle as the sausage is extruded from the nozzle into the casing.

7 After all the sausage has been stuffed into the casing, twist or tie the sausage into uniform links of the desired size.

1 Sliding the casing over the nozzle of the sausage stuffer.

2 Knotting and piercing the casing with a skewer.

3 Supporting and guiding the casing off the end of the nozzle as the sausage is extruded from the machine into the casing.

4 Twisting the sausage into uniform links.

▶ **andouille (an-DOO-ee)** a very spicy smoked pork sausage, popular in Cajun cuisine

▶ **chorizo (chor-EE-zoh)** a coarse, spicy pork sausage flavored with ground chiles and removed from its casing before cooking; used in Mexican and Spanish cuisines

▶ **mortadella (mohr-tah-DEH-lah)** an Italian smoked sausage made with ground beef, pork and pork fat, flavored with coriander and white wine; it is air-dried and has a delicate flavor; also a large American bologna-type pork sausage studded with pork fat and garlic

▶ **pepperoni (peh-peh-ROH-nee)** a hard, thin, air-dried Italian sausage seasoned with red and black pepper

▶ **soppressata (soh-preh-SAH-tah)** a hard, aged Italian salami, sometimes coated with cracked peppercorns or herbs

▶ SALT-CURING, BRINING AND SMOKING

Curing, brining and smoking are ancient techniques for preserving food. Today, foods such as hams, corned beef and smoked salmon are salt-cured, brined or smoked primarily for flavor. Cured meats have a characteristic pink color caused by the reaction of sodium nitrite, which is added during processing, with the naturally occurring myoglobin protein in the meat.

SALT-CURING

Salt-curing is the process of surrounding a food with salt or a mixture of salt, sugar, nitrite-based curing salt, herbs and spices. Salt-curing dehydrates the food, inhibits bacterial growth and adds flavor. It is most often used with pork products and fish. Salt-curing is not a quick procedure—and the time involved adds money to production costs. For example, country-style hams are salt-cured. Proper curing requires approximately one and a half days per pound of ham, which means three weeks for the average ham.

Some salt-cured hams such as Smithfield and prosciutto are not actually cooked. The curing process preserves the meat and makes it safe to consume raw. Gravlax (page 887) is a well-known salmon dish prepared by salt-curing salmon fillets with a mixture of salt, sugar, pepper and dill.

BRINING

A brine is actually a very salty marinade. Most brines have approximately 20% salinity, which is equivalent to 1 pound (450 grams) of salt per gallon (4 liters) of water. As with dry-salt cures, brines can also contain sugar, nitrites, herbs and spices. Brining is sometimes called pickling.

Today, most cured meats are prepared in large production facilities where the brine is injected into the meat for rapid and uniform distribution. Commercially brined corned beef is cured by this process, as are most common hams. After brining, hams are further processed by smoking.

SMOKING

There are two basic methods of smoking foods: cold smoking and hot smoking. The principal difference is that hot smoking actually cooks the food, while cold smoking does not.

Both are done in a **smoker** specifically designed for this purpose. Smokers can be gas or electric; they vary greatly in size and operation. But they have several things in common. All consist of a chamber that holds the food being smoked, a means of burning wood to produce smoke and a heating element.

Different types of wood can be used to smoke food. Specific woods are selected to impart specific flavors. Hickory is often used for pork products; alder is excellent for smoked salmon. Maple, chestnut, juniper, mesquite and many other woods are also used. Resinous woods such as pine give food a bitter flavor and should be avoided.

Cold smoking is the process of exposing foods to smoke at temperatures of 50°F to 85°F (10°C to 29°C). Meat, poultry, game, fish, shellfish, cheese, nuts and even vegetables can be cold-smoked successfully. Most cold-smoked meats are generally salt-cured or brined first. Salt-curing or brining adds flavor, allows the nitrites (which give the ham, bacon and other smoked meats their distinctive pink color) to penetrate the flesh and, most important, extracts moisture from the food, allowing the smoke to penetrate more easily. Cold-smoked foods are actually still raw. Some, such as smoked salmon (lox), are eaten without further cooking. Most, such as bacon and hams, must be cooked before eating.

Hot smoking is the process of exposing foods to smoke at temperatures of 200°F to 250°F (93°C to 121°C). As with cold smoking, a great variety of foods can be prepared by hot smoking. Meats, poultry, game, fish and shellfish that are hot-smoked also benefit from salt-curing or brining. Although most hot-smoked foods are fully cooked when removed from the smoker, many are used in other recipes that call for further cooking.

PORK PRODUCTS

Preparing hams and curing and smoking pork products are a traditional part of charcuterie. Although most bacon and ham are now produced in large commercial facilities, the chef still works with these products and must be able to identify them properly.

Most bacon comes from a hog's fatty belly.

Common bacon is produced by brining and cold-smoking trimmed pork belly. It is available in slab or sliced form. Sliced bacon is purchased by count (number of slices) per pound; thick-sliced bacon runs 10–14 slices per pound, while thin-sliced bacon may contain as many as 28–32 slices per pound.

Canadian bacon is produced from a boneless pork loin, trimmed so that only a thin layer of fat remains on its surface. It is then brined and smoked.

Pancetta (pan-CHEH-tuh) is an Italian pork-belly bacon that is not smoked. It is salt-cured, peppered and often rolled into a cylinder shape. It can be sliced into rounds and fried; it is diced, rendered and combined with sauce to make fettuccine carbonara.

A fresh ham is a hog's hind leg; it is a primal cut. Many processed products produced from the primal fresh ham are also called ham.

Ham, in the United States, describes a variety of processed pork products, most of which come from the primal fresh ham. **Boneless** or **formed hams** are produced by separating a primal ham into its basic muscles, defatting the meat, curing it, stuffing the meat into casings of various sizes and shapes and cooking it. Boneless or formed hams either are smoked or have chemical smoke flavoring added during the curing process. The quality of boneless or formed hams varies greatly. The best hams are formed from only one or two large muscles and have low fat content and no added water other than that used during the curing process. Hams of lesser quality are formed from many small pieces of muscle and have a higher fat and water content. Many boneless or formed hams are listed in *The Meat Buyers Guide* and are indexed by the NAMP/IMPS system.

Country ham is a specialty of the southeastern United States. Country hams are dry-cured, smoked and hung to air-dry for a period ranging from several weeks to more than a year. During drying, a mold develops on the ham rind that must be scrubbed off before the ham is cooked. It is best cooked by first soaking, then slow simmering. The most famous country hams are Virginia hams; those from Smithfield, Virginia, are considered the finest. Only hams produced in rural areas can be called country hams; others must be labeled country-style ham.

Prosciutto (proh-SHOO-toh) is the Italian word for ham. What we call prosciutto in this country is called **Parma** in Italy. Parma ham, produced near that Italian city, is made from hogs fed on the whey of cheese processed nearby. It is salt-cured and air-dried but not smoked. The curing process makes it safe and wholesome to consume raw. Several domestic varieties of prosciutto are produced, varying widely in quality. Imported prosciuttos are much larger than the domestic varieties because Italian hogs are larger when butchered.

Sliced Bacon

Canadian Bacon

Pancetta

IMPS No. 501, Ham short shank, cured and smoked

IMPS No. 510, Ham, boneless, skinless, cured and smoked, fully cooked

Prosciutto

Westphalian ham is dry-cured, brined and then smoked with beechwood. Authentic Westphalian hams are produced in the Westphalia region of Germany and are quite similar to prosciutto. They are sold bone-in or boneless. Their characteristic flavor is derived from the juniper berries used in the curing process and the beechwood used for smoking.

▶ SAUCE CHAUD-FROID

Sauce chaud-froid (shoh-FRAWH) (French for "hot-cold") is prepared hot but served cold. Traditionally used to coat meats, poultry or fish that were eaten cold, sauce chaud-froid is now more typically used to coat a whole poached salmon or whole roasted poultry item, which is then further decorated and used as a centerpiece. As with aspic jelly, chaud-froid that is to be eaten should be fairly firm when cold, gelled at room temperature but tender enough to melt quickly in the mouth when eaten. Chaud-froid used for decorative purposes only should have a heavier gelatin content and be quite firm, which makes it easier to work with.

A classic sauce chaud-froid is a mixture of one part cream and two parts stock (veal, chicken and/or fish) strengthened with gelatin. Depending on the stock used, this coating ranges in color from cream to beige. A more modern sauce chaud-froid (also known as a mayonnaise chaud-froid or mayonnaise collée) is based on mayonnaise; it is easier to make than the classic sauce and provides a whiter product, which is more desirable when used for centerpieces.

RECIPE 27.6   **MAYONNAISE CHAUD-FROID**

Yield: 2 qt. (2 lt)

Aspic jelly (firm to very firm)	1 qt.	1 lt
Mayonnaise (commercially made)	1 lb.	450 g
Sour cream	1 lb.	450 g

1 Melt the aspic jelly.
2 In a stainless steel bowl, combine the mayonnaise with the sour cream and mix until smooth.
3 Stir the aspic jelly into the mayonnaise and sour cream mixture until smooth.
4 Warm the sauce over a double boiler, stirring gently with a spoon until smooth and all the air bubbles disappear.

▶ PROCEDURE FOR COATING FOODS WITH SAUCE CHAUD-FROID

1 Cook (usually by poaching or roasting), trim and otherwise prepare the item to be decorated.
2 Place the item on a cooling rack over a clean sheet pan and refrigerate until ready to decorate. (Sauce that drips into the clean pan can be reused.)
3 Warm an ample amount of sauce chaud-froid in a stainless steel bowl over a double boiler until it is completely melted. Stir the sauce gently with a spoon rather than a whisk in order to prevent air bubbles from forming.
4 When the sauce is warm and smooth, remove the bowl from the double boiler and place it in an ice bath.
5 Using the back of a large ladle, stir the sauce by spinning the bowl and holding the ladle stationary. This should be done almost continuously while the sauce cools. Do not scrape the solidified chaud-froid from the sides of the bowl, as lumps will form.

1 Scoring the skin of the fish.

2 Removing the skin.

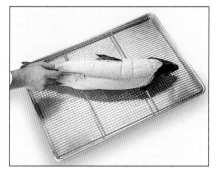

3 Removing the dark flesh and preparing the fish for the first coating of sauce chaud-froid.

4 Glazing the fish with the sauce chaud-froid.

5 Decorating the fish with vegetable flowers.

6 The decorated fish ready for service.

6 When the sauce has cooled to room temperature, remove the item to be decorated from the refrigerator and place it on the work table.

7 Coat the item with the sauce in a single, smooth motion. Use a ladle if the item is small; if it is large, pour the sauce directly from the bowl. The sauce should adhere to the cold food, and the coating should be free of bubbles or runs.

8 Repeat as necessary, reusing the sauce that drips onto the sheet pan, until the desired thickness is achieved.

9 Using a paring knife, carefully cut away any sauce from areas that are to be left uncoated.

10 Decorate the item as desired with vegetable flowers or other garnishes. If desired, finish the item by coating the vegetable garnishes with a layer of clear aspic jelly, using the same procedure.

CONCLUSION

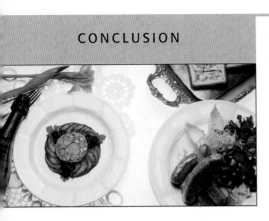

The classic art of charcuterie is as popular today as ever. Consumers regularly enjoy high-quality pâtés, sausages, hams and other charcuterie products.

Although production procedures have changed as new technologies and equipment have developed, the basic principles remain the same: Terrines, pâtés and sausages can be produced only from high-quality forcemeats, and temperature control is fundamental to the proper production of forcemeats and other charcuterie products.

Armed with a basic knowledge of the procedures used for charcuterie, you can use your imagination and creativity to produce a variety of charcuterie products.

QUESTIONS FOR DISCUSSION

1 Explain why the art of charcuterie is relevant to the training of modern chefs.

2 Compare the three styles of forcemeat.

3 In what way is a terrine different from a pâté? How does a pâté differ from a pâté en croûte?

4 Describe the differences and the similarities between a ballotine and a galantine.

5 Describe the typical procedure for making sausages. Why is the selection of casings important?

6 Explain the difference between hot smoking and cold smoking. Describe a food typically prepared by each of these methods.

SMOKED DUCK AND FOIE GRAS GALANTINE ON A PEAR GALETTE

RECIPE 27.7

Note: This dish appears in the chapter opening photograph.

CHEF LELAND ATKINSON, Washington, DC

Yield: 1 Galantine

Duck breast, 10 oz. (300 g), boneless, skinless	1	1
Duck meat, lean	1 lb.	450 g
Pork butt, boneless, cubed	8 oz.	240 g
Pâté spice	2 tsp.	10 ml
Salt	1 Tbsp.	15 ml
Orange zest	1 Tbsp.	15 ml
Fresh thyme	1 tsp.	5 ml
Fresh ginger	1 tsp.	5 ml
Juniper berries, crushed	10	10
Port	4 fl. oz.	120 ml
Olive oil	1 fl. oz.	30 ml
Fatback, cubed	8 oz.	240 g
Foie gras pâté, diced	3 oz.	90 g
Ham, medium dice	2 oz.	60 g
Pistachios, chopped	2 oz.	60 g
Fatback, slab	as needed	as needed
Smoker marinade:		
Brown sugar	2 oz.	60 g
Garlic, chopped	1 tsp.	5 ml
Lemon juice	3 fl. oz.	90 ml
Walnut oil	6 fl. oz.	180 ml
Salt and pepper	TT	TT
Galette (per order):		
Pear	1	1
Clarified butter	1 tsp.	5 ml
Sugar	½ tsp.	3 ml
Italian parsley	as needed	as needed

CHEF LELAND ATKINSON

Chef Leland Atkinson began his career at age 14, washing dishes, breading tons of fried chicken and watching remarkable black cooks work their magic at Tom Flynn's Plantation Style Restaurant in Stone Mountain, Georgia. He soon moved on, completing an ACF apprenticeship with Omni International Hotels in Atlanta, Georgia, in 1981. He has worked in a variety of hotels and restaurants, including the Ritz-Carlton Buckhead Hotel in Atlanta, the Four Seasons Olympic Hotel in Seattle and Mark Miller's Red Sage in Washington, D.C. Chef Atkinson is the author of "¡Cocina! A Hands-On Guide to the Techniques of Southwestern Cooking," which won the 1996 Julia Child Cookbook Award in the Food Reference Category.

For the past 10 years Chef Atkinson's hobby has been working as a part-time member of the White House culinary staff, assisting Chef Walter Schieb and his staff with state dinners and gala receptions.

Chef Atkinson advises young cooks that restraint can be the toughest discipline to develop. He says, "Use the best ingredients that you can find, and then stay out of their way. Keep it simple. Don't try to show the sum total of your knowledge on every plate."

1 Cut the duck breast into several long strips.

2 Marinate the duck breast, duck meat and pork in the pâté spice, salt, orange zest, thyme, ginger, juniper berries and port for 2 days.

3 Remove the strips of duck breast from the marinade and sauté in the olive oil to brown. Remove, drain and reserve.

4 Grind the remaining duck meat, pork and marinade ingredients and the cubed fatback in a chilled grinder, first through the large die then through the small die.

5 Place the ground meat in a stainless steel bowl over an ice bath. Fold in the foie gras, ham and pistachios.

6 Slice the fatback slab into thin sheets. Spread a piece of plastic wrap on the work surface and lay out the slices of fatback in a large rectangle with the edges overlapping slightly.

7 Place the forcemeat and duck breast strips along the length of the fatback rectangle so that when the galantine is rolled up the strips of duck will be arranged in the center. Use the plastic wrap to roll the galantine into a large cylinder.

8 Roll the cylinder in heavy-duty aluminum foil and poach until it reaches an internal temperature of 140°F (60°C). Remove and chill the galantine for at least 6 hours.

9 Combine the smoker marinade ingredients in a blender. Unwrap the galantine, brush it with the smoker marinade and chill for 1 hour. Place the galantine in a smoker and cold-smoke for 2 hours. Remove and chill before slicing.

10 For each galette, core the pear and slice ⅛ inch (3 millimeters) thick. Add the clarified butter to a warm sauté pan and arrange the pear slices in the pan by overlapping them to form a circle. Sprinkle the pear slices with the sugar. Sauté the galette, using a spatula to carefully turn it over when browned on the first side.

11 Place a pear galette on a plate and place a slice of galantine directly in the center of the galette. Garnish with Italian parsley or as desired. May be accompanied by Cherry Confit (page 821).

Approximate values per 4-oz. (120-g) serving: **Calories** 280, **Total fat** 22 g, **Saturated fat** 8 g, **Cholesterol** 100 mg, **Sodium** 290 mg, **Total carbohydrates** 5 g, **Protein** 17 g, **Vitamin C** 10%, **Iron** 20%

LAMB SAUSAGE WITH TRICOLOR BEAN SALAD

RECIPE 27.8

Note: This dish appears in the chapter opening photograph.

CHEF LELAND ATKINSON, Washington, DC

Yield: 12 Links, 4 oz. (120 g) each

Lamb shoulder	3 lb.	1.5 kg
Salt	1 Tbsp.	15 ml
Garlic, chopped	2 tsp.	10 g
Paprika	1 Tbsp.	15 ml
Cayenne pepper	½ tsp.	2 ml
Black pepper	½ tsp.	2 ml
Cumin, ground	1 Tbsp.	15 ml
Fresh cilantro, chopped	2 Tbsp.	30 ml
Tricolor Bean Salad (recipe follows)	as needed	as needed
Baby lettuces, assorted	12 heads	12 heads
Belgian endive	2 heads	2 heads
Olive oil	as needed	as needed
Red wine vinegar	as needed	as needed

1 Cut the meat in small cubes.

2 Combine the meat with the seasonings and herbs and refrigerate for 1 hour.

3 Grind the meat through a medium die directly into casings.

4 Grill or sauté the sausage links.

5 Present the cooked links with a portion of the Tricolor Bean Salad garnished with baby greens and Belgian endive. Accent with drizzled olive oil and red wine vinegar.

Approximate values per 4-oz. (120-g) serving of sausage: **Calories** 330, **Total fat** 19 g, **Saturated fat** 7 g, **Cholesterol** 135 mg, **Sodium** 680 mg, **Total carbohydrates** 1 g, **Protein** 37 g, **Iron** 20%

TRICOLOR BEAN SALAD

Yield: 24 oz. (700 g)

Dijon mustard	2 Tbsp.	30 ml
Garlic, minced	1 tsp.	5 ml
Red onion, small dice	1 oz.	30 g
Jalapeños, seeded and minced	2	2
Red wine vinegar	2 Tbsp.	30 ml
Olive oil	3 Tbsp.	45 ml
Black beans, cooked	4 oz.	120 g
Black-eyed peas, cooked	4 oz.	120 g
Plum tomatoes, concassée	3	3
Fresh cilantro, chopped	1 bunch	1 bunch
Salt and pepper	TT	TT

1 Combine the mustard, garlic, onion, jalapeños and red wine vinegar in a mixing bowl.

2 Slowly whisk in the olive oil in a steady stream.

3 Add the beans, black-eyed peas, tomato concassée and cilantro and season with salt and pepper. Refrigerate 1 hour to allow the flavors to blend.

Approximate values per 1-oz. (30-g) serving: **Calories** 30, **Total fat** 2 g, **Saturated fat** 0 g, **Cholesterol** 0 mg, **Sodium** 125 mg, **Total carbohydrates** 2 g, **Protein** 1 g, **Claims**—low fat; low sodium; low calorie

VEGETABLE TERRINE IN BRIOCHE

RECIPE 27.9

Note: This dish appears in the chapter opening photograph.

CHEF LELAND ATKINSON, WASHINGTON, DC

Yield: 1 Terrine, 12 × 4 × 3 in.
(30 × 10 × 7.5 cm)

Chicken breast meat, lean	2 lb.	900 g
Egg whites	3	3
Heavy cream	4 fl. oz.	120 ml
Brandy	2 fl. oz.	60 ml
Nutmeg, ground	TT	TT
Salt and pepper	TT	TT
Carrots, medium dice	3 oz.	90 g
Broccoli florets	8 oz.	250 g
Shiitake mushrooms, trimmed	12–18	12–18
Olive oil	1 fl. oz.	30 ml
Red bell peppers, medium dice	2 oz.	60 g
Leeks, white part only, medium dice	2 oz.	60 g
Fresh chives, basil and parsley, chopped	4 Tbsp.	60 ml
Brioche dough	1 lb.	450 g
Egg yolks, beaten	2	2
Eggs	2	2
Water	2 Tbsp.	30 ml
Madeira aspic	as needed	as needed

1 Dice or grind the chicken and place it in the bowl of a cold food processor and process.

2 Add the egg whites and then the cream and brandy in a steady stream while the motor is running.

3 Season the mousseline with nutmeg, salt and pepper and poach a small amount to test for texture and seasonings.

4 Adjust the seasonings and transfer to a metal mixing bowl in an ice bath.

5 Separately blanch the carrots and broccoli; drain and blot dry on a paper towel.

6 Sauté the mushrooms in olive oil. Drain and chill. In the same pan, sauté the bell peppers and leeks. Remove from the stove and add the herbs. Fold the carrots, peppers, leeks and herbs into the mousseline.

7 Roll the brioche dough out to approximately 1/8 inch (3 millimeters) thick and refrigerate until well chilled.

8 Line a buttered pâté mold with the chilled brioche, reserving the excess for the top and garnish.

9 Fill the mold one-quarter full with the mousseline. Layer the mushrooms over the mousseline and then cover them with another layer of mousseline, followed by the broccoli. Repeat this process until the mold is filled, finishing with a layer of mousseline.

10 Fold the ends of the brioche over the filling and brush with the beaten egg yolks.

11 Make a top from the remaining brioche and place it over the mold; cut a vent and insert a foil funnel into the vent.

12 Beat the eggs with the water to make an egg wash. Brush the exposed brioche with the egg wash and bake at 425°F (220°C) until the internal temperature reaches 125°F (52°C), approximately 35–40 minutes.

13 When cold, fill the pâté with Madeira aspic, if needed.

Approximate values per slice: **Calories** 450, **Total fat** 20 g, **Saturated fat** 6 g, **Cholesterol** 185 mg, **Sodium** 520 mg, **Total carbohydrates** 35 g, **Protein** 34 g, **Vitamin A** 45%, **Vitamin C** 150%, **Claims**—high fiber

RECIPE 27.10 **BASIC GAME FORCEMEAT**

Yield: 4 lb. 8 oz. (2 kg)

Venison, cubed	1 lb. 8 oz.	675 g
Veal, cubed	1 lb. 8 oz.	675 g
Brandy	4 fl. oz.	120 ml
Salt and pepper	TT	TT
Dried thyme	1 tsp.	5 ml
Pork fatback, cubed	1 lb.	450 g
Eggs	3	3
Game stock, cold	1 pt.	450 ml
Fresh parsley, chopped	1 oz.	30 g
Green peppercorns	1/2 oz.	15 g

1 Combine the venison and veal with the brandy, salt, pepper and thyme; marinate for several hours or overnight.

2 Grind the marinated meat and marinade ingredients in a chilled meat grinder once through a large die and then once through a small die; refrigerate.

3 Grind the fatback once through the small die.

4 Emulsify the fat with the ground meats in the bowl of a cold food processor. This can be done in several batches. Place the forcemeat in a stainless steel bowl over an ice bath.

5 Add the eggs, stock, parsley and peppercorns to the forcemeat in several batches; work them in by hand.

6 Additional garnishes may be added as desired. The forcemeat can be used to make a variety of pâtés or terrines.

Approximate values per 1-oz. (30-g) serving: **Calories** 100, **Total fat** 7 g, **Saturated fat** 3 g, **Cholesterol** 40 mg, **Sodium** 110 mg, **Total carbohydrates** 1 g, **Protein** 7 g

SALMON AND SEA BASS TERRINE
WITH SPINACH AND BASIL

RECIPE 27.11

Yield: 1 Terrine, 12 × 4 × 3 in.
(30 × 10 × 7.5 cm)

Salmon fillet, boneless, skinless	1 lb. 8 oz.	700 g
Egg whites	3	3
Salt and white pepper	TT	TT
Cayenne pepper	TT	TT
Heavy cream	24 fl. oz.	700 ml
Fresh basil leaves	12	12
Truffles, brunoise (optional)	¾ oz.	22 g
Spinach leaves, cleaned	6 oz.	180 g
Sea bass fillet	12 oz.	350 g

1 Grind the salmon through the large die of a well-chilled meat grinder.

2 Place the salmon in the bowl of a food processor and process until smooth.

3 Add the egg whites, one at a time, pulsing the processor to incorporate. Scrape down the bowl and season with salt, white pepper and cayenne pepper.

4 With the machine running, add the cream in a steady stream. Scrape down the bowl again and process the mousseline until it is smooth and well mixed.

5 Blanch the basil leaves and refresh. Chop them finely.

6 Remove the mousseline from the bowl of the processor. Fold in the basil leaves and truffles and refrigerate.

7 Blanch and refresh the spinach leaves.

8 Spread the spinach leaves on a piece of plastic wrap, completely covering a rectangle approximately the length and width of the terrine mold.

9 Cut the sea bass fillet into strips approximately 1 inch (2.5 centimeters) wide and place end to end on the spinach leaves. Season with salt and white pepper.

10 Use the plastic wrap to wrap the spinach leaves tightly around the fish fillets.

11 Grease a terrine and line it with plastic wrap.

12 Half-fill the lined terrine with the salmon mousseline.

13 Carefully unwrap the spinach and sea bass fillets and place them down the center of the terrine. Fill the terrine with the remaining mousseline.

14 Tap the terrine mold firmly to remove any air pockets, then fold the plastic wrap over the top.

15 Cover and bake the terrine in a water bath at 300°F (150°C) to an internal temperature of 140°F (60°C), approximately 1½ hours.

16 Cool the terrine well, unmold, slice or decorate and serve as desired.

Approximate values per 3.5-oz. (105-g) slice: **Calories** 210, **Total fat** 16 g, **Saturated fat** 8 g, **Cholesterol** 75 mg, **Sodium** 180 mg, **Total carbohydrates** 1 g, **Protein** 15 g, **Vitamin A** 25%

LIVER TERRINE

RECIPE 27.12

Yield: 1 Terrine, 12 × 4 × 3 in.
(30 × 10 × 7.5 cm)

Pork liver	1 lb. 4 oz.	600 g
Fatback, diced	12 oz.	360 g
Onions, diced	6 oz.	180 g
Eggs	2	2
Salt	1 Tbsp.	15 ml
Green peppercorns	½ tsp.	2 ml

Continued

Allspice, ground	½ tsp.	2 ml
Cloves, ground	¼ tsp.	1 ml
Ginger, ground	¼ tsp.	1 ml
Cream sauce	8 fl. oz.	250 ml
Brown veal stock	6 fl. oz.	180 ml
Fatback, sliced	as needed	as needed

1 Trim and dice the liver.
2 Grind the liver and diced fatback through a grinder with a fine die.
3 Add the onions and pass the liver and fatback through the grinder again.
4 Beat together by hand the eggs, salt, green peppercorns, allspice, cloves and ginger.
5 Combine the cream sauce and brown veal stock, add the egg mixture and mix well.
6 Add the ground liver mixture and beat until smooth.
7 Line a terrine with slices of fatback. Fill the mold with the forcemeat and cover with the overhanging slices of fatback.
8 Cover the terrine with its lid or aluminum foil and bake in a water bath at 350°F (180°C) to an internal temperature of 150°F (66°C), approximately 1½ hours.
9 Cool, unmold, slice and serve as desired.

Approximate values per 4-oz. (120-g) serving: **Calories** 490, **Total fat** 46 g, **Saturated fat** 20 g, **Cholesterol** 265 mg, **Sodium** 800 mg, **Total carbohydrates** 5 g, **Protein** 14 g, **Vitamin A** 250%, **Iron** 45%

RECIPE 27.13   **VEGETABLE TERRINE**

Yield: 1 Terrine, 8 × 4 × 3 in.
(20 × 10 × 7.5 cm)

Carrots, diced	1 pt.	500 ml
Cauliflower florets	1 qt.	1 lt
Broccoli florets	1 pt.	500 ml
Cream cheese	3 oz.	90 g
Eggs, separated	3	3
Almonds, ground	2 Tbsp.	30 ml
Salt and pepper	TT	TT
Nutmeg, grated	¼ tsp.	1 ml
Lemon juice	1 tsp.	5 ml
Fresh mint, chopped	1 Tbsp.	15 ml

1 Cook each vegetable separately in a steamer until tender, but not mushy.
2 Purée each vegetable separately in a food processor with 1 ounce (30 grams) of cream cheese and 1 egg yolk.
3 Add the ground almonds to the carrot purée and season with salt and pepper.
4 Add the nutmeg and lemon juice to the cauliflower purée and season with salt and pepper.
5 Add the mint to the broccoli purée and season with salt and pepper.
6 Whip the egg whites to stiff peaks. Fold one-third of the whipped egg whites into each of the vegetable purées.
7 Layer the three purées in a terrine mold. Place the terrine in a water bath and bake at 325°F (160°C) until firm, approximately 45 minutes. Chill for service.

Approximate values per 1-in. (2.5-cm) slice: **Calories** 114, **Total fat** 7 g, **Saturated fat** 3 g, **Cholesterol** 91 mg, **Sodium** 87 mg, **Total carbohydrates** 8.5 g, **Protein** 6 g, **Vitamin A** 171%, **Vitamin C** 87%

ROASTED RED PEPPER MOUSSE

RECIPE 27.14

Yield: 1 ½ pt. (700 ml)

Onions, small dice	3 oz.	90 g
Garlic, chopped	1 tsp.	5 ml
Olive oil	1 fl. oz.	30 ml
Red bell peppers, roasted and peeled, small dice	10 oz.	300 g
Salt and pepper	TT	TT
Chicken stock	8 fl. oz.	225 ml
Granulated gelatin	1 Tbsp.	15 ml
Dry white wine	2 fl. oz.	60 ml
Heavy cream, whipped	6 fl. oz.	180 ml

1. Sauté the onions and garlic in the olive oil until tender, approximately 2 minutes.
2. Add the bell peppers, salt, pepper and chicken stock. Bring to a boil, lower to a simmer and cook for 5 minutes.
3. Soften the gelatin in the white wine, then add it to the bell pepper mixture. Purée the bell pepper mixture in a blender or food processor and strain through a china cap.
4. Place the bell pepper purée over an ice bath. Stir until cool but do not allow the gelatin to set. Fold in the whipped cream. Pour the mousse into aspic-lined or well-oiled timbales or molds and refrigerate several hours or overnight.
5. Unmold the mousse and serve as desired.

Variations: Substitute yellow bell peppers for part or all of the red bell peppers.

Broccoli Mousse—Substitute 8 ounces (225 grams) of blanched, chopped broccoli for the red bell peppers.

Approximate values per 1-oz. (30-g) serving: **Calories** 60, **Total fat** 6 g, **Saturated fat** 2.5 g, **Cholesterol** 15 mg, **Sodium** 200 mg, **Total carbohydrates** 2 g, **Protein** 1 g, **Vitamin C** 25%

SALMON MOUSSE

RECIPE 27.15

Yield: 1 lb. 8 oz. (650 g)

Salmon, boneless, skinless	12 oz.	360 g
Fish velouté, warm	8 fl. oz.	250 ml
Heavy cream	8 fl. oz.	250 ml
Granulated gelatin	1 ½ Tbsp.	23 ml
White wine	4 fl. oz.	120 ml
Salt and white pepper	TT	TT
Cayenne pepper	TT	TT

1. Steam the salmon and transfer it to a food processor while still warm. Add the warm velouté in a steady stream while the machine is running.
2. Whip the cream to soft peaks and reserve.
3. Add the gelatin to the wine and allow it to rest for 5 minutes. Heat the gelatin mixture to a simmer.
4. Transfer the salmon and velouté to a mixing bowl and stir in the gelatin mixture. Season with salt, white pepper and cayenne.
5. When the mixture has cooled to near room temperature, use a rubber spatula to fold in the whipped cream until just mixed. The mousse is now ready to be formed into timbales or molded into various shapes as desired.

Approximate values per 1-oz. (30-g) serving: **Calories** 100, **Total fat** 6 g, **Saturated fat** 3 g, **Cholesterol** 25 mg, **Sodium** 480 mg, **Total carbohydrates** 6 g, **Protein** 5 g, **Vitamin A** 4%

RECIPE 27.16

CHEF JACK SHOOP, CMC, CCE

Yield: 1 Galantine, 8–10 Servings,
4 oz. (120 g) each

Onion, diced	2 Tbsp.	30 ml
Whole butter	1 Tbsp.	15 ml
Lobster meat	4 oz.	120 g
White bread, crust removed	2 slices	2 slices
Egg white	1	1
Heavy cream	9 fl. oz.	270 ml
Sea salt	TT	TT
White pepper	TT	TT
Nutmeg, ground	TT	TT
Fresh dill, chopped	1 tsp.	5 ml
Turbot fillets, skinned, 6 oz. (180 g) each	4	4
Spiny lobster tails, blanched, meat removed and cut into long strips	2	2

1 Sauté the onion in the butter without browning, then allow it to cool.
2 Dice the lobster meat and place in a stainless bowl over ice. Add the cooled onion, slices of white bread, egg white and 1 fluid ounce (30 milliliters) of the cream. Season with salt, white pepper and nutmeg and combine the ingredients well.
3 Grind the mixture very fine in a food processor, then sieve through a strainer if necessary.
4 In a stainless bowl over an ice bath, beat in the remaining heavy cream and stir in the dill.
5 Flatten the turbot fillets with a meat mallet. Season the fillets with salt and white pepper.
6 Place the fillets touching side by side, skin side up, on a large piece of heavy plastic wrap.
7 Spread the forcemeat on the fillets and lay the lobster strips down the center of the assembly.
8 Use the plastic wrap to help roll the galantine, then tie the ends of the wrap with twine.
9 Poach the galantine in fish broth or salted water for about 30 minutes. Cool overnight in the poaching liquid.
10 To serve, slice and plate with salad greens, diced tomatoes and a balsamic vinaigrette.

Approximate values per 4-oz. (120-g) serving: **Calories** 163, **Total fat** 9 g, **Saturated fat** 5 g, **Cholesterol** 74 mg, **Sodium** 215 mg, **Total carbohydrates** 4 g, **Protein** 17 g

RECIPE 27.17

Yield: 20 oz. (600 g)

Chicken livers, trimmed	1 lb.	450 g
Chicken fat or butter	2 oz.	60 g
Eggs, hard-cooked	2	2
Onions, small dice	6 oz.	180 g
Kosher salt and pepper	TT	TT

1 Sautéing the chicken livers.   **2** Chopping the cooked livers.   **3** The finished chopped chicken liver.

1 Sauté the livers in the chicken fat or butter until lightly browned with a slightly pink interior.

2 Chop the livers with a chef's knife, blending in the eggs and onions. Season to taste with kosher salt and pepper.

3 The final product should be slightly coarse and peppery. Blend in additional chicken fat or butter if necessary to make the mixture hold together.

4 Pack into a serving bowl, cover well and chill for 24 hours. Serve with crackers, toast or matzos and sliced radishes.

Approximate values per 1-oz. (30-g) serving: **Calories** 60, **Total fat** 4 g, **Saturated fat** 1 g, **Cholesterol** 105 mg, **Sodium** 240 mg, **Total carbohydrates** 1 g, **Protein** 4 g, **Vitamin A** 70%

RABBIT PÂTÉ EN CROÛTE   RECIPE 27.18

Yield: 1 Pâté, 3 × 3.5 × 16 in.
(7.5 × 8.7 × 40 cm)

Rabbit meat, boneless, large dice	2 lb.	1 kg
Pork butt, large dice	1 lb.	450 g
Marinade:		
Pâté spice	1 Tbsp.	15 ml
Orange zest	2 Tbsp.	30 ml
Lime zest	1 Tbsp.	15 ml
Brandy	4 fl. oz.	120 ml
Fresh thyme	1 bunch	1 bunch
Juniper berries	6	6
Salt and pepper	TT	TT
Fatback, large dice	1 lb.	450 g
Eggs	4	4
Pistachios, chopped coarse	8 oz.	250 g
Ham, diced	6 oz.	180 g
Black olives, chopped coarse	2 oz.	60 g
Rabbit loins, browned lightly in oil	4	4
Rabbit livers, browned lightly in oil	6	6
Pâté dough	1 lb. 8 oz.	700 g

1 Combine the rabbit meat and pork butt with the marinade ingredients and marinate several hours or overnight.

2 Freeze the fatback.

3 Remove the thyme and juniper berries from the marinated meat mixture and grind the meat and the remaining marinade ingredients in a well-chilled grinder once through the large die, then through the medium die. Hold the mixture in an ice bath.

4 Grind the fatback through the medium die and add to the meat mixture.

5 Place the meat mixture and fat in a chilled food processor and process until emulsified.

6 Over an ice bath, incorporate the eggs into the forcemeat.

7 Fold the pistachios, ham and olives into the forcemeat.

8 Follow the procedure for preparing a pâté en croûte using the rabbit loins and livers as garnishes running the length of the pâté.

Approximate values per 5-oz. (150-g) slice: **Calories** 520, **Total fat** 39 g, **Saturated fat** 12 g, **Choles-terol** 155 mg, **Sodium** 230 mg, **Total carbohydrates** 14 g, **Protein** 29 g, **Vitamin A** 80%, **Iron** 20%

RECIPE 27.19   TEX-MEX TURKEY SAUSAGE

Yield: 4 lb. (1.8 kg)

Canola oil	4 Tbsp.	60 ml
Onions, chopped fine	12 oz.	360 g
Garlic, minced	1 Tbsp.	15 ml
Jalapeño, chopped	1 Tbsp.	15 ml
Turkey breast meat, trimmed of fat	2 lb.	1 kg
Veal, lean	8 oz.	250 g
White wine vinegar	2 fl. oz.	60 ml
Water	8 fl. oz.	250 ml
Fresh cilantro, chopped	4 oz.	120 g
White pepper	1 tsp.	5 ml
Chilli powder	1 tsp.	5 ml
Cumin, ground	½ tsp.	2 ml
Salt	1 tsp.	5 ml

1 Heat the oil and sauté the onions, garlic and jalapeño until the onions are translucent; remove and chill well.

2 Grind the turkey and veal in a cold meat grinder, once through the large die and then through the medium die. Working over an ice bath, combine the meats, vinegar, water and seasonings. Add the sautéed vegetables.

3 Blend well, then cook a small portion to test the flavor and texture. Adjust the seasonings.

4 Stuff into casings or portion into 2-ounce (60-gram) patties and broil. Serve with papaya salsa.

Approximate values per 2-oz. (60-g) serving: **Calories** 80, **Total fat** 2.5 g, **Saturated fat** 0 g, **Choles-terol** 30 mg, **Sodium** 115 mg, **Total carbohydrates** 3 g, **Protein** 12 g, **Vitamin A** 8%, **Vitamin C** 8% **Iron** 15%, **Claims**—low fat; low sodium

---

RECIPE 27.20   SPICY ITALIAN SAUSAGE

Yield: 5 lb. (2.2 kg)

Pork butt	5 lb.	2.2 kg
Salt	1½ Tbsp.	23 ml
Black pepper	1½ tsp	7 ml
Fennel seeds	1½ tsp.	7 ml
Paprika	1 Tbsp.	15 ml
Red pepper, crushed	1½ tsp.	7 ml
Coriander, ground	¾ tsp.	4 ml
Water, cold	5 fl. oz.	150 ml

1 Cut the pork into 2-inch (5-centimeter) cubes.
2 Combine the pork with the remaining ingredients except the water.
3 Grind the meat once through the coarse die of a well-chilled grinder.
4 Add the water and mix well.
5 Stuff the sausage into casings.

Approximate values per 4-oz. (120-g) serving: **Calories** 220, **Total fat** 9 g, **Saturated fat** 3 g, **Cholesterol** 80 mg, **Sodium** 260 mg, **Total carbohydrates** 0 g, **Protein** 36 g

CHORIZO   RECIPE 27.21

Yield: 7 lb. 8 oz. (3.4 kg)

Pork, lean	5 lb.	2.2 kg
Fatback	2 lb. 8 oz.	1.1 kg
Red pepper flakes	1 tsp.	5 ml
Garlic, chopped	1 oz.	30 g
Cumin, ground	3 Tbsp.	45 ml
Cayenne pepper	2 Tbsp.	30 ml
Salt	4 tsp.	20 ml
Paprika	5 Tbsp.	75 ml
Red wine vinegar	3 fl. oz.	90 ml

1 Cut the pork and fatback in 1-inch (2.5-centimeter) pieces. Grind the pork once using a medium die. Grind half of the pork a second time together with the fatback through a fine die.
2 Combine all the ingredients in the bowl of a mixer using the paddle attachment. The sausage may be used in bulk or formed into links as desired.

Approximate values per 1-oz. (30-g) serving: **Calories** 120, **Total fat** 10 g, **Saturated fat** 4 g, **Cholesterol** 25 mg, **Sodium** 90 mg, **Total carbohydrates** 0 g, **Protein** 5 g

DUCK PROSCIUTTO WITH FRESH MANGO   RECIPE 27.22

Chef Steven Chiappetti, Chicago, IL

Yield: 2 Servings

Muscovy duck breasts	2	2
Kosher salt	1 c.	250 ml
Sugar	4 oz.	120 g
Molasses	2 Tbsp.	30 ml
Red wine vinegar	2 fl. oz.	60 ml
Olive oil	2 fl. oz.	60 ml
Fresh mango	1	1
Mâche lettuce	2 bunches	2 bunches

1 Rinse the duck breasts under cold water and trim off the excess fat. Place the duck breasts on a sheet pan and refrigerate until ready to use.
2 In a medium-sized bowl, combine the salt, 1/4 cup (60 milliliters) of sugar and the molasses. Rub this mixture on the duck breasts. Cover and refrigerate the duck for 48 hours.
3 Rinse the duck well under cold water and refrigerate another 48 hours before serving.
4 To make the dressing, boil the remaining sugar and red wine vinegar in a small pan until thick. Remove from the heat and let cool. Whisk in the olive oil.

5 Peel and finely dice the mango.

6 Place a tablespoon of diced mango on a each plate.

7 Slice the duck breast paper-thin and fan over the mango.

8 Arrange the mâche lettuce next to the mango and drizzle the olive oil and red wine reduction dressing over the plate.

Approximate values per serving: **Calories** 550, **Total fat** 30 g, **Saturated fat** 4.5 g, **Cholesterol** 155 mg, **Sodium** 3610 mg, **Total carbohydrates** 41 g, **Protein** 30 g, **Vitamin A** 70%, **Vitamin C** 100%, **Iron** 40%

RECIPE 27.23 — GRAVLAX

Yield: approximately 5 lb. (2.2 kg)

Salmon, drawn, 10–12 lb.	1	1
Kosher salt	8 oz.	250 g
White peppercorns, cracked	1 oz.	30 g
Fresh dill, chopped	2 bunches	2 bunches
Sugar	8 oz.	250 g

1 Fillet the salmon, removing the pin bones but leaving the skin attached.

2 To make the salt cure, combine the salt, white peppercorns, dill and sugar.

3 Coat the salmon fillets with the salt cure and wrap each fillet separately in plastic wrap.

4 Place the fillets in a hotel pan and place another hotel pan on top. Place two #10 cans in the top hotel pan to weigh it down and press the fish.

5 Refrigerate the salmon for 2–3 days.

6 Unwrap the gravlax, scrape off the salt cure and slice the gravlax very thin.

Approximate values per 1-oz. (30-g) serving: **Calories** 110, **Total fat** 4.5 g, **Saturated fat** 1 g, **Cholesterol** 30 mg, **Sodium** 1130 mg, **Total carbohydrates** 3 g, **Protein** 16 g, **Claims**—low saturated fat

1 Coating the salmon fillet with the salt cure.

2 Wrapping the fillets in plastic wrap.

3 Weighting down a pan placed on top of the wrapped fish.

4 Slicing the cured gravlax thinly.

EATING IS NOT MERELY A MATERIAL PLEASURE.
EATING WELL GIVES A SPECTACULAR JOY TO LIFE AND
CONTRIBUTES IMMENSELY TO GOODWILL AND HAPPY
COMPANIONSHIP. IT IS OF GREAT IMPORTANCE TO
THE MORALE.

—Elsa Schiaparelli, Italian fashion designer
  (1890–1973)

28

HORS D'OEUVRE AND CANAPÉS

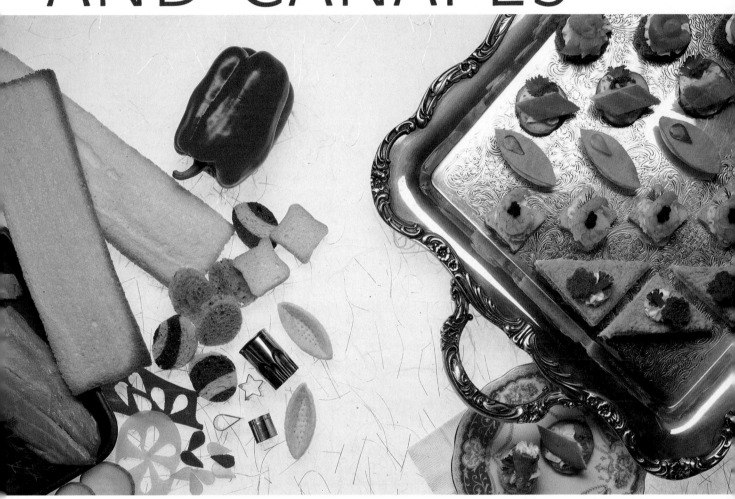

PREP CHEF, INC., Phoenix, AZ
Chef Sidney Brodsky

AFTER STUDYING THIS
CHAPTER, YOU WILL BE
ABLE TO:

▶ prepare and serve a variety of
cold and hot hors d'oeuvre,
including canapés

▶ choose hors d'oeuvre, including
canapés, that are appropriate
for the meal or event

Hors d'oeuvre, whether hot or cold, are very small portions of foods served before the meal to whet the appetite. Hors d'oeuvre and canapés can be passed elegantly by waiters or displayed on buffets. Appetizers, or starters, whether hot or cold, are generally the first course or introduction to a meal; they are more typically served with dinner than with lunch. Sometimes there is very little difference between an hors d'oeuvre and an appetizer.

Preparing hors d'oeuvre, including canapés, uses skills from almost every work station. Because they can consist of meat, poultry, fish, shellfish, vegetables, potatoes, grains, pasta, fruits, baked goods and sauces, they require a detailed knowledge of these foods and how they are prepared.

The French term *hors d'oeuvre* translates as "outside the work." Its usage was correct under the classic kitchen brigade system, for it was the service staff's responsibility to prepare small tidbits for guests to enjoy while the kitchen prepared the meal. Today, however, the kitchen staff prepares the hors d'oeuvre as well as the meals. Cold hors d'oeuvre (a final s is added as an Americanized plural) are usually prepared by the garde-manger; hot ones are prepared in the main kitchen.

There are really only two limitations on the type of food and manner of preparation that can be used for hors d'oeuvre: the chef's imagination and the foods at his or her disposal. There are, however, a few guidelines.

▶ GUIDELINES FOR PREPARING HORS D'OEUVRE
1 They should be small, one to two bites.
2 They should be flavorful and well seasoned without being overpowering.
3 They should be visually attractive.
4 They should complement whatever foods may follow without duplicating their flavors.

▶ COLD HORS D'OEUVRE

Cold hors d'oeuvre are divided here into five broad categories based upon preparation method, principal ingredient or presentation style. They are canapés, caviars, crudités, dips and sushi. These categories may vary somewhat from classical teachings, but they are completely appropriate for modern menus and food service operations.

CANAPÉS

Canapés are tiny, open-faced sandwiches. They are constructed from a base, a spread and one or more garnishes.

The most common **canapé base** is a thin slice of bread cut into an interesting shape and toasted. Although most any variety of bread can be used, spiced, herbed or otherwise flavored breads may be inappropriate for some spreads or garnishes. Melba toasts, crackers and slices of firm vegetables such as cucumbers or zucchini are also popular canapé bases. Whatever item is used, the base must be strong enough to support the weight of the spread and garnish without falling apart when handled.

The **canapé spread** provides much of the canapé's flavor. Spreads are usually flavored butters, cream cheese or a combination of the two. Several examples of spreads are listed in Table 28.1. Each of the spreads is made by adding the desired amount of the main ingredient (chopped or puréed as appropriate) and seasonings to softened butter or cream cheese and mixing until combined. Quantities and proportions vary according to individual tastes. Other canapé spreads include bound salads (for example, tuna or egg), finely chopped shrimp or liver mousse. Any of a number of ingredients can be combined for spreads, provided the following guidelines are followed.

▶ GUIDELINES FOR PREPARING CANAPÉ SPREADS

1 The spread's texture should be smooth enough to produce attractive designs if piped through a pastry bag fitted with a decorative tip.

2 The spread's consistency should be firm enough to hold its shape when piped onto the base, yet soft enough to stick to the base and hold the garnishes in place.

3 The spread's flavor should complement the garnishes and be flavorful enough to stimulate the appetite without being overpowering.

A spread may be a substantial portion of the canapé as well as its distinguishing characteristic. Or it can be applied sparingly and used more as a means of gluing the garnish to the base than as a principal ingredient.

Canapés with bread bases tend to become soggy quickly from both the moisture in the spread and the moisture in the refrigerator where they are stored. Using a spread made with butter will help keep the bread bases crispier, as will buttering the base with a thin coat of softened plain butter before piping on the spread. The best way to ensure a crisp base is to make the canapés as close to service time as possible.

Table 28.1   A SELECTION OF CANAPÉ SPREADS AND SUGGESTED GARNISHES

SPREAD	SUGGESTED GARNISHES
Anchovy butter	Hard-cooked eggs, capers, green or black olive slices
Blue cheese	Grape half, walnuts, roast beef roulade, pear slice, currants, watercress
Caviar butter	Caviar, lemon, egg slice, chives
Deviled ham	Cornichons, mustard butter, sliced radish
Horseradish butter	Smoked salmon, roast beef, smoked trout, marinated herring, capers, parsley
Lemon butter	Shrimp, crab, caviar, salmon, chives, parsley, black olive slices
Liver pâté	Truffle slice, cornichon
Mustard butter	Smoked meats, pâté, dry salami coronet, cornichon
Pimento cream cheese	Smoked oyster, sardine, pimento, parsley
Shrimp butter	Poached bay scallops, shrimp, caviar, parsley
Tuna salad	Capers, cornichons, sliced radish

Salmon Rosette Canapés

Salami Cornet Canapés

Shrimp and Caviar Canapés

The variety of **canapé garnishes** is vast. The garnish can dominate or complement the spread, or it can be a simple sprig of parsley intended to provide visual appeal but little flavor. Although several ingredients can be used to garnish the same canapé, remember the limitations imposed by the canapé's size and purpose. Traditional garnishes can be made by shaping thinly sliced smoked salmon into rosettes, or thin slices of salami into cornets, into which additional spread can be piped. The natural shape of a boiled, peeled shrimp also makes an attractive canapé garnish.

▶ PROCEDURE FOR PREPARING CANAPÉS

This procedure can be adapted and used with a variety of ingredients to produce a variety of canapés. If the canapé base is a bread crouton, begin with Step 1. If some other product is used as the base, prepare that base and begin with Step 4.

1 Trim the crust from an unsliced loaf of bread. Slice the bread lengthwise approximately ⅓ inch (8 millimeters) thick.

2 Cut the bread slices into the desired shapes using a serrated bread knife or canapé cutter. See Figure 28.1.

3 Brush the bread shapes with melted butter and bake in a 350°F (180°C) oven until they are toasted and dry. Remove and cool. Alternatively, the entire bread slice can be buttered and toasted, then cut into shapes.

4 If desired, spread each base with a thin layer of softened plain butter.

5 Apply the spread to the base. If a thin layer is desired, use a palette knife. If a thicker or more decorative layer is desired, pipe the spread onto the base using a pastry bag and decorative tip. Alternatively, the entire bread slice can be buttered, toasted, cooled, covered with a spread and then cut into the desired shapes.

6 Garnish the canapé as desired.

7 If desired, glaze each canapé with a thin coating of aspic jelly. The aspic jelly can be applied with a small spoon or a spray bottle designated for that purpose.

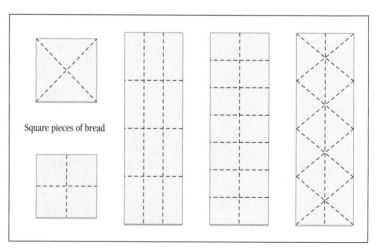

Square pieces of bread

FIGURE 28.1 ▶ Bread can be sliced into several basic shapes to avoid waste.

1 Slicing bread into the desired shapes.

2 Applying the spread to the base with a palette knife.

3 Piping the spread onto the base.

4 Coating the entire slice of toasted bread with a spread before cutting it into canapés.

5 Garnishing the canapés.

6 Spraying the finished canapés with aspic.

BARQUETTES, TARTLETS AND PROFITEROLES

Barquettes, tartlets and profiteroles are all adaptations of the basic canapé. A **barquette** is a tiny boat-shaped shell made from a savory dough such as pâte brisée. A **tartlet** is simply a round version of a barquette. A **profiterole** is a small puff made from pâte à choux. These three items can be prepared like canapés by filling them with flavored spreads and garnishing as desired.

▶ PROCEDURE FOR PREPARING BARQUETTES

1 Rolling out the pastry dough.

2 Pressing the dough into the barquette shells.

3 Pricking the dough with a fork to allow steam to escape during baking.

4 Placing a second barquette shell on top of the dough to prevent it from rising as it bakes.

Beluga Caviar

OTHER TYPES OF CANAPÉS

Vegetables such as cherry tomatoes, blanched snow peas, mushroom caps and Belgian endive leaves are sometimes used as canapé bases. They are filled and garnished in the same manner as barquettes, tartlets and profiteroles.

CAVIAR

Caviar, considered by many to be the ultimate hors d'oeuvre, is the salted roe (eggs) of the sturgeon fish. In the United States, only sturgeon roe can be labeled simply "caviar." Roe from other fish must be qualified as such on the label (for example, salmon caviar or lumpfish caviar).

Sevruga Caviar

Most of the world's caviar comes from sturgeon harvested in the Caspian Sea and imported from Russia and Iran. Imported sturgeon caviar, classified according to the sturgeon species and the roe's size and color, includes beluga, osetra and sevruga as well as pressed caviar. **Beluga** is the most expensive caviar, and comes from the largest species (the sturgeon can weigh up to 1750 pounds/800 kilograms); the dark gray and well-separated eggs are the largest and most fragile kind. **Osetra** is considered by some connoisseurs to be the best caviar; the eggs are medium-sized, golden yellow to brown and quite oily. **Sevruga** is harvested from small sturgeon; the eggs are quite small and light to dark gray. **Pressed caviar** is a processed caviar made from osetra and sevruga roes. The eggs are cleaned, packed in linen bags and hung to drain; as salt and moisture drain away, the natural shape of the eggs is destroyed and the eggs are pressed together. Approximately 3 pounds (1.3 kilograms) of roe produce only 1 pound (450 grams) of pressed caviar; pressed caviar has a spreadable, jamlike consistency.

Osetra Caviar

Most of the caviar consumed in the United States, however, comes from either domestic sturgeon or other fish and is labeled American sturgeon caviar, golden whitefish caviar, lumpfish caviar or salmon caviar. **American sturgeon caviar** is not considered to be of the same quality as Russian or Iranian caviars; nevertheless, roe from sturgeon harvested in the coastal waters of the American northwest and the Tennessee River is becoming increasingly popular, due in part to its relatively low price. **Golden whitefish caviar** is a small and very crisp roe; it is a natural golden color and comes from whitefish native to the northern Great Lakes. **Lumpfish caviar** is readily available and reasonably priced; it is produced from lumpfish harvested in the North Atlantic. The small and very crisp eggs are dyed black, red or gold; the food coloring is not stable, however, and when used to garnish foods, colored lumpfish caviar tends to bleed. **Salmon caviar,** the eggs of the chum and silver salmon, is a very popular garnish. The eggs are large with a good flavor and natural orange color.

American Salmon Roe

PURCHASING AND STORING CAVIARS

Although all caviar is processed with salt, some caviar is labeled **malassol,** which means "little salt." Caviar should smell fresh, with no off-odors. The eggs should be whole, not broken, and they should be crisp and pop when pressed with the tongue. Excessive oiliness may be caused by a large number of broken eggs. The best way to test caviar's quality is to taste it. Remember, price alone does not necessarily indicate quality.

Most caviar can be purchased fresh or pasteurized in tins or jars ranging from 1 ounce (28 grams) to more than 4 pounds (2 kilograms). Some caviars are also available frozen. (Frozen caviar should be used only as a garnish and should not be served by itself.) In order to ensure the freshest possible product, always purchase caviar in small quantities as often as possible based on your needs.

Fresh caviar should be stored at 32°F (0°C). Because most refrigerators are considerably warmer than that, store the caviar on ice in the coldest part of the refrigerator and change the ice often. If properly handled, fresh caviar will last one to two weeks before opening and several days after opening. Pasteurized caviar does not require refrigeration until it is opened and will last several days in the refrigerator after opening.

SERVING CAVIARS

Fine caviar should be served in its original container or a nonmetal bowl on a bed of crushed ice, accompanied only by lightly buttered toasts or blinis and sour cream. Connoisseurs prefer china, bone or other nonmetal utensils for serving caviar because metal reacts with the caviar, producing off-flavors.

Lesser-quality caviars are often served on ice, accompanied by minced onion, chopped hard-cooked egg whites and yolks (separately), lemon, sour cream and buttered toasts.

Lumpfish and other nonsturgeon caviars are usually not served by themselves. Rather, they are used as ingredients in or garnishes for other dishes.

CRUDITÉS

Crudité, a French word meaning "raw thing," generally refers to raw or slightly blanched vegetables served as an hors d'oeuvre. Although almost any vegetable will do, the most commonly used are broccoli, cauliflower, carrots, celery, asparagus and green beans, all of which are often blanched, and cucumbers, zucchini, yellow squash, radishes, green onions, cherry tomatoes, Belgian endive leaves, mushrooms, peppers and jicama, which are served raw.

When preparing crudités, use only the freshest and best-looking produce available. Because they are displayed and eaten raw, blemishes and imperfections cannot be disguised. Vegetables, both blanched and raw, should be cut into attractive shapes. Crudités are usually served with one or more dips.

DIPS

Dips can be served hot or cold and as an accompaniment to crudités, crackers, chips, toasts, breads or other foods.

Cold dips often use mayonnaise, sour cream or cream cheese as a base. The methods for preparing mayonnaise-based and sour cream–based dips are identical to those for making mayonnaise-based salad dressings discussed in Chapter 24, Salads and Salad Dressings. The principal difference is that dips are normally thicker than dressings.

To use cream cheese as a base, first soften it by mixing it in an electric mixer with a paddle attachment. Then add the flavoring ingredients such as chopped cooked vegetables, chopped cooked fish or shellfish, herbs, spices, garlic or onions. Adjust the consistency of the dip by adding milk, buttermilk, cream, sour cream or other appropriate liquid.

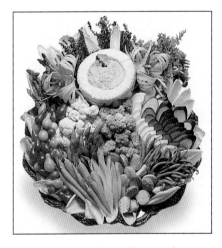

Artful Array of Crudités and Dip

Some cold dips such as guacamole and hummus use purées of fruits, vegetables or beans as the base.

Hot dips often use a béchamel, cream sauce or cheese sauce as a base and usually contain a dominant flavoring ingredient such as chopped spinach or shellfish.

Dips can be served in small bowls or hollowed-out cabbages, squash, pumpkins or other vegetables. Hot dips are often served in chafing dishes.

The combinations of ingredients and seasonings that can be used to make dips as well as the foods that are dipped in them are limited only by the chef's imagination.

RECIPE 28.1 CLAM DIP

Yield: 3 pt. (1.5 lt)

Cream cheese	1 lb.	450 g
Worcestershire sauce	2 Tbsp.	30 ml
Dijon mustard	1 Tbsp.	15 ml
Sour cream	1 lb.	450 g
Canned clams, drained	1 lb.	450 g
Lemon juice	2 Tbsp.	30 ml
Salt and pepper	TT	TT
Tabasco sauce	TT	TT
Green onions, sliced	2 oz.	60 g

1 Soften the cream cheese in the bowl of an electric mixer, using the paddle attachment.
2 Add the Worcestershire sauce, Dijon mustard and sour cream; mix until smooth.
3 Add the clams and lemon juice and season with salt, pepper and Tabasco.
4 Add the green onions and mix well.

Approximate values per 2-Tbsp. (30-ml) serving: **Calories** 70, **Total fat** 5 g, **Saturated fat** 3.5 g, **Cholesterol** 20 mg, **Sodium** 55 mg, **Total carbohydrates** 1 g, **Protein** 4 g, **Iron** 15%, **Claims—** low sodium; low sugar

SUSHI

Generally, **sushi** refers to cooked or raw fish and shellfish rolled in or served on seasoned rice. **Sashimi** is raw fish eaten without rice. In Japan, the word *sushi* (or **zushi**) refers only to the flavored rice. Each combination of rice and another ingredient or ingredients has a specific name. These include *nigiri zushi* (rice with raw fish), *norimaki zushi* (rice rolled in seaweed), *fukusa zushi* (rice wrapped in omelet), *inari zushi* (rice in fried bean curd) and *chirashi zushi* (rice with fish, shellfish and vegetables). Although a Japanese sushi master spends years perfecting style and technique, many types of sushi can be produced in any professional kitchen with very little specialized equipment.

INGREDIENTS

Fish

The key to good sushi and sashimi is the freshness of the fish. All fish must be of the highest quality and absolutely fresh, preferably no more than one day out of the water. Ahi and yellowfin tuna, salmon, flounder and sea bass are typically used for sushi. Cooked shrimp and eel are also popular.

Rice

Sushi rice is prepared by adding seasonings such as vinegar, sugar, salt and rice wine (sake or mirin) to steamed short-grain rice. The consistency of the rice is very important. It must be sticky enough to stay together when formed into finger-shaped oblongs, but not too soft.

Seasonings

Seasonings include the following:

▶ Shoyu—Japanese soy sauce, which is lighter and more delicate than the Chinese variety.

▶ Wasabi—A strong aromatic root, purchased as a green powder. It is sometimes called green horseradish, although it is not actually related to the common horseradish.

▶ Pickled ginger—fresh ginger pickled in vinegar, which gives it a pink color.

▶ Nori—A dried seaweed purchased in sheets; it adds flavor and is sometimes used to contain the rolled rice and other ingredients.

ZUSHI (SUSHI RICE)

RECIPE 28.2

Yield: 2 lb. (1 kg)

Short-grain rice	1 lb.	450 g
Water	20 fl. oz.	600 ml
Rice vinegar	2 fl. oz.	60 ml
Granulated sugar	3 Tbsp.	45 ml
Salt	2½ tsp.	12 ml
Mirin	2 Tbsp.	30 ml

1 Wash the rice and allow it to drain for 30 minutes.

2 Combine the rice and water in a saucepan. Bring to a boil, lower to a simmer, cover and steam for 20 minutes.

3 Combine the rice vinegar, sugar, salt and mirin and add to the rice. Mix well and cool to room temperature.

Approximate values per 1-oz. (30-g) serving: **Calories** 60, **Total fat** 0 g, **Saturated fat** 0 g, **Cholesterol** 0 mg, **Sodium** 140 mg, **Total carbohydrates** 13 g, **Protein** 1 g, **Claims**—fat free

NIGIRI ZUSHI

RECIPE 28.3

Yield: 24 Pieces

Sushi-quality fish fillets such as ahi, salmon, flounder or sea bass	1 lb.	450 g
Wasabi powder	1 oz.	30 g
Water	1 fl. oz.	30 ml
Sushi rice	2 lb.	900 g
Pickled ginger, sliced	2 oz.	60 g
Shoyu	3 fl. oz.	90 ml

1 Trim the fish fillets of any skin, bone, imperfections or blemishes. Cut the fillets into 24 thin slices, approximately 2 inches by 1 inch (5 centimeters by 2.5 centimeters).

2 Mix the wasabi powder and water to form a paste.

3 With your hands, form a 1½-ounce (50-gram) portion of rice into a finger-shaped mound.

4 Rub a small amount of wasabi on one side of a slice of fish.

5 Holding the rice mound in one hand, press the fish, wasabi side down, onto the rice with the fingers of the other hand.

6 Serve with additional wasabi, pickled ginger and shoyu.

Approximate values per piece: **Calories** 80, **Total fat** 2 g, **Saturated fat** 0 g, **Cholesterol** 10 mg, **Sodium** 310 mg, **Total carbohydrates** 11 g, **Protein** 5 g, **Claims**—low fat; low cholesterol; no sugar

1 Forming a finger-shaped rice mound.

2 Pressing the fish onto the rice.

RECIPE 28.4

Yield: 36 Pieces

Dried shiitake mushrooms	4	4
Water, hot	8 fl. oz.	250 ml
Shoyu	4 fl. oz.	120 ml
Brown sugar	1 Tbsp.	15 ml
Cucumber	½	½
Sushi-quality fish fillets such as ahi, salmon, flounder or sea bass	5 oz.	150 g
Nori	3 sheets	3 sheets
Sushi rice	18 oz.	500 g
Wasabi paste	4 Tbsp.	60 ml
Pickled ginger	2 oz.	60 g

1 Soak the mushrooms in hot water for 20 minutes. Remove the mushrooms and reserve 4 ounces (120 grams) of the liquid. Trim off the mushroom stems.

2 Julienne the mushroom caps. Combine the reserved soaking liquid with 2 tablespoons (30 milliliters) of the shoyu and the brown sugar. Simmer the caps in this liquid and reduce au sec. Remove from the heat and refrigerate.

3 Peel and seed the cucumber; cut it into strips the size of pencils, approximately 6 inches (15 centimeters) long.

4 Trim the fish fillets of any skin, bone, imperfections or blemishes. Cut the fillets into strips the same size as the cucumbers.

5 Cut the sheets of nori in half and place one half sheet on a napkin or bamboo rolling mat. Divide the rice into six equal portions; spread one portion over each half sheet of nori, leaving a ½-inch (1.2-centimeter) border of nori exposed.

6 Spread 1 teaspoon (5 milliliters) of wasabi paste evenly on the rice.

7 Lay one-sixth of the mushrooms, cucumber and fish strips in a row down the middle of the rice.

8 Use the napkin or bamboo mat to roll the nori tightly around the rice and garnishes.

9 Slice each roll into six pieces and serve with the remaining shoyu, pickled ginger and wasabi.

Approximate values per piece: **Calories** 40, **Total fat** 0 g, **Saturated fat** 0 g, **Cholesterol** 5 mg, **Sodium** 220 mg, **Total carbohydrates** 6 g, **Protein** 2 g, **Vitamin C** 15%, **Claims**—fat free; low cholesterol; low calorie

1 Preparing the garnishes for the sushi roll.

2 Spreading the rice over the nori.

3 Adding the garnishes in a row down the middle of the rice.

4 Rolling the nori around the rice and garnishes.

5 Slicing the roll into six pieces.

▶ Hot Hors d'Oeuvre

To provide a comprehensive list of hot hors d'oeuvre would be virtually impossible; therefore, we discuss just a few of the more commonly encountered ones that can be easily made in most any kitchen.

FILLED PASTRY SHELLS

Because savory (unsweetened) barquettes and tartlets, éclair puffs and bouchées can hold a small amount of liquid, they are often baked then filled with warm meat, poultry or fish purées or ragoûts, garnished and served hot. They become soggy quickly, however, and must be prepared at the last possible minute before service.

BROCHETTES

Hors d'oeuvre brochettes are small skewers holding a combination of meat, poultry, game, fish, shellfish or vegetables. The foods are typically marinated, then baked, grilled or broiled, and are usually served with a dipping sauce. Brochettes can be small pieces of boneless chicken breast marinated in white wine and grilled; beef cubes glazed with teriyaki sauce; lamb or chicken satay (saté) with peanut sauce or rabbit and shiitake mushrooms skewered on a sprig of fresh rosemary.

In order to increase visual appeal, the main ingredients should be carefully cut and consistent in size and shape. The ingredients are normally diced, but strips of meat and poultry can also be threaded onto the skewers.

As hors d'oeuvre, the skewers should be very small, slightly larger than a toothpick. When assembling brochettes, leave enough exposed skewer so that diners can pick them up easily. Wooden skewers have a tendency to burn during cooking. Soaking them in water before assembling helps reduce the risk of burning.

RABBIT AND SHIITAKE SKEWERS

RECIPE 28.5

Yield: 12 Skewers

Rabbit	1	1
Shiitake mushrooms	2 lb.	1 kg
Fresh rosemary	12 sprigs	12 sprigs
Salt and pepper	TT	TT
Olive oil	2 fl. oz.	60 ml

1 Bone the rabbit and cut the pieces into ½-inch (1.2-centimeter) cubes. One rabbit should produce 36 cubes.

2 Wash the mushrooms. Trim and discard the stems.

3 Cut enough of the mushrooms into ½-inch (1.2-centimeter) dice to produce 24 pieces.

4 Skewer three pieces of rabbit and two pieces of mushroom alternately onto each rosemary sprig.

5 Season the skewers and the remaining mushrooms with salt and pepper and brush with olive oil. Grill the skewers and the mushroom caps over medium heat, being careful not to burn the rosemary sprigs.

6 Slice the mushroom caps and arrange a portion of sliced mushrooms and two rabbit skewers on each plate.

Approximate values per skewer: **Calories** 160, **Total fat** 8 g, **Saturated fat** 1.5 g, **Cholesterol** 30 mg, **Sodium** 20 mg, **Total carbohydrates** 11 g, **Protein** 12 g

MEATBALLS

Meatballs made from ground beef, veal, pork or poultry and served in a sauce buffet style are a popular hot hors d'oeuvre. One of the best known is the Swedish meatball. It is made from ground beef, veal and pork bound with eggs and bread crumbs and served in a velouté or cream sauce seasoned with dill. Other sauces that can be used in the same manner are mushroom sauce, red wine sauce or any style of tomato sauce.

RECIPE 28.6

SWEDISH MEATBALLS

Yield: 4 lb. 8 oz. (2 kg)

Onions, small dice	8 oz.	250 g
Whole butter	2 oz.	60 g
Ground beef	2 lb.	1 kg
Ground pork	2 lb.	1 kg
Bread crumbs, fresh	4 oz.	120 g
Eggs	3	3
Salt	1 Tbsp.	15 ml
Black pepper	TT	TT
Nutmeg, ground	TT	TT
Allspice, ground	TT	TT
Lemon zest, grated	1 tsp.	5 ml
Demi-glace, hot	1 qt.	1 lt
Heavy cream, hot	8 fl. oz.	250 ml
Fresh dill, chopped	2 Tbsp.	30 ml

1 Sauté the onions in the butter without coloring. Remove and cool.

2 Combine the onions with all of the ingredients except the demi-glace, cream and dill. Mix well.

3 Portion the meat with a #20 scoop; form into balls with your hands and place on a sheet pan.

4 Bake the meatballs at 400°F (200°C) until firm, approximately 15 minutes. Remove the meatballs from the pan with a slotted spoon, draining well, and place in a hotel pan.

5 Combine the demi-glace, cream and dill; pour over the meatballs.

6 Cover the meatballs and bake at 350°F (180°C) until done, approximately 20 minutes. Skim off the grease from the surface and serve.

Approximate values per 5-oz. (150-g) serving: **Calories** 250, **Total fat** 16 g, **Saturated fat** 7 g, **Cholesterol** 105 mg, **Sodium** 420 mg, **Total carbohydrates** 7 g, **Protein** 20 g, **Calcium** 30%

RUMAKI

Traditionally, rumaki were made by wrapping chicken livers in bacon and broiling or baking them. Today, however, many other foods prepared in the same fashion are called rumaki. For example, blanched bacon can be wrapped around olives, pickled watermelon rind, water chestnuts, pineapple, dates or scallops. These morsels are then broiled, baked or fried and served piping hot.

1 Rolling rumaki.

2 The finished rumaki.

RUMAKI

RECIPE 28.7

Yield: 60 Pieces

Chicken livers	1 lb.	450 g
Marinade:		
Brown sugar	1 Tbsp.	15 ml
Water, hot	1 Tbsp.	15 ml
Dark soy sauce	1 Tbsp.	15 ml
Garlic, minced	1 Tbsp.	15 ml
Bacon, sliced thin	30 slices	30 slices
Water chestnuts, sliced	60 slices	60 slices

1 Trim the livers and cut into 60 equal-sized pieces. Place the livers in a stainless steel bowl.

2 Combine the marinade ingredients. Pour the marinade over the livers and refrigerate for 1 hour.

3 Cut the bacon slices in half, spread them on a sheet pan and parcook at 375°F (180°C) for approximately 5 minutes. Pour off and discard the excess fat.

4 Drain the livers. Roll one piece of liver and one water chestnut slice in one piece of bacon and secure with a toothpick. Place on a baking rack over a sheet pan with the seam side down.

5 Bake the rumaki in a 400°F (200°C) convection oven until the bacon is crisp and the liver is cooked, approximately 10 minutes. Do not overcook or the rumaki will be dry. Serve hot.

Approximate values per piece: **Calories** 60, **Total fat** 5 g, **Saturated fat** 1.5 g, **Cholesterol** 30 mg, **Sodium** 170 mg, **Total carbohydrates** 1 g, **Protein** 4 g, **Vitamin A** 10%

STUFFED WONTON SKINS

Wonton skins are an Asian noodle dough used to produce a wide variety of hors d'oeuvre such as a miniature version of the traditional egg roll or a puff filled with a mixture of seasoned cream cheese and crab. Or they can be stuffed with a wide variety of pork, chicken, shellfish and vegetables before cooking. As hors d'oeuvre, stuffed wonton skins can be steamed, but they are more often pan-fried or deep-fried.

RECIPE 28.8 STUFFED WONTONS WITH APRICOT SAUCE

Yield: 24 Pieces

Cream cheese	8 oz.	250 g
Crab meat	8 oz.	250 g
Garlic, chopped	1 tsp.	5 ml
Green onions, sliced	1 oz.	30 g
Salt and pepper	TT	TT
Worcestershire sauce	TT	TT
Sesame oil	TT	TT
Wonton skins	24	24
Apricot Sauce (recipe follows)	as needed	as needed

1 Place the cream cheese in the bowl of a mixer and mix until soft.
2 Add the crab meat, garlic and green onions. Season with salt and pepper, Worcestershire sauce and a drop or two of sesame oil.
3 Place several wonton skins on a work surface. Brush the edges with water. Place 1 tablespoon (15 milliliters) of the cream cheese mixture in the center of each skin. Fold the wonton skin in half to form a triangle; seal the edges.
4 Using the swimming method, deep-fry the wontons at 350°F (180°C) for 10 seconds. Remove the wontons, drain well and refrigerate.
5 At service time, deep-fry the wontons at 350°F (180°C) until crisp, approximately 1 minute. Serve with Apricot Sauce.

Approximate values per piece, with sauce: **Calories** 130, **Total fat** 8 g, **Saturated fat** 2.5 g, **Cholesterol** 20 mg, **Sodium** 105 mg, **Total carbohydrates** 11 g, **Protein** 4 g

APRICOT SAUCE

Yield: 8 oz. (250 g)

Apricot preserves	8 oz.	250 g
Fresh ginger, grated	1 Tbsp.	15 ml
Dry mustard	1 tsp.	5 ml
Red wine vinegar	1 Tbsp.	15 ml

1 Combine all ingredients and heat until the preserves melt and the flavors blend.

Approximate values per 1-oz. (30-g) serving: **Calories** 70, **Total fat** 0 g, **Saturated fat** 0 g, **Cholesterol** 0 mg, **Sodium** 10 mg, **Total carbohydrates** 19 g, **Protein** 0 g, **Claims**—fat free

OTHER HOT HORS D'OEUVRE

Other types of hot hors d'oeuvre include layers of phyllo dough wrapped around various fillings; vegetables such as mushrooms that are stuffed and baked; tiny red potatoes filled with sour cream and caviar or Roquefort cheese and walnuts; tiny artichoke or clam fritters or any of the hundreds of varieties of chicken wings that are seasoned or marinated, baked, fried, broiled or grilled and served with a cool and soothing or outrageously spicy sauce.

The secret is to let your imagination be your guide, to keep the ingredients harmonious and, if the hors d'oeuvre are to precede dinner, not to allow them to duplicate the foods to be served or overpower them with excessively spicy flavors.

▶ SERVING HORS D'OEUVRE

Hors d'oeuvre are not served only as a precursor to dinner. At many events, the only foods served may be butlered hors d'oeuvre, an hors d'oeuvre buffet or a combination of the two. Whether the hors d'oeuvre are being served before dinner or as dinner, butler style or buffet style, they must always be attractively prepared and displayed.

All events have themes and varying degrees of formality. Long buffets with overflowing baskets of crudités and sweet potato chips with dips presented in hollowed squashes and cabbages may be appropriate for one event, while elegant silver trays of carefully prepared canapés passed among guests by white-gloved, tuxedoed service staff may be appropriate for another. When preparing and serving hors d'oeuvre, always keep the event's theme in mind and plan accordingly.

When choosing hors d'oeuvre, select an assortment that contrasts flavors, textures and styles. There are no limits to the variety of hors d'oeuvre that can be served, but three to four cold and three to four hot selections are sufficient for most occasions. The following is a sample selection of hot and cold hors d'oeuvre that contrast flavors, textures and styles as well as types of food.

Cold

- ▶ Canapés of smoked salmon on brioche
- ▶ Barquettes filled with Roquefort cheese and garnished with grapes
- ▶ Tiny tortilla cups filled with grilled chicken and spicy tomato salsa

Hot

- ▶ Tiny pouches of shrimp wrapped in phyllo dough (page 919)
- ▶ Date and chorizo rumaki (page 915)
- ▶ Rabbit and shiitake skewers (page 901)
- ▶ Small chèvre tarts (page 918)

BUTLER SERVICE

Butler service hors d'oeuvre, or "passed" hors d'oeuvre, are presented to guests on trays by the service staff. The hors d'oeuvre can be hot or cold and should be very small to make it easier for the guests to eat them without the aid of a knife or fork. Hot and cold hors d'oeuvre should be passed separately so that they can be kept at the correct temperatures. For a one-hour cocktail reception before a dinner, three to five hors d'oeuvre per person is usually sufficient. If hors d'oeuvre are the only food being served, however, four to five pieces per person per hour may be more appropriate.

BUFFET SERVICE

An hors d'oeuvre buffet should be beautiful and appetizing. It may consist of a single table to serve a small group of people or several huge multilevel displays designed to feed thousands. Colors, flavors and textures must all be taken into account when planning the menu.

Both hot and cold hors d'oeuvre may be served on buffets. Hot hors d'oeuvre are often kept hot by holding them in chafing dishes. Alternatively, hot hors d'oeuvre can be displayed on trays or platters; the trays and platters, however, must be replaced frequently to ensure that the food stays hot. Cold hors d'oeuvre can be displayed on trays, mirrors, platters, baskets, leaves, papers or other serving pieces to create the desired look.

ARRANGING BUFFET PLATTERS

When displaying hors d'oeuvre and other foods on mirrors, trays or platters, the foods should be displayed in a pattern that is pleasing to the eye and flows toward the guest or from one side to the other. An easy and attractive method for accomplishing this is to arrange the items on a mirror or tray with an attractive centerpiece. The food can be placed in parallel diagonal lines, alternating the various styles and shapes. Three alternative arrangements are shown in the following photographs. Be careful not to make the tray or mirror too fussy or cluttered, however; often the best approach is to keep it simple.

The preparation of hors d'oeuvre provides an opportunity for the chef to demonstrate his or her creativity, knowledge of food and skills in presentation and garnishing. Because hors d'oeuvre often serve as the guests' introduction to the foods you serve, it is especially important that these foods be properly prepared and of the highest quality.

CONCLUSION

QUESTIONS FOR DISCUSSION

1 Discuss four guidelines that should be followed when preparing hors d'oeuvre.

2 Identify and describe the three parts of a canapé.

3 Describe the differences between beluga, osetra and sevruga caviars, and explain how these differ from domestic caviars.

4 Create an hors d'oeuvre menu for a small cocktail party. Include three hot and three cold items, and explain the reasons for your selections.

RECIPE 28.9

CURRIED CHICKEN CANAPÉS

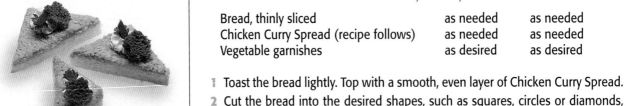

PREP CHEF, INC., PHOENIX, AZ
Chef Sidney Brodsky

Bread, thinly sliced	as needed	as needed
Chicken Curry Spread (recipe follows)	as needed	as needed
Vegetable garnishes	as desired	as desired

1 Toast the bread lightly. Top with a smooth, even layer of Chicken Curry Spread.

2 Cut the bread into the desired shapes, such as squares, circles or diamonds, being sure to wipe the knife blade clean after each cut. Garnish each canapé as desired.

CHICKEN CURRY SPREAD

Yield: 25 Servings

Chicken breasts, boneless, skinless, cooked	1 lb.	450 g
Cream of coconut	½ c.	120 ml
Mayonnaise	½ c.	120 ml
Curry powder	1½ Tbsp.	45 ml
Lemon juice	1 Tbsp.	30 ml
Salt and white pepper	TT	TT

1 Cut the chicken into small pieces and place in a food processor. Pulse until a fine texture is obtained.

2 Add the remaining ingredients and mix until blended. Refrigerate until needed, but use within 2 days.

Variation: For a mixure that can be piped into barquettes or used as a garnish, process the chicken until very smooth and add 2–3 ounces (60–90 grams) of plain cream cheese.

Approximate values per 1-oz. (30-g) serving: **Calories** 80, **Total fat** 6 g, **Saturated fat** 2 g, **Cholesterol** 20 mg, **Sodium** 40 mg, **Total carbohydrates** 1 g, **Protein** 6 g

CHEF SIDNEY BRODSKY

After washing dishes at his school cafeteria while still a student, Chef Brodsky completed a three-year American Culinary Federation apprenticeship at the Canterbury Golf Club in Shaker, Ohio. He then attended culinary school at Cuyahoga Community College, Cleveland, earning an AOS degree in Restaurant and Food Service Management in 1986.

Chef Brodsky is now the chef and owner of Phoenix's James Gerald Foods, which specializes in preparing fresh, unique hors d'oeuvre and canapés for commercial clients such as hotels, resorts and caterers.

Having taught garde-manger at Scottsdale Community College in Scottsdale, Arizona, Chef Brodsky encourages students to "look for and focus on the details in all that you do."

RECIPE 28.10

BUCKWHEAT BLINI

Blini may be used as a canapé base and are frequently topped with crème fraîche and garnished with caviar.

Yield: 24 Blini

Granulated sugar	2 tsp.	10 ml
Dry yeast	¼ oz.	7 g
Milk, lukewarm	14 fl. oz.	420 ml
Buckwheat flour	4 oz.	120 g
All-purpose flour	3 oz.	90 g

Salt	½ tsp.	2 ml
Unsalted butter, melted	3 Tbsp.	45 ml
Vegetable oil	2 Tbsp.	30 ml
Egg yolks	3	3
Egg whites	2	2

1 Stir the sugar and yeast into the milk and let stand until foamy, approximately 5 minutes.
2 Whisk in the flours, salt, butter, oil and egg yolks. Beat until smooth.
3 Cover the batter and allow it to rise in a warm place until doubled, approximately 1 hour.
4 Beat the egg whites to stiff peaks, then fold them into the risen batter.
5 Lightly oil and preheat a large sauté pan. Drop 2 tablespoons (30 milliliters) of batter into the sauté pan, spacing the blini at least 1 inch (2.5 centimeters) apart. Cook until the bottom of each blini is golden, approximately 1 minute. Turn the blini and cook an additional 30 seconds. Remove from the pan and keep warm for service.

Approximate values per blini: **Calories** 70, **Total fat** 4 g, **Saturated fat** 1.5 g, **Cholesterol** 35 mg, **Sodium** 60 mg, **Total carbohydrates** 7 g, **Protein** 2 g

POACHED SEA SCALLOP, SMOKED SALMON AND CAVIAR CANAPÉS

RECIPE 28.11

THE BROWN PALACE HOTEL, Denver, CO
Executive Chef Mark Black

Yield: 10 Canapés

Sour cream	4 oz.	120 g
Chives, minced	1 Tbsp.	15 ml
Fresh lemon juice	1 fl. oz.	30 ml
Court bouillon	1 qt.	1 lt
Sea scallops, size U-10	10	10
Bread canapé bases, round, toasted	10	10
Smoked salmon, sliced thin	6 oz.	180 g
Caviar	¼ oz.	8 g
Green onion, sliced on the bias	1	1

1 Combine the sour cream, chives and lemon juice. Mix well and refrigerate until service.
2 Bring the court bouillon to a simmer. Add the scallops and poach for 5 minutes, remove and refrigerate.
3 Once cooled, slice each scallop horizontally into three even slices.
4 Spread the canapé bases with a small amount of the sour cream mixture.
5 To assemble each canapé, place one scallop slice on a base and top with a small amount of sour cream. Place a small amount of the smoked salmon on the scallop slice and top with a small amount of sour cream. Add a second layer of scallop slice, sour cream, salmon and sour cream and then place the third slice of scallop on top. Garnish the canapé with caviar and green onion and serve.

Approximate values per canapé: **Calories** 90, **Total fat** 3.5 g, **Saturated fat** 1.5 g, **Cholesterol** 20 mg, **Sodium** 450 mg, **Total carbohydrates** 6 g, **Protein** 8 g

RECIPE 28.12   SEARED RABBIT WITH RASPBERRY MUSTARD

THE BROWN PALACE HOTEL, Denver, CO
Executive Chef Mark Black

Yield: 6 Canapés

Rabbit loins, silverskin removed	2	2
Salt and pepper	TT	TT
Vegetable oil	as needed	as needed
Dijon mustard	1 oz.	30 ml
Fresh raspberries	1½ oz.	45 g
Lingonberries	1 Tbsp.	15 ml
Honey	½ tsp.	3 ml
Brioche croutons, 1-in. (2.5-cm) rounds	6	6
Cream cheese, softened	as needed	as needed
Yellow bell pepper	as needed	as needed
Fresh chervil	as needed	as needed

1 Season the rabbit loins with salt and pepper. Sear them in a small amount of oil in a hot sauté pan. Remove from the pan and cool.
2 Combine the mustard, raspberries, lingonberries and honey and purée in a food processor until smooth.
3 Cut the rabbit into 12 slices.
4 Lightly spread the mustard mixture on the brioche croutons. Place two slices of rabbit on top of the mustard. Pipe a garnish of cream cheese on each and garnish with bell pepper and fresh chervil.

Approximate values per canapé: **Calories** 60, **Total fat** 2.3 g, **Saturated fat** 1 g, **Cholesterol** 23 mg, **Sodium** 42 mg, **Total carbohydrates** 1 g, **Protein** 8 g

RECIPE 28.13   TOSTADITAS OF GULF CRAB WITH GUACAMOLE

CAFÉ ANNIE, Houston, TX
Chef-Owner Robert Del Grande
Executive Chef Ben Berryhill

Yield: 36 Pieces

Gulf crab meat, fresh	1 lb.	450 g
Mayonnaise	2 Tbsp.	30 ml
Heavy cream	2 Tbsp.	30 ml
Salt	1 tsp.	5 ml
Chipotle sauce (optional)	1 Tbsp.	15 ml
Guacamole:		
Hass avocados, ripe, medium dice	2	2
White onions, minced	4 oz.	120 g
Serrano chiles, stems removed, minced	2	2
Cilantro leaves, minced	2 Tbsp.	30 ml
Olive oil	2 tsp.	10 ml
Fresh lime juice	1 tsp.	5 ml
Kosher salt	1 tsp.	5 ml
Black pepper	¼ tsp.	1 ml
Tomato, chopped	1	1
Tortilla triangles, fried crisp	36	36

1 Check the crab meat for any small pieces of shell. In a small mixing bowl, combine the mayonnaise, heavy cream, salt and chipotle sauce (if desired). Mix until blended and smooth. Add the crab meat and toss to coat the crab. Do not overmix. Refrigerate until ready to use.

2 To prepare the guacamole, combine all of the guacamole ingredients except the tomato. Stir the ingredients together with a spoon to form a coarse mixture. Do not overmix; leave bits of avocado intact. At service time, stir in the tomato.

3 To serve, place a small spoonful of guacamole on each crisp tortilla chip. Top the guacamole with a small spoonful of crab meat. If desired, garnish each tostadita with a few drops of chipotle sauce.

Approximate values per piece: **Calories** 50, **Total fat** 3.5 g, **Saturated fat** 0.5 g, **Cholesterol** 10 mg, **Sodium** 180 mg, **Total carbohydrates** 2 g, **Protein** 3 g

KALAMATA OLIVE AND ASIAGO CROSTINI

RECIPE 28.14

LES GOURMETTES COOKING SCHOOL, Phoenix, AZ
Barbara Fenzl, CCP

Yield: 12 pieces

French bread	½ loaf	½ loaf
Fresh basil leaves, chopped	50	50
Tomato concassée	4 oz.	120 g
Garlic, chopped	2 tsp.	10 ml
Kalamata olives, pitted, chopped	15	15
Asiago, grated	2 oz.	60 g

1 Slice the bread ¼ inch (6 millimeters) thick.

2 Combine the remaining ingredients and mix well.

3 Spread ½ tablespoon (8 milliliters) of the mixture on each slice of bread. Place under the broiler or salamander until hot and the cheese is melted, approximately 2 minutes.

Approximate values per piece: **Calories** 60, **Total fat** 2 g, **Saturated fat** 1 g, **Cholesterol** 5 mg, **Sodium** 180 mg, **Total carbohydrates** 8 g, **Protein** 2 g, **Claims**—low fat; low cholesterol; no sugar

HUMMUS

RECIPE 28.15

Yield: 1 qt. (1 lt)

Chickpeas, cooked	1 lb.	450 g
Tahini	8 oz.	225 g
Garlic, chopped	2 tsp.	10 ml
Cumin, ground	½ tsp.	2 ml
Lemon juice	4 fl. oz.	120 ml
Salt	1 tsp.	5 ml
Cayenne pepper	TT	TT
Olive oil	2 fl. oz.	60 g
Fresh parsley, chopped	2 tsp.	10 ml

1 Combine the chickpeas, tahini, garlic, cumin and lemon juice in a food processor; process until smooth. Season with salt and cayenne.

2 Spoon the hummus onto a serving platter and smooth the surface. Drizzle the olive oil over the hummus and garnish with the chopped parsley. Serve with warm pita bread that has been cut into quarters.

Approximate values per 2-fl.-oz. (60-ml) serving: **Calories** 210, **Total fat** 16 g, **Saturated fat** 1 g, **Cholesterol** 0 mg, **Sodium** 250 mg, **Total carbohydrates** 10 g, **Protein** 7 g, **Iron** 8%

► **tahini** (tah-HEE-nee) a thick, oily paste made from crushed sesame seeds

RECIPE 28.16

BABA GHANOUSH

Yield: 5 c. (1.2 lt)

Eggplants	3	3
Virgin olive oil	4 fl. oz.	120 ml
Salt and pepper	TT	TT
Fresh lemon juice	4 fl. oz.	120 ml
Garlic cloves	6	6
Tahini	7 oz.	210 g

1 Cut the eggplants in half and score the cut surface of each half from edge to edge in a crosshatch pattern approximately ½ inch (1.2 centimeters) deep.

2 Brush the cut surfaces with 2 fluid ounces (60 milliliters) of olive oil, season with salt and pepper and place cut side down on a sheet pan. Roast in a 350°F (180°C) oven until very soft, approximately 45 minutes.

3 Cool the eggplants and scoop out the flesh. Purée the flesh in a food processor with the lemon juice, garlic, tahini, salt and pepper. Add the remaining olive oil and blend in. Adjust the seasonings. Serve in a bowl, drizzled with additional olive oil, if desired, and accompanied by pita bread or crudités.

Approximate values per 2-Tbsp. (30-ml) serving: **Calories** 60, **Total fat** 5 g, **Saturated fat** 0.5 g, **Cholesterol** 0 mg, **Sodium** 0 mg, **Total carbohydrates** 3 g, **Protein** 1 g

RECIPE 28.17

TAPENADE

Yield: 12 fl. oz. (350 ml)

Garlic cloves	4	4
Kalamata olives, pitted	1 pt.	450 ml
Anchovies	1 oz.	30 g
Capers	2 Tbsp.	30 ml
Fresh thyme	1 tsp.	5 ml
Fresh rosemary	1 tsp.	5 ml
Fresh oregano	1 tsp.	5 ml
Fresh lemon juice	3 Tbsp.	45 ml
Extra virgin olive oil	2 fl. oz.	60 ml

1 Place all of the ingredients in the bowl of a food processor and process until the mixture forms a coarse paste. Refrigerate.

Approximate values per tablespoon (15 ml): **Calories** 35, **Total fat** 3.5 g, **Saturated fat** 0 g, **Cholesterol** 0 mg, **Sodium** 160 mg, **Total carbohydrates** 1 g, **Protein** 0 g

RECIPE 28.18

GUACAMOLE

Yield: 1 qt. (1 lt)

Avocados	6	6
Lemon juice	2½ fl. oz.	75 ml
Green onions, sliced	4 Tbsp.	60 ml
Fresh cilantro, chopped	3 Tbsp.	45 ml
Tomatoes, seeded, diced	3 Tbsp.	45 ml
Garlic, chopped	1 tsp.	5 ml
Dried oregano	½ tsp.	2 ml
Jalapeños, seeded, chopped	1	1
Salt	TT	TT

1 Cut each avocado in half. Remove the seed and scoop out the pulp.

2 Add the lemon juice to the avocado pulp and mix well, mashing the avocado pulp.

3 Add the remaining ingredients. Season with salt and mix well.

Approximate values per 2-fl.-oz. (60-ml) serving: **Calories** 120, **Total fat** 12 g, **Saturated fat** 0 g, **Cholesterol** 0 mg, **Sodium** 25 mg, **Total carbohydrates** 1 g, **Protein** 2 g, **Vitamin C** 15%, **Claims**—no saturated fat; no cholesterol; no sugar; high fiber

ORANGE SOY VINAIGRETTE

RECIPE 28.19

SAN JOAQUIN DELTA COLLEGE, STOCKTON, CA
John D. Britto, CEC, CCE

This vinaigrette may be used as a dip for egg rolls, fried fish or calamari or served as a salad dressing.

Yield: 10 Servings

Rice vinegar	8 fl. oz.	240 ml
Chile flakes	1 tsp.	5 ml
Granulated sugar	3 Tbsp.	45 ml
Orange oil	½ tsp.	2 ml
Sesame oil	2 tsp.	10 ml
Soy sauce	1 Tbsp.	15 ml
Orange zest, minced	4 tsp.	20 ml
Water	as needed	as needed
Green onion tops, sliced very thin on the bias	2 Tbsp.	30 ml
Sesame seeds	2 tsp.	10 ml
Fresh cilantro, chopped	2 tsp.	10 ml

1 Combine the vinegar, chile flakes, sugar, oils, soy sauce and orange zest in a small saucepan. Bring to a boil and cook just until the sugar dissolves.

2 Taste the mixture and adjust the strength by adding 4 to 8 fluid ounces (120 to 240 milliliters) of water.

3 Cool the mixture, then add the green onions, sesame seeds and cilantro. Stir to combine, cover and chill until ready to use.

Approximate values per 1-fl.-oz. (30-ml) serving: **Calories** 45, **Total fat** 1.5 g, **Saturated fat** 0 g, **Cholesterol** 0 mg, **Sodium** 105 mg, **Total carbohydrates** 8 g, **Protein** 0 g, **Claims**—low fat; no cholesterol

SPINACH AND ARTICHOKE DIP

RECIPE 28.20

Yield: 4 lb. 6 oz. (2 kg)

Onions, medium dice	3 oz.	90 g
Garlic, chopped	2 tsp.	10 ml
Clarified butter	1 fl. oz.	30 ml
Frozen chopped spinach, thawed	1 lb. 8 oz.	700 g
Artichoke hearts, canned, chopped coarse	1 lb.	450 g
Cream sauce	1 qt.	1 lt
Worcestershire sauce	2 tsp.	10 ml
Parmesan, grated	6 oz.	180 g
Salt and pepper	TT	TT
Tabasco sauce	TT	TT

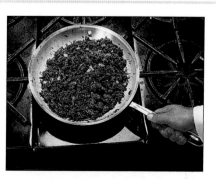

1 Sautéing the onions, garlic and spinach.

1 Sauté the onion and garlic in the butter until tender without coloring.
2 Add the spinach and sauté until hot.
3 Add the artichoke hearts, cream sauce, Worcestershire sauce and 4 ounces (120 grams) of the Parmesan. Mix well.
4 Season with salt, pepper and Tabasco sauce.
5 Transfer the dip to a half-size hotel pan. Top with the remaining Parmesan and bake at 350°F (180°C) until hot and browned on top, approximately 20 minutes.

Approximate values per 2-oz. (60-g) serving: **Calories** 110, **Total fat** 6 g, **Saturated fat** 3.5 g, **Cholesterol** 15 mg, **Sodium** 250 mg, **Total carbohydrates** 8 g, **Protein** 5 g, **Vitamin A** 20%

2 Serving the dip from a chafing dish.

RECIPE 28.21

LAMB SATAY

Yield: 16 Skewers

Lamb leg meat, boned, trimmed	2 lb.	1 kg
Vegetable oil	2 fl. oz	60 ml
Lemongrass, chopped	2 Tbsp.	30 ml
Garlic, chopped	1 Tbsp.	15 ml
Red pepper flakes, crushed	1 tsp.	5 ml
Curry powder	1 Tbsp.	15 ml
Honey	1 Tbsp.	15 ml
Fish sauce	1 Tbsp.	15 ml
Peanut Sauce (page 241)	as needed	as needed

1 Cut the lamb into 2-ounce (60-gram) strips approximately 4 inches (10 centimeters) long. Lightly pound the strips with a mallet. Thread the strips onto 6-inch (15-centimeter) bamboo skewers that have been soaked in water.
2 To make the marinade, combine all of the ingredients except the Peanut Sauce in the bowl of a food processor and purée until smooth.
3 Brush the meat with the marinade and allow to marinate for 1 hour.
4 Grill the skewers until done, approximately 2 minutes. Serve with Peanut Sauce.

Variations: Beef or chicken satay can be made by substituting well-trimmed beef or boneless, skinless chicken meat for the lamb.

Approximate values per skewer: **Calories** 118, **Total fat** 7 g, **Saturated fat** 2 g, **Cholesterol** 37 mg, **Sodium** 40 mg, **Total carbohydrates** 2 g, **Protein** 12 g

RECIPE 28.22

GRILLED SHRIMP WITH PROSCIUTTO AND BASIL

Yield: 12 Pieces

Shrimp, 16–20 count, peeled and deveined	12	12
Dry white wine	4 fl. oz.	120 ml
Rice wine vinegar	2 fl. oz.	60 ml
Dried thyme	2 tsp.	10 ml
Onions, minced	2 oz.	60 g
Cumin, ground	1 Tbsp.	15 ml
Salt and pepper	TT	TT
Vegetable oil	6 fl. oz.	180 ml
Dried basil	2 tsp.	10 ml

Garlic cloves, chopped	2	2
Prosciutto slices	3	3
Fresh basil leaves	6	6

1　Combine all the ingredients except the prosciutto and fresh basil in a stainless steel bowl. Marinate for 30 minutes.
2　Remove the shrimp from the marinade and drain them well.
3　Cut each slice of prosciutto into quarters.
4　Wrap each shrimp first with half a basil leaf, then with a piece of prosciutto; secure with a toothpick.
5　Grill until done, remove the toothpick and serve hot or cold.

Approximate values per piece: **Calories** 220, **Total fat** 15 g, **Saturated fat** 2 g, **Cholesterol** 170 mg, **Sodium** 250 mg, **Total carbohydrates** 2 g, **Protein** 18 g, **Iron** 15%

DATE AND CHORIZO RUMAKI　　　　　　　RECIPE 28.23

Yield: 32 Pieces

Bacon, sliced thin	16 slices	16 slices
Chorizo (page 887)	8 oz.	250 g
Cream cheese	4 oz.	120 g
Whole dates, pitted	32	32

1　Partially cook the bacon on a sheet pan in a 350°F (180°C) oven for approximately 5 minutes.
2　Cook the chorizo to render the excess fat. If the chorizo is in links, remove the meat from the casings before cooking.
3　Remove the cooked chorizo from the pan and drain in a mesh strainer or china cap to remove excess fat. Then blend the cream cheese into the meat.
4　Cut the dates open, butterfly style. Stuff each date with a portion of the chorizo mixture.
5　Wrap each date with a half slice of bacon, securing with a toothpick.
6　Arrange the rumaki on a rack placed over a sheet pan. Bake at 350°F (180°C) until the bacon is crisp and the dates are hot, approximately 15 to 20 minutes.

Approximate values per piece: **Calories** 90, **Total fat** 5 g, **Saturated fat** 2.5 g, **Cholesterol** 15 mg, **Sodium** 150 mg, **Total carbohydrates** 7 g, **Protein** 3 g

RED POTATOES WITH WALNUTS
AND GORGONZOLA　　　　　　　RECIPE 28.24

Yield: 80 Pieces

New red potatoes	40	40
Salt and pepper	TT	TT
Fresh thyme	2 tsp.	10 ml
Olive oil	2 fl. oz.	60 ml
Cream cheese	8 oz.	250 g
Gorgonzola	3 oz.	90 g
Bacon, medium dice, cooked	1 oz.	30 g
Sour cream	4 oz.	120 g
Walnuts, chopped coarse	1½ oz.	45 g
Worcestershire sauce	TT	TT
Tabasco sauce	TT	TT
Chives, minced	3 Tbsp.	45 ml

1 Cut the potatoes in half and scoop out a portion of the inside with a Parisienne scoop.

2 Toss the potatoes with the salt, pepper, thyme and olive oil. Arrange the potatoes on a sheet pan with their flat surfaces down and bake at 400°F (200°C) until brown and cooked through, approximately 15 minutes.

3 Soften the cream cheese in the bowl of an electric mixer. Add the Gorgonzola, bacon, sour cream and walnuts. Mix until smooth. Season with the Worcestershire and Tabasco sauces.

4 Using a pastry bag and plain tip, fill each hot potato half with the cold cheese mixture and sprinkle with chopped chives.

Variation: Fill the cooked potatoes with crème fraîche, top with caviar and sprinkle with sliced chives instead of using the bacon-and-cheese mixture.

Approximate values per piece: **Calories** 50, **Total fat** 3 g, **Saturated fat** 1 g, **Cholesterol** 5 mg, **Sodium** 35 mg, **Total carbohydrates** 6 g, **Protein** 1 g, **Claims**—low fat; low cholesterol; low sodium; no sugar

1 Scooping out the potato halves.

2 Filling the potato halves with the cheese mixture.

3 Garnishing the finished potato hors d'oeuvre.

RECIPE 28.25

TRICOLOR POTATO CANAPÉS WITH CRÈME FRAÎCHE AND CAVIAR

THE BROWN PALACE HOTEL, Denver, CO

Executive Chef Mark Black

Yield: 6 Servings

Russet potatoes	3	3
Red potatoes	3	3
Purple potatoes	3	3
Saffron threads	1/2 tsp.	3 ml
Crème fraîche	4 fl. oz.	120 ml
Beluga caviar	1/8 oz.	4 g
Chives	as needed	as needed

1 Cut each potato crosswise into 1 1/4-inch- (3-centimeter-) thick slices. Using a 3/4-inch (2-centimeter) round fluted cutter, cut rounds from the potato slices. Using a Parisienne scoop, scoop a cavity in the top of each round.

2 Simmer each type of potato separately in a small amount of salted water, adding saffron to the water with the russet potato rounds. Simmer the potato rounds until tender, approximately 8 to 10 minutes. Remove from the water and chill.

3 Fill the cavities of the chilled potatoes with crème fraîche. Top each potato with caviar and garnish with chives.

Approximate values per 5-oz. (150-g) serving: **Calories** 160, **Total fat** 4 g, **Saturated fat** 2.5 g, **Cholesterol** 10 mg, **Sodium** 25 mg, **Total carbohydrates** 28 g, **Protein** 3 g, **Vitamin C** 15%

STUFFED MUSHROOM CAPS   RECIPE 28.26

Yield: 48 Pieces

White mushrooms, medium	60	60
Clarified butter	2 fl. oz.	60 ml
Onions, minced	4 oz.	120 g
Flour	1 Tbsp.	15 ml
Heavy cream	4 fl. oz.	120 ml
Ham, cooked, chopped	4 oz.	120 g
Fresh parsley, chopped	2 Tbsp.	30 ml
Salt and pepper	TT	TT
Swiss cheese, shredded	2 oz.	60 g

1 Wash the mushrooms. Remove and chop the stems and 12 of the caps.
2 Sauté the whole mushroom caps in 1 ounce (30 grams) of the clarified butter until partially cooked but still firm. Remove from the pan and reserve.
3 Add the remaining butter to the pan. Sauté the onions and chopped mushrooms until dry.
4 Add the flour and cook for 1 minute. Add the cream; bring to a simmer and cook for 2 minutes.
5 Add the ham and parsley, season to taste with salt and pepper; stir to combine. Remove from the pan and cool slightly.
6 Stuff the mushroom caps with the ham mixture and sprinkle with shredded Swiss cheese.
7 Bake the mushrooms at 350°F (180°C) until hot, approximately 10 to 15 minutes.

Approximate values per piece: **Calories** 30, **Total fat** 2.5 g, **Saturated fat** 1.5 g, **Cholesterol** 10 mg, **Sodium** 35 mg, **Total carbohydrates** 1 g, **Protein** 1 g, **Claims**—low fat; low cholesterol; low sodium; low calorie; no sugar

ESCARGOT IN GARLIC BUTTER   RECIPE 28.27

Yield: 48 Pieces

Snails, canned	48	48
Butter, softened	1 lb.	450 g
Shallots, minced	2 Tbsp.	30 ml
Garlic, chopped	2 tsp.	10 ml
Fresh parsley, chopped	3 Tbsp.	45 ml
Salt and pepper	TT	TT
Mushroom caps, medium	48	48

1 Drain and rinse the snails.
2 Combine the butter, shallots, garlic, parsley, salt and pepper in a mixer or food processor and mix or process until well blended.
3 Sauté the mushroom caps in a small amount of the garlic butter until cooked but still firm. Remove from the heat.

▶ **escargot** (ays-skahr-go) French for snail; those used for culinary purposes are land snails (genus *Helix*); the most popular are the large Burgundy snails and the smaller but more flavorful common or garden snail known as *petit gris*

4 Place a snail in each cap and top with a generous amount of the garlic butter.

5 Bake the mushrooms and snails at 450°F (230°C) for 5 to 7 minutes and serve hot.

Variation: Prepare 48 small bouchées from puff pastry. Sauté the snails in a generous amount of the garlic butter and place one snail in each bouchée. Drizzle the snail with the garlic butter and serve.

Approximate values per piece: **Calories** 63, **Total fat** 6 g, **Saturated fat** 4 g, **Cholesterol** 19 mg, **Sodium** 64 mg, **Total carbohydrates** 0.5 g, **Protein** 1 g, **Vitamin A** 6%

RECIPE 28.28   **CHÈVRE TARTS**

Yield: 12 Tarts

Tomato concassée	4 oz.	120 g
Black pepper	TT	TT
Parmesan, grated	3 oz.	90 g
Puff pastry	8 oz.	250 g
Olive oil	as needed	as needed
Pesto Sauce (page 237)	2 fl. oz.	60 ml
Goat cheese (chèvre), Montrachet style	4 oz.	120 g
Zucchini, shredded	4 oz.	120 g

1 Season the tomato concassée with the pepper and sprinkle with 2 tablespoons (30 milliliters) of the Parmesan.

2 Roll out the puff pastry until it is approximately ¼ inch (6 millimeters) thick, then cut it into 12 circles, approximately 2½ inches (6.2 centimeters) in diameter.

3 Brush mini-muffin tins with olive oil and line them with the puff pastry circles.

4 Add 1 teaspoon (5 milliliters) of Pesto Sauce to each tart.

5 Add ⅓ ounce (10 grams) of goat cheese to each tart.

6 Add enough shredded zucchini to each tart to nearly fill it.

7 Top each tart with the tomato concassée and sprinkle with the remaining Parmesan.

8 Bake at 375°F (190°C) until the tarts are brown on top and the dough is cooked, approximately 15 to 20 minutes.

Approximate values per tart: **Calories** 210, **Total fat** 15 g, **Saturated fat** 4.5 g, **Cholesterol** 15 mg, **Sodium** 270 mg, **Total carbohydrates** 11 g, **Protein** 7 g, **Vitamin A** 20%

1 Lining mini-muffin tins with puff pastry dough.

2 Filling the tarts.

3 The baked tarts.

SPANAKOPITTA

Yield: 90 Pieces

Onions, small dice	4 oz.	120 g
Unsalted butter, melted	6 oz.	180 g
Fresh spinach, cooked and cooled, or frozen spinach, thawed	24 oz.	700 g
Fresh mint, chopped	1 Tbsp.	15 ml
Feta, crumbled	1 lb.	450 g
Eggs, beaten	3	3
Salt and pepper	TT	TT
Phyllo dough	1 lb.	450 g

1 Stacking the layers of buttered phyllo pastry.

1 Sauté the onions in 1 tablespoon (15 milliliters) of the butter until tender. Remove and cool.
2 Combine the cooled onions, spinach, mint, feta and eggs. Season with salt and pepper and mix well.
3 Spread one sheet of phyllo dough on the work surface; brush with melted butter. Place another sheet of phyllo on top of the first; brush it with butter. Place a third sheet of phyllo on top of the second and brush it with butter as well.
4 Cut the dough into 2-inch- (5-centimeter-) wide strips.
5 Place 1 tablespoon (15 milliliters) of the spinach mixture on the end of each strip of phyllo.
6 Starting with the end of the dough strip with the spinach mixture, fold one corner of the dough over the spinach mixture to the opposite side of the strip to form a triangle. Continue folding the dough, keeping it in a triangular shape, like point-folding a flag.
7 Place the phyllo triangles on a sheet pan and brush with melted butter. Bake at 375°F (190°C) until brown and crispy, approximately 20 minutes.

Approximate values per piece: **Calories** 45, **Total fat** 3 g, **Saturated fat** 2 g, **Cholesterol** 15 mg, **Sodium** 105 mg, **Total carbohydrates** 3 g, **Protein** 2 g, **Vitamin A** 8%, **Claims**—low fat; low cholesterol; no sugar

2 Placing the filling on the pastry.

3 Folding the pastry and filling into triangles.

SHRIMP CRUMPLE

Yield: 24 Pieces

Rice vinegar	1 Tbsp.	15 ml
Cayenne pepper	TT	TT
Garlic, minced	1 tsp.	5 ml
Fresh ginger, minced	1 tsp.	5 ml
Orange juice	1 Tbsp.	15 ml
Salt and pepper	TT	TT
Fresh thyme	TT	TT
Papaya	½	½
Shrimp, 16–20 count, peeled and deveined	12	12
Phyllo dough	6 sheets	6 sheets
Whole butter, melted	as needed	as needed

1 To make the marinade, combine the vinegar, cayenne, garlic, ginger and orange juice in a bowl. Stir to combine; season with salt, pepper and thyme.

2 Peel and seed the papaya and cut into medium dice. Place the papaya in a bowl and pour a small amount of marinade over it.

3 Split the shrimp and add them to the marinade.

4 Spread one sheet of phyllo dough on a work surface and brush it with butter. Lay another sheet on top of the first and brush it with butter. Place a third sheet of phyllo on top of the second and brush it with butter as well.

5 Prepare a second stack of phyllo with the three remaining sheets. Cut each stack of phyllo dough into 12 squares.

6 Place one half shrimp in the center of each square of phyllo dough and place several pieces of papaya on each shrimp. Gather the dough around the shrimp and papaya to form a small pouch.

7 Repeat with the remaining shrimp.

8 Bake the phyllo pouches at 350°F (180°C) until the phyllo is browned and the shrimp is cooked, approximately 15 to 20 minutes.

Approximate values per piece: **Calories** 60, **Total fat** 1 g, **Saturated fat** 0 g, **Cholesterol** 85 mg, **Sodium** 125 mg, **Total carbohydrates** 4 g, **Protein** 9 g, **Vitamin C** 15%

RECIPE 28.31

SAMOSAS
(DEEP-FRIED INDIAN TURNOVERS)

Yield: 30 Samosas

Pastry:

All-purpose flour	9 oz.	270 g
Salt	1 tsp.	5 ml
Garam masala	1 tsp.	5 ml
Peppercorns, cracked	1 tsp.	5 ml
Turmeric	1 tsp.	5 ml
Vegetable oil	1½ Tbsp.	23 ml
Water, warm	7 fl. oz.	200 ml

Filling:

Potatoes, peeled, small dice	4 oz.	120 g
Clarified butter or ghee	1 Tbsp.	15 ml
Ground lamb, lean	12 oz.	360 g
Fresh ginger juice	2 tsp.	10 ml
Garlic, minced	1 tsp.	5 ml
Onions, small dice	2 oz.	60 g
Garam masala	2 tsp.	10 ml
Chilli powder	1 tsp.	5 ml
Turmeric	1 tsp.	5 ml
Salt	1 tsp.	5 ml
Green peas	3 oz.	90 g
Fresh lemon juice	1 Tbsp.	15 ml
Fresh cilantro, chopped	2 Tbsp.	30 ml

1 In an electric mixer fitted with a dough hook attachment, combine the flour, salt, garam masala, peppercorns and turmeric and mix thoroughly. With the mixer at medium speed, add the oil, then add enough of the warm water to make a stiff dough. Knead the dough in the mixer until it is completely smooth and pliable. Cover the dough with a damp cloth and allow it to rest for 20 minutes.

2 Blanch the potatoes in salted water until nearly tender. Remove, refresh and reserve the potatoes.

3 Heat the clarified butter or ghee in a sauté pan and sauté the ground lamb until it begins to brown. Add the ginger juice, garlic and onions and sauté for approximately 5 minutes. Add the garam masala and other spices, salt, potatoes and peas and gently cook until the potatoes and peas are tender, approximately 5 minutes. Stir in the lemon juice and cook until the liquid evaporates. Stir in the cilantro. Transfer the filling to a sheet pan to cool completely.

4 Roll the dough into a rope and cut into 15 evenly sized pieces. Roll each piece out to a round approximately 5 inches (12 centimeters) in diameter, then cut each round in half. Place a spoonful of the filling toward one half of each piece of pastry. Run a wet finger around the edge and fold over to make a triangular pastry with one curved side. Pinch the edges together, then press the edges with the tines of a fork to seal them.

5 Using the basket method, deep-fry the turnovers at 350°F (180°C) until done, approximately 3 minutes. Drain and serve hot with chutney.

Variation: *Vegetarian Samosas*—Omit the lamb. Add 2 ounces (60 grams) of chopped unsalted peanuts and 6 ounces (180 grams) of chopped mushrooms in Step 3. Increase the amount of onion to 4 ounces (120 grams).

Approximate values per samosa: **Calories** 60, **Total fat** 2 g, **Saturated fat** 0.5 g, **Cholesterol** 10 mg, **Sodium** 160 mg, **Total carbohydrates** 8 g, **Protein** 3 g

CHA GIO
(DEEP-FRIED VIETNAMESE SPRING ROLLS)

RECIPE 28.32

Yield: 1 lb. (450 g) filling,
approximately 32 rolls

Cellophane noodles	2 oz.	60 g
Vegetable oil	2	2
Garlic cloves, minced	1 Tbsp.	15 ml
Shrimp, raw, peeled, deveined and chopped	4 oz.	120 g
Pork, minced	4 oz.	120 g
Carrot, grated	1	1
Green onions, sliced	3	3
Mung bean sprouts	1 oz.	30 g
Fish sauce	2 tsp.	10 ml
Vietnamese chile sauce	1 Tbsp.	15 ml
Cornstarch	2 tsp.	10 ml
Water, cold	2 tsp.	10 ml
Spring roll wrappers	32	32

1 Soak the cellophane noodles in boiling water for 5 minutes. Drain and cut into 1- to 2-inch (2.5- to 5-centimeter) pieces.

2 Heat a wok or sauté pan and add the oil. Stir-fry the garlic for a few seconds. Add the shrimp and pork and stir-fry, breaking up any large lumps. Add the carrots, green onions, bean sprouts, fish sauce, chile sauce and drained noodles. Cook until the carrots are slightly softened. Remove from the heat and cool completely.

3 Mix the cornstarch and water together in a small bowl. Moisten the spring roll wrappers with water and keep them covered with a damp towel to prevent them from drying out.

1 Soaking the spring roll wrappers.

2 Filling the spring roll wrappers.

3 Folding the wrapper around the filling.

4 Sealing the spring roll with water

4 Place approximately 1 tablespoon (30 milliliters) of filling in the center of a wrapper. Fold the sides over toward the middle and roll up into a cigar shape. Brush the edge with the water-and-cornstarch mixture to seal.

5 Using the swimming method, deep-fry the spring rolls at 325°F (165°C) until hot and crispy, approximately 45 seconds. Drain on absorbent paper and serve with Nuoc Cham, page 243.

Approximate values per roll: **Calories** 60, **Total fat** 2 g, **Saturated fat** 0 g, **Cholesterol** 10 mg, **Sodium** 70 mg, **Total carbohydrates** 7 g, **Protein** 2 g, **Vitamin A** 15%

RECIPE 28.33

BLUE CORN AND SHRIMP TAMALES

Yield: 16 Pieces

Fresh blue corn masa	1 lb.	450 g
Baking powder	½ tsp.	2 ml
Shortening	4 oz.	120 g
Salt	TT	TT
Onions, small dice	5 oz.	150 g
Red bell pepper, small dice	2 oz.	60 g
Green bell pepper, small dice	2 oz.	60 g
Garlic, chopped	1 tsp.	5 ml
Vegetable oil	2 Tbsp.	30 ml
Salt and pepper	TT	TT
Shrimp, 16–20 count, peeled and deveined	16	16
Dried corn husks	as needed	as needed

1 Combine the masa, baking powder and shortening in a bowl of an electric mixer, season with salt and mix until the masa pulls away from the sides of the bowl.

2 Sauté the onions, bell peppers and garlic in the vegetable oil until tender; season with salt. Remove from the heat and cool.

3 Cut the shrimp in half lengthwise.

4   To assemble the tamales, use a rubber spatula to spread 5 ounces (150 grams) of the masa mixture lengthwise on a 16-inch × 12-inch (40-centimeter × 30-centimeter) piece of parchment paper to form a 4-inch × 12-inch (10-centimeter × 30-centimeter) band of masa. Spread 1½ ounces (45 grams) of the vegetable mixture in a line lengthwise down the center of the masa.

5   Place eight shrimp halves, end to end, on top of each row of the vegetable mixture. Roll the parchment paper so that the masa completely encircles the shrimp and vegetable mixture. Twist the ends of the paper to seal. Repeat three more times to make four rolls. Freeze the rolls.

6   Unwrap each frozen roll and cut into four pieces. Wrap each piece tightly in dried corn husks that have been soaked in water, tying each end with thin strands of husk. Steam the tamales for 30 to 45 minutes. Allow the steamed tamales to rest for 10 minutes after cooking so that the masa becomes firm. Serve warm.

Approximate values per piece: **Calories** 280, **Total fat** 11 g, **Saturated fat** 3 g, **Cholesterol** 185 mg, **Sodium** 200 mg, **Total carbohydrates** 22 g, **Protein** 21 g, **Vitamin A** 25%, **Iron** 35%

1 Arranging vegetables and shrimp on the masa.

2 Rolling the tamale in parchment paper.

3 Wrapping pieces of tamale in corn husks.

No one who cooks, cooks alone. Even at her most solitary, a cook in the kitchen is surrounded by generations of cooks past, the advice and menus of cooks present, the wisdom of cookbook writers.

—Laurie Colwin, American writer (1944–1992)

PRINCIPLES OF THE BAKESHOP

AFTER STUDYING THIS CHAPTER, YOU WILL BE ABLE TO:

▶ recognize and select ingredients used in a bakeshop

▶ control the development of gluten

▶ cook sugar correctly

▶ understand the baking process

▶ recognize many of the specialized tools and equipment used in the bakeshop

▶ **formula** standard term used throughout the industry for a bakeshop recipe

Flour, sugar, eggs, milk, butter, flavorings—with this simple list of ingredients you can produce a seemingly endless variety of goods, from breads to sauces to pastries. But to produce consistently good brioche, Bavarians, biscuits or the like, you must pay careful attention to the character and quantity of each ingredient, the way the ingredients are combined and how heat is applied to them. Unlike, for example, a cut of meat that can be grilled, roasted, sautéed or braised and still be the same cut of meat, bakeshop products depend on careful, precise preparation for their very identity.

Accurate measurements are critical in the bakeshop. It is equally important to follow bakeshop **formulas** carefully and completely. Unlike other types of cooking, baking mistakes often cannot be discovered until the product is finished, by which time it is too late to correct them. For example, if you omit the salt when preparing a stew, the mistake can be corrected by adding salt at service time. If you omit the salt from a loaf of bread, however, the mistake cannot be corrected after the bread has baked, and its texture and flavor may be ruined. It is probably more important to follow a written formula, measure ingredients precisely and combine them accurately in the bakeshop than anywhere else in the kitchen.

In order to provide you with a thorough introduction to the skills needed in a bakeshop, we focus on preparing the types of breads and desserts usually found in a small retail shop or restaurant. Because this book is not designed for large wholesale or commercial bakeries, mixes, stabilizers and mechanical preparation and shaping skills are not included.

▶ INGREDIENTS

Although substituting ingredients may have little or no effect on some dishes (you can use carrots instead of turnips in a stew, for instance), this is not the case with baked goods. Different flours, fats, liquids and sweeteners function differently. Bread flour and cake flour are not the same, nor are shortening and butter. If you substitute one ingredient for another, the results will be different.

Understanding ingredients, why they function the way they do and how to adjust for their differences will make your baking experiences more successful and consistent. This chapter discusses flours, sugar and other sweeteners, fats, thickeners and flavorings such as chocolate, extracts and liquors. Dairy products, also common in baked goods, are discussed in Chapter 8, Dairy Products, and eggs are discussed in Chapter 21, Eggs and Breakfast.

FLOURS

WHEAT FLOUR

The most frequently used—and therefore the most important—ingredient in the bakeshop is wheat flour (Fr. *farine*). Flour provides bulk and structure to baked goods. It is also used to thicken liquids in items such as puddings and pie fillings and to prevent foods from sticking during preparation and baking.

Flour is produced by milling wheat kernels (berries). As discussed in Chapter 23, Potatoes, Grains and Pasta, a wheat kernel has an outer covering called bran. It is composed of several layers that protect the endosperm, which contains starches and proteins. The innermost part is the germ, which contains fat and serves as the wheat seed (see Figure 23.1). During milling, the kernels first pass through metal rollers to crack them, then the bran and germ are removed through repeated stages of sifting and separation. The remaining endosperm is then ground into flour. Flour derived from the portion of the endosperm closer to the germ is finer; flour derived from the portion of the endosperm nearer the bran is coarser and darker.

The character of the wheat determines the character of the flour. Wheats are classified as *soft* or *hard* depending on the kernel's hardness. The harder the wheat kernel, the higher its protein content. Soft wheat yields a soft flour with a low protein content. Soft flour, also called weak flour, is best for tender products such as cakes. Hard wheat yields a hard flour with a high protein content. Hard flour, also known as strong flour, is used for yeast breads.

Various types of flour are created by mixing or blending flours from different sources. **All-purpose flour,** a blend of hard and soft flours, is designed for use in a wide range of foods. It is also referred to throughout this book because it is readily available in quantities appropriate for small food service operations. Large bakeshops rarely use all-purpose flour; instead, they choose flours specifically milled and blended for industrial uses.

Aging and Bleaching

Any flour develops better baking qualities if allowed to rest for several weeks after milling. Freshly milled flour produces sticky doughs and products with less volume than those made with aged flour. During aging, flour turns white through a natural oxidation process referred to as bleaching.

Natural aging and bleaching are somewhat unpredictable, time-consuming processes, however, so chemicals are now used to do both. Potassium bromate and chlorine dioxide gas rapidly age flour. Chlorine dioxide and other chemicals bleach flour by removing yellow pigments in order to obtain a uniform white color. Bleaching destroys small amounts of the flour's naturally occurring vitamin E, which is replaced in fortified or enriched products.

Composition of Flour

Flour consists primarily of five nutrients: fat, minerals, moisture, starches and proteins. Fat and minerals each generally account for less than 1 percent of flour's content. The moisture content of flour is also relatively low—when packaged, it cannot exceed 15 percent under government standards. But its actual moisture content varies depending on climatic conditions and storage. In damp areas, flour absorbs moisture from the atmosphere.

Starches comprise 63 to 77 percent of flour, and are necessary for the absorption of moisture during baking. This process, known as **gelatinization,** occurs primarily at temperatures above 140°F (60°C). Starches also provide food for yeast during **fermentation.**

Flour proteins are important because of their gluten-forming potential. **Gluten** is the tough, rubbery substance created when wheat flour is mixed with water. Gluten strands are both plastic (that is, they change shape under pressure) and elastic (they resume their original shape when that pressure is removed).

▶ **gluten** an elastic network of proteins created when wheat flour is moistened and manipulated

Table 29.1	PROTEIN CONTENT OF FLOURS	
TYPE OF FLOUR	**PERCENT PROTEIN**	**USES**
Cake	7–9.5	Tender cakes
Pastry	7.5–12	Biscuits, pie crusts
All-purpose	10–13	General baking
Bread	12–15	Yeast breads
Whole-wheat	13–14	Breads
High-gluten	41–42	To increase protein content of weaker flours for bread making

Gluten is responsible for the volume, texture and appearance of baked goods. It provides structure and enables dough to retain the gases given off by leavening agents. Without gluten, there could be no raised breads: The gases created by yeast fermentation or chemical leaveners would simply escape if there were no network of gluten strands to trap them in the dough.

The higher a flour's protein content, the greater that flour's gluten-forming potential. The proteins responsible for gluten formation are *glutenin* and *gliadin*. Flour does not contain gluten; only a dough or batter can contain gluten. Gluten is produced when glutenin and gliadin are moistened and manipulated, as when they are stirred or kneaded. Generally, the longer a substance is mixed, the more gluten will develop. Products requiring a dough that can be kneaded and shaped, such as French rolls, require a flour with a higher protein content than products meant to be tender, such as cakes or muffins.

Table 29.1 lists the protein content and uses for several common flours. Remember that substituting one type of flour for another will result in a changed and probably less desirable product.

SPECIALTY FLOURS

Whole-Wheat Flour

Whole-Wheat Flour

Whole-wheat flour, also referred to as graham flour, is made by milling the entire wheat kernel, including the bran and germ. Whole-wheat flour has a nutty, sweet flavor and brown, flecked color. Products made with whole-wheat flour will be denser, with less volume than those made with white flour. Whole-wheat flour has a reduced shelf life because fats in the germ can become rancid during storage.

Self-Rising Flour

Self-rising flour is an all-purpose flour to which salt and a chemical leavener, usually baking powder, have been added. It is not recommended for professional use. Chemicals lose their leavening ability over time and may cause inconsistent results. Furthermore, different formulas call for different ratios of salt and leaveners; no commercial blend is appropriate for all purposes.

Nonwheat Flours

Nonwheat flours, also referred to as composite flours, are made from grains, seeds or beans. Corn, soybeans, rice, oats, buckwheat, potatoes and other items provide flours, but none of them contain the gluten-forming proteins of wheat flour. Composite flours are generally blended with a high-protein wheat flour for baking. Substituting a composite flour for wheat flour changes the flavor and texture of the product.

Rye Flour

Rye flour is commonly used in bread baking. It is milled from the rye berry much as wheat flour is milled from the wheat berry. Rye flour comes in four grades or colors: white, medium, dark and pumpernickel. White rye flour is made from only the center of the rye berry. Medium and dark rye flours are made from the whole rye berry after the bran is removed. Pumpernickel is made by grinding the entire rye berry, including the bran. All rye flours have a warm, pungent flavor similar to caraway and a gray-brown color. Although rye flour contains proteins, they will not form gluten, so a bread made with 100% rye flour will be dense and flat. Therefore, rye flour is usually blended with a high-protein wheat flour to produce a more acceptable product.

NUTRITION

Flours are generally high in carbohydrates and low in fat. The grains from which they are milled are often rich in vitamins and minerals. Some of these nutrients, however, are lost during milling. In enriched flours, thiamin, riboflavin, niacin and iron are added at levels set by the government.

PURCHASING AND STORING

Most flours are purchased in 50- and 100-pound bags. They should be stored in a lit, ventilated room at temperatures no higher than 80°F (27°C). Flour can be stored in a refrigerator or freezer if necessary to prevent the onset of rancidity. Refrigeration may cause the flour to absorb moisture, however, which will limit the flour's ability to absorb additional moisture during actual use.

An open bag of flour should be transferred to a closed container to prevent contamination. Even unopened bags of flour should not be stored near items with strong odors, as flour readily absorbs odors.

SUGAR AND SWEETENERS

Sugar (Fr. *sucre*) and other sweeteners serve several purposes in the bakeshop: They provide flavor and color, tenderize products by weakening gluten strands, provide food for yeasts, serve as a preservative and act as a creaming or foaming agent to assist with leavening.

SUGAR

Sugars are carbohydrates. They are classified as either (1) single or simple sugars (monosaccharides), such as glucose and fructose, which occur naturally in honey and fruits, or (2) double or complex sugars (disaccharides), which may occur naturally, such as lactose in milk, or in refined sugars.

The sugar most often used in the kitchen is **sucrose,** a refined sugar obtained from both the large tropical grass called sugar cane *(Saccharum officinarum)* and the root of the sugar beet *(Beta vulgaris)*. Sucrose is a disaccharide, composed of one molecule each of glucose and fructose. The chemical composition of beet and cane sugars is identical. The two products taste, look, smell and react the same. Sucrose is available in many forms: white granulated, light or dark brown granulated, molasses and powdered.

▶ **sucrose** the chemical name for common refined sugar; it is a disaccharide, composed of one molecule each of glucose and fructose

Sugar Manufacturing

Common refined or table sugar is produced from sugar cane or sugar beets. The first step in sugar production is to crush the cane or beet to extract the juice. This juice contains tannins, pigments, proteins and other undesirable components that must be removed through refinement. Refinement begins by dissolving the juice in water, then boiling it in large steam evaporators. The solution is then crystallized in heated vacuum pans. The uncrystallized liquid by-product, known as molasses, is separated out in a centrifuge. The remaining crystallized product, known as raw sugar, contains many impurities; the USDA considers it unfit for direct use in food.

Raw sugar is washed with steam to remove some of the impurities. This yields a product known as turbinado sugar. Refining continues as the turbinado is heated, liquefied, centrifuged and filtered. Chemicals may be used to bleach

SUGAR: A SWEET AND SORDID PAST

Few foods have so murky an early history as sugar, now one of the most commonplace of foods. Neither botanists nor anthropologists know precisely where sugar cane first grew or when sugar was first extracted from it.

Nevertheless, there are records of a crude sugar being used as a sweetener in India more than 2500 years ago. Sugar cane was being cultivated in the Middle East by the 6th century A.D. and spread from there to North Africa and Spain. Egyptians were manufacturing sugar commercially by the 10th century A.D.

Western Europeans first encountered sugar in the Middle East during the 12th-century Crusades. During the succeeding centuries, sugar remained a rare luxury in Europe. The small amounts available were traded by spice merchants and dispensed by apothecaries. At first, sugar was used only as a medicine, a condiment or, occasionally, a preservative. English cookbooks dating from the late 1300s illustrate an indiscriminate use of sugar as a condiment for meats, fish and vegetables. Like spices, sugar was used to show a person's wealth and position.

When Columbus landed in the West Indies, he found an environment perfectly suited for growing sugar cane, so he brought sugar cane cuttings to the New World on his second voyage in 1493. Huge sugar cane plantations soon flourished in the New World, built and worked by enslaved Africans and their descendants.

By the 18th century, European and American middle classes were able to afford sugar by the pound. Sugar was now being used principally as a sweetener, particularly in connection with three other imports: coffee, tea and chocolate. Sugar, in fact, had become one of the principal components of a vast and complex trade network involving molasses from the West Indies, distilled rum from New England, finished goods from Europe and slaves from Africa.

Early sugars bore little resemblance to the white granulated substance we use today. Until vacuum pans and centrifuges were invented in the late 19th century, pure sugars were unobtainable. All contained varying amounts of molasses and other impurities. Most of the world's sugar was sold only in large, brown cones. The price of sugar depended on its whiteness and fineness, with the whitest sugar being the most costly.

After two centuries of prosperity, the sugar cane industry began to decline in the 19th century. Several factors contributed to this: abolition of slavery, discovery of alternative sweeteners and falling sugar prices.

If cane sugar was an ancient plant exploited in the New World, then beet sugar is a modern plant fully realized in the Old World. Although the ability to refine a crude sweetener from root vegetables had been known for centuries, scientists and chefs mistakenly believed that sugar could be obtained only from plants grown in tropical heat. It was not until 1747 that a German chemist, Andreas Marggraf, proved otherwise. He isolated sucrose—the same substance produced from sugar cane—from white beets. His research, however, did not have a commercial application until cane sugar supplies were threatened. During the Napoleonic Wars, the British blockade of European ports cut off supplies of cane sugar. At Napoleon's urging, research into manufacturing beet sugar progressed. The first beet sugar factory was built in France in 1812. Soon France, Germany and Belgium were virtually self-sufficient in sugar production.

Consumers accepted this new sugar with few complaints; most were totally unaware of any difference. Today, about 40 percent of the world's sugar is manufactured from beets, primarily in Russia, Germany and the United States.

and purify the liquid sugar. Finally, the clear liquid sugar is recrystallized in vacuum pans as granulated white sugar.

Pure sucrose is sold in granulated and powdered forms and is available in several grades. Because there are no government standards regulating grade labels, various manufacturers' products may differ slightly.

Turbinado Sugar

Turbinado sugar, sometimes called Demerara sugar, is the closest consumable product to raw sugar. It is partially refined, light brown in color, with coarse crystals and a caramel flavor. It is sometimes used in beverages and certain baked goods. Because of its high and variable moisture content, turbinado sugar is not recommended as a substitute for granulated or brown sugar.

Sanding Sugar

Sanding sugar has a large, coarse crystal structure that prevents it from dissolving easily. It is used almost exclusively for decorating cookies and pastries.

Granulated Sugar

This is the all-purpose sugar used throughout the kitchen. The crystals are a fine, uniform size suitable for a variety of purposes.

Cube Sugar

Sugar cubes are formed by pressing moistened granulated sugar into molds and allowing it to dry. Cube sugar is most often used for beverage service.

Clockwise from top left: Demerara sugar cubes, light brown sugar, powdered sugar, sugar cubes, brown sugar crystals, granulated sugar

Brown Sugar

Brown sugar is simply regular refined sugar with some of the molasses returned to it. Light brown sugar contains approximately 3.5 percent molasses; dark brown sugar contains about 6.5 percent. Molasses adds moisture and a distinctive flavor. Brown sugar can be substituted for refined sugar, measure for measure, in any formula where its flavor is desired. Because of the added moisture, brown sugar tends to lump, trapping air into pockets. It should be measured by weight or, if measured by volume, it should be packed firmly into the measuring cup in order to remove any air pockets. Always store brown sugar in an airtight container to prevent it from drying and hardening.

Superfine or Castor Sugar

Superfine sugar is granulated sugar with a smaller-sized crystal. Also known as castor sugar, it can be produced by processing regular granulated sugar in a food processor for a few moments. Superfine sugar dissolves quickly in liquids and produces light and tender cakes.

Powdered or Confectioner's Sugar

Powdered sugar (Fr. *sucre en poudre*) is made by grinding granulated sugar crystals through varying degrees of fine screens. Powdered sugar cannot be made in a food processor. It is widely available in three degrees of fineness: 10X is the finest and most common; 6X and 4X are progressively coarser. Because of powdered sugar's tendency to lump, 3 percent cornstarch is added to absorb moisture. Powdered sugar is most often used in icings and glazes and for decorating baked products.

LIQUID SWEETENERS

Except for leavening, liquid sweeteners can be used to achieve the same benefits as sugar in baked goods. Most of these liquids have a distinctive flavor as well as sweetness. Some liquid sweeteners are made from sugar cane; others are derived from other plants, grains or bees.

Corn Syrup

Corn syrup is produced by extracting starch from corn kernels and treating it with acid or an enzyme to develop a sweet syrup. This syrup is extremely thick or viscous and less sweet-tasting than honey or refined sugar. Its viscosity gives foods a thick, chewy texture. Corn syrup is available in light and dark forms; the dark syrup has caramel color and flavor added. Corn syrup is a **hygroscopic** (water-attracting) sweetener, which means it will attract water from the air on humid days and lose water through evaporation more slowly than granulated sugar. Thus, it keeps products moister and fresher longer.

Honey

Honey (Fr. *miel*) is a strong sweetener consisting of fructose and glucose. It is created by honey bees from nectar collected from flowers. Its flavor and color vary depending on the season, the type of flower the nectar came from and its age. Commercial honey is often a blend, prepared to be relatively neutral and consistent. Like corn syrup, honey is highly hygroscopic. Its distinctive flavor is found in several ethnic foods such as baklava and halvah, and beverages such as Drambuie and Benedictine.

Honey

Maple Syrup

Maple syrup is made from the sap of sugar maple trees. Sap is collected during the spring, then boiled to evaporate its water content, yielding a sweet brown syrup. One sugar maple tree produces about 12 gallons of sap each season; 30–40 gallons of sap will produce 1 gallon of syrup. Pure maple syrup must weigh not less than 11 pounds per gallon; it is graded according to color, flavor and sugar content. The more desirable products, Grades AA and A, have a light amber color and delicate flavor. Pure maple syrup is expensive, but it does add a distinct flavor to baked goods, frostings and, of course, pancakes and waffles.

Maple-flavored syrups, often served with pancakes, are usually corn syrups with artificial colorings and flavorings added.

Molasses

As mentioned earlier, molasses (Fr. *mélasse*) is the liquid by-product of sugar refining. Edible molasses is derived only from cane sugar, as beet molasses has an unpleasant odor and bitter flavor. *Unsulfured molasses* is not a true by-product of sugar making. It is intentionally produced from pure cane syrup and is preferred because of its lighter color and milder flavor. *Sulfured molasses* is a by-product and contains some of the sulfur dioxide used in secondary sugar processing. It is darker and has a strong, bitter flavor.

The final stage of sucrose refinement yields *blackstrap molasses,* which is somewhat popular in the American South. Blackstrap molasses is very dark and thick, with a strong, unique flavor that is unsuitable for most purposes.

Sorghum molasses is produced by cooking down the sweet sap of a brown corn plant known as sorghum, which is grown for animal feed. The flavor and appearance of sorghum molasses are almost identical to unsulfured sugar cane molasses.

Molasses

NUTRITION

Sweeteners are carbohydrates. They are high in calories and contain no fiber, protein, fat, vitamin A or vitamin C. They contain only trace amounts of thiamin, riboflavin and niacin.

COOKING SUGAR

Sugar can be incorporated into a prepared item in its dry form or first liquefied into a syrup. **Sugar syrups** (not to be confused with liquid sweeteners such as molasses) take two forms: **simple syrups,** which are mixtures of sugar and water, and **cooked syrups,** which are made of melted sugar cooked until it reaches a specific temperature.

Simple Sugar Syrups

Simple or stock syrups are solutions of sugar and water. They are used to moisten cakes and to make sauces, sorbets, and beverages.

The syrup's density or concentration is dictated by its intended purpose. Cold water will dissolve up to double its weight in sugar; heating the solution forms denser, more concentrated syrups. A hydrometer, which measures specific gravity and shows degrees of concentration on the Baumé scale, is the most accurate guide to density. The higher the number, the greater the density of the solution.

Simple syrups can be prepared without the aid of a hydrometer, however. To make a simple sugar syrup, specific amounts of water and sugar are combined in a saucepan and brought to a boil. Once the solution boils, it is important not to stir, as this may cause recrystallization or lumping. For successful simple sugar syrups, the following formulas must be followed precisely.

Using a Baumé hydrometer.

▶ Light syrup—Boil 2 parts water with 1 part sugar for 1 minute. This concentration would measure 17°–20° on the Baumé scale. A light syrup can be used for making sorbet or moistening spongecake.

▶ Medium syrup—Boil 1 part sugar with 1½ parts water for 1 minute. This concentration would measure 21°–24° on the Baumé scale. A medium syrup can be used for candying citrus peel.

▶ Heavy syrup—Boil equal parts water and sugar for 1 minute. This concentration would measure 28°–30° on the Baumé scale, and the solution should be at 220°F (104°C). Heavy syrup is a basic, all-purpose syrup kept on hand in many bakeshops.

SAFETY ALERT

Be extremely careful when working with hot sugar syrups. Because sugar can be heated to very high temperatures, these syrups can cause severe burns. Do not touch liquefied or caramelized sugar with your bare hand until it has cooled completely.

Cooked Sugars

Caramel sauce, meringue, buttercream, candy and other confections often need liquid sugar that will be firm when cool or have a cooked caramel flavor. For these purposes, sugar needs to be cooked to temperatures far higher than simple syrups. A small amount of water is generally added at the beginning to help the sugar dissolve evenly. As the mixture boils, the water evaporates, the solution's temperature rises and its density increases. The syrup's concentration depends on the amount of water remaining in the final solution: The less water, the harder the syrup will become when cool.

The sugar's temperature indicates its concentration. If there is a great deal of water present, the temperature will not rise much above 212°F (100°C). As water evaporates, however, the temperature will rise until it reaches 320°F (160°C), the point at which all water is evaporated. At temperatures above 320°F (160°C), the pure sugar begins to brown or caramelize. As sugar caramelizes, its sweetening power decreases dramatically. At approximately 375°F (190°C), sugar will burn, developing a bitter flavor. If allowed to continue cooking, sugar will ignite.

Sugar solutions are unstable because of their molecular structure. They can recrystallize because of agitation or uneven heat distribution. To prevent recrystallization:

Caramelizing sugar.

1 Always use a heavy, clean saucepan, preferably copper.
2 Stir the solution to make sure all sugar crystals dissolve before it reaches a boil. Do not stir the solution after it begins boiling, however.
3 An **interferent** may be added when the solution begins to boil. Cream of tartar, vinegar, glucose (a monosaccharide) and lemon juice are known as interferents because they interfere with the formation of sugar crystals. Some formulas specify which interferent to use, although most are used in such small quantities that their flavor cannot be detected.
4 Brush down the sides of the pan with cold water to wash off crystals that may be deposited there. These sugar crystals may seed the solution, causing more crystals (lumps) to form if not removed. Instead of using a brush to wash away crystals, you can cover the pan for a few moments as soon as the solution comes to a boil. Steam will condense on the cover and run down the sides of the pan, washing away the crystals.

Brushing sugar crystals from the side of the pan.

The concentration of sugar syrup should be determined with a candy thermometer that measures very high temperatures. If a thermometer is not available, use the traditional but less accurate ice-water test: Spoon a few drops of the hot sugar into a bowl of very cold water. Check the hardness of the cooled sugar with your fingertips. Each stage of cooked sugar is named according to its firmness when cool—for example, soft ball or hard crack.

Table 29.2 lists the various stages of cooked sugar and the temperature for each. Each stage is also identified by the ice-water test result. Note that even a few degrees makes a difference in the syrup's concentration.

Soft ball stage.

Hard ball stage.

Hard crack stage.

Table 29.2	STAGES OF COOKED SUGAR	
STAGE	**TEMPERATURE**	**ICE-WATER TEST—ONE DROP:**
Thread	236°F (110°C)	Spins a 2-inch (5-centimeter) thread when dropped
Soft ball	240°F (116°C)	Forms a soft ball
Firm ball	246°F (119°C)	Forms a firm ball
Hard ball	260°F (125°C)	Forms a hard, compact ball
Soft crack	270°F (132°C)	Separates into a hard, but not brittle, thread
Hard crack	300°F (149°C)	Separates into a hard, brittle sheet
Caramel	338°F (170°C)	Liquid turns brown in the pan

FATS

Fat is the general term for butter, lard, shortening, oil and margarine. Fats provide flavor and color, add moisture and richness, assist with leavening, help extend a product's shelf life and shorten gluten strands.

The flavor and texture of a baked good depends on the type of fat used and the manner in which it is incorporated with other ingredients. In pastry doughs, solid fat shortens or tenderizes the gluten strands; in bread doughs, fat increases loaf volume and lightness; in cake batters, fat incorporates air bubbles and helps leaven the mixture. Fats should be selected based on their flavor, melting point and ability to form emulsions.

Most bakeshop ingredients combine completely with liquids; fats do not. Fats will not dissolve but will break down into smaller and smaller particles through mixing. With proper mixing, these fat particles are distributed, more or less evenly, throughout the other ingredients.

All-Purpose Shortening

Any fat is a shortening in baking because it shortens gluten strands and tenderizes the product. What is generally referred to as shortening, however, is a type of solid, white, generally flavorless fat, specially formulated for baking. Shortenings are made from animal fats and/or vegetable oils that are solidified through hydrogenation. These products are 100 percent fat with a relatively high melting point. Solid shortenings are ideal for greasing baking pans because they are flavorless and odorless.

Emulsified Shortening

Emulsifiers may be added to regular shortening to assist with moisture absorption and retention as well as leavening. Emulsified shortenings, also known as high-ratio shortenings, are used in the commercial production of cakes and frostings where the formula contains a large amount of sugar. If a formula calls for an emulsified shortening, use it. If you substitute any other fat, the product's texture suffers.

Lard

Lard

Lard (Fr. *saindoux*) is rendered pork fat. It is a solid white product of almost 100 percent pure fat; it contains only a small amount of water. Lard yields flaky, flavorful pastries, such as pie crusts, but is rarely used commercially because it turns rancid quickly.

Butter and Margarine

Butter is prized in the bakeshop for its flavor; however, it melts at a relatively low temperature of approximately 93°F (33°C) and burns easily. Unsalted butter is preferred for baking because it tends to be fresher, and additional salt might

Table 29.3	MELTING POINT OF FATS*	
Butter, whole		92°F–98°F (33°C–36°C)
Butter, clarified		92°F–98°F (33°C–36°C)
Cocoa butter		88°F–93°F (31°C–34°C)
Lard		89°F–98°F (32°C–36°C)
Margarine, solid		94°F–98°F (34°C–36°C)
Shortening, all-purpose vegetable		120°F (49°C)
Shortening, emulsified vegetable		115°F (46°C)
Shortening, heavy-duty fryer		97°F–107°F (36°C–42°C)

*The melting point of any fat depends upon its specific ratio of fatty acids. Natural products such as butter and lard will vary more from one lot to the next than will manufactured products such as margarine.

This information was obtained from a variety of manufacturers and assumes that the fat is pure and previously unused.

interfere with product formulas. Margarine melts at a slightly higher temperature than butter, making it useful for some rolled-in doughs such as puff pastry or danish. For detailed information on butter and margarine, see Chapter 8, Dairy Products.

Oil

Unlike butter and other fats, oil blends thoroughly throughout a mixture. It therefore coats more of the proteins, and the gluten strands produced are much shorter, a desirable result in fine-textured products such as muffins or chiffon cakes. For baking, select a neutral-flavored oil unless the distinctive taste of olive oil is desired, as in some breads. Never substitute oil in a formula requiring a solid shortening. For detailed information on oil, see Chapter 7, Kitchen Staples.

NUTRITION

Fats are high in calories and contain varying levels of saturated fats. Although they have no carbohydrates, a few fats such as butter have trace amounts of protein and minerals. Butter is also high in vitamin A. Fats are also useful for carrying fat-soluble vitamins.

THICKENERS

Starches are often used as thickening agents in bakeshop products. Cornstarch, arrowroot and flour can be used as thickeners for pastry creams, sauces, custards and fruit fillings. These thickeners are discussed in Chapter 11, Stocks and Sauces.

One of the most commonly used thickeners in the bakeshop is **gelatin,** a natural product derived from collagen, an animal protein. It is available in two forms: granulated gelatin and sheet (also called leaf) gelatin. A two-step process is necessary to use either form: The gelatin must first be softened in a cold liquid, then dissolved in a hot liquid.

Granulated gelatin is available in bulk or in ¼-ounce (7-gram) envelopes (slightly less than 1 tablespoon). One envelope is enough to set 1 pint (500 milliliters) of liquid. Granulated gelatin should be softened in a cold liquid for at least five minutes, then heated gently to dissolve. The initial softening in a cold liquid is necessary to separate the gelatin molecules so that they will not lump together when the hot liquid is added.

Sheet or leaf gelatin is available in 1-kilogram boxes, sometimes further packaged in sheets containing five or six envelopes. The sheets are produced in varying thicknesses and weights. They must be separated and soaked in ice water until very soft, at least 15 minutes. They are then removed from the water and stirred into a hot liquid until completely dissolved.

Granulated Gelatin

PROCEDURE FOR USING SHEET GELATIN

1 Gelatin sheets are submerged in ice water for several minutes to soften.

2 Softened gelatin sheets are then removed from the ice water and incorporated into a hot liquid.

Pearl Tapioca

Granulated and sheet gelatin can be substituted weight for weight in any formula. Sheet gelatin, though more expensive, is preferred for its lack of flavor and color. It also tends to dissolve more readily and evenly and has a longer shelf life than the granulated product.

Once incorporated into a product such as a Bavarian, gelatin can be frozen, or melted and reset once or twice, without a loss of thickening ability. Because it scorches easily, gelatin and mixtures containing gelatin should not be allowed to boil. Products thickened with gelatin, such as mousse or custard, will become rubbery after a few days in the refrigerator.

Although less commonly encountered in professional bakeshops, **tapioca** can be used to thicken a variety of pastry products. Tapioca is a starch produced from the root of the tropical cassava (manioc) plant. It is available as a flour or as balls, referred to as pearls. Tapioca flour can be used in the same manner as cornstarch to thicken soups, sauces and fruit mixtures. Pearl tapioca is used to thicken milk for tapioca pudding, or to thicken fruit pie fillings. Most pearl tapioca must be soaked in a cold liquid for several hours before cooking. Instant tapioca, which is smaller, needs to soak for only 20 to 30 minutes before cooking.

FLAVORINGS

Many spices and flavorings are used in the bakeshop. The most popular spices such as cinnamon, cloves, nutmeg and allspice are discussed in Chapter 7, Kitchen Staples. Here we discuss emulsions and extracts, vanilla, chocolate and alcoholic beverages.

EMULSIONS AND EXTRACTS

Emulsions and extracts are liquid flavoring agents derived from various oils.

Emulsions are flavoring oils mixed into water with the aid of emulsifiers. Lemon and orange are the most common emulsions. Emulsions are much stronger than extracts and should be used carefully and sparingly.

Extracts are mixtures of flavoring oils and ethyl alcohol. Vanilla, almond and lemon are frequently used extracts. An extract may be made with pure flavoring oils or with artificial flavors and colors. Contents are regulated by the FDA, and package labels must indicate any artificial ingredients.

Emulsions and extracts are highly volatile. They should be stored in sealed containers in a cool area away from direct light.

VANILLA

Vanilla (Fr. *vanille*) is the most frequently used flavoring in the bakeshop. It comes from the pod fruit, called a bean, of a vine in the orchid family. Vanilla beans are purchased whole, individually or by the pound. They should be soft

Scraping seeds from the interior of a vanilla bean.

and pliable, with a rich brown color and good aroma. The finest vanilla comes from Tahiti and Madagascar.

To use a vanilla bean, cut it open lengthwise with a paring knife. Scrape out the moist seeds with the knife's tip and stir them into the mixture being flavored. The seeds do not dissolve and will remain visible as small black or brown flecks. After all the seeds have been removed, the bean can be stored in a covered container with sugar to create vanilla sugar.

Vanilla beans should be stored in an airtight container in a cool, dark place. During storage, the beans may develop a white coating. This is not mold, but rather crystals of vanilla flavor known as **vanillin.** It should not be removed.

Pure vanilla extract is an easy and less expensive way to give bakeshop products a true vanilla flavor. It is dark brown and aromatic, and comes in several strengths referred to as folds. The higher the number of folds, the stronger the flavor of the extract. Any product labeled "vanilla extract" must not contain artificial flavorings and must be at least 35 percent alcohol by volume.

Vanilla extract should be stored at room temperature in a closed, opaque container. It should not be frozen.

Artificial or imitation vanilla flavoring is made with synthetic vanillin. Artificial flavoring is available in a clear form, which is useful for white buttercreams where the dark brown color of pure vanilla extract would be undesirable. Although inexpensive, artificial vanilla is, at best, weaker and less aromatic than pure extract. It can also impart a chemical or bitter taste to foods.

CHOCOLATE

Chocolate is one of the most popular flavorings—perhaps *the* most popular—for candies, cookies, cakes and pastries. Chocolate is also served as a beverage and is an ingredient in the traditional spicy Mexican molé sauce. Chocolate is available in a variety of forms and degrees of sweetness.

Chocolate Production

Chocolate (Fr. *chocolat*) begins as yellow fruit pods dangling from the trunk and main branches of the tropical cacao tree. Each pod contains about 40 almond-sized cocoa beans. After the pods ripen, the beans are placed in the sun for several days to dry and ferment. They are then cleaned, dried, cured and roasted to develop flavor and reduce bitterness. Next, the beans are crushed to remove their shells, yielding the prized chocolate **nib.**

Nibs are shipped to manufacturers worldwide where they can be further roasted. They are crushed into a thick (nonalcoholic) paste known as **chocolate liquor** or **chocolate mass.** Chocolate mass contains about 53 percent fat, known as **cocoa butter.** The chocolate mass is further refined depending on the desired product. If **cocoa powder** is to be produced, virtually all the cocoa butter is removed. A variety of other products are created by adding more cocoa butter, sugar, milk solids and flavorings to the chocolate mass. Most manufacturers of fine chocolates use the Swiss technique of **conching** to increase smoothness. Conching involves stirring large vats of blended chocolate with a heavy roller or paddle to smooth out sugar crystals and mellow the flavor, a process that may last from a few hours to three days.

Cocoa Beans

Tasting Chocolates

There are three types of cocoa beans: a very hardy, abundant African variety used as a base bean, and two flavorful, aromatic varieties used for flavor. Unlike wine or coffee, you cannot taste processed chocolate and tell which beans were used. Most chocolates are blends, created by their manufacturer to be unique yet consistent. Varietal chocolates, those made from one type of bean grown in one specific area, have become trendy, though expensive, for both chocolate bars and baking chocolates.

Roasting greatly affects the final flavor of chocolate. Generally, German and Spanish manufacturers use a high (or strong) roast; Swiss and American makers use a low (or mild) roast.

FROM CACAO TO CHOCOLATE CHIPS

To understand the history of chocolate, a chef or chocoholic must first understand the fundamental difference between its original use as a beverage and its later transformation into a candy.

The cacao tree (called *Theobroma cacao;* in Greek, *theobroma* means "food of the gods") originated in the river valleys of South America and was carried into what is now Mexico by the Mayans before the 7th century A.D. It was cultivated by Mayans, Aztecs and Toltecs not only as a source of food but also as currency. Chocolate was consumed only as a treasured drink. Cacao beans were roasted, crushed to a paste and steeped in water, then thickened with corn flour to create a cold, bitter beverage. Sometimes honey, vanilla or spices, including chiles, were added. The Aztec emperor Montezuma was so enamored with the beverage that he reportedly consumed 50 cups at each meal.

Columbus brought cacao beans to Spain from his fourth voyage to the New World in 1504. (The common term *cocoa* is actually a western European mispronunciation of the proper term *cacao,* caused by confusion with another New World delicacy, the coconut.) But almost 20 years passed before Spanish conquistadors, led by Cortez, understood the beans' value. With Montezuma's encouragement, Cortez and his soldiers slowly acquired a taste for the bitter beverage, spurred on by the intoxicating effects of caffeine.

Cortez's most important contribution to the history of chocolate was to take beans with him when he left Mexico. He planted them on the islands he passed on his return to Spain: Trinidad, Haiti and Fernando Po, from which the giant African cocoa industry grew. Through Cortez's farsighted efforts, Spain controlled all aspects of the cocoa trade until well into the 18th century.

The Spanish began drinking chocolate at home during the 16th century. It was usually mixed with two other expensive imports, sugar and vanilla, and frothed with a carved wooden swizzle stick known as a *molinet.* This thick, cold drink was made from tablets of crushed cocoa beans produced and sold by monks. The Spanish believed that cocoa cured all ills and supplied limitless stamina. In the early 17th century, cocoa beverages, now served hot, crept into France via royal marriages.

Cocoa spread through the rest of Europe by different routes. The Dutch, who had poached on Spanish trade routes for many years, eventually realized the value of the unusual beans they found on Spanish ships. Holland soon became the most important cocoa port outside Spain. From there, a love of cocoa spread to Germany, Scandinavia and Italy. In 1655, England acquired Jamaica and its own cocoa plantations.

Until the Industrial Revolution, cocoa was made by hand using mortar and pestle or stone-grinding disks to crush the cocoa nibs. By the 1700s, cocoa factories had opened throughout Europe. James Baker opened the first cocoa factory in the United States in 1765.

Conrad van Houten, a Dutch chemist, patented "chocolate powder" in 1825. His work marked the beginning of a shift from drinking to eating chocolate. It also paved the way for everything we know as chocolate today. Van Houten developed a screw press that removed most of the cocoa butter from the bean, leaving a brown, flaky powder, essentially the same substance as modern cocoa powder.

Eventually, it was discovered that the extra cocoa butter resulting from the production of cocoa powder could be added to ground beans to make the paste more malleable, smoother and more tolerant of added sugar. The English firm of Fry and Sons introduced the first eating chocolate in 1847. Their recipe was the same then as today: crushed cocoa beans, cocoa butter and sugar.

In 1876, Swiss chocolatier Daniel Peter invented solid milk chocolate using the new condensed milk created by baby-food manufacturer Henri Nestlé. Pennsylvania cocoa manufacturer Milton Hershey introduced his milk chocolate bars in 1894, followed by Hershey's Kisses in 1907. Nestlé Foods introduced the chocolate chip, perfect for cookies, in 1939.

Chocolate Chef, sculpted by Pastry Chef Rubin Foster.

Refining is also a matter of national taste. Swiss and German chocolate are the smoothest, followed by English chocolates. American chocolate is noticeably more grainy.

Chocolate quality is actually the product of several factors besides flavor. All these factors should be evaluated when selecting chocolates:

1 Appearance—color should be even and glossy, without any discoloration.

2 Smell—should be chocolatey with no off-odors or staleness.

3 Break—should snap cleanly without crumbling.

4 Texture—should melt quickly and evenly on the tongue.

Unsweetened Chocolate

Unsweetened chocolate is pure hardened chocolate liquor without any added sugar or milk solids. It is frequently used in baking and is sometimes referred to

MELTING CHOCOLATE

Two important rules for melting chocolate:

1 Chocolate must never exceed 120°F or there will be a loss of flavor.

2 Water—even a drop in the form of steam—must never touch the chocolate.

When a droplet of water enters melted chocolate, the chocolate becomes lumpy (a process called *seizing*). There must be a minimum of 1 tablespoon water per ounce of chocolate to keep seizing from occurring.

If seizing does occur, the addition of fat such as vegetable shortening, clarified butter, or cocoa butter will somewhat restore the chocolate to a workable condition.

For melting chocolate, unlined copper is the traditional "chocolate pot" because it is so responsive to changes in temperature. Aluminum or heatproof glass also works well. Ideally, chocolate should be heated to 120°F, the point at which all the different fat fractions in the cocoa butter are melted.

When melting chocolate or cocoa butter, temperatures exceeding 120°F adversely affect the flavor. There are many acceptable methods for melting dark chocolate. If the heat source does not exceed 120°F it is fine to add the dark chocolate in large pieces and leave it to melt unmonitored. When the heat source is capable of bringing the chocolate over 120°F, however, the chocolate should be finely chopped or grated to ensure uniformity of melting. The chocolate must be carefully watched and stirred to avoid overheating. If using a double boiler, water in the lower container should not exceed 140°F and the upper container should not touch the water. The chocolate should be stirred constantly.

Milk and white chocolate must always be stirred frequently while melting because they contain milk solids which seed (lump) if left undisturbed.

Remove chocolate from the heat source when it reaches 115°F as the temperature may continue to rise, and stir vigorously to prevent overheating and to distribute the cocoa butter evenly.

Always melt chocolate uncovered as moisture could condense on the lid, drop back in the chocolate, and cause seizing.

—from *The Cake Bible* by ROSE LEVY BERANBAUM

---

as "baking chocolate." Unsweetened chocolate is approximately 53 percent cocoa butter and 47 percent cocoa solids. Its flavor is pure and chocolatey, but the absence of sugar makes it virtually inedible as is.

Bittersweet and Semisweet Chocolates

Both bittersweet and semisweet chocolates contain at least 35 percent chocolate liquor plus additional cocoa butter, sugar, flavorings and sometimes emulsifiers. Generally, semisweet chocolate will be sweeter than bittersweet chocolate, but there are no precise definitions, so flavor and sweetness will vary from brand to brand. Both are excellent eating chocolates and can usually be substituted measure for measure in any formula. **Couverture** (koo-vehr-TYOOR) refers to high-quality chocolate containing at least 32 percent cocoa butter. Professionals generally prefer couverture chocolates, which are available in a range of flavors. They have a glossy appearance and can be used to create a thin, smooth coating on confections and pastries.

Sweet Chocolate

Government standards require that sweet chocolate contain not less than 15 percent chocolate liquor and varying amounts of sugar, milk solids, flavorings and emulsifiers. As the name implies, sweet chocolate is sweeter, and thus less chocolatey, than semisweet chocolate.

Milk Chocolate

The favorite eating chocolate in the United States is milk chocolate. It contains sugar, vanilla, perhaps other flavorings and, of course, milk solids. The milk solids that make the chocolate milder and sweeter than other chocolates also make it less suitable for baking purposes. Do not substitute milk chocolate for dark chocolate in any product that must be baked, as the milk solids tend to burn. If melted slowly and carefully, milk chocolate can be used in glazes, mousses or candies.

Clockwise from lower left: semisweet chips, disks of chocolate liquor, block of bittersweet chocolate, block of milk chocolate, disks of white chocolate, alkalized cocoa powder

Dutch-Processed Cocoa Powder (left) and American-Style Non-Alkalized Cocoa Powder

Cocoa Powder

The brown powder left after the fat (cocoa butter) is removed from cocoa beans is known as cocoa powder. It does not contain any sweeteners or flavorings and is used primarily in baked goods. Alkalized or Dutch-processed cocoa powder has been treated with an alkaline solution, such as potassium carbonate, to raise the powder's pH from 5.5 to 7 or 8. Alkalized powder is darker and milder than nonalkalized powder and has a reduced tendency to lump. Either can be used in baked goods, however.

Cocoa Butter

Chocolate liquor is approximately 53 percent fat, known as cocoa butter. Cocoa butter has long been prized for its resistance to rancidity and its use as a cosmetic. Cocoa butter has a very precise melting point, just below body temperature. Fine chocolatiers use high percentages of cocoa butter to give their chocolates melt-in-the-mouth quality.

White Chocolate

This ivory-colored substance is not the product of an albino cocoa bean. It is actually a confectionery product that does not contain any chocolate solids or liquor. (Thus it is usually labeled white confectionery or coating in the United States.) The finest white chocolates contain cocoa butter, sugar, milk solids, vanilla or other flavors. Other products replace all or part of the cocoa butter with vegetable oils. These confectionery products will be less expensive than those containing pure cocoa butter, but their flavor and texture will be noticeably inferior. White chocolate melts at a lower temperature than dark chocolate and burns easily. It is excellent for mousses, sauces, and candy making but is less often used in baked products.

Imitation Chocolate

A less-expensive product substituted in many prepared foods, imitation chocolate is made with vegetable oils instead of cocoa butter. The resulting product melts at a higher temperature. Products containing imitation chocolate should be labeled "chocolate flavored."

Nutrition

Chocolate is high in calories and fat. It contains minimal amounts of vitamin A and trace amounts of other vitamins as well as some sodium, phosphorous, potassium and other minerals.

TO TEMPER OR NOT TO TEMPER

The number-one mystique that surrounds chocolate has to do with tempering. From the dessert maker and pastry chef's point of view, I take a radical position: I do not think it is necessary or practical to temper. But what are we talking about anyway?

Briefly, tempering is a process of slowly raising and lowering the temperature of melted chocolate, stirring constantly, until the complex fat crystals in the cocoa butter stabilize and "behave" in concert with each other. At a cool room temperature, chocolate that has been tempered will dry rapidly to a hard and shiny piece that breaks with a snap. It shrinks slightly as it dries, enabling it to release easily from a mold. A tempered chocolate piece keeps at room temperature for months without losing its luster or snap. Any bar of chocolate that you purchase to eat or to melt has been tempered. Once melted or exposed to heat, however, it loses its temper, though it can be retempered.

Chocolate that is melted but not tempered will dry slowly, at room temperature, to a soft, almost cakey texture. It will stick inside a mold. Untempered chocolate "blooms"—that is, it becomes dull and streaky, or it takes on a mottled appearance—unless it is refrigerated immediately.

Candy makers almost always temper the chocolate they use. But dessert chefs have little need to temper. There is no reason to temper the chocolate used in cake and torte batters, buttercreams, and most ganaches. The same is true for mousses, custards, and creams. Chocolate that will be stored in the refrigerator or consumed quickly need not be tempered. Chocolate glazes, properly handled, do not require tempering to remain shiny for the short life of the dessert.

—from Cocolat: Extraordinary Chocolate Desserts by ALICE MEDRICH

Storing Chocolate

All chocolates should be stored at a cool, consistent temperature, away from strong odors and moisture. Dark chocolate, white chocolate and cocoa powder can be kept for up to one year without loss of flavor. Milk chocolate will not keep as well because it contains milk solids.

Chocolate may develop grayish-white spots during storage. This is called **bloom;** it results from the migration of cocoa butter crystals to the surface when temperatures change. Generally, bloom does not affect the flavor or function of chocolate and will disappear when the chocolate is melted.

ALCOHOLIC BEVERAGES

Liquors, liqueurs, wines and **brandies** are frequently used flavorings in the bakeshop. Liquors such as rum, bourbon or whiskey can be used for their own distinctive flavors or to blend with other flavors such as chocolate and coffee. Liqueurs are selected for their specific flavors: for example, kirsch for cherry, amaretto for almond, Kahlúa for coffee, crème de cassis for black currant and crème de cacao for chocolate. They are used to either add or enhance flavors. Wine, both still and sparkling, is used as a flavoring (for example, in sabayon sauce) or as a cooking medium (for example, pears poached in red wine). Brandy, especially the classic orange-flavored Grand Marnier, is another common bakeshop flavoring. Brandy complements fruits and rounds off the flavor of custards and creams.

When selecting an alcoholic beverage for baking, make quality your first concern. Only high-quality products will enhance the flavor and aroma of your baked goods.

▶ MEASURING INGREDIENTS

The precise, accurate measurement of ingredients is extremely important for bakeshop products. As a result, baking formulas often use weight, even for liquid ingredients. Measuring ingredients by weight is more accurate and, once you learn the basic procedures, it will be faster than measuring by volume. It is also important to remember that most foods do not weigh their volume. In other words, 1 cup of flour equals 8 fluid ounces of flour (a measure of volume) but *it does not contain* 8 ounces of flour by weight. For best results use the measurement specified in each recipe.

Because accurate weights are so important, balance scales are commonly employed in the bakeshop. Procedures for using these scales are shown in Chapter 9, Mise en Place.

▶ MIXING METHODS

An important step in the production of all baked goods is the mixing of ingredients. The techniques used to mix or combine ingredients affect the baked good's final volume, appearance and texture. There are several mixing methods: **beating, blending, creaming, cutting, folding, kneading, sifting, stirring** and **whipping.** These terms are used throughout this part of the text, especially in procedure discussions and formulas. Use the designated mixing method as well as the appropriate equipment or tool to ensure a good-quality finished product.

▶ THE BAKING PROCESS

Baked goods are made from doughs and batters. A **dough** has a low water content. The water-protein complex known as gluten forms the continuous medium into which other ingredients are embedded. A dough is usually pre-

▶ **liquor** an alcoholic beverage made by distilling grains, vegetables or other foods; includes rum, whiskey and vodka

▶ **liqueur** a strong, sweet, syrupy alcoholic beverage made by mixing or redistilling neutral spirits with fruits, flowers, herbs, spices or other flavorings; also known as a cordial

▶ **wine** an alcoholic beverage made from the fermented juice of grapes; may be sparkling (effervescent) or still (noneffervescent) or fortified with additional alcohol

▶ **brandy** an alcoholic beverage made by distilling wine or the fermented mash of grapes or other fruits

▶ **beating** vigorously agitating foods to incorporate air or develop gluten; use a spoon or electric mixer with its paddle attachment

▶ **blending** mixing two or more ingredients until evenly distributed; use a spoon, rubber spatula, whisk or electric mixer with its paddle attachment

▶ **creaming** vigorously combining fat and sugar while incorporating air; use an electric mixer with its paddle attachment on medium speed

▶ **cutting** incorporating solid fat into dry ingredients only until lumps of the desired size remain; use pastry cutters, fingers or an electric mixer with its paddle attachment

▶ **folding** very gently incorporating ingredients, such as whipped cream or whipped eggs with dry ingredients or a batter; use a rubber spatula

▶ **kneading** working a dough to develop gluten; use hands or an electric mixer with its dough hook. If done by hand, the dough must be vigorously and repeatedly folded and turned in a rhythmic pattern.

▶ **sifting** passing one or more dry ingredients through a wire mesh to remove lumps and combine and aerate ingredients; use a rotary or drum sifter or mesh strainer

▶ **stirring** gently mixing ingredients by hand until blended; use a spoon, whisk or rubber spatula

▶ **whipping** beating vigorously to incorporate air; use a whisk or an electric mixer with its whip attachment pared by beating, blending, cutting or kneading and is often stiff enough to cut into various shapes.

A **batter** generally contains more fat, sugar and liquids than a dough. Gluten development is minimized, and liquid forms the continuous medium in which other ingredients are disbursed. A batter bakes into softer, moister and more crumbly products. A batter is usually prepared by blending, creaming, stirring or whipping and is generally thin enough to pour.

The changes that occur in a dough or batter as it bakes seem mysterious and complex. A pourable liquid becomes a tender, light cake; a sticky mass becomes soft, chewy cookies; a soft, elastic dough becomes firm, crusty French bread. Yet the same physical changes that occur during baking cause all these results. Namely, gases form and are trapped within the dough or batter; starches, proteins and sugars cook; fats melt; moisture evaporates and staling begins.

By learning to control these changes, you are also learning to control the final product. Control can be exerted in the selection of ingredients and the methods by which those ingredients are combined, as well as the baking temperature and duration.

GASES FORM

A baked good's final texture is determined by the amount of leavening or rise that occurs both before and during baking. This rise is caused by the gases present in the dough or batter. These gases are carbon dioxide, air and steam. Air and carbon dioxide are present in doughs and batters before they are heated. Other gases are formed when heat is applied. For example, steam is created as the moisture in a dough is heated; yeast and baking powder rapidly release additional carbon dioxide when placed in a hot oven. These gases then expand and leaven the product. Additional information on baking powder and baking soda is found in Chapter 30, Quick Breads; additional information on yeast is found in Chapter 31, Yeast Breads.

GASES ARE TRAPPED

The stretchable network of proteins created in a batter or dough either by egg proteins or gluten traps gases in the product. Without an appropriate network of proteins, the gases would just escape without causing the mixture to rise.

STARCHES GELATINIZE

When starch granules reach a temperature of approximately 140°F (60°C), they absorb additional moisture—up to 10 times their own weight—and expand. This contributes to the baked good's structure.

PROTEINS COAGULATE

Gluten and dairy and egg proteins begin to coagulate (solidify) when the dough or batter reaches a temperature of 160°F (71°C). This process provides most of the baked good's structure.

Proper baking temperatures are important for controlling the point at which proteins coagulate. If the temperature is too high, proteins will solidify before the gases in the product have expanded fully, resulting in a product with poor texture and volume. If the temperature is too low, gases will escape before the proteins coagulate, resulting in a product that may collapse.

FATS MELT

As fats melt, steam is released and fat droplets are dispersed throughout the product. These fat droplets coat the starch (flour) granules, thus moistening and tenderizing the product by keeping the gluten strands short. Shortenings melt at

Table 29.4	LEAVENING AGENTS IN BAKED GOODS	
LEAVENING AGENT	**PRESENT IN**
Air	All products, especially those containing whipped eggs or creamed fat
Steam	All products when liquids evaporate or fats melt
Carbon dioxide	Products containing baking soda, baking powder, baking ammonia or yeast

different temperatures. It is important to select a fat with the proper melting point for the product being prepared. See Table 29.3.

WATER EVAPORATES

Throughout the baking process, the water contained in the liquid ingredients will turn to steam and evaporate. This steam is a useful leavener. As steam is released the dough or batter dries out starting from the outside and resulting in the formation of a crust.

SUGARS CARAMELIZE

As sugars are heated above 320°F (160°C), they caramelize, adding flavor and causing the product to darken. Sugars are found in eggs, dairy products and other ingredients, not just in refined sugar and liquid sweeteners.

CARRYOVER BAKING

The physical changes in a baked good do not stop when it is removed from the oven. The residual heat contained in the hot baking pan and the product itself continues the baking process as the product cools. That is why a cookie or biscuit may seem a bit underbaked when removed from the oven; it will finish baking as it cools.

STALING

Staling is a change in a baked good's texture and aroma caused by both moisture loss and changes in the structure of the starch granules. Stale products have lost their fresh aroma and are firmer, drier and more crumbly than fresh goods.

Staling is not just a general loss of moisture into the atmosphere; it is also a change in the location and distribution of water molecules within the product. This process, known as **starch retrogradation,** occurs as starch molecules cool, becoming more dense and expelling moisture.

In breads, this moisture migrates from the interior to the drier crust, causing the crust to become tough and leathery. If the product is not well wrapped, moisture will escape completely into the surrounding air. In humid conditions, unwrapped bread crusts absorb moisture from the atmosphere, resulting in the same loss of crispness. The flavor and texture of breads can be revived by reheating them to approximately 140°F (60°C), the temperature at which starch gelatinization occurs. Usually, products can be reheated only once without causing additional quality loss.

The retrogradation process is temperature-dependent. It occurs most rapidly at temperatures of approximately 40°F (4°C). Therefore, baked products should not be refrigerated unless they contain perishable components such as cream fillings. It is better to store products frozen or at room temperature.

FIGURE 29.1 ▶ Clockwise from center back: cake turntable, cake pans, flan ring, tartlet pans, connoli forms, offset spatulas, flat cake spatula, blade for slashing breads, flower nail, rectangular tartlet pans, piping bag and tips, metal spatula, dough cutter, rolling pin, springform pan, copper sugar pot (on cooling rack), nest of round cutters

Products containing fats and sugars, which retain moisture, tend to stay fresh longer. Commercial bakeries usually add chemical emulsifiers, modified shortening or special sweeteners to retard staling, but these additives are not as practical for small-scale production.

▶ BAKESHOP TOOLS AND EQUIPMENT

As a beginning cook, you may find the tools of the bakeshop a bit complex. Indeed, the tools required for a professional pâtisserie are quite specialized. A well-rounded chef need not be concerned with possessing every gadget available, but should recognize and be familiar with most of the items shown in Figure 29.1. Although many of these hand tools will make a task easier, most can be improvised by a creative chef. Several of the items shown, such as the springform pans, tartlet pans and petit four molds, are used for shaping or holding batters and doughs. The various spatulas are used for spreading icings or fillings. The piping tools and cake comb are used for decorating and finishing baked goods.

When purchasing tools and equipment, look for quality and durability. As your baking skills grow, so will your equipment selection.

Bakeshop ovens may be conventional, convection or steam injection models. Convection ovens can reduce cooking time, but the air currents may damage delicate products such as spongecake or puff pastry. Steam injection ovens use conventional heat flow but allow the baker to automatically add steam to the cooking chamber as needed to produce crisp-crusted breads. Although expensive, steam injection ovens are a necessity for commercial bakeries and most larger restaurant and hotel bakeshops. Baking instructions in the following chapters are based on the use of a conventional oven. If a convection oven is used instead, remember that the temperature and baking time may need to be reduced.

CONCLUSION

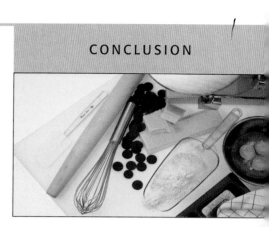

Of the many stations of the kitchen, the bakeshop often requires the most conscientious attention to detail. The correct use of flour, thickeners, sugar, fat, chocolate and other flavorings is essential. During preparation and baking, doughs and batters go through many physical changes. One of the most important is the development of gluten, the elastic network of wheat proteins created when doughs and batters are prepared, which gives baked goods body and structure. You should understand the changes baked goods undergo and learn to control or adjust them as needed.

QUESTIONS FOR DISCUSSION

1 What is gluten? How is it produced, and why is it important in the preparation of baked goods?

2 Discuss four functions of sugar and other sweeteners in baked goods.

3 Describe several steps that can be taken to prevent crystals from forming in sugar solutions.

4 Describe the effect of fat on gluten strands. Why is fat an important ingredient in baked goods?

5 Explain the difference between chocolate liquor and semisweet chocolate. Can these two types of chocolate be used interchangeably in most recipes? Explain your answer.

6 List and describe the nine steps in the baking process.

7 Assume that you were recently hired as the bread baker for a new bakery and deli. You must now research and find suppliers for several specialized bakery products for use in your kitchen. Find two or three Web sites that will assist you in this task. Also find the names of two schools or institutes that you might wish to attend for advanced training in retail baking techniques.

GOOD BREAD IS THE MOST FUNDAMENTALLY SATISFY-
ING OF ALL FOODS; AND GOOD BREAD WITH FRESH
BUTTER, THE GREATEST OF FEASTS.

—James Beard, American food writer and
 teacher (1903–1985)

QUICK BREADS

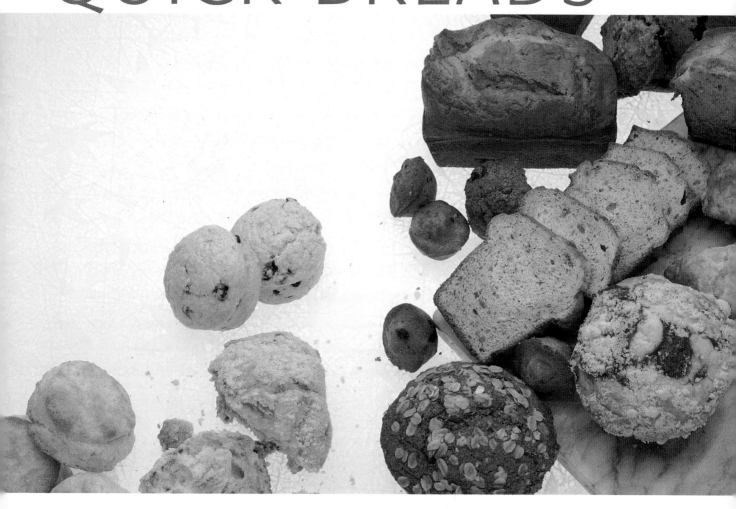

AFTER STUDYING THIS
CHAPTER, YOU WILL BE
ABLE TO:

▶ use chemical leavening agents
properly

▶ prepare a variety of quick
breads using the biscuit
method, muffin method and
creaming method

Buttermilk biscuits, blueberry muffins, banana nut bread and currant scones are all quick breads. Why they are called quick breads is obvious: They are quick to make and quick to bake. With only a few basic ingredients and no yeast, almost any food service operation can provide its customers with fresh muffins, biscuits, scones and loaf breads.

The variety of ingredients is virtually limitless: cornmeal, whole wheat, fruits, nuts, spices and vegetables all yield popular products. And the use of these products is not limited to breakfast service—they are equally appropriate for lunch, snacks and buffets.

▶ CHEMICAL LEAVENING AGENTS

Quick breads are made with chemical leavening agents, principally baking soda and baking powder. This sets them apart from breads that are made with yeast and require additional time for fermentation and proofing. Understanding how chemical leavening agents operate is essential to successfully producing quick breads.

Chemical leavening agents release gases (primarily carbon dioxide) through chemical reactions between acids and bases contained in the formula. These gases form bubbles or air pockets throughout the dough or batter. As the product bakes, these gases expand causing the product to rise. The dough or batter then sets around these air pockets, giving the quick bread its rise and texture.

BAKING SODA

Sodium bicarbonate ($NaHCO_3$) is more commonly known as household baking soda. Baking soda is an alkaline compound (a base), which releases carbon dioxide gas (CO_2) if both an acid and moisture are present. Heat is not necessary for this reaction to occur. Therefore, products made with baking soda must be baked at once, before the carbon dioxide has a chance to escape from the batter or dough.

Acids commonly used with baking soda are buttermilk, sour cream, lemon juice, honey, molasses and fresh fruit. Generally, the amount of baking soda used in a formula is only the amount necessary to neutralize the acids present. If more leavening action is needed, baking powder, not more baking soda, should be used. Too much baking soda causes the product to taste soapy or bitter; it may also cause a yellow color and brown spots to develop.

BAKING POWDER

Baking powder is a mixture of sodium bicarbonate and one or more acids, generally cream of tartar ($KHC_4H_4O_6$) and/or sodium aluminum sulfate ($Na_2SO_4 \cdot Al_2[SO_4]_3$). Baking powder also contains a starch to prevent lumping and balance the chemical reactions. Because baking powder contains both the acid and the base necessary for the desired chemical reaction, the quick bread formula does not need to contain any acid. Only moisture is necessary to induce the release of gases.

There are two types of baking powder: single-acting and double-acting. An excess of either type produces undesirable flavors, textures and colors in baked products.

Single-acting baking powder requires only the presence of moisture to start releasing gas. This moisture is supplied by the eggs, milk, water or other liquids in the formula. As with baking soda, products using single-acting baking powder must be baked immediately.

Double-acting baking powder is more popular. With double-acting baking powder, there is a small release of gas upon contact with moisture and a second, stronger release of gas when heat is applied. Products made with double-acting baking powder need not be baked immediately, but can sit for a short time without loss of leavening ability. All formulas in this book rely on double-acting baking powder.

Both baking soda and baking powder are sometimes used in one formula. This is because baking soda can release CO_2 only to the extent that there is also an acid present in the formula. If the soda/acid reaction alone is insufficient to leaven the product, baking powder is needed for additional leavening.

BAKING AMMONIA

Baking ammonia (ammonia bicarbonate or ammonia carbonate) is also used as a leavening agent in some baked goods, primarily cookies and crackers. Baking ammonia releases ammonia and carbon dioxide very rapidly when heated. It is suitable for low-moisture products with large surface areas that are baked at high temperatures, such as crackers. Consequently, it is rarely used in quick breads.

PURCHASING AND STORING

Purchase chemical leaveners in the smallest unit appropriate for your operation. Although a large can of baking powder may cost less than several small ones, if not used promptly the contents of a larger container can deteriorate, causing waste or unusable baked goods.

Chemical leavening agents should always be kept tightly covered. Not only is there a risk of contamination if left open, but they can also absorb moisture from the air and lose their effectiveness. They should be stored in a cool place, as heat deteriorates them. A properly stored and unopened container of baking powder or baking soda has a shelf life of several years.

▶ MIXING METHODS

Quick breads are generally mixed by either the **biscuit method,** the **muffin method** or the **creaming method.** The mixing method employed is directly related to the type and consistency of fat used in the formula. Cold solid fats, such as butter, lard or vegetable shortening, are used in the biscuit method to produce flaky products. Fats that are soft but not liquid are used in the high-fat creaming method. And liquid fats, such as oil or melted butter, are used in the muffin method to produce very moist, tender products.

MODERN SCIENCE

The practice of mixing an acid and an alkali to leaven bread began, appropriately enough, during the Industrial Revolution, a period of rapid development in scientific thought and technological ability. The first commercial leaveners were marketed in 1850. Sodium bicarbonate was first marketed as baking soda in 1867 under the brand name Arm & Hammer. The first double-acting baking powder was available in 1889 under the brand name Calumet.

Table 30.1	QUICK BREAD MIXING TECHNIQUES		
MIXING TECHNIQUE	**FAT**	**RESULT**
Biscuit method	Solid (chilled)	Flaky dough
Muffin method	Liquid (oil or melted butter)	Soft, tender, cakelike texture
Creaming method	Softened (room temperature)	Rich, tender, cakelike texture

BISCUITS AND SCONES: A GENEALOGY

Biscuit is a French word used to describe any dry, flat cake, whether sweet or savory. It was, perhaps, originally coined to describe twice-baked cakes (*bis* = twice + *cuit* = cooked). Crusader chronicles, for example, mention soldiers eating a "bread called 'bequis' because it is cooked twice" and still, today, the Reims biscuit is returned to the oven for further baking after it is removed from its tin.

Over the centuries, the French began to use the term *biscuit* generically and appended modifiers to identify the particular type of dry, flat cake. For example, a *biscuit de guerre* was the very hard, barely risen product of flour and water used from the time of the Crusades to the era of Louis XIV as an army ration (*guerre* is French for "war"); *biscuit de Savoie* is a savory sponge-cake; *biscuit de pâtisserie* is a sweet biscuit.

To the British, a biscuit is what Americans call a cracker or cookie. Yet there appears to be no British quick bread quite comparable to the American biscuit–the closest relative would be the scone. But because a scone contains eggs and butter, it is much richer than a biscuit.

Elizabeth Alston, in *Biscuits and Scones*, proposes that the biscuit is an American variant of the scone. She theorizes that early British colonists in America brought with them traditional scone recipes. Unable to find or afford the necessary fresh butter and eggs, these practical bakers substituted lard and omitted the eggs. What they created, however, were not mock scones, but rather a new product, different from scones but still delicious. Alston further speculates that French cooks initially called the new American product "biscuit de something" and eventually dropped the "de something."

BISCUIT METHOD

The biscuit method is used for biscuits, shortcakes and scones and is very similar to the technique used to make flaky pie doughs. The goal is to create a baked good that is light, flaky and tender.

▶ PROCEDURE FOR PREPARING PRODUCTS WITH THE BISCUIT METHOD

1 Measure all ingredients.

2 Sift the dry ingredients together.

3 Cut in the fat, which should be in a solid form.

4 Combine the liquid ingredients, including any eggs.

5 Add the liquid ingredients to the dry ingredients. Mix just until the ingredients are combined. Do not overmix, as this causes toughness and inhibits the product's rise.

6 Place the dough on the bench and knead it lightly 10 or 15 times (approximately 20 to 30 seconds). The dough should be soft and slightly elastic, but not sticky. Too much kneading toughens the biscuits.

7 The dough is now ready for makeup and baking.

▶ MAKEUP OF BISCUIT-METHOD PRODUCTS

1 Roll out the dough on a floured surface to a thickness of ½ to ¾ inch (1.2 to 1.8 centimeters). Be careful to roll it evenly. Biscuits should double in height during baking.

2 Cut into the desired shapes. Cut straight down; do not twist the cutters, as this inhibits rise. Space cuts as close together as possible to minimize scraps.

3 Position the biscuits on a lightly greased or paper-lined sheet pan. If placed with sides nearly touching, the biscuits will rise higher and have softer sides. Place farther apart for crusty sides.

4 Reworking and rerolling the dough may cause tough, misshapen biscuits. Nevertheless, it may be possible to reroll scraps once by pressing the dough together gently without kneading.

5 Tops may be brushed with egg wash before baking or with melted butter after baking. Bake immediately in a hot oven.

6 Cool the finished products on a wire rack.

COUNTRY BISCUITS

RECIPE 30.1

Yield: 36 Biscuits

Method: Biscuit

All-purpose flour	2 lb. 8 oz.	1.2 kg
Salt	¾ oz.	21 g
Granulated sugar	2 oz.	60 g
Baking powder	2 oz.	60 g
Unsalted butter, cold	14 oz.	420 g
Milk	1 lb. 8 oz.	720 ml

1 Sift the dry ingredients together, making sure they are blended thoroughly.

2 Cut in the butter. The mixture should look mealy; do not overmix.

3 Add the milk and stir, combining only until the mixture holds together.

4 Transfer the dough to a lightly floured work surface; knead until it forms one mass, approximately five or six kneadings.

5 Roll out the dough to a thickness of ½ inch (1.2 centimeters). Cut with a floured cutter and place the biscuits on a paper-lined sheet pan.

6 Bake at 425°F (220°C) until the tops are light brown, the sides almost white and the interiors still moist, approximately 10 to 15 minutes. Internal heat will continue to cook the biscuits after they are removed from the oven.

7 Remove the biscuits to a wire rack to cool.

Approximate values per biscuit: **Calories** 210, **Total fat** 10 g, **Saturated fat** 6 g, **Cholesterol** 25 mg, **Sodium** 240 mg, **Total carbohydrates** 27 g, **Protein** 4 g, **Vitamin A** 10%

1 Sifting the dry ingredients together.

2 Cutting in the fat.

3 Kneading the dough.

4 Cutting the biscuits.

MUFFIN METHOD

Muffins are any small, cakelike baked good made in a muffin tin (pan). Batters for muffins and loaf quick breads are generally interchangeable. For example, banana muffin batter may be baked in a loaf pan, provided the baking time is altered.

When preparing baked goods by the muffin method, the goal is to produce a tender product with an even shape and an even distribution of fruits, nuts or other ingredients. The most frequent problem encountered with muffin-method products is overmixing. This causes toughness and may cause holes to form inside the baked product, a condition known as **tunneling.**

▶ PROCEDURE FOR PREPARING PRODUCTS
  WITH THE MUFFIN METHOD

1 Measure all ingredients.

2 Sift the dry ingredients together.

3 Combine the liquid ingredients, including melted fat or oil. Melted butter or shortening may resolidify when combined with the other liquids; this is not a cause for concern.

4 Add the liquid ingredients to the dry ingredients and stir just until combined. Do not overmix. The batter will be lumpy.

5 The batter is now ready for makeup and baking.

▶ MAKEUP OF MUFFIN-METHOD PRODUCTS

1 Muffin pans and loaf pans should be greased with butter, shortening or a commercial pan grease. Paper liners may be used and will prevent sticking if the batter contains fruits or vegetables. Paper liners, however, inhibit rise.

2 A portion scoop is a useful tool for ensuring uniform-sized muffins. Be careful not to drip or spill batter onto the edge of the muffin cups; it will burn and cause sticking.

3 Allow muffins and loaf breads to cool for several minutes before attempting to remove them from the pan.

4 Cool the finished products on a wire rack.

RECIPE 30.2   **BLUEBERRY MUFFINS**

Yield: 12 Muffins		**Method:** Muffin
All-purpose flour	8 oz.	250 g
Granulated sugar	5 oz.	150 g
Baking powder	2 tsp.	10 ml
Salt	¼ tsp.	1 ml
Eggs	2	2
Milk	8 fl. oz.	250 ml
Unsalted butter, melted	2 oz.	60 g
Vanilla extract	1 tsp.	5 ml
Blueberries	¾ c.	180 ml
Lemon zest	1 Tbsp.	15 ml

1 Sift the dry ingredients together.

2 Stir together the liquid ingredients, including the melted butter.

3 Stir the liquid mixture into the dry ingredients. Do not overmix. The batter should be lumpy.

4 Gently fold in the blueberries and lemon zest.

5 Portion into greased or paper-lined muffin cups and bake at 350°F (180°C) until light brown and set in the center, approximately 18 minutes.

6 Cool the muffins in the pan for several minutes before removing.

1 Combining the liquid ingredients.

2 Folding in the blueberries.

3 Portioning the batter.

Variations: *Cranberry Orange Muffins*–Substitute fresh orange zest for the lemon zest and 4 ounces (120 grams) of dried cranberries for the blueberries.

Pecan Spice Muffins–Omit the blueberries and lemon zest. Add 4 ounces (120 grams) of chopped pecans, ½ teaspoon (2 milliliters) of cinnamon and ¼ teaspoon (1 milliliter) each of nutmeg and ground ginger to the batter.

Approximate values per muffin: **Calories** 180, **Total fat** 6 g, **Saturated fat** 3 g, **Cholesterol** 50 mg, **Sodium** 150 mg, **Total carbohydrates** 29 g, **Protein** 4 g

CREAMING METHOD

The creaming method is comparable to the mixing method used for many butter cakes. The softened fat and sugar should be properly creamed to incorporate air, which will help leaven the product as it bakes. The final product will be cake-like, with a fine texture. There is less danger of overmixing with this method because the higher fat content shortens gluten strands and tenderizes the batter.

▶ PROCEDURE FOR PREPARING PRODUCTS
WITH THE CREAMING METHOD

1 Measure all ingredients.

2 Sift the dry ingredients together.

3 Combine the softened fat and sugar in a mixer bowl. Cream until the color lightens and the mixture fluffs.

4 Add eggs gradually, mixing well.

5 Add the dry and liquid ingredients to the creamed fat alternately. In other words, a portion of the flour is added to the fat and incorporated, then a portion of the liquid is added and incorporated. These steps are repeated until all the liquid and dry ingredients are incorporated. By adding the liquid and dry ingredients alternately, you avoid overmixing the batter and prevent the butter and sugar mixture from curdling.

6 The batter is now ready for makeup and baking.

▶ MAKEUP OF CREAMING-METHOD PRODUCTS

Panning and baking procedures are the same as those for quick breads prepared with the muffin method.

 SOUR CREAM MUFFINS   RECIPE 30.3

Yield: 15 Muffins   **Method:** Creaming

Unsalted butter, room temperature	8 oz.	225 g
Granulated sugar	8 oz.	225 g
Eggs	2	2
All-purpose flour	10 oz.	300 g
Baking powder	1 tsp.	5 ml
Baking soda	1 tsp.	5 ml
Salt	1 tsp.	5 ml
Sour cream	10 oz.	300 g
Vanilla extract	1 tsp.	5 ml

1 Cream the butter and sugar until light and fluffy. Add the eggs.

2 Sift the dry ingredients together.

3 Stir the dry ingredients and sour cream, alternately, into the butter mixture. Stir in the vanilla.

1 Creaming the butter and sugar.

2 Adding the sour cream.

3 Topping the muffins with streusel.

4 Portion and bake at 350°F (180°C) until light brown and set, approximately 20 minutes.

5 Allow the muffins to cool briefly in the pan before removing.

▶ **streusel** a crumbly mixture of fat, flour, sugar and sometimes nuts and spices, used to top baked goods

Variations: Sour cream muffins can be topped with **streusel** or flavored with a wide variety of fruits or nuts by adding approximately 4–6 ounces (1 cup or 120–180 grams) fresh or frozen drained fruit to the batter. Blueberries, dried cherries, candied fruits, pecans and diced pears yield popular products. To make basic spice muffins, add ½ teaspoon (2 milliliters) each of cinnamon and nutmeg.

Approximate values per muffin: **Calories** 290, **Total fat** 17 g, **Saturated fat** 10 g, **Cholesterol** 70 mg, **Sodium** 260 mg, **Total carbohydrates** 31 g, **Protein** 4 g, **Vitamin A** 15%

RECIPE 30.4

STREUSEL TOPPING

Yield: 5 lb. 4 oz. (2.5 kg)

All-purpose flour	2 lb.	900 g
Cinnamon, ground	¼ oz.	7 g
Salt	1 tsp.	5 ml
Brown sugar	8 oz.	225 g
Granulated sugar	1 lb. 8 oz.	680 g
Whole butter, cold	1 lb. 4 oz.	560 g

1 Combine the dry ingredients. Cut in the butter until the mixture is coarse and crumbly.

2 Sprinkle on top of muffins or quick breads prior to baking. Streusel topping will keep for several weeks under refrigeration and may be frozen for longer storage. There is no need to thaw before use.

Approximate values per 1-oz. (30-g) serving: **Calories** 190, **Total fat** 8 g, **Saturated fat** 5 g, **Cholesterol** 20 mg, **Sodium** 45 mg, **Total carbohydrates** 29 g, **Protein** 2 g

Table 30.2 TROUBLESHOOTING CHART

PROBLEM	CAUSE	SOLUTION
Soapy or bitter flavor	Chemical leaveners not properly mixed into batter	Sift chemicals with dry ingredients
	Too much baking soda	Adjust formula
Elongated holes (tunneling)	Overmixing	Do not mix until smooth; mix only until moistened
Crust too thick	Too much sugar	Adjust formula
	Oven temperature too low	Adjust oven
Flat top with only a small peak in center	Oven temperature too low	Adjust oven
Cracked, uneven top	Oven temperature too high	Adjust oven
No rise; dense product	Old batter	Bake promptly
	Damaged leavening agents	Store new chemicals properly
	Overmixing	Do not overmix

First you must master the three mixing methods used in producing quick breads (biscuit, muffin and creaming) and understand the interaction between chemical leaveners and other ingredients. Then, with an imaginative use of flavoring ingredients, you can successfully produce a wide array of fresh-baked breads for almost any food service operation.

CONCLUSION

QUESTIONS FOR DISCUSSION

1 Name two chemical leavening agents, and explain how they cause batters and doughs to rise.
2 List three common methods used for mixing quick breads. What is the significance of the type of fat used for each of these mixing methods?
3 What is the most likely explanation for discolored and bitter-tasting biscuits? What is the solution?
4 What happens when muffin batter has been overmixed?
5 Visit the Web sites for King Arthur Flour and White Lily Foods to learn more about the varieties of flours and flavoring ingredients that are available for use in biscuits and muffins. What are each of these companies famous for? How do the products of these two regional flour manufacturers differ?

RECIPE 30.5

SARAH R. LABENSKY, CCP

Chef Sarah Labensky is founding director of the Culinary Arts Institute at Mississippi University for Women (and smart men, too!). She teaches cooking courses and administers MUW's four-year baccalaureate degree program in culinary arts. Before joining MUW, she was a professor of culinary arts at Scottsdale (Arizona) Community College and had worked as a pastry chef and caterer.

Her career has not always been focused on the kitchen, however. Chef Sarah was once a practicing attorney with a J.D. degree from Vanderbilt University School of Law.

She is the principal author of this textbook and *On Baking: A Textbook of Baking and Pastry Fundamentals,* as well as a co-author of *Webster's New World Dictionary of Culinary Arts.*

Yield: 24 Scones   **Method:** Biscuit

All-purpose flour	1 lb.	450 g
Granulated sugar	1½ oz.	45 g
Baking powder	1 Tbsp.	15 ml
Baking soda	1 tsp.	5 ml
Salt	1 tsp.	5 ml
Unsalted butter, cold	4 oz.	120 g
Egg yolks	2	2
Half-and-half	11 fl. oz.	330 ml

1 Combine all ingredients using the biscuit method.
2 Roll out the dough to a thickness of approximately ½ inch (1.2 centimeters). Cut as desired.
3 Bake at 400°F (200°C) for approximately 10 minutes.
4 Brush the tops with butter while hot.

Variations: Add ½ cup (125 milliliters) of raisins, sultanas or currants to the dry ingredients.

Approximate values per scone: **Calories** 130, **Total fat** 6 g, **Saturated fat** 3.5 g, **Cholesterol** 35 mg, **Sodium** 160 mg, **Total carbohydrates** 17 g, **Protein** 3 g

RECIPE 30.6

Yield: 48 Large Pieces   **Method:** Biscuit

All-purpose flour	4 lb.	1.8 kg
Baking powder	3¾ oz.	110 g
Salt	2 tsp.	10 ml
Granulated sugar	13 oz.	390 g
Unsalted butter, cold	1 lb. 12 oz.	840 g
Eggs	7	7
Milk	18 fl. oz.	540 ml
Whole butter, melted	as needed	as needed
Granulated sugar	as needed	as needed

1 Combine all ingredients using the biscuit method.
2 Cut into 3-inch (7.5-centimeter) circles and space 2 inches (5 centimeters) apart on a paper-lined sheet pan.
3 Bake at 400°F (200°C) until lightly browned, approximately 15 to 18 minutes.
4 Remove from the oven and brush the tops with melted butter, then sprinkle with granulated sugar.

Approximate values per 3-oz. (90-g) serving: **Calories** 310, **Total fat** 15 g, **Saturated fat** 9 g, **Cholesterol** 65 mg, **Sodium** 250 mg, **Total carbohydrates** 38 g, **Protein** 5 g, **Vitamin A** 15%

BASIC BERRY MUFFINS

RECIPE 30.7

STOUFFER STANFORD COURT HOTEL, San Francisco, CA
Former Executive Chef Ercolino Crugnale

Yield: 60 Muffins   **Method:** Muffin

Eggs	8	8
Heavy cream	1 qt.	1 lt
Lemon zest, finely grated	from 2 lemons	from 2 lemons
Nutmeg, ground	¼ tsp.	1 ml
Granulated sugar	1 lb. 4 oz.	600 g
Baking powder	6 Tbsp.	90 ml
Cake flour	3 lb.	1.3 kg
Kosher salt	1 Tbsp.	15 ml
Berries or nuts*	1–1½ qt.	1–1.5 lt
Unsalted butter, melted	1 lb.	450 g

1 Whip the eggs, cream and zest together by hand.

2 Sift the dry ingredients together. Add the berries or nuts, tossing to coat them evenly with the flour mixture.

3 Add the dry ingredients to the egg mixture and stir until about two-thirds mixed. Add the melted butter and finish mixing.

4 Portion into greased muffin tins and bake at 375°F (190°C) for approximately 15 to 18 minutes.

Approximate values per muffin: **Calories** 260, **Total fat** 13 g, **Saturated fat** 8 g, **Cholesterol** 70 mg, **Sodium** 135 mg, **Total carbohydrates** 31 g, **Protein** 3 g, **Vitamin A** 15%, **Claims**—low sodium

*Blueberries, blackberries, raspberries, chopped pecans or walnuts may be used, as desired.

MORNING GLORY MUFFINS

RECIPE 30.8

Yield: 18 Muffins   **Method:** Muffin

All-purpose flour	1 lb.	450 g
Granulated sugar	18 oz.	530 g
Baking soda	4 tsp.	20 ml
Cinnamon, ground	4 tsp.	20 ml
Carrots, grated	14 oz.	420 g
Raisins	6 oz.	180 g
Pecan pieces	4 oz.	120 g
Coconut, shredded	4 oz.	120 g
Apple, unpeeled, grated	6 oz.	180 g
Eggs	6	6
Corn oil	12 fl. oz.	360 ml
Vanilla extract	4 tsp.	20 ml

1 Sift the dry ingredients together and set aside.

2 Combine the carrots, raisins, pecans, coconut and apple.

3 Whisk together the eggs, oil and vanilla.

4 Toss the carrot mixture into the dry ingredients. Then add the liquid ingredients, stirring just until combined.

5 Bake in well-greased muffin tins at 350°F (170°C) until done, approximately 25 minutes.

Approximate values per muffin: **Calories** 520, **Total fat** 27 g, **Saturated fat 5** g, **Cholesterol** 70 mg, **Sodium** 310 mg, **Total carbohydrates** 63 g, **Protein** 6 g, **Vitamin A,** 45% **Claims**—good source of fiber

---

RECIPE 30.9   **BASIC BRAN MUFFINS**

Yield: 24 Muffins   **Method:** Muffin

Toasted wheat bran	6 oz.	180 g
All-purpose flour	12 oz.	360 g
Granulated sugar	4 oz.	120 g
Baking powder	4 tsp.	20 ml
Salt	1 tsp.	5 ml
Milk	12 fl. oz.	360 ml
Honey	3 oz.	90 g
Molasses	3 oz.	90 g
Eggs	2	2
Vanilla extract	1 tsp.	5 ml
Unsalted butter, melted	4 oz.	120 g

1 Combine all ingredients using the muffin method.

2 Scoop into greased or paper-lined muffin tins. Bake at 350°F (170°C) until lightly brown and firm, approximately 20 minutes.

Variations: Up to 6 ounces (180 grams) of raisins or chopped nuts may be added to the batter if desired.

Approximate values per muffin: **Calories** 170, **Total fat** 5 g, **Saturated** fat 2.5 g, **Cholesterol** 30 mg, **Sodium** 110 mg, **Total carbohydrates** 26 g, **Protein** 4 g, **Claims**—low sodium; good source of fiber

---

RECIPE 30.10   **ZUCCHINI BREAD**

Yield: 2 Loaves, 9 in. × 5 in.   **Method:** Muffin
(24 cm × 12 cm)

Whole eggs	3	3
Corn oil	8 fl. oz.	225 ml
Granulated sugar	1 lb. 2 oz.	510 g
Vanilla extract	1 tsp.	5 ml
Cinnamon, ground	2 tsp.	10 ml
Salt	1 tsp.	5 ml
Baking soda	1 tsp.	5 ml
Baking powder	½ tsp.	2 ml
All-purpose flour	14 oz.	420 g
Zucchini, coarsely grated	11 oz.	330 g
Pecans, chopped	4 oz.	120 g

1 Combine all ingredients using the muffin method.

2 Bake in two greased loaf pans at 350°F (170°C), approximately 1 hour.

Approximate values per 2-oz. (60-g) serving: **Calories** 260, **Total fat** 16 g, **Saturated fat** 2 g, **Cholesterol** 30 mg, **Sodium** 190 mg, **Total carbohydrates** 27 g, **Protein** 2 g

IRISH SODA BREAD

RECIPE 30.11

Yield: 1 Round Loaf, 8 in. (20 cm)   **Method:** Muffin

Currants	2 oz.	60 g
Irish whiskey	1½ fl. oz.	45 ml
All-purpose flour, sifted	12 oz.	360 g
Salt	1 tsp.	5 ml
Baking powder	1½ tsp.	7 ml
Baking soda	1 tsp.	5 ml
Brown sugar	1 Tbsp.	15 ml
Lowfat buttermilk	1 pt.	500 ml

1 Soak the currants in the whiskey until plump, at least 1 hour.

2 Sift the dry ingredients together. Stir in the currants and whiskey.

3 Stir in the buttermilk, making a stiff batter.

4 Spread the batter in a greased 8-inch (20-centimeter) round cake pan. Bake at 350°F (170°C) until well browned and firm, approximately 45 minutes.

Approximate values per 3-oz. (90-g) serving: **Calories** 150, **Total fat** 1 g, **Saturated fat** 0 g, **Cholesterol** 0 mg, **Sodium** 480 mg, **Total carbohydrates** 31 g, **Protein** 5 g, **Calcium** 10%, **Claims**— low fat; no cholesterol; no saturated fat

 ## BASIC CORN MUFFINS

RECIPE 30.12

Yield: 30 Muffins   **Method:** Muffin

Yellow cornmeal	12 oz.	360 g
All-purpose flour	12 oz.	360 g
Granulated sugar	10 oz.	300 g
Baking powder	1 Tbsp.	15 ml
Baking soda	1 tsp.	5 ml
Salt	¾ tsp.	3 ml
Buttermilk	24 fl. oz.	720 ml
Eggs	6	6
Unsalted butter, melted	6 oz.	180 g

1 Combine all ingredients using the muffin method.

2 Portion into greased muffin tins, filling two-thirds full.

3 Bake at 375°F (190°C) until done, approximately 20 to 25 minutes.

Variation: *Southern-Style Cornbread*—Omit the sugar. Pour the batter into cast-iron skillets or molds that are preheated and well greased with shortening or bacon fat. Bake at 425°F (220°C) until golden.

Approximate values per muffin: **Calories** 180, **Total fat** 6 g, **Saturated fat** 3.5 g, **Cholesterol** 55 mg, **Sodium** 140 mg, **Total carbohydrates** 28 g, **Protein** 4 g

RECIPE 30.13

HUSH PUPPIES
(DEEP-FRIED CORNBREAD)

Yield: 60 Pieces, 2 in. (5 cm) each   **Method:** Muffin

Yellow cornmeal	1 lb.	450 g
All-purpose flour	8 oz.	225 g
Baking powder	1 Tbsp.	15 ml
Salt	1 Tbsp.	15 ml
Black pepper	1 Tbsp.	15 ml
Granulated sugar	2 oz.	60 g
Onions, minced	8 oz.	225 g
Eggs	4	4
Milk	1 pt.	450 ml

1 Combine all ingredients using the muffin method.
2 Drop small scoops (using a #60 or #70 portion scoop) into deep fat at 375°F (190°C). Using the swimming method, deep-fry until golden brown.
3 Remove from the fat and drain. Serve immediately.

Approximate values per piece: **Calories** 70, **Total fat** 3 g, **Saturated fat** 1 g, **Cholesterol** 5 mg, **Sodium** 120 mg, **Total carbohydrates** 10 g, **Protein** 1 g

1 Scooping the hush puppy batter into the deep-fat fryer.

2 Draining the cooked hush puppies.

RECIPE 30.14

BLUE CORN MUFFINS

Yield: 60 Muffins   **Method:** Creaming

All-purpose shortening	1 lb.	450 g
Granulated sugar	1 lb. 8 oz.	680 g
Blue cornmeal	1 lb.	450 g
Whole eggs	1 pt.	450 ml
All-purpose flour	2 lb.	900 g
Baking powder	1¼ oz.	35 g
Salt	1½ oz.	45 g
Vanilla extract	1 Tbsp.	15 ml
Honey	12 fl. oz.	340 ml
Buttermilk	1 qt.	1 lt

1 Using a mixer fitted with the paddle attachment, cream the shortening, sugar and cornmeal until light and fluffy. Add the eggs. Mix on low speed for 1 minute.

2 Sift the remaining dry ingredients together.

3 Stir the vanilla and honey into the buttermilk.

4 Add the dry ingredients and buttermilk mixture, alternately, to the creamed mixture. Mix on low speed for 2 minutes, scraping down the bowl as necessary.

5 Portion into well-greased muffin pans. Bake at 325°F (160°C) until done, approximately 15 minutes.

Approximate values per muffin: **Calories** 230, **Total fat** 9 g, **Saturated fat** 2.5 g, **Cholesterol** 25 mg, **Sodium** 310 mg, **Total carbohydrates** 35 g, **Protein** 4 g

Note: Blue cornmeal is derived from variegated Indian corn. Its natural blue-gray color is a result of a high lysine content. Blue corn has a stronger flavor than white or yellow corn and is popular in southwestern cuisine.

LEMON TEA BREAD

RECIPE 30.15

Yield: 12 Muffins or 1 Loaf   **Method:** Creaming

Unsalted butter, softened	3 oz.	90 g
Granulated sugar	10 oz.	300 g
Eggs	2	2
Milk	4 fl. oz.	120 ml
All-purpose flour	6 oz.	180 g
Baking powder	1 tsp.	5 ml
Salt	½ tsp.	2 ml
Lemon zest	1 Tbsp.	15 ml
Lemon juice	4 fl. oz.	120 ml

1 Cream the butter with 7 ounces (210 grams) of the sugar. Add the eggs and milk. Mix well.

2 Sift the flour, baking powder and salt together and add to the butter mixture. Fold in the lemon zest. Portion into lightly greased pans.

3 Bake at 350° (170°C) until a tester comes out clean, approximately 35 to 40 minutes for a large loaf or 12 to 15 minutes for muffins. Remove the bread from the pan(s) and place on a cooling rack.

4 Combine the remaining 3 ounces (90 grams) of sugar with the lemon juice. Heat until the sugar dissolves and the mixture is hot. Slowly pour or brush the glaze over the hot bread.

Approximate values per muffin: **Calories** 220, **Total fat** 7 g, **Saturated fat** 4 g, **Cholesterol** 50 mg, **Sodium** 115 mg, **Total carbohydrates** 36 g, **Protein** 3 g

SOUR CREAM COFFEECAKE

RECIPE 30.16

Yield: 1 Tube Cake, 10 in. (25 cm)   **Method:** Creaming

Filling:		
All-purpose flour	1½ Tbsp.	27 ml
Cinnamon, ground	1 Tbsp.	15 ml
Brown sugar	6 oz.	180 g
Pecans, chopped	4 oz.	120 g
Unsalted butter, melted	1 oz.	30 g

continued

Unsalted butter	4 oz.	120 g
Granulated sugar	8 oz.	225 g
Eggs	2	2
Sour cream	8 oz.	225 g
Cake flour, sifted	7 oz.	210 g
Salt	¼ tsp.	1 ml
Baking powder	1 tsp.	5 ml
Baking soda	1 tsp.	5 ml
Vanilla extract	1 tsp.	5 ml

1 To make the filling, blend all the filling ingredients together in a small bowl. Set aside.

2 To make the cake batter, cream the butter and sugar. Add the eggs, one at a time, beating well after each addition. Add the sour cream. Stir until smooth.

3 Sift the sifted flour, salt, baking powder and baking soda together twice. Stir into the batter. Stir in the vanilla extract.

4 Spoon half of the batter into a greased tube pan. Top with half of the filling. Cover the filling with the remaining batter and top with the remaining filling. Bake at 350°F (180°C) for 35 minutes.

Approximate values per serving: **Calories** 490, **Total fat** 26 g, **Saturated fat** 11 g, **Cholesterol** 85 mg, **Sodium** 220 mg, **Total carbohydrates** 59 g, **Protein** 5 g, **Vitamin A** 15%

RECIPE 30.17   **POPOVERS**

CONNECTICUT CULINARY INSTITUTE, FARMINGTON, CT

Chef Jamie Roraback

Yield: 20 Popovers

Beef fat or vegetable oil	12 fl. oz.	360 ml
All-purpose flour	8 oz.	225 g
Salt	1 tsp.	5 ml
Eggs	6	6
Whole milk	1 pt.	475 ml
Whole butter, melted	3 oz.	90 g

1 Place 20 4-ounce (120-milliliter) greased ramekins or popover tins on a sheet pan and drop 1 tablespoon (15 milliliters) of beef fat or vegetable oil in the bottom of each ramekin. Place the ramekins in a 425°F (220°C) oven until the fat smokes.

2 Sift the flour and salt together into a large bowl. In a separate bowl, whisk together the eggs, milk and butter. Pour the liquid ingredients into the dry ingredients and whip until smooth.

3 Remove the ramekins from the oven and fill each approximately two-thirds full with batter. Bake at 425°F (220°C) for 20 minutes without opening the oven door. After 20 minutes, lower the heat to 375°F (190°C) and bake for approximately 10 more minutes.

4 Remove the popovers from the oven, unmold and serve.

5 For crispier popovers, slit the sides of the unmolded popovers to allow the steam to escape. Place on a sheet pan and return them to the oven until the tops are firm, crisp and brown, approximately 10 minutes.

Variation: *Onion*—Sauté 4 tablespoons (60 milliliters) of finely chopped onion in 1 tablespoon (15 milliliters) of butter until tender. Sprinkle the onions over the batter just before baking.

Approximate values per popover: **Calories** 250, **Total fat** 21 g, **Saturated fat** 11 g, **Cholesterol** 95 mg, **Sodium** 150 mg, **Total carbohydrates** 10 g, **Protein** 4 g

BREAD DEALS WITH LIVING THINGS, WITH GIVING LIFE, WITH GROWTH, WITH THE SEED, THE GRAIN THAT NURTURES. IT IS NOT COINCIDENCE THAT WE SAY BREAD IS THE STAFF OF LIFE.

—Lionel Poilane, France's most celebrated baker (1946–)

YEAST BREADS

AFTER STUDYING THIS
CHAPTER, YOU WILL BE
ABLE TO:

▶ select and use yeast

▶ perform the 10 steps involved
in yeast bread production

▶ mix yeast doughs using the
straight dough method and the
sponge method

▶ prepare rolled-in doughs

Although few baked goods intimidate novice bakers as much as yeast breads, few baked goods are actually as forgiving or as comforting to prepare. By mastering a few basic procedures and techniques, you can offer your customers delicious, fresh yeast products.

Yeast breads can be divided into two categories: lean doughs and rich doughs. Lean doughs, such as those used for French and Italian breads, contain little or no sugar or fat. Rich doughs, such as brioche and some multigrain breads, contain significantly more sugar and fat. Laminated or rolled-in doughs, so called because the fat is rolled into the dough in layers, are a type of rich dough used for baked goods such as croissants and sweetened Danish pastries.

The study of yeast breads could well occupy this entire text and an entire course. The focus here is narrowed to an understanding of fundamental techniques and procedures for making the most common styles of yeast breads for a small retail shop or restaurant. Most of the formulas in this chapter yield only one or two loaves or a few dozen rolls. Although most of these formulas can be increased successfully if necessary, you can best develop proper judgment skills by first preparing small quantities. We discuss hands-on mixing and makeup techniques, leaving the science of commercial (that is, mechanical) bread production to others.

▶ YEAST

Yeast is a living organism: a one-celled fungus. Various strains of yeast are present virtually everywhere. Yeast feeds on carbohydrates, converting them to carbon dioxide and alcohol in an organic process known as **fermentation**:

Yeast + Carbohydrates = Alcohol + Carbon Dioxide

When yeast releases carbon dioxide gas during bread making, the gas becomes trapped in the dough's gluten network. The trapped gas leavens the bread, providing the desired rise and texture. The small amount of alcohol produced by fermentation evaporates during baking.

As with most living things, yeast is very sensitive to temperature. It prefers temperatures between 90°F and 110°F (32°C and 43°C). At temperatures below 34°F (2°C), it becomes dormant; above 138°F (59°C), it dies.

Salt is used in bread making because it conditions gluten, making it stronger and more elastic. Salt also affects yeast fermentation. Because salt inhibits the growth of yeast, it helps control the dough's rise. Too little salt and not only will the bread taste bland, it will rise too rapidly. Too much salt, however, and the yeast will be destroyed. By learning to control the amount of food for the yeast and the temperatures of fermentation, you can learn to control the texture of your yeast-leavened products.

TYPES OF YEAST

Baker's yeast is available in two forms: compressed and active dry. (You may also encounter a product called brewer's yeast; it is a nutritional supplement with no leavening ability.)

▶ **fermentation** the process by which yeast converts sugar into alcohol and carbon dioxide; it also refers to the time that yeast dough is left to rise—that is, the time it takes for carbon dioxide gas cells to form and become trapped in the gluten network

Table 31.1	TEMPERATURES FOR YEAST DEVELOPMENT	
TEMPERATURE		**YEAST DEVELOPMENT**
34°F	2°C	Inactive
60°F–70°F	16°C–21°C	Slow action
70°F–90°F	21°C–32°C	Best temperature for growth of fresh yeast
105°F–115°F	41°C–46°C	Best temperature for growth of dry yeast
125°F–130°F	52°C–54°C	Best temperature for activating instant yeast
138°F	59°C	Yeast dies

COMPRESSED YEAST

Compressed yeast is a mixture of yeast and starch with a moisture content of approximately 70 percent. Also referred to as **fresh yeast,** compressed yeast must be kept refrigerated. It should be creamy white and crumbly with a fresh, yeasty smell. Do not use compressed yeast that has developed a sour odor, brown color or slimy film.

Compressed yeast is available in 0.6-ounce (17-gram) cubes and 1-pound (450-gram) blocks. Under proper storage conditions, compressed yeast has a shelf life of 2 to 3 weeks.

ACTIVE DRY YEAST

Active dry yeast differs from compressed yeast in that virtually all the moisture has been removed by hot air. The absence of moisture renders the organism dormant and allows the yeast to be stored without refrigeration for several months. When preparing doughs, dry yeast is generally rehydrated in a lukewarm (approximately 110°F [43°C]) liquid before being added to the other ingredients.

Dry yeast is available in ¼-ounce (7-gram) packages and 1- or 2-pound (500-gram or 1-kilogram) vacuum-sealed bags. It should be stored in a cool, dry place and refrigerated after opening.

INSTANT YEAST

Instant or **quick-rise dry yeast** is also available. It should be blended with the dry ingredients in a bread formula, then activated with hot (approximately 125°F–130°F [52°C–54°C]) water. It dramatically speeds the rising process. Instant yeast can be substituted measure for measure for regular dry yeast. Instant yeast is still a living organism and will be destroyed at temperatures above 138°F (59°C).

SUBSTITUTING YEASTS

The flavors of dry and compressed yeasts are virtually indistinguishable, but dry yeast is approximately twice as strong. Because too much yeast can ruin bread, always remember to reduce by half the specified weight of compressed yeast when substituting dry yeast in a formula. Likewise, if a formula specifies dry yeast, double the amount when substituting compressed yeast. All the formulas in this text requiring yeast use regular active dry yeast.

SOURDOUGH STARTER

Prior to commercial yeast production, bakers relied on starters to leaven their breads. Early starters were simple but magical mixtures of flour and a liquid (water, potato broth, milk) left to capture wild yeasts from the air and then ferment. Only a portion of the starter was used at a time. The rest was kept for later use, replenished periodically with additional flour and liquid so that the magic could continue.

Compressed Yeast

Dry Yeast

Today, starters are generally fortified with yeast to provide consistency and reliability; they are prized for the unique, sour flavors they impart. Prepared dry cultures are often used commercially to give bread a "sourdough" flavor without requiring the time and space necessary to develop and maintain an active starter.

RECIPE 31.1

Sourdough Starter

SOURDOUGH STARTER

Yield: 1 qt. (1 lt)

Active dry yeast	1 tsp.	5 ml
Water, warm	4 fl. oz.	120 ml
Water, room temperature	14 fl. oz.	420 ml
All-purpose flour	2 lb.	1 kg

1 Combine the yeast and warm water. Let stand until foamy, approximately 10 minutes.
2 Stir in the 14 fluid ounces (420 milliliters) of room-temperature water, then add the flour, 2 ounces (60 grams) at a time.
3 Blend by hand or with the paddle attachment of an electric mixer on low speed for 2 minutes.
4 Place the starter in a warmed bowl and cover with plastic wrap. Let stand at room temperature overnight. The starter should triple in volume but still be wet and sticky. Refrigerate until ready to use.
5 Each time a portion of the starter is used, it must be replenished. To replenish the starter, stir in equal amounts by volume of flour and warm water. Then allow the mixture to ferment at room temperature for several hours or overnight before refrigerating.

Approximate values per fluid ounce (30 ml): **Calories** 100, **Total fat** 0 g, **Saturated fat** 0 g, **Cholesterol** 0 mg, **Sodium** 0 mg, **Total carbohydrates** 22 g, **Protein** 3 g

Note: If liquid rises to the top of the starter, it can be stirred back into the mixture. If the starter develops a pink or yellow film, it has been contaminated and must be discarded.

▶ PRODUCTION STAGES FOR YEAST BREADS

The production of yeast breads can be divided into 10 stages:

1 Scaling the ingredients
2 Mixing and kneading the dough
3 Fermenting the dough
4 Punching down the dough
5 Portioning the dough
6 Rounding the portions
7 Shaping the portions
8 Proofing the products
9 Baking the products
10 Cooling and storing the finished products

STAGE 1: SCALING THE INGREDIENTS

As with any other bakeshop product, it is important to scale or measure ingredients accurately when making a yeast bread. Be sure that all necessary ingredients are available and at the proper temperature before starting.

The amount of flour required in a yeast bread may vary depending upon the humidity level, storage conditions of the flour and the accuracy with which other ingredients are measured. The amount of flour stated in most formulas is to be used as a guide; experience teaches when more or less flour is actually needed.

STAGE 2: MIXING AND KNEADING THE DOUGH

The way ingredients are combined affects the outcome of the bread. A dough must be mixed properly in order to combine the ingredients uniformly, distribute the yeast and develop the gluten. If the dough is not mixed properly, the bread's texture and shape suffer.

Yeast breads are usually mixed by either the **straight dough method** or the **sponge method.** A third method used for rich, flaky doughs is discussed later in the section on **rolled-in doughs.**

Once the ingredients are combined, the dough must be kneaded to develop gluten, the network of proteins that gives a bread its shape and texture. Kneading can be done by hand or by an electric mixer with its dough hook attachment. Dough should be kneaded until it is smooth and moderately elastic. The presence of a few blisterlike air bubbles on the dough's surface also signals that kneading is complete. Because fat and sugar slow gluten development, rich, sweet doughs are generally kneaded longer than lean doughs. Overkneading results in dough that is, at best, difficult to shape and, in extreme cases, sticky and inelastic. Overkneading is rarely a problem, however, except when using a high-speed mixer or food processor.

▶ PROCEDURE FOR KNEADING DOUGH BY HAND

1 First, bring a portion of the dough toward you.

2 Then push the dough away from you with your fist.

3 Repeat until the dough is properly kneaded.

STRAIGHT DOUGH METHOD

The simplest and most common method for mixing yeast doughs is known as the straight dough method. With this method, all ingredients are simply com-

THE RISE OF YEAST BREADS

How and when the first yeast-leavened breads came into being, no one knows. Perhaps some wild yeasts–the world is full of them–drifted into a dough as it awaited baking. Perhaps some ancient baker substituted fermented ale or beer for water one day. In any case, the resulting bread was different, lighter and more appetizing.

Based on models, images and writings found in excavated tombs, we can be fairly certain that the ancient Egyptians saved a bit of fermented dough from one day's baking to add to the next day's. This use of sourdough starter continues today, enjoying widespread popularity.

Other cultures developed their own leavening methods. The Greeks and Romans prepared a wheat porridge with wine, which caused their doughs to ferment. The Gauls and Iberians added the foamy head from ale to their doughs. Both methods resulted in lighter breads that retained their fresh textures longer.

Since ancient times, bread baking has been one of the first household tasks readily turned over to professionals. The first cooks to work outside homes during the Greek and Roman empires were bakers. The bakery trade flourished during the Middle Ages, with a wide variety of breads being produced. Yeast-leavened breads remained the exception, not the norm, until well into the 17th century, however.

The first real collection of bread recipes is found in Nicolas Bonnefon's *Les Délices de la campagne,* published in 1654. Bonnefon's instructions, meant for those dissatisfied with commercial products of the time, included the use of beer yeast. By the end of the 17th century, published works included recipes for breads leavened with sourdough starter and the yeasts used in breweries.

Louis Pasteur finally identified yeast as a living organism in 1857. Soon after, a process for distilling or manufacturing baker's yeast was developed. By 1868, commercial baking yeast was available in stores.

bined and mixed. The yeast may or may not be combined first with a warm liquid. Be careful that the temperature of the liquid ingredients does not exceed 138°F (59°C) or the yeast will die.

Once the ingredients are combined, the dough is kneaded until it is smooth and elastic. Kneading time varies according to the kneading method used and the type of dough being produced. The straight dough method is illustrated by the recipe for Soft Yeast Dinner Rolls (page 973).

SPONGE METHOD

The sponge method of mixing yeast doughs has two stages. During the first stage the yeast, liquid and approximately half the flour are combined to make a thick batter known as a **sponge.** The sponge is allowed to rise until bubbly and doubled in size. During the second stage, the fat, salt, sugar and remaining flour are added. The dough is kneaded and allowed to rise again. These two fermentations give sponge method breads a somewhat different flavor and a lighter texture than breads made with the straight dough method.

Do not confuse sponge method breads with sourdough starters. The sponge method is most often used to improve the texture of heavy doughs such as rye. Unlike a sourdough starter, the first-stage sponge is prepared only for the specific formula and is not reserved for later use. The sponge method is illustrated by the recipe for Light Rye Bread (page 975).

STAGE 3: FERMENTING THE DOUGH

As mentioned earlier, fermentation is the process by which yeast converts sugar into alcohol and carbon dioxide. Fermentation also refers to the time that yeast dough is left to rise—that is, the time it takes for carbon dioxide gas to form and become trapped in the gluten network. Note that *fermentation* refers to the rise given to the entire mass of yeast dough, while *proofing* refers to the rise given to shaped yeast products just prior to baking.

For fermentation, place the kneaded dough into a lightly oiled container large enough to allow the dough to expand. The surface of the dough may be oiled to prevent drying. Cover the dough and place it in a warm place—that is, at temperatures between 75°F and 85°F (24°C and 29°C). It is better to allow the dough to rise slowly in a cool place than to rush fermentation.

Fermentation is complete when the dough has approximately doubled in size and no longer springs back when pressed gently with two fingers. The time necessary varies depending on the type of dough, the temperature of the room and the temperature of the dough.

STAGE 4: PUNCHING DOWN THE DOUGH

After fermentation, the dough is gently folded down to expel and redistribute the gas pockets with a technique known as **punching down.** Punching down dough also helps even out the dough's temperature and relaxes the gluten.

STAGE 5: PORTIONING THE DOUGH

The dough is now ready to be divided into portions. For loaves, the dough is scaled to the desired weight. For individual rolls, you can first shape the dough into an even log, then cut off portions with a chef's knife or dough cutter. Weighing the cut dough pieces on a portion scale ensures even-sized portions. When portioning, work quickly and keep the dough covered to prevent it from drying out.

STAGE 6: ROUNDING THE PORTIONS

The portions of dough must be shaped into smooth, round balls in a technique known as **rounding.** Rounding stretches the outside layer of gluten into a smooth coating. This helps hold in gases and makes it easier to shape the dough. Unrounded rolls rise unevenly and have a rough, lumpy surface.

STAGE 7: SHAPING THE PORTIONS

Lean doughs and some rich doughs can be shaped into a variety of forms: large loaves, small loaves, free-form or country-style rounds or individual dinner rolls. Table 31.2 identifies common pan sizes and the approximate weight of the dough used to fill them. Some shaping techniques are shown here. Other doughs, particularly brioche, croissant and Danish, are usually shaped in very specific ways. Those techniques are discussed and illustrated with their specific formulas.

Cloverleaf rolls

Bow knot rolls

Loaves in a bannaton

Boule loaves

STAGE 8: PROOFING THE PRODUCTS

Proofing is the final rise of shaped or panned yeast products before baking. The temperature should be between 95°F and 115°F (35°C and 46°C), slightly higher than the temperature for fermentation. Some humidity is also desirable to prevent the dough from drying or forming a crust. Temperature and humidity can be controlled with a special cabinet known as a **proof box.**

Proofing should continue until the product doubles in size and springs back slowly when lightly touched. Underproofing results in poor volume and texture. Overproofing results in a sour flavor, poor volume and a paler color after baking.

▶ **bagel** a dense, donut-shaped yeast roll; it is cooked in boiling water, then baked, which gives it a shiny glaze and chewy texture

▶ **bun** any of a variety of small, round yeast rolls; can be sweet or savory

▶ **club roll** a small oval-shaped roll made of crusty French bread

▶ **kaiser roll** a large round yeast roll with a crisp crust and a curved pattern stamped on the top; used primarily for sandwiches

Table 31.2	PAN SIZE	
PAN	**APPROXIMATE SIZE**	**WEIGHT OF DOUGH***
Sandwich loaf	16 in. × 4 in. × 4½ in.	4 lb.
Pullman	13 in. × 4 in. × 3 in.	3 lb.
Large	9 in. × 5 in. × 3 in.	2 lb.
Medium	8 in. × 4 in. × 2 in.	1 lb. 8 oz.
Small	7 in. × 3 in. × 2 in.	1 lb.
Miniature	5 in. × 3 in. × 2 in.	8 oz.

*Weights given are approximate; variations may occur based on the type of dough used as well as the temperature and time of proofing.

STAGE 9: BAKING THE PRODUCTS

As yeast breads bake, a variety of chemical and physical changes turn the dough into an edible product. These changes are discussed in Chapter 29, Principles of the Bakeshop.

Because of the expansion of gases, yeast products experience a sudden rise when first placed in a hot oven. This rise is known as **oven spring.** As the dough's temperature increases, the yeast dies, the gluten fibers become firm, the starches gelatinize, the moisture evaporates and, finally, the crust forms and turns brown.

Before baking, products can be washed and then, if desired, slashed.

WASHES

The appearance of yeast breads can be altered by applying a glaze or **wash** to the dough before baking. The crust is made shiny or matte, hard or soft, darker or lighter by the proper use of washes. Washes are also used to attach seeds, wheat germ, oats or other toppings to the dough's surface.

The most commonly used wash is an egg wash, composed of whole egg and water. Yeast products can also be topped with plain water, a mixture of egg and milk, plain milk or richer glazes containing sugar and flavorings. Even a light dusting of white flour can be used to top dough. (This is commonly seen with potato rolls.)

Avoid using too much wash, as it can burn or cause the product to stick to the pan. Puddles or streaks of egg wash on the dough will cause uneven browning.

Washes may be applied before or after proofing. If applied after proofing, be extremely careful not to deflate the product.

Occasionally, a formula will specify that melted butter or oil be brushed on the product after baking. Do not, however, apply egg washes to already baked products, as the egg will remain raw and the desired effect will not be achieved.

SLASHING

The shape and appearance of some breads can be improved by cutting their tops with a sharp knife or razor just before baking. This is referred to as **slashing** or **docking.** Hard-crusted breads are usually slashed to allow for continued rising and the escape of gases after the crust has formed. Breads that are not properly slashed will burst or break along the sides. Slashing can also be used to make an attractive design on the product's surface.

STEAM INJECTION

The crisp crust desired for certain breads and rolls is achieved by introducing moisture into the oven during baking. Professional bakers' ovens have built-in steam injection jets to provide moisture as needed. To create steam in any oven, you can spray or mist the bread with water several times during baking, place

Table 31.3	WASHES FOR YEAST PRODUCTS
WASH	**USE**
Whole egg and water	Shine and color
Whole egg and milk	Shine and color with soft crust
Egg white and water	Shine with a firm crust
Water	Crisp crust
Flour	Texture and contrast
Milk or cream	Color with a soft crust

ice cubes on the oven floor to melt or keep a pan of hot water on the oven's lowest rack. Rich doughs, which do not form crisp crusts, are baked without steam.

DETERMINING DONENESS

Baking time is determined by a variety of factors: the product's size, the oven thermostat's accuracy and the desired crust color. Larger items require a longer baking time than smaller ones. Lean dough products bake faster and at higher temperatures than rich dough products.

Bread loaves can be tested for doneness by tapping them on the bottom and listening for a hollow sound. This indicates that air, not moisture, is present inside the loaf. If the bottom is damp or heavy, the loaf probably needs more baking time. The texture and color of the crust are also a good indication of doneness, particularly with individual rolls. As you bake a variety of yeast products, you will develop the experience necessary to determine doneness without strict adherence to elapsed time.

STAGE 10: COOLING AND STORING THE FINISHED PRODUCTS

The quality of even the finest yeast products suffers if they are cooled or stored improperly. Yeast products should be cooled at room temperature and away from drafts. Yeast breads and rolls should be removed from their pans for cooling. Allow loaves to cool completely before slicing.

Once cool, yeast products should be stored at room temperature or frozen for longer storage. Do not refrigerate baked goods, as refrigeration promotes staling. Do not wrap Italian or French loaves, as this causes crusts to lose the desired crispness.

SOFT YEAST DINNER ROLLS

RECIPE 31.2

Yield: 75 Rolls   **Method:** Straight dough

Water, warm	1 lb. 4 oz.	560 ml
Active dry yeast	2 oz.	60 g
Bread flour	2 lb. 12 oz.	1.2 kg
Salt	1 oz.	30 g
Granulated sugar	4 oz.	120 g
Nonfat dry milk powder	2 oz.	60 g
Shortening	2 oz.	60 g
Unsalted butter, softened	2 oz.	60 g
Eggs, whole	2	2
Egg wash	as needed	as needed

1 Combine the water and yeast in a small bowl. Combine the remaining ingredients (except the egg wash) in the bowl of an electric mixer.

2 Add the water-and-yeast mixture to the remaining ingredients; stir to combine.

3 Knead with a dough hook on second speed for 10 minutes.

4 Transfer the dough to a lightly greased bowl, cover and place in a warm spot. Let rise until doubled, approximately 1 hour.

5 Punch down the dough. Let it rest a few minutes to allow the gluten to relax.

6 Divide the dough into 1¼-ounce (35-gram) portions and round. Shape as desired and arrange on paper-lined sheet pans. Proof until doubled in size.

7 Carefully brush the proofed rolls with egg wash. Bake at 400°F (200°C) until medium brown, approximately 12 to 15 minutes.

Approximate values per roll: **Calories** 90, **Total fat** 1.5 g, **Saturated fat** 0.5 g, **Cholesterol** 10 mg, **Sodium** 160 mg, **Total carbohydrates** 15 g, **Protein** 3 g **Claims**—low fat; low saturated fat; low cholesterol

1 Mixing the soft yeast dough: **(a)** Combining the ingredients in a mixer bowl with the dough hook attached.

(b) Adding the yeast-and-water mixture.

2 Kneading the dough.

3 The dough before rising.

4 Punching down the risen dough: **(a)** Pressing down on the center of the dough with your fist.

(b) Folding the edges of the dough in toward the center.

5 Scaling the dough.

6 Rounding the rolls.

7 Egg-washing the rolls.

LIGHT RYE BREAD

Yield: 2 Large Loaves   **Method:** Sponge

Unbleached wheat flour	1 lb.	450 g
Medium rye flour	8 oz.	225 g
Dark molasses	3 oz.	90 g
Water, warm	1 lb. 4 oz.	560 ml
Active dry yeast	½ oz.	15 g
Nonfat dry milk powder	1½ oz.	45 g
Caraway seeds, crushed	2 Tbsp.	30 ml
Kosher salt	1 Tbsp.	15 ml
Unsalted butter, melted	1 Tbsp.	15 ml
Egg wash	as needed	as needed

1 Rye bread sponge.

1. Stir the flours together and set aside.

2. To make the sponge, combine the molasses, water and yeast. Add 8 ounces (225 grams) of the flour mixture. Stir vigorously for 3 minutes. Cover the bowl and set aside to rise until doubled and very bubbly, approximately 1 hour.

3. Stir the milk powder, caraway seeds, salt and butter into the sponge.

4. Gradually add the remaining flour to the sponge. When the dough is too stiff to mix by hand, transfer the dough to a mixer fitted with a dough hook.

5. Continue adding flour until the dough is stiff but slightly tacky. Knead for 5 minutes on low speed.

6. Transfer the dough to a lightly greased bowl, cover and place in a warm place until doubled, approximately 45 to 60 minutes.

7. Punch down the dough and divide into two pieces. Shape each piece into a round loaf and place on a sheet pan that has been dusted with cornmeal or lightly oiled. Brush the loaves with egg wash and let rise until doubled, approximately 45 minutes.

8. Slash the tops with a razor or knife. Bake at 375°F (190°C) until golden brown and crusty, approximately 25 minutes.

Approximate values per ¹⁄₁₀-loaf slice: **Calories** 160, **Total fat** 1.5 g, **Saturated fat** 0 g, **Cholesterol** 15 mg, **Sodium** 370 mg, **Total carbohydrates** 31 g, **Protein** 6 g, **Claims**—low fat; no saturated fat; low cholesterol

2 Mixing the rye dough.

3 Shaping the rye loaves.

▶ ROLLED-IN DOUGHS

Baked goods made with rolled-in (laminated) doughs include croissants, Danish pastries and nonyeast-leavened puff pastry. (Puff pastry is discussed in Chapter 32, Pies, Pastries and Cookies.) The dough is so named because the fat is incorporated through a process of rolling and folding. Products made with a rolled-in dough have a distinctive flaky texture created by the repeated layering of fat and dough. As the dough bakes, moisture is released from the fat in the form of steam. The steam is then trapped between the layers of dough, causing them to rise and separate.

MAKING ROLLED-IN DOUGHS

Rolled-in doughs are made following most of the 10 production stages discussed earlier. The principal differences are (1) the butter is incorporated through a turning process after the dough base is fermented and punched down; (2) rolled-in doughs are portioned somewhat differently from other yeast doughs; and (3) the portions are shaped without rounding.

Butter is often used for rolled-in products because of its flavor. Unfortunately, butter is hard to work with because it cracks and breaks when cold and becomes too soft to roll at room temperature. Margarine, shortening or specially formulated high-moisture fats, however, can be used—sometimes in combination with butter—in order to reduce costs or to make it easier to work with the dough.

The dough base should not be kneaded too much, as gluten will continue to develop during the rolling and folding process. An electric dough sheeter can be used to roll the dough. This saves time and ensures a more consistent product.

▶ PROCEDURE FOR PREPARING ROLLED-IN DOUGHS

1 Mix the dough and allow it to rise.

2 Prepare the butter or shortening.

3 Roll out the dough evenly, then top it with the butter.

4 Fold the dough around the butter, enclosing it completely.

5 Roll out the dough into a rectangle, about ¼ to ½ inch (0.6 to 1.2 centimeters) thick. Always be sure to roll at right angles; do not roll haphazardly or in a circle as you would pastry doughs.

6 Fold the dough in thirds. Be sure to brush off any excess flour from between the folds. This completes the first turn. Chill the dough for 20 to 30 minutes.

7 Roll out the dough and fold it in the same manner a second and third time, allowing the dough to rest between each turn. After completing the third turn, wrap the dough carefully and allow it to rest for several hours or overnight before shaping and baking.

RECIPE 31.4 | CROISSANTS |

THE CULTURED CROISSANT

A croissant brings to mind a Parisian sidewalk café and a steaming cup of café crème. It is, however, a truly international delicacy. The croissant was created by bakers in Budapest, Hungary, to celebrate the city's liberation from Turkey in 1686; its shape was derived from the crescent moon of the Turkish flag. The delicacy was soon adopted as a breakfast pastry by both the French and the Italians. The first machine for mass-producing croissants was designed by a Japanese firm and manufactured in Italy. Although croissants became popular in the United States only during the late 20th century, Americans now consume millions of croissants each year.

Yield: 60 Rolls		**Method:** Rolled-in dough
Bread flour	2 lb. 4 oz.	1 kg
Salt	1 oz.	30 g
Granulated sugar	6 oz.	180 g
Milk	21 fl. oz.	625 ml
Active dry yeast	1 oz.	30 g
Unsalted butter, softened	1 lb. 8 oz.	680 g
Egg wash	as needed	as needed

1 Stir the flour, salt and sugar together in a mixer bowl fitted with a dough hook.

2 Warm the milk to approximately 90°F (32°C). Stir in the yeast.

3 Add the milk-and-yeast mixture to the dry ingredients. Stir until combined, then knead on second speed for 10 minutes.

4 Place the dough in a large floured bowl, cover and let rise until doubled in size, approximately 1 hour.

5 Prepare the butter while the dough is rising. Place the butter in an even layer between two large pieces of plastic wrap and roll into a flat rectangle, approximately 8 inches × 11 inches (20 centimeters × 27.5 centimeters) and chill.

6 After the dough has risen, punch it down. Roll out the dough into a large rectangle, about ½ inch (1.2 centimeters) thick and large enough to enclose the

rectangle of butter. Place the unwrapped butter in the center of the dough and fold the dough around the butter, enclosing it completely.

7 Roll out the block of dough into a long rectangle, about 1 inch (2.5 centimeters) thick. Fold the dough in thirds, as if folding a letter. This completes the first turn. Wrap the dough in plastic and chill for approximately 20 to 30 minutes.

8 Repeat the rolling and folding process two more times, chilling the dough between each turn. When finished, wrap the dough well and chill it overnight before shaping and baking.

9 To shape the dough into croissant rolls, cut off one-quarter of the block at a time, wrapping the rest and returning it to the refrigerator. Roll each quarter of dough into a large rectangle, about ¼ inch (6 millimeters) thick.

10 Cut the dough into uniform triangles. Starting with the large end, roll each triangle into a crescent and place on a paper-lined sheet pan.

11 Brush lightly with egg wash. Proof until doubled, but do not allow the dough to become so warm that the butter melts.

12 Bake at 375°F (190°C) until golden brown, approximately 12 to 15 minutes.

Approximate values per roll: **Calories** 200, **Total fat** 12 g, **Saturated fat** 7 g, **Cholesterol** 40 mg, **Sodium** 230 mg, **Total carbohydrates** 19 g, **Protein** 3 g, **Vitamin A** 10%

1 Rolling out the butter between two sheets of plastic wrap.

2 Folding the dough around the butter, which has been placed in the center.

3 Brushing the excess flour from the rolled-out dough.

4 Folding the dough in thirds.

5 The finished croissant dough.

6 Cutting the dough into triangles.

7 Baked croissants.

Table 31.4 **TROUBLESHOOTING CHART**

PROBLEM	CAUSE	SOLUTION
Cannonball of dough	Too much flour forced into the dough	Gradually add water; adjust formula
Crust too pale	Oven temperature too low	Adjust oven
	Dough overproofed	Proof only until almost doubled, then bake immediately
Crust too dark	Oven too hot	Adjust oven
	Too much sugar in the dough	Adjust formula or measure sugar carefully
Top crust separates from rest of loaf	Dough improperly shaped	Shape dough carefully
	Crust not slashed properly	Slash dough to a depth of ½ in. (1.2 cm)
	Dough dried out during proofing	Cover dough during proofing
Sides of loaf are cracked	Bread expanded after crust had formed	Slash top of loaf before baking
Dense texture	Not enough yeast	Adjust formula or measure salt carefully
	Not enough fermentation time	Let dough rise until doubled or as directed
	Too much salt	Adjust formula or measure salt carefully
Ropes of undercooked dough running through the product	Insufficient kneading	Knead dough until it is smooth and elastic or as directed
	Insufficient rising time	Allow adequate time for rising
	Oven too hot	Adjust oven
Free-form loaf spreads and flattens	Dough too soft	Add flour
Large holes in bread	Too much yeast	Adjust formula or measure yeast carefully
	Overkneaded	Knead only as directed
	Inadequate punch-down	Punch down properly to knead out excess air before shaping
Blisters on crust	Too much liquid	Measure ingredients carefully
	Improper shaping	Knead out excess air before shaping
	Too much steam in oven	Reduce amount of steam or moisture in oven

CONCLUSION

Fresh yeast breads are a popular and inexpensive addition to any menu and are surprisingly easy to prepare. By understanding and appreciating the importance of each of the 10 production stages described in this chapter, you will be able to create and adapt formulas to suit your specific operation and needs.

QUESTIONS FOR DISCUSSION

1 Describe the characteristics of lean and rich doughs, and give an example of each.

2 Explain the differences between active dry yeast and compressed yeast. Describe the correct procedures for working with these yeasts.

3 Explain the differences between a sponge and a sourdough starter. How is each of these items used?

4 Describe the straight dough mixing method, and give two examples of products made with this procedure.

5 Briefly describe the procedure for making a rolled-in dough, and give two examples of products made from rolled-in doughs.

6 List the 10 production stages for yeast breads. Which of these production stages would also apply to quick-bread production? Explain your answer.

7 Locate a professional organization for bread bakers. What services are available to its members?

8 Locate two recipes each for typical French, German and Italian yeast breads and determine whether they are made with the straight dough, sponge or rolled-in method.

RECIPE 31.5

FRENCH BREAD

Yield: 5 lb. (2.2 kg) **Method:** Straight dough

Water, warm	1 qt.	1 lt
Active dry yeast	1 oz.	30 g
Bread flour	3 lb. 12 oz.	1.8 kg
Salt	1 oz.	30 g

1 Combine the water and yeast in a mixer bowl. Add the remaining ingredients and mix on low speed with a dough hook until all the flour is incorporated.

2 Increase to second speed and knead the dough until it is smooth and elastic.

3 Let the dough rise until doubled. Punch down, divide, shape and slash as desired. Let rise again until doubled.

4 Place a pan of water in the oven to generate steam while the dough rises.

5 Bake at 400°F (200°C) until the crust is well developed and golden brown and the bread is baked through, approximately 12 minutes for rolls and 30 minutes for small loaves.

Approximate values per 1½-oz. (45-g) serving: **Calories** 80, **Total fat** 0 g, **Saturated fat** 0 g, **Cholesterol** 0 mg, **Sodium** 135 mg, **Total carbohydrates** 16 g, **Protein** 3 g, **Claims**—fat free; low sodium; no sugar

1 The dough is portioned and then rolled into baguettes in two stages.

2 The proofed loaves are slashed to allow steam to escape.

3 The finished baguettes.

RECIPE 31.6

WHITE SANDWICH BREAD

Yield: 2 Large Loaves **Method:** Straight dough

Water, warm	12 fl. oz.	360 ml
Nonfat dry milk powder	1¼ oz.	35 g
Granulated sugar	1 oz.	30 g
Salt	2 tsp.	10 ml
Active dry yeast	½ oz.	15 g
Bread flour	1 lb. 8 oz.	680 g
Unsalted butter, softened	1 oz.	30 g
Eggs	2	2

1 Combine the water, milk powder, sugar, salt, yeast and 12 ounces (360 grams) of the flour. Blend well. Add the butter and eggs and beat for 2 minutes.

2 Stir in the remaining flour, 2 ounces (60 grams) at a time. Knead for 8 minutes.

3 Place the dough in a lightly greased bowl, cover and let rise at room temperature until doubled, approximately 1 to 1½ hours.

4 Shape into loaves and let rise until doubled.

5 Bake at 400°F (200°C) if free-form or small loaves; bake at 375°F (190°C) if larger loaves. Bake until brown and hollow sounding, approximately 35 minutes for small loaves and 50 minutes for large loaves.

Variation: *Whole-Wheat Bread*—Substitute up to 12 ounces (360 grams) of whole-wheat flour for an equal amount of the bread flour.

Approximate values per 2-oz. (60-g) serving: **Calories** 150, **Total fat** 2 g, **Saturated fat** 1 g, **Cholesterol** 25 mg, **Sodium** 250 mg, **Total carbohydrates** 28 g, **Protein** 6 g, **Vitamin A** 4%, **Claims**—low fat

---

ENGLISH MUFFIN LOAVES

RECIPE 31.7

Yield: 2 Large Loaves   **Method:** Straight dough

Active dry yeast	½ oz.	15 g
Granulated sugar	1 Tbsp.	15 ml
Baking soda	¼ tsp.	1 ml
Salt	2 tsp.	10 ml
All-purpose flour	1 lb. 8 oz.	720 g
Milk	1 pt.	500 ml
Water	4 fl. oz.	120 ml
Cornmeal	as needed	as needed

1 Stir together the yeast, sugar, baking soda, salt and 12 ounces (360 grams) of the flour.

2 Combine the milk and water and heat to 120°F (49°C).

3 Stir the warm liquids into the dry ingredients, beating well. Add enough of the remaining flour to make a stiff batter.

4 Spoon the batter into loaf pans that have been greased and dusted with cornmeal. Proof until doubled.

5 Bake at 400°F (200°C) until golden brown and done, approximately 25 minutes.

6 Remove the bread from the pans immediately and cool.

Approximate values per ¹⁄₁₂-loaf slice: **Calories** 119, **Total fat** 1 g, **Saturated fat** 0.5 g, **Cholesterol** 3 mg, **Sodium** 202 mg, **Total carbohydrates** 23 g, **Protein** 4 g

---

POTATO CHEDDAR CHEESE BREAD

RECIPE 31.8

STOUFFER STANFORD COURT HOTEL, SAN FRANCISCO, CA
Former Executive Chef Ercolino Crugnale

Yield: 7 Loaves, 1 lb. 4 oz. (600 g) each   **Method:** Straight dough

Active dry yeast	2 oz.	60 g
Water, warm (100°F/38°C)	8 fl. oz.	225 ml
Bread flour	4 lb. 8 oz.	2.2 kg
Potatoes, boiled, peeled and puréed	2 lb.	1 kg

Continued

Kosher salt	1½ oz.	45 g
Cracked pepper	1 oz.	30 g
Unsalted butter, melted	3 oz.	90 g
Cheddar, grated	1 lb.	500 g
Water, room temperature	1 pt.	500 ml

1 Dissolve the yeast in the warm water and set aside.
2 Combine the flour, potatoes, salt, pepper, butter and cheese. Blend on low speed for 2 to 3 minutes.
3 Slowly add the room-temperature water and the yeast mixture. Mix on medium speed for 8 to 10 minutes.
4 Allow the dough to rise in a warm spot until doubled, approximately 2 hours. Punch down the dough and divide into loaves.
5 Proof in a flour-dusted **banneton** until doubled in size, approximately 45 minutes. Remove the proofed dough from the banneton and bake at 350°F (180°C) until brown, approximately 20 to 30 minutes.

▶ **banneton** (BAN-tahn) a traditional woven basket, often lined with canvas, in which yeast bread is placed to rise before baking. The basket leaves marks in the dough. Heavy plastic versions are available for commercial food service use.

Approximate values per 1½-oz. (45-g) serving: **Calories** 150, **Total fat** 3.5 g, **Saturated fat** 2 g, **Cholesterol** 10 mg, **Sodium** 280 mg, **Total carbohydrates** 25 g, **Protein** 6 g, **Calcium** 10%, **Claims**—low cholesterol

---

RECIPE 31.9   **WHOLE-WHEAT BREAD**

Yield: 2 Large Loaves or 35 Dinner Rolls

Method: Straight dough

Salt	2 tsp.	10 ml
Nonfat dry milk powder	1¼ oz.	35 g
Whole-wheat flour	1 lb. 10 oz.	780 g
Water, hot	18 fl. oz.	540 ml
Active dry yeast	½ oz.	15 g
Honey	3 oz.	90 g
Unsalted butter, softened	1 oz.	30 g
Whole butter, melted	as needed	as needed

1 In a large mixer bowl, combine the salt and milk powder with 12 ounces (360 grams) of the flour.
2 Stir in the hot water, yeast, honey and softened butter. Beat until combined into a thick batterlike dough.
3 Add the remaining flour 2 ounces (60 grams) at a time. Knead for approximately 8 minutes.
4 Place the dough in a lightly greased bowl and cover. Let rise in a warm place until doubled.
5 Punch down, portion and shape as desired.
6 Let the shaped dough rise until doubled. Bake at 375°F (190°C) until firm and dark brown, approximately 1 hour for loaves and 20 minutes for rolls. Brush the top of the loaves or rolls with melted butter after baking if desired.

Approximate values per 1½-oz. (45-g) serving: **Calories** 170, **Total fat** 2 g, **Saturated fat** 1 g, **Cholesterol** 5 mg, **Sodium** 250 mg, **Total carbohydrates** 32 g, **Protein** 6 g, **Claims**—low fat; low saturated fat; low cholesterol; good source of fiber

MULTIGRAIN SOURDOUGH BREAD   RECIPE 31.10

Yield: 2 Loaves, 9 in. × 5 in.
(22 cm × 13 cm)   **Method:** Straight dough

Cracked wheat	4½ oz.	135 g
Water, hot	8 fl. oz.	225 ml
Whole butter, melted	2 oz.	60 g
Molasses	2 Tbsp.	30 ml
Honey	2 Tbsp.	30 ml
Salt	1 tsp.	5 ml
Nonfat dry milk powder	2 oz.	60 g
Flax seeds	2 oz.	60 g
Sunflower seeds, roasted	2 oz.	60 g
Sourdough starter (p. 968)	2½ c.	590 ml
Active dry yeast	1 tsp.	5 ml
Whole-wheat flour	10 oz.	300 g
Bread flour	10–12 oz.	300–360 g
Egg wash	as needed	as needed

1 Combine the cracked wheat and hot water in the bowl of an electric mixer. Add the butter, molasses, honey, salt and milk powder. Set aside to cool.

2 When the mixture has cooled to lukewarm, stir in the flax seeds, sunflower seeds, starter and yeast. Stir in the whole-wheat flour gradually, then add the bread flour. When the dough begins to stiffen, attach the bowl to a mixer fitted with a dough hook and continue adding the bread flour. Knead until the dough is smooth and elastic, approximately 5 minutes.

3 Place the dough in a lightly oiled bowl, cover and let rise to double.

4 Punch down the risen dough, cover and allow it to double again.

5 After the second rise, punch down the dough and divide into two portions. Place the dough into two well-greased loaf pans, cover and let it double again.

6 Brush the surface of each loaf with egg wash and make two or three cuts across the top of each loaf. Bake at 375°F (190°C) until done, approximately 30 minutes.

Approximate values per ¹⁄₁₆-loaf slice: **Calories** 150, **Total fat** 3.5 g, **Saturated fat** 1 g, **Cholesterol** 5 mg, **Sodium** 90 mg, **Total carbohydrates** 26 g, **Protein** 5 g, **Iron** 10%, **Claim**—good source of fiber and iron

 BREADSTICKS   RECIPE 31.11

Yield: 24 Breadsticks   **Method:** Straight dough

Active dry yeast	½ oz.	15 g
Water, warm	10 fl. oz.	300 ml
Granulated sugar	1 oz.	30 g
Olive oil	4 fl. oz.	120 ml
Salt	2 tsp.	10 ml
Bread flour	1 lb. 2 oz.	540 g
Egg wash	as needed	as needed
Sesame seeds	3 Tbsp.	45 ml

1 Rolling breadstick dough.

2 Twisting breadstick dough.

1 Stir the yeast, water and sugar together in a mixer bowl.
2 Blend in the oil, salt and 8 ounces (225 grams) of the flour.
3 Gradually add the remaining flour. Knead the dough until it is smooth and cleans the sides of the bowl, approximately 5 minutes.
4 Remove the dough from the bowl and allow it to rest for a few minutes. Roll the dough into a rectangle, about ¼ inch (6 millimeters) thick.
5 Cut the dough into 24 even pieces. Roll each piece into a rope and twist; bring the ends together, allowing the sides to curl together. Place on a paper-lined sheet pan.
6 Brush with egg wash and top with sesame seeds. Let the sticks rise until doubled, approximately 20 minutes.
7 Bake at 375°F (190°C) until golden brown, approximately 12 to 15 minutes.

Variations: *Garlic Breadsticks*—Knead 1 ounce (30 grams) grated Parmesan and 2 tablespoons (30 milliliters) minced garlic into the dough.

Herbed Breadsticks—Knead 3 tablespoons (45 milliliters) chopped fresh herbs such as basil, parsley, dill and oregano into the dough.

Approximate values per breadstick: **Calories** 60, **Total fat** 5 g, **Saturated fat** 1 g, **Cholesterol** 10 mg, **Sodium** 190 mg, **Total carbohydrates** 2 g, **Protein** 1 g, **Claims**—low saturated fat; low cholesterol

RECIPE 31.12

FOCACCIA (ROMAN FLATBREAD)

Topping the flatbread dough with crushed rosemary.

Yield: 1 Sheet Pan, 12 in. × 18 in. (30 cm × 45 cm)

Method: Straight dough

Granulated sugar	1 Tbsp.	15 ml
Active dry yeast	1 Tbsp.	15 ml
Water, lukewarm	12 fl. oz.	360 ml
All-purpose flour	1 lb. 2 oz.	540 g
Kosher salt	2 tsp.	10 ml
Onion, chopped fine	3 oz.	90 g
Olive oil	2 tsp.	10 ml
Fresh rosemary, crushed	2 Tbsp.	30 ml

1 Combine the sugar, yeast and water. Stir to dissolve the yeast. Stir in the flour 4 ounces (120 grams) at a time.
2 Stir in 1½ teaspoons (7 milliliters) of the salt and the onion. Mix well, then knead on a lightly floured board until smooth.
3 Place the dough in an oiled bowl, cover and let rise until doubled.
4 Punch down the dough, then flatten it onto an oiled sheet pan. It should be no more than 1 inch (2.5 centimeters) thick. Brush the top of the dough with the olive oil. Let the dough proof until doubled, approximately 15 minutes.
5 Sprinkle the crushed rosemary and remaining ½ teaspoon (2 milliliters) of salt on top of the dough. Bake at 400°F (200°C) until lightly browned, approximately 20 minutes.

Approximate values per 1-oz. (30-g) serving: **Calories** 100, **Total fat** 0.5 g, **Saturated fat** 0 g, **Cholesterol** 0 mg, **Sodium** 230 mg, **Total carbohydrates** 21 g, **Protein** 3 g, **Claims**—low fat; no saturated fat; no cholesterol

PIZZA DOUGH

RECIPE 31.13

Yield: 1 Large or 8 Individual Pizzas   **Method:** Straight dough

Active dry yeast	1 Tbsp.	15 ml
Water, warm	2 fl. oz.	60 ml
Bread flour	14 oz.	420 g
Water, cool	6 fl. oz.	180 ml
Salt	1 tsp.	5 ml
Olive oil	1 fl. oz.	30 ml
Honey	1 Tbsp.	15 ml

1 Stir the yeast into the warm water to dissolve. Add the flour.

2 Stir the remaining ingredients into the flour mixture. Knead with a dough hook or by hand until smooth and elastic, approximately 5 minutes.

3 Place the dough in a lightly greased bowl and cover. Allow the dough to rise in a warm place for 30 minutes. Punch down the dough and divide into portions. The dough may be wrapped and refrigerated for up to two days.

4 On a lightly floured surface, roll the dough into very thin rounds and top as desired. Bake at 400°F (200°C) until crisp and golden brown, approximately 8 to 12 minutes.

Approximate values per 2-oz. (60-g) serving: **Calories** 220, **Total fat** 4 g, **Saturated fat** 0.5 g, **Cholesterol** 0 mg, **Sodium** 290 mg, **Total carbohydrates** 41 g, **Protein** 6 g, **Claims**—low saturated fat; no cholesterol

SAN FRANCISCO
SOURDOUGH BREAD

RECIPE 31.14

STOUFFER STANFORD COURT HOTEL, SAN FRANCISCO, CA
Former Executive Chef Ercolino Crugnale

Yield: 1 Loaf   **Method:** Straight dough

Active dry yeast	½ oz.	15 g
Water, warm (120°F/49°C)	8 fl. oz.	225 ml
Sourdough starter (page 968)	1 c.	225 ml
Bread flour	1 lb.	450 g
Kosher salt	1 Tbsp.	15 ml
Cornmeal	as needed	as needed
Egg white, beaten	1	1

1 Sprinkle the dry yeast over 2 fluid ounces (60 milliliters) of the warm water and set aside until dissolved and foamy.

2 In the bowl of a mixer fitted with a dough hook, combine the Sourdough Starter and the remaining warm water. Add 6 ounces (180 grams) of the bread flour.

3 Stir until a dough forms, then add the yeast mixture. Knead for 5 minutes on medium speed.

4 Add the remaining flour and the salt. Knead until the dough is smooth and elastic, approximately 10 minutes.

5 Place the dough in a lightly greased bowl and cover with a damp cloth. Let rise in a warm place, about 80°F–90°F (27°C–32°C), until doubled.

6 Punch down the dough and shape it into a round loaf. Place the loaf on a greased and cornmeal-dusted sheet pan.

7 Let the loaf rise in a warm place, covered with a damp cloth, until it has risen to 2½ times its original size.

8 Brush the risen loaf with the beaten egg white and score the top of the loaf with a sharp knife.

9 Bake at 450°F (230°C), with a pan of boiling water underneath the oven rack, for 10 minutes.

10 Reduce the oven temperature to 375°F (190°C), remove the water and continue baking until the loaf is well browned, approximately 35 to 45 minutes.

Approximate values per 2-oz. (60-g) serving: **Calories** 135, **Total fat** 0.5 g, **Saturated fat** 0 g, **Cholesterol** 0 mg, **Sodium** 355 mg, **Total carbohydrates** 27 g, **Protein** 4 g, **Claims**—low fat; no saturated fat; no cholesterol

---

RECIPE 13.15   CHALLAH

Challah (HAH-la) is the traditional bread for Jewish Sabbaths and celebrations. Rich with eggs and flavored with honey, it is braided into oval loaves and topped with poppy or sesame seeds. Challah is excellent for toast or sandwiches.

1 Rolling challah dough into ropes.

2 Braiding challah dough.

Yield: 2 Large Loaves   **Method:** Straight dough

Honey	6 fl. oz.	180 ml
Salt	1 Tbsp.	15 ml
Bread flour	1 lb. 12 oz.	800 g
Active dry yeast	½ oz.	15 g
Water, warm	14 fl. oz.	400 ml
Eggs	4	4
Unsalted butter, melted	4 oz.	120 g
Egg wash	as needed	as needed
Sesame or poppy seeds	as needed	as needed

1 Stir together the honey, salt and 8 ounces (225 grams) of the flour in a mixer bowl. Add the yeast, water, eggs and butter. Stir until smooth.

2 Using the dough hook, knead the dough on second speed, adding the remaining flour 2 ounces (60 grams) at a time until smooth and elastic, approximately 5 minutes.

3 Place the dough in a lightly greased bowl, cover and let rise until doubled, approximately 1 to 1½ hours.

4 Punch down the dough and divide into six equal portions. Roll each portion into a long strip, about 1 inch (2.5 centimeters) in diameter and 12 inches (30 centimeters) long. Lay three strips side by side and braid. Pinch the ends together and tuck them under the loaf. Place the loaf on a paper-lined sheet pan. Braid the three remaining pieces of dough in the same manner.

5 Brush the loaves with egg wash and sprinkle with sesame or poppy seeds. Proof until doubled, approximately 45 minutes.

6 Bake at 350°F (170°C) until the loaves are golden brown and sound hollow when thumped, approximately 40 minutes.

Approximate values per 2-oz. (30-g) serving: **Calories** 156, **Total fat** 4 g, **Saturated fat** 2 g, **Cholesterol** 44 mg, **Sodium** 145 mg, **Total carbohydrates** 25 g, **Protein** 6 g

BRIOCHE

RECIPE 13.16

Brioche (bree-ohsh) is a rich, tender bread made with lots of eggs and butter. The high ratio of fat makes this dough difficult to work with, but the flavor is well worth the extra effort. Brioche is traditionally made in fluted pans and has a cap or topknot of dough; this shape is known as brioche à tête. The dough may also be baked in a loaf pan, making it perfect for toast or canapés.

Yield: 3 Large Loaves or 60 Rolls, 3 in. (7.5 cm)

Method: Straight dough

All-purpose flour	4 lb. 7 oz.	2 kg
Eggs	24	24
Salt	1¾ oz.	50 g
Granulated sugar	7 oz.	210 g
Active dry yeast	1¾ oz.	50 g
Water, warm	7 fl. oz.	210 ml
Unsalted butter, room temperature	3 lb.	1.3 kg

1 Combining the ingredients for brioche.

1 Place the flour, eggs, salt and sugar into the bowl of a large mixer fitted with a dough hook. Stir the ingredients together.

2 Combine the yeast and water and add to the other ingredients.

3 Knead for 20 minutes on second speed. The dough will be smooth, shiny and moist. It should not form a ball.

4 Slowly add the butter to the dough. Knead only until all the butter is incorporated. Remove the dough from the mixer and place it into a bowl dusted with flour. Cover and let rise at room temperature until doubled.

5 Punch down the dough, cover well and refrigerate overnight.

6 Shape the chilled dough as desired. Place the shaped dough in well-greased pans and proof at room temperature until doubled. Do not proof brioche in a very warm place; the butter may melt out of the dough before proofing is complete.

7 Bake at 375°F (190°C) until the brioche is a dark golden brown and sounds hollow. Baking time will vary depending on the temperature of the dough and the size of the rolls or loaves being baked.

Variation: *Raisin Brioche*—Gently warm 3 fluid ounces (90 milliliters) of rum with 6 ounces (180 grams) of raisins. Set aside until the raisins are plumped. Drain off the remaining rum and add the raisins to the dough after the butter is incorporated.

Approximate values per 4-oz. (120-g) serving: **Calories** 475, **Total fat** 30 g, **Saturated fat** 17 g, **Cholesterol** 192 mg, **Sodium** 138 mg, **Total carbohydrates** 43 g, **Protein** 9 g, **Vitamin A** 30%, **Iron** 16%

2 Adding the yeast-and-water mixture to the dough.

3 Brioche dough after kneading for 20 minutes.

4 Adding the butter to the brioche dough.

5 The finished brioche dough ready for fermentation.

6 Shaping brioche à tête.

7 Panning the rolls.

8 A finished loaf of brioche baked in a pullman pan.

RECIPE 31.17

JUMBO CINNAMON BUNS

Yield: 24 Large Rolls

Method: Straight dough

Dough:

Water, warm	1 qt.	1 lt
All-purpose flour	5 lb.	2250 g
Granulated sugar	12 oz.	360 g
Active dry yeast	1 oz.	30 g
Dry milk powder	1¼ oz.	37 g
Salt	¼ oz.	7 g
Whole butter, softened	10 oz.	300 g

Filling:

Whole butter, softened	6 oz.	180 g
Cinnamon, ground	¼ oz.	7 g
Brown sugar	6 oz.	180 g
Raisins	4 oz.	120 g
Powdered Sugar Glaze (recipe follows)	11 fl. oz.	325 ml

1 In a large mixer bowl, combine all the dough ingredients. Knead the dough until it is smooth.

2 Place the dough in a lightly oiled bowl, cover and let rise until doubled.

3 Punch down the dough and roll it out on a lightly floured surface. Shape into a rectangle, approximately 18 inches × 30 inches (45 centimeters × 75 centimeters).

4 To make the filling, spread the softened butter over the surface of the dough. Combine the cinnamon, brown sugar and raisins and sprinkle this mixture over the butter, covering the dough evenly.

5 Starting with the longer side, roll the dough into a spiral. Cut into 24 pieces, each approximately 1½ inches (3.7 centimeters) thick. Place the rolls, cut side up, on a paper-lined sheet pan and allow them to rise until doubled.

6 Bake at 300°F (150°C) oven until golden brown and done, approximately 30 minutes.

7 Cool slightly, then top with Powdered Sugar Glaze.

Approximate values per roll: **Calories** 656, **Total fat** 16 g, **Saturated fat** 10 g, **Cholesterol** 42 mg, **Sodium** 132 mg, **Total carbohydrates** 117 g, **Protein** 11 g, **Vitamin A** 11%, **Iron** 27%

POWDERED SUGAR GLAZE

Yield: 11 fl. oz. (325 ml)

Powdered sugar, sifted	1 lb.	450 g
Vanilla extract	2 tsp.	10 ml
Lemon juice	2 tsp.	10 ml
Water, warm	2 Tbsp.	30 ml

1 Combine all the ingredients in a small bowl. Stir to blend thoroughly and dissolve any lumps. Cover and store at room temperature.

Approximate values per 1-fl.-oz. (30-ml) serving: **Calories** 160, **Total fat** 0 g, **Saturated fat** 0 g, **Cholesterol** 0 mg, **Sodium** 0 mg, **Total carbohydrates** 41 g, **Protein** 0 g

PECAN STICKY BUNS

RECIPE 31.18

Yield: 12–15 Buns

Method: Straight dough

Active dry yeast	1 oz.	30 g
Sugar	2 oz.	60 g
Salt	½ tsp.	2 ml
Milk	1 Tbsp.	15 ml
Buttermilk	5½ fl. oz.	165 ml
Vanilla extract	1 tsp.	5 ml
Lemon zest, grated	1 Tbsp.	15 ml
Lemon juice	1 tsp.	5 ml
Egg yolks	2	2
All-purpose flour	14 oz.	420 g
Unsalted butter, very soft	8 oz.	225 g
Topping:		
Honey	6 fl. oz.	180 ml
Brown sugar	6 oz.	180 g
Pecans, chopped	3 oz.	90 g
Filling:		
Cinnamon	1 tsp.	5 ml
Pecans, chopped	3 oz.	90 g
Brown sugar	4 oz.	120 g
Unsalted butter, melted	3 oz.	90 g

1 Brushing melted butter over the sticky bun dough.

2 Rolling up the filling in the sticky bun dough.

3 Cutting and panning the sticky buns.

1 Stir the yeast, sugar, salt and milk together in a small bowl. Set aside.

2 Stir the buttermilk, vanilla, lemon zest and lemon juice together and add to the yeast mixture.

3 Add the egg yolks, flour and softened butter to the liquid mixture. Turn out onto a lightly floured board and knead until the butter is evenly distributed and the dough is smooth. Cover and let rise until doubled.

4 Prepare the topping and filling mixtures while the dough is rising. To make the topping, cream the honey and sugar together. Stir in the pecans. This mixture will be very stiff. To make the filling, stir the cinnamon, pecans and sugar together.

5 Lightly grease muffin cups, then distribute the topping mixture evenly, about 1 tablespoon (15 milliliters) per muffin cup. Set the pans aside at room temperature until the dough is ready.

6 Punch down the dough and let it rest 10 minutes. Roll out the dough into a rectangle about ½ inch (1.2 centimeters) thick. Brush with the melted butter and top evenly with the filling mixture.

7 Starting with either long edge, roll up the dough. Cut into slices about ¾ to 1 inch (1.8 to 2.5 centimeters) thick. Place a slice in each muffin cup over the topping.

8 Let the buns proof until doubled, approximately 20 minutes. Bake at 350°F (170°C) until very brown, approximately 25 minutes. Immediately invert the muffin pans onto paper-lined sheet pans to let the buns and their topping slide out.

Approximate values per bun: **Calories** 480, **Total fat** 26 g, **Saturated fat** 11 g, **Cholesterol** 75 mg, **Sodium** 100 mg, **Total carbohydrates** 55 g, **Protein** 5 g, **Vitamin A** 15%, **Iron** 15%

RECIPE 31.19   **DANISH PASTRIES**

Danish pastry was actually created by a French baker more than 350 years ago. He forgot to knead butter into his bread dough and attempted to cover the mistake by folding in softened butter. This rich, flaky pastry is now popular worldwide for breakfasts, desserts and snacks. The dough may be shaped in a variety of ways and is usually filled with jam, fruit, cream or marzipan.

DOUGH FOR DANISH PASTRIES

Yield: 36 Pastries   **Method:** Rolled-in dough

Active dry yeast	½ oz.	15 g
All-purpose flour	1 lb. 4 oz.	600 g
Granulated sugar	4 oz.	120 g
Water, warm	4 fl. oz.	120 ml
Milk, warm	4 fl. oz.	120 ml
Eggs, room temperature	2	2
Salt	1 tsp.	5 ml
Vanilla extract	1 tsp.	5 ml
Cinnamon, ground	½ tsp.	2 ml
Unsalted butter, melted	1½ oz.	45 g
Unsalted butter, cold	1 lb.	450 g
Egg wash	as needed	as needed

1 Kneading the cold butter with the flour.

2 Spreading the butter over two thirds of the rolled-out dough.

3 Folding the dough in thirds to cover the butter.

4 Rolling out the dough.

5 Folding the dough in thirds to complete a turn.

6 Cutting rectangles of Danish dough.

7 Piping cream cheese filling onto Danish dough.

8 Shaping snails from Danish dough.

1 In a large bowl, stir together the yeast and 12 ounces (340 grams) of the flour. Add the sugar, water, milk, eggs, salt, vanilla, cinnamon and melted butter. Stir until well combined.

2 Add the remaining flour gradually, kneading the dough by hand or with a mixer fitted with a dough hook. Knead until the dough is smooth and only slightly tacky to the touch, approximately 2 to 3 minutes.

3 Place the dough in a bowl that has been lightly dusted with flour. Cover and refrigerate for 1 to 1½ hours.

4 Prepare the remaining butter while the dough is chilling. Start by sprinkling flour over the work surface and placing the cold butter on the flour. Then pound the butter with a rolling pin until the butter softens. Using a pastry

scraper or the heel of your hand, knead the butter and flour until the mixture is spreadable. The butter should still be cold. If it begins to melt, refrigerate it until firm. Keep the butter chilled until the dough is ready.

5 On a lightly floured surface, roll out the dough into a large rectangle, about ½ inch (1.2 centimeters) thick. Brush away any excess flour.

6 Spread the chilled butter evenly over two-thirds of the dough. Fold the unbuttered third over the center, then fold the buttered third over the top. Press the edges together to seal in the butter.

7 Roll the dough into a rectangle about 12 inches × 18 inches (30 centimeters × 45 centimeters). Fold the dough in thirds as before. This rolling and folding (called a turn) must be done a total of six times. Chill the dough between turns as necessary. After the final turn, wrap the dough well and refrigerate for at least 4 hours or overnight.

8 Shape and fill the danish dough as desired. Place the shaped pastries on a paper-lined baking sheet and allow to proof for approximately 15 to 20 minutes.

9 Brush the pastries with egg wash and sprinkle lightly with sugar if desired. Bake at 400°F (200°C) for 5 minutes. Decrease the oven temperature to 350°F (170°C) and bake until light brown, approximately 12 to 15 minutes.

Approximate values per pastry, without filling: **Calories** 85, **Total fat** 1.5 g, **Saturated fat** 0 g, **Cholesterol** 15 mg, **Sodium** 65 mg, **Total carbohydrates** 15.5 g, **Protein** 2 g

FILLINGS FOR DANISH PASTRIES

CREAM CHEESE FILLING

Yield: 26 oz. (780 g)

Cream cheese	1 lb.	450 g
Granulated sugar	8 oz.	225 g
Salt	¼ tsp.	1 ml
Vanilla extract	1 tsp.	5 ml
Flour	2 Tbsp.	30 ml
Egg yolk	1	1
Lemon extract	1 tsp.	5 ml
Lemon zest	2 tsp.	10 ml

1 Beat the cream cheese until light and fluffy. Stir in the remaining ingredients.

Approximate values per 1-oz. (30-g) serving: **Calories** 100, **Total fat** 6 g, **Saturated fat** 4 g, **Cholesterol** 25 mg, **Sodium** 75 mg, **Total carbohydrates** 10 g, **Protein** 1 g

ALMOND CREAM FILLING

Yield: 2 lb. (900 g)

Almond paste	20 oz.	600 g
Unsalted butter, soft	8 oz.	240 g
Salt	½ tsp.	2 ml
Vanilla	2 tsp.	10 ml
Egg whites	4	4

1 Blend the almond paste and butter until smooth. Add the salt and vanilla, and then the egg whites. Blend well.

Approximate values per 1-oz. (30-g) serving: **Calories** 130, **Total fat** 11 g, **Saturated fat** 4 g, **Cholesterol** 15 mg, **Sodium** 45 mg, **Total carbohydrates** 9 g, **Protein** 2 g

Yield: 2 lb. (900 g)

Dried apricots	8 oz.	225 g
Orange juice	1 pt.	450 ml
Granulated sugar	6 oz.	180 g
Salt	¼ tsp.	1 ml
Unsalted butter	2 oz.	60 g

1 Place the apricots and orange juice in a small saucepan. Cover and simmer until the apricots are very tender, approximately 25 minutes. Stir in the sugar and salt. When the sugar is dissolved, add the butter and remove from the heat.

2 Purée the mixture in a blender until smooth. Cool completely before using.

Approximate values per 1-oz. (30-g) serving: **Calories** 60, **Total fat** 1.5 g, **Saturated fat** 1 g, **Cholesterol** 5 mg, **Sodium** 20 mg, **Total carbohydrates** 13 g, **Protein** 0 g, **Vitamin A** 20%, **Vitamin C** 15%, **Claims**—low fat; low sodium; good source of vitamins A and C

THE PIE IS AN ENGLISH INSTITUTION WHICH, PLANTED ON AMERICAN SOIL, FORTHWITH RAN RAMPANT AND BURST FORTH INTO AN UNTOLD VARIETY OF GENERA AND SPECIES.

—*Harriet Beecher Stowe, American novelist (1811–1896)*

32

PIES, PASTRIES AND COOKIES

HOUSTON COMMUNITY COLLEGE, Houston, TX
Pastry Chef Eddy Van Damme

Mention pastries to diners and most conjure up images of buttery dough baked to crisp flaky perfection and filled or layered with rich cream, ripe fruit or smooth custard. Mention pastries to novice chefs and most conjure up images of sophisticated, complex and intimidating work. Although the diners are correct, the novice chefs are not. Pastry making is the art of creating containers for various fillings. Taken one step at a time, most pastries are nothing more than selected building blocks or components assembled in a variety of ways to create traditional or unique desserts.

Perhaps the most important (and versatile) building block is the dough. Pastries can be made with flaky dough, mealy dough, sweet dough, puff pastry, éclair dough, meringue or phyllo. See Table 32.1. Because pies, tarts and cookies are constructed from some of these same doughs (principally pie dough and sweet dough), they, as well as pie fillings, are discussed in the section on pies and tarts; puff pastry, éclair paste and baked meringue are discussed in the section on classic pastries. The cream, custard and mousse fillings used in some of the recipes at the end of this chapter are discussed in Chapter 34, Custards, Creams, Frozen Desserts and Dessert Sauces. Cakes and frostings are covered in Chapter 33, Cakes and Frostings.

▶ PIES AND TARTS

A **pie** is composed of a sweet or savory filling in a baked crust. It can be open-faced (without a top crust) or, more typically, topped with a full or lattice crust. A pie is generally made in a round, slope-sided pan and cut into wedges for service. A **tart** is similar to a pie except it is made in a shallow, straight-sided pan, often with fluted edges. A tart can be almost any shape; round, square, rectangular and petal shapes are the most common. It is usually open-faced and derives much of its beauty from an attractive arrangement of glazed fruit, piped cream or chocolate decorations.

CRUSTS

Pie crusts and tart shells can be made from several types of doughs or crumbs. **Flaky dough, mealy dough** and **crumbs** are best for pie crusts; **sweet dough** is usually used for tart shells. A pie crust or tart shell can be shaped and completely baked before filling (known as **baked blind**) or filled and baked simultaneously with the filling.

FLAKY AND MEALY DOUGHS

Flaky and mealy pie doughs are quick, easy and versatile. Flaky dough, sometimes known as **pâte brisée,** takes its name from its final baked texture. It is best for pie top crusts and lattice coverings and may be used for prebaked shells that will be filled with a cooled filling shortly before service. Mealy dough takes its name from its raw texture. It is used whenever a soggy crust would be a problem (for example, as the bottom crust of a custard or fruit pie) because it is

Table 32.1 CLASSIFICATION OF PASTRY DOUGHS

DOUGH	FRENCH NAME	CHARACTERISTICS AFTER BAKING	USE
Flaky dough	Pâte brisée	Very flaky; not sweet	Prebaked pie shells; pie top crusts
Mealy dough	Pâte brisée	Moderately flaky; not sweet	Custard, cream or fruit pie crusts; quiche crusts
Sweet dough	Pâte sucrée	Very rich; crisp; not flaky	Tart and tartlet shells
Éclair paste	Pâte à choux	Hollow with crisp exterior	Cream puffs; éclairs; savory products
Puff pastry	Pâte feuilletée	Rich but not sweet; hundreds of light, flaky layers	Tart and pastry cases; cookies; layered pastries; savory products
Meringue	Meringue	Sweet; light; crisp or soft depending on preparation	Topping or icing; baked as a shell or component for layered desserts; cookies
Phyllo	Phyllo	Very thin, crisp, flaky layers; bland	Middle Eastern pastries and savory dishes, especially hors d'oeuvre; baklava

sturdier and resists sogginess better than flaky dough. Both flaky and mealy doughs are too delicate for tarts that will be removed from the pan for service. Sweet dough, described later, is better for these types of tarts.

Flaky and mealy doughs contain little or no sugar and can be prepared from the same formula with only a slight variation in mixing method. For both types of dough, a cold fat, such as butter or shortening, is cut into the flour. The amount of flakiness in the baked crust depends on the size of the fat particles in the dough. The larger the pieces of fat, the flakier the crust will be. This is because the flakes are actually the sides of fat pockets created during baking by the melting fat and steam. When preparing flaky dough, the fat is left in larger pieces, about the size of peas or peanuts. When preparing mealy dough, the fat is blended in more thoroughly, until the mixture resembles coarse cornmeal. Because the resulting fat pockets are smaller, the crust is less flaky.

The type of fat used affects both the dough's flavor and flakiness. Butter contributes a delicious flavor, but does not produce as flaky a crust as other fats. Butter is also more difficult to work with than other fats because of its lower melting point and its tendency to become brittle when chilled. All-purpose vegetable shortening produces a flaky crust but contributes nothing to its flavor. The flakiest pastry is made with lard. Because some people dislike its flavor for sweet pies, lard is more often used for pâté en croûte or other savory preparations. Some chefs prefer to use a combination of butter with either shortening or lard. Oil is not an appropriate substitute as it disperses too thoroughly through the dough; when baked, the crust will be extremely fragile but without any flakiness.

After the fat is cut into the flour, water or milk is added to form a soft dough. Less water is needed for mealy dough because more flour is already in contact with the fat, reducing its ability to absorb liquid. Cold water is normally used for both flaky and mealy doughs. The water should be well chilled to prevent softening the fat. Milk may be used to increase richness and nutritional value. It will produce a darker, less crisp crust, however. If dry milk powder is used, it should be dissolved in water first.

Hand mixing is best for small to moderate quantities of dough. You retain better control over the procedure when you can feel the fat being incorporated. It is very difficult to make flaky dough with an electric mixer or food processor, as machines tend to cut the fat in too thoroughly. Overmixing develops too much gluten, making the dough elastic and difficult to use. If an electric mixer must be used for large quantities, use the paddle attachment at the lowest speed and be sure the fat is well chilled, even frozen.

OF TARTS AND TORTES

The names given to desserts can be rather confusing. One country or region calls an item a *torte* while another region calls the same item a *gâteau*. The following definitions are based on classic terms. You will, no doubt, encounter variations depending on your location and the training of those with whom you work.

Cake—In American and British usages, *cake* refers to a broad range of pastries, including layer cakes, coffee cakes and gâteaux. *Cake* may refer to almost everything that is baked, tender, sweet and sometimes frosted. But to the French, *le cake* is a loaf-shaped fruitcake, similar to an American pound cake with the addition of fruit, nuts and rum.

Gâteau—(pl. *gâteaux*) To the French, *gâteau* refers to various pastry items made with puff pastry, éclair paste, short dough or sweet dough. In America, *gâteau* often refers to any cake-type dessert.

Pastry—*Pastry* may refer to a group of doughs made primarily with flour, water and fat. *Pastry* can also refer to foods made with these doughs or to a large variety of fancy baked goods.

Tart—A *tart* is a pastry shell filled with sweet or savory ingredients. Tarts have straight, shallow sides and are usually prepared open-face. In France and Britain, the term **flan** is sometimes used to refer to the same items. A **tartlet** is a small, individual-sized tart.

Torte—In Central and Eastern European countries, a *torte* (pl. *torten*) is a rich cake in which all or part of the flour is replaced with finely chopped nuts or bread crumbs. Other cultures refer to any round sweet cake as a torte.

▶ PROCEDURE FOR PREPARING FLAKY AND MEALY DOUGHS

1 Sift flour, salt and sugar (if used) together in a large bowl.

2 Cut the fat into the flour.

3 Gradually add a cold liquid, mixing gently until the dough holds together. Do not overmix.

4 Cover the dough with plastic wrap and chill thoroughly before using.

5 Remember that rerolled scraps will be tough and elastic.

RECIPE 32.1   **BASIC PIE DOUGH**

Yield: 5 lb. (2.2 kg)

Pastry flour	3 lb.	1300 g
Salt	4 tsp.	20 ml
Granulated sugar (optional)	2 oz.	60 g
All-purpose shortening	1 lb. 8 oz.	680 g
Water, cold*	8 fl. oz.	250 ml

1 Sift the flour, salt and sugar together in a large bowl.

2 Cut the shortening into the flour mixture until the desired consistency (flaky or mealy) is reached.

3 Gradually add the cold water, mixing gently until the dough holds together. Do not overmix or add too much water.

4 Cover the dough with plastic wrap and chill thoroughly before using.

*The amount of water needed varies depending upon the manner in which the fat is incorporated. Mealy dough will probably not require this entire amount.

Approximate values per 1-oz. (30-g) serving: **Calories** 140, **Total fat** 9 g, **Saturated fat** 2.5 g, **Cholesterol** 0 mg, **Sodium** 120 mg, **Total carbohydrates** 14 g, **Protein** 1 g, **Claims**—no cholesterol; low sodium

1 Cutting the fat into the flour coarsely for flaky dough.

2 Cutting the fat into the flour finely for mealy dough.

3 The finished dough.

SWEET DOUGH

Sweet dough or **pâte sucrée** is a rich, nonflaky dough used for sweet tart shells. It is sturdier than flaky or mealy dough because it contains egg yolks and the fat is blended in thoroughly. It is also more cookielike than classic pie dough and has the rich flavor of butter. It creates a crisp but tender crust and is excellent for tartlets as well as for straight-sided tarts that will be removed from their pans before service. The raw dough may be kept refrigerated for up to two weeks or frozen up to three months.

▶ PROCEDURE FOR PREPARING SWEET DOUGH

1 Cream softened butter. Add sugar and beat until the mixture is light and fluffy.

2 Slowly add eggs, blending well.

3 Slowly add flour, mixing only until incorporated. Overmixing toughens the dough.

4 Cover the dough with plastic wrap and chill thoroughly before using.

5 Scraps may be rerolled once or twice, provided the dough is still cool, nongreasy and pliable. If too much gluten develops, the crust will shrink and toughen.

SWEET DOUGH · RECIPE 32.2

Yield: 7 lb. (3.1 kg)

Unsalted butter, softened	1 lb. 8 oz.	675 g
Powdered sugar	1 lb. 5 oz.	580 g
Egg yolks	1 lb.	450 g
Whole eggs	2	2
All-purpose flour	3 lb. 8 oz.	1600 g

1 Cream the butter and powdered sugar in a large mixer bowl using the paddle attachment.

2 Combine the egg yolks and whole eggs. Slowly add the eggs to the creamed butter. Mix until smooth and free of lumps, scraping down the sides of the bowl as needed.

3 With the mixer on low speed, slowly add the flour to the butter-and-egg mixture. Mix only until incorporated; do not overmix. The dough should be firm, smooth and not sticky.

1 Mixing sweet dough.

2 The finished sweet dough.

4 Dust a half-sheet pan with flour. Pack the dough into the pan evenly. Wrap well in plastic wrap and chill until firm.

5 Work with a small portion of the chilled dough when shaping tart shells or other products.

Approximate values per 1-oz. (30-g) serving: **Calories** 120, **Total fat** 5 g, **Saturated fat** 3 g, **Cholesterol** 15 mg, **Sodium** 0 mg, **Total carbohydrates** 16 g, **Protein** 2 g, **Vitamin A** 4%

SHAPING CRUSTS

Crusts are shaped by rolling out the dough to fit into a pie pan or tart shell (mold) or to sit on top of fillings. Mealy, flaky and sweet doughs are all easier to roll out and work with if well chilled, as chilling keeps the fat firm and prevents stickiness. When rolling and shaping the dough, work on a clean, flat surface (wood or marble is best). Lightly dust the work surface, rolling pin and dough with pastry flour before starting to roll the dough. Also, work only with a manageable amount at a time: usually one crust's worth for a pie or standard-sized tart or enough for 10 to 12 tartlet shells.

Roll out the dough from the center, working toward the edges. Periodically, lift the dough gently and rotate it. This keeps the dough from sticking and helps produce an even thickness. If the dough sticks to the rolling pin or work surface, sprinkle on a bit more flour. Too much flour, however, makes the crust dry and crumbly and causes gray streaks.

▶ PROCEDURE FOR ROLLING AND SHAPING DOUGH FOR PIE CRUSTS AND TART SHELLS

1 A typical pie crust or tart shell should be rolled to a thickness of approximately ⅛ inch (3 millimeters); it should also be at least 2 inches (5 centimeters) larger in diameter than the baking pan.

2 Carefully roll the dough up onto a rolling pin. Position the pin over the pie pan or tart shell and unroll the dough, easing it into the pan or shell. Trim the edges as necessary and flute as desired. Bake or fill as desired.

▶ PROCEDURE FOR ROLLING AND SHAPING DOUGH FOR TARTLET SHELLS

1 A typical crust for tartlets should be approximately ⅛ inch (3 millimeters) thick.

2 Roll the dough out as described earlier. Then roll the dough up onto the rolling pin.

1 Lay out a single layer of tartlet shells. Unroll the dough over the shells, pressing the dough gently into each one.

2 Roll the rolling pin over the top of the shells. The edge of the shells will cut the dough. Be sure the dough is pressed against the sides of each shell. Bake or fill as desired.

▶ PROCEDURE FOR ROLLING AND SHAPING DOUGH FOR TOP CRUSTS

1 Roll the dough out as before, making the circle large enough to hang over the pan's edge. The dough may be lifted into place by rolling it onto the rolling pin, as with the bottom crust. Slits or designs can be cut from the top crust to allow steam to escape.

2 Seal the top crust to the bottom crust with egg wash or water. Crimp as desired.

▶ PROCEDURE FOR ROLLING AND SHAPING DOUGH FOR LATTICE CRUSTS

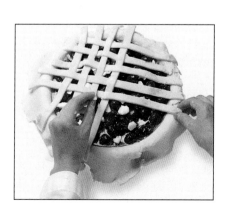

1 Roll the dough out as before. Using a ruler as a guide, cut even strips of the desired width, typically ½ inch (1.2 centimeters).

2 Using an over-under-over pattern, weave the strips together on top of the filling. Be sure the strips are evenly spaced for an attractive result. Crimp the lattice strips to the bottom crust to seal. Streusel topping is also used for some pies, particularly fruit pies. A standard recipe is given in Chapter 30, Quick Breads.

BAKING CRUSTS

Pie crusts can be filled and then baked, or baked and then filled. Unfilled baked crusts can be stored at room temperature for two to three days or wrapped in plastic wrap and frozen for as long as three months.

▶ PROCEDURE FOR BAKING UNFILLED CRUSTS (BAKED BLIND)

1 Roll the dough out to the desired thickness and line the pie pan or tart mold. Add a crimped edge or border if desired.

2 **Dock** the dough with a fork.

▶ **docking** pricking small holes in an unbaked dough or crust to allow steam to escape and to prevent the dough from rising when baked

3 Cover the dough with baking parchment or greased aluminum foil (greased side down). Press the paper or foil against the edge or walls of the shell. Allow a portion of the paper or foil to extend above the pan.

4 Fill the pan with baking weights or dry rice or beans. These will prevent the crust from rising.

5 Bake the weighted crust at 350°F (180°C) for 10 to 15 minutes.

6 Remove the weights and paper and return the crust to the oven. Bake until golden brown and fully cooked, approximately 10 to 15 minutes.

7 Allow to cool, then fill as desired or store.

Making a crumb crust.

CRUMB CRUSTS

A quick and tasty bottom crust can be made from finely ground cookie crumbs moistened with melted butter. Crumb crusts can be used for unbaked pies such as those with cream or chiffon fillings, or they can be baked with their fillings, as with cheesecakes.

Chocolate cookies, graham crackers, gingersnaps, vanilla wafers and macaroons are popular choices for crumb crusts. Some breakfast cereals such as corn flakes or bran flakes are also used. Ground nuts and spices can be added for flavor. Whatever cookies or other ingredients are used, be sure they are ground to a fine, even crumb. If packaged crumbs are unavailable, a food processor, blender or rolling pin can be used.

The typical ratio for a crumb crust is one part melted butter, two parts sugar and four parts crumbs. For example, 8 ounces (250 grams) graham crackers mixed with 4 ounces (120 grams) sugar and 2 ounces (60 grams) melted butter produces enough crust to line one 9- or 10-inch (22- or 25-centimeter) pan. The amount of sugar may need to be adjusted depending on the type of crumbs used, however; for example, chocolate sandwich cookies need less sugar than graham crackers. If the mixture is too dry to stick together, gradually add more melted butter. Press the mixture into the bottom of the pan and chill or bake it before filling.

FILLINGS

Fillings make pies and tarts distinctive and flavorful. Four types of fillings are discussed here: **cream, fruit, custard** and **chiffon.** There is no one correct presentation or filling-and-crust combination. The apples in an apple pie, for example, may be sliced, seasoned and topped with streusel; caramelized, puréed and blended with cream; chopped and covered with a flaky dough lattice; or poached, arranged over pastry cream and brushed with a shiny glaze. Only an understanding of the fundamental techniques for making fillings—and some imagination—ensures success.

CREAM FILLINGS

A cream filling is really nothing more than a flavored pastry cream. Pastry cream is a type of starch-thickened egg custard discussed in Chapter 34, Custards, Creams, Frozen Desserts and Dessert Sauces. When used as a pie filling, pastry cream should be thickened with cornstarch so that it is firm enough to hold its shape when sliced. Popular flavors are chocolate, banana, coconut and lemon.

A cream filling is fully cooked on the stove top, so a prebaked or crumb crust is needed. The crust can be filled while the filling is still warm, or the filling can be chilled and piped into the crust later. A cream pie is often topped with meringue, which is then browned quickly in an oven or under a broiler.

BASIC CREAM PIE

RECIPE 32.3

Yield: 2 Pies, 9 in. (22 cm)   **Method:** Cream Filling

Granulated sugar	1 lb.	500 g
Milk	2 qt.	2 lt
Egg yolks	8	8
Eggs	4	4
Cornstarch	5 oz.	150 g
Unsalted butter	4 oz.	120 g
Vanilla extract	1 fl. oz.	30 ml
Flaky pie dough shells, baked	2	2
Meringue	as needed	as needed

1 Filling a baked pie shell with chocolate custard.

1 In a heavy saucepan, dissolve 8 ounces (250 grams) of the sugar in the milk. Bring just to a boil.

2 Meanwhile, whisk the egg yolks and whole eggs together in a large bowl.

3 Sift the cornstarch and the remaining sugar onto the eggs. Whisk until smooth.

4 Temper the egg mixture with approximately half of the hot milk. Stir the warmed egg mixture back into the remaining milk and return it to a boil, stirring constantly.

5 Stirring constantly and vigorously, allow the cream to boil until thick, approximately 30 seconds. Remove from the heat and stir in the butter and vanilla. Stir until the butter is melted and incorporated.

6 Pour the cream into the pie shells.

7 The pies can be topped with meringue while the filling is still warm. The meringue is then lightly browned in a 425°F (210°C) oven. Chill the pies for service.

2 Topping with meringue.

Variations: *Chocolate Cream Pie*—Melt 12 ounces (340 grams) bittersweet chocolate. Fold the melted chocolate into the hot cream after adding the butter and vanilla.

Banana Cream Pie—Layer 12 ounces (340 grams) sliced bananas (about three medium bananas) into the baked shell with the warm cream. Do not purée the bananas, as this will make the filling runny.

Coconut Cream Pie I—Substitute 12 fluid ounces (340 milliliters) of cream of coconut for 12 fluid ounces (340 milliliters) of milk and 4 ounces (120 grams) of sugar. Top the pie with meringue and shredded coconut.

Coconut Cream Pie II—Stir 8 ounces (250 grams) toasted coconut into the warm cream.

Approximate values per serving: **Calories** 220, **Total fat** 9 g, **Saturated fat** 5 g, **Cholesterol** 130 mg, **Sodium** 55 mg, **Total carbohydrates** 29 g, **Protein** 5 g, **Vitamin A** 10%

FRUIT FILLINGS

A fruit filling is a mixture of fruit, fruit juice, spices and sugar thickened with a starch. Apple, cherry, blueberry and peach are traditional favorites. The fruit can be fresh, frozen or canned. (See Chapter 25, Fruits, for comments on selecting the best fruits for fillings.) The starch can be flour, cornstarch, tapioca or a packaged commercial instant or pregelatinized starch. The ingredients for a fruit filling are most often combined using one of three methods: **cooked fruit, cooked juice** or **baked.**

Cooked Fruit Fillings

The cooked fruit filling method is often used when the fruits need to be softened by cooking (for example, apples or rhubarb) or are naturally rather dry. A cooked fruit filling should be combined with a prebaked or crumb crust.

▶ PROCEDURE FOR PREPARING COOKED FRUIT FILLINGS

1 Combine the fruit, sugar and some juice or liquid in a heavy, nonreactive saucepan and bring to a boil.

2 Dissolve the starch (usually cornstarch) in a cold liquid, then add to the boiling fruit.

3 Stirring constantly, cook the fruit-and-starch mixture until the starch is clear and the mixture is thickened.

4 Add any other flavorings and any acidic ingredients such as lemon juice. Stir to blend.

5 Remove from the heat and cool before filling a prebaked pie or crumb crust.

RECIPE 32.4 | **APPLE-CRANBERRY PIE**

Yield: 1 Pie, 9 in. (22 cm) | **Method:** Cooked Fruit Filling

Fresh tart apples such as Granny Smiths, peeled, cored and cut in 1-in. (2.5-cm) cubes	1 lb.	450 g
Brown sugar	4 oz.	120 g
Granulated sugar	4 oz.	120 g
Orange zest	1 Tbsp.	15 ml
Cinnamon, ground	1 tsp.	5 ml
Salt	1/4 tsp.	1 ml
Cornstarch	2 tsp.	10 ml
Orange juice	3 fl. oz.	90 ml

Fresh cranberries, rinsed	1 pt.	500 ml
Mealy dough pie shell, partially baked	1	1
Streusel Topping (page 954)	4 oz.	120 g

1 Combine the apples, brown sugar, granulated sugar, orange zest, cinnamon and salt in a large, nonreactive saucepan.

2 Dissolve the cornstarch in the orange juice and add it to the apples.

3 Cover and simmer until the apples begin to soften, stirring occasionally. Add the cranberries, cover and continue simmering until the cranberries begin to soften, approximately 2 minutes.

4 Place the apple-cranberry mixture in the pie shell and cover with the prepared streusel topping. Bake at 400°F (200°C) until the filling is bubbling hot and the topping is lightly browned, approximately 20 minutes.

Variation: *Apple-Rhubarb Pie*—Substitute cleaned rhubarb, cut into 1-inch (2.5-centimeter) chunks, for the cranberries. Add ⅛ teaspoon (0.5 milliliter) nutmeg.

Approximate values per serving: **Calories** 290, **Total fat** 8 g, **Saturated fat** 2 g, **Cholesterol** 0 mg, **Sodium** 200 mg, **Total carbohydrates** 53 g, **Protein** 2 g, **Claims**—no cholesterol; good source of fiber

Cooked Juice Fillings

The cooked juice filling method is used for juicy fruits such as berries, especially when they are canned or frozen. This method is also recommended for delicate fruits that cannot withstand cooking, such as strawberries, pineapple and blueberries. Because only the juice is cooked, the fruit retains its shape, color and flavor better. A cooked juice filling should be combined with a prebaked or crumb crust.

▶ PROCEDURE FOR PREPARING COOKED JUICE FILLINGS

1 Drain the juice from the fruit. Measure the juice and add water if necessary to create the desired volume.

2 Combine the liquid with sugar in a nonreactive saucepan and bring to a boil.

3 Dissolve the starch in cold water, then add it to the boiling liquid. Cook until the starch is clear and the juice is thickened.

4 Add any other flavoring ingredients.

5 Pour the thickened juice over the fruit and stir gently.

6 Cool the filling before placing it in a precooked pie shell.

 BLUEBERRY PIE FILLING RECIPE 32.5

Yield: 8 lb. (3.6 kg) **Method:** Cooked Juice Filling

Canned blueberries, #10 can, unsweetened	1	1
Granulated sugar	1 lb. 12 oz.	840 g
Cornstarch	4½ oz.	135 g
Water	8 fl. oz.	225 ml
Cinnamon, ground	½ tsp.	2 ml
Lemon juice	2 Tbsp.	30 ml
Lemon zest, grated fine	1 Tbsp.	15 ml

1 Drain the juice from the canned blueberries, reserving both the fruit and the juice.

2 Measure the juice and, if necessary, add enough water to provide 1 quart (1 liter) of liquid. Bring to a boil, add the sugar and stir until dissolved.

3 Dissolve the cornstarch in 8 fluid ounces (225 milliliters) of water.

4 Add the cornstarch to the boiling juice and return to a boil. Cook until the mixture thickens and clears. Remove from the heat.

5 Add the cinnamon, lemon juice, lemon zest and reserved blueberries. Stir gently to coat the fruit with the glaze.

6 Allow the filling to cool to room temperature, then use it to fill prebaked pie shells or other pastry items.

Approximate values per 1-oz. (30-g) serving: **Calories** 40, **Total fat** 0 g, **Saturated fat** 0 g, **Cholesterol** 0 mg, **Sodium** 0 mg, **Total carbohydrates** 10 g, **Protein** 0 g, **Claims**—fat free; no cholesterol; no sodium; low calorie

Baked Fruit Fillings

The baked fruit filling method is a traditional technique in which the fruit, sugar, flavorings and starch are combined in an unbaked shell. The dough and filling are then baked simultaneously. Results are not always consistent with this technique, however, as thickening is difficult to control.

▶ PROCEDURE FOR PREPARING BAKED FRUIT FILLINGS

1 Combine the starch, spices and sugar.

2 Peel, core, cut and drain the fruit as desired or as directed in the recipe.

3 Toss the fruit with the starch mixture, coating well.

4 Add a portion of juice to moisten the fruit. Small lumps of butter are also often added.

5 Fill an unbaked shell with the fruit mixture. Cover with a top crust, lattice or streusel and bake.

RECIPE 32.6

CHERRY PIE

Dotting the cherry filling with butter.

Yield: 2 Pies, 9 in. (22 cm) **Method:** Baked Fruit Filling

Tapioca	1½ oz.	45 g
Salt	1 pinch	1 pinch
Granulated sugar	1 lb.	450 g
Almond extract	½ tsp.	2 ml
Canned pitted cherries, drained, liquid reserved	3 lb.	1.3 kg
Mealy dough pie shells, unbaked	2	2
Unsalted butter	1 oz.	30 g
Egg wash	as needed	as needed
Sanding sugar	as needed	as needed

1 Stir the tapioca, salt and granulated sugar together. Add the almond extract and cherries.

2 Stir in up to 8 fluid ounces (250 milliliters) of the liquid drained from the cherries, adding enough liquid to moisten the mixture thoroughly.

3 Allow the filling to stand for 30 minutes. Then stir gently and place the filling in the unbaked pie shells.

4 Cut the butter into small pieces. Dot the filling with the butter.

5 Place a top crust or a lattice crust over the filling; seal and flute the edges. If using a full top crust, cut several slits in the dough to allow steam to escape. Brush the top crust or lattice with an egg wash and sprinkle with sanding sugar.

6 Place on a preheated sheet pan and bake at 400°F (200°C) for 50 to 60 minutes.

Approximate values per ⅛-pie serving: **Calories** 340, **Total fat** 9 g, **Saturated fat** 3 g, **Cholesterol** 5 mg, **Sodium** 170 mg, **Total carbohydrates** 63 g, **Protein** 2 g

CUSTARD FILLINGS

A custard pie has a soft filling that bakes along with the crust. Popular examples include pumpkin, egg custard and pecan pies. As explained in Chapter 34, Custards, Creams, Frozen Desserts and Dessert Sauces, custards are liquids thickened by coagulated egg proteins. To make a custard pie, an uncooked liquid containing eggs is poured into a pie shell. When baked, the egg proteins coagulate, firming and setting the filling.

The procedure for making custard pies is simple: Combine the ingredients and bake. But there is often a problem: baking the bottom crust completely without overcooking the filling. For the best results, start baking the pie near the bottom of a hot oven at 400°F (200°C). After 10 minutes, lower the heat to 325°F–350°F (160°C–180°C) to finish cooking the filling slowly.

To determine the doneness of a custard pie:

1 Shake the pie gently. It is done if it is no longer liquid. The center should show only a slight movement.

2 Insert a thin knife about 1 inch (2.5 centimeters) from the center. The filling is done if the knife comes out clean.

CONVENIENCE PRODUCTS

Prepared or canned pie fillings are available in a variety of fruit and custard flavors. These products offer convenience and the ability to serve fruit pies out of season. The ratio of fruit to pregelled liquid varies greatly from brand to brand, however. Most commercial fillings are stabilized to permit any additional cooking needed to assemble the final product. Shelf life tends to be extremely long, often without the need for refrigeration. Dry custard mixes are also available, needing only the addition of water or milk to produce a cream pie filling.

PUMPKIN PIE

RECIPE 32.7

Yield: 4 Pies, 9 in. (22 cm)   **Method:** Custard Filling

Eggs, beaten slightly	4	4
Pumpkin purée	2 lb.	900 g
Granulated sugar	12 oz.	360 g
Salt	1 tsp.	5 ml
Nutmeg, ground	½ tsp.	2 ml
Cloves, ground	½ tsp.	2 ml
Cinnamon, ground	2 tsp.	10 ml
Ginger, ground	1 tsp.	5 ml
Evaporated milk	24 fl. oz.	720 ml
Flaky dough pie shells, unbaked	4	4

1 Combine the eggs and pumpkin. Blend in the sugar.

2 Add the salt and spices, and then the evaporated milk. Whisk until completely blended and smooth.

3 Allow the filling to rest for 15 to 20 minutes before filling the pie shells. This allows the starch in the pumpkin to begin absorbing liquid, making it less likely to separate after baking.

4 Pour the filling into the unbaked pie shells. Place in the oven on a preheated sheet pan at 400°F (200°C). Bake for 15 minutes. Lower the oven temperature to 350°F (180°C) and bake until a knife inserted near the center comes out clean, approximately 40 to 50 minutes.

Approximate values per ⅛-pie serving: **Calories** 210, **Total fat** 10 g, **Saturated fat** 2.5 g, **Cholesterol** 30 mg, **Sodium** 230 mg, **Total carbohydrates** 25 g, **Protein** 4 g, **Vitamin A** 6%

CHIFFON FILLINGS

A chiffon filling is created by adding gelatin to a stirred custard or a fruit purée. Whipped egg whites are then folded into the mixture. The filling is placed in a prebaked crust and chilled until firm. These preparations are the same as those for chiffons, mousses and Bavarians discussed in Chapter 34, Custards, Creams, Frozen Desserts and Dessert Sauces.

Table 32.2 SUGGESTIONS FOR ASSEMBLING PIES

FILLING	CRUST	TOPPING	GARNISH
Vanilla or lemon cream	Prebaked flaky dough or crumb	None, meringue or whipped cream	Crumbs from the crust
Chocolate cream	Prebaked flaky dough or crumb	None, meringue or whipped cream	Crumbs from the crust or shaved chocolate
Banana cream	Prebaked flaky dough	Meringue or whipped cream	Dried banana chips
Coconut cream	Prebaked flaky dough	Meringue or whipped cream	Shredded coconut
Fresh fruit	Unbaked mealy dough, or sweet dough if shallow tart	Lattice, full crust or streusel	Sanding sugar or cut-out designs if lattice or top crust is used
Canned or frozen fruit	Unbaked mealy dough	Lattice, full crust or streusel	Sanding sugar or cut-out designs if lattice or top crust is used
Chiffon or mousse	Crumb or prebaked, sweetened flaky dough	None or whipped cream	Crumbs, fruit or shaved chocolate
Custard (e.g., pecan or pumpkin)	Unbaked mealy dough	None	Whipped cream
Vanilla pastry cream	Prebaked sweet dough	Fresh fruit	Glaze

ASSEMBLING PIES AND TARTS

The various types of pie fillings can be used to fill almost any crust or shell, provided the crust is prebaked as necessary. The filling can then be topped with meringue or whipped cream as desired. Garnishes such as toasted coconut, cookie crumbs and chocolate curls are often added for appearance and flavor.

Table 32.3 TROUBLESHOOTING CHART FOR PIES

PROBLEM	CAUSE	SOLUTION
Crust shrinks	Overmixing	Adjust mixing technique
	Overworking dough	Adjust rolling technique
	Not enough fat	Adjust formula
Soggy crust	Wrong dough used	Use mealier dough
	Oven temperature too low	Adjust oven
	Not baked long enough	Adjust baking time
Crumbly crust	Not enough liquid	Adjust formula
	Too much fat	Adjust formula
Tough crust	Not enough fat	Adjust formula
	Overmixing	Adjust mixing technique
Runny filling	Insufficient starch	Adjust formula
	Starch insufficiently cooked	Allow starch to gelatinize completely
Lumpy cream filling	Starch not incorporated properly	Stir filling while cooking
	Filling overcooked	Adjust cooking time
Custard filling "weeps" or separates	Too many eggs	Reduce egg content or add starch to the filling
	Eggs overcooked	Reduce oven temperature or baking time

STORING PIES AND TARTS

Pies and tarts filled with cream or custard must be kept refrigerated to retard bacterial growth.

Unbaked fruit pies or unbaked pie shells may be frozen for up to two months. Freezing baked fruit pies is not recommended, but they may be stored for 2 to 3 days at room temperature or in the refrigerator. Custard, cream and meringue-topped pies should be stored in the refrigerator for no more than 2 to 3 days. They should not be frozen, as the eggs will separate, making the product runny.

▶ CLASSIC PASTRIES

Puff pastry, éclair paste and **meringue** are classic components of French pastries; they are used to create a wide variety of dessert and pastry items. Many combinations are traditional. Once you master the skills necessary to produce these products, however, you will be free to experiment with other flavors and assembly techniques.

PUFF PASTRY

Puff pastry is one of the bakeshop's most elegant and sophisticated products. Also known as **pâte feuilletée,** it is a rich, buttery dough that bakes into hundreds of light, crisp layers.

Puff pastry is used for both sweet and savory preparations. It can be baked and then filled, or filled first and then baked. Puff pastry may be used to wrap beef (for beef Wellington), pâté (for pâté en croûte) or almond cream (for an apple tart). It can be shaped into shells or cases known as vol-au-vents or bouchées and filled with shellfish in a cream sauce or berries in a pastry cream. Puff pastry is essential for napoleons, pithiviers and tartes tatin.

Like croissant and Danish dough (discussed in Chapter 31, Yeast Breads), puff pastry is a rolled-in dough. But unlike those doughs, puff pastry does not contain any yeast or chemical leavening agents. Fat is rolled into the dough in horizontal layers; when baked, the fat melts, separating the dough into layers. The fat's moisture turns into steam, which causes the dough to rise and the layers to further separate.

Butter is the preferred fat because of its flavor and melt-in-the-mouth quality. But butter is rather difficult to work with as it becomes brittle when cold and melts at a relatively low temperature. Therefore, specially formulated puff pastry shortenings are used to compensate for butter's shortcomings. They do not, however, provide the true flavor of butter.

MAKING PUFF PASTRY

The procedure described here for making and folding puff pastry dough is just one of several. All methods, however, depend upon the proper layering of fat and dough through a series of turns to give the pastry its characteristic flakiness and rise.

Some chefs prefer to prepare a dough called *blitz* or *quick puff pastry*. It does not require the extensive rolling and folding procedure used for true puff pastry. Blitz puff pastry is less delicate and flaky but may be perfectly acceptable for some uses. A formula for it is given at the end of this chapter.

▶ PROCEDURE FOR PREPARING PUFF PASTRY

1 Prepare the dough base (**detrempe**) by combining the flour, water, salt and a small amount of fat. Do not overmix. Overmixing results in greater gluten formation, and too much gluten can make the pastry undesirably tough.

CONVENIENCE PRODUCTS

Commercially prepared puff pastry is readily available in unbaked frozen sheets or precut into a variety of shapes. Some convenience doughs, especially those made with butter, provide excellent results. Their expense may be offset by the ability to offer a consistent product at a tiny fraction of the labor cost. Keep these frozen doughs well wrapped to prevent drying and freezer burn, and prepare according to package directions.

Fully baked, ready-to-use éclair paste (pâte à choux) items such as éclair and cream puff shells are also available commercially, in both frozen and shelf-stable forms. These are useful when time or labor cost is a concern; just follow package directions for storage and recrisping. High-quality fillings and glazes can then be added to create excellent finished pastries.

▶ **detrempe** a paste made with flour and water during the first stage of preparing a pastry dough, especially rolled-in doughs

2 Wrap the detrempe and chill for several hours or overnight. This allows the gluten to relax and the flour to absorb the liquid.

3 Shape the butter into a rectangle of even thickness; wrap and chill until ready to use.

4 Allow the detrempe and butter to sit at room temperature until slightly softened and of the same consistency.

5 Roll out the detrempe into a rectangle of even thickness.

6 Place the butter in the center of the dough. Fold the dough around the butter, enclosing it completely.

7 Roll out the block of dough and butter into a long, even rectangle. Roll only at right angles so that the layered structure is not destroyed.

8 Fold the dough like a business letter: Fold the bottom third up toward the center so that it covers the center third, then fold the top third down over the bottom and middle thirds. This completes the first turn.

9 Rotate the block of dough one quarter turn (90 degrees) on the work surface. Roll out again into a long, even rectangle.

10 Fold the dough in thirds again, like a business letter. This completes the second turn. Wrap the dough and chill for approximately 30 minutes. The resting period allows the gluten to relax; the chilling prevents the butter from becoming too soft.

11 Repeat the rolling and folding process, chilling between every one or two turns, until the dough has been turned a total of five times.

12 Wrap well and chill overnight. Raw dough may be refrigerated for a few days or frozen for 2 to 3 months.

13 Shape and bake as needed. Baked, unfilled puff pastry can be stored at room temperature for 2 to 3 days.

RECIPE 32.8   **PUFF PASTRY**

1 Mise en place for puff pastry. The detrempe is shown on the left.

2 Folding the dough around the butter.

Yield: 2 lb. (1 kg)   **Method:** Rolled-in Dough

All-purpose flour	13 oz.	390 g
Salt	1½ tsp.	7 ml
Unsalted butter, cold	3 oz.	90 g
Water, cold	7 fl. oz.	210 ml
Unsalted butter, softened	10 oz.	300 g

1 To form the detrempe, sift the flour and salt together in a large bowl. Cut the cold butter into small pieces and then cut the pieces into the flour until the mixture resembles coarse cornmeal.

2 Make a well in the center of the mixture and add all the water at once. Using a rubber spatula or your fingers, gradually draw the flour into the water. Mix until all the flour is incorporated. Do not knead. The detrempe should be sticky and shaggy-looking.

Note: The detrempe can be made in a food processor. To do so, combine the flour, salt and pieces of cold butter in a food processor bowl fitted with the metal blade. Process until a coarse meal is formed. With the processor running, slowly add the water. Turn the machine off as soon as the dough comes together to form a ball. Proceed with the remainder of the recipe.

3 Turn the detrempe out onto a lightly floured surface. Knead the dough a few times by hand, rounding it into a ball. Wrap the dough tightly in plastic and chill overnight.

4 To roll in the butter, first prepare the softened butter by placing it between two sheets of plastic wrap. Use a rolling pin to roll the softened butter into a rectangle, approximately 5 inches × 8 inches (12.5 centimeters × 20 centimeters). It is important that the detrempe and butter be of almost equal consistency. If necessary, allow the detrempe to sit at room temperature to soften or chill the butter briefly to harden.

5   On a lightly floured board, roll the detrempe into a rectangle approximately 12 inches × 15 inches (30 centimeters × 37.5 centimeters). Lift and rotate the dough as necessary to prevent sticking.

6   Use a dry pastry brush to brush away any flour from the dough's surface. Loose flour can cause gray streaks and can prevent the puff pastry from rising properly when baked.

7   Peel one piece of plastic wrap from the butter. Position the butter in the center of the rectangle and remove the remaining plastic. Fold the four edges of the detrempe over the butter enclosing it completely. Stretch the dough if necessary; it is important that none of the butter be exposed.

8   With the folded side facing up, press the dough several times with a rolling pin. Use a rocking motion to create ridges in the dough. Place the rolling pin in each ridge and slowly roll back and forth to widen the ridge. Repeat until all the ridges are doubled in size.

9   Using the ridges as a starting point, roll the dough out into a smooth, even rectangle approximately 8 inches × 24 inches (20 centimeters × 60 centimeters). Be careful to keep the corners of the dough as right angles.

10   Use a dry pastry brush to remove any loose flour from the dough's surface. Fold the dough in thirds, like a business letter. If one end is damaged or in worse condition, fold it in first; otherwise, start at the bottom. This completes the first turn.

11   Rotate the block of dough 90 degrees so that the folded edge is on your left and the dough faces you like a book. Roll out the dough again, repeating the ridging technique. Once again, the dough should be in a smooth, even rectangle of approximately 8 inches × 24 inches (20 centimeters × 60 centimeters).

12   Fold the dough in thirds again, completing the second turn. Cover the dough with plastic wrap and chill for at least 30 minutes.

13   Repeat the rolling and folding technique until the dough has had a total of five turns. Do not perform more than two turns without a resting and chilling period. Cover the dough completely and chill overnight before shaping and baking.

3 Rolling out the dough.

4 Folding the dough in thirds.

Approximate values per 1-oz. (30-g) serving: **Calories** 120, **Total fat** 9 g, **Saturated fat** 6 g, **Cholesterol** 25 mg, **Sodium** 110 mg, **Total carbohydrates** 9 g, **Protein** 1 g, **Vitamin A** 8%

Note: It is not necessary to work with the entire block of dough when making bouchées, cookies or the like. Cut the block into thirds or quarters and work with one of these portions at a time, keeping the rest chilled until needed.

SHAPING PUFF PASTRY

Once puff pastry dough is prepared, it can be shaped into containers of various sizes and shapes. **Bouchées** are small puff pastry shells often used for hors d'oeuvre or appetizers. **Vol-au-vents** are larger, deeper shells, often filled with savory mixtures for a main course. Although they may be simply round or square, special vol-au-vent cutters are available in the shape of fish, hearts or petals. **Feuilletées** are square, rectangular or diamond-shaped puff pastry boxes. They can be filled with a sweet or savory mixture.

When making straight cuts in puff pastry, press the tip of your knife into the dough and cut by pressing down on the handle. Do not drag the knife through the dough or you will crush the layers and prevent the dough from rising properly.

▶ **bouchées (boo-SHAY)** small puff pastry shells that can be filled and served as bite-size hors d'oeuvre or petit fours

▶ **vol-au-vents** deep, individual portion-sized puff pastry shells, often shaped as a heart, fish or fluted circle; they are filled with a savory mixture and served as an appetizer or main course

▶ **feuilletées (fuh-YETS)** square, rectangular or diamond-shaped puff pastry boxes; may be filled with a sweet or savory mixture

1 A vol-au-vent cutter looks like a double cookie cutter with one cutter about 1 inch (2.5 centimeters) smaller than the other. To cut the pastry, simply position the cutter and press down.

2 To shape with rings, use two rings, one approximately 1 inch (2.5 centimeters) smaller in diameter than the other. The larger ring is used to cut two rounds. One will be the base and is set aside. The smaller ring is then used to cut out an interior circle from the second round, leaving a border ring of dough. (The scrap of dough from the dough ring's center has no further use in making vol-au-vents.)

▶ PROCEDURE FOR SHAPING VOL-AU-VENTS AND BOUCHÉES

1 Roll out the puff pastry dough to a thickness of approximately ¼ inch (6 millimeters).

2 Cut the desired shape and size using a vol-au-vent cutter or rings.

3 Place the vol-au-vent or bouchée on a paper-lined sheet pan. If you used rings, place the base on the paper-lined sheet pan, brush lightly with water, then top it with the dough ring; score the edge with the back of a paring knife. Chill for 20 to 30 minutes to allow the dough to relax before baking.

4 Brush with egg-wash if desired and dock the center with a fork.

▶ PROCEDURE FOR SHAPING FEUILLETÉES

1 Roll out the puff pastry dough into an even rectangle, approximately ⅛ to ¼ inch (3 to 6 millimeters) thick.

2 Using a sharp paring knife or chef's knife, cut squares that are about 2 inches (5 centimeters) larger than the desired interior of the finished feuilletée.

3 Fold each square in half diagonally. Cut through two sides of the dough, about ½ inch (1.2 centimeters) from the edge. Cut a V, being careful not to cut through the corners at the center fold.

4 Open the square and lay it flat. Lift opposite sides of the cut border at the cut corners and cross them.

5 Brush water on the edges to seal the dough. Place the feuilletées on a paper-lined sheet pan.

6 Score the edges with the back of a paring knife. Chill for 20 to 30 minutes to allow the dough to relax before baking.

7 Brush with egg-wash if desired and dock the center with a fork.

Puff pastry scraps cannot be rerolled and used for products needing a high rise. The additional rolling destroys the layers. Scraps (known as rognures), however, can be used for cookies such as palmiers (page 1032), turnovers, decorative crescents (fleurons), tart shells, napoleons (page 1031) or any item for which rise is less important than flavor and flakiness. Most puff pastry products bake best in a hot oven, about 400°F–425°F (200°C–220°C).

ÉCLAIR PASTE

Éclair paste, also known as **pâte à choux,** bakes up into golden brown, crisp pastries. Inside these light pastries are mostly air pockets with a bit of moist dough. They can be filled with sweet cream, custard, fruit or even savory mixtures. The dough is most often piped into rounds for **cream puffs,** fingers for **éclairs** or rings for **Paris-Brest.** Éclair paste may also be piped or spooned into specific shapes and deep-fried for doughnut-type products known as **beignets, churros** and **crullers.**

MAKING ÉCLAIR PASTE

Éclair paste is unique among doughs because it is cooked before baking. The cooking occurs when the flour is added to a boiling mixture of water, milk and butter. This process breaks down the starches in the flour, allowing them to absorb the liquid, speeding gelatinization. Eggs are added to the flour mixture for leavening. The dough produced is batterlike with a smooth, firm texture; it does not have the dry, crumbly texture of other doughs. Without this technique, the dough would not puff up and develop the desired large interior air pockets when baked.

▶ PROCEDURE FOR PREPARING ÉCLAIR PASTE

1 Combine the liquid ingredients and butter and bring to a boil.

2 Add all the flour to the saucepan as soon as the water-and-butter mixture comes to a boil. If the liquid is allowed to boil, evaporation occurs; this can create an imbalance in the liquid-to-flour ratio.

3 Stir vigorously until the liquid is absorbed. Continue cooking the dough until it forms a ball that comes away from the sides of the pan, leaving only a thin film of dough in the pan.

4 Transfer the dough to a mixing bowl. Add the eggs one at a time, beating well after each addition. This may be done in a mixer with the paddle attachment or by hand. The number of eggs used varies depending on the

▶ **cream puffs** baked rounds of éclair paste cut in half and filled with pastry cream, whipped cream, fruit or other filling

▶ **profiteroles** small baked rounds of éclair paste filled with ice cream and topped with chocolate sauce

▶ **croquembouche** a pyramid of small puffs, each filled with pastry cream; a French tradition for Christmas and weddings, it is held together with caramelized sugar and decorated with spun sugar or marzipan flowers

▶ **éclairs** baked fingers of éclair paste filled with pastry cream; the top is then coated with chocolate glaze or fondant

▶ **Paris-Brest** rings of baked éclair paste cut in half horizontally and filled with light pastry cream and/or whipped cream; the top is dusted with powdered sugar or drizzled with chocolate glaze

▶ **beignets** squares or strips of éclair paste deep-fried and dusted with powdered sugar

▶ **churros** a Spanish and Mexican pastry in which sticks of éclair paste flavored with cinnamon are deep-fried and rolled in sugar while still hot

▶ **crullers** a Dutch pastry in which a loop or strip of twisted éclair paste is deep-fried size of each egg and the moisture content of the flour mixture. Stop adding eggs when the dough just begins to fall away from the beaters.

5 The finished dough should be smooth and pliable enough to pipe through a pastry bag; it should not be runny.

6 Pipe the dough as desired and bake immediately. A high oven temperature is necessary at the start of baking; it is then lowered gradually to finish baking and drying the product. Do not open the oven door during the first half of the baking period.

7 Allow the dough to bake until completely dry. If the products are removed from the oven too soon, they will collapse.

8 Baked éclair paste can be stored, unfilled, for several days at room temperature or frozen for several weeks. Once filled, the pastry should be served within 2 or 3 hours, as it quickly becomes soggy.

RECIPE 32.9	ÉCLAIR PASTE (PÂTE À CHOUX)	

Yield: 2 lb. (1 kg) Dough

Milk*	8 fl. oz.	225 ml
Water	8 fl. oz.	225 ml
Salt	1½ tsp.	7 ml
Granulated sugar	2 tsp.	10 ml
Unsalted butter	7½ oz.	225 g
All-purpose flour	8 oz.	450 g
Eggs	7–9	7–9

1 Preheat the oven to 425°F (220°C). Line a sheet pan with parchment. Have a pastry bag with a large plain tip ready.

2 Place the milk, water, salt, sugar and butter in a saucepan. Bring to a boil. Make sure the butter is fully melted.

3 Remove from the heat and immediately add all the flour. Vigorously beat the dough by hand. Put the pan back on the heat and continue beating the dough until it comes away from the sides of the pan. The dough should look relatively dry and should just begin to leave a film on the saucepan.

4 Transfer the dough to a mixing bowl and allow it to cool briefly to a temperature of approximately 130°F (54°C) or lower. Using the mixer's paddle attachment, begin beating in the eggs one at a time.

5 Continue to add the eggs one by one until the mixture is shiny but firm. It may not be necessary to use all nine eggs. The dough should pull away from the sides of the bowl in thick threads; it will not clear the bowl.

1 Heating the butter and milk.

2 Adding the flour to the hot liquid.

3 Stirring the dough to dry it.

4 The finished batter after the eggs are incorporated.

5 Piping éclairs.

6 Put a workable amount of dough into the pastry bag and pipe onto the sheet pan in the desired shapes at once.

7 Bake immediately, beginning at 425°F (220°C) for 10 minutes, then lowering the heat to 375°F (190°C) for another 10 minutes. Continue gradually lowering the oven temperature every few minutes until it reaches about 200°F (90°C) or until the shapes are brown and dry inside. Open the oven door as little as possible to prevent rapid changes in the oven's temperature.

8 Cool completely, then fill as desired. Leftovers can be frozen or stored at room temperature.

*For a crisper product, replace the milk with water.

Approximate values per 1-oz. (30-g) serving: **Calories** 90, **Total fat** 7 g, **Saturated fat** 4 g, **Cholesterol** 60 mg, **Sodium** 180 mg, **Total carbohydrates** 6 g, **Protein** 2 g, **Vitamin A** 8%

MERINGUES

Meringues are egg whites whipped with sugar. The texture—hard or soft—depends on the ratio of sugar to egg whites.

A low sugar content in comparison with the egg whites creates a **soft meringue.** Soft meringues can be folded into a mousse or Bavarian to lighten it, or used in a spongecake or soufflé. Meringues with only a small amount of sugar will always be soft; they will not become crisp no matter how they are used.

Hard meringues are made with egg whites and an equal part or more, by weight, of sugar. They can be incorporated into a buttercream or pastry cream or used to top a pie or baked Alaska. These toppings are usually placed briefly under a broiler to caramelize the sugar, creating an attractive brown surface.

Hard meringues with twice as much sugar, by weight, as egg whites can be piped into disks or other shapes and dried in an oven. A low oven temperature evaporates the eggs' moisture, leaving a crisp, sugary, honeycomblike structure. Disks of baked meringue can be used as layers in a torte or cake. Cups or shells of baked meringue can be filled with cream, mousse, ice cream or fruit. Often baked meringues also contain ground nuts (and are then known as dacquoise), cocoa powder or other flavorings.

MAKING MERINGUES

There are three methods for making meringues: **common, Swiss** and **Italian.** Regardless of which preparation method is used, the final product should be smooth, glossy and moist. A meringue should never be dry or spongelike. Review the procedure for whipping egg whites given in Chapter 21, Eggs and Breakfast.

Table 32.4   MERINGUES

TYPE	RATIO OF SUGAR TO EGGS WHITES BY WEIGHT	PREPARATION	USE
Common–hard	Twice as much or more	Whip or fold sugar into whipped egg whites	Baked
Common–soft	Equal parts or less	Whip or fold sugar into whipped egg whites	Pie topping soufflé; cake ingredient
Swiss	Varies	Warm egg whites with sugar, then whip	Buttercream; pie topping; baked
Italian	Varies	Hot sugar syrup poured into whipped egg whites	Buttercream; frosting; crème Chiboust; baked

Table 32.5 **TROUBLESHOOTING CHART FOR MERINGUES**

PROBLEM	CAUSE	SOLUTION
Weeps or beads of sugar syrup are released	Old eggs	Use fresher eggs or add sarch or stabilizer
	Egg whites overwhipped	Whip only until stiff peaks form
	Not enough sugar	Increase sugar
	Not baked long enough	Increase baking time
	Browning too rapidly	Do not dust with sugar before baking; reduce oven temperature
	Moisture in the air	
		Do not refrigerate baked meringue
Fails to attain any volume or stiffness	Fat present	Start over with clean bowls and utensils
	Sugar added too soon	Allow egg whites to reach soft peaks before adding sugar
Lumps	Not enough sugar	Add additional sugar gradually or start over
	Overwhipping	Whip only until stiff peaks form
Not shiny	Not enough sugar	Add additional sugar gradually or start over
	Overwhipping	Whip only until stiff peaks form

Common Meringues

Common meringues are made by first beating egg whites to a soft foam (soft peaks). Granulated sugar is then slowly beaten or folded into the egg whites. The final product may be hard or soft depending on the ratio of sugar to egg whites.

Swiss Meringues

Swiss meringues are made by combining unwhipped egg whites with sugar and warming the mixture over a bain marie to a temperature of approximately 100°F (38°C). The syrupy solution is then whipped until cool and stiff. The final product may be hard or soft depending on the ratio of sugar to egg whites. Swiss meringues are extremely stable but rather difficult to prepare. If the mixture gets too hot, it will not whip properly; the result will be syrupy and runny. Swiss meringue is often used as a topping or in buttercream.

Italian Meringues

Italian meringues are made by slowly pouring a hot sugar syrup into whipped egg whites. The heat from the syrup cooks the egg whites, adding stability. Be sure that the sugar syrup reaches the correct temperature and that it is added to the egg whites in a slow, steady stream. Italian meringues are used in buttercream (see Chapter 33, Cakes and Frostings) or folded into pastry cream to produce crème Chiboust. They may be flavored and used as a cake filling and frosting called boiled icing.

RECIPE 32.10 ITALIAN MERINGUE

Yield: Approx. 2 gal. (8 lt)

Granulated sugar	28 oz.	840 g
Water	as needed	as needed
Egg whites, room temperature	14 oz.	420 g

1 Place 18 ounces (540 grams) of the sugar in a heavy saucepan and add enough water to moisten the sugar thoroughly. Attach a candy thermometer to the pan and bring the sugar to a boil over high heat.

2 Place the egg whites in the bowl of an electric mixer fitted with the whip attachment. As the temperature of the boiling sugar approaches 220°F (104°C), begin whipping the egg whites. When the whites form soft peaks, gradually add the remaining 10 ounces (300 grams) of sugar. Lower the mixer speed and continue whipping.

3 When the sugar reaches the soft ball stage (238°F/115°C), pour it into the whites, with the mixer running. Pour in a steady stream between the side of the bowl and the beater. Continue whipping the whites at medium speed until they are cool.

Approximate values per cup (225 ml): **Calories** 102, **Total fat** 0 g, **Saturated fat** 0 g, **Cholesterol** 0 mg, **Sodium** 16 mg, **Total carbohydrates** 25 g, **Protein** 1 g, **Claims**—fat free; no cholesterol; low sodium

PHYLLO DOUGH

Phyllo (fee-low), also spelled *filo* or *fillo,* is from the Greek *phyllon,* meaning "thin sheet or leaf." Although its name is Greek, its origin is unknown. Indians, Turks, Syrians, Yugoslavs and Austrians all claim it as their own. Somewhat blandly flavored, phyllo sheets are brushed with melted butter or oil, stacked and then used in many Mediterranean, Middle Eastern and Central Asian dishes as a tart crust or a wrapper for various sweet or savory fillings.

Phyllo dough is made from flour, water, a bit of oil and eggs. The dough must be stretched tissue-paper thin, using techniques that can take years to master. Fortunately, excellent commercially prepared phyllo is available in frozen sheets. Sheets of phyllo can stick together if thawed too quickly, so thaw frozen dough slowly for a day or so in the refrigerator. Then temper the package of dough at room temperature for at least one hour before opening. (Unused phyllo should not be refrozen; it will keep for several days in the refrigerator if tightly wrapped.)

When ready to use, open the package and unfold the stack of leaves. Place them flat on a sheet pan or work surface and cover with a sheet of plastic wrap topped with a damp towel. Remove one leaf at a time from the stack, keeping the remainder well covered to prevent them from drying out. Brush melted butter or oil over the sheet's entire surface. Chopped nuts, sugar, cocoa powder or bread crumbs can be dusted over the butter or oil for additional flavor. Repeat with additional leaves until the desired number of layers have been prepared and stacked together. The number of layers will depend on the thickness of the sheets and their use. Generally, a filled tart or casserole requires more leaves than a folded or wrapped hors d'oeuvre. Cut the stacked phyllo with scissors or a very sharp knife and use as directed in the recipe. Recipes using phyllo dough are found at the end of this chapter and in Chapter 28, Hors d'Oeuvre and Canapés.

▶ COOKIES

Cookies are small, flat pastries usually eaten alone (although not singularly) as a snack or as a petit four with coffee at the end of a meal. The proliferation of cookie shops in malls and office buildings attests to the popularity of freshly baked cookies. They are indeed one of America's best-loved foods.

Part of the pleasure of cookies comes from their versatility. They may be eaten as a midmorning snack or as the elegant end to a formal dinner. Cookies also provide the finishing touch to a serving of ice cream, custard or fruit. Flavors are limited only by the baker's imagination; chocolate, oatmeal, cornmeal, fresh and dried fruit and nuts all find their way into several types of cookies. Several cookie formulas are given at the end of this chapter.

Drop Cookies

Icebox Cookies

Bar Cookies

Cut-Out or Rolled Cookies

MIXING METHODS

Most cookie doughs are mixed by the creaming method used for quick breads and cake batters. (See Chapter 30, Quick Breads, and Chapter 33, Cakes and Frostings.) Because cookie dough contains less liquid than these batters, the liquid and flour need not be added alternately, however. Cookies can be leavened with baking soda, baking powder or just air and steam. Most cookies are high in fat, which contributes flavor and tenderness and extends shelf life. Overdevelopment of gluten is usually not a problem with cookies because of their high fat and low moisture contents. But careless mixing can cause the dough to become tough and dense instead of tender and flaky.

▶ PROCEDURE FOR MIXING COOKIE DOUGHS

1 Cream the fat and sugar together to incorporate air and to blend the ingredients completely.
2 Add the eggs gradually, scraping down the bowl as needed.
3 Stir in the liquid ingredients.
4 Stir in the flour, salt, spices and leaveners.
5 Fold in any nuts, chocolate chips or chunky ingredients by hand.

MAKEUP METHODS

Cookie varieties are usually classified by the way in which the individual cookies are prepared. This section describes six preparation or makeup techniques: **drop, icebox, bar, cut-out** or **rolled, pressed** and **wafer.** Some doughs can be made up by more than one method. For example, chocolate chip cookie dough can be (1) baked in sheets and cut into bars, (2) dropped in mounds or (3) rolled into logs, chilled and sliced like icebox cookies. Regardless of the makeup method used, uniformity of size and shape is important for appearance and baking time. Cookies should also be evenly spaced on sheet pans for proper air circulation and crust formation.

DROP COOKIES

Drop cookies are made from a soft dough that is spooned or scooped into mounds for baking. Chunky cookies such as chocolate chip, oatmeal raisin and nut jumbles are common examples. Although a uniform appearance is not as important for drop cookies as for other types, uniform size and placement results in uniform baking time. A portion scoop is recommended for portioning the dough. Drop cookies tend to be thick with a soft or chewy texture.

ICEBOX COOKIES

Icebox cookies are made from dough that is shaped into logs or rectangles, chilled thoroughly, then sliced into individual pieces and baked as needed. Icebox cookies can be as simple as a log of chocolate chip dough or as sophisticated as elegant pinwheel and checkerboard cookies assembled with two colors of short dough. This method usually produces uniform, waferlike cookies with a crisp texture.

BAR COOKIES

Bar cookie dough is pressed or layered in shallow pans and cut into portions after baking, usually squares or rectangles to avoid waste or scraps. This category, also known as sheet cookies, contains a wide variety of layered or fruit-filled products. Brownies, often considered a bar cookie, are discussed in Chapter 33, Cakes and Frostings.

CUT-OUT OR ROLLED COOKIES

Cut-out or rolled cookies are made from a firm dough that is rolled out into a sheet and then cut into various shapes before baking. A seemingly infinite selection of cookie cutters is available, or you can use a paring knife or pastry wheel to cut the dough into the desired shapes. Always start cutting cookies from the edge of the dough, working inward. Cut the cookies as close to each other as possible to avoid scraps. Cut-out cookies are usually baked on an ungreased pan to keep the dough from spreading.

Cut-out cookies are often garnished or decorated with nuts, glaze, fruit or candies. Raw cookies should be decorated as soon as they are placed on the pan. If the dough is allowed to stand, the surface will dry out and the garnish will not adhere properly.

PRESSED COOKIES

Also referred to as bagged or **spritz cookies,** these products are made with a soft dough that is forced through a pastry tip or **cookie press.** Pressed cookies are usually small, with a distinct, decorative shape. The task of piping out dozens of identical cookies may seem daunting, but the skill can be mastered with practice and an understanding of doughs. Doughs for pressed cookies often use eggs as their only liquid. Eggs, which are a toughener, contribute body and help the cookies retain their shape. Using too much fat or too soft a flour (that is, one low in protein) can cause the cookies to spread and lose their shape.

WAFER COOKIES

Wafer cookies are extremely thin and delicate. They are made with a thin batter that is poured or spread onto a baking sheet and baked. Then, while still hot, the wafer is molded into a variety of shapes. The most popular shapes are the tightly rolled cigarette, the curved tuile and the cup-shaped tulipe. Wafer batter is sweet and buttery and is often flavored with citrus zest or ground nuts.

COOKIE TEXTURES

The textures associated with cookies—crispness, softness, chewiness or spread—are affected by various factors, including the ratio of ingredients in the dough, the oven's temperature and the pan's coating. Understanding these factors allows you to adjust formulas or techniques to achieve the desired results. See Table 32.6.

STORING COOKIES

Most cookies can be stored for up to 1 week in an airtight container. Do not store crisp cookies and soft cookies in the same container, however. The crisp cookies will absorb moisture from the soft cookies, ruining the texture of both. Do not store strongly flavored cookies, such as spice, with those that are milder, such as shortbread.

Most cookies freeze well if wrapped airtight to prevent moisture loss or freezer burn. Raw dough can also be frozen, either in bulk or shaped into individual portions.

Pressed Cookies

Wafer Cookies

▶ **cookie press** also known as a cookie gun; a hollow tube fitted with a plunger and an interchangeable decorative tip or plate. Soft cookie dough is pressed through the tip to create shapes or patterns.

THE STORY BEHIND THE CHIP

History was made in 1930 when Ruth Wakefield, innkeeper of the Toll House Inn in Whitman, Massachusetts, cut up a semisweet chocolate bar and added the pieces to cookie dough. She was disappointed, however, that the pieces kept their shape when baked—until her first bite, that is.

Mrs. Wakefield contacted Nestlé Foods Corporation, which published her cookie recipe on the wrapper of their semisweet chocolate bars. The recipe's popularity led Nestlé to create and begin selling chocolate chips in 1939.

Today's cookie maker can now choose from milk, white, sweet or bitter chocolate chips, along with mint, butterscotch, peanut butter, cinnamon and other flavor chips, offered in several sizes from a variety of manufacturers.

Table 32.6 COOKIE TEXTURES

DESIRED TEXTURE	FAT	SUGAR	LIQUID	FLOUR	SIZE OR SHAPE	BAKING
			CONTENT OF			
Crispness	High	High; use granulated sugar	Low	Strong	Thin dough	Well done; cool on baking sheet
Softness	Low	Low; use hydro-scopic sugars	High	Weak	Thick dough	Use parchment-lined pan; under-bake
Chewiness	~~High~~ *Low*	High; use hydro-scopic sugars	High	Strong	Not relevant; chilled dough	Underbake; cool on rack
Spread	High	High; use coarse granulated sugar	High; especially from eggs	Weak	Not relevant; room-temperature dough	Use greased pan; low temperature

CONCLUSION

Pastry making is the backbone of dessert preparation. A wide variety of pastry doughs can be prepared from flour, fat and a liquid. Proper mixing, rolling and shaping techniques are crucial to the success of the finished product. With a selection of properly prepared doughs and fillings, you can prepare an endless variety of tempting desserts.

QUESTIONS FOR DISCUSSION

1 How does the type of pie filling influence the selection of a pie crust? What type of crust would be best for a pie made with fresh, uncooked fruit? Explain your answer.

2 How does rolling fat into a dough in layers (as with puff pastry) produce a flaky product? Why isn't sweet dough (which contains a high ratio of butter) flaky?

3 Explain the difference between a cream pie filling and a custard pie filling. Give two examples of each type of filling.

4 List and describe three ways of preparing fruit fillings for pies.

5 Why is it said that éclair paste is the only dough that is cooked before it is baked? Why is this step necessary? List three ways of using éclair paste in making classic desserts.

6 Explain the differences and similarities between common, Swiss and Italian meringues.

7 List and describe four makeup methods for cookie doughs.

8 When was the Oreo cookie first sold? How many are now sold annually? How can you explain their popularity?

Several of the formulas given in the following pages are combinations of the pastry items presented in this chapter and the creams, custards and other dessert products covered in other chapters. For example, the Strawberry Napoleon is made with the puff pastry discussed in this chapter, the pastry cream and créme Chantilly discussed in Chapter 34, Custards, Creams, Frozen Desserts and Dessert Sauces and the fondant glaze discussed in Chapter 33, Cakes and Frostings. As a student, your first goal should be to learn to prepare a variety of pastry components. You can then combine and assemble them appropriately into both classic and modern desserts.

CHOCOLATE TART WITH FRESH BERRIES

RECIPE 32.11

Note: This dish appears in the chapter opening photograph.

HOUSTON COMMUNITY COLLEGE, Houston, TX
Pastry Chef Eddy Van Damme

Yield: 2 Tarts, 8 in. (20 cm)

Shortbread Tart Dough (page 1024), made with hazelnut flour	10 oz.	300 g
Egg wash	as needed	as needed
Flourless Chocolate Spongecake (recipe follows)	2 rounds	2 rounds
Raspberry Ganache (recipe follows)	1 lb. 7 oz.	700 g
Fresh raspberries and strawberries	4–5 pt.	2–2.4 lt
Neutral glaze	1 Tbsp.	15 ml

1 Roll out the hazelnut Shortbread Tart Dough to a thickness of a ⅛ inch (3 millimeters) and line two 8-inch (20-centimeter) tart rings or pans with it, gently pressing the dough into place.

2 Place paper and pie weights in the shells. Bake at 375°F (190°C) until the edges are lightly golden, approximately 8 minutes. Remove the paper and weights from the shells, brush them with egg wash and bake until golden brown, approximately 12 to 15 minutes. Set aside to cool.

3 Place a 7-inch (17-centimeter) round of Flourless Chocolate Spongecake in the bottom of each cooled tart shell.

4 Using a ladle, fill each tart to the rim with Raspberry Ganache. Refrigerate until set.

5 Cover the entire surface of the tart with fresh berries.

6 Place the neutral glaze in a parchment-paper piping cone and pipe a drop of "dew" on each berry.

Approximate values per ⅛-tart serving: **Calories** 420, **Total fat** 24 g, **Saturated fat** 13 g, **Cholesterol** 145 mg, **Sodium** 95 mg, **Total carbohydrates** 50 g, **Protein** 6 g, **Vitamin A** 15%, **Vitamin C** 70%, **Iron** 15%

PASTRY CHEF EDDY VAN DAMME, Houston Community College, Houston, TX

A native of Belgium, Chef Eddy Van Damme knew that his future lay in the pastry shop by the time he was only 7 years old. Inspired by his mother and an uncle, he began baking at home, making cookies, cakes and even éclairs by age 10. He started working weekends in a pastry shop at age 12, where he learned many of the skills that must become second nature to any successful patisserie. Chef Van Damme has also worked at Bundervoet, one of the finest pastry shops in Belgium; attended pastry school at Piva in Antwerp, Belgium, and has taken many courses at the LeNôtre and Cacao Barry schools in Paris.

When Chef Van Damme immigrated to the United States in the 1980s, he headed straight for Houston, Texas. He has been in charge of the pastry program at Houston Community College for more than a decade. His awards include five 5 A.C.F. gold medals in pastry competitions, Best of Show at the 10th Annual Culinary Classic in Louisiana and the Chancellor's Medallion for teaching excellence. He is a co-author of *On Baking: A Textbook of Baking and Pastry Fundamentals.*

FLOURLESS CHOCOLATE SPONGECAKE

Yield: 3 Rounds, 7 in. (17 cm)

Egg whites	6 oz.	180 g
Granulated sugar	6½ oz.	195 g
Egg yolks	4½ oz.	135 g
Vanilla extract	1 tsp.	5 ml
Cocoa powder sifted	2 oz.	60 g

1 Using a mixer fitted with the whip attachment, beat the egg whites to soft peaks. Add the sugar and continue whipping to stiff peaks.

2 In a separate bowl, whip the egg yolks to a thick ribbon.

3 When both mixtures have reached the proper consistency, add one-third of the whipped yolks to the egg whites, folding them together using a balloon whisk. Heavy streaks may remain in the batter.

4 Add the remaining egg yolks and gently fold together. Some streaks may remain in the batter.

5 Add the vanilla and cocoa powder and gently fold together until no streaks remain in the batter.

6 Using a piping bag fitted with a large plain tip, pipe the batter onto parchment-lined sheet pans in a tight spiral pattern in order to form three 7-inch- (17-centimeter-) diameter rounds.

7 Bake at 360°F (180°C) until the cake springs back when gently touched, approximately 25 minutes. Cool completely. Any unneeded cake rounds can be wrapped tightly in plastic wrap and frozen for later use.

Approximate values per round: **Calories** 470, **Total fat** 16 g, **Saturated fat** 6 g, **Cholesterol** 545 mg, **Sodium** 115 mg, **Total carbohydrates** 73 g, **Protein** 17 g, **Vitamin A** 15%, **Iron** 25%

RASPBERRY GANACHE

Yield: 1 lb. 7 oz. (700 g)

Semisweet chocolate	9 oz.	270 g
Raspberry purée, unsweetened, seedless	10 fl. oz.	300 g
Pectin	½ tsp.	2 ml
Granulated sugar	1½ oz.	45 g
Unsalted butter, melted	2 oz.	60 g

1 Chop the chocolate into pea-size bits, place in a bowl and set aside.

2 Heat the raspberry purée to 120°F (50°C) in a nonreactive pan.

3 Thoroughly mix the pectin and sugar. Whisk it into the raspberry purée and bring to a boil.

4 Pour approximately 2 fluid ounces (60 milliliters) of the hot purée into the bowl of chocolate. Combine with a spatula, adding the remaining purée in four increments.

5 Stir in the butter. If lumps form or if the chocolate fails to melt completely, place the bowl over a bain marie until completely melted and smooth. Use immediately.

Approximate values per 2-Tbsp (30-ml) serving: **Calories** 80, **Total fat** 5 g, **Saturated fat** 3 g, **Cholesterol** 5 mg, **Sodium** 0 mg, **Total carbohydrates** 10 g, **Protein** 1 g

PURPLE FIG TART WITH MINTED CHEESE MOUSSE

RECIPE 32.12

Note: This dish appears in the chapter opening photograph.

HOUSTON COMMUNITY COLLEGE, HOUSTON, TX
Pastry Chef Eddy Van Damme

Yield: 12 Tarts, 2½ in. (7.5 cm)

Shortbread Tart Dough (page 1024), made with almond flour	24 oz.	720 g
Egg wash	as needed	as needed
Minted Cheese Mousse (recipe follows)	1 lb. 10 oz.	780 g
Fresh purple figs	30	30
Orange Glaze (recipe follows)	4 oz.	120 g

1 Roll out the almond Shortbread Tart Dough to a thickness of ⅛ inch (3 millimeters). Using a round cutter, cut circles slightly wider than the tart forms. Line the tart forms with the dough, gently pressing the dough into place.

2 Place paper and pie weights in the shells and bake at 375°F (190°C) until the edges of the tarts are lightly golden, approximately 6 minutes. Remove the paper and weights from the shells, brush the shells with egg wash and bake until golden brown, approximately 12 to 15 minutes.

3 Using a pastry bag fitted with a medium plain tip, pipe the Minted Cheese Mousse into the tart shells. Chill until the filling has set.

4 Slice the figs in half and arrange in pyramid style on the tarts.

5 Brush the fruit with the Orange Glaze.

Approximate values per tart: **Calories** 440, **Total fat** 27 g, **Saturated fat** 16 g, **Cholesterol** 110 mg, **Sodium** 140 mg, **Total carbohydrates** 50 g, **Protein** 5 g, **Vitamin A** 25%

MINTED CHEESE MOUSSE

Yield: 1 lb. 10 oz. (780 g)

Cream cheese or mascarpone	10 oz.	300 g
Granulated sugar	4 oz.	120 g
Water	2 fl. oz.	60 ml
Mint compound (or 20 mint leaves)	1 Tbsp.	15 ml
Heavy cream	10 fl. oz.	300 ml

1 Cut the cream cheese or mascarpone into medium cubes, place in a bowl and soften in a microwave oven until the cheese is 90°F (32°C).

2 Boil the water and sugar for 1 minute. Remove from the heat and cool, then use a spatula to incorporate into the softened cheese.

3 Whip the mint compound and heavy cream to soft peaks. (Or cut the mint leaves into a fine chiffonade, add to the heavy cream and whip to soft peaks.) Fold the cream into the cheese mixture and use immediately.

ORANGE GLAZE

Yield: 4 oz. (120 g)

Neutral glaze	2½ oz.	75 g
Orange juice	1½ fl. oz.	45 ml

1 Combine the ingredients using a spatula.

RECIPE 32.13

SHORTBREAD TART DOUGH

HOUSTON COMMUNITY COLLEGE, HOUSTON, TX
Pastry Chef Eddy Van Damme

Yield: 4 lb. 7 oz. (2.1 kg)

Egg yolks, hard-boiled	5 oz.	150 g
Unsalted butter	1 lb. 8 oz.	675 g
Powdered sugar	11 oz.	330 g
Vanilla extract	1 Tbsp.	15 ml
Salt	1½ tsp.	8 ml
Almond or hazelnut flour	4½ oz.	135 g
Pastry flour	1 lb. 10 oz.	750 g

1 Press the egg yolks through a sieve using a plastic pastry scraper. Set aside.
2 Using an electric mixer fitted with the paddle attachment, cream the butter. Add the powdered sugar, combining well.
3 Add the vanilla, salt and almond or hazelnut flour, then the sieved egg yolks, and mix until combined.
4 Add all of the pastry and mix on low speed just until combined. Do not overmix.
5 Wrap the dough in plastic and chill for several hours or overnight.
6 When ready to use, roll out the chilled dough on a lightly floured board. The dough may be crumbly and difficult to work with, which is normal. Simply press the dough back together with your fingertips.

Approximate values per 2-oz. (60-g) serving: **Calories** 227, **Total fat** 19 g, **Saturated fat** 10 g, **Cholesterol** 93 mg, **Sodium** 103 mg, **Total carbohydrates** 25 g, **Protein** 4 g

RECIPE 32.14

QUICHE DOUGH

Yield: 8 lb. (3.6 kg)

All-purpose flour	4 lb. 7 oz.	2 kg
Salt	1½ oz.	45 g
Unsalted butter, cold	2 lb. 3 oz.	1 kg
Eggs	12	12

1 Combine the flour and salt in a mixer bowl fitted with a paddle attachment. Cut in the butter until the mixture looks like coarse cornmeal.
2 Whisk the eggs together to blend, then add them slowly to the dry ingredients. Blend only until the dough comes together in a ball.
3 Remove from the mixer, cover and chill until ready to use.

Approximate values per 1-oz. (30-g) serving: **Calories** 120, **Total fat** 7 g, **Saturated fat** 4 g, **Cholesterol** 35 mg, **Sodium** 140 mg, **Total carbohydrates** 12 g, **Protein** 2 g

RECIPE 32.15

LEMON MERINGUE PIE

Yield: 2 Pies, 9 in. (22 cm)   **Method:** Cream Filling

Granulated sugar	1 lb. 4 oz.	600 g
Cornstarch	3 oz.	90 g
Salt	1 pinch	1 pinch
Water, cold	24 fl. oz.	750 ml
Egg yolks	10	10

Lemon juice, fresh	8 fl. oz.	250 ml
Lemon zest, grated	2 Tbsp.	60 ml
Unsalted butter	1 oz.	60 g
Flaky dough pie shells, baked	2	2
Egg whites	8 oz.	250 g
Granulated sugar	8 oz.	250 g

1 To make the filling, combine the 1 pound 4 ounces (600 grams) of sugar, cornstarch, salt and water in a heavy saucepan. Cook over medium-high heat, stirring constantly, until the mixture becomes thick and almost clear.

2 Remove from the heat and slowly whisk in the egg yolks. Stir until completely blended. Return to the heat and cook, stirring constantly, until thick and smooth.

3 Stir in the lemon juice and zest. When the liquid is completely incorporated, remove the filling from the heat. Add the butter and stir until melted.

4 Set the filling aside to cool briefly. Fill the pie shells with the lemon filling.

5 To prepare the meringue, whip the egg whites until soft peaks form. Slowly add the 8 ounces (250 grams) of sugar while whisking constantly. The meringue should be stiff and glossy, not dry or spongy looking.

6 Mound the meringue over the filling, creating decorative patterns with a spatula. Be sure to spread the meringue to the edge of the crust so that all of the filling is covered.

7 Place the pies in a 400°F (200°C) oven until the meringue is golden brown, approximately 5 to 8 minutes. Let cool at room temperature, then refrigerate. Serve the same day.

Approximate values per ⅛-pie serving: **Calories** 400, **Total fat** 12 g, **Saturated fat** 4 g, **Cholesterol** 135 mg, **Sodium** 310 mg, **Total carbohydrates** 67 g, **Protein** 5 g, **Vitamin C** 10%

FRESH STRAWBERRY PIE

RECIPE 32.16

Yield: 2 Pies, 9 in. (22 cm) **Method:** Cooked Juice

Granulated sugar	1 lb. 7 oz.	700 g
Water	8 fl. oz.	450 ml
Cornstarch	2½ oz.	75 g
Water, cold	12 fl. oz.	360 ml
Salt	½ tsp.	2 ml
Lemon juice	4 Tbsp.	60 ml
Red food coloring	as needed	as needed
Fresh strawberries, rinsed and sliced in half	2 qt.	2 lt
Flaky dough pie shells, baked	2	2
Whipped cream	as needed	as needed

1 Bring the sugar and 8 fluid ounces (225 milliliters) of water to a boil.

2 Dissolve the cornstarch in the cold water and add to the boiling liquid. Cook over low heat until clear, approximately 5 minutes.

3 Stir in the salt, lemon juice and enough red food coloring to produce a bright red color.

4 Pour this glaze over the strawberries and toss gently to coat them. Spoon the filling into the prepared pie shells. Chill thoroughly and top with whipped cream for service.

Approximate values per ⅛-pie serving: **Calories** 330, **Total fat** 8 g, **Saturated fat** 2 g, **Cholesterol** 0 mg, **Sodium** 200 mg, **Total carbohydrates** 63 g, **Protein** 2 g, **Vitamin C** 80%

RECIPE 32.17

FREEFORM APPLE PIES

CONNECTICUT CULINARY INSTITUTE, FARMINGTON, CT
Chef Jamie Roraback

Yield: 4 Pies   **Method:** Baked Fruit

Dough:		
Unsalted butter	8 oz.	240 g
All-purpose flour	8 oz.	240 g
Salt	1 tsp.	5 ml
Water, ice cold	3 fl. oz.	90 ml
Filling:		
Apples, peeled, cored, large dice	3	3
Unsalted butter	1 oz.	30 g
Granulated sugar	2 oz.	60 g
Cinnamon, ground	¼ tsp.	2 ml
Vanilla extract	1 Tbsp.	15 ml
Apple brandy	2 fl. oz.	60 ml
Egg wash:		
Egg	1	1
Milk	2 Tbsp.	30 ml
Sanding sugar	as needed	as needed

▶ **sanding sugar** granulated sugar with a large, coarse crystal structure that prevents it from dissolving easily; used for decorating cookies and pastries

1 To prepare the dough, cut the butter into medium dice and place it in the freezer for 5 minutes. Sift the flour with the salt. Toss the butter with the flour and salt and then place the mixture in the bowl of a food processor. Pulse until the butter chunks are the size of very small peas. Then, in a continuous stream, drizzle in the ice water and pulse just until the dough barely comes together. Do not overmix.

2 Turn the dough out onto a work surface. Knead it gently and quickly. Divide the dough into four small rounds. Place the rounds on a sheet pan, cover them with plastic wrap and refrigerate for approximately 20 minutes before rolling out.

3 To prepare the filling, heat a sauté pan over high heat, add the apples and let them brown slightly. Add the butter and let it melt so that it loosens and frees the apples from the bottom of the pan. Then cook for approximately 1 minute, add the sugar and let it brown, stirring occasionally. Add the cinnamon and vanilla. Remove from the heat, add the apple brandy, return to the heat and flambé. Cool the filling before assembling the pies.

4 Prepare the egg wash by whipping the egg together with the milk.

5 On a floured surface, roll out each round of dough into a circle approximately 8 inches (20 centimeters) wide. Place an appropriate-size plate or other circular object on top of the rolled-out dough and cut out a circle.

6 Place one-quarter of the apple filling in the center of each dough round, leaving exposed 1½ inches (3.7 centimeters) of dough along the edges. Fold this border over the filling in approximately five or six folds, each fold slightly overlapping the previous one. Place the pies on a sheet pan and using a pastry brush, glaze each pie (dough only) with egg wash. Sprinkle sanding sugar over the pies after glazing.

7 Place the pies in the freezer until frozen. (Freezing will help prevent the butter running from the high-butter-content crust during baking.)

8 Preheat the oven to 400°F (200°C). While the pies are baking, rotate them occasionally. Bake until the apples are tender and the crust is evenly browned, approximately 20 minutes. Serve at room temperature, dusted with powdered sugar and accompanied by whipped cream or ice cream.

Approximate values per ½-pie serving: **Calories** 420, **Total fat** 27 g, **Saturated fat** 16 g, **Cholesterol** 95 mg, **Sodium** 300 mg, **Total carbohydrates** 36 g, **Protein** 4 g, **Vitamin A** 20%

BLACKBERRY COBBLER

RECIPE 32.18

A cobbler is a homestyle baked fruit dessert, usually made with a top crust of flaky pie dough, biscuit dough or streusel topping. The finished product will be slightly runny and is often served warm in a bowl or rimmed dish, accompanied by whipped cream or ice cream.

Yield: 10 Servings	**Method:** Baked Fruit	
IQF blackberries	2 qt.	2 lt
Granulated sugar	8 oz.	450 g
Tapioca, instant	2 oz.	60 g
Water	10 fl. oz.	300 ml
Unsalted butter	2 oz.	60 g
Lemon zest	1 Tbsp.	15 ml

1 Combine all the ingredients, tossing the berries gently until well coated with the other ingredients.

2 Transfer to a lightly buttered half-sized hotel pan, then set aside for at least 30 minutes before baking.

3 The cobbler can be topped with Basic Pie Dough (page 998), Country Biscuit dough (page 951) or Streusel Topping (page 954) before baking.

4 Bake at 350°F (180°C) until the berry mixture bubbles and the crust is appropriately browned, approximately 40 to 50 minutes.

Approximate values per 6-oz. (180-g) serving: **Calories** 210, **Total fat** 5 g, **Saturated fat** 3 g, **Cholesterol** 20 mg, **Sodium** 10 mg, **Total carbohydrates** 39 g, **Protein** 1 g, **Vitamin C** 45%

PECAN PIE WITH OATMEAL STOUT ICE CREAM AND GINGER CARAMEL SAUCE

RECIPE 32.19

CAFÉ ALLEGRE, ORLANDO, FL
Chef Kevin Fonzo

Yield: 1 Pie, 10 in. (24 cm)	**Method:** Custard Filling	
Eggs	5	5
Dark corn syrup	1⅓ c.	320 ml
Granulated sugar	1⅓ c.	320 ml
Vanilla extract	1 tsp.	5 ml
Whole butter, melted	3 Tbsp.	45 ml
Oatmeal stout	4 fl. oz.	120 ml
Pecan pieces	3 c.	720 ml
10-inch pie crust, unbaked	1	1

1 Beat the eggs thoroughly. Add the corn syrup, sugar, vanilla, butter and stout. Mix until well blended.

2 Fold in the pecans and pour the mixture into the pie crust.

3 Bake at 350°F (180°C) until set, approximately 45 to 55 minutes.

4 Allow the pie to cool completely before service.

Approximate values per ⅛-pie serving: **Calories** 800, **Total fat** 45 g, **Saturated fat** 8 g, **Cholesterol** 145 mg, **Sodium** 210 mg, **Total carbohydrates** 91 g, **Protein** 8 g

OATMEAL STOUT ICE CREAM

Yield: 3 qt.

Milk	1 qt.	1 lt
Heavy cream	1 qt.	1 lt
Oatmeal stout	8 fl. oz.	225 ml
Dark corn syrup	½ c.	120 ml
Granulated sugar	8 oz.	225 g
Egg yolks	2	2
Vanilla beans, split	2	2

1 In a medium-sized saucepot, heat the milk and cream.

2 In a separate saucepot, bring the oatmeal stout to a boil and reduce by half. Add the corn syrup and remove from heat.

3 In a small mixing bowl, combine the sugar, egg yolks and vanilla beans. Mix well.

4 When the cream mixture comes to a boil, temper it into the egg mixture. Once all of the cream mixture is incorporated into the egg mixture, strain it.

5 Allow the mixture to cool completely. Gently stir the stout reduction into the cooled custard.

6 Freeze the custard in an ice cream freezer.

Approximate values per ½-c. (120-ml) serving: **Calories** 215, **Total fat** 15 g, **Saturated fat** 9 g, **Cholesterol** 121 mg, **Sodium** 37 mg, **Total carbohydrates** 17 g, **Protein** 3 g, **Vitamin A** 18%

GINGER CARAMEL SAUCE

Yield: 3 c. (720 ml)

Granulated sugar	1 lb.	500 g
Water	⅓ c.	75 ml
Lemon juice	½ tsp.	2 ml
Fresh ginger, peeled and chopped	6 oz.	180 g
Heavy cream	12 fl. oz.	360 ml
Unsalted butter	2 oz.	60 g

1 Bring the sugar, water and lemon juice to a boil in a small saucepan.

2 Cook over medium heat until the syrup turns a golden amber color. Add the ginger.

3 Remove the saucepan from the heat and slowly add the cream.

4 Return the pan to the heat and cook for 2 to 3 more minutes.

5 Add the butter and stir to melt. Serve the sauce warm.

Approximate values per 1-fl. oz. (30-ml) serving: **Calories** 90, **Total fat** 4.5 g, **Saturated fat** 3 g, **Cholesterol** 15 mg, **Sodium** 15 mg, **Total carbohydrates** 12 g, **Protein** 0 g

---

RECIPE 32.20

FRESH BERRY TART

Yield: 1 Tart, 9 in. (22 cm)

Sweet Dough (page 999) tart shell, 9 in. (22 cm), fully baked	1	1
Pastry Cream (page 1093)	1 pt.	500 ml
Fresh berries such as strawberries, blackberries, blueberries or raspberries	3 pt.	1.5 lt
Apricot glaze	as needed	as needed

1 Arranging the fruit over the pastry cream.

2 Brushing the apricot glaze over the fruit.

1 Fill the cool tart shell with Pastry Cream.

2 Arrange the berries over the Pastry Cream in an even layer. Be sure to place the berries so that the Pastry Cream is covered.

3 Heat the apricot glaze and brush over the fruit to form a smooth coating.

Approximate values per ⅙-tart serving: **Calories** 135, **Total fat** 3 g, **Saturated fat** 1 g, **Cholesterol** 2 mg, **Sodium** 62 mg, **Total carbohydrates** 26 g, **Protein** 2 g

FRENCH APPLE TART

RECIPE 32.21

Note: The amount of each ingredient, the yield and the baking time will depend on the capacity and number of tart molds used. This procedure can be used for individual tartlets or large round, rectangular or daisy-shaped tart pans.

Sweet Dough (page 999)	as needed
Almond Cream (page 1031)	as needed
Tart apples, peeled, cored and sliced thin	as needed
Unsalted butter, melted	as needed
Granulated sugar	as needed
Apricot glaze	as needed

1 Line the tart forms with Sweet Dough. Do not prick the dough.

2 Pipe in an even layer of Almond Cream.

3 Arrange the apples in overlapping rows, covering the Almond Cream completely.

4 Brush the top of the apples with melted butter and sprinkle lightly with granulated sugar.

5 Bake at 375°F (190°C) until the crust is done and the apples are light brown.

6 Allow the tart to cool to room temperature. Brush the top with apricot glaze.

Approximate values per 4-oz. (120-g) serving: **Calories** 395, **Total fat** 17 g, **Saturated fat** 7 g, **Cholesterol** 234 mg, **Sodium** 98 mg, **Total carbohydrates** 56 g, **Protein** 7 g, **Vitamin A** 12%

QUICK PUFF PASTRY

RECIPE 32.22

Adapted from *NICK MALGIERI'S PERFECT PASTRY*

Yield: 1 lb. 4 oz. (560 g)

Unbleached all-purpose flour	6¼ oz.	180 g
Cake flour	1¼ oz.	37 g
Unsalted butter	8 oz.	225 g

Continued

Salt	½ tsp.	2 ml
Water, very cold	4 fl. oz.	120 ml

1 To mix the dough, place the all-purpose flour in a 2-quart (2-liter) mixer bowl and sift the cake flour over it. Thoroughly stir the two flours together.

2 Slice 1 ounce (30 grams) of the butter into thin pieces and add to the bowl. Rub in the butter by hand, tossing and squeezing in the butter until no visible pieces remain.

3 Cut the remaining butter into ½-inch (1.2-centimeter) cubes. Add the butter cubes to the flour mixture. Toss with a rubber spatula just to separate and distribute the butter. Do not rub the butter into the flour.

4 Dissolve the salt in the water. Make a well in the flour-and-butter mixture and add the water. Toss gently with the spatula until the dough is evenly moistened. Add drops of water, if necessary, to complete the moistening. Press and squeeze the dough in a bowl to form a rough cylinder.

5 To turn the dough, first lightly flour the work surface and the dough. Using the palm of your hand, press down on the dough three or four times to shape the dough into a rough rectangle.

6 Press and pound the dough with a rolling pin to form an even rectangle about ½ inch (1.2 centimeters) thick. Roll the dough back and forth along its length once or twice until it is an even rectangle about ¼ inch (6 millimeters) thick. At this stage, pieces of butter are likely to stick to the work surface. If the dough does stick, loosen it with a long spatula or scraper. Clean the surface to minimize further sticking.

7 Fold both ends of the dough in toward the center, then fold them in toward the center again to make four layers. The folded package of dough will resemble a book. Position the package of dough so that the "spine" is on the left.

8 Lightly flour the work surface and the dough and repeat the pressing as before. Roll the dough along its length as before, then roll several times along its width to form a rectangle approximately 6 inches × 18 inches (15 centimeters × 45 centimeters). Fold the dough, both ends in toward the center, then over again as before. Repeat the process once more so that the dough will have three double turns.

9 Wrap the dough well in plastic and chill for at least 1 hour before using.

10 The dough can be refrigerated for about 3 days or frozen for up to 1 month. Defrost frozen dough in the refrigerator overnight before using it.

Approximate values per 3-oz. (90-g) serving: **Calories** 480, **Total fat** 37 g, **Saturated fat** 23 g, **Cholesterol** 100 mg, **Sodium** 240 mg, **Total carbohydrates** 31 g, **Protein** 5 g, **Vitamin A** 35%

RECIPE 32.23

FRESH PEACH TART WITH ALMOND CREAM

VINCENT ON CAMELBACK, Phoenix, AZ
Chef Vincent Guerithault

Yield: 8 Servings

Puff pastry	6 oz.	180 g
Almond Cream (recipe follows)	1 lb. 8 oz.	750 g
Fresh peaches, peeled, pitted and sliced	6–8	6–8
Unsalted butter, melted	3 oz.	90 g
Granulated sugar	2 Tbsp.	30 ml
Powdered sugar	as needed	as needed

1 Roll out the puff pastry into a strip, approximately 6 inches × 22 inches (the length of a sheet pan); (15 centimeters × 55 centimeters) and ⅛ inch (3 millimeters) thick. Lay the dough on a sheet pan lined with parchment paper.

2 Using a large plain tip, pipe four rows of almond cream down the length of the puff pastry. Leave a ¾-inch (18-millimeter) margin along both long edges of the dough.

3 Arrange the peach slices over the almond cream, overlapping slightly.

4 Brush the peaches with the melted butter and evenly sprinkle the granulated sugar over them.

5 Bake at 400°F (200°C) until the dough is done and the peaches are lightly browned, approximately 20 to 30 minutes.

6 Serve warm, dusted with powdered sugar and accompanied by vanilla ice cream.

Approximate values per serving: **Calories** 140, **Total fat** 9 g, **Saturated fat** 5 g, **Cholesterol** 25 mg, **Sodium** 0 mg, **Total carbohydrates** 15 g, **Protein** 1 g, **Vitamin A** 10%

ALMOND CREAM (FRANGIPANE)

Yield: 3 lb. (1.3 kg)

Unsalted butter, softened	8 oz.	225 g
Granulated sugar	1 lb.	450 g
Eggs	8 oz.	225 g
All-purpose flour	5 oz.	150 g
Almonds, ground	12 oz.	360 g

1 Cream the butter and sugar. Slowly add the eggs, scraping down the sides of the bowl as necessary.

2 Stir the flour and almonds together, then add to the butter mixture. Blend until no lumps remain.

3 Almond cream may be stored under refrigeration for up to 3 weeks.

Approximate values per 1-oz. (30-g) serving: **Calories** 140, **Total fat** 8 g, **Saturated fat** 3 g, **Cholesterol** 30 mg, **Sodium** 5 mg, **Total carbohydrates** 13 g, **Protein** 2 g

STRAWBERRY NAPOLEON   RECIPE 32.24

Yield: 10 Servings

Puff pastry, 4-in. × 15-in. (10-cm × 37-cm) strips, docked and baked	3	3
Pastry Cream (page 1093)	1 pt.	500 ml
Fresh strawberries, sliced	1 qt.	1 lt
Crème Chantilly (page 1099)	1 pt.	500 ml
Basic Sugar Glaze (page 1065)	as needed	as needed
Dark chocolate, melted	1 oz.	30 g

1 Allow the puff pastry to cool completely before assembling.

2 Place a strip of puff pastry on a cake cardboard for support. Pipe on a layer of Pastry Cream, leaving a clean margin of almost ½ inch (1.2 centimeters) on all four sides.

3 Top the cream with a layer of berries.

4 Spread on a thin layer of Créme Chantilly and top with a second layer of puff pastry. Repeat the procedure for the second layer of puff pastry and chill.

5 Prepare the Basic Sugar Glaze. Place the melted chocolate in a piping cone. When ready to glaze, place the third strip of puff pastry on an icing rack, flat side up. Pour the Basic Sugar Glaze down the length of the pastry and spread evenly with a metal cake spatula. Allow the excess to drip over the sides.

6 Immediately pipe thin lines of chocolate across the glaze. Use a toothpick to pull a spiderweb pattern in the glaze. Chill to set the glaze, then place the top in position on the napoleon.

Approximate values per 5-oz. (150-g) serving: **Calories** 320, **Total fat** 20 g, **Saturated fat** 9 g, **Cholesterol** 115 mg, **Sodium** 65 mg, **Total carbohydrates** 29 g, **Protein** 4 g, **Vitamin A** 15%, **Vitamin C** 60%

RECIPE 32.25 PALMIERS

1 Folding the dough toward the center from both edges.

| Puff pastry | as needed | as needed |
| Granulated sugar | as needed | as needed |

1 Roll out the puff pastry into a very thin rectangle. The length is not important, but the width should be at least 7 inches (17.5 centimeters).

2 Using a rolling pin, gently press the granulated sugar into the dough on both sides.

3 Make a 1-inch (2.5-centimeter) fold along the long edges of the dough toward the center. Sprinkle on additional sugar.

4 Make another 1-inch (2.5-centimeter) fold along the long edges of the dough toward the center. The two folds should almost meet in the center. Sprinkle on additional sugar.

5 Fold one side on top of the other. Press down gently with a rolling pin or your fingers so that the dough adheres. Chill for 1 hour.

6 Cut the log of dough in thin slices. Place the cookies on a paper-lined sheet pan and bake at 400°F (200°C) until the edges are brown, approximately 8 to 12 minutes.

Approximate values per 1-oz. (30-g) serving: **Calories** 130, **Total fat** 5 g, **Saturated fat** 1 g, **Cholesterol** 0 mg, **Sodium** 35 mg, **Total carbohydrates** 19 g, **Protein** 1 g

2 Slicing the log of dough into individual cookies.

RECIPE 32.26 CHOCOLATE ÉCLAIRS

1 Using a piping bag to fill the éclairs with pastry cream.

Yield: 20 Éclairs

Baked Éclair shells, 4 in. (10 cm) long, made from Éclair Paste (page 1014)	20	20
Vanilla Pastry Cream (page 1093)	1 qt.	1 lt
Chocolate glaze:		
Unsweetened chocolate	4 oz.	120 g
Semisweet chocolate	4 oz.	120 g
Unsalted butter	4 oz.	120 g
White corn syrup	4 tsp.	20 ml
White chocolate, melted (optional)	as needed	as needed

1 Use a paring knife or skewer to cut a small hole into the end of each baked, cooled éclair shell.

2 Pipe the Vanilla Pastry Cream into each shell using a piping bag fitted with a small plain tip. Be sure that the cream fills the full length of each shell. Refrigerate the filled éclairs.

3 To prepare the chocolate glaze, melt all the ingredients together over a bain marie. Remove from the heat and allow to cool until slightly thickened, stirring occasionally.

4 In a single, smooth stroke, drag the top of each filled éclair through the glaze. Only the very top of each pastry should be coated with chocolate.

5 Melted white chocolate may be piped onto the wet glaze, then pulled into patterns using a toothpick. Keep the finished éclairs refrigerated and serve within 8 to 12 hours.

2 Dipping the éclairs in chocolate glaze.

Approximate values per éclair, **Calories** 410, **Total fat** 31 g, **Saturated fat** 17 g, **Cholesterol** 110 mg, **Sodium** 230 mg, **Total carbohydrates** 27 g, **Protein** 5 g, **Vitamin A** 20%

BAKED MERINGUE

RECIPE 32.27

Yield: 6 lb. 8 oz. (3 kg)

Egg whites	2 lb. 3 oz.	1 kg
Granulated sugar	4 lb. 6 oz.	2 kg
Coffee extract (optional)	2½ fl. oz.	75 ml

1 Whip the egg whites to soft peaks. With the mixer running at medium speed, slowly add the sugar and continue whipping until very stiff and glossy.

2 If desired, whip in the coffee extract.

3 Spread or pipe the meringue into the desired shapes on parchment-lined sheet pans.

4 Bake at 200°F (120°C) for 5 hours or overnight in a nonconvection oven. The baked meringues should be firm and crisp but not browned.

5 Use in assembling dessert or pastry items.

Approximate values per serving: **Calories** 80, **Total fat** 0 g, **Saturated fat** 0 g, **Cholesterol** 0 mg, **Sodium** 15 mg, **Total carbohydrates** 20 g, **Protein** 1 g

CHOCOLATE DÉLICE

RECIPE 32.28

Yield: 1 Cake, 8 in. (20 cm)

Ganache (recipe follows)	7 oz.	210 g
Classic Dacquoise (recipe follows),		
8-in. (20 cm) disks	3	3
Créme Chantilly (recipe follows)	2 qt.	2 lt
Candied Almonds (recipe follows)	as needed	as needed

1 Spread an even layer of ganache over two of the dacquoise disks.

2 Top one disk with approximately ³/₄ cup (170 milliliters) of Créme Chantilly. Place the second disk on top, chocolate side up. Top with another ³/₄ cup (170 milliliters) of Créme Chantilly. Position the third disk on top, flat side up.

3 Spread the remaining Créme Chantilly over the top and sides.

1 Piping out the meringue disks.

2 Layering the ganache-covered dacquoise.

3 Frosting the délice.

4 Sprinkle Candied Almonds over the top and sides of the cake.

5 Freeze to firm the cream, approximately 1 hour. Remove from freezer and refrigerate for service.

Approximate values per ⅛-cake serving: **Calories** 490, **Total fat** 32.5 g, **Saturated fat** 13 g, **Cholesterol** 50 mg, **Sodium** 35 mg, **Total carbohydrates** 39 g, **Protein** 10 g, **Vitamin A** 16%

CLASSIC DACQUOISE

Yield: 3 Disks, 8 in. (20 cm)

Blanched almonds	2 oz.	60 g
Granulated sugar	6 oz.	180 g
Egg whites	3 oz.	90 g

1 Preheat oven to 225°F (110°C). Line a baking sheet with parchment. Draw three 8-inch (20-centimeter) circles on the parchment.

2 Grind the nuts in a food processor. They should be the consistency of cornmeal and as dry as possible. Combine with 2 ounces (60 grams) of the sugar and set aside.

3 Whip the egg whites on medium speed until foamy. Increase the speed and gradually add 1 ounce (30 grams) of the sugar.

4 Continue whipping until the egg whites form soft peaks. Gradually add the remaining sugar.

5 Continue whipping until smooth and glossy, approximately 2 minutes.

6 Sprinkle the almond-sugar mixture over the meringue and fold together by hand.

7 Using a pastry bag with a plain tip, pipe the meringue onto the parchment paper to form three 8-inch (20-centimeter) rounds.

8 Bake until firm and crisp but not brown, approximately 60–75 minutes. Cool completely.

Approximate values per serving: **Calories** 100, **Total fat** 2.5 g, **Saturated fat** 0 g, **Cholesterol** 0 mg, **Sodium** 15 mg, **Total carbohydrates** 16 g, **Protein** 2 g, **Claims**–low fat; low saturated fat; no cholesterol; very low sodium

GANACHE

Yield: 7 oz. (210 g)

Semisweet chocolate	4 oz.	120 g
Heavy cream	3 fl. oz.	90 ml

1 Chop the chocolate into small pieces and place in a bowl.

2 Heat the cream just to boiling. Pour the cream over the chocolate and stir until the mixture is glossy and smooth. Allow to cool slightly before using.

Approximate values per serving: **Calories** 130, **Total fat** 10 g, **Saturated fat** 6 g, **Cholesterol** 15 mg, **Sodium** 0 mg, **Total carbohydrates** 10 g, **Protein** 1 g, **Vitamin A** 6%

CRÉME CHANTILLY

Yield: 2 qt. (2 lt)

Heavy cream	1 qt.	1 lt
Granulated sugar	3 oz.	90 g
Vanilla extract	1 tsp.	5 ml

1 Whip all the ingredients together until soft peaks form.

Approximate values per serving: **Calories** 100, **Total fat** 10 g, **Saturated fat** 6 g, **Cholesterol** 35 mg, **Sodium** 10 mg, **Total carbohydrates** 3 g, **Protein** 1 g, **Vitamin A** 10%

CANDIED ALMONDS

Egg whites	2	2
Granulated sugar	2 oz.	60 g
Sliced almonds	8 oz.	250 g

1 Preheat oven to 325°F (160°C).

2 Whisk the egg whites and sugar together. Add the almonds. Toss with a rubber spatula to coat the nuts completely.

3 Spread the nuts in a thin layer on a lightly greased baking sheet. Bake until lightly toasted and dry, approximately 15 to 20 minutes. Watch closely to prevent burning.

4 Stir the nuts with a metal spatula every 5 to 7 minutes during baking.

5 Cool completely. Store in an airtight container for up to 10 days.

Approximate values per serving: **Calories** 160, **Total fat** 10 g, **Saturated fat** 1 g, **Cholesterol** 0 mg, **Sodium** 10 mg, **Total carbohydrates** 10 g, **Protein** 6 g, **Claims**—no saturated fat; no cholesterol; very low sodium

GREEK CUSTARD PIE (GALACTOBOUREKO)

RECIPE 32.29

SKORPIOS II, LAKE WORTH, FL

Yield: 1 Pan, 9 in. × 12 in.
(22 cm × 30 cm) 16 Servings

Milk	1 qt.	1 lt
Granulated sugar	4 oz.	120 g
Semolina flour	¾ c.	180 ml
Unsalted butter	2 oz.	60 g
Orange zest, finely grated	1 Tbsp.	15 ml
Vanilla extract	2 tsp.	10 ml
Eggs, beaten	5	5
Clarified butter	6 fl. oz.	180 ml
Phyllo dough, thawed		
(approx. 24 sheets)	1 lb.	500 g
Egg wash	as needed	as needed
Spiced syrup:		
Water	4 fl. oz.	120 ml
Granulated sugar	4 oz.	120 g
Honey	2 fl. oz.	60 ml
Cinnamon sticks	1	1
Whole cloves	3	3

1 In a large saucepan, combine the milk and sugar. Bring to a boil, stirring to dissolve the sugar. Gradually whisk in the semolina. Continue whisking until the mixture thickens and becomes smooth, approximately 2 minutes.

2 Add the 2 ounces (60 grams) of unsalted butter, stirring to melt. Remove from the heat and stir in the orange zest and vanilla. Cool the custard to room temperature, then whisk in the beaten eggs.

3 Brush the baking dish with clarified butter. Spread out the phyllo dough on a work surface and cover with a damp towel and then with plastic wrap to prevent it from drying out. Place one sheet of phyllo in the baking dish. Brush with clarified butter and top with another sheet of phyllo. Repeat until 12 sheets of phyllo have been placed in the baking pan.

4 Spread the custard evenly over the phyllo. Top the custard with the remaining phyllo, brushing clarified butter between each sheet. Brush the top layer with egg wash. Cut through the phyllo top to mark servings.

5 Bake at 350°F (180°C) until the phyllo is a deep golden brown and the custard is set, approximately 55 minutes.

6 Prepare the syrup by combining all the ingredients in a small saucepan. Bring to a simmer, stirring to dissolve the sugar. Allow the syrup to boil for 5 minutes. Remove from the heat and set aside to cool, then remove the cloves and cinnamon.

7 When the pie is removed from the oven, immediately begin pouring the syrup slowly over the pie, allowing the syrup to soak in before adding more. Chill the pie before cutting for service.

Approximate values per serving: **Calories** 360, **Total fat** 18 g, **Saturated fat** 10 g, **Cholesterol** 105 mg, **Sodium** 190 mg, **Total carbohydrates** 42 g, **Protein** 7 g, **Vitamin A** 15%

RECIPE 32.30

PEACH AND BLUEBERRY NAPOLEON

PESCE RESTAURANT, Houston, TX

Milan Villavicencio

Yield: 10 Servings

Peaches	7	7
Blueberries	2 pt.	1 lt
Orange Muscat wine	8 fl. oz.	240 ml
Phyllo Crisps (recipe follows)	30	30
Muscat Pastry Cream (recipe follows)	as needed	as needed
Powdered sugar	as needed	as needed
Raspberry Sauce (page 1107)	1 pt.	450 ml

1 Split the peaches in half and discard the pits. Cut each half into six wedges.

2 Macerate the peach wedges and blueberries in the wine.

3 To assemble each napoleon, place a Phyllo Crisp in the center of a plate. Pipe Muscat Pastry Cream along the edges of the crisp. Arrange four peach wedges and approximately six blueberries on the crisp and pipe a dollop of pastry cream on top of the fruit. Place another crisp on top of the pastry cream and fruit, pipe more pastry cream and add more fruit to this second layer. Top with a third crisp and dust with powdered sugar.

4 Drizzle Raspberry Sauce around the napoleon on the plate and garnish with additional blueberries.

Approximate values per serving: **Calories** 790, **Total fat** 31 g, **Saturated fat** 17 g, **Cholesterol** 355 mg, **Sodium** 170 mg, **Total carbohydrates** 111 g, **Protein** 10 g, **Vitamin A** 35%, **Vitamin C** 20%, **Calcium** 15%

PHYLLO CRISPS

Yield: 10 Servings

Whole butter, melted	4 oz.	120 g
Phyllo dough, 12-in. × 17-in. (30-cm × 42-cm) sheets	8	8
Powdered sugar	8 oz.	240 g

1 Line a full-sized sheet pan with parchment paper and brush with melted butter. Dust with powdered sugar and place two sheets of phyllo dough side by side on the pan.

2 Brush the phyllo sheets with butter and dust with powdered sugar. Place a second phyllo sheet on top of each of the first sheets, brush them with butter and dust with powdered sugar. Continue until there are two stacks of phyllo dough, each four layers high.

3 Using a pastry wheel, cut each stack of phyllo into four columns and four rows, creating 16 small rectangular stacks of phyllo dough from each large stack.

4 Cover the phyllo stacks with parchment paper and another sheet pan. Bake at 325°F (160°C) until brown, approximately 15 minutes. Remove and cool.

Approximate values per crisp: **Calories** 70, **Total fat** 3 g, **Saturated fat** 2 g, **Cholesterol** 10 mg, **Sodium** 25 mg, **Total carbohydrates** 10 g, **Protein** 0 g

MUSCAT PASTRY CREAM

Yield: 10 Servings, 5 fl. oz. (150 ml) each

Milk	1 pt.	500 ml
Vanilla bean, seeded	½	½
Cornstarch	2 oz.	60 g
Granulated sugar	8 oz.	225 g
Salt	⅛ tsp.	0.5 ml
Whole eggs	2	2
Egg yolks	4	4
Orange Muscat wine	2 fl. oz.	60 ml
Heavy cream, cold	12 fl. oz.	360 ml

1 Reserve 2 fluid ounces (60 milliliters) of the milk. Place the remaining milk in a saucepot and add the vanilla bean and its seeds. Scald the milk.

2 Combine the cornstarch with 7 ounces (210 grams) of the sugar, the salt and the reserved milk and whisk until smooth. Add the eggs and yolks and mix until they are incorporated and the mixture is smooth.

3 Temper the cornstarch mixture with some of the scalded milk and return the mixture to the saucepot with the remaining milk. Whisk and cook over medium heat until the mixture has thickened and begins to boil.

4 Remove the pastry cream from the heat and pour into a hotel pan. Lay plastic wrap over the surface of the pastry cream and refrigerate until completely cold.

5 Whip the chilled pastry cream until smooth, approximately 1 minute. Add the wine and whip to combine.

6 Whip the heavy cream with the remaining sugar to stiff peaks. Combine the whipped pastry cream and the whipped cream and whip together, scraping down the bowl as necessary. Refrigerate until ready to use.

Approximate values per 5-fl.-oz. (150-ml) serving: **Calories** 370, **Total fat** 22 g, **Saturated fat** 11 g, **Cholesterol** 330 mg, **Sodium** 90 mg, **Total carbohydrates** 36 g, **Protein** 8 g, **Vitamin A** 20%, **Calcium** 10%

LINZER TART

RECIPE 32.31

CHEFS SUSAN FENIGER AND MARY SUE MILLIKEN

Yield: 8–10 Servings

Unsalted butter, softened	8 oz.	225 g
Granulated sugar	8 oz.	225 g
Egg yolks	2	2
Orange zest	2 Tbsp.	30 ml
Lemon zest	1 Tbsp.	15 ml

Continued

All-purpose flour	11 oz.	330 g
Hazelnuts, ground fine	6 oz.	180 g
Baking powder	1 tsp.	5 ml
Cinnamon, ground	2 tsp.	10 ml
Cloves, ground	½ tsp.	2 ml
Salt	¼ tsp.	1 ml
Raspberry preserves	6 oz.	180 g

1 To make the dough, cream together the butter and sugar until light and fluffy. Add the egg yolks and the orange and lemon zests. Beat until well combined.

2 In another bowl, mix together all the remaining ingredients except the preserves. Add the dry mixture all at once to the creamed mixture and mix briefly, until just combined. (This dough looks more like cookie dough than pastry.) Wrap in plastic and chill until firm, at least 4 hours or overnight.

3 Divide the dough in half. On a generously floured board, briefly knead one piece of dough and flatten it with the palm of your hand. Gently roll the dough out ¼ inch (6 millimeters) thick and use it to line a 9- or 10-inch (22- or 25-centimeter) tart pan with a removable bottom. This rich dough patches easily. Chill for approximately 10 minutes.

4 Roll out the second piece of dough to form a 12-inch × 4-inch (30-centimeter × 10-centimeter) rectangle. Using a sharp knife or pastry wheel, cut lengthwise strips, approximately ⅓ inch (8 millimeters) wide.

5 Remove the lined tart shell from the refrigerator and spread the raspberry preserves evenly over it. To create the lattice pattern with the pastry strips, first lay some strips in parallel lines, ½ inch (1.2 centimeters) apart. Then lay a second row of strips at a 45-degree angle to the first. Press the strips to the edge of the crust to seal.

6 Bake at 350°F (180°C) until the crust is golden brown and the filling is bubbly in center, approximately 45 minutes. Set aside to cool.

Approximate values per ¹/₁₀-tart serving: **Calories** 300, **Total fat** 29 g, **Saturated fat** 12 g, **Cholesterol** 90 mg, **Sodium** 65 mg, **Total carbohydrates** 7 g, **Protein** 4 g, **Vitamin A** 20%, **Claims—** low sodium; good source of fiber

RECIPE 32.32

CHOCOLATE BEIGNETS

HERBSAINT BAR AND RESTAURANT, New Orleans, LA
Chef Donald Link

Beignets (ben-YEA), are leavened, deep-fried doughnutlike pastries smothered in powdered sugar. They are served piping hot 24 hours a day in New Orleans' French Quarter. Chef Link has added chocolate to the traditional formula for this dessert presentation.

Yield: 60 Pieces   **Method:** Deep-Frying

Chocolate ganache filling:		
Dark chocolate	1 lb.	450 g
Heavy cream	1 pt.	450 ml
Whole butter	4 oz.	120 g
Dried cherries	2 oz.	60 g
Flour	26 oz.	780 g
Cocoa powder	1¾ oz.	50 g
Granulated sugar	4 oz.	120 g
Salt	½ tsp.	2 g
Granulated yeast	2 Tbsp.	30 ml
Milk, warm	6 fl. oz.	180 ml
Eggs	7	7

Whole butter	5 oz.	150 g
Egg wash	as needed	as needed
Powdered sugar	as needed	as needed

1 To make the ganache, chop the chocolate into small pieces and place in the bowl of a small electric mixer. Bring the cream to a boil and pour over the chocolate. Allow the chocolate and cream to sit for 5 minutes. Using the whisk attachment, mix on low speed, adding the butter in chunks, until the mixture comes together and is shiny. Allow the filling to rest at room temperature until it begins to firm. Then pipe the ganache into ½-ounce (15-gram) "kisses" using a large plain piping tip.

2 Steep the cherries in hot water for 5 minutes, then drain and chop.

3 Combine the flour with the cocoa powder and sift together, then combine with the sugar and salt.

4 Combine the yeast with the warm milk. Add the yeast and milk to the dry ingredients in the bowl of a small electric mixer fitted with a dough hook. Mix the ingredients at low speed, adding the eggs one at a time. Mix the dough until gluten develops, approximately 7 to 10 minutes. Allow the dough to rest for 5 minutes. Then mix on medium speed, adding the butter a small piece at a time. Let the butter mix in after each addition. When all of the butter has been added and the dough is pulling away from the sides of the bowl, add the cherries and mix until incorporated. Allow the dough to rest in the refrigerator for 30 minutes before using.

5 Roll a portion of the dough into a long rectangle, approximately 2 inches (5 centimeters) wide and ⅛ inch (3 millimeters) thick. Mark a centerline down the length of the dough with the back of a chef's knife. Brush the dough with egg wash. Place the ganache kisses on the lower half of the dough, spaced approximately 2 inches (5 centimeters) apart. Fold the upper half of the dough over the truffles. Press the dough together around the ganache, ravioli-style. Cut the dough between the truffles to form individual pillows. Place the beignets on a parchment-covered sheet pan and freeze.

6 Using the double-basket method, deep-fry the frozen beignets at 325°F (160°C) for approximately 3 to 4 minutes. Drain, toss in powdered sugar and serve.

Approximate values per 3-piece serving: **Calories** 870, **Total fat** 54 g, **Saturated fat** 30 g, **Cholesterol** 225 mg, **Sodium** 170 mg, **Total carbohydrates** 93 g, **Protein** 17 g, **Vitamin A** 30%, **Calcium** 10%, **Iron** 35%

 ## CHOCOLATE JUMBLE COOKIES
RECIPE 32.33

Yield: 33 Cookies, 1 oz. (30 g) each   **Method:** Drop Cookies

Coffee or espresso	2 fl. oz.	60 ml
Unsweetened chocolate	2 oz.	60 g
Flour, sifted	4½ oz.	135 g
Salt	¼ tsp.	1 ml
Unsalted butter	3 oz.	90 g
Vanilla extract	½ tsp.	3 ml
Granulated sugar	8 oz.	240 g
Eggs	2	2
Walnuts, chopped	6 oz.	180 g
Milk chocolate chips	6 oz.	180 g

1 Combine the coffee and chocolate and melt over a bain marie.

2 Stir the flour and salt together and set aside.

3 Cream the butter, vanilla and sugar together until fluffy. Add the eggs one at a time. Add the chocolate, stirring to blend well.

4 Stir the flour into the chocolate mixture, then fold in the nuts and chocolate chips. Refrigerate the dough for at least 1 hour before baking.

5 Portion into 1-ounce (30-gram) mounds using a #20 portion scoop. Place on parchment-lined baking sheets and bake at 375°F (190°C) until set, approximately 12 minutes.

Approximate values per cookie: **Calories** 130, **Total fat** 8 g, **Saturated fat** 3 g, **Cholesterol** 20 mg, **Sodium** 25 mg, **Total carbohydrates** 14 g, **Protein** 2 g

---

RECIPE 32.34   SPICED OATMEAL COOKIES

Yield: 36 Cookies	**Method:** Drop Cookies	
All-purpose shortening	6 oz.	180 g
Brown sugar	6 oz.	180 g
Granulated sugar	6 oz.	180 g
Eggs	2	2
Orange juice concentrate	2 Tbsp.	30 ml
All-purpose flour	7 oz.	210 g
Baking soda	1 tsp.	5 ml
Baking powder	1 tsp.	5 ml
Salt	1 tsp.	5 ml
Cinnamon, ground	1 tsp.	5 ml
Allspice, ground	½ tsp.	2 ml
Nutmeg, ground	½ tsp.	2 ml
Regular oats	1 pt.	500 ml
Dark raisins	6 oz.	180 g
Golden raisins	6 oz.	180 g

1 Cream the shortening and sugars until light and fluffy. Add the eggs and orange juice concentrate.

2 Sift the dry ingredients together and add them to the creamed mixture.

3 Blend in the oats and raisins.

4 Portion the dough onto lightly greased sheet pans and bake at 325°F (160°C) until almost firm, approximately 12 minutes.

Approximate values per cookie: **Calories** 150, **Total fat** 5 g, **Saturated fat** 1.5 g, **Cholesterol** 10 mg, **Sodium** 105 mg, **Total carbohydrates** 24 g, **Protein** 2 g, **Claims**—low cholesterol; low sodium

---

RECIPE 32.35   CHOCOLATE CHIP COOKIES

Yield: 48 Cookies, 3½ oz. (100 g) each	**Method:** Icebox Cookies	
Granulated sugar	8 oz.	225 g
Brown sugar	12 oz.	360 g
Vegetable shortening	1 lb.	450 g
Eggs	4	4
Vanilla extract	2 tsp.	10 ml
All-purpose flour	1 lb. 4 oz.	600 g
Baking soda	2 tsp.	10 ml
Salt	2 tsp.	10 ml
Pecans, chopped	8 oz.	225 g
Chocolate chips	2 lb.	900 g

1 Cream the sugars and shortening in a mixer fitted with a flat paddle. Beat until light, approximately 5 minutes at medium speed.

2 Add the eggs to the creamed mixture one at a time. Add the vanilla.

3 Stir the dry ingredients together and add to the creamed mixture.

4 Stir in the pecans and chips.

5 Divide the dough onto two pieces on parchment paper. Wrap the dough in the paper and roll each portion into a log. (The diameter of the logs will be the approximate diameter of the finished cookies.) Wrap the paper tightly and twist the ends to close. Chill until completely firm. When ready to bake, cut each log into ½-inch (1.2-centimeter) slices. Arrange the slices on a parchment-lined sheet pan and bake at 350°F (180°C) for 10 to 12 minutes.

Approximate values per 2-oz. (60-g) cookie: **Calories** 310, **Total fat** 20 g, **Saturated fat** 7 g, **Cholesterol** 20 mg, **Sodium** 160 mg, **Total carbohydrates** 35 g, **Protein** 3 g

CHERRY-ALMOND FLORENTINES

RECIPE 32.36

HOUSTON COMMUNITY COLLEGE, Houston, TX
Pastry Chef Eddy Van Damme

Yield: 40 Cookies

Method: Bar cookies

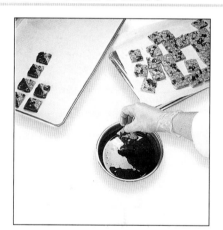

Sweet Dough (page 999), chilled	1 lb.	450 g
Sugar	6 oz.	180 g
Glucose or corn syrup	2 oz.	60 g
Water	3 fl. oz.	90 ml
Butter, cubed	5 oz.	150 g
Honey	2½ oz.	75 g
Heavy cream, boiling	3 fl. oz.	90 ml
Vanilla extract	1 tsp.	5 ml
Almonds, sliced, toasted	11 oz.	330 g
Dried cherries	2 oz.	60 g
Semisweet couverture, tempered	as needed	as needed

1 Roll chilled Sweet Dough ⅛ inch (3 millimeters) thick and slightly larger than a half-size sheet pan. Line the bottom and sides of the sheet pan with the dough. Prick the dough with a fork.

2 Bake blind at 375°F (190°C) until blonde in color, approximately 8 to 11 minutes. Remove from the oven and set aside to cool.

3 Boil the sugar, glucose and water to a golden caramel, approximately 325°F (163°C).

4 Add the butter and honey to the caramel, then add the boiling cream. Bring the mixture to a full boil.

5 Remove from heat and add the vanilla, almonds and cherries. While still warm, spread the mixture onto the prebaked crust in a thin, even layer.

6 Bake at 375°F (190°C) for approximately 20 minutes or until the center has set and is golden brown.

7 Cool completely, then cut into squares. Dip one corner of each piece in tempered semisweet chocolate.

Approximate values per cookie: **Calories** 160, **Total fat** 10 g, **Saturated fat** 3.5 g, **Cholesterol** 15 mg, **Sodium** 0 mg, **Total carbohydrates** 15 g, **Protein** 3 g

RECIPE 32.37

SUGAR COOKIES

Yield: 36 Cookies **Method:** Cut-out Cookies

All-purpose flour	12 oz.	360 g
Baking powder	2 tsp.	10 ml
Mace, ground	¼ tsp.	1 ml
Unsalted butter, softened	4 oz.	120 g
Granulated sugar	8 oz.	250 g
Vanilla extract	1 tsp.	5 ml
Egg	1	1

1 Stir together the flour, baking powder and mace. Set aside.

2 Cream the butter and sugar until light and fluffy. Blend in the vanilla. Add the egg and beat again until fluffy. Gradually add the flour mixture, beating just until well combined.

3 Wrap the dough in plastic wrap and refrigerate until firm, approximately 1 to 2 hours.

4 Work with half of the dough at a time, keeping the remainder refrigerated. On a lightly floured board, roll out the dough to a thickness of approximately ⅛ inch (3 millimeters). Cut as desired with cookie cutters. Carefully transfer the cookies to lightly greased baking sheets.

5 Bake at 325°F (160°C) until golden brown, approximately 10 to 12 minutes. Let stand for 1 minute, then transfer to wire racks to cool.

Approximate values per cookie: **Calories** 90, **Total fat** 3 g, **Saturated fat** 1.5 g, **Cholesterol** 15 mg, **Sodium** 0 mg, **Total carbohydrates** 14 g, **Protein** 1 g, **Claims**—low fat; low cholesterol; no sodium

RECIPE 32.38

GINGERBREAD COOKIES

Yield: 12 Cookies **Method:** Cut-out Cookies

Unsalted butter, softened	4 oz.	120 g
Brown sugar	4 oz.	120 g
Molasses	6 fl. oz.	180 ml
Egg	1	1
All-purpose flour	12 oz.	360 g
Baking soda	1 tsp.	5 ml
Salt	½ tsp.	2 ml
Ginger, ground	2 tsp.	10 ml
Cinnamon, ground	1 tsp.	5 ml
Nutmeg, ground	½ tsp.	2 ml
Cloves, ground	½ tsp.	2 ml

1 Cream the butter and sugar until light and fluffy. Add the molasses and egg and beat to blend well; set aside.

2 Stir together the remaining ingredients. Gradually add the flour mixture to the butter mixture, beating until just blended. Gather the dough into a ball and wrap in plastic wrap; refrigerate for at least 1 hour.

3 On a lightly floured board, roll out the gingerbread to a thickness of ¼ inch (6 millimeters). Cut out the cookies with a floured cutter and transfer to greased baking sheets.

4 Bake at 325°F (160°C) until the cookies are lightly browned around the edges and feel barely firm when touched, approximately 10 minutes. Transfer to wire racks to cool. Decorate as desired with Royal Icing (page 1066).

Approximate values per cookie: **Calories** 260, **Total fat** 8 g, **Saturated fat** 5 g, **Cholesterol** 40 mg, **Sodium** 220 mg, **Total carbohydrates** 41 g, **Protein** 4 g, **Vitamin A** 8%

SPRITZ COOKIES

RECIPE 32.39

Yield: 84 Cookies   **Method:** Pressed Cookies

Unsalted butter, softened	8 oz.	250 g
Granulated sugar	4 oz.	120 g
Salt	¼ tsp.	1 ml
Vanilla extract	1 tsp.	5 ml
Egg	1	1
Cake flour, sifted	10 oz.	300 g

1 Cream the butter and sugar until light and fluffy. Add the salt, vanilla and egg; beat well.
2 Gradually add the flour, beating until just blended. The dough should be firm but neither sticky nor stiff.
3 Press or pipe the dough onto an ungreased sheet pan using a cookie press or a piping bag fitted with a large star tip.
4 Bake at 350°F (177°C) until lightly browned around the edges, approximately 10 minutes. Transfer to wire racks to cool.

Approximate values per cookie: **Calories** 40, **Total fat** 2.5 g, **Saturated fat** 1.5 g, **Cholesterol** 10 mg, **Sodium** 10 mg, **Total carbohydrates** 4 g, **Protein** 0 g, **Claims**—low fat; low cholesterol; very low sodium; low calorie

LACY PECAN COOKIES

RECIPE 32.40

Yield: 100 Cookies, 3 in. (7.5 cm)   **Method:** Wafer Cookies

Brown sugar	3 lb.	1.3 kg
Unsalted butter	2 lb. 8 oz.	1.1. kg
Dark corn syrup	3 lb. 12 oz.	1.7 kg
All-purpose flour	3 lb.	1.3 kg
Pecans, finely chopped	2 lb. 8 oz.	1.1 kg

1 Combine the sugar, butter and corn syrup in a large, heavy saucepan. Bring to a boil.
2 Mix the flour and nuts together.
3 As soon as the sugar mixture comes to a boil, start timing it. Let it boil for 3 minutes. Remove from the heat and stir in the flour-nut mixture. Pour into a hotel pan and cool completely.
4 Use a small portion scoop to make equal-sized balls of dough. Flatten out the balls of dough and place on a silicon baking mat or paper-lined sheet pans.
5 Bake at 325°F (160°C) until very dark brown and no longer moist in center, approximately 15 to 18 minutes. Remove from oven and shape as desired.

Approximate values per serving: **Calories** 320, **Total fat** 17 g, **Saturated fat** 6 g, **Cholesterol** 25 mg, **Sodium** 20 mg, **Total carbohydrates** 38 g, **Protein** 2 g

1 Portioning the batter on a sheet pan lined with a silicon mat.

2 Shaping the baked cookies over a rolling pin while still hot.

RECIPE 32.41　　　　　　　　　　TULIPE COOKIES

Yield: 4 lb. 8 oz. (2 kg) Batter;
enough for 30 cups, 3 in. (7.5 cm)　　　**Method:** Wafer Cookie

Unsalted butter	1 lb.	500 g
Powdered sugar	1 lb.	500 g
All-purpose flour	1 lb.	500 g
Egg whites	1 lb. 8 oz.	750 ml

1 Melt the butter and place in a mixer bowl fitted with the paddle attachment. Add the sugar and blend until almost smooth.

2 Add the flour and blend until smooth. With the mixer running, add the egg whites very slowly. Beat until blended, but do not incorporate air into the batter.

3 Strain the dough through a china cap and set aside to cool completely.

4 Coat several sheet pans with melted butter or line with silicon mats. Spread the dough into 6-inch (15-centimeter) circles on the pans. Bake at 400°F (200°C) until the edges are brown and the dough is dry, approximately 12 to 18 minutes.

5 To shape into cups, lift the hot cookies off the sheet pan one at a time with an offset spatula. Immediately place over an inverted glass and top with a ramekin or small bowl. The cookies cool very quickly, becoming firm and crisp. The cookie bowls can be used for serving ice cream, crème brûlée, fruit or other items.

Approximate values per 2½-oz. (75-g) serving: **Calories** 240, **Total fat** 12 g, **Saturated fat** 8 g, **Cholesterol** 35 mg, **Sodium** 40 mg, **Total carbohydrates** 37 g, **Protein** 4 g, **Vitamin A** 10%

1 Spreading the batter into circles on a sheet pan lined with a silicon mat.

2 Shaping the baked wafer cookies into cups while still hot.

MADELEINES   RECIPE 32.42

Madeleines are cookies made from spongecake or genoise batter. They are traditionally shaped as small fluted fans using special molds. Madeleines are popular petits fours served with tea or coffee, as their somewhat dry, spongy texture is excellent for dipping into a hot beverage. Unlike the classic that launched Marcel Proust on his "Remembrance of Things Past," this recipe incorporates brown butter (beurre noisette) for additional flavor.

Yield: 12 Large Cookies	**Method:** Spongecake Cookies	
Unsalted butter	4 oz.	120 g
Eggs	2	2
Granulated sugar	3 oz.	90 g
Lemon zest, grated fine	1 tsp.	5 ml
Lemon juice	¼ tsp.	1 ml
Vanilla extract	¼ tsp.	1 ml
Baking powder	⅛ tsp.	0.5 ml
Cake flour, sifted	3 oz.	90 g

1 Melt the butter over medium heat; continue cooking until the milk solids turn a golden-brown color. Set aside to cool.

2 Whisk the eggs and sugar over a bain marie until warm (98°F/38°C). Remove from the heat and whisk in the lemon zest, lemon juice and vanilla.

3 Sift the baking powder and flour together; stir into the egg mixture. Stir in the melted and cooled butter. Cover the bowl and allow to rest for 1 hour at room temperature.

4 Butter and flour the madeleine shells. Spoon or pipe the batter into the shells, filling each three-fourths full.

5 Bake at 450°F (230°C) until the cookies rise in the center and are very light brown on the bottom and edges, approximately 3 to 4 minutes for 1½-inch (3.7-centimeter) madeleines and 10 to 12 minutes for 3-inch (7.5-centimeter) madeleines. They should spring back when touched lightly in the center. Remove the madeleines from the oven, invert the pan over a wire cooling rack, and tap lightly to release the cookies from the pan.

Approximate values per cookie: **Calories** 110, **Total fat** 7 g, **Saturated fat** 4 g, **Cholesterol** 45 mg, **Sodium** 10 mg, **Total carbohydrates** 10 g, **Protein** 1 g, **Vitamin A** 6%

1 Piping the batter into greased and floured molds.

2 The finished madeleines.

ANYONE CAN MAKE YOU ENJOY THE FIRST BITE OF A
DISH, BUT ONLY A REAL CHEF CAN MAKE YOU ENJOY
THE LAST.

—*François Minot*

33

CAKES
AND FROSTINGS

HYATT REGENCY SCOTTSDALE AT GAINEY RANCH, Scottsdale, AZ
Former Executive Pastry Chef Judy Doherty

AFTER STUDYING THIS CHAPTER, YOU WILL BE ABLE TO:

▶ prepare a variety of cakes
▶ prepare a variety of frostings
▶ assemble cakes using basic finishing and decorating techniques

Cakes are popular in most bakeshops because a wide variety of finished products can be created from only a few basic cake, filling and frosting formulas. Many of these components can even be made in advance and assembled into finished desserts as needed. Cakes are also popular because of their versatility: They can be served as unadorned sheets in a high-volume cafeteria or as the elaborate centerpiece of a wedding buffet.

Cake making need not be difficult or intimidating, but it does require an understanding of ingredients and mixing methods. This chapter begins by explaining how typical cake ingredients interact. Each of the traditional mixing methods is then explained and illustrated with a recipe. Information on panning batters, baking temperatures, determining doneness and cooling methods follows. The second portion of this chapter presents mixing methods and formulas for a variety of frostings and icings. The third section covers cake assembly and presents some simple and commonly used cake decorating techniques. A selection of popular cake formulas concludes the chapter.

▶ CAKES

Most cakes are created from liquid batters with high fat and sugar contents. The baker's job is to combine all the ingredients to create a structure that will support these rich ingredients, yet keep the cake as light and delicate as possible. As with other baked goods, it is impossible to taste a cake until it is fully cooked and too late to alter the formula. Therefore, it is extremely important to study any formula before beginning and to follow it with particular care and attention to detail.

INGREDIENTS

Good cakes begin with high-quality ingredients (see Chapter 29, Principles of the Bakeshop). However, even the finest ingredients must be combined in the proper balance. Too much flour and the cake may be dry; too much egg and the cake will be tough and hard. Changing one ingredient may necessitate a change in one or more of the other ingredients.

Each ingredient performs a specific function and has a specific effect on the final product. Cake ingredients can be classified by function as tougheners, tenderizers, moisteners, driers, leaveners and flavorings. Some ingredients fulfill more than one of these functions. For example, eggs contain water, so they are moisteners, and they contain protein, so they are tougheners. By understanding the function of various ingredients, you should be able to understand why cakes are made in particular ways and why a preparation sometimes fails. With additional experience, you should be able to recognize and correct flawed formulas and develop your own cake formulas.

TOUGHENERS

Flour, milk and eggs contain protein. Protein provides structure and toughens the cake. Too little protein and the cake may collapse; too much protein and the cake may be tough and coarse-textured.

TENDERIZERS

Sugar, fats and egg yolks shorten gluten strands, making the cake tender and soft. These ingredients also improve the cake's keeping qualities.

MOISTENERS

Liquids such as water, milk, juice and eggs bring moisture to the mixture. Moisture is necessary for gluten formation and starch gelatinization, as well as for improving a cake's keeping qualities.

DRIERS

Flour, starches and milk solids absorb moisture, giving body and structure to the cake.

LEAVENERS

Cakes rise because gases in the batter expand when heated. Cakes are leavened by the air trapped when fat and sugar are creamed together, by carbon dioxide released from baking powder and baking soda and by air trapped in beaten eggs. All cakes rely on natural leaveners—steam and air—to create the proper texture and rise. Because baking soda and baking powder are also used in some cake formulas, you should review the material on chemical leaveners in Chapter 30, Quick Breads.

FLAVORINGS

Flavorings such as extracts, cocoa, chocolate, spices, salt, sugar and butter provide cakes with the desired flavors. Acidic flavoring ingredients such as sour cream, chocolate and fruit also provide the acid necessary to activate baking soda.

Cake ingredients should be at room temperature, approximately 70°F (21°C), before mixing begins. If one ingredient is too cold or too warm, it may affect the batter's ability to trap and hold the gases necessary for the cake to rise.

MIXING METHODS

Even the finest ingredients will be wasted if the cake batter is not mixed correctly. When mixing any cake batter, your goals are to combine the ingredients uniformly, incorporate air cells and develop the proper texture.

All mixing methods can be divided into two categories: high fat—those that create a structure that relies primarily on **creamed fat**—and egg foam—those that create a structure that relies primarily on **whipped eggs.** Within these broad categories are several mixing methods or types of cakes. Creamed-fat cakes include **butter cakes** (also known as **creaming method cakes**) and **high-ratio cakes.** Whipped-egg cakes include **genoise, spongecakes, angel food cakes** and **chiffon cakes.** See Table 33.1. Although certain general procedures are used to prepare each cake type, there are, of course, variations. Follow specific formula instructions precisely.

CREAMED FAT

Creamed-fat cakes include most of the popular American-style cakes: poundcakes, layer cakes, coffeecakes and even brownies. All are based on high-fat formulas containing chemical leaveners. A good high-fat cake has a fine grain, cells of uniform size and a crumb that is moist rather than crumbly. Crusts should be thin and tender.

Creamed-fat cakes can be divided into two classes: butter cakes and high-ratio cakes.

Table 33.1 CAKES

CATEGORY	MIXING METHOD/TYPE OF CAKE	KEY FORMULA CHARACTERISTICS	TEXTURE
Creamed fat (high fat)	Butter (creaming method)	High-fat formula; chemical leavener used	Fine grain; air cells of uniform size; moist crumb; thin and tender crust
	High-ratio (two-stage)	Emulsified shortening; two-part mixing method	Very fine grain; moist crumb; relatively high rise
Whipped egg (egg foam)	Genoise	Whole eggs are whipped with sugar; no chemical leaveners	Dry and spongy
	Sponge	Egg yolks are mixed with other ingredients, then whipped egg whites are folded in	Moister and more tender than genoise
	Angel food	No fat; large quantity of whipped egg whites; high percentage of sugar	Tall, light and spongy
	Chiffon	Vegetable oil used; egg yolks mixed with other ingredients, then whipped egg whites folded in; baking power may be added	Tall, light and fluffy; moister and richer than angel food

▶ **creaming** vigorously combining fat and sugar while incorporating air

POUNDCAKES

Poundcakes are the original high-fat, creaming method cake. They are called pound-cakes because early formulas specified one pound each of butter, eggs, flour and sugar. Poundcakes should have a close grain and compact texture but still be very tender. They should be neither heavy nor soggy.

As bakers experimented with pound-cake formulas, they reduced the amount of eggs and fat, substituting milk instead. These changes led to the development of the modern butter cake.

Butter Cakes

Butter cakes, also known as creaming method cakes, begin with softened butter or shortening **creamed** to incorporate air cells. Because of their high fat content, these cakes usually need the assistance of a chemical leavener to achieve the proper rise.

Modern-day butter cakes—the classic American layer cakes, popular for birthdays and special occasions—are made with the creaming method. These cakes are tender yet sturdy enough to handle rich buttercreams or fillings. High-fat cakes are too soft and delicate, however, to use for roll cakes or to slice into extremely thin layers.

When making butter cakes, the fat should be creamed at low to moderate speeds to prevent raising its temperature. An increased temperature could cause a loss of air cells.

▶ PROCEDURE FOR PREPARING BUTTER CAKES (CREAMING METHOD)

1 Preheat the oven and prepare the pans.
2 Sift the dry ingredients together and set aside.
3 Cream the butter or shortening until it is light and fluffy. Add the sugar and cream until the mixture is fluffy and smooth.
4 Add the eggs slowly, beating well after each addition.
5 Add the dry and liquid ingredients alternately.
6 Divide the batter into prepared pans and bake immediately.

RECIPE 33.1 CLASSIC POUNDCAKE

Yield: 2 Loaves, 8 in. × 4 in. (20 cm × 10 cm)　　　**Method:** Creaming

Cake flour	1 lb.	500 g
Baking powder	2 tsp.	10 ml
Salt	½ tsp.	2 ml

Unsalted butter, softened	1 lb.	500 g
Granulated sugar	12 oz.	340 g
Eggs	9	9
Vanilla extract	1 tsp.	5 ml
Lemon extract	1 tsp.	5 ml

1 Sift the cake flour, baking powder and salt together; set aside.
2 Cream the butter and sugar until light and fluffy. Add the eggs one at a time, beating well after each addition. Stir in the extracts.
3 Fold in the dry ingredients by hand. Divide the batter into greased loaf pans.
4 Bake at 325°F (160°C) until golden brown and springy to the touch, approximately 1 hour and 10 minutes.

Variation: *French-Style Fruitcake*—Add 6 ounces (180 grams) finely diced nuts, raisins and candied fruit to the batter. Substitute vanilla extract for the lemon extract and add 3 tablespoons (45 milliliters) rum to the batter. After baking, brush the warm cake with additional rum.

Approximate values per 3-oz. (90-g) serving: **Calories** 350, **Total fat** 21 g, **Saturated fat** 12 g, **Cholesterol** 145 mg, **Sodium** 90 mg, **Total carbohydrates** 35 g, **Protein** 5 g, **Vitamin A** 20%

1 Creaming the butter.

2 Folding in the flour.

3 Panning the batter.

High-Ratio Cakes

Commercial bakeries often use a special two-stage mixing method to prepare large quantities of a very liquid cake batter. These formulas require special emulsified shortenings and are known as two-stage cakes because the liquids are added in two stages or portions. If emulsified shortenings are not available, do not substitute all-purpose shortening or butter, as those fats cannot absorb the large amounts of sugar and liquid in the formula.

Because they contain a high ratio of sugar and liquid to flour, these cakes are often known as high-ratio cakes. They have a very fine, moist crumb and relatively high rise. High-ratio cakes can be used interchangeably with modern butter cakes but are rarely prepared outside high-volume bakeries such as those found in supermarkets.

WHIPPED EGG

Cakes based on whipped egg foams include European-style genoise as well as spongecakes, angel food cakes and chiffon cakes. Some formulas contain chemical leaveners, but the air whipped into the eggs (whether whole or separated) is the primary leavening agent. Egg-foam cakes contain little or no fat.

Genoise

Genoise is the classic European-style cake. It is based on whole eggs whipped with sugar until very light and fluffy. Chemical leaveners are not used. A small amount of oil or melted butter is sometimes added for flavor and moisture. Genoise is often baked in a thin sheet and layered with buttercream, puréed fruit, jam or chocolate filling to create multilayered specialty desserts, sometimes known as torten. Because genoise is rather dry, it is usually soaked with a flavored sugar syrup (see Chapter 29, Principles of the Bakeshop) or liquor for additional flavor and moisture.

▶ PROCEDURE FOR PREPARING GENOISE

1 Preheat the oven and prepare the pans.
2 Sift the flour with any additional dry ingredients.
3 Combine the whole eggs and sugar in a large bowl and warm over a double boiler to a temperature of 100°F (38°C).
4 Whip the egg-and-sugar mixture until very light and tripled in volume.
5 Fold the sifted flour into the whipped eggs carefully but quickly.
6 Fold in oil or melted butter if desired.
7 Divide into pans and bake immediately.

RECIPE 33.2   **CLASSIC GENOISE**

Yield: 3 Full-Size Sheet Pans		**Method:** Whipped Egg
Cake flour	1 lb. 8 oz.	680 g
Eggs	30	30
Granulated sugar	1 lb. 8 oz.	680 g
Unsalted butter, melted (optional)	4 oz.	120 g

1 Sift the flour and set aside.
2 Whisk the eggs and sugar together in a large mixer bowl. Place the bowl over a bain marie and warm the eggs to approximately 100°F (38°C). Stir frequently to avoid cooking the eggs.
3 When the eggs are warm, remove the bowl from the bain marie and attach to a mixer fitted with a whip attachment. Whip the egg-and-sugar mixture at medium speed until tripled in volume.
4 Quickly fold the flour into the egg mixture by hand. Be careful not to deflate the batter.
5 Pour the melted, cooled butter around the edges of the batter and fold in quickly.
6 Divide the batter immediately into parchment-lined pans. Bake at 350°F (180°C) until light brown and springy to the touch, approximately 8 minutes.

1 Whipped eggs.

2 Folding in the flour.

3 Adding the melted butter.

4 Panning the batter.

Variation: *Chocolate Genoise*—Sift 3½ ounces (100 grams) of cocoa powder with the flour.

Approximate values per 2-oz. (60-g) serving: **Calories** 140, **Total fat** 4 g, **Saturated fat** 2 g, **Cholesterol** 110 mg, **Sodium** 30 mg, **Total carbohydrates** 21 g, **Protein** 4 g, **Vitamin A** 6%

Spongecakes

Spongecakes (Fr. *biscuits*) are made with separated eggs. A batter is prepared with egg yolks and other ingredients, and then egg whites are whipped to firm peaks with a portion of the sugar and folded into the batter. Spongecakes are primarily leavened with air, but baking powder may be included in the formula. As with genoise, oil or melted butter may be added if desired.

Spongecakes are extremely versatile. They can be soaked with sugar syrup or a liquor and assembled with butter cream as a traditional layer cake. Or they can be sliced thinly and layered, like genoise, with a jam, custard, chocolate or cream filling.

▶ PROCEDURE FOR PREPARING SPONGECAKES

1 Preheat the oven and prepare the pans.
2 Separate the eggs. Whip the egg whites with a portion of the sugar.
3 Sift the dry ingredients together and combine with the liquid ingredients, including the egg yolks, as directed.
4 Carefully fold the whipped egg whites into the batter.
5 Pour the batter into the pans and bake immediately.

  CLASSIC SPONGECAKE   RECIPE 33.3

Yield: 2 Rounds, 9 in. (22 cm)   **Method:** Whipped Egg

Cake flour, sifted	6 oz.	180 g
Granulated sugar	11 oz.	330 g
Eggs	10	10
Vanilla extract	1½ tsp.	7 ml
Cream of tartar	1½ tsp.	7 ml

1 The eggs whipped to ribbon stage.

1 Line the bottom of two springform pans with parchment. Do not grease the sides of the pans.
2 Sift the flour and 6 ounces (180 grams) of the sugar together and set aside.
3 Separate the eggs, placing the yolks and the whites in separate mixing bowls. Whip the yolks on high speed until thick, pale and at least doubled in volume, approximately 3 to 5 minutes. Whip in the vanilla extract. The yolks should be whipped "to ribbon," that is, until they fall from the beater in thick ribbons that slowly disappear into the surface.
4 Place the bowl of egg whites on the mixer and, using a clean whip attachment, beat until foamy. Add the cream of tartar and 2 tablespoons (30 grams) of the sugar. Whip at medium speed until the whites are glossy and stiff but not dry.
5 Remove the bowl from the mixer. Pour the egg yolks onto the whipped whites. Quickly fold the two mixtures together by hand. Sprinkle the remaining sugar over the mixture and fold in lightly.
6 Sprinkle one-third of the sifted flour over the batter and fold in. Repeat the procedure until all the flour is incorporated. Do not overmix; fold just until incorporated.
7 Pour the batter into the prepared pans, smoothing the surface as needed. Bake immediately at 375°F (190°C) until the cake is golden brown and

2 Folding the flour into the batter.

3 Panning the batter.

spongy, approximately 30 minutes. A toothpick inserted in the center will be completely clean when removed.

8 Allow the cakes to rest in their pans until completely cool, approximately 2 hours.

9 To remove the cakes from their pans, run a thin metal spatula around the edge of each pan. When the cake is completely cool, it can be frosted or wrapped in plastic wrap and frozen for 2 to 3 months.

Approximate values per 2-oz. (60-g) serving: **Calories** 130, **Total fat** 2.5 g, **Saturated fat** 1 g, **Cholesterol** 105 mg, **Sodium** 30 mg, **Total carbohydrates** 23 g, **Protein** 4 g, **Claims**–low fat; low saturated fat; very low sodium

Angel Food Cakes

Angel food cakes are tall, light cakes made without fat and leavened with a large quantity of whipped egg whites. Angel food cakes are traditionally baked in ungreased tube pans, but large loaf pans can also be used. The pans are left ungreased so that the batter can cling to the sides as it rises. The cakes should be inverted as soon as they are removed from the oven and left in the pan to cool. This technique allows gravity to keep the cakes from collapsing or sinking as they cool.

Although they contain no fat, angel food cakes are not low in calories, as they contain a high percentage of sugar. The classic angel food cake is pure white, but flavorings, ground nuts or cocoa powder may be added for variety. Although angel food cakes are usually not frosted, they may be topped with a fruit-flavored or chocolate glaze. They are often served with fresh fruit, a fruit compote or whipped cream.

▶ PROCEDURE FOR PREPARING ANGEL FOOD CAKES

1 Preheat the oven.

2 Sift the dry ingredients together.

3 Whip the egg whites with a portion of the sugar until stiff and glossy.

4 Gently fold the dry ingredients into the egg whites.

5 Spoon the batter into an ungreased pan and bake immediately.

6 Allow the cake to cool inverted in its pan.

RECIPE 33.4

CHOCOLATE ANGEL FOOD CAKE

1 Folding the egg white and cocoa mixture into the whipped egg whites.

Yield: 1 Tube Cake, 10 in. (25 cm)   **Method:** Whipped egg

Cocoa powder, alkalized	1 oz.	30 g
Water, warm	2 fl. oz.	60 ml
Vanilla extract	2 tsp.	10 ml
Granulated sugar	12 oz.	360 g
Cake flour, sifted	3½ oz.	100 g
Salt	¼ tsp.	1 g
Egg whites	16	16
Cream of tartar	2 tsp.	10 ml

1 Combine the cocoa powder and water in a bowl. Add the vanilla and set aside.

2 In another bowl, combine 5 ounces (150 grams) of the sugar with the flour and salt.

3 Whip the egg whites until foamy, add the cream of tartar and beat to soft peaks. Gradually beat in the remaining sugar. Continue beating until the egg whites are stiff but not dry.

4 Whisk approximately 1 cup (225 milliliters) of the whipped egg whites into the cocoa mixture. Fold this into the remaining egg whites.

5 Sift the dry ingredients over the whites and fold in quickly but gently.

2 Folding in the flour.

3 Cooling the cake upside down in its pan.

4 Removing the cake from the pan.

6 Pour the batter into an ungreased tube pan and smooth the top with a spatula. Bake immediately at 350°F (180°C) until the cake springs back when lightly touched and a cake tester comes out clean, approximately 40 to 50 minutes. The cake's surface will have deep cracks.

7 Remove the cake from the oven and immediately invert the pan onto the neck of a bottle. Allow the cake to rest upside down until completely cool.

8 To remove the cake from the pan, run a thin knife or spatula around the edge of the pan and the edge of the interior tube. If a two-piece tube pan was used, the cake and tube portion are lifted out of the pan. Use a knife or spatula to loosen the bottom of the cake, then invert it onto a cake cardboard or serving platter.

Variation: *Vanilla Angel Food Cake*—Omit the cocoa powder and warm water from the formula. Increase the amount of vanilla extract to 1 tablespoon (15 milliliters) and fold it in at the end of Step 5.

Lemon Angel Food Cake—Omit the cocoa powder and warm water from the formula. Add 2 teaspoons (10 milliliters) fresh lemon zest to the sugar and flour mixture. Add 1 teaspoon (5 milliliters) lemon extract, folding it and the vanilla extract in at the end of Step 5.

Approximate values per serving: **Calories** 210, **Total fat** 0.5 g, **Saturated fat** 0 g, **Cholesterol** 0 mg, **Sodium** 150 mg, **Total carbohydrates** 44 g, **Protein** 7 g, **Claims**—low fat; no saturated fat; no cholesterol

Chiffon Cakes

Although chiffon cakes are similar to angel food cakes in appearance and texture, the addition of egg yolks and vegetable oil makes them moister and richer. Chiffon cakes are usually leavened with whipped egg whites but may contain baking powder as well. Like angel food cakes, chiffon cakes are baked in an ungreased pan to allow the batter to cling to the pan as it rises. Chiffon cakes can be frosted with a light butter cream or whipped cream or topped with a glaze. Lemon and orange chiffon cakes are the most traditional, but formulas containing chocolate, nuts or other flavorings are also common.

▶ PROCEDURE FOR PREPARING CHIFFON CAKES

1 Preheat the oven.
2 Whip the egg whites with a portion of the sugar until almost stiff. Set aside.
3 Sift the dry ingredients together. Add the liquid ingredients, including oil.
4 Fold the whipped egg whites into the batter.
5 Spoon the batter into an ungreased pan and bake immediately.
6 Allow the cake to cool inverted in its pan.

A HOLLYWOOD CLASSIC

Chiffon cake is one of the few desserts whose history can be traced with absolute certainty. According to Gerry Schremp in her book *Kitchen Culture: Fifty Years of Food Fads,* a new type of cake was invented by Henry Baker, a California insurance salesman, in 1927. Dubbed chiffon, it was as light as angel food and as rich as poundcake. For years he kept the formula a secret, earning fame and fortune by selling his cakes to Hollywood restaurants. The cake's secret ingredient—vegetable oil—became public knowledge in 1947 when Baker sold the formula to General Mills, which promoted it on packages of cake flour. Chiffon cakes, in a variety of flavors, became extremely popular nationwide.

RECIPE 33.5

ORANGE CHIFFON CAKE

Yield: 1 Tube Cake, 10 in. (25 cm)   **Method:** Whipped Egg

Cake flour, sifted	8 oz.	225 g
Granulated sugar	12 oz.	360 g
Baking powder	1 Tbsp.	15 ml
Salt	1 tsp.	5 ml
Vegetable oil	4 fl. oz.	120 ml
Egg yolks	6	6
Water, cool	2 fl. oz.	60 ml
Orange juice	4 fl. oz.	120 ml
Orange zest	1 Tbsp.	15 ml
Vanilla extract	1 Tbsp.	15 ml
Egg whites	8 oz.	250 g
Glaze:		
Powdered sugar, sifted	3 oz.	90 g
Orange juice	2 Tbsp.	30 ml
Orange zest	2 tsp.	10 ml

1. Sift together the flour, 6 ounces (170 grams) of sugar and the baking powder and salt.
2. In a separate bowl mix the oil, yolks, water, juice, zest and vanilla. Add the liquid mixture to the dry ingredients.
3. In a clean bowl, beat the egg whites until foamy. Slowly beat in the remaining 6 ounces (170 grams) of sugar. Continue beating until the egg whites are stiff but not dry.
4. Stir one-third of the egg whites into the batter to lighten it. Fold in the remaining egg whites.
5. Pour the batter into an ungreased 10-inch (25-centimeter) tube pan. Bake at 325°F (160°C) until a toothpick comes out clean, approximately 1 hour.
6. Immediately invert the pan over the neck of a wine bottle. Allow the cake to hang upside down until completely cool, then remove from the pan.
7. Stir the glaze ingredients together in a small bowl and drizzle over the top of the cooled cake.

Variation: *Lemon Chiffon Cake*—Substitute 2 fluid ounces (60 milliliters) fresh lemon juice and 2 fluid ounces (60 milliliters) water for the orange juice. Substitute lemon zest for the orange zest. Top with Basic Sugar Glaze (page 1065).

Approximate values per ¹/₁₀-cake serving: **Calories** 370, **Total fat** 15 g, **Saturated fat** 2.5 g, **Cholesterol** 130 mg, **Sodium** 280 mg, **Total carbohydrates** 54 g, **Protein** 6 g, **Vitamin C** 10%

CONVENIENCE PRODUCTS

Packaged cake mixes are a tremendous time-saver for commercial food service operations. Almost any operation can serve a variety of cakes made by relatively unskilled employees using prepared mixes. The results are consistent and the texture and flavor are acceptable to most consumers. Indeed, a well-prepared packaged mix cake is preferable to a poorly prepared cake made from scratch. Most packaged cake mixes can be adapted to include flavorings, nuts, spices or fruits, which can improve the product's overall quality. Frostings, fillings and attractive decorations complete these items.

The convenience of mixes is not without cost, however. Packaged cake mixes are often more expensive than the ingredients needed for an equal number of cakes made from scratch. Cakes made from mixes are also softer and more cottony than scratch cakes, and their flavor tends to be more artificial. Mixing techniques vary, so follow package directions carefully.

PANNING, BAKING AND COOLING

PREPARING PANS

In order to prevent cakes from sticking, most baking pans are coated with fat, a nonstick baking parchment or both. Pans should be prepared before the batter is mixed so that they may be filled and the cakes baked as soon as the batter is finished. If the batter stands while the pans are prepared, air cells within the batter will deflate and volume may be lost.

Solid shortening is better than butter for coating pans because it does not contain any water; butter and margarine contain water and this may cause the cake to stick in places. Solid shortening is also less expensive, tasteless and odorless. Finally, solid shortening does not burn as easily as butter, and it holds a dusting of flour better.

Pan release sprays are useful but must be applied carefully and completely. Although relatively expensive, sprays save time and are particularly effective when used with parchment pan liners.

In kitchens where a great deal of baking is done, it may be more convenient to prepare quantities of pan coating to be kept available for use as needed. Pan coating is a mixture of equal parts oil, shortening and flour that can be applied to cake pans with a pastry brush. It is used whenever pans need to be greased and floured. Pan coating will not leave a white residue on the cake's crust, as a dusting of flour often does.

PAN COATING

RECIPE 33.6

Yield: 1 ½ qt. (1.5 lt)

Vegetable oil	1 lb.	500 g
All-purpose shortening	1 lb.	500 g
Bread flour	1 lb.	500 g

1 Combine all the ingredients in a mixer fitted with the paddle attachment. Blend on low speed for 5 minutes or until smooth.

2 Store in an airtight container at room temperature for up to 2 months.

3 Apply to baking pans in a thin, even layer using a pastry brush.

Pan coating is not appropriate for all cakes, however. Those containing chocolate, raisins or fruit should still be baked in pans lined with parchment paper in order to prevent sticking.

Angel food and chiffon cakes are baked in ungreased, unlined pans because these fragile cakes need to cling to the sides of the pan as they rise. Sponge-cakes and genoise are often baked in pans with a paper liner on the bottom and ungreased sides. Although the ungreased sides give the batter a surface to cling to, the paper liner makes removing the cake from the pan easier.

FILLING PANS

Pans should be filled no more than one-half to two-thirds full. This allows the batter to rise during baking without spilling over the edges.

Pans should be filled to uniform depths. High-fat and egg-foam cake batters can be ladled into each pan according to weight. High-ratio cake batter is so liquid that it can be measured by volume and poured into each pan. Filling the pans uniformly prevents both uneven layers and over- or underfilled pans. If

Table 33.2	PAN PREPARATIONS
PAN PREPARATION	**USED FOR**
Ungreased	Angel food and chiffon cakes
Ungreased sides; paper on bottom	Genoise layers
Greased and papered	High-fat cakes, sponge sheets
Greased and coated with flour	High-fat cakes, chocolate cakes, anything in a Bundt or shaped pan
Greased, floured and lined with paper	Cakes containing melted chocolate, fruit chunks or fruit or vegetable purées

Table 33.3 **CAKE PAN SIZES**		
PAN SHAPE AND SIZE	**QUANTITY OF BATTER***	**NO. OF SERVINGS FOR 2-LAYER CAKE**
Round, 2 in. deep		
6 in.	1 pt.	6
8 in.	3 c.	12
10 in.	1½ qt.	20
12 in.	1 qt. + 3½ c.	30
14 in.	2½ qt.	40
Square, 2 in. deep		
8 in.	1 qt.	16
10 in.	1½ qt.	20
12 in.	2½ qt.	36
14 in.	3 qt. + 1½ c.	48
Rectangular, 2 in. deep		
6 in. × 8 in.	2½ c.	12
9 in. × 13 in.	2 qt.	24
16 in. × 12 in.	2 qt. + 3 c.	36

*Quantities given are approximate and are based on filling the pans two-thirds full of batter. The weight of cake batter needed to properly fill a pan will vary depending on the type of batter, additional flavor ingredients and the amount of air incorporated by the cook.

you are baking three 8-inch layers to be stacked for one presentation and the amount of batter is different in each pan, the baking times will vary and the final product will be uneven.

Cake batter should always be spread evenly in the pan. Use an offset spatula. Do not work the batter too much, however, as this destroys air cells and prevents the cake from rising properly.

BAKING

Temperatures

Always preheat the oven before preparing the batter. If the finished batter must wait while the oven reaches the correct temperature, valuable leavening will be lost and the cake will not rise properly.

Most cakes are baked at temperatures between 325°F and 375°F (160°C and 190°C). The temperature must be high enough to create steam within the batter and cause that steam and other gases in the batter to expand and rise quickly. If the temperature is too high, however, the cake may rise unevenly and the crust may burn before the interior is completely baked. The temperature must also be low enough that the batter can set completely and evenly without drying out. If the temperature is too low, however, the cake will not rise sufficiently and may dry out before baking completely.

If no temperature is given in a formula or you are altering the dimensions of the baking pan from those specified, use common sense in setting the oven temperature. The larger the surface area, the higher the temperature can usually be. Tall cakes, such as Bundt or tube cakes, should be baked at a lower temperature than thin layer or sheet cakes. Tube or loaf cakes take longer to bake than thin sheet cakes; butter cakes, because they contain more liquid, take longer to bake than genoise or spongecake.

Altitude Adjustments

As you learned in Chapter 10, Principles of Cooking, altitude affects the temperatures at which foods cook. The decreased atmospheric pressure at altitudes above 3000 feet affects the creation of steam and the expansion of hot air in cake batters. These factors must be considered when making cakes. Because gases expand more easily at higher altitudes, your cake may rise so much that its structure cannot support it and the cake collapses.

Therefore, the amount of leavening should be decreased at higher altitudes. Chemical leaveners should usually be reduced by one-third at 3500 feet and by two-thirds at altitudes over 5000 feet. Eggs should be underwhipped to avoid incorporating too much air, which would also create too much rise. In general, oven temperatures should also be increased by 25°F (4°C) at altitudes over 3500 feet to help set the cake's structure rapidly.

Because the boiling point decreases at higher altitudes, more moisture will evaporate from your cake during baking. This may cause dryness and an excessive proportion of sugar, which shows up as white spots on the cake's surface. Correct this by reducing every 8 ounces (225 grams) of sugar by ½ ounce (15 grams) at 3000 feet and by 1½ ounces (45 grams) at 7000 feet.

Attempting to adjust typical (that is, sea-level) formulas for high altitudes is somewhat risky, especially in a commercial operation. Furthermore, different types of cakes will need different adjustment techniques. Try to find and use formulas developed especially for your area, or contact the local offices of your state's department of agriculture or the agricultural extension service for detailed assistance.

Determining Doneness

In addition to following the baking time suggested in a formula, several simple tests can be used to determine doneness. Whichever tests are used, avoid opening the oven door to check the cake's progress. Cold air or a drop in oven temperature can cause the cake to fall. Use a timer to note the minimum suggested baking time. Then, and only then, should you use the following tests to evaluate the cake's doneness:

▶ Appearance—The cake's surface should be a light to golden brown. Unless noted otherwise in the formula, the edges should just begin to pull away from the pan. The cake should not jiggle or move beneath its surface.

▶ Touch—Touch the cake lightly with your finger. It should spring back quickly without feeling soggy or leaving an indentation.

▶ Cake tester—If appearance and touch indicate that the cake is done, test the interior by inserting a toothpick, bamboo skewer or metal cake tester into the cake's center. With most cakes, the tester should come out clean. If wet crumbs cling to the tester, the cake probably needs to bake a bit longer.

If a formula provides particular doneness guidelines, they should be followed. For example, some flourless cakes are fully baked even though a cake tester will not come out clean.

COOLING

Generally, a cake is allowed to cool for 10 to 15 minutes in its pan after taking it out of the oven. This helps prevent the cake from cracking or breaking after it is removed from its pan.

To remove the partially cooled cake from its pan, run a thin knife or spatula blade between the pan and the cake to loosen it. Place a wire rack, cake cardboard or sheet pan over the cake and invert. Then remove the pan. The cake can be left upside down to cool completely or inverted again to cool top side up. Wire racks are preferred for cooling cakes because they allow air to circulate, speeding the cooling process and preventing steam from making the cake soggy.

BROWNIES

Where do you draw the line between cakes and brownies? The decision must be a matter of texture and personal preference, for the preparation methods are nearly identical. Brownies are generally chewy and fudgy, sweeter and denser than even the richest of butter cakes.

Brownies are a relatively inexpensive and easy way for a food service operation to offer its customers a fresh-baked dessert. Although not as sophisticated as an elaborate gâteau, a well-made brownie can always be served with pride (and a scoop of ice cream).

Brownies are prepared using the same procedures as those for high-fat cakes. Good brownies are achieved with a proper balance of ingredients: A high percentage of butter to flour produces a dense, fudgy brownie; less butter produces a more cakelike brownie. Likewise, the higher the ratio of sugar, the gooier the finished brownie. In some formulas, the fat is creamed to incorporate air, as with butter cakes. In others, the fat is first melted and combined with other liquid ingredients. Brownies are rarely made with whipped egg whites, however, as this makes their texture too light and cakelike.

Each customer and cook has his or her own idea of the quintessential brownie. Some are cloyingly sweet, with a creamy texture and an abundance of chocolate; others are bitter and crisp. Some are frosted; others need only a dusting of powdered sugar. Baked brownies can be frozen for two to three months if well wrapped.

Table 33.4 TROUBLESHOOTING CHART FOR CAKES

PROBLEM	CAUSE	SOLUTION
Batter curdles during mixing	Ingredients too warm or too cold	Eggs must be at room temperature and added slowly
	Incorrect fat used	Use correct ingredients
	Fat inadequately creamed before liquid was added	Add a portion of the flour, then continue adding the liquid
Cake lacks volume	Flour too strong	Use a weaker flour
	Old chemical leavener	Replace with fresh leavener
	Egg foam underwhipped	Use correct mixing method; do not deflate eggs during folding
	Oven too hot	Adjust oven temperature
Crust burst or cracked	Too much flour or too little liquid	Adjust formula
	Oven too hot	Adjust oven temperature
Cake shrinks after baking	Weak internal structure	Adjust formula
	Too much sugar or fat for the batter to support	Adjust formula
	Cake not fully cooked	Test cake for doneness before removing from oven
	Cake cooled too rapidly	Cool away from drafts
Texture is dense or heavy	Too little leavening	Adjust formula
	Too much fat or liquid	Cream fat or whip eggs properly
	Oven too cool	Adjust oven temperature
Texture is coarse with an open grain	Overmixing	Alter mixing method
	Oven too cool	Adjust oven temperature
Poor flavor	Poor ingredients	Check flavor and aroma of all ingredients
	Unclean pans	Do not grease pans with rancid fats
Uneven shape	Butter not incorporated evenly	Incorporate fats completely
	Batter spread unevenly	Spread batter evenly
	Oven rack not level	Adjust oven racks
	Uneven oven temperature	Adjust oven temperature

Angel food and chiffon cakes should be turned upside down immediately after they are removed from the oven. They are left to cool completely in their pans to prevent the cake from collapsing or shrinking. The top of the pan should not touch the countertop, so that air can circulate under the inverted pan.

All cakes should be left to cool away from drafts or air currents that might cause them to collapse. Cakes should not be refrigerated to speed the cooling process, as rapid cooling can cause cracking. Prolonged refrigeration also causes cakes to dry out.

▶ FROSTING

Frosting, also known as **icing,** is a sweet decorative coating used as a filling between the layers or as a coating over the top and sides of a cake. It is used to add flavor and to improve a cake's appearance. Frosting can also extend a cake's shelf life by forming a protective coating.

There are seven general types of frosting: **buttercream, foam, fudge, fondant, glaze, royal icing** and **ganache.** See Table 33.5. Each type can be produced with a number of formulas and in a range of flavorings.

Table 33.5 FROSTINGS

FROSTING	PREPARATION	TEXTURE/FLAVOR
Buttercream	Mixture of sugar and fat (usually butter); can contain egg yolks or egg whites	Rich but light; smooth, fluffy
Foam	Meringue made with hot sugar syrup	Light, fluffy; very sweet
Fudge	Cooked mixture of sugar, butter and water or milk; applied warm	Heavy, rich and candylike
Fondant	Cooked mixture of sugar and water; applied warm	Thick, opaque; sweet
Glaze	Confectioner's sugar with liquid	Thin; sweet
Royal icing	Uncooked mixture of confectioner's sugar and egg whites	Hard and brittle when dry; chalky
Ganache	Blend of melted chocolate and cream	Rich, smooth; intense chocolate flavor

Because frosting is integral to the flavor and appearance of many cakes, it should be made carefully using high-quality ingredients and natural flavors and colors. A good frosting is smooth; it is never grainy or lumpy. It should complement the flavor and texture of the cake without overpowering it.

BUTTERCREAM

A buttercream is a light, smooth, fluffy mixture of sugar and fat (butter, margarine or shortening). It may also contain egg yolks for richness or whipped egg whites for lightness. A good buttercream will be sweet, but not cloying; buttery, but not greasy.

Buttercreams are popular and useful for most types of cakes and may be flavored or colored as desired. They may be stored, covered, in the refrigerator for several days but must be softened before use.

Although there are many types of buttercream and many formula variations, we discuss the three most popular styles: **simple, Italian** and **French.**

SIMPLE BUTTERCREAM

Simple buttercream, sometimes known as **American-style buttercream,** is made by creaming butter and powdered sugar together until the mixture is light and smooth. Cream, pasteurized eggs and flavorings may be added as desired. Simple buttercream requires no cooking and is quick and easy to prepare.

If cost is a consideration, hydrogenated all-purpose shortening can be substituted for a portion of the butter, but the flavor and mouth-feel will be different. Buttercream made with shortening tends to feel greasier and heavier because shortening does not melt on the tongue like butter. It will be more stable than pure butter buttercream, however, and is necessary when a pure white frosting is desired

▶ PROCEDURE FOR PREPARING SIMPLE BUTTERCREAMS

1 Cream softened butter or shortening until the mixture is light and fluffy.

2 Beat in egg, if desired.

3 Beat in sifted powdered sugar, scraping down the sides of the bowl as needed.

4 Beat in the flavoring ingredients.

RECIPE 33.7

SIMPLE BUTTERCREAM

Yield: 2 lb. (1 kg)

Lightly salted butter, softened	1 lb.	450 g
Pasteurized egg (optional)	2 oz.	60 g
Powdered sugar, sifted	2 lb.	900 g
Vanilla extract	2 tsp.	10 ml

1 Using a mixer fitted with the paddle attachment, cream the butter until light and fluffy.
2 Beat in the egg if desired. Gradually add the sugar, frequently scraping down the sides of the bowl.
3 Add the vanilla and continue beating until the frosting is smooth and light.

Variations: *Light Chocolate Buttercream*—Dissolve 1 ounce (30 grams) sifted cocoa powder in 2 fluid ounces (60 milliliters) cool water. Add to the buttercream along with the vanilla.

Lemon Buttercream—Decrease the vanilla extract to 1 teaspoon (5 milliliters). Add 1 teaspoon (5 milliliters) lemon extract and the finely grated zest of one lemon.

Approximate values per 1-oz. (30-g) serving: **Calories** 170, **Total fat** 6 g, **Saturated fat** 4 g, **Cholesterol** 25 mg, **Sodium** 70 mg, **Total carbohydrates** 28 g, **Protein** 0 g, **Vitamin A** 10%

ITALIAN BUTTERCREAM

Italian buttercream, also known as **meringue buttercream,** is based on an Italian meringue, that is, whipped egg whites cooked with hot sugar syrup. (See Chapter 32, Pies, Pastries and Cookies.) Softened butter is then whipped into the cooled meringue, and the mixture is flavored as desired. This type of buttercream is extremely soft and light. It can be used on most types of cakes and is particularly popular for multilayered genoise and spongecakes.

▶ PROCEDURE FOR PREPARING ITALIAN BUTTERCREAMS

1 Whip the egg whites until soft peaks form.
2 Beat granulated sugar into the egg whites and whip until firm and glossy.
3 Meanwhile, combine additional sugar with water and cook to soft ball stage (240°F/116°C).
4 With the mixer on medium speed, pour the sugar syrup into the whipped egg whites. Pour slowly and carefully to avoid splatters.
5 Continue whipping the egg-white-and-sugar mixture until completely cool.
6 Whip softened, but not melted, butter into the cooled egg-white-and-sugar mixture.
7 Add flavoring ingredients as desired.

RECIPE 33.8

ITALIAN BUTTERCREAM

Yield: 5 lb. (2.2 kg)

Egg whites	14 oz.	400 g
Granulated sugar	1 lb. 11 oz.	750 g
Water	as needed	as needed
Lightly salted butter, softened but not melted	2 lb. 12 oz.	1250 g

1 All ingredients should be at room temperature before beginning.

2 Place the egg whites in a mixer bowl. Have 9 ounces (250 grams) of the sugar nearby.

3 Place 1 pound 2 ounces (500 grams) of the sugar in a heavy saucepan with enough water to moisten. Bring to a boil over high heat.

4 As the sugar syrup's temperature approaches soft ball stage (240°F/116°C), begin whipping the egg whites. Watch the sugar closely so that the temperature does not exceed 240°F (116°C).

5 When soft peaks form in the egg whites, gradually add the 9 ounces (250 grams) of sugar to them. Reduce the mixer speed to medium and continue whipping the egg whites to stiff peaks.

6 When the sugar syrup reaches soft ball stage, immediately pour it into the whites while the mixer is running. Pour the syrup in a steady stream between the side of the bowl and the beater. If the syrup hits the beater, it will splatter and cause lumps. Continue beating at medium speed until the egg whites are completely cool. At this point, the product is known as Italian meringue.

7 Gradually add the softened butter to the Italian meringue. When all the butter is incorporated, add flavoring ingredients as desired.

Variation: *Chocolate Italian Buttercream*—Add 1 tablespoon (15 milliliters) vanilla extract to the buttercream, then stir in 10 ounces (300 grams) melted and cooled bittersweet chocolate.

Approximate values per 1-oz. (30-g) serving: **Calories** 175, **Total fat** 13 g, **Saturated fat** 8 g, **Cholesterol** 34 mg, **Sodium** 140 mg, **Total carbohydrates** 16 g, **Protein** 1 g, **Vitamin A** 10%

FRENCH BUTTERCREAM

French buttercream, also known as **mousseline buttercream,** is similar to Italian buttercream except that the hot sugar syrup is whipped into beaten egg yolks (not egg whites). Softened butter and flavorings are added when the sweetened egg yolks are fluffy and cool. An Italian meringue such as the one created in the preceding formula is sometimes folded in for additional body and lightness. French buttercream is perhaps the most difficult type of buttercream to master, but it has the richest flavor and smoothest texture. Like a meringue buttercream, mousseline buttercream may be used on almost any type of cake.

▶ PROCEDURE FOR PREPARING FRENCH BUTTERCREAMS

1 Prepare a sugar syrup and cook to soft ball stage (240°F/116°C).

2 Beat egg yolks to a thin ribbon.

3 Slowly beat the sugar syrup into the egg yolks.

4 Continue beating until the yolks are pale, stiff and completely cool.

5 Gradually add softened butter to the cooled yolks.

6 Fold in Italian meringue.

7 Stir in flavoring ingredients.

1 Adding the sugar syrup to the whipped egg whites.

2 Adding the softened butter to the cooled Italian meringue.

3 The finished Italian buttercream.

FRENCH BUTTERCREAM   RECIPE 33.9

Yield: 2 qt. (2 lt)

Granulated sugar	1 lb. 10 oz.	800 g
Water	8 fl. oz.	250 ml
Egg yolks	16	16
Lightly salted butter, softened but not melted	3 lb.	1500 g
Italian Meringue (page 1016)	1 qt.	1 lt

1 Combine the sugar and water in a small saucepan and bring to a boil. Continue boiling until the syrup reaches 240°F (116°C).

2 Meanwhile, beat the egg yolks in a mixer fitted with a wire whisk on low speed. When the sugar syrup reaches 240°F (116°C), pour it slowly into the egg yolks, gradually increasing the speed at which they are whipped. Continue beating at medium-high speed until the mixture is very pale, stiff and cool.

3 Gradually add the softened butter to the egg mixture, frequently scraping down the sides of the bowl.

4 Fold in the Italian meringue with a spatula. Stir in flavoring extracts as desired.

Approximate values per 1-oz. (30-g) serving: **Calories** 230, **Total fat** 20 g, **Saturated fat** 12 g, **Cholesterol** 105 mg, **Sodium** 190 mg, **Total carbohydrates** 12 g, **Protein** 1 g, **Vitamin A** 20%

FOAM FROSTING

Foam frosting, sometimes known as **boiled icing,** is simply an Italian meringue (made with hot sugar syrup). Foam frosting is light and fluffy but very sweet. It may be flavored with extract, liqueur or melted chocolate.

Foam frosting is rather unstable. It should be used immediately and served the day it is prepared. Refrigeration often makes the foam weep beads of sugar. Freezing causes it to separate or melt.

An easy foam frosting can be made by following the formula for Italian Meringue (page 1016). As soon as the meringue has cooled to room temperature, it can be flavored as desired.

FUDGE FROSTING

A fudge frosting is a warmed mixture of sugar, butter and water or milk. It is heavy, rich and candylike. It is also stable and holds up well. A fudge frosting should be applied warm and allowed to dry on the cake or pastry. When dry, it will have a thin crust and a moist interior. A fudge frosting can be vanilla- or chocolate-based and is used on cupcakes, layer cakes and sheet cakes.

▶ PROCEDURE FOR PREPARING FUDGE FROSTINGS

1 Blend sifted powdered sugar with corn syrup, beating until the sugar is dissolved and the mixture is smooth.

2 Blend in warm melted shortening and/or butter.

3 Blend in hot liquids. Add extracts or flavorings.

4 Use fudge frosting while still warm.

RECIPE 33.10

Cocoa Fudge Frosting

BASIC FUDGE FROSTING

Yield: 3 lb. (1500 g)

Powdered sugar, sifted	3 lb.	1500 g
Salt	¼ tsp.	1 ml
Light corn syrup	2 fl. oz.	60 ml
Shortening, melted	4 oz.	120 g
Water, hot (140°F/60°C)	10 fl. oz.	300 ml
Vanilla extract	2 Tbsp.	30 ml

1 Blend the sugar, salt and corn syrup. Beat until smooth.

2 Add the melted shortening and blend well.

3 Add the hot water and vanilla and blend well. If the fudge is too stiff, it may be thinned with a simple sugar syrup. Use before the icing cools.

Variation: *Cocoa Fudge Frosting*—Sift 4 ounces (120 grams) cocoa powder with the powdered sugar. Add 2 ounces (60 grams) melted unsalted butter with the shortening.

Approximate values per 1-oz. (30-g) serving: **Calories** 140, **Total fat** 2.5 g, **Saturated fat** 0.5 g, **Cholesterol** 0 mg, **Sodium** 15 mg, **Total carbohydrates** 30 g, **Protein** 0 g, **Claims**—low fat; low saturated fat; no cholesterol; very low sodium

FONDANT

Fondant is a thick, opaque sugar paste commonly used for glazing napoleons, petits fours and other pastries as well as some cakes. It is a cooked mixture of sugar and water, with **glucose** or corn syrup added to encourage the correct type of sugar crystallization. Poured over the surface being coated, fondant quickly dries to a shiny, nonsticky coating. It is naturally pure white and can be tinted with food coloring. Fondant can also be flavored with melted chocolate.

Fondant is rather tricky to make, so it is usually purchased prepared. To use, thin it with water or simple syrup and carefully warm to 100°F (38°C). Commercially prepared fondant will keep for several months at room temperature in an airtight container. The surface of the fondant should be coated with simple syrup, however, to prevent a crust from forming.

Rolled fondant is a very stiff doughlike type of fondant that is used for covering cakes and for making flowers and other decorations. As the name implies, it is rolled out to the desired thickness, then draped over a cake or torte to create a very smooth, flat coating. After the fondant dries, the cake may be decorated with royal icing or buttercream. Rolled fondant is available in a ready-to-use form. It can be flavored or colored if desired. Be sure to keep the fondant tightly wrapped in plastic and stored in an air tight container to prevent it from drying out and cracking.

▶ **glucose** a thick, sweet syrup made from cornstarch, composed primarily of dextrose; light corn syrup can usually be substituted for it in baked goods or candy making

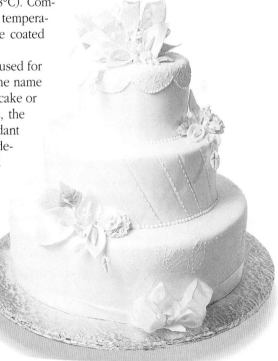

GLAZE

A glaze is a thin coating meant to be poured or dripped onto a cake or pastry. A glaze is usually too thin to apply with a knife or spatula. It is used to add moisture and flavor to cakes on which a heavy frosting would be undesirable— for example, a chiffon or angel food cake.

Flat icing or water icing is a specific type of glaze used on Danish pastries and coffeecakes. It is pure white and dries to a firm gloss.

Wedding Cake Covered with Rolled Fondant

▶ PROCEDURE FOR PREPARING SUGAR GLAZES

1 Blend sifted powdered sugar with a small amount of liquid and flavorings.
2 Use immediately.

BASIC SUGAR GLAZE   RECIPE 33.11

Yield: 12 oz. (340 g)

Powdered sugar, sifted	9½ oz.	270 g
Light cream or milk	2 fl. oz.	60 ml
Unsalted butter, melted	1 oz.	30 g
Vanilla extract	2 tsp.	10 ml

CONVENIENCE PRODUCTS

A wide selection of prepared icings, glazes and toppings are available. Often, chocolate and vanilla fudge icing bases are purchased and then flavored or colored as needed. Foam frostings can be purchased in powder form, to which you simply add water and whip. Even prepared "buttercreams" are available, although they contain little or no real butter.

Prepared icings are often exceedingly sweet and overpowered by artificial flavors and chemical preservatives. These products save time and offer consistent results but often cost more than their counterparts made from scratch. They should be used only after balancing the disadvantages against the benefits for your particular operation.

1 Stir the ingredients together in a small bowl until smooth.

2 Adjust the consistency by adding more cream or milk to thin the glaze if necessary.

3 Adjust the flavor as necessary. (Another extract, such as lemon or almond, may be used if desired.)

4 Use immediately, before the glaze begins to dry.

Approximate values per 1-oz. (30-g) serving: **Calories** 110, **Total fat** 2 g, **Saturated fat** 1.5 g, **Cholesterol** 5 mg, **Sodium** 0 mg, **Total carbohydrates** 23 g, **Protein** 0 g, **Claims**—low fat; low cholesterol; no sodium

ROYAL ICING

Royal icing, also known as **decorator's icing,** is similar to flat icing except it is much stiffer and becomes hard and brittle when dry. It is an uncooked mixture of powdered sugar and egg whites. It can be dyed with food coloring pastes.

Royal icing is used for making decorations, particularly intricate flowers or lace patterns. Prepare royal icing in small quantities, and always keep any unused portion covered with a damp towel to prevent hardening.

▶ PROCEDURE FOR PREPARING ROYAL ICING

1 Combine egg white and lemon juice, if used.

2 Beat in sifted powdered sugar until the correct consistency is reached.

3 Beat until very smooth and firm enough to hold a stiff peak.

4 Color as desired with paste food colorings.

5 Store covered with a damp cloth and plastic wrap.

RECIPE 33.12

ROYAL ICING

Yield: 6 oz. (180 g)

Powdered sugar	6 oz.	180 g
Egg white, room temperature	1	1
Lemon juice	¼ tsp.	1 ml

1 Sift the sugar and set aside.

2 Place the egg white and lemon juice in a stainless steel bowl.

3 Add 4 ounces (120 grams) of the sugar and beat with an electric mixer or metal spoon until blended. The mixture should fall from a spoon in heavy globs. If it pours, it is too thin and will need the remaining 2 ounces (60 grams) of sugar.

4 Once the consistency is correct, continue beating for 3 to 4 minutes. The icing should be white, smooth and thick enough to hold a stiff peak. Food coloring paste can be added at this time if desired.

5 Cover the icing with a damp towel and plastic wrap to prevent it from hardening.

Approximate values per 1-oz. (30-g) serving: **Calories** 120, **Total fat** 0 g, **Saturated fat** 0 g, **Cholesterol** 0 mg, **Sodium** 10 mg, **Total carbohydrates** 28 g, **Protein** 1 g, **Claims**—fat free; no saturated fat; no cholesterol; very low sodium

GANACHE

Ganache is a sublime blending of pure chocolate and cream. It can also include butter, liqueur or other flavorings. Any bittersweet, semisweet or dark chocolate may be used; the choice depends on personal preference and cost considerations.

Depending on its consistency, ganache may be used as a candy or as a filling, frosting or glaze-type coating on cakes or pastries. The ratio of chocolate to cream determines how thick the cooled ganache will be. Equal parts by weight of chocolate and cream generally are best for frostings and fillings. Increasing the percentage of chocolate produces a thicker ganache. Warm ganache can be poured over a cake or pastry and allowed to harden as a thin glaze, or the ganache can be cooled and whipped to create a rich, smooth frosting. If it becomes too firm, ganache can be remelted over a bain marie.

► PROCEDURE FOR PREPARING GANACHE

1 Melt finely chopped chocolate with cream in a double broiler. Alternatively, bring cream just to a boil; then pour it over finely chopped chocolate and allow the cream's heat to gently melt the chocolate.

2 Whichever method is used, cool the cream and chocolate mixture over an ice bath.

Do not attempt to melt chocolate and then add cool cream. This will cause the chocolate to resolidify and lump.

CHOCOLATE GANACHE

RECIPE 33.13

Yield: 2.2 lb. (1 kg)

Bittersweet chocolate	1 lb. 1 oz.	500 g
Heavy cream	17 fl. oz.	500 ml
Almond or coffee liqueur	1 fl. oz.	30 ml

1 Chop the chocolate into small pieces and place in a large metal bowl.
2 Bring the cream just to a boil, then immediately pour it over the chocolate, whisking to blend. Stir gently until all the chocolate has melted.
3 Stir in the liqueur.
4 Allow to cool, stirring frequently with a rubber spatula until the desired consistency is achieved.

Approximate values per 1-oz. (30-g) serving: **Calories** 130, **Total fat** 10 g, **Saturated fat** 6 g, **Cholesterol** 20 mg, **Sodium** 5 mg, **Total carbohydrates** 8 g, **Protein** 1 g, **Vitamin A** 6%

1 Pouring the hot cream over the chopped chocolate.

CHOCOLATE TRUFFLES

Ganache, is also the foundation of one of the world's most sophisticated candies: the chocolate truffle. Truffles take their name from the rough, black, highly prized fungus they resemble, but there the similarity ends. Chocolate truffles should have a rich, creamy ganache center with a well-balanced, refined flavor.

To prepare chocolate truffles a ganache is flavored as desired, then allowed to harden. Once firm, the ganache is scooped into balls and rolled in cocoa powder, confectioner's sugar or melted chocolate. The classic French truffle is a small, irregularly shaped ball of bittersweet chocolate dusted with cocoa powder. Americans, however, seem to prefer larger candies, coated with melted chocolate and decorated with nuts or additional chocolate. The following recipe can be prepared in either style.

2 Cool, firm ganache.

Table 33.6 TROUBLESHOOTING CHART FOR FROSTINGS

PROBLEM	CAUSE	SOLUTION
Frosting breaks or curdles	Fat added too slowly or eggs too hot when fat was added	Add shortening or sifted confectioner's sugar
Frosting is lumpy	Confectioner's sugar not sifted	Sift dry ingredients
	Ingredients not blended	Use softened fat
	Sugar syrup lumps in frosting	Add sugar syrups carefully
Frosting is gritty	Granulated sugar not dissolved	Cook sugar syrups properly; cook fudge frostings as directed
Frosting is too stiff	Not enough liquid	Adjust formula; add small amount of water or milk to thin the frosting
	Too cold	Bring frosting to room temperature
Frosting will not adhere to cake	Cake too hot	Cool cake completely
	Frosting too thin	Adjust frosting formula

RECIPE 33.14 DARK CHOCOLATE TRUFFLES

Shaping chocolate truffles.

Yield: 150 Medium-Sized Truffles

Dark chocolate	2 lb.	1 kg
Unsalted butter	1 lb.	500 g
Heavy cream	1 pt.	500 ml
Brandy, bourbon or liqueur	4 fl. oz.	120 ml

1 Chop the chocolate and butter into small pieces and place in a large metal bowl.
2 Bring the cream to a boil. Immediately pour the hot cream over the chocolate and butter. Stir until the chocolate and butter are completely melted.
3 Stir in the brandy. Pour the ganache into a flat, shallow, ungreased pan and chill until firm.
4 Shape the ganache into rough balls using a melon ball cutter. Immediately drop each ball into a pan of sifted cocoa powder or confectioner's sugar, rolling it around to coat completely.
5 Truffles can be stored in the refrigerator for 7 to 10 days. Allow them to soften slightly at room temperature before serving.

Approximate values per truffle: **Calories** 70, **Total fat** 6 g, **Saturated fat** 3.5 g, **Cholesterol** 10 mg, **Sodium** 0 mg, **Total carbohydrates** 4 g, **Protein** 0 g

▶ ASSEMBLING AND DECORATING CAKES

Much of a cake's initial appeal lies in its appearance. This is true whether the finished cake is a simple sheet cake topped with swirls of buttercream or an elaborate wedding cake with intricate garlands and bouquets of pulled sugar roses. Any cake assembled and decorated with care and attention to detail is preferable to a carelessly assembled or garishly overdecorated one.

Thousands of decorating styles or designs are possible, of course. This section describes a few simple options that can be prepared by beginning pastry cooks using a minimum of specialized tools. In planning your cake's design, consider the flavor, texture and color of the components used as well as the number of guests or portions that must be served. Consider who will be cutting and eating the cake and how long the dessert must stand before service.

ADVANCED PÂTISSERIE

Sugar can be used to create a number of doughs, pastes and syrups used for artistic and decorative work. Mastering even some of these products takes years of experience and practice. Although formulas and preparation methods are beyond the scope of this book, it is important that all pastry cooks be able to recognize and identify certain decorative sugar products.

Blown sugar—a boiled mixture of sucrose, glucose and tartaric acid that is colored and shaped (in a manner very similar to glass blowing) using an air pump. It is used for making pieces of fruit and containers such as bowls and vases.

Gum paste—a smooth dough made of sugar and gelatin; it dries relatively slowly, becoming very firm and hard. The paste can be colored and rolled out, cut and shaped, or molded. It is used for making flowers, leaves and small figures.

Marzipan—a mixture of almond paste and sugar that may be colored and used like modeling clay for sculpting small fruits, flowers or other objects. Marzipan can also be rolled out and cut into various shapes or used to cover cakes or pastries.

Nougat—a candy made of caramelized sugar and almonds that can be molded into shapes or containers. Unlike other sugar decorations, nougat remains deliciously edible.

Pastillage—a paste made with sugar, cornstarch and gelatin. It can be rolled into sheets, then cut into shapes. It dries in a very firm and sturdy form, like plaster. Naturally pure white, it can be painted with cocoa or food colorings. Pastillage is used for showpieces and large decorative items.

Pulled sugar—a doughlike mixture of sucrose, glucose and tartaric acid that is colored, then shaped by hand. Pulled sugar is used for making birds, flowers, leaves, bows and other items.

Spun sugar—long, fine, hairlike threads of sugar made by flicking dark caramelized sugar rapidly across dowels. Mounds or wreaths of these threads are used to decorate ice cream desserts, croquembouche and gâteaux.

ASSEMBLING CAKES

Before a cake can be decorated, it must be assembled and coated with frosting. Most cakes can be assembled in a variety of shapes and sizes; sheet cakes, round layer cakes and rectangular layer cakes are the most common. When assembling any cake, the goal is to fill and stack the cake layers evenly and to apply an even coating of frosting that is smooth and free of crumbs.

Most of the photographs used in this section show the assembly and decoration of a wedding cake. The finished cake is shown in the photograph that introduces this chapter. The complete formula is found on page 1075.

▶ PROCEDURE FOR ASSEMBLING CAKES

1 Begin by leveling the cake and trimming the edges as needed with a serrated knife.

2 Split the cake horizontally into thin layers if desired. Use cake boards to support each layer as it is removed. Brush away any loose crumbs with a dry pastry brush or your hand.

3 Position the bottom layer on a cake board. Place the layer on a revolving cake stand, if available. Pipe a border of buttercream around the cake, then top the layer with a mound of filling. Use a cake spatula to spread it evenly.

4 Position the next cake layer over the filling and continue layering and filling the cake as desired.

5 Place a mound of frosting in the center of the cake top. Push it to the edge of the cake with a cake spatula. Do not drag the frosting back and forth or lift the spatula off the frosting, as these actions tend to pick up crumbs.

6 Cover the sides with excess frosting from the top, adding more as necessary. Hold the spatula upright against the side of the cake and, pressing gently, turn the cake stand slowly. This smooths and evens the sides. When the sides and top are smooth, the cake is ready to be decorated as desired.

SIMPLE DECORATING TECHNIQUES

An extremely simple yet effective way to decorate a frosted cake is with a garnish of chopped nuts, fruit, toasted coconut, shaved chocolate or other foods arranged in patterns or sprinkled over the cake. Be sure to use a garnish that complements the cake and frosting flavors or reflects one of the cake's ingredients. For example, finely chopped pecans would be an appropriate garnish for a carrot cake that contains pecans; shaved chocolate would not.

Side masking is the technique of coating only the sides of a cake with garnish. The top may be left plain or decorated with icing designs or a message. Be sure to apply the garnish while the frosting is still damp enough for it to adhere.

Stencils can be used to apply patterns of finely chopped garnishes, confectioner's sugar or cocoa powder to the top of a cake. A design can be cut from cardboard, or thin plastic forms can be purchased. Even simple strips of parchment paper can be used to create an attractive pattern. If using a stencil on a

Side masking—coating the sides of a carrot cake with chopped pecans.

Stencils—creating a design with confectioner's sugar and strips of parchment paper.

frosted cake, allow the frosting to set somewhat before laying the stencil on top of it. After the garnishes have been sprinkled over the stencil, carefully lift the stencil to avoid spilling the excess garnish and messing the pattern.

A **cake** or **baker's comb** or a serrated knife can be used to create patterns on a cake iced with buttercream, fudge or ganache. Hold the comb against the side of a frosted cake and rotate the cake slowly and evenly to create horizontal lines in the icing.

PIPING TECHNIQUES

More elaborate and difficult decorations can be produced with the aid of a piping bag and an assortment of pastry tips. With these tools, frosting or royal icing can be used to create borders, flowers and messages. Before applying any decorations, however, plan a design or pattern that is appropriate for the size and shape of the item being decorated.

When used properly, colored frostings can bring cake decorations to life. Buttercream, royal icing and fondant are easily tinted using paste food coloring. Liquid food colorings are not recommended as they may thin the frosting too much. Always add coloring gradually with a toothpick. Frosting colors tend to darken as they sit. It is easy to add more later to darken the color if necessary, but it is difficult to lighten the color if too much is added.

Piping bags made from plastic, nylon or plastic-coated canvas are available in a range of sizes. A disposable piping cone can also be made from parchment paper.

Most decorations and designs are made by using a piping bag fitted with a pastry tip. Pastry tips are available with dozens of different openings and are referred to by standardized numbers. Some commonly used tips are shown here. You can produce a variety of borders and designs by changing the pressure, the angle of the bag and the distance between the tip and the cake surface.

Cake comb—creating a pattern on a frosted cake.

Tip Patterns

MAKING A PARCHMENT-PAPER CONE

A disposable piping bag or cone is easily made from parchment paper. Begin with an equilateral triangle of uncreased paper. Shape it into a cone as shown, folding the top edges together to hold the shape. The point of the cone can be cut as desired. Paper cones are especially useful for writing messages or piping melted chocolate.

1 Wrapping opposite ends of the parchment triangle.

2 Folding the ends together to seal.

3 Cutting the tip of the filled parchment cone.

▷ PROCEDURE FOR FILLING A PIPING BAG

1 Select the proper size piping bag for your task. Insert the desired tip.

2 Fold down the top of the bag, then fill approximately half full with frosting. Do not overfill the bag.

3 Be sure to close the open end tightly before you start piping. Hold the bag firmly in your palm and squeeze from the top. Do not squeeze from the bottom or you may force the contents out the wrong end. Use the fingers of your other hand to guide the bag as you work.

PIPED-ON DECORATING TECHNIQUES

Instead of leaving the sides of a frosted cake smooth or coating them with chopped nuts or crumbs, you can pipe on frosting designs and patterns. A simple but elegant design is the basket weave, shown here.

Applying a basket weave pattern to the sides of the wedding cake.

Applying a shell border to the wedding cake.

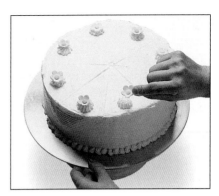

Placing royal icing flowers onto cake portions.

Normally, a border pattern will be piped around the base of the cake and along the top edge. Borders should be piped on after nuts or any other garnishes are applied.

Each slice or serving of cake can be marked with its own decoration. For example, a rosette of frosting or a whole nut or piece of fruit could be used as shown. This makes it easier to portion the cake evenly.

Delicate flowers such as roses can be piped, allowed to harden, then placed on the cake in attractive arrangements. Royal icing is particularly useful for making decorations in advance because it dries very hard and lasts indefinitely.

► PROCEDURE FOR PIPING BUTTERCREAM ROSES

1 Using a #104 tip, pipe a mound of icing onto a rose nail.

2 Pipe a curve of icing around the mound to create the center of the rose.

3 Pipe three overlapping petals around the center.

4 Pipe five more overlapping petals around the first three petals.

5 Place the finished rose on the cake.

The key to success with a piping bag is practice, practice, practice. Use plain all-purpose shortening piped onto parchment paper to practice and experiment with piping techniques. Once you are comfortable using a piping bag, you can apply these newfound skills directly to cakes and pastries.

STORING CAKES

Unfrosted cake layers or sheets can be stored at room temperature for 2 or 3 days if well covered. Frosted or filled cakes are usually refrigerated to prevent spoilage. Simple buttercreams or sugar glazes, however, can be left at room temperature for 1 or 2 days. Any cake containing custard filling or whipped cream must be refrigerated. Cakes made with foam-type frosting should be eaten the day they are prepared.

Cakes can usually be frozen with great success; this makes them ideal for baking in advance. Unfrosted layers or sheets should be well covered with plastic wrap and frozen at 0°F (−18°C) or lower. High-fat cakes will keep for up to 6 months; egg foam cakes begin to deteriorate after 2 or 3 months.

Frostings and fillings do not freeze particularly well, often losing flavor or changing texture when frozen. Buttercreams made with egg whites or sugar syrups tend to develop crystals and graininess. Foam frostings weep, expelling beads of sugar and becoming sticky. Fondant will absorb moisture and separate from the cake. If you must freeze a filled or frosted cake, it is best to freeze it unwrapped first, until the frosting is firm. The cake can then be covered with plastic wrap without damaging the frosting design. Leave the cake wrapped until completely thawed. It is best to thaw cakes in the refrigerator; do not refreeze a thawed cake.

CONCLUSION

The ability to produce good cakes and frostings depends on using the right balance of high-quality ingredients and combining them with the proper techniques. When preparing cakes and frostings, always combine flavors and textures with care; apply frostings, garnishes and decorations with care as well. Avoid overly rich, cloyingly sweet or garishly decorated products. With study and practice, you can learn the mixing techniques and assembly skills necessary for producing good cakes. With additional practice, you will develop the decorating and garnishing skills of a fine pastry chef.

QUESTIONS FOR DISCUSSION

1 Cake ingredients can be classified by function into six categories. List them and give an example of each.

2 What is the primary leavening agent in cakes made with the foaming method? How is this similar to or different from cakes made with the creaming method?

3 What is the difference between a spongecake and a classic genoise?

4 Describe the procedures for making three types of frosting or icing as discussed in this chapter.

5 List the steps employed in assembling and frosting a three-layer cake.

6 Wedding cakes vary greatly from one region or culture to another. Investigate the various types or styles of cakes traditionally served at weddings in three or four different cultures. Which recipes in this book would be appropriate for a wedding cake?

VANILLA RASPBERRY WEDDING CAKE WITH WHITE CHOCOLATE BUTTERCREAM

RECIPE 33.15

Note: This dish appears in the chapter opening photograph.

HYATT REGENCY SCOTTSDALE AT GAINEY RANCH, Scottsdale, AZ
Former Executive Pastry Chef Judy Doherty

Yield: 1 Three-Tier Wedding Cake,
80 Servings*

Vanilla Cake (recipe follows):		
8-in. (20-cm) round	1	1
10-in. (25-cm) round	1	1
14-in. (35-cm) round	1	1
Raspberry Syrup (recipe follows)	1 pt.	500 ml
Diplomat Cream Filling (recipe follows)	as needed	as needed
Fresh raspberries	6 dry pt.	3 lt.
White Chocolate Buttercream (recipe follows)	as needed	as needed
Royal icing or pulled sugar roses	as desired	

1 Working with one vanilla cake round at a time, slice each round into three horizontal layers. Brush the bottom layer with Raspberry Syrup and then top it with Diplomat Cream Filling and fresh raspberries. Place the middle layer on top of the filled bottom layer and top it with Diplomat Cream Filling and fresh raspberries. Then place the top layer on the middle layer to complete the tier.

2 Repeat with each of the other two cake tiers.

3 Apply a thin coating of White Chocolate Buttercream to the top and sides of each tier. Spread additional buttercream on the tops, smoothing it with a cake spatula. Then pipe additional buttercream to the sides of each tier in a basketweave design. Pipe a border along the top edge of each tier.

4 Stack the tiers and pipe a border along the bottom edge of each tier. Then decorate the assemblage with icing roses and garlands.

* This assembly is illustrated by photographs appearing throughout this chapter.

Approximate values per 6-oz. (180-g) serving: **Calories** 600, **Total fat** 28 g, **Saturated fat** 7 g, **Cholesterol** 240 mg, **Sodium** 520 mg, **Total carbohydrates** 75 g, **Protein** 10 g, **Vitamin A** 10%, **Calcium** 20%

VANILLA CAKE

Yield: 3 Cake Rounds, 8 in. (20 cm), 10 in. (25 cm) and 14 in. (35 cm)   **Method:** Two-Stage

Cake flour	1 lb. 14 oz.	850 g
Granulated sugar	2 lb. 8 oz.	1130 g
Baking powder	2½ oz.	70 g
Eggs	28	28
Salt	1 oz.	28 g
Fluid Flex	1 lb. 4 oz.	570 g
Milk	1 pt.	450 ml

1 Prepare the cake pans—one 8-inch (20-centimeter) pan, one 10-inch (25-centimeter) pan and one 14-inch (35-centimeter) pan—by spraying with pan release and lining with parchment paper.

2 Combine the flour, sugar, baking powder, eggs and salt in a large mixer bowl. Whip on high speed for 8 minutes.

3 Add the Fluid Flex (an emulsifier for spongecakes) and milk. Mix for 8 more minutes at medium speed.

4 Divide the batter between the prepared cake pans. Fill each pan halfway.

5 Bake at 350°F (180°C) for 35 to 60 minutes, depending upon tier size. The cake is done when it springs back when lightly touched in the center. Allow to cool, then remove from the pans and freeze.

RASPBERRY SYRUP

Yield: 1 qt. (1 lt)

Water	1 pt.	450 ml
Granulated sugar	1 lb.	450 g
Raspberry liqueur	2 fl. oz.	60 ml

1 Bring the water and sugar to a boil, then cool to room temperature. Add the raspberry liqueur.

DIPLOMAT CREAM FILLING

Yield: 5 qt. (5 lt)

Pastry cream, chilled	1 gal.	4 lt
Raspberry liqueur	4 fl. oz.	120 ml
Gelatin	1½ oz.	42 g
Water	6 fl. oz.	170 ml
Whipped cream	1 qt.	1 lt

1 Place the pastry cream in a large mixer bowl and whip on high speed until smooth. Add the raspberry liqueur.

2 Soften the gelatin in the water, then place over a low flame and heat to dissolve.

3 Add 1 pint (450 milliliters) of the raspberry-flavored pastry cream to the gelatin. Place over a low flame and whip by hand until smooth and the gelatin is incorporated. Add this mixture to the rest of the pastry cream.

4 Fold in the whipped cream.

Approximate values per 1-oz. (30-g) serving: **Calories** 40, **Total fat** 2 g, **Saturated fat** 1 g, **Cholesterol** 30 mg, **Sodium** 10 mg, **Total carbohydrates** 5 g, **Protein** 1 g

WHITE CHOCOLATE BUTTERCREAM

Yield: 17 lb. (7.7 kg)

Granulated sugar	5 lb. 8 oz.	2500 g
Water	22 fl. oz.	625 ml
Egg whites	1 lb. 12 oz.	800 g
Unsalted butter, softened	7 lb.	3150 g
White crème de cacao	9 fl. oz.	260 ml
White chocolate, melted	1 lb. 8 oz.	680 g

1 Cook the sugar and water to 242°F (117°C), then pour into a measuring container with a handle for easier pouring.

2 Start whipping the egg whites when the sugar reaches 235°F (113°C).

3 When the whites are whipped to firm peaks, add the hot sugar syrup slowly while continuing to whip at low speed. Whip until completely cool.

4 Add the butter and whip until smooth.

5 Add the crème de cacao to the white chocolate. Whip until smooth, then add the chocolate to the buttercream.

Approximate values per 1-oz. (30-g) serving: **Calories** 140, **Total fat** 11 g, **Saturated fat** 7 g, **Cholesterol** 25 mg, **Sodium** 10 mg, **Total carbohydrates** 10 g, **Protein** 1 g, **Vitamin A** 8%

CARROT CAKE WITH
CREAM CHEESE FROSTING

RECIPE 33.16

Yield: 4 Sheet Cakes or 12 Rounds, 10 in. (25 cm)   **Method:** Creaming

Vegetable oil	3 lb. 8 oz.	1750 g
Granulated sugar	3 lb. 11 oz.	1850 g
Eggs	1 lb. 12 oz.	875 g
Carrots, shredded	5 lb.	2500 g
Crushed pineapple, with juice	3 lb. 4 oz.	1625 g
Baking soda	1½ oz.	45 g
Cinnamon, ground	2 oz.	60 g
Pumpkin pie spice	1½ oz.	45 g
Salt	1½ oz.	45 g
Baking powder	1¼ oz.	40 g
Cake flour	4 lb. 10 oz.	2300 g
Coconut, shredded	1 lb.	500 g
Walnut pieces	1 lb.	500 g

1 Blend the oil and sugar in a large mixer bowl fitted with the paddle attachment. Add the eggs, beating to incorporate.

2 Blend in the carrots and pineapple.

3 Sift the dry ingredients together, then add them to the batter. Stir in the coconut and walnuts.

4 Divide the batter into greased and floured pans.

5 Bake at 340°F (170°C) until springy to the touch and a cake tester comes out almost clean.

6 Allow the cakes to cool, then fill and frost as desired with Cream Cheese Frosting.

Approximate values per serving: **Calories** 390, **Total fat** 22 g, **Saturated fat** 4 g, **Cholesterol** 40 mg, **Sodium** 490 mg, **Total carbohydrates** 44 g, **Protein** 5 g, **Vitamin A** 100%

CREAM CHEESE FROSTING

Yield: 12½ lb. (5.5 kg)

Unsalted butter, softened	12 oz.	350 g
Cream cheese, softened	3 lb.	1500 g
Margarine	12 oz.	350 g
Vanilla extract	1 fl. oz.	30 ml
Powdered sugar, sifted	6 lb.	3000 g

1 Cream the butter and cream cheese until smooth. Add the margarine and beat well.

2 Beat in the vanilla extract. Slowly add the sugar, scraping down the bowl frequently. Beat until smooth.

Approximate values per serving: **Calories** 130, **Total fat** 6 g, **Saturated fat** 3 g, **Cholesterol** 15 mg, **Sodium** 45 mg, **Total carbohydrates** 17 g, **Protein** 1 g, **Vitamin A** 6%

RECIPE 33.17

MARBLE CAKE

Yield: 1 Sheet Cake, 18 in. × 24 in. (45 cm × 60 cm)　　　**Method:** Creaming

Cake flour, sifted	1 lb. 11 oz.	1300 g
Baking powder	2½ Tbsp.	45 ml
Salt	1½ tsp.	7 ml
Unsalted butter	12 oz.	360 g
Granulated sugar	1 lb. 11 oz.	1300 g
Milk	24 fl. oz.	720 ml
Vanilla extract	1 tsp.	5 ml
Dark chocolate, melted	4½ oz.	135 g
Baking soda	¼ tsp.	1 ml
Coffee extract	2 tsp.	10 ml
Egg whites	12	12
Cocoa Fudge Frosting (page 1065)	as needed	as needed

1 Sift the flour, baking powder and salt together; set aside.

2 Cream the butter and sugar until light and fluffy.

3 Combine the milk and vanilla.

4 Add the dry ingredients to the creamed butter alternately with the milk. Stir the batter only until smooth.

5 Separate the batter into two equal portions. Add the melted chocolate, baking soda and coffee extract to one portion.

6 Whip the egg whites until stiff but not dry. Fold half of the whites into the vanilla batter and half into the chocolate batter.

7 Spoon the batters onto a greased sheet pan, alternating the two colors. Pull a paring knife through the batter to swirl the colors together.

8 Bake at 350°F (180°C) until a tester comes out clean, approximately 25 minutes.

9 Allow the cake to cool, then cover the top with Cocoa Fudge Frosting.

Approximate values per 5-oz. (150-g) serving: **Calories** 480, **Total fat** 17 g, **Saturated fat** 11 g, **Cholesterol** 40 mg, **Sodium** 250 mg, **Total carbohydrates** 75 g, **Protein** 7 g, **Vitamin A** 15%, **Calcium** 15%

RECIPE 33.18

GERMAN CHOCOLATE CAKE

Yield: 1 Layer Cake, 9 in. (22 cm)　　　**Method:** Creaming

Sweet baking chocolate	8 oz	225 g
Water, boiling	4 fl. oz.	120 ml
Unsalted butter	8 oz	225 g
Granulated sugar	1 lb.	450 g
Eggs, separated	4	4
Vanilla extract	1 tsp.	5 ml
Cake flour	10 oz.	300 g
Baking soda	1 tsp.	5 ml

Salt	½ tsp.	2 ml
Buttermilk	8 fl. oz.	225 ml
Coconut Pecan Frosting (recipe follows)	2½ c.	600 ml

1 Chop the chocolate and melt it with the boiling water over a bain marie.

2 In a mixer fitted with a paddle attachment, cream together the butter and sugar until light and fluffy.

3 Add the egg yolks, one at a time, to the butter, then stir in the vanilla and the melted chocolate.

4 Sift the dry ingredients together and add them alternately with the buttermilk, beating well after each addition.

5 Whip the egg whites to stiff peaks and fold into the batter.

6 Divide the batter into three 9-inch (22-centimeter) layer pans that have been greased and lined with parchment paper.

7 Bake at 350°F (180°C) until set and just beginning to pull away from the sides, approximately 30 to 40 minutes. When the cake has cooled completely, spread the Coconut Pecan Frosting between each layer and on top. The sides of this cake are traditionally left unfrosted.

Approximate values per ¹⁄₁₂-cake serving: **Calories** 840, **Total fat** 47 g, **Saturated fat** 24 g, **Cholesterol** 210 mg, **Sodium** 240 mg, **Total carbohydrates** 101 g, **Protein** 10 g, **Vitamin A** 25%, **Calcium** 15%, **Iron** 20%

COCONUT PECAN FROSTING

Yield: 2½ c. (600 ml),
enough for 1 three-layer cake

Evaporated milk	8 fl. oz.	225 ml
Granulated sugar	8 oz.	225 g
Egg yolks	3	3
Unsalted butter	4 oz.	120 g
Vanilla extract	1 tsp.	5 ml
Coconut, flaked	1⅓ c.	300 ml
Pecans, chopped	4 oz.	120 g

1 Combine the milk, sugar, egg yolks and butter in a saucepan over medium heat. Cook, stirring constantly, until the mixture thickens, approximately 12 minutes.

2 Remove from the heat and add the vanilla, coconut and pecans. Beat until cool and spreadable.

SACHER TORTE

RECIPE 33.19

Yield: 2 Cakes, 9 in. (22 cm)	**Method:** Creaming	
All-purpose flour	10 oz.	280 g
Cocoa powder, alkalized	3 oz.	80 g
Unsalted butter	12½ oz.	360 g
Granulated sugar	18 oz.	520 g
Eggs, separated	14	14
Hazelnuts, toasted and ground	3 oz.	90 g
Apricot jam	18 oz.	520 g
Apricot glaze	as needed	as needed
Chocolate Glaze (page 1065)	as needed	as needed

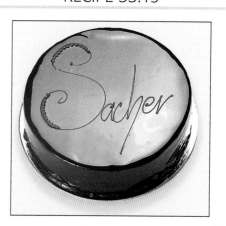

1 Grease two 9-inch (22-centimeter) springform pans lightly with butter and line with parchment paper.

2 Sift the flour and cocoa powder together twice; set aside.

3 Cream the butter and 7 ounces (200 grams) of the sugar together until light and fluffy. Gradually add the egg yolks and beat well.

4 Fold in the sifted flour and cocoa and the hazelnuts by hand.

5 Whip the egg whites to soft peaks, then gradually add the remaining sugar and continue whipping until stiff, glossy peaks form.

6 Lighten the batter with about one-quarter of the egg whites, then fold in the remaining whites.

7 Pour the batter into the prepared pans and bake at 350°F (180°C) until the cakes are set, approximately 35 to 45 minutes.

8 Cool the cakes for 5 minutes before removing from the pans.

9 Cool completely, then cut each cake horizontally into three layers. Spread apricot jam on each layer and restack them, creating two three-layer cakes.

10 Heat the apricot glaze until spreadable. Pour it over the top and sides of each cake.

11 Allow the apricot glaze to cool completely, then pour the chocolate glaze over the top and sides of each cake to create a smooth, glossy coating.

Approximate values per ¹⁄₁₀-cake serving: **Calories** 450, **Total fat** 21 g, **Saturated fat** 10 g, **Cholesterol** 185 mg, **Sodium** 60 mg, **Total carbohydrates** 56 g, **Protein** 7 g, **Vitamin A** 20%

RECIPE 33.20

BLACKSTRAP MOLASSES TORTE WITH CASSIS POACHED PEARS

THE BROWN PALACE, Denver, CO.

Pastry Chef Sky Globe

Yield: 3 Tortes, 10 in. (25 cm)

Cassis Poached Pears (recipe follows)	10	10
Blackstrap Molasses Banana Cake (recipe follows)	2	2
Five-Spice Mascarpone Mousse (recipe follows)	6 lb.	2.7 kg
Neutral glaze	as needed	as needed
Star anise, whole	as needed	as needed
Cloves, whole	as needed	as needed
Cinnamon sticks	as needed	as needed

1 Drain and towel-dry the Cassis Poached Pears. Reserve the poaching liquid.

2 Trim the bottom and top from the Blackstrap Molasses Banana Cakes. Cut each cake into three even layers, for a total of six layers. Cover and set aside.

3 Grease three 10-inch × 3-inch (25-centimeter × 7.5-centimeter) cake rings and place on sheet pans.

4 Place one layer of cake in each ring. Lightly brush the layers with the poaching liquid. Thinly slice 8 of the poached pears and fan the slices over the banana cake, dividing them equally among the three cakes. Cover the banana cakes completely with the pears.

5 Divide half of the Five-Spice Mascarpone Mousse equally among the three cakes. Spread the mousse evenly to completely cover the pear slices.

6 Top with the remaining layers of banana cake and brush the top layers with a liberal amount of the poaching liquid. Divide the remaining mousse among the three cakes and spread in a smooth, even layer over the top of each torte. Place the tortes in the freezer for 1 to 4 hours.

7 Remove the tortes from the freezer and remove the cake rings. Coat the top of each torte with neutral glaze and garnish with the pears, whole star anise, whole cloves and cinnamon sticks.

Approximate values per ¹/₁₀-cake serving: **Calories** 450, **Total fat** 20 g, **Saturated fat** 7 g, **Cholesterol** 60 mg, **Sodium** 490 mg, **Total carbohydrates** 62 g, **Protein** 5 g, **Calcium** 20%, **Iron** 30%

CASSIS POACHED PEARS

Yield: 10 Pears

Method: Poaching

Cassis purée	9 oz.	270 g
Water	5 fl. oz.	150 ml
Granulated sugar	6 oz.	180 g
Cassis liquor	3 fl. oz.	90 ml
Vanilla bean	1	1
Cinnamon stick	1	1
Black peppercorns	3	3
Star anise	1	1
Pears	10	10

1 Combine all of the ingredients (except the pears) and bring to a boil.
2 Peel the pears. Cut each pear in half and scoop out the core.
3 Reduce the poaching liquid to a simmer and add the pears to the liquid. Cover and poach until the pears are tender, approximately 10 minutes. Remove from the heat and cool.

Approximate values per pear: **Calories** 200, **Total fat** 1 g, **Saturated fat** 0 g, **Cholesterol** 0 mg, **Sodium** 0 mg, **Total carbohydrates** 47 g, **Protein** 1 g, **Vitamin C** 70%, **Claims**—low fat; no sodium; high in fiber and vitamin C

BLACKSTRAP MOLASSES BANANA CAKE

Yield: 2 Cakes, 10 in. (25 cm)

Method: Creaming

Whole butter	5 oz.	150 g
Brown sugar	1 lb.	450 g
Shortening	9 oz.	270 g
Bananas, mashed	8 oz.	240 g
Blackstrap molasses	8 fl. oz.	240 ml
Eggs	4	4
Rum	3 fl. oz.	90 ml
Salt	¹/₂ oz.	15 g
Cake flour	14¹/₂ oz.	435 g
Pastry flour	12¹/₂ oz.	375 g
Baking powder	1 oz.	30 g
Baking soda	¹/₂ tsp.	3 ml
Cinnamon, ground	1¹/₂ tsp.	8 ml
Cloves, ground	¹/₂ tsp.	3 ml
Nutmeg, ground	¹/₄ tsp.	1 ml

1 Cream the butter, sugar and shortening until light and fluffy. Add the bananas and molasses and mix to incorporate.
2 Scrape down the bowl. Mix in the eggs and rum. Scrape down the bowl and mix on medium speed for 5 minutes.
3 Sift the remaining dry ingredients together and add them to the bowl. Whip on high speed for 5 minutes.

4 Divide the batter between two well-greased 10-inch (25-centimeter) cake pans. Bake at 350°F (180°C) until a toothpick inserted near the center comes out clean, approximately 45 minutes. Turn the cakes out onto cardboard circles while still warm. Cool completely before slicing.

FIVE-SPICE MASCARPONE MOUSSE

Yield: 6 lb. (2.8 kg)

Honey	7 oz.	210 g
Granulated sugar	8 oz.	240 g
Water	2 fl. oz.	60 ml
Egg whites	16 oz.	450 g
Gelatin	½ oz.	15 g
Mascarpone	4 lb. 2 oz.	1.8 kg
Five-spice powder	2 Tbsp.	30 ml
Molasses	2 fl. oz.	60 ml

1 Combine the honey, sugar and 1 ounce (30 milliliters) of the water in a heavy-bottomed saucepan. Stir over low heat to dissolve the sugar. Increase the heat and cook to a light caramel stage.

2 Mix the egg whites at low speed until they form soft peaks. Then slowly pour in the caramelized sugar, being careful not to let the sugar touch the whip or the side of the bowl.

3 Add the gelatin to the remaining 1 ounce (30 milliliters) of water and allow to bloom. Melt the gelatin over low heat. Add the warm gelatin to the egg whites and whip to stiff peaks.

4 Combine the mascarpone, five-spice powder and molasses. Stir a small portion of the whipped egg whites into the mascarpone mixture. Fold the remaining egg whites into the mixture in several steps until they are completely incorporated.

Approximate values per ounce (30 g): **Calories** 100, **Total fat** 9 g, **Saturated fat** 4.5 g, **Cholesterol** 25 mg, **Sodium** 20 mg, **Total carbohydrates** 5 g, **Protein** 2 g

---

RECIPE 33.21

BÛCHE DE NOËL

Yield: 10–12 Servings

Classic Genoise (page 1052), freshly baked	½ sheet	½ sheet
Simple syrup	as needed	as needed
Buttercream, coffee, chocolate or vanilla	1 qt.	1 lt

1 Roll up the warm genoise in a spiral, starting with the long side. Wrap in parchment paper and cool.

2 Carefully unroll the cake. Brush the interior with simple syrup and coat with buttercream, leaving a 1-inch (2.5-centimeter) unfrosted rim around each edge.

3 Reroll the cake tightly and position it with the seam down on a cake cardboard.

4 Cut one end from the cake on a diagonal. Place the cut piece on top of the log, securing with toothpicks.

5 Pipe additional buttercream onto the cake log using a large star tip. Pipe the buttercream on the ends in a spiral pattern. Decorate as desired with buttercream flowers, baked meringue mushrooms or marzipan figures.

Approximate values per serving: **Calories** 650, **Total fat** 21 g, **Saturated fat** 6 g, **Cholesterol** 0 mg, **Sodium** 330 mg, **Total carbohydrates** 115 g, **Protein** 2 g, **Vitamin C** 70%, **Claims**—no cholesterol

1 Rolling the cake filled with buttercream.

2 Attaching the cut end to the log.

3 Piping on the buttercream.

  LADYFINGERS

RECIPE 33.22

Yield: 80 Cookies, 4 in. (10 cm) each   **Method:** Spongecake

Cornstarch	3 oz.	90 g
Bread flour	4 oz.	120 g
Eggs, separated	6	6
Granulated sugar	6 oz.	180 g
Lemon juice	½ tsp.	2 ml

1 Sift the cornstarch and flour together.

2 Whip the egg yolks with 2 ounces (60 grams) of the sugar until thick and creamy.

3 Whip the egg whites until foamy. Gradually add 2 ounces (60 grams) of the sugar and the lemon juice. Continue whipping to soft peaks, then add the remaining sugar gradually and whip to stiff peaks.

4 Fold approximately one-quarter of the egg whites into the whipped yolks to lighten them, then gently fold in the remaining whites. Fold in the flour mixture.

5 Place the batter into a pastry bag fitted with a large plain tip. Pipe 4-inch- (10-centimeter-) long cookies onto paper-lined sheet pans.

6 Bake immediately at 425°F (220°C) until lightly browned, approximately 8 minutes.

Approximate values per cookie: **Calories** 20, **Total fat** 0 g, **Saturated fat** 0 g, **Cholesterol** 15 mg, **Sodium** 0 mg, **Total carbohydrates** 4 g, **Protein** 1 g, **Claims**—fat free; no saturated fat; low cholesterol; no sodium; low calorie

CHOCOLATE FLOURLESS CAKE

RECIPE 33.23

VINCENT ON CAMELBACK, PHOENIX, AZ
Chef Vincent Guerithault

Yield: 21 Servings   **Method:** Egg Foam

Unsalted butter	1 lb.	450 g
Dark chocolate	27 oz.	800 g
Eggs, separated	20	20
Granulated sugar	7 oz.	200 g
Powdered sugar	as needed	as needed

1 Melt the butter and chocolate over a bain marie.

2 Whisk the egg yolks into the melted chocolate.

3 Whip the egg whites until shiny. Add the granulated sugar and whip until very stiff. Fold into the chocolate. Pour the batter into a full-sized hotel pan that is lined with buttered parchment.

4 Bake at 400°F (200°C) for 10 minutes. Lower the oven temperature to 350°F (180°C) and continue baking until done, approximately 40 minutes. A cake tester will not come out clean, even though the cake will be done.

5 Invert the cake onto the back of a sheet pan. Cool completely, and then dust with powdered sugar.

Approximate values per 4-oz. (120-g) serving: **Calories** 470, **Total fat** 35 g, **Saturated fat** 20 g, **Cholesterol** 250 mg, **Sodium** 65 mg, **Total carbohydrates** 32 g, **Protein** 8 g, **Vitamin A** 25%

CHOCOLATE SOUFFLÉ CAKE WITH PEANUT BUTTER HONEY CENTER AND BURNT BLOOD-ORANGE SAUCE

RECIPE 33.24

THE BROWN PALACE HOTEL, Denver, CO

Sky Goble, Pastry Chef

Yield: 6 Servings

Chocolate Soufflé Cake (recipe follows)	6	6
Grand Marnier Flambé Bananas (recipe follows)	as needed	as needed
Candied Orange Peel (recipe follows)	24 pieces	24 pieces
Burnt Blood-Orange Sauce (recipe follows)	9 fl. oz.	270 ml
Banana Twists (recipe follows)	6	6

1 Heat the Chocolate Soufflé Cakes in a 350°F (180°C) oven until warm, approximately 5 to 10 minutes.

2 For each serving, place nine Grand Marnier Flambé Banana disks in one layer in the center of a plate and place the warm soufflé cake on top of them.

3 Place small piles of diced flambé bananas at 12, 3, 6 and 9 o'clock positions on the plate. Place a Candied Orange Peel on top of each pile of bananas.

4 Drizzle Burnt Blood-Orange Sauce between the piles of bananas. Garnish each plate with a Banana Twist.

Approximate values per serving: **Calories** 1080, **Total fat** 48 g, **Saturated fat** 24 g, **Cholesterol** 185 mg, **Sodium** 140 mg, **Total carbohydrates** 160 g, **Protein** 12 g, **Vitamin A** 20%, **Vitamin C** 40%, **Iron** 20%

CHOCOLATE SOUFFLÉ CAKE WITH PEANUT BUTTER HONEY CENTER

Yield: 6 Servings

Peanut butter honey center:		
Peanut butter	3 oz.	90 g
Honey	3 Tbsp.	45 ml
Peanut oil	1 Tbsp.	15 ml
Chocolate soufflé cake:		
Pastry flour	4 oz.	120 g
Salt	1 pinch	1 pinch
Whole butter	4 oz.	120 g

Egg yolks	2 oz.	60 g
Dark couverture, melted	9 oz.	270 g
Strong coffee	2 fl. oz.	60 ml
Vanilla extract	½ Tbsp.	8 g
Egg whites	3½ oz.	105 g
Granulated sugar	3¾ oz.	110 g

1 Combine the peanut butter, honey and peanut oil and mix well. Freeze the mixture overnight. Remove from the freezer, form the mixture into six balls and return them to the freezer.

2 Cream the flour, salt and butter. Blend in the egg yolks. Add the melted chocolate, then the coffee and vanilla.

3 Whip the egg whites to soft peaks, then add the sugar and continue whipping to medium-firm peaks. Fold the whites into the batter.

4 Grease six molds, approximately 2½ inches × 2½ inches (7 centimeters × 7 centimeters). Fill each mold halfway with the soufflé mix. Add a frozen ball of the peanut butter mixture and then fill each mold to the top with the soufflé mix. Bake at 350°F (180°C) until done, approximately 15 minutes. Chill and remove from the molds.

GRAND MARNIER FLAMBÉ BANANAS

Yield: 6 Servings

Bananas	3	3
Granulated sugar	2 oz.	60 g
Water	1 Tbsp.	15 ml
Whole butter	½ oz.	15 g
Half-and-half	2 fl. oz.	60 ml
Grand Marnier	2 fl. oz.	60 ml

1 Peel the bananas. Cut a total of 54 thin slices, then dice the remainder.

2 Combine the sugar and water. Bring to a boil and cook until it caramelizes. Add the butter and half-and-half and stir very carefully.

3 Add the sliced and diced bananas. Add the Grand Marnier and flambé. Remove from the heat and set aside.

CANDIED ORANGE PEEL

Yield: 24 Pieces

Water	16 fl. oz.	450 ml
Granulated sugar	8 oz.	240 g
Oranges	as needed	as needed

1 Combine 8 fluid ounces (240 milliliters) of the water with the sugar in a small saucepan.

2 Bring the remaining water to a boil in a second small saucepan. Cut 24 strips of orange zest with a channel knife. Blanch the zest in the boiling water for 30 seconds, drain and add the orange peel to the sugar mixture and simmer until the peel is translucent, approximately 15 minutes.

3 Remove the peel from the liquid and spread on a sheet pan to cool.

BURNT BLOOD-ORANGE SAUCE

Yield: 9 fl. oz. (270 ml)

Granulated sugar	4 oz.	120 g
Corn syrup	2 Tbsp.	30 ml
Water	1 Tbsp.	15 ml
Fresh lemon juice	¼ tsp.	2 ml
Whole butter	1 oz.	30 ml
Blood orange purée	3 oz.	90 g

1 Combine the sugar, corn syrup, water and lemon juice over low heat until the sugar is dissolved. Turn the heat to high and boil the mixture, occasionally brushing the sides of the pan with the liquid to prevent crystals from forming. Cook the sugar to a caramel stage.

2 Add the butter. Carefully add the blood orange purée. Stir until well combined and set aside to cool.

Approximate values per 1-fl.-oz. (30-ml) serving: **Calories** 80, **Total fat** 2.5 g, **Saturated fat** 1.5 g, **Cholesterol** 5 mg, **Sodium** 0 mg, **Total carbohydrates** 16 g, **Protein** 0 g

BANANA TWISTS

Banana, green-tip	1	1

1 Peel the banana. Slice the banana lengthwise in very thin slices using an electric slicer or mandoline. Place the slices on a sheet pan lined with a silicon mat or parchment paper and dry in a 200°F (90°C) oven for 1½ to 2 hours.

2 While they are still warm, wrap the banana slices around a clean piece of PVC pipe and allow to cool.

RECIPE 33.25

CLASSIC BROWNIES

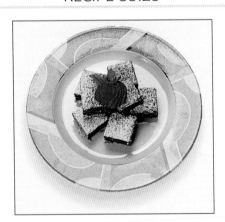

Yield: 1 Sheet Pan   **Method:** Egg Foam

Unsweetened chocolate	2 lb.	1000 g
Unsalted butter	2 lb.	1000 g
Eggs	20	20
Granulated sugar	5 lb. 12 oz.	2.6 kg
Vanilla extract	2 fl. oz.	60 ml
All-purpose flour	1 lb. 10 oz.	800 g
Pecan pieces	1 lb.	500 g

1 Melt the chocolate with the butter over a double boiler.

2 While the chocolate is melting, whip the eggs and sugar in a large mixer bowl fitted with the paddle attachment for 10 minutes.

3 Add the melted chocolate and vanilla to the eggs. Stir to blend completely. Stir in the flour and nuts.

4 Spread the batter evenly onto a parchment-lined and buttered sheet pan. The pan will be very full. Bake at 325°F (160°C) for 40 minutes, rotating the pan after the first 20 minutes.

5 Allow to cool completely before cutting. Dust the brownies with confectioner's sugar if desired.

Approximate values per 2-in. (5-cm) square: **Calories** 343, **Total fat** 18 g, **Saturated fat** 9 g, **Cholesterol** 70 mg, **Sodium** 16 mg, **Total carbohydrates** 41 g, **Protein** 4 g

APPLESAUCE BROWNIES

RECIPE 33.26

Yield: 1 Sheet Pan

Unsweetened chocolate	4 oz.	120 g
Cake flour, sifted	1 lb.	450 g
Cocoa powder	9 oz.	270 g
Salt	2 tsp.	10 ml
Egg whites	12	12
Whole eggs	8	8
Granulated sugar	2 lb. 2 oz.	1 kg
Light corn syrup	2 lb.	900 g
Unsweetened applesauce	1½ pt.	670 ml
Canola oil	7 fl. oz.	210 ml
Vanilla extract	2 Tbsp.	30 ml

1 Coat a sheet pan with spray pan release.
2 Melt the chocolate over a bain marie and set aside.
3 Sift the flour, cocoa powder and salt together and set aside.
4 Whisk the egg whites and eggs together. Add the sugar, corn syrup, applesauce, oil and vanilla. Whisk in the chocolate.
5 Fold the flour mixture into the egg mixture. Pour into the prepared pan and bake at 350°F (180°C) until a cake tester comes out clean, approximately 25 minutes.

Approximate values per 2-in. (5-cm) square: **Calories** 150, **Total fat** 5 g, **Saturated fat** 0.8 g, **Cholesterol** 19 mg, **Sodium** 82 mg, **Total carbohydrates** 26 g, **Protein** 2 g

PRALINE SQUARES

RECIPE 33.27

Yield: 1 Sheet Pan, 12 in. × 18 in. (30 cm × 45 cm) (30 squares)

Method: Creaming

Unsalted butter, softened	8 oz.	225 g
Brown sugar	1 lb. 4 oz.	570 g
Eggs	5	5
Vanilla extract	1 tsp.	5 ml
Hazelnut extract	1 tsp.	5 ml
Flour	12 oz.	360 g
Baking powder	1 Tbsp.	15 ml
Salt	½ tsp.	2 ml
Pecans, chopped	8 oz.	225 g
Powdered sugar	as needed	as needed

1 Using a mixer fitted with a paddle attachment, cream the butter and sugar on medium speed until light, approximately 3 minutes.
2 Add the eggs, one at a time, then add the extracts.
3 Stir the dry ingredients together and gradually add them to the creamed mixture on low speed. Stir in the nuts.
4 Spread the batter into a lightly greased pan and bake at 325°F (160°C) until golden brown and set, approximately 40 minutes.
5 Cool in the pan, then cut into squares and dust with powdered sugar.

Approximate values per square: **Calories** 220, **Total fat** 11 g, **Saturated fat** 4.5 g, **Cholesterol** 50 mg, **Sodium** 105 mg, **Total carbohydrates** 28 g, **Protein** 3 g

WHAT DOES COOKERY MEAN? IT MEANS THE KNOWLEDGE OF MEDEA AND OF CIRCE, AND OF CALYPSO, AND SHEBA. IT MEANS KNOWLEDGE OF ALL HERBS, AND FRUITS, AND BALMS AND SPICES. . . . IT MEANS THE ECONOMY OF YOUR GREAT-GRANDMOTHER AND THE SCIENCE OF MODERN CHEMISTRY, AND FRENCH ART, AND ARABIAN HOSPITALITY. IT MEANS, IN FINE, THAT YOU ARE TO SEE IMPERATIVELY THAT EVERYONE HAS SOMETHING NICE TO EAT.

—*John Ruskin, English critic and theorist (1819–1900)*

CUSTARDS, CREAMS, FROZEN DESSERTS AND DESSERT SAUCES

34

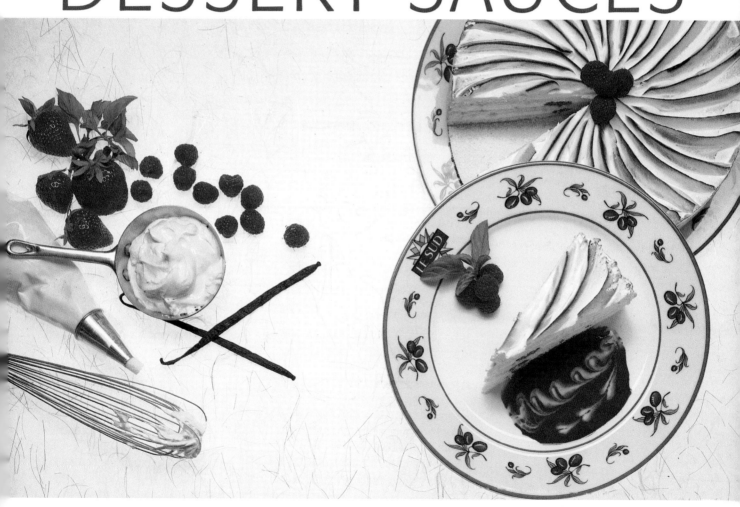

CHEF JACK SHOOP, CMC, CCE

AFTER STUDYING THIS
CHAPTER, YOU WILL BE
ABLE TO:

▶ prepare a variety of custards
and creams

▶ prepare a variety of ice creams,
sorbets and frozen dessert
items

▶ prepare a variety of dessert
sauces

▶ use these products in preparing
and serving other pastry and
dessert items

The bakeshop is responsible for more than just quick breads, yeast breads, pies, pastries, cookies and cakes. It also produces many delightfully sweet concoctions that are not baked and often not even cooked. These include sweet custards, creams, frozen desserts and dessert sauces. Sweet custards are cooked mixtures of eggs, sugar and milk; flour or cornstarch may be added. Sweet custards can be flavored in a variety of ways and eaten hot or cold. Some are served alone as a dessert or used as a filling, topping or accompaniment for pies, pastries or cakes. Creams include whipped cream and mixtures lightened with whipped cream such as Bavarians, chiffons and mousses. Frozen desserts include ice cream and sorbet as well as the still-frozen mousses called semifreddi.

Sauces for these desserts, including fruit purées, caramel sauces and chocolate syrup, are also made in the bakeshop and are discussed in this chapter. Indeed, many of the items presented in this chapter are components, meant to be combined with pastries (Chapter 32) or cakes (Chapter 33) to form complete desserts. Guidelines for assembling desserts are given at this chapter's end.

▶ CUSTARDS

A **custard** is any liquid thickened by the coagulation of egg proteins. A custard's consistency depends on the ratio of eggs to liquid and the type of liquid used. The more eggs used, the thicker and richer the final product will be. The richer the liquid (cream versus milk, for example), the thicker the final product. Most custards, with the notable exception of pastry creams, are not thickened by starch.

A custard can be stirred or baked. A **stirred custard** tends to be soft, rich and creamy. A **baked custard,** typically prepared in a bain marie, is usually firm enough to unmold and slice.

STIRRED CUSTARDS

A stirred custard is cooked on the stove top either directly in a saucepan or over a double boiler. It must be stirred throughout the cooking process to prevent curdling (overcooking).

A stirred custard can be used as a dessert sauce, incorporated into a complex dessert or eaten alone. The stirred custards most commonly used in food service operations are **vanilla custard sauce** and **pastry cream.** Other popular stirred custards are lemon curd (page 1117) and **sabayon** (page 1094).

VANILLA CUSTARD SAUCE

Vanilla custard sauce (Fr. *crème anglaise*) is made with egg yolks, sugar and milk or half-and-half. Usually flavored with vanilla bean or pure vanilla extract, a custard sauce can also be flavored with liquor, chocolate, ground nuts or extracts.

It is prepared on the stove top over direct heat. When making a custard sauce, be extremely careful to stir the mixture continually and not allow it to boil, or it will curdle. A properly made custard sauce should be smooth and thick enough to coat the back of a spoon. It should not contain any noticeable bits of cooked egg.

A custard sauce can be served with cakes, pastries, fruits and soufflés and is often used for decorating dessert plates. It may be served hot or cold. It is also used as the base for many ice creams.

A very thick version of custard sauce can be made using heavy cream and additional egg yolks. Its consistency is more like a **pudding** than a sauce. This custard is often served over fruit in a small ramekin or other container and then topped with caramelized sugar for a dessert known as **crème brûlée** (burnt cream). See the recipe on page 1096.

PASTRY CREAM

Pastry cream (Fr. *crème pâtissière*) is a stirred custard made with egg yolks, sugar and milk and thickened with starch (flour, cornstarch or a combination of the two). Because the starch protects the egg yolks from curdling, pastry cream can be boiled. In fact, it must be boiled to fully gelatinize the starch and eliminate the taste of raw starch.

Pastry cream can be flavored with chocolate, liquors, extracts or fruits. (Pudding is nothing more than a flavored pastry cream.) It is used for filling éclairs, cream puffs, napoleons, fruit tarts and other pastries. Pastry cream thickened with cornstarch is also the filling for cream pies (see Chapter 32, Pies, Pastries and Cookies). Pastry cream is thick enough to hold its shape without making pastry doughs soggy.

Pastry cream can be rather heavy. It can be lightened by folding in whipped cream to produce a **mousseline,** or Italian meringue can be folded in to produce a **crème Chiboust.**

▶ PROCEDURE FOR PREPARING VANILLA CUSTARD SAUCE
AND PASTRY CREAM

1 Place milk and/or cream in a heavy, nonreactive saucepan; add vanilla bean if desired.

2 In a mixing bowl, whisk together the egg yolks, sugar and starch (if used). Do not use an electric mixer, as it incorporates too much air.

3 Bring the liquid just to a boil. **Temper** the egg mixture with approximately one-third of the hot liquid.

4 Pour the tempered eggs into the remaining hot liquid and return the mixture to the heat. The stove's temperature can be as hot as you dare: The lower the temperature, the longer the custard will take to thicken; the higher the temperature, the greater the risk of curdling.

5 Cook, stirring constantly, until thickened. Custard sauce should reach a temperature of 185°F (85°C). Pastry cream should be allowed to boil for a few moments.

6 Immediately remove the cooked custard from the hot saucepan to avoid overcooking. Butter or other flavorings can be added at this time.

7 Cool over an ice bath. Store in a clean, shallow container, cover and refrigerate.

▶ PROCEDURE FOR SALVAGING CURDLED
VANILLA CUSTARD SAUCE

1 Strain the sauce into a bowl. Place the bowl over an ice bath and whisk vigorously.

2 If this does not smooth out the overcooked sauce, place the sauce in a blender and process for a few moments.

▶ **pudding** a thick, spoonable dessert custard, usually made with eggs, milk, sugar and flavorings and thickened with flour or another starch

▶ **crème brûlée** (krehm broo-lay) French for burnt cream; used to describe a rich dessert custard topped with a crust of caramelized sugar

▶ **mousseline** (moos-uh-leen) a cream or sauce lightened by folding in whipped cream

▶ **crème chiboust** (krehm chee-boos) a vanilla pastry cream lightened by folding in Italian meringue; traditionally used in a gâteau St. Honoré

▶ **tempering** heating gently and gradually; refers to the process of slowly adding a hot liquid to eggs to raise their temperature without causing them to curdle

SAFETY ALERT

EGGS

Eggs are high-protein foods that are easily contaminated by bacteria such as *Salmonella* that cause food-borne illnesses. Because custards cannot be heated to temperatures high enough to destroy these bacteria without first curdling the eggs, it is especially important that sanitary guidelines be followed in preparing the egg products discussed in this chapter.

1 Cleanliness is important: Wash your hands thoroughly before beginning; be sure to use clean, sanitized bowls, utensils and storage containers.

2 When breaking or separating eggs, do not allow the exterior of the eggshell to come into contact with the raw egg.

3 Heat the milk to just below a boil before combining it with the eggs. This reduces the final cooking time.

4 Chill the finished product quickly in an ice bath and refrigerate immediately.

5 Do not use your fingers to taste the custard.

6 Do not store any custard mixture, cooked or uncooked, at room temperature.

RECIPE 34.1

VANILLA CUSTARD SAUCE
(CRÈME ANGLAISE)

Yield: 40 fl. oz. (1200 ml)   **Method:** Stirred Custard

Half-and-half	1 qt.	1 lt
Vanilla bean, split	1	1
Egg yolks	12	12
Granulated sugar	10 oz.	300 g

1 Using a heavy nonreactive saucepan, bring the half-and-half and vanilla bean just to a boil.

2 Whisk the egg yolks and sugar together in a mixing bowl. Temper the egg mixture with approximately one-third of the hot half-and-half, then return the entire mixture to the saucepan with the remaining half-and-half.

3 Cook the sauce over medium heat, stirring constantly, until it is thick enough to coat the back of a spoon. Do not allow the sauce to boil.

4 As soon as the sauce thickens, remove it from the heat and pour it through a fine mesh strainer into a clean bowl. Chill the sauce over an ice bath, then cover and keep refrigerated. The sauce should last 3 to 4 days.

Variations: *Chocolate Custard Sauce*—Stir 6 ounces (180 grams) of finely chopped dark chocolate into the strained custard while it is still warm. The heat of the custard will melt the chocolate.

Coffee Custard Sauce—Add 2 tablespoons (30 milliliters) of coffee (café) extract or compound to the warm custard.

Frangelico Custard Sauce—Omit the vanilla bean. Stir in ½ teaspoon (2 milliliters) of vanilla and 2–3 tablespoons (30–45 milliliters) of Frangelico, to taste.

Pistachio Custard Sauce—Omit the vanilla bean. Place 4 ounces (120 grams) of finely chopped pistachio nuts in the saucepan with the barely boiling half-and-half. Remove from the heat, cover and steep for up to 1 hour. Uncover the mixture, reheat and continue preparing the sauce as directed. The ground nuts will be strained out in Step 4.

Approximate values per 1-fl.-oz. (30-ml) serving: **Calories** 80, **Total fat** 4.5 g, **Saturated fat** 2.5 g, **Cholesterol** 75 mg, **Sodium** 15 mg, **Total carbohydrates** 8 g, **Protein** 2 g, **Vitamin A** 6%

1 Mise en place for vanilla sauce.

2 Tempering the eggs.

3 The properly cooked sauce.

4 Straining the sauce into a bowl.

PASTRY CREAM
(CRÈME PÂTISSIÈRE)

RECIPE 34.2

Yield: 1 qt. (1 lt)		**Method:** Stirred Custard
Cake flour	4 oz.	120 g
Granulated sugar	12 oz.	360 g
Milk	1 qt.	1 lt
Egg yolks	12	12
Vanilla bean, split	1	1
Unsalted butter	2 oz.	60 g

1 Sift the flour and sugar together.

2 Whisk 8 fluid ounces (225 milliliters) of the milk into the egg yolks. Then add the flour and sugar and whisk until completely smooth.

3 Heat the remaining milk with the vanilla bean in a heavy nonreactive saucepan. As soon as the milk comes to a boil, whisk approximately one-third of it into the egg-and-flour mixture and blend completely. Pour the egg mixture into the saucepan with the rest of the milk.

4 Stir constantly until the custard thickens. As it thickens, the custard will go through a lumpy stage. Although you should not be alarmed, you should increase the speed of your stirring. Continue to stir vigorously, and it will smooth out and thicken just before coming to a boil.

5 Allow the pastry cream to boil for approximately 1 minute, stirring constantly.

6 Remove the pastry cream from the heat and immediately pour it into a clean mixing bowl.

7 Fold in the butter until melted. Do not overmix, as this will thin the custard.

8 Cover by placing plastic wrap on the surface of the custard. Chill over an ice bath. Remove the vanilla bean just before using the pastry cream.

1 Stirring the pastry cream as it comes to a boil.

2 Folding butter into the cooked pastry cream.

Variations: *Mousseline Pastry Cream*—Whip 8 fluid ounces (225 milliliters) of plain whipping cream to stiff peaks. Fold into the chilled pastry cream.

Chocolate Pastry Cream—Stir 4 ounces (120 grams) of finely chopped dark chocolate into the strained custard while it is still warm. The heat of the custard will melt the chocolate.

Coffee Pastry Cream—Add 2 tablespoons (30 milliliters) of coffee (café) extract or compound to the warm custard.

Coconut Pastry Cream—Replace 16 fluid ounces (500 milliliters) of the milk with an equal amount of unsweetened canned coconut milk.

Approximate values per 1-fl.-oz. (30-ml) serving: **Calories** 110, **Total fat** 4.5 g, **Saturated fat** 2 g, **Cholesterol** 90 mg, **Sodium** 20 mg, **Total carbohydrates** 15 g, **Protein** 2 g, **Vitamin A** 6%

SABAYON

Sabayon (sah-bay-own; It. *zabaglione*) is a foamy, stirred custard sauce made by whisking eggs, sugar and wine over low heat. The egg proteins coagulate, thickening the mixture, while the whisking incorporates air to make it light and fluffy. Usually a sweet wine is used; marsala and champagne are the most popular choices.

The mixture can be served warm, or it can be chilled and lightened with whipped cream or whipped egg whites. Sabayon may be served alone or as a sauce or topping with fruit or pastries such as spongecake or ladyfingers.

▶ PROCEDURE FOR PREPARING SABAYON

1 Combine egg yolks, sugar and wine in the top of a double boiler.

2 Place the double boiler over low heat and whisk constantly until the sauce is foamy and thick enough to form a ribbon when the whisk is lifted.

3 Remove from the heat and serve immediately, or whisk over an ice bath until cool. If allowed to sit, the hot mixture may separate.

4 Whipped egg whites or whipped cream may be folded into the cooled sabayon.

RECIPE 34.3

CHAMPAGNE SABAYON

The thickened sabayon.

Yield: 1 qt. (1 lt)	**Method:** Stirred Custard	
Egg yolks	8	8
Granulated sugar	4 oz.	120 g
Salt	¼ tsp.	1 ml
Marsala wine	2 fl. oz.	60 ml
Dry champagne	6 fl. oz.	180 ml
Heavy cream (optional)	8 fl. oz.	225 ml

1 Combine the egg yolks, sugar and salt in a stainless steel bowl.

2 Add the marsala and champagne to the egg mixture.

3 Place the bowl over a pan of barely simmering water. Whisk vigorously until the sauce is thick and pale yellow, approximately 10 minutes. Serve immediately.

4 To prepare a sabayon mousseline, place the bowl of sabayon over an ice bath and continue whisking until completely cold. Whip the cream to soft peaks and fold it into the cold sabayon.

Approximate values per 1-fl.-oz. (30-ml) serving: **Calories** 50, **Total fat** 4 g, **Saturated fat** 2 g, **Cholesterol** 60 mg, **Sodium** 25 mg, **Total carbohydrates** 4 g, **Protein** 1 g, **Vitamin A** 6%

BAKED CUSTARDS

A baked custard is based on the same principle as a stirred custard: A liquid thickens by the coagulation of egg proteins. However, with a baked custard, the thickening occurs in an oven. The container of custard is usually placed in a water bath (bain marie) to protect the eggs from curdling. Even though the water bath's temperature will not exceed 212°F (100°C), care must be taken not to bake the custards for too long or at too high a temperature. An overbaked custard will be watery or curdled; a properly baked custard should be smooth-textured and firm enough to slice.

Baked custards include simple mixtures of egg yolks, sugar and milk such as crème caramel as well as custard mixtures in which other ingredients are suspended, for example, cheesecake, rice pudding, bread pudding and quiche.

CRÈME CARAMEL

Crème caramel, crème renversée and flan all refer to an egg custard baked over a layer of caramelized sugar and inverted for service. The caramelized sugar produces a golden-brown surface on the inverted custard and a thin caramel sauce.

TOFFEE CARAMEL FLAN

RECIPE 34.4

Yield: 10 Ramekins, 6 oz. (180 ml)   **Method:** Baked Custard

Granulated sugar	1 lb. 4 oz.	600 g
Water	8 fl. oz.	250 ml
Milk	24 fl. oz.	720 ml
Heavy cream	24 fl. oz.	720 ml
Cinnamon sticks	2	2
Vanilla bean, split	1	1
Whole eggs	8	8
Egg yolks	4	4
Brown sugar	6 oz.	180 g
Molasses	1 Tbsp.	15 ml
Amaretto liqueur	2 Tbsp.	30 ml

Filling the ramekins for flans.

1 Combine the granulated sugar with the water in a small heavy saucepan; bring to a boil. Cook until the sugar reaches a deep golden brown. Immediately pour about 2 tablespoons (30 milliliters) of the sugar into each of the ramekins. Tilt each ramekin to spread the caramel evenly along the bottom. Arrange the ramekins in a 2-inch-deep hotel pan and set aside.

2 Combine the milk, cream, cinnamon sticks and vanilla bean in a large saucepan. Bring just to a boil, cover and remove from the heat. Allow this mixture to **steep** for about 30 minutes.

3 Whisk the eggs, egg yolks, brown sugar, molasses and amaretto together in a large bowl.

4 Uncover the milk mixture and return it to the stove top. Bring just to a boil. Temper the egg-and-sugar mixture with approximately one-third of the hot milk. Whisk in the remaining hot milk.

5 Strain the custard through a fine mesh strainer. Pour into the caramel-lined ramekins, filling to just below the rim.

6 Pour enough warm water into the hotel pan to reach halfway up the sides of the ramekins. Bake at 325°F (160°C) for approximately 30 to 40 minutes. The custards should be almost set, but still slightly soft in the center.

7 Completely chill the baked custards before serving. To unmold, run a small knife around the edge of the custard, invert onto the serving plate and give the ramekin a firm sideways shake. Garnish with fresh fruit or caramelized almonds.

▶ **steep** to soak food in a hot liquid in order to either extract its flavor or soften its texture

Approximate values per serving: **Calories** 670, **Total fat** 33 g, **Saturated fat** 19 g, **Cholesterol** 355 mg, **Sodium** 120 mg, **Total carbohydrates** 82 g, **Protein** 10 g, **Vitamin A** 40%, **Calcium** 20%

CRÈME BRÛLÉE

Crème brûlée (krehm broo-LAY) can be made as either a stirred or a baked custard. Neither version should be considered superior, however; they are simply different. The stirred or stovetop method is quicker, but requires constant attention and a practiced feel for the custard's consistency. The finished custard will be heavier, creamier and softer than its baked counterpart. The baked version is served in the ramekin or bowl in which it was baked. Unlike crème caramel or flan, baked crème brûlée is not inverted or removed from its baking dish for service. A formula for the baked version follows; a stirred version appears on page 1112.

Gentle heat is important for both methods. Overcooked stirred custard will curdle, turning into scrambled eggs. Overcooked baked custard will become watery, its texture marred with small bubbles.

CLASSIC CUSTARD

James Beard called crème brûlée "one of the greatest desserts in the realm of cooking." The secret to crème brûlée's success probably lies in its comfort-food familiarity. It is a rich, creamy concoction of egg yolks, sugar and cream served very cold and topped with a crisp, crunchy layer of deeply caramelized sugar. The contrast of textures and flavors satisfies multiple taste desires.

Despite its French name, crème brûlée (literally, burnt cream) is most likely a product of Great Britain. Perhaps the earliest recipe for burnt cream appears in a 17th-century cookbook from Dorset, England. Numerous sources credit a member of the faculty at Trinity College in Cambridge, England, with successfully introducing this caramelized custard to his peers in the mid-1800s.

Burnt cream was also popular in America, with recognizable versions appearing in Thomas Jefferson's personal recipe collection and in several cookbooks from the 1800s.

Considered a trendy dessert for upscale American restaurants in the 1980s, crème brûlée now appears on all types of menus and is equally at home in neighborhood diners and four-star, white-tablecloth eateries.

Additional flavors and textures can be added to the custard in several ways:

1 Placing a layer of fresh berries or fruit compote under the custard
2 Incorporating fruit, nuts or liqueurs directly into the custard
3 Adding flavoring compounds and extracts to the custard
4 Infusing the heavy cream with nuts, herbs, spices, tea or other flavorings before making the custard

If fruit purées or other liquids are used, the quantity of cream will have to be adjusted or else the custard may be too watery or unable to set properly.

RECIPE 34.5

BAKED CRÈME BRÛLÉE

Yield: 10 Servings, 4 oz. (120 g) each   **Method:** Baked Custard

Heavy cream	1 qt.	1 lt
Vanilla bean, split	½	½
Granulated sugar	4 oz.	120 g
Egg yolks	10	10
Granulated sugar	as needed	as needed

1 Heat the cream and the vanilla bean in a medium saucepan over medium-high heat until bubbles appear along the sides of the pan.
2 Quickly whisk the sugar into the egg yolks.
3 When the cream is hot, slowly pour it into the yolk mixture. Whisk until well combined.
4 Strain the mixture through a fine sieve into a pitcher or large measuring cup. Scrape the vanilla bean with the tip of a paring knife to remove the remaining seeds; stir the seeds into the custard.
5 Preheat the oven to 325°F (160°C). Arrange the ramekins in a 2-inch- (5-cm-) deep hotel pan or baking dish. Pour the custard into the ramekins. Set the pan of ramekins inside the preheated oven, then carefully pour enough water into the pan to come two-thirds of the way up the sides of the ramekins. Bake until just set, approximately 45 to 50 minutes. Start checking the custards early; baking time will depend on the thickness and depth of your ramekins. The custard should be set, not soupy, with only a small area of jiggle in the center.
6 When the custards are done, carefully remove the baking dish from the oven and allow the ramekins to cool in the water bath. When the ramekins are cool enough to handle, remove them from the water, cover with plastic wrap, and refrigerate for at least 4 hours or up to 2 days before service.

7 At service, sprinkle the top of each custard with granulated sugar then immediately caramelize the sugar with a blowtorch or under a broiler.

Approximate values per serving: **Calories** 430, **Total fat** 40 g, **Saturated fat** 24 g, **Cholesterol** 345 mg, **Sodium** 45 mg, **Total carbohydrates** 14 g, **Protein** 5 g, **Vitamin A** 35%

CHEESECAKE

Cheesecakes, which are almost as old as western civilization, have undergone many changes and variations since the ancient Greeks devised the first known recipe. Americans revolutionized the dessert with the development of cream cheese in 1872.

Cheesecake is a baked custard that contains a smooth cheese, usually a soft, fresh cheese such as cream, ricotta, cottage or farmer cheese. A cheesecake may be prepared without a crust, or it may have a base or sides of short dough, cookie crumbs, ground nuts or spongecake. The filling can be dense and rich (New York style) or light and fluffy (Italian style). Fruit, nuts and flavorings may also be included in the filling. Cheesecakes are often topped with fruit or sour cream glaze. Recipes for both dense and light cheesecakes are at the end of this chapter.

Some cheesecakes are unbaked and rely on gelatin for thickening; others are frozen. These are not really custards, however, but are more similar to the chiffons or mousses discussed later.

BREAD PUDDING

Bread pudding is a home-style dessert in which chunks of bread, flavorings and raisins or other fruit are mixed with an egg custard and baked. The result is somewhat of a cross between a cake and a pudding. It is often served with custard sauce, ice cream, whipped cream or a whiskey-flavored butter sauce. Bread pudding is a delicious way to use stale or leftover bread or overripe fruit. A recipe for bread pudding with bourbon sauce appears at the end of this chapter.

SOUFFLÉS

A soufflé is made with a custard base that is lightened with whipped egg whites and then baked. The air in the egg whites expands to create a light, fluffy texture and tall rise. A soufflé is not as stable as a cake or other pastry item, however, and will collapse very quickly when removed from the oven.

Soufflés can be prepared in a wide variety of sweet and savory flavors. The flavorings can be incorporated into the custard, as in the following recipe. Alternatively, an unflavored pastry cream can be used as the base; the liqueur, fruit or chocolate is then added to each portion separately.

When making a soufflé, the custard base and egg whites should be at room temperature. First, the egg whites will whip to a better volume, and second, if the base is approximately the same temperature as the egg whites, the two mixtures can be more easily incorporated. The egg whites are whipped to stiff peaks with a portion of the sugar for stability. The whipped egg whites are then gently folded into the base immediately before baking.

A soufflé is baked in a straight-sided mold or individual ramekin. The finished soufflé should be puffy with a lightly browned top. It should rise well above the rim of the baking dish. A soufflé must be served immediately, before it collapses. A warm custard sauce (crème anglaise) is often served as an accompaniment to a sweet soufflé.

A frozen soufflé is not a true soufflé. Rather, it is a creamy custard mixture thickened with gelatin, lightened with whipped egg whites or whipped cream and placed in a soufflé dish wrapped with a paper or acetate collar. When the collar is removed, the mixture looks as if it has risen above the mold like a hot soufflé.

▷ PROCEDURE FOR PREPARING BAKED SOUFFLÉS

1 Butter the mold or ramekins and dust with granulated sugar. Preheat the oven to approximately 425°F (220°C).

2 Prepare the custard base. Add flavorings as desired.

3 Whip the egg whites and sugar to stiff peaks. Fold the whipped egg whites into the base.

4 Pour the mixture into the prepared mold or ramekins and bake immediately.

RECIPE 34.6

CHOCOLATE SOUFFLÉS

Yield: 8 Servings

Orange juice	1 pt.	500 ml
Eggs, separated	8	8
Granulated sugar	4 oz.	120 g
All-purpose flour	3 oz.	90 g
Bittersweet chocolate, chopped fine	8 oz.	225 g
Orange liqueur	2 fl. oz.	60 ml
Butter, melted	as needed	as needed
Granulated sugar	as needed	as needed

1 To prepare the base, heat the orange juice to lukewarm in a heavy saucepan.

2 Whisk the egg yolks with 3 ounces (90 grams) of the sugar in a large mixing bowl. Whisk in the flour and warm orange juice, then return the mixture to the saucepan.

3 Cook over medium-low heat, stirring constantly, until the custard is thick. Do not allow it to boil. Remove from the heat.

4 Stir in the chocolate until completely melted. Stir in the liqueur. Cover this base mixture with plastic wrap to prevent a skin from forming. Hold for use at room temperature. (Unused base can be kept overnight in the refrigerator; it should be brought to room temperature before mixing with the egg whites.)

5 To prepare the soufflés, brush individual-serving-sized ramekins with melted butter and dust with granulated sugar.

6 Preheat the oven to 425°F (220°C). Place a sheetpan in the oven, onto which you will place the soufflés for baking. (This makes it easier to remove the hot soufflé cups from the oven.)

7 Whip the egg whites to stiff peaks with the remaining 1 ounce (30 grams) of sugar. Fold the whites into the chocolate base and spoon the mixture into the prepared ramekins. The ramekins should be filled to within ¼ inch (6 mil-

1 Folding the whipped egg whites into the chocolate base.

2 Filling the ramekins.

3 The finished soufflé, ready for service.

limeters) of the rim. Smooth the top of each soufflé with a spatula and bake immediately.

8 The soufflés are done when well risen and golden brown on top and the edges appear dry, approximately 12 minutes. Do not touch a soufflé to test doneness.

9 Sprinkle the soufflés with powdered sugar if desired and serve immediately.

Approximate values per serving: **Calories** 350, **Total fat** 15 g, **Saturated fat** 8 g, **Cholesterol** 210 mg, **Sodium** 65 mg, **Total carbohydrates** 48 g, **Protein** 10 g, **Vitamin A** 10%, **Vitamin C** 50%

▶ CREAMS

Creams (Fr. *crèmes*) include light, fluffy or creamy-textured dessert items made with whipped egg whites or whipped cream. Some, such as **Bavarian creams** and **chiffons,** are thickened with gelatin. Others, such as **mousses** and **crèmes Chantilly,** are softer and lighter. The success of all, however, depends on properly whipping and incorporating egg whites or heavy cream.

You should review the material on whipping cream found in Chapter 8, Dairy Products. Note that whipping cream has a butterfat content of 30 to 40 percent. When preparing any whipped cream, be sure that the cream, the mixing bowl and all utensils are well chilled and clean. A warm bowl can melt the butterfat, destroying the texture of the cream. Properly whipped cream should increase two to three times in volume.

CRÈME CHANTILLY

Crème Chantilly is simply heavy cream whipped to soft peaks and flavored with sugar and vanilla. It can be used for garnishing pastry or dessert items, or it can be folded into cooled custard or pastry cream and used as a component in a pastry.

When making crème Chantilly, the vanilla extract and sugar should be added after the cream begins to thicken. Either granulated or powdered sugar may be used; there are advantages and disadvantages to both. Granulated sugar assists in forming a better foam than powdered sugar, but it may cause the cream to feel gritty. Powdered sugar dissolves more quickly and completely than granulated sugar, but does nothing to assist with foaming. Whichever sugar is used, it should be added just before the whipping is complete to avoid interfering with the cream's volume and stability.

CRÈME CHANTILLY (CHANTILLY CREAM)

RECIPE 34.7

Yield: 2–2 ½ qt. (2–2 ½ lt)

Heavy cream, chilled	1 qt.	1 lt
Powdered sugar	3 oz.	90 g
Vanilla extract	2 tsp.	10 ml

1 Place the cream in a chilled mixing bowl. Using a balloon whisk, whisk the cream until slightly thickened.

2 Add the sugar and vanilla and continue whisking to the desired consistency. The cream should be smooth and light, not grainy. Do not overwhip.

Properly whipped Crème Chantilly.

CHARLOTTE, SWEET CHARLOTTE

The original charlotte was created during the 18th century and named for the wife of King George III of England. It consisted of an apple compote baked in a round mold lined with toast slices. A few decades later, the great French chef Carême adopted the name but altered the concept in response to a kitchen disaster. When preparing a grand banquet for King Louis XVIII, he found that his gelatin supply was insufficient for the Bavarian creams he was making, so Carême steadied the sides of his sagging desserts with ladyfingers. The result became known as charlotte russe, probably due to the reigning fad for anything Russian. A fancier version, known as charlotte royale, is made with pinwheels or layers of spongecake and jam instead of ladyfingers. The filling for either should be a classic Bavarian cream.

3 Crème Chantilly may be stored in the refrigerator for several hours. If the cream begins to soften, gently rewhip as necessary.

Approximate values per 1-fl.-oz. (30-ml) serving: **Calories** 60, **Total fat** 6 g, **Saturated fat** 3.5 g, **Cholesterol** 20 mg, **Sodium** 5 mg, **Total carbohydrates** 2 g, **Protein** 0 g

BAVARIAN CREAM

A Bavarian cream (Fr. *bavarois*) is prepared by first thickening custard sauce with gelatin, then folding in whipped cream. The final product is poured into a mold and chilled until firm enough to unmold and slice. Although a Bavarian cream can be molded into individual servings, it is often poured into a round mold lined with spongecake or ladyfingers to create the classic dessert known as a **charlotte.**

Bavarians can be flavored by adding chocolate, puréed fruit, chopped nuts, extracts or liquors to the custard sauce base. Layers of fruit or liquor-soaked spongecake can also be added for flavor and texture.

When thickening a dessert cream with gelatin, it is important to use the correct amount of gelatin. If not enough gelatin is used or it is not incorporated completely, the cream will not become firm enough to unmold. If too much gelatin is used, the cream will be tough and rubbery. The recipes given here use sheet gelatin, although an equal amount by weight of granulated gelatin can be substituted. Refer to Chapter 29, Principles of the Bakeshop, for information on using gelatin.

▶ PROCEDURE FOR PREPARING BAVARIAN CREAMS

1 Prepare a custard sauce of the desired flavor.
2 While the custard sauce is still quite warm, stir in softened gelatin. Make sure the gelatin is completely incorporated.
3 Chill the custard until almost thickened, then fold in the whipped cream.
4 Pour the Bavarian into a mold or charlotte form. Chill until set.

RECIPE 34.8   **FRESH FRUIT BAVARIAN**

Yield: 1 Mold, 1 qt. (1 lt)

Fresh fruit such as 2 kiwis, 1 banana
     or ½ pint (225 ml) raspberries, blueberries or wild strawberries

Honey	1 Tbsp.	15 ml
Kirsch or brandy	2 Tbsp.	30 ml
Egg yolks	4	4
Granulated sugar	4 oz.	120 g
Milk	8 fl. oz.	250 ml
Vanilla bean	½	½
Gelatin, softened	½ oz.	14 g
Heavy cream	12 fl. oz.	360 ml

1 Adding gelatin to the custard base.

2 Folding in the whipped egg whites.

1 Lightly spray the bottom of a 1-quart (1-liter) mold with pan release spray. If a smooth mold is being used, line it with a sheet of plastic wrap, allowing the wrap to extend beyond the mold's edges.

2 Peel and thinly slice the fruit if necessary. Mix the honey and the kirsch or brandy and pour over the fruit. Chill while preparing the Bavarian cream.

3 Prepare a vanilla custard sauce using the egg yolks, sugar, milk and vanilla. Remove from the saucepan.

4 Add softened gelatin to the hot custard. Chill until thick, but do not allow the custard to set.

5 Whip the cream until stiff and fold it into the chilled and thickened custard. Pour about one-third of this mixture (the Bavarian cream) into the mold. Arrange half of the fruit on top. Pour half of the remaining Bavarian cream on top of the fruit and top with the remaining fruit. Fill with the rest of the Bavarian cream. Chill until completely set, approximately 2 hours.

6 Unmold onto a serving dish. Garnish the top with additional fruit and whipped cream as desired.

Note: Gelatin may separate in the freezer, so quick chilling is not recommended. Products made with gelatin keep well for 1 to 2 days but stiffen with age.

Variation: *Charlotte*—Line a 1–1½-quart (1–1.5-liter) charlotte mold with ladyfingers (page 1083), then fill with layers of fruit and Bavarian cream. Invert onto a serving platter when firm and garnish with whipped cream.

Approximate values per 3.5-oz. (105-g) serving: **Calories** 230, **Total fat** 15 g, **Saturated fat** 9 g, **Cholesterol** 135 mg, **Sodium** 30 mg, **Total carbohydrates** 19 g, **Protein** 3 g, **Vitamin A** 20%, **Vitamin C** 25%

CHIFFON

A chiffon is similar to a Bavarian except that whipped egg whites instead of whipped cream are folded into the thickened base. The base may be a custard or a fruit mixture thickened with cornstarch. Although a chiffon may be molded like a Bavarian, it is most often used as a pie or tart filling.

▶ PROCEDURE FOR PREPARING CHIFFONS

1 Prepare the base, which is usually a custard or a fruit mixture thickened with cornstarch.

2 Add gelatin to the warm base.

3 Fold in whipped egg whites.

4 Pour into a mold or pie shell and chill.

LIME CHIFFON   RECIPE 34.9

Yield: 1 Pie, 10 in. (25 cm), 8 Servings

Granulated gelatin	¼ oz.	7 g
Water	5 fl. oz.	150 ml
Granulated sugar	7 oz.	210 g
Fresh lime juice	3 fl. oz.	90 ml
Lime zest	1 Tbsp.	15 ml
Eggs, separated	4	4

1 Soften the gelatin in 1 fluid ounce (30 milliliters) of the water.

2 Combine 4 ounces (120 grams) of the sugar, the remaining water, lime juice, zest and egg yolks in a bowl over a pan of simmering water.

3 Whisk the egg-and-lime mixture together vigorously until it begins to thicken. Add the softened gelatin and continue whipping until very thick and foamy.

4 Remove from the heat, cover and refrigerate until cool and as thick as whipping cream.

5 Meanwhile, whip the egg whites to soft peaks. Whip in the remaining sugar and continue whipping until stiff but not dry.

6 Fold the whipped egg whites into the egg-and-lime mixture. Pour into a prepared pie crust or serving dishes and chill for several hours, until firm.

Variations: *Lemon Chiffon*—Substitute lemon juice and lemon zest for the lime juice and zest.

Orange Chiffon—Substitute orange juice for the lime juice and for 4 fluid ounces (120 milliliters) of the water. Substitute orange zest for the lime zest. Reduce the amount of sugar in the egg yolk mixture to 1 ounce (30 grams).

Approximate values per serving: **Calories** 140, **Total fat** 2.5 g, **Saturated fat** 1 g, **Cholesterol** 105 mg, **Sodium** 35 mg, **Total carbohydrates** 26 g, **Protein** 4 g, **Claims**—low fat; low saturated fat; low sodium

MOUSSE

The term *mousse* applies to an assortment of dessert creams not easily classified elsewhere. A mousse is similar to a Bavarian or chiffon in that it is lightened with whipped cream, whipped egg whites or both. A mousse is generally softer than these other products, however, and only occasionally contains a small amount of gelatin. A mousse is generally too soft to mold.

A mousse may be served alone as a dessert or used as a filling in cakes or pastry items. Sweet mousses can be based on a custard sauce, melted chocolate or puréed fruit.

Savory mousses are discussed in Chapter 27, Charcuterie.

▶ PROCEDURE FOR PREPARING MOUSSES

1 Prepare the base, which is usually a custard sauce, melted chocolate or puréed fruit.

2 If gelatin is used, it is softened first, then dissolved in the warm base.

3 Fold in whipped egg whites, if used. If the base is slightly warm when the egg whites are added, their proteins will coagulate, making the mousse firmer and more stable.

CONVENIENCE PRODUCTS

Commercially prepared powders and mixes can be used to make a wide assortment of puddings, custards, mousses, gelatin desserts and creams. The advantages to these products are speed, quality control and reduced labor costs. Packaged mixes are simply prepared according to the directions provided by the manufacturer. The pastry cook can often improve on the final product by adding whipped cream, fruit or an appropriate garnish. As with other convenience products, quality varies from merely adequate to very good. Sample and experiment with several brands to select the best for your operation.

Table 34.1 CREAM (CRÈME) COMPONENTS

FOR A:	BEGIN WITH A BASE OF:	THICKEN WITH:	THEN FOLD IN:
Bavarian	Custard	Gelatin	Whipped cream
Chiffon	Custard or starch-thickened fruit	Gelatin	Whipped egg whites
Mousse	Melted chocolate, puréed fruit or custard	Nothing or gelatin	Whipped cream, whipped egg whites or both

4 Allow the mixture to cool completely, then fold in whipped cream, if used. Note that the egg whites are folded in before any whipped cream. Although the egg whites may deflate somewhat during folding, if the cream is added first it may become overwhipped when the egg whites are added, creating a grainy or coarse product.

 ## CLASSIC CHOCOLATE MOUSSE RECIPE 34.10

Yield: 1½–2 qt. (1.5–2 lt)

Bittersweet chocolate	15 oz.	440 g
Unsalted butter	9 oz.	280 g
Egg yolks	7	7
Egg whites	11	11
Granulated sugar	2½ oz.	70 g
Heavy cream	8 fl. oz.	250 ml

1 Melt the chocolate and butter in a double boiler over low heat. Stir until no lumps remain.

2 Allow the mixture to cool slightly, then whisk in the egg yolks one at a time.

3 Beat the egg whites until soft peaks form. Slowly beat in the sugar and continue beating until stiff peaks form. Fold the whipped egg whites into the chocolate mixture.

4 Whip the cream to soft peaks. Allow the mousse to cool, then fold in the whipped cream. Make sure no streaks of egg white or cream remain.

5 Spoon the mousse into serving bowls or chill completely and pipe into bowls or baked tartlet shells. The mousse may be used as a cake or pastry filling.

Approximate values per 3-fl.-oz. (90-ml) serving: **Calories** 370, **Total fat** 31 g, **Saturated fat** 18 g, **Cholesterol** 215 mg, **Sodium** 50 mg, **Total carbohydrates** 16 g, **Protein** 7 g, **Vitamin A** 25%

1 Folding in the whipped egg whites. **2** Folding in the whipped cream.

▶ FROZEN DESSERTS

Frozen desserts include **ice cream** and **gelato** and desserts assembled with ice cream such as baked Alaska, bombés and parfaits. Frozen fruit purées, known as **sorbets** and **sherbets,** are also included in this category. Still-frozen desserts, known as **semifreddi,** are made from custards or mousses that are frozen without churning.

When making any frozen mixture, remember that cold dulls flavors. Although perfect at room temperature, flavors seem weaker when the mixture is cold. Thus, it may be necessary to oversweeten or overflavor creams or custards that will be frozen for service. Although liquors and liqueurs are common flavoring ingredients, alcohol drastically lowers a liquid mixture's freezing point. Too much alcohol will prevent the mixture from freezing; thus any liqueurs or liquors must be used in moderation.

ICE CREAM AND GELATO

Ice cream and gelato are custards that are churned during freezing. They can be flavored with a seemingly endless variety of fruits, nuts, extracts, liqueurs and the like. Gelato is an Italian-style ice cream. It is denser than American-style products because less air is incorporated during churning.

▶ **overrun** the amount of air churned into an ice cream

The USDA requires that products labeled "ice cream" contain not less than 10 percent milk fat and 20 percent milk solids, and have no more than 50 percent **overrun.** "Ice milk" refers to products that do not meet the standards for ice cream. Low-fat products made without cream or egg yolks are also available for the calorie conscious. Frozen yogurt uses yogurt as its base. Although touted as a nutritious substitute for ice cream, frozen yogurt may have whole milk or cream added for richness and smoothness.

One hallmark of good ice cream and gelato is smoothness. The ice crystals that would normally form during freezing can be avoided by incorporating air through constant stirring or churning. The air causes the mixture to expand. Gelato is denser because it has little incorporated air. Good-quality ice creams and sorbets have enough air to make them light; inferior products often contain excessive overrun. The difference becomes obvious when equal volumes are weighed.

Many food service operations use ice cream makers that have internal freezing units to chill the mixture while churning it. Most commercial machines are

ICE CREAM: FROM ANCIENT CHINA TO DOUBLE-FUDGE-BROWNIE-CHOCOLATE-CHIP WITH COOKIE DOUGH AND TOASTED ALMOND SLIVERS

Despite claims to the contrary, it is impossible to identify any one country as having invented ice cream. More likely, it was invented in several places around the world at various times.

Early ancestors of today's ice creams were flavored water ices, which have been popular in China since prehistoric times. They have also been popular in the Mediterranean and Middle East since the Golden Age of Greece. In fact, Alexander the Great had a penchant for wine-flavored ices, made with ice brought down from the mountains by runners. The Roman emperor Nero served his guests mixtures of fruit crushed with snow and honey. The Saracens brought their knowledge of making flavored ices with them when they migrated to Sicily in the 9th century. And 12th-century Crusaders returned to western Europe with memories of Middle Eastern sherbets.

The Italians are said to have developed gelato from a recipe brought back from China by Marco Polo in the 13th century. Somehow the dish spread to England by the 15th century, where it was recorded that King Henry V served it at his coronation banquet. Catherine de Medici brought the recipe with her when she married the future king of France in 1533. A different flavor was served during each of the 34 days of their marriage festivities.

Ice cream was first sold to the public in Paris during the late 17th century. It was available at fashionable cafés serving another new treat: coffee. French chefs quickly developed many elaborate desserts using ice creams, including bombés, coupes and parfaits.

Many of this country's founders—Thomas Jefferson, Alexander Hamilton and James and Dolley Madison—were confirmed ice cream ad-

dicts. George Washington spent more than $200, a very princely sum, for ice cream during the summer of 1790.

The mechanized ice cream freezer was invented in 1846, setting the stage for mass production and wide availability. By the late 19th century, ice cream parlors were popular gathering places. (Some of today's ice cream parlors still take their décor from "Gay Nineties" motifs.)

Despite the disappearance of most ice cream wagons, soda fountains and lunch counters, all of which were popular ice cream purveyors for much of the 20th century, ice cream sales have never waned. Today, more than 80 percent of all ice cream is sold in supermarkets or convenience stores. The public's demand for high-fat, homemade-style "super-premium" ice creams with rich and often-elaborate flavor combinations shows no sign of declining.

suitable for churning either ice cream or sorbet. Follow the manufacturer's directions for using and cleaning any ice cream maker.

▶ PROCEDURE FOR PREPARING ICE CREAMS

1 Place the milk and/or cream in a heavy saucepan. If vanilla bean is being used, it may be added at this time.

2 Whisk the egg yolks and sugar together in a mixing bowl.

3 Bring the liquid just to a boil. Temper the egg mixture with approximately one-third of the hot liquid.

4 Pour the tempered eggs into the remaining hot liquid and return the mixture to the heat.

5 Cook, stirring constantly, until warm.

6 Remove the cooked custard sauce from the hot saucepan immediately. If left in the hot saucepan, it will overcook. Flavorings may be added at this time.

7 Cool the cooked custard sauce over an ice bath. Store covered and refrigerated until ready to process.

8 Process according to the machine manufacturer's directions.

ICE CREAM BASE

RECIPE 34.11

Yield: 2 qt. (2 lt)

Whole milk	1½ qt.	1500 ml
Heavy cream	1 pt.	500 ml
Vanilla bean (optional)	1	1
Egg yolks	16	16
Granulated sugar	20 oz.	600 g

1 Combine the milk and cream in a heavy saucepan and bring to a boil. Add the vanilla bean, if desired.

2 Whisk the egg yolks and sugar together in a mixing bowl.

3 Temper the eggs with one-third of the hot milk. Return the egg mixture to the saucepan.

4 Cook over medium heat until slightly thickened. Pour through a fine mesh strainer into a clean bowl.

5 Chill the cooked ice cream base completely before processing.

Variations: *Chocolate Ice Cream*—Add approximately 9 ounces (250 grams) of finely chopped bittersweet chocolate per quart (liter) of ice cream base. Add the chocolate to the hot mixture after it has been strained. Stir until completely melted.

Cappuccino Ice Cream—Steep the hot milk and cream with the vanilla bean and two or three cinnamon sticks. After the ice cream base is made, stir in 2 tablespoons (30 milliliters) coffee extract.

Brandied Cherry Ice Cream—Drain the liquid from one 16-ounce (500-gram) can of tart, pitted cherries. Soak the cherries in 3 tablespoons (45 milliliters) brandy. Prepare the ice cream base as directed, omitting the vanilla bean. Add the brandy-soaked cherries to the cooled custard before processing.

Approximate values per 6-fl.-oz. (180-ml) serving: **Calories** 370, **Total fat** 20 g, **Saturated fat** 11 g, **Cholesterol** 270 mg, **Sodium** 65 mg, **Total carbohydrates** 41 g, **Protein** 7 g, **Vitamin A** 25%

SHERBETS AND SORBETS

Sherbet and sorbet are frozen mixtures of fruit juice or fruit purée. Sherbet contains milk and/or eggs for creaminess; sorbet contains neither.

Sorbet can be prepared in a wide variety of fruit (and even some vegetable) flavors; it is often flavored with an alcoholic beverage. It is served as a first course, a palate refresher between courses or a dessert. Because of its milk content, sherbet tends to be richer than a sorbet, so it is generally reserved for dessert.

Sorbet and sherbet may be made with fresh, frozen or canned fruit. Granulated sugar or sugar syrup is added for flavor and body. The ratio of sugar to fruit purée or juice depends to some extent on the natural sweetness of the specific fruit as well as personal preference. If too much sugar is used, however, the mixture will be soft and syrupy. If too little sugar is used, the sorbet will be very hard and grainy. Egg whites may also be added during churning for improved texture and body.

RECIPE 34.12

GRAPEFRUIT SORBET

▶ **sundae** a great and gooey concoction of ice cream, sauces (hot fudge, marshmallow and caramel, for example), toppings (nuts, candies and fresh fruit to name a few) and whipped cream

▶ **baked Alaska** ice cream set on a layer of spongecake and encased in meringue, then baked until the meringue is warm and golden

▶ **bombé** two or more flavors of ice cream, or ice cream and sherbet, shaped in a spherical mold; each flavor is a separate layer that forms the shell for the next flavor

▶ **coupe** another name for an ice cream sundae, especially one served with a fruit topping

▶ **coulis** (coo-lee) a sauce made from a purée of fruits or vegetables

▶ **parfait** ice cream served in a long, slender glass with alternating layers of topping or sauce

▶ **marquise** a frozen mousse-like dessert, usually chocolate

▶ **neapolitan** a three-layered loaf or cake of ice cream; each layer is a different flavor and a different color, a typical combination being chocolate, vanilla and strawberry

Yield: 1½ qt. (1.5 lt)

| Fresh grapefruit juice | 1 qt. | 1 lt |
| Granulated sugar | 8 oz. | 250 g |

1 Combine the juice and sugar.
2 Process in an ice cream maker according to the manufacturer's directions.
3 Pack into a clean container and freeze until firm.

Variations: *Mango Sorbet*—Combine 2.2 pounds (1 kilogram) of mango purée with 8 fluid ounces (240 milliliters) of medium sugar syrup (page 932).

Raspberry Sorbet—Combine 2.2 pounds (1 kilogram) of puréed, strained raspberries with 1 pound (500 grams) granulated sugar and 1 fluid ounce (30 milliliters) lemon juice.

Approximate values per 3-fl.-oz. (90-ml) serving: **Calories** 94, **Total fat** 0 g, **Saturated fat** 0 g, **Cholesterol** 0 mg, **Sodium** 1 mg, **Total carbohydrates** 23 g, **Protein** 0.5 g, **Vitamin C** 36%, **Claims**—no fat; no cholesterol; very low sodium; low calorie

SERVING SUGGESTIONS FOR ICE CREAMS AND SORBETS

Ice creams and sorbets are usually served by the scoop, often in cookie cones. Or they can be served as **sundaes.** More formal presentations include **baked Alaska, bombés, coupes** and **parfaits.**

STILL-FROZEN DESSERTS

Still-frozen desserts (It. *semifreddi*) are made with frozen mousse, custard or cream. Layers of spongecake and/or fruit may be added for flavor and texture. Because these mixtures are frozen without churning, air must be incorporated by folding in relatively large amounts of whipped cream or meringue. The air helps keep the mixture smooth and prevents it from becoming too hard.

Still-frozen products include frozen soufflés, **marquise,** mousses and **neapolitans.** The Chocolate Hazelnut Marquise recipe at the end of this chapter (page 1121) is an example of a still-frozen dessert.

▶ DESSERT SAUCES

Pastries and desserts are often accompanied by sweet sauces. Dessert sauces provide moisture, flavor and texture and enhance plate presentation. Vanilla Custard Sauce (page 1092) is the principal dessert sauce. It can be flavored and colored with chocolate, coffee extract, liquor or fruit compound as desired. Other dessert sauces include fruit purées, caramel sauce and chocolate syrup.

FRUIT PURÉES

Many types of fruit can be puréed for dessert sauces; strawberries, raspberries, blackberries, apricots, mangoes and papayas are popular choices. They produce thick sauces with strong flavors and colors. Fresh or individually quick-frozen (IQF) fruits are recommended. Several commercial brands of prepared fruit purées are available. The best use only natural fruits and are excellent for making sauces and sorbets. They provide consistent flavor and color, reduce preparation time, and make out-of-season or hard-to-obtain tropical fruits available at a reasonable price.

Puréed fruit sauces, also known as **coulis,** can be cooked or uncooked. Cooking thickens the sauces by reduction and allows any starch thickener to gelatinize. They can also be sweetened with granulated sugar or a sugar syrup. The amount of sweetener will vary depending upon the fruit's natural sweetness and personal preference.

RASPBERRY SAUCE

RECIPE 34.13

Raspberry Sauce

Yield: 1 qt. (1 lt)

Raspberries, fresh or IQF	2 lb.	1 kg
Granulated sugar	1 lb.	500 g
Lemon juice	1 fl. oz.	30 ml

1 Purée the berries and strain through a fine chinois.
2 Stir in the sugar and lemon juice. Adjust the flavor with additional sugar if necessary.

Approximate values per 1-fl.-oz. (30-ml) serving: **Calories** 70, **Total fat** 0 g, **Saturated fat** 0 g, **Cholesterol** 0 mg, **Sodium** 0 mg, **Total carbohydrates** 17 g, **Protein** 0 g, **Claims**–fat free; no saturated fat; no cholesterol; no sodium

CARAMEL SAUCE

Caramel sauce is a mixture of caramelized sugar and heavy cream. A liqueur or citrus juice may be used for added flavor. Review the material on caramelizing sugar in Chapter 29, Principles of the Bakeshop, before making caramel sauce.

CARAMEL SAUCE

RECIPE 34.14

Yield: 4 qt. (4 lt)

Granulated sugar	4 lb. 8 oz.	2 kg
Water	1 pt.	500 ml
Lemon juice	2 fl. oz.	60 ml
Heavy cream, room temperature	2 qt.	2 lt
Unsalted butter, cut into pieces	5 oz.	150 g

Caramel Sauce

1 Combine the sugar and water in a large heavy saucepan. Stir to moisten the sugar completely. Place the saucepan on the stove top over high heat and bring to a boil. Brush down the sides of the pan with water to remove any sugar granules.

2 When the sugar comes to a boil, add the lemon juice. Do not stir the sugar, as this may cause lumping. Continue boiling until the sugar caramelizes, turning a dark golden brown and producing a rich aroma.

3 Remove the saucepan from the heat. Gradually add the cream. Be extremely careful, as the hot caramel may splatter. Whisk in the cream to blend.

4 Add the pieces of butter. Stir until the butter melts completely. If necessary, return the sauce to the stove to reheat enough to melt the butter.

5 Strain the sauce and cool completely at room temperature. The sauce may be stored for several weeks under refrigeration. Stir before using.

Approximate values per 1-fl.-oz. (30-ml) serving: **Calories** 130, **Total fat** 7 g, **Saturated fat** 4 g, **Cholesterol** 25 mg, **Sodium** 5 mg, **Total carbohydrates** 16 g, **Protein** 0 g, **Vitamin A** 8%

CHOCOLATE SYRUP

Chocolate syrup or sauce can be prepared by adding finely chopped chocolate to warm vanilla custard sauce. A darker syrup can also be made with unsweetened chocolate or cocoa powder. Fudge-type sauces, like the one at the end of this chapter (page 1122), are really just variations on ganache, discussed in Chapter 33, Cakes and Frostings.

RECIPE 34.15   DARK CHOCOLATE SYRUP

Dark Chocolate Syrup

Yield: 1 pt. (500 ml)

Cocoa powder	2 oz.	60 g
Water	12 fl. oz.	340 ml
Granulated sugar	8 oz.	250 g
Unsalted butter	3 oz.	90 g
Heavy cream	1 fl. oz.	30 ml

1 Mix the cocoa powder with just enough water to make a smooth paste.

2 Bring the sugar and remaining water to a boil in a small, heavy saucepan. Immediately add the cocoa paste, whisking until smooth.

3 Simmer for 15 minutes, stirring constantly, then remove from the heat.

4 Stir the butter and cream into the warm cocoa mixture. Serve warm or at room temperature.

Approximate values per 1-fl.-oz. (30-ml) serving: **Calories** 120, **Total fat** 6 g, **Saturated fat** 3 g, **Cholesterol** 15 mg, **Sodium** 0 mg, **Total carbohydrates** 16 g, **Protein** 1 g, **Vitamin A** 6%

▶ ASSEMBLING DESSERTS

As noted previously, many pastries and other desserts are assembled from the baked doughs discussed in Chapter 32, Pies, Pastries and Cookies; the cakes, icings and glazes discussed in Chapter 33, Cakes and Frostings, and the creams, custards and other products discussed in this chapter. Many of these desserts are classic presentations requiring the precise arrangement of specific components. But once you begin to master the basic skills presented in these chapters, you can use your creativity, taste and judgment to combine these components into a wide selection of new, unique and tempting desserts.

Assembled pastries and other desserts generally consist of three principal components: the base, the filling and the garnish. The **base** is the dough, crust or cake product that provides structure and forms the foundation for the final product. The **filling** refers to whatever is used to add flavor, texture and body to the final product. The **garnish** is any glaze, fruit, sauce or accompaniment used to complete the dish.

▶ GUIDELINES FOR ASSEMBLING DESSERTS

1 There should be a proper blend of complementary and contrasting flavors. For example, pears, red wine and blue cheese go well together, as do chocolate and raspberries. Do not combine flavors simply for the sake of originality, however.

2 There should be a proper blend of complementary and contrasting textures. For example, crisp puff pastry, soft pastry cream and tender strawberries are combined for a strawberry napoleon.

3 There should be a proper blend of complementary and contrasting colors. For example, a garnish of red raspberries and green mint adds life to a brown-on-brown chocolate torte.

4 Garnishes should not be overly fussy or garish.

5 The base should be strong enough to hold the filling and garnish without collapsing, yet thin or tender enough to cut easily with a fork.

6 The filling or garnish may cause the base to become soft or even soggy. This may or may not be desirable. If you want a crisp base, assemble the product very close to service. If you want this softening to occur, assemble the product in advance of service.

7 Consider the various storage and keeping qualities of the individual components. It may be best to assemble or finish some products at service time.

8 The final construction should not be so elaborate or fragile that it cannot be portioned or served easily or attractively.

9 Consider whether the product would be better prepared as individual portions or as one large item. This may depend on the desired plate presentation and the ease and speed with which a large product can be cut and portioned for service.

If pastry doughs are the backbone of dessert preparations, then custards, creams, mousses and the like are the heart. The skills and techniques presented in this chapter are essential to successful pastry production. Many of these skills, such as whipping cream or preparing custards, will be useful in other areas of the kitchen as well. Once you have mastered these skills as well as those discussed in Chapter 32, Pies, Pastries and Cookies, and Chapter 33, Cakes and Frostings, you will be able to prepare a wide variety of tempting desserts.

CONCLUSION

QUESTIONS FOR DISCUSSION

1 Eggs and dairy products are susceptible to bacterial contamination. What precautions should be taken to avoid food-borne illnesses when preparing custards?

2 Explain why pastry cream should be boiled and why custard sauce should not be boiled.

3 Identify three desserts that are based on a baked custard.

4 Compare a classically prepared Bavarian, chiffon, mousse and souffle. How are they similar? How are they different?

5 Describe the procedure for making a typical still-frozen dessert. What is the purpose of including whipped cream or whipped egg whites?

6 Explain three ways in which sweet sauces can be used in preparing or presenting a dessert.

 7 Locate the Web sites of three manufacturers or distributors of prepared dessert sauces. How do you think these products compare with sauces that you could make from scratch? What additional information—not available on the Internet—would you need in order to make a decision about using these sauces?

LONGCHAMP   RECIPE 34.16

Note: This dish appears in the chapter opening photograph.

CHEF JACK SHOOP, CMC

Yield: 1 Cake, 10 in. (24 cm)

Ladyfingers (page 1083)	as needed	as needed
Genoise (page 1052), cut into a 10-in. (24-cm) circle	1 layer	1 layer
Kirsch (cherry brandy)	3½ fl. oz.	100 ml
Simple syrup, cool	1 qt.	1 lt
Kirsch Mousse (recipe follows)	as needed	as needed
Fresh raspberries	1 pt.	480 ml
Italian Meringue (page 1016)	as needed	as needed

1 Place a 10-inch (24-centimeter) metal ring that is 1¾ inches (4.5 centimeters) high over a cardboard circle. Line the ring completely with Ladyfingers. Cut the ladyfingers level with the top of the ring. Place the genoise inside the ring to form the bottom of the cake.

2 Prepare a Kirsch-flavored syrup by combining the Kirsch and the simple syrup. Brush the genoise and the ladyfingers with this syrup. Reserve the remaining Kirsch-flavored syrup for another use.

3 Fill the cake with Kirsch Mousse, sprinkling in raspberries as the cake is filled so that the fruit is evenly distributed. The cake should be filled to the top of the ring. Smooth the top of the mousse with an offset spatula.

4 Freeze the cake until set.

5 Spread a thin layer of Italian Meringue over the mousse. Decorate the top of the cake with Italian Meringue piped through a pastry bag fitted with a Saint-Honoré tip. Pipe the meringue from the center, curving outward to the edge of the cake. Brown the top of the meringue with a propane torch.

6 Remove the metal ring and garnish the cake with fresh raspberries.

Approximate values per ¹/₁₂-cake serving: **Calories** 690, **Total fat** 30 g, **Saturated fat** 17 g, **Cholesterol** 267 mg, **Sodium** 171 mg, **Total carbohydrates** 89 g, **Protein** 10 g, **Vitamin A** 25%, **Vitamin C** 35%, **Calcium** 10%

KIRSCH MOUSSE

Yield: 2 qt. (2 lt)

Gelatin sheets	9	9
Kirsch	3½ fl. oz.	100 ml
Heavy cream	1 qt.	1 lt
Pastry cream	35 oz.	1 kg

1 Soften the gelatin in ice water.

2 Bring the Kirsch to a simmer over low heat. Remove from the heat, add the gelatin and stir until it is completely dissolved.

3 Stir the gelatin mixture into the heavy cream, then whip the cream to soft peaks.

4 Fold the whipped cream into the pastry cream and chill until ready to use.

Approximate values per serving: **Calories** 480, **Total fat** 36 g, **Saturated fat** 22 g, **Cholesterol** 245 mg, **Sodium** 96 mg, **Total carbohydrates** 27 g, **Protein** 8 g, **Vitamin A** 29%, **Vitamin C** 41%, **Calcium** 12%

RECIPE 34.17

CRÈME BRÛLÉE

VINCENT ON CAMELBACK, PHOENIX, AZ
Chef Vincent Guerithault

Yield: 3½ qt. (3.5 lt)   **Method:** Stirred Custard

Heavy cream	2 qt.	2 lt
Vanilla beans, split	2	2
Egg yolks	50	50
Granulated sugar	20 oz.	600 g
Fresh berries	as needed	as needed
Tulipe Cookie cups (page 1044)	as needed	as needed
Granulated sugar	as needed	as needed

1 Place the cream and the vanilla beans in a large, heavy saucepan. Heat just to a boil.

2 Whisk the egg yolks and sugar together until smooth and well blended.

3 Temper the egg mixture with one-third of the hot cream. Return the egg mixture to the saucepan and cook, stirring constantly, until very thick. Do not allow the custard to boil.

4 Remove from the heat and strain into a clean bowl. Cool over an ice bath, stirring occasionally.

5 To serve, place fresh berries in the bottom of each Tulipe Cookie cup. Top with several spoonsful of custard.

6 Sprinkle granulated sugar over the top of the custard and caramelize with a propane torch. Serve immediately.

Variation: *Passion Fruit Crème Brûlée*—Replace ½ quart (500 milliliters) of the cream with ½ quart (500 milliliters) of frozen, thawed passion fruit purée.

Coffee Crème Brûlée—Omit the vanilla bean. Add 2–3 tablespoons (30–45 milliliters) of coffee extract or compound to the finished custard.

Ginger Crème Brûlée—Omit the vanilla bean. Peel and coarsely chop a 2-inch (10-centimeter) piece of fresh ginger. Steep the ginger in the warm cream for 30 minutes, and then proceed with the recipe. The ginger will be strained out in Step 4.

Approximate values per 5-fl.-oz. (150-ml) serving: **Calories** 460, **Total fat** 36 g, **Saturated fat** 20 g, **Cholesterol** 480 mg, **Sodium** 135 mg, **Total carbohydrates** 26 g, **Protein** 7 g, **Vitamin A** 50%

RECIPE 34.18

CRÈME CHIBOUST

Yield: 1 pt. (500 ml)   **Method:** Stirred Custard

Gelatin sheets	3	3
Milk	6 fl. oz.	180 ml
Vanilla bean	½	½
Egg yolks	3	3

Granulated sugar	3 Tbsp.	45 ml
Cornstarch	2 Tbsp.	30 ml
Italian Meringue:		
Granulated sugar	6 oz.	180 g
Water	3 Tbsp.	45 ml
Egg whites	3	3
Cream of tartar	⅛ tsp.	0.5 ml

1 Soak the gelatin in ice water.

2 Prepare a pastry cream by heating the milk and vanilla bean just to a boil. Whisk the egg yolks, 3 tablespoons (45 milliliters) of sugar and the cornstarch together. Temper with one-third of the hot milk, then return the mixture to the saucepan and cook over moderate heat until thick. The pastry cream should be allowed to boil briefly to properly gelatinize the starch. Remove the cream from the heat and transfer to a clean bowl.

3 Stir the softened gelatin into the hot cream. Cover and set aside but do not chill or allow the cream to set while preparing the Italian meringue.

4 Prepare an Italian meringue using the remaining ingredients.

5 Quickly and thoroughly incorporate one-third of the meringue into the warm pastry cream with a spatula. Gently fold in the remaining meringue.

Approximate values per 1-fl.-oz. (30-ml) serving: **Calories** 80, **Total fat** 1.5 g, **Saturated fat** 0.5 g, **Cholesterol** 40 mg, **Sodium** 20 mg, **Total carbohydrates** 14 g, **Protein** 3 g, **Claims**—low fat; low saturated fat; very low sodium

 ## CHOCOLATE POT AU CRÈME RECIPE 34.19

Yield: 8 Servings, 4 oz. (120 ml) each **Method:** Baked Custard

Milk	1 pt.	500 ml
Bittersweet chocolate	8 oz.	225 g
Granulated sugar	7 oz.	210 g
Vanilla extract	1 tsp.	5 ml
Coffee liqueur	2 Tbsp.	30 ml
Egg yolks	7	7

1 Heat the milk just to a simmer. Add the chocolate and sugar. Stir constantly until the chocolate melts; do not allow the mixture to boil. Remove from the heat and add the vanilla and liqueur.

2 Whisk the egg yolks together, then slowly whisk them into the chocolate mixture.

3 Pour the custard into ramekins. Place the ramekins in a hotel pan and add enough hot water to reach halfway up the sides of the ramekins.

4 Bake at 325°F (160°C) until the custards are almost set in the center, approximately 30 minutes. Remove from the water bath and refrigerate until thoroughly chilled. Serve garnished with whipped cream and chocolate shavings.

Approximate values per serving: **Calories** 360, **Total fat** 16 g, **Saturated fat** 9 g, **Cholesterol** 195 mg, **Sodium** 40 mg, **Total carbohydrates** 46 g, **Protein** 6 g, **Vitamin A** 10%, **Calcium** 10%

 ## PISTACHIO CITRUS CHEESECAKE RECIPE 34.20

Yield: 4 Cakes, 10 in. (25 cm) each

Unsalted butter, melted	as needed	as needed
Pistachios, chopped fine	16 oz.	450 g
Cream cheese, softened	6 lb. 10 oz.	3.7 kg

Continued

All-purpose flour	3½ oz.	100 g
Granulated sugar	2 lb. 5 oz.	1 kg
Eggs	18	18
Heavy cream	10 fl. oz.	300 ml
Lemon zest, grated fine	4 Tbsp.	60 ml
Orange zest, grated fine	4 Tbsp.	60 ml

1 Brush the sides and bottoms of four cake pans (do not use springform pans) with melted butter. Coat with an even layer of pistachio nuts.

2 Beat the cream cheese until smooth. Add the flour and sugar and beat to incorporate completely.

3 Add the eggs slowly, then stir in the cream. Stir in the zests and pour the batter into prepared pans.

4 Place the cake pans in a water bath and bake at 325°F (160°C) until set, approximately 45 minutes.

5 Cool to room temperature before inverting onto a serving tray or cake card-board. The nut crust becomes the top of the cakes.

Approximate values per ¹/₁₀-cake serving: **Calories** 470, **Total fat** 34 g, **Saturated fat** 19 g, **Cholesterol** 190 mg, **Sodium** 250 mg, **Total carbohydrates** 32 g, **Protein** 10 g, **Vitamin A** 40%

RECIPE 34.21

NEW YORK–STYLE CHEESECAKE

Yield: 2 Cakes, 10 in. (25 cm) each

Cream cheese, softened	3 lb. 6 oz.	1.6 kg
Cake flour	2 oz.	60 g
Granulated sugar	18 oz.	540 g
Eggs	8	8
Heavy cream	5 fl. oz.	150 ml
Vanilla extract	1 Tbsp.	15 ml

1 Beat the cheese until smooth. Beat in the flour and sugar.

2 Blend in the eggs slowly, then add the cream and vanilla.

3 Pour the batter into well-buttered springform pans. Bake at 300°F (150°C) until set, approximately 1 to 1½ hours.

4 Cool completely before removing the sides of each pan.

Approximate values per ¹/₁₀-cake serving: **Calories** 450, **Total fat** 32 g, **Saturated fat** 20 g, **Cholesterol** 180 mg, **Sodium** 260 mg, **Total carbohydrates** 31 g, **Protein** 9 g, **Vitamin A** 40%

RECIPE 34.22

CHOCOLATE MOLE CHEESECAKE

SENCHA, Colorado Springs, CO

Chef Brent Beavers

Yield: 1 Cheescake, 10 in. (25 cm)

Cream cheese, room temperature	3 lb.	1.4 kg
Cocoa powder	2 oz.	60 g
Granulated sugar	12 oz.	360 g
Cumin, ground	1 tsp.	5 ml
Kosher salt	1 pinch	1 pinch
Eggs, large	6	6
Chipotle Adobo (recipe follows)	4 tsp.	20 ml
Sour Cherry Sauce (recipe follows)	as needed	as needed

1 Beat the cream cheese until smooth.

2 Sift together the cocoa powder, sugar, cumin and salt. Add the sugar mixture to the cream cheese and mix on low speed, scraping down the bowl as necessary to prevent lumps.

3 Slowly add the eggs and Chipotle Adobo, scraping down the bowl as necessary.

4 Pour the batter into a buttered springform pan and bake at 300°F (150°C) until set, approximately 1 to 1½ hours.

5 Cool completely before removing from the pan. Serve the cheesecake with Sour Cherry Sauce.

Approximate values per ¹⁄₁₂-cake serving: **Calories** 560, **Total fat** 43 g, **Saturated fat** 26 g, **Cholesterol** 230 mg, **Sodium** 380 mg, **Total carbohydrates** 35 g, **Protein** 13 g, **Vitamin A** 40%, **Calcium** 10%, **Iron** 15%

CHIPOTLE ADOBO

Yield: 8 fl. oz. (240 ml)

Chipotle peppers, dried	3 oz.	90 g
White onion, chopped	8 oz.	240 g
Champagne vinegar	4 fl. oz.	120 ml

1 In a small saucepan, simmer the peppers and onion in the vinegar until tender, approximately 10 minutes. Purée the mixture in a food processor until it forms a paste.

SOUR CHERRY SAUCE

Yield: 5 c. (1.1 lt)

Fresh cherries, pitted	1 lb.	450 g
Champagne vinegar	6 fl. oz.	180 ml
Cloves, ground	½ tsp.	3 ml
Simple syrup	2 pt.	450 ml

1 Soak the cherries in the vinegar with the ground cloves for 30 minutes. Combine the mixture with the simple syrup, bring to a simmer and reduce by half. Cool and serve.

Approximate values per 1-fl.-oz. (30-ml) serving: **Calories** 100, **Total fat** 0 g, **Saturated fat** 0 g, **Cholesterol** 0 mg, **Sodium** 30 mg, **Total carbohydrates** 26 g, **Protein** 0 g

BREAD PUDDING WITH BOURBON SAUCE

RECIPE 34.23

Yield: 20 Servings　　　　**Method:** Baked Custard

Raisins	8 oz.	250 g
Brandy	4 fl. oz.	120 ml
Unsalted butter, melted	2 oz.	60 g
White bread, day-old	24 oz.	720 g
Heavy cream	2 qt.	2 lt
Eggs	6	6
Granulated sugar	1 lb. 10 oz.	800 g
Vanilla extract	2 Tbsp.	30 ml
Bourbon Sauce (recipe follows)	as needed	as needed

1 Combine the raisins and brandy in a small saucepan. Heat just to a simmer, cover and set aside.

2 Use a portion of the butter to thoroughly coat a 2-inch- (5-centimeter-) deep hotel pan. Reserve the remaining butter.

3 Tear the bread into chunks and place in a large bowl. Pour the cream over the bread and set aside until soft.

4 Beat the eggs and sugar until smooth and thick. Add the vanilla, the remaining melted butter and the raisins and brandy.

5 Toss the egg mixture with the bread gently to blend. Pour into the hotel pan and bake at 350°F (180°C) until browned and almost set, approximately 45 minutes.

6 Serve warm with 2–3 tablespoons (30–45 milliliters) of the Bourbon Sauce.

Approximate values per serving: **Calories** 700, **Total fat** 44 g, **Saturated fat** 26 g, **Cholesterol** 270 mg, **Sodium** 260 mg, **Total carbohydrates** 67 g, **Protein** 9 g, **Vitamin A** 50%, **Calcium** 10%, **Iron** 10%

BOURBON SAUCE

Yield: 1 qt. (1 lt)

Unsalted butter	8 oz.	250 g
Granulated sugar	1 lb.	500 g
Eggs	2	2
Bourbon	8 fl. oz.	250 ml

1 Melt the butter; stir in the sugar and eggs and simmer to thicken.

2 Add the bourbon and hold in a warm place for service.

Approximate values per 1-fl.-oz. (30-ml) serving: **Calories** 150, **Total fat** 8 g, **Saturated fat** 5 g, **Cholesterol** 40 mg, **Sodium** 50 mg, **Total carbohydrates** 19 g, **Protein** 1 g, **Vitamin A** 8%

RECIPE 34.24

CHERRY CLAFOUTI

Clafouti is a country-style dessert from the Loire region of France and is similar to a quiche. Stone fruits such as cherries, peaches or plums are baked in an egg custard, then served piping hot or at room temperature.

Yield: 1 Cake, 10 in. (25 cm)

Dark cherries, fresh or canned, pitted	1 lb.	500 g
Eggs	4	4
Milk	12 fl. oz.	360 ml
Granulated sugar	2 oz.	60 g
Vanilla extract	1 tsp.	5 ml
All-purpose flour	2 oz.	60 g
Powdered sugar	as needed	as needed

1 Drain the cherries and pat them completely dry with paper towels. Arrange them evenly on the bottom of a buttered 10-inch (25-centimeter) pan. Do not use a springform pan or removable-bottom tartlet pan.

2 Make the custard by whisking the eggs and milk together. Add the sugar, vanilla and flour and continue whisking until all the lumps are removed.

3 Pour the custard over the cherries and bake at 325°F (160°C) for 1 to 1½ hours. The custard should be lightly browned and firm to the touch when done.

4 Dust with powdered sugar and serve the clafouti while still warm.

Approximate values per ¹⁄₁₀-cake serving: **Calories** 170, **Total fat** 3.5 g, **Saturated fat** 1.5 g, **Cholesterol** 90 mg, **Sodium** 4.5 mg, **Total carbohydrates** 30 g, **Protein** 5 g, **Vitamin A** 6%

LEMON CURD

RECIPE 34.25

Yield: 1½ qt. (1.5 lt)

Eggs	12	12
Egg yolks	4	4
Granulated sugar	2 lb.	900 g
Unsalted butter, cubed	1 lb.	450 g
Lemon zest	from 8 lemons	from 8 lemons
Fresh lemon juice	12 fl. oz.	360 ml

1 Whisk everything together in a large bowl.
2 Place the bowl over a pan of simmering water and cook, stirring frequently, until very thick, approximately 20 to 25 minutes.
3 Strain, cover and chill completely. Serve with scones or use as a filling for tartlets or layer cakes.

Approximate values per 1-fl.-oz. (30-ml) serving: **Calories** 170, **Total fat** 9 g, **Saturated fat** 5 g, **Cholesterol** 90 mg, **Sodium** 20 mg, **Total carbohydrates** 20 g, **Protein** 2 g, **Vitamin A** 10%

WHITE CHOCOLATE FRANGELICO BAVARIAN

RECIPE 34.26

Yield: 4 qt. (4 lt)

Heavy cream	2 qt.	2 lt
White chocolate, chopped	2 lb.	1 kg
Gelatin sheets	8	8
Frangelico (hazelnut liqueur)	10 fl. oz.	300 ml
Vanilla extract	2 tsp.	10 ml

1 Bring 1 quart (1 liter) of the cream just to a boil. Immediately pour over the chopped chocolate. Stir until the chocolate melts.
2 Place the gelatin in ice water to soften.
3 Gently heat the Frangelico just to a simmer. Remove from the heat and stir in the gelatin, one softened sheet at a time.
4 Add the gelatin mixture to the chocolate. Stir to blend well. Cool over an ice bath, stirring frequently.
5 Whip the remaining cream with the vanilla to stiff peaks.
6 Fold the whipped cream into the chocolate mixture. Chill until ready to use.

Approximate values per 4-fl.-oz. (120-ml) serving: **Calories** 400, **Total fat** 32 g, **Saturated fat** 21 g, **Cholesterol** 90 mg, **Sodium** 50 mg, **Total carbohydrates** 22 g, **Protein** 5 g, **Vitamin A** 25%

CHOCOLATE CHIFFON PIE

RECIPE 34.27

Yield: 2 Pies, 9 in. (22 cm)

Gelatin, sheets or powder	½ oz.	15 g
Milk	20 fl. oz.	600 ml
Unsweetened chocolate	4 oz.	120 g
Granulated sugar	6 oz.	180 g
Salt	¼ tsp.	1 ml

Continued

Eggs, separated	6	6
Vanilla extract	2 tsp.	10 ml
Crumb-crust pie shells, 9 in. (22 cm)	2	2
Whipped cream	as needed for garnish	
Chocolate shavings	as needed for garnish	

1 Soften the gelatin and set aside.
2 Combine the milk and chocolate in a heavy saucepan and warm over low heat until the chocolate melts.
3 Add 4 ounces (120 grams) of the sugar, the salt and the egg yolks. Continue cooking, stirring constantly, until the mixture thickens.
4 Remove from the heat and add the gelatin, stirring until completely dissolved. Pour the mixture into a bowl and chill until very thick.
5 Whip the egg whites to soft peaks. Add the vanilla and the remaining sugar and whip to stiff peaks. Fold the whites into the chocolate.
6 Mound the chiffon into the pie shells and chill for several hours before serving. Garnish with unsweetened whipped cream and chocolate shavings.

Approximate values per ¹⁄₁₀-pie serving: **Calories** 210, **Total fat** 12 g, **Saturated fat** 4.5 g, **Cholesterol** 70 mg, **Sodium** 160 mg, **Total carbohydrates** 21 g, **Protein** 5 g

RECIPE 34.28   **RASPBERRY MOUSSE**

Yield: 1 qt. (1 lt)

Gelatin sheets	6	6
Raspberries, puréed	12 oz.	360 g
Granulated sugar	3 oz.	90 g
Raspberry brandy	2 Tbsp.	30 ml
Heavy cream	8 fl. oz.	250 ml

1 Soften the gelatin in ice water and set aside.
2 Place the raspberry purée, sugar and brandy in a nonreactive saucepan and warm just to dissolve the sugar. Remove from the heat and strain through a fine chinois.
3 Add the gelatin, stirring until it is dissolved. Chill the mixture until thick but not set.
4 Whip the cream to soft peaks and fold it into the raspberry mixture.

Approximate values per 3-fl.-oz. (90-ml) serving: **Calories** 180, **Total fat** 11 g, **Saturated fat** 7 g, **Cholesterol** 40 mg, **Sodium** 15 mg, **Total carbohydrates** 16 g, **Protein** 5 g, **Vitamin A** 10%

RECIPE 34.29   **CHOCOLATE ICE CREAM**

CHRISTOPHER'S FERMIER BRASSERIE AND PAOLA'S WINE BAR, Phoenix, AZ
Chef-Owner Christopher Gross

Yield: 10 Servings

Egg yolks	5	5
Granulated sugar	5 oz.	150 g
Cocoa powder	1½ oz.	45 g

Milk	1 pt.	500 ml
Heavy cream	3 fl. oz.	90 ml
Semisweet chocolate, chopped	4 oz.	120 g

1 Whisk the egg yolks, sugar and cocoa powder together.

2 Combine the milk and cream and bring to a boil. Temper the egg mixture with a portion of the hot milk; return the mixture to the saucepan and continue cooking, stirring constantly, until the custard thickens.

3 Remove from the heat and add the chocolate. Stir until the chocolate melts, then strain and chill.

4 Process the custard in an ice cream maker according to the manufacturer's directions.

Approximate values per 3-oz. (90-g) serving: **Calories** 210, **Total fat** 11 g, **Saturated fat** 7 g, **Cholesterol** 125 mg, **Sodium** 40 mg, **Total carbohydrates** 27 g, **Protein** 4 g

CARAMEL ICE CREAM

RECIPE 34.30

CHEFS SUSAN FENIGER AND MARY SUE MILLIKIN

Yield: 1½ qt. (1½ lt)

Half-and-half	20 fl. oz.	600 ml
Heavy cream	12 fl. oz.	360 ml
Egg yolks	9	9
Granulated sugar	6 oz.	180 g
Vanilla extract	2 tsp.	10 ml
Sour cream	8 oz.	225 g
Caramel Chunks (recipe follows)	as needed	as needed

1 Combine the half-and-half and heavy cream in a medium-heavy saucepan. Bring to a boil.

2 Whisk together the egg yolks and sugar until thick and pale yellow. Pour into the boiling cream and stir to combine. Remove from the heat.

3 Add the vanilla and stir. Strain into a large container and chill over an ice bath, stirring occasionally.

4 Stir in the sour cream and pour into an ice cream maker. Process according to the manufacturer's directions.

5 When the ice cream is done, fold in the Caramel Chunks. Store in the freezer for 1 to 2 days.

Approximate values per serving: **Calories** 310, **Total fat** 24 g, **Saturated fat** 14 g, **Cholesterol** 225 mg, **Sodium** 45 mg, **Total carbohydrates** 18 g, **Protein** 5 g, **Vitamin A** 30%, **Claims**—low sodium

CARAMEL CHUNKS

| Granulated sugar | 8 oz. | 225 g |
| Water | 4 fl. oz. | 120 ml |

1 Combine the sugar and water in a heavy saucepan. Cook over moderate heat until the color turns deep brown and the aroma is strong, approximately 10 to 15 minutes.

2 Immediately, and with great care, pour the hot caramel onto a greased sheet pan. Set aside until cool, then crack into ½-inch (1.2-centimeter) pieces.

RECIPE 34.31

HONEY ICE CREAM

BISHOP'S RESTAURANT, Vancouver, BC

Chefs Michael Allemeier and Dennis Green

Yield: 1 qt. (1 lt)

Heavy cream	1 pt.	500 ml
Light cream	1 pt.	500 ml
Egg yolks	8	8
Honey	4 fl. oz.	120 ml

1 In a nonreactive saucepan, combine the heavy and light cream and heat just to a simmer.
2 In a large mixing bowl, beat the egg yolks and honey together until pale, slightly thickened and at the ribbon stage. Slowly add the heated cream, whisking continuously, so as not to cook the yolks.
3 Return the mixture to the saucepan and cook over low heat, stirring constantly, until the mixture coats the back of a spoon.
4 Remove from the heat and cool over an ice bath. Pour into an ice cream maker and process according to the manufacturer's directions.

Approximate values per 3$\frac{1}{2}$-fl.-oz. (105-ml) serving: **Calories** 275, **Total fat** 22 g, **Saturated fat** 13 g, **Cholesterol** 210 mg, **Sodium** 48 mg, **Total carbohydrates** 15 g, **Protein** 6 g, **Vitamin A** 30%, **Calcium** 10%

RECIPE 34.32

SOYNUT TOFU ICE CREAM

Adapted from *SOY DESSERTS* BY PATRICIA GREENBERG, CCP ReganBooks, 2000

Yield: 1 qt. (1 lt), 12 Servings

Soynuts	1$\frac{1}{2}$ c.	360 ml
Tofu, soft	2 lb.	1 kg
Granulated sugar	5 oz.	150 g
Soy milk	12 fl. oz.	360 ml
Almond extract	1 tsp.	5 ml

1 In a food processor, grind the soynuts to a course consistency. Add the tofu and sugar and purée.
2 With the processor running, add the soy milk and extract and continue to process until the mixture is smooth. Pour into an ice cream maker and process according to the manufacturer's directions.

Variation: *Lemon-Ginger-Soy Ice Cream*—Omit the soynuts and the almond extract. Add 2 ounces (60 grams) of crystallized ginger, the zest of three lemons and $\frac{1}{2}$ teaspoon (3 milliliters) of lemon extract. Process the ginger and lemon zest with the tofu as directed in Step 2.

Approximate values per serving: **Calories** 159, **Total fat** 5.6 g, **Saturated fat** 0 g, **Cholesterol** 0 mg, **Sodium** 12 mg, **Total carbohydrates** 15 g, **Protein** 11.8 g

LEMON SORBET

RECIPE 34.33

VINCENT ON CAMELBACK, PHOENIX, AZ

Chef Vincent Guerithault

Yield: 1½ qt. (1.5 lt)

Lemon juice	1 pt.	500 ml
Water	1 pt.	500 ml
Granulated sugar	1 lb.	500 g

1 Combine all the ingredients in a large bowl. Stir until the sugar dissolves completely.

2 Pour the mixture into an ice cream/sorbet machine and process according to the manufacturer's directions.

3 The finished sorbet will be rather soft. Pack it into a storage container and freeze at a temperature of 0°F (−18°C) or lower until firm.

Approximate values per ½-fl.-oz. (45-ml) serving: **Calories** 25, **Total fat** 0 g, **Saturated fat** 0 g, **Cholesterol** 0 mg, **Sodium** 0 mg, **Total carbohydrates** 6 g, **Protein** 0 g, **Claims**—fat free; no sodium; low calorie

 ## STRAWBERRY SORBET

RECIPE 34.34

THE RITZ-CARLTON, CHICAGO, IL

Executive Chef George Bumbaris and Chef Sarah Stegner

Yield: 8 Servings, 4 oz. (120 g) each

Granulated sugar	4 oz.	120 g
Pectin	1 tsp.	5 ml
Medium sugar syrup (page 932)	8 fl. oz.	225 ml
Strawberries, puréed	1 lb.	450 g
Fresh lemon juice	1 Tbsp.	15 ml

1 Mix the sugar and pectin together, add the syrup and bring to a boil. Remove from the heat and cool completely.

2 Add the puréed berries and lemon juice; strain. Adjust the flavor with additional sugar or lemon juice as needed.

3 Pour the mixture into an ice cream/sorbet machine and process according to the manufacturer's directions.

Approximate values per 4-oz. (120-g) serving: **Calories** 196, **Total fat** 0 g, **Saturated fat** 0 g, **Cholesterol** 0 mg, **Sodium** 1.5 mg, **Total carbohydrates** 48 g, **Protein** 0 g, **Vitamin C** 54%, **Claims**—no fat; no cholesterol; very low sodium; high fiber

CHOCOLATE HAZELNUT MARQUISE
 ## WITH FRANGELICO SAUCE

RECIPE 34.35

Yield: 12 Servings

Dark chocolate	1 lb.	500 g
Unsalted butter	4 oz.	120 g
Hazelnuts, roasted, skinned and chopped coarse	4 oz.	120 g
Eggs, separated	6	6
Frangelico (hazelnut liqueur)	2 fl. oz.	60 ml

Continued

Salt	1 pinch	1 pinch
Frangelico Sauce (page 1092)	as needed	as needed
Hazelnuts, roasted and		
chopped coarse	as needed for garnish	
Raspberries	as needed for garnish	
Fresh mint	as needed for garnish	

1 Line a terrine mold with melted butter and parchment paper.
2 Melt the chocolate and butter over a bain marie. Remove from the heat and stir in the nuts, egg yolks and Frangelico. Set aside to cool to room temperature. Do not use an ice bath, as the chocolate will solidify.
3 Whip the egg whites with the salt until stiff but not dry. Fold the whipped whites into the chocolate mixture.
4 Pour the mixture into the terrine mold and freeze overnight.
5 Remove the marquise from the mold and peel off the paper. (Work quickly because this melts quickly.) While still frozen, use a hot knife to slice the loaf into ⅓-inch- (8-millimeter-) thick slices. Return the marquise to freeze until just before service.
6 Serve two slices on a pool of Frangelico Sauce. Garnish with coarsely chopped hazelnuts, fresh raspberries and fresh mint.

Approximate values per serving: **Calories** 380, **Total fat** 28 g, **Saturated fat** 14 g, **Cholesterol** 125 mg, **Sodium** 35 mg, **Total carbohydrates** 25 g, **Protein** 6 g, **Vitamin A** 10%

RECIPE 34.36   **BUTTERSCOTCH SAUCE**

Yield: 2 qt. (2 lt)

Granulated sugar	1 lb. 8 oz.	720 g
Light corn syrup	2 lb. 4 oz.	1 kg
Unsalted butter	4 oz.	120 g
Heavy cream	10 fl. oz.	300 ml
Scotch whisky	4 fl. oz.	120 ml

1 Cook the sugar to a dark brown caramel. Add the corn syrup.
2 Remove the sugar from the heat and slowly add the butter and the cream, stirring until the butter is completely melted.
3 Stir in the Scotch and cool.

Approximate values per 1-fl.-oz. (30-ml) serving: **Calories** 120, **Total fat** 3 g, **Saturated fat** 2 g, **Cholesterol** 23 mg, **Sodium** 20 mg, **Total carbohydrates** 23 g, **Protein** 0 g, **Vitamin A** 4%, **Claims**—low fat; low cholesterol; very low sodium

RECIPE 34.37   **CHOCOLATE FUDGE SAUCE**

Yield: 1 gal. (4 lt)

Heavy cream	2 qt.	2 lt
Light corn syrup	6 fl. oz.	180 ml
Granulated sugar	8 oz.	225 g
Bittersweet chocolate	4 lb.	2 kg

1 Combine the cream, corn syrup and sugar in a saucepan and bring just to a boil, stirring frequently.
2 Chop the chocolate and place in a large bowl.

3 Pour the hot cream over the chocolate and stir until completely melted.

4 Store well covered and refrigerated. Gently rewarm over a bain marie if desired.

Approximate values per 1-fl.-oz. (30-ml) serving: **Calories** 130, **Total fat** 9 g, **Saturated fat** 6 g, **Cholesterol** 20 mg, **Sodium** 10 mg, **Total carbohydrates** 10 g, **Protein** 1 g, **Vitamin A** 6%

ESPRESSO SAUCE

RECIPE 34.38

CHRISTOPHER'S FERMIER BRASSERIE AND PAOLA'S WINE BAR, Phoenix, AZ

Chef-Owner Christopher Gross

Yield: 1½ pt. (700 ml)

Egg yolks	8	8
Granulated sugar	3½ oz.	100 g
Half-and-half	1 pt.	450 ml
Espresso beans, whole	3 oz.	90 g
Vanilla bean	½	½

1 Whisk the egg yolks and sugar together in a medium bowl.

2 Bring the half-and-half, espresso beans and vanilla bean to a simmer in a heavy saucepan.

3 Temper the egg yolks with a portion of the hot half-and-half, then return the mixture to the saucepan. Cook over low heat, stirring constantly, until the sauce is thick enough to coat the back of a spoon. Strain and cool over an ice bath.

Approximate values per 1-fl.-oz. (30-ml) serving: **Calories** 60, **Total fat** 4 g, **Saturated fat** 2 g, **Cholesterol** 75 mg, **Sodium** 10 mg, **Total carbohydrates** 5 g, **Protein** 2 g, **Vitamin A** 6%

APPENDIX I

The American Cheese Society

304 West Liberty Street, Suite 201
Louisville, KY 40202
(502) 583-3783
http://www.cheesesociety.org

American Culinary Federation, Inc. (ACF)

10 San Bartola Drive
St. Augustine, FL 32086
(800) 624-9458
http://www.acfchefs.org

The American Dietetic Association (ADA)

216 West Jackson Blvd.
Chicago, IL 60606-6995
(312) 899-0040
http://www.eatright.org

American Institute of Baking (AIB)

P.O. Box 3999
Manhattan, KS 66505-3999
(800) 633-5137
http://www.aibonline.org

The American Institute of Wine & Food (AIWF)

304 West Liberty Street, Suite 201
Louisville, KY 40202
(502) 992-1022
http://www.aiwf.org

Chefs Collaborative

441 Stuart Street, #712
Boston, MA 02116
(617) 236-5200
http://www.chefnet.com/cc2000.html

Club Managers Association of America (CMAA)

1733 King Street
Alexandria, VA 22314
(703) 739-9500
http://www.cmaa.org

International Association of Culinary Professionals (IACP)

304 West Liberty Street, Suite 201
Louisville, KY 40202
(502) 581-9786
http://www.iacp.com

International Food Service Executives Association

15724 Edgewood Street
Livonia, MI 48154-2312
(734) 542-9412
http://www.ifsea.org

The James Beard Foundation

167 West 12th Street
New York, NY 10011
(800) 36-BEARD
http://www.jamesbeard.org

Les Dames d'Escoffier International

P.O. Box 4961
Louisville, KY 40204
(502) 456-1851
http://www.ldei.org

National Ice Carving Association

P.O. Box 3593
Oak Brook, IL 60522-3593
(630) 871-8431
http://www.nica.org

National Restaurant Association

1200 17th Street, NW
Washington, DC 20036
(202) 331-5900
http://www.restaurant.org

Oldways Preservation & Exchange Trust

266 Beacon Street
Boston, MA 02116
(617) 421-5500
http://www.oldwayspt.org

Personal Chefs Network

(877) 905-CHEF
http://www.personalchefsnetwork.com

Research Chefs Association

5775 Peachtree-Dunwoody Road, Building G, Suite 500
Atlanta, GA 30342
(404) 252-3663
http://www.researchchef.org

Share Our Strength (SOS)

733 15th Street, NW, Suite 640
Washington, DC 20005
(800) 969-4767
http://www.strength.org

Slow Food USA

434 Broadway, 7th Floor
New York, NY 10013
(212) 965-5640
http://www.slowfood.usa.org

The Southern Foodways Alliance

Center for the Study of Southern Culture
P.O. Box 1848
University, MS 38677
(662) 915-5993
http://www.southernfoodways.com

U.S. Pastry Alliance

434 Broadway, 7th Floor
New York, NY 10013
(888) A-PASTRY
http://www.uspastry.org

U.S. Personal Chef Association

481 Rio Rancho Blvd. NE
Rio Rancho, NM 87124
(800) 995-2138
http://www.uspca.com

Women Chefs and Restaurateurs (WCR)

304 West Liberty Street, Suite 201
Louisville, KY 40202
(502) 581-0300
http://www.chefnet.com/wcr

APPENDIX II

MEASUREMENT CONVERSION CHART

FORMULAS FOR EXACT MEASURES

	WHEN YOU KNOW:	MULTIPLY BY:	TO FIND:
Mass	ounces	28.35	grams
(Weight)	pounds	0.45	kilograms
	grams	0.035	ounces
	kilograms	2.2	pounds
Volume (Capacity)	teaspoons	5.0	milliliters
	tablespoons	15.0	milliliters
	fluid ounces	29.57	milliliters
	cups	0.24	liters
	pints	0.47	liters
	quarts	0.95	liters
	gallons	3.785	liters
	milliliters	0.034	fluid ounces
Temperature	Fahrenheit	$5/9$ (after subtracting 32)	Celsius
	Celsius	$9/5$ (then add 32)	Fahrenheit

ROUNDED MEASURES FOR QUICK REFERENCE

1 oz.		= 30 g
4 oz.		= 120 g
8 oz.		= 225 g
16 oz.	= 1 lb.	= 450 g
32 oz.	= 2 lb.	= 900 g
36 oz.	= $2^{1}/4$ lb.	= 1000 g (1 kg)
$1/4$ tsp.	= $1/24$ fl. oz.	= 1 ml
$1/2$ tsp.	= $1/12$ fl. oz.	= 2 ml
1 tsp.	= $1/6$ fl. oz.	= 5 ml
1 Tbsp.	= $1/2$ fl. oz.	= 15 ml
1 c.	= 8 fl. oz.	= 250 ml
2 c. (1 pt.)	= 16 fl. oz.	= 500 ml
4 c. (1 qt.)	= 32 fl. oz.	= 1 lt
4 qt. (1 gal.)	= 128 fl. oz.	= $3^{3}/4$ lt
32°F	= 0°C	
122°F	= 50°C	
212°F	= 100°C	

CONVERSION GUIDELINES

1 gallon	=	4 quarts
		8 pints
		16 cups (8 fluid ounces)
		128 fluid ounces
1 fifth bottle	=	approximately $1\frac{1}{2}$ pints or exactly 26.5 fluid ounces
1 measuring cup	=	holds 8 fluid ounces (a coffee cup generally holds 6 fluid ounces)
1 large egg white	=	1 ounce (average)
1 lemon	=	1 to $1\frac{1}{4}$ fluid ounces of juice
1 orange	=	3 to $3\frac{1}{2}$ fluid ounces of juice

SCOOP SIZES

SCOOP MEASURE	LEVEL MEASURE
6	$\frac{2}{3}$ cup
8	$\frac{1}{2}$ cup
10	$\frac{2}{5}$ cup
12	$\frac{1}{3}$ cup
16	$\frac{1}{4}$ cup
20	$3\frac{1}{5}$ tablespoons
24	$2\frac{2}{3}$ tablespoons
30	$2\frac{1}{5}$ tablespoons
40	$1\frac{3}{5}$ tablespoons

The number of the scoop determines the number of servings in each quart of a mixture; for example, with a No. 16 scoop, 1 quart of mixture will yield 16 servings.

LADLE SIZES

SIZE	PORTION OF A CUP	NUMBER PER QUART	NUMBER PER LITER
1 fl. oz	$\frac{1}{8}$	32	34
2 fl. oz.	$\frac{1}{4}$	16	17
$2\frac{2}{3}$ fl. oz.	$\frac{1}{3}$	12	13
4 fl. oz.	$\frac{1}{2}$	8	8.6
6 fl. oz.	$\frac{3}{4}$	$5\frac{1}{3}$	5.7

Various standard cans—(left to right, front row) No ¼, No. ½ flat, (middle row) No. ½, No. 1 tall, No. 300, (back row) No. 5, No. 3 cylinder, No. 10

CANNED-GOOD SIZES

SIZE	NO. OF CANS PER CASE	AVERAGE WEIGHT	AVERAGE NO. OF CUPS PER CAN
No. ½	8	8 oz.	1
No. 1 tall (also known as 303)	2 & 4 doz.	16 oz.	2
No. 2	2 doz.	20 oz.	$2\frac{1}{2}$
No. 2½	2 doz.	28 oz.	$3\frac{1}{2}$
No. 3	2 doz.	33 oz.	4
No. 3 cylinder	1 doz.	46 oz.	$5\frac{2}{3}$
No. 5	1 doz.	3 lb. 8 oz.	$5\frac{1}{2}$
No. 10	6	6 lb. 10 oz.	13

APPENDIX III

▶ FRESH PRODUCE AVAILABILITY CHART

The availability of fresh, locally grown produce depends on local climate and growing conditions. Gardeners in central Arizona may be enjoying vine-ripened tomatoes in March, while gardeners in Michigan or New England may still be buried under snow. Just looking at what's available in the produce department of your local supermarket, you may not be able to tell if it is July or January. That's because consumers have become accustomed to having the same foods available all year. Modern transportation and storage methods allow us to have out-of-season foods anytime, anywhere. But though we depend on and enjoy this convenience, it contributes to hidden costs that are not usually considered. These include loss of farmlands and natural resources involved in the marketing and movement of these foods.

Chefs across the country are now shopping for fruits and vegetables at local farmer's markets and working with local farmers who grow products especially for their kitchens. While any good produce wholesalers or even supermarkets will carry out-of-season, imported produce, the taste will be inferior and the cost will be much higher.

Locally grown, in-season products appeal to restaurant patrons and demonstrate your concern for both food quality and the viability of local farmers and foragers.

Chefs can also work with local farmers before planting begins to determine what specialty items grow well in the area and to encourage farmers to grow products that the restaurant agrees to purchase at harvest. Many states now have programs to assist and encourage chefs and farmers to work together. It's a shift from demand-driven (chef) to supply-driven (farm) choices.

With only 2 percent of the U.S. population farming the land, few Americans give a second thought to the sources of their food. Many of us may have lost our connection to agriculture, but none of us has lost our dependence on that connection. By creating markets for local agriculture, we can ensure that farmland remains active and viable. What happens to farmers remains crucial to our nation's well-being. Even if we never set foot on a farm, our connection to the farmer and the land is there every time we buy a loaf of bread, munch an apple, plan a daily special or design a restaurant's menu.

The following chart is intended as only a general guide to the best availability of freshly harvested produce items grown in the continental United States. State departments of agriculture can provide charts of local produce availability and information on local farmer's markets and sustainable agriculture programs.

PRODUCT	JAN	FEB	MAR	APR	MAY	JUN	JUL	AUG	SEP	OCT	NOV	DEC
	WINTER DEC 21–MAR19		SPRING MAR 20–JUN 20			SUMMER JUN 21–SEP 21			AUTUMN SEP 22–DEC 20			
Apples								×	×	×	×	
Apricots						×	×					
Artichokes			×	×	×							
Asparagus				×	×	×						

PRODUCT	JAN	FEB	MAR	APR	MAY	JUN	JUL	AUG	SEP	OCT	NOV	DEC
Avocados, Hass				×	×	×	×	×	×	×		
Beans, green					×	×	×	×	×			
Beets								×	×	×		
Blueberries					×	×	×	×				
Broccoli	×	×	×						×	×	×	×
Brussels sprouts	×	×							×	×	×	×
Cabbage	×	×	×	×	×				×	×	×	×
Cantaloupe						×	×	×	×			
Cauliflower	×	×	×	×	×				×	×	×	×
Celery root	×	×	×	×						×	×	×
Cherries					×	×	×	×				
Chestnuts									×	×	×	×
Citrus	×	×	×	×	×	×			×	×	×	×
Collards			×	×	×	×						
Corn						×	×	×				
Cranberries									×	×	×	×
Cucumbers					×	×	×	×				
Dates										×	×	×
Eggplants						×	×	×	×			
Figs						×	×	×	×	×		
Grapes						×	×	×	×	×	×	
Greens			×	×	×	×						
Kohlrabi						×	×					
Leeks	×	×	×							×	×	×
Lettuce			×	×	×	×	×	×	×			
Lychees						×	×					
Mangos					×	×	×	×				
Mushrooms, morels			×	×	×							
Mushrooms, truffles	×	×									×	×
Okra					×	×	×	×	×			
Onions						×	×	×	×			
Onions, sweet			×	×	×							
Papayas			×	×	×	×						
Peaches					×	×	×	×				
Pears	×	×	×	×						×	×	×
Peas, English				×	×							
Peas, field							×	×				
Pecans											×	×
Peppers, bell						×	×	×	×			
Peppers, chile									×	×	×	×
Persimmons										×	×	×
Pineapples			×	×	×	×	×	×				
Plums						×	×	×	×			
Pomegranates									×	×	×	×
Potatoes								×	×	×		
Prickly pears									×	×	×	×
Pumpkins									×	×	×	

PRODUCT	JAN	FEB	MAR	APR	MAY	JUN	JUL	AUG	SEP	OCT	NOV	DEC
Raspberries						×	×	×	×			
Rhubarb		×	×	×	×							
Spinach	×	×	×	×	×					×	×	×
Squash, summer				×	×	×	×	×	×			
Squash, winter	×	×	×							×	×	×
Strawberries		×	×	×	×	×						
Tomatoes						×	×	×	×			
Turnips				×	×					×	×	
Watermelons						×	×	×				

BIBLIOGRAPHY
and Recommended Reading

General Interest

Bickel, Walter, ed. and trans. *Hering's Dictionary of Classical and Modern Cookery.* 13th English ed. London: Virtue, 1994.

Davidson, Alan. *The Oxford Companion to Food.* Oxford, England: Oxford University Press, 1999.

Escoffier, Auguste. *The Escoffier Cook Book and Guide to the Fine Art of Cookery for Connoisseurs, Chefs, Epicures.* (Trans. of *Le Guide culinaire.*) New York: Crown, 1969.

Kamman, Madeleine. *The New Making of a Cook.* New York: Morrow, 1997.

Labensky, Steven, Gaye G. Ingram and Sarah R. Labensky. *Webster's New World Dictionary of Culinary Arts.* Upper Saddle River, N.J.: Prentice Hall, 1997.

Larousse Gastronomique. English ed. New York: Potter, 2001.

Molt, Mary. *Food for Fifty.* 11th ed. Upper Saddle River, N.J.: Prentice Hall, 2001.

Pepin, Jacques. *The Art of Cooking.* New York: Knopf, 1987.

———. *La Technique.* New York: Pocket Books, 1987.

Peterson, James. *Essentials of Cooking.* New York: Artisan, 2000.

Point, Fernand. *Fernand Point: Ma Gastronomie.* English ed. Wilton, Conn.: Lyceum Books, 1974.

Saulnier, Louis. *Le Répertoire de la Cuisine.* Revised ed. New York: Barron's Educational Series, 1976.

Willan, Anne. *La Varenne Pratique.* New York: Crown, 1989.

Food History

Coe, Sophie D. and Michael D. Coe. *The True History of Chocolate.* New York: Thames and Hudson, 1996.

Cooper, Ann. *A Woman's Place Is in the Kitchen: The Evolution of Women Chefs.* Stamford, Conn.: Thomson, 1997.

Fussell, Betty. *The Story of Corn.* New York: Knopf, 1992.

Kurlansky, Mark. *Cod: A Biography of the Fish That Changed the World.* New York: Walker, 1997.

Lovegren, Sylvia. *Fashionable Food: Seven Decades of Food Fads.* New York: Macmillan General Reference, 1995.

Mintz, Sidney W. *Sweetness and Power: The Place of Sugar in Modern History.* New York: Viking Press, 1995.

Norman, Barbara. *Tales of the Table: A History of Western Cuisine.* Englewood Cliffs, N.J.: Prentice-Hall, 1972.

Revel, Jean-François. *Culture and Cuisine.* (Trans. of *Un Festin en paroles.*) New York: Da Capo Press, 1982.

Rupp, Rebecca. *Blue Corn and Square Tomatoes.* Pownal, Vt.: Garden Way, 1987.

Schlossberg, Eli W. *The World of Orthodox Judaism.* Northvale, N.J.: Aronson, 1996.

Shapiro, Laura. *Perfection Salad: Women and Cooking at the Turn of the Century.* New York: Farrar, Straus and Giroux, 1986.

Tannahill, Reay. *Food in History.* Revised ed. New York: Crown, 1995.

Toussaint-Samat, Maguelonne. *A History of Food.* Trans. by Anthea Bell. Cambridge, Mass.: Blackwell, 1992.

Wheaton, Barbara Ketcham. *Savoring the Past: The French Kitchen and Table from 1300 to 1789.* Reprint ed. New York: Touchstone Books, 1996.

Willan, Anne. *Great Cooks and Their Recipes: From Taillevent to Escoffier.* Boston: Little, Brown, 1992.

Sanitation and Safety

International Life Sciences Institute. *A Simple Guide to Understanding and Applying the Hazard Analysis Critical Control Point Concept.* Washington, D.C.: ILSI Press, 1993.

Loken, Joan K. *The HACCP Food Safety Manual.* Wiley, 1995.

McSwane, David, Nancy Rue, and Richard Linton. *Essentials of Food Safety and Sanitation.* Updated 2nd ed. Upper Saddle River, N.J.: Prentice Hall, 2002.

National Assessment Institute. *Handbook for Safe Food Service Management.* 2nd ed. Upper Saddle River, N.J.: Prentice Hall, 1998.

National Restaurant Association Educational Foundation. *ServSafe Coursebook.* New York: Wiley, 2001.

Nutrition

Baskette, Michael, and Eleanor Mainella. *The Art of Nutritional Cooking.* 2nd ed. Upper Saddle River, N.J.: Prentice Hall, 1999.

Freyberg, Nicholas, and Willis A. Gortner. *The Food Additives Book.* New York: Bantam Books, 1982.

Food Costing and Business Skills

Cullen, Noel. *Life beyond the Line: A Front-of-the-House Companion for Culinarians.* Upper Saddle River, N.J.: Prentice Hall, 2001.

Drysdale, John, and Jennifer Adams Aldrich. *Profitable Menu Planning.* 3rd ed. Upper Saddle River, N.J.: Prentice Hall, 2002.

Labensky, Sarah R. *Applied Math for Food Service.* Upper Saddle River, N.J.: Prentice Hall, 1998.

Miller, Jack E. *Menu Pricing and Strategy.* 4th ed. New York: Van Nostrand Reinhold, 1996.

Schmidt, Arno. *Chef's Book of Formulas, Yields, and Sizes.* 2nd ed. New York: Van Nostrand Reinhold, 1996.

Tools

Bridge, Fred, and Jean F. Tibbetts. *The Well-Tooled Kitchen.* New York: Morrow, 1991.

Williams, Chuck, ed. *Williams-Sonoma Kitchen Companion.* New York: Time-Life Books, 2000.

Wolf, Burton, ed. *The New Cooks' Catalogue.* New York: Knopf, 2000.

General Ingredients

DeMers, John. *The Community Kitchen's Complete Guide to Gourmet Coffee.* New York: Simon & Schuster, 1986.

Dowell, Philip, and Adrian Bailey. *Cook's Ingredients.* New York: Morrow, 1980.

Jordan, Michele Anna. *The Good Cook's Book of Oil & Vinegar.* Reading, Mass.: Addison-Wesley, 1992.

Morris, Sallie, and Lesley Mackley. *The Spice Ingredients Cookbook.* New York: Lorenz Books, 1997.

Norman, Jill. *The Complete Book of Spices.* American ed. New York: Viking Studio Books, 1991.

Ortiz, Elisabeth Lambert. *The Encyclopedia of Herbs, Spices and Flavorings.* 1st American ed. New York: Dorling Kindersley, 1992.

Schapira, Joel, and Karl Schapira. *The Book of Coffee and Tea.* New York: St. Martin's Press, 1975.

Ward, Susie, et al. *The Gourmet Atlas.* New York: Macmillan, 1997.

Dairy and Cheese

Jenkins, Steven. *Steven Jenkins' Cheese Primer.* New York: Workman, 1996.

Lambert, Paula. *The Cheese Lover's Cookbook & Guide.* New York: Simon & Schuster, 2000.

Marquis, Vivienne, and Patricia Haskell. *The Cheese Book.* New York: Simon & Schuster, 1985.

Masui, Kazuko, and Tomoko Yamada. *French Cheeses.* New York: Dorling Kindersley, 1996.

Werlin, Laura. *The New American Cheese.* New York: Stewart, Tabori & Chang, 2000.

Food Science

Corriher, Shirley O. *Cookwise.* New York: Morrow, 1997.

McGee, Harold. *On Food and Cooking.* New York: Scribner, 1984.

McWilliams, Margaret. *Foods: Experimental Perspectives.* 4th ed. Upper Saddle River, N.J.: Prentice Hall, 2001.

Parsons, Russ. *How to Read a French Fry.* Boston: Houghton Mifflin, 2001.

Stocks, Sauces and Soups

Clayton, Bernard. *The Complete Book of Soups and Stews.* New York: Simon & Schuster, 1987.

Davis, Deidre. *A Fresh Look at Saucing Foods.* Reading, Mass.: Addison-Wesley, 1993.

Editors of *Cook's Illustrated* Magazine. *The Best Recipe: Soup and Stew.* Boston: Boston Common Press, 2001.

Kafka, Barbara. *Soup: A Way of Life.* New York: Artisan, 1998.

Larousse, David Paul. *The Sauce Bible: Guide to the Saucier's Craft.* New York: Wiley, 1993.

Peterson, James. *Sauces: Classical and Contemporary Sauce Making.* 2nd ed. New York: 1998.

Sokolov, Raymond A. *The Saucier's Apprentice.* New York: Knopf, 1976.

Meat

Aidells, Bruce, and Denis Kelly. *The Complete Meat Cookbook.* New York: Houghton Mifflin, 1998.

Ellis, Merle. *The Great American Meat Cookbook.* New York: Knopf, 1996.

Knox, Luc, and Keith Richmond. *The World Encyclopedia of Meat, Game and Poultry.* New York: Lorenz Books, 2000.

The Meat Buyers Guide. Reston, Va.: National Association of Meat Purveyors, 1990.

Game

Cameron, Angus, and Judith Jones. *The L. L. Bean Game and Fish Cookbook*. New York: Random House, 1983.

Hibler, Jane. *Wild about Game: 150 Recipes for Cooking Farm-Raised and Wild Game from Alligator and Antelope to Venison and Wild Turkey*. New York: Broadway Books, 1998.

Little, Carolyn. *The Game Cookbook*. Wiltshire, England: Crowood Press, 1988.

Marrone, Teresa. *Dressing and Cooking Wild Game*. New York: Prentice Hall, 1987.

Webster, Harold W., Jr. *The Complete Venison Cookbook*. Brandon, Miss.: Quail Ridge Press, 1996.

Fish and Shellfish

Cronin, Isaac, Jay Harlow, and Paul Johnson. *The California Seafood Cookbook*. Berkeley, Calif.: Aris Books, 1983.

Howarth, A. Jan. *The Complete Fish Cookbook*. New York: St. Martin's Press, 1983.

King, Shirley. *Fish, The Basics*. Rev. and Updated ed. New York: Chapters, 1996.

———. *Saucing the Fish*. New York: Simon & Schuster, 1986.

Loomis, Susan Herrmann. *The Great American Seafood Cookbook*. New York: Workman, 1988.

McClane, A. J. *The Encyclopedia of Fish Cookery*. New York: Holt, Rinehart and Winston, 1989.

Peterson, James. *Fish and Shellfish*. New York: Morrow, 1998.

The Seafood Handbook: Seafood Standards. Rockland, Maine: Seafood Business Magazine, 1991.

The Seafood List: FDA Guide to Acceptable Market Names for Food Fish Sold in Interstate Commerce. Washington, D.C.: Center for Food Safety and Applied Nutrition, 2001.

Eggs and Breakfast Cookery

Bristow, Linda Kay. *Bread and Breakfast*. San Ramon, Calif.: 101 Productions, 1985.

Eggcyclopedia. 2nd ed. Park Ridge, Ill.: American Egg Board, 1989.

Fox, Margaret S., and John Bear. *Morning Food from Café Beaujolais*. Berkeley, Calif.: Ten Speed Press, 1994.

Jamison, Cheryl A., and Bill Jamison. *A Real American Breakfast: The Best Meal of the Day, Any Time of the Day*. New York: Morrow, 2002.

Vegetables and Fruits

Andrews, Jean. *Peppers: The Domesticated Capsicums*. Austin, Tex.: University of Texas Press, 1984.

Brown, Marlene. *International Produce Cookbook and Guide*. Los Angeles: HP Books, 1989.

Davidson, Alan. *Fruit: A Connoisseur's Guide and Cookbook*. New York: Simon & Schuster, 1991.

DeWitt, Dave, and Nancy Gerlach. *The Whole Chile Pepper Book*. Boston: Little, Brown, 1990.

Greenburg, Patricia. *The Whole Soy Cookbook*. New York: Random House, 1998.

Holthaus, Fusako. *Tofu Cookery*. Tokyo: Kodansha International, 1992.

Ingram, Christine. *The New Guide to Vegetables*. New York: Hermes House, 1997.

Miller, Mark, with John Harrisson. *The Great Chile Book*. Berkeley, Calif.: Ten Speed Press, 1991.

Murdich, Jack. *Buying Produce*. New York: Morrow, 1986.

Nathan, Amy. *Salad*. San Francisco, Calif.: Chronicle Books, 1985.

Payne, Rolce Redard, and Dorrit Speyer Senior. *Cooking with Fruit*. New York: Crescent Books, 1995.

Peterson, James, and Justin Schwartz. *Vegetables*. New York: Morrow, 1998.

Routhier, Nicole. *Nicole Routhier's Fruit Cookbook*. New York: Workman, 1996.

Schmidt, Jimmy. *Cooking for All Seasons*. New York: Macmillan, 1991.

Schneider, Elizabeth. *Uncommon Fruits and Vegetables: A Commonsense Guide*. New York: Morrow, 1998.

Grains and Pasta

Bugialli, Giuliano. *On Pasta*. New York: Simon & Schuster, 1988.

Della Croce, Julia. *Pasta Classica*. Reprint ed. San Francisco, Calif.: Chronicle Books, 1996.

Greene, Bert. *The Grains Cookbook*. New York: Workman, 1988.

Kummer, Corby. "Pasta." *The Atlantic,* 258, no. 1 (July 1986): 35–47.

Leblang, Bonnie Tandy, and Joanne Lamb Hayes. *Rice*. New York: Harmony Books, 1991.

Spier, Carol. *Food Essentials: Grains and Pasta*. New York: Crescent Books, 1993.

Charcuterie

Editors of Time-Life Books. *The Good Cook: Terrines, Pâtés and Galantines*. London: Time-Life International (Nederland) B.V., 1981.

Ehlert, Friedrich W., et al. *Pâtés and Terrines*. Reprint ed. London: Hearst Books, 1990.

Grigson, Jane. *The Art of Charcuterie*. Reprint ed. New York: Echo Press, 1991.

Breads

Albright, Barbara, and Leslie Weiner. *Mostly Muffins*. New York: St. Martin's Press, 1984.

Alston, Elizabeth. *Biscuits and Scones*. New York: Potter, 1988.

Clayton, Bernard. *Bernard Clayton's New Complete Book of Breads*. Revised ed. New York: Fireside Books, 1995.

David, Elizabeth. *English Bread and Yeast Cookery*. Notes by Karen Hess. American ed. New York: Viking Press, 1980.

Hensperger, Beth. *The Bread Bible: Beth Hensperger's 300 Favorite Recipes*. San Francisco, Calif.: Chronicle Books, 1999.

Ortiz, Joe. *The Village Baker: Classic Regional Breads from Europe and America*. Berkeley, Calif.: Ten Speed Press, 1993.

Reinhart, Peter. *Crust & Crumb*. Berkeley, Calif.: Ten Speed Press, 1998.

Pastries and Desserts

Bloom, Carole. *The International Dictionary of Desserts, Pastries, and Confections*. New York: Hearst Books, 1995.

Braker, Flo. *The Simple Art of Perfect Baking*. Shelburne, Vt.: Chapters, 1992.

Daley, Regan. *In the Sweet Kitchen: The Definitive Baker's Companion*. New York: Artisan, 2001.

Fletcher, Helen S. *The New Pastry Cook*. New York: Morrow, 1986.

Friberg, Bo. *The Professional Pastry Chef*. 4th ed. New York: Wiley, 2002.

Healy, Bruce, and Paul Bugat. *Mastering the Art of French Pastry*. Woodbury, N.Y.: Barron's, 1984.

Heatter, Maida. *Maida Heatter's Book of Great Desserts*. Kansas City: Andrews McMeel, 1999.

Hyman, Philip, and Mary Hyman, trans. *The Best of Gaston Lenotre's Desserts*. Woodbury, N.Y.: Barron's, 1983.

London, Sheryl, and Mel London. *Fresh Fruit Desserts: Classic and Contemporary*. New York: Prentice Hall, 1990.

Purdy, Susan G. *A Piece of Cake*. Reprint. New York: Macmillan, 1993.

Silverton, Nancy. *Desserts by Nancy Silverton*. New York: Harper & Row, 1986.

Teubner, Christian, ed. *The Chocolate Bible*. New York: Penguin Studio, 1997.

Hors D'Oeuvre and Buffets

Aloni, Nicole. *Secrets from a Caterer's Kitchen*. Tucson, Ariz.: HP Books, 2001.

Janericco, Terence. *The Book of Great Hors d'Oeuvre*. New York: Wiley, 1990.

Larousse, David Paul. *The Professional Garde Manger*. New York: Wiley, 1996.

Sanders, Ed, et al. *Catering Solutions*. Upper Saddle River, N.J.: Prentice Hall, 2000.

Schmidt, Arno, and Inja Nam. *The Book of Hors d'Oeuvres and Canapes*. New York: Van Nostrand Reinhold, 1996.

Simmons, Bob, and Coleen Simmons. *Tapas Fantasticas: Appetizers with a Spanish Flair*. San Leandro, Calif.: Bristol, 1999.

International Cuisines

Bayless, Rick, with Deann Groen Bayless. *Authentic Mexican: Regional Cooking from the Heart of Mexico*. New York: Morrow, 1987.

Bugialli, Giuliano. *The Fine Art of Italian Cooking*. New York: Random House, 1990.

Casas, Penelope. *The Foods and Wines of Spain*. New York: Knopf, 1991.

Downer, Lesley. *At the Japanese Table*. San Francisco, Calif.: Chronicle Books, 1993.

Field, Carol. *Celebrating Italy*. New York: Morrow, 1990.

Gin, Maggie. *Regional Cooking of China*. San Francisco, Calif.: 101 Productions, 1984.

Harris, Jessica. *The Africa Cookbook: Tastes of a Continent*. New York: Simon & Schuster, 1998.

Hazan, Marcella. *Essentials of Classic Italian Cooking*. New York: Knopf, 1993.

Jaffrey, Madhur. *An Invitation to Indian Cooking*. New York: Vintage Books, 1973.

Kasper, Lynn Rossetto. *The Splendid Table: Recipes from Emilia-Romagna, the Heartland of Northern Italian Food*. New York: Morrow, 1992.

Kennedy, Diana. *The Cuisines of Mexico*. Revised ed. New York: Harper & Row, 1986.

Lo, Kenneth. *The Encyclopedia of Chinese Cooking*. New York: Bristol Books, 1997.

McDermott, Nancie. *Real Thai: The Best of Thailand's Regional Cooking*. San Francisco, Calif.: Chronicle Books, 1992.

Pham, Mai. *Pleasures of the Vietnamese Table*. New York: HarperCollins, 2001.

Roden, Claudia. *The New Book of Middle Eastern Food*. New York: Knopf, 2000.

Rojas-Lombardi, Felipe. *The Art of South American Cooking*. New York: HarperCollins, 1991.

Rose, Evelyn. *The New Complete International Jewish Cookbook*. New York: Carroll & Graf, 1992.

Routhier, Nicole. *Foods of Vietnam*. New York: Stewart, Tabori & Chang, 1989.

Rozin, Elisabeth. *Ethnic Cuisine: How to Create the Authentic Flavors of 30 International Cuisines*. Reprint ed. New York: Penguin Books USA, 1992.

Solomon, Charmaine. *The Complete Asian Cookbook*. Revised ed. Boston: Tuttle, 1992.

———. *Encyclopedia of Asian Food*. Boston: Periplus Editions, 1998.

Toomre, Joyce. *Classic Russian Cooking: Elena Molokhovets' A Gift to Young Housewives*. Translated, introduced and annotated by Joyce Toomre. Bloomington, Ind.: Indiana University Press, 1992.

Von Bremzen, Anya, and John Welchman. *Please to the Table: The Russian Cookbook*. New York: Workman, 1990.

Garnishing

Budgen, June. *The Book of Garnishes*. Los Angeles: HP Books, 1986.

Haydock, Robert, and Yukiko Haydock. *Japanese Garnishes*. New York: Holt, Rinehart and Winston, 1980.

Huang, Su-Huei. *Great Garnishes*. Monterey Park, Calif.: Wei-Chuan, 1990.

Lynch, Francis Talyn. *Garnishing: A Feast for Your Eyes.* Los Angeles: HP Books, 1987.

Rosen, Harvey. *How to Garnish.* Lakewood, N.J.: International Culinary Consultants, 1998.

Texido, Amy. *Glorious Garnishes: Crafting Easy & Spectacular Food Decorations.* Ashville, N.C.: Lark Books, 1996.

Books by Contributing Chefs

Ash, John, and Sid Goldstein. *American Game Cooking.* Reading, Mass.: Addison-Wesley, 1991.

Atkinson, Leland. *Cocina! A Hands-On Guide to the Techniques of Southwestern Cooking.* Berkeley, Calif.: Ten Speed Press, 1996.

Beranbaum, Rose Levy. *The Cake Bible.* New York: Morrow, 1988.

Bishop, John. *Bishop's: The Cookbook.* Vancouver, Canada: Douglas & McIntyre, 1997.

Brennan, Pip, Jimmy Brennan, and Ted Brennan. *Breakfast at Brennan's and Dinner, Too.* New Orleans, La.: Brennan's Inc., 1994.

Carpenter, Hugh, and Teri Sandison. *Chopstix: Quick Cooking with Pacific Flavors.* New York: Stewart, Tabori & Chang, 1990.

Golden, Harris. *Golden's Kitchen: The Artistry of Cooking and Dining on the Light Side.* Revised 2nd ed. Phoenix, Ariz.: Quail Run Books, 1989.

Guerithault, Vincent. *Vincent's Cookbook.* Berkeley, Calif.: Ten Speed Press, 1994.

Lukins, Sheila. *Sheila Lukins USA Cookbook.* New York: Workman, 1997.

Malgieri, Nick. *Nick Malgieri's Perfect Pastry.* New York: Macmillan, 1989.

Medrich, Alice. *Cocolat.* New York: Warner Books, 1990.

Miller, Mark. *Coyote Cafe.* Berkeley, Calif.: Ten Speed Press, 1989.

Milliken, Mary Sue, and Susan Feniger. *City Cuisine.* New York: Morrow, 1989.

Portale, Alfred. *Alfred Portale's Gotham Bar and Grill Cookbook.* New York: Doubleday, 1997.

Puck, Wolfgang. *The Wolfgang Puck Cookbook: Recipes from Spago, Chinois and Points East and West.* New York: Random House, 1996.

Richard, Michel. *Michel Richard's Home Cooking with a French Accent.* New York: Morrow, 1993.

Roberts, Michael. *Secret Ingredients.* New York: Bantam Books, 1988.

Smith, Andrew F. *The Tomato in America: Early History, Culture and Cookery.* Reprint ed. Champaign, Ill.: University of Illinois Press, 2001.

Somerville, Annie. *Fields of Greens: New Vegetarian Recipes from the Celebrated Greens Restaurant.* New York: Bantam Books, 1993.

Susser, Allen. *Allen Susser's New World Cuisine and Cookery.* New York: Doubleday, 1995.

Tropp, Barbara. *China Moon Cookbook.* New York: Workman, 1992.

GLOSSARY

Acid—foods such as citrus juice, vinegar and wine that have a sour or sharp flavor (most foods are slightly acidic); acids have a pH of less than 7

Acidulation—the browning of cut fruit caused by the reaction of an enzyme (polyphenoloxidase) with the phenolic compounds present in these fruits; this browning is often mistakenly attributed to exposure to oxygen

Additives—substances added to many foods to prevent spoilage or to improve appearance, texture, flavor or nutritional value; they may be synthetic materials copied from nature (for example, sugar substitutes) or naturally occurring substance (for example, lecithin). Some food additives may cause allergic reactions in sensitive people

Adobo seasoning—a commercial spice blend; although several brands are available, most include dried chiles, Mexican oregano, cumin, black pepper, garlic powder and onion powder

Aerobic bacteria—those that thrive on oxygen

Aging—(1) the period during which freshly killed meat is allowed to rest so that the effects of rigor mortis dissipate; (2) the period during which freshly milled flour is allowed to rest so that it will whiten

and produce less sticky doughs; the aging of flour can be chemically accelerated

Airline breast—a boneless chicken breast with the first wing bone attached

À la—(ah lah) French for "in the manner or style of"; used in relation to a food, it designates a style of preparation or presentation

À la carte—(ah lah kart) (1) a menu on which each food and beverage is listed and priced separately; (2) foods cooked to order as opposed to foods cooked in advance and held for later service

À la grecque—(ah lah grehk) a preparation style in which vegetables are marinated in olive oil, lemon juice and herbs, then served cold

Albumen—the principal protein found in egg whites

Al dente—(ahl DEN-tay) Italian for "to the tooth"; used to describe cooked foods (usually vegetables and pasta) that are prepared firm to the bite, not soft or mushy

Alkali—also known as a base, any substance with a pH higher than 7; baking soda is one of the few alkaline foods

Alkaloid—a number of bitter organic substances with alkaline prop-

erties; found most often in plants and sometimes used in drugs

Allemande—(ah-leh-MAHND) a sauce made by adding lemon juice and a liaison to a velouté made from veal or chicken stock; used to make several small sauces of the velouté family

Allumette—(al-yoo-MEHT) (1) a matchstick cut of ⅛ inch × ⅛ inch × 2 inches (3 millimeters × 3 millimeters × 5 centimeters) usually used for potatoes; (2) a strip of puff pastry with a sweet or savory filling

American service—restaurant service in which the waiter takes the orders and brings the food to the table; the food is placed on dishes (plated) in the kitchen, making it a relatively fast method for seated service

Amino acid—the basic molecular component of proteins; each of the approximately two dozen amino acids contains oxygen, hydrogen, carbon and nitrogen atoms

Anadromous—a fish that migrates from a saltwater habitat to spawn in fresh water

Anaerobic bacteria—those that are able to live and grow without the presence of oxygen

Angus beef, Certified—a brand created in 1978 to distinguish the highest-quality beef produced from descendants of the black, hornless Angus cattle of Scotland

Animal husbandry—the business, science and practice of raising domesticated animals

Anterior—at or toward the front of an object or place; opposite of posterior

Appetizers—also known as first courses, usually small portions of hot or cold foods intended to whet the appetite in anticipation of the more substantial courses to follow

Aquafarming—also known as aquaculture, the business, science and practice of raising large quantities of fish and shellfish in tanks, ponds or ocean pens

Aromatic—an item added to enhance the natural aromas of a food; aromatics include most flavorings, such as herbs and spices, as well as some vegetables

Aspic; aspic jelly—a clear jelly usually made from a clarified stock thickened with gelatin; used to coat foods, especially charcuterie items, and for garnish

As-purchased (A.P.)—the condition or cost of an item as it is purchased or received from the supplier

Au gratin—(oh GRAH-tan) foods with a browned or crusted top; often made by browning a food with a bread-crumb, cheese and/or sauce topping under a broiler or salamander

Au jus—(oh zhew) roasted meats, poultry or game served with their natural, unthickened juices

Au sec—(oh sek) cooked until nearly dry

Bacteria—single-celled microorganisms, some of which can cause diseases, including food-borne diseases

Bain marie—(bane mah-ree) (1) a hot-water bath used to gently cook food or keep cooked food hot; (2) a container for holding food in a hot-water bath

Baking—a dry-heat cooking method in which foods are surrounded by hot, dry air in a closed environment; similar to roasting, the term *baking* is usually applied to breads, pastries, vegetables and fish

Baking powder—a mixture of sodium bicarbonate and one or more acids, generally cream of tartar and/or sodium aluminum sulfate, used to leaven baked goods; it releases carbon dioxide gas if moisture is present in a formula. Single-acting baking powder releases carbon dioxide gas in the presence of moisture only; double-acting baking powder releases some carbon dioxide gas upon contact with moisture, and more gas is released when heat is applied.

Baking soda—sodium bicarbonate, an alkaline compound that releases carbon dioxide gas when combined with an acid and moisture; used to leaven baked goods

Ballotine—(bahl-lo-teen) similar to a galantine; usually made by stuffing a deboned poultry leg with forcemeat; it is then poached or braised and normally served hot

Banneton—(BAN-tahn) a traditional woven basket, often lined with canvas, in which yeast bread is placed to rise before baking

Barbecue—(1) to cook foods over dry heat created by the burning of hardwood or hardwood charcoals; (2) a tangy tomato- or vinegar-based sauce used for grilled foods; (3) foods cooked by this method and/or with this sauce

Barding—tying thin slices of fat, such as bacon or pork fatback, over meats or poultry that have little to no natural fat covering in order to protect and moisten them during roasting

Baste—to moisten foods during cooking (usually grilling, broiling or roasting) with melted fat, pan drippings, a sauce or other liquids to prevent drying and to add flavor

Batonnet—(bah-toh-nah) foods cut into matchstick shapes of ¼ inch ×

¼ inch × 2 inches (6 millimeters × 6 millimeters × 5 centimeters)

Batter—(1) a semiliquid mixture containing flour or other starch used to make cakes and breads. The gluten development is minimized and the liquid forms the continuous medium in which other ingredients are disbursed; generally contains more fat, sugar and liquids than a dough; (2) a semiliquid mixture of liquid and starch used to coat foods for deep-frying.

Baumé scale—(boh-may) see **Hydrometer**

Bavarian cream—a sweet dessert mixture made by thickening custard sauce with gelatin and then folding in whipped cream; the final product is poured into a mold and chilled until firm

Beard—a clump of dark threads found on a mussel

Béarnaise—(bare-NAYZ) a sauce made of butter and egg yolks and flavored with a reduction of vinegar, shallots, tarragon and peppercorns

Beating—a mixing method in which foods are vigorously agitated to incorporate air or develop gluten; a spoon or electric mixer with its paddle attachment is used

Béchamel—(bay-shah-MELL) a leading sauce made by thickening milk with a white roux and adding seasonings

Beefalo—the product of crossbreeding a bison (American buffalo) and a domestic beef animal.

Berry—(1) the kernel of certain grains such as wheat; (2) small, juicy fruits that grow on vines and bushes

Beurre blanc—(burr BLANHK) French for "white butter"; an emulsified butter sauce made from shallots, white wine and butter

Beurre composé—(burr kom-poh-ZAY) see **Compound butter**

Beurre manié—(burr man-YAY) a combination of equal amounts by weight of flour and soft, whole butter; it is whisked into a simmering sauce at the end of the cooking process for quick thickening and added sheen and flavor

Beurre noir—(burr NWAR) French for "black butter"; whole butter cooked until dark brown (not black); sometimes flavored with vinegar or lemon juice

Beurre noisette—(burr nwah-ZEHT) French for "brown butter"; whole butter heated until it turns light brown, giving off a nutty aroma

Beurre rouge—(burr ROOGE) French for "red butter"; an emulsified butter sauce made from shallots, red wine and butter

Biological hazard—a danger to the safety of food caused by disease-causing microorganisms such as bacteria, molds, yeasts, viruses or fungi

Biscuit method—a mixing method used to make biscuits, scones and flaky doughs; it involves cutting cold fat into the flour and other dry ingredients before any liquid is added

Bisque—(bisk) a soup made from shellfish; classic versions are thickened with rice

Bivalves—mollusks such as clams, oysters and mussels that have two bilateral shells attached at a central hinge

Blanching—very briefly and partially cooking a food in boiling water or hot fat; used to assist preparation (for example, to loosen peels from vegetables), as part of a combination cooking method, to remove undesirable flavors or to prepare a food for freezing

Blanquette—(blahn-KEHT) a white stew made of a white sauce and meat or poultry that is simmered without first browning

Blending—a mixing method in which two or more ingredients are combined just until they are evenly distributed

Bloom—(1) a white, powdery layer that sometimes appears on chocolate if the cocoa butter separates; (2) a measure of gelatin's strength

Blue cheese—(1) a generic term for any cheese containing visible blue-green molds that contribute a characteristic tart, sharp flavor and aroma; also known as a blue-veined cheese or bleu; (2) a group of Roquefort-style cheeses made in the United States and Canada from cow's or goat's milk rather than ewe's milk and injected with molds that form blue-green veins; also known as blue mold cheese or blue-veined cheese

Boiling—a moist-heat cooking method that uses convection to transfer heat from a hot (approximately 212°F/100°C) liquid to the food submerged in it; the turbulent waters and higher temperatures cook foods more quickly than do poaching or simmering

Bordelaise—(bor-dil-AYZ) a brown sauce flavored with a reduction of red wine, shallots, pepper and herbs and garnished with marrow

Bouchées—(boo-SHAY) small puff pastry shells that can be filled and served as bite-size hors d'oeuvre or petit fours

Bound salad—a salad composed of cooked meats, poultry, fish, shellfish, pasta or potatoes combined with a dressing

Bouquet garni—(boo-KAY gar-NEE) fresh herbs and vegetables tied into a bundle with twine and used to flavor stocks, sauces, soups and stews

Bouquetière—(boo-kuh-TYEHR) a garnish (bouquet) of carefully cut and arranged fresh vegetables

Boxed beef—industry terminology for primal and subprimal cuts of beef that are vacuum-sealed and packed into cardboard boxes for shipping from the packing plant to retailers and food service operations

Braising—a combination cooking method in which foods are first

browned in hot fat, then covered and slowly cooked in a small amount of liquid over low heat; braising uses a combination of simmering and steaming to transfer heat from the liquid (conduction) and the air (convection) to the foods

Bran—the tough outer layer of a cereal grain and the part highest in fiber

Brandy—an alcoholic beverage made by distilling the fermented mash of grapes or other fruits

Brawn—also called an aspic terrine, made from simmered meats packed into a terrine and covered with aspic

Brazier; brasier—a pan designed for braising; usually round with two handles and a tight-fitting lid

Breading—(1) a coating of bread or cracker crumbs, cornmeal or other dry meal applied to foods that will typically be deep-fried or pan-fried; (2) the process of applying this coating

Brigade—a system of staffing a kitchen so that each worker is assigned a set of specific tasks; these tasks are often related by cooking method, equipment or the types of foods being produced

Brine—a mixture of salt, water and seasonings used to preserve foods

Brioche—(bree-OHSH) a rich yeast bread containing large amounts of eggs and butter

Brochettes—(bro-SHETTS) skewers, either small hors d'oeuvre or large entrée size, threaded with meat, poultry, fish, shellfish and/or vegetables and grilled, broiled or baked, sometimes served with a dipping sauce

Broiling—a dry-heat cooking method in which foods are cooked by heat radiating from an overhead source

Broth—a flavorful liquid obtained from the long simmering of meats and/or vegetables

Brown sauce—see **Espagnole**

Brown stew—a stew in which the meat is first browned in hot fat

Brown stock—a richly colored stock made of chicken, veal, beef or game bones and vegetables, all of which are caramelized before they are simmered in water with seasonings

Brunch—a late-morning to early-afternoon meal that takes the place of both breakfast and lunch; a brunch menu often offers breakfast foods as well as almost anything else

Brunoise—(BROO-nwaz) (1) foods cut into cubes of ⅛ inch × ⅛ inch × ⅛ inch (3 millimeters × 3 millimeters × 3 millimeters); a 1/16-inch (1.5-millimeter) cube is referred to as a **fine brunoise;** (2) foods garnished with vegetables cut in this manner

Buffet service—restaurant service in which diners generally serve themselves foods arranged on a counter or table or are served by workers assigned to specific areas of the buffet. Usually buffet-service-style restaurants charge by the meal; restaurants offering buffet service that charge by the dish are known as cafeterias.

Butcher—(1) to slaughter and/or dress or fabricate animals for consumption; (2) the person who slaughters and fabricates animals

Butler service—restaurant service in which servers pass foods (typically hors d'oeuvre) or drinks arranged on trays

Buttercream—a light, smooth, fluffy frosting of sugar, fat and flavorings; egg yolks or whipped egg whites are sometimes added. There are three principal kinds: simple, Italian and French.

Butterfly—to slice boneless meat, poultry, fish or shrimp nearly in half lengthwise so that it spreads open like a book; used to increase surface area and speed cooking

Cafeteria—see **Buffet service**

Caffeine—an alkaloid found in coffee beans, tea leaves and cocoa beans that acts as a stimulant

Cake—in American usage, refers to a broad range of pastries, including layer cakes, coffeecakes and gâteaux; can refer to almost anything that is baked, tender, sweet and sometimes frosted

Calf—(1) a young cow or bull; (2) the meat of calves slaughtered when they are older than five months

Calorie—the unit of energy measured by the amount of heat required to raise 1000 grams of water one degree Celsius; it is also written as kilocalorie or kcal and is used as a measure of food energy

Canapé—(KAN-ah-pay) a tiny open-faced sandwich served as an hors d'oeuvre; usually composed of a small piece of bread or toast topped with a savory spread and garnish

Capon—(kay-pahn) the class of surgically castrated male chickens; they have well-flavored meat and soft, smooth skin

Capsaicin—(kap-SAY-ee-zin) an alkaloid found in a chile pepper's placental ribs that provides the pepper's heat

Caramelization—the process of cooking sugars; the browning of sugar enhances the flavor and appearance of foods

Carbohydrates—a group of compounds composed of oxygen, hydrogen and carbon that supply the body with energy (4 calories per gram); carbohydrates are classified as simple (including certain sugars) and complex (including starches and fiber)

Carotenoid—a naturally occurring pigment that predominates in red and yellow vegetables such as carrots and red peppers

Carryover cooking—the cooking that occurs after a food is removed from a heat source; it is accom-plished by the residual heat remaining in the food

Cartilage—also known as gristle, a tough, elastic, whitish connective tissue that helps give structure to an animal's body

Carve—to cut cooked meat or poultry into portions

Casings—membranes used to hold forcemeat for sausages; they can be natural animal intestines or manufactured from collagen extracted from cattle hides

Casserole—(1) a heavy dish, usually ceramic, for baking foods; (2) foods baked in a casserole dish

Caul fat—a fatty membrane from pig or sheep intestines; it resembles fine netting and is used to bard roasts and pâtés and to encase forcemeat for sausages

Cellulose—a complex carbohydrate found in the cell wall of plants; it is edible but indigestible by humans

Cephalopods—mollusks with a single, thin internal shell called a pen or cuttlebone, well-developed eyes, a number of arms that attach to the head and a saclike fin-bearing mantle; include squid and octopus

Chafing dish—a metal dish with a heating unit (flame or electric) used to keep foods warm at tableside or during buffet service

Chalazae cords—thick, twisted strands of egg white that anchor the yolk in place

Charcuterie—(shahr-COO-tuhr-ree) the production of pâtés, terrines, galantines, sausages and similar foods

Cheesecloth—a light, fine mesh gauze used to strain liquids and make sachets

Chef de cuisine—(chef duh quizine) also known simply as chef; the person responsible for all kitchen operations, developing menu items and setting the kitchen's tone and tempo

Chef de partie—(chef duh par-tee) also known as station chef; produces the menu items under the direct supervision of the chef or sous-chef

Chef's knife—an all-purpose knife used for chopping, slicing and mincing; its tapering blade is 8–14 inches (20–35 centimeters) long

Chemical hazard—a danger to the safety of food caused by chemical substances, especially cleaning agents, pesticides and toxic metals

Chèvre—(SHEHV-ruh) French for "goat"; generally refers to a cheese made from goat's milk

Chiffonade—(chef-fon-nahd) (1) to finely slice or shred leafy vegetables or herbs; (2) the finely cut leafy vegetables or herbs often used as a garnish or bedding

Chile—a member of the capsicum plant family; may be used fresh or dried or dried and ground into a powder

Chili—a stewlike dish containing chiles

Chilli—a commercial spice powder containing a blend of seasonings

China cap—a cone-shaped strainer made of perforated metal

Chinois—(sheen-WAH) a conical strainer made of fine mesh, used for straining and puréeing foods

Chlorophyll—a naturally occurring pigment that predominates in green vegetables such as cabbage

Cholesterol—a fatty substance found in foods derived from animal products and in the human body; it has been linked to heart disease

Chop—(1) a cut of meat, including part of the rib; (2) to cut an item into small pieces where uniformity of size and shape is neither feasible nor necessary

Choux pastry—(shoo paste-re) see **Éclair paste**

Chowder—a hearty soup made from fish, shellfish and/or vegetables, usually containing milk and potatoes and often thickened with roux

Chutney—a sweet-and-sour condiment made of fruits and/or vegetables cooked in vinegar with sugar and spices; some chutneys are reduced to a purée, while others retain recognizable pieces of their ingredients

Cider—mildly fermented apple juice; nonalcoholic apple juice may also be labeled cider

Citrus—fruits characterized by a thick rind, most of which is a bitter white pith (albedo) with a thin exterior layer of colored skin (zest); their flesh is segmented and juicy and varies from bitter to tart to sweet

Clarification—(1) the process of transforming a broth into a clear consommé by trapping impurities with a clearmeat consisting of the egg white protein albumen, ground meat, an acidic product, mirepoix and other ingredients; (2) the clearmeat used to clarify a broth

Clarified butter—purified butterfat; the butter is melted and the water and milk solids are removed

Classic cuisine—a late 19th- and early 20th-century refinement and simplification of French *grande cuisine*. Classic (or classical) cuisine relies on the thorough exploration of culinary principles and techniques, and emphasizes the refined preparation and presentation of superb ingredients

Clean—to remove visible dirt and soil

Clearmeat—see **Clarification**

Clear soups—unthickened soups, including broths, consommés and broth-based soups

Coagulation—the irreversible transformation of proteins from a liquid or semiliquid state to a drier, solid state; usually accomplished through the application of heat

Cocoa butter—the fat found in cocoa beans and used in fine chocolates

Coconut cream—(1) a coconut-flavored liquid made like coconut milk but with less water; it is creamier and thicker than coconut milk; (2) the thick fatty portion that separates and rises to the top of canned or frozen coconut milk. Do not substitute cream of coconut for true coconut cream.

Coconut milk—a coconut-flavored liquid made by pouring boiling water over shredded coconut; may be sweetened or unsweetened. Do not substitute cream of coconut for coconut milk.

Coconut water—the thin, slightly opaque liquid contained within a fresh coconut/

Cojita—(ko-HEE-ta) an aged, hard, salty Mexican cow's-milk cheese; similar to feta, although not soaked in brine

Colander—a perforated bowl, with or without a base or legs, used to strain foods

Collagen—a protein found in nearly all connective tissue; it dissolves when cooked with moisture

Combination cooking methods—cooking methods, principally braising and stewing, that employ both dry-heat and moist-heat procedures

Composed salad—a salad prepared by arranging each of the ingredients (the base, body, garnish and dressing) on individual plates in an artistic fashion

Compound butter—also known as a beurre composé, a mixture of softened whole butter and flavorings used as a sauce or to flavor and color other sauces

Compound sauces—see **Small sauces**

Concassée—(kon-kaas-SAY) peeled, seeded and diced tomato

Concasser—(kon-kaas) to pound or chop coarsely; usually used for tomatoes or parsley

Concentrate—also known as a fruit paste or compound; a reduced fruit purée, without a gel structure, used as a flavoring

Condiment—traditionally, any item added to a dish for flavor, including herbs, spices and vinegars; now also refers to cooked or prepared flavorings such as prepared mustards, relishes, bottled sauces and pickles

Conduction—the transfer of heat from one item to another through direct contact

Confit—(kohn-FEE) meat or poultry (often lightly salt-cured) slowly cooked and preserved in its own fat and served hot

Connective tissues—tissue found throughout an animal's body that binds together and supports other tissues such as muscles

Consommé—(kwang-soh-MAY) a rich stock or broth that has been clarified with clearmeat to remove impurities

Contaminants—biological, chemical or physical substances that can be harmful when consumed in sufficient quantities

Contamination—the presence, generally unintentional, of harmful organisms or substances

Convection—the transfer of heat caused by the natural movement of molecules in a fluid (whether air, water or fat) from a warmer area to a cooler one; mechanical convection is the movement of molecules caused by stirring

Conversion factor (C.F.)—the number used to increase or decrease ingredient quantities and recipe yields

Cookery—the art, practice or work of cooking

Cookies—small, sweet, flat pastries; usually classified by preparation or makeup techniques as drop, icebox, bar, cutout, pressed and wafer

Cooking—(1) the transfer of energy from a heat source to a food; this energy alters the food's molecu-

lar structure, changing its texture, flavor, aroma and appearance; (2) the preparation of food for consumption

Cooking medium—the air, fat, water or steam in which a food is cooked

Coring—the process of removing the seeds or pit from a fruit or fruit-vegetable

Cost of goods sold—the total cost of food items sold during a given period; calculated as beginning inventory plus purchases minus ending inventory

Cost per portion—the amount of the total recipe cost divided by the number of portions produced from that recipe; the cost of one serving

Coulis—(koo-lee) a sauce made from a purée of vegetables and/or fruit; may be served hot or cold

Count—the number of individual items in a given measure of weight or volume

Court bouillon—(kort boo-yon) water simmered with vegetables, seasonings and an acidic product such as vinegar or wine; used for simmering or poaching fish, shellfish or vegetables

Cows—female cattle after their first calving, principally raised for milk and calf production

Cracking—a milling process in which grains are broken open

Cream filling—a pie filling made of flavored pastry cream thickened with cornstarch

Creaming—a mixing method in which softened fat and sugar are vigorously combined to incorporate air

Cream of coconut—a canned commercial product consisting of thick, sweetened coconut-flavored liquid; used for baking and in beverages

Creams—also known as crèmes; include light, fluffy or creamy-textured dessert foods made with whipped cream or whipped egg

whites, such as Bavarian creams, chiffons, mousses and crème Chantilly

Cream sauce—a sauce made by adding cream to a béchamel sauce

Cream soup—a soup made from vegetables cooked in a liquid that is thickened with a starch and puréed; cream is then incorporated to add richness and flavor

Crème anglaise—(khrem ahn-GLEHZ) also known as crème à l'anglaise; see **Vanilla custard sauce**

Crème caramel—(khrem kair-ah-MEHL) like crème renversée (rehn-vehr-SAY) and flan, a custard baked over a layer of caramelized sugar and inverted for service

Crème Chantilly—(khrem shan-TEE) heavy cream whipped to soft peaks and flavored with sugar and vanilla; used to garnish pastries or desserts or folded into cooled custard or pastry cream for fillings

Crème Chiboust—(khrem chee-BOOS) a pastry cream lightened by folding in Italian meringue

Crème pâtissière—(khrem pah-tees-SYEHR) see **Pastry cream**

Crêpe—(krayp) a thin, delicate unleavened griddlecake made with a very thin egg batter cooked in a very hot sauté pan; used in sweet and savory preparations

Critical control point—under the HACCP system, any step during the processing of a food when a mistake can result in the transmission, growth or survival of pathogenic bacteria

Croissant—(krwah-SAHN) a crescent-shaped roll made from a rich, rolled-in yeast dough

Croquette—(crow-keht) a food that has been puréed or bound with a thick sauce (usually béchamel or velouté), made into small shapes and then breaded and deep-fried

Cross-contamination—the transfer of bacteria or other contaminants from one food, work surface or piece of equipment to another

Croûte, en—(awn KROOT) describes a food encased in a bread or pastry crust

Crouton—(KROO-tawn) a bread or pastry garnish, usually toasted or sautéed until crisp

Crudités—(croo-dee-TAYS) generally refers to raw or blanched vegetables served as an hors d'oeuvre and often accompanied by a dip

Crustaceans—shellfish characterized by a hard outer skeleton or shell and jointed appendages; include lobsters, crabs and shrimp

Cuisine—the ingredients, seasonings, cooking procedures and styles attributable to a particular group of people; the group can be defined by geography, history, ethnicity, politics, culture or religion

Cuisson—(kwee-sohn) the liquid used for shallow poaching

Curdling—the separation of milk or egg mixtures into solid and liquid components; caused by overcooking, high heat or the presence of acids

Curing salt—a mixture of salt and sodium nitrite that inhibits bacterial growth; used as a preservative, often for charcuterie items

Custard—any liquid thickened by the coagulation of egg proteins; its consistency depends on the ratio of eggs to liquid and the type of liquid used; custards can be baked in the oven or cooked in a bain marie or on the stove top

Cutlet—a relatively thick, boneless slice of meat

Cutting—(1) reducing a food to smaller pieces; (2) a mixing method in which solid fat is incorporated into dry ingredients until only lumps of the desired size remain

Cutting loss—the unavoidable and unrecoverable loss of food during fabrication; the loss is usually the result of food particles sticking to the cutting board or the evaporation of liquids

Cuttlebone—also known as the pen, the single, thin internal shell of cephalopods

Cycle menu—a menu that changes every day for a certain period and then repeats the same daily items in the same order (for example, on a seven-day cycle, the same menu is used every Monday)

Dairy products—include cow's milk and foods produced from cow's milk such as butter, yogurt, sour cream and cheese; sometimes other milks and products made from them are included (e.g., goat's milk cheese)

Decline phase—a period during which bacteria die at an accelerated rate, also known as the negative growth phase

Decoction—(1) boiling a food until its flavor is removed; (2) a procedure used for brewing coffee

Decorator's icing—see **Royal icing**

Deep-frying—a dry-heat cooking method that uses convection to transfer heat to a food submerged in hot fat; foods to be deep-fried are usually first coated in batter or breading

Deglaze—to swirl or stir a liquid (usually wine or stock) in a sauté pan or other pan to dissolve cooked food particles remaining on the bottom; the resulting mixture often becomes the base for a sauce

Degrease—to skim the fat from the top of a liquid such as a sauce or stock

Demi-glace—(deh-me glass) French for "half-glaze"; a mixture of half brown stock and half brown sauce reduced by half

Detrempe—(day-trup-eh) a paste made with flour and water during the first stage of preparing a pastry dough, especially rolled-in doughs

Deveining—the process of removing a shrimp's digestive tract

Deviled—describes meat, poultry or other food seasoned with mustard, vinegar and other spicy seasonings

Diagonals—elongated or oval-shaped slices of cylindrical vegetables or fruits

Dice—(1) to cut foods into cubes: ¼ inch (6 millimeters) for small, ½ inch (1.2 centimeters) for medium and ¾ inch (2 centimeters) for large; (2) the cubes of cut food

Dip—a thick, creamy sauce, served hot or cold, to accompany crudités, crackers, chips or other foods, especially as an hors d'oeuvre; dips are often based on sour cream, mayonnaise or cream cheese

Direct contamination—the contamination of raw foods in their natural setting or habitat

Diver scallops—scallops that are harvested from the ocean by divers who hand-pick each one; diver scallops tend to be less gritty than those harvested by dragging, and hand-harvesting is more ecologically friendly

Docking—pricking small holes in an unbaked dough or crust to allow steam to escape and to prevent the dough from rising when baked

Dough—a mixture of flour and other ingredients used in baking; has a low moisture content, and gluten forms the continuous medium into which other ingredients are embedded; it is often stiff enough to cut into shapes

Drawn—a market form for fish in which the viscera is removed

Dredging—coating a food with flour or finely ground crumbs; usually done prior to sautéing or frying or as the first step of the standardized breading procedure

Dress—to trim or otherwise prepare an animal carcass for consumption

Dressed—a market form for fish in which the viscera, gills, fins and scales are removed

Drupes—see **Stone fruits**

Dry-heat cooking methods— cooking methods, principally broiling, grilling, roasting and baking, sautéing, pan-frying and deep-frying, that use air or fat to transfer heat through conduction and convection; dry-heat cooking methods allow surface sugars to caramelize

Drying—a preservation method in which the food's moisture content is dramatically reduced; drying changes the food's texture, flavor and appearance

Duchesse potatoes—(duh-shees) a purée of cooked potatoes, butter and egg yolks, seasoned with salt, pepper and nutmeg; can be eaten as is or used to prepare several classic potato dishes

Dumpling—any of a variety of small starchy products made from doughs or batters that are simmered or steamed; can be plain or filled

Durum wheat—a species of very hard wheat with a particularly high amount of protein; it is used to make couscous or milled into semolina, which is used for making pasta

Duxelles—(dook-SEHL) a coarse paste made of finely chopped mushrooms sautéed with shallots in butter

Éclair paste—(ay-clahr) also known as pâte à choux; a soft dough that produces hollow baked products with crisp exteriors; used for making éclairs, cream puffs and savory products

Edible portion (E.P.)—the amount of a food item available for consumption or use after trimming or fabrication; a smaller, more convenient portion of a larger or bulk unit

Egg wash—a mixture of beaten eggs (whole eggs, yolks or whites) and a liquid, usually milk or water, used to coat doughs before baking to add sheen

Elastin—a protein found in connective tissues, particularly ligaments and tendons; it often appears as the white or silver covering on meats known as silverskin; elastin does not dissolve when cooked

Émincé—(eh-manss-say) a small, thin boneless piece of meat

Emulsification—the process by which generally unmixable liquids, such as oil and water, are forced into a uniform distribution

Emulsion—(1) a uniform mixture of two unmixable liquids; (2) flavoring oils such as orange and lemon, mixed into water with the aid of emulsifiers

Endosperm—the largest part of a cereal grain and a source of protein and carbohydrates (starch); the part used primarily in milled products

Entrée—(ahn-tray) the main dish of an American meal, usually meat, poultry, fish or shellfish accompanied by a vegetable and starch; in France, the first course, served before the fish and meat courses

Enzymes—proteins that aid specific chemical reactions in plants and animals

Escalope—(eh-SKAL-ohp) see **Scallop**

Escargot—(ays-skahr-go) French for "snail"; those used for culinary purposes are land snails (genus *Helix*)

Espagnole—(ess-spah-nyol) also known as brown sauce, a leading sauce made of brown stock, mirepoix and tomatoes thickened with brown roux; often used to produce demi-glace

Essence—a sauce made from a concentrated vegetable juice

Essential nutrients—nutrients that must be provided by food because the body cannot or does not produce them in sufficient quantities

Ethnic cuisine—the cuisine of a group of people having a common cultural heritage, as opposed to the cuisine of a group of people bound together by geography or political factors

Ethylene gas—a colorless, odorless hydrocarbon gas naturally emitted from fruits and fruit-vegetables that encourages ripening

Evaporation—the process by which heated water molecules move faster and faster until the water turns to a gas (steam) and vaporizes; evaporation is responsible for the drying of foods during cooking

Extracts—concentrated mixtures of ethyl alcohol and flavoring oils such as vanilla, almond and lemon

Extrusion—the process of forcing pasta dough through perforated plates to create various shapes; pasta dough that is not extruded must be rolled and cut

Fabricate—to cut a large item into smaller portions; often refers to the butchering of fish or shellfish

Fabricated cuts—individual portions of meat cut from a subprimal

Facultative bacteria—those that can adapt and will survive with or without oxygen

Fancy—(1) fish that has been previously frozen; (2) a quality grade for fruits, especially canned or frozen

Fatback—fresh pork fat from the back of the pig, used primarily for barding

Fats—(1) a group of compounds composed of oxygen, hydrogen and carbon atoms that supply the body with energy (9 calories per gram); fats are classified as saturated, monounsaturated or polyunsaturated; (2) the general term for butter, lard, shortening, oil and margarine used as cooking media or ingredients

Fermentation—the process by which yeast converts sugar into alcohol and carbon dioxide; it also refers to the time that yeast dough is left to rise

Feuilleté—(fuh-YET) square, rectangular or diamond-shaped puff pastry boxes; may be filled with a sweet or savory mixture

Fiber—also known as dietary fiber; indigestible carbohydrates found in grains, fruits and vegetables; fiber aids digestion

FIFO—first in, first out; a system of rotating inventory, particularly perishable and semiperishable goods, in which items are used in the order in which they are received

Filé—(fee-lay) a seasoning and thickening agent made from dried, ground sassafras leaves

Filet, fillet—(fee-lay) (1) filet: a boneless tenderloin of meat; (2) fillet: the side of a fish removed intact, boneless or semiboneless, with or without skin; (3) to cut such a piece

Fish velouté—a velouté sauce made from fish stock

Flambé—(flahm-BAY) food served flaming; produced by igniting brandy, rum or other liquor

Flash-frozen—describes food that has been frozen very rapidly using metal plates, extremely low temperatures or chemical solutions

Flatfish—fish with asymmetrical, compressed bodies that swim in a horizontal position and have both eyes on the top of the head; include sole, flounder and halibut

Flavonoid—a naturally occurring pigment that predominates in red, purple and white vegetables such as cauliflower, red cabbage and beets

Flavoring—an item that adds a new taste to a food and alters its natural flavors; flavorings include herbs, spices, vinegars and condiments. The terms *seasoning* and *flavoring* are often used interchangeably.

Fleuron—(fluh-rawng) a crescent-shaped piece of puff pastry used as a garnish

Flour—a powdery substance of varying degrees of fineness made by milling grains such as wheat, corn or rye

Foamed milk—milk that is heated and frothed with air and steam generated by an espresso machine; it

will be slightly cooler than steamed milk

Foie gras—(fwah grah) liver of specially fattened geese

Fold—a measurement of the strength of vanilla extract

Folding—incorporating light, airy ingredients into heavier ingredients by gently moving them from the bottom of the bowl up over the top in a circular motion, usually with a rubber spatula

Fond—(fahn) (1) French for "stock"; (2) French for "bottom"; the concentrated juices, drippings and bits of food left in pans after foods are roasted or sautéed; it is used to flavor sauces made directly in the pans in which the foods were cooked

Fondant—(FAHN-dant) a sweet, thick opaque sugar paste commonly used for glazing pastries such as napoleons or making candies

Fond lié—(fahn lee-ay) see **Jus lié**

Fondue—a Swiss specialty made with melted cheese, wine and flavorings; eaten by dipping pieces of bread into the hot mixture with long forks

Food cost—the cost of the materials that go directly into the production of menu items

Food cost percentage—the ratio of the cost of foods served to the food sales dollars during a given period

Food Guide Pyramid—a dietary guide that prioritizes and proportions food choices among six general food groups

Forcemeat—a preparation made from uncooked ground meats, poultry, fish or shellfish, seasoned, and emulsified with fat; commonly prepared as country-style, basic and mousseline and used for charcuterie items

Formula—a recipe; the term is most often used in the bakeshop

Frangipane—(fran-juh-pahn) a sweet almond and egg filling cooked inside pastry

Free-range chickens—chickens allowed to move freely and forage for food; as opposed to chickens raised in coops

Free-range veal—the meat of calves that are allowed to roam freely and eat grasses and other natural foods; this meat is pinker and more strongly flavored than that of milk-fed calves

Freezer burn—the surface dehydration and discoloration of food that result from moisture loss at below-freezing temperatures

French dressing—classically, a vinaigrette dressing made from oil, vinegar, salt and pepper. In the United States the term also refers to a commercially prepared dressing that is creamy, tartly sweet and red-orange in color.

Frenching—a method of trimming racks or individual chops of meat, especially lamb, in which the excess fat is cut away leaving the eye muscle intact; all meat and connective tissue are removed from the rib bone

French service—restaurant service in which one waiter (a captain) takes the order, does the tableside cooking and brings the drinks and food; the secondary or back waiter serves bread and water, clears each course, crumbs the table and serves the coffee

Fresh-frozen—describes a food that has been frozen while still fresh

Fricassee—(FRIHK-uh-see) a white stew in which the meat is cooked in fat without browning before the liquid is added

Frittata—(free-tah-ta) an open-faced omelet of Spanish-Italian heritage

Frosting—also known as icing, a sweet decorative coating used as a filling between the layers or as a coating over the top and sides of a cake

Fruit—the edible organ that develops from the ovary of a flowering plant and contains one or more seeds (pips or pits)

Frying—a dry-heat cooking method in which foods are cooked in hot fat; includes sautéing and stir-frying, pan-frying and deep-frying

Fumet—(foo-may) a stock made from fish bones or shellfish shells and vegetables simmered in a liquid with flavorings

Fungi—a large group of plants ranging from single-celled organisms to giant mushrooms; the most common are molds and yeasts

Fusion cuisine—the blending or use of ingredients and/or preparation methods from various ethnic, regional or national cuisines in the same dish; also known as transnational cuisine

Galantine—(GAL-uhn-teen) similar to a ballotine; a charcuterie item made from a forcemeat of poultry, game or suckling pig usually wrapped in the skin of the bird or animal and poached in an appropriate stock; often served cold, usually in aspic

Game—birds and animals hunted for sport or food; many game birds and animals are now ranch-raised and commercially available

Game hen—the class of young or immature progeny of Cornish chickens or of a Cornish chicken and White Rock chicken; they are small and very flavorful

Ganache—(ga-nosh) a rich blend of chocolate and heavy cream and, optionally, flavorings, used as a pastry or candy filling or frosting

Garde-manger—(gar mawn-zhay) (1) also known as the pantry chef, the cook in charge of cold food production, including salads and salad dressings, charcuterie items, cold appetizers and buffet items; (2) the work area where these foods are prepared

Garnish—(1) food used as an attractive decoration; (2) a subsidiary food used to add flavor or character to the main ingredient in a dish (for example, noodles in chicken noodle soup)

Gastrique—(gas-streek) caramelized sugar deglazed with vinegar; used to flavor tomato or savory fruit sauces

Gastronomy—the art and science of eating well

Gâteau—(gah-toe) (1) in American usage, refers to any cake-type dessert; (2) in French usage, refers to various pastry items made with puff pastry, éclair paste, short dough or sweet dough

Gaufrette potatoes—(goh-FREHT) thin, fried, lattice-cut slices of potato

Gelatin—a flavorless, odorless and brittle mixture of proteins (especially collagen) extracted from boiling bones, connective tissue and other animal parts; when dissolved in a hot liquid and then cooled, it forms a jellylike substance used as a thickener and stabilizer

Gelatinization—the process by which starch granules are cooked; they absorb moisture when placed in a liquid and heated; as the moisture is absorbed, the product swells, softens and clarifies slightly

Gelato—(jah-laht-to) an Italian-style ice cream that is denser than American-style ice cream

Genoise—(zhen-waahz) (1) a form of whipped-egg cake that uses whole eggs whipped with sugar; (2) a French spongecake

Germ—the smallest portion of a cereal grain and the only part that contains fat

Ghee—a form of clarified butter in which the milk solids remain with the fat and are allowed to brown; originating in India and now used worldwide as an ingredient and cooking medium, it has a long shelf life, a high smoke point and a nutty, caramel-like flavor

Giblets—the collective term for edible poultry viscera, including gizzards, hearts, livers and necks.

Gizzard—a bird's second stomach

Glaçage—(glah-sahge) browning or glazing a food, usually under a salamander or broiler

Glace de poisson—(glahss duh pwah-sawng) a syrupy glaze made by reducing a fish stock

Glace de viande—(glahss duh vee-awnd) a dark, syrupy meat glaze made by reducing a brown stock

Glace de volaille—(glahss duh vo-lahy) a light brown, syrupy glaze made by reducing a chicken stock

Glaze—(1) any shiny coating applied to food or created by browning; (2) the dramatic reduction and concentration of a stock; (3) a thin, flavored coating poured or dripped onto a cake or pastry

Gliaden—see **Gluten**

Global cuisine—foods (often commercially produced items) or preparation methods that have become ubiquitous throughout the world; for example, curries and French-fried potatoes

Glucose—an important energy source for the body; also known as blood sugar; (2) a thick, sweet syrup made from cornstarch

Gluten—an elastic network of proteins created when wheat flour is moistened and manipulated; it gives structure and strength to baked goods and is responsible for their volume, texture and appearance. The proteins necessary for gluten formation are glutenin and gliaden.

Glutenin—see **Gluten**

Gourmand—a connoisseur of fine food and drink, often to excess

Gourmet—a connoisseur of fine food and drink

Gourmet foods—foods of the highest quality, perfectly prepared and beautifully presented

Grading—a series of voluntary programs offered by the U.S. Department of Agriculture to designate a food's overall quality

Grains—(1) grasses that bear edible seeds, including corn, rice and wheat; (2) the fruit (that is, the seed or kernel) of such grasses

Gram—the basic unit of weight in the metric system; equal to approximately 1/30 of an ounce

Grande cuisine—the rich, intricate and elaborate cuisine of the 18th- and 19th-century French aristocracy and upper classes. It is based upon the rational identification, development and adoption of strict culinary principles.

Grate—to cut a food into small, thin shreds by rubbing it against a serrated metal plate known as a grater

Gravy—a sauce made from meat or poultry juices combined with a liquid and thickening agent; usually made in the pan in which the meat or poultry was cooked

Green meats—freshly slaughtered meats that have not had sufficient time to age and develop tenderness and flavor

Gremolada—(greh-moa-LAH-dah) an aromatic garnish of chopped parsley, garlic and lemon zest used for osso buco

Grilling—a dry-heat cooking method in which foods are cooked by heat radiating from a source located below the cooking surface; the heat can be generated by electricity or by burning gas, hardwood or hardwood charcoals

Grind—to pulverize or reduce food to small particles using a mechanical grinder or food processor

Grinding—a milling process in which grains are reduced to a powder; the powder can be of differing degrees of fineness or coarseness

Gristle—see **Cartilage**

Grosse piece—a centerpiece consisting of a large piece of the principal food offered; for example, a large wheel of cheese with slices of the cheese cascading around it

Gum paste—a smooth dough of sugar and gelatin that can be colored and used to make decorations, especially for pastries

HACCP—see **Hazard Analysis Critical Control Points**

Halal—describes food prepared in accordance with Muslim dietary laws

Hanging—the practice of allowing eviscerated (drawn or gutted) game to age in a dry, well-ventilated place; hanging helps tenderize the flesh and strengthen its flavor

Hazard Analysis Critical Control Points (HACCP)—a rigorous system of self-inspection used to manage and maintain sanitary conditions in all types of food service operations; it focuses on the flow of food through the food service facility to identify any point or step in preparation (known as a critical control point) where some action must be taken to prevent or minimize a risk or hazard

Heimlich maneuver—the first-aid procedure for choking victims in which sudden upward pressure is applied to the upper abdomen in order to force any foreign object from the windpipe

Herb—any of a large group of aromatic plants whose leaves, stems or flowers are used as a flavoring; used either dried or fresh

High-ratio cake—a form of creamed-fat cake that uses emulsified shortening and has a two-stage mixing method

Hollandaise—(ohll-uhn-daze) an emulsified sauce made of butter, egg yolks and flavorings (especially lemon juice)

Homogenization—the process by which milk fat is prevented from separating out of milk products

Hors d'oeuvre—(ohr durv) very small portions of hot or cold foods served before the meal to stimulate the appetite

Hotel pan—a rectangular, stainless steel pan with a lip allowing it to rest in a storage shelf or steam table; available in several standard sizes

Hull—also known as the husk, the outer covering of a fruit, seed or grain

Hulling—a milling process in which the hull or husk is removed from grains

Hybrid—the result of crossbreeding different species that are genetically unalike; often a unique product

Hybrid menu—a menu combining features of a static menu with a cycle menu or a market menu of specials

Hydrogenation—the process used to harden oils; hydrogen atoms are added to unsaturated fat molecules, making them partially or completely saturated and thus solid at room temperature

Hydrometer—a device used to measure specific gravity; it shows degrees of concentration on the Baumé scale

Hygroscopic—describes a food that readily absorbs moisture from the air

Icing—see **Frosting**

IMPS/NAMP—see **NAMP/IMPS**

Incidental food additives—those inadvertently or unintentionally added to foods during processing, such as pesticide residues on fruits

Induction cooking—a cooking method that uses a special coil placed below the stove top's surface in combination with specially designed cookware to generate heat rapidly with an alternating magnetic field

Infection—in the food safety context, a disease caused by the ingestion of live pathogenic bacteria that continue their life processes in the consumer's intestinal tract

Infrared cooking—a heating method that uses an electric or ceramic element heated to such a high temperature that it gives off waves of radiant heat that cook the food

Infusion—(1) the extraction of flavors from a food at a temperature below boiling; (2) a group of coffee brewing techniques, including steeping, filtering and dripping; (3) the liquid resulting from this process

Instant-read thermometer—a thermometer used to measure the internal temperature of foods; the stem is inserted in the food, producing an instant temperature readout

Intentional food additives—those added to foods on purpose, such as the chemicals used to ensure longer shelf life or food colorings

Intoxication—in the food safety context, a disease caused by the toxins that bacteria produce during their life processes

Inventory—the listing and counting of all foods in the kitchen, storerooms and refrigerators

IQF (individually quick-frozen)—describes the technique of rapidly freezing each individual item of food such as slices of fruit, berries or pieces of fish before packaging; IQF foods are not packaged with syrup or sauce

Irradiation—a preservation method used for certain fruits, vegetables, grains, spices, meat and poultry in which ionizing radiation sterilizes the food, slows ripening and prevents sprouting

Jam—a fruit gel made from fruit pulp and sugar

Jelly—a fruit gel made from fruit juice and sugar

Juice—the liquid extracted from any fruit or vegetable

Julienne—(ju-lee-en) (1) to cut foods into stick-shaped pieces, approximately 1/8 inch × 1/8 inch × 2 inches (3 millimeters × 3 millimeters × 5 centimeters); a **fine julienne** has dimensions of 1/16 inch × 1/16 inch × 2 inches (1.5 millimeters × 1.5 millimeters × 5 centimeters); (2) the stick-shaped pieces of cut food

Jus lié—(zhoo lee-ay) also known as fond lié; a sauce made by thickening brown stock with cornstarch or similar starch; often used like a demi-glace, especially to produce small sauces

Kneading—working a dough to develop gluten

Kobe beef—an exclusive type of beef traditionally produced in Kobe, Japan, from Wagyu cattle fed a special diet

Kosher—describes food prepared in accordance with Jewish dietary laws

Lactose—a disaccharide that occurs naturally in mammalian milk; milk sugar

Lag phase—a period, usually following transfer from one place to another, during which bacteria do not experience much growth

Lamb—the meat of sheep slaughtered under the age of one year

Lard—the rendered fat of hogs

Larding—inserting thin slices of fat, such as pork fatback, into low-fat meats in order to add moisture

Lardon—diced, blanched, fried bacon

Leading sauces—also known as mother sauces, the foundation for the entire classic repertoire of hot sauces; the five leading sauces (béchamel, velouté, espagnole [also known as brown], tomato and hollandaise) are distinguished by the liquids and thickeners used to make them; they can be seasoned and garnished to create a wide variety of small or compound sauces

Leavener—an ingredient or process that produces or incorporates gases in a baked product in order to increase volume, provide structure and give texture

Lecithin—a natural emulsifier found in egg yolks

Legumes—(lay-gyooms) (1) French for "vegetables"; (2) a large group of vegetables with double-seamed seed pods; depending upon the variety, the seeds, pod and seeds together, or the dried seeds are eaten

Liaison—(lee-yeh-zon) a mixture of egg yolks and heavy cream used to thicken and enrich sauces

Liqueur—a strong, sweet, syrupy alcoholic beverage made by mixing or redistilling neutral spirits with fruits, flowers, herbs, spices or other flavorings; also known as a cordial

Liquor—an alcoholic beverage made by distilling grains, vegetables or other foods; includes rum, whiskey and vodka

Liter—the basic unit of volume in the metric system, equal to slightly more than a quart

Log phase—a period of accelerated growth for bacteria

Lozenges—diamond-shaped pieces, usually of firm vegetables

Macaroni—(1) any dried pasta made with wheat flour and water; (2) in the United States, refers to an elbow-shaped pasta tube

Macerate—to soak foods in a liquid, usually alcoholic, to soften them

Macronutrients—the nutrients needed in large quantities: carbohydrates, proteins, fats and water

Madeira—(muh-DEH-rah) a Portuguese fortified wine heated during aging to give it a distinctive flavor and brown color

Maître d'hotel (maître d')—(may-tr doh-tel) (1) the leader of the dining room brigade, also known as the dining room manager; oversees the dining room or "front of the house" staff; (2) a compound butter flavored with chopped parsley and lemon juice

Mandoline—a stainless steel, hand-operated slicing device with adjustable blades

Marbling—whitish streaks of inter- and intramuscular fat

Marinade—the liquid used to marinate foods; it generally contains herbs, spices and other flavoring ingredients as well as an acidic product such as wine, vinegar or lemon juice

Marinate—to soak a food in a seasoned liquid in order to tenderize the food and add flavor to it

Market menu—a menu based upon product availability during a specific period; it is written to use foods when they are in peak season or readily available

Marmalade—a citrus jelly that also contains unpeeled slices of citrus fruit

Marsala—(mar-SAH-lah) a flavorful fortified sweet-to-semidry Sicilian wine

Marzipan—(MAHR-sih-pan) a paste of ground almonds, sugar and egg whites used to fill and decorate pastries

Matignon—a standard mirepoix plus diced smoked bacon or smoked ham and, depending on the dish, mushrooms and herbs; sometimes called an edible mirepoix, it is usually cut more uniformly than a standard mirepoix and left in the finished dish as a garnish

Matzo—thin, crisp unleavened bread made only with flour and water; can be ground into meal that is used for matzo balls and pancakes

Mayonnaise—a thick, creamy sauce consisting of oil and vinegar emulsified with egg yolks, usually used as a salad dressing

Meal—(1) the coarsely ground seeds of any edible grain such as corn or oats; (2) any dried, ground substance (such as bonemeal)

Mealy potatoes—also known as starchy potatoes; those with a high starch content and thick skin; they are best for baking

Medallion—a small, round piece of meat or fish

Melting—the process by which certain foods, especially those high in fat, gradually soften and then liquefy when heated

Menu—a list of foods and beverages available for purchase

Meringue—(muh-reng) a foam made of beaten egg whites and sugar

Metabolism—all the chemical reactions and physical processes that occur continuously in living cells and organisms

Meter—the basic unit of length in the metric system, equal to slightly more than 1 yard

Mezzaluna—a two-handled knife with one or more thick, crescent-shaped blades used to chop and mince herbs and vegetables

Micronutrients—the nutrients needed only in small amounts; vitamins and minerals

Microorganisms—single-celled organisms as well as tiny plants and animals that can be seen only through a microscope

Microwave cooking—a heating method that uses radiation generated by a special oven to penetrate the food; it agitates water molecules, creating friction and heat; this energy then spreads throughout the food by conduction (and by convection in liquids)

Mignonette—(mee-nyohn-EHT) a small cut or medallion of meat

Milk-fed veal—also known as formula-fed veal; the meat of calves fed only a nutrient-rich liquid and kept tethered in pens; this meat is whiter and more mildly flavored than that of free-range calves

Milling—the process by which grain is ground into flour or meal

Mince—to cut a food item into very small pieces

Minerals—inorganic micronutrients necessary for regulating body functions and proper bone and tooth structures

Mirepoix—(meer-pwa) a mixture of coarsely chopped onions, carrots and celery used to flavor stocks, stews and other foods; generally, a mixture of 50 percent onions, 25 percent carrots and 25 percent celery, by weight, is used

Mise en place—(meez on plahs) French for "putting in place"; refers to the preparation and assembly of all necessary ingredients and equipment

Miso—(ME-so) a thick paste made by salting and fermenting soybeans

and rice or barley; generally used as a flavoring

Mix—to combine ingredients in such a way that they are evenly dispersed throughout the mixture

Moist-heat cooking methods—cooking methods, principally simmering, poaching, boiling and steaming, that use water or steam to transfer heat through convection; moist-heat cooking methods are used to emphasize the natural flavors of foods

Mojo criollo—a citrus and herb marinade used in Latino cuisines; several bottled brands are available from Hispanic markets

Molding—the process of shaping foods, particularly grains and vegetables bound by sauces, into attractive, hard-edged shapes by using metal rings, circular cutters or other forms

Molds—(1) algaelike fungi that form long filaments or strands; for the most part, molds affect only food appearance and flavor; (2) containers used for shaping foods

Mollusks—shellfish characterized by a soft, unsegmented body, no internal skeleton and a hard outer shell

Monounsaturated fats—see **Unsaturated fats**

Monter au beurre—(mohn-tay ah burr) to finish a sauce by swirling or whisking in butter (raw or compound) until it is melted; used to give sauces shine, flavor and richness

Mortar and pestle—a hard bowl (the mortar) in which foods such as spices are ground or pounded into a powder with a club-shaped tool (the pestle)

Mother sauces—(French *sauce mère*), see **Leading sauces**

Mousse—(moose) a soft, creamy food, either sweet or savory, lightened by adding whipped cream, beaten egg whites or both

Mousseline—(moose-uh-leen) (1) a delicately flavored forcemeat based on white meat, fish or shellfish lightened with cream and egg whites; (2) a sauce or cream lightened by folding in whipped cream

Muesli—(MYOOS-lee) a breakfast cereal made from raw or toasted cereal grains, dried fruits, nuts and dried milk solids and usually eaten with milk or yogurt; sometimes known as granola

Muffin method—a mixing method used to make quick-bread batters; it involves combining liquid fat with other liquid ingredients before adding them to the dry ingredients

Muscles—animal tissues consisting of bundles of cells or fibers that can contract and expand; they are the portions of a carcass usually consumed

Mushrooms—members of a broad category of plants known as fungi; they are often used and served like vegetables

Mutton—the meat of sheep slaughtered after they reach the age of one year

NAMP/IMPS—the Institutional Meat Purchasing Specifications (IMPS) published by the U.S. Department of Agriculture; the IMPS are illustrated and described in *The Meat Buyer's Guide* published by the National Association of Meat Purveyors (NAMP)

Nappe—(nap) (1) the consistency of a liquid, usually a sauce, that will coat the back of a spoon; (2) to coat a food with sauce

National cuisine—the characteristic cuisine of a nation

Navarin—(nah-veh-rahng) a brown ragoût generally made with turnips, other root vegetables, onions, peas and lamb

Nectar—the diluted, sweetened juice of peaches, apricots, guavas, black currants or other fruits, the juice of which would be too thick or too tart to drink straight

New American cuisine—a late-20th-century movement that began in California but has spread across the United States; it stresses the use of fresh, locally grown, seasonal produce and high-quality ingredients simply prepared in a fashion that preserves and emphasizes natural flavors

Noisette—(nwah-zet) (1) a small, usually round, portion of meat cut from the rib or loin; (2) French for "hazelnut"

Noodles—flat strips of pasta-type dough made with eggs; may be fresh or dried

Nouvelle cuisine—French for "new cooking"; a mid-20th-century movement away from many classic cuisine principles and toward a lighter cuisine based on natural flavors, shortened cooking times and innovative combinations

Nut—(1) the edible single-seed kernel of a fruit surrounded by a hard shell; (2) generally, any seed or fruit with an edible kernel in a hard shell

Nutrients—the chemical substances found in food that nourish the body by promoting growth, facilitating body functions and providing energy; there are six categories of nutrients: proteins, carbohydrates, fats, water, minerals and vitamins

Nutrition—the science that studies nutrients

Oblique cuts—also known as roll cuts; small pieces of food, usually vegetables, with two angle-cut sides

Offal—(OFF-uhl) also called variety meats; edible entrails (for example, the heart, kidneys, liver, sweetbreads and tongue) and extremities (for example, oxtail and pig's feet) of an animal

Oignon brûlée—(ohn-nawng brew-LAY) French for "burnt onion"; made by charring onion halves; used to flavor and color stocks and sauces

Oignon piqué—(ohn-nawng pee-KAY) French for "pricked onion"; a

bay leaf tacked with a clove to a peeled onion; used to flavor sauces and soups

Oil—a type of fat that remains liquid at room temperature

Organic farming—a method of farming that does not rely on synthetic pesticides, fungicides, herbicides or fertilizers

Oven spring—the rapid rise of yeast goods in a hot oven, resulting from the production and expansion of trapped gases

Overrun—the amount of air churned into an ice cream

Paillarde—(pahy-lahrd) a scallop of meat pounded until thin; usually grilled

Panada; panade—(pah-nahd) (1) something other than fat added to a forcemeat to enhance smoothness, aid emulsification or both; it is often béchamel, rice or crustless white bread soaked in milk; (2) a mixture for binding stuffings and dumplings, notably quenelles, often choux pastry, bread crumbs, frangipane, puréed potatoes or rice

Pan-broiling—a dry-heat cooking method that uses conduction to transfer heat to a food resting directly on a cooking surface; no fat is used and the food remains uncovered

Pan-dressed—a market form for fish in which the viscera, gills and scales are removed and the fins and tail are trimmed

Pan-frying—a dry-heat cooking method in which food is placed in a moderate amount of hot fat

Pan gravy—a sauce made by deglazing pan drippings from roast meat or poultry and combining them with a roux or other starch and stock

Papillote, en—(awn pa-pee-yote) a cooking method in which food is wrapped in paper or foil and then heated so that the food steams in its own moisture

Parboiling—partially cooking a food in a boiling or simmering liquid; similar to blanching but the cooking time is longer

Parchment (paper)—heat-resistant paper used throughout the kitchen for tasks such as lining baking pans, wrapping foods to be cooked en papillote and covering foods during shallow poaching

Parcooking—partially cooking a food by any cooking method

Paring knife—a short knife used for detail work, especially cutting fruits and vegetables; it has a rigid blade approximately 2–4 inches (5–10 centimeters) long

Parisienne; Parisian—(1) the smaller scoop on a two-scoop melon ball cutter; (2) small spheres of fruit or vegetables cut with a tiny melon ball cutter

Parstock (par)—the amount of stock necessary to cover operating needs between deliveries

Pasta—(1) an unleavened paste or dough made from wheat flour (often semolina), water and eggs; the dough can be colored and flavored with a wide variety of herbs, spices or other ingredients and cut or extruded into a wide variety of shapes and sizes; it can be fresh or dried and is boiled for service; (2) general term for any macaroni product or egg noodle

Pasteurization—the process of heating something to a prescribed temperature for a specific period in order to destroy pathogenic bacteria

Pastillage—(pahst-tee-azh) a paste made of sugar, cornstarch and gelatin; it may be cut or molded into decorative shapes

Pastry cream—also known as crème pâtissière, a stirred custard made with egg yolks, sugar and milk and thickened with starch; used for pastry and pie fillings

Pâte—(paht) French for "dough"

Pâté—(pah-TAY) traditionally, a fine savory meat filling wrapped in pastry, baked and served hot or cold; as opposed to a terrine, which

was a coarsely ground and highly seasoned meat mixture baked in an earthenware mold and served cold; today, the words *pâté* and *terrine* are generally used interchangeably

Pâte à choux—(paht ah shoo) see **Éclair paste**

Pâte au pâté—(paht ah pah-TAY) a specially formulated pastry dough used for wrapping pâté when making pâté en croûte

Pâte brisée—(paht bree-zay) a dough that produces a very flaky baked product containing little or no sugar; flaky dough is used for prebaked pie shells or crusts; mealy dough is a less flaky product used for custard, cream or fruit pie crusts

Pâté en croûte—(pah-tay awn croot) a pâté baked in pastry dough such as pâte au pâté

Pâte feuilletée—(paht fuh-yuh-tay) also known as puff pastry; a rolled-in dough used for pastries, cookies and savory products; it produces a rich and buttery but not sweet baked product with hundreds of light, flaky layers

Pâte sucrée—(paht soo-kray) a dough containing sugar that produces a very rich, crisp (not flaky) baked product; also known as sweet dough, it is used for tart shells

Pathogen—any organism that causes disease; usually refers to bacteria

Pâtissier—(pah-tees-sir-yair) a pastry chef; the person responsible for all baked items, including breads, pastries and desserts

Paupiette—(po-pee-et) a thin slice of meat, poultry or fish spread with a savory stuffing and rolled, then braised or poached

Paysanne—(pahy-sahn) foods cut into flat square, round or triangular items with dimensions of ½ inch × ½ inch × ⅛ inch (1.2 centimeters × 1.2 centimeters × 3 millimeters)

Pearling—a milling process in which all or part of the hull, bran and germ are removed from the grain

Pectin—a gelatinlike carbohydrate obtained from certain fruits; used to thicken jams and jellies

Persillade—(payr-se-yad) (1) a food served with or containing parsley; (2) a mixture of bread crumbs, parsley and garlic used to coat meats, usually lamb

pH—a measurement of the acid or alkali content of a solution, expressed on a scale of 0 to 14.0. A pH of 7.0 is considered neutral or balanced. The lower the pH value, the more acidic the substance. The higher the pH value, the more alkaline the substance

Physical hazard—a danger to the safety of food caused by particles such as glass chips, metal shavings, bits of wood or other foreign matter

Pickle—(1) to preserve food in a brine or vinegar solution; (2) food that has been preserved in a seasoned brine or vinegar, especially cucumbers. Pickled cucumbers are available whole, sliced, in wedges, or chopped as a relish, and may be sweet, or sour, dill-flavored or hot and spicy.

Pigment—any substance that gives color to an item

Pilaf—a cooking method for grains in which the grains are lightly sautéed in hot fat and then a hot liquid is added; the mixture is simmered without stirring until the liquid is absorbed

Poaching—a moist-heat cooking method that uses convection to transfer heat from a hot (approximately 160°F–180°F [71°C–82°C] liquid to the food submerged in it

Polyunsaturated fats—see **Unsaturated fats**

Pomes—members of the *Rosaceae* family; tree fruits with a thin skin and firm flesh surrounding a central core containing many small seeds (called pips or carpels); include apples, pears and quince

Pork—the meat of hogs, usually slaughtered under the age of one year

Posterior—at or toward the rear of an object or place; opposite of anterior

Potentially hazardous foods—foods on which bacteria can thrive

Poultry—the collective term for domesticated birds bred for eating; they include chickens, ducks, geese, guineas, pigeons and turkeys

Preserve—(1) a fruit gel that contains large pieces or whole fruits; (2) to extend the shelf life of a food by subjecting it to a process such as irradiation, canning, vacuum-packing, drying or freezing and/or by adding preservatives

Primal cuts—the primary divisions of muscle, bone and connective tissue produced by the initial butchering of the carcass; primals are further broken down into smaller, more manageable cuts

Prix fixe—(pree feks) French for "fixed price"; refers to a menu offering a complete meal for a set price; also known as *table d'hôte*

Professional cooking—a system of cooking based on a knowledge of and appreciation for ingredients and procedures

Profiterole—(pro-feet-uh-roll) small round pastry made from éclair paste filled with a savory filling and served as an hors d'oeuvre or filled with ice cream topped with sauce and served as a dessert

Proofing—the rise given shaped yeast products just prior to baking

Proteins—a group of compounds composed of oxygen, hydrogen, carbon and nitrogen atoms necessary for manufacturing, maintaining and repairing body tissues and as an alternative source of energy (4 calories per gram); protein chains are constructed of various combinations of amino acids

Puff pastry—see **Pâte feuilletée**

Pulled sugar—a doughlike mixture of sucrose, glucose and tartaric acid that can be colored and shaped by hand

Pulses—dried seeds from a variety of legumes

Pumpernickel—(1) coarsely ground rye flour; (2) bread made with this flour

Purée—(pur-ray) (1) to process food to achieve a smooth pulp; (2) food that is processed by mashing, straining or fine chopping to achieve a smooth pulp

Purée soup—a soup usually made from starchy vegetables or legumes; after the main ingredient is simmered in a liquid, the mixture, or a portion of it, is puréed

Putrefactives—bacteria that spoil food without rendering it unfit for human consumption

Quality grades—a guide to the eating qualities of meat—its tenderness, juiciness and flavor—based on an animal's age and the meat's color, texture and degree of marbling

Quenelle—(kuh-nehl) a small, dumpling-shaped portion of a mousseline forcemeat poached in an appropriately flavored stock; it is shaped by using two spoons

Quiche—a savory tart or pie consisting of a custard baked in a pastry shell with a variety of flavorings and garnishes

Quick bread—a bread, including loaves and muffins, leavened by chemical leaveners or steam rather than yeast

Radiation cooking—a heating process that does not require physical contact between the heat source and the food being cooked; instead, energy is transferred by waves of heat or light striking the food. Two kinds of radiant heat used in the kitchen are infrared and microwave.

Raft—a crust formed during the process of clarifying consommé; it is composed of the clearmeat and impurities from the stock, which rise to the top of the simmering stock and release additional flavors

Ragoût—(rah-goo) (1) traditionally, a well-seasoned, rich stew containing meat, vegetables and wine; (2) any stewed mixture

Ramekin—a small, ovenproof dish, usually ceramic

Rancidity—a chemical change in fats caused by exposure to air, light or heat that results in objectionable flavors and odors

Ratites—a family of flightless birds with small wings and flat breastbones; they include the ostrich, emu and rhea

Recipe—a set of written instructions for producing a specific food or beverage; also known as a formula

Recovery time—the length of time it takes hot fat to return to the desired cooking temperature after food is submerged in it

Red fish—a name applied to various species of fish around the world. In the United States it generally refers to a member of the drum family found in the Southern Atlantic and the Gulf of Mexico. It has a reddish-bronze skin; firm, ivory flesh with a mild flavor and a typical market weight of 2–8 lb. (0.9–3.6 kg), and is also known as channel bass, red drum and red bass.

Red rice—an unmilled, short- or long-grain rice from the Himalayas; it has a russet-colored bran and an earthy, nutty flavor

Reduction—cooking a liquid such as a sauce until its quantity decreases through evaporation; typically done to concentrate flavors and thicken liquids

Refreshing—see **Shocking**

Regional cuisine—a set of recipes based on local ingredients, traditions and practices; within a larger geographical, political, cultural or social unit, regional cuisines are often variations of each other that blend together to create a national cuisine

Relish—a cooked or pickled sauce usually made with vegetables or fruits and often used as a condiment

Remouillage—(rhur-moo-yahj) French for "rewetting"; a stock produced by reusing the bones left from making another stock

Render—(1) to melt and clarify fat; (2) to cook meats in order to remove the fat

Respiration rate—the speed with which the cells of a fruit use up oxygen and produce carbon dioxide during ripening

Ricer—a sievelike utensil with small holes through which soft food is forced; it produces particles about the size of a grain of rice

Rillette—(ree-yeh) meat or poultry slowly cooked, mashed and preserved in its own fat; served cold and usually spread on toast

Ripe—(1) fully grown and developed fruit; the fruit's flavor, texture and appearance are at their peak and the fruit is ready to eat; (2) an unpleasant odor indicating that a food, especially meat, poultry, fish or shellfish, may be past its prime

Risers—covered boxes used on a buffet to add height or as a base for platters, trays or displays

Risotto—(re-zot-toe) (1) a cooking method for grains in which the grains are lightly sautéed in butter and then a liquid is gradually added; the mixture is simmered with near-constant stirring until the still-firm grains merge with the cooking liquid; (2) a Northern Italian rice dish prepared this way

Roasting—a dry-heat cooking method that heats food by surrounding it with hot, dry air in a closed environment or on a spit over an open fire; similar to baking, the term *roasting* is usually applied to meats, poultry, game and vegetables

Roe—(roh) fish eggs

Roll cuts—see **Oblique cuts**

Rolled-in dough—a dough in which a fat is incorporated in many layers by using a rolling and folding procedure; it is used for flaky baked goods such as croissants, puff pastry and Danish pastry

Rondeau—(ron-doe) a shallow, wide, straight-sided pot with two loop handles

Rondelles—(ron-dellz) also called rounds; 1/8-inch- (3-millimeter-) thick, disk-shaped slices of cylindrical vegetables or fruits

Rotate stock—to use products in the order in which they were received; all perishable and semiperishable goods, whether fresh, frozen, canned or dry, should be used according to the first in, first out (FIFO) principle

Rotisserie—cooking equipment that slowly rotates meat or other foods in front of a heating element

Roulade—(roo-lahd) (1) a slice of meat, poultry or fish rolled around a stuffing; (2) a filled and rolled spongecake

Round fish—fish with round, oval or compressed bodies that swim in a vertical position and have eyes on both sides of their heads; include salmon, swordfish and cod

Rounding—the process of shaping dough into smooth, round balls; used to stretch the outside layer of gluten into a smooth coating

Roux—(roo) a cooked mixture of equal parts flour and fat, by weight, used as a thickener for sauces and other dishes; cooking the flour in fat coats the starch granules with the fat and prevents them from lumping together or forming lumps when introduced into a liquid

Royal icing—also known as decorator's icing, an uncooked mixture of confectioner's sugar and egg whites that becomes hard and brittle when dry; used for making intricate cake decorations

Rub—a mixture of fresh or dried herbs and spices ground together; it can be used dried, or it can be mixed with a little oil, lemon juice, prepared mustard or ground fresh garlic or ginger to make a wet rub

Russian service—restaurant service in which the entrée, vegetables and starches are served from a platter onto the diner's plate by a waiter

Sabayon—(sa-by-on) also known as zabaglione; a foamy, stirred custard sauce made by whisking eggs, sugar and wine over low heat

Sachet d'épices; sachet—(sah-shay day-pea-say) French for "bag of spices"; aromatic ingredients tied in a cheesecloth bag and used to flavor stocks and other foods; a standard sachet contains parsley stems, cracked peppercorns, dried thyme, bay leaf, cloves and, optionally, garlic

Salad—a single food or a mix of different foods accompanied or bound by a dressing

Salad dressing—a sauce for a salad; most are based on a vinaigrette, mayonnaise or other emulsified product

Salad greens—a variety of leafy vegetables that are usually eaten raw

Salamander—a small broiler used primarily for browning or glazing the tops of foods

Salsa—(sahl-sah) Spanish for "sauce"; (1) generally, a cold chunky mixture of fresh herbs, spices, fruits and/or vegetables used as a sauce for meat, poultry, fish or shellfish; (2) in Italian usage, a general term for pasta sauces

Salt-curing—the process of surrounding a food with salt or a mixture of salt, sugar, nitrite-based curing salt, herbs and spices; salt-curing dehydrates the food, inhibits bacterial growth and adds flavor

Sanding sugar—granulated sugar with a large, coarse crystal structure that prevents it from dissolving easily; used for decorating cookies and pastries

Sanitation—the creation and maintenance of conditions that will prevent food contamination or foodborne illness

Sanitize—to reduce pathogenic organisms to safe levels

Sashimi—(sah-shee-mee) raw fish eaten without rice; usually served as the first course of a Japanese meal

Saturated fats—fats found mainly in animal products and tropical oils; usually solid at room temperature; the body has more difficulty breaking down saturated fats than either monounsaturated or polyunsaturated fats

Sauce—generally, a thickened liquid used to flavor and enhance other foods

Sausage—a seasoned forcemeat usually stuffed into a casing; a sausage can be fresh, smoked and cooked, dried or hard

Sautéing—(saw-tay-ing) a dry-heat cooking method that uses conduction to transfer heat from a hot pan to food with the aid of a small amount of hot fat; cooking is usually done quickly over high temperatures

Sauteuse—(saw-toose) the basic sauté pan with sloping sides and a single long handle

Sautoir—(saw-twahr) a sauté pan with straight sides and a single long handle

Savory—(1) describes spiced or seasoned, as opposed to sweet, foods; (2) (savoury) a highly seasoned last course of a traditional English dinner

Scald—to heat a liquid, usually milk, to just below the boiling point

Scallop—(French *escalope*) a thin, boneless slice of meat

Score—to cut shallow gashes across the surface of a food before cooking

Scoville Heat Units—a subjective rating for measuring a chile's heat; the sweet bell pepper usually rates 0 units, the tabasco pepper rates from 30,000 to 50,000 units and the habanero pepper rates from 100,000 to 300,000 units

Seafood—an inconsistently used term encompassing some or all of

the following: saltwater fish, freshwater fish, saltwater shellfish, freshwater shellfish and other edible marine life

Sear—to brown food quickly over high heat; usually done as a preparatory step for combination cooking methods

Season—(1) traditionally, to enhance flavor by adding salt; (2) more commonly, to enhance flavor by adding salt and/or pepper as well as herbs and spices; (3) to mature and bring a food (usually beef or game) to a proper condition by aging or special preparation; (4) to prepare a pot, pan or other cooking surface to prevent sticking

Seasoning—an item added to enhance the natural flavors of a food without dramatically changing its taste; salt is the most common seasoning, although all herbs and spices are often referred to as seasonings

Seitan—(SAY-tan) a form of wheat gluten; it has a firm, chewy texture and a bland flavor; traditionally simmered in a broth of soy sauce or tamari with ginger, garlic and kombu (seaweed)

Semi à la carte—describes a menu on which some foods (usually appetizers and desserts) and beverages are priced and ordered separately, while the entrée is accompanied by and priced to include other dishes such as a salad, starch or vegetable

Semifreddi—(seh-mee-frayd-dee) also known as still-frozen desserts; items made with frozen mousse, custard or cream into which large amounts of whipped cream or meringue are folded in order to incorporate air; layers of spongecake and/or fruits may be added for flavor and texture; include frozen soufflés, marquise, mousses and neapolitans

Semolina—see **Durum wheat**

Sfoglia—(sfo-glee-ah) a thin, flat sheet of pasta dough that can be cut into ribbons, circles, squares or other shapes

Shallow poaching—a moist-heat cooking method that combines poaching and steaming; the food (usually fish) is placed on a vegetable bed and partially covered with a liquid (cuisson) and simmered

Shellfish—aquatic invertebrates with shells or carapaces

Sherbet—a frozen mixture of fruit juice or fruit purée that contains milk and/or eggs for creaminess

Shocking—submerging a food in cold water to quickly cool it and prevent further cooking, also known as shocking; usually used for vegetables

Shortening—(1) a white, flavorless, solid fat formulated for baking or deep-frying; (2) any fat used in baking to tenderize the product by shortening gluten strands

Shred—to cut into thin but irregular strips

Shuck—(1) a shell, pod or husk; (2) to remove the edible portion of a food (for example, clam meat, peas or an ear of corn) from its shell, pod or husk

Side masking—the technique of coating only the sides of a cake with garnish

Sifting—(1) shaking a dry, powdered substance through a sieve or sifter to remove lumps and incorporate air; (2) mixing together powdery substances by sifting

Silverskin—the tough connective tissue that surrounds certain muscles; see **Elastin**

Simmering—(1) a moist-heat cooking method that uses convection to transfer heat from a hot (approximately 185°F–205°F [85°C–96°C]) liquid to the food submerged in it; (2) maintaining the temperature of a liquid just below the boiling point

Skim—to remove fat and impurities from the surface of a liquid during cooking

Slice—to cut an item into relatively broad, thin pieces

Slurry—a mixture of raw starch and cold liquid used for thickening

Small sauces—also known as compound sauces; made by adding one or more ingredients to a leading sauce; they are grouped together into families based on their leading sauce; some small sauces have a variety of uses, while others are traditional accompaniments for specific foods

Smoke point—the temperature at which a fat begins to break down and smoke

Smoking—any of several methods for preserving and flavoring foods by exposing them to smoke; includes cold smoking (in which the foods are not fully cooked) and hot smoking (in which the foods are cooked)

Smørbrød—(SMURR-brur) Norwegian cold open-faced sandwiches. Similarly, the Swedish term *smörgåsbord* (SMORE-guhs-bohrd) refers to a buffet or bread-and-butter table of salads, open-faced sandwiches, pickled or marinated fish, sliced meats and cheeses.

Solid pack—canned fruits or vegetables with little or no water added

Sorbet—(sore-bay) a frozen mixture of fruit juice or fruit purée; similar to sherbet but without milk products

Soufflé—(soo-flay) either a sweet or savory fluffy dish made with a custard base lightened with whipped egg whites and then baked; the whipped egg whites cause the dish to puff when baked

Sous-chef—(soo-shef) a cook who supervises food production and who reports to the executive chef; he or she is second in command of a kitchen

Specifications; specs—standard requirements to be followed in procuring items from suppliers

Spice—any of a group of strongly flavored or aromatic portions of plants (other than leaves) used as flavorings, condiments or aromatics;

usually used in dried form, either whole or ground

Springform pan—a circular baking pan with a separate bottom and a side wall held together with a clamp that is released to free the baked product

Spring lamb—the meat of sheep slaughtered before they have fed on grass or grains

Spun sugar—a decoration made by flicking dark caramelized sugar rapidly over a dowel to create long, fine, hairlike threads

Squab—the class of young pigeon used in food service operations

Staling—also known as starch retrogradation; a change in the distribution and location of water molecules within baked products; stale products are firmer, drier and more crumbly than fresh baked goods

Standard breading procedure—the procedure for coating foods with crumbs or meal by passing the food through flour, then an egg wash and then the crumbs; it gives foods a relatively thick, crisp coating when deep-fried or pan-fried

Standardized recipe—a recipe producing a known quality and quantity of food for a specific operation

Staples—(1) certain foods regularly used throughout the kitchen; (2) certain foods, usually starches, that help form the basis for a regional or national cuisine and are principal components in the diet

Starch—(1) complex carbohydrates from plants that are edible and either digestible or indigestible (fiber); (2) a rice, grain, pasta or potato accompaniment to a meal

Starch retrogradation—see **Staling**

Starchy potatoes—see **Mealy potatoes**

Static menu—a menu offering patrons the same foods every day

Station chef—the cook in charge of a particular department in a kitchen

Steak—(1) a cross-section slice of a round fish with a small section of the bone attached; (2) a cut of meat, either with or without the bone

Steamed milk—milk that is heated with steam generated by an espresso machine; it should be approximately 150°F to 170°F (65°C to 76°C)

Steamer—(1) a set of stacked pots with perforations in the bottom of each pot; they fit over a larger pot filled with boiling or simmering water and are used to steam foods; (2) a perforated insert made of metal or bamboo placed in a pot and used to steam foods; (3) a type of soft-shell clam from the East Coast; (4) a piece of gas or electric equipment in which foods are steamed in a sealed chamber

Steaming—a moist-heat cooking method in which heat is transferred from steam to the food being cooked by direct contact; the food to be steamed is placed in a basket or rack above a boiling liquid in a covered pan

Steel—a tool, usually made of steel, used to hone or straighten knife blades

Steep—to soak food in a hot liquid in order to either extract its flavor or impurities or soften its texture

Steers—male cattle castrated prior to maturity and principally raised for beef

Sterilize—to destroy all living microorganisms

Stewing—a combination cooking method similar to braising but generally involving smaller pieces of meat that are first blanched or browned, then cooked in a small amount of liquid that is served as a sauce

Stir-frying—a dry-heat cooking method similar to sautéing in which foods are cooked over very high heat using little fat while stirring constantly and briskly; often done in a wok

Stirring—a mixing method in which ingredients are gently mixed by hand until blended, usually with a spoon, whisk or rubber spatula

Stock—(French *fond*) a clear, unthickened liquid flavored by soluble substances extracted from meat, poultry or fish and their bones as well as from a mirepoix, other vegetables and seasonings

Stone fruits—members of the genus *Prunus,* also known as drupes; tree or shrub fruits with a thin skin, soft flesh and one woody stone or pit; include apricots, cherries, nectarines, peaches and plums

Straight dough method—a mixing method for yeast breads in which all ingredients are simply combined and mixed

Strain—to pour foods through a sieve, mesh strainer or cheesecloth to separate or remove the liquid component

Streusel—(stroo-zel) a crumbly mixture of fat, flour, sugar and sometimes nuts and spices; used to top baked goods

Subcutaneous fat—also known as exterior fat; the fat layer between the hide and muscles

Submersion poaching—a poaching method in which the food is completely covered with the poaching liquid

Subprimal cuts—the basic cuts produced from each primal

Sucrose—the chemical name for refined or table sugar, it is refined from the raw sugars found in the large tropical grass called sugar cane and the root of the sugar beet

Sugar—a carbohydrate that provides the body with energy and gives a sweet taste to foods

Sugar syrups—either simple syrups (thin mixtures of sugar and water) or cooked syrups (melted sugar cooked until it reaches a specific temperature)

Suprême—(su-prem) (1) a sauce made by adding cream to a velouté made from chicken stock; it is used to make several compound sauces

of the velouté family; (2) a boneless, skinless chicken breast with the first wing segment attached; (3) an intact segment of citrus fruit with all membrane removed

Sushi—(szu-she) cooked or raw fish or shellfish rolled in or served on seasoned rice

Sweat—to cook a food (typically vegetables) in a small amount of fat, usually covered, over low heat without browning until the food softens and releases moisture; sweating allows the food to release its flavor more quickly when cooked with other foods

Sweetbreads—the thymus glands of a calf or lamb

Syrup—sugar that is dissolved in liquid, usually water, and often flavored with spices or citrus zest

Syrup pack—canned fruits with a light, medium or heavy syrup added

Table d'hôte—(tab-bluh dote) see **Prix fixe**

Tagarishi—a Japanese spice that is available at Asian markets

Tahini—(tah-HEE-nee) a thick, oily paste made from crushed sesame seeds

Tang—the portion of a knife's blade that extends inside the handle

Tart—a sweet or savory filling in a baked crust made in a shallow, straight-sided pan without a top crust

Tartlet—a small, single-serving tart

Tempeh—(TEHM-pay) fermented whole soybeans mixed with a grain such as rice or millet; it has a chewy consistency and a yeasty, nutty flavor

Temperature danger zone—the broad range of temperatures between 40°F and 140°F (4°C and 60°C) at which bacteria multiply rapidly

Tempering—(1) heating gently and gradually; refers to the process of slowly adding a hot liquid to eggs or other foods to raise their

temperature without causing them to curdle; (2) a process for melting chocolate during which the temperature of the cocoa butter is carefully stabilized; this keeps the chocolate smooth and glossy

Terrine—(teh-reen) (1) traditionally, a loaf of coarse forcemeat cooked in a covered earthenware mold and without a crust; today, the word is used interchangeably with *pâté;* (2) the mold used to cook such items, usually a rectangle or oval shape and made of ceramic

Thickening agents—ingredients used to thicken sauces; include starches (flour, cornstarch and arrowroot), gelatin and liaisons

Timbale—(tim-bull) (1) a small pail-shaped mold used to shape foods; (2) a preparation made in such a mold

Tisanes—(teh-zahns) beverages made from herbal infusions that do not contain any tea

Tofu—also known as bean curd; it is created from soymilk using a method similar to the way animal milk is separated into curds and whey in the production of cheese

Tomato sauce—a leading sauce made from tomatoes, vegetables, seasonings and white stock; it may or may not be thickened with roux

Toque—(toke) the tall white hat worn by chefs

Torte—in Central and Eastern European usage, refers to a rich cake in which all or part of the flour is replaced with finely chopped nuts or bread crumbs

Tossed salad—a salad prepared by placing the greens, garnishes and salad dressing in a large bowl and tossing to combine

Total recipe cost—the total cost of ingredients for a particular recipe; it does not reflect overhead, labor, fixed expenses or profit

Tourner—(toor-nay) French for "to turn"; to cut foods, usually vegetables, into football-shaped pieces with seven equal sides and blunt ends

Toxins—by-products of living bacteria that can cause illness if consumed in sufficient quantities

Tranche—(tranch) an angled slice cut from fish fillets

Tripe—the edible lining of a cow's stomach

Truffles—(1) flavorful tubers that grow near the roots of oak or beech trees; (2) rich chocolate candies made with ganache

Truss—to tie poultry with butcher's twine into a compact shape for cooking

Tube pan—a deep round baking pan with a hollow tube in the center

Tuber—the fleshy root, stem or rhizome of a plant from which a new plant will grow; some, such as potatoes, are eaten as vegetables

Tunneling—the holes that may form in baked goods as the result of overmixing

Unit cost—the price paid to acquire one of the specified units, calculated as total cost divided by number of units

Univalves—single-shelled mollusks with a single muscular foot, such as abalone

Unsaturated fats—fats that are normally liquid (oils) at room temperature; they may be monounsaturated (from plants such as olives and avocados) or polyunsaturated (from grains and seeds such as corn, soybeans and safflower as well as from fish)

Vanilla custard sauce—also known as crème anglaise; a stirred custard made with egg yolks, sugar and milk or half-and-half and flavored with vanilla; served with or used in dessert preparations

Vanillin—(1) whitish crystals of vanilla flavor that often develop on vanilla beans during storage; (2) synthetic vanilla flavoring

Variety—the result of breeding plants of the same species that have different qualities or characteristics; the new plant often combines features from both parents

Variety meats—see **Offal**

Veal—the meat of calves under the age of nine months

Vegan—(VEE-gun) a vegetarian who does not eat dairy products, eggs, honey or any other animal product; vegans usually also avoid wearing and using animal products such as fur, leather or wool

Vegetable—any herbaceous plant (one with little or no woody tissue) that can be partially or wholly eaten; vegetables can be classified as cabbages, fruit-vegetables, gourds and squashes, greens, mushrooms and truffles, onions, pods and seeds, roots and tubers and stalks

Vegetarian—a person who does not eat any meat, poultry, game, fish, shellfish or animal by-products such as gelatin or animal fats; may not eat dairy products and eggs

Velouté—(veh-loo-tay) a leading sauce made by thickening a white stock (either fish, veal or chicken) with roux

Venison—meat from any member of the deer family, including antelope, elk, moose, reindeer, red-tailed deer, white-tailed deer, mule deer and axis deer; it is typically a lean, dark red meat with a mild aroma

Vent—(1) to allow the circulation or escape of a liquid or gas; (2) to cool a pot of hot liquid by setting the pot on blocks in a cold water bath and allowing cold water to circulate around it

Vinaigrette—(vin-nay-greht) a temporary emulsion of oil and vinegar (usually three parts oil to one part vinegar) seasoned with herbs, salt and pepper; used as a salad dressing or sauce

Vinegar—a thin, sour liquid used as a preservative, cooking ingredient and cleaning solution

Viruses—the smallest known form of life; they invade the living cells of a host and take over those cells' genetic material, causing the cells to produce more viruses; some viruses can enter a host through the ingestion of food contaminated with those viruses

Viscera—internal organs

Vitamins—compounds present in foods in very small quantities; they do not provide energy but are essential for regulating body functions

Vol-au-vents—(vul-oh-vanz) deep, individual portion-sized puff pastry shells; often filled with a savory mixture and served as an appetizer or a main course

Volume—the space occupied by a substance; volume measurements are commonly expressed as liters, teaspoons, tablespoons, cups, pints and gallons

Wash—a glaze applied to dough before baking; a commonly used wash is made with whole egg and water

Water bath—see **Bain marie**

Water pack—canned fruits with water or fruit juice added

Waxy potatoes—those with a low starch content and thin skin; they are best for boiling

Weight—the mass or heaviness of a substance; weight measurements are commonly expressed as grams, ounces and pounds

Whetstone—a dense, grained stone used to sharpen or hone a knife blade

Whipping—a mixing method in which foods are vigorously beaten in order to incorporate air; a whisk or an electric mixer with its whip attachment is used

White stew—see **Fricassee** and **Blanquette**

White stock—a light-colored stock made from chicken, veal, beef or fish bones simmered in water with vegetables and seasonings

Whitewash—a thin mixture or slurry of flour and cold water used like cornstarch for thickening

Whole butter—butter that is not clarified, whipped or reduced in fat content; it may be salted or unsalted

Wine—an alcoholic beverage made from the fermented juice of grapes; may be sparkling (effervescent) or still (noneffervescent) or fortified with additional alcohol

Work section—see **Work station**

Work station—a work area in the kitchen dedicated to a particular task, such as broiling or salad making; work stations using the same or similar equipment for related tasks are grouped together into work sections

Yeasts—microscopic fungi whose metabolic processes are responsible for fermentation; they are used for leavening bread and in cheese, beer and wine making

Yield—(1) the total amount of a food item created or remaining after trimming or fabrication; (2) the total amount of a product made from a specific recipe

Yield grades—a grading program for meat that measures the amount of usable meat on a carcass

Zabaglione—see **Sabayon**

Zest—the thin, colored part of a citrus peel

Zushi—(zhoo-she) the seasoned rice used for sushi

INDEX

[Note: Recipes are in boldface type and are listed by title and under main ingredient, cooking method, or category of food. Thus Grilled Potato Salad may be found under Potatoes, Grilling, and Salads. Some dishes, like Jambalaya, are also listed as unique entries.]

Abalone, 506
Aboyeur, 8
Acapulco Catfish Grill, 542
Acapulco Spice Blend, 542
Acesulfame-K, 47
Acetic acid, 132
Achiote Paste, 483–484
Achiote-Basted Rack of Venison with Smoked Corn Pudding, 483
Acid/alkali balance
　and bacteria growth, 21
　reactions and, 644–645
Acidity
　of coffee, 136
　of olive oil, 129
Acidulated water, 41
Acidulation, 808
Acorn squash, 626
Active dry yeast, 967
Additives, 48
Adrian, Christine, 442
Aerobic bacteria, 21
Agnolotti, 710
AIDS, 25
Aïoli, 755
　Cilantro Aïoli, 849
　Sun-Dried Tomato and Basil Aïoli, 770
　Tarragon Aïoli, 661
À la carte, 56
À la nage, 206
Albacore, 504
Albin, Christian, 350, 562, 578, 720
Albufera sauce, 215
Albumen, 588
Alcoholic beverages, in the bakeshop, 941
Al dente, 711
Aleppo pepper, 116
Alfalfa sprouts, 749
Allemande Sauce, 214
Allemeier, Michael, 281, 367, 823, 1120
Allergic reactions, 49
All-purpose flour, 927
All-purpose shortening, 934
Allspice, 116
Allumette, 102
Almond Cream, 1031
Almond Cream Filling, 992
Almonds, 126
　Candied Almonds, 1035
Alston, Elizabeth, 950
Altitude, boiling point and, 189
Aluminum, in cookware, 76–77
American buffalo. *See* Bison (American buffalo)

American cheddar, 155
American red snapper, 502–503
American service, 10
American sturgeon caviar, 896
Amino acids, 39
Ammonia bicarbonate, 949
Anadromous, 500
Anaerobic bacteria, 21
Anaheim peppers, 622
Achiote Paste, 483–484
Andouille sausage, 872
Angler fish, 502
Anisakiasis, 22
Anise, 116
Anise pepper, 120
Anjou pears, 800
Annato seeds, 116
Anodized aluminum
　in cookware, 77
Antelope, 476
　Braised Antelope in Sour Cream, 488–489
Antibiotics, 24
Antimony, 24
Apples
　Apple-Cranberry Pie, 1004–1005
　Apple Fritters, 814
　Apple Gelée, 472
　Apple Horseradish Sauce, 243
　Apple Salsa, 541
　Applesauce, 823–824
　Applesauce Brownies, 1087
　Baked Apples, 812
　Braised Red Cabbage with Apples, 681–682
　coring, 799
　dried, 809
　Freeform Apple Pie, 1026
　French Apple Tart, 1029
　varieties, 798–799
Apprentices, 9
　in the kitchen brigade, 10
Apricots, 801
　Apricot and Bourbon Grilled Chicken, 443
　Apricot Filling (for Danish pastries), 993
　Apricot Mustard, 459–460
　Apricot Sauce (for dipping), 904
　dried, 809
Aquafarming, 500
Arabica coffee beans, 134, 137
Area chefs, 10
Aril, 120
Arizona Baked Corn, 663
Aroma, coffee, 136
Aromatics, 112
Arrowroot, 210
Arteriosclerosis
　fats and, 39
Artesian-well water, 41
Artichokes, 637
　Artichoke Soup, 280
　Artichokes Stuffed with Italian Sausage, 683

　Spinach and Artichoke Dip, 912–913
Artlip, Mike, 274, 327, 396, 400, 402
Arugula, 748
Asafetida, 116
Ascorbic acid. *See* Vitamins, table of
Ash, John, 460, 485, 490, 776
Asiago cheese, 156
Asian Chicken Salad, 781
Asian noodles, 707
Asian pears, 800
Asparagus, 638
　Stir-Fried Asparagus with Shitake Mushrooms, 649
　Tomato and Asparagus Salad with Fresh Mozzarella, 762
Aspartame, 47
Aspic jelly, 864, 868
Aspics, 864
As purchased (A.P.), 62
Assam tea, 138
Assistants *(demi-chefs),* 10
Atkinson, Leland, 234, 325, 353, 376, 447, 457, 463, 561, 579, 877, 878, 879
Atlantic cod, 500–501
Atlantic hard-shell clams, 507
Atlantic mackerel, 502
Atlantic oysters, 508
Atlantic salmon, 503
Au jus, 227, 295
Aunt Ruthie's Pot Roast, 306
Aurora sauce, 214
Avocado, 619–620
　Avocado Relish, 232
　Avocado Salsa, 242
　Guacamole, 912–913
　Pink Grapefruit and Avocado Salad, 776
　Shrimp and Avocado Omelet, 594–595

Baba Ghanoush, 911
Baby lettuces, 747
Baby vegetables, 639
Back waiters *(chefs de rang),* 10
Bacon
　BLT sandwich, 835
　Canadian-style, 600
　Club Sandwich, 848
　curing and smoking, 873–874
　Smoked Bacon and Quinoa Pilaf, 494
Bacteria
　classification of, 17
　illnesses from, 18
　intoxications and infections, 17–18
　prevention and, 18–21
Bagel, 971
Bain marie, 87
Baked Alaska, 1106
Baked Apples, 812
Baked Barley with Mushrooms, 732
Baked Beans, 664